Responding to Literature

to

Literature

Second Edition

JUDITH A. STANFORD

Rivier College

Mayfield Publishing Company
Mountain View, California
London · Toronto

LIBRARY OF CONGRESS CATALOGING-IN-PUBLICATION DATA
Responding to literature / [edited by] Judith A. Stanford.—2nd ed.
    p.   cm.
  Includes bibliographical references and index.
  ISBN 1-55934-538-1
    1. College readers. 2. English literature—Rhetoric.
  3. Literature—Collections.   I. Stanford, Judith A.
  PE1417.R4745   1996
  808'.0668—dc20   95-40985
                                      CIP

Manufactured in the United States of America
10 9 8 7 6 5 4

Mayfield Publishing Company
1280 Villa Street
Mountain View, California 94041

Sponsoring editor, Janet M. Beatty; production, Mary Forkner Douglas, Rogue
Valley Publications; manuscript editor, Sally Peyrefitte; text designer, David Bullen;
cover image, Lou Beach; cover designer and art director, Jeanne M. Schreiber; manufacturing manager, Randy Hurst. The text was set in 10.5/12 Bembo by Thompson
Type and printed on 30# Nyalite by The Banta Company.

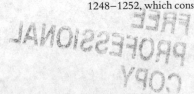

For Jan Beatty, editor and friend

PREFACE

Samuel Johnson's renowned biographer, James Boswell, reported a heated exchange of literary opinions that took place one late winter afternoon over cups of steaming, black coffee. Incensed by the proffered opinion that he "ought" to have read some particular work, Johnson replied, "A man ought to read just as inclination leads him; for what he reads as a task will do him little good." Most of us would agree with Johnson; what we read through our own motivation usually means more to us and stays with us longer than does something we are forced to read. Yet how do we discover what we want to read? Perhaps we walk into a bookstore and browse through the latest paperbacks, or we may listen to the recommendations of family members and friends. But these methods have their limits. At bookstores, for instance, many readers look only for writers with whom they are familiar or look only for the most recent arrivals in one particular section—perhaps mystery, science fiction, or romance.

Responding to Literature, second edition, encourages readers to explore a richly diverse selection of literature, including the essay. Four introductory chapters use student papers to illustrate ways of responding to writing about literature. Eight thematically arranged chapters follow, each with five or six stories, ten or more poems, one or two plays, and two essays.

Responding to Literature, second edition, helps readers to develop a wide range of possibilities as they decide what they will read in the future. The text offers this encouragement to readers through these key features.

- *Emphasis on the reader's personal response.* The text stresses the importance of the reader's interaction with and response to what he or she reads. Chapter 1 explores the difference between reading as a choice and reading as a requirement; this emphasis on the reader's engagement with the literary work is reflected throughout the text.
- *Examples of student writing.* Chapters 1, 2, and 4 provide many examples of students' notes, journal entries, sample drafts, and revised papers, including numerous examples of writers working collaboratively.
- *Informal introduction to literary terms.* Chapter 2 offers four works—a story, a poem, a brief play, and an essay—and student-written responses to them that incorporate key literary terms in a natural, informal way. The chapter stresses the similarities among literary genres, showing students, for example, that once they know how to talk about character in short stories, they also know how to discuss character in drama and persona in poetry. The emphasis is always on how readers find meaning in a work—how they bring their own knowledge, experiences, and insights to bear on what they read.

v

• *Introduction to the concept of genre and to major approaches to literary criticism.* In Chapter 3—new to the second edition—readers learn how understanding genre and the major approaches to literary criticism can provide new ways of considering literature.

• *Emphasis on the writing process.* Chapter 4 devotes special attention to the writing process, including strategies for discovering and exploring ideas, considering the audience, drafting, revising, and editing. This chapter provides six examples of students writing in different ways as they respond to Dylan Thomas's "Do Not Go Gentle into That Good Night" and Joan Aleshire's "Slipping." The six papers—a personal response, a comparison, an analysis, an explication, an evaluation, and a researched response—are accompanied by explanations of each student's process. Set off from the text throughout are summaries of many flexible, yet clear, guidelines for writing about literature. Chapter 4 also offers examples of students preparing for and participating in conferences with the instructor as well as with a writing center tutor.

• *Balance of new and classic selections.* The selections include an unusually strong representation of fresh voices—including women, minorities, and writers from other countries—as well as many familiar favorites.

• *Thought-provoking questions about the works.* The "Considerations" and "Connections" sections following the pieces in the thematic chapters provide ways of thinking and writing about the selections that lead readers away from a single "correct" interpretation and, instead, suggest multiple possibilities—always, of course, to be supported by evidence in the work itself.

• *Full-color section inviting students to make connections between literature and art.* Sixteen poems are paired with the works of art that inspired them (or vice versa); students are asked to reflect on their responses to both visual and verbal works.

• *Black and white photographs leading students to discuss each theme.* Each thematic chapter is introduced by a carefully selected photograph intended as a way to open a discussion of the theme the picture represents.

• An appendix on MLA documentation provides numerous illustrations of the 1995 MLA guidelines.

• An exceptionally thorough Instructor's Manual provides sections on teaching the first class and encouraging interaction in the classroom. The 250-page manual includes suggested responses for each discussion or writing topic in *Responding to Literature.*

NEW TO THE SECOND EDITION OF *RESPONDING TO LITERATURE*

• *Listening to Other Voices.* This section of Chapter 3 invites students to become part of the larger conversation about literature. Literary scholarship is approached as a way of seeing new possibilities, including formalist, reader-response, feminist, Marxist, psychoanalytic, and new historical criticism.

In addition, students learn about reviews, interviews with writers, and writers' commentaries on their own works—all as useful sources that provide invitations to new ideas about literature.

• *Expanded sample essays.* Each "Writing about Literature" section now includes a completed draft of the paper, clearly highlighted for easy access so that students and instructors may more readily refer to these examples.

• *Critical commentaries.* Each thematic chapter includes a "Commentary"— a review, scholarly essay, interview, or comment by an author on his or her own work. These commentaries give students examples of the "other voices" introduced in Chapter 3 and invite students to discuss or write in response to the ideas and insights these voices offer.

• *New selections and a new thematic chapter.* In this edition, twenty new short stories, thirty-seven new poems, seven new plays, and a new thematic section, "Roots, Identity, and Culture," offer students the opportunity to think, discuss, and write about questions that are central to leading the examined life: Who Am I? Where Did I Come From? Where Am I Going?

• *Expanded Art and Poetry section.* The first edition included eight poems paired with art; this new edition includes sixteen.

• *New Chapter—Three American Poets.* This chapter offers opportunity for in-depth study of the works of Robert Frost, Elizabeth Bishop, and Gwendolyn Brooks. Introductory sections provide biographical and critical background that establish an historical and aesthetic context, encouraging students to see connections between the poets' work and the times and places in which they lived.

• *Biographical Notes.* In the thematic chapters, each writer's work is now introduced with a brief biographical note that provides a context for the selection. Students are thus given a sense that literature does not exist in a vacuum but, rather, that it connects with the writer's life and times.

ACKNOWLEDGMENTS

My own teaching and the inspiration for this text owe much to the writing of Louise Rosenblatt, Robert Scholes, Robert DiYanni, Nancie Atwell, and Mike Rose. Rebecca Burnett inspires me as a teacher, a researcher, and most of all as a true friend. Lynn Quitman Troyka deserves special thanks for encouraging me in many ways, especially in the world of textbook publishing. Writing and Learning Center faculty as well as many English department faculty members at Rivier College have inspired me with lively literary discussions, a generous willingness to share ideas, and a keen understanding of the importance of positive reinforcement. Joan O'Brien of the Sylvan Learning Center in Chelmsford, Massachusetts, stands out as a true educator and a great friend; her encouragement and support have been extremely valuable. I thank my husband, Don, and my sons, Aaron and David, for being people who like to read and who share with me their thoughts about what they read. My mother, Arline Dupras, earns praise not only for the endless support she gave researching and typing, but most especially for being the person who first taught me that reading is joyful.

The reviewers of this edition, as well as those of the first edition, offered helpful and wise suggestions which I greatly appreciate. Reviewers for the first edition include: Thomas Dukes, University of Akron; Cynthia A. Eby, James Madison University; Leonard Engel, Quinnipiac College; Jennifer W. Thompson, University of Kansas; James Wanless, Henry Ford Community College. Reviewers for the second edition include: Elizabeth Addison, Western Carolina University; Melissa E. Barth, Appalachian State University; Denise David, Niagara County Community College; Ruth Elowitz, Chabot College; Anita R. Guynn, University of South Carolina, Columbia; John Heyda, Miami University; Anna Jackson, Southern Illinois University, Carbondale; Pansy J. Jackson, Virginia State University; Maggy Lindgren, University of Cincinnati; Elizabeth C. Mitchell, Ocean County College; Alan B. Shaw, Monroe Community College; Camille Taylor, College of Lake County; Cyrilla Vessey, Northern Virginia Community College; and Bertha L. Wise, Oklahoma City Community College.

I extend thanks and gratitude to all students whose writing and discussion contributed to this book. Kathleen Fencil and Darold Rorabacher deserve special mention for their research, which inspired the inclusion of Gwendolyn Brooks and Elizabeth Bishop in Chapter 13, Three American Poets.

April Wells-Hayes at Mayfield and Mary Douglas at Rogue Valley Publications worked with amazing speed and grace during the production of the book while Pamela Trainer attended to the difficult task of obtaining permissions. I thank Tom Broadbent for his continued interest in this project and for the ideas he shared over an unforgettable dinner in Boston. Finally, I thank Senior Editor Jan Beatty. This edition, even more than the first, reflects her vision, warmth, and wit. Knowing that with this edition I am saying goodbye to Jan as an editor (but not as a friend) brings to mind Frost's line, "Nothing gold can stay." And so, with deep gratitude, I dedicate the second edition to Jan Beatty.

CONTENTS

13 *Three American Poets* 1209

ALTERNATE CONTENTS
BY GENRE

Fiction

Poetry

Drama

Essays

1

Why Read Literature?

At the first meeting of a course called "Literature and Writing," a professor asked students to respond to a question written on the forms she distributed to them. She explained that some students would receive Form A and some Form B. The question on each form was different, although the two questions differed by only one word.

Form A asked students, "Why do you read literature? (For the purposes of this response, please consider 'literature' to mean any and all fiction, poetry, drama, and essays.)"

Form B asked students, "Why do we read literature? (For the purposes of this response, please consider 'literature' to mean any and all fiction, poetry, drama, and essays.)"

Exercise

Before you read further, consider the two questions. Do you see any real difference between them? How would you respond to each question? Take a few minutes to jot down your thoughts. Then compare your responses with those that follow.

WHY DO YOU READ LITERATURE?

Students responded to this question in a wide variety of ways. The following comments are representative:

I read mostly fiction for pleasure. Poetry and drama I don't read much. When I read, I like to escape—to get away from all the pressures of everyday life. So, I don't want to read about a lot of the same troubles I have. And no unhappy endings. *Karin Estes*

I don't read what you call literature except that you said "any and all fiction, poetry, drama, or essays." So, if "any and all" can mean Stephen King (which a teacher I had said was not literature) then that's what I read. And the reason is his books always hold my interest because I get interested in the characters' lives. Then, when they get into totally weird situations, it's like I can really believe that. I don't know why I like to read stuff that scares me, but I do. I also like this kind of movie. *Jeff Pedino*

Literature to me has always meant a place to find someone else who goes through the same things I do. But seeing them and their problems or situations more in an objective way. When I was in middle school, I read a lot of Judy Blume's novels. I liked that she was honest and wrote about real feelings people have instead of what was some fantasy of how people should feel. She wasn't always teaching a lesson. Also, in high school I read *Tess of the D'Urbervilles* by Thomas Hardy. I thought Hardy was really honest, too, and Tess is not just the perfect little heroine. Then I read three more novels by Hardy because I liked how he wrote. I do that. Read a lot of one author when I find someone I like. *Kate Anstrom*

I read literature for two reasons: (1) it's assigned by a teacher, and (2) it's something that interests me. Most of the time these are not the same thing. Forget poetry, which is always a big puzzle to me. I don't want to have to figure out hidden meanings. I don't read drama because who buys drama in a book store? I like novels or short stories in some magazines. Adventures that move fast and have a good plot really keep my interest (mysteries are sometimes good, too, when you don't figure out on the second page who the killer was). *Dave Willette*

WHY DO WE READ LITERATURE?

The responses to this question were not so widely varied, but they were very different from the responses to the first question. Here are two samples; nearly all students gave a variation on one of these two themes:

We read literature to find the beauty of words of great writers. Literature teaches us the truth about our lives. We learn good values from literature like Shakespeare. *Elayne Mercier*

Literature is very important to read because those writers have lasted through a lot of years, and so what they say must be important. Otherwise they would have been forgotten. We read literature because it is an important part of our education. Like history is one part and math is one part and literature is one part. *Rick McDougal*

BRIDGING THE GAP

The differences students saw between personal reading (and the reasons for it) and "school reading" (and the reasons for it) show up clearly in these different responses. When answering the universally phrased question "Why do we read literature?" students dutifully answered with language that echoed pat textbook phrases, such as "beauty of words," "truth about our lives," and "lasted through . . . years." Few students mentioned whether they themselves found literature beautiful; few wondered why literature had "lasted through the years." Almost no one commented on any personal, individual reading choices. The only author consistently mentioned by name was Shakespeare.

By contrast, students' responses to the more individual question ("Why do you read literature?") varied widely and showed that literature was important to them for many different reasons. In addition, they noted some of the problems they encountered with traditionally defined "literature." For example, when Jeff Pedino comments that a teacher did not consider Stephen King's writing literature, he's beginning to search for a definition. In essence, Jeff is asking, "What makes a story, novel, poem, play, or essay 'literature'?"

Note, also, Dave Willette's comment that he doesn't enjoy poetry because he doesn't like reading that is a "puzzle." Dave cuts right to the heart of an issue that had always bothered him—the feeling that reading literature (and especially poetry) was basically a grueling search through a maze of difficult words to find a hidden meaning.

Some students made observations about their reading patterns. For instance, Kate Anstrom likes to read many novels by the same author (she mentions Judy Blume and Thomas Hardy). Kate's response is interesting because she bridges the gap between literature that is read in school and outside of school. She read *Tess of the D'Urbervilles* for a class and liked the novel because she thought Hardy was honest. He created a heroine who was far from perfect.

So, Kate makes a connection between her values (it's clear that truth, honesty, and realism are important to her) and the literature she reads. She looks at assigned books in a personal way and thus makes them part of her world. Of course, there's a reciprocal exchange involved, too. Hardy and his characters become part of Kate's world, but she also becomes part of theirs. When she reads Hardy's novels, she sees, senses, and experiences nineteenth-century England in a direct and detailed way. She doesn't read with detachment but instead becomes deeply involved with Hardy's creation.

This text invites you to make personal connections with various selections of literature that other readers have found important to their lives. A work of literature exists on the printed page, but it gains life and meaning only when individual readers bring their knowledge, beliefs, feelings, and values to the reading experience. You are not expected to like or to enjoy everything you read in this text (or everything that you read anywhere): no reader could honestly claim to do that. But you should be able to *respond* to every work that you read. Having a genuine response—and being willing to explore that response—is the key to opening new possibilities in whatever you read, in or out of class, both now and in the future.

RESPONDING TO WHAT YOU READ

The great thing about responding to literature is that there are no absolute answers. A response is a beginning point. You read a work through, keeping your mind and spirit open, and then jot down what you thought and felt as you read it. An initial response might include any of the following:

  • A question (about the meaning of a word or sentence, the choice of a word, the reason why a particular character appears in the work; the reason the author chose to begin or end as he or she did)
  • A comment on what you think the work is about and why you are interested or not interested in that idea
  • An observation about a particular description, or line, or sentence to which you had a strong reaction (you liked it; you disliked it; it made you angry, happy, sad, puzzled, uncomfortable)
  • A connection between this work and something else you have read, experienced, or observed in your own life

Remember that a response is a place to begin. Just as we often change our first impressions of a person or situation, readers often revise initial responses to a work of literature.

Exercise

Read the following poem by Robert Frost, and then write down your responses. You don't have to interpret the poem (although interpretation can certainly be one part of response). Don't worry about what you are "supposed to get" from the reading. Just notice your reactions and then write them down. When you are finished, compare your responses to the students' comments that follow Frost's poem. If possible, compare your comments to those of students in your class.

ROBERT FROST (1874–1963)

The Road Not Taken

Two roads diverged in a yellow wood,
And sorry I could not travel both
And be one traveler, long I stood
And looked down one as far as I could
To where it bent in the undergrowth;   5

Then took the other, as just as fair,
And having perhaps the better claim,
Because it was grassy and wanted wear;
Though as for that the passing there
Had worn them really about the same,   10

And both that morning equally lay
In leaves no step had trodden black.
Oh, I kept the first for another day!
Yet knowing how way leads on to way,
I doubted if I should ever come back.   15

I shall be telling this with a sigh
Somewhere ages and ages hence:
Two roads diverged in a wood, and I—
I took the one less traveled by,
And that has made all the difference.   20

Sample Student Responses to "The Road Not Taken"

This person is standing in the woods, and it's probably fall because the leaves are yellow. This is a nice time to take a walk, and it's a question which way he wants to go, because he would like to see all of the woods. He can go on only one path today. But I can't figure out why he says in lines 14 and 15 that he couldn't come back. Why does he doubt he'll come back if he wants to see what's on the other path? *Janice Angstrom, age 18*

This is not a poem about Frost just taking some walk in the woods. It's about him making a choice to be a poet. Then in the last verse he is glad he made that choice, and he says it has made all the difference in his life. *Gilbert Brown, age 21*

I see this as a poem about choices. The poet might be thinking about one choice, but I think it could mean many different possible decisions. I don't think the choice seems too big at first because I notice lines 9 and 10 say that the paths really had been traveled almost the same amount. To me, this is like a lot of life decisions. They may seem small at the time, but as Frost says, one way leads on to another, and you can't go back and relive your life. *Anita Juarez, age 35*

In the poem, the poet is sorry he made a certain choice in his life. He calls the poem "The Road Not Taken," so he is looking at the choice he didn't make and thinking about it for some reason. Maybe wondering what life would be like if he took that other road. And that is why he sighs in the last stanza. He is regretting what he lost out on. I can understand this because I do this, too. I look back and see some choices I made—like dropping out of school and going into the army—and I can see what I missed. *David Furman, age 28*

Commentary

You may find one or more of these responses similar to yours, or they all may be very different. Some of the observations may have surprised you. And certainly you noticed that two of the student writers had reactions that were nearly opposite. Gilbert Brown thinks that the speaker in the poem is glad he made a certain choice, whereas David Furman thinks that the speaker regrets the choice.

Suppose those two students compared their responses to Frost's poem. Noticing the difference in their reactions, they might reread "The Road Not Taken." David Furman has already offered some evidence to back up what he says: he notes that the title focuses on the path that was not followed, and he reads the sigh as sad. But Gilbert Brown might well ask whether a sigh is always sad. A sigh might show pleasure, contentment, relief, or any number of other emotions. How can these two commentators resolve their differences?

The answer is that they don't have to find a single resolution. Both readings of this poem are possible. By listening to a number of responses and then rereading the work to see what evoked those responses, readers often discover multiple possibilities, new ways of looking at the work that they had not previously considered.

Of course, there is always the chance that returning to the work will cause a reader to rethink an initial reaction. For instance, how would Gilbert Brown support his idea that the poem is about Frost's decision to be a poet? Nothing in the poem directly backs up this reading; to the contrary, lines 9 and 10 suggest that the choice involves two rather similar alternatives. Nevertheless, nothing in the poem definitely rules out the possibility that the choice relates to careers. Gilbert Brown might decide, however, to broaden the scope of his initial reaction.

Notice that David Furman relates strongly to what he sees as the speaker's regret. David's response shows that he regrets several life choices he made, and so he believes that the speaker in the poem must be experiencing this emotion, too. Even if David Furman modifies his reading to include other possibilities (for example, that the speaker in the poem might be proud of or pleased with his choice), that revision does not lessen the importance of the personal connection David has made with the poem. His reading remains a possibility, but now he also sees a fuller context than he did at first.

And what about Janice Angstrom? She sees the poem as basically about taking a walk in the woods. Is she wrong or imperceptive? No. Her reading is a very useful first step. She sees clearly the picture the poet paints and, in addition, she sees that part of the picture is puzzling. In lines 14 and 15, Janice recognizes an element of contradiction. If the speaker in the poem were simply talking about a woodland walk, he would not be so concerned about being unable to backtrack and explore another path. Janice, then, uses her literal first response to raise questions that lead to a nonliteral reading of the poem. Janice shows that she is perceptive by recognizing those questions and by being willing to pursue them.

Anita Juarez makes an intriguing observation when she notes that lines 9 and 10 suggest that the choice was not between extreme opposites. The paths are almost equally worn, so the choice is probably not between, for instance, nonconformity and conformity. Because of her own experiences, Anita sees a valuable insight in Frost's poem: it's frequently the apparently minor decisions in life that end up making "all the difference." Because of her initial reaction to "The Road Not Taken," she decided to read the poem more closely and to use it for the following assignment:

> Choose a poem to which you have a strong personal response. Then reread the poem and come to class prepared with notes to help you explain your response. Be sure to refer to specific lines and stanzas in the poem as you explain your thoughts and feelings.

Exercise

After reading the example that follows, choose a poem from any of the thematic chapters of this text (Chapters 5 through 12) and take notes as though you were preparing for the assignment given to Anita.

CLOSE ACTIVE READING

Once you've read a work of literature—poem, story, novel, or play—and noted your initial response, you may decide (or be asked) to read more closely. As you read, you check on your first reactions, and you consider the reactions you've heard others express. Close active reading always means reading with a pen or pencil (rather than a highlighter) in your hand. You might use a highlighter during your first reading to mark passages that impress, puzzle, delight, or outrage you, but a close reading requires actually interacting with the work—writing down your questions and observations as you go.

Here is how Anita Juarez marked "The Road Not Taken":

The Road (Not) Taken

Why not "The Road Taken"?

Two roads diverged in a (yellow wood,) —*Why yellow? Could be fall or spring— New beginnings?*
And sorry I could not travel both
And be one traveler, long I stood
And looked down one as far as I could
To where it bent in the undergrowth; — *maybe hard to get past.*   5

Then took the other, as just as fair, — *are they the same?*
And having perhaps the better claim,
Because it was grassy and wanted wear;
Though as for that the passing there
Had worn them really about the same, *Again — seems similar*   10

And both that morning equally lay
In leaves no step had trodden black.
Oh, I kept the first for another day!
Yet knowing how way leads on to way, / *Like a lot of choices in life — lead you in many directions.*
I doubted if I should ever come back. /   15

Happy or Sad About // Choices?

I shall be telling this with a sigh
Somewhere ages and ages hence:
Two roads diverged in a wood, and I—
I took the one less traveled by,
And that has made all the difference.   20

Sample Oral Response to "The Road Not Taken"

Using these notes as a guide, Anita Juarez gave the following informal oral response in class:

When I read this poem, I thought right away of the choice I made in high school not to study foreign languages. In the poem, the speaker makes his choice in either fall or spring—when the woods are yellow. I see both these seasons as times of new beginnings. In spring, everything new is growing. In fall (at least for students) it's the start of a new school year. I made my choice one fall when a guidance director told me I was not "college material" and recommended that I drop my French class. September should have been a beginning, but I saw it as an end to my dream for college. It's only now that I can begin to think it was—in a way—a beginning, too.

Dropping French was desirable because I didn't do well in languages, but taking a language was also desirable because you had to take a language to get into college. So, like the speaker in the poem, I made a choice between two possibilities—and just as the poem says, both these two choices had been made before by many people. As Frost says, "the passing there/Had worn them really about the same."

What really interested me about the poem is the way it says that "way leads on to way." Because I decided not to take a language, I knew I couldn't go to college—back then you had to have a language to get into college. So, after high school, I went to work at Sears, and at work I met my husband. So, working at Sears was what got me to meet that particular man. And then marrying him, I had children (that were of course different from those I might have had if I married somebody else). I could keep going on, but you get the idea about how "way led on to way" in my life.

In the poem the person doubts that he will "ever come back." Well, at first when I read this, I thought that in a way I have come back because now I am starting college, which I couldn't do out of high school. But I really know it's still not the same, because I am a different person than I was then. All those "ways that lead to other ways" have made me—or maybe helped me to become—somebody new. So, this is not about going back to an old fork in the road but being at a new one.

You can't really tell whether in the last stanza the speaker is entirely happy, entirely sad, or some mixture. But you can see he knows now how important life's choices can be. He knows he'll think back over one particular choice even when he is an old man ("somewhere ages and ages hence"). I feel the same way. Reading this poem has made me look at some of the choices I've made, and I know I'll still be looking at them years from now. And, whether for better or worse, those choices will have "made all the difference."

Commentary

Anita Juarez read "The Road Not Taken" carefully and related the speaker's experience to her own choices in life. Her observations show that she became genuinely interested in Frost's theme and was able to appreciate his poem more fully by bringing something of herself to her reading. You may think her commentary is very different from what you have previously thought of as "literary analysis." Certainly, her ideas are expressed informally and personally, yet she has indeed "analyzed" the poem (looked at how parts of it work to create the whole).

Chapter 2 introduces and explains terms that are useful when you talk or write about literature, Chapter 3 suggests two ways of extending the conversation about literature, and Chapter 4 demonstrates and explains six ways of writing about literature. As you read Chapters 2, 3, and 4, remember that all real enjoyment and understanding of literature begin with your engagement as a reader and your willingness to discover and explore the kinds of responses introduced in this chapter.

Exercise

Using the notes you took for the exercise on page 7, plan an oral response similar to the one you just read. Remember to refer to specific parts of the poem to explain why you had the responses you describe.

KEEPING A READING JOURNAL

In addition to taking notes, keeping a reading journal is one of the best ways to explore your responses to literature as well as to discover ideas for papers you may write. The comments on pages 5 and 6 come from students' journals, as do the paragraphs that introduce each new section in Chapter 2 (see pages 24, 29, 37, 42, 48).

There are many different ways of keeping such a journal. If you write a journal for your class, the instructor may ask you to write a certain number of entries each week and may specify how long those entries should be. The instructor may also suggest topics or approaches to help you determine the focus of some or all of the entries.

For journal entries that you plan yourself, consider the possibilities presented in the Guidelines box.

GUIDELINES
Keeping a Reading Journal

1. After you read a work, jot down several questions that come to mind. Then choose one question and explore it more fully.
2. List the emotions (anger, pity, envy, admiration, astonishment, and so on) the work evoked. Then explain the reasons you think you felt these emotions.
3. Copy one sentence, one line, or one phrase that struck you as especially beautiful, puzzling, enlightening, and so on. Then discuss how and why the sentence, line, or phrase evoked this response.
4. Write a letter to the author asking questions or making observations about the work.
5. Write a letter to one of the characters (or to the speaker in a poem) describing your response to a choice or decision he or she made.
6. Explain why you could—or couldn't—identify with a particular character or situation in the work.
7. Jot down your initial impression of a work. Then reread and write another entry describing new or changed impressions.
8. Make notes during class discussion of a particular work. Then respond to a comment made either by the instructor or by another student.

2

Joining the Conversation: Ways of Talking about Literature

People who start a new job or a new sport often find themselves surrounded by unfamiliar language. "Byte," "hard disk," and "system error" may not mean much to a newly hired office worker, but the new employee soon learns the terminology along with the practical steps required to use the office computer. Saying "monitor" instead of "the thing that looks like a TV" simplifies communication. The novice skier is in a similar situation. Someone who has never skied probably doesn't know or care about the difference between "new powder" and "packed, granular snow." As soon as a person rents skis and takes the first lesson, however, understanding the words that describe the condition of the ski slopes becomes important. It's much easier to warn a fellow skier of danger on the slopes by mentioning "moguls" than by describing "bumps and ridges with hard, icy coverings." In addition, learning new words to describe kinds of snow makes skiers more conscious of the natural world around them. They become aware of subtle distinctions they might not have noticed before.

Like computer users and skiers, many people who talk and write about literature use specialized terminology. Understanding the terms that describe various aspects of literature enriches the reader's experience. This vocabulary not only provides a shortcut for talking or writing about literature but also often suggests new ways of looking at poetry, fiction, drama, and nonfiction and at the connections between our lives and the literary works we read.

To begin learning about the language of literature, read the following selections. Each represents one genre of literature: fiction, poetry, drama, and nonfiction. As you read, make notes in the margins to keep track of your responses to each selection. (For note-taking suggestions, see Chapter 1, page 4). Following each selection are suggestions for writing to develop your responses further.

PATRICIA GRACE (1937–   )

Butterflies

The grandmother plaited her granddaughter's hair and then she said, "Get your lunch. Put it in your bag. Get your apple. You come straight back after school, straight home here. Listen to the teacher," she said. "Do what she say."

Her grandfather was out on the step. He walked down the path with her and out onto the footpath. He said to a neighbor, "Our granddaughter goes to school. She lives with us now."

"She's fine," the neighbor said. "She's terrific with her two plaits in her hair."

"And clever," the grandfather said. "Writes every day in her book."

"She's fine," the neighbor said.   5

The grandfather waited with his granddaughter by the crossing and then he said, "Go to school. Listen to the teacher. Do what she say."

When the granddaughter came home from school her grandfather was hoeing around the cabbages. Her grandmother was picking beans. They stopped their work.

"You bring your book home?" the grandmother asked.

"Yes."

"You write your story?"   10

"Yes."

"What's your story?"

"About the butterflies."

"Get your book then. Read your story."

The granddaughter took her book from her schoolbag and opened it.   15

"I killed all the butterflies," she read. "This is me and this is all the butterflies."

"And your teacher like your story, did she?"

"I don't know."

"What your teacher say?"

"She said butterflies are beautiful creatures. They hatch out and fly in   20
the sun. The butterflies visit all the pretty flowers, she said. They lay their
eggs and then they die. You don't kill butterflies, that's what she said."

The grandmother and the grandfather were quiet for a long time, and
their granddaughter, holding the book, stood quite still in the warm garden.

"Because you see," the grandfather said, "your teacher, she buy all her
cabbages from the supermarket and that's why."

Responding to "Butterflies"

1. Describe the relationship between the granddaughter and grandparents.
   Compare it to your own relationship to your grandparents or to other
   grandchild–grandparent relationships you know of.
2. What can you tell about the place where these people live? Can you make
   any guesses about the time period in which they live?
3. Even though the schoolteacher does not appear in the story, can you tell
   anything about her? What kind of a person do you think she is? How
   effective do you think she is as a teacher? Why?
4. What is your response to the advice the grandfather gives the granddaughter as she sets out for school? Do you think the grandfather might change
   his advice in response to his granddaughter's experience? Explain.
5. What was your response to the connection the grandfather makes between cabbages and butterflies? Explain.

LANGSTON HUGHES (1902–1967)

Theme for English B

The instructor said,

   Go home and write
   a page tonight.

   And let that page come out of you—
   Then, it will be true.   5

I wonder if it's that simple?

I am twenty-two, colored, born in Winston-Salem.
I went to school there, then Durham, then here
to this college on the hill above Harlem.
I am the only colored student in my class.   10
The steps from the hill lead down to Harlem,
through a park, then I cross St. Nicholas,

Eighth Avenue, Seventh, and I come to the Y,
the Harlem Branch Y, where I take the elevator
up to my room, sit down, and write this page: 15

It's not easy to know what is true for you or me
at twenty-two, my age. But I guess I'm what
I feel and see and hear. Harlem, I hear you:
hear you, hear me—we two—you, me talk on this page.
(I hear New York, too.) Me—who?   20

Well, I like to eat, sleep, drink, and be in love.
I like to work, read, learn, and understand life.
I like a pipe for a Christmas present,
or records—Bessie, bop, or Bach.

I guess being colored doesn't make me not like   25
the same things other folks like who are other races.
So will my page be colored that I write?
Being me, it will not be white.
But it will be
a part of you, instructor.   30
You are white—
yet a part of me, as I am a part of you.
That's American.
Sometimes perhaps you don't want to be a part of me.
Nor do I often want to be a part of you.   35
But we are, that's true!
As I learn from you,
I guess you learn from me—
although you're older—and white—
and somewhat more free.   40

This is my page for English B.

Responding to "Theme for English B"

1. Describe the thoughts and feelings that run through the speaker's mind as he considers the assignment for his English course. Does his process in any way remind you of the way you think about course assignments? Or do you work entirely differently? Explain.
2. What places seem significant to the speaker? How are they significant? For example, what differences does he suggest between the places he has lived (and the place he now lives) and the place he attends his classes? What comparisons can you make between places where you have lived and places where you have attended school?
3. What does the poem tell you about the speaker? Make two lists, one describing what might be called external facts (the speaker's age, for ex-

ample) and the other describing the inner speaker (his hopes, fears, motivations, personality traits, and so on).

4. What do you make of the question "So will my page be colored that I write?" (line 27)? What is the speaker's answer to his own question? What is your response to this answer?

5. If you were the instructor and received this poem in response to the assignment suggested in lines 2–5, how would you grade the paper? What comments would you write to explain your thoughts and feelings to the student?

WENDY WASSERSTEIN (1950–   )

The Man in a Case

Characters
BYELINKOV
VARINKA

Scene *A small garden in the village of Mironitski. 1898.*

(BYELINKOV *is pacing. Enter* VARINKA *out of breath.*)

BYELINKOV: You are ten minutes late.

VARINKA: The most amazing thing happened on my way over here. You know the woman who runs the grocery store down the road. She wears a black wig during the week, and a blond wig on Saturday nights. And she has the daughter who married an engineer in Moscow who is doing very well thank you and is living, God bless them, in a three-room apartment. But he really is the most boring man in the world. All he talks about is his future and his station in life. Well, she heard we were to be married and she gave me this basket of apricots to give to you.

BYELINKOV: That is a most amazing thing!

VARINKA: She said to me, "Varinka, you are marrying the most honorable man in the entire village. In this village he is the only man fit to speak with my son-in-law."

BYELINKOV: I don't care for apricots. They give me hives.

VARINKA: I can return them. I'm sure if I told her they give you hives she would give me a basket of raisins or a cake.

BYELINKOV: I don't know this woman or her pompous son-in-law. Why would she give me her cakes?

VARINKA: She adores you!

BYELINKOV: She is emotionally loose.

VARINKA: She adores you by reputation. Everyone adores you by reputation. I tell everyone I am to marry Byelinkov, the finest teacher in the county.

BYELINKOV: You tell them this?

VARINKA: If they don't tell me first.

BYELINKOV: Pride can be an imperfect value.

VARINKA: It isn't pride. It is the truth. You are a great man!

BYELINKOV: I am the master of Greek and Latin at a local school at the end of the village of Mironitski.

(VARINKA kisses him.)

VARINKA: And I am to be the master of Greek and Latin's wife!

BYELINKOV: Being married requires a great deal of responsibility. I hope I am able to provide you with all that a married man must properly provide a wife.

VARINKA: We will be very happy.

BYELINKOV: Happiness is for children. We are entering into a social contract, an amicable agreement to provide us with a secure and satisfying future.

VARINKA: You are so sweet! You are the sweetest man in the world!

BYELINKOV: I'm a man set in his ways who saw a chance to provide himself with a small challenge.

VARINKA: Look at you! Look at you! Your sweet round spectacles, your dear collar always starched, always raised, your perfectly pressed pants always creasing at right angles perpendicular to the floor, and my most favorite part, the sweet little galoshes, rain or shine, just in case. My Byelinkov, never taken by surprise. Except by me.

BYELINKOV: You speak about me as if I were your pet.

VARINKA: You are my pet! My little school mouse.

BYELINKOV: A mouse?

VARINKA: My sweetest dancing bear with galoshes, my little stale babka.

BYELINKOV: A stale babka?

VARINKA: I am not Pushkin.°

BYELINKOV *(Laughs)*: That depends what you think of Pushkin.

VARINKA: You're smiling. I knew I could make you smile today.

BYELINKOV: I am a responsible man. Every day I have for breakfast black bread, fruit, hot tea, and every day I smile three times. I am halfway into my translation of the *Aeneid*° from classical Greek hexameter° into Russian alexandrines.° In twenty years I have never been late to school. I am a responsible man, but no dancing bear.

Pushkin: A Russian poet and prose writer (1799–1837). Aeneid: Epic poem written by Vergil (70–19 B.C.). *hexameter:* A line of verse having six metric units. *alexandrine:* A line of verse having six metric units.

VARINKA: Dance with me.

BYELINKOV: Now? It is nearly four weeks before the wedding!

VARINKA: It's a beautiful afternoon. We are in your garden. The roses are
in full bloom.

BYELINKOV: The roses have beetles.

VARINKA: Dance with me!

BYELINKOV: You are a demanding woman.

VARINKA: You chose me. And right. And left. And turn. And right. And
left.

BYELINKOV: And turn. Give me your hand. You dance like a school
mouse. It's a beautiful afternoon! We are in my garden. The roses are
in full bloom! And turn. And turn. *(Twirls* VARINKA *around)*

VARINKA: I am the luckiest woman!

(BYELINKOV stops dancing.)

Why are you stopping?

BYELINKOV: To place a lilac in your hair. Every year on this day I will
place a lilac in your hair.

VARINKA: Will you remember?

BYELINKOV: I will write it down. *(Takes a notebook from his pocket)* Dear
Byelinkov, don't forget the day a young lady, your bride, entered your
garden, your peace, and danced on the roses. On that day every year
you are to place a lilac in her hair.

VARINKA: I love you.

BYELINKOV: It is convenient we met.

VARINKA: I love you.

BYELINKOV: You are a girl.

VARINKA: I am thirty.

BYELINKOV: But you think like a girl. That is an attractive attribute.

VARINKA: Do you love me?

BYELINKOV: We've never spoken about housekeeping.

VARINKA: I am an excellent housekeeper. I kept house for my family on
the farm in Gadyatchsky. I can make a beetroot soup with tomatoes
and aubergines which is so nice. Awfully, awfully nice.

BYELINKOV: You are fond of expletives.

VARINKA: My beet soup, sir, is excellent!

BYELINKOV: Please don't be cross. I too am an excellent housekeeper. I
have a place for everything in the house. A shelf for each pot, a cubby
for every spoon, a folder for favorite recipes. I have cooked for myself
for twenty years. Though my beet soup is not outstanding, it is
sufficient.

VARINKA: I'm sure it's very good.

BYELINKOV: No. It is awfully, awfully not. What I am outstanding in,
however, what gives me greatest pleasure, is preserving those things

which are left over. I wrap each tomato slice I haven't used in a wet cloth and place it in the coolest corner of the house. I have had my shoes for seven years because I wrap them in the galoshes you are so fond of. And every night before I go to sleep I wrap my bed in quilts and curtains so I never catch a draft.

VARINKA: You sleep with curtains on your bed?

BYELINKOV: I like to keep warm.

VARINKA: I will make you a new quilt.

BYELINKOV: No. No new quilt. That would be hazardous.

VARINKA: It is hazardous to sleep under curtains.

BYELINKOV: Varinka, I don't like change very much. If one works out the arithmetic, the final fraction of improvement is at best less than an eighth of value over the total damage caused by disruption. I never thought of marrying till I saw your eyes dancing among the familiar faces at the headmaster's tea. I assumed I would grow old preserved like those which are left over, wrapped suitably in my case of curtains and quilts.

VARINKA: Byelinkov, I want us to have dinners with friends and summer country visits. I want people to say, "Have you spent time with Varinka and Byelinkov? He is so happy now that they are married. She is just what he needed."

BYELINKOV: You have already brought me some happiness. But I never was a sad man. Don't ever think I thought I was a sad man.

VARINKA: My sweetest darling, you can be whatever you want! If you are sad, they'll say she talks all the time, and he is soft-spoken and kind.

BYELINKOV: And if I am difficult?

VARINKA: Oh, they'll say he is difficult because he is highly intelligent. All great men are difficult. Look at Lermontov, Tchaikovsky, Peter the Great.

BYELINKOV: Ivan the Terrible.

VARINKA: Yes, him too.

BYELINKOV: Why are you marrying me? I am none of these things.

VARINKA: To me you are.

BYELINKOV: You have imagined this. You have constructed an elaborate romance for yourself. Perhaps you are the great one. You are the one with the great imagination.

VARINKA: Byelinkov, I am a pretty girl of thirty. You're right, I am not a woman. I have not made myself into a woman because I do not deserve that honor. Until I came to this town to visit my brother I lived on my family's farm. As the years passed I became younger and younger in fear that I would never marry. And it wasn't that I wasn't pretty enough or sweet enough, it was just that no man ever looked at me and saw a wife. I was not the woman who would be there when he came home. Until I met you I thought I would lie all my life and say I never married because I never met a man I loved. I will love you, Byelinkov. And I will help you to love me. We deserve the life everyone else has. We deserve not to be different.

BYELINKOV: Yes. We are the same as everyone else.

VARINKA: Tell me you love me.

BYELINKOV: I love you.

VARINKA *(Takes his hands)*: We will be very happy. I am very strong. *(Pauses)* It is time for tea.

BYELINKOV: It is too early for tea. Tea is at half past the hour.

VARINKA: Do you have heavy cream? It will be awfully nice with apricots.

BYELINKOV: Heavy cream is too rich for teatime.

VARINKA: But today is special. Today you placed a lilac in my hair. Write in your note pad. Every year we will celebrate with apricots and heavy cream. I will go to my brother's house and get some.

BYELINKOV: But your brother's house is a mile from here.

VARINKA: Today it is much shorter. Today my brother gave me his bicycle to ride. I will be back very soon.

BYELINKOV: You rode to my house by bicycle! Did anyone see you?

VARINKA: Of course. I had such fun. I told you I saw the grocery store lady with the son-in-law who is doing very well thank you in Moscow, and the headmaster's wife.

BYELINKOV: You saw the headmaster's wife!

VARINKA: She smiled at me.

BYELINKOV: Did she laugh or smile?

VARINKA: She laughed a little. She said, "My dear, you are very progressive to ride a bicycle." She said, "You and your fiancé Byelinkov must ride together sometime. I wonder if he'll take off his galoshes when he rides a bicycle."

BYELINKOV: She said that?

VARINKA: She adores you. We had a good giggle.

BYELINKOV: A woman can be arrested for riding a bicycle. That is not progressive, it is a premeditated revolutionary act. Your brother must be awfully, awfully careful on behalf of your behavior. He has been careless—oh so careless—in giving you the bicycle.

VARINKA: Dearest Byelinkov, you are wrapping yourself under curtains and quilts! I made friends on the bicycle.

BYELINKOV: You saw more than the headmaster's wife and the idiot grocery woman.

VARINKA: She is not an idiot.

BYELINKOV: She is a potato-vending, sausage-armed fool!

VARINKA: Shhhh! My school mouse. Shhh!

BYELINKOV: What other friends did you make on this bicycle?

VARINKA: I saw students from my brother's classes. They waved and shouted, "Anthropos in love! Anthropos in love!!"

BYELINKOV: Where is that bicycle?

VARINKA: I left it outside the gate. Where are you going?

BYELINKOV *(Muttering as he exits)*: Anthropos in love, anthropos in love.

VARINKA: They were cheering me on. Careful, you'll trample the roses.

BYELINKOV *(Returning with the bicycle)*: Anthropos is the Greek singular for man. Anthropos in love translates as the Greek and Latin master in love. Of course they cheered you. Their instructor, who teaches them the discipline and contained beauty of the classics, is in love with a sprite on a bicycle. It is a good giggle, isn't it? A very good giggle! I am returning this bicycle to your brother.

VARINKA: But it is teatime.

BYELINKOV: Today we will not have tea.

VARINKA: But you will have to walk back a mile.

BYELINKOV: I have my galoshes on. *(Gets on the bicycle)* Varinka, we deserve not to be different. *(Begins to pedal. The bicycle doesn't move.)*

VARINKA: Put the kickstand up.

BYELINKOV: I beg your pardon.

VARINKA *(Giggling)*: Byelinkov, to make the bicycle move, you must put the kickstand up.

(BYELINKOV *puts it up and awkwardly falls off the bicycle as it moves.)*

(Laughing) Ha ha ha. My little school mouse. You look so funny! You are the sweetest dearest man in the world. Ha ha ha!

(Pause)

BYELINKOV: Please help me up. I'm afraid my galosh is caught.

VARINKA *(Trying not to laugh)*: Your galosh is caught! *(Explodes in laughter again)* Oh, you are so funny! I do love you so. *(Helps* BYELINKOV *up)* You were right, my pet, as always. We don't need heavy cream for tea. The fraction of improvement isn't worth the damage caused by the disruption.

BYELINKOV: Varinka, it is still too early for tea. I must complete two stanzas of my translation before late afternoon. That is my regular schedule.

VARINKA: Then I will watch while you work.

BYELINKOV: No. You had a good giggle. That is enough.

VARINKA: Then while you work I will work too. I will make lists of guests for our wedding.

BYELINKOV: I can concentrate only when I am alone in my house. Please take your bicycle home to your brother.

VARINKA: But I don't want to leave you. You look so sad.

BYELINKOV: I never was a sad man. Don't ever think I was a sad man.

VARINKA: Byelinkov, it's a beautiful day, we are in your garden. The roses are in bloom.

BYELINKOV: Allow me to help you on to your bicycle. *(Takes* VARIN-
KA's *hand as she gets on the bike)*
VARINKA: You are such a gentleman. We will be very happy.
BYELINKOV: You are very strong. Good day, Varinka.

>   *(VARINKA pedals off.* BYELINKOV, *alone in the garden, takes out his
>   pad and rips up the note about the lilac, strews it over the garden, then
>   carefully picks up each piece of paper and places them all in a small envelope as
>   lights fade to black.)*

Responding to *The Man in a Case*

1. Describe the relationship between the man and woman in the play. What
   seems important to each of them? Do any things seem important to them
   both? Explain. Does their relationship remind you of any relationships
   you know about? Describe the differences and similarities you see.
2. Did you find it important to know that this play takes place in 1898?
   Where do you think the village of Mironitski is located? Was knowing
   the location in any way connected to your response to the play?
3. Were you more sympathetic to one of the characters than to the other?
   Or did you find them both equally appealing (or lacking in appeal)?
   Explain.
4. What did you make of the bicycle episode? Why is Byelinkov so upset
   about Varinka's riding the bicycle? What is her response? How does this
   episode relate to other episodes in the play?
5. Write a short scene that takes place between Varinka and Byelinkov two
   weeks after the day of the play's action. What future do you predict for
   them? Why?

E. B. WHITE (1899–1985)

Education

I have an increasing admiration for the teacher in the country school
where we have a third-grade scholar in attendance. She not only undertakes
to instruct her charges in all the subjects of the first three grades, but she
manages to function quietly and effectively as a guardian of their health, their
clothes, their habits, their mothers, and their snowball engagements. She has
been doing this sort of Augean task° for twenty years, and is both kind and

---

Augean task: A very difficult task. (King Augeas of Elis set the Greek hero Hercules to the task
of cleaning the royal stables, which had been neglected for thirty years.)

wise. She cooks for the children on the stove that heats the room, and she can cool their passions or warm their soup with equal competence. She conceives their costumes, cleans up their messes, and shares their confidences. My boy already regards his teacher as his great friend, and I think tells her a great deal more than he tells us.

The shift from city school to country school was something we worried about quietly all last summer. I have always rather favored public school over private school, if only because in public school you meet a greater variety of children. This bias of mine, I suspect, is partly an attempt to justify my own past (I never knew anything but public schools) and partly an involuntary defense against getting kicked in the shins by a young ceramist on his way to the kiln. My wife was unacquainted with public schools, never having been exposed (in her early life) to anything more public than the washroom of Miss Winsor's. Regardless of our backgrounds, we both knew that the change in schools was something that concerned not us but the scholar himself. We hoped it would work out all right. In New York our son went to a medium-priced private institution with semi-progressive ideas of education, and modern plumbing. He learned fast, kept well, and we were satisfied. It was an electric, colorful, regimented existence with moments of pleasurable pause and giddy incident. The day the Christmas angel fainted and had to be carried out by one of the Wise Men was educational in the highest sense of the term. Our scholar gave imitations of it around the house for weeks afterward, and I doubt if it ever goes completely out of his mind.

His days were rich in formal experience. Wearing overalls and an old sweater (the accepted uniform of the private seminary), he sallied forth at morn accompanied by a nurse or a parent and walked (or was pulled) two blocks to a corner where the school bus made a flag stop. This flashy vehicle was as punctual as death: seeing us waiting at the cold curb, it would sweep to a halt, open its mouth, suck the boy in, and spring away with an angry growl. It was a good deal like a train picking up a bag of mail. At school the scholar was worked on for six or seven hours by a half a dozen teachers and a nurse, and was revived on orange juice in mid-morning. In a cinder court he played games supervised by an athletic instructor, and in a cafeteria he ate lunch worked out by a dietitian. He soon learned to read with gratifying facility and discernment and to make Indian weapons of a semi-deadly nature. Whenever one of his classmates fell low of a fever the news was put on the wires and there were breathless phone calls to physicians, discussing periods of incubation and allied magic.

In the country all one can say is that the situation is different, and somehow more casual. Dressed in corduroys, sweatshirt, and short rubber boots, and carrying a tin dinner-pail, our scholar departs at crack of dawn for the village school, two and a half miles down the road, next to the cemetery. When the road is open and the car will start, he makes the journey by motor, courtesy of his old man. When the snow is deep or the motor is dead or both, he makes it on the hoof. In the afternoons he walks or hitches all or part of the way home in fair weather, gets transported in foul. The schoolhouse is a two-room frame building, bungalow type, shingles stained a burnt brown with weather-resistant stain. It has a chemical toilet in the basement and two teachers above stairs. One takes the first three grades, the other the fourth, fifth, and sixth. They have little or no time for individual instruction, and no time at all for the esoteric. They teach what they know themselves, just as fast and as hard as they can manage. The pupils sit still at their desks in class, and do their milling around outdoors during recess.

There is no supervised play. They play cops and robbers (only they call   5
it "Jail") and throw things at one another—snowballs in winter, rose hips in fall. It seems to satisfy them. They also construct darts, pinwheels, and "pick-up sticks" (jackstraws), and the school itself does a brisk trade in penny candy, which is for sale right in the classroom and which contains "surprises." The most highly prized surprise is a fake cigarette, made of cardboard, fiend-ishly lifelike.

The memory of how apprehensive we were at the beginning is still strong. The boy was nervous about the change too. The tension, on that first fair morning in September when we drove him to school, almost blew the windows out of the sedan. And when later we picked him up on the road, wandering along with his little blue lunch-pail, and got his laconic report "All right" in answer to our inquiry about how the day had gone, our relief was vast. Now, after almost a year of it, the only difference we can discover in the two school experiences is that in the country he sleeps better at night— and *that* probably is more the air than the education. When grilled on the subject of school-in-country *vs.* school-in-city, he replied that the chief dif-ference is that the day seems to go so much quicker in the country. "Just like lightning," he reported.

Responding to "Education"

1. Make a list of the details the speaker provides to explain why he has "an increasing admiration for the teacher in the country school." Do you agree that these qualities are admirable? Explain.

2. How do the physical facilities of the city school compare with those of the country school? Which school would you prefer to attend (or to teach in)? Discuss your reasons.

3. Read paragraph 3 carefully and explain your response to the speaker's description of the school bus that takes his son to the city school.

4. In the final paragraph, the speaker says, "Now, after almost a year of it, the only difference we can discover in the two school experiences is that in the country he sleeps better at night—and *that* probably is more the air than the education." To what extent do the details in the rest of the essay suggest that the speaker does or does not favor one school over the other?

Do you find evidence to suggest that the "third-grade scholar" prefers one school to the other?

5. The speaker says that he "always rather favored public school over private school." What is your response to this judgment? Have you attended private schools? Public schools? Both? What differences do you believe exist between public and private schools?

THE VOCABULARY OF LITERATURE

As you look at your own responses to the four selections you've just read, you'll almost certainly find comments about actions and events, about people and places, about ideas and values. In addition, you'll probably note questions about the significance of particular objects, about the choice of certain words, or the use of references to people, places, and events outside the work itself.

Each of the following sections begins with observations, evaluations, or questions written by students—mostly freshmen and sophomores—who had just read the same selections you have. The commentary following their responses suggests how these students have provided insights both into the works themselves and into ways of reading, writing, thinking, and talking about literature.

ACTIONS AND EVENTS

In "Butterflies," the granddaughter is at a big point in her life—starting school. You can tell it's near the beginning because she writes a story in only two sentences. Also, you get the impression she has drawn a picture when she says, "This is me." Usually you only draw pictures like that very early in your school years. You can see she is not in agreement with her teacher because of the killing of the butterflies, which the teacher didn't understand. And I don't understand this, really. Why would the granddaughter want to kill butterflies? *Lisa Tisico*

I think the student in this poem ["Theme for English B"] is walking all the time that he is talking. In the lines where he talks about the steps that lead down the hill and "through a park" and then he even shows taking the elevator. Well, I guess once he's off the elevator and in his room, he's not walking then. But I liked the verse where he is walking because I could picture this. Probably because this is how I do a lot of my planning for classes and other things. I walk a lot and I am always putting my mind in gear and thinking while I do this. *Jim Belanger*

At first I thought that *The Man in a Case* was just all talking, but when I went back to read again, it was full of action. I love the way Varinka gets Byelinkov to dance. He is so stuffy and talks about how he is "a responsible man, but no dancing bear." Then two minutes later, he is dancing (and I could picture him like a dancing bear because Varinka counts off the steps like a bear trainer). This shows you that they really do seem to have fun together. But later the action with the bicycle makes everything fall apart. He is so jealous of her because she is free and not afraid to do things like riding a bicycle when she could be arrested or when other people might not approve. *Bonnie Dederian*

I can really understand the feelings of the third-grade kid that the father talks about [in E. B. White's essay]. Changing schools is hard because you're the new kid and you have to get to know everything, like the teacher, the other kids, and how things are done, all over again. My father is in the military, so we moved all the time. The best part of the essay for me was when the father tells that the kid thinks his day goes by "Just like lightning." You can tell he must like that school because time usually goes by very slowly in school, and especially when you're young. *Ryan Berker*

When readers react to literature, among the first aspects they notice are actions and events. You can see how natural this response is when you think about talking to a friend who recommends a new film. You'd almost certainly ask some version of this question: "What's it about?" And your friend would almost certainly respond by giving you a brief summary of what happens in the film or perhaps (like Bonnie Dederian in her response to *The Man in a Case*) by singling out particular actions that seemed especially interesting, entertaining, moving, frightening, or significant in some way.

Plot

When you tell what happens in a film or in a work of literature, you are describing the **plot,** the sequence of events that take place. Most readers begin by describing *external* actions, those that, through the writer's description, we can see and hear. For instance, in her response to "Butterflies," Lisa Tisico begins by writing about the granddaughter's starting school and the drawing she includes in her story of killing butterflies. These are external plot actions. But Lisa also asks questions that indicate her interest in *internal* actions, those events that take place inside the mind and heart. For example, she sees that the granddaughter does not agree with the teacher; in addition, Lisa wonders why the child would want to kill butterflies. So, looking at the external actions carefully led Lisa to think about the internal changes that might be happening.

Structure

The sequence of external and internal actions and events in a literary work creates its **structure,** the pattern the plot follows. In most traditional plays and works of fiction, the plot structure is something like this:

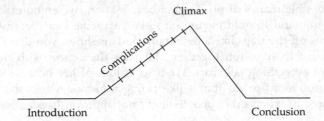

The work usually opens with an **introduction** that lets us know whom the action will concern and where the action will take place. Next, we are given a **complication** or a series of complications (small or large problems, sometimes comic, sometimes serious). For instance, in *The Man in a Case,* after Byelinkov and Varinka greet each other, they almost immediately have a series of small disagreements. He claims not to like the apricots she has received as a gift for him. She offers to return the apricots and try to exchange them for a different gift. He responds by attacking the character of the woman who gave Varinka the apricots.

It's easy to see that these two are not an entirely compatible couple, and most readers begin to wonder about the wisdom of their engagement. These early complications are revealed primarily through conversation, but, as Bonnie Dederian notes in her comment on this play, their incompatibility becomes even more obvious through two key actions in the play. The first action is the dance. Byelinkov protests that he is not a dancing bear, yet Varinka is able to lead him into a romantic, gently humorous noonday waltz in the garden. Now the two characters seem to come together, yet almost immediately they get into another squabble, this time over housekeeping styles. As Varinka talks about her fantasy of a marriage in which she and her husband will have "the life everyone has," Byelinkov appears to agree with her. So far in this play, the complications seem to follow a pattern of disagreement followed by reconciliation followed by new disagreement and further reconciliation.

The episode of the bicycle, however—which Bonnie Dederian sees as the action "that makes everything fall apart"—takes the play beyond complications and to the **climax** (the point of greatest tension or the turning point). Varinka has braved the law against women riding bicycles as well as the possible bad opinion of people who might see her. Byelinkov is shocked and particularly upset that some of his students have seen Varinka; he fears that they will laugh at him for being engaged to such a free-spirited woman. The turning point comes when Byelinkov tries to take charge by riding the bicycle back to the house of Varinka's brother. However, Byelinkov simply embarrasses himself by showing that he has no idea how to ride the bicycle. When Varinka first laughs and then rushes to help in response to his pleas, Byelinkov sends her away. Whether they will marry or not remains to be seen; however, the **conclusion,** the ending of the play, shows him ripping up and scattering the pieces of the note reminding him to put lilacs in Varinka's hair. Byelinkov must wonder if he will ever again be able to feel totally in control of his life or whether he'll be able to rely so completely on his carefully kept lists and notes.

Conflict

As you read a literary work and think about the structure of the plot— and particularly as you focus on the complications and climax—keep in mind that nearly all fiction and drama, and many poems, focus on a **conflict,** a struggle between opposing forces. The conflict or conflicts in a literary work are usually reflected or accompanied by the external and internal action. For instance, in Langston Hughes's poem "Theme for English B," the speaker starts by introducing a complication: he has been assigned a topic for a theme. As Jim Belanger notes in his response to the poem, the first verse shows the speaker walking and thinking as he struggles to decide how to write this theme. The external actions (walking and taking the elevator) suggest the internal action (thoughts moving along and then suddenly upward with the idea of what to write in response to the assignment). The conflict here takes place *within the speaker's mind.* The speaker wonders what he can write that will fulfill the assignment, that his instructor will understand, and that will still remain true to himself.

In addition to conflicts inside the mind, literary works may also focus on conflicts *between individuals* (as with Varinka and Byelinkov), *between an individual and a social force* (a community, school, church, workplace), and *between an individual and a natural force* (disease, fire, flood, cold, famine). It's important to note that conflicts do not necessarily belong in just one cate- gory. For instance, in "Theme for English B," the speaker is definitely expe- riencing an internal conflict, yet he also demonstrates the conflicts he feels between himself and various social forces (for example, the discrepancy be- tween his world and the world of his white instructor).

Sometimes you find conflict even in works of nonfiction, where you might not expect it. For example, Ryan Berker's comment on E. B. White's "Education" suggests some of the conflicts the third-grader might face as he changes schools. And, of course, the essay focuses on the conflict between the values and procedures of the public school and the values and procedures of the private school.

Whatever the nature of the conflict, it often forces characters to make a decision: to act or not to act, to behave according to a personal moral code or an external moral code, to compromise or to refuse to compromise, to grow and change or to remain more or less the same. The point at which characters make these choices is usually the climactic moment of the story, poem, or play. The effects or implications of this choice usually represent the conclusion of the literary work.

Irony of Situation

The actions and events in a work may generate a sense of irony. **Irony of situation** is a difference between what a character says and what a char- acter does. For example, Bonnie Dederian notes that Byelinkov claims he is not a dancing bear yet a minute later is, in fact, performing just like the animal he claims to disdain. The discrepancy between what Byelinkov says and what he does is ironic. In this case, the irony is comic, but sometimes the ironic discrepancy can be sad or tragic. If a character claims to be brave, for instance, yet fails to act bravely in a crucial moment, that discrepancy is ironic. This irony, however, might well shock or sadden readers rather than amuse them.

Irony of situation also occurs when a character expects one thing to happen and instead something else happens. For instance, in "Butterflies," the granddaughter expected that her story of the butterflies would please her teacher. The teacher's reaction, however, was very different from the one the child expected. The grandfather's final comment, "Because, you see, your teacher, she buy all her cabbages from the supermarket and that's why," underlines the irony. To the child, the butterflies are pests whose eggs will hatch into worms that destroy the cabbage crop. When she kills butterflies in her grandfather's garden, she is acting practically and usefully. To the teacher, who does not have to grow her own food, the butterflies are simply beautiful creatures of nature.

Terms Related to Actions and Events

Plot: The sequence of events and actions in a literary work.

Structure: The pattern formed by the events and actions in a literary work. Traditional elements of structure are introduction, complications, climax, and conclusion.

Introduction: The beginning of a work, which usually suggests the setting (time and place) and shows one or more of the main characters.

Complications: Events or actions that establish the conflict in a literary work.

Climax: The turning point, often signified by a character's making a significant decision or taking action to resolve a conflict.

Conflict: A struggle between internal and external forces in a literary work.

Conclusion: The ending of a work, which often shows the effects of the climactic action or decision.

Irony of situation: A discrepancy between what is said and what is done or between what is expected and what actually happens.

Exercises: Actions and Events

1. Think about a television program or a film you have seen recently that shows a character facing a conflict. Describe the conflict, its resolution, and your response to that resolution. For instance, would you have made the same choice or choices as the character? Why? Do you find the character's reaction to the conflict realistic? Explain.

2. Think of an ironic situation you have observed or experienced. Briefly describe the situation and then explain why you see it as ironic. Do you consider this ironic situation comic, sad, annoying, enlightening? Explain. Remember that irony always requires a discrepancy between two things (what is said and what is done, for instance).

3. Read any one of the following works from this book.

   "Telephone Conversation," page 415
   "The Revolt of 'Mother,'" page 555
   "The Loudest Voice," page 921
   "Traveling through the Dark," page 1172
   "Graduation in Stamps," page 332
   Trifles, page 608

Then describe the complications that lead one character or speaker to the climactic action or decision. Explain your response to each complication. Do you see one particular complication as more important than any others? Why? Speculate on what might have happened if the character or speaker had responded differently than he or she did to any of the complications you identified.

PEOPLE

The grandfather and grandmother [in "Butterflies"] seem like very wise people to me even though they don't speak correct English. They try to give their granddaughter good advice, and I noticed that both of them tell her to do what the teacher says. What's really good and what makes me say they are wise is that when the granddaughter comes home they ask her about school and they really listen. They are quiet with her when they find out what the teacher said about the butterflies. I think this is because they know she must feel bad or at least confused. What's also good, and shows the grandfather to be wise, is that in the end he makes a comment about why the teacher said what she did. You get the feeling that maybe he will be thinking hard about his advice to "listen to the teacher." *Mark James*

You think about this poem ["Theme for English B"] and you don't right away think about a person or character because it's like the poet, Langston Hughes, is describing something that happened. But when you think about it, this could be something that happened to Hughes or not. Because a poem can be made up—and I think a lot of them are—just like the story we read about the butterflies, which didn't necessarily happen to the author. So when I stopped thinking about just the poet, I started to think about the person that was created in the poem. And you know a lot about him. He is black (but he says "colored," which isn't a word I'd expect him to use), he is 22 years old, and he is taking a class called "English B" that sounds to me like a freshman course from the assignment. So, he's a little old to be starting college, and he mentions his age again in line 16, so maybe he thinks about it a lot. He's on his own, too. Lives at the "Y"—not at home or in a dorm. Maybe being older and on your own would make you especially think about being free, which he talks about. But he doesn't feel completely free—you can see that in line 40 when he says his English instructor is "more free" than he is. *Carlene Indreasano*

At first I was totally sympathetic with Varinka [in the play *The Man in a Case*]. If I ask myself who I would rather spend the afternoon with, there's no contest. Varinka has a good sense of humor and a spirit of adventure (she's not afraid to ride the bicycle, even though it's illegal). Also, she seems to love life—she wants to enjoy apricots and dancing and flowers. Byelinkov, on the other hand, is just depressing. He is too concerned with what his students think—too uptight, not liking to have fun. But then I thought about some of the questions he asks Varinka about why she is marrying him. She sees him one way, and he sees himself another way. He may be boring, but he has a right to be himself, so by the end I have some sympathy for Byelinkov and I can see why he rips up the note—but I did wonder why he picked up the pieces again—maybe just he's so concerned with neatness? *Nathalie LaRochelle*

The father in "Education" has a good sense of humor, and you can see that he laughs at himself as well as at other people. He makes fun of the way parents in New York got on the telephone to each other and to the doctor whenever one of the children in the school got sick. But he also is sort of making fun of himself because he tells about things like picking his son up after his first day at the new school and being deeply relieved when he said his day had been "all right." Underneath almost every sentence, you can feel a father who cares a lot and thinks a lot about his son. *Dora DiFonzo*

Most of us are interested in other people. When we meet someone for the first time, we notice certain things: how the person looks, speaks, and acts, for example. We make judgments according to what we notice. Sometimes, as we get to know the person better, those evaluations are affirmed. Sometimes they are challenged. Interest in other people is more than just idle curiosity. We base our most important life decisions—whom we will work with, whom we will live with, whom we will love—on what we learn from observing, talking with, and interacting with other people.

It's not surprising, then, that when we watch television programs, see movies, or read literature, most of us pay close attention to the people—the

characters—whose lives unfold before us. To stay interested in a film, a novel, a short story, or a play, we must find the characters interesting in some way. Some characters fascinate us by being very different—by living in a distant place or a time long past or by being wildly glamorous or consummately evil. Sometimes characters may capture our minds and hearts because they are people we can relate to. They may face circumstances similar to our own or may act in ways that make us feel as though we are looking in a mirror. Frequently a character intrigues us by displaying a special quality or style: a unique sense of humor, a gift for the absurd, or a profoundly wise way of looking at the world.

Characters: Listening and Observing

Just as we respond to the people in our lives according to what we notice when we look at them and when we listen to them, readers respond to the speech, actions, and appearance of literary characters.

LISTENING Sometimes characters speak with others **(dialogue).** For example, as Mark James observes, the grandparents in "Butterflies" speak kindly to their granddaughter. They show they want the best for her by encouraging her to do well in school. And they ask questions that indicate their concern when she returns from school. We learn a great deal about the grandparents from listening to what they say. It is also interesting to note Mark's comment that the grandparents "don't speak correct English." Debates about what is and is not "correct" English have been going on for centuries and will continue to go on, but, nonetheless, Mark has noticed something important. The grandparents speak a **dialect,** a language that is different from the form taught in school. Noticing the grandparents' speech patterns leads to seeing a gentle irony in their wisdom. They may not know how to speak the "proper" English of the schools, but unlike the schoolteacher, who buys "all her cabbages from the supermarket," they understand the point of their granddaughter's story. Further, they grasp the reason behind the teacher's different interpretation.

When characters speak to each other, they reveal certain qualities about themselves and about their relationships with the characters to whom they speak. The conversation between the grandparents and granddaughter provides one example; the dialogue between Varinka and Byelinkov provides another. He speaks primarily in an orderly, controlled manner, whereas she tends to be as extravagant in her language as she is in her behavior: to Varinka everything is "awfully, awfully nice" or "excellent" or "awfully not." We can learn a great deal about Varinka's and Byelinkov's personalities just by noticing how they speak to each other; understanding their personalities leads to questions about their relationship, their conflicts, their hopes for the future.

In addition to speaking to others, characters sometimes talk to an absent or unspeaking listener **(monologue).** In a play, a character may address thoughts directly to the audience, or the character may speak thoughts aloud without any acknowledgment that an audience is there **(soliloquy).** Such a strategy gives the audience a chance to hear the uncensored thoughts of the character, thoughts that have not been shaped by the interaction with another character in the play.

The character in "Theme for English B" reveals everything we know about him through a monologue: musings that he addresses to his instructor. The reader has a chance to "hear" the thoughts of this character (sometimes called the *persona* or *speaker*) and to learn certain things about him. Carlene Indreasano notices that the speaker mentions twice that he is twenty-two. Wondering why age might be important to him, she links his age with his concern for freedom. You may have noticed other details that the speaker reveals through his monologue, and you may have had a response quite different from Carlene's. For instance, many readers note the questions of race and of nationality that the speaker raises in lines 25–35. The point here is not that everyone should notice the same details—or that some details are necessarily more important than others—but rather that "listening" carefully to what the speaker says leads to learning more about him, to asking questions, and to speculating on the significance of the experience he describes.

OBSERVING Hearing what characters say leads to insights into who they are: what they believe, what they fear, what they hope for, and how they think about themselves and others. Observing characters provides further information. Just as you notice certain external characteristics about a person you meet, readers notice those qualities about a literary character. We know, for instance, that the granddaughter in "Butterflies" wears her hair in "two plaits" (braids) and that she carries a schoolbag, so we can create a picture of her in our minds. We know from Varinka's description that Byelinkov wears round spectacles, perfectly pressed pants, and galoshes (whether or not it's raining). These details allow us not only to visualize Byelinkov but also to make some inferences about his personality.

If you've ever indulged in "people watching" (perhaps at an airport or in a supermarket), you are probably an expert at noticing characteristics (such as age, hair color, manner of dress) and at observing gestures, body movements, and other actions. Nathalie LaRochelle notes two significant actions in *The Man in a Case*. Varinka rides a bicycle (suggesting to Nathalie that Varinka has "a spirit of adventure"), and Byelinkov rips up the note he has written to remind himself to place lilacs in Varinka's hair. Byelinkov's action raises a question for Nathalie and leads her to think further about his **motivation** (the reason behind the action).

Seeing a play is like people watching. Your understanding of the characters is enriched by seeing their dress, gestures, and so on. When you read plays, it's important not to skip the **stage directions** (parenthetical notes by the playwright, at the beginning of the play or just before or just after a speech). These directions indicate what the characters are doing, describe their significant gestures and tone of voice, and often tell as much about the characters as do their words.

Although it may seem easier to notice gestures and movements of characters in plays or in works of fiction than in poetry, the speaker's words often indicate actions. In "Theme for English B," for example, the speaker's walk from the college "on the hill above Harlem" to his room at "the Harlem Branch Y" suggests the physical distance he must travel each day and also may hint at the distance he feels between himself and his white instructor.

By observing literary characters astutely and listening carefully to their words and thoughts, we bring them closer to our own lives. In much the same way, getting to know a person better may bring joy, pain, complication, challenge, frustration, and fulfillment.

Characters: Growing and Changing

In life, all of us grow and change every day. We often don't notice day-to-day changes because they are so small, but if we haven't seen someone for a while—for a year or two or even a few months—we usually notice differences, both in physical appearance and in the way the person thinks, speaks, and acts. To observe changes accurately, and to speculate on what brought about those changes, we have to know a person fairly well.

So it is with literary characters. Many times, a story, play, or poem shows a character who changes—a **dynamic character.** To be interested in the change, we need to know the character fairly well. He or she must come alive for us. To capture our interest, the author must create a **round** (well-developed) **character** rather than a **flat character** who shows only one or two characteristics. When Mark James talks about the grandparents in "Butterflies," he focuses on the qualities he observes: they try to give their granddaughter good advice; they listen to her; they show they are sensitive to her feelings by being quiet with her. Finally, Mark notes that the grandparents, particularly the grandfather, change at the end of the story. The grandfather sees that the teacher does not necessarily have all the right answers, or at least the only right answers. She does not know that butterflies can be harmful to cabbages, so she misunderstands the granddaughter's story. As Mark suggests, the grandfather's final comment strongly suggests that he will rethink his advice to "listen to the teacher."

Although "Butterflies" is a very short story, the grandfather comes alive as a round, dynamic character. The teacher, by contrast, is a flat character. She shows herself only in her single, rather rigid comment to the granddaughter. Flat characters are nearly always **static;** that is, they do not change. Round characters, however, may be either static or dynamic. And noting whether a round character changes or remains the same can lead you to ask significant questions about the work you are reading.

For example, consider Nathalie LaRochelle's observations about Byelinkov. She notices some negative qualities about Byelinkov, but she is also sympathetic to the questions he asks about Varinka's reasons for marrying him. She sees that Byelinkov is more than just a stereotypical fussy old schoolmaster; he shows more than one side to his character. When Nathalie comments on Byelinkov's action at the end of the play—ripping up the note and scattering the pieces—she wonders why he picks the pieces up again. She pushes the question further, speculating that the gathering up might reflect nothing more than Byelinkov's concern with neatness. According to this reading, Byelinkov has not been changed by the events of the afternoon. Now suppose the gathering up indicates that he wants to save the note, that he regrets his rejection both of Varinka and of the romantic gesture the note represents. If so, Byelinkov has grown and developed, and your response to him and to the play might be quite different from your response during the first reading.

Like our readings of the comments and actions of people we meet in everyday life, no single reading of literary characters' words or gestures is necessarily "correct." No single observation represents the "final answer." Instead, multiple possibilities exist. The important thing to remember is that all those possibilities must be suggested—and supported—by details in the text. Obviously we draw on our own life experiences and observations when we think about literary characters, but it's essential to keep in mind that the information that leads to our responses comes from what the work itself offers.

Characters: Point of View

Suppose you hear a friend talk angrily about an argument with a roommate and later hear the roommate describe the same disagreement. What are the chances that the two reports will be the same? Almost none. Accounts such as these are bound to be very different, primarily because they are being told from two distinct **points of view.** What information is offered? What is withheld? Which words are repeated? Which are suppressed? What significance is the incident given? The answers to all these questions depend on who is describing the argument. When you form your own opinion about the disagreement, you take into account who is recounting the incident. In much the same way, readers think carefully about point of view in literary works.

AUTHOR AND SPEAKER Distinguishing author from speaker in a literary work is essential. Unlike roommates describing an argument, poets, playwrights, writers of fiction, and sometimes even writers of nonfiction are not necessarily telling personal stories. Although **authors** often do write about incidents or people from their own lives, they write through a created voice that is not necessarily identical to their own.

Carlene Indreasano points out this distinction between author and speaker. In her comment on "Theme for English B," she says that the events in the poem "could be something that happened to Hughes [the poet] or not." Carlene is absolutely right. In fact, Hughes did attend Columbia University (which does sit "on the hill above Harlem"), but it does not matter whether or not he received the assignment described and responded to it in the way described. What matters is that Hughes has created a **speaker (persona)** who describes receiving and responding to an assignment that asks students to "Go home and write / a page tonight. / And let that page come out of you— / Then, it will be true."

NARRATOR Just as the voice in a poem is called the speaker, the voice that tells a story (in a novel or short fiction) is called the **narrator.** (Sometimes a play has a narrator. Usually, however, a play unfolds directly from the characters' dialogue, along with the playwright's stage directions.)

In fiction, the narrator is sometimes **omniscient** (all-knowing), moving freely into the minds of all the characters. An omniscient narrator can report not only what characters look like, what they do, and what they say but also what they think. A variation is the **limited omniscient** narrator, who sees into the mind of only one character. Obviously, when the thoughts of only one character are reported, readers know more about that character than any other and see the events of the story—as well as the other characters—through that character's eyes.

Sometimes the narrator is also a character in the story. In this case, the narrator uses the **first person** ("I" or "we"). First-person narrators can, of course, report only what is in their own minds or what they see or hear. Omniscient, limited omniscient, and first-person narrators may also make evaluations—for example, they may state that a character is brave or silly or that an action was wise or foolhardy. As readers, we must consider the source of such judgments. Is the narrator **reliable** or **unreliable?** Is there reason to think that the narrator is suppressing information, is lying outright, or is simply incapable of seeing and understanding certain facts? Even if the narrator is reliable, keep in mind that the events are reported from that person's point of view—a different viewpoint might lead to a very different story. Consider, for example, how different the episode in "Butterflies" would be if it were told from the point of view of the teacher.

Sometimes the narrator is **objective,** like a sound camera that reports what it sees and hears. This point of view is used in the story "Butterflies." We are told what the characters do and say, but we are not taken inside their minds. Objective point of view leaves all evaluation and judgment to the reader. Even so, the narrator still has a great deal of power. This particular objective narrator, for example, shows us only the girl and her grandparents; we do not get to see the teacher and to observe for ourselves her response to the girl's story. It's always essential, then, to recognize that the speaker in a poem and the narrator (or characters) in a work of fiction or in drama show us only one way of looking at an experience, an object, a person, or an emotion. There are many other ways—left unexplored except in our own imaginations—of looking at that same experience, object, person, or emotion.

PEOPLE IN NONFICTION Nonfiction—essays, articles, letters, journals, documents—does not usually have fictional characters, yet in every work of nonfiction there is at least one very important point of view: the author's. Identifying and understanding the author's point of view help suggest the work's meaning. For instance, Dora DiFonzo notes that the father who talks about his son in "Education" uses humor. Yet behind the humor, Dora thinks, lie deep concern and—perhaps—a serious comment about the effect of school experiences not only on the child but also on the parents.

Terms Related to People

Characters: The fictional people who are part of the action of a literary work.

Dialogue: A conversation between two or more fictional characters.

Dialect: A variety of a language different from that generally taught in school; may include distinctive pronunciations of words, original vocabulary, or grammatical constructions that are not considered standard.

Monologue: A speech by one character addressed to a silent or absent listener.

Soliloquy: A speech by one character in a play, given while the character is alone on the stage or standing apart from other characters and intended to represent the inner thoughts of the character.

Motivation: The reason or reasons that cause a character to think, act, or speak in a certain way.

Stage directions: Comments by the playwright to provide actors (or readers) with information about actions and ways of speaking specific lines.

Dynamic character: A character who changes in some significant way during the course of the work.

Round character: A character who shows many different facets; often presented in depth and with great detail.

Flat character: A character who usually has only one outstanding trait or feature.

Static character: A character who does not change in any significant way during the course of the work.

Point of view: The position from which the details of the work are reported or described.

Author/speaker/persona/narrator: The *author* is the person who writes the literary work. Do not confuse the author with the *speaker* or *persona,* the voice that is heard in a poem, or the *narrator,* the voice that tells a work of fiction (or sometimes frames a play).

Omniscient narrator: A narrator who knows everything and can report both external actions and conversations as well as the internal thoughts of all characters and who often provides evaluations and judgments of characters and events.

Limited omniscient narrator: A narrator who can report external actions and conversations but who can describe the internal thoughts of only one character. A limited omniscient narrator may offer evaluations and judgments of characters and events.

First-person narrator: A narrator who is also a character in the work and who uses "I" or "we" to tell the story. First-person narrators can report their own thoughts but not the thoughts of others. They may offer evaluations and judgments of characters and events.

Reliable/unreliable narrators: A reliable narrator convinces readers that he or she is reporting events, actions, and conversations accurately and without prejudice. An unreliable narrator raises suspicions in the minds of readers that events, actions, and conversations may be reported inaccurately and that evaluations may reflect intentional or unintentional prejudice.

Objective narrator: A narrator who, like a camera, shows external events and conversations but cannot look inside the minds of characters or offer evaluations and judgments.

Exercises: People

1. Describe your first impressions of a person you now know well, noting what caused you to have these impressions. Then explain your current view of this person. Discuss what events, conversations, actions, or inter-actions either confirmed or changed your initial impression.

2. Think of a film you have seen or a book you have read in which the characters changed significantly. Explain what the characters were like both before and after the change. What motivated the change? What was your response to the change?

3. Read (or reread) any of the works listed in Exercise 3, page 29. Think about how the point of view of the speaker, narrator, or characters affects your response to that work. Try rewriting one section of the work from a different point of view. For example, if the poem or story uses the first-person point of view, try changing every instance of "I" to "he" or "she." Or, if the story or poem is told from an omniscient point of view, try retelling it through the eyes of one of the characters (consider minor characters as well as major characters). Explain how you think the work would change if it were told from this new point of view.

PLACES AND TIMES

This story ["Butterflies"] makes me very confused. I can see the grandparents are farmers who probably grow their own food or maybe sell food, so it seems like they are in an isolated place. Also, I thought maybe this happened a long time ago because in some ways it sounds like a fairy tale or any story that might start like: "In a faraway place, long ago. . . ." But then they talk about the supermarket, so it's got to be modern and not too isolated. And I don't get the part about the teacher buying her cabbages in supermarkets. What does that have to do with the butterflies? *Lara Zoufally*

First I look at the introductory sentence under "Scene" [in *The Man in a Case*], and I see "1898" which, right away, makes me know I am not going to like this play because I like to read modern things. Then, I don't know where Mironitski is (but I figure that out from "Moscow" in the first speech of Varinka—Russia). So now I am totally turned off because it's also a country I don't know much about and am not really interested in. What is funny is that as I read even though there are things I don't know—like "little stale babka"—basically, Byelinkov and Varinka could be this couple I know! She is really crazy and does things that are wild and slightly illegal (driving too fast, etc.). He is—I know this is unbelievable—just like B. Even to the round glasses and the "being neat" stuff. But these people are still together, so maybe there's hope for V and B at the end. (He *could* learn to ride a bike!!!) So how much difference is there between love in Russia (1898) and love in the U.S. (1993)? *Tanya Elizah*

Places and Times in "Theme for English B": I would say the time is both past and present. You start in the present, jump to the past, then back to the present. Places? Well, the speaker is in one place—walking from his college to his room at the Harlem Branch Y—but, on the other hand, there is another place, too, which is inside his mind when he thinks back to the past. I looked up Winston-Salem and it's in the South, and there is also a Durham, N.C., so Durham could be (and probably is) south, too. I think this is important—the North and the South all together because the speaker seems to come to a point about being American and having all the parts (people and parts of the country, I think he means) connected. They have to interact whether they want to or not. *Paul Medino*

This essay ["Education"] must have been written quite a few years ago because I don't think that now even way out in the country they have schools where the teachers have to cook on a stove in the classroom (except for homemaking classes, I mean). And I think it would be a fire hazard to heat a school with a stove. But other than those things, both of the schools seemed like places that could exist today. I liked the way the author seemed to make the point that it didn't matter that the city school had all this fancy equipment. The country school was better because of the people. I think that's true now. There's too much push for more money to build schools and to make the *place* better, but what needs more attention is the people. *Ray Conover*

"Where do you come from?" You can expect new acquaintances to ask this question. Learning where others were born or grew up or discovering where they have lived or traveled helps us understand them better. In some cases, a new friend comes from a place where customs and values are different from ours. For instance, most people in the United States believe that not looking another person in the eye indicates shame or deceit. In some cultures, however, looking directly at another individual is a sign of boldness and lack of respect.

Time can be as important as place in determining the way a person thinks and acts. Consider the way people from different generations characteristically think about circumstances and ideas. For instance, many people who lived through the Great Depression of the 1930s attach more importance to saving money and achieving job security than people who have not experienced widespread poverty and unemployment. Although not all people who live in a particular time think exactly the same way, recognizing the influence of time helps us understand and appreciate the differences we observe in our daily lives.

In reading literature, it is just as important as it is in daily life to think about time and place, the **setting** of the work.

Place

Lara Zoufally raises important questions about the setting of "Butterflies." She notices that the grandparents seem to live in a somewhat isolated place where they farm and grow their own vegetables. But, Lara notes, they can't be too isolated because the grandfather talks about supermarkets. When Lara read this journal entry aloud in class, another student, Rolf Jensen, responded to her final question, "What does that have to do with the butterflies?" He explained that certain butterflies lay eggs on cabbages. The eggs hatch into caterpillars that eat the cabbages. For a farm family, killing the butterflies is a useful—even necessary—act. Like the teacher in the story, Lara (and many readers) may not immediately see the irony in the teacher's response to the granddaughter's story. Rolf, who grew up in a family that farmed, was able to provide the information, related to the setting, that made the story meaningful for Lara.

In addition to talking with others, readers can sometimes uncover information about setting by finding out something about the author's background. Reference books, such as *Contemporary Authors, Dictionary of Literary Biography,* and *American Authors, 1600–1900,* are useful resources. For instance, if you knew that Patricia Grace, the author of "Butterflies," is a Maori New Zealander, you could read about the Maori population. Although you can't assume that Grace is definitely writing about the Maori culture, you might find details that suggest a larger context for the grandparents' way of speaking, for their value of education, and for their relationship with their granddaughter.

So, as you read "Butterflies," it's helpful to think about the location—a somewhat isolated farm—and it's interesting to speculate that the farm may be part of a Maori village in New Zealand. Smaller details of setting are also important. For instance, in "Theme for English B," the speaker describes "the steps from the hill" that lead to the Harlem Y, where he takes the elevator (another detail of setting) and goes to his room (yet another setting). Paul Medino also notes an intriguing aspect of the setting in "Theme for English B." Much of the setting is inside the speaker's mind. The speaker recalls the Southern cities where he was born and went to school. Later, he talks directly to Harlem (lines 18 and 19) as though it were a person. The **exterior** (outside) **setting** in this poem in many ways reflects and enhances our understanding of the **interior setting:** the setting inside the speaker's mind and heart.

Sometimes place is the main focus of a work. For example, in E. B. White's "Education," the two schools, and their surroundings, are central. Details of setting fill the essay. The "cold curbs" and "cinder court" in the city contrast sharply with the country roads and unsupervised playground in the country. The settings imply the more important spiritual difference suggested by the author's final paragraph: his son now sleeps better, and his school day goes by "like lightning."

Time

Tanya Elizah was disappointed when she read the **stage directions** at the beginning of *The Man in a Case* and discovered that the play took place not only in a location she had never heard of but also during a time that she believed would not interest her. She discovered, however, that the conversations, conflicts, and actions of the characters transcended their own time. Varinka and Byelinkov reminded her of people she knew, leading her to ask how much difference there is between love in 1898 Russia and love in the present-day United States.

If Tanya had pursued this question, she might have noticed that, in spite of the many similarities, there are also real differences. In the United States today, a woman would hardly be regarded as revolutionary for riding a bicycle—and even if she were, there are few laws today that forbid to women actions allowed to men. Also, although there are certainly women today who are eager to marry, few of them would spend their twenties living on their parents' farm, apparently engaged in no occupation other than hoping that some man would finally look at them and "see a wife." Varinka's passive way of living seems to contradict her lively, unconventional spirit unless we remember that, in 1898, women of the upper and middle classes had very limited options. Most either married or were dependents of any male relative who would take them in.

The stage directions (essential to the understanding of a play) often provide details of setting; you can learn other details from the comments and observations the characters make. For example, Varinka and Byelinkov both talk about the lilacs and roses in bloom in the garden, so we can infer that the play takes place in the spring. How might this point be significant? Consider, for example, how the drama would change if it took place in a cavernous, dark, wood-paneled living room lit only by the flames in a large fireplace and if Byelinkov placed a sprig of holly instead of lilacs in Varinka's hair.

Writers understand the power of time and often use time in special ways. For instance, Paul Medino says that the time in "Theme for English B" is "both past and present," noting that the poem begins "in the present, jump[s] to the past, then back to the present." The events in the poem do not take place in chronological order, with the speaker telling us about his birth, his early education, then about his present education. Instead, the poem begins in the present, with the instructor's assignment; then there is a **flashback,** a description of events that occurred earlier. Whenever a writer chooses to change time sequence—to work with a structure other than chronological order—the reader should ask why. How is my response affected by the way time is used in this work? For instance, what if the instructor's words (and the question in line 6) were not given until after line 10?

Terms Related to Places and Times

Setting: The time and place of a literary work. Setting includes social, political, and economic background as well as geographic, physical locations.
Exterior setting: Aspects of setting that exist outside of the characters.
Interior setting: Aspects of setting that exist inside the minds and hearts of the characters.
Stage directions: Comments by the playwright to provide actors (or readers) with information about the times and places in which the play is set.
Flashback: An interruption in the chronological order of a work by description of earlier occurrences.

Exercises: Places and Times

1. Write a paragraph or two about an event that took place before you were born (for example, the passage of the 19th amendment, which gave women the right to vote; the Vietnam War; President Kennedy's assassination). Then interview someone who was alive then and remembers the event. After the interview, write another paragraph indicating anything new that you have learned, explaining which of your ideas and impressions were confirmed and which were changed.
2. Think about films and television programs you have seen recently. Then discuss one whose setting strikes you as especially important. First, explain the place and the time and then describe how the setting relates to the characters and their actions. What would happen if these characters and their story were transported to another time or place?
3. Read (or reread) any of the works listed in Exercise 3, page 29. Explain when and where the work takes place. How can you identify times and locations? Think about how the setting affects your response to that work. What aspects of the work would be greatly changed if the setting were changed? Do any aspects seem "timeless" and "placeless" (aspects

that would be meaningful and important in nearly any place or time)? Explain.

WORDS AND IMAGES, SOUNDS AND PATTERNS

You [the instructor] said "Theme for English B" is a poem, but it seems more like a speech or maybe a journal entry to me. The assignment from the speaker's teacher (lines 2–5) is like a poem with rhyme words at the end of lines. Also, I noticed a few other rhymes like "write"/ "white" (lines 27–28), "true"/"you" (lines 36–37), and "me"/"free"/ "B" (line 38 and lines 40–41). But most of this "Theme," when you read it out loud and don't look at the way the lines are set up on the page, could be just a regular paragraph. So why is it a poem? Because it begins and ends with the rhyming lines? *Terence Sullivan*

The butterflies mean one thing to the grandparents and the grand-daughter and something else to the teacher. Now, I think I am sup-posed to sympathize with the granddaughter, and I do feel sorry for her that her teacher didn't like her story. But the teacher's view of butterflies is more like my own. I think they are beautiful, and I was really shocked to think about the granddaughter drawing a picture of killing them. When she said that, it really gave me a strange feeling because I thought it was very odd and not what I expected. So to the granddaughter the butterflies are one thing and to the teacher another (and I feel more or less like the teacher, but I see the granddaughter's reason). So who is right here about butterflies? This is something to think about. *Naomi Rousseau*

Just look at the way Byelinkov and Varinka talk and you know they are two opposite people. Varinka just goes on and on and uses lots of cute expressions like calling Byelinkov a "little school mouse" and talking about his "perfectly pressed pants" and his "sweet little galoshes." Bye-linkov tells her, "You are fond of expletives" (which according to my dictionary means a word or phrase that is not needed for the sense of a sentence). Byelinkov likes to talk in short sentences and to give advice: "Pride can be an imperfect value" and "Being married requires a great deal of responsibility." Varinka likes to compare Byelinkov to things, like a mouse, a dancing bear, and a stale babka and to famous people in Russian history like Lermontov, Tchaikovsky, and Peter the Great. She sees that the roses are beautiful, but he sees beetles in the roses. To my mind, he talks about translating Greek and Latin poetry—which he probably thinks is beautiful—but Varinka sees things around her as beautiful and special and Byelinkov doesn't even really seem to look at those things. *Maureen Wimselski*

The absolute best thing in this essay [E. B. White's "Education"] is the school bus in the city. It's hilarious but it also shows a kind of terror. First White says the bus is "punctual as death." Then the school bus proceeds to "open its mouth" and apparently eat up the boy. Then it takes off like a vicious animal "with an angry growl." To me this says it all. Going to that school is like death—or like getting eaten up by a beast. You can just feel the dread of the kid (or maybe it's the father's dread, maybe he remembers his own school days). *Gerald Stryker*

One of the things that gives life to a fictional character is the way that character speaks. We come to identify certain words and expressions with that particular character.

Style

A character's style, then, is established by the way that person speaks and acts. Of course, authors choose the words and phrases that make up their characters' speech, describe their actions, and create the setting in which they speak and act. We need to keep this in mind when we consider exactly what it is that distinguishes the **style** of one writer from that of another. And, of course, it's essential to ask how a writer's style affects your response to that person's literary work. Why do you like one style better than another? Why does one style bore, puzzle, or annoy you whereas another delights, informs, and makes you want to read on? How does the author's style relate to the meaning or meanings you discover in the work or to the questions the work raises?

Tone

Tone, the attitude of the author to the characters and situations in the work, is closely related to style. For example, Gerald Stryker notes that, in "Education," E. B. White uses humorous images that are tinged with seriousness (even terror). The yellow city school bus that "swallows" the child in the story is funny, but White's words also suggest that a child can be overwhelmed by the trappings and demands of certain kinds of schooling. The tone here is complex, and it suggests the complexity the author sees in his subject.

Diction

Diction (choice of words) helps to establish a writer's style and tone. Some writers, for example, choose to use many descriptive words, whereas some use almost none. Consider the contrast between the speeches Wendy Wasserstein gives her characters in *The Man in a Case* and the language of the narrator and characters in Patricia Grace's "Butterflies." Wasserstein's play is filled with language that appeals to all the senses **(imagery);** we can easily conjure up the scent of the lilacs and roses; the anticipated delicious apricots and cream; the picture of Byelinkov wrapped in his "quilts and curtains" as he retires for the night. In contrast, Grace's story focuses on only one image: that of the butterflies. The description is spare and, as Lara Zoufally (page 37) notes, the story "sounds like a fairy tale or any story that might start like: 'In a faraway place, long ago. . . .'" Lara notices, then, that the language of "Butterflies" makes it sound like one of those childhood tales, perhaps a fable. The story's language raises questions about its meaning. Does it have a simple moral—or lesson—as a fable does? Or is Patricia Grace's story more complex than that?

Syntax

Syntax is the arrangement of words in phrases or sentences and the arrangement of phrases or sentences in paragraphs (fiction), speeches (plays), or lines and stanzas (poetry). Choices related to syntax are aspects of a writer's style. Terence Sullivan raises an important question when he notes that much of "Theme for English B" sounds like a paragraph of regular prose. Unless you look at the arrangement of the sentences and phrases into lines and stanzas, you might not be aware that you are reading a poem. Why does Langston Hughes choose this syntax to write about this experience? The speaker, after all, describes an assignment to which most students would respond by writing a carefully planned essay with an opening paragraph, thesis statement, body, and conclusion. Why, then, does he respond with a poem?

Rhythm and Rhyme

Closely connected to the syntax of a work—and also part of a writer's style—are **rhythm** (the pattern of sound) and **rhyme** (the matching of final sounds in two or more words). The rhythms of many parts of "Theme for English B," for example, are the rhythms of everyday prose speech. Yet, as Terence Sullivan notes, the instructor's assignment at the beginning sounds like a traditional poem. You can read these lines aloud in an exaggerated way to hear the regular beat:

> Go home and write
> a page tonight.
> And let that page come out of you—
> Then, it will be true.

It's intriguing that the instructor's words have such a regular pattern, seeming to lead logically to the speaker/student's otherwise unconventional essay poem. Perhaps this student sees and hears the world in terms of poetic sound and patterns?

Terence Sullivan also comments on rhyme; he wonders if a poem that doesn't rhyme in a regular pattern is really a poem, raising the question of how to distinguish between poetry and prose. Terence notes that the poem begins and ends with rhyming lines, creating, in a sense, bookends of strong end rhymes to frame the rest of the poem. In addition to using end rhymes, the poet also uses internal rhyme. Look at lines 16 and 17, for instance.

> It's not easy to know what is **true** for **you** or me
> at twenty-**two,** my age.

And the next three lines have six one-syllable words that rhyme with "you"; the repetition of these words and, of course, the fact that they rhyme contribute to a subtle, insistent poetic rhythm even while the speaker seems simply to be conversing in everyday speech.

Notice also, in line 24, the list of records the speaker likes: "Bessie, bop, or Bach." These choices represent a wide range of musical taste, and notice also that the words sound musical as you pronounce them. The identical initial sounds create **alliteration.**

Of course, alliteration is not a device used strictly by poets: the romantic Varinka, as Maureen Wimselski notes, describes Byelinkov's "perfectly pressed pants." The rhythmic sound of the initial *p*'s underlines the extravagance of her speech and makes many readers smile in sympathy at Byelinkov's complaint that she is "fond of expletives."

Figurative Language

As they work, writers choose whether and when to use **figurative language:** words or expressions that carry more than their literal meaning. Wendy Wasserstein, for instance, fills Varinka's speeches with **metaphors** (comparisons of unlike objects). Varinka calls Byelinkov "my little school mouse," "my sweetest dancing bear," and "my little stale babka." Byelinkov also makes comparisons, but his are less direct; he uses **similes** (comparisons of unlike things using the words "like" or "as"), such as "You speak about me as if I were your pet" and "You dance like a school mouse."

Sometimes the writer's figurative language allows a reader to see an object in a new way. For example, in "Theme for English B," the speaker uses an **apostrophe** (he speaks directly to an inanimate object or place) when he says: "I feel and see and hear. Harlem, I hear you." The apostrophe seems to show that he feels connected to Harlem, perhaps as he would feel connected to a close friend or relative. During class discussion of this work, Terence Sullivan (whose response to the poem appears on page 42) wondered why, when the speaker says he also hears New York, he does not choose to speak directly to that city as he does to Harlem.

Personification means giving an inanimate object the characteristics of a person or animal. E. B. White's beastlike school bus is an excellent example of this kind of figurative language. We can see the bus bearing down on its innocent victim, and we certainly get the impression that city schooling, for White, has more to do with being a helpless captive than a willing participant.

A writer sometimes repeats a word or image so many times in a literary work that you begin to wonder why. Why, for instance, does Patricia Grace call her story "Butterflies" and use butterflies as the central image? Naomi Rousseau writes that the "butterflies mean one thing to the grandparents and the granddaughter and something else to the teacher." And, to the reader, the butterflies may come to have a meaning different from either of those two. The butterflies, then, become a **symbol,** standing for more than just winged creatures that lay eggs on cabbages. The butterflies may indicate the great diversity of ways to look at the world around us; they may suggest the need not to limit ourselves, but to stay open to many possibilities.

Verbal Irony

Just as there can be discrepancies between what a character says and what a character does or between what a character believes to be true and what the reader knows to be true (irony of situation, page 27), so, too, can there be discrepancies between what a character or author says and what he or she means **(verbal irony).** For example, when Varinka compares Byelinkov to Lermontov, Tchaikovsky, and Peter the Great (all respected Russian men), Byelinkov adds, "Ivan the Terrible." Of course, Byelinkov does not really mean he is like the merciless tyrant; he is being ironic. But Varinka either doesn't pick up on the irony or replies with an ironic statement of her own, "Yes, him too." Whether Varinka is intentionally ironic or not, the discrepancies underline the enormous differences between these two would-be lovers.

Allusions

To understand the irony just described, you have to know that Lermontov, Tchaikovsky, and Peter the Great are all admired figures from Russian history and that Ivan the Terrible (whose name should give him away) was a ruthless czar. When writers use **allusions** (references to events, people, and places outside the work itself), you can usually figure out what is going on from the context. However, if you are interested in adding an extra dimension to your reading, it's easy enough to find the references in a dictionary or encyclopedia. *Webster's New World Dictionary,* for instance, would let you know that Lermontov was a Russian poet and novelist, Tchaikovsky a composer, and Peter the Great a czar. Knowing these specific definitions underlines the extent of Varinka's exaggerations; she considers—or perhaps wishes—her fiancé to be the equal of the most outstanding writers, composers, and rulers of their country.

Terms Related to Words and Images, Sounds and Patterns

Style: The way an author chooses words; arranges them in lines, sentences, paragraphs, or stanzas; and conveys meaning through the use of imagery, rhythm, rhyme, figurative language, irony, and other devices.

Tone: The attitude of the author toward the subject of the work.

Diction: Choice of words.

Imagery: Words that appeal to the five senses: touch, taste, sight, hearing, and smell.

Syntax: The way words are arranged in phrases or sentences and the way phrases or sentences are arranged in paragraphs (fiction), speeches (plays), or lines and stanzas (poetry).

Rhythm: Pattern of sound.

Rhyme: The matching of final sounds in two or more words.

Alliteration: The repetition of identical initial sounds in neighboring words or syllables.

Figurative language: Words or expressions that carry more than their literal meaning.

Metaphor: Comparison of two unlike things.

Simile: Comparison of two unlike things, using the words "like" or "as."

Apostrophe: Addressing an inanimate object or place as if it were alive.

Personification: Giving an inanimate object the qualities of a person or animal.

Symbol: In a literary work, an object, action, person, or animal that stands for something more than its literal meaning.

Verbal irony: A discrepancy between what is said and what is meant or between what is said and what the reader knows to be true.

Allusion: A reference to a person, place, object, or event outside the work itself.

Exercises: Words and Images, Sounds and Patterns

1. Think of three friends or acquaintances who speak in a distinctive way. Imagine a conversation between these three people (even though they may not know each other). Write the conversation and then explain briefly what special qualities you notice in the way these three people speak. What would make you recognize these people if you could hear but not see them?

2. For one day, carry a small notebook with you and write down every example of figurative language you see or hear. Keep your mind open to all kinds of possibilities: explanations in textbooks, the language of sports reporters, the speeches of politicians, the exaggerations of advertising. And, of course, stay alert to overheard conversations as well as to your own speech. At the end of the day, write a brief comment describing your discoveries and your response to those discoveries.

3. Read, reread, or reconsider any of the works listed in Exercise 3, page 29. Try reading a section (a stanza, a paragraph or two) aloud and (if possible) have someone else read the same section aloud so that you can listen. What do you notice about sounds, images, words, patterns? Describe your response to the author's (or a character's) diction, to a particularly striking or strange image, to an intriguing use of figurative language, or to the rhythm (or rhyme) of a work.

IDEAS

The following excerpts from journal entries show the ideas students discovered as they read, discussed, and thought about "Butterflies," *The Man in a Case,* and "Theme for English B." The italicized sentences represent general statements that could apply beyond the work itself.

"Butterflies" shows how easy—and how dangerous—it is to look at the world around you in just one way. The teacher sees only the beauty in the butterfly and doesn't even consider any other possibility. Because she doesn't know about, or try to find out about, another possibility, her student goes home very puzzled and unhappy. *Lara Zoufally*

The butterflies symbolize destruction to the grandparents and beauty to the teacher. Who is right? Neither. *People see things according to their own perspective and sometimes this causes problems in communication.* Sure, maybe the teacher should have asked the granddaughter about her picture without making such a judgment. But, on the other hand, the grandparents maybe need to look more carefully and see that even though the butterflies cause problems, they are also beautiful. *Naomi Rousseau*

"Theme for English B" has ideas both of separation and of connection. The speaker is physically apart from his instructor. The instructor is at the college on the hill in NYC, and the speaker is back in his room in Harlem. But the speaker is writing an assignment for the instructor, so even though there's separation, there's connection. And I think this is very important and what is meant by "As I learn from you, / I guess you learn from me." The instructor learns from the student while the student learns from the teacher because both have different experiences and knowledge to give. *What is meant here is that everyone can gain from listening to someone else who is different from themselves. Paul Medino*

As the speaker walks and walks to his room in Harlem, it seems like his thoughts are walking, too. And you get the impression that those thoughts walk all over America. He's looking at what it means to be a black person in America, and he's arguing that white people have to see that black people are just as American as they are. Even for people who may not like it. As he says, the instructor is "a part of me, as I am a part of you." *Whites had better realize that blacks are part of America too, and that there has to be some kind of connection between the two parts. Mark James*

Varinka makes fun of Byelinkov for being so stuffy and wearing ga-loshes all the time. True, he has a rather rigid way of looking at things, but Varinka is also rigid. For instance, she wants to get married to have "the life everyone else has" and to "not be different." And she wants Byelinkov to fit into one specific role—a hero, like Peter the Great. *To me, people have to let others be themselves. Love doesn't come from trying to change someone. You have to accept people as they are.* Nathalie LaRochelle

I kept thinking and thinking about the title: *The Man in a Case.* I saw the line where Byelinkov says that he thought he "would grow old preserved like those which are left over, wrapped suitably in my case of curtains and quilts." I realized that later Varinka tells him, "You are wrapping yourself under curtains and quilts." So, to me, some of the curtains and quilts were the real ones on his bed, but they were also a metaphor. Those curtains and quilts are like a cocoon, an outer case, that Byelinkov has to protect himself against experiences of the world. But you get the impression that Byelinkov will never "hatch" out into maturity. *Protection like that has a cost. Insulation against experiences of the world—even something simple like eating peaches and cream for lunch—means that a person may lose the chance of human connection (of love, in this case).* Maureen Wimselski

White may say that the only difference he sees in the two schools is that his son "sleeps better at night." It's clear to me, however, that he's really saying something quite different. *A simple and uncomplicated schooling is better in every way than a school that has too many trend-setting new programs.* In the city, his son gets "worked on," but in the country it seems to be the boy who does the work and the teacher is just there to help. She gives him food for his body and food for his mind. It's simple and direct—not planned by a dietician or other fancy experts. Marianne Bachmann

After reading a work carefully, with mind and spirit fully open to actions, events, people, places, times, sounds, images, words, and patterns, a reader may well feel overwhelmed. "What does it all mean?" "What's the point?" "What am I supposed to get from this?" "What's the lesson here?" "What's the author trying to say?" These questions—and others—often nag insistently at us, giving us the sense that even though the work evoked a definite response, something more has been left undiscovered.

These questions lead you to consider **theme,** the central idea you seek as you read a work and think about it. The theme of a work is a generalization: an idea that can be broadly applied both to the work itself and to real-life situations outside the work. For example, consider Maureen Wimselski's statement: *"Protection like that has a cost. Insulation against experiences of the world—even something simple like eating peaches and cream for lunch—means that a person may lose the chance of human connection (of love, in this case)."* The italicized words represent a general statement of theme that could apply to people and circumstances very different from those in Wasserstein's play. The details from the play are examples that demonstrate how Maureen arrived at her larger idea, her statement of theme.

It's important to understand that "meaning" is not fixed in literature. Two people reading the same work may see different themes. One person reading a work at age twenty and the same work at age thirty or forty-five may see different themes. Literary scholars reading the same work frequently see different themes. So, questions such as "What am I supposed to get from this?" do not have a specific, easily defined answer. Although it's interesting—and often helpful—to know what others think about a work, their ideas should not define what any other reader is "supposed to get" from the work.

Some literary works, such as fables and biblical parables, do have a lesson or a moral that is directly stated by the writer. Most works, however, convey their meaning indirectly. Whether or not there is something to be learned—and what that something is—depends on what the reader discovers in the work and on how those discoveries interact with what the reader already knows, thinks, or feels about the subject of the work. Sometimes a work of literature causes us to think differently about something; sometimes it reinforces what we already believe, adding new details to support our current beliefs and emotions; sometimes we encounter a work whose main idea offends or angers us. A reader who is affronted by a work is likely to see a very different theme than the reader whose values are reaffirmed by the same work.

What a writer intended to say is not necessarily what the work "says" to various readers. So the question "What is the writer trying to say?" is not really very helpful. For example, a writer may convey one thing to an audience from her or his own time and something quite different to an audience reading the same work a century later. The reader—not the author—defines the theme, although, of course, the reader's ideas relate directly to what the author has written.

As you read the students' responses at the beginning of this section, you almost certainly noticed that those who commented on the same works had quite different views. For instance, Lara Zoufally focused on the teacher's narrow view in "Butterflies," whereas Naomi Rousseau thought that both the grandparents and the teacher lacked something in the way they looked at butterflies. As you read the story, you might have discovered still another theme. Notice that both Lara and Naomi use specific details and examples from the story to support their generalization (their statement of theme). Because they offer evidence from their reading, it's easy to see how they arrived at their ideas. Direct references to the work make these statements of theme convincing and thought-provoking.

As you think about a work and the main idea it conveys to you, remember to support your observations with specific references to the work. Don't be intimidated by the thought that the theme must be some hidden secret. Instead, look at what you know about the work, what you have felt, what you have observed as you read. Work from the strength of what you do know rather than assuming that you are faced with a mysterious puzzle.

CHAPTER 5

Exercises: Theme

1. Choose a film that you have seen more than once and that you think is worth seeing again. Write a paragraph or two explaining why you feel so strongly about this film. As part of your explanation, include a brief discussion of the film's theme.

2. Write a response to one of the students' comments at the beginning of this section. Explain why you agree or disagree with the way that student sees the work in question.

3. Read, reread, or rethink any of the selections listed in Exercise 3, page 29. Write a response that includes your view of the work's theme. Be sure to make specific references to the work to explain what you say.

3

Continuing the Conversation: Considering Genre and Listening to Other Voices

Chapter 2 introduces terms people use to talk about literature. This chapter suggests two other useful ways to expand the conversation about literature. First, four short sections describe the major literary genres: fiction, poetry, drama, and the essay. Next, the text introduces ways of listening to the voices of other people who have read and commented on literary works in which you have an interest.

Genre is a French term used in literary criticism to indicate a type or form of literature. Understanding the history of the four major literary genres and considering various strategies for reading them should add to your pleasure as well as your understanding of fiction, poetry, drama, and essays. Understanding genre also provides you with new ways to talk and write about literature.

AN INTRODUCTION TO SHORT FICTION

Cave paintings showing the outcome of a hunting expedition or imagining the exploits of a fantastic beast testify to the ancient roots of the human love for stories. From the time when people first discovered how to communicate through spoken words or written symbols, they have instructed, amazed, warned, and entertained each other with tales—both true and fictional.

Early Forms of Fiction

ALLEGORY Allegories are stories in which each character, action, and setting stands for one specific meaning. For example, in John Bunyan's allegory *A Pilgrim's Progress,* a character named Christian represents the virtues associated with the ideal member of that faith. In the allegory, Christian passes through a landscape of temptations and dangers with areas symbolically named the "Slough of Despond," the "City of Destruction," and the "Valley of Humiliation" before he reaches the "Celestial City." Allegories, which are intended to teach moral lessons, may also be written as poetry and drama.

MYTH Myths often tell the stories of ancient deities, sometimes describing their exploits, sometimes explaining how a particular god or goddess came into being. Other myths address the mysteries of nature, including the creation of the universe and its diverse inhabitants. Ancient people probably invented myths as a way to make sense of the world in which they lived. For instance, gods and goddesses were described as experiencing human emotions—hate, jealousy, love, passion, despair—and as facing the human conflicts these feelings create.

LEGEND Legends recount the amazing achievements of fictional characters or exaggerate the exploits of people who actually lived. For example, the story of Paul Bunyan is apparently based on a real man, but his size, his blue ox (Babe), and his astounding feats are inventions of those who told and retold tales of the resourceful lumberjack. Legends—which often include the entertaining tall tale—frequently praise and confirm traits that a society particularly values. For instance, Paul Bunyan works hard, never backs down from a fight, and knows how to enjoy a party—all qualities that were greatly admired during the early years of the American westward expansion.

FAIRY TALE Like myths, fairy tales focus on supernatural beings and events. They are not peopled by gods and goddesses, however, but by giants, trolls, fairy godmothers, and talking animals who happily coexist with humans—both royalty and common folk. Fairy tales do not attempt to explain the natural world or to affirm national values but instead focus on the struggle between clearly defined good and evil. In fairy tales, good always prevails over evil, although—in those that have not been censored to suit modern sensibilities—the "good" is often achieved by rather terrifying means. Figures of evil drop into pots of boiling oil, are flayed alive, or are cooked into (evidently tasty) pies.

FABLE The best-known fables are those that were told by the Greek slave Aesop. Fables usually feature animals who can talk and, in general, act just as rationally (and just as irrationally) as humans. Unlike myths, legends, and fairy tales—but like allegories—fables state an explicit lesson. For instance, nearly everyone knows the story of the race between the boastful Hare who runs quickly ahead of the plodding Tortoise, stops for a rest, and is beaten to the finish line by his slow yet determined rival. "Slow but steady wins the race," Aesop told his listeners, stating specifically the moral he wished to teach.

PARABLE Like fables, parables teach a lesson or explain a complex spiritual concept. Unlike a fable, which tells a story that demonstrates the stated moral, a parable is a narrative that serves as an analogy for the principle being taught. For example, the New Testament contains many parables that suggest the relationship between God and humans. In one parable, God is depicted as a Good Shepherd who looks for one lost sheep in a flock of one hundred. In another parable, God is compared to a father who rejoices at the return of a son who has strayed.

Modern Short Fiction

All of these early forms of short fiction still exist today. In the nineteenth century, however, a new form evolved. It was exemplified by the work of writers such as Guy De Maupassant in France; Anton Chekhov in Russia; George Eliot and Thomas Hardy in Great Britain; and Edgar Allan Poe, Nathaniel Hawthorne, Herman Melville, Mary Wilkins Freeman, and Sarah Orne Jewett in the United States.

THE REALISTIC SHORT STORY The nineteenth-century **realistic short story** differed from early forms of fiction in many ways. Nineteenth-century realistic short stories focused on scenes and events of everyday life. Ordinary men, women, and children—not fabulous gods, powerful giants, and talking animals—inhabited these stories. Characters were developed more fully; rather than representing one primary trait, the central figures of short stories exhibited the complexities and contradictions of real people. Plots became more intricate to suggest the workings of characters' souls and minds and to depict their external actions. Settings became more than briefly sketched backdrops; times and places were described in vivid detail. Most importantly, realistic short stories moved away from teaching one particular moral or lesson. Although the theme of a short story often suggested certain values, readers were expected to find meaning for themselves. The author no longer served up a moral or a lesson in a direct and obvious way.

The realistic short story, as it evolved from the nineteenth century to the twentieth, usually focuses on a conflict experienced by a character or group of characters. Often, by facing that conflict, the characters come to know themselves (and other people) more fully. A short story that shows a young person moving from innocence to experience is called a **story of initiation.** A related form is the **story of epiphany,** in which a character experiences a conflict that leads to a sudden insight or profound understanding. (The word "epiphany" comes from the name of the Christian feast day celebrating the revelation of the infant Jesus to the Magi. These wise men, who had traveled from the East, returned to their own countries deeply moved and changed by what they had seen in Bethlehem.)

THE NONREALISTIC SHORT STORY The nineteenth century also saw the development of the **nonrealistic short story.** For example, many of Nathaniel Hawthorne's stories introduced supernatural beings, strange settings, or plot events that could not be explained by the traditional laws of nature. (See, for example, "Young Goodman Brown" page 634.) Although these nonrealistic stories often incorporated elements of earlier forms of short fiction (for instance, characters—human or animal—with unusual powers), they shared certain qualities with the realistic short story. Their characters were more fully developed and had spiritual and psychological depth; their plots were more complex; and their settings were more fully described. Most importantly, their themes often led the reader to speculate, wonder, and question rather than to accept a directly stated moral or lesson.

In the twentieth century, writers such as Donald Barthelme ("Me and Miss Mandible," page 904) and María Luisa Bombal ("New Islands," page 650) continue the tradition of the nonrealistic short story. Unbound by realistic dimensions of time and space, unfettered by the laws of physics or even by the conventions of human psychology, these writers push their own imaginations—and the imaginations of their readers—in new, and sometimes unsettling, directions. Reading nonrealistic fiction requires what the nineteenth-century poet Samuel Taylor Coleridge called "the willing suspension of disbelief"—the willingness to read, enjoy, and ponder settings, plots, and characters that seem strange and unconventional. Even more so than realistic fiction, nonrealistic stories lead in many diverse directions rather than toward a single theme.

A Word about Fiction and Truth

What distinguishes true stories from fiction? An easy answer is that true stories tell about events that actually happened to people who actually lived, whereas fiction tells about events and people who are imaginary. It's often difficult, however, to make such neat distinctions clearly. For example, consider a short story set during a recent time in a familiar city. As you read, you may recognize the names of streets and remember some of the events of the era. Although most of the characters who inhabit this familiar city are imagined, occasionally one of those fictional characters meets—or refers to—a person who was alive at the time the story takes place. To what extent, then, is this story true? Are only the parts that can be verified by your own observation (street names, for example) or through historical reports (assassinations, wars, economic upheavals) true? Or are the created characters—their actions, their conflicts, their emotions—also true in some sense? And what about stories that take place entirely outside the realm of what we currently recognize as reality—for example, stories set in the future or in an imagined country with no familiar patterns or rules? In what ways might such stories tell the "truth"? Consider such possibilities as human emotions, conflicts, and interactions that the story portrays.

As you read the short stories that follow, think about the people you meet, the places they live, the conflicts they face. Sort out for yourself what truths these people, places, and conflicts have to offer. Consider how those truths fit—or do not fit—with your life, your hopes, your fears, your values.

✣ GUIDELINES
Short Fiction

These considerations provide guidelines for reading, thinking about, and writing about short fiction. Although not every consideration applies to every story, these guidelines can help you read more deeply and experience the story more fully.

1. Read the opening paragraphs carefully several times. Jot down questions, predictions, and expectations for the rest of the story. After you finish reading the story, look back at your early responses. To what extent were your questions answered and your predictions and expectations fulfilled?

2. As you read, list the conflicts in the story (consider major as well as minor characters). Note how the characters face and resolve (or do not resolve) those conflicts. Then discuss the implications of the characters' actions (or inaction).

3. To continue thinking about conflict, identify a character who faces a difficult choice, perhaps a moral decision. What would you do under the same or similar circumstances? Compare your imagined response to the character's response.

4. Describe the setting of the story in detail. Remember to consider the following: (a) large elements of place (city, state, section of country, nation); (b) small elements of place (a bedroom, a business office, a battlefield); (c) large elements of time (century, part of century); (d) small elements of time (day, night, season of the year, holiday). How important is setting to the meaning you find in the story? How would the story be changed if any (or several) of the elements of setting were changed?

5. Consider the viewpoint from which the story is told. How would the story change if that viewpoint were different? Try retelling any part of the story through the eyes of a different character or through the eyes of an objective observer.

6. Read the story once quickly, then jot down your responses, impressions, and questions. Wait several days, then reread the story slowly and carefully. Return to your original responses, impressions, and questions to consider what you now have to add or to change. Note the reasons for making these changes and additions.

7. Note any objects, animals, gestures, or aspects of nature that are mentioned repeatedly or receive unusual emphasis. What do these elements contribute to your experience of the story? In what ways might they add to the meaning(s) you see?

(continued)

Short Fiction (*continued*)

8. Think about the comparisons and contrasts you see in the story. For example, are there two characters who face the same situation yet act very differently? Consider also comparisons you can make between the characters, setting, conflicts, and action in two different stories. What significance can you see in the differences and similarities you've discovered?

9. Compare any situation, character, choice, or decision in the story to some aspect of your own life. Explain how the story is different from or similar to your own experience.

10. Write a continuation of the story. For example, imagine what will happen immediately after the ending scene. Or project what one or more of the characters might be like in five or ten years. Explain the thinking that led you to your speculations.

AN INTRODUCTION TO POETRY

Long before humans could read or write, they created, understood, and valued poetry. Historic events, natural catastrophes, and dramatic predictions were remembered and embellished in the verses of song-makers, court poets, and minstrels, who also invented ballads recording the universal emotions evoked by lovers' quarrels, forbidden romance, and family fights.

The works of early poets were recited or sung; the audience gathered in groups and listened. These ancient settings suggest the important connection between the sound of a poem and the meaning it creates. More than any other qualities, rhythm and structural patterns distinguish poetry from prose. Today, most poetry is read silently and alone. To bring poetry to life, however, we must reach back into the past to revive its music.

Suggestions for Reading Poetry

When you first approach a poem, try reading it aloud. Stay alert to the ways the words sound as you pronounce them. You may notice rhyme or alliteration (see page 45), although not every poem uses these sound devices.

ENJAMBMENT Listen carefully to how the lines flow together. Be aware of **enjambment:** the carrying over of meaning and sound from one line to the next, with no pause between lines. Consider this example from Sappho's "To me he seems like a god."

> To me he seems like a god
> as he sits facing you and
> hears you near as you speak
> softly and laugh

in a sweet echo that jolts
the heart in my ribs.

Although there are six lines, there is only one sentence. If you come to a full stop at the end of each line as you read, the poem will sound disjointed and the meaning will be obscured. Do *not* read these lines like this:

To me he seems like a god *(long pause)*
as he sits facing you and *(long pause)*
hears you near as you speak *(long pause)*

Rather, read them like this:

To me he seems like a god *(very brief pause)* as he sits facing you and *(very brief pause)* hears you near as you speak *(very brief pause)* softly and laugh *(very brief pause)* in a sweet echo that jolts *(very brief pause)* the heart in my ribs.

Notice that when you pay attention to the enjambment, the lines flow together and become more coherent. The sound and meaning work together rather than against each other.

At this point you may well wonder why poets bother to write lines rather than standard sentences and paragraphs. Often, poets use enjambed lines because they want the reader to pause (but only for an instant) so that the next words (those that begin the next line) will be particularly noticed.

Enjambment, then, lets the poet emphasize a phrase or idea or (sometimes) surprise the reader with the thought on the next line. Look at enjambed lines with aroused curiosity and read them with a sense of discovery. Try to discover why the poet chose to end the line at this particular point rather than at another.

Once you understand how enjambment works, you'll be able to read poetry aloud smoothly and with enjoyment. Try, also, to keep it in mind as you read poetry silently. Learn to "hear" with your mind so that every experience with poetry, whether actually voiced or not, combines sound and meaning.

SYNTAX The **syntax** (the arrangement of words in a sentence) of poetry is sometimes different from the syntax of prose. Consider, for example, these lines from W. H. Auden's "Unknown Citizen":

Except for the War till the day he retired
He worked in a factory and never got fired

Most speakers would use this word order:

Except for the War, he worked in a factory till the day he retired and never got fired.

The poet inverts the expected order of the phrases and clauses within the sentence to focus our attention both on the length of the citizen's working time ("till the day he retired") and on his steadiness ("never got fired"). In addition, the inversion allows for the rhyme of "retired" and "fired," which further emphasizes the length of the citizen's work life.

Pay attention to the syntax as you read, especially if you are pondering the meaning of some lines. Often, experimenting with ways to rearrange the words and phrases will lead you to see meanings you had not noticed before.

STRUCTURE   Although poetry was originally a strictly oral art form, for centuries it has also been a visual form. When asked how they differentiate prose from poetry, many readers say, "The way it looks on the page" or "The way the lines are arranged."

Closed Form   In many traditional forms of poetry, the lines and stanzas must be arranged according to established patterns. Japanese haiku is one example. Each haiku must have seventeen syllables (in the original Japanese), generally divided into three lines. Here is a haiku:

> The piercing chill I feel:
> my dead wife's comb, in our bedroom,
> under my heel . . .
>
> Taniguchi Buscon
(translated by Harold G. Henderson)

Other examples of traditional poetic forms are the ode and the sonnet. When you read closed-form poetry, ask yourself why the poet chose this form and how the form contributes to the meaning the work conveys to you.

Open Form   Many readers think of closed form as an inherent part of poetry. And, indeed, for centuries poems from all cultures and in all languages conformed to set rules of line, stanza, and/or syllable length and often had set rhyme patterns. In the nineteenth century, however, poets began to experiment, resisting the limitations they believed were imposed by traditional poetic forms.

These poets determined the length of their own lines and stanzas, used unexpected rhythms and rhymes, and frequently did away with rhyme entirely. For an example of open-form poetry, read e.e. cummings's "Buffalo Bill's" (page 1167).

When you read such a poem, ask yourself why the poet chose not to use a traditional form. How would the meaning of the poem be changed if the same images and themes were set in a carefully rhymed sonnet, for example, rather than an unrhymed series of lines that are uniquely arranged?

Types of Poetry

Although not all poems fit neatly into categories, the two major types of poems are **narrative** and **lyric.** Narrative poems tell stories. They often present a significant episode or series of episodes in the life of one primary character (or, sometimes, two primary characters). Lyric poems express the feelings, musings, or emotions of a single character (the speaker).

NARRATIVE POETRY Examples of narrative poems include long **epics** (such as Homer's *Iliad* or Milton's *Paradise Lost*) as well as short **ballads** (such as "Lord Randal," page 833). Nearly all narrative poems stress action and suggest a conflict. Many focus on a moral choice or difficult decision. For examples of modern narrative poems, see William Stafford's "Traveling through the Dark" (page 1172), Seamus Heaney's "Mid-Term Break" (page 203), or Kristine Batey's "Lot's Wife" (page 687).

LYRIC POETRY The word "lyric" comes from the lyre, the Greek instrument used for musical accompaniment of poetry, which was often sung or chanted. Although a lyric poem may depict an outward action, it generally focuses on inward reactions, insights, or responses. Lyric poems are written in many forms, including the following:

Italian (or Petrarchan) Sonnet The **Italian sonnet** is divided into two parts, an **octave** (eight lines) with the rhyme scheme *abbaabba* and a **sestet** (six lines) with the rhyme scheme *cdecde* (or some variation). The octave usually develops an idea or image, and the sestet comments on this idea or image. For an example, see William Wordsworth's "The world is too much with us" (page 411).

English (or Shakespearean) Sonnet The **English sonnet** falls into three **quatrains** (four lines) and a concluding **couplet** (two lines). The rhyme scheme is *abab cdcd efef gg*. The first three quatrains usually develop an idea or image, and the closing couplet comments on this idea or image. For an example, see Shakespeare's "Let me not to the marriage of true minds" (page 694).

Open Form Open-form lyric poems do not follow any particular pattern or structure.

GUIDELINES
Poetry

These considerations provide guidelines for reading, thinking about, and writing about poetry. Although not every consideration applies to every poem, these guidelines can help you read more deeply and experience the poem more fully.

1. After reading and thinking about a poem, read it aloud several times to an audience (at least two or three people). With each reading, use a different tone of voice and emphasize different lines and words. Discuss with your audience how the different readings changed the poem for them. Explain your discoveries about the possible ways to read this poem.
2. Write a brief character sketch of the speaker in the poem. What values do you think the speaker holds? What is your response to

(continued)

Poetry (*continued*)

these values? Refer to specific details in the poem to support your evaluation.

3. Using Christopher Marlowe's "The Passionate Shepherd to His Love" (page 692) and Sir Walter Raleigh's "The Nymph's Reply to the Shepherd" (page 693) as models, write your own "reply" to any of the poems in this anthology. Reply in poetry or in prose.

4. Consider two or three poems that treat the same theme (perhaps in one of the thematic anthology sections. Compare and explain the significant differences and similarities you see in your responses to these poems.

5. Consider a poem in which the speaker describes or addresses another person. Imagine how that person might respond to the poem. For example, consider how the man described in Sappho's "To me he seems like a god" (page 692) might react to his deification or how the mother might respond to her child's description of her in "The Youngest Daughter" (page 418).

6. Find a poem with figures of speech (metaphors, similes, personifications) you find particularly intriguing, puzzling, moving, affirming (or whatever) and explain your response. As you write, focus specifically on one or two figures of speech. Explain the meanings they suggest as well as the emotions they evoke.

7. Read a poem whose title caught your attention. Discuss the connection you see between the poem and its title. Were you disappointed, surprised, pleased by the relationship between the poem and its title? Explain whether and why your expectations were fulfilled, disappointed, or exceeded.

8. Consider the final stanza or lines of a poem carefully. Then suggest an alternative ending. Explain why you would make the changes you have indicated.

9. Discover a poem that describes a character, place, action, conflict, or decision that relates in some way to a person, place, action, conflict, or decision in your own life. Compare your experience to the experience described in the poem.

10. After reading the works of several poets, choose one you would like to know more about. Read biographical information as well as more of the poet's works. Then choose *one* aspect of the poet's life that particularly intrigues you and that you see reflected in the poet's work. Write a paper explaining what you have discovered.

AN INTRODUCTION TO DRAMA

Since the days of ancient Greece, people have created, watched, and participated in drama. Drama makes events and emotions—whether realistic or fantastic—come to life before the eyes of the audience. More than any other literary form, drama is a visual experience. Whether we read it or see it on stage, a play leaves pictures in our minds. These pictures, along with the echoes of the characters' (and, of course, the playwright's) words, create the emotions and ideas that together make up that play's themes.

Suggestions for Reading Drama

Reading drama, of course, is not exactly the same as seeing a play performed. Some qualities are lost—yet others are gained—when you read the playwright's descriptions and dialogue without the intervening interpretation of directors and actors.

DIALOGUE For some people, reading plays is difficult because they find the structure of the dialogue (the characters' conversations with others, with themselves, or with the audience) hard to follow. Although it may seem artificial to have the character's name at the beginning of each speech, it is obviously essential to know who is talking.

With a little practice, you can adjust to this distraction by training yourself to "read through" the characters' names. Try simply to note the name, rather than actually reading it as part of the speech. Consider the name almost as you would a mark of punctuation. It's there to guide you, but you don't consciously think about it any more than you consciously note a period, apostrophe, or comma when you come across those guides to meaning.

If you find this strategy unworkable, try providing your own transitional words to link the name to the speech. For instance, consider these speeches from *Antigone:*

> ISMENE: Why do you speak so strangely?
> ANTIGONE: Listen, Ismene:
>   Kreon buried our brother Eteocles
>   With military honors.

To get rid of the artificial introductory names, read the speeches this way:

> Ismene *says,* "Why do you speak so strangely?"
> Antigone *answers,* "Listen, Ismene . . ."

Using this strategy, you create a bridge from the name of the character to the words the character says.

STAGE DIRECTIONS Playwrights provide stage directions that explain details of setting and give information about the way characters speak and move. For some readers, stage directions divert attention from the dialogue, causing them to lose their train of thought. Yet it is necessary to be aware of stage directions to understand fully how the playwright envisioned both setting and action.

Some people read a play at least twice, once paying close attention to the stage directions and once simply noting the stage directions as brief guides but not stopping to read them in detail. They try to hold the information in their minds from the first reading, and, during the second reading, they use the stage directions to start "creating" or "directing" their own version of the play.

Some students read the play in short sections—by scenes or parts of scenes. They read the stage directions for a scene first (without paying much attention to the dialogue). Then they return to read the dialogue, this time integrating what they learned about setting and action from their reading of the stage directions.

LIST OF CHARACTERS At the beginning of most plays, the playwright gives a list of characters and often a brief description of each. Read this list before you start reading the play; you'll get a head start on understanding the relationships and dynamics between characters. Reading the list of characters also alerts you to watch for the entrance of each individual and helps you become aware of the role—however important or minor—each plays in the drama.

Traditional Forms of Drama

Traditional forms of drama are still performed and enjoyed. In addition, modern playwrights often adapt, incorporate, or rebel against elements of traditional drama as they write today's plays.

GREEK DRAMA Formal competitions among Greek playwrights began in approximately 530 B.C. These competitions continued to be held for several centuries, always in connection with religious celebrations dedicated to Dionysus, the god of wine who symbolized life-giving power. Greek plays were performed in large, outdoor, semicircular amphitheaters that held as many as 15,000 people.

These audiences, of course, understood the conventions of Greek theater. For example, the **chorus** (usually representing the voice of the community) danced and sang in the **orchestra** (a round area at the foot of the amphitheater). On an elevated stage behind the orchestra, the actors—wearing masks that symbolized their primary characteristics and, in addition, amplified their voices—performed their roles. Although Greek theaters did not have elaborate sets, they did have one rather spectacular stage device, the **deus ex machina** (god from the machine). By means of elaborate mechanisms, actors were lowered from above to the stage to play the role of gods meting out punishments or rewards to the human characters.

Scenes end with the dances and songs of the chorus (the **ode**), which sometimes comment on the action of the scene or provide background information clarifying the action of the scene. As the chorus sang one part of their observation (the **strophe**), they moved from right to left on the stage; as they sang another part (the **antistrophe**), they moved to the right.

Greek plays are short in comparison to five-act Shakespearean plays or modern three-act plays. Because the audience was familiar with the myths and legends on which most of the plays are based, the playwrights did not have to spend time explaining many of the background circumstances. Most Greek plays can be acted in about an hour and a half.

For an example of a Greek tragedy, read Sophocles' *Antigone* (page 1077) or *Oedipus Rex* (page 423).

ELIZABETHAN DRAMA William Shakespeare's plays exemplify the drama written during the reign of Queen Elizabeth I of England (1558–1603). Shakespeare wrote tragedy, comedy, and history; he captures the large, spectacular actions of kings, queens, and other highborn characters (and the people who serve them) as well as the romances and intrigues that are part of their lives.

Elizabethans followed Greek tradition by barring women from the stage. Adolescent boys played the parts of young heroines such as Juliet, and male character actors eagerly sought the parts of older women.

Although currently there is much speculation about the design of Elizabethan theaters, most scholars agree that early Elizabethan plays were performed in makeshift locations such as inn yards or open spaces between buildings such as the Inns at Court, which was a London law college. When theaters were built, they were usually octagonal on the outside. Inside, they were circular. The audience sat on both sides as well as in front of the raised stage. As in the Greek theater, there was little scenery or stage setting, except for the booms and machinery used to lower actors who came as messengers or agents of supernatural forces. Unlike Greek theaters, however, Elizabethan theaters had a second-level balcony, doors at the back for entrances and exits, a curtained alcove, and a trap door in the stage floor for surprise entrances of ghosts and spirits. Although the huge Greek amphitheaters could accommodate many thousands of theater-goers, most Elizabethan theaters could house no more than about 1000 to 2000, including 500 to 800 **groundlings** (common folk who could not afford seats and thus stood at the foot of the stage). The composition of the Elizabethan audiences—ranging from the illiterate groundlings to the highly educated nobility—presented a challenge to the playwright. Successful plays usually melded action, humor, and violence with philosophical insights and evocative poetry. For an example of such a play, read *Hamlet* (page 209).

Modern Forms of Drama

Following the flourishing drama during the Elizabethan period, playwrights—particularly in England and in France—focused on comedy. These eighteenth- and nineteenth-century playwrights frequently satirized the failings and foibles of society in witty dramas depicting romantic intrigues and entanglements. During this same time in the United States, playwrights developed the tradition of **melodrama,** plays with stereotyped villains and heroes representing extremes of good and evil.

REALISTIC DRAMA Reacting against both stylized comedy and exaggerated melodrama, some late nineteenth- and early twentieth-century dramatists began to develop a new form: the **realistic drama.** These dramatists worked to present everyday life—crises, conflicts, and emotional responses to which ordinary people could relate.

Dramatists writing in the realistic tradition depict problems with work, with family relationships, with community politics. Ghosts do not pop up from the floor of the realistic stage to introduce problems into the characters' lives, nor do gods descend from above to solve those problems. Instead, the difficulties the characters face seem to follow logically from events and decisions with which most members of the audience can identify. Most can also relate to—if not agree with—the responses characters have to the conflicts in their lives.

Settings and props in the realistic theater are more important than in earlier forms of drama, because the dramatist seeks to create the illusion of real life. Often the stage is like a room with the fourth wall removed. The audience is invited to watch ordinary people and listen to them conversing in ordinary language rather than in polished poetry, stylized witty exchanges, or highly dramatic pronouncements.

Examples of realistic drama in this anthology include Ibsen's *A Doll House*° (page 697), Glaspell's *Trifles* (page 608), and Wilson's *Fences* (page 466).

THEATER OF THE ABSURD In the second half of the twentieth century, a number of playwrights rejected the conventions of realistic drama. Instead of a sequence of logically connected events, absurdist drama offers actions that lead in no predictable direction. The motivations of characters are contradictory or absent altogether. Conversations and speeches ramble disjointedly, leaping first one way and then another for no apparent reason.

Rather than suggesting coherent themes, absurdist dramas invite the audience to ask questions about the world in which we live. Martin Esslin, who first called these dramas "theater of the absurd," offers the following insights:

> The Theater of the Absurd shows the world as an incomprehensible place. The spectators see the happenings on the stage entirely from the outside, without ever understanding the full meaning of these strange patterns of events, as newly arrived visitors might watch life in a country of which they have not yet mastered the language.
> (*The Theater of the Absurd,* New York: Doubleday, 1969)

In this anthology, Arrabal's *Picnic on the Battlefield* (page 1065) provides a fine example of absurdist drama.

°Ibsen's title is sometimes translated from the Norwegian as *A Doll's House.*

Types of Drama

Whether ancient or modern, plays represent a wide range of emotions and views of the world. Although most plays contain both serious and comic elements, they usually fit into one of two major dramatic categories: **tragedy,** which focuses on life's sorrows and serious problems, and **comedy,** which focuses on life's joys and humorous absurdities.

TRAGEDY Traditionally, the tragic play looks at the life of a royal figure or highly respected official. During the course of the drama, this character's fortunes change drastically from good to bad. Having enjoyed high status in society, the **tragic hero** meets his or her downfall for one (or a combination) of these three reasons: fate or coincidence beyond the control of the character, a flaw in character, or a mistake in judgment.

Because the traditional tragic hero is a noble character, his or her fall has been regarded as particularly moving to the audience. After all, if someone as brave, stalwart, wise (and so on) as the tragic hero can fall prey to random accidents, character flaws, or poor judgment, how much more vulnerable must we ordinary mortals be. In the *Poetics,* Aristotle suggested that watching the tragic hero's downfall (the **catastrophe,** which generally involves the death not only of the hero but also of other, often innocent, individuals) inspires in us the emotions of pity and terror. By watching the tragic hero move steadily toward disaster, and by seeing the drama's **resolution** (the conclusion, in which order is generally restored to the society at large), we viewers may experience **catharsis** (profound relief from the tension of the play and a sense that we have gained insight and enlightenment, rather than simply entertainment, from the drama). For classic examples of traditional tragic heroes, consider the title characters in Sophocles' *Antigone* or Shakespeare's *Othello.*

Modern plays that are sometimes termed tragedies do not always follow the conventions of traditional tragedy strictly. For instance, the main character may not be highborn but may instead be a rather ordinary person like Nora in Ibsen's *A Doll House.* Also, like *A Doll House,* a modern tragedy may not end with the main character's physical death but rather with the death of a way of life. Some scholars argue that these modern plays are not true tragedies and that their main characters are not true tragic heroes. *A Doll House* (page 697) provides an opportunity to consider the nature of modern tragic drama and modern tragic characters.

COMEDY Unlike traditional tragic drama, which focuses on the lives of noble, highborn characters, comic drama shows us the lives of ordinary people. Like the characters in tragedies, these people encounter conflicts, challenges, and difficulties. Yet their problems are seldom deeply serious—or if they are serious, they are treated in a lighthearted way.

The humor in comic plots has many sources. **Satiric comedy** exposes the foibles and shortcomings of humanity, inviting us not only to laugh at the often-exaggerated stage examples but also to pay attention to our own idiosyncrasies and follies. Satiric comedy may be light and witty, but often its humor is rather dark and biting. We laugh at the characters, yet we cannot help but see the selfishness and egotism in their plights. The source of satiric humor is often both verbal and visual. Writers of satiric comedy use sharp words and cutting phrases as well as pratfalls and fisticuffs to inspire laughter in their audience.

In **romantic comedy,** by contrast, the source of humor is frequently mistaken identity and unexpected discoveries as well as romping stage chases, mock fistfights, and other physical actions. Unlike satiric comedy, romantic comedy does not aim at chastising and improving human behavior but rather at inviting the gentle laughter of self-recognition. Romantic comedy seeks to delight the audience rather than to teach a lesson. Shakespeare's comedies, such as *As You Like It,* typify romantic comedy.

Whether the comic drama is satiric or romantic, it differs in major ways from tragedy. Whereas tragedy moves toward the main characters' downfall, comedy moves toward the improvement of the main characters' fortunes. Tragedy usually ends with death and then with restoration of order; comedy concludes with reconciliation, often through the marriage of the main characters as well as the marriage of minor or supporting characters.

TRAGICOMEDY More common among modern dramas than the comedy is the **tragicomedy:** a play that mixes elements of comedy and tragedy. For instance, Glaspell's *Trifles* (page 608) focuses on a tragedy, a woman's murder of her husband. Yet the bumbling sheriff and his male cohorts become darkly comic figures as they make fun of the two women who manage to solve the crime that stumps all the men. Other plays in this anthology that combine comedy and tragedy include Wilson's *Fences* (page 466) and Howe's *Painting Churches* (page 839).

Tragicomedy takes many forms. Sometimes, as with *Trifles,* the play is primarily tragic yet is relieved by moments of humor. Sometimes humor dominates the play, yet serious themes lie behind the comic words and actions. Consider, for example, Fierstein's *On Tidy Endings* (page 1174) with its witty exchanges between the characters yet with underlying themes relating to loss and death.

✳ GUIDELINES
Drama

1. Find one scene (or part of one scene) that you find particularly strange, intriguing, puzzling, powerful, or moving. Briefly summarize the scene and explain your response. As you explain, indicate the relationship between the scene you are discussing and the rest of the play.
2. Compare the primary qualities of two characters in the play. Explain why you find their similarities and differences significant.

3. Describe your initial response to one of the play's main characters (after reading the first act or scene); then explain your response after you finished reading (and rereading) the entire play. Evaluate the events, actions, and speeches in the play that either confirmed your first response or caused you to change it.

4. List all the conflicts you see in the play, whether they are experienced by major or minor characters. Then consider how these conflicts might be related. How are they similar? How are they different? How does the characters' resolution of conflicts contribute to the play's resolution?

5. Rewrite a significant scene (or part of a scene) from the play in short story form. Provide detailed descriptions of the characters' inner feelings and thoughts as well as the setting in which the action takes place.

6. Watch a live or filmed performance of one of the plays (or a film based on the play). Compare your responses to the play as you read it to your responses as you viewed the stage or film version. Notice particularly aspects the stage or film directors have chosen to change. For example, are any characters eliminated? Added? Are scenes omitted? Added? Evaluate the effect of these decisions.

7. Explicate the opening dialogue of any of the plays. Consider each line—and the language within each line—very carefully. What tone does this dialogue establish? What expectations do these lines raise concerning the play's conflicts and themes?

8. Consider the conflicts and choices of any character. Explain your response to the way the character deals with conflict. Draw on your own experiences and observations as you evaluate this character's decisions and actions (or failure to make decisions or to act).

9. Write either an alternative ending for one of the plays or an additional scene to take place at a specified time after the current final scene. Explain the reasons for your changes or for your speculations concerning the futures of the characters. Refer to specific details in the play as you make this explanation.

10. Read either biographical background on the playwright, reviews of performances of the play, or critical essays analyzing and evaluating the play. Choose one or two new insights about the play that you have gained from your reading and explain those insights. How has your research changed, challenged, affirmed, or enriched your initial reading of the play?

AN INTRODUCTION TO NONFICTION

Nonfiction is often defined as prose works that are factual. Under this definition, all prose works other than imaginative literature (novels, short stories, poetry, and drama) are considered nonfiction. Essays, transcriptions of speeches, letters, documents, and journals are nonfiction. So are recipes, corporate reports, and grant proposals. But are all of these forms literature?

For centuries, most readers and scholars have agreed that one particular type of essay—the **belle lettre** (French for "beautiful letter")—deserves to be called literature. These essays often pursue philosophical subjects using language with the figures we traditionally think of as literary, such as metaphor, simile, and personification. Virginia Woolf's "Professions for Women" (page 621) (which in its original form was a speech) exemplifies the *belle lettre* essay.

But what about other forms of nonfiction? Most people would immediately reject recipes, corporate reports, and grant proposals as examples of literature, perhaps because these forms of writing are meant simply to convey information rather than to intrigue both the minds and emotions of readers; perhaps because these forms deal primarily with facts rather than ideas, ideals, and emotions; perhaps because the language of these forms is usually literal rather than figurative; perhaps because these forms tend to avoid ambiguity and complication rather than suggest them; perhaps because these forms generally provide answers and certainties rather than raising questions and possibilities.

This series of "perhaps," then, suggests a possible definition for literary works.

1. They deal with ideas, ideals, and emotions.
2. Their language is often figurative.
3. They suggest ambiguity and complication.
4. They raise questions and possibilities.

It is important to realize that readers and scholars have proposed many different definitions of literature. (During your lifetime of reading, you may develop your own definition of literature, and it may be different both from the one suggested here and from those of other readers.) Many forms that have not traditionally been called literary meet the four criteria in the preceding list. Certain transcriptions of speeches, letters, documents, and journals may be read as literature.

Consider, for example, Lincoln's Gettysburg address or John F. Kennedy's inaugural address. What makes these speeches memorable and important? (Consider not only their original audiences but also those who hear them repeated or who read transcripts.) The answer is complex: Certainly the sensitive and striking choice of language (Lincoln, for example, begins with "Fourscore and seven years ago" rather than with the more common "eighty-seven years ago"); certainly the powerful rhythm (both Lincoln and Kennedy make use of parallel structure: "Government of the people, by the people, for the people shall not perish from the earth" and "Ask not what your country can do for you; ask what you can do for your country"); certainly the thought-provoking themes offered and the complex questions raised. We might say, then, that these speeches can be called literature.

Suggestions for Reading Speeches

When you read speeches, try to picture the original audience. How has the speech-giver chosen his or her words to reach that audience? Imagine the possible responses of that audience to the speech. Consider, too, that many speakers are aware that their speeches will be reported by the press or—at the very least—repeated by those who have heard them. What elements of the speech might appeal to an even wider audience than those originally addressed? Keep in mind, too, that one of the best ways to appreciate a transcript of a speech is to read it aloud—or to listen to it being read aloud. Chief Seattle's "My People" (page 528) is an example of a speech.

Suggestions for Reading Letters

Like speeches, letters are addressed to an audience. When you read letters, keep in mind the original audience. Some letters were intended to be read by only one other person. Others were written for a far larger audience. Consider how the different audiences affect how the writer treats his or her subject.

Suggestions for Reading Documents

As you read a document—for example, the Declaration of Independence—consider its purpose. Consider also how effective you think the document might have been in accomplishing that purpose.

Ask yourself, also, how responses to the document may have changed from the time it was written to the present. Consider why and how readers' responses might have changed (or stayed nearly the same).

Suggestions for Reading Journals and Diaries

Unlike nearly any other writings, journals and diaries were usually originally composed for an audience of only one: the writer. Journals may jump from subject to subject without any clear connection because the writer is not trying to communicate ideas or emotions to a group of readers but is, instead, exploring those ideas or emotions for personal reasons.

Reading journals and diaries gives us the opportunity to look directly into the hearts and minds of writers; to observe the ideas, images, and emotions they treasure for themselves; and to see the early stages of the creative process. Frederick Douglass's "Learning to Read and Write" was originally part of a journal that Douglass later revised to become his autobiography.

Suggestions for Reading Essays

As you respond to an essay, consider what its central purpose seems to be. Is it written primarily to describe a person or place? Or does it, perhaps, tell a true story (a **narrative**)? What significance do you see in the description or in the narrative? How does that description or narrative relate to your own observations and experiences?

An essay may make significant comparisons or contrasts; it may explain the reasons something happened or explore the effects of a particular event or action. Some essays contemplate or speculate on an idea, exploring many possibilities without insisting on one final conclusion. Many other essays, in one way or another, argue for or against a point of view, a solution to a problem, or a new way of thinking about the world.

Whatever the essay's purpose, look carefully at the writer's choice of words as well as the way he or she structures both the essay itself and its sentences and paragraphs. Then consider how well you believe the writer has fulfilled his or her purpose. Consider also the details, reasons, and examples the writer supplies to support generalizations. Do you find them convincing? Intriguing? Weak? Insufficient?

Notice the questions and complexities stated or implied by the writer as well as answers or solutions that are offered. Think carefully about your own response to these questions, complexities, answers, and solutions.

 **GUIDELINES**
Nonfiction

Speeches

1. Imagine that you are a member of the audience first hearing the speech. Describe the setting, the speaker, and your response to the speech.
2. Write a speech in response to the speech you have read. In your speech, pose questions or suggest alternatives to the views you have read.

Letters

1. Assume that you are the person (or one of the persons) to whom the letter was originally addressed. Write a response to the writer. Refer to specific details in the letter as you plan your response.
2. Write a character sketch of the person who wrote the letter. What do the details of the letter (content as well as style) suggest to you about this person? Use specific examples from the letter to support your character analysis.

Documents

1. Imagine that you are one of the drafters of the document. Describe the process of planning and writing the document. Project the arguments and disagreements that might have been part of this process and explain how they were resolved. (You may want to research some of the historical background relating to the document.)

2. Write a document styled on the one you read, but relating to a current political issue.

Journals

1. Write the entry (or series of entries) you imagine might follow the one(s) you have read. Try to capture the writer's style as you build on his or her ideas and emotions.
2. Write a letter to the journal's author explaining your responses to what you have read.

Essays

1. Explain what you see as the author's purpose in writing the essay. How effectively has the author accomplished that purpose? Explain.
2. Find a passage or sentence you find particularly thought-provoking. Copy the passage or sentence and then write your response to it.
3. Identify the point of view taken by the writer. Compose a response written from a different point of view.
4. Describe the values you believe are exemplified by the points raised, the questions asked, or the views asserted in the essay. Write an evaluation of those values, explaining how they compare or contrast to your own.
5. Write a letter to the author of the essay explaining your response to specific parts of the essay (for instance, to specific examples or to a specific argument or proposal). Begin this assignment by making a list of five to ten questions you would like to ask the author if you could speak to him or her privately.

CONSIDERING OTHER VOICES

Listening to the voices of others who read, talk about, and write about literary works provides an opportunity to expand your enjoyment and understanding of these works. Some voices—professors and class members, friends and relatives—are close and easily accessible. Other voices must be sought out, usually from printed sources. Such voices include authors who have written about their own works or who have been interviewed about their works. Still other voices come from critical reviews of dramas or of collections of poetry, fiction, or essays and from scholarly journals or books in which professors of literature share their views of the literature they study and teach. In this textbook, each of the thematic chapters provides a "Commentary," a voice or voices that suggest new ways of looking at one of the works in that chapter.

Listening to the voices of others can enable you to develop your own literary conversation in ways you may not previously have considered. As you listen to various voices, you will notice that they do not always agree. For example, Flannery O'Connor in "A Reasonable Use of the Unreasonable" (page 818) explains why she disagrees with the way some teachers have explained her short story "A Good Man Is Hard to Find." When you read voices that disagree with each other, you are confronted with the importance of your own ability to make judgments about the literature you read. Because even "experts" disagree, you need to develop strategies for reading their comments, returning to the text, and then making up your own mind.

Note that if you do consult other sources and refer to their views in your own writing, you must give proper documentation (see pages 1239–1247). Failure to acknowledge the use of other people's ideas, opinions, and judgments in your own writing constitutes plagiarism.

Authors' Commentaries and Interviews

Many authors write commentaries or provide interviews with insights about their works. Although one should not necessarily accept an author's statement about the meaning of his or her work without closely examining the evidence in the work itself (as W. K. Wimsatt warned in his 1964 book, *The Verbal Icon*), it is usually extremely interesting and helpful to hear what an author has to say. Sometimes authors discuss the origins of their ideas; sometimes they address what they believe to be mistaken interpretations of their works; sometimes they explain points that many readers have found puzzling or difficult to understand. For authors who have been writing during the past seventy years or so, the *New York Times Index* and the *Humanities Index* (which indexes various literary magazines and scholarly journals) can provide sources for tracking down such commentaries and interviews. In this text, the "Interview with August Wilson" (page 525), Gilman's "On Writing 'The Yellow Wallpaper'" (page 589), O'Connor's "A Reasonable Use of the Unreasonable" (page 818), and Faulkner's "The Meaning of 'A Rose for Emily'" (page 1140) provide examples of commentaries and interviews that shed light on the author's work.

Reviews

Most major newspapers and many magazines offer reviews of newly published works, newly compiled anthologies, and new productions of plays. A highly useful source of such reviews is the *New York Times Index*. If you know the year in which a work was published or in which a new production of a play began, you can use this index to discover whether the *New York Times* published a review. These reviews are written for the general, educated reader and so will probably not use the highly specialized vocabulary of scholarly literary criticism. In this textbook, Walter Kerr's article on Claire Bloom's performance as Nora in *A Doll House* (page 754) provides an example of the voices you can discover through reading reviews.

Scholarly Criticism

Although scholars have been reading, thinking about, and writing about literature for hundreds of years, it is only in the twentieth century that such commentary has been divided into complex, separate schools. To locate scholarly criticism of works in which you are interested, consult the card catalogue of your library, the *Humanities Index,* and the *MLA International Bibliography.* (The indexes, especially the *MLA,* can be a bit complicated to use at first; you may need to ask a librarian for help. Once you know the process, however, you'll have easy access to an amazing number of new voices.)

As you continue with the study of literature, you'll hear references to various ways of reading texts, such as **formalist, reader response, socio-logical, psychoanalytic,** and **new historical.** Although these terms may seem daunting, they simply describe many different paths to follow in pursuit of the pleasure, revelation, illumination, and elevation of spirit and mind that come from reading deeply, fully, and well. Many of the most outstanding scholars who write about literature do not adhere to only one way of reading texts but rather consider the many possibilities. They draw from these many ways of reading literature to create the most sensible, helpful critical commentaries possible.

Brief definitions of these various approaches follow. The definitions are intended only as starting points, as ways to begin thinking about the study of literature. If you are interested in learning more, you might begin by consulting a literary handbook, such as *A Glossary of Literary Terms* by M. H. Abrams, which can help you find more extensive discussions about various aspects of literary criticism as well as bibliographies for further reading.

FORMALIST CRITICISM Formalist criticism, sometimes called new criticism, looks at a work as existing by itself. Formalists pay little attention to biographical or historical information; instead, they use a process called *close reading* to look at the various parts of the work in detail. Close reading, also called *explication,* requires a careful analysis of the various elements within a work. While explicating a work, a reader watches for ambiguities (apparent contradictions) within a text and works to explain how these ambiguities ultimately lead to the text's theme. In this book, Michael W. Murphy's explication of "Do Not Go Gentle Into That Good Night" (page 80), which appeared in the journal *Explicator,* provides an example of formalist criticism.

READER-RESPONSE CRITICISM Reader-response criticism, as you might expect, focuses on the meaning that is created when a reader interacts with a text. This way of reading does not assume that there is one single "correct" reading of a text but rather that multiple readings, which are equally defensible, can be derived from any given work. One of the points made by reader-response theorists is that all written texts have what German critic Wolfgang Iser calls "gaps"—places where details or inferences are not provided by the writer but instead must come from the reader. How readers fill in those gaps may differ according to their age, gender, socioeconomic background, occupation, religion, and so on. In this book, Judith Fetterley's "Reading about Reading: 'The Yellow Wallpaper'" (page 590) provides an example of reader-response criticism.

SOCIOLOGICAL CRITICISM Sociological criticism, in direct opposition to formalist criticism, argues that literature is profoundly affected both by the societal forces that surround authors and by the societal forces that surround readers. Sociological criticism is often divided into two schools: feminist and Marxist.

Feminist criticism notes that our civilization has been predominantly male-centered and that, therefore, literature reflects **patriarchal** (male-dominated) themes. Feminist critics read classics with an eye toward paying fair mind to female values, ideals, and points of view. In this textbook, Carolyn Heilbrun's essay "The Character of Hamlet's Mother" (page 322) demonstrates this approach to feminist criticism. Feminist criticism also addresses the omission of women writers from the **canon** (the standard group of works that have been accepted as great literature). Through the work of feminist critics, such writers as Charlotte Perkins Gilman (page 575), Susan Glaspell (page 608), and Kate Chopin (page 645) have come to prominence. Their works, previously paid little attention and—in some cases—suppressed, are now widely anthologized and available to many readers.

Marxist criticism is named for social and economic reformer Karl Marx (1818–1883). Marx described the process by which, he believed, wealthy capitalists oppressed the working classes and created an unfair distribution of power. Literary critics who subscribe to Marx's theories read literary texts to discover evidence of the way social, political, and economic forces have shaped not only the destinies of living people but also the themes of imaginative literature written by authors who were and are part of capitalist societies. In this textbook, Barbara Christian's essay "Alice Walker: The Black Woman as Wayward" (page 1001) looks both at feminist issues and at Marxist, class-related issues.

PSYCHOANALYTIC CRITICISM Psychoanalytic criticism views the themes, conflicts, and characterizations of a work primarily as a reflection of the needs, emotions, states of mind, and subconscious desires of the author. Psychoanalytic critics apply to characters in literary texts the principles established by Sigmund Freud (1856–1936) for understanding human behavior. For example, many psychoanalytic critics, beginning with Freud himself, have studied *Hamlet*. In the excerpt from *The Interpretation of Dreams* (page 320), you can see how Freud uses his theories of repression and the subconscious mind to explain why Oedipus kills his father whereas Hamlet continually delays killing Claudius, even after he is convinced that the ghost of his father has correctly named Claudius as his killer.

NEW HISTORICISM New-historicist criticism is related to sociological criticism and reader-response criticism in that its proponents point out the impact of the politics, ideologies, and social customs of the author's world to the themes, images, and characterizations of his or her work. The new-historicist view notes that an important element is omitted when we read a work as though it existed in a vacuum, completely unrelated to the conditions and influences of the historical events that were taking place when it was written. In addition to making this connection between history and literature, new historicists note that no historical event remains absolutely fixed; new discoveries and new interpretations change the way we look at and interpret history and, therefore, the way we look at history in relation to literary works. Leonard Tennenhouse's commentary on "Power in *Hamlet*" (page 321) provides an example of the way new-historical criticism can provide insights into literature.

4

Writing about Literature

At first I hated that we have to keep journals for this class, but after a while what I noticed is that when I write about some poem or story that we've read, I find out ideas I didn't know I had. *Maurine Buckley*

For me reading has always been my best pleasure. Even when I was only five or six, people were always saying, "She's always got her nose in a book." Writing about what I read is not that hard for me. What I like best is starting a paper with what I think is a great idea and then finding out while I'm writing that a lot of other ideas are in my head, too. So it's a way to think about what I've read. *Nadine Nuñez*

No way will I ever "enjoy" writing a paper, but I do have to say that one thing that happens is this: When I start really thinking about an idea I have for a paper, and listening hard to class discussion, and pushing thoughts around in my brain and then trying out writing them, I sometimes find that I've changed my mind from my first reaction to the story, poem, or whatever. This is a big step because I don't usually change my mind. So for me, writing in this class has made me see that an idea might start out in one direction, but when you really think about it, it might take you some place entirely different. *Tim Janning*

Maurine, Nadine, and Tim, students in an introductory course called "Literature and Writing," reacted to writing about literature in different ways. Nadine found putting her ideas in writing rather easy. Maurine and Tim at first saw writing as an obstacle: a requirement to be dutifully carried out. As the semester progressed, however, they all discovered an important insight that Nadine suggests: Writing is a way of thinking. Maurine found that her journal entries helped her to discover ideas she didn't know she had; Tim saw that the mental energy required to really think through a topic for a paper often led him to modify his initial way of reading and responding to a work.

The value, then, of writing about literature is the same as the value of writing honestly and with emotional and intellectual vigor about any subject: the hard work brings new ways of understanding, of thinking and feeling. Both the process of writing and the final product provide the satisfaction of learning new ways to perceive, to speculate, to wonder, and to know.

This chapter explains strategies for and approaches to writing about literature by using samples of students' spoken and written responses to the following two poems. You'll find the samples of students' writing more meaningful if you take time now to read the poems and to respond to them through both discussion and writing.

DYLAN THOMAS (1914–1953)

Do Not Go Gentle into That Good Night

Do not go gentle into that good night,
Old age should burn and rave at close of day;
Rage, rage against the dying of the light.

Though wise men at their end know dark is right,
Because their words had forked no lightning they   5
Do not go gentle into that good night.

Good men, the last wave by, crying how bright
Their frail deeds might have danced in a green bay,
Rage, rage against the dying of the light.

Wild men who caught and sang the sun in flight,   10
And learn, too late, they grieved it on its way,
Do not go gentle into that good night.

Grave men, near death, who see with blinding sight
Blind eyes could blaze like meteors and be gay,
Rage, rage against the dying of the light.   15

And you, my father, there on the sad height,
Curse, bless, me now with your fierce tears, I pray,
Do not go gentle into that good night.
Rage, rage against the dying of the light.

Responding to "Do Not Go Gentle into That Good Night"

1. Given the details of the poem, how do you picture the speaker in the poem? How do you picture his father?
2. What advice does the speaker in this poem give to his father? What is your response to this advice?
3. Imagine that you are the father, hearing this advice. What might you say in a letter answering your son?
4. Read the poem aloud and, if possible, listen to the poem being read aloud. Try using a different tone of voice or emphasizing different phrases. Notice whether—and how—your response to the poem changes with these variations.

JOAN ALESHIRE (1947–   )

Slipping

Age comes to my father as a slow
slipping: the leg that weakens, will
barely support him, the curtain of mist
that falls over one eye. Years, like
pickpockets, lift his concentration,   5
memory, fine sense of direction. The car,
as he drives, drifts from lane to lane
like a raft on a river, speeds and slows
for no reason, keeps missing turns.

As my mother says, "He's never liked   10
to talk about feelings," but tonight
out walking, as I slow to match his pace—
his left leg trailing a little like
a child who keeps pulling on your hand—he says,
"I love you so much." Darkness, and the sense   15
we always have that each visit may be
the last, have pushed away years of restraint.

A photograph taken of him teaching—
white coat, stethoscope like a pet snake
around his neck, chair tipped back   20
against the lecture-room wall—shows
a man talking, love of his work lighting
his face—in a way we seldom saw at home.
I answer that I love him, too, but
hardly knowing him, what I love   25
is the way reserve has slipped from
his feeling, like a screen suddenly
falling, exposing someone dressing or
washing: how wrinkles ring a bent neck,
how soft and mutable is the usually hidden flesh.   30

Responding to "Slipping"

1. How did you respond to the description of the father in the first stanza? Was this response changed or reinforced after you finished reading the poem? Explain.
2. How do you imagine the relationships among the family members described in this poem? What facts about their lives do the details of the poem show? What can you infer from those details?
3. Explain your response to the speaker's attitude regarding the changes in her father.
4. Try writing this poem as though it were a prose paragraph. Copy the sentences and punctuation exactly as they appear, but arrange the sentences in a paragraph rather than in lines. Pay attention to the length of the sentences as you write them and to the way some of the sentences are punctuated with dashes. Does reading the new arrangement change your response to the poem? Explain.

THE PROCESS OF WRITING ABOUT LITERATURE

Understanding the Assignment

When you are writing about literature for a class, your writing assignments originate—at least to some extent—from your instructor. It's important to have a clear notion of what you are being asked to do. An assignment may be quite open ("Write an essay responding to any work we have read this semester"), or it may be structured in a number of ways. Read or listen to the assignment carefully before you begin planning how you will fulfill it.

Thinking about the Assignment

Keep in mind the following questions as you begin thinking about an assignment:

1. Does the assignment ask that your subject be a specific work or works?
2. Does the assignment ask that you focus on a specific genre (poetry, fiction, drama, essay)?
3. Does the assignment ask that you focus on a particular aspect of the literary work or works (for example, on the images of war or on the concept of honor)?
4. Does the assignment specify an audience, real (for instance, will you be reading part or all of the paper to the class?) or imagined (for example, will you be writing a fictional letter from one character to another?)?
5. Does the assignment ask for a particular approach or organization? For example, are you being asked to compare? To explicate? To evaluate? (These approaches and methods of organization are explained and demonstrated on pages 84–143.)
6. Does the assignment specify a length? (The focus of a two-page paper will be quite different from that of a ten-page paper.)
7. Does the assignment ask for (or allow) research?
8. Does the assignment ask that you discover a topic for yourself?

Keeping these questions in mind, read the following assignment. The instructor wants students to write a paper of two to four pages (typewritten, double-spaced). When they submit their papers, students are to give a brief talk (three to five minutes) explaining the most significant point of the paper.

Assignment Topics (Choose One)

1. Briefly summarize your response to one of these poems and then, using a personal narrative, explain that response, making references to the poem that show its connection to your narrative.
2. Explore the similarities and differences you see between these poems. Then write a paper explaining what you discovered and what significance you find in these similarities and differences.
3. Explain how the figurative language in one of the poems suggests the relationship between the speaker and his or her father.
4. What, exactly, does the speaker say in each poem? And how does he or she say it? Look carefully at the language in the poems. Then choose one poem and explain how the central idea of the poem unfolds as you read from one stanza to the next.
5. Consider the values and beliefs suggested by each of these poems. Choose one of the poems and explain those values and beliefs as well as your evaluation of them. Do you agree with them completely? Question them? Explain.
6. Discover a question related to Thomas's "Do Not Go Gentle" and do research to explore that question. In your paper, refer to at least three sources.

Writing to Respond

A response paper can take many different directions, but remember that part of the point of the paper is to help those who read it understand the connections you made. Why did this particular poem, short story, play, or essay evoke a sad memory or recall a triumph? What details affected you strongly? You need to show your audience exactly what you felt as you were reading the work. Avoid simply announcing that you liked or didn't like what you read. Showing means finding examples that will make sense to your readers. For this reason, you should reread the work carefully several times to find telling examples. To write a strong response paper, you need to make clear and frequent references to the work that evoked the thoughts and feelings you'll be discussing.

Topic 1

Briefly summarize your response to one of these poems and then, using a personal narrative, explain that response, making references to the poem that show its connection to your narrative.

This assignment asks for the reader's response, that is, for the personal and individual feelings and thoughts evoked by the experience of reading either Thomas's or Aleshire's poem. In this case, the topic asks for an example from the reader's experience that will support, develop, and explain that response.

DISCOVERING IDEAS: JOURNAL ENTRIES After reading the assignment sheet, Karen Angstrom decided that she would like to work with the first assignment. She read both poems twice and then wrote the following journal entry about her response to "Slipping." (For more information on journals, see page 10.)

> OK, first time through I kept thinking about this daughter who seems like she's glad her father is old and weak because now he tells her he loves her. I felt sympathy for the daughter. But the second time through, her response began to seem selfish to me. She seemed to me to be willing to have her father old and weak as long as he would say that he loved her. But what about how the father felt inside? Maybe he was acting the way he was because he was scared. The poem talks about the screen falling down, which seems to me like the person's protection against the world. That made me think about Mr. Gagnon and the way he was after his stroke—how he lost his protection. The poem looks from the daughter's point of view and she sees the change as positive. But from the point of view of the person who is changing, losing part of what has been yourself has to be frightening. And I definitely see that as negative. So I see another side to this poem.

This journal entry shows Karen's changing response as she read "Slipping." In addition, she keeps the writing topic she has chosen in mind, remembering that she has to include a personal narrative to explain her response. As she thinks about her second reading, she focuses on one particular image (the screen suddenly falling) that triggered a strong memory for her and leads her to the observation that "losing part of what has been yourself has to be frightening."

CONSIDERING AUDIENCE After deciding to write about Aleshire's poem and to use the story of Mr. Gagnon to illustrate her response, Karen thought about the audience for her paper (and for the oral response that was part of the assignment). Her instructor would be reading the paper; both the instructor and her classmates would be listening to her report. Everyone in this audience would be familiar with "Slipping," so Karen knew she wouldn't have to give a detailed summary of the poem.

No one in her audience, however, knew Mr. Gagnon, a man who had lived in Karen's neighborhood for as long as she could remember. She knew she would have to give some background information to help her audience understand why the changes in Mr. Gagnon after his surgery were so important to her and how having known Mr. Gagnon affected her response to the poem.

Karen also thought about the different views various classmates held. She knew that some would not share her response to "Slipping." She realized she would need to choose her words and examples carefully to express herself honestly without alienating readers or listeners whose responses to the poem were different from her own. Her purpose in writing the paper was not to make her audience angry but rather to show clearly her own thoughts and feelings.

NARROWING THE TOPIC Having decided on a general topic—the way the change in Mr. Gagnon related to her response to "Slipping"—Karen realized that she needed to find a more specific focus before she began drafting her paper. To explore possibilities, she made the following lists:

"Slipping"
    father used to be full of energy
    "love of work lighting his face"
    now losing physical abilities
        can't drive
        can't walk easily
    used to be reserved about emotions
    now exposes emotions
    can't (or doesn't) control feelings

Mr. Gagnon
    always full of energy and life
    never praised or said thanks
    brain tumor

surgery not successful
changing—every day worse
exposing emotions he never would have
pain from exposing
no control over feelings

As Karen looked at these lists, she paid special attention to the idea of exposing emotions and to the sense of losing control. She then made another list, this time with possible subjects for her response essay.

emotions and old age
old age: changing emotions
emotions, control, and self

Karen decided that the third topic best fit her response both to the poem and to her former neighbor, Mr. Gagnon. She knew that she wanted to explore a view of the changes brought by old age and illness that differed from the view suggested by Aleshire.

DEVISING A PRELIMINARY THESIS STATEMENT Once Karen had a narrowed topic in mind, she thought about what she wanted to say about this subject. She came up with these possibilities. Remember that a **thesis statement** makes an assertion; it does not simply announce a subject but instead indicates what the writer plans to say about the subject. Remember also that a preliminary thesis statement is tentative. You may revise it or even change it completely during the drafting process. The benefit of having a preliminary thesis is that it provides the sense of a central idea as you begin writing.

When a person's "reserve has slipped from feeling," the main emotion revealed may be fear.
Losing control because of sickness or old age may make a person emotional because of fear.
Losing control over your life is frightening.

The first thesis seemed strongest to Karen because it focuses specifically on what she wanted to say about her response to the poem. The assertion in the second statement is not as clear or as straightforward as the first, and the third thesis is too broad and general. Also, the first thesis is strengthened by the specific reference to the poem, which supports the central idea she proposes.

PLANNING AND ORGANIZING While evaluating possible thesis statements, Karen saw what direction she wanted to take. Also, she'd made a list of ideas to discuss in her response to the poem and in the narrative about Mr. Gagnon that would explain her response. She now thought about how to organize her material, how to present it most effectively to her audience. The opening paragraph, she decided, would briefly describe her response to Aleshire's poem. The story of Mr. Gagnon's relationship with her and her brother Cory would follow. It seemed logical to give the details in chrono-logical order, beginning with Mr. Gagnon before he became sick and then explaining the changes after his surgery.

To help keep this organization clearly in mind, Karen wrote an infor-mal outline.

1. Introduction (My response to "Slipping"—details on what the fa-
     ther has lost—driving, work, etc.)
2. Mr. Gagnon
     When I was young—always there, welcoming us, but also grouchy;
       never saying thanks
     Mr. G's illness and surgery
     Visiting Mr. G—his change
3. Conclusion???

DRAFTING After doing the preliminary reading, writing, and think-ing described here, Karen realized that she knew how she wanted to start her paper and she had a plan for developing the narrative example. She did not, however, know how she was going to conclude.

At this point, writing a draft—putting her explorations together on paper—seemed the best strategy.

CHANGES
Karen Angstrom

The daughter in Joan Aleshire's poem "Slipping" is seeing her father become more open to expressing emotions as he becomes older. "Like a screen suddenly falling." The daughter sees this change as positive, and my first response was to agree with her view, then I thought about the changes the father has gone through. He can't do the things he loved anymore. Work as a teacher. Drive a car safely. Walk without limping. Everything that used to make up this man's self seems to be gone. Yes, he says words of love, but when a person's "reserve has slipped from feeling," because of old age or illness, the main emotion which is revealed may be fear.

There was a man in our neighborhood who reminds me of the father in "Slipping." He, too, loved to work. He sang at the top of his voice (usually off tune) whenever he worked outside and he was always demanding that we join in. Both in his songs and in his projects. "In the good old SUMMER-TI-IME," my brother Cory and I would bellow as we helped him rig up a pulley to lift stones over his garden fence. "Let me call you SWE-EE-THEART," we'd try to harmonize as we built a birdfeeder designed to completely baffle squirrels. Mr. G was always busy and was always trying to figure out some new way to do something.

When Cory and I worked with him, he didn't have too much patience. There might be a tool that we'd drop or we'd put something together wrong, he'd have some sharp comment for us. Sometimes he'd send us home. Or even tell us to "get lost." There were many years, however, when we were fascinated by his strange inventions, and we'd always go back when we got one of his semi-grouchy invitations to "stop staring at me and get over here to help." As we got older, we really were able to help, but Mr. Gagnon never said thank you. I guess he never thought about it. Because Cory and I were always there, willing to come.

One day, when I was twelve years old, I realized I hadn't seen Mr. G for two or three days. I was told by my mother that he'd been sick. A brain tumor was diagnosed by the doctors, they wanted to operate. I felt sick myself thinking about it. Mr. G didn't want the surgery because he was told all the things that could happen. His eyesight or his ability to walk could be lost. Not to mention his memory. Finally, however, he had the surgery.

When he came home, my mom, Cory, and I went to visit. It was horrible. Mr. G had been in the hospital for two weeks and he had lost lots of weight. Mrs. G said that he had bad dreams both when he was awake and when he was asleep. He just stared at us. He looked scared. Then he croaked in a little, tinny voice "Who's that? Who's that?" We said our names, and he called for me to come over. He grabbed at my hand and started to tell me how glad he was to see me; how much he liked Cory and me. He thanked us for coming to see him. And kept saying over and over to please come back.

Unlike the speaker in the poem, I didn't feel good about this change. There were times that I used to wish that Mr. G would at least ac-knowledge the good things Cory and I did. But, now as he talked, it just seemed that he didn't have any of himself left. I suppose, in a way, I was seeing behind a screen that suddenly fell away. I was seeing an intimate part of Mr. G, but I felt like he was forced into showing this part of himself. It wasn't like he just decided he wanted to express that he liked us. It seemed like he was forced into it by his sickness. It was the weakness and the fear of not being strong again. The fear that we wouldn't come to visit now that he was changed.

The speaker in "Slipping" says that what she loves about her aging father is "the way reserve has slipped from his feeling." But is emotion expressed under these circumstances really something to celebrate?

REVISING FOCUS: TITLES, OPENINGS, CONCLUSIONS After Karen had written her draft, she put it away for several days and then looked at it again with a fresh mind and "new eyes." As she read, Karen liked very much the way she had described Mr. Gagnon. For example, she saw that the specific details she had used—the songs he taught and the projects he worked on—showed the reader his life and energy.

But she was not happy with her title. She felt it was too general and did not really reflect what she hoped to say in the paper. Also, she thought the opening paragraph was somewhat confusing. She didn't explain the first quote she used; it just seemed to hang there without really making much sense. In addition, her tentative thesis needed added detail to make clear that the changing emotions she discussed resulted from the weakening that often accompanies aging and illness.

Karen also recognized that her conclusion was much too brief. Her question was a starting place, but she needed to develop her response more fully. Her list for revising looked like this:

1. Title—needs to be more specific
2. Opening paragraph
   Explain quote better
   Revise thesis
3. Conclusion—expand (maybe try answering question?)

EDITING FOCUS: "TO BE," EXPLETIVES, PASSIVE VOICE As Karen reread her paper, she noticed that some of her sentences seemed awkward. They just didn't sound right as she read them aloud. With some help from a tutor at the writing center on her campus, she saw three problems she could correct:

1. Overuse of forms of the verb "to be." Karen replaced them with active verbs where possible.

   Mr. G. was always busy and was always trying to figure out some new way to do something.
   Edited: Mr. G. always kept busy trying to figure out some new way to do something.

2. Overuse of expletives such as "there is" and "there are."

   There was a man in our neighborhood who reminds me of the father in "Slipping."
   Edited: Mr. Gagnon, a man from our neighborhood, reminds me of the father in "Slipping."

3. Overuse of passive-voice constructions. (In passive-voice constructions, the subject of the sentence is acted upon; in active voice, the subject acts.)

   A brain tumor was diagnosed by the doctors.
   Edited: The doctors had diagnosed a brain tumor.

PROOFREADING FOCUS: FRAGMENTS AND COMMA SPLICES
The tutor at the writing center also told Karen that some of her sentences were confusing because they were fragments or comma splices.

Fragment: Drive a car safely
Edited: He can't drive a car safely.

Comma splice: The daughter sees this change as positive, and my first response was to agree with her view, then I thought about the changes the father has gone through.
Edited: The daughter sees this change as positive, and my first response was to agree with her view. Then I thought about the changes the father has gone through.

Exercise

Keeping in mind the revising, editing, and proofreading focuses just discussed, as well as your own evaluation of the draft, try rewriting Karen's paper. Think carefully about the reasons for the changes you make. Then compare your final version with the one that follows. Of course, each person's revision of this paper will be different. The point is not to duplicate Karen's final paper but to think about the differences and similarities between the choices she made and the choices you made.

Final Copy: Writing to Respond

CHANGES: FOR BETTER OR WORSE?
Karen Angstrom

The daughter in Joan Aleshire's poem "Slipping" notices her father becoming more open to expressing emotions as he becomes older. She says his normal reserve is "like a screen suddenly falling." The daughter sees this change as positive, and my first response was to agree with her view. Then I thought about the changes the father has gone through. He can't do the things he loved anymore. He can't work as a teacher or drive a car safely or walk without limping. Everything that used to make up this man's self seems to be gone. Yes, he says words of love, but when a person's "reserve has slipped from feeling," because of old age or illness, the main emotion revealed may be fear.

Mr. Gagnon, a man from our neighborhood, reminds me of the father in "Slipping." Like the father, Mr. G, too, loved to work. He sang at the top of his voice (usually off tune) whenever he worked outside, and he frequently demanded that my brother Cory and I join him, both in his songs and in his projects. "In the good old SUM-MER-TI-IME," my brother and I would bellow as we helped Mr. G rig up a pulley to lift stones over his garden fence. "Let me call you SWE-EE-THEART," we'd try to harmonize as we built a birdfeeder designed to completely baffle squirrels. Mr. G always kept busy trying to figure out some new way to do something.

When Cory and I worked with him, he didn't have too much patience. If we dropped a tool or put something together wrong, he'd have some sharp comment for us. Sometimes he'd send us home or even tell us to "get lost." Nevertheless, for many years, we were fascinated by his strange inventions, and we'd always go back when we got one of his semi-grouchy invitations to "stop staring at me and get over here to help." As we got older, we really were able to help. We unloaded countless boxes of supplies from his old station wagon and picked up hundreds of scraps to store in what he called his "useful junk" pile. During all these years, Mr. Gagnon never said thank you or told us that we did a good job. He never told us he was glad to see us, either. I guess he never thought about it since Cory and I were always there, willing to come.

One day, when I was twelve years old, I realized I hadn't seen Mr. G for two or three days. My mother told me that he'd been sick. The doctors diagnosed a brain tumor, and they wanted to operate. I felt sick myself thinking about it. When he was told all the possible side-effects of the operation, Mr. G didn't want the surgery. He could have lost his eyesight or his ability to walk, not to mention his memory. Finally, however, he had the surgery.

When he came home, my mom, Cory, and I went to visit. It was horrible. Mr. G had been in the hospital for two weeks, and he had lost lots of weight. Mrs. G said that he had bad dreams both when he was awake and when he was asleep. He just stared at us, looking scared. Then he croaked in a little, tinny voice: "Who's that? Who's that?" We said our names, and he called for me to come over. He grabbed at my hand and started to tell me how glad he was to see me. He repeated several times how much he liked Cory and me. He thanked us for coming to see him and kept saying over and over to please come back.

Unlike the speaker in the poem, I didn't feel good about this change. Sometimes I used to wish that Mr. G would at least acknowledge the good things Cory and I did. But, now as he talked, it just seemed that he didn't have any of himself left. I suppose, in a way, like the daughter in "Slipping," I was seeing behind a screen that had suddenly fallen away. I was seeing an intimate part of Mr. G, but I felt like he was forced into showing this part of himself. He didn't have the chance to decide for himself that he wanted to express that he liked us. He seemed forced by his weakness, and the fear of not being strong again, to talk about his feelings. I believed he feared that we wouldn't come to visit now that he could no longer create intriguing projects or order us around.

The speaker in "Slipping" says that what she loves about her aging father is "the way reserve has slipped from his feeling." But is emotion expressed under these circumstances really something to celebrate? I don't think so. Yes, "years of restraint" may have been pushed away, yet the force that pushes them may be fear rather than love. The person who stands exposed like "someone dressing or washing" has lost all of his privacy and all of his personal power. That person has no more real self.

Exercise

Read a work from the anthology sections of this book and then, using the process demonstrated with Karen's paper, plan and write a response. Begin by briefly summarizing your response to the work and then use a personal narrative to explain that response. Make references to the story, poem, play, or essay that show its connection to your narrative.

As you write your response, keep the following guidelines in mind.

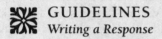

GUIDELINES
Writing a Response

1. Read the work several times, making marginal notes and writing journal entries to explore your responses.
2. Focus on one response that seems particularly strong.
3. Explain that response, using examples from your own experience, but also make certain to refer to the work so that the connections between your experience and the work are clear.
4. Remember that a response asks for your own ideas and feelings, not simply a summary of the ideas and feelings in the work.

Writing to Compare

The second assignment topic asks the reader to make comparisons between "Slipping" and "Do Not Go Gentle."

Topic 2

Explore the similarities and differences you see between these poems. Then write a paper explaining what you discovered and what significance you find in these similarities and differences.

As Walter Johnson considered this topic, he thought that it was relatively simple to see several things that were the same about the two poems as well as several things that were different. But the topic also asked for an explanation of the significance of the similarities and differences. This step—making meaning from the comparisons and contrasts—seemed more difficult.

DISCOVERING IDEAS: DISCUSSION Walter read the poems several times and made these lists of similarities and differences to bring to a scheduled small-group discussion of paper topics.

	"Do Not Go Gentle"	"Slipping"
SUBJECT	old age of speaker's father	same
RHYME	regular rhyme pattern	no rhyme
IMAGES	mostly visual—(lots about light)	visual and physical—leg weakens, walking slowly; screen falling
SETTING	on a mountain? ("sad height"?)	in familiar places; walking near home; thinking of photograph (probably at home)—picture shows father at work
IDEA	changes in father seen as negative; he should fight old age (the "good night")	changes in father positive; becomes more loving, less reserved

Walter's instructor assigned him to a group of four students; all of them were working on the comparison topic. Several had brought lists of their own. Everyone agreed that finding the significance was the most difficult part of the assignment. The following edited excerpt from a taped transcript of their discussion illustrates the way talking about literature can lead to discovering possibilities for writing.

Walter: One poem—"Do Not Go Gentle"—says that the changes in old age are bad, but in "Slipping" the person seems to see those changes as good. So they're completely opposite.

Anna: Well, I don't see—I don't think that—in "Do Not Go" what you have to look at is that he says "*good* night." Why is old age—or, I think it's death—a "good night" if it's bad? But I agree he wants his father to fight it.

Tomás: Same thing to me about "Slipping." You can't—in my opinion, you can't just say that she—the person who's talking in the poem—is saying something like, "Old age is really great and it makes people change in a good way." I mean it's definitely under pretty awful circumstances. Like the guy— her father—is losing his memory and he can't even drive a car right. So I would say *some* changes in old age can be good.

Michelle: But what Anna was saying, I think "good night" could be just like saying "good-bye." So that it would be: "Don't go without a fight into that last 'good-bye.'" Don't just go through these changes without resisting what you lose.

Walter: Right. I can see what Anna says, but he says "rage, rage against the dying of the light" so many times. And like I wrote on the list here with the rhyme words—so many of them rhyme with "light"—it's like he really wants to emphasize that. To emphasize that the father should fight against the light going away—the light, I think, is like his life—his normal life. It's a metaphor or symbol—whatever—for life.

Anna: I can agree—but what I'm just saying—it's not the opposite of what you're saying—it's just that you can't totally ignore the "good" part.

Tomás: So does it matter whether this guy thinks that old age can be a little bit good or not? What I noticed was the way he was giving advice to his father. He's like really making a lot of decisions for his father, I think. Or trying to make them.

Walter: The person in "Slipping," she's not telling her father what to do—she's just glad he is changed.

Michelle: Right. The speaker in "Do Not Go Gentle" seems like he can't accept the changes in his father—or in anyone who gets old and is facing death. The daughter in "Slipping," you can see she's accepting the changes—and she even appreciates some of the changes.

CONSIDERING AUDIENCE, NARROWING THE TOPIC, AND DEVISING A PRELIMINARY THESIS After thinking about this discussion, Walter realized he needed to be careful not to make sweeping generalizations he couldn't support. For instance, he saw that Anna had a reasonable point about the ambiguity of the phrase "good night." To make what he said convincing to other students (and, of course, to the instructor) he could not simply say that one poem showed the changes of old age as bad and the other showed those changes as good.

The last part of the discussion printed here seemed particularly useful for discovering a specific topic and formulating a preliminary thesis. Walter thought about the speaker in "Do Not Go Gentle" giving advice to his father and compared that to the speaker in "Slipping" describing her thoughts. She seems to be much more accepting of the changes of old age than does the speaker in Thomas's poem.

This insight led to the following preliminary thesis:

> The speakers in Joan Aleshire's poem "Slipping" and Dylan Thomas's poem "Do Not Go Gentle into That Good Night" raise questions about the responses of those who must watch someone they love face the changes of old age.

PLANNING AND ORGANIZING Walter now had a central idea to work with, and he had the list he'd made to bring to the group discussion. In addition, he had other notes written in the margins of the poem as well as notes taken in class and during and after the small-group discussion.

When he thought about organizing the information, he remembered from his composition course that there are two standard ways to write about comparisons and contrasts. He could talk about one poem first and then talk about the second, referring back to the first to note similarities and differences. Or he could talk about one point he wanted to make and discuss each poem in relationship to that point, then go on to a new point once again, discussing each poem in relationship to that point, and so on. Instead of deciding on one structure and then drafting, Walter decided to try writing two outlines to see which organization would work best with the ideas and information he had gathered.

RESPONSES
I. Introduction—responses of person watching a parent face the changes of old age
II. "Do Not Go Gentle"
    A. Speaker's tone—giving advice
    B. Rhyme and rhythm—emphasizes pattern; speaker wants order; wants listener to do what speaker wants
    C. Setting—general, symbolic, applies to many "old men" (people?) in various circumstances
    D. Images—mostly visual; focus on seeing, and on past actions
III. "Slipping"
    A. Speaker's tone—explaining, reassuring
    B. No rhyme—rhythm close to ordinary talking; not like planned speech
    C. Setting—real-life (a walk outside family house; a photo of the father in his classroom)
    D. Images—appeal to both sight and touch—more intimate
IV. Conclusion: Speakers' responses different; themes of poems go in different directions. Contradictory? Agreeing in any way?

RESPONSES
I. Introduction—responses of person watching a parent face the changes of old age
II. Speaker's tone
    A. "Do Not Go Gentle"—giving advice, resisting
    B. "Slipping"—accepting
III. Rhyme and rhythm
    A. "Do Not Go Gentle"—emphasizes pattern; speaker wants order; wants listener to do what speaker wants
    B. "Slipping"—no rhyme—rhythm seems close to ordinary talking—not like planned speech
IV. Setting
    A. "Do Not Go Gentle"—general, applies to many "old men" (people?) in various circumstances
    B. "Slipping"—specific: one father; individual experiences (teaching, going for walks)

V. Images
    A. "Do Not Go Gentle"—mostly visual; focuses on seeing, and
        on past actions
    B. "Slipping"—appeals to both sight and touch—more intimate
VI. Conclusion: Speakers' responses different; themes of poems go in
    different directions. Contradictory? Agreeing in any way?

DRAFTING After thinking about both possibilities for organizing, Walter decided to try the first arrangement. Like most successful writers, he revises throughout the process of working on the assignment. For instance, looking at the two outlines convinced him that his title needed to be more specific. He needed to connect his idea of responses to the theme he was working with, and so he came up with "Responses: Raging versus Slipping."

Note, too, that he doesn't expect to resolve every question about his topic completely before he starts drafting. For example, his outlines show that he still has questions about the paper's conclusion.

RESPONSES: RAGING VERSUS SLIPPING
Walter Johnson

The speakers in Joan Aleshire's poem "Slipping" and Dylan Thomas's poem "Do Not Go Gentle into That Good Night" describe their responses as their fathers face the changes of old age. The speakers in these two poems look at their aging parents in very different ways.

In "Do Not Go Gentle" the speaker is talking to his father and is telling him to fight against "the dying of the light." The speaker sounds like he is giving a speech that is meant to convey the conviction to his father, and a larger audience would be informed as well, that it's important to "rage, rage" against the changes of old age. This is advice given to all old men, not just to one old man. Then each of the stanzas that follows talks about one category of old men and showed that no matter what they may have done in life, in the end they all fight the changes that lead to death. They did not give in easily.

The regular rhythm and rhyme in the poem contributes to making it sound like an argument. This repetition emphasizes the speaker's plea. It sounds like a carefully planned speech that is designed to be very convincing to anyone who hears it, not just the father who is not spoken to directly until the last stanza.

It's hard to tell where this speaker is. He isn't clearly in a house or a work place or any building. In the middle four stanzas, the men described are related to parts of nature but these seemed to be general and not specific places. The father in the final stanza is on a "sad height," which doesn't seem like a real mountain. Instead, it may be a metaphor for the final place humans reach just before they die. All these setting elements emphasized that the speaker was arguing for an approach to old age that he thinks is best for many men. Of course, it was also best for his father as well.

Most of the images in the poem are visual. They are things you see or think about. Things you feel or experience are not pictured. For example, the speaker talks about words that "forked no lightning" and deeds that "might have danced in a green bay." The speaker talked about past deeds rather than about the present experience of aging and (possibly) illness that these old men, and the speaker's father, now face.

The speaker's tone in "Slipping" is explanatory and accepting. The speaker is describing the changes in her father with understanding. She sympathizes with her father and understands what he is facing, but she doesn't wish him back the way he was. She expresses, instead, her love for his new way of expressing his emotions.

In "Slipping" there are no rhymes, and the rhythm seems like an ordinary conversation and not like a planned speech that is making an argument. The speaker even uses direct quotations, giving the exact words of her mother and father.

In "Slipping" the settings are from real life. The father is shown driving a car, taking a walk with his daughter, and there is a picture of him teaching in his classroom.

The images in "Slipping" are personal and appeal to both sight and touch. The father's leg "trailing a little" and the "curtain of mist" that obscures his sight make the changes he faces specific. He is compared to "a child who keeps pulling on your hand," and his feelings are exposed like someone who was dressing behind a screen that suddenly falls down.

The speakers, who clearly love the aging fathers, have very different responses to the changes they see. The speaker in "Do Not Go Gentle" takes the responsibility for his father's life on his own shoulders. He tells his father how to approach old age. It seems like the speaker just thinks about death as the ultimate enemy which everyone should fight. On the other hand, the speaker in "Slipping" sees both the negative aspects of the changes and also the positive aspects. The speaker in "Do Not Go Gentle" rages against accepting his father's changes. On the other hand, the speaker in Aleshire's poem just slips into this new phase of life.

REVISING FOCUS: TRANSITIONS, DEVELOPMENT OF IDEAS   When Walter read his paper to Anna, Tomás, and Michelle during an in-class workshop, he asked about the organization of his paper. As he reread his paper, the meaning didn't seem to flow smoothly from paragraph to paragraph. He wondered whether he should have used the organization shown in the second outline (page 95). Here's an excerpt from an edited transcript of the tape made during the discussion that followed:

Anna: I don't know—to me, the other organization—where you discuss each little bit separately—that could be just as jumpy.

Tomás: The main thing for me was that when you got to the part on "Slipping," it seemed really like a surprise. I didn't really see where you led in to it.

Michelle: We were talking the last time about similarities and differences—which is the subject or—well—the approach to the paper. But I don't see that.

Walter: Don't see what?

Michelle: Don't see that you are comparing. It's like two separate papers—except for the first paragraph and the conclusion.

After thinking about the comments of his writing group, Walter saw that he had not connected his thoughts clearly. He had not shown his readers how he got from one idea to the next. He knew that he needed to work on **transitions:** words, phrases, and sentences that provide a bridge from one paragraph to the next or from one section of the paper to the next. He had to show the relationship among his ideas and examples.

In addition, he noticed that some of his paragraphs seemed too short. As he read them, he saw that he needed to expand and explain his ideas more fully. He needed to be more specific: to give details, reasons, and examples that would convey his thoughts accurately to his audience.

EDITING FOCUS: NOMINALIZATIONS, PARALLEL STRUC-TURE The writing group also noticed several sentences that needed to be edited. Most of the sentences either used some form of the verb "to be" too much (see page 89) or relied too heavily on nouns that were formed from verbs (nominalizations). As an example, Tomás pointed out this sentence from the second paragraph:

> The speaker sounds like he is giving a speech that is meant to convey the conviction to his father, and a larger audience would be informed as well, that it's important to "rage, rage" against the changes of old age.

Notice that Walter uses some form of the verb "to be" three times. When a sentence sounds wordy and plodding, you can often improve it by getting rid of excess "to be" verbs. In addition, this sentence uses the nominalization "convey the conviction" instead of the simpler, more direct, active form of the verb "convince." Here's the sentence as Walter edited it.

> The speaker sounds like he is giving a speech meant to convince his father, and a larger audience would be informed as well, to "rage, rage" against the changes of old age.

Walter can improve the structure of this sentence further by using parallel phrases instead of the awkward "his father, and a larger audience would be informed as well."

The speaker sounds like he is giving a speech meant to convince not only his father but also a larger audience to "rage, rage" against the changes of old age.

Notice that the edited sentence is much leaner and sleeker than the original; the edited sentence uses thirty words, whereas the original uses forty.

PROOFREADING FOCUS: SUBJECT–VERB AGREEMENT, TENSE AGREEMENT As the writing group gave final consideration to Walter's paper, Michelle suggested that he proofread for two other problems:

1. Problem with subject-verb agreement.

   Plural subject   *Singular verb*
   The regular *rhythm and rhyme* in the poem *contributes* to making it sound like an argument.

   Plural subject   *Plural verb*
   Edited: The regular *rhythm* and *rhyme* in the poem *contribute* to making it sound like an argument.

2. Problem with verb tense agreement. Verbs should all be in the same tense unless there is a reason to indicate a change to another time. Generally, papers about literature are written in present tense. In this sentence, "showed" marks an unneeded switch from present to past tense:

   Present
   Then each of the stanzas that follows *talks* about one category of

   Past   *Present perfect*
   old men and *showed* that no matter what they *may have done* in life,

   Present
   in the end they all *fight* the changes that lead to death.

   Edited: Then each of the stanzas that follows *talks* about one category of old man and *shows* that, no matter what they *may have done* in life, in the end they all *fight* the changes that lead to death.

Exercise

Keeping in mind the revising, editing, and proofreading focuses just discussed as well as your own evaluation of the draft, try rewriting Walter's paper. Think carefully about the reasons for the changes you make. Then compare your final version with the one that follows. Of course, each person's revision of this paper will be different. The point is not to duplicate Walter's final paper but to think about the differences and similarities between the choices he made and the choices you made.

Final Copy: Writing to Compare

RESPONSES: RAGING VERSUS SLIPPING
Walter Johnson

The speakers in Joan Aleshire's poem "Slipping" and Dylan Thomas's poem "Do Not Go Gentle into That Good Night" describe their responses as their fathers experience the changes of old age. Thomas's speaker sees his father as representative of all men facing old age and urges his father to fight old age. Aleshire's speaker, on the other hand, looks at her father's changes in a more personal way and sees some of the changes as being in some ways positive.

In "Do Not Go Gentle" the speaker talks to his father and tells him to struggle against "the dying of the light." The speaker sounds like he is giving a speech meant to convince not only his father but also a larger audience to "rage, rage" against death. For instance, he says in the first stanza, "Old age should burn and rave at close of day." Here the speaker advises all old men, not just one old man. Then each stanza that follows talks about one category of old man and shows that, no matter what they may have done in life, in the end they all fight death. They do not give in easily.

The regular rhythm and rhyme in the poem contribute to making it sound like an argument. Of the nineteen lines in the poem, thirteen either end with the word "light" or "night" or with a word that rhymes with "light" or "night." This repetition emphasizes the speaker's plea. It sounds like a carefully planned speech designed to convince not just the father, who is not directly addressed until the last stanza, but anyone who hears it.

The setting of the poem also indicates a larger audience than just the father. It's hard to tell where this speaker is. He isn't clearly in a building or in a specific outdoor location. In the middle four stanzas, the men described relate to parts of nature (lightning, a green bay, the sun, meteors) but these seem to be general and not specific places. The father in the final stanza stands on a "sad height," which doesn't seem like a real mountain but instead like a metaphor for the final place humans reach just before they die. All these setting elements emphasize that the speaker argues for an approach to old age that he considers best for many men as well as for his father.

The speaker's approach to old age seems to be highly idealistic and philosophical. Most of the images in the poem are visual. They show things you see or think about rather than things you feel or experience, for example, words that "forked no lightning" and deeds that "might have danced in a green bay." The speaker talks about past deeds rather than about the present experience of aging and (possibly) illness that these old men, and the speaker's father, now face.

In contrast to the formal, arguing tone of "Do Not Go Gentle," the speaker's tone in "Slipping" explains and accepts. The speaker describes the changes in her father with understanding. She sees that his legs can "barely support him" and that he is losing his memory. These details show that she sympathizes with her father and recognizes what he is facing, but she doesn't wish him back the way he was. She expresses, instead, her love for his new way of expressing his emotions. She describes this openness with a gentle image, noting "how soft and mutable is the usually hidden flesh."

The rhyme and rhythm also contrast sharply with those of "Do Not Go Gentle." In Thomas's poem, the rhythm and rhyme are regular and repetitive. In "Slipping," there are no rhymes, and the rhythm seems like everyday speech and not like a planned formal argument. The speaker even uses direct quotations, giving the exact words of her mother ("He's never liked to talk about feelings") and her father ("I love you"). This dialogue gives an intimate view of a specific family rather than the formal picture conveyed by the language of "Do Not Go Gentle."

In "Do Not Go Gentle," there's no clear picture of the speaker's location, and his examples also have general, idealized settings. In "Slipping," however, the setting comes from real life. The father is shown driving a car, taking a walk with his daughter, and teaching in his classroom. Even the metaphor the daughter uses to describe his changes—the screen falling—gives a picture of a dressing room, like the ones in a doctor's office.

The images in "Slipping" also show the difference between this poem and "Do Not Go Gentle." While Thomas's images are visual and can be applied generally to large groups of men, the images in "Slipping" are personal and appeal to both sight and touch. The father's leg "trailing a little" and the "curtain of mist" that obscures his sight make the changes he faces specific. His trailing leg is compared to "a child who keeps pulling on your hand," and his feelings are exposed like someone who was dressing behind a screen that suddenly falls down. Both images give a physical sense of someone who has lost power.

The speakers, who clearly love their aging fathers, have very different responses to the changes they see. The speaker in "Do Not Go Gentle" takes the responsibility for his father's life on his own shoulders. He tells his father how to approach old age. It seems like the speaker just thinks about death as the ultimate enemy that everyone should fight. On the other hand, the speaker in "Slipping" sees both the negative and the positive aspects of the changes. The father no longer has the pleasure of his work, but he now has found a relationship with his family, which never seemed to be possible before. The speaker in "Do Not Go Gentle" rages against accepting his father's changes, whereas the speaker in Aleshire's poem seems, like her father, to slip gently into this new phase of life.

Exercise

Read several works from any one of the thematic chapters of this book (Chapters 5 through 12). Then, using the process demonstrated with Walter's paper, choose two works and plan and write a comparison. Keep in mind the principles presented in the following Guidelines box.

> ### ❋ GUIDELINES
> *Writing a Comparison*
>
> 1. As you plan the paper by doing preliminary reading, writing, and thinking, remember that listing and outlining are useful strategies for planning a comparison paper.
> 2. Remember that a comparison should be made for a purpose. A comparison should not simply list the similarities and differences discovered during planning sessions.
> 3. Note which similarities or differences seem most significant and decide which you will emphasize.
> 4. Decide how you will organize your paper—for example, the "whole-subject" approach, the "point-by-point" approach, or a combination of these approaches.
> 5. Open with a paragraph that focuses on the purpose and point of the comparison. For example, do *not* say
>   > In this paper "Slipping" will be compared to "Do Not Go Gentle into That Good Night."
>   >
>   > *or*
>   >
>   > There are many similarities and differences between "Slipping" and "Do Not Go Gentle into That Good Night."
>
>   *Do* say, for example,
>   > The speakers in Joan Aleshire's poem "Slipping" and Dylan Thomas's poem "Do Not Go Gentle into That Good Night" describe their responses as their fathers face the changes of old age.
> 6. Develop each subject (or each point) in a separate paragraph (or a series of carefully related and logically linked paragraphs).
> 7. Make certain that transitions between paragraphs and between sections of the paper show the connections—the comparisons and contrasts—you want to make.
> 8. Develop a conclusion that offers an analysis, evaluates the evidence the body of your paper provides, or in some other way shows the significance of the comparison you have made.

Writing to Analyze

When you analyze, you look at parts (or at a part) in relationship to the whole to which they belong. For example, a United States history exam might ask you to discuss and explain the significance of the economic causes of the American Revolution. Such a question requires that you look at part (the economic causes) of a whole (the American Revolution) and that you explain how knowing about that part contributes to understanding the whole. When you analyze a work of literature, you look carefully at its parts—or at one particular part—to see what they contribute to the meaning the whole work holds for you. For instance, you might look carefully at the language of a poem, a particular character in a short story, or a significant scene in a play. The third assignment topic asks for such an approach.

Topic 3

Explain how the figurative language in one of the poems suggests the relationship between the speaker and his or her father.

As Catherine Hupel considered this topic, she noticed that "Slipping" was divided into three stanzas. She knew that she was being asked to look at one element—figurative language—and to talk about how that element worked to create the poem's meaning. Looking at the parts in relation to the whole called for analysis, so she decided to look at each stanza to see how the figurative language helped to develop the speaker's view of her father.

DISCOVERING IDEAS: LISTING AND GROUPING   Catherine began by making the following lists:

Stanza 1: Father's aging is like "Slow slipping"
               Eyes blinded "curtain of mist" (cataract?)
               Years (father's aging) like "pickpockets"
               Father drives car "like raft on river"
                      "drifts from lane to lane"

Stanza 2: Father's leg "trails like a child"

Stanza 3: Father in photo: "Stethoscope like a pet snake"
               Father's reserve has fallen "like a screen"

After making the list, Catherine saw that these figures of speech were all similes (comparisons using "like" or "as"). She noticed that several of the images suggested something hidden or stealthy. She noticed, too, that some of the similes had a negative connotation, whereas others were dreamlike. She grouped the similes as follows:

hidden/stealthy	negative	dreamlike
curtain of mist	pickpockets	slow slipping
pickpockets	pet snake	curtain of mist
		drifts . . . like a raft

Catherine knew that dividing the images into these lists would help her to plan her paper. She also noted that not every image fit neatly. For instance, "curtain of mist" and "pickpockets" seemed to belong in two categories, whereas "like a child" did not seem to fit any category.

CONSIDERING AUDIENCE, NARROWING THE TOPIC, AND DEVISING A PRELIMINARY THESIS Catherine knew that other students in the class would be reading her draft as part of the revision process. She also knew that some of them might not see the similes as falling into the categories she had created. For instance, she knew that not everyone would see "pet snake" as negative, so she realized she had to convince her readers that her analysis was plausible, even though they might not agree with her conclusions. Considering her evaluation of her audience, Catherine decided to narrow her focus to the ambivalent feelings she believed the speaker's similes revealed. Catherine developed the following tentative thesis:

> Although the speaker in Joan Aleshire's poem "Slipping" clearly loves her father, some of the figurative language in the poem suggests a darker side to their new closeness.

PLANNING, ORGANIZING, AND DRAFTING At first, Catherine thought she would organize her paper by going through the poem and discussing each stanza. However, as she thought about her thesis, she decided that the most effective way to convince her audience would be to discuss the speaker's positive feelings first and then to show that the figurative language also suggested negative aspects. Here is Catherine's next-to-final draft:

LOVE AND LOSS IN "SLIPPING"
Catherine Hupel

Joan Aleshire's poem demonstrates the strong emotions the speaker feels for her father. She describes with kind understanding the symptoms of his aging and indicates her pleasure at feeling closer to her father than she has in the past. Nevertheless, although the speaker clearly loves her father, some of the figurative language in the poem suggests a darker side to their new closeness.

It is easy to identify images and figures of speech that show the speaker's caring for her father. For example, in the first stanza, she describes her father's losses with such phrases as "slow slipping" and "curtain of mist." These phrases clearly show his changes, yet the words are also gentle, even dreamlike, suggesting her sympathy for him.

The speaker goes on to describe her father's weak leg. It drags behind "like / a child who keeps pulling on your hand." She also notes that her father is now more open to her and that he finds a sense of pleasure in visits where "years of restraint" have been "pushed away." In fact, she describes this change with a simile: The "reserve has slipped / from his feeling like a screen suddenly / falling." Now they are able to say to each other the words "I love you."

In spite of the positive feelings expressed, much of the figurative language shows negative emotions that underlie the speaker's picture of her father. For example, even the title "Slipping" can mean so many things. "To slip" can mean to lose physical and mental health, which is what is literally meant. On the other hand, we also think of "to slip" as meaning to make a mistake. Perhaps the father has been "slipping" even before his old age. A simile that would confirm this interpretation is the comparison of his stethoscope (in his picture as a younger man) to "a pet snake." The snake is shown in the Bible as a tempter.

Other images that give a dark feeling to the poem include the comparison to the years as "pickpockets." The father has his strength stolen, but the daughter has also had something stolen from her by time— the chance to really know her father well. The comparison of the father's car when he drives to a "raft on a river" suggests a sense of moving away and a lack of direction. It seems that he missed some turns earlier in his life as well, when his face was lighted by "love of his work" in a way the narrator "seldom saw at home."

The image of the father's left leg "trailing a little like / a child who keeps pulling on your hand" may reflect the way the speaker believes her father saw her when she was a child. Finally, the simile that suggests that the father's uncustomary loss of restraint is "like a screen suddenly / falling" has ambiguous meaning. When a screen falls down, it reveals whatever is behind it. That may be good or it may be bad. The speaker says that she loves the fact that he is no longer so reserved. Yet she also is able to see all the wrinkles and flaws.

The figurative language of the poem suggests that the speaker has gained something positive from being with her aging father: she has had a small glimpse into his heart. On the other hand, she has also had to recognize and face up to all that she has lost because this moment of closeness has been so long coming.

REVISING FOCUS: USING AND EXPLAINING EXAMPLES   As Catherine read her draft, she recognized that sometimes her ideas were not fully explained. For example, consider her second paragraph:

It is easy to identify images and figures of speech that show the speaker's caring for her father. For example, in the first stanza, she describes her father's losses with phrases like "slow slipping" and "curtain of mist." These phrases clearly show his changes, yet the words are also gentle, even dreamlike, suggesting her sympathy for him.

In this paragraph, Catherine gives examples of images and figures of speech in her second sentence, but she doesn't really show how these examples relate to the statement in her first sentence. Here's how she revised this paragraph:

> It is easy to identify images and figures of speech that show the speaker's caring for her father. For example, in the first stanza, she shows the gradual losses that her father must endure. These losses include physical weakness in the legs, the ability to remember and to concentrate, and the ability to drive safely. She describes these losses with phrases like "slow slipping" and "curtain of mist." These phrases clearly show his changes, yet the words are also gentle, even dreamlike, suggesting her sympathy for him.

Exercise

Compare the rest of Catherine's next-to-final draft with the final paper (page 107). Identify places where she has amplified and explained her examples. Then explain why you think she made these choices. What has been gained by the revisions she made? Keep in mind the principles presented in the Guidelines box on page 109.

EDITING FOCUS: WORD CHOICE In an earlier draft of her paper (not included here), Catherine had written the following sentences. As she read this draft, some of the words she had chosen did not sound quite right to her. These words are indicated in the examples that follow by boldface type. She checked with a dictionary, and in a few cases asked her professor's advice, and then replaced the word she had used with one that reflected the meaning she had intended.

1. *Original:* Joan Aleshire's poem **denotes** the strong emotions the speaker feels for her father.
   Edited: Joan Aleshire's poem **demonstrates** the strong emotions the speaker feels for her father.
2. *Original:* For example, in the first stanza, she shows the **graduated** losses that her father must endure.
   Edited: For example, in the first stanza, she shows the **gradual** losses that her father must endure.
3. *Original:* Finally, the simile that suggests that the father's **unaccustomary** loss of restraint is "like a screen suddenly / falling" has ambiguous meanings.
   Edited: Finally, the simile that suggests that the father's **uncustomary** loss of restraint is "like a screen suddenly / falling" has ambiguous meanings.

Exercise

Check the words in these examples in a dictionary, and explain why you think Catherine made the choices shown in the edited sentences.

PROOFREADING FOCUS: MISPLACED MODIFIERS In an early draft, not shown here, Catherine had written this sentence:

Although loving her father, the figurative language in the poem suggests a darker side to their new closeness.

As she read the sentence, she could see that something was wrong. After talking with a tutor at the campus writing center, Catherine saw that she had written a sentence with a misplaced modifier. The introductory phrase "although loving her father" should describe the word or phrase that follows it. Of course, "although loving her father" does not describe "the figurative language"; it describes the speaker. Catherine revised the sentence this way:

Nevertheless, although the speaker loves her father, some of the figurative language in the poem suggests a darker side to their new closeness.

Exercise

Identify and revise the misplaced modifiers in the following paragraph: Driving his car in a dangerous way, the lives of the father and others could have been threatened. The daughter's thoughts only should have been about the safety of her father and others on the road with him. Instead, while continuing to drive erratically, the daughter seems to be doing nothing to keep her father off the road.

Final Copy: Writing to Analyze

After revising, editing, and proofreading, Catherine submitted to her professor the following draft of her paper.

LOVE AND LOSS IN "SLIPPING"
Catherine Hupel

Joan Aleshire's poem demonstrates the strong emotions the speaker feels for her father. She describes with kind understanding the symptoms of his aging and indicates her pleasure at feeling closer to her father than she has in the past. Nevertheless, although the speaker clearly loves her father, some of the figurative language in the poem suggests a darker side to their new closeness.

It is easy to identify images and figures of speech that show the speaker's caring for her father. For example, in the first stanza, she shows the gradual losses that her father must endure. These losses include physical weakness in the legs, the ability to remember and to concentrate, and the ability to drive safely. She describes these losses with such phrases as "slow slipping" and "curtain of mist." These phrases clearly show his changes, yet the words are also gentle, even dreamlike, suggesting her sympathy for him.

The speaker goes on to describe her father's weak leg in a somewhat playful way. It drags behind "like / a child who keeps pulling on your hand." She also notes that her father is now more open to her and that he finds a sense of pleasure in visits where "years of restraint" have been "pushed away." In fact, she describes this change with a simile: The "reserve has slipped / from his feeling like a screen suddenly / falling." Now she is able to see her father more fully than ever before, and they are able to say to each other the words, "I love you."

In spite of the positive feelings expressed, much of the figurative language shows negative emotions that underlie the speaker's picture of her father. For example, even the title "Slipping" can mean so many things. "To slip" can mean to lose physical and mental health, which is what is literally meant. On the other hand, we also think of "to slip" as meaning to make a mistake. Perhaps the father has been "slipping" even before his old age. A simile that would confirm this interpretation is the comparison of his stethoscope (in his picture as a younger man) to "a pet snake." The snake is shown in the Bible as a tempter. Perhaps the father was always tempted by his work, which is represented by his stethoscope, to stay away from his family. He seems to have withheld any expressions of love toward them until now.

Other images that give a dark feeling to the poem include the comparison to the years as "pickpockets," that is, sneak thieves. Time has stolen the father's strength, but it has also stolen something from the daughter—the chance to know her father well. The comparison of the father's car to a "raft on a river" suggests a sense of moving away and a lack of direction. True, this is happening to the father now in his old age, but it seems that he missed some turns earlier in his life as well, when his face was lighted by "love of his work" in a way the narrator "seldom saw at home."

The image of the father's left leg "trailing a little like / a child who keeps pulling on your hand" may reflect the way the speaker believes her father saw her when she was a child. She may believe that he saw her as a force slowing him down and keeping him away from the work he loved. Finally, the simile that suggests that the father's uncustomary loss of restraint is "like a screen suddenly / falling" has ambiguous meaning. When a screen falls down, it reveals whatever is behind it. That may be good, or it may be bad. The speaker says that she loves the fact that he is no longer so reserved. Yet she also is able to see all the wrinkles and flaws.

The figurative language of the poem suggests that the speaker has gained something positive from being with her aging father: she has had a small glimpse into his heart. On the other hand, she has also had to recognize and face up to all that she has lost because this moment of closeness has been so long coming.

✳ GUIDELINES
Writing an Analysis

1. An analysis looks at parts (or at a part) in relationship to the whole to which they belong.
2. A literary analysis often focuses on one or more elements of literature, including—but not limited to—the following:

   > sound (rhyme and rhythm)
   > structure (patterns of lines and stanzas; organization and structure of paragraphs and/or dialogue)
   > figurative language (such as metaphors, similes, personification, symbols)
   > development of characters
   > development of plot and action (particularly conflict/resolution)
   > irony

3. An analysis shows how the element or elements being considered contribute to the whole meaning of the work; each part of the discussion, therefore, must relate to a clear central idea.
4. An analysis is not a paraphrase (a restatement of the ideas of the work in your own words); instead, it is an explanation of the way a work communicates (see page 110).

Writing to Explicate

Explication is one form of analysis. The word "explicate" comes from the Latin *explicare,* which means to unfold. When you write a paper that unfolds the meaning of a work, you are writing an explication. The fourth assignment topic asks for such an approach.

Topic 4

What, exactly, does the speaker say in "Do Not Go Gentle"? And how does he say it? How does the central idea of the poem unfold as you read from one stanza to the next?

Matt Cejak chose this topic. He noticed that the first part of the topic seemed relatively easy; he didn't think he'd have much trouble describing what the speaker says. He also felt confident that he could talk about the central idea of the poem (as required by the last part of the topic). Explaining both how the speaker conveys his meaning and how each stanza relates to the central idea of the poem seemed more difficult.

DISCOVERING IDEAS: PARAPHRASING To make certain he had a sense of what was going on in each stanza, Matt decided to write a **paraphrase.** That is, he decided to write a series of short paragraphs, putting each stanza into his own words.

Paraphrase of "Do Not Go Gentle" (by Dylan Thomas)
1. People who are old should not be resigned to dying. They should fight against it.
2. People who are wise may know that death is the right thing, but (????something about lightning???not sure) they still resist dying.
3. People who are good (seems to mean morally upright?) realize that their time on earth is nearly through, but they think about the things they have done and that makes them fight against death.
4. "Wild men" (outlaws? rebels? nonconformists? crazy people?) who did strange and brave things and acted like they didn't care if they were doing things that might kill them find out at the end of their lives that they regret having to give up life. They then fight against death.
5. Serious (sad?) men who are near death and nearly blind (with disease or old age?) realize (or think) they could still act in some special way (like meteors). These people fight death, too.
6. (Talks directly to his father) You are facing death. I want you to give me your blessing, even though you may curse me with your angry tears, so that you can fight against death.

As he read over the paraphrase, Matt saw that he had a place to begin. But he also saw that working on the explication was going to be harder than he had thought. The paraphrase of "Do Not Go Gentle" seemed matter-of-fact and overly simple. It had none of the energy of the original poem. In addition, the paraphrase raised questions: some of the stanzas were hard to put into prose. They didn't easily yield one thought or idea.

Matt looked closely again at the poem and compared it to his paraphrase. He made this list of what the paraphrase lacked:

1. sound—rhyme, rhythm
2. pattern—repetition, arrangement and number of lines in stanzas
3. figurative language—metaphors, symbols
4. many possible meanings to phrases and sentences

Matt decided to use this list as a guide when he drafted his explication. As he discussed each stanza, he would consider how each of the elements helped to convey meaning.

CONSIDERING AUDIENCE, NARROWING THE TOPIC, AND DEVISING A PRELIMINARY THESIS At this point, Matt thought about focusing his topic more clearly and about finding a preliminary thesis. Everything he came up with seemed too obvious. For example, here are some possibilities he tried:

> Dylan Thomas's poem "Do Not Go Gentle into That Good Night" describes the words of a son pleading with his father to fight death.
> The speaker in Dylan Thomas's poem "Do Not Go Gentle into That Good Night" urges his father to fight against the ending of his life.
> In the poem "Do Not Go Gentle into That Good Night" by Dylan Thomas the idea is given that death is a force to fight.

Matt liked the third possibility better than the other two because the idea seemed more widely applicable than the other two, but he was not really satisfied. Looking back at the topic he'd chosen for this paper, he realized that none of his possible theses really addressed the question of how the ideas and feelings in the poem were conveyed.

Thinking of his instructor as an important part of the audience for this paper, Matt realized that he needed to work on all parts of the topic. Although he was not happy with any of his possible theses, he decided to write a draft to see whether he could discover a clear focus during writing.

PLANNING AND ORGANIZING Because Matt was still not sure where he was going, he had trouble planning the organization of the draft. He didn't have any idea how to write an opening paragraph because he still didn't have a clear preliminary thesis. He remembered, however, that an explication is an unfolding of the meaning of a work. So, he decided to start by discussing the first stanza and then move chronologically through the other five stanzas. He hoped this process would help him to discover how the poem "worked"; then he could return during the revision process to write an introduction.

DRAFTING Matt began work on the draft, keeping in mind the four elements he'd listed as crucial to the way the poem conveys meaning.

EXPLICATION: "DO NOT GO GENTLE"
Matthew Cejak

In the first stanza, three lines give the speaker's plea to old people not to die easily. They should fight and be angry at "close of day." The first and third lines of the stanza rhyme—"night" and "light." The word "rage" is repeated twice. "Night" is a metaphor for death, and "day" or "light" are metaphors for life.

In the second stanza, there are three lines again. They have the same rhyme pattern as the first stanza. In this stanza, the speaker talks about wise men who "know dark is right." When they spoke during their lifetime maybe they didn't really get their message across. They didn't speak like lightning. So they don't want to die, they want to continue to live. The last line repeats the first line of the first stanza.

REVISING FOCUS: SUMMARIZING VERSUS ANALYZING At this point, Matt stopped and reread what he had written. He was happy with some aspects and unhappy with others. He had gone beyond the paraphrase he had written earlier and was paying attention to the list he'd made of elements to consider, but the draft still didn't seem to address the "how" part of the assignment. At this point, Matt asked his instructor for a conference. To prepare for the office conference, Matt consulted the guidelines the instructor had distributed at the beginning of the term.

GUIDELINES
Preparing for a Writing Conference

1. Gather all preliminary work (notes, drafts, books with your annotations, and so on) to bring with you.
2. List the strong points of your paper.
3. List the weak points of your paper. Focus first on large issues, such as organization or use of examples, rather than finer points, such as word choice or punctuation.
4. List approaches you have considered to revise the weaknesses you see.
5. Make a list of questions about your writing project.
6. Make your questions precise.

   Not this: How can I get a better grade on this paper?
   But this: This statement, I know, is too general. How can I make my point more specific?

The following conversation is an edited transcript of Matt's conference with his instructor:

Matt: I can't get started—I know this is wrong.
Instructor: Well, actually, you have a good start here. You've got a lot on paper. Try reading what you've written in this draft out loud.
Matt: (After finishing reading) I know it's not—not enough—or, somehow, doesn't answer the "how" part. But—
Instructor: I think you're right—do you see why?
Matt: No! If I saw why—I would—If I saw why, I'd change it.
Instructor: (Laughs) Right—yes—I see your point. OK. This time, listen to me read what you've said. Tell me what you're learning—new insights into the poem—whatever. *(Reads the draft)*
Matt: What it sounds like to me is a summary of the notes—here—I did this paraphrase and then this list.

Instructor: Good stuff here, Matt. You've done a lot of work—but now you need to go further. You said the word yourself. You've got mostly summary—either summary of meaning or summary of various elements. Take this paragraph, for instance:

> In the first stanza, three lines give the speaker's plea to old people not to die easily. They should fight and be angry at "close of day." The first and third lines of the stanza rhyme "night" and "light." The word "rage" is repeated twice. "Night" is a metaphor for death, and "day" or "light" are metaphors for life.

What's the point here?

Matt: I guess—mmm—it's just to tell what the aspects of the poem are.

Instructor: Can you put any of these sentences together—work on them in a connected way? How do they relate?

Matt: Well, I talk about "night" and "day" or "light" being metaphors and then there's this part about "night" and "light" rhyming and this part where I quote "close of day"—so—maybe—something about how they go together? Why they go together?

Instructor: Sounds like a good plan—let me hear you talk a little more about your idea.

Matt: Well, how about that "night" and "day" are really important to the poem and that this repeating—and the metaphor—and the rhyme—I would say maybe that's how Thomas makes you really notice the importance.

Instructor: See—now you're really getting away from summary and into the analysis—the explication. Good. See—you say "that's *how* Thomas makes you notice. . . ."

After talking with his instructor, Matt knew what direction he wanted his paper to take. He had to make the hard decision to discard most of the first draft. Keeping in mind the idea of making connections and of analyzing rather than summarizing, Matt wrote this second draft. He still was not sure of his central idea, so he again followed his plan of explicating each stanza in chronological order, planning to go back and write an introductory paragraph later.

EXPLICATION: "DO NOT GO GENTLE"
Matthew Cejak

The first stanza begins with the speaker's plea, addressed to old people. They should fight against going "into that good night," a metaphor for death. The words in this stanza set a tone of heat and passion. Those who face death should "burn," "rave," and "rage." The repetition of the word "rage" emphasizes the importance the speaker places on this fight against death.

The second stanza gives the first of three examples demonstrating why the speaker believes old people should resist death. Wise men may know that "dark"—another metaphor for death—"is right." But when these wise men spoke during their lifetime maybe they didn't really get their message across. They didn't speak like lightning. So they don't want to die, they want to continue to live. "Lightning" relates to "light" in the first stanza; both indicate something powerful and good. The lightning may be powerful words, while the light represents life itself. In this stanza, the rhyme scheme of the poem begins to underline the speaker's insistence on life. Like in the first stanza, the first and third lines rhyme. And all four of these lines (1, 3, 4, and 6) rhyme, too. The rhyme emphasizes the relationship between "light" (life) and "night" (death) and the struggle between the two.

"Good men" serve as the example in stanza 3. They don't want to die because they think back on the actions of their lives, and they realize that these actions may not have been fully appreciated. These actions are described as "frail deeds." The word "frail" suggests the weakness often associated with old age, and the "good men" think about how those actions "might have danced in a green bay." This phrase shows the men's actions as lively and sparkling, like light on the water in a bay. Once again, the idea of light is emphasized as good and the idea of dark (death) as bad. The deeds could have been "bright" and so these "good men" fight against letting their light go out. The importance of life is stressed by the rhyming of "bright" and "light" at the ends of the first and last lines in the stanza.

"Wild men" are shown in the fourth stanza as the example of old people who fight death. They seem to be people who grabbed on to parts of life, and yet also let those same parts of life go with no regrets. They "caught" the sun, which may be a metaphor for a very intense and beautiful part of life, but they sang "the sun in flight." This singing indicates that they were able to say good-bye to these intense, beautiful times with joy. But now they realize that they also feel sorrow. They feel the loss of these strong experiences. Once again, the image of light (the sun) is good. It represents power, energy, and life. Like the "wise men" wishing their words had been like lightning, and like the "good men" imagining their deeds dancing "in a green bay," the "wild men" seem to have a strong connection with the physical part of nature (in this case the sun). The final line repeats the ending line of the second stanza and the first line of the first stanza: "Do not go gentle into that good night." The repetition ties this example in with the others and shows that yet one more category of old people fight the ending of life.

The final example of those who "rage, rage against the dying of the light" are grave men. It's interesting to note that "grave" means serious, yet "grave" here could also maybe suggest the nearness to burial—the grave of the dead. These grave men may be nearly blind, but the speaker says they see with "blinding sight." This means that even though they might not have all their senses working in the same way as a younger person, they can still *see* meaning in life. Here again the imagery relates to a beautiful, strong, and spectacular part of nature—meteors. The blind eyes of the grave men could still "blaze" with commitment to the power of life.

The poem concludes with a stanza that returns to the plea of the first stanza. In the middle four stanzas that give examples, the lines "Rage, rage against the dying of the light" and "Do not go gentle into that good night" have been used to complete sentences of description. For example, "Good men rage against the dying of the light" or "Wild men do not go gentle into that good night." Now these lines are addressed directly to the speaker's father, so they would read more like this, "Father, I am asking you not to 'go gentle into that good night,'" or "Father, I am pleading with you to 'rage, rage against the dying of the light.'" The opening request is backed up by a series of examples, leading to a stronger plea (the only four-line stanza in the poem). The speaker builds an argument that he hopes will encourage his father to stay strong and brave even in the face of death. The frequent rhymes emphasize the opposing forces of "light"/"bright" (life) and "night" (death) and the repetition of the speaker's pleas ("Do not go . . ." and "Rage, rage . . .") underline the urgency of his message to his father.

Matt was much happier with this draft. He read it through and decided that what he talked about most was the repetition and the emphasis that repetition gave to the poem. He revised his title and—after several tries—wrote this opening paragraph to make the focus of his paper clear:

THE POWER OF SOUND AND SIGHT IN "DO NOT GO GENTLE"
Matthew Cejak

Dylan Thomas's poem "Do Not Go Gentle into That Good Night" gives a man's plea to his father to fight death. Images of strength, power, and life fill the poem, showing nature's beauty and energy and giving reasons for the father to fight death. The poem's rhythm and sound seem to oppose death, too. The rhymes and repetition of lines build a lively pattern to the speaker's final argument.

EDITING FOCUS: CONCISENESS One of the earlier versions of Matt's opening paragraph looked like this:

In Dylan Thomas's poem "Do Not Go Gentle into That Good Night," he writes about the plea a man is making to his father to mount a gallant battle against the trials and tribulations of the finality of death. The poem is filled with images of strength, power, and life. These images show to the reader the beauty and energy of nature and give reasons for the father to fight the grim reaper. As a matter of fact, the poem has a rhythm and sound that seem to oppose the ghastly specter of death, too. The rhymes and repetition of lines build a lively pattern to the speaker's final argument.

With his instructor's help, Matt identified the following problems. Matt edited to make certain that he conveyed his meaning as directly and clearly as possible.

1. Unneeded words and phrases.

   Wordy: As a matter of fact, the poem has a rhythm and sound that seem to oppose the ghastly specter of death, too.
   Edited: The poem's rhythm and sound seem to oppose death, too.

2. Unnecessary repetition. Matt combined sentences, trying to eliminate repetition.

   Wordy: The poem is filled with images of strength, power, and life. These images show to the reader the beauty and energy of nature and give reasons for the father to fight the grim reaper.
   Edited: Images of strength, power, and life fill the poem, showing nature's beauty and energy and giving reasons for the father to fight death.

3. Clichés and overused phrases.

   Wordy: fight the grim reaper
   Edited: fight death

4. Redundancy.

   Wordy: the finality of death.
   Edited: death. (Death is obviously final, so "finality of death" is ineffectively repetitious.)

Exercise

Compare the two versions of Matt's paragraph on pages 115–116. Then, editing for conciseness, revise the following early version of another paragraph from Matt's paper. When you have completed the revision, compare your editing decisions with the editing decisions demonstrated by the second paragraph of Matt's paper, page 119.

The second stanza gives the first of three examples the speaker gives for the purpose of demonstrating why he believes old people should resist death. Wise men may know that "dark is right." Like "night" in the first stanza, "dark" is a metaphor for death. But these wise men, when they spoke during their lifetime maybe they didn't really get their message across. They didn't speak like lightning. So they don't want to die. Instead, continuing in life is their heart's desire. "Lightning" relates to "light" in the first stanza. Good is implied by these words, and they also suggest strong power. The lightning may be powerful words. Light, on the other hand, represents the liveliness of life itself. In this stanza, the type of rhyme scheme of the poem begins to underline the insistence of the speaker on life. As in the first stanza, the first and third lines rhyme. And all four of these lines (1, 3, 4, and 6) rhyme, too. The rhyme emphasizes the relationship between "light" (life) and "night" (death) and the struggle that is continually going on between these two archenemies.

PROOFREADING FOCUS: APOSTROPHES, QUOTATION MARKS TO INDICATE WORDS USED IN A SPECIAL WAY As he completed his draft, Matt noticed that he had questions about the use of apostrophes. In addition, when he discussed a word from the poem, he was not certain whether to underline it, put it in quotation marks, or use no punctuation.

A quick check with a grammar handbook told him that apostrophes are required in the following situations:

- To form possessive nouns:

Singular: One author's opinion.
Plural: Two authors' opinions.

Note: Do not use apostrophes with possessive pronouns such as "his," "hers," "theirs," and "ours."

Note: When a word does not form the plural by adding "s" or "es," form the possessive simply by adding apostrophe "s."
No: The childrens' story.
Yes: The children's story.

- To form contractions:

"were not" becomes "weren't"

Note: "It's" is the contraction for "it is"; "its" is a possessive pronoun. (The bird left its nest.)

Note: Do not use apostrophes with verbs that are not part of contractions.
No: He read's well.
Yes: He reads well.

The handbook gave the following rule for punctuating words used in special situations:

- Words being referred to as words can be either underlined (italicized, in printed material) or enclosed in quotation marks.

"Light" is used as a metaphor for life.

or

Light is used as a metaphor for life.

Be consistent throughout the paper; use either quotation marks or underlining, not a combination.

Exercises

1. Applying these rules, proofread and correct the following earlier versions of sentences from Matt's paper. Add apostrophes where needed; delete incorrectly used apostrophes. Add either quotation marks or underlining to words used as words (be consistent; use either quotation marks or underlining, not both).

   The first stanza begins with the speakers plea, addressed to old people.
   The repetition of the word rage emphasizes the importance the
     speaker places on this fight against death.
   They didnt speak like lightning.
   This phrase shows the mens' actions as lively and sparkling, like light
     on the water in a bay.
   It represent's power, energy, and life.
   Its interesting to note that grave means serious, yet "grave" here could
     also maybe suggest the nearness to burial.
   Now these lines are addressed directly to the speakers' father.

2. Keeping in mind the revising, editing, and proofreading strategies described in this chapter (as well as other strategies you know), combine Matt's first paragraph (pages 115–116) with his draft (pages 113–115) to make a strong, unified essay. Be prepared to explain the choices you make as you revise, edit, and proofread. Compare your final copy with the version that follows. Of course, each person's revision of this paper will be different. The point is not to duplicate Matt's final paper but to think about the differences and similarities between your version and his.

Final Copy: Writing to Explicate

THE POWER OF SOUND AND SIGHT IN "DO NOT GO GENTLE"
Matthew Cejak

Dylan Thomas's poem "Do Not Go Gentle into That Good Night" is a man's plea to his father to fight death. Images of strength, power, and life fill the poem, showing nature's beauty and energy and giving reasons for the father to fight death. The poem's rhythm and sound seem to oppose death, too. The rhymes and repetition of lines build a lively pattern to the speaker's final argument.

The first stanza begins with the speaker's plea, addressed to old people. He urges them to fight against going "into that good night," a metaphor for death. The words in this stanza set a tone of heat and passion. Those who face death should "burn," "rave," and "rage." The repetition of the word "rage" emphasizes the importance the speaker places on this fight against death.

The second stanza gives the first of three examples demonstrating why the speaker believes old people should resist death. Wise men may know that "dark"—another metaphor for death—"is right." But when these wise men spoke during their lifetime, maybe they didn't really get their message across. They didn't speak like lightning. So they don't want to die; they want to continue to live. "Lightning" relates to "light" in the first stanza; both indicate something powerful and good. The lightning may refer to powerful words, whereas the light represents life itself. In this stanza, the rhyme scheme of the poem begins to underline the speaker's insistence on life. As in the first stanza, the first and third lines rhyme. And all four of these lines (1, 3, 4, and 6) rhyme, too. The rhyme emphasizes the relationship between "light" (life) and "night" (death) and the struggle between the two.

The phrase "Good men" serves as the example in stanza 3. They don't want to die, because as they think back on the actions of their lives they realize that these actions may not have been fully appreciated. These actions are described as "frail deeds." The word "frail" suggests the weakness often associated with old age, and the "good men" think about how those actions "might have danced in a green bay." This phrase shows the men's actions as lively and sparkling, like light on the water in a bay. Once again, the idea of light is emphasized as good, and the idea of dark (death) as bad. The deeds could have been "bright," and so these "good men" fight against letting their light go out. The importance of life is stressed by the rhyming of "bright" and "light" at the ends of the first and last lines in the stanza.

"Wild men" are shown in the fourth stanza as old people who fight death. They seem to be people who grabbed on to parts of life and yet also let those same parts of life go with no regrets. They "caught . . . the sun" (a metaphor for a very intense and beautiful part of life), but they sang "the sun in flight." This singing indicates that they were able to say good-bye with joy to these intense, beautiful times. Now, however, they realize that they also feel sorrow. They feel the loss of these strong experiences. Once again, the image of light (the sun) is good, representing power, energy, and life. Like the "wise men," wishing their words had been like lightning, and like the "good men," imagining their deeds dancing "in a green bay," the "wild men" seem to have a strong connection with the physical part of nature (in this case the sun). The final line repeats the ending line of the second stanza and the first line of the first stanza: "Do not go gentle into that good night." The repetition ties this example in with the others and shows yet one more category of old people who fight the ending of life.

The final example of those who "rage, rage against the dying of the light" is grave men. It's interesting to note that "grave" means serious, yet "grave" here could also maybe suggest the nearness to burial—the grave of the dead. These grave men may be nearly blind, but the speaker says they see with "blinding sight." This means that even though they might not have all their senses working in the same way as a younger person, they can still *see* meaning in life. Here again the imagery relates to a beautiful, strong, and spectacular part of nature—meteors. The blind eyes of the grave men could still "blaze" with commitment to the power of life.

The poem concludes with a stanza that returns to the plea of the first stanza. In the middle four stanzas that give examples, the lines "Rage, rage against the dying of the light" and "Do not go gentle into that good night" have been used to complete sentences of description. For example, "Good men rage against the dying of the light" or "Wild men do not go gentle into that good night." Now these lines are addressed directly to the speaker's father, so they would read more like this, "Father, I am asking you not to 'go gentle into that good night,'" or "Father, I am pleading with you to 'rage, rage against the dying of the light.'" It is clear now that the opening request is backed up by a series of examples, leading to a stronger plea (the only four-line stanza in the poem). The speaker builds an argument that he hopes will encourage his father to stay strong and brave even in the face of death. The frequent rhymes emphasize the opposing forces of "light"/"bright" (life) and "night" (death) and the repetition of the speaker's pleas ("Do not go . . ." and "Rage, rage . . .") underline the urgency of his message to his father.

Exercise

Read several poems from the poetry any thematic section (Chapters 5–12) and then, using the process demonstrated with Matt's paper, plan and write an explication. Keep in mind the principles presented in the following Guidelines box.

❖ GUIDELINES
Writing an Explication

1. An analysis, or explication, "unfolds" the poem (or section of a short story, novel, play, or essay). That is, it explains in detail how the work communicates to the reader.
2. An explication considers significant details and suggestions in the poem, including—but not limited to—these elements:

> sound (rhyme and rhythm)
> structure (patterns of lines and stanzas)
> figurative language (metaphors, similes, symbols)
> irony
> definitions of words

3. An explication shows how each part contributes to the whole meaning of the work; each part of the discussion, therefore, must relate to a clear central idea.
4. An explication is not a paraphrase (a restatement of the ideas of the work in your own words); instead, it is an explanation of the way a work communicates.
5. An explication is easy to organize; working chronologically from first to last stanza of a poem (or from beginning to end of a section from a short story, novel, essay, or play) makes the most sense.
6. An explication begins with an introduction indicating the main idea of the work and suggesting the direction of the explication.
7. An explication concludes with a paragraph that sums up the meaning that has been unfolded for the reader.

Writing to Evaluate

A literary work can be judged in many ways. For instance, a reader may evaluate a work by asking questions such as these: "Is this poem beautiful?" "Are the motives of the characters in this short story convincing?" "Are the ideas in this play worthy of close, careful attention?" "What are the values supported by this work? And do I subscribe to those values?"

You are probably prompted to ask a question of your own: "According to what standards?" Any evaluation—whether of a literary work, a scientific theory, or a historical event—must be based on criteria. The next question, of course, is "Who sets these criteria?" The answers to these questions are not simple. Each reader must develop his or her own standards for evaluation, but where do these criteria come from? They come from what we have learned, what we have experienced, what we have observed or heard—not only in school but also at home, in our communities, in our religious institutions, at work.

A topic such as number 5 requires an evaluation of the values and beliefs expressed by the work, and—more importantly—asks the reader to examine his or her own values and beliefs as a means of judging the work.

Topic 5

Consider the values and beliefs suggested by each of these poems. Choose one of the poems and explain those values and beliefs as well as your evaluation of them. Do you agree with them completely? Question them? Explain.

DISCOVERING IDEAS: INTERVIEWING After reading both poems, Joann Epstein wrote this journal entry:

> I read "Do Not Go Gentle" first and I thought how much this son loved his father, that he didn't want him to just die with no fight. I was thinking right away that I would write the paper on the values in this poem which I can relate to—not so much my father, but my grandfather—I really want him to keep going even though he does have emphysema. I hate to see him slow down. Then I read "Slipping." This was a hard poem for me to read because you can see she loves her father, but she in some ways really likes seeing him slow down. Now, this to me is almost the exact opposite of the idea in Thomas's poem. It's saying, "Don't fight the changes of old age, just accept them and look for the good." I didn't agree with this because I think you should always fight for every bit of life. But the more I thought about it, the more I wondered which way I would want my relatives to think or act if I was the person who was getting old.

After writing this journal entry and thinking about the topic for a while, Joann still wasn't sure what her own criteria were for judging the values suggested by the two poems. She decided to work on "Slipping" because she saw that the poem supported the ideas of love and commitment (which she also believed in). But the means of showing love—accepting and even welcoming debilitating changes—was something she found difficult to understand.

To think further about the issues raised by the poem, Joann decided to interview Norma Heath, a nurse who worked with elderly patients and their families at the hospital where Joann held a part-time job. She chose Norma because in the past they'd had conversations about some patients in the hospital. Joann knew Norma believed that families often distressed hospitalized relatives by pushing for more treatment rather than accepting the changes brought on by illness. To prepare Norma for the interview, Joann asked her to read the poem. She also wrote a list of questions she wanted to ask. After asking permission, Joann taped the interview so that she could review it at home and make certain she was accurate if she decided to quote Norma. The following is a transcript of part of that tape:

Joann: So, what did you think of the poem?
Norma: I'm not a great one for poetry—but this one I liked—I kept reading it—especially the last lines.
Joann: Why the last lines?
Norma: I think—I guess—well, for me the screen seems like the ones we have in some of the exam rooms. And it falls, and you really see the whole

truth about this man—who, I think, was a doctor in his professional life. So he was used to examining people and seeing—maybe "the truth" about them. But nobody saw him in that way.

Joann: I see what you mean. But I still think it's weird that his daughter is, like, loving this change. Because, to me, what it shows is that her father is really not her father—I mean the way she always knew him. He's like weaker, but she likes that just because now he says he loves her.

Norma: To me it makes total sense—and I'm not sure what you mean by weaker. You mean the father is physically weak or emotionally weak because he says he loves her?

Joann: No, I—of course I don't mean to say "I love you" is emotionally weak, but it's because he's physically weak that he says it. I mean, would he say that if he still was totally well? I think the physical weakness has, sort of, broken him down.

Norma: I'm not sure I agree. Yes, his body is weak. But sometimes the inner change is not like breaking down. More like letting something go. Letting something go that has been preventing strength—hmm—preventing strong feelings. Like the poem says here "reserve has slipped" away from him. Now his loving of his daughter can be seen. And he is lucky she can accept that. And she's not just totally cynical about it.

Joann: What do you mean by totally cynical?

Norma: Well, some families, they just ignore changes like that because it's like they feel it's just another symptom of the person getting old. Or else they get angry with the person and it's like, "Well, it's too late!" I see a lot of bitterness.

Joann: But this daughter seems happy—she's not angry or bitter.

Norma: That's what I get—and I tell you, I wish we had more daughters like her who could say, "what I love" is this or that about some change they see in their parent—mother or father.

After the interview—and after spending more time rereading and rethinking the poem—Joann thought more about the speaker in the poem and about the implications of her responses to her father's changes. Norma's comment about the change showing strength rather than weakness really intrigued her.

CONSIDERING AUDIENCE, NARROWING THE TOPIC, AND DEVISING A PRELIMINARY THESIS Joann decided to focus on emotional strength as a central concept for evaluating the poem. She came up with this list of questions:

What does the poem say about emotional strength?
Who shows emotional strength?
Why is this person (or persons) showing emotional strength?
What is the definition of emotional strength in this poem?
What is my definition of emotional strength?
What does the poem say about the relationship between emotional strength and love?

What do I think about the relationship between emotional strength
and love?

Joann knew that several people in the class had a strongly negative
response to the values expressed in the poem. Just as she at first had questioned the daughter's motives for admiring the changes in her father, many
students had seen her reaction as selfish. Joann realized that she was going to
propose an alternative reading. She knew that she would have to work hard
to find evidence that was convincing. She also knew she had to express her
ideas so that people who did not share her views would not feel personally
attacked.

Joann had no trouble coming up with a preliminary thesis. She knew
she wanted to focus on the concept of emotional strength.

> Both the speaker and the father in Joan Aleshire's poem "Slipping"
> show emotional strength and love as they face the changes brought
> by his aging.

PLANNING AND ORGANIZING When she was ready to draft,
Joann thought about how she wanted to start her essay and where she would
go with it. She decided to focus on the questions she had listed and to use
images and ideas from the poem to explore those questions. She rewrote the
questions as statements and reordered the questions like this:

> Introduction: focus on relationship of emotional strength and love.
> 1. Both father and daughter show emotional strength.
> 2. They show emotional strength in different ways and for a different
>   reason.
>   A. Father: physical changes cause him to drop his guard; wants
>   to tell what has always been there.
>   B. Daughter: accepts changes; does not act angry or judgmental.
> 3. Emotional strength means being able to change and to accept
>   change.
> 4. Having the ability to change and accept change is a necessary part
>   of loving and being loved.

DRAFTING Using the notes she had taken during the interview,
notes she had made on a copy of the poem, journal entries, and the outline,
Joann wrote several drafts. Here is her final copy:

Final Copy: Writing to Evaluate

LOVE AND STRENGTH
Joann Epstein

In Joan Aleshire's poem "Slipping," a daughter describes the changes
old age has brought to her father. The father gradually loses his physical

abilities and, in addition, becomes less reserved. The daughter accepts the physical changes and welcomes her father's loss of restraint. Although both the speaker and the father are weak in some ways, they also show emotional strength and love as they face the changes brought by his aging.

Many images in the first two stanzas suggest the father's physical weakness: "the leg that weakens . . . the curtain of mist that falls over one eye"; the lost concentration and "fine sense of direction." In addition, he has become dependent on other family members. When he takes a walk with his daughter, she has to slow down "to match his pace." She describes him as being similar to "a child who keeps pulling on your hand."

Another change that might be seen as weakening is the way he no longer keeps his feelings inside himself. For much of his life, this man has saved his emotional energy for his work. His daughter explains that a familiar photograph of him, teaching with his

> chair tipped back
> against the lecture-room wall—shows
> a man talking, love of his work lighting
> his face—in a way we seldom saw at home.

Now instead of putting his emotions into his work, he freely tells his daughter, "I love you so much." So his ability to keep up his reserve with his family is no longer there. True, in a way he has weakened, but also he now shows real feelings for his daughter, which is a kind of emotional strength. It's as if the weakening of the body has allowed his strong feelings to come out. They were simply trapped inside.

The daughter, too, shows her emotional strength. Recalling her mother's observation that "[your father] never liked / to talk about feelings," the speaker honestly describes the father she knew when she was growing up as someone who didn't show too much affection at home. However, she doesn't seem bitter and angry, which would show weakness. Instead, she loves her father the way he is now. She doesn't berate him for what happened in the past. Also, even though it seems like her father didn't spend too much time with the family in the past, she is still willing to take walks with him and to talk to him. She doesn't hold a grudge or retaliate by rejecting him.

The father has grown stronger in family relationships even though his body has grown weaker. The daughter shows that she is strong because she accepts the love her father has begun to express. Both the father and the daughter use the emotional strength brought about by his aging to express the connection they feel to each other. Both say, "I love you," which are words they may not have spoken out loud before.

REVISING FOCUS: LOGIC While she was drafting, Joann saw that she needed to work on presenting her ideas logically. She isolated these particular problems in earlier drafts of the final copy you just read.

1. Making **absolute statements** that could not be supported. For instance, she used words such as "all," "every," and "none" when she should have acknowledged exceptions.

   Illogical: All the images in the first two stanzas suggest the father's physical weakness. (Not every image in these stanzas suggests physical weakness; for example, the image of the darkness pushing "away years of restraint" suggests an emotional, not a physical change.)
   Revised: Many of the images in the first two stanzas suggest the father's physical weakness.

2. Using a **question-begging approach,** that is, stating that something "is obvious" or that "everyone knows" something rather than providing evidence to support the point.

   Illogical: It's obvious that the daughter, too, shows emotional strength. She really understands her father and herself. (It's not obvious to the reader of the paper; evidence is needed to demonstrate the daughter's emotional strength and to demonstrate—rather than simply announce—her understanding of her father and herself.)
   Revised: The daughter, too, shows her emotional strength. She honestly describes the father she knew when she was growing up as someone who didn't show too much affection at home. However, she doesn't seem bitter and angry, which would show weakness. Instead, she loves her father the way he is now. She doesn't berate him for what happened in the past. Also, even though it seems like her father didn't spend too much time with the family in the past, she is still willing to take walks with him and to talk to him. She doesn't hold a grudge or retaliate by rejecting him. (Here details and examples provide evidence to show the reader the validity of the draft paragraph's initial sentence and to replace the broad generalization of the second sentence in the draft version.)

3. Using a **non sequitur.** This Latin term means "it does not follow" and describes conclusions drawn from evidence that cannot logically support them—for example, saying that a certain point in a work of literature is true because the speaker states that it is so. (Because some speakers are unreliable, their statements cannot be taken as truth.)

   Illogical: She honestly describes the father she knew when she was growing up as someone who didn't show too much affection at home. Of course, because he is her father, she knows that he really did love her and she is not bitter or angry. (It is not necessarily true

that "because he is her father" she would know that he loved her. The mere fact of parenthood does not ensure love.)
Revised: She honestly describes the father she knew when she was growing up as someone who didn't show too much affection at home. However, she doesn't seem bitter and angry, which would show weakness. Instead, she loves her father the way he is now. (Here the transitional sentence beginning with "however" shows the logical relationship between the ideas expressed in the sentences that precede and follow it.)

The three fallacies in the preceding list are examples of problems with logic that can make a paper unclear or undermine an essential point. Consult an English handbook to review other possible problems with logic as well as strategies for revision.

EDITING FOCUS: INTEGRATING AND PUNCTUATING QUOTATIONS As Joann read through an early draft of her paper, she realized that she had problems with the quotations she had used. She edited her paper to conform to the following rules:

1. Make clear whose ideas you are quoting and whom you are talking about:

   Unclear: The poem talks about slowing down "to match his pace" and being similar to "a child who keeps pulling on your hand."
   Edited: When the father takes a walk with his daughter, she has to slow down "to match his pace." She describes his leg as dragging like "a child who keeps pulling on your hand."

2. Use quotation marks around short quotations (four lines or fewer) that are combined with your own sentences.

   When he takes a walk with his daughter, she has to slow down "to match his pace."

3. When you cite fewer than three lines of poetry, run the words or phrases into your own sentences. Indicate line breaks with a slash (/).

   Recalling her mother's observation that "[your father] never liked / to talk about feelings," the speaker honestly describes the father she knew when she was growing up as someone who didn't show too much affection at home.

4. Set off long quotations (more than four lines) in a separate block (called an extract) indented several spaces. Do not use quotation marks around the extract.

   His daughter explains that a familiar photograph of him, teaching with his

> chair tipped back
> against the lecture-room wall—shows
> a man talking, love of his work lighting
> his face—in a way we seldom saw at home.

5. Integrate quotations into your own sentences to show the relationship of the quotation to the point you are making.

   Unclear: Now, he puts his emotions into his family instead of his
   work. "I love you so much."
   Edited: Now instead of putting his emotions into his work, he freely
   tells his daughter, "I love you so much."

   Unclear: Another change relates to his work.
   > A photograph taken of him teaching—
   > white coat, stethoscope like a pet snake
   > around his neck, chair tipped back
   > against the lecture-room wall—shows
   > a man talking, love of his work lighting
   > his face—in a way we seldom saw at home.

   Edited: Another change that might be seen as weakening is the way
   he no longer keeps his feelings inside himself. For much of his life,
   this man has saved his emotional energy for his work. His daughter
   explains that a familiar photograph of him, teaching with his
   > chair tipped back
   > against the lecture-room wall—shows
   > a man talking, love of his work lighting
   > his face—in a way we seldom saw at home.

6. Use the ellipsis (three spaced periods) to show that words are
   omitted.

   Many images in the first two stanzas suggest the father's physical
   weakness: "the leg that weakens . . . the curtain of mist that falls
   over one eye."

7. Use brackets to indicate a minor change that makes a quotation
   grammatically compatible with the rest of your sentence.

   Original: As the daughter watches her father's changes, it's clear that
   "what I love is the way reserve has slipped from / feeling."
   Edited: As the daughter watches her father's changes, it's clear that
   "what [she loves] is the way reserve has slipped from / [his] feeling."

8. Check carefully to make certain that quotations are accurate.

9. To make your quotations effective, use them sparingly. Overly long
   quotations often obscure the meaning they are intended to convey.

PROOFREADING FOCUS: PRONOUN REFERENCE, PRO-
NOUN AGREEMENT, TREATMENT OF TITLES While proofreading,
Joann realized she needed to work on revising pronoun references. For ex-
ample, here's a sentence from an earlier draft of paragraph 4.

> Her mother says that her father "never liked / to talk about feel-
> ings." She honestly describes him as someone who didn't show too
> much affection at home.

To whom does "her" in the phrase "her father" refer? To the mother or to
the daughter? Almost certainly it refers to the daughter, but the reference
needs to be made clear.

> *Edited:* Recalling her mother's observation that "[your father] never
> liked / to talk about feelings," the speaker honestly describes the
> father she knew when she was growing up as someone who didn't
> show too much affection at home.

Of course, this sentence can also be revised in other ways—but the proofreading issue here is that a pronoun cannot convey its meaning accurately if
the reader cannot tell who or what that pronoun represents.

Another problem with pronouns in the paper was their agreement with
the nouns to which they referred.

> It's as if the weakening of the body has allowed his strong feelings to
> come out. It was simply trapped inside. ("It" is singular, and the
> word referred to, "feelings," is plural. Pronouns must agree in num-
> ber with the words to which they refer.)
> *Edited:* It's as if the weakening of the body has allowed his strong
> feelings to come out. They were simply trapped inside.

As Joann proofread, she realized she wasn't sure how to treat titles, so
she checked an English handbook and found these rules:

> *Treatment of Titles*
> 1. When citing a poem, short story, or essay, put the title in quotation
>   marks.
>
>   In Joan Aleshire's poem "Slipping," a daughter describes the changes
>   old age has brought to her father.
>
> 2. When citing a novel or a play, underline the title (or use italics).
>
>   Dickens's novel A Tale of Two Cities is often required reading for
>   high school sophomores.
>   *or*
>   Dickens's novel *A Tale of Two Cities* is often required reading for
>   high school sophomores.

3. When writing the title of your own paper, do not underline it or put it in quotation marks.

Love and Strength

4. Always capitalize the first word in a title as well as all other important words. Do not capitalize small, unimportant words such as "and," "the," "an," "a," "of," "to," "in," and so on.

Dylan Thomas published "Do Not Go Gentle into That Good Night" in 1952.

Exercise

Read several works from the anthology chapters (Chapters 5 through 12) and then, using the process demonstrated with Joann's paper, plan and write an evaluation of the beliefs and values expressed in one of the works. Keep the principles presented in the following Guidelines box in mind.

 GUIDELINES
Writing an Evaluation of Beliefs and Values

1. Identify the beliefs and values expressed in the work, making note of specific details that demonstrate these beliefs and values.
2. Think about the criteria you will use to evaluate those beliefs and values.
3. Consider what questions might be raised concerning those beliefs and values. (If you share those values, imagine the response of someone who does not.)
4. To expand your thinking, consider interviewing others who might be particularly interested in the values and beliefs expressed in the work.
5. Decide whether your evaluation will support or question (perhaps even refute) the values and beliefs expressed in the work.
6. List your reasons for supporting, questioning, or refuting these values and beliefs.
7. Remember to reread the work frequently to make certain you are responding to values and beliefs actually expressed there.
8. Make certain the opening section of the paper makes clear both the values and beliefs expressed in the work and the approach you are taking toward those values and beliefs.
9. Make certain the conclusion sums up the evaluation—the reasons you support and subscribe to (or do not support and subscribe to) the beliefs and values expressed in the work.

Writing a Research Paper

The sixth assignment topic calls for research. Here it is:

Topic 6

Discover a question related to Thomas's "Do Not Go Gentle" and do research to explore that question. In your paper, refer to at least three sources.

A paper that requires research can lead in many directions. In some courses, particularly the physical or social sciences, research may include experiments or observations you design and carry out yourself. Another research strategy is the interview: talking to experts who know about the subject you are considering. For this assignment, library resources—books, journals, newspapers—are most useful.

As Toni Jackmon considered writing about "Do Not Go Gentle," she became curious about many things. She wondered if the final stanza really did address Thomas's father. She wondered what relationship he had had with his father. In addition, she was confused about the different kinds of men who "do not go gentle" into death. What did wise men, good men, wild men, or grave men have to do with the father in the poem?

Toni saw that she did not yet have one question to explore, as the assignment asked. She decided to do some reading, hoping that her research would help her to focus on one particular consideration.

DISCOVERING IDEAS: RESEARCHING Toni went to the library and made an appointment to talk to a reference librarian. During her appointment with the librarian, David Bauer, she discovered many possibilities. The resources David suggested fell primarily into four categories:

1. **Special encyclopedias, reference works, handbooks, and general histories.** For Toni's project, David suggested the following:

   Annual Bibliography of English Language and Literature
   Dictionary of Literary Biography
   Dictionary of National Biography [British]

2. **Periodicals** (journals and magazines; in this case, journals and magazines relating to the field of English literature). David suggested that, to find articles relating to Dylan Thomas, Toni should use **periodical indexes** (guides compiled by organizations that research the most important journals and magazines in any field of study and then publish indexes listing articles alphabetically according to their subject matter). For information on literary topics, David suggested these indexes:

   Humanities Index
   MLA International Bibliography

3. **Newspapers.** With David's help, Toni learned how to use the *New York Times Index* and also the microfilm reader/copier, because copies of the *Times* are stored on microfilm.
4. **Books.** Toni was already familiar with this source and knew how to use the library's card catalogue to find books relating to Thomas's work. David provided her with more options, however, by explaining the process of **interlibrary loan** so that Toni could have access to books not held by her library.

Toni decided to begin by reading some background information on Thomas. She used the *Dictionary of Literary Biography* and (at David's suggestion) she also checked the *New York Times Index* for 1953 (the year of Thomas's death), looking under the topic "Deaths" to find his obituary.

She discovered that Thomas apparently had a happy childhood growing up in Wales. Although he experienced the usual conflicts with his parents, the family remained close. "Do Not Go Gentle," she learned, was written during the months of Thomas's father's final illness, but what interested her more were the details of Thomas's own battle with alcoholism and his subsequent early death at the age of 39. She also found that he had published a volume of poetry called *Death and Entrances,* which suggested to her that death was a frequent theme in Thomas's work.

Toni then decided to look for information specifically related to "Do Not Go Gentle." She found a book, William York Tindall's *A Reader's Guide to Dylan Thomas,* that gave a reading of the poem. She was surprised to see that Tindall thought the "grave men" were poets and decided to look further to find out how other scholars might have interpreted the kinds of men Thomas said did not "go gentle" to their deaths.

Toni could not find any further references to this theme in the books she read. She turned next to the *Humanities Index* and discovered the titles of several articles that looked promising. After reading the articles, she decided that the most relevant was "Thomas' 'Do Not Go Gentle into That Good Night'" by Michael W. Murphy.

THOMAS' "DO NOT GO GENTLE INTO THAT GOOD NIGHT"
Michael W. Murphy, University of Wisconsin, Green Bay

Although there is widespread agreement about the theme of Dylan Thomas' "Do Not Go Gentle into That Good Night" (the need to affirm life emotionally at the hour of death, even when one rationally recognizes that death is both natural and inevitable), the references in the poem to "wise men," "good men," "wild men," and "grave men" have caused considerable difficulty. The only two critics who have ventured to explicate the references (most commentators simply ignore them) differ essentially in their interpretations: Clark Emery identifies the wise men as "philosophers who had thundered but lit no fires";

the good men as "saints, who at last see abstinence as *contra naturam*"; the wild men as "poets, whose best intentions were reversed"; and the grave men as "sober-sides, who realize they have lived half-lives" (*The World of Dylan Thomas,* p. 54). William York Tindall, on the other hand, agrees that the wise men are some kind of philosophers but interprets the good men as "moralists, Puritans perhaps, who, having avoided dancing waters in life's 'green bay,' cannot accept death after such a life," and considers the grave men, not the wild men, to be the poets; the wild men are "men of action and lovers of living" (*A Reader's Guide to Dylan Thomas,* p. 205). Both Emery's and Tindall's interpretations are not only unjustifiably narrow but, more importantly, fail to take account of the careful play of opposites—"my dialectical method," Thomas called it—which characterizes this poem, as it does so many of his others.

The contrast between the wise men of the second tercet and the good men of the third is specifically indicated by the placement of "words" and "deeds" in parallel positions in these stanzas as well as by the explicit contrast of "dark" and "bright" and the implicit contrast of the sky (where the lightning would appear) and the water ("green bay"). The wise men who have spent their lives preaching wisdom are contrasted with the good men who have spent their lives practicing it. Both rage against death because their work has not accomplished anything. The words of the wise have gone unheeded; they have not sparked or generated any change in the actions of men or brought any light into the world. The deeds of the good men have been similarly ignored, engulfed by the waves of the rough sea of life. Had that sea been more serene—"a green bay"—the frail deeds would have remained afloat, serving as a visible example for others to follow (like the "woodtongued virtue" of Ann Jones that Thomas called upon to "Babble like a bellbuoy" in "After the Funeral").

The fourth and fifth tercets present another pair of contrasting types, and again an active way of life is opposed to a more passive way, with neither proving satisfactory. Again, too, the contrast is expressed in terms of light and dark—or day and night—imagery, the wild men being associated with the light (the sun) and the grave men with the dark (blindness and meteors, which are only visible at night). The wild men are those who have taken a hedonistic, *carpe diem* (cf. "caught . . . the sun") approach to life, only to discover that it is time which has caught them, rather than *vice-versa*—a theme which occurs frequently in Thomas' poetry, most memorably at the end of "Fern Hill": "Time held me green and dying / Though I sang in my chains like the sea." Thus the songs the wild men sang extolling the sun appear now, in retrospect, to have been elegies lamenting its passing. In contrast to the Dionysian wild men, the grave men are the sober-minded Apollonians who have taken such an ascetic approach to life that all the joys of life have passed them by. Now, nearing death (the pun on "grave" is typical of Thomas), they are suddenly struck—like Saul on the road to Damascus—with a blinding revelation: though they are afflicted with all the infirmities of old age, not even blindness could keep them from enjoying life fully (and thus dying with meteor-like splendor) if they could only live a little longer.

Taken all together, the references to the wise, good, wild, and grave men suggest that life is always too brief and incomplete for everyone, regardless of how he has lived. Thus no one should "go gentle into that good night," especially someone like Thomas' father, who presumably represents a combination of all the types described in the poem.

Toni was particularly pleased to note that Murphy mentioned the reading by Tindall. She was a little surprised that another scholar Murphy mentioned, Clark Emery, thought that the "wild men" were poets. Here's the journal entry she wrote:

> When I read Tindall, and he said the grave men were poets, I was surprised because I didn't think of any of these people as having specific roles in life. They seemed like personality types. Then, in the article that I found, Michael W. Murphy quotes Clark Emery as saying that the wild men were "poets, whose best intentions were reversed." I know in class we keep talking about different readings, but it still threw me off guard to see this difference. Then Murphy has a whole other idea. I'm going to reread the poem (for the fifth time!!) to see if I see any poets there!

This journal entry shows how Toni used the research process to refine her questions about "Do Not Go Gentle" and about Thomas himself. She realized that she wanted to focus on the interpretation of the wise, good, wild, and grave men.

CONSIDERING AUDIENCE, NARROWING THE TOPIC, AND DEVISING A PRELIMINARY THESIS Toni realized that her instructor would probably be familiar with the background material and the literary criticism she had discovered, but most of the other students in the class would not. She knew that she would have to explain the views she was discussing, yet she also wanted to avoid simply summarizing the critical views she had read. She knew that the focus of the paper should be to pursue her own examination of this question she formulated: Do the wise, good, wild, and grave men, and their actions, relate in some way to poets and poetry?

Several rereadings of the poem, plus consideration of Michael Murphy's article and the ideas of several other scholars, led Toni to decide that there could very well be a poet—or rather several poets—in the poem. She was especially struck by Murphy's contention that the interpretation of any one of the groups of men as "poet" was too narrow, and she was also intrigued by his final statement that Thomas's father "presumably represents a combination of all the types described in the poem."

Here are several note cards she made as she worked toward developing a preliminary thesis statement. Note that Toni carefully put all the publishing information at the top of the first note card from a source. On subsequent note cards she simply used the author's last name. She used quotation marks to make clear which words were directly taken from the source. She also noted the page from which she took direct quotes. Toni needed all of this information to document her research properly.

Michael W. Murphy
"Thomas's 'Do Not Go Gentle into That Good Night'"
Explication, 28, Feb. 1970, 55.

Claims interpretations seeing one group of men as poets "unjustifiably narrow."

Morphy, 55

(p.55)
"Thus no one should 'go gentle into That good night,' especially someone like Thomas's father, who presumably represents a combination of all the types described in the poem."

Why "presumably"? Why do these types relate mainly to Thomas's father? Maybe instead to poet → Then to all of us?

> Horace Gregory, " The Black-Stock-
> inged Bait and Dylan Thomas " in
> <u>Critical Essays on Dylan Thomas</u>
> ed. Georg Gaston, G.K. Hall,
> Boston, 1989, 118-129
>
> (p.120) " denial of Spiritual death "
> " In one sense, the poem stands
>   as Thomas's own epitaph. "

After thinking about the research she had gathered, Toni developed this preliminary thesis statement:

Dylan Thomas's men are described as wise, good, wild, and grave. They could share qualities with poets. On the other hand, their lives and their views of life also represent us all.

PLANNING AND ORGANIZING Toni decided to begin her paper by discussing some of the proposed interpretations of Thomas's wise, good, wild, and grave men. Then, after stating her own view in her thesis, she planned to move through the poem stanza by stanza, showing why she thought each type of man could represent both a poet and also a broad range of humans.

Toni did not have a conclusion firmly in mind, but she thought she might use, in some context, the phrase from Horace Gregory's article suggesting that the poem could stand "as Thomas's own epitaph."

DRAFTING Toni began her paper by considering the proposed interpretations, discovered through her research, of wise, good, wild, and grave men.

William York Tindall describes the grave men in "Do Not Go Gentle" as poets. On the other hand, it may be that the wild men are the poets, but "Although there is widespread agreement about the theme of Dylan Thomas' "Do Not Go Gentle into That Good Night" (the need to affirm life emotionally at the hour of death, even when one rationally recognizes that death is both natural and inevitable), the references in the poem to "wise men," "good men," and "wild men" and "grave men" have caused considerable difficulty." "Taken all together, the references to the wise, good, wild, and grave men suggest that life is always too brief and incomplete for everyone, regardless of how he has lived. Thus no one should "go gentle into that good night," especially someone like Thomas' father who presumably represents a combination of all the types described in the poem" (55). These interpretations all seem too narrow. Dylan Thomas's men are described as wise, good, wild, and grave. They could share qualities with poets. On the other hand, their lives and their views of life also represent us all.

REVISING FOCUS: USING QUOTATIONS EFFECTIVELY As she read over the paragraph, Toni found it confusing. It was hard to tell where the quotations started and ended. In fact, the paragraph seemed to be mostly quotations. Also, she saw that it wasn't clear whether William York Tindall was responsible for all the quotes and ideas or whether they came from other writers.

The following rules helped Toni with the revision process:

1. When quoted words appear within short quotations, enclose the quoted words in single quotation marks.

   Michael Murphy believes the poem argues that "no one should 'go gentle into that good night,' especially someone like Thomas' father" (55).

2. Document all direct quotations and paraphrases (someone else's ideas put in your own words). That is, give credit by indicating the source either in an introduction to the quotation or paraphrase or in parentheses following the quotation or paraphrase. Give the page number of the source in parentheses following the quotation or paraphrase.

   Clark Emery identifies the wild men as "poets, whose best intentions were reversed" (54).

   or

   On the other hand, the wild men may be identified as "poets, whose best intentions were reversed" (Emery, 54).

3. List your references according to an established format. For papers in the humanities (for example, English, music, art, foreign languages), document your sources according to the Modern Language Association (MLA) format. See the Appendix, pages 1239–1247, for explanations and examples.

In addition to these points, Toni recognized another essential principle relating to quotations: *Do not overquote*. She saw that she needed to rely more on her own words and ideas, using the possibilities she had discovered in her research as ways to discover and explore—rather than replace—her own thoughts.

Keeping in mind the new approach she wanted to take—using primarily her own ideas and using quotations and paraphrases sparingly—Toni wrote this revision.

WE ARE ALL POETS
Toni Jackmon

In *A Reader's Guide to Dylan Thomas,* William York Tindall describes the grave men in "Do Not Go Gentle" as poets (205). Clark Emery beleives that the wild men are the poets (Murphy 55). Michael Murphy, on the other hand, does not identify any of the men as poets. He sees all of the men mentioned in stanzas 2–4 as having a broader interpretation, suggesting "that life is always too brief and incomplete for everyone, regardless of how he has lived" (55). Even Murphy's interpretation, however, seems too narrow. Dylan Thomas's men are described as wise, good, wild, and grave. They could share qualities with poets. On the other hand, there lives and there views of life also represent us all.

The wise men may be like poets. These would be poets who have not been heard. Their "words had forked no lightning." Of course they would not want to die in that situation. They would hope for a chance to have their words make a difference. The wise men do not need to just stand for poets, however. They could stand for any person who felt that he or she had not really had a chance to do anything in life that might make an inpact on others. People who felt they had not yet done something significant or useful might feel this way. They certainly would fight death.

The good men, too, could be poets. The "frail deeds" might refer to writing poems. Line 8 says that those deeds "might have danced in a green bay." This could mean that the poems had the possibility to cause a beautiful responce. They could have been bright, and they could have danced. For some reason they didn't. Many people besides poets also feel this way. They see their work and their actions as not having caused the reaction they would have hoped for.

The wild men might be poets who spent most of their time "singing" (writing) about the sun. The sun represents beautiful things in life. Maybe they didn't really take the time to appreciate those beautiful things. They didn't stop to think that nothing can last forever. Beauty started to go. Then they greived. These poets are certainly like many people. These are people who don't take the time to appreciate what they have. Then at the end of their lives they want want to fight death. They want to live longer to have a chance to appreciate "the sun in flight." Now they understand what they loose when that sun (beauty) has gone from them.

Thomas describes the grave men as seeing "with blinding sight." We often think of poets as being able to see things that others cannot see. The grave men, too, could be poets. These poets might be near death. They still, however, have the ability to see special things. They want to live so they can continue to enlighten others. This enlightenment of others is what could be meant by "blind eyes could blaze like meteors." Their knowledge could shine out still. So it's easy to see how the images in this stanza could apply specificaly to poets. It's also easy to see how they could apply to most people. Most of us beleive that we are special individuals. As special, unique beings we have special ways of seeing. Each of us sees the world in a slightly different way. In old age, near death, our phsyical sight might be failing. We would probably still, however, beleive that we had a special way to "see" (understand) the world around us. This beleif in being unique is one of the things that would keep a person fightting against dying.

It makes sence that Dylan Thomas, a poet, might have chosen examples of men who could be seen as poets. Horace Gregory suggests this possibility when he says that "Do Not Go Gentle" could be read "as Thomas's own epitaph" (129). On the other hand, a poet does not have to be somebody who stands entirely apart from the rest of humanity. The examples also suggest that those who fight against death could be any of us who look back and see our actions as incomplete or as unappreciated. Those who fight could be any of us who failed to stop to fully acknowledge the beauty in our lives or any or us who consider our view of the world to be unique and special. Perhaps, in a way, we are all poets. Thomas may be speaking to us all when he says, "Do not go gentle into that good night."

Works Cited

Gregory, Horace. "The Black–Stockinged Bait and Dylan Thomas." *Critical Essays on Dylan Thomas.* Ed. Georg Gaston. Boston: G. K. Hall, 1989, 125–132.

Murphy, Michael. "Thomas' 'Do Not Go Gentle into That Good Night'" *Explicator* 28 (1970): 55.

Tindall, William York. *A Reader's Guide to Dylan Thomas.* New York: Macmillan, 1962.

EDITING FOCUS: COMBINING SENTENCES Reading her revised draft, Toni was happy with the way she had used quotations, but felt that many of her sentences did not seem to flow together smoothly. Working with her instructor, she revised again according to the following rules for combining sentences:

1. Reduce information in one sentence to a group of words you can include in another sentence.

   Dylan Thomas was born and grew up in Wales. He was a poet. *Edited:* The poet Dylan Thomas was born and grew up in Wales.

2. Make one sentence into a clause; join the remaining sentence and the clause to show the relationship between the two.

Dylan Thomas was married to a woman named Caitlin. She wrote a book about their life together.
Edited: Dylan Thomas was married to a woman named Caitlin, who wrote a book about their life together.

3. Join two short sentences with a word that shows the relationship between the two.

Dylan Thomas traveled widely to give poetry readings. His heart remained in Wales, however.
Edited: Dylan Thomas traveled widely to give poetry readings, but his heart remained in Wales.

Keeping these rules in mind, Toni edited her second paragraph this way:

The wise men may be like poets who have not been heard. Because their "words had forked no lightning," they do not want to die, but hope for a chance to have their words make a difference. The wise men do not need to stand just for poets, however. They could stand for any person who felt that he or she had not really had a chance to do anything in life that might make an inpact on others— people who felt they had not yet done something significant or useful might fight death.

Exercise

Edit the rest of Toni's paper, using the preceding sentence-combining strategies.

PROOFREADING FOCUS: SPELLING After working on her sentence structure, Toni ran a spelling checker program that was part of her word processing software. Although she found several spelling mistakes, she knew that she couldn't rely on it to find every mistake. She kept in mind the following points for using a spelling checker effectively:

1. Remember that a spelling checker cannot tell the difference between words that sound alike but are spelled differently (for instance, "their," "there," and "they're").
2. Remember that a spelling checker cannot read in context. For instance, it won't mark "run" as an error in "the run [sun] rose early."
3. Keep a notebook beside your computer. When your spelling checker discovers an error, write the correct version of the word in your notebook. Every time the spelling checker finds that same word incorrectly spelled, put a checkmark next to it in your notebook. If you accumulate five checkmarks, practice writing the word until you learn how to spell it.

4. Use your list of misspelled words to evaluate patterns of errors. For example, you may frequently misspell words with *ie* or *ei* in them. Or you may have problems knowing whether to double a letter when adding an ending to a word. If you notice patterns like these, check an English handbook and learn the rules that will help to avoid such errors.

Exercises

1. Proofread Toni's paper for spelling errors. First, read the paper backward, beginning with the last sentence. Reading this way helps you to focus on spelling rather than on the meaning of the sentences. Then read the paper from beginning to end to pick up errors that depend on context. List the corrected versions of words that are misspelled, noting any patterns of errors that you discover.
2. After proofreading Toni's paper, compare your changes with the final copy that follows these exercises. Remember, you may have made some changes different from hers. Check with your professor to see whether your changes reflect accurate proofreading.
3. Choose a poem, short story, or play from the anthology section. Then, using the process demonstrated with Toni's paper (as well as any other strategies explained in this chapter), plan and write a paper that integrates your ideas with the ideas of others (discovered through library research). Keep in mind the principles presented in the Guidelines box on page 143.

Final Copy: Research Paper

WE ARE ALL POETS
Toni Jackmon

In *A Reader's Guide to Dylan Thomas,* William York Tindall describes the grave men in "Do Not Go Gentle" as poets (205). Clark Emery believes that the wild men are the poets (Murphy 55). Michael Murphy, on the other hand, does not identify any of the men as poets. He sees all of the men mentioned in stanzas 2–4 as having a broader interpretation, suggesting "that life is always too brief and incomplete for everyone, regardless of how he has lived" (55). Even Murphy's interpretation, however, seems too narrow. Dylan Thomas's men are described as wise, good, wild, and grave: qualities they could share with poets. On the other hand, their lives and their views of life also represent us all.

The wise men may be like poets who have not been heard. Because their "words had forked no lightning," they do not want to die, but hope for a chance to have their words make a difference. The wise men do not need to stand just for poets, however. They could stand for any person who felt that he or she had not really had a chance to do anything in life that might make an impact on others. People who felt they had not yet done something significant or useful might fight death.

The good men, too, could be poets. The "frail deeds" might refer to writing poems. Line 8 says that those deeds "might have danced in a green bay," which could mean that the poems had the possibility to cause a beautiful response. These poems could have been bright, and they could have danced, but for some reason they didn't. Many people besides poets also feel this way, failing to see their work and their actions as causing the reaction they would have wished.

The wild men might be poets who spent most of their time "singing" (writing) about the sun, which represents beautiful things in life. Maybe they didn't really take the time to appreciate those beautiful things. Perhaps they didn't stop to think that nothing can last forever, but when beauty started to go, they grieved. These poets are certainly like many people who don't take the time to appreciate what they have. Then at the end of their lives, they want to fight death, to live longer, and to have a chance to appreciate "the sun in flight." Now they understand what they will lose when that sun (beauty) has gone from them.

Thomas describes the grave men as seeing "with blinding sight." We often think of poets as being able to see things that others cannot see. The grave men, too, could be poets who, although near death, have the ability to see special things. They want to live so they can continue to enlighten others so that their "blind eyes could blaze like meteors." The poets' knowledge could shine out still, so it's easy to see how the images in this stanza could apply specifically to poets. On the other hand, it's also easy to see how these images could apply to most people, since most of us believe that we are special individuals. As unique beings we have particular ways of seeing. Each of us sees the world in a slightly different way. In old age, near death, our physical sight might be failing, but we would probably still believe that we had a special way to "see" (understand) the world around us. This belief in being unique is one of the things that would keep a person fighting against dying.

It makes sense that Dylan Thomas, a poet, might have chosen examples of men who could be seen as poets. Horace Gregory suggests this possibility when he says that "Do Not Go Gentle" could be read "as Thomas's own epitaph" (129). On the other hand, a poet does not have to be somebody who stands entirely apart from the rest of humanity. The examples also suggest that those who fight against death could be any of us who look back and see our actions as incomplete or as unappreciated. Those who fight could be any of us who failed to stop to fully acknowledge the beauty in our lives or any of us who consider our view of the world to be unique and special. Perhaps, in a way, we are all poets. Thomas may be speaking to us all when he says, "Do not go gentle into that good night."

Works Cited

Gregory, Horace. "The Black-Stockinged Bait and Dylan Thomas." *Critical Essays on Dylan Thomas*. Ed. Georg Gaston. Boston: G. K. Hall, 1989, 125–132.

Murphy, Michael. "Thomas' 'Do Not Go Gentle into That Good Night.'" *Explicator* 28 (1970): 55.

Tindall, William York. *A Reader's Guide to Dylan Thomas*. New York: Macmillan, 1962.

✺ GUIDELINES
Writing a Research Paper

1. Begin by reading the work carefully and by thinking of questions that outside reading might help you answer.
2. Become familiar with library resources.

   Books (and the cataloguing system used by your library)
   Specialized dictionaries and encyclopedias
   Periodical indexes
   > *Humanities Index*
   > *MLA International Bibliography*
   Newspaper indexes: *New York Times Index*

3. Skim the sources you discover to find which might help to answer or focus your questions.
4. Decide on a preliminary thesis.
5. Take notes from sources that will help you to explore this thesis. (Make certain to note carefully bibliographic information, including author, title, date and place of publication, publisher, and page numbers, from each source.)
6. Organize your information and begin to draft.
7. Remember to use quotations and paraphrases sparingly. Your ideas, not those of your sources, should dominate the paper.
8. Lead in to quotations and paraphrases smoothly, so that the reader knows why they are important.
9. Provide accurate documentation for quoted and paraphrased material. (See Appendix, pages 1242–1244.)
10. Provide an accurate list of works cited. (See Appendix, pages 1245–1247.)

SUMMARY

Strategies for Discovering and Exploring Ideas

1. Write journal entries about the work (pages 84, 122, and 134).
2. Discuss the work with others (page 93).
3. Make lists of questions or observations about the work (pages 87, 93, and 103).
4. Write a paraphrase of a poem or of a complex section of a story, play, or essay (page 110).
5. Interview someone who has special interest or expertise in the theme or subject of the work (page 122).
6. Research the ideas of others on the work (page 131).

Strategies for Evaluating Your Audience

1. Consider the readers' interests (page 85).
2. Consider the readers' knowledge (pages 94, 134).
3. Consider the readers' opinions (pages 104, and 123–124).
4. Consider the readers' values (page 123).

Strategies for Revising

1. Give the paper an accurate, inviting title (page 89).
2. Open with a paragraph that indicates the paper's purpose and intrigues the reader (page 89).
3. Conclude with a paragraph that follows logically from the rest of the paper and that does more than summarize (page 89).
4. Use clear transitions to show the relationship between sections of the paper, between paragraphs, and between sentences (page 97).
5. Use evidence—details, reasons, and examples—from the work to support your ideas (pages 98 and 105).
6. Keep summaries of works very short (no more than a few sentences at most). Know the difference between summarizing and discussing your own ideas (page 112).
7. Make sure your ideas are logically presented (page 126).
8. Make sure the organization of your paper is clear (pages 86, 94, 104, 124, and 136).
9. Use quotations and paraphrases effectively. Lead in to quotations and paraphrases smoothly (pages 127 and 128).
10. Use quotations and paraphrases sparingly to support your points. Your own ideas should form the core of the paper (page 137).

Strategies for Editing

1. Avoid overuse of the verb "to be," expletives, passive voice, and nominalizations (pages 89 and 98).

2. Make careful word choices (page 106).
3. Use parallel structure effectively (page 98).
4. Be concise (pages 115–116).
5. Integrate quotations well and punctuate them accurately (page 127).
6. Combine sentences to eliminate wordiness, repetition, and choppy structure (page 139).

Strategies for Proofreading

1. Rewrite fragments and comma splices as complete sentences (pages 89–90).
2. Make subjects and verbs agree (page 99).
3. Make verb tenses agree (page 99).
4. Identify and revise misplaced modifiers (page 107).
5. Make sure that pronoun references are clear (page 129).
6. Make pronouns agree with the nouns to which they refer (page 129).
7. Punctuate lines of poetry correctly (page 127).
8. Use apostrophes correctly (page 117).
9. Use quotation marks correctly (page 127).
10. Format titles correctly (page 129).
11. Check for spelling or typographical errors (page 140).

5

Innocence and Experience

JAMES JOYCE (1882–1941)

Araby

Born in a suburb of Dublin, Ireland, James Joyce received his early education at schools run by Jesuit priests. Joyce had a troubled childhood: his father's heavy drinking and resulting unemployment led the family into serious economic difficulties. Nevertheless, Joyce was able to attend University College in Dublin. After his graduation in 1902, he moved to Paris. Although he returned for a brief time to Ireland to stay with his mother during her final illness, he left again in 1904, believing that he had to leave his childhood home to examine his complex thoughts and responses to his native land and to find the freedom needed "to forge in the smithy of my soul the uncreated conscience of my race." He spent the rest of his life living in major European cities—Trieste, Zurich, and Paris—while writing Dubliners, *the collection of short stories in which "Araby" appears (written between 1904 and 1907; published in 1914);* Portrait of the Artist as a Young Man, *an autobiographical novel (1916);* Ulysses *(1922); and* Finnegans Wake *(1939).*

North Richmond Street, being blind, was a quiet street except at the hour when the Christian Brothers' School set the boys free. An uninhabited house of two stories stood at the blind end, detached from its neighbors in a square ground. The other houses of the street, conscious of decent lives within them, gazed at one another with brown imperturbable faces.

The former tenant of our house, a priest, had died in the back drawing-room. Air, musty from having been long enclosed, hung in all the rooms, and the waste room behind the kitchen was littered with old useless papers. Among these I found a few paper-covered books, the pages of which were curled and damp: *The Abbot,* by Walter Scott, *The Devout Communicant* and *The Memoirs of Vidoca.* I liked the last best because its leaves were yellow. The wild garden behind the house contained a central apple-tree and a few straggling bushes under one of which I found the late tenant's rusty bicycle-pump. He had been a very charitable priest: in his will he had left all his money to institutions and the furniture of his house to his sister.

When the short days of winter came dusk fell before we had well eaten our dinners. When we met in the street the houses had grown somber. The space of sky above us was the color of ever-changing violet and towards it the lamps of the street lifted their feeble lanterns. The cold air stung us and we played till our bodies glowed. Our shouts echoed in the silent street. The career of our play brought us through the dark muddy lanes behind the houses where we ran the gantlet of the rough tribes from the cottages, to the back doors of the dark dripping gardens where odors arose from the ashpits, to the dark odorous stables where a coachman smoothed and combed the horse or shook music from the buckled harness. When we returned to the street light from the kitchen windows had filled the areas. If my uncle was

seen turning the corner we hid in the shadow until we had seen him safely
housed. Or if Mangan's sister came out on the doorstep to call her brother
in to his tea we watched her from our shadow peer up and down the street.
We waited to see whether she would remain or go in and, if she remained,
we left our shadow and walked up to Mangan's steps resignedly. She was
waiting for us, her figure defined by the light from the half-opened door.
Her brother always teased her before he obeyed and I stood by the railings
looking at her. Her dress swung as she moved her body and the soft rope of
her hair tossed from side to side.

Every morning I lay on the floor in the front parlor watching her door.
The blind was pulled down to within an inch of the sash so that I could not
be seen. When she came out on the doorstep my heart leaped. I ran to the
hall, seized my books and followed her. I kept her brown figure always in
my eye and, when we came near the point at which our ways diverged, I
quickened my pace and passed her. This happened morning after morning. I
had never spoken to her, except for a few casual words, and yet her name
was like a summons to all my foolish blood.

Her image accompanied me even in places the most hostile to romance.   5
On Saturday evenings when my aunt went marketing I had to go to carry
some of the parcels. We walked through the flaring streets, jostled by drunken
men and bargaining women, amid the curses of laborers, the shrill litanies
of shop-boys who stood on guard by the barrels of pigs' cheeks, the nasal
chanting of street-singers, who sang a *come-all-you* about O'Donovan Rossa,
or a ballad about the troubles in our native land. These noises converged in
a single sensation of life for me: I imagined that I bore my chalice safely
through a throng of foes. Her name sprang to my lips at moments in strange
prayers and praises which I myself did not understand. My eyes were often
full of tears (I could not tell why) and at times a flood from my heart seemed
to pour itself out into my bosom. I thought little of the future. I did not
know whether I would ever speak to her or not or, if I spoke to her, how I
could tell her of my confused adoration. But my body was like a harp and
her words and gestures were like fingers running upon the wires.

One evening I went into the back drawing-room in which the priest
had died. It was a dark rainy evening and there was no sound in the house.
Through one of the broken panes I heard the rain impinge upon the earth,
the fine incessant needles of water playing in the sodden beds. Some distant
lamp or lighted window gleamed below me. I was thankful that I could see
so little. All my senses seemed to desire to veil themselves and, feeling that I
was about to slip from them, I pressed the palms of my hands together until
they trembled, murmuring: *O love! O love!* many times.

At last she spoke to me. When she addressed the first words to me I
was so confused that I did not know what to answer. She asked me was I
going to *Araby.* I forget whether I answered yes or no. It would be a splendid
bazaar, she said; she would love to go.

—And why can't you? I asked.

While she spoke she turned a silver bracelet round and round her wrist. She could not go, she said, because there would be a retreat that week in her convent. Her brother and two other boys were fighting for their caps and I was alone at the railings. She held one of the spikes, bowing her head towards me. The light from the lamp opposite our door caught the white curve of a neck, lit up her hair that rested there and, falling, lit up the hand upon the railing. It fell over one side of her dress and caught the white border of a petticoat, just visible as she stood at ease.

—It's well for you, she said.   10

—If I go, I said, I will bring you something.

What innumerable follies laid waste my waking and sleeping thoughts after that evening! I wished to annihilate the tedious intervening days. I chafed against the work of school. At night in my bedroom and by day in the classroom her image came between me and the page I strove to read. The syllables of the word *Araby* were called to me through the silence in which my soul luxuriated and cast an Eastern enchantment over me. I asked for leave to go to the bazaar on Saturday night. My aunt was surprised and hoped it was not some Freemason affair. I answered few questions in class, I watched my master's face pass from amiability to sternness; he hoped I was not beginning to idle. I could not call my wandering thoughts together. I had hardly any patience with the serious work of life which, now that it stood between me and my desire, seemed to me child's play, ugly monotonous child's play.

On Saturday morning I reminded my uncle that I wished to go to the bazaar in the evening. He was fussing at the hall-stand, looking for the hat-brush, and answered me curtly:

—Yes, boy, I know.

As he was in the hall I could not go into the front parlor and lie at the   15
window. I left the house in bad humor and walked slowly towards the school. The air was pitilessly raw and already my heart misgave me.

When I came home to dinner my uncle had not yet been home. Still it was early. I sat staring at the clock for some time and, when its ticking began to irritate me, I left the room. I mounted the staircase and gained the upper part of the house. The high cold empty gloomy rooms liberated me and I went from room to room singing. From the front window I saw my companions playing below in the street. Their cries reached me weakened and indistinct and, leaning my forehead against the cool glass, I looked over at the dark house where she lived. I may have stood there for an hour, seeing nothing but the brown-clad figure cast by my imagination, touched discreetly by the lamplight at the curved neck, at the hand upon the railings and at the border below the dress.

When I came downstairs again I found Mrs. Mercer sitting at the fire. She was an old garrulous woman, a pawnbroker's widow, who collected used stamps for some pious purpose. I had to endure the gossip of the tea-table. The meal was prolonged beyond an hour and still my uncle did not come.

Mrs. Mercer stood up to go: she was sorry she couldn't wait any longer, but it was after eight o'clock and she did not like to be out late, as the night air was bad for her. When she had gone I began to walk up and down the room, clenching my fists. My aunt said:

—I'm afraid you may put off your bazaar for this night of Our Lord.

At nine o'clock I heard my uncle's latchkey in the halldoor. I heard him talking to himself and heard the hall-stand rocking when it had received the weight of his overcoat. I could interpret these signs. When he was midway through his dinner I asked him to give me the money to go to the bazaar. He had forgotten.

—The people are in bed and after their first sleep now, he said.   20

I did not smile. My aunt said to him energetically:

—Can't you give him the money and let him go? You've kept him late enough as it is.

My uncle said he was very sorry he had forgotten. He said he believed in the old saying: *All work and no play makes Jack a dull boy.* He asked me where I was going and, when I had told him a second time he asked me did I know *The Arab's Farewell to His Steed.* When I left the kitchen he was about to recite the opening lines of the piece to my aunt.

I held a florin tightly in my hand as I strode down Buckingham Street towards the station. The sight of the streets thronged with buyers and glaring with gas recalled to me the purpose of my journey. I took my seat in a third-class carriage of a deserted train. After an intolerable delay the train moved out of the station slowly. It crept onward among ruinous houses and over the twinkling river. At Westland Row Station a crowd of people pressed to the carriage doors; but the porters moved them back, saying that it was a special train for the bazaar. I remained alone in the bare carriage. In a few minutes the train drew up beside an improvised wooden platform. I passed out on to the road and saw by the lighted dial of a clock that it was ten minutes to ten. In front of me was a large building which displayed a magical name.

I could not find any sixpenny entrance and, fearing that the bazaar   25
would be closed, I passed in quickly through a turnstile, handing a shilling to a weary-looking man. I found myself in a big hall girdled at half its height by a gallery. Nearly all the stalls were closed and the greater part of the hall was in darkness. I recognized a silence like that which pervades a church after a service. I walked into the center of the bazaar timidly. A few people were gathered about the stalls which were still open. Before a curtain, over which the words *Café Chantant* were written in colored lamps, two men were counting money on a salver. I listened to the fall of the coins.

Remembering with difficulty why I had come I went over to one of the stalls and examined porcelain vases and flowered tea-sets. At the door of the stall a young lady was talking and laughing with two young gentlemen. I remarked their English accents and listened vaguely to their conversation.

—O, I never said such a thing!

—O, but you did!

—O, but I didn't!

—Didn't she say that? 30

—Yes. I heard her.

—O, there's a . . . fib!

Observing me the young lady came over and asked me did I wish to buy anything. The tone of her voice was not encouraging; she seemed to have spoken to me out of a sense of duty. I looked humbly at the great jars that stood like eastern guards at either side of the dark entrance to the stall and murmured:

—No, thank you.

The young lady changed the position of one of the vases and went 35 back to the two young men. They began to talk of the same subject. Once or twice the young lady glanced at me over her shoulder.

I lingered before her stall, though I knew my stay was useless, to make my interest in her wares seem the more real. Then I turned away slowly and walked down the middle of the bazaar. I allowed the two pennies to fall against the sixpence in my pocket. I heard a voice call from one end of the gallery that the light was out. The upper part of the hall was now completely dark.

Gazing up into the darkness I saw myself as a creature driven and derided by vanity; and my eyes burned with anguish and anger.

Considerations

1. Compare the adult narrator who tells the story with the younger self he describes. What differences do you see in the two? Similarities?
2. List several details relating to the story's setting and consider how those details relate to the changes the narrator experiences.
3. What does the narrator expect to find at Araby? What drives him so intensely to the bazaar? Why is he so intensely disappointed?
4. What is your response to the final passage describing the narrator's experience when he finally arrives at Araby?
5. Describe an experience in which you anticipated an event with pleasure but found the actual event disappointing. Provide specific details that show what you hoped for and why those hopes were not realized. In addition, show the difference between the way you looked at this experience as a child and the way you look at it now.

WAKAKO YAMAUCHI (1924–   )

And the Soul Shall Dance

> *Wakako Yamauchi was born in Westmoreland, California, in 1924, to par-*
> *ents who had immigrated from Japan. While growing up on the family farm,*
> *Yamauchi spent every minute of leisure reading voraciously, imagining herself*
> *as part of the varied worlds created in the books she read. In 1942, Yamauchi*
> *and her family were interned in Arizona as a result of the United States*
> *government's World War II policy to "relocate" West Coast residents of Japa-*
> *nese ancestry. Although she met and became friends with the Japanese-*
> *American writer Hisaye Yamamoto during her time in the internment camp,*
> *she herself did not begin to write until several years later. Many of Yamauchi's*
> *stories, including "And the Soul Shall Dance," deal with the struggles between*
> *Japanese immigrant parents and their American-born children. Her published*
> *stories include "Songs My Mother Taught Me" (1977), "Boatmen on Toneh*
> *River" (1983), "Surviving the Wasteland Years" (1988), "Makapoo Bay"*
> *(1989), and "Maybe" (1990).*

It's all right to talk about it now. Most of the principals are dead, except, of course, me and my younger brother, and possibly Kiyoko Oka, who might be near forty-five now, because, yes, I'm sure of it, she was fourteen then. I was nine, and my brother about four, so he hardly counts at all. Kiyoko's mother is dead, my father is dead, my mother is dead, and her father could not have lasted all these years with his tremendous appetite for alcohol and pickled chilies—those little yellow ones, so hot they could make your mouth hurt; he'd eat them like peanuts and tears would surge from his bulging thyroid eyes in great waves and stream down the dark coarse terrain of his face.

My father farmed then in the desert basin resolutely named Imperial Valley, in the township called Westmoreland; twenty acres of tomatoes, ten of summer squash, or vice versa, and the Okas lived maybe a mile, mile and a half, across an alkaline road, a stretch of greasewood, tumbleweed and white sand, to the south of us. We didn't hobnob much with them, because you see, they were a childless couple and we were a family: father, mother, daughter, and son, and we went to the Buddhist church on Sundays where my mother taught Japanese, and the Okas kept pretty much to themselves. I don't mean they were unfriendly; Mr. Oka would sometimes walk over (he rarely drove) on rainy days, all dripping wet, short and squat under a soggy newspaper, pretending to need a plow-blade or a file, and he would spend the afternoon in our kitchen drinking sake and eating chilies with my father. As he got progressively drunker, his large mouth would draw down and with the stream of tears, he looked like a kindly weeping bullfrog.

Not only were they childless, impractical in an area where large families were looked upon as labor potentials, but there was a certain strangeness about them. I became aware of it the summer our bathhouse burned down, and my father didn't get right down to building another, and a Japanese without a bathhouse . . . well, Mr. Oka offered us the use of his. So every night that summer we drove to the Okas for our bath, and we came in frequent contact with Mrs. Oka, and this is where I found the strangeness.

Mrs. Oka was small and spare. Her clothes hung on her like loose skin and when she walked, the skirt about her legs gave her a sort of webbed look. She was pretty in spite of the boniness and the dull calico and the barren look; I know now that she couldn't have been over thirty. Her eyes were large and a little vacant, although once I saw them fill with tears; the time I insisted we take the old Victrola over and we played our Japanese records for her. Some of the songs were sad, and I imagined the nostalgia she felt, but my mother said the tears were probably from yawning or from the smoke of her cigarettes. I thought my mother resented her for not being more hospitable; indeed, never a cup of tea appeared before us, and between them the conversation of women was totally absent: the rise and fall of gentle voices, the arched eyebrows, the croon of polite surprise. But more than this, Mrs. Oka was *different*.

Obviously she was shy, but some nights she disappeared altogether. She   5
would see us drive into her yard and then lurch from sight. She was gone all evening. Where could she have hidden in that two-roomed house—where in that silent desert? Some nights she would wait out our visit with enormous forbearance, quietly pushing wisps of stray hair behind her ears and waving gnats away from her great moist eyes, and some nights she moved about with nervous agitation, her khaki canvas shoes slapping loudly as she walked. And sometimes there appeared to be welts and bruises on her usually smooth brown face, and she would sit solemnly, hands on lap, eyes large and intent on us. My mother hurried us home then: "Hurry, Masako, no need to wash well; hurry."

You see, being so poky, I was always last to bathe. I think the Okas bathed after we left because my mother often reminded me to keep the water clean. The routine was to lather outside the tub (there were buckets and pans and a small wooden stool), rinse off the soil and soap, and then soak in the tub of hot hot water and contemplate. Rivulets of perspiration would run down the scalp.

When my mother pushed me like this, I dispensed with ritual, rushed a bar of soap around me and splashed about a pan of water. So hastily toweled, my wet skin strapped the clothes to me, impeding my already clumsy progress. Outside, my mother would be murmuring her many apologies and my father, I knew, would be carrying my brother whose feet were already sandy. We would hurry home.

I thought Mrs. Oka might be insane and I asked my mother about it, but she shook her head and smiled with her mouth drawn down and said that Mrs. Oka loved her sake. This was unusual, yes, but there were other unusual women we knew. Mrs. Nagai was brought by her husband from a geisha house; Mrs. Tani was a militant Christian Scientist; Mrs. Abe, the midwife, was occult. My mother's statement explained much: sometimes Mrs. Oka was drunk and sometimes not. Her taste for liquor and cigarettes was a step in the realm of men; unusual for a Japanese wife, but at that time, in that place, and to me, Mrs. Oka loved her sake in the way my father loved his, in the way of Mr. Oka, and the way I loved my candy. That her psychology may have demanded this anesthetic, that she lived with something unendurable, did not occur to me. Nor did I perceive the violence of emotions that the purple welts indicated—or the masochism that permitted her to display these wounds to us.

In spite of her masculine habits, Mrs. Oka was never less than a woman. She was no lady in the area of social amenities; but the feminine in her was innate and never left her. Even in her disgrace, she was a small broken sparrow, slightly floppy, too slowly enunciating her few words, too carefully rolling her Bull Durham, cocking her small head and moistening the ocher tissue. Her aberration was a protest of the life assigned her; it was obstinate, but unobserved, alas, unheeded. "Strange" was the only concession we granted her.

Toward the end of summer, my mother said we couldn't continue bath-   10
ing at the Okas'; when winter set in we'd all catch our death from the commuting and she'd always felt dreadful about our imposition on Mrs. Oka. So my father took the corrugated tin sheets he'd found on the highway and had been saving for some other use and built up our bathhouse again. Mr. Oka came to help.

While they raised the quivering tin walls, Mr. Oka began to talk. His voice was sharp and clear above the low thunder of the metal sheets.

He told my father he had been married in Japan previously to the present Mrs. Oka's older sister. He had a child by the marriage, Kiyoko, a girl. He had left the two to come to America intending to send for them soon, but shortly after his departure, his wife passed away from an obscure stomach ailment. At the time, the present Mrs. Oka was young and had foolishly become involved with a man of poor reputation. The family was anxious to part the lovers and conveniently arranged a marriage by proxy and sent him his dead wife's sister. Well that was all right, after all, they were kin, and it would be good for the child when she came to join them. But things didn't work out that way, year after year he postponed calling for his daughter, couldn't get the price of fare together, and the wife—ahhh, the wife, Mr. Oka's groan was lost in the rumble of his hammering.

He cleared his throat. The girl was now fourteen, he said, and begged to come to America to be with her own real family. Those relatives had forgotten the favor he'd done in accepting a slightly used bride, and now tormented his daughter for being forsaken. True, he'd not sent much money, but if they knew, if they only knew how it was here.

"Well," he sighed, "who could be blamed? It's only right she be with me anyway."

"That's right," my father said.   15

"Well, I sold the horse and some other things and managed to buy a third-class ticket on the Taiyo-Maru. Kiyoko will get here the first week of September." Mr. Oka glanced toward my father, but my father was peering into a bag of nails. "I'd be much obliged to you if your wife and little girl," he rolled his eyes toward me, "would take kindly to her. She'll be lonely."

Kiyoko-san came in September. I was surprised to see so very nearly a woman; short, robust, buxom: the female counterpart of her father; thyroid eyes and protruding teeth, straight black hair banded impudently into two bristly shucks, Cuban heels and white socks. Mr. Oka brought her proudly to us.

"Little Masako here," for the first time to my recollection, he touched me; he put his rough fat hand on the top of my head, "is very smart in school. She will help you with your school work, Kiyoko," he said.

I had so looked forward to Kiyoko-san's arrival. She would be my soul mate; in my mind I had conjured a girl of my own proportion: thin and tall, but with the refinement and beauty I didn't yet possess that would surely someday come to the fore. My disappointment was keen and apparent. Kiyoko-san stepped forward shyly, then retreated with a short bow and small giggle, her fingers pressed to her mouth.

My mother took her away. They talked for a long time—about Japan, about enrollment in American school, the clothes Kiyoko-san would need, and where to look for the best values. As I watched them, it occurred to me that I had been deceived: this was not a child, this was a woman. The smile pressed behind her fingers, the way of her nod, so brief, like my mother when father scolded her: the face was inscrutable, but something—maybe spirit—shrank visibly, like a piece of silk in water. I was disappointed; Kiyoko-san's soul was barricaded in her unenchanting appearance and the smile she fenced behind her fingers. 20

She started school from third grade, one below me, and as it turned out, she quickly passed me by. There wasn't much I could help her with except to drill her on pronunciation—the "L" and "R" sounds. Every morning walking to our rural school: land, leg, library, loan, lot; every afternoon returning home: ran, rabbit, rim, rinse, roll. That was the extent of our communication; friendly but uninteresting.

One particularly cold November night—the wind outside was icy; I was sitting on my bed, my brother's and mine, oiling the cracks in my chapped hands by lamplight—someone rapped urgently at our door. It was Kiyoko-san; she was hysterical, she wore no wrap, her teeth were chattering, and except for the thin straw zori, her feet were bare. My mother led her to the kitchen, started a pot of tea, and gestured to my brother and me to retire. I lay very still but because of my brother's restless tossing and my father's snoring, was unable to hear much. I was aware, though, that drunken and savage brawling had brought Kiyoko-san to us. Presently they came to the bedroom. I feigned sleep. My mother gave Kiyoko-san a gown and pushed me over to make room for her. My mother spoke firmly: "Tomorrow you

will return to them; you must not leave them again. They are your people."
I could almost feel Kiyoko-san's short nod.

All night long I lay cramped and still, afraid to intrude into her hulking back. Two or three times her icy feet jabbed into mine and quickly retreated. In the morning I found my mother's gown neatly folded on the spare pillow. Kiyoko-san's place in bed was cold.

She never came to weep at our house again but I know she cried: her eyes were often swollen and red. She stopped much of her giggling and routinely pressed her fingers to her mouth. Our daily pronunciation drill petered off from lack of interest. She walked silently with her shoulders hunched, grasping her books with both arms, and when I spoke to her in my halting Japanese, she absently corrected my prepositions.

Spring comes early in the Valley; in February the skies are clear though   25
the air is still cold. By March, winds are vigorous and warm and wild flowers dot the desert floor, cockleburs are green and not yet tenacious, the sand is crusty underfoot, everywhere there is a smell of things growing and the first tomatoes are showing green and bald.

As the weather changed, Kiyoko-san became noticeably more cheerful. Mr. Oka who hated so to drive could often be seen steering his dusty old Ford over the road that passes our house, and Kiyoko-san sitting in front would sometimes wave gaily to us. Mrs. Oka was never with them. I thought of these trips as the westernizing of Kiyoko-san: with a permanent wave, her straight black hair became tangles of tiny frantic curls; between her textbooks she carried copies of *Modern Screen* and *Photoplay*, her clothes were gay with print and piping, and she bought a pair of brown suede shoes with alligator trim. I can see her now picking her way gingerly over the deceptive white peaks of alkaline crust.

At first my mother watched their coming and going with vicarious pleasure. "Probably off to a picture show; the stores are all closed at this hour," she might say. Later her eyes would get distant and she would muse, "They've left her home again; Mrs. Oka is alone again, the poor woman."

Now when Kiyoko-san passed by or came in with me on her way home, my mother would ask about Mrs. Oka—how is she, how does she occupy herself these rainy days, or these windy or warm or cool days. Often the answers were polite: "Thank you, we are fine," but sometimes Kiyoko-san's upper lip would pull over her teeth, and her voice would become very soft and she would say, "Drink, always drinking and fighting." And those times my mother would invariably say, "Endure, soon you will be marrying and going away."

Once a young truck driver delivered crates at the Oka farm and he dropped back to our place to tell my father that Mrs. Oka had lurched behind his truck while he was backing up, and very nearly let him kill her. Only the daughter pulling her away saved her, he said. Thoroughly unnerved, he stopped by to rest himself and talk about it. Never, never, he said in wide-eyed wonder, had he seen a drunken Japanese woman. My father nodded gravely, "Yes, it's unusual," he said and drummed his knee with his fingers.

Evenings were longer now, and when my mother's migraines drove me   30
from the house in unbearable self-pity, I would take walks in the desert. One night with the warm wind against me, the dune primrose and yellow poppies closed and fluttering, the greasewood swaying in languid orbit, I lay on the white sand beneath a shrub and tried to disappear.

A voice sweet and clear cut through the half-dark of the evening:

Red lips press against a glass
Drink the purple wine
    And the soul shall dance

Mrs. Oka appeared to be gathering flowers. Bending, plucking, standing, searching, she added to a small bouquet she clasped. She held them away; looked at them slyly, lids lowered, demure, then in a sudden and sinuous movement, she broke into a stately dance. She stopped, gathered more flowers, and breathed deeply into them. Tossing her head, she laughed—softly, beautifully, from her dark throat. The picture of her imagined grandeur was lost to me, but the delusion that transformed the bouquet of tattered petals and sandy leaves, and the aloneness of a desert twilight into a fantasy that brought such joy and abandon made me stir with discomfort. The sound broke Mrs. Oka's dance. Her eyes grew large and her neck tense—like a cat on the prowl. She spied me in the bushes. A peculiar chill ran through me. Then abruptly and with childlike delight, she scattered the flowers around her and walked away singing:

Falling, falling, petals on a wind . . .

That was the last time I saw Mrs. Oka. She died before the spring harvest. It was pneumonia. I didn't attend the funeral, but my mother said it was sad. Mrs. Oka looked peaceful, and the minister expressed the irony of the long separation of Mother and Child and the short-lived reunion; hardly a year together, she said. We went to help Kiyoko-san address and stamp those black-bordered acknowledgments.

When harvest was over, Mr. Oka and Kiyoko-san moved out of the Valley. We never heard from them or saw them again and I suppose in a large city, Mr. Oka found some sort of work, perhaps as a janitor or a dishwasher and Kiyoko-san grew up and found someone to marry.

Considerations

1. Read the first paragraph, and write a brief prediction about the story's possible themes based only on the images and short character sketches you find there. Then read the story and explain how your initial responses changed or developed.

2. At the end of paragraph 4, the narrator characterizes Mrs. Oka as "*different*." What effect is created by printing the word in italics? As you read the description of Mrs. Oka, what details suggest that she is or is not, in your own definition, "different." From whom is she different? Do you see the narrator's designation of "different" as negative, positive, or neutral? Explain.

3. Describe the narrator's response to and interactions with Kiyoko-san. What is Kiyoko-san's role in the narrator's growth from innocence to experience?

4. Toward the end of the story, the narrator's mother advises Kiyoko-san, "Endure, soon you will be marrying and going away." How would you evaluate this advice? What advice would you have given Kiyoko-san, under the same circumstances? Suggest possible outcomes both for the advice of the narrator's mother and for the advice you would have given.

5. Read paragraph 32 carefully, and consider the possible themes for this story suggested by the images in the narrator's description and in the poem Mrs. Oka sings.

LOUISE ERDRICH (1954–   )

The Red Convertible
Lyman Lamartine

> *Louise Erdrich is the daughter of a German-born father and a Chippewa mother, who were both working for the Bureau of Indian Affairs in North Dakota when she was born in 1954. During most of her childhood, Erdrich's maternal grandfather was tribal chair of the Turtle Mountain Band of Chippewa. Erdrich received her bachelor of arts from Dartmouth and her master of arts from Johns Hopkins University. She has taught in the Poetry in the Schools Program in North Dakota and currently lives with her husband, Michael Dorris, a professor of Native American studies at Dartmouth College. Erdrich's publications include* Jacklight, *a collection of poetry (1984);* The Beet Queen, *a novel (1986); and* Love Medicine, *a novel that won the National Book Critics Circle Award in 1984. "The Red Convertible" is a chapter from* Love Medicine.

I was the first one to drive a convertible on my reservation. And of course it was red, a red Olds. I owned that car along with my brother Henry Junior. We owned it together until his boots filled with water on a windy night and he bought out my share. Now Henry owns the whole car, and his youngest brother Lyman (that's myself), Lyman walks everywhere he goes.

How did I earn enough money to buy my share in the first place? My own talent was I could always make money. I had a touch for it, unusual in a Chippewa. From the first I was different that way, and everyone recognized it. I was the only kid they let in the American Legion Hall to shine shoes, for example, and one Christmas I sold spiritual bouquets for the mission door to door. The nuns let me keep a percentage. Once I started, it seemed the more money I made the easier the money came. Everyone encouraged it. When I was fifteen I got a job washing dishes at the Joliet Café, and that was where my first big break happened.

It wasn't long before I was promoted to busing tables, and then the short-order cook quit and I was hired to take her place. No sooner than you know it I was managing the Joliet. The rest is history. I went on managing. I soon became part owner, and of course there was no stopping me then. It wasn't long before the whole thing was mine.

After I'd owned the Joliet for one year, it blew over in the worst tornado ever seen around here. The whole operation was smashed to bits. A total loss. The fryalator was up in a tree, the grill torn in half like it was paper. I was only sixteen. I had it all in my mother's name, and I lost it quick, but before I lost it I had every one of my relatives, and their relatives, to dinner, and I also bought that red Olds I mentioned, along with Henry.

The first time we saw it! I'll tell you when we first saw it. We had gotten a 5
ride up to Winnipeg, and both of us had money. Don't ask me why, because
we never mentioned a car or anything, we just had all our money. Mine was
cash, a big bankroll from the Joliet's insurance. Henry had two checks—a
week's extra pay for being laid off, and his regular check from the Jewel
Bearing Plant.

We were walking down Portage anyway, seeing the sights, when we
saw it. There it was, parked, large as life. Really as *if* it was alive. I thought
of the word *repose,* because the car wasn't simply stopped, parked, or whatever. That car reposed, calm and gleaming, a FOR SALE sign in its left front
window. Then, before we had thought it over at all, the car belonged to us
and our pockets were empty. We had just enough money for gas back home.

We went places in that car, me and Henry. We took off driving all one
whole summer. We started off toward the Little Knife River and Mandaree
in Fort Berthold and then we found ourselves down in Wakpala somehow,
and then suddenly we were over in Montana on the Rocky Boy, and yet the
summer was not even half over. Some people hang on to details when they
travel, but we didn't let them bother us and just lived our everyday lives here
to there.

I do remember this one place with willows. I remember I laid under
those trees and it was comfortable. So comfortable. The branches bent down
all around me like a tent or a stable. And quiet, it was quiet, even though
there was a powwow close enough so I could see it going on. The air was
not too still, not too windy either. When the dust rises up and hangs in the
air around the dancers like that, I feel good. Henry was asleep with his arms
thrown wide. Later on, he woke up and we started driving again. We were
somewhere in Montana, or maybe on the Blood Reserve—it could have
been anywhere. Anyway it was where we met the girl.

All her hair was in buns around her ears, that's the first thing I noticed about
her. She was posed alongside the road with her arm out, so we stopped.
That girl was short, so short her lumber shirt looked comical on her, like a
nightgown. She had jeans on and fancy moccasins and she carried a little
suitcase.

"Hop on in," says Henry. So she climbs in between us. 10
"We'll take you home," I says. "Where do you live?"
"Chicken," she says.
"Where the hell's that?" I ask her.
"Alaska."
"Okay," says Henry, and we drive. 15
We got up there and never wanted to leave. The sun doesn't truly set
there in summer, and the night is more a soft dusk. You might doze off,
sometimes, but before you know it you're up again, like an animal in nature.
You never feel like you have to sleep hard or put away the world. And things

would grow up there. One day just dirt or moss, the next day flowers and long grass. The girl's name was Susy. Her family really took to us. They fed us and put us up. We had our own tent to live in by their house, and the kids would be in and out of there all day and night. They couldn't get over me and Henry being brothers, we looked so different. We told them we knew we had the same mother, anyway.

One night Susy came in to visit us. We sat around in the tent talking of this and that. The season was changing. It was getting darker by that time, and the cold was even getting just a little mean. I told her it was time for us to go. She stood up on a chair.

"You never seen my hair," Susy said.

That was true. She was standing on a chair, but still, when she un-clipped her buns the hair reached all the way to the ground. Our eyes opened. You couldn't tell how much hair she had when it was rolled up so neatly. Then my brother Henry did something funny. He went up to the chair and said, "Jump on my shoulders." So she did that, and her hair reached down past his waist, and he started twirling, this way and that, so her hair was flung out from side to side.

"I always wondered what it was like to have long pretty hair," Henry   20 says. Well we laughed. It was a funny sight, the way he did it. The next morning we got up and took leave of those people.

On to greener pastures, as they say. It was down through Spokane and across Idaho then Montana and very soon we were racing the weather right along under the Canadian border through Columbus, Des Lacs, and then we were in Bottineau County and soon home. We'd made most of the trip, that summer, without putting up the car hood at all. We got home just in time, it turned out, for the army to remember Henry had signed up to join it.

I don't wonder that the army was so glad to get my brother that they turned him into a Marine. He was built like a brick outhouse anyway. We liked to tease him that they really wanted him for his Indian nose. He had a nose big and sharp as a hatchet, like the nose on Red Tomahawk, the Indian who killed Sitting Bull, whose profile is on signs all along the North Dakota highways. Henry went off to training camp, came home once during Christ-mas, then the next thing you know we got an overseas letter from him. It was 1970, and he said he was stationed up in the northern hill country. Whereabouts I did not know. He wasn't such a hot letter writer, and only got off two before the enemy caught him. I could never keep it straight, which direction those good Vietnam soldiers were from.

I wrote him back several times, even though I didn't know if those letters would get through. I kept him informed all about the car. Most of the time I had it up on blocks in the yard or half taken apart, because that long trip did a hard job on it under the hood.

I always had good luck with numbers, and never worried about the draft myself. I never even had to think about what my number was. But

Henry was never lucky in the same way as me. It was at least three years before Henry came home. By then I guess the whole war was solved in the government's mind, but for him it would keep on going. In those years I'd put his car into almost perfect shape. I always thought of it as his car while he was gone, even though when he left he said, "Now it's yours," and threw me his key.

"Thanks for the extra key," I'd said. "I'll put it up in your drawer just   25
in case I need it." He laughed.

When he came home, though, Henry was very different, and I'll say this: the change was no good. You could hardly expect him to change for the better, I know. But he was quiet, so quiet, and never comfortable sitting still anywhere but always up and moving around. I thought back to times we'd sat still for whole afternoons, never moving a muscle, just shifting our weight along the ground, talking to whoever sat with us, watching things. He'd always had a joke, then, too, and now you couldn't get him to laugh, or when he did it was more the sound of a man choking, a sound that stopped up the throats of other people around him. They got to leaving him alone most of the time, and I didn't blame them. It was a fact: Henry was jumpy and mean.

I'd bought a color TV set for my mom and the rest of us while Henry was away. Money still came very easy. I was sorry I'd ever bought it though, because of Henry. I was also sorry I'd bought color, because with black-and-white the pictures seem older and farther away. But what are you going to do? He sat in front of it, watching it, and that was the only time he was completely still. But it was the kind of stillness that you see in a rabbit when it freezes and before it will bolt. He was not easy. He sat in his chair gripping the armrests with all his might, as if the chair itself was moving at a high speed and if he let go at all he would rocket forward and maybe crash right through the set.

Once I was in the room watching TV with Henry and I heard his teeth click at something. I looked over, and he'd bitten through his lip. Blood was going down his chin. I tell you right then I wanted to smash that tube to pieces. I went over to it but Henry must have known what I was up to. He rushed from his chair and shoved me out of the way, against the wall. I told myself he didn't know what he was doing.

My mom came in, turned the set off real quiet, and told us she had made something for supper. So we went and sat down. There was still blood going down Henry's chin, but he didn't notice it and no one said anything, even though every time he took a bite of his bread his blood fell onto it until he was eating his own blood mixed in with the food.

While Henry was not around we talked about what was going to   30
happen to him. There were no Indian doctors on the reservation, and my mom couldn't come around to trusting the old man, Moses Pillager, because

he courted her long ago and was jealous of her husbands. He might take revenge through her son. We were afraid that if we brought Henry to a regular hospital they would keep him.

"They don't fix them in those places," Mom said; "they just give them drugs."

"We wouldn't get him there in the first place," I agreed, "so let's just forget about it."

Then I thought about the car.

Henry had not even looked at the car since he'd gotten home, though like I said, it was in tip-top condition and ready to drive. I thought the car might bring the old Henry back somehow. So I bided my time and waited for my chance to interest him in the vehicle.

One night Henry was off somewhere. I took myself a hammer. I went 35 out to that car and I did a number on its underside. Whacked it up. Bent the tail pipe double. Ripped the muffler loose. By the time I was done with the car it looked worse than any typical Indian car that has been driven all its life on reservation roads, which they always say are like government promises—full of holes. It just about hurt me, I'll tell you that! I threw dirt in the carburetor and I ripped all the electric tape off the seats. I made it look just as beat up as I could. Then I sat back and waited for Henry to find it.

Still, it took him over a month. That was all right, because it was just getting warm enough, not melting, but warm enough to work outside.

"Lyman," he says, walking in one day, "that red car looks like shit."

"Well it's old," I says. "You got to expect that."

"No way!" says Henry. "That car's a classic! But you went and ran the piss right out of it, Lyman, and you know it don't deserve that. I kept that car in A-one shape. You don't remember. You're too young. But when I left, that car was running like a watch. Now I don't even know if I can get it to start again, let alone get it anywhere near its old condition."

"Well you try," I said, like I was getting mad, "but I say it's a piece of 40 junk."

Then I walked out before he could realize I knew he'd strung together more than six words at once.

After that I thought he'd freeze himself to death working on that car. He was out there all day, and at night he rigged up a little lamp, ran a cord out the window, and had himself some light to see by while he worked. He was better than he had been before, but that's still not saying much. It was easier for him to do the things the rest of us did. He ate more slowly and didn't jump up and down during the meal to get this or that or look out the window. I put my hand in the back of the TV set, I admit, and fiddled around with it good, so that it was almost impossible now to get a clear picture. He didn't look at it very often anyway. He was always out with that car or going off to get parts for it. By the time it was really melting outside, he had it fixed.

I had been feeling down in the dumps about Henry around this time. We had always been together before. Henry and Lyman. But he was such a loner now that I didn't know how to take it. So I jumped at the chance one day when Henry seemed friendly. It's not that he smiled or anything. He just said, "Let's take that old shitbox for a spin." Just the way he said it made me think he could be coming around.

We went out to the car. It was spring. The sun was shining very bright. My only sister, Bonita, who was just eleven years old, came out and made us stand together for a picture. Henry leaned his elbow on the red car's windshield, and he took his other arm and put it over my shoulder, very carefully, as though it was heavy for him to lift and he didn't want to bring the weight down all at once.

"Smile," Bonita said, and he did.   45

That picture. I never look at it anymore. A few months ago, I don't know why, I got his picture out and tacked it on the wall. I felt good about Henry at the time, close to him. I felt good having his picture on the wall, until one night when I was looking at television. I was a little drunk and stoned. I looked up at the wall and Henry was staring at me. I don't know what it was, but his smile had changed, or maybe it was gone. All I know is I couldn't stay in the same room with that picture. I was shaking. I got up, closed the door, and went into the kitchen. A little later my friend Ray came over and we both went back into that room. We put the picture in a brown bag, folded the bag over and over tightly, then put it way back in a closet.

I still see that picture now, as if it tugs at me, whenever I pass that closet door. The picture is very clear in my mind. It was so sunny that day Henry had to squint against the glare. Or maybe the camera Bonita held flashed like a mirror, blinding him, before she snapped the picture. My face is right out in the sun, big and round. But he might have drawn back, because the shadows on his face are deep as holes. There are two shadows curved like little hooks around the ends of his smile, as if to frame it and try to keep it there—that one, first smile that looked like it might have hurt his face. He has his field jacket on and the worn-in clothes he'd come back in and kept wearing ever since. After Bonita took the picture, she went into the house and we got into the car. There was a full cooler in the trunk. We started off, east, toward Pembina and the Red River because Henry said he wanted to see the high water.

The trip over there was beautiful. When everything starts changing, drying up, clearing off, you feel like your whole life is starting. Henry felt it, too. The top was down and the car hummed like a top. He'd really put it back in shape, even the tape on the seats was very carefully put down and glued back in layers. It's not that he smiled again or even joked, but his face looked to me as if it was clear, more peaceful. It looked as though he wasn't thinking of anything in particular except the bare fields and windbreaks and houses we were passing.

The river was high and full of winter trash when we got there. The sun was still out, but it was colder by the river. There were still little clumps of dirty snow here and there on the banks. The water hadn't gone over the banks yet, but it would, you could tell. It was just at its limit, hard swollen, glossy like an old gray scar. We made ourselves a fire, and we sat down and watched the current go. As I watched it I felt something squeezing inside me and tightening and trying to let go all at the same time. I knew I was not just feeling it myself; I knew I was feeling what Henry was going through at that moment. Except that I couldn't stand it, the closing and opening. I jumped to my feet. I took Henry by the shoulders and I started shaking him. "Wake up," I says, "wake up, wake up, wake up!" I didn't know what had come over me. I sat down beside him again.

His face was totally white and hard. Then it broke, like stones break all   50
of a sudden when water boils up inside them.

"I know it," he says. "I know it. I can't help it. It's no use."

We start talking. He said he knew what I'd done with the car. It was obvious it had been whacked out of shape and not just neglected. He said he wanted to give the car to me for good now, it was no use. He said he'd fixed it just to give it back and I should take it.

"No way," I says. "I don't want it."

"That's okay," he says, "you take it."

"I don't want it, though," I says back to him, and then to emphasize,   55
just to emphasize, you understand, I touch his shoulder. He slaps my hand off.

"Take that car," he says.

"No," I say. "Make me," I say, and then he grabs my jacket and rips the arm loose. That jacket is a class act, suede with tags and zippers. I push Henry backwards, off the log. He jumps up and bowls me over. We go down in a clinch and come up swinging hard, for all we're worth, with our fists. He socks my jaw so hard I feel like it swings loose. Then I'm at his rib cage and land a good one under his chin so his head snaps back. He's dazzled. He looks at me and I look at him and then his eyes are full of tears and blood and at first I think he's crying. But no, he's laughing. "Ha! Ha!" he says. "Ha! Ha! Take good care of it."

"Okay," I says. "Okay, no problem. Ha! Ha!"

I can't help it, and I start laughing, too. My face feels fat and strange, and after a while I get a beer from the cooler in the trunk, and when I hand it to Henry he takes his shirt and wipes my germs off. "Hoof-and-mouth disease," he says. For some reason this cracks me up, and so we're really laughing for a while, and then we drink all the rest of the beers one by one and throw them in the river and see how far, how fast, the current takes them before they fill up and sink.

"You want to go on back?" I ask after a while. "Maybe we could snag   60
a couple nice Kashpaw girls."

He says nothing. But I can tell his mood is turning again.

"They're all crazy, the girls up here, every damn one of them."

"You're crazy too," I say, to jolly him up. "Crazy Lamartine boys!"

He looks as though he will take this wrong at first. His face twists, then clears, and he jumps up on his feet. "That's right!" he says. "Crazier 'n hell. Crazy Indians!"

I think it's the old Henry again. He throws off his jacket and starts   65
springing his legs up from the knees like a fancy dancer. He's down doing something between a grass dance and a bunny hop, no kind of dance I ever saw before, but neither has anyone else on all this green growing earth. He's wild. He wants to pitch whoopee! He's up and at me and all over. All this time I'm laughing so hard, so hard my belly is getting tied up in a knot.

"Got to cool me off!" he shouts all of a sudden. Then he runs over to the river and jumps in.

There's boards and other things in the current. It's so high. No sound comes from the river after the splash he makes, so I run right over. I look around. It's getting dark. I see he's halfway across the water already, and I know he didn't swim there but the current took him. It's far. I hear his voice, though, very clearly across it.

"My boots are filling," he says.

He says this in a normal voice, like he just noticed and he doesn't know what to think of it. Then he's gone. A branch comes by. Another branch. And I go in.

By the time I get out of the river, off the snag I pulled myself onto, the   70
sun is down. I walk back to the car, turn on the high beams, and drive it up the bank. I put it in first gear and then I take my foot off the clutch. I get out, close the door, and watch it plow softly into the water. The headlights reach in as they go down, searching, still lighted even after the water swirls over the back end. I wait. The wires short out. It is all finally dark. And then there is only the water, the sound of it going and running and going and running and running.

Considerations

1. As you read this story, make a list of at least ten phrases or sentences that give you insight into the character of the narrator, Lyman Lamartine. Then write a short essay describing Lyman. Use some (or all) of the phrases or sentences you listed as evidence to demonstrate the points you are making about Lyman.

2. In the final sentence of the opening paragraph, Lyman uses third person to describe himself. What effect does this choice of language create? How would the rest of the story be changed if it were told in third, rather than first, person?

3. Note the setting of each section of the story (time and place). How do the narrator's descriptions of time and place relate to the story's themes? For example, what is the effect of the jump ahead in time in paragraph

46, where the narrator describes his responses to the photograph taken by his sister?

4. What significance do you see in the fact that Lyman and Henry are Native Americans? Does this part of their background contribute to your own response to their actions and choices? Explain.

5. How does the red convertible serve as a symbol that relates to the story's central conflicts and resolutions (or lack of resolutions)?

_____

RALPH ELLISON (1914–1994)

Battle Royal

Born in Oklahoma City in 1914, Ralph Ellison was raised primarily by his widowed mother, who supported herself and her son by working as a household servant. After graduating from high school, Ellison followed his desire to study music by enrolling at Tuskegee Institute. After three years, he left Tuskegee and went to Harlem, hoping to further his knowledge of music composition and the visual arts. During his years in Harlem, he met African-American authors such as Langston Hughes and Richard Wright, who encouraged him to try his hand at writing fiction. He began to publish stories, essays, and reviews in 1939, and his writing career was briefly interrupted while he served in the Merchant Marine during World War II. After the war, he published the novel Invisible Man, *which received the National Book Award in 1952. He taught at Yale, Harvard, Rutgers, and New York University. "Battle Royal" is the first chapter in* Invisible Man.

It goes a long way back, some twenty years. All my life I had been looking for something, and everywhere I turned someone tried to tell me what it was. I accepted their answers too, though they were often in contradiction and even self-contradictory. I was naive. I was looking for myself and asking everyone except myself questions which I, and only I, could answer. It took me a long time and much painful boomeranging of my expectations to achieve a realization everyone else appears to have been born with: That I am nobody but myself. But first I had to discover that I am an invisible man!

And yet I am no freak of nature, nor of history. I was in the cards, other things having been equal (or unequal) eighty-five years ago. I am not ashamed of my grandparents for having been slaves. I am only ashamed of myself for having at one time been ashamed. About eighty-five years ago they were told that they were free, united with others of our country in everything pertaining to the common good, and, in everything social, separate like the fingers of the hand. And they believed it. They exulted in it. They stayed in their place, worked hard, and brought up my father to do the same. But my grandfather is the one. He was an odd old guy, my grandfather, and I am told I take after him. It was he who caused the trouble. On his deathbed he called my father to him and said, "Son, after I'm gone I want you to keep up the fight. I never told you, but our life is a war and I have been a traitor all my born days, a spy in the enemy's country ever since I give up my gun back in the Reconstruction. Live with your head in the lion's mouth. I want you to overcome 'em with yeses, undermine 'em with grins, agree 'em to death and destruction, let 'em swoller you till they vomit or bust wide open." They thought the old man had gone out of his mind. He had been the meekest of men. The younger children were rushed from the room, the shades drawn and the flame of the lamp turned so low that it sputtered on the wick like the old man's breathing. "Learn it to the young-uns," he whispered fiercely; then he died.

But my folks were more alarmed over his last words than over his dying. It was as though he had not died at all, his words caused so much anxiety. I was warned emphatically to forget what he had said and, indeed, this is the first time it has been mentioned outside the family circle. It had a tremendous effect upon me, however. I could never be sure of what he meant. Grandfather had been a quiet old man who never made any trouble, yet on his deathbed he had called himself a traitor and a spy, and he had spoken of his meekness as a dangerous activity. It became a constant puzzle which lay unanswered in the back of my mind. And whenever things went well for me I remembered my grandfather and felt guilty and uncomfortable. It was as though I was carrying out his advice in spite of myself. And to make it worse, everyone loved me for it. I was praised by the most lily-white men of the town. I was considered an example of desirable conduct—just as my grandfather had been. And what puzzled me was that the old man had defined it as *treachery*. When I was praised for my conduct I felt a guilt that in some way I was doing something that was really against the wishes of the white folks, that if they had understood they would have desired me to act just the opposite, that I should have been sulky and mean, and that that really would have been what they wanted, even though they were fooled and thought they wanted me to act as I did. It made me afraid that some day they would look upon me as a traitor and I would be lost. Still I was more afraid to act any other way because they didn't like that at all. The old man's words were like a curse. On my graduation day I delivered an oration in which I showed that humility was the secret, indeed, the very essence of progress. (Not that I believed this—how could I, remembering my grandfather?—I only believed that it worked.) It was a great success. Everyone praised me and I was invited to give the speech at a gathering of the town's leading white citizens. It was a triumph for our whole community.

It was in the main ballroom of the leading hotel. When I got there I discovered that it was on the occasion of a smoker, and I was told that since I was to be there anyway I might as well take part in the battle royal to be fought by some of my schoolmates as part of the entertainment. The battle royal came first.

All of the town's big shots were there in their tuxedos, wolfing down the buffet foods, drinking beer and whiskey and smoking black cigars. It was a large room with a high ceiling. Chairs were arranged in neat rows around three sides of a portable boxing ring. The fourth side was clear, revealing a gleaming space of polished floor. I had some misgivings over the battle royal, by the way. Not from a distaste for fighting, but because I didn't care too much for the other fellows who were to take part. They were tough guys who seemed to have no grandfather's curse worrying their minds. No one could mistake their toughness. And besides, I suspected that fighting a battle royal might detract from the dignity of my speech. In those pre-invisible days

5

I visualized myself as a potential Booker T. Washington. But the other fellows didn't care too much for me either, and there were nine of them. I felt superior to them in my way, and I didn't like the manner in which we were all crowded together into the servants' elevator. Nor did they like my being there. In fact, as the warmly lighted floors flashed past the elevator we had words over the fact that I, by taking part in the fight, had knocked one of their friends out of a night's work.

We were led out of the elevator through a rococo hall into an anteroom and told to get into our fighting togs. Each of us was issued a pair of boxing gloves and ushered out into the big mirrored hall, which we entered looking cautiously about us and whispering, lest we might accidentally be heard above the noise of the room. It was foggy with cigar smoke. And already the whiskey was taking effect. I was shocked to see some of the most important men of the town quite tipsy. They were all there—bankers, lawyers, judges, doctors, fire chiefs, teachers, merchants. Even one of the more fashionable pastors. Something we could not see was going on up front. A clarinet was vibrating sensuously and the men were standing up and moving eagerly forward. We were a small tight group, clustered together, our bare upper bodies touching and shining with anticipatory sweat; while up front the big shots were becoming increasingly excited over something we still could not see. Suddenly I heard the school superintendent, who had told me to come, yell, "Bring up the shines, gentlemen! Bring up the little shines!"

We were rushed up to the front of the ballroom, where it smelled even more strongly of tobacco and whiskey. Then we were pushed into place. I almost wet my pants. A sea of faces, some hostile, some amused, ringed around us, and in the center, facing us, stood a magnificent blonde—stark naked. There was a dead silence. I felt a blast of cold air chill me. I tried to back away, but they were behind me and around me. Some of the boys stood with lowered heads, trembling. I felt a wave of irrational guilt and fear. My teeth chattered, my skin turned to goose flesh, my knees knocked. Yet I was strongly attracted and looked in spite of myself. Had the price of looking been blindness, I would have looked. The hair was yellow like that of a circus kewpie doll, the face heavily powdered and rouged, as though to form an abstract mask, the eyes hollow and smeared a cool blue, the color of a ba-boon's butt. I felt a desire to spit upon her as my eyes brushed slowly over her body. Her breasts were firm and round as the domes of East Indian temples, and I stood so close as to see the fine skin texture and beads of pearly perspiration glistening like dew around the pink and erected buds of her nipples. I wanted at one and the same time to run from the room, to sink through the floor, or go to her and cover her from my eyes and the eyes of the others with my body; to feel the soft thighs, to caress her and destroy her, to love her and murder her, to hide from her, and yet to stroke where below the small American flag tattooed upon her belly her thighs formed a capital V. I had a notion that of all in the room she saw only me with her impersonal eyes.

And then she began to dance, a slow sensuous movement; the smoke of a hundred cigars clinging to her like the thinnest of veils. She seemed like a fair bird–girl girdled in veils calling to me from the angry surface of some gray and threatening sea. I was transported. Then I became aware of the clarinet playing and the big shots yelling at us. Some threatened us if we looked and others if we did not. On my right I saw one boy faint. And now a man grabbed a silver pitcher from a table and stepped close as he dashed ice water upon him and stood him up and forced two of us to support him as his head hung and moans issued from his thick bluish lips. Another boy began to plead to go home. He was the largest of the group, wearing dark red fighting trunks much too small to conceal the erection which projected from him as though in answer to the insinuating low-registered moaning of the clarinet. He tried to hide himself with his boxing gloves.

And all the while the blonde continued dancing, smiling faintly at the big shots who watched her with fascination, and faintly smiling at our fear. I noticed a certain merchant who followed her hungrily, his lips loose and drooling. He was a large man who wore diamond studs in a shirtfront which swelled with the ample paunch underneath, and each time the blonde swayed her undulating hips he ran his hand through the thin hair of his bald head and, with his arms upheld, his posture clumsy like that of an intoxicated panda, wound his belly in a slow and obscene grind. This creature was completely hypnotized. The music had quickened. As the dancer flung herself about with a detached expression on her face, the men began reaching out to touch her. I could see their beefy fingers sink into the soft flesh. Some of the others tried to stop them and she began to move around the floor in graceful circles, as they gave chase, slipping and sliding over the polished floor. It was mad. Chairs went crashing, drinks were spilt, as they ran laughing and howling after her. They caught her just as she reached a door, raised her from the floor, and tossed her as college boys are tossed at a hazing, and above her red, fixed-smiling lips I saw the terror and disgust in her eyes, almost like my own terror and that which I saw in some of the other boys. As I watched, they tossed her twice and her soft breasts seemed to flatten against the air and her legs flung wildly as she spun. Some of the more sober ones helped her to escape. And I started off the floor, heading for the ante-room with the rest of the boys.

Some were still crying and in hysteria. But as we tried to leave we were stopped and ordered to get into the ring. There was nothing to do but what we were told. All ten of us climbed under the ropes and allowed ourselves to be blindfolded with broad bands of white cloth. One of the men seemed to feel a bit sympathetic and tried to cheer us up as we stood with our backs against the ropes. Some of us tried to grin. "See that boy over there?" one of the men said. "I want you to run across at the bell and give it to him right in the belly. If you don't get him, I'm going to get you. I don't like his looks." Each of us was told the same. The blindfolds were put on. Yet even then I had been going over my speech. In my mind each word was as bright as flame. I felt the cloth pressed into place, and frowned so that it would be loosened when I relaxed.

But now I felt a sudden fit of blind terror. I was unused to darkness. It was as though I had suddenly found myself in a dark room filled with poisonous cottonmouths. I could hear the bleary voices yelling insistently for the battle royal to begin.

"Get going in there!"

"Let me at the big nigger!"

I strained to pick up the school superintendent's voice, as though to squeeze some security out of that slightly more familiar sound.

"Let me at those black sonsabitches!" someone yelled.   15

"No, Jackson, no!" another voice yelled. "Here, somebody, help me hold Jack."

"I want to get at that ginger-colored nigger. Tear him limb from limb," the first voice yelled.

I stood against the ropes trembling. For in those days I was what they called ginger-colored, and he sounded as though he might crunch me between his teeth like a crisp ginger cookie.

Quite a struggle was going on. Chairs were being kicked about and I could hear voices grunting as with a terrific effort. I wanted to see, to see more desperately than ever before. But the blindfold was as tight as a thick skin-puckering scab and when I raised my gloved hands to push the layers of white aside a voice yelled, "Oh, no you don't, black bastard! Leave that alone!"

"Ring the bell before Jackson kills him a coon!" someone boomed in   20
the sudden silence. And I heard the bell clang and the sound of feet scuffling forward.

A glove smacked against my head. I pivoted, striking out stiffly as someone went past, and felt the jar ripple along the length of my arm to my shoulder. Then it seemed as though all nine of the boys had turned upon me at once. Blows pounded me from all sides while I struck out as best I could. So many blows landed upon me that I wondered if I were not the only blindfolded fighter in the ring, or if the man called Jackson hadn't succeeded in getting me after all.

Blindfolded, I could no longer control my motions. I had no dignity. I stumbled about like a baby or a drunken man. The smoke had become thicker and with each new blow it seemed to sear and further restrict my lungs. My saliva became like hot bitter glue. A glove connected with my head, filling my mouth with warm blood. It was everywhere. I could not tell if the moisture I felt upon my body was sweat or blood. A blow landed hard against the nape of my neck. I felt myself going over, my head hitting the floor. Streaks of blue light filled the black world behind the blindfold. I lay prone, pretending that I was knocked out, but felt myself seized by hands and yanked to my feet. "Get going, black boy! Mix it up!" My arms were like lead, my head smarting from blows. I managed to feel my way to the ropes and held on, trying to catch my breath. A glove landed in my mid-section and I went over again, feeling as though the smoke had become a knife jabbed into my guts. Pushed this way and that by the legs milling around me, I finally pulled erect and discovered that I could see the black, sweat-washed forms weaving in the smoky-blue atmosphere like drunken dancers weaving to the rapid drumlike thuds of blows.

Everyone fought hysterically. It was complete anarchy. Everybody fought everybody else. No group fought together for long. Two, three, four, fought one, then turned to fight each other, were themselves attacked. Blows landed below the belt and in the kidney, with the gloves open as well as closed, and with my eye partly opened now there was not so much terror. I moved carefully, avoiding blows, although not too many to attract attention, fighting from group to group. The boys groped about like blind, cautious crabs crouching to protect their mid-sections, their heads pulled in short against their shoulders, their arms stretched nervously before them, with their fists testing the smoke-filled air like the knobbed feelers of hypersensitive snails. In the corner I glimpsed a boy violently punching the air and heard him scream in pain as he smashed his hand against a ring post. For a second I saw him bent over holding his hand, then going down as a blow caught his unprotected head. I played one group against the other, slipping in and throwing a punch then stepping out of range while pushing the others into the melee to take the blows blindly aimed at me. The smoke was agonizing and there were no rounds, no bells at three minute intervals to relieve our exhaustion. The room spun around me, a swirl of lights, smoke, sweating bodies surrounded by tense white faces. I bled from both nose and mouth, the blood spattering upon my chest.

The men kept yelling, "Slug him, black boy! Knock his guts out!"

"Uppercut him! Kill him! Kill that big boy!"

Taking a fake fall, I saw a boy going down heavily beside me as though we were felled by a single blow, saw a sneaker-clad foot shoot into his groin as the two who had knocked him down stumbled upon him. I rolled out of range, feeling a twinge of nausea.

The harder we fought the more threatening the men became. And yet, I had begun to worry about my speech again. How would it go? Would they recognize my ability? What would they give me?

I was fighting automatically when suddenly I noticed that one after another of the boys was leaving the ring. I was surprised, filled with panic, as though I had been left alone with an unknown danger. Then I understood. The boys had arranged it among themselves. It was custom for the two men left in the ring to slug it out for the winner's prize. I discovered this too late. When the bell sounded two men in tuxedos leaped into the ring and re-moved the blindfold. I found myself facing Tatlock, the biggest of the gang. I felt sick at my stomach. Hardly had the bell stopped ringing in my ears than it clanged again and I saw him moving swiftly toward me. Thinking of nothing else to do I hit him smash on the nose. He kept coming, bringing

25

the rank sharp violence of stale sweat. His face was a black blank of a face, only his eyes alive—with hate of me and aglow with a feverish terror from what had happened to us all. I became anxious. I wanted to deliver my speech and he came at me as though he meant to beat it out of me. I smashed him again and again, taking his blows as they came. Then on a sudden impulse I struck him lightly and as we clinched, I whispered, "Fake like I knocked you out, you can have the prize."

"I'll break your behind," he whispered hoarsely.

"For *them?*"   30

"For *me,* sonofabitch."

They were yelling for us to break it up and Tatlock spun me half around with a blow, and as a joggled camera sweeps in a reeling scene, I saw the howling red faces crouching tense beneath the cloud of blue-gray smoke. For a moment the world wavered, unraveled, flowed, then my head cleared and Tatlock bounced before me. The fluttering shadow before my eyes was his jabbing left hand. Then falling forward, my head against his damp shoulder, I whispered.

"I'll make it five dollars more."

"Go to hell!"

But his muscles relaxed a trifle beneath my pressure and I breathed.   35
"Seven?"

"Give it to your ma," he said, ripping me beneath the heart.

And while I still held him I butted him and moved away. I felt myself bombarded with punches. I fought back with hopeless desperation. I wanted to deliver my speech more than anything else in the world, because I felt only these men could judge truly my ability, and now this stupid clown was ruining my chances. I began fighting carefully now, moving in to punch him and out again with my greater speed. A lucky blow to his chin and I had him going too—until I heard a loud voice yell, "I got my money on the big boy."

Hearing this, I almost dropped my guard. I was confused: Should I try to win against the voice out there? Would not this go against my speech, and was not this a moment for humility, for nonresistance? A blow to my head as I danced about sent my right eye popping like a jack-in-the-box and settled my dilemma. The room went red as I fell. It was a dream fall, my body languid and fastidious as to where to land, until the floor became impatient and smashed up to meet me. A moment later I came to. An hypnotic voice said FIVE emphatically. And I lay there, hazily watching a dark red spot of my own blood shaping itself into a butterfly, glistening and soaking into the soiled gray world of the canvas.

When the voice drawled TEN I was lifted up and dragged to a chair. I sat dazed. My eye pained and swelled with each throb of my pounding heart and I wondered if now I would be allowed to speak. I was wringing wet, my mouth still bleeding. We were grouped along the wall now. The other boys ignored me as they congratulated Tatlock and speculated as to how much they would be paid. One boy whimpered over his smashed hand. Looking up front, I saw attendants in white jackets rolling the portable ring away and placing a small square rug in the vacant space surrounded by chairs. Perhaps, I thought, I will stand on the rug to deliver my speech.

Then the M.C. called to us, "Come on up here boys and get your 40 money."

We ran forward to where the men laughed and talked in their chairs, waiting. Everyone seemed friendly now.

"There it is on the rug," the man said. I saw the rug covered with coins of all dimensions and a few crumpled bills. But what excited me, scattered here and there, were the gold pieces.

"Boys, it's all yours," the man said. "You get all you grab."

"That's right, Sambo," a blond man said, winking at me confidentially.

I trembled with excitement, forgetting my pain. I would get the gold 45 and the bills, I thought. I would use both hands. I would throw my body against the boys nearest me to block them from the gold.

"Get down around the rug now," the man commanded, "and don't anyone touch it until I give the signal."

"This ought to be good," I heard.

As told, we got around the square rug on our knees. Slowly the man raised his freckled hand as we followed it upward with our eyes.

I heard, "These niggers look like they're about to pray!"

Then, "Ready," the man said. "Go!" 50

I lunged for a yellow coin lying on the blue design on the carpet, touching it and sending a surprised shriek to join those rising around me. I tried frantically to remove my hand but could not let go. A hot, violent force tore through my body, shaking me like a wet rat. The rug was electrified. The hair bristled up on my head as I shook myself free. My muscles jumped, my nerves jangled, writhed. But I saw that this was not stopping the other boys. Laughing in fear and embarrassment, some were holding back and scooping up the coins knocked off by the painful contortions of the others. The men roared above us as we struggled.

"Pick it up, goddammit, pick it up!" someone called like a bass-voiced parrot. "Go on, get it!"

I crawled rapidly around the floor, picking up the coins, trying to avoid the coppers and to get greenbacks and the gold. Ignoring the shock by laughing, as I brushed the coins off quickly, I discovered that I could contain the electricity—a contradiction, but it works. Then the men began to push us onto the rug. Laughing embarrassedly, we struggled out of their hands and kept after the coins. We were all wet and slippery and hard to hold. Suddenly I saw a boy lifted into the air, glistening with sweat like a circus seal, and dropped, his wet back landing flush upon the charged rug, heard him yell and saw him literally dance upon his back, his elbows beating a frenzied tattoo upon the floor, his muscles twitching like the flesh of a horse stung by many flies. When he finally rolled off, his face was gray and no one stopped him when he ran from the floor amid booming laughter.

"Get the money," the M.C. called. "That's good hard American cash!"

And we snatched and grabbed, snatched and grabbed. I was careful not   55
to come too close to the rug now, and when I felt the hot whiskey breath
descend upon me like a cloud of foul air I reached out and grabbed the leg
of a chair. It was occupied and I held on desperately.

"Leggo nigger! Leggo!"

The huge face wavered down to mine as he tried to push me free. But
my body was slippery and he was too drunk. It was Mr. Colcord, who
owned a chain of movie houses and "entertainment palaces." Each time he
grabbed me I slipped out of his hands. It became a real struggle. I feared the
rug more than I did the drunk, so I held on, surprising myself for a moment
by trying to topple *him* upon the rug. It was such an enormous idea that I
found myself actually carrying it out. I tried not to be obvious, yet when I
grabbed his leg, trying to tumble him out of the chair, he raised up roaring
with laughter, and, looking at me with soberness dead in the eye, kicked me
viciously in the chest. The chair leg flew out of my hand and I felt myself
going and rolled. It was as though I had rolled through a bed of hot coals. It
seemed a whole century would pass before I would roll free, a century in
which I was seared through the deepest levels of my body to the fearful
breath within me and the breath seared and heated to the point of explosion.
It'll all be over in a flash, I thought as I rolled clear. It'll all be over in a flash.

But not yet, the men on the other side were waiting, red faces swollen
as though from apoplexy as they bent forward in their chairs. Seeing their
fingers coming toward me I rolled away as a fumbled football rolls off the
receiver's fingertips, back into the coals. That time I luckily sent the rug
sliding out of place and heard the coins ringing against the floor and the boys
scuffling to pick them up and the M.C. calling, "All right, boys, that's all. Go
get dressed and get your money."

I was limp as a dish rag. My back felt as though it had been beaten
with wires.

When we had dressed the M.C. came in and gave us each five dollars,   60
except Tatlock, who got ten for being last in the ring. Then he told us to
leave. I was not to get a chance to deliver my speech, I thought. I was going
out into the dim alley in despair when I was stopped and told to go back. I
returned to the ballroom, where the men were pushing back their chairs and
gathering in groups to talk.

The M.C. knocked on a table for quiet. "Gentlemen," he said, "we
almost forgot an important part of the program. A most serious part, gentlemen. This boy was brought here to deliver a speech which he made at his
graduation yesterday . . ."

"Bravo!"

"I'm told that he is the smartest boy we've got out there in Greenwood.
I'm told that he knows more big words than a pocket-sized dictionary."

Much applause and laughter.

"So now, gentlemen, I want you to give him your attention."   65

There was still laughter as I faced them, my mouth dry, my eye throbbing. I began slowly, but evidently my throat was tense, because they began shouting, "Louder! Louder!"

"We of the younger generation extol the wisdom of that great leader and educator," I shouted, "who first spoke these flaming words of wisdom. 'A ship lost at sea for many days suddenly sighted a friendly vessel. From the mast of the unfortunate vessel was seen a signal: "Water, water; we die of thirst!" The answer from the friendly vessel came back: "Cast down your bucket where you are." The captain of the distressed vessel, at last heeding the injunction, cast down his bucket, and it came up full of fresh sparkling water from the mouth of the Amazon River.' And like him I say, and in his words, 'To those of my race who depend upon bettering their condition in a foreign land, or who underestimate the importance of cultivating friendly relations with the Southern white man, who is his next-door neighbor, I would say: "Cast down your bucket where you are"—cast it down in making friends in every manly way of the people of all races by whom we are surrounded. . . .'"

I spoke automatically and with such fervor that I did not realize that the men were still talking and laughing until my dry mouth, filling up with blood from the cut, almost strangled me. I coughed, wanting to stop and go to one of the tall brass, sand-filled spittoons to relieve myself, but a few of the men, especially the superintendent, were listening and I was afraid. So I gulped it down, blood, saliva, and all, and continued. (What powers of endurance I had during those days! What enthusiasm! What a belief in the rightness of things!) I spoke even louder in spite of the pain. But still they talked and still they laughed, as though deaf with cotton in dirty ears. So I spoke with greater emotional emphasis. I closed my ears and swallowed blood until I was nauseated. The speech seemed a hundred times as long as before, but I could not leave out a single word. All had to be said, each memorized nuance considered, rendered. Nor was that all. Whenever I uttered a word of three or more syllables a group of voices would yell for me to repeat it. I used the phrase "social responsibility" and they yelled:

"What's that word you say, boy?"

"Social responsibility," I said. 70

"What?"

"Social . . ."

"Louder."

". . . responsibility."

"More!" 75

"Respon—"

"Repeat!"

"—sibility."

The room filled with the uproar of laughter until, no doubt, distracted by having to gulp down my blood, I made a mistake and yelled a phrase I had often seen denounced with newspaper editorials, heard debated in private.

"Social . . ."   80
"What?" they yelled.
". . . equality—"
The laughter hung smokelike in the sudden stillness. I opened my eyes
puzzled. Sounds of displeasure filled the room. The M.C. rushed forward.
They shouted hostile phrases at me. But I did not understand.
A small dry mustached man in the front row blared out, "Say that
slowly, son!"
"What sir?"   85
"What you just said!"
"Social responsibility, sir," I said.
"You weren't being smart, were you, boy?" he said, not unkindly.
"No, sir!"
"You sure that about 'equality' was a mistake?"   90
"Oh, yes, sir," I said. "I was swallowing blood."
"Well, you had better speak more slowly so we can understand. We
mean to do right by you, but you've got to know your place at all times. All
right, now, go on with your speech."
I was afraid. I wanted to leave but I wanted also to speak and I was
afraid they'd snatch me down.
"Thank you, sir," I said, beginning where I had left off, and having
them ignore me as before.
Yet when I finished there was a thunderous applause. I was surprised   95
to see the superintendent come forth with a package wrapped in white tissue
paper, and, gesturing for quiet, address the men.
"Gentlemen, you see that I did not overpraise this boy. He makes a
good speech and some day he'll lead his people in the proper paths. And I
don't have to tell you that that is important in these days and times. This is
a good, smart boy, and so to encourage him in the right direction, in the
name of the Board of Education I wish to present him a prize in the form of
this . . ."
He paused, removing the tissue paper and revealing a gleaming calfskin
briefcase.
". . . in the form of this first-class article from Shad Whitmore's shop."
"Boy," he said, addressing me, "take this prize and keep it well. Consider it a badge of office. Prize it. Keep developing as you are and some day
it will be filled with important papers that will help shape the destiny of your
people."
I was so moved that I could hardly express my thanks. A rope of bloody 100
saliva forming a shape like an undiscovered continent drooled upon the
leather and I wiped it quickly away. I felt an importance that I had never
dreamed.
"Open it and see what's inside," I was told.
My fingers a-tremble, I complied, smelling the fresh leather and finding
an official-looking document inside. It was a scholarship to the state college
for Negroes. My eyes filled with tears and I ran awkwardly off the floor.

I was so overjoyed; I did not even mind when I discovered that the gold pieces I had scrambled for were brass pocket tokens advertising a certain make of automobile.

When I reached home everyone was excited. Next day the neighbors came to congratulate me. I even felt safe from grandfather, whose deathbed curse usually spoiled my triumphs. I stood beneath his photograph with my briefcase in hand and smiled triumphantly into his stolid black peasant's face. It was a face that fascinated me. The eyes seemed to follow everywhere I went.

That night I dreamed I was at a circus with him and that he refused to laugh at the clowns no matter what they did. Then later he told me to open my briefcase and read what was inside and I did, finding an official envelope stamped with the state seal; and inside the envelope I found another and another, endlessly, and I thought I would fall of weariness. "Them's years," he said. "Now open that one." And I did and in it I found an engraved document containing a short message in letters of gold. "Read it," my grandfather said. "Out loud." 105

"To Whom It May Concern," I intoned. "Keep This Nigger-Boy Running."

I awoke with the old man's laughter ringing in my ears.

(It was a dream I was to remember and dream again for many years after. But at that time I had no insight into its meaning. First I had to attend college.)

Considerations

1. "Battle Royal" can be divided into six sections. Identify these sections and explain what the narrator learns in each section and how he changes in response to what he learns.
2. Consider the deathbed scene that opens the story. What lesson does the grandfather try to teach his grandchildren? What motivates him to change during the last moments of his life from "a quiet old man who never made any trouble" to an agitator whose words sound, in his family's ears, radical and alarming? Why is the family so disturbed by the final message? Why do they tell the children to forget what he said?
3. What achievement led to the narrator's invitation to speak before the town's white citizens? What are his expectations of the evening? What does he learn from the contrast between his expectations and the reality of the "battle royal"?
4. What lesson do the white men teach by their responses to the blond stripper?
5. Discuss the significance of the "slip" the narrator makes when he finally delivers his speech. Consider the relationship between the slip and the response of the audience. Pay particular attention to the white superintendent of schools and to the prize he awards the narrator.

JAMAICA KINCAID (1950–   )

The Circling Hand

Born in 1950 in St. John's, Antigua, Jamaica Kincaid grew up as the cherished only child of her mother and carpenter father. According to Kincaid, her mother—like the narrator's mother in "The Circling Hand"—kept "everything I ever wore, and basically until I was quite grown up was sort of a museum to me." Kincaid was educated at the Princess Margaret School in Antigua and later attended college in New Hampshire. She found her college courses disappointing, however, and left to educate herself. As part of her plan for self-education, she began writing and published stories in Rolling Stone, Paris Review, *and* The New Yorker. *She has been a staff writer at* The New Yorker *since 1978. Although she lives and works in New York City, Kincaid's West Indian roots continue to be a major source of characters and themes for her fiction. "The Circling Hand" appears as a chapter in her 1985 autobiographical novel,* Annie John.

During my holidays from school, I was allowed to stay in bed until long after my father had gone to work. He left our house every weekday at the stroke of seven by the Anglican church bell. I would lie in bed awake, and I could hear all the sounds my parents made as they prepared for the day ahead. As my mother made my father his breakfast, my father would shave, using his shaving brush that had an ivory handle and a razor that matched; then he would step outside to the little shed he had built for us as a bathroom, to quickly bathe in water that he had instructed my mother to leave outside overnight in the dew. That way, the water would be very cold, and he believed that cold water strengthened his back. If I had been a boy, I would have gotten the same treatment, but since I was a girl, and on top of that went to school only with other girls, my mother would always add some hot water to my bathwater to take off the chill. On Sunday afternoons, while I was in Sunday school, my father took a hot bath; the tub was half filled with plain water, and then my mother would add a large caldronful of water in which she had just boiled some bark and leaves from a bay-leaf tree. The bark and leaves were there for no reason other than that he liked the smell. He would then spend hours lying in this bath, studying his pool coupons or drawing examples of pieces of furniture he planned to make. When I came home from Sunday school, we would sit down to our Sunday dinner.

My mother and I often took a bath together. Sometimes it was just a plain bath, which didn't take very long. Other times, it was a special bath in which the barks and flowers of many different trees, together with all sorts of oils were boiled in the same large caldron. We would then sit in this bath in a darkened room with a strange-smelling candle burning away. As we sat in this bath, my mother would bathe different parts of my body; then she would do the same to herself. We took these baths after my mother had consulted with her obeah woman, and with her mother and a trusted friend, and all three of them had confirmed that from the look of things around our house—the way a small scratch on my instep had turned into a small sore, then a large sore, and how long it had taken to heal; the way a dog she knew, and a friendly dog at that, suddenly turned and bit her; how a porcelain bowl she had carried from one eternity and hoped to carry into the next suddenly slipped out of her capable hands and broke into pieces the size of grains of sand; how words she spoke in jest to a friend had been completely misunderstood—one of the many women my father had loved, had never married, but with whom he had had children was trying to harm my mother and me by setting bad spirits on us.

When I got up, I placed my bedclothes and my nightie in the sun to air out, brushed my teeth, and washed and dressed myself. My mother would then give me my breakfast, but since, during my holidays, I was not going to school, I wasn't forced to eat an enormous breakfast of porridge, eggs, an orange or half a grapefruit, bread and butter, and cheese. I could get away with just some bread and butter and cheese and porridge and cocoa. I spent the day following my mother around and observing the way she did everything. When we went to the grocer's, she would point out to me the reason she bought each thing. I was shown a loaf of bread or a pound of butter from at least ten different angles. When we went to market, if that day she wanted to buy some crabs she would inquire from the person selling them if they came from near Parham, and if the person said yes my mother did not buy the crabs. In Parham was the leper colony, and my mother was convinced that the crabs ate nothing but the food from the lepers' own plates. If we were then to eat the crabs, it wouldn't be long before we were lepers ourselves and living unhappily in the leper colony.

How important I felt to be with my mother. For many people, their wares and provisions laid out in front of them, would brighten up when they saw her coming and would try hard to get her attention. They would dive underneath their stalls and bring out goods even better than what they had on display. They were disappointed when she held something up in the air, looked at it, turning it this way and that, and then, screwing up her face, said, "I don't think so," and turned and walked away—off to another stall to see if someone who only last week had sold her some delicious christophine had something that was just as good. They would call out after her turned back that next week they expected to have eddoes or dasheen or whatever, and my mother would say, "We'll see," in a very disbelieving tone of voice. If then we went to Mr. Kenneth, it would be only for a few minutes, for he knew exactly what my mother wanted and always had it ready for her. Mr. Kenneth had known me since I was a small child, and he would always remind me of little things I had done then as he fed me a piece of raw liver he had set aside for me. It was one of the few things I liked to eat, and, to boot, it pleased my mother to see me eat something that was so good for me, and she would tell me in great detail the effect the raw liver would have on my red blood corpuscles.

We walked home in the hot midmorning sun mostly without event.   5
When I was much smaller, quite a few times while I was walking with my
mother she would suddenly grab me and wrap me up in her skirt and drag
me along with her as if in a great hurry. I would hear an angry voice saying
angry things, and then, after we had passed the angry voice, my mother
would release me. Neither my mother nor my father ever came straight out
and told me anything, but I had put two and two together and I knew that
it was one of the women that my father had loved and with whom he had
had a child or children, and who never forgave him for marrying my mother
and having me. It was one of those women who were always trying to harm
my mother and me, and they must have loved my father very much, for not
once did any of them ever try to hurt him, and whenever he passed them on
the street it was as if he and these women had never met.

When we got home, my mother started to prepare our lunch (pumpkin
soup with droppers, banana fritters with salt fish stewed in antroba and tomatoes, fungie with salt fish stewed in antroba and tomatoes, or pepper pot,
all depending on what my mother had found at market that day). As my
mother went about from pot to pot, stirring one, adding something to the
other, I was ever in her wake. As she dipped into a pot of boiling something
or other to taste for correct seasoning, she would give me a taste of it also,
asking me what I thought. Not that she really wanted to know what I
thought, for she had told me many times that my taste buds were not quite
developed yet, but it was just to include me in everything. While she made
our lunch, she would also keep an eye on her washing. If it was a Tuesday
and the colored clothes had been starched, as she placed them on the line I
would follow, carrying a basket of clothespins for her. While the starched
colored clothes were being dried on the line, the white clothes were being
whitened on the stone heap. It was a beautiful stone heap that my father had
made for her; an enormous circle of stone, about six inches high, in the
middle of our yard. On it the soapy white clothes were spread out; as the
sun dried them, bleaching out all stains, they had to be made wet again by
dousing them with buckets of water. On my holidays, I did this for my
mother. As I watered the clothes, she would come up behind me, instructing
me to get the clothes thoroughly wet, showing me a shirt that I should turn
over so that the sleeves were exposed.

Over our lunch, my mother and father talked to each other about the
houses my father had to build; how disgusted he had become with one of
his apprentices, or with Mr. Oatie; what they thought of my schooling so
far; what they thought of the noises Mr. Jarvis and his friends made for so
many days when they locked themselves up inside Mr. Jarvis's house and
drank rum and ate fish they had caught themselves and danced to the music
of an accordion that they took turns playing. On and on they talked. As they
talked, my head would move from side to side, looking at them. When my
eyes rested on my father, I didn't think very much of the way he looked. But
when my eyes rested on my mother, I found her beautiful. Her head looked
as if it should be on a sixpence. What a beautiful long neck, and long plaited

hair, which she pinned up around the crown of her head because when her hair hung down it made her too hot. Her nose was the shape of a flower on the brink of opening. Her mouth, moving up and down as she ate and talked at the same time, was such a beautiful mouth I could have looked at it forever if I had to and not mind. Her lips were wide and almost thin, and when she said certain words I could see small parts of big white teeth—so big, and pearly, like some nice buttons on one of my dresses. I didn't much care about what she said when she was in this mood with my father. She made him laugh so. She could hardly say a word before he would burst out laughing. We ate our food, I cleared the table, we said goodbye to my father as he went back to work, I helped my mother with the dishes, and then we settled into the afternoon.

When my mother, at sixteen, after quarreling with her father, left his house on Dominica and came to Antigua, she packed all her things in an enormous wooden trunk that she had bought in Roseau for almost six shillings. She painted the trunk yellow and green outside, and she lined the inside with wallpaper that had a cream background with pink roses printed all over it. Two days after she left her father's house, she boarded a boat and sailed for Antigua. It was a small boat, and the trip would have taken a day and a half ordinarily, but a hurricane blew up and the boat was lost at sea for almost five days. By the time it got to Antigua, the boat was practically in splinters, and though two or three of the passengers were lost overboard, along with some of the cargo, my mother and her trunk were safe. Now, twenty-four years later, this trunk was kept under my bed, and in it were things that had belonged to me, starting from just before I was born. There was the chemise, made of white cotton, with scallop edging around the sleeves, neck, and hem, and white flowers embroidered on the front—the first garment I wore after being born. My mother had made that herself, and once, when we were passing by, I was even shown the tree under which she sat as she made this garment. There were some of my diapers, with their handkerchief hemstitch that she had also done herself; there was a pair of white wool booties with matching jacket and hat; there was a blanket in white wool and a blanket in white flannel cotton; there was a plain white linen hat with lace trimming; there was my christening outfit; there were two of my baby bottles: one in the shape of a normal baby bottle, and the other shaped like a boat, with a nipple on either end; there was a thermos in which my mother had kept a tea that was supposed to have a soothing effect on me; there was the dress I wore on my first birthday: a yellow cotton with green smocking on the front; there was the dress I wore on my second birthday: pink cotton with green smocking on the front; there was also a photograph of me on my second birthday wearing my pink dress and my first pair of earrings, a chain around my neck, and a pair of bracelets, all specially made of gold from British Guiana; there was the first pair of shoes I grew out of after I knew how to walk; there was the dress I wore when I first went to school, and the first notebook in which I wrote; there were the sheets for my crib and the sheets for my first bed; there was my first straw hat, my first straw basket—decorated with flowers—my grandmother had sent me from Dominica; there were my report cards, my certificates of merit from school, and my certificates of merit from Sunday school.

From time to time, my mother would fix on a certain place in our house and give it a good cleaning. If I was at home when she happened to do this, I was at her side, as usual. When she did this with the trunk, it was a tremendous pleasure, for after she had removed all the things from the trunk, and aired them out, and changed the camphor balls, and then refolded the things and put them back in their places in the trunk, as she held each thing in her hand she would tell me a story about myself. Sometimes I knew the story first hand, for I could remember the incident quite well; sometimes what she told me had happened when I was too young to know anything; and sometimes it happened before I was even born. Whichever way, I knew exactly what she would say, for I had heard it so many times before, but I never got tired of it. For instance, the flowers on the chemise, the first garment I wore after being born, were not put on correctly, and that is because when my mother was embroidering them I kicked so much that her hand was unsteady. My mother said that usually when I kicked around in her stomach and she told me to stop I would, but on that day I paid no attention at all. When she told me this story, she would smile at me and say, "You see, even then you were hard to manage." It pleased me to think that, before she could see my face, my mother spoke to me in the same way she did now. On and on my mother would go. No small part of my life was so unimportant that she hadn't made a note of it, and now she would tell it to me over and over again. I would sit next to her and she would show me the very dress I wore on the day I bit another child my age with whom I was playing. "Your biting phase," she called it. Or the day she warned me not to play around the coal pot, because I liked to sing to myself and dance around the fire. Two seconds later, I fell into the hot coals, burning my elbows. My mother cried when she saw that it wasn't serious, and now, as she told me about it, she would kiss the little black patches of scars on my elbows.

As she told me the stories, I sometimes sat at her side, leaning against   10 her, or I would crouch on my knees behind her back and lean over her shoulder. As I did this, I would occasionally sniff at her neck, or behind her ears, or at her hair. She smelled sometimes of lemons, sometimes of sage, sometimes of roses, sometimes of bay leaf. At times I would no longer hear what it was she was saying; I just liked to look at her mouth as it opened and closed over words, or as she laughed. How terrible it must be for all the people who had no one to love them so and no one whom they loved so, I thought. My father, for instance. When he was a little boy, his parents, after kissing him goodbye and leaving him with his grandmother, boarded a boat and sailed to South America. He never saw them again, though they wrote to him and sent him presents—packages of clothes on his birthday and at

Christmas. He then grew to love his grandmother, and she loved him, for she took care of him and worked hard at keeping him well fed and clothed. From the beginning, they slept in the same bed, and as he became a young man they continued to do so. When he was no longer in school and had started working, every night, after he and his grandmother had eaten their dinner, my father would go off to visit his friends. He would then return home at around midnight and fall asleep next to his grandmother. In the morning, his grandmother would awake at half past five or so, a half hour before my father, and prepare his bath and breakfast and make everything proper and ready for him, so that at seven o'clock sharp he stepped out the door off to work. One morning, though, he overslept, because his grand-mother didn't wake him up. When he awoke, she was still lying next to him. When he tried to wake her, he couldn't. She had died lying next to him sometime during the night. Even though he was overcome with grief, he built her coffin and made sure she had a nice funeral. He never slept in that bed again, and shortly afterward he moved out of that house. He was eigh-teen years old then.

When my father first told me this story, I threw myself at him at the end of it, and we both started to cry—he just a little, I quite a lot. It was a Sunday afternoon; he and my mother and I had gone for a walk in the botanical gardens. My mother had wandered off to look at some strange kind of thistle, and we could see her as she bent over the bushes to get a closer look and reach out to touch the leaves of the plant. When she returned to us and saw that we had both been crying, she started to get quite worked up, but my father quickly told her what had happened and she laughed at us and called us her little fools. But then she took me in her arms and kissed me, and she said that I needn't worry about such a thing as her sailing off or dying and leaving me all alone in the world. But if ever after that I saw my father sitting alone with a faraway look on his face, I was filled with pity for him. He had been alone in the world all that time, what with his mother sailing off on a boat with his father and his never seeing her again, and then his grandmother dying while lying next to him in the middle of the night. It was more than anyone should have to bear. I loved him so and wished that I had a mother to give him, for, no matter how much my own mother loved him, it could never be the same.

When my mother got through with the trunk, and I had heard again and again just what I had been like and who had said what to me at what point in my life, I was given my tea—a cup of cocoa and a buttered bun. My father by then would return home from work, and he was given his tea. As my mother went around preparing our supper, picking up clothes from the stone heap, or taking clothes off the clothesline, I would sit in a corner of our yard and watch her. She never stood still. Her powerful legs carried her from one part of the yard to the other, and in and out of the house. Sometimes she might call out to me to go and get some thyme or basil or some other herb for her, for she grew all her herbs in little pots that she kept in a corner of our little garden. Sometimes when I gave her the herbs, she might stoop down and kiss me on my lips and then on my neck. It was in such a paradise that I lived.

The summer of the year I turned twelve, I could see that I had grown taller; most of my clothes no longer fit. When I could get a dress over my head, the waist then came up to just below my chest. My legs had become more spindlelike, the hair on my head even more unruly than usual, small tufts of hair had appeared under my arms, and when I perspired the smell was strange, as if I had turned into a strange animal. I didn't say anything about it, and my mother and father didn't seem to notice, for they didn't say anything, either. Up to then, my mother and I had many dresses made out of the same cloth, though hers had a different, more grownup style, a boat neck or a sweetheart neckline, and a pleated or gored skirt, while my dresses had high necks with collars, a deep hemline, and, of course, a sash that tied in the back. One day, my mother and I had gone to get some material for new dresses to celebrate her birthday (the usual gift from my father), when I came upon a piece of cloth—a yellow background, with figures of men, dressed in a long-ago fashion, seated at pianos that they were playing, and all around them musical notes flying off into the air. I immediately said how much I loved this piece of cloth and how nice I thought it would look on us both, but my mother replied, "Oh, no. You are getting too old for that. It's time you had your own clothes. You just cannot go around the rest of your life looking like a little me." To say that I felt the earth swept away from under me would not be going too far. It wasn't just what she said, it was the way she said it. No accompanying little laugh. No bending over and kissing my little wet forehead (for suddenly I turned hot, then cold, and all my pores must have opened up, for fluids just flowed out of me). In the end, I got my dress with the men playing their pianos, and my mother got a dress with red and yellow overgrown hibiscus, but I was never able to wear my own dress or see my mother in hers without feeling bitterness and hatred, directed not so much toward my mother as toward, I suppose, life in general.

As if that were not enough, my mother informed me that I was on the verge of becoming a young lady, so there were quite a few things I would have to do differently. She didn't say exactly just what it was that made me on the verge of becoming a young lady, and I was so glad of that, because I didn't want to know. Behind a closed door, I stood naked in front of a mirror and looked at myself from head to toe. I was so long and bony that I more than filled up the mirror, and my small ribs pressed out against my skin. I tried to push my unruly hair down against my head so that it would lie flat, but as soon as I let it go it bounced up again. I could see the small tufts of hair under my arms. And then I got a good look at my nose. It had suddenly spread across my face, almost blotting out my cheeks, taking up my whole face, so that if I didn't know I was me standing there I would have wondered about that strange girl—and to think that only so recently my nose had been a small thing, the size of a rosebud. But what could I do? I thought of begging my mother to ask my father if he could build for me a set of clamps into which I could screw myself at night before I went to sleep and which would surely cut back on my growing. I was about to ask her this when I remembered that a few days earlier I had asked in my most pleasing, winning way for a look through the trunk. A person I did not recognize answered in a voice I did not recognize, "Absolutely not! You and I don't have time for that anymore." Again, did the ground wash out from under me? Again, the answer would have to be yes, and I wouldn't be going too far.

Because of this young-lady business, instead of days spent in perfect   15
harmony with my mother, I trailing in her footsteps, she showering down on me her kisses and affection and attention, I was now sent off to learn one thing and another. I was sent to someone who knew all about manners and how to meet and greet important people in the world. This woman soon asked me not to come again, since I could not resist making farting-like noises each time I had to practice a curtsy, it made the other girls laugh so. I was sent for piano lessons. The piano teacher, a shriveled-up old spinster from Lancashire, England, soon asked me not to come back, since I seemed unable to resist eating from the bowl of plums she had placed on the piano purely for decoration. In the first case, I told my mother a lie—I told her that the manners teacher had found that my manners needed no improvement, so I needn't come anymore. This made her very pleased. In the second case, there was no getting around it—she had to find out. When the piano teacher told her of my misdeed, she turned and walked away from me, and I wasn't sure that if she had been asked who I was she wouldn't have said, "I don't know," right then and there. What a new thing this was for me: my mother's back turned on me in disgust. It was true that I didn't spend all my days at my mother's side before this, that I spent most of my days at school, but before this young-lady business I could sit and think of my mother, see her doing one thing or another, and always her face bore a smile for me. Now I often saw her with the corners of her mouth turned down in disapproval of me. And why was my mother carrying my new state so far? She took to pointing out that one day I would have my own house and I might want it to be a different house from the one she kept. Once, when showing me a way to store linen, she patted the folded sheets in place and said, "Of course, in your own house you might choose another way." That the day might actually come when we would live apart I had never believed. My throat hurt from the tears I held bottled up tight inside. Sometimes we would both forget the new order of things and would slip into our old ways. But that didn't last very long.

In the middle of all these new things, I had forgotten that I was to enter a new school that September. I had then a set of things to do, preparing for school. I had to go to the seamstress to be measured for new uniforms, since my body now made a mockery of the old measurements. I had to get shoes, a new school hat, and lots of new books. In my new school, I needed a different exercise book for each subject, and in addition to the usual— English, arithmetic, and so on—I now had to take Latin and French, and attend classes in a brand-new science building. I began to look forward to my new school. I hoped that everyone there would be new, that there would be no one I had ever met before. That way, I could put on a new set of airs; I could say I was something that I was not, and no one would ever know the difference.

On the Sunday before the Monday I started at my new school, my mother became cross over the way I had made my bed. In the center of my bedspread, my mother had embroidered a bowl overflowing with flowers and two lovebirds on either side of the bowl. I had placed the bedspread on my bed in a lopsided way so that the embroidery was not in the center of my bed, the way it should have been. My mother made a fuss about it, and I could see that she was right and I regretted very much not doing that one little thing that would have pleased her. I had lately become careless, she said, and I could only silently agree with her.

I came home from church, and my mother still seemed to hold the bedspread against me, so I kept out of her way. At half past two in the afternoon, I went off to Sunday school. At Sunday school, I was given a certificate for best student in my study-of-the-Bible group. It was a surprise that I would receive the certificate on that day, though we had known about the results of the test weeks before. I rushed home with my certificate in hand, feeling that with this prize I would reconquer my mother—a chance for her to smile on me again.

When I got to our house, I rushed into the yard and called out to her, but no answer came. I then walked into the house. At first, I didn't hear anything. Then I heard sounds coming from the direction of my parents' room. My mother must be in there, I thought. When I got to the door, I could see that my mother and father were lying in their bed. It didn't interest me what they were doing—only that my mother's hand was on the small of my father's back and that it was making a circular motion. But her hand! It was white and bony, as if it had long been dead and had been left out in the elements. It seemed not to be her hand, and yet it could only be her hand, so well did I know it. It went around and around in the same circular motion, and I looked at it as if I would never see anything else in my life again. If I were to forget everything else in the world, I could not forget her hand as it looked then. I could also make out that the sounds I had heard were her kissing my father's ears and his mouth and his face. I looked at them for I don't know how long.

When I next saw my mother, I was standing at the dinner table that I 20 had just set, having made a tremendous commotion with knives and forks as I got them out of their drawer, letting my parents know that I was home. I had set the table and was now half standing near my chair, half draped over the table, staring at nothing in particular and trying to ignore my mother's presence. Though I couldn't remember our eyes having met, I was quite sure that she had seen me in the bedroom, and I didn't know what I would say if she mentioned it. Instead, she said in a voice that was sort of cross and sort of something else, "Are you going to just stand there doing nothing all day?" The something else was new; I had never heard it in her voice before. I couldn't say exactly what it was, but I know that it caused me to reply, "And what if I do?" and at the same time to stare at her directly in the eyes. It must have been a shock to her, the way I spoke. I had never talked back to her before. She looked at me, and then, instead of saying some squelching thing that would put me back in my place, she dropped her eyes and walked away. From the back, she looked small and funny. She carried her hands limp at her sides. I was sure I could never let those hands touch me again; I was sure I could never let her kiss me again. All that was finished.

I was amazed that I could eat my food, for all of it reminded me of things that had taken place between my mother and me. A long time ago, when I wouldn't eat my beef, complaining that it involved too much chewing, my mother would first chew up pieces of meat in her own mouth and then feed it to me. When I had hated carrots so much that even the sight of them would send me into a fit of tears, my mother would try to find all sorts of ways to make them palatable for me. All that was finished now. I didn't think that I would ever think of any of it again with fondness. I looked at my parents. My father was just the same, eating his food in the same old way, his two rows of false teeth clop-clopping like a horse being driven off to market. He was regaling us with another one of his stories about when he was a young man and played cricket on one island or the other. What he said now must have been funny, for my mother couldn't stop laughing. He didn't seem to notice that I was not entertained.

My father and I then went for our customary Sunday-afternoon walk. My mother did not come with us. I don't know what she stayed home to do. On our walk, my father tried to hold my hand, but I pulled myself away from him, doing it in such a way that he would think I felt too big for that now.

That Monday, I went to my new school. I was placed in a class with girls I had never seen before. Some of them had heard about me, though, for I was the youngest among them and was said to be very bright. I liked a girl named Albertine, and I liked a girl named Gweneth. At the end of the day, Gwen and I were in love, and so we walked home arm in arm together.

When I got home, my mother greeted me with the customary kiss and inquiries. I told her about my day, going out of my way to provide pleasing details, leaving out, of course, any mention at all of Gwen and my overpowering feelings for her.

Considerations

1. Describe several of the items the speaker's mother stores in her trunk. What do these items represent to the speaker? To her mother?
2. How does the speaker's relationship with her mother change? List specific events that demonstrate the change and explain their significance.
3. What role does the speaker's father play in her life? At the end of the story, why does she pull away from her father as they walk together?
4. Choose any incident in the story and retell it from the mother's point of view. As you do this, explicate the mother's reasons for changing so greatly in the way she treats her daughter.
5. Suppose someone gave you a memory trunk and asked you to store in it five items emblematic of significant events, people, or places in your life. What items would you select? Describe the items and explain their significance both at the time you acquired them and to your life today.

A. E. HOUSMAN (1859–1936)

When I was one-and-twenty

> *Although he failed his final examinations at Oxford in 1881, A. E. Housman was regarded as an excellent student. Later he earned a master of arts and became a professor of Latin at Cambridge University. Housman, who believed that poetry should appeal more to the heart than to the mind, often wrote on themes related to the transitory quality of youth and romantic love.*

When I was one-and-twenty
   I heard a wise man say,
'Give crowns and pounds and guineas
   But not your heart away;
Give pearls away and rubies   5
   But keep your fancy free.'
But I was one-and-twenty,
   No use to talk to me.

When I was one-and-twenty
   I heard him say again,   10
'The heart out of the bosom
   Was never given in vain;
'Tis paid with sighs a plenty
   And sold for endless rue.'
And I am two-and-twenty,   15
   And oh, 'tis true, 'tis true.

Considerations

1. Compare the advice given by the wise man in stanza 1 to the advice he gives in stanza 2. Is he saying the same thing both times? Or do you see the meaning as different? What might he mean, for instance, by "keep your fancy free"?
2. How does the attitude of the speaker change from stanza 1 to stanza 2? Pay particular attention to the last two lines in each stanza. What are the implications of the change?
3. Imagine the speaker at thirty-two (or at forty or at sixty-five). To what extent and in what ways do you think this early lesson might affect his later life? Create several possible scenarios.

COUNTEE CULLEN (1903–1946)

Incident

> *Along with Langston Hughes, Richard Wright, and Jean Toomer, Countee Cullen was a major figure in the Harlem Renaissance of the 1920s. Most of his work focuses on themes related to race and class structure. He published five volumes of poetry and a novel,* One Way to Heaven *(1932), which is set in Harlem in the 1920s and depicts conflicts and contrasts between wealthy and poor African Americans.*

Once riding in old Baltimore,
    Heart-filled, head-filled with glee,
I saw a Baltimorean
    Keep looking straight at me.

Now I was eight and very small,   5
    And he was no whit bigger,
And so I smiled, but he poked out
    His tongue and called me, "Nigger."

I saw the whole of Baltimore
    From May until December: 10
Of all the things that happened there
    That's all that I remember.

Considerations

1. Read this poem aloud. How do the rhythm and rhyme in the poem relate to the picture given of the speaker and of his experience?

2. What is the significance of the final stanza? Why is this the only event that the speaker remembers about his eight-month stay in Baltimore?
3. Describe an incident from your past that you remember as vividly as the speaker remembers this one. Focus on one particular moment lasting no more than five or ten minutes. Explain both what happened and why it was so significant that you can still recall it in detail.

EDWIN ARLINGTON ROBINSON (1869–1935)

Richard Cory

Edwin Arlington Robinson was born and raised in Gardiner, Maine, and he worked there as a freelance writer after attending Harvard. Robinson's poetry draws heavily on his experiences and observations during his years living in his hometown; many of the characters he depicts in his poems are based on people he met or heard about during his years in Maine.

Whenever Richard Cory went downtown,
We people on the pavement looked at him;
He was a gentleman from sole to crown,
Clean favored, and imperially slim.

And he was always quietly arrayed,   5
And he was always human when he talked;
But still he fluttered pulses when he said,
"Good-morning," and he glittered when he walked.

And he was rich—yes, richer than a king—
And admirably schooled in every grace: 10
In fine, we thought that he was everything
To make us wish that we were in his place.

So on we worked, and waited for the light,
And went without the meat, and cursed the bread;
And Richard Cory, one calm summer night,   15
Went home and put a bullet through his head.

Considerations

1. Explain how the townspeople might represent the view of innocence whereas Richard Cory represents experience. Then explain how the

townspeople might represent the voice of experience whereas Cory remains in some ways innocent.
2. Why does Richard Cory commit suicide?
3. Look carefully at the images the speaker uses to describe Cory. What do these images suggest about the speaker's view toward his subject?

BETTIE SELLERS (1926–   )

In the Counselor's Waiting Room

> *Born in Florida, Bettie Sellers earned her master's degree from the University of Georgia and later became an English instructor at Young Harris College in Georgia. She has published two anthologies of poetry,* Westward from Bald Mountain *(1974) and* Spring Onions and Cornbread *(1977).*

The terra cotta girl
with the big flat farm feet
traces furrows in the rug
with her toes,
reads an existentialist paperback   5
from psychology class,
finds no ease there
from the guilt of loving
the quiet girl down the hall.
Their home soil has seen to this visit,   10
their Baptist mothers,
who weep for the waste of sturdy hips
ripe for grandchildren.

Considerations

1. What conflict (or conflicts) do you see in the poem? Why are the Baptist mothers so upset with their daughters? What values clash?
2. Consider the implications of the two settings—the college that the "terra cotta girl" and "the quiet girl down the hall" attend and the "home soil" of the Baptist mothers.
3. Why are these people sitting in a counselor's waiting room? What might motivate the girl (or girls) to be there? Their mothers?

MAY SWENSON (1919–1989)

The Centaur°

> *Born and raised in Logan, Utah, May Swenson later became a reporter for the*
> *Salt Lake City* Desert News *before moving to New York City to become*
> *an editor for New Directions Press in 1959. Poet Elizabeth Bishop said of*
> *Swenson that she is "one of the few good poets who write good poems about*
> *nature."*

The summer that I was ten—
Can it be there was only one
summer that I was ten? It must

have been a long one then—
each day I'd go out to choose   5
a fresh horse from my stable

which was a willow grove
down by the old canal.
I'd go on my two bare feet.

But when, with my brother's jack-knife,   10
I had cut me a long limber horse
with a good thick knob for a head,

and peeled him slick and clean
except a few leaves for the tail,
and cinched my brother's belt   15

around his head for a rein,
I'd straddle and canter him fast
up the grass bank to the path,

trot along in the lovely dust
that talcumed over his hoofs,   20
hiding my toes, and turning

his feet to swift half-moons.
The willow knob with the strap
jouncing between my thighs

Centaur: A creature, half man, half horse, in Greek mythology; most centaurs followed Dionysus,
the god of wine and celebration, but some were teachers of humans.

was the pommel and yet the poll
of my nickering pony's head.
My head and my neck were mine,

25

yet they were shaped like a horse.
My hair flopped to the side
like the mane of a horse in the wind.

30

My forelock swung in my eyes,
my neck arched and I snorted.
I shied and skittered and reared,
stopped and raised my knees,
pawed at the ground and quivered.
My teeth bared as we wheeled

35

and swished through the dust again.
I was the horse and the rider,
and the leather I slapped to his rump

spanked my own behind.
Doubled, my two hoofs beat
a gallop along the bank,

40

the wind twanged in my mane,
my mouth squared to the bit.
And yet I sat on my steed

45

quiet, negligent riding,
my toes standing the stirrups,
my thighs hugging his ribs.

At a walk we drew up to the porch.
I tethered him to a paling.
Dismounting, I smoothed my skirt

50

and entered the dusky hall.
My feet on the clean linoleum
left ghostly toes in the hall.

Where have you been? said my mother.
Been riding, I said from the sink,
and filled me a glass of water.

55

What's that in your pocket? she said.
Just my knife. It weighted my pocket
and stretched my dress awry.

60

Go tie back your hair, said my mother,
and Why is your mouth all green?
Rob Roy, he pulled some clover
as we crossed the field, I told her.

Considerations

1. Why does the speaker's tenth summer seem so long to her? Suggest as many possibilities as you can; provide details from the poem to support your ideas.
2. What is the significance of the conversation between mother and daughter in the final lines of the poem? Consider carefully the imagery the speaker uses to describe herself as you respond and, in addition, consider the meaning of the title.
3. Imagine that you are the speaker's mother. Then write a journal entry describing your daughter during her tenth summer. Use details and images from the poem to support your projection of the mother's thoughts and feelings.

ANNE SEXTON (1928–1975)

Snow White and the Seven Dwarfs

> Described as a confessional poet, Anne Sexton often used details from her personal life experiences to create images relating to larger themes and issues. Published in 1971, "Snow White and the Seven Dwarfs" is typical of Sexton's exploration of conflicts related to women at various stages in their lives.

No matter what life you lead
the virgin is a lovely number:
cheeks as fragile as cigarette paper,
arms and legs made of Limoges,
lips like Vin Du Rhône,   5
rolling her china-blue doll eyes
open and shut.
Open to say,
Good Day Mama,
and shut for the thrust   10
of the unicorn.
She is unsoiled.
She is as white as a bonefish.

Once there was a lovely virgin
called Snow White.
Say she was thirteen.   15
Her stepmother,
a beauty in her own right,
though eaten, of course, by age,
would hear of no beauty surpassing her own.   20
Beauty is a simple passion,
but, oh my friends, in the end
you will dance the fire dance in iron shoes.
The stepmother had a mirror to which she referred—
something like the weather forecast—   25
a mirror that proclaimed
the one beauty of the land.
She would ask,
Looking glass upon the wall,
who is fairest of us all?   30
And the mirror would reply,
You are fairest of us all.
Pride pumped in her like poison.

Suddenly one day the mirror replied,
Queen, you are full fair, 'tis true,   35
but Snow White is fairer than you.
Until that moment Snow White
had been no more important
than a dust mouse under the bed.
But now the queen saw brown spots on her hand   40
and four whiskers over her lip
so she condemned Snow White
to be hacked to death.
Bring me her heart, she said to the hunter,
and I will salt it and eat it.   45
The hunter, however, let his prisoner go
and brought a boar's heart back to the castle.
The queen chewed it up like a cube steak.
Now I am fairest, she said,
lapping her slim white fingers.   50

Snow White walked in the wildwood
for weeks and weeks.
At each turn there were twenty doorways
and at each stood a hungry wolf,
his tongue lolling out like a worm.   55
The birds called out lewdly,

talking like pink parrots,
and the snakes hung down in loops,
each a noose for her sweet white neck.
On the seventh week   60
she came to the seventh mountain
and there she found the dwarf house.
It was as droll as a honeymoon cottage
and completely equipped with
seven beds, seven chairs, seven forks   65
and seven chamber pots.
Snow White ate seven chicken livers
and lay down, at last, to sleep.

The dwarfs, those little hot dogs,
walked three times around Snow White,   70
the sleeping virgin. They were wise
and wattled like small czars.
Yes. It's a good omen,
they said, and will bring us luck.
They stood on tiptoes to watch   75
Snow White wake up. She told them
about the mirror and the killer-queen
and they asked her to stay and keep house.
Beware of your stepmother,
they said.   80
Soon she will know you are here.
While we are away in the mines
during the day, you must not
open the door.

Looking glass upon the wall . . .   85
The mirror told
and so the queen dressed herself in rags
and went out like a peddler to trap Snow White.
She went across seven mountains.
She came to the dwarf house   90
and Snow White opened the door
and bought a bit of lacing.
The queen fastened it tightly
around her bodice,
as tight as an Ace bandage,   95
so tight that Snow White swooned.
She lay on the floor, a plucked daisy.
When the dwarfs came home they undid the lace
and she revived miraculously.

She was as full of life as soda pop.   100
Beware of your stepmother,
they said.
She will try once more.

Looking glass upon the wall . . .
Once more the mirror told   105
and once more the queen dressed in rags
and once more Snow White opened the door.
This time she bought a poison comb,
a curved eight-inch scorpion,
and put it in her hair and swooned again.   110
The dwarfs returned and took out the comb
and she revived miraculously.
She opened her eyes as wide as Orphan Annie.
Beware, beware, they said,
but the mirror told,   115
the queen came,
Snow White, the dumb bunny,
opened the door
and she bit into a poison apple
and fell down for the final time.   120
When the dwarfs returned
they undid her bodice,
they looked for a comb,
but it did no good.
Though they washed her with wine   125
and rubbed her with butter
it was to no avail.
She lay as still as a gold piece.

The seven dwarfs could not bring themselves
to bury her in the black ground   130
so they made a glass coffin
and set it upon the seventh mountain
so that all who passed by
could peek in upon her beauty.
A prince came one June day   135
and would not budge.
He stayed so long his hair turned green
and still he would not leave.
The dwarfs took pity upon him
and gave him the glass Snow White—   140
its doll's eyes shut forever—
to keep in his far-off castle.

As the prince's men carried the coffin
they stumbled and dropped it
and the chunk of apple flew out   145
of her throat and she woke up miraculously.

And thus Snow White became the prince's bride.
The wicked queen was invited to the wedding feast
and when she arrived there were
red-hot iron shoes,   150
in the manner of red-hot roller skates,
clamped upon her feet.
First your toes will smoke
and then your heels will turn black
and you will fry upward like a frog,   155
she was told.
And so she danced until she was dead,
a subterranean figure,
her tongue flicking in and out
like a gas jet.   160
Meanwhile Snow White held court,
rolling her china-blue doll eyes open and shut
and sometimes referring to her mirror
as women do.

WILLIAM BLAKE (1757–1827)

*William Blake earned his living as an engraver and painter. As a working
artisan, he experienced the inequities of socioeconomic conditions in late
eighteenth- and early nineteenth-century England. "The Lamb" and "The
Tyger" were first published in 1794 as part of Blake's Songs of Experience.*

The Lamb

   Little Lamb, who made thee?
   Dost thou know who made thee?
Gave thee life & bid thee feed,
By the stream & o'er the mead;
Gave thee clothing of delight,   5
Softest clothing wooly bright;
Gave thee such a tender voice,
Making all the vales rejoice!
   Little Lamb who made thee?
   Dost thou know who made thee?   10

Little Lamb I'll tell thee,
Little Lamb I'll tell thee!
He is calléd by thy name,
For he calls himself a Lamb:
He is meek & he is mild, 15
He became a little child:
I a child & thou a lamb,
We are calléd by his name.
Little Lamb God bless thee.
Little Lamb God bless thee. 20

The Tyger

Tyger! Tyger! burning bright
In the forests of the night,
What immortal hand or eye
Could frame thy fearful symmetry?

In what distant deeps or skies 5
Burnt the fire of thine eyes?
On what wings dare he aspire?
What the hand, dare seize the fire?

And what shoulder, & what art,
Could twist the sinews of thy heart? 10
And when thy heart began to beat,
What dread hand? & what dread feet?

What the hammer? what the chain?
In what furnace was thy brain?
What the anvil? what dread grasp 15
Dare its deadly terrors clasp?

When the stars threw down their spears,
And water'd heaven with their tears,
Did he smile his work to see?
Did he who made the Lamb make thee? 20

Tyger! Tyger! burning bright
In the forests of the night,
What immortal hand or eye
Dare frame thy fearful symmetry?

GERARD MANLEY HOPKINS (1844–1889)

Spring and Fall
To a Young Child

> *Gerard Manley Hopkins, a convert to Roman Catholicism who became a Jesuit priest, wrote innovative poetry that experimented with rhythms and line patterns. His poems often celebrate the beauty of God's world, although his later poems, like "Spring and Fall" (1880), also show a sense both of darkness and of the fragility of human life.*

Márgarét, are you gríeving
Over Goldengrove unleaving?
Leáves, líke the things of man, you
With your fresh thoughts care for, can you?
Ah! ás the heart grows older   5
It will come to such sights colder
By and by, nor spare a sigh
Though worlds of wanwood leafmeal lie;
And yet you will weep and know why.
Now no matter, child, the name: 10
Sórrow's spríngs áre the same.
Nor mouth had, no nor mind, expressed
What heart heard of, ghost guessed:
It ís the blight man was born for,
It is Margaret you mourn for.   15

SEAMUS HEANEY (1939–   )

Mid-Term Break

> *Seamus Heaney's poetry is rooted both in his native Northern Ireland and in his own life experiences. His volumes of verse include* Door into the Dark *(1969),* North *(1975), and* Field Work *(1979). Many of his critical and autobiographical pieces in prose appear in the collection* Preoccupations *(1980).*

I sat all morning in the college sick bay
Counting bells knelling classes to a close.
At two o'clock our neighbors drove me home.

In the porch I met my father crying—
He had always taken funerals in his stride—   5
And Big Jim Evans saying it was a hard blow.

The baby cooed and laughed and rocked the pram
When I came in, and I was embarrassed
By old men standing up to shake my hand

And tell me they were "sorry for my trouble,"   10
Whispers informed strangers I was the eldest,
Away at school, as my mother held my hand

In hers and coughed out angry tearless sighs.
At ten o'clock the ambulance arrived
With the corpse, stanched and bandaged by the nurses.   15

Next morning I went up into the room. Snowdrops
And candles soothed the bedside; I saw him
For the first time in six weeks. Paler now,

Wearing a poppy bruise on his left temple,
He lay in the four foot box as in his cot.   20
No gaudy scars, the bumper knocked him clear.

A four foot box, a foot for every year.

MURIEL STUART (1889–1987)

In the Orchard

'I thought you loved me.' 'No, it was only fun.'
'When we stood there, closer than all?' 'Well, the harvest moon
Was shining and queer in your hair, and it turned my head.'
'That made you?' 'Yes.' 'Just the moon and the light it made
Under the tree?' 'Well, your mouth, too.' 'Yes, my mouth?'   5
'And the quiet there that sang like the drum in the booth.
You shouldn't have danced like that.' 'Like what?' 'So close,
With your head turned up, and the flower in your hair, a rose
That smelt all warm.' 'I loved you. I thought you knew
I wouldn't have danced like that with any but you.'   10
'I didn't know. I thought you knew it was fun.'
'I thought it was love you meant.' 'Well, it's done.' 'Yes, it's done.
I've seen boys stone a blackbird, and watched them drown
A kitten . . . it clawed at the reeds, and they pushed it down
Into the pool while it screamed. Is that fun, too?'   15
'Well, boys are like that . . . Your brothers . . .' 'Yes, I know.
But you, so lovely and strong! Not you! Not you!'
'They don't understand it's cruel. It's only a game.'

'And are girls fun, too?' 'No, still in a way it's the same.
It's queer and lovely to have a girl . . .' 'Go on.'   20
'It makes you mad for a bit to feel she's your own,
And you laugh and kiss her, and maybe you give her a ring,
But it's only in fun.' 'But I gave you everything.'
'Well, you shouldn't have done it. You know what a fellow thinks
When a girl does that.' 'Yes, he talks of her over his drinks   25
And calls her a—' 'Stop that now. I thought you knew.'
'But it wasn't with anyone else. It was only you.'
'How did I know? I thought you wanted it too.
I thought you were like the rest. Well, what's to be done?'
'To be done?' 'Is it all right?' 'Yes.' 'Sure?' 'Yes, but why?'   30
'I don't know. I thought you were going to cry.
You said you had something to tell me.' 'Yes, I know.
It wasn't anything really . . . I think I'll go.'
'Yes, it's late. There's thunder about, a drop of rain
Fell on my hand in the dark. I'll see you again   35
At the dance next week. You're sure that everything's right?'
'Yes,' 'Well, I'll be going.' 'Kiss me . . .' 'Good night.' . . . 'Good night.'

RITA DOVE (1952–   )

Grape Sherbet

Rita Dove was born in Akron, Ohio, in 1952 and educated at Miami University of Ohio, Universität Tübingen in Germany (as a Fulbright/Hays fellow), and the University of Iowa. She has published the poetry collections The Yellow House on the Corner *(1980),* Museum *(1983),* Thomas and Beulah *(1986),* Grace Notes *(1989),* Selected Poems *(1993), and* Mother Love *(1995), the short story collection* Fifth Sunday *(1985), the novel* Through the Ivory Gate *(1992), the verse drama* The Darker Face of the Earth *(1994), and essays under the title* The Poet's World *(1995). In 1987 she received the Pulitzer Prize in poetry, and from 1993 to 1995 she served as Poet Laureate of the United States and Consultant in Poetry at the Library of Congress. She is Commonwealth Professor of English at the University of Virginia and lives near Charlottesville, Virginia, with her husband and daughter.*

The day? Memorial.
After the grill
Dad appears with his masterpiece—
swirled snow, gelled light.
We cheer. The recipe's   5
a secret and he fights

a smile, his cap turned up
so the bib resembles a duck.

That morning we galloped
through the grassed-over mounds   10
and named each stone
for a lost milk tooth. Each dollop
of sherbet, later,
is a miracle,
like salt on a melon that makes it sweeter.   15

Everyone agrees—it's wonderful!
It's just how we imagined lavender
would taste. The diabetic grandmother
stares from the porch,
a torch   20
of pure refusal.

We thought no one was lying
there under our feet,
we thought it
was a joke. I've been trying   25
to remember the taste,
but it doesn't exist.
Now I see why
you bothered,
father.   30

JOHN KEATS (1795–1821)

Ode on a Grecian Urn

*Born in London, John Keats was sent to the Reverend John Clarke's private
school at Enfield, where he studied with Charles Cowden Clarke, the son of
the headmaster. It was Clarke who first sparked Keats's love of literature,
music, and theater. After the death of both his parents, Keats's guardian removed him from school and apprenticed him to a surgeon. During his appren-
ticeship, Keats wrote thirty-three poems, which were published in 1817, the
year he qualified as an apothecary-surgeon. The publication of his poems provided the encouragement he needed to reject the practice of medicine and write
poetry full time. In 1820, Keats published his second collection of poems,
Lamia, Isabells, The Eve of St. Agnes, and Other Poems. Suffering from
tuberculosis, he was ordered to Rome, whose climate was believed to be benefi-
cial. In spite of these efforts to relieve the effects of tuberculosis, however, Keats
died at age twenty-six.*

I

Thou still unravish'd bride of quietness,
   Thou foster-child of silence and slow time,
Sylvan° historian, who canst thus express
   A flowery tale more sweetly than our rhyme:
What leaf-fring'd legend haunts about thy shape   5
   Of deities or mortals, or of both,
      In Tempe or the dales of Arcady?°
   What men or gods are these? What maidens loath?
What mad pursuit? What struggle to escape?
      What pipes and timbrels? What wild ecstasy?   10

II

Heard melodies are sweet, but those unheard
   Are sweeter; therefore, ye soft pipes, play on;
Not to the sensual ear, but, more endear'd,
   Pipe to the spirit ditties of no tone:
Fair youth, beneath the trees, thou canst not leave   15
   Thy song, nor ever can those trees be bare;
      Bold Lover, never, never canst thou kiss,
Though winning near the goal—yet, do not grieve;
      She cannot fade, though thou hast not thy bliss,
   Forever wilt thou love, and she be fair!   20

III

Ah, happy, happy boughs! that cannot shed
   Your leaves, nor ever bid the Spring adieu;
And, happy melodist, unwearied,
   Forever piping songs forever new;
More happy love! more happy, happy love!   25
   Forever warm and still to be enjoy'd,
      Forever panting, and forever young;
All breathing human passion far above,
   That leaves a heart high-sorrowful and cloy'd,
      A burning forehead, and a parching tongue.   30

IV

Who are these coming to the sacrifice?
   To what green altar, O mysterious priest,

---

3 *Sylvan:* Related to woods. 7 *Tempe . . . Arcady:* Beautiful, wooded areas in Greece.

Lead'st thou that heifer lowing at the skies,
    And all her silken flanks with garlands drest?
What little town by river or sea shore,   35
    Or mountain-built with peaceful citadel,
        Is emptied of this folk, this pious morn?
And, little town, thy streets forevermore
    Will silent be; and not a soul to tell
        Why thou art desolate, can e'er return.   40

V

O Attic shape! Fair attitude! with brede°
    Of marble men and maidens overwrought,°
With forest branches and the trodden weed;
    Thou, silent form, dost tease us out of thought
As doth eternity: Cold Pastoral!   45
    When old age shall this generation waste,
        Thou shalt remain, in midst of other woe
    Than ours, a friend to man, to whom thou say'st,
"Beauty is truth, truth beauty,"—that is all
        Ye know on earth, and all ye need to know.   50

41 *brede:* Intertwined pattern. 42 *overwrought:* Decorated.

WILLIAM SHAKESPEARE (1564–1616)

Hamlet

Although there is little direct evidence relating to Shakespeare's childhood and adolescence, it is almost certain that he was educated at the free grammar school in his native Stratford-on-Avon, England. As Shakespeare entered his teens, his father experienced serious financial setbacks, and William apparently had to leave school to help support the family. At eighteen, he married Anne Hathaway, with whom he had three children. Sometime after the birth of his children, Shakespeare left Stratford-on-Avon and went to London, where he began his career as an actor and playwright. By 1594, he had gained both wealth and prestige, performing at court for Queen Elizabeth I. During the 1590s, he wrote a series of sonnets, many of which address themes of love. His dramas include comedies such as As You Like It *(1599),* A Midsummer's Night Dream *(1595), and* Twelfth Night *(1599). Shakespeare's best-known tragedies are* Hamlet *(1602),* Othello *(1604),* King Lear *(1605), and* Macbeth *(1606).* Richard the Third *(1592) and* Henry the IV, Parts I and II *(1590) are among his plays based on historical political struggles of England's ruling families. In 1611, he retired to Stratford, where he lived until his death in 1616. After his burial, his grave was marked by a stone bearing an inscription (supposedly dictated by Shakespeare himself) that warns all who come "Bleste Be Ye Man Yt Spares Thes Stones / And Curst Be He Yt Moves My Bones."*

Characters

CLAUDIUS, *King of Denmark*
HAMLET, *son of the late King Hamlet, and nephew to the present King*
POLONIUS, *Lord Chamberlain*
HORATIO, *friend to Hamlet*
LAERTES, *son to Polonius*
VOLTIMAND,
CORNELIUS,
ROSENCRANTZ, *courtiers*
GUILDENSTERN,
OSRIC,
GENTLEMAN,
PRIEST, OR DOCTOR OF DIVINITY
MARCELLUS, *officers*
BERNARDO,
FRANCISCO, *a soldier*
REYNALDO, *servant to Polonius*
PLAYERS
TWO CLOWNS, *grave-diggers*
FORTINBRAS, *Prince of Norway*
CAPTAIN

ENGLISH AMBASSADORS
GERTRUDE, *Queen of Denmark, mother to Hamlet*
OPHELIA, *daughter to Polonius*
LORDS, LADIES, OFFICERS, SOLDIERS, SAILORS,
    MESSENGERS, AND OTHER ATTENDANTS
GHOST *of Hamlet's father*

Scene *Denmark*

ACT I
SCENE I°

(*Enter* BERNARDO *and* FRANCISCO, TWO SENTINELS,
[*meeting*].)

BERNARDO: Who's there?
FRANCISCO: Nay, answer me.° Stand and unfold yourself.
BERNARDO: Long live the King!
FRANCISCO: Bernardo?
BERNARDO: He.
FRANCISCO: You come most carefully upon your hour.   5
BERNARDO: 'Tis now struck twelve. Get thee to bed, Francisco.
FRANCISCO: For this relief much thanks. 'Tis bitter cold,
    And I am sick at heart.
BERNARDO: Have you had quiet guard?
FRANCISCO: Not a mouse stirring.   10
BERNARDO: Well, good night.
    If you do meet Horatio and Marcellus,
    The rivals° of my watch, bid them make haste.

(*Enter* HORATIO *and* MARCELLUS.)

FRANCISCO: I think I hear them. Stand, ho! Who is there?
HORATIO: Friends to this ground.
MARCELLUS: And liegemen to the Dane.°   15
FRANCISCO: Give you° good night.
MARCELLUS: O, farewell, honest soldier.
    Who hath relieved you?
FRANCISCO: Bernardo hath my place.
    Give you good night.
                                                (*Exit* FRANCISCO.)
MARCELLUS: Holla, Bernardo!

ACT I, SCENE I. *Location:* Elsinore castle. A guard platform. 2 *me:* Francisco emphasizes that *he* is the sentry currently on watch. 13 *rivals:* Partners. 15 *liegemen to the Dane:* Men sworn to serve the Danish king. 16 *Give you:* God give you.

BERNARDO: Say,
    What, is Horatio there?
HORATIO: A piece of him.
BERNARDO: Welcome, Horatio. Welcome, good Marcellus.   20
HORATIO: What, has this thing appear'd again tonight?
BERNARDO: I have seen nothing.
MARCELLUS: Horatio says 'tis but our fantasy,
    And will not let belief take hold of him
    Touching this dreaded sight, twice seen of us.   25
    Therefore I have entreated him along
    With us to watch the minutes of this night,
    That if again this apparition come
    He may approve° our eyes and speak to it.
HORATIO: Tush, tush, 'twill not appear.
BERNARDO: Sit down awhile,   30
    And let us once again assail your ears,
    That are so fortified against our story,
    What we have two nights seen.
HORATIO: Well, sit we down,
    And let us hear Bernardo speak of this.
BERNARDO: Last night of all,   35
    When yond same star that's westward from the pole°
    Had made his° course t' illume that part of heaven
    Where now it burns, Marcellus and myself,
    The bell then beating one—

(Enter GHOST.*)*

MARCELLUS: Peace, break thee off! Look where it comes again!   40
BERNARDO: In the same figure, like the King that's dead.
MARCELLUS: Thou art a scholar.° Speak to it, Horatio.
BERNARDO: Looks 'a° not like the King? Mark it, Horatio.
HORATIO: Most like. It harrows me with fear and wonder.
BERNARDO: It would be spoke to.
MARCELLUS: Speak to it,° Horatio.   45
HORATIO: What art thou that usurp'st this time of night,
    Together with that fair and warlike form
    In which the majesty of buried Denmark°
    Did sometimes° march? By heaven I charge thee, speak!
MARCELLUS: It is offended.
BERNARDO: See, it stalks away.   50

---

29 *approve:* Corroborate. 36 *pole:* Polestar. 37 *his:* Its. 42 *scholar:* One learned in Latin and able
to address spirits. 43 *'a:* He. 45 *It . . . it:* A ghost could not speak until spoken to. 48 *buried*
Denmark: The buried king of Denmark. 49 *sometimes:* Formerly.

HORATIO: Stay! Speak, speak. I charge thee, speak.　　*(Exit GHOST.)*
MARCELLUS: 'Tis gone, and will not answer.
BERNARDO: How now, Horatio? You tremble and look pale.
　　Is not this something more than fantasy?
　　What think you on 't?　　　　　　　　　　　　　　　　　　　　55
HORATIO: Before my God, I might not this believe
　　Without the sensible° and true avouch
　　Of mine own eyes.
MARCELLUS:　　　　　　Is it not like the King?
HORATIO: As thou art to thyself.
　　Such was the very armor he had on　　　　　　　　　　　　60
　　When he the ambitious Norway° combated.
　　So frown'd he once when, in an angry parle,°
　　He smote the sledded° Polacks° on the ice.
　　'Tis strange.
MARCELLUS: Thus twice before, and jump° at this dead hour,　　65
　　With martial stalk hath he gone by our watch.
HORATIO: In what particular thought to work I know not,
　　But, in the gross and scope° of mine opinion,
　　This bodes some strange eruption to our state.
MARCELLUS: Good now,° sit down, and tell me, he that knows,　　70
　　Why this same strict and most observant watch
　　So nightly toils° the subject° of the land,
　　And why such daily cast° of brazen cannon,
　　And foreign mart° for implements of war,
　　Why such impress° of shipwrights, whose sore task　　　　75
　　Does not divide the Sunday from the week.
　　What might be toward,° that this sweaty haste
　　Doth make the night joint-laborer with the day?
　　What is 't that can inform me?
HORATIO:　　　　　　　　　　　That can I,
　　At least, the whisper goes so. Our last king,　　　　　　80
　　Whose image even but now appear'd to us,
　　Was, as you know, by Fortinbras of Norway,
　　Thereto prick'd on° by a most emulate° pride,
　　Dar'd to the combat; in which our valiant Hamlet—
　　For so this side of our known world esteem'd him—　　　85
　　Did slay this Fortinbras; who, by a seal'd compact,
　　Well ratified by law and heraldry,

---

57 *sensible:* Confirmed by the senses.　61 *Norway:* King of Norway.　62 *parle:* Parley.　63 *sledded:* Traveling on sleds; *Polacks:* Poles.　65 *jump:* Exactly.　68 *gross and scope:* General view.　70 *Good now:* An expression denoting entreaty or expostulation.　72 *toils:* Causes to toil; *subject:* Subjects. 73 *cast:* Casting.　74 *mart:* Buying and selling.　75 *impress:* Impressment, conscription.　77 *toward:* in preparation.　83 *prick'd on:* incited; *emulate:* Ambitious.

Did forfeit, with his life, all those his lands
Which he stood seiz'd° of, to the conqueror;
Against the° which a moi'ty competent°   90
Was gaged° by our king, which had return'd
To the inheritance of Fortinbras
Had he been vanquisher, as, by the same comart°
And carriage° of the article design'd,
His fell to Hamlet. Now, sir, young Fortinbras,   95
Of unimproved° mettle hot and full,
Hath in the skirts° of Norway here and there
Shark'd up° a list of lawless resolutes°
For food and diet° to some enterprise
That hath a stomach° in 't, which is no other—   100
As it doth well appear unto our state—
But to recover of us, by strong hand
And terms compulsatory, those foresaid lands
So by his father lost. And this, I take it,
Is the main motive of our preparations,   105
The source of this our watch, and the chief head°
Of this post-haste and romage° in the land.
BERNARDO: I think it be no other but e'en so.
Well may it sort° that this portentous figure
Comes armed through our watch so like the King   110
That was and is the question of these wars.
HORATIO: A mote° it is to trouble the mind's eye.
In the most high and palmy° state of Rome,
A little ere the mightiest Julius fell,
The graves stood tenantless and the sheeted° dead   115
Did squeak and gibber in the Roman streets;
As° stars with trains of fire and dews of blood,
Disasters° in the sun; and the moist star°
Upon whose influence Neptune's° empire stands°
Was sick almost to doomsday° with eclipse.   120
And even the like precurse° of fear'd events,

---

89 *seiz'd:* Possessed. 90 *Against the:* In return for; *moi'ty competent:* Sufficient portion. 91 *gaged:* Engaged, pledged. 93 *comart:* Joint bargain (?). 94 *carriage:* Import, bearing. 96 *unimproved:* Not turned to account (?) or untested (?). 97 *skirts:* Outlying regions, outskirts. 98 *Shark'd up:* Got together in haphazard fashion; *resolutes:* desperadoes. 99 *food and diet:* No pay but their keep. 100 *stomach:* Relish of danger. 106 *head:* Source. 107 *romage:* Bustle, commotion. 109 *sort:* Suit. 112 *mote:* Speck of dust. 113 *palmy:* Flourishing. 115 *sheeted:* Shrouded. 117 *As:* This abrupt transition suggests that matter is possibly omitted between lines 116 and 117. 118 *Disasters:* Unfavorable signs of aspects; *moist star:* Moon, governing tides. 119 *Neptune:* God of the sea; *stands:* Depends. 120 *sick . . . doomsday:* See Matt. 24:29 and Rev. 6:12. 121 *precurse:* Heralding, foreshadowing.

As harbingers° preceding still° the fates
And prologue to the omen° coming on,
Have heaven and earth together demonstrated
Unto our climatures° and countrymen.   125

(Enter GHOST.*)*

But soft, behold! Lo where it comes again!
I'll cross° it, though it blast me. Stay, illusion!
If thou hast any sound, or use of voice,
Speak to me!   *(It spreads his arms.)*
If there be any good thing to be done   130
That may to thee do ease and grace to me,
Speak to me!
If thou art privy to thy country's fate,
Which, happily,° foreknowing may avoid,
O, speak!   135
Or if thou hast uphoarded in thy life
Extorted treasure in the womb of earth,
For which, they say, you spirits oft walk in death,   *(The cock crows.)*
Speak of it. Stay, and speak! Stop it, Marcellus.
MARCELLUS: Shall I strike at it with my partisan?°   140
HORATIO: Do, if it will not stand.   *(They strike at it.)*
BERNARDO: 'Tis here!
HORATIO: 'Tis here!
MARCELLUS: 'Tis gone.   *(Exit* GHOST.*)*
We do it wrong, being so majestical,
To offer it the show of violence;
For it is, as the air, invulnerable,
And our vain blows malicious mockery.   145
BERNARDO: It was about to speak when the cock crew.
HORATIO: And then it started like a guilty thing
Upon a fearful summons. I have heard,
The cock, that is the trumpet to the morn,
Doth with his lofty and shrill-sounding throat   150
Awake the god of day, and, at his warning,
Whether in sea or fire, in earth or air,
Th' extravagant and erring° spirit hies
To his confine; and of the truth herein   155
This present object made probation.°

---

122 *harbingers:* Forerunners; *still:* Continually. 123 *omen:* Calamitous event. 125 *climatures:*
Regions. 127 *cross:* Meet, face directly. 134 *happily:* Haply, perchance. 140 *partisan:* Long-
handled spear. 154 *extravagant and erring:* Wandering. (The words have similar meaning.) 156
probation: Proof.

MARCELLUS: It faded on the crowing of the cock.
　　Some say that ever 'gainst° that season comes
　　Wherein our Savior's birth is celebrated,
　　The bird of dawning singeth all night long,　　　　　　　　160
　　And then, they say, no spirit dare stir abroad;
　　The nights are wholesome, then no planets strike,°
　　No fairy takes,° nor witch hath power to charm,
　　So hallowed and so gracious° is that time.
HORATIO: So have I heard and do in part believe it.　　　165
　　But, look, the morn, in russet mantle clad,
　　Walks o'er the dew of yon high eastward hill.
　　Break we our watch up, and by my advice
　　Let us impart what we have seen tonight
　　Unto young Hamlet; for, upon my life,　　　　　　　　　170
　　This spirit, dumb to us, will speak to him.
　　Do you consent we shall acquaint him with it,
　　As needful in our loves, fitting our duty?
MARCELLUS: Let's do 't, I pray, and I this morning know
　　Where we shall find him most conveniently.　　　　*(Exeunt.)°* 175

SCENE II°

(Flourish. Enter CLAUDIUS, *King of Denmark,* GERTRUDE *the
Queen,* COUNCILORS, POLONIUS *and his son* LAERTES,
HAMLET, *cum aliis° [including* VOLTIMAND *and* CORNELIUS*].)*

KING: Though yet of Hamlet our dear brother's death
　　The memory be green, and that it us befitted
　　To bear our hearts in grief and our whole kingdom
　　To be contracted in one brow of woe,
　　Yet so far hath discretion fought with nature　　　　　5
　　That we with wisest sorrow think on him,
　　Together with remembrance of ourselves.
　　Therefore our sometime sister, now our queen,
　　Th' imperial jointress° to this warlike state,
　　Have we, as 'twere with a defeated joy—　　　　　　　10
　　With an auspicious and a dropping eye,
　　With mirth in funeral and with dirge in marriage,
　　In equal scale weighing delight and dole—
　　Taken to wife. Nor have we herein barr'd
　　Your better wisdoms, which have freely gone　　　　　15
　　With this affair along. For all, our thanks.

---

158 *'gainst:* Just before. 162 *strike:* Exert evil influence. 163 *takes:* Bewitches. 164 *gracious:* Full
of goodness. 175 s.d. *Exeunt:* Latin for "they go out." ACT I, SCENE II. *Location:* The castle;
cum aliis: With others. 9 *jointress:* Woman possessed of a joint tenancy of an estate.

Now follows that you know° young Fortinbras,
Holding a weak supposal° of our worth,
Or thinking by our late dear brother's death
Our state to be disjoint and out of frame,   20
Colleagued with° this dream of his advantage,°
He hath not fail'd to pester us with message
Importing° the surrender of those lands
Lost by his father, with all bands° of law,
To our most valiant brother. So much for him.   25
Now for ourself and for this time of meeting.
Thus much the business is: we have here writ
To Norway, uncle of young Fortinbras—
Who, impotent and bed-rid, scarcely hears
Of this his nephew's purpose—to suppress   30
His° further gait° herein, in that the levies,
The lists, and full proportions are all made
Out of his subject;° and we here dispatch
You, good Cornelius, and you, Voltimand,
For bearers of this greeting to old Norway,   35
Giving to you no further personal power
To business with the King, more than the scope
Of these delated° articles allow.   *(Gives a paper.)*
Farewell, and let your haste commend your duty.
CORNELIUS, VOLTIMAND: In that, and all things, will we show our duty. 40
KING: We doubt it nothing. Heartily farewell.
                    (Exit VOLTIMAND *and* CORNELIUS.*)*
And now, Laertes, what's the news with you?
You told us of some suit; what is 't, Laertes?
You cannot speak of reason to the Dane°
And lose your voice.° What wouldst thou beg, Laertes,   45
That shall not be my offer, not thy asking?
The head is not more native° to the heart,
The hand more instrumental° to the mouth,
Than is the throne of Denmark to thy father.
What wouldst thou have, Laertes?
LAERTES: My dread lord,   50
Your leave and favor to return to France,
From whence though willingly I came to Denmark
To show my duty in your coronation,

---

17 *know:* Be informed (that). 18 *weak supposal:* Low estimate. 21 *Colleagued with:* Joined to, allied with; *dream . . . advantage:* Illusory hope of success. 23 *Importing:* Pertaining to. 24 *bands:* Contracts. 31 *His:* Fortinbras's; *gait:* Proceeding. 31–33 *in that . . . subject:* Since the levying of troops and supplies is drawn entirely from the King of Norway's own subjects. 38 *delated:* Detailed. (Variant of "dilated.") 44 *the Dane:* The Danish King. 45 *lose your voice:* Waste your speech. 47 *native:* Closely connected, related. 48 *instrumental:* Serviceable.

    Yet now I must confess, that duty done,
    My thoughts and wishes bend again toward France   55
    And bow them to your gracious leave and pardon.°
KING: Have you your father's leave? What says Polonius?
POLONIUS: H'ath, my lord, wrung from me my slow leave
    By laborsome petition, and at last
    Upon his will I seal'd my hard° consent.   60
    I do beseech you, give him leave to go.
KING: Take thy fair hour, Laertes. Time be thine,
    And thy best graces spend it at thy will!
    But now, my cousin° Hamlet, and my son—
HAMLET: A little more than kin, and less than kind.°   65
KING: How is it that the clouds still hang on you?
HAMLET: Not so, my lord. I am too much in the sun.°
QUEEN: Good Hamlet, cast thy nighted color off,
    And let thine eye look like a friend on Denmark.
    Do not forever with thy vailed° lids   70
    Seek for thy noble father in the dust.
    Thou know'st 'tis common,° all that lives must die,
    Passing through nature to eternity.
HAMLET: Ay, madam, it is common.
QUEEN: If it be,
    Why seems it so particular with thee?   75
HAMLET: Seems, madam! Nay, it is. I know not "seems."
    'Tis not alone my inky cloak, good mother,
    Nor customary suits of solemn black,
    Nor windy suspiration of forc'd breath,
    No, nor the fruitful° river in the eye,   80
    Nor the dejected havior of the visage,
    Together with all forms, moods, shapes of grief,
    That can denote me truly. These indeed seem,
    For they are actions that a man might play.
    But I have that within which passes show;   85
    These but the trappings and the suits of woe.
KING: 'Tis sweet and commendable in your nature, Hamlet,
    To give these mourning duties to your father.
    But you must know your father lost a father,
    That father lost, lost his, and the survivor bound   90
    In filial obligation for some term

---

56 *leave and pardon:* Permission to depart. 60 *hard:* Reluctant. 64 *cousin:* Any kin not of the immediate family. 65 *A little . . . kind:* Closer than an ordinary nephew (since I am stepson), and yet more separated in natural feeling (with pun on "kind," meaning affectionate and natural, lawful). (This line is often read as an aside, but it need not be.) 67 *sun:* The sunshine of the King's royal favor (with pun on "son"). 70 *vailed:* Downcast. 72 *common:* Of universal occurrence. (But Hamlet plays on the sense of "vulgar" in line 74.) 80 *fruitful:* Abundant.

To do obsequious° sorrow. But to persever°
In obstinate condolement° is a course
Of impious stubbornness. 'Tis unmanly grief.
It shows a will most incorrect to heaven,   95
A heart unfortified, a mind impatient,
An understanding simple and unschool'd.
For what we know must be and is as common
As any the most vulgar thing to sense,°
Why should we in our peevish opposition   100
Take it to heart? Fie, 'tis a fault to heaven,
A fault against the dead, a fault to nature,
To reason most absurd, whose common theme
Is death of fathers, and who still hath cried,
From the first corse° till he that died today,   105
"This must be so." We pray you, throw to earth
This unprevailing° woe, and think of us
As of a father; for let the world take note,
You are the most immediate° to our throne,
And with no less nobility of love   110
Than that which dearest father bears his son
Do I impart toward you. For your intent
In going back to school in Wittenberg,°
It is most retrograde° to our desire,
And we beseech you, bend you° to remain   115
Here in the cheer and comfort of our eye,
Our chiefest courtier, cousin, and our son.
QUEEN: Let not thy mother lose her prayers, Hamlet.
   I pray thee stay with us, go not to Wittenberg.
HAMLET: I shall in all my best obey you, madam.   120
KING: Why, 'tis a loving and a fair reply.
   Be as ourself in Denmark. Madam, come.
   This gentle and unforc'd accord of Hamlet
   Sits smiling to my heart, in grace whereof
   No jocund° health that Denmark drinks today   125
   But the great cannon to the clouds shall tell,
   And the King's rouse° the heaven shall bruit again,°
   Respeaking earthly thunder.° Come away.

(Flourish. Exeunt all but HAMLET.*)*

---

92 *obsequious:* Suited to obsequies or funerals; *persever:* Persevere. 93 *condolement:* Sorrowing. 99
As . . . sense: As the most ordinary experience. 105 *corse:* Corpse. 107 *unprevailing:* Unavailing.
109 *most immediate:* Next in succession. 113 *Wittenberg:* Famous German university founded in
1502. 114 *retrograde:* Contrary. 115 *bend you:* Incline yourself. 125 *jocund:* Merry. 127 *rouse:*
Draft of liquor; *bruit again:* Loudly echo. 128 *thunder:* Of trumpet and kettledrum, sounded
when the King drinks; see I.iv.8–12.

HAMLET: O, that this too too sullied° flesh would melt,
          Thaw, and resolve itself into a dew!   130
          Or that the Everlasting had not fix'd
          His canon° 'gainst self-slaughter! O God, God,
          How weary, stale, flat, and unprofitable
          Seem to me all the uses of this world!
          Fie on 't, ah, fie! 'Tis an unweeded garden   135
          That grows to seed. Things rank and gross in nature
          Possess it merely.° That it should come to this!
          But two months dead—nay, not so much, not two.
          So excellent a king, that was to° this
          Hyperion° to a satyr; so loving to my mother   140
          That he might not beteem° the winds of heaven
          Visit her face too roughly. Heaven and earth,
          Must I remember? Why, she would hang on him
          As if increase of appetite had grown
          By what it fed on, and yet, within a month—   145
          Let me not think on 't. Frailty, thy name is woman!—
          A little month, or ere those shoes were old
          With which she followed my poor father's body,
          Like Niobe,° all tears, why she, even she—
          O God, a beast, that wants discourse of reason,°   150
          Would have mourn'd longer—married with my uncle,
          My father's brother, but no more like my father
          Than I to Hercules. Within a month,
          Ere yet the salt of most unrighteous tears
          Had left the flushing in her galled° eyes,   155
          She married. O, most wicked speed, to post
          With such dexterity to incestuous° sheets!
          It is not nor it cannot come to good.
          But break, my heart, for I must hold my tongue.

          (Enter HORATIO, MARCELLUS, and BERNARDO.)

HORATIO: Hail to your lordship!
HAMLET: I am glad to see you well.   160
          Horatio!—or I do forget myself.
HORATIO: The same, my lord, and your poor servant ever.

---

129 *sullied:* Defiled. 132 *canon:* Law. 137 *merely:* Completely. 139 *to:* In comparison to. 140
Hyperion: Titan sun-god, father of Helios. 141 *beteem:* Allow. 149 *Niobe:* Tantalus's daughter,
Queen of Thebes, who boasted that she had more sons and daughters than Leto; for this, Apollo
and Artemis, children of Leto, slew her fourteen children. She was turned by Zeus into a stone
which continually dropped tears. 150 *wants . . . reason:* Lacks the faculty of reason. 155 *galled:*
Irritated, inflamed. 157 *incestuous:* In Shakespeare's day, the marriage of a man like Claudius to
his deceased brother's wife was considered incestuous.

HAMLET: Sir, my good friend; I'll change° that name with you.
　　And what make° you from Wittenberg, Horatio?
　　Marcellus?   165
MARCELLUS: My good lord.
HAMLET: I am very glad to see you.　　　　　　　　*(To* BERNARDO.)
　　　　　　　　　　　Good even, sir.—
　　But what, in faith, make you from Wittenberg?
HORATIO: A truant disposition, good my lord.
HAMLET: I would not hear your enemy say so,   170
　　Nor shall you do my ear that violence
　　To make it truster of your own report
　　Against yourself. I know you are no truant.
　　But what is your affair in Elsinore?
　　We'll teach you to drink deep ere you depart.   175
HORATIO: My lord, I came to see your father's funeral.
HAMLET: I prithee do not mock me, fellow student;
　　I think it was to see my mother's wedding.
HORATIO: Indeed, my lord, it followed hard° upon.
HAMLET: Thrift, thrift, Horatio! The funeral bak'd meats   180
　　Did coldly furnish forth the marriage tables.
　　Would I had met my dearest° foe in heaven
　　Or° ever I had seen that day, Horatio!
　　My father!—Methinks I see my father.
HORATIO: Where, my lord?
HAMLET:　　　　　　　　　In my mind's eye, Horatio.   185
HORATIO: I saw him once. 'A° was a goodly king.
HAMLET: 'A was a man, take him for all in all,
　　I shall not look upon his like again.
HORATIO: My lord, I think I saw him yesternight.
HAMLET: Saw? Who?   190
HORATIO: My lord, the King your father.
HAMLET:　　　　　　　　　　　　　　The King my father.
HORATIO: Season your admiration° for a while
　　With an attent° ear, till I may deliver,
　　Upon the witness of these gentlemen,
　　This marvel to you.
HAMLET:　　　　　　　For God's love, let me hear!   195
HORATIO: Two nights together had these gentlemen,
　　Marcellus and Bernardo, on their watch,
　　In the dead waste and middle of the night,
　　Been thus encount'red. A figure like your father,
　　Armed at point° exactly, cap-a-pe,°   200

---

163 *change:* Exchange (i.e., the name of friend).　164 *make:* Do.　179 *hard:* Close.　182 *dearest:* Direst.　183 *Or:* Ere, before.　186 *'A:* He.　192 *Season your admiration:* Restrain your astonishment. 193 *attent:* Attentive.　200 *at point:* Completely; *cap-a-pe:* From head to foot.

Appears before them, and with solemn march
Goes slow and stately by them. Thrice he walk'd
By their oppress'd and fear-surprised eyes
Within his truncheon's° length, whilst they, distill'd
Almost to jelly with the act° of fear,   205
Stand dumb and speak not to him. This to me
In dreadful secrecy impart they did,
And I with them the third night kept the watch,
Where, as they had delivered, both in time,
Form of the thing, each word made true and good,   210
The apparition comes. I knew your father;
These hands are not more like.

HAMLET: But where was this?

MARCELLUS: My lord, upon the platform where we watch.

HAMLET: Did you not speak to it?

HORATIO: My lord, I did,
But answer made it none. Yet once methought   215
It lifted up it° head and did address
Itself to motion, like as it would speak;
But even then the morning cock crew loud,
And at the sound it shrunk in haste away,
And vanish'd from our sight.

HAMLET: 'Tis very strange.   220

HORATIO: As I do live, my honor'd lord, 'tis true,
And we did think it writ down in our duty
To let you know of it.

HAMLET: Indeed, indeed, sirs. But this troubles me.
Hold you the watch tonight?

ALL: We do, my lord.   225

HAMLET: Arm'd, say you?

ALL: Arm'd, my lord.

HAMLET: From top to toe?

ALL: My lord, from head to foot.

HAMLET: Then saw you not his face?

HORATIO: O, yes, my lord. He wore his beaver° up.   230

HAMLET: What, looked he frowningly?

HORATIO: A countenance more
In sorrow than in anger.

HAMLET: Pale or red?

HORATIO: Nay, very pale.

HAMLET: And fix'd his eyes upon you?

HORATIO: Most constantly.

HAMLET: I would I had been there.

---

204 *truncheon:* Officer's staff. 205 *act:* Action, operation. 216 *it:* Its. 230 *beaver:* Visor on the
helmet.

HORATIO: It would have much amaz'd you.   235
HAMLET: Very like, very like. Stay'd it long?
HORATIO: While one with moderate haste might tell° a hundred.
MARCELLUS, BERNARDO: Longer, longer.
HORATIO: Not when I saw 't.
HAMLET: His beard was grizzl'd,—no?
HORATIO: It was, as I have seen it in his life,   240
    A sable silver'd.°
HAMLET: I will watch tonight.
    Perchance 'twill walk again.
HORATIO: I warr'nt it will.
HAMLET: If it assume my noble father's person,
    I'll speak to it, though hell itself should gape
    And bid me hold my peace. I pray you all,   245
    If you have hitherto conceal'd this sight,
    Let it be tenable° in your silence still,
    And whatsomever else shall hap tonight,
    Give it an understanding, but no tongue.
    I will requite your loves. So, fare you well.   250
    Upon the platform, 'twixt eleven and twelve,
    I'll visit you.
ALL: Our duty to your honor.
HAMLET: Your loves, as mine to you. Farewell.

                            (Exeunt [all but HAMLET*].)*

    My father's spirit in arms! All is not well.
    I doubt° some foul play. Would the night were come!   255
    Till then sit still, my soul. Foul deeds will rise,
    Though all the earth o'erwhelm them, to men's eyes.   *(Exit.)*

SCENE III°

(Enter LAERTES *and* OPHELIA, *his sister.)*

LAERTES: My necessaries are embark'd. Farewell.
    And, sister, as the winds give benefit
    And convoy is assistant,° do not sleep
    But let me hear from you.
OPHELIA: Do you doubt that?
LAERTES: For Hamlet, and the trifling of his favor,   5
    Hold it a fashion and a toy in blood,°
    A violet in the youth of primy° nature,
    Forward,° not permanent, sweet, not lasting,

---

237 *tell:* Count. 241 *sable silver'd:* Black mixed with white. 247 *tenable:* Held tightly. 255 *doubt:* Suspect. ACT I, SCENE III. *Location:* Polonius's chambers. 3 *convoy is assistant:* Means of conveyance are available. 6 *toy in blood:* Passing amorous fancy. 7 *primy:* In its prime, springtime. 8 *Forward:* Precocious.

The perfume and suppliance° of a minute—
No more.

OPHELIA: No more but so?

LAERTES: Think it no more.   10
For nature crescent° does not grow alone
In thews° and bulk, but, as this temple° waxes,
The inward service of the mind and soul
Grows wide withal.° Perhaps he loves you now,
And now no soil° nor cautel° doth besmirch   15
The virtue of his will;° but you must fear,
His greatness weigh'd,° his will is not his own.
For he himself is subject to his birth.
He may not, as unvalued persons do,
Carve° for himself; for on his choice depends   20
The safety and health of this whole state,
And therefore must his choice be circumscrib'd
Unto the voice and yielding° of that body
Whereof he is the head. Then if he says he loves you,
It fits your wisdom so far to believe it   25
As he in his particular act and place
May give his saying deed,° which is no further
Than the main voice of Denmark goes withal.
Then weigh what loss your honor may sustain
If with too credent° ear you list° his songs,   30
Or lose your heart, or your chaste treasure open
To his unmaster'd importunity.
Fear it, Ophelia, fear it, my dear sister,
And keep you in the rear of your affection,
Out of the shot° and danger of desire.   35
The chariest° maid is prodigal enough
If she unmask her beauty to the moon.
Virtue itself scapes not calumnious strokes.
The canker galls° the infants of the spring
Too oft before their buttons° be disclos'd,°   40
And in the morn and liquid dew° of youth
Contagious blastments° are most imminent.
Be wary then; best safety lies in fear.
Youth to itself rebels, though none else near.

---

9 *suppliance:* Supply, filler. 11 *crescent:* Growing, waxing. 12 *thews:* Bodily strength; *temple:* Body. 14 *Grows wide withal:* Grows along with it. 15 *soil:* Blemish; *cautel:* deceit. 16 *will:* desire. 17 *greatness weigh'd:* High position considered. 20 *Carve:* Choose pleasure. 23 *Voice and yielding:* Assent, approval. 27 *deed:* Effect. 30 *credent:* Credulous; *list:* Listen to. 35 *shot:* Range. 36 *chariest:* Most scrupulously modest. 39 *canker galls:* Cankerworm destroys. 40 *buttons:* Buds; *disclos'd:* Opened. 41 *liquid dew:* Time when dew is fresh. 42 *blastments:* Blights.

OPHELIA: I shall the effect of this good lesson keep   45
  As watchman to my heart. But, good my brother,
  Do not, as some ungracious pastors do,
  Show me the steep and thorny way to heaven,
  Whiles, like a puff'd° and reckless libertine,
  Himself the primrose path of dalliance treads,   50
  And recks° not his own rede.°

  (Enter POLONIUS.*)*

LAERTES: O, fear me not.
  I stay too long. But here my father comes.
  A double blessing is a double° grace;
  Occasion° smiles upon a second leave.
POLONIUS: Yet here, Laertes? Aboard, aboard, for shame!   55
  The wind sits in the shoulder of your sail,
  And you are stay'd for. There—my blessing with thee!
  And these few precepts in thy memory
  Look thou character.° Give thy thoughts no tongue,
  Nor any unproportion'd thought his° act.   60
  Be thou familiar,° but by no means vulgar.°
  Those friends thou hast, and their adoption tried,°
  Grapple them to thy soul with hoops of steel,
  But do not dull thy palm with entertainment
  Of each new-hatch'd, unfledg'd courage.° Beware   65
  Of entrance to a quarrel, but, being in,
  Bear't that° th' opposed may beware of thee.
  Give every man thy ear, but few thy voice;
  Take each man's censure,° but reserve thy judgment.
  Costly thy habit as thy purse can buy,   70
  But not express'd in fancy; rich, not gaudy,
  For the apparel oft proclaims the man,
  And they in France of the best rank and station
  Are of a most select and generous chief° in that.
  Neither a borrower nor a lender be,   75
  For loan oft loses both itself and friend,
  And borrowing dulleth edge of husbandry.°
  This above all: to thine own self be true,
  And it must follow, as the night the day,
  Thou canst not then be false to any man.   80
  Farewell. My blessing season° this in thee!

49 *puff'd:* Bloated. 51 *recks:* Heeds; *rede:* Counsel. 53 *double:* I.e., Laertes has already bidden his
father good-by. 54 *Occasion:* Opportunity. 59 *character:* Inscribe. 60 *his:* Its. 61 *familiar:* Sociable;
vulgar: common. 62 *tried:* Tested. 65 *courage:* Young man of spirit. 67 *Bear't that:* Manage it
so that. 69 *censure:* Opinion, judgment. 74 *generous chief:* Noble eminence (?). 77 *husbandry:*
Thrift. 81 *season:* Mature.

LAERTES: Most humbly do I take my leave, my lord.
POLONIUS: The time invests° you. Go, your servants tend.°
LAERTES: Farewell, Ophelia, and remember well
    What I have said to you.   85
OPHELIA: 'Tis in my memory lock'd,
    And you yourself shall keep the key of it.
LAERTES: Farewell.   *(Exit* LAERTES.*)*
POLONIUS: What is 't, Ophelia, he hath said to you?
OPHELIA: So please you, something touching the Lord Hamlet.   90
POLONIUS: Marry,° well bethought.
    'Tis told me he hath very oft of late
    Given private time to you, and you yourself
    Have of your audience been most free and bounteous.
    If it be so—as so 'tis put on° me,   95
    And that in way of caution—I must tell you
    You do not understand yourself so clearly
    As it behooves my daughter and your honor.
    What is between you? Give me up the truth.
OPHELIA: He hath, my lord, of late made many tenders°   100
    Of his affection to me.
POLONIUS: Affection? Pooh! You speak like a green girl,
    Unsifted° in such perilous circumstance.
    Do you believe his tenders, as you call them?
OPHELIA: I do not know, my lord, what I should think.   105
POLONIUS: Marry, I will teach you. Think yourself a baby
    That you have ta'en these tenders° for true pay,
    Which are not sterling.° Tender° yourself more dearly,
    Or—not to crack the wind° of the poor phrase,
    Running it thus—you'll tender me a fool.°   110
OPHELIA: My lord, he hath importun'd me with love
    In honorable fashion.
POLONIUS: Ay, fashion° you may call it. Go to, go to.
OPHELIA: And hath given countenance° to his speech, my lord,
    With almost all the holy vows of heaven.   115
POLONIUS: Ay, springes° to catch woodcocks.° I do know,
    When the blood burns, how prodigal the soul
    Lends the tongue vows. These blazes, daughter,
    Giving more light than heat, extinct in both

---

83 *invests:* Besieges; *tend:* Attend, wait.   91 *Marry:* By the Virgin Mary (a mild oath).   95 *put on:* Impressed on, told to.   100 *tenders:* Offers.   103 *Unsifted:* Untried.   107 *tenders:* With added meaning here of "promises to pay."   108 *sterling:* Legal currency; *Tender:* Hold.   109 *crack the wind:* Run it until it is broken, winded.   110 *tender me a fool:* (1) Show yourself to me as a fool; (2) show me up as a fool; (3) present me with a grandchild ("fool" was a term of endearment for a child).   113 *fashion:* Mere form, pretense.   114 *countenance:* Credit, support.   116 *springes:* Snares; *woodcocks:* Birds easily caught; here used to connote gullibility.

Even in their promise, as it is a-making, 120
You must not take for fire. From this time
Be something scanter of your maiden presence.
Set your entreatments° at a higher rate
Than a command to parle.° For Lord Hamlet,
Believe so much in him° that he is young, 125
And with a larger tether may he walk
Than may be given you. In few,° Ophelia,
Do not believe his vows, for they are brokers,°
Not of that dye° which their investments° show,
But mere implorators° of unholy suits, 130
Breathing° like sanctified and pious bawds,
The better to beguile. This is for all:
I would not, in plain terms, from this time forth
Have you so slander° any moment leisure
As to give words or talk with the Lord Hamlet. 135
Look to 't, I charge you. Come your ways.

OPHELIA: I shall obey, my lord. *(Exeunt.)*

SCENE IV°

(Enter HAMLET, HORATIO, *and* MARCELLUS.)

HAMLET: The air bites shrewdly; it is very cold.

HORATIO: It is a nipping and an eager air.

HAMLET: What hour now?

HORATIO: I think it lacks of twelve.

MARCELLUS: No, it is struck.

HORATIO: Indeed? I heard it not.
It then draws near the season 5
Wherein the spirit held his wont to walk.

              (A flourish of trumpets, and two pieces° go off within.)
What does this mean, my lord?

HAMLET: The King doth wake° tonight and takes his rouse,°
Keeps wassail,° and the swagg'ring up-spring° reels;
And as he drains his draughts of Rhenish° down, 10

---

123 *entreatments:* Negotiations for surrender (a military term). 124 *parle:* Discuss terms with the enemy. (Polonius urges his daughter, in the metaphor of military language, not to meet with Hamlet and consider giving in to him merely because he requests an interview.) 125 *so . . . him:* This much concerning him. 127 *In few:* Briefly. 128 *brokers:* Go-betweens, procurers. 129 *dye:* Color or sort; *investments:* Clothes (i.e., they are not what they seem). 130 *mere implorators:* Out and out solicitors. 131 *Breathing:* Speaking. 134 *slander:* Bring disgrace or reproach upon. ACT I, SCENE IV. *Location:* The guard platform. 6 s.d. *pieces:* I.e., of ordnance, cannon. 8 *wake:* Stay awake and hold revel; *rouse:* Carouse, drinking bout. 9 *wassail:* Carousal; *up-spring:* Wild German dance. 10 *Rhenish:* Rhine wine.

The kettle-drum and trumpet thus bray out
The triumph of his pledge.°
HORATIO: Is it a custom?
HAMLET: Ay, marry, is 't,
But to my mind, though I am native here
And to the manner° born, it is a custom   15
More honor'd in the breach than the observance.°
This heavy-headed revel east and west°
Makes us traduc'd and tax'd of° other nations.
They clepe° us drunkards, and with swinish phrase°
Soil our addition;° and indeed it takes   20
From our achievements, though perform'd at height,°
The pith and marrow of our attribute.
So, oft it chances in particular men,
That for some vicious mole of nature° in them,
As in their birth—wherein they are not guilty,   25
Since nature cannot choose his° origin—
By the o'ergrowth of some complexion,°
Oft breaking down the pales° and forts of reason,
Or by some habit that too much o'er-leavens°
The form of plausive° manners, that these men,   30
Carrying, I say, the stamp of one defect,
Being nature's livery,° or fortune's star,°
Their virtues else, be they as pure as grace,
As infinite as man may undergo,
Shall in the general censure take corruption   35
From that particular fault. The dram of eale°
Doth all the noble substance of a doubt°
To his own scandal.°

(Enter GHOST.)

HORATIO: Look, my lord, it comes!
HAMLET: Angels and ministers of grace defend us!
Be thou a spirit of health° or goblin damn'd,   40

---

12 *triumph . . . pledge:* His feat in draining the wine in a single draft. 15 *manner:* Custom (of drinking). 16 *More . . . observance:* Better neglected than followed. 17 *east and west:* I.e., everywhere. 18 *tax'd of:* Censured by. 19 *clepe:* Call; *with swinish phrase:* By calling us swine. 20 *addition:* Reputation. 21 *at height:* Outstandingly. 24 *mole of nature:* Natural blemish in one's constitution. 26 *his:* Its. 27 *complexion:* Humor (i.e., one of the four humors or fluids thought to determine temperament). 28 *pales:* Palings, fences (as of a fortification). 29 *o'er-leavens:* Induces a change throughout (as yeast works in dough). 30 *plausive:* Pleasing. 32 *nature's livery:* Endowment from nature; *fortune's star:* Mark placed by fortune. 36 *dram of eale:* Small amount of evil (?). 37 *of a doubt:* A famous crux, sometimes emended to "oft about" or "often dout," i.e., often erase or do out, or to "antidote," counteract. 38 *To . . . scandal:* To the disgrace of the whole enterprise. 40 *of health:* Of spiritual good.

Bring with thee airs from heaven or blasts from hell,
Be thy intents wicked or charitable,
Thou com'st in such a questionable° shape
That I will speak to thee. I'll call thee Hamlet,
King, father, royal Dane. O, answer me!   45
Let me not burst in ignorance; but tell
Why thy canoniz'd° bones, hearsed° in death,
Have burst their cerements;° why the sepulcher
Wherein we saw thee quietly interr'd
Hath op'd his ponderous and marble jaws   50
To cast thee up again. What may this mean,
That thou, dead corse, again in complete steel
Revisits thus the glimpses of the moon,°
Making night hideous, and we fools of nature°
So horridly to shake our disposition   55
With thoughts beyond the reaches of our souls?
Say, why is this? Wherefore? What should we do?

                    (GHOST beckons HAMLET.)

HORATIO: It beckons you to go away with it,
    As if it some impartment° did desire
    To you alone.
MARCELLUS: Look with what courteous action   60
    It waves you to a more removed ground.
    But do not go with it.
HORATIO: No, by no means.
HAMLET: It will not speak. Then I will follow it.
HORATIO: Do not, my lord.
HAMLET: Why, what should be the fear?
    I do not set my life at a pin's fee,°   65
    And for my soul, what can it do to that,
    Being a thing immortal as itself?
    It waves me forth again. I'll follow it.
HORATIO: What if it tempt you toward the flood, my lord,
    Or to the dreadful summit of the cliff   70
    That beetles o'er° his° base into the sea,
    And there assume some other horrible form
    Which might deprive your sovereignty of reason,°
    And draw you into madness? Think of it.
    The very place puts toys of desperation,°   75

---

43 *questionable:* Inviting question or conversation. 47 *canoniz'd:* Buried according to the canons of the church; *hearsed:* Coffined. 48 *cerements:* Grave-clothes. 53 *glimpses of the moon:* Earth by night. 54 *fools of nature:* Mere men, limited to natural knowledge. 59 *impartment:* Communication. 65 *fee:* Value. 71 *beetles o'er:* Overhangs threateningly; *his:* Its. 73 *deprive . . . reason:* Take away the rule of reason over your mind. 75 *toys of desperation:* Fancies of desperate acts, i.e., suicide.

Without more motive, into every brain
That looks so many fathoms to the sea
And hears it roar beneath.
HAMLET: It waves me still.
     Go on, I'll follow thee.
MARCELLUS: You shall not go, my lord.   *(They try to stop him.)*
HAMLET: Hold off your hands!   80
HORATIO: Be rul'd, you shall not go.
HAMLET: My fate cries out,
     And makes each petty artery° in this body
     As hardy as the Nemean lion's° nerve.°
     Still am I call'd. Unhand me, gentlemen.
     By heaven, I'll make a ghost of him that lets° me!   85
     I say, away! Go on. I'll follow thee.   *(Exeunt* GHOST *and* HAMLET.*)*
HORATIO: He waxes desperate with imagination.
MARCELLUS: Let's follow. 'Tis not fit thus to obey him.
HORATIO: Have after. To what issue° will this come?
MARCELLUS: Something is rotten in the state of Denmark.   90
HORATIO: Heaven will direct it.°
MARCELLUS: Nay, let's follow him.   *(Exeunt.)*

SCENE V°

(Enter GHOST *and* HAMLET.*)*

HAMLET: Whither wilt thou lead me? Speak. I'll go no further.
GHOST: Mark me.
HAMLET: I will.
GHOST: My hour is almost come,
     When I to sulph'rous and tormenting flames
     Must render up myself.
HAMLET: Alas, poor ghost!
GHOST: Pity me not, but lend thy serious hearing   5
     To what I shall unfold.
HAMLET: Speak. I am bound to hear.
GHOST: So art thou to revenge, when thou shalt hear.
HAMLET: What?
GHOST: I am thy father's spirit,   10
     Doom'd for a certain term to walk the night,
     And for the day confin'd to fast° in fires,
     Till the foul crimes° done in my days of nature
     Are burnt and purg'd away. But that° I am forbid

---

82 *artery:* Sinew. 83 *Nemean lion:* One of the monsters slain by Hercules in his twelve labors; *nerve:* Sinew. 85 *lets:* Hinders. 89 *issue:* Outcome. 91 *it:* The outcome. ACT I, SCENE V. *Location:* The battlements of the castle. 12 *fast:* Do penance. 13 *crimes:* Sins. 14 *But that:* Were it not that.

To tell the secrets of my prison-house,   15
I could a tale unfold whose lightest word
Would harrow up thy soul, freeze thy young blood,
Make thy two eyes, like stars, start from their spheres,°
Thy knotted and combined locks° to part,
And each particular hair to stand an end,°   20
Like quills upon the fearful porpentine.°
But this eternal blazon° must not be
To ears of flesh and blood. List, list, O, list!
If thou didst ever thy dear father love—

HAMLET: O God!   25

GHOST: Revenge his foul and most unnatural murder.

HAMLET: Murder?

GHOST: Murder most foul, as in the best it is,
But this most foul, strange, and unnatural.

HAMLET: Haste me to know 't, that I, with wings as swift   30
As meditation or the thoughts of love,
May sweep to my revenge.

GHOST: I find thee apt;
And duller shouldst thou be than the fat weed
That roots itself in ease on Lethe° wharf,°
Wouldst thou not stir in this. Now, Hamlet, hear.   35
'Tis given out that, sleeping in my orchard,
A serpent stung me. So the whole ear of Denmark
Is by a forged process° of my death
Rankly abus'd.° But know, thou noble youth,
The serpent that did sting thy father's life   40
Now wears his crown.

HAMLET: O my prophetic soul!
My uncle!

GHOST: Ay, that incestuous, that adulterate° beast,
With witchcraft of his wits, with traitorous gifts—
O wicked wit and gifts, that have the power   45
So to seduce!—won to his shameful lust
The will of my most seeming-virtuous queen.
O Hamlet, what a falling-off was there!
From me, whose love was of that dignity
That it went hand in hand even with the vow   50

---

18 *spheres:* Eye sockets, here compared to the orbits or transparent revolving spheres in which, according to Ptolemaic astronomy, the heavenly bodies were fixed. 19 *knotted . . . locks:* Hair neatly arranged and confined. 20 *an end:* on end. 21 *fearful porpentine:* Frightened porcupine. 22 *eternal blazon:* Revelation of the secrets of eternity. 34 *Lethe:* The river of forgetfulness in Hades; *wharf:* Bank. 38 *forged process:* Falsified account. 39 *abus'd:* Deceived. 43 *adulterate:* Adulterous.

I made to her in marriage, and to decline
Upon a wretch whose natural gifts were poor
To those of mine!
But virtue, as it never will be moved,
Though lewdness court it in a shape of heaven,°   55
So lust, though to a radiant angel link'd,
Will sate itself in a celestial bed,
And prey on garbage.
But, soft, methinks I scent the morning air.
Brief let me be. Sleeping within my orchard,   60
My custom always of the afternoon,
Upon my secure° hour thy uncle stole,
With juice of cursed hebona° in a vial,
And in the porches of my ears did pour
The leprous° distillment, whose effect   65
Holds such an enmity with blood of man
That swift as quicksilver it courses through
The natural gates and alleys of the body,
And with a sudden vigor it doth posset°
And curd, like eager° droppings into milk,   70
The thin and wholesome blood. So did it mine,
And a most instant tetter° bark'd° about,
Most lazar-like,° with vile and loathsome crust,
All my smooth body.
Thus was I, sleeping, by a brother's hand   75
Of life, of crown, of queen, at once dispatch'd,°
Cut off even in the blossoms of my sin,
Unhous'led,° disappointed,° unanel'd,°
No reck'ning made, but sent to my account
With all my imperfections on my head.   80
O, horrible! O, horrible, most horrible!
If thou hast nature° in thee, bear it not.
Let not the royal bed of Denmark be
A couch for luxury° and damned incest.
But, howsomever thou pursues this act,   85
Taint not thy mind, nor let thy soul contrive
Against thy mother aught. Leave her to heaven

---

55 *shape of heaven:* Heavenly form. 62 *secure:* Confident, unsuspicious. 63 *hebona:* Poison. (The word seems to be a form of "ebony," though it is perhaps thought to be related to "henbane," a poison, or to "ebenus," yew.) 65 *leprous:* Causing leprosy-like disfigurement. 69 *posset:* Coagulate, curdle. 70 *eager:* Sour, acid. 72 *tetter:* Eruption of scabs; *bark'd:* Covered with a rough covering, like bark on a tree. 73 *lazar-like:* Leper-like. 76 *dispatch'd:* Suddenly deprived. 78 *Unhous'led:* Without having received the sacrament of Holy Communion; *disappointed:* Unready (spiritually) for the last journey; *unanel'd:* Without having received extreme unction. 82 *nature:* The promptings of a son. 84 *luxury:* Lechery

And to those thorns that in her bosom lodge,
To prick and sting her. Fare thee well at once.
The glow-worm shows the matin° to be near,   90
And 'gins to pale his uneffectual fire.°
Adieu, adieu, adieu! Remember me.   *(Exit.)*
HAMLET: O all you host of heaven! O earth! What else?
And shall I couple° hell? O fie! Hold, hold, my heart,
And you, my sinews, grow not instant old,   95
But bear me stiffly up. Remember thee!
Ay, thou poor ghost, whiles memory holds a seat
In this distracted globe.° Remember thee!
Yea, from the table° of my memory
I'll wipe away all trivial fond° records,   100
All saws° of books, all forms,° all pressures° past
That youth and observation copied there,
And thy commandment all alone shall live
Within the book and volume of my brain,
Unmix'd with baser matter. Yes, by heaven!   105
O most pernicious woman!
O villain, villain, smiling, damned villain!
My tables—meet it is I set it down,
That one may smile, and smile, and be a villain.
At least I am sure it may be so in Denmark.   *(Writing.)* 110
So, uncle, there you are. Now to my word;
It is "Adieu, adieu! Remember me."
I have sworn 't.

(Enter HORATIO *and* MARCELLUS.*)*

HORATIO: My lord, my lord!
MARCELLUS: Lord Hamlet!
HORATIO: Heavens secure him!
HAMLET: So be it!   115
MARCELLUS: Illo, ho, ho, my lord!
HAMLET: Hillo, ho, ho,° boy! Come, bird, come.
MARCELLUS: How it 't, my noble lord?
HORATIO: What news, my lord?
HAMLET: O, wonderful!
HORATIO: Good my lord, tell it.
HAMLET: No, you will reveal it.   120
HORATIO: Not I, my lord, by heaven.

90 *matin:* Morning. 91 *uneffectual fire:* Cold light. 94 *couple:* Add. 98 *globe:* Head. 99 *table:* Writing tablet. 100 *fond:* Foolish. 101 *saws:* Wise sayings; *forms:* Images; *pressures:* Impressions stamped. 117 *Hillo, ho, ho:* A falconer's call to a hawk in air. Hamlet is playing upon Marcellus's "Illo," i.e., "halloo."

MARCELLUS: Nor I, my lord.

HAMLET: How say you, then, would heart of man once think it?
But you'll be secret?

HORATIO, MARCELLUS: Ay, by heaven, my lord.

HAMLET: There's never a villain dwelling in all Denmark
But he's an arrant° knave.   125

HORATIO: There needs no ghost, my lord, come from the grave
To tell us this.

HAMLET: Why, right, you are in the right.
And so, without more circumstance° at all,
I hold it fit that we shake hands and part,
You, as your business and desire shall point you—   130
For every man hath business and desire,
Such as it is—and for my own poor part,
Look you, I'll go pray.

HORATIO: These are but wild and whirling words, my lord.

HAMLET: I am sorry they offend you, heartily;   135
Yes, faith, heartily.

HORATIO: There's no offense, my lord.

HAMLET: Yes, by Saint Patrick,° but there is, Horatio,
And much offense too. Touching this vision here,
It is an honest° ghost, that let me tell you.
For your desire to know what is between us,   140
O'ermaster 't as you may. And now, good friends,
As you are friends, scholars, and soldiers,
Give me one poor request.

HORATIO: What is 't, my lord? We will.

HAMLET: Never make known what you have seen tonight.   145

HORATIO, MARCELLUS: My lord, we will not.

HAMLET: Nay, but swear 't.

HORATIO: In faith,
My lord, not I.

MARCELLUS: Nor I, my lord, in faith.

HAMLET: Upon my sword.°   *(Holds out his sword.)*

MARCELLUS: We have sworn, my lord, already.

HAMLET: Indeed, upon my sword, indeed.   (GHOST *cries under the stage.)*

GHOST: Swear.   150

HAMLET: Ha, ha, boy, say'st thou so? Art thou there, truepenny?°
Come on, you hear this fellow in the cellarage.
Consent to swear.

---

125 *arrant:* Thoroughgoing.   128 *circumstance:* Ceremony.   137 *Saint Patrick:* The keeper of purgatory and patron saint of all blunders and confusion.   139 *honest:* I.e., a real ghost and not an evil spirit.   148 *sword:* The hilt in the form of a cross.   151 *truepenny:* Honest old fellow.

HORATIO: Propose the oath, my lord.

HAMLET: Never to speak of this that you have seen,
Swear by my sword.   155

GHOST *(beneath)*: Swear.

HAMLET: Hic et ubique?° Then we'll shift our ground.

(He moves to another spot.)

Come hither, gentlemen,
And lay your hands again upon my sword.
Swear by my sword   160
Never to speak of this that you have heard.

GHOST *(beneath)*: Swear by his sword.

HAMLET: Well said, old mole! Canst work i' th' earth so fast?
A worthy pioner!° Once more remove, good friends.   *(Moves again.)*

HORATIO: O day and night, but this is wondrous strange!   165

HAMLET: And therefore as a stranger give it welcome.
There are more things in heaven and earth, Horatio,
Than are dreamt of in your philosophy.°
But come;
Here, as before, never, so help you mercy,   170
How strange or odd soe'er I bear myself—
As I perchance hereafter shall think meet
To put an antic° disposition on—
That you, at such times seeing me, never shall,
With arms encumb'red° thus, or this headshake,   175
Or by pronouncing of some doubtful phrase,
As "Well, well, we know," or "We could, an if° we would,"
Or "If we list° to speak," or "There be, an if they might,"
Or such ambiguous giving out,° to note°
That you know aught of me—this do swear,   180
So grace and mercy at your most need help you.

GHOST *(beneath)*: Swear.   *(They swear.)*

HAMLET: Rest, rest, perturbed spirit! So, gentlemen,
With all my love I do commend me to you;
And what so poor a man as Hamlet is   185
May do, t' express his love and friending to you,
God willing, shall not lack. Let us go in together,
And still° your fingers on your lips, I pray.
The time is out of joint. O cursed spite,
That ever I was born to set it right!   *(They wait for him to leave first.)* 190
Nay, come, let's go together.   *(Exeunt.)*

---

157 *Hic et ubique:* Here and everywhere (Latin). 164 *pioner:* Pioneer, digger, miner. 168 *your philosophy:* This subject called "natural philosophy" or "science" that people talk about. 173 *antic:* Fantastic. 175 *encumb'red:* Folded or entwined. 177 *an if:* If. 178 *list:* Were inclined. 179 *giving out:* Profession of knowledge; *note:* Give a sign, indicate. 188 *still:* Always.

ACT II
SCENE I°

(Enter old POLONIUS, *with his man [*REYNALDO*].)*

POLONIUS: Give him this money and these notes, Reynaldo.
REYNALDO: I will, my lord.
POLONIUS: You shall do marvel's° wisely, good Reynaldo,
    Before you visit him, to make inquire
    Of his behavior.
REYNALDO: My lord, I did intend it.   5
POLONIUS: Marry, well said, very well said. Look you, sir,
    Inquire me first what Danskers° are in Paris,
    And how, and who, what means,° and where they keep,°
    What company, at what expense; and finding
    By this encompassment° and drift° of question   10
    That they do know my son, come you more nearer
    Than your particular demands will touch it.°
    Take° you, as 'twere, some distant knowledge of him,
    As thus, "I know his father and his friends,
    And in part him." Do you mark this, Reynaldo?   15
REYNALDO: Ay, very well, my lord.
POLONIUS: "And in part him, but," you may say, "not well.
    But, if 't be he I mean, he's very wild,
    Addicted so and so," and there put on° him
    What forgeries° you please—marry, none so rank   20
    As may dishonor him take heed of that,
    But, sir, such wanton,° wild, and usual slips,
    As are companions noted and most known
    To youth and liberty.
REYNALDO: As gaming, my lord.
POLONIUS: Ay, or drinking, fencing, swearing,   25
    Quarreling, drabbing°—you may go so far.
REYNALDO: My lord, that would dishonor him.
POLONIUS: Faith, no, as you may season° it in the charge.
    You must not put another scandal on him
    That he is open to incontinency;°   30
    That's not my meaning. But breathe his faults so quaintly°
    That they may seem the taints of liberty,°

ACT II, SCENE I. *Location:* Polonius's chambers. 3 *marvel's:* Marvelous(ly). 7 *Danskers:* Danes.
8 *what means:* What wealth (they have); *keep:* Dwell. 10 *encompassment:* Roundabout talking;
drift: Gradual approach or course. 11–12 *come . . . it:* You will find out more this way than by
asking pointed questions (*particular demands*). 13 *Take:* Assume, pretend. 19 *put on:* Impute to.
20 *forgeries:* Invented tales. 22 *wanton:* Sportive, unrestrained. 26 *drabbing:* Whoring. 28 *season:*
Temper, soften. 30 *incontinency:* Habitual loose behavior. 31 *quaintly:* Delicately, ingeniously.
32 *taints of liberty:* Faults resulting from freedom.

    The flash and outbreak of a fiery mind,
    A savageness in unreclaimed° blood,
    Of general assault.°

REYNALDO: But, my good lord—   35

POLONIUS: Wherefore should you do this?

REYNALDO: Ay, my lord,
    I would know that.

POLONIUS: Marry, sir, here's my drift,
    And, I believe, it is a fetch of wit.°
    You laying these slight sullies on my son,
    As 'twere a thing a little soil'd i' th' working,°   40
    Mark you,
    Your party in converse,° him you would sound,°
    Having ever° seen in the prenominate crimes°
    The youth you breathe° of guilty, be assur'd
    He closes with you in this consequence:°   45
    "Good sir," or so, or "friend," or "gentleman,"
    According to the phrase or the addition°
    Of man and country.

REYNALDO: Very good, my lord.

POLONIUS: And then, sir, does 'a this—'a does—what was I about to say?
    By the mass, I was about to say something.   50
    Where did I leave?

REYNALDO: At "closes in the consequence."

POLONIUS: At "closes in the consequence," ay, marry.
    He closes thus: "I know the gentleman;
    I saw him yesterday, or th' other day,
    Or then, or then, with such, or such, and, as you say,   55
    There was 'a gaming, there o'ertook in 's rouse,°
    There falling out° at tennis," or perchance,
    "I saw him enter such a house of sale,"
    Videlicet,° a brothel, or so forth. See you now,
    Your bait of falsehood takes this carp° of truth;   60
    And thus do we of wisdom and of reach,°
    With windlasses° and with assays of bias,°
    By indirections find directions° out.

---

34 *unreclaimed:* Untamed. 35 *general assault:* Tendency that assails all unrestrained youth. 38 *fetch of wit:* Clever trick. 40 *soil'd i' th' working:* Shopworn. 42 *converse:* Conversation; *sound:* Sound out. 43 *Having ever:* If he has ever; *prenominate crimes:* Before-mentioned offenses. 44 *breathe:* Speak. 45 *closes . . . consequence:* Follows your lead in some fashion as follows. 47 *addition:* Title. 56 *o'ertook in 's rouse:* Overcome by drink. 57 *falling out:* Quarreling. 59 *Videlicet:* Namely. 60 *carp:* A fish. 61 *reach:* Capacity, ability. 62 *windlasses:* Circuitous paths (literally, circuits made to head off the game in hunting); *assays of bias:* Attempts through indirection (like the curving path of the bowling ball which is biased or weighted to one side). 63 *directions:* The way things really are.

So by my former lecture and advice
Shall you my son. You have me, have you not?   65
REYNALDO: My lord, I have.
POLONIUS: God buy ye; fare ye well.
REYNALDO: Good my lord.
POLONIUS: Observe his inclination in yourself.°
REYNALDO: I shall, my lord.
POLONIUS: And let him ply° his music.
REYNALDO: Well, my lord.   70
POLONIUS: Farewell.   *(Exit* REYNALDO.*)*

(Enter OPHELIA.*)*

                    How now, Ophelia, what's the matter?
OPHELIA: O, my lord, my lord, I have been so affrighted!
POLONIUS: With what, i' th' name of God?
OPHELIA: My lord, as I was sewing in my closet,°
    Lord Hamlet, with his doublet° all unbrac'd,°   75
    No hat upon his head, his stockings fouled,
    Ungart'red, and down-gyved to his ankle,°
    Pale as his shirt, his knees knocking each other,
    And with a look so piteous in purport
    As if he had been loosed out of hell   80
    To speak of horrors—he comes before me.
POLONIUS: Mad for thy love?
OPHELIA: My lord, I do not know,
    But truly I do fear it.
POLONIUS: What said he?
OPHELIA: He took me by the wrist and held me hard.
    Then goes he to the length of all his arm,   85
    And, with his other hand thus o'er his brow,
    He falls to such perusal of my face
    As 'a would draw it. Long stay'd he so.
    At last, a little shaking of mine arm
    And thrice his head thus waving up and down,   90
    He rais'd a sigh so piteous and profound
    As it did seem to shatter all his bulk°
    And end his being. That done, he lets me go,
    And, with his head over his shoulder turn'd,
    He seem'd to find his way without his eyes,   95
    For out o' doors he went without their helps,
    And, to the last, bended their light on me.

---

68 *in yourself:* In your own person (as well as by asking questions). 70 *let him ply:* See that he
continues to study. 74 *closet:* Private chamber. 75 *doublet:* Close-fitting jacket; *unbrac'd:* Unfastened. 77 *down-gyved to his ankle:* Fallen to the ankles (like gyves or fetters). 92 *bulk:* Body.

POLONIUS: Come, go with me. I will go seek the King.
  This is the very ecstasy° of love,
  Whose violent property° fordoes° itself   100
  And leads the will to desperate undertakings
  As oft as any passion under heaven
  That does afflict our natures. I am sorry.
  What, have you given him any hard words of late?
OPHELIA: No, my good lord, but, as you did command,   105
  I did repel his letters and denied
  His access to me.
POLONIUS: That hath made him mad.
  I am sorry that with better heed and judgment
  I had not quoted° him. I fear'd he did but trifle
  And meant to wrack thee; but, beshrew my jealousy!°   110
  By heaven, it is as proper to our age°
  To cast beyond° ourselves in our opinions
  As it is common for the younger sort
  To lack discretion. Come, go we to the King.
  This must be known, which, being kept close,° might move   115
  More grief to hide than hate to utter love.°
  Come.   *(Exeunt.)*

SCENE II°

(Flourish. Enter KING *and* QUEEN, ROSENCRANTZ, *and*
GUILDENSTERN *[with others].)*

KING: Welcome, dear Rosencrantz and Guildenstern.
  Moreover that° we much did long to see you,
  The need we have to use you did provoke
  Our hasty sending. Something have you heard
  Of Hamlet's transformation—so call it,   5
  Sith° nor th' exterior nor° the inward man
  Resembles that° it was. What it should be,
  More than his father's death, that thus hath put him
  So much from th' understanding of himself,
  I cannot dream of. I entreat you both   10
  That, being of so young days° brought up with him,

---

99 *ecstasy:* Madness. 100 *property:* Nature; *fordoes:* Destroys. 109 *quoted:* Observed. 110 *beshrew my jealousy:* A plague upon my suspicious nature. 111 *proper . . . age:* Characteristic of us (old) men. 112 *cast beyond:* Overshoot, miscalculate. 115 *close:* Secret; 115–16 *might . . . love:* Might cause more grief (to others) by hiding the knowledge of Hamlet's strange behavior to Ophelia than hatred by telling it. ACT II, SCENE II. *Location:* The castle. 2 *Moreover that:* Besides the fact that. 6 *Sith:* Since; *nor . . . nor:* Neither . . . nor. 7 *that:* What. 11 *of . . . days:* From such early youth.

And sith so neighbor'd to his youth and havior,
That you vouchsafe your rest° here in our court
Some little time, so by your companies
To draw him on to pleasures, and to gather   15
So much as from occasion you may glean,
Whether aught to us unknown afflicts him thus,
That, open'd,° lies within our remedy.
QUEEN: Good gentlemen, he hath much talk'd of you,
And sure I am two men there is not living   20
To whom he more adheres. If it will please you
To show us so much gentry° and good will
As to expend your time with us awhile
For the supply and profit° of our hope,
Your visitation shall receive such thanks   25
As fits a king's remembrance.
ROSENCRANTZ: Both your Majesties
Might, by the sovereign power you have of us,
Put your dread pleasures more into command
Than to entreaty.
GUILDENSTERN: But we both obey,
And here give up ourselves in the full bent°   30
To lay our service freely at your feet,
To be commanded.
KING: Thanks, Rosencrantz and gentle Guildenstern.
QUEEN: Thanks, Guildenstern and gentle Rosencrantz.
And I beseech you instantly to visit   35
My too much changed son. Go, some of you,
And bring these gentlemen where Hamlet is.
GUILDENSTERN: Heavens make our presence and our practices
Pleasant and helpful to him!
QUEEN: Ay, amen!
                    (*Exeunt* ROSENCRANTZ *and* GUILDENSTERN
                                with some ATTENDANTS.)

(*Enter* POLONIUS.)

POLONIUS: Th' ambassadors from Norway, my good lord,   40
Are joyfully return'd.
KING: Thou still° hast been the father of good news.
POLONIUS: Have I, my lord? I assure my good liege
I hold my duty, as I hold my soul,
Both to my God and to my gracious king;   45

---

13 *vouchsafe your rest:* Please to stay. 18 *open'd:* Revealed. 22 *gentry:* Courtesy. 24 *supply and profit:* Aid and successful outcome. 30 *in . . . bent:* To the utmost degree of our capacity. 42 *still:* Always.

And I do think, or else this brain of mine
Hunts not the trail of policy so sure
As it hath us'd to do, that I have found
The very cause of Hamlet's lunacy.
KING: O, speak of that! That do I long to hear.   50
POLONIUS: Give first admittance to th' ambassadors.
My news shall be the fruit° to that great feast.
KING: Thyself do grace to them, and bring them in.   *(Exit* POLONIUS.*)*
He tells me, my dear Gertrude, he hath found
The head and source of all your son's distemper.   55
QUEEN: I doubt° it is no other but the main,°
His father's death, and our o'erhasty marriage.

(Enter AMBASSADORS *[*VOLTIMAND *and* CORNELIUS, *with*
POLONIUS*].)*

KING: Well, we shall sift him.—Welcome, my good friends!
Say, Voltimand, what from our brother Norway?
VOLTIMAND: Most fair return of greetings and desires.   60
Upon our first,° he sent out to suppress
His nephew's levies, which to him appear'd
To be a preparation 'gainst the Polack,
But, better look'd into, he truly found
It was against your Highness. Whereat griev'd   65
That so his sickness, age, and impotence
Was falsely borne in hand,° sends out arrests
On Fortinbras, which he, in brief, obeys,
Receives rebuke from Norway, and in fine°
Makes vow before his uncle never more   70
To give th' assay° of arms against your Majesty.
Whereon old Norway, overcome with joy,
Gives him three score thousand crowns in annual fee,
And his commission to employ those soldiers,
So levied as before, against the Polack,   75
With an entreaty, herein further shown,   *(Giving a paper.)*
That it might please you to give quiet pass
Through your dominions for this enterprise,
On such regards of safety and allowance°
As therein are set down.
KING: It likes° us well;   80

---

52 *fruit:* Dessert. 56 *doubt:* Fear, suspect; *main:* Chief point, principal concern. 61 *Upon our first:*
At our first words on the business. 67 *borne in hand:* Deluded, taken advantage of. 69 *in fine:* In
the end. 71 *assay:* Trial. 79 *On . . . allowance:* With such pledges of safety and provisos. 80
likes: Pleases.

And at our more consider'd° time we'll read,
Answer, and think upon this business.
Meantime we thank you for your well-took labor.
Go to your rest; at night we'll feast together.
Most welcome home!   *(Exeunt* AMBASSADORS.*)*
POLONIUS: This business is well ended.   85
My liege, and madam, to expostulate°
What majesty should be, what duty is,
Why day is day, night night, and time is time,
Were nothing but to waste night, day, and time.
Therefore, since brevity is the soul of wit,°   90
And tediousness the limbs and outward flourishes,
I will be brief. Your noble son is mad.
Mad call I it, for, to define true madness,
What is 't but to be nothing else but mad?
But let that go.
QUEEN: More matter, with less art.   95
POLONIUS: Madam, I swear I use no art at all.
That he is mad, 'tis true; 'tis true 'tis pity,
And pity 'tis 'tis true—a foolish figure,°
But farewell it, for I will use no art.
Mad let us grant him, then, and now remains   100
That we find out the cause of this effect,
Or rather say, the cause of this defect,
For this effect defective comes by cause.°
Thus it remains, and the remainder thus.
Perpend.°   105
I have a daughter—have while she is mine—
Who, in her duty and obedience, mark,
Hath given me this. Now gather, and surmise.
(Reads the letter.) "To the celestial and my soul's idol,
the most beautified Ophelia"—   110
That's an ill phrase, a vile phrase; "beautified" is a vile
phrase. But you shall hear. Thus: *(Reads.)*
"In her excellent white bosom, these, etc."
QUEEN: Came this from Hamlet to her?
POLONIUS: Good madam, stay awhile; I will be faithful.   *(Reads.)* 115
"Doubt° thou the stars are fire,
    Doubt that the sun doth move,
Doubt truth to be a liar,
    But never doubt I love.

---

81 *consider'd:* Suitable for deliberation. 86 *expostulate:* Expound. 90 *wit:* Sound sense or judgment. 98 *figure:* Figure of speech. 103 *For . . . cause:* I.e., for this defective behavior, this
madness has a cause. 105 *Perpend:* Consider. 116 *Doubt:* Suspect, question.

O dear Ophelia, I am ill at these numbers.° I have   120
not art to reckon° my groans. But that I love thee
best, O most best, believe it. Adieu.
   Thine evermore, most dear lady, whilst this
    machine° is to him, Hamlet."
This in obedience hath my daughter shown me,   125
And, more above,° hath his solicitings,
As they fell out° by time, by means, and place,
All given to mine ear.
KING: But how hath she
 Receiv'd his love?
POLONIUS: What do you think of me?
KING: As of a man faithful and honorable.   130
POLONIUS: I would fain prove so. But what might you think,
 When I had seen this hot love on the wing—
 As I perceiv'd it, I must tell you that,
 Before my daughter told me—what might you,
 Or my dear Majesty your Queen here, think,   135
 If I had play'd the desk or table-book,°
 Or given my heart a winking,° mute and dumb,
 Or look'd upon this love with idle sight?°
 What might you think? No, I went round° to work,
 And my young mistress thus I did bespeak:°   140
 "Lord Hamlet is a prince, out of thy star;°
 This must not be." And then I prescripts gave her,
 That she should lock herself from his resort,
 Admit no messengers, receive no tokens.
 Which done, she took the fruits of my advice;   145
 And he, repelled—a short tale to make—
 Fell into a sadness, then into a fast,
 Thence to a watch,° thence into a weakness,
 Thence to a lightness,° and, by this declension,°
 Into the madness wherein now he raves,   150
 And all we mourn for.
KING: Do you think this?
QUEEN: It may be, very like.
POLONIUS: Hath there been such a time—I would fain know that—
 That I have positively said "'Tis so,"

120 *ill . . . numbers:* Unskilled at writing verses. 121 *reckon:* (1) Count, (2) number metrically, scan. 124 *machine:* Body. 126 *more above:* Moreover. 127 *fell out:* Occurred. 136 *play'd . . . table-book:* Remained shut up, concealing the information. 137 *winking:* Closing of the eyes. 138 *with idle sight:* Complacently or uncomprehendingly. 139 *round:* Roundly, plainly. 140 *bespeak:* Address. 141 *out of thy star:* Above your sphere, position. 148 *watch:* State of sleeplessness. 149 *lightness:* Light-headedness; *declension:* Decline, deterioration.

When it prov'd otherwise?

KING: Not that I know.   155

POLONIUS *(pointing to his head and shoulder):* Take this from this, if this be
  otherwise.
  If circumstances lead me, I will find
  Where truth is hid, though it were hid indeed
  Within the center.°

KING: How may we try it further?

POLONIUS: You know, sometimes he walks four hours together   160
  Here in the lobby.

QUEEN: So he does indeed.

POLONIUS: At such a time I'll loose my daughter to him.
  Be you and I behind an arras° then.
  Mark the encounter. If he love her not
  And be not from his reason fall'n thereon,°   165
  Let me be no assistant for a state,
  But keep a farm and carters.

KING: We will try it.

(Enter HAMLET *reading on a book.)*

QUEEN: But look where sadly the poor wretch comes reading.

POLONIUS: Away, I do beseech you both, away.
  I'll board° him presently.
        (Exeunt KING *and* QUEEN *with* ATTENDANTS.*)*
         O, give me leave.   170
  How does my good Lord Hamlet?

HAMLET: Well, God-a-mercy.°

POLONIUS: Do you know me, my lord?

HAMLET: Excellent well. You are a fishmonger.°

POLONIUS: Not I, my lord.   175

HAMLET: Then I would you were so honest a man.

POLONIUS: Honest, my lord?

HAMLET: Ay, sir. To be honest, as this world goes, is to be one man pick'd
  out of ten thousand.

POLONIUS: That's very true, my lord.   180

HAMLET: For if the sun breed maggots in a dead dog, being a good kissing
  carrion°—Have you a daughter?

POLONIUS: I have, my lord.

---

159 *center:* Middle point of the earth (which is also the center of the Ptolemaic universe).   163
arras: Hanging, tapestry.   165 *thereon:* On that account.   170 *board:* Accost.   172 *God-a-mercy:*
Thank you.   174 *fishmonger:* Fish merchant (with connotation of "bawd," "procurer"[?]).   180–82
good kissing carrion: A good piece of flesh for kissing, or for the sun to kiss.

HAMLET: Let her not walk i' th' sun.° Conception° is a blessing, but as
your daughter may conceive, friend, look to 't.   185
POLONIUS *(aside)*: How say you by that? Still harping on my daughter.
Yet he knew me not at first; 'a said I was a fishmonger. 'A is far gone.
And truly in my youth I suff'red much extremity for love, very near
this. I'll speak to him again.—What do you read, my lord?
HAMLET: Words, words, words.   190
POLONIUS: What is the matter,° my lord?
HAMLET: Between who?
POLONIUS: I mean, the matter that you read, my lord.
HAMLET: Slanders, sir; for the satirical rogue says here that old men have
gray beards, that their faces are wrinkled, their eyes purging° thick   195
amber and plum-tree gum, and that they have a plentiful lack of wit,
together with most weak hams. All which, sir, though I most power-
fully and potently believe, yet I hold it not honesty° to have it thus set
down, for you yourself, sir, shall grow old as I am, if like a crab you
could go backward.   200
POLONIUS *(aside)*: Though this be madness, yet there is method in 't.—
Will you walk out of the air, my lord?
HAMLET: Into my grave.
POLONIUS: Indeed, that's out of the air. *(Aside.)* How pregnant° sometimes his replies are! A happiness° that often madness hits on, which   205
reason and sanity could not so prosperously° be deliver'd of. I will leave
him, and suddenly contrive the means of meeting between him and
my daughter.—My honorable lord, I will most humbly take my leave
of you.
HAMLET: You cannot, sir, take from me any thing that I will more will-   210
ingly part withal—except my life, except my life, except my life.

(Enter GUILDENSTERN *and* ROSENCRANTZ.*)*

POLONIUS: Fare you well, my lord.
HAMLET: These tedious old fools!°
POLONIUS: You go to seek the Lord Hamlet; there he is.
ROSENCRANTZ *(to* POLONIUS*)*: God save you, sir! *(Exit* POLONIUS.*)*   215
GUILDENSTERN: My honor'd lord!
ROSENCRANTZ: My most dear lord!
HAMLET: My excellent good friends! How dost thou, Guildenstern? Ah,
Rosencrantz! Good lads, how do you both?
ROSENCRANTZ: As the indifferent° children of the earth.   220

---

184 *i' th' sun:* With additional implication of the sunshine of princely favors; *Conception:* (1)
Understanding, (2) pregnancy. 191 *matter:* Substance (but Hamlet plays on the sense of "basis
for a dispute"). 195 *purging:* Discharging. 198 *honesty:* Decency. 204 *pregnant:* Full of meaning.
205 *happiness:* Felicity of expression. 206 *prosperously:* Successfully. 213 *old fools:* I.e., old men
like Polonius. 220 *indifferent:* Ordinary.

GUILDENSTERN: Happy in that we are not over-happy. On Fortune's cap
    we are not the very button.

HAMLET: Nor the soles of her shoe?

ROSENCRANTZ: Neither, my lord.

HAMLET: Then you live about her waist, or in the middle of her favors?   225

GUILDENSTERN: Faith, her privates° we.

HAMLET: In the secret parts of Fortune? O, most true; she is a strumpet.°
    What news?

ROSENCRANTZ: None, my lord, but the world's grown honest.

HAMLET: Then is doomsday near. But your news is not true. Let me   230
    question more in particular. What have you, my good friends, deserv'd
    at the hands of Fortune that she sends you to prison hither?

GUILDENSTERN: Prison, my lord?

HAMLET: Denmark's a prison.

ROSENCRANTZ: Then is the world one.   235

HAMLET: A goodly one, in which there are many confines,° wards,° and
    dungeons, Denmark being one o' th' worst.

ROSENCRANTZ: We think not so, my lord.

HAMLET: Why then 'tis none to you, for there is nothing either good or
    bad but thinking makes it so. To me it is a prison.   240

ROSENCRANTZ: Why then, your ambition makes it one. 'Tis too narrow
    for your mind.

HAMLET: O God, I could be bounded in a nutshell and count myself a
    king of infinite space, were it not that I have bad dreams.

GUILDENSTERN: Which dreams indeed are ambition, for the very sub-   245
    stance of the ambitious° is merely the shadow of a dream.

HAMLET: A dream itself is but a shadow.

ROSENCRANTZ: Truly, and I hold ambition of so airy and light a quality
    that it is but a shadow's shadow.

HAMLET: Then are our beggars bodies,° and our monarchs and out-   250
    stretch'd° heroes the beggars' shadows. Shall we to th' court? For, by
    my fay,° I cannot reason.

ROSENCRANTZ, GUILDENSTERN: We'll wait upon° you.

HAMLET: No such matter. I will not sort° you with the rest of my
    servants, for, to speak to you like an honest man, I am most dreadfully   255
    attended.° But, in the beaten way° of friendship, what make° you at
    Elsinore?

---

226 *privates:* Close acquaintances (with sexual pun on "private parts"). 227 *strumpet:* Prostitute
(a common epithet for indiscriminate Fortune). 236 *confines:* Places of confinement; *wards:* Cells.
245–46 *the very . . . ambitious:* That seemingly very substantial thing which the ambitious pursue.
250 *bodies:* Solid substances rather than shadows (since beggars are not ambitious). 250–51
outstretch'd: (1) Far-reaching in their ambition, (2) elongated as shadows. 252 *fay:* Faith. 253 *wait*
upon: Accompany, attend. 254 *sort:* Class, associate. 255–56 *dreadfully attended:* Waited upon in
slovenly fashion. 256 *beaten way:* Familiar path; *make:* Do.

ROSENCRANTZ: To visit you, my lord, no other occasion.

HAMLET: Beggar that I am, I am even poor in thanks; but I thank you, and sure, dear friends, my thanks are too dear a halfpenny.° Were you 260 not sent for? Is it your own inclining? Is it a free visitation? Come, come, deal justly with me. Come, come; nay, speak.

GUILDENSTERN: What should we say, my lord?

HAMLET: Why, anything, but to th' purpose. You were sent for; and there is a kind of confession in your looks which your modesties have not 265 craft enough to color. I know the good King and Queen have sent for you.

ROSENCRANTZ: To what end, my lord?

HAMLET: That you must teach me. But let me conjure° you, by the rights of our fellowship, by the consonancy of our youth,° by the obligation 270 of our ever-preserv'd love, and by what more dear a better proposer° could charge° you withal, be even° and direct with me, whether you were sent for, or no?

ROSENCRANTZ (aside to GUILDENSTERN): What say you?

HAMLET (aside): Nay then, I have an eye of° you.— If you love me, hold 275 not off.

GUILDENSTERN: My lord, we were sent for.

HAMLET: I will tell you why; so shall my anticipation prevent your discovery,° and your secrecy to the King and Queen molt no feather.° I have of late—but wherefore I know not—lost all my mirth, for- 280 gone all custom of exercises; and indeed it goes so heavily with my disposition that this goodly frame, the earth, seems to me a sterile promontory; this most excellent canopy, the air, look you, this brave° o'erhanging firmament, this majestical roof fretted° with golden fire, why, it appeareth nothing to me but a foul and pestilent 285 congregation of vapors. What a piece of work is a man! How noble in reason, how infinite in faculties, in form and moving how ex- press° and admirable, in action how like an angel, in apprehension how like a god! The beauty of the world, the paragon of animals! And yet, to me, what is this quintessence° of dust? Man delights not 290 me—no, nor woman neither, though by your smiling you seem to say so.

260 *dear a halfpenny:* Expensive at the price of a halfpenny, i.e., of little worth. 269 *conjure:* Adjure, entreat. 270 *consonancy of our youth:* The fact that we are of the same age. 271 *better proposer:* More skillful propounder. 272 *charge:* Urge; *even:* Straight, honest. 275 *of:* On. 278– 79 *prevent your discovery:* Forestall your disclosure. 279 *molt no feather:* Not diminish in the least. 284 *brave:* Splendid; *fretted:* Adorned (with fretwork, as in a vaulted ceiling). 287–88 *express:* Well-framed (?), exact (?). 290 *quintessence:* The fifth essence of ancient philosophy, beyond earth, water, air, and fire, supposed to be the substance of the heavenly bodies and to be latent in all things.

ROSENCRANTZ: My lord, there was no such stuff in my thoughts.

HAMLET: Why did you laugh then, when I said "man delights not me"?

ROSENCRANTZ: To think, my lord, if you delight not in man, what 295
lenten entertainment° the players shall receive from you. We coted°
them on the way, and hither are they coming, to offer you service.

HAMLET: He that plays the king shall be welcome; his Majesty shall have
tribute of me. The adventurous knight shall use his foil and target,° the
lover shall not sigh gratis, the humorous man° shall end his part in 300
peace, the clown shall make those laugh whose lungs are tickle o' th'
sere,° and the lady shall say her mind freely, or the blank verse shall
halt° for 't. What players are they?

ROSENCRANTZ: Even those you were wont to take such delight in, the
tragedians of the city. 305

HAMLET: How chances it they travel? Their residence,° both in reputation
and profit, was better both ways.

ROSENCRANTZ: I think their inhibition° comes by the means of the
innovation.°

HAMLET: Do they hold the same estimation they did when I was in the 310
city? Are they so follow'd?

ROSENCRANTZ: No, indeed, are they not.

HAMLET: How comes it? Do they grow rusty?

ROSENCRANTZ: Nay, their endeavor keeps in the wonted° pace. But
there is, sir, an aery° of children, little eyases,° that cry out on the top 315
of question,° and are most tyrannically° clapp'd for 't. These are now
the fashion, and so berattle° the common stages°—so they call them—
that many wearing rapiers° are afraid of goose-quills° and dare scarce
come thither.

HAMLET: What, are they children? Who maintains 'em? How are they 320
escoted?° Will they pursue the quality° no longer than they can sing?°
Will they not say afterwards, if they should grow themselves to com-
mon° players—as it is most like, if their means are no better—their

---

296 *lenten entertainment:* Meager reception (appropriate to Lent); *coted:* Overtook and passed
beyond. 299 *foil and target:* Sword and shield. 300 *humorous man:* Eccentric character, dominated
by one trait or "humor." 301–2 *tickle o' th' sere:* Easy on the trigger, ready to laugh easily. (*Sere*
is part of a gunlock.) 303 *halt:* Limp. 306 *residence:* Remaining in one place, i.e., in the city.
308 *inhibition:* Formal prohibition (from acting plays in the city). 309 *innovation:* I.e., the new
fashion in satirical plays performed by boy actors in the "private" theaters; or possibly a political
uprising; or the strict limitations set on the theater in London in 1600. 314 *wonted:* Usual. 315
aery: Nest; *eyases:* Young hawks. 315–16 *cry . . . question:* Speak shrilly, dominating the controversy (in decrying the public theaters). 316 *tyrannically:* Outrageous. 317 *berattle:* Berate; *common
stages:* Public theaters. 318 *many wearing rapiers:* Many men of fashion, who were afraid to
patronize the common players for fear of being satirized by the poets who wrote for the children;
goose-quills: pens of satirists. 321 *escoted:* maintained; *quality:* (Acting) profession; *no longer . . .
sing:* Only until their voices change. 322–23 *common:* Regular, adult.

writers do them wrong, to make them exclaim against their own
succession?°   325

ROSENCRANTZ: Faith, there has been much to do° on both sides; and
the nation holds it no sin to tarre° them to controversy. There was, for
a while, no money bid for argument° unless the poet and the player
went to cuffs in the question.°

HAMLET: Is 't possible?   330

GUILDENSTERN: O, there has been much throwing about of brains.

HAMLET: Do the boys carry it away?°

ROSENCRANTZ: Ay, that they do, my lord—Hercules and his load° too.

HAMLET: It is not very strange; for my uncle is King of Denmark, and
those that would make mouths° at him while my father liv'd, give   335
twenty, forty, fifty, a hundred ducats° apiece for his picture in little.°
'Sblood,° there is something in this more than natural, if philosophy
could find it out.   (A flourish of trumpets within.)

GUILDENSTERN: There are the players.

HAMLET: Gentlemen, you are welcome to Elsinore. Your hands, come   340
then. Th' appurtenance of welcome is fashion and ceremony. Let me
comply° with you in this garb,° lest my extent° to the players, which,
I tell you, must show fairly outwards,° should more appear like enter-
tainment° than yours. You are welcome. But my uncle-father and aunt-
mother are deceiv'd.   345

GUILDENSTERN: In what, my dear lord?

HAMLET: I am but mad north-north-west.° When the wind is southerly I
know a hawk from a handsaw.°

(Enter POLONIUS.)

POLONIUS: Well be with you, gentlemen!

HAMLET: Hark you, Guildenstern, and you too; at each ear a hearer. That   350
great baby you see there is not yet out of his swaddling-clouts.°

ROSENCRANTZ: Happily° he is the second time come to them; for they
say an old man is twice a child.

HAMLET: I will prophesy he comes to tell me of the players; mark it.—
You say right, sir, o' Monday morning, 'twas then indeed.   355

---

325 *succession:* Future careers. 326 *to do:* Ado. 327 *tarre:* Set on (as dogs). 328 *argument:* Plot
for a play. 329 *went . . . question:* Came to blows in the play itself. 332 *carry it away:* Win the
day. 333 *Hercules . . . load:* Thought to be an allusion to the sign of the Globe Theatre, which
was Hercules bearing the world on his shoulder. 335 *mouths:* Faces. 336 *ducats:* Gold coins;
in little: In miniature. 337 *'Sblood:* By His (God's, Christ's) blood. 342 *comply:* Observe the
formalities of courtesy; *garb:* Manner; *my extent:* The extent of my showing courtesy. 343 *show
fairly outwards:* Look cordial to outward appearances. 343–44 *entertainment:* A (warm) reception. 347 *north-north-west:* Only partly, at times. 348 *hawk, handsaw:* Mattock (or "hack") and
a carpenter's cutting tool respectively; also birds, with a play on "hernshaw" or heron. 351
swaddling-clouts: Cloths in which to wrap a newborn baby. 352 *Happily:* Haply, perhaps.

POLONIUS: My lord, I have news to tell you.

HAMLET: My lord, I have news to tell you. When Roscius° was an actor
   in Rome—

POLONIUS: The actors are come hither, my lord.

HAMLET: Buzz,° buzz!   360

POLONIUS: Upon my honor—

HAMLET: Then came each actor on his ass—

POLONIUS: The best actors in the world, either for tragedy, comedy, history, pastoral, pastoral-comical, historical-pastoral, tragical-historical,
   tragical-comical-historical-pastoral, scene individable,° or poem un-   365
   limited.° Seneca° cannot be too heavy, nor Plautus° too light. For the
   law of writ and the liberty,° these are the only men.

HAMLET: O Jephthah, judge of Israel,° what a treasure hadst thou!

POLONIUS: What a treasure had he, my lord?

HAMLET: Why,   370
   "One fair daughter, and no more,
      The which he loved passing° well."

POLONIUS *(aside)*: Still on my daughter.

HAMLET: Am I not i' th' right, old Jephthah?

POLONIUS: If you call me Jephthah, my lord, I have a daughter that I love   375
   passing well.

HAMLET: Nay, that follows not.

POLONIUS: What follows, then, my lord?

HAMLET: Why,
   "As by lot, God wot,"°   380
   and then, you know,
   "It came to pass, as most like° it was."
   The first row° of the pious chanson° will show you more, for look
   where my abridgement° comes.

(Enter the PLAYERS.*)*

You are welcome, masters; welcome, all. I am glad to see thee well.   385
Welcome, good friends. O, old friend! Why, thy face is valanc'd° since
I saw thee last. Com'st thou to beard° me in Denmark? What, my
young lady° and mistress? By 'r lady, your ladyship is nearer to heaven

---

357 *Roscius:* A famous Roman actor who died in 62 B.C. 360 *Buzz:* An interjection used to
denote stale news. 365 *scene individable:* A play observing the unity of place. 365–66 *poem
unlimited:* A play disregarding the unities of time and place. 366 *Seneca:* Writer of Latin tragedies;
Plautus: Writer of Latin comedy. 367 *law . . . liberty:* Dramatic composition both according to
rules and without rules, i.e., "classical" and "romantic" dramas. 368 *Jephthah . . . Israel:* Jephthah
had to sacrifice his daughter; see Judges 11. Hamlet goes on to quote from a ballad on the theme.
372 *passing:* Surpassingly. 380 *wot:* Knows. 382 *like:* Likely, probable. 383 *row:* Stanza; *chanson:*
Ballad, song. 384 *my abridgement:* Something that cuts short my conversation; also, a diversion.
386 *valanc'd:* Fringed (with a beard). 387 *beard:* Confront (with obvious pun). 388 *young lady:*
Boy playing women's parts.

than when I saw you last, by the altitude of a chopine.° Pray God your
voice, like a piece of uncurrent° gold, be not crack'd within the ring.°   390
Masters, you are all welcome. We'll e'en to 't like French falconers, fly
at anything we see. We'll have a speech straight.° Come, give us a taste
of your quality; come, a passionate speech.

FIRST PLAYER: What speech, my good lord?

HAMLET: I heard thee speak me a speech once, but it was never acted, or,   395
    if it was, not above once, for the play, I remember, pleas'd not the
    million; 'twas caviary to the general.° But it was—as I receiv'd it, and
    others, whose judgments in such matters cried in the top of° mine—
    an excellent play, well digested in the scenes, set down with as much
    modesty as cunning.° I remember one said there were no sallets° in the   400
    lines to make the matter savory, nor no matter in the phrase that might
    indict° the author of affectation, but call'd it an honest method, as
    wholesome as sweet, and by very much more handsome than fine.°
    One speech in 't I chiefly lov'd: 'twas Aeneas' tale to Dido, and there-
    about of it especially when he speaks of Priam's slaughter.° If it live in   405
    your memory, begin at this line: let me see, let me see—
    "The rugged Pyrrhus,° like th' Hyrcanian beast"°—
    'Tis not so. It begins with Pyrrhus:
    "The rugged Pyrrhus, he whose sable° arms,
    Black as his purpose, did the night resemble   410
    When he lay couched in the ominous horse,°
    Hath now this dread and black complexion smear'd
    With heraldry more dismal.° Head to foot
    Now is he total gules,° horridly trick'd°
    With blood of fathers, mothers, daughters, sons,   415
    Bak'd and impasted° with the parching streets,°
    That lend a tyrannous and a damned light
    To their lord's° murder. Roasted in wrath and fire,
    And thus o'er-sized° with coagulate gore,
    With eyes like carbuncles, the hellish Pyrrhus   420

---

389 *chopine:* Thick-soled shoe of Italian fashion. 390 *uncurrent:* Not passable as lawful coinage.
390 *crack'd . . . ring:* Changed from adolescent to male voice, no longer suitable for women's
roles. (Coins featured rings enclosing the sovereign's head; if the coin was cracked within this
ring, it was unfit for currency.) 392 *straight:* At once. 397 *caviary to the general:* Caviar to the
multitude, i.e., a choice dish too elegant for coarse tastes. 398 *cried in the top of:* Spoke with
greater authority than. 400 *cunning:* Skill; *sallets:* Salad, i.e., spicy improprieties. 402 *indict:*
Convict. 403 *fine:* Elaborately ornamented, showy. 405 *Priam's slaughter:* The slaying of the
ruler of Troy, when the Greeks finally took the city. 407 *Pyrrhus:* A Greek hero in the Trojan
War, also known as Neoptolemus, son of Achilles; *Hyrcanian beast:* I.e., the tiger. 409 *sable:* Black
(for reasons of camouflage during the episode of the Trojan horse). 411 *ominous horse:* Trojan
horse, by which the Greeks gained access to Troy. 413 *dismal:* Ill-omened. 414 *gules:* Red (a
heraldic term); *trick'd:* Adorned, decorated. 416 *impasted:* Crusted, like a thick paste; *with . . .
streets:* By the parching heat of the streets (because of the fires everywhere). 418 *their lord's:*
Priam's. 419 *o'er-sized:* Covered as with size or glue.

Old grandsire Priam seeks."
So proceed you.
POLONIUS: 'Fore God, my lord, well spoken, with good accent and good
discretion.
FIRST PLAYER: "Anon he finds him
Striking too short at Greeks. His antique sword,   425
Rebellious to his arm, lies where it falls,
Repugnant° to command. Unequal match'd,
Pyrrhus at Priam drives, in rage strikes wide,
But with the whiff and wind of his fell° sword
Th' unnerved father falls. Then senseless Ilium,°   430
Seeming to feel this blow, with flaming top
Stoops to his° base, and with a hideous crash
Takes prisoner Pyrrhus' ear. For, lo! His sword,
Which was declining on the milky head
Of reverend Priam, seem'd i' th' air to stick.   435
So as a painted° tyrant Pyrrhus stood,
And, like a neutral to his will and matter,°
Did nothing.
But, as we often see, against° some storm,
A silence in the heavens, the rack° stand still,   440
The bold winds speechless, and the orb below
As hush as death, anon the dreadful thunder
Doth rend the region,° so, after Pyrrhus' pause,
Aroused vengeance sets him new a-work,
And never did the Cyclops'° hammers fall   445
On Mars's armor forg'd for proof eterne°
With less remorse than Pyrrhus' bleeding sword
Now falls on Priam.
Out, out, thou strumpet Fortune! All you gods,
In general synod,° take away her power!   450
Break all the spokes and fellies° from her wheel,
And bowl the round nave° down the hill of heaven,
As low as to the fiends!"
POLONIUS: This is too long.
HAMLET: It shall to the barber's with your beard.—Prithee say on. He's   455
for a jig° or a tale of bawdry, or he sleeps. Say on; come to Hecuba.°

---

427 *Repugnant:* Disobedient, resistant.   429 *fell:* Cruel.   430 *senseless Ilium:* Insensate Troy.   432
his: Its.   436 *painted:* Painted in a picture.   437 *like . . . matter:* As though poised indecisively
between his intention and its fulfillment.   439 *against:* Just before.   440 *rack:* Mass of clouds.   443
region: Sky.   445 *Cyclops:* Giant armor makers in the smithy of Vulcan.   446 *proof eterne:* Eternal
resistance to assault.   450 *synod:* Assembly.   451 *fellies:* Pieces of wood forming the rim of a
wheel.   452 *nave:* Hub.   456 *jig:* Comic song and dance often given at the end of a play; *Hecuba:*
Wife of Priam.

FIRST PLAYER: "But who, ah woe! had seen the mobled° queen"—
HAMLET: "The mobled queen?"
POLONIUS: That's good. "Mobled queen" is good.
FIRST PLAYER: "Run barefoot up and down, threat'ning the flames   460
    With bisson rheum,° a clout° upon that head
    Where late the diadem stood, and for a robe,
    About her lank and all o'er-teemed° loins,
    A blanket, in the alarm of fear caught up—
    Who this had seen, with tongue in venom steep'd,   465
    'Gainst Fortune's state° would treason have pronounc'd.°
    But if the gods themselves did see her then
    When she saw Pyrrhus make malicious sport
    In mincing with his sword her husband's limbs,
    The instant burst of clamor that she made,   470
    Unless things mortal move them not at all,
    Would have made milch° the burning eyes of heaven,
    And passion in the gods."
POLONIUS: Look whe'er° he has not turn'd his color and has tears in 's
    eyes. Prithee, no more.   475
HAMLET: 'Tis well; I'll have thee speak out the rest of this soon. Good my lord,
    will you see the players well bestow'd?° Do you hear, let them be well us'd,
    for they are the abstract° and brief chronicles of the time. After your death
    you were better have a bad epitaph than their ill report while you live.
POLONIUS: My lord, I will use them according to their desert.   480
HAMLET: God's bodkin,° man, much better! Use every man after his de-
    sert, and who shall scape whipping? Use them after your own honor
    and dignity. The less they deserve, the more merit is in your bounty.
    Take them in.
POLONIUS: Come, sirs.   485
HAMLET: Follow him, friends. We'll hear a play tomorrow. *(As they start to*
    leave, HAMLET *detains the* FIRST PLAYER.*)* Dost thou hear me, old
    friend? Can you play the Murder of Gonzago?
FIRST PLAYER: Ay, my lord.
HAMLET: We'll ha 't tomorrow night. You could, for need, study a speech   490
    of some dozen or sixteen lines, which I would set down and insert in
    't, could you not?
FIRST PLAYER: Ay, my lord.
HAMLET: Very well. Follow that lord, and look you mock him not.—My
    good friends, I'll leave you till night. You are welcome to Elsinore.   495
                                 (Exeunt POLONIUS *and* PLAYERS.*)*

---

457 *mobled:* Muffled.   461 *bisson rheum:* Blinding tears; *clout:* Cloth.   463 *o'er-teemed:* Worn out
with bearing children.   466 *state:* Rule, managing; *pronounc'd:* Proclaimed.   472 *milch:* Milky,
moist with tears.   474 *whe'er:* Whether.   477 *bestow'd:* Lodged.   478 *abstract:* Summary account.
481 *God's bodkin:* By God's (Christ's) little body, "bodykin" (not to be confused with "bodkin,"
dagger).

ROSENCRANTZ: Good my lord!
            (Exeunt ROSENCRANTZ *and* GUILDENSTERN.*)*
HAMLET: Ay, so, God buy you.—Now I am alone.
    O, what a rogue and peasant slave am I!
    Is it not monstrous that this player here,
    But in a fiction, in a dream of passion,   500
    Could force his soul so to his own conceit°
    That from her working all his visage wann'd,°
    Tears in his eyes, distraction in his aspect,
    A broken voice, and his whole function suiting
    With forms to his conceit?° And all for nothing!   505
    For Hecuba!
    What's Hecuba to him, or he to Hecuba,
    That he should weep for her? What would he do,
    Had he the motive and the cue for passion
    That I have? He would drown the stage with tears   510
    And cleave the general ear with horrid speech,
    Make mad the guilty and appall the free,°
    Confound the ignorant, and amaze indeed
    The very faculties of eyes and ears. Yet I,
    A dull and muddy-mettled° rascal, peak,°   515
    Like John-a-dreams,° unpregnant of° my cause,
    And can say nothing—no, not for a king
    Upon whose property° and most dear life
    A damn'd defeat was made. Am I a coward?
    Who calls me villain? Breaks my pate across?   520
    Plucks off my beard, and blows it in my face?
    Tweaks me by the nose? Gives me the lie° i' th' throat,
    As deep as to the lungs? Who does me this?
    Ha, 'swounds, I should take it; for it cannot be
    But I am pigeon-liver'd,° and lack gall   525
    To make oppression bitter, or ere this
    I should have fatted all the region kites°
    With this slave's offal. Bloody, bawdy villain!
    Remorseless, treacherous, lecherous, kindless° villain!
    O, vengeance!   530
    Why, what an ass am I! This is most brave,
    That I, the son of a dear father murder'd,

---

501 *conceit:* Conception. 502 *wann'd:* Grew pale. 504–5 *his whole . . . conceit:* His whole being responded with actions to suit his thought. 512 *free:* Innocent. 515 *muddy-mettled:* Dull-spirited; *peak:* Mope, pine. 516 *John-a-dreams:* Sleepy dreaming idler; *unpregnant of:* Not quickened by. 518 *property:* The crown; perhaps also character, quality. 522 *Gives me the lie:* Calls me a liar. 525 *pigeon-liver'd:* The pigeon or dove was popularly supposed to be mild because it secreted no gall. 527 *region kites:* Kites (birds of prey) of the air, from the vicinity. 529 *kindless:* Unnatural.

Prompted to my revenge by heaven and hell,
Must, like a whore, unpack my heart with words,
And fall a-cursing, like a very drab,°   535
A stallion!° Fie upon 't, foh! About,° my brains!
Hum, I have heard
That guilty creatures sitting at a play
Have by the very cunning of the scene
Been struck so to the soul that presently°   540
They have proclaim'd their malefactions;
For murder, though it have no tongue, will speak
With most miraculous organ. I'll have these players
Play something like the murder of my father
Before mine uncle. I'll observe his looks;   545
I'll tent° him to the quick. If 'a do blench,°
I know my course. The spirit that I have seen
May be the devil, and the devil hath power
T' assume a pleasing shape; yea, and perhaps
Out of my weakness and my melancholy,   550
As he is very potent with such spirits,°
Abuses° me to damn me. I'll have grounds
More relative° than this. The play's the thing
Wherein I'll catch the conscience of the King.   (Exit.)

ACT III
SCENE I°

(Enter KING, QUEEN, POLONIUS, OPHELIA,
ROSENCRANTZ, GUILDENSTERN, LORDS.)

KING: And can you, by no drift of conference,°
    Get from him why he puts on this confusion,
    Grating so harshly all his days of quiet
    With turbulent and dangerous lunacy?
ROSENCRANTZ: He does confess he feels himself distracted,   5
    But from what cause 'a will by no means speak.
GUILDENSTERN: Nor do we find him forward° to be sounded,°
    But with a crafty madness keeps aloof
    When we would bring him on to some confession
    Of his true state.
QUEEN: Did he receive you well?   10

---

535 *drab:* Prostitute. 536 *stallion:* Prostitute (male or female); *About:* About it, to work. 540
presently: At once. 546 *tent:* Probe; *blench:* Quail, flinch. 551 *spirits:* Humors (of melancholy).
552 *Abuses:* Deludes. 553 *relative:* Closed related, pertinent. ACT III, SCENE I. *Location:* The
castle. 1 *drift of conference:* Direction of conversation. 7 *forward:* Willing; *sounded:* Tested deeply.

ROSENCRANTZ: Most like a gentleman.
GUILDENSTERN: But with much forcing of his disposition.°
ROSENCRANTZ: Niggard of question,° but of our demands
    Most free in his reply.
QUEEN: Did you assay° him
    To any pastime?   15
ROSENCRANTZ: Madam, it so fell out that certain players
    We o'er-raught° on the way. Of these we told him,
    And there did seem in him a kind of joy
    To hear of it. They are here about the court,
    And, as I think, they have already order   20
    This night to play before him.
POLONIUS: 'Tis most true,
    And he beseech'd me to entreat your Majesties
    To hear and see the matter.
KING: With all my heart, and it doth much content me
    To hear him so inclin'd.   25
    Good gentlemen, give him a further edge,°
    And drive his purpose into these delights.
ROSENCRANTZ: We shall, my lord.
               (Exeunt ROSENCRANTZ *and* GUILDENSTERN.*)*
KING: Sweet Gertrude, leave us too,
    For we have closely° sent for Hamlet hither,
    That he, as 'twere by accident, may here   30
    Affront° Ophelia.
    Her father and myself, lawful espials,°
    Will so bestow ourselves that seeing, unseen,
    We may of their encounter frankly judge,
    And gather by him, as he is behav'd,   35
    If 't be th' affliction of his love or no
    That thus he suffers for.
QUEEN: I shall obey you.
    And for your part, Ophelia, I do wish
    That your good beauties be the happy cause
    Of Hamlet's wildness. So shall I hope your virtues   40
    Will bring him to his wonted way again,
    To both your honors.
OPHELIA: Madam, I wish it may.   *(Exit* QUEEN.*)*
POLONIUS: Ophelia, walk you here.—Gracious,° so please you,
    We will bestow ourselves. *(To* OPHELIA.*)* Read on this book,
                             (Gives her a book.)

---

12 *disposition:* Inclination. 13 *question:* Conversation. 14 *assay:* Try to win. 17 *o'er-raught:*
Overtook and passed. 26 *edge:* Incitement. 29 *closely:* Privately. 31 *Affront:* Confront, meet. 32
espials: Spies. 43 *Gracious:* Your Grace (i.e., the King).

That show of such an exercise° may color°   45
Your loneliness. We are oft to blame in this—
'Tis too much prov'd°—that with devotion's visage
And pious action we do sugar o'er
The devil himself.
KING *(aside)*: O, 'tis too true!   50
How smart a lash that speech doth give my conscience!
The harlot's cheek, beautied with plast'ring art,
Is not more ugly to° the thing° that helps it
Than is my deed to my most painted word.
O heavy burden!   55
POLONIUS: I hear him coming. Let's withdraw, my lord.

(KING and POLONIUS withdraw.°)

(Enter HAMLET. OPHELIA pretends to read a book.)

HAMLET: To be, or not to be, that is the question:
Whether 'tis nobler in the mind to suffer
The slings and arrows of outrageous fortune,
Or to take arms against a sea of troubles,   60
And by opposing end them. To die, to sleep—
No more—and by a sleep to say we end
The heart-ache and the thousand natural shocks
That flesh is heir to. 'Tis a consummation
Devoutly to be wish'd. To die, to sleep;   65
To sleep, perchance to dream. Ay, there's the rub,°
For in that sleep of death what dreams may come
When we have shuffled° off this mortal coil,°
Must give us pause. There's the respect°
That makes calamity of so long life.°   70
For who would bear the whips and scorns of time,
Th' oppressor's wrong, the proud man's contumely,°
The pangs of despis'd° love, the law's delay,
The insolence of office,° and the spurns°
That patient merit of th' unworthy takes,   75
When he himself might his quietus° make
With a bare bodkin?° Who would fardels° bear,
To grunt and sweat under a weary life,
But that the dread of something after death,

45 *exercise:* Act of devotion. (The book she reads is one of devotion.); *color:* Give a plausible appearance to. 47 *too much prov'd:* Too often shown to be true, too often practiced. 53 *to:* Compared to; *thing:* I.e., the cosmetic. 56 s.d. *withdraw:* The King and Polonius may retire behind an arras. The stage directions specify that they "enter" again near the end of the scene. 66 *rub:* Literally, an obstacle in the game of bowls. 68 *shuffled:* Sloughed, cast; *coil:* Turmoil. 69 *respect:* Consideration. 70 *of . . . life:* So long-lived. 72 *contumely:* Insolent abuse. 73 *despis'd:* Rejected. 74 *office:* Officialdom; *spurns:* Insults. 76 *quietus:* Acquittance; here, death. 77 *bodkin:* Dagger; *fardels:* Burdens.

The undiscover'd country from whose bourn°   80
No traveler returns, puzzles the will,
And makes us rather bear those ills we have
Than fly to others that we know not of?
Thus conscience does make cowards of us all
And thus the native hue° of resolution   85
Is sicklied o'er with the pale cast° of thought,
And enterprises of great pitch° and moment°
With this regard° their currents° turn awry,
And lose the name of action.—Soft you now,
The fair Ophelia. Nymph, in thy orisons°   90
Be all my sins rememb'red.
OPHELIA: Good my lord,
    How does your honor for this many a day?
HAMLET: I humbly thank you; well, well, well.
OPHELIA: My lord, I have remembrances of yours,
    That I have longed long to re-deliver.   95
    I pray you, now receive them.   *(Offers tokens.)*
HAMLET: No, not I, I never gave you aught.
OPHELIA: My honor'd lord, you know right well you did,
    And with them words of so sweet breath compos'd
    As made these things more rich. Their perfume lost,   100
    Take these again, for to the noble mind
    Rich gifts wax poor when givers prove unkind.
    There, my lord.   *(Gives tokens.)*
HAMLET: Ha, ha! Are you honest?°
OPHELIA: My lord?   105
HAMLET: Are you fair?°
OPHELIA: What means your lordship?
HAMLET: That if you be honest and fair, your honesty° should admit no
    discourse° to your beauty.
OPHELIA: Could beauty, my lord, have better commerce° than with   110
    honesty?
HAMLET: Ay, truly; for the power of beauty will sooner transform honesty
    from what it is to a bawd than the force of honesty can translate beauty
    into his likeness. This was sometime° a paradox,° but now the time°
    gives it proof. I did love you once.   115
OPHELIA: Indeed, my lord, you made me believe so.

---

80 *bourn:* Boundary. 85 *native hue:* Natural color, complexion. 86 *cast:* Shade of color. 87 *pitch:* Height (as of a falcon's flight); *moment:* Importance. 88 *regard:* Respect, consideration; *currents:* Courses. 90 *orisons:* Prayers. 104 *honest:* (1) Truthful, (2) chaste. 106 *fair:* (1) Beautiful, (2) just, honorable. 108 *your honesty:* Your chastity. 109 *discourse:* Familiar dealings. 110 *commerce:* Dealings. 114 *sometime:* Formerly; *paradox:* A view opposite to commonly held opinion; *the time:* The present age.

HAMLET: You should not have believ'd me, for virtue cannot so inoculate°
our old stock but we shall relish of it.° I lov'd you not.

OPHELIA: I was the more deceiv'd.

HAMLET: Get thee to a nunn'ry.° Why wouldst thou be a breeder of sin- 120
ners? I am myself indifferent honest;° but yet I could accuse me of such
things that it were better my mother had not borne me: I am very
proud, revengeful, ambitious, with more offenses at my beck° than I
have thoughts to put them in, imagination to give them shape, or time
to act them in. What should such fellows as I do crawling between 125
earth and heaven? We are arrant knaves, all; believe none of us. Go thy
ways to a nunn'ry. Where's your father?

OPHELIA: At home, my lord.

HAMLET: Let the doors be shut upon him, that he may play the fool
nowhere but in 's own house. Farewell. 130

OPHELIA: O, help him, you sweet heavens!

HAMLET: If thou dost marry, I'll give thee this plague for thy dowry: be
thou as chaste as ice, as pure as snow, thou shalt not escape calumny.
Get thee to a nunn'ry, farewell. Or, if thou wilt needs marry, marry a
fool, for wise men know well enough what monsters° you° make of 135
them. To a nunn'ry, go, and quickly too. Farewell.

OPHELIA: Heavenly powers, restore him!

HAMLET: I have heard of your paintings too, well enough. God hath given
you one face, and you make yourselves another. You jig,° and amble,
and you lisp, you nickname God's creatures, and make your wantonness 140
your ignorance.° Go to, I'll no more on 't; it hath made me mad. I say,
we will have no moe marriage. Those that are married already—all but
one—shall live. The rest shall keep as they are. To a nunn'ry, go.

(Exit.)

OPHELIA: O, what a noble mind is here o'erthrown!
The courtier's, soldier's, scholar's, eye, tongue, sword, 145
Th' expectancy and rose of the fair state,°
The glass of fashion and the mold of form,°
Th' observ'd of all observers,° quite, quite down!
And I, of ladies most deject and wretched,
That suck'd the honey of his music vows, 150
Now see that noble and most sovereign reason,
Like sweet bells jangled, out of time and harsh,

---

117 *inoculate:* Graft, be engrafted to. 118 *but . . . it:* That we do not still have about us a taste of
the old stock; i.e., retain our sinfulness. 120 *nunn'ry:* (1) Convent, (2) brothel. 121 *indifferent
honest:* Reasonably virtuous. 123 *beck:* Command. 135 *monsters:* An allusion to the horns of a
cuckold; *you:* You women. 139 *jig:* Dance and sing affectedly and wantonly. 140–41 *make . . .
ignorance:* Excuse your affection on the grounds of your ignorance. 146 *Th' expectancy . . . state:*
The hope and ornament of the kingdom made fair (by him). 147 *The glass . . . form:* The mirror
of fashion and the pattern of courtly behavior. 148 *observ'd . . . observers:* The center of attention
and honor in the court.

That unmatch'd form and feature of blown° youth
Blasted with ecstasy.° O, woe is me,
T' have seen what I have seen, see what I see!   155

(Enter KING *and* POLONIUS.*)*

KING: Love? His affections do not that way tend;
Nor what he spake, though it lack'd form a little,
Was not like madness. There's something in his soul,
O'er which his melancholy sits on brood,
And I do doubt° the hatch and the disclose°   160
Will be some danger; which for to prevent,
I have in quick determination
Thus set it down: he shall with speed to England,
For the demand of° our neglected tribute.
Haply the seas and countries different   165
With variable° objects shall expel
This something-settled° matter in his heart,
Whereon his brains still beating puts him thus
From fashion of himself.° What think you on 't?
POLONIUS: It shall do well. But yet do I believe   170
The origin and commencement of his grief
Sprung from neglected love.—How now, Ophelia?
You need not tell us what Lord Hamlet said;
We heard it all.—My lord, do as you please,
But, if you hold it fit, after the play   175
Let his queen mother all alone entreat him
To show his grief. Let her be round° with him;
And I'll be plac'd, so please you, in the ear
Of all their conference. If she find him not,
To England send him, or confine him where   180
Your wisdom best shall think.
KING: It shall be so.
Madness in great ones must not unwatch'd go.   *(Exeunt.)*

SCENE II°

(Enter HAMLET *and three of the* PLAYERS.*)*

HAMLET: Speak the speech, I pray you, as I pronounc'd it to you, trip-
pingly on the tongue. But if you mouth it, as many of our players° do,
I had as lief the town-crier spoke my lines. Nor do not saw the air too

---

153 *blown:* Booming. 154 *ecstasy:* Madness. 160 *doubt:* Fear; *disclose:* Disclosure. 164 *For . . .
of:* To demand. 166 *variable:* Various. 167 *something-settled:* Somewhat settled. 169 *From . . .
himself:* Out of his natural manner. 177 *round:* Blunt. ACT III, SCENE II. *Location:* The castle.
2 *our players:* Indefinite use; i.e., "players nowadays."

much with your hand, thus, but use all gently; for in the very torrent, tempest, and, as I may say, whirlwind of your passion, you must acquire 5
and beget a temperance that may give it smoothness. O, it offends me to the soul to hear a robustious° periwig-pated° fellow tear a passion to tatters, to very rags, to split the ears of the groundlings,° who for the most part are capable of° nothing but inexplicable dumb-shows and noise. I would have such a fellow whipp'd for o'er-doing Termagant.° 10
It out-herods Herod.° Pray you, avoid it.

FIRST PLAYER: I warrant your honor.

HAMLET: Be not too tame neither, but let your own discretion be your tutor. Suit the action to the word, the word to the action, with this special observance, that you o'erstep not the modesty of nature. For 15
anything so o'erdone is from° the purpose of playing, whose end, both at the first and now, was and is, to hold, as 't were, the mirror up to nature, to show virtue her feature, scorn her own image, and the very age and body of the time his° form and pressure.° Now this overdone, or come tardy off,° though it makes the unskillful laugh, cannot but 20
make the judicious grieve, the censure of which one° must in your allowance o'erweigh a whole theater of others. O, there be players that I have seen play, and heard others praise, and that highly, not to speak it profanely, that, neither having th' accent of Christians nor the gait of Christian, pagan, nor man, have so strutted and bellow'd that I have 25
thought some of nature's journeymen° had made men and not made them well, they imitated humanity so abominably.

FIRST PLAYER: I hope we have reform'd that indifferently° with us, sir.

HAMLET: O, reform it altogether. And let those that play your clowns speak no more than is set down for them; for there be of them° that 30
will themselves laugh, to set on some quantity of barren° spectators to laugh too, though in the mean time some necessary question of the play be then to be consider'd. That's villainous, and shows a most pitiful ambition in the fool that uses it. Go, make you ready.

(Exeunt PLAYERS.*)*

(Enter POLONIUS, GUILDENSTERN, *and* ROSENCRANTZ.*)*

How now, my lord? Will the King hear this piece of work? 35

---

7 *robustious:* Violent, boisterous; *periwig-pated:* Wearing a wig. 8 *groundlings:* Spectators who paid least and stood in the yard of the theater. 9 *capable of:* Susceptible to being influenced by. 10 *Termagant:* A god of the Saracens; a character in the St. Nicholas play, where one of his worshipers, leaving him in charge of goods, returns to find them stolen; whereupon he beats the god or idol, which howls vociferously. 11 *Herod:* Herod of Jewry. (A character in *The Slaughter of the Innocents* and other cycle plays. The part was played with great noise and fury.) 16 *from:* Contrary to. 19 *his:* Its; *pressure:* Stamp, impressed character. 20 *come tardy off:* Inadequately done. 21 *the censure . . . one:* The judgment of even one of whom. 26 *journeymen:* Laborers not yet masters in their trade. 28 *indifferently:* Tolerably. 30 *of them:* Some among them. 31 *barren:* I.e., of wit.

POLONIUS: And the Queen too, and that presently.°
HAMLET: Bid the players make haste.   *(Exit* POLONIUS.*)*
     Will you two help to hasten them?
ROSENCRANTZ: Ay, my lord.   *(Exeunt they two.)*
HAMLET: What ho, Horatio!

(Enter HORATIO.*)*

HORATIO: Here, sweet lord, at your service.   40
HAMLET: Horatio, thou art e'en as just a man
     As e'er my conversation cop'd withal.°
HORATIO: O, my dear lord—
HAMLET: Nay, do not think I flatter;
     For what advancement may I hope from thee
     That no revenue hast but thy good spirits,   45
     To feed and clothe thee? Why should the poor be flatter'd?
     No, let the candied° tongue lick absurd pomp,
     And crook the pregnant° hinges of the knee
     Where thrift° may follow fawning. Dost thou hear?
     Since my dear soul was mistress of her choice   50
     And could of men distinguish her election,
     Sh' hath seal'd thee for herself, for thou hast been
     As one, in suff'ring all, that suffers nothing,
     A man that Fortune's buffets and rewards
     Hast ta'en with equal thanks; and blest are those   55
     Whose blood° and judgment are so well commeddled°
     That they are not a pipe for Fortune's finger
     To sound what stop° she please. Give me that man
     That is not passion's slave, and I will wear him
     In my heart's core, ay, in my heart of heart,   60
     As I do thee.— Something too much of this.—
     There is a play tonight before the King.
     One scene of it comes near the circumstance
     Which I have told thee of my father's death.
     I prithee, when thou seest that act afoot,   65
     Even with the very comment of thy soul°
     Observe my uncle. If his occulted° guilt
     Do not itself unkennel in one speech,
     It is a damned° ghost that we have seen,
     And my imaginations are as foul   70
     As Vulcan's stithy.° Give him heedful note,

36 *presently:* At once. 42 *my . . . withal:* My contact with people provided opportunity for
encounter with. 47 *candied:* Sugared, flattering. 48 *pregnant:* Compliant. 49 *thrift:* Profit. 56
blood: Passion; *commeddled:* Commingled. 58 *stop:* Hole in a wind instrument for controlling the
sound. 66 *very . . . soul:* Inward and sagacious criticism. 67 *occulted:* Hidden. 69 *damned:* In
league with Satan. 71 *stithy:* Smithy, place of stiths (anvils).

For I mine eyes will rivet to his face,
And after we will both our judgments join
In censure of his seeming.°
HORATIO: Well, my lord.
If 'a steal aught the whilst this play is playing,   75
And scape detecting, I will pay the theft.

*(Flourish. Enter trumpets and kettledrums, KING, QUEEN,
POLONIUS, OPHELIA, ROSENCRANTZ, GUILDENSTERN,
and other LORDS, with GUARDS carrying torches.)*

HAMLET: They are coming to the play. I must be idle. Get you a place.
                                    (The KING, QUEEN, and COURTIERS sit.)
KING: How fares our cousin Hamlet?
HAMLET: Excellent, i' faith, of the chameleon's dish:° I eat the air, promise-
cramm'd. You cannot feed capons so.   80
KING: I have nothing with° this answer, Hamlet. These words are not
mine.°
HAMLET: No, nor mine now. *(To POLONIUS.)* My lord, you played once
i' th' university, you say?
POLONIUS: That did I, my lord; and was accounted a good actor.   85
HAMLET: What did you enact?
POLONIUS: I did enact Julius Caesar. I was killed i' th' Capitol; Brutus
kill'd me.
HAMLET: It was a brute part of him to kill so capital a calf there. Be the
players ready?   90
ROSENCRANTZ: Ay, my lord; they stay upon your patience.
QUEEN: Come hither, my dear Hamlet, sit by me.
HAMLET: No, good mother, here's metal more attractive.
POLONIUS *(to the KING)*: O, ho, do you mark that?
HAMLET: Lady, shall I lie in your lap?   *(Lying down at OPHELIA's feet.)* 95
OPHELIA: No, my lord.
HAMLET: I mean, my head upon your lap?
OPHELIA: Ay, my lord.
HAMLET: Do you think I meant country° matters?
OPHELIA: I think nothing, my lord.   100
HAMLET: That's a fair thought to lie between maids' legs.
OPHELIA: What is, my lord?
HAMLET: Nothing.
OPHELIA: You are merry, my lord.
HAMLET: Who, I?   105

---

74 *censure of his seeming:* Judgment of his appearance or behavior. 79 *chameleon's dish:* Chameleons
were supposed to feed on air. Hamlet deliberately misinterprets the King's "fares" as "feeds." By
his phrase *eat the air* he also plays on the idea of feeding himself with the promise of succession,
of being the "heir." 81 *have . . . with:* Make nothing of. 81–82 *are not mine:* Do not respond to
what I asked. 99 *country:* With a bawdy pun.

OPHELIA: Ay, my lord.

HAMLET: O God, your only jig-maker.° What should a man do but be merry? For look you how cheerfully my mother looks, and my father died within 's° two hours.

OPHELIA: Nay, 'tis twice two months, my lord. 110

HAMLET: So long? Nay then, let the devil wear black, for I'll have a suit of sables.° O heavens! Die two months ago, and not forgotten yet? Then there's hope a great man's memory may outlive his life half a year. But, by 'r lady, 'a must build churches, then, or else shall 'a suffer not thinking on,° with the hobby-horse, whose epitaph is "For, O, for, O, 115 the hobby-horse is forgot."°

(The trumpets sound. Dumb show follows.)

Enter a KING *and a* QUEEN *very lovingly; the* QUEEN *embracing him, and he her. She kneels and makes show of protestation unto him. He takes her up, and declines his head upon her neck. He lies him down upon a bank of flowers. She, seeing him asleep, leaves him. Anon comes in another man, takes off his crown, kisses it, pours poison in the sleeper's ears, and leaves him. The* QUEEN *returns; finds the* KING *dead, makes passionate action. The* POISONER, *with some three or four, come in again, seem to condole with her. The dead body is carried away. The* POISONER *woos the* QUEEN *with gifts; she seems harsh awhile but in the end accepts love.*

(Exeunt.)

OPHELIA: What means this, my lord?

HAMLET: Marry, this' miching mallecho;° it means mischief.

OPHELIA: Belike° this show imports the argument° of the play.

(Enter PROLOGUE*.)*

HAMLET: We shall know by this fellow. The players cannot keep counsel;° 120 they'll tell all.

OPHELIA: Will 'a tell us what this show meant?

HAMLET: Ay, or any show that you will show him. Be not you° asham'd to show, he'll not shame to tell you what it means.

OPHELIA: You are naught, you are naught.° I'll mark the play. 125

PROLOGUE: For us, and for our tragedy,
Here stooping° to your clemency,
We beg your hearing patiently.

(Exit.)

---

107 *only jig-maker:* Very best composer of jigs (song and dance). 109 *within 's:* Within this. 111–12 *suit of sables:* Garments trimmed with the fur of the sable and hence suited for a wealthy person, not a mourner (with a pun on *sable,* black). 114–15 *suffer . . . on:* Undergo oblivion. 115–16 *"For . . . forgot":* Verse of a song occurring also in *Love's Labor's Lost,* III.I.30. The hobby-horse was a character made up to resemble a horse, appearing in the Morris dance and such May-game sports. This song laments the disappearance of such customs under pressure from the Puritans. 118 *this' miching mallecho:* This is sneaking mischief. 119 *Belike:* Probably; *argument:* Plot. 120 *counsel:* Secret. 123 *Be not you:* If you are not. 125 *naught:* Indecent. 127 *stooping:* Bowing.

HAMLET: Is this a prologue, or the posy of a ring?°

OPHELIA: 'Tis brief, my lord.   130

HAMLET: As woman's love.

(Enter two PLAYERS *as* KING *and* QUEEN.)

PLAYER KING: Full thirty times hath Phoebus' cart° gone round
    Neptune's salt wash° and Tellus'° orbed ground,
    And thirty dozen moons with borrowed° sheen
    About the world have times twelve thirties been,   135
    Since love our hearts and Hymen° did our hands
    Unite commutual° in most sacred bands.

PLAYER QUEEN: So many journeys may the sun and moon
    Make us again count o'er ere love be done!
    But, woe is me, you are so sick of late,   140
    So far from cheer and from your former state.
    That I distrust you. Yet, though I distrust,°
    Discomfort you, my lord, it nothing° must.
    For women's fear and love hold quantity;°
    In neither aught, or in extremity.   145
    Now, what my love is, proof° hath made you know,
    And as my love is siz'd, my fear is so.
    Where love is great, the littlest doubts are fear;
    Where little fears grow great, great love grows there.

PLAYER KING: Faith, I must leave thee, love, and shortly too;   150
    My operant° powers their functions leave to do.°
    And thou shalt live in this fair world behind,
    Honor'd, belov'd; and haply one as kind
    For husband shalt thou—

PLAYER QUEEN: O, confound the rest!
    Such love must needs be treason in my breast.   155
    In second husband let me be accurst!
    None wed the second but who kill'd the first.

HAMLET: Wormwood, wormwood.

PLAYER QUEEN: The instances° that second marriage move°
    Are base respects of thrift,° but none of love.   160
    A second time I kill my husband dead,
    When second husband kisses me in bed.

PLAYER KING: I do believe you think what now you speak,

---

129 *posy . . . ring:* Brief motto in verse inscribed in a ring. 132 *Phoebus' cart:* The sun god's chariot. 133 *salt wash:* The sea; *Tellus:* Goddess of the earth, of the *orbed ground.* 134 *borrowed:* Reflected. 136 *Hymen:* God of matrimony. 137 *commutual:* Mutually. 142 *distrust:* Am anxious about. 143 *nothing:* Not at all. 144 *hold quantity:* Keep proportion with one another. 146 *proof:* Experience. 151 *operant:* Active; *leave to do:* Cease to perform. 159 *instances:* Motives; *move:* Motivate. 160 *base . . . thrift:* Ignoble considerations of material prosperity.

But what we do determine oft we break.
Purpose is but the slave to memory,°   165
Of violent birth, but poor validity,°
Which now, like fruit unripe, sticks on the tree,
But fall unshaken when they mellow be.
Most necessary 'tis that we forget
To pay ourselves what to ourselves is debt.°   170
What to ourselves in passion we propose,
The passion ending, doth the purpose lose.
The violence of either grief or joy
Their own enactures° with themselves destroy.
Where joy most revels, grief doth most lament;   175
Grief joys, joy grieves, on slender accident.
This world is not for aye,° nor 'tis not strange
That even our loves should with our fortunes change;
For 'tis a question left us yet to prove,
Whether love lead fortune, or else fortune love.   180
The great man down, you mark his favorite flies;
The poor advanc'd makes friends of enemies.
And hitherto doth love on fortune tend;
For who not needs° shall never lack a friend,
And who in want° a hollow friend doth try,°   185
Directly seasons him° his enemy.
But, orderly to end where I begun,
Our wills and fates do so contrary run
That our devices still° are overthrown;
Our thoughts are ours, their ends° none of our own.   190
So think thou wilt no second husband wed,
But die thy thoughts when thy first lord is dead.
PLAYER QUEEN: Nor earth to me give food, nor heaven light,
Sport and repose lock from me day and night,
To desperation turn my trust and hope,   195
An anchor's cheer° in prison be my scope!°
Each opposite° that blanks° the face of joy
Meet what I would have well and it destroy!
Both here and hence° pursue me lasting strife,
If, once a widow, ever I be wife!   200

---

165 *Purpose . . . memory:* Our good intentions are subject to forgetfulness. 166 *validity:* Strength, durability. 169–70 *Most . . . debt:* It's inevitable that in time we forget the obligations we have imposed on ourselves. 174 *enactures:* Fulfillments. 177 *aye:* Ever. 184 *who not needs:* He who is not in need (of wealth). 185 *who in want:* He who is in need; *try:* Test (his generosity). 186 *seasons him:* Ripens him into. 189 *devices still:* Intentions continually. 190 *ends:* Results. 196 *anchor's cheer:* Anchorite's or hermit's fare; *my scope:* The extent of my happiness. 197 *opposite:* Adverse thing; *blanks:* Causes to blanch or grow pale. 199 *hence:* In the life hereafter.

HAMLET: If she should break it now!

PLAYER KING: 'Tis deeply sworn. Sweet, leave me here awhile;
My spirits grow dull, and fain I would beguile
The tedious day with sleep.   *(Sleeps.)*

PLAYER QUEEN: Sleep rock thy brain,
And never come mischance between us twain!   *(Exit.)* 205

HAMLET: Madam, how like you this play?

QUEEN: The lady doth protest too much, methinks.

HAMLET: O, but she'll keep her word.

KING: Have you heard the argument?° Is there no offense in 't?

HAMLET: No, no, they do but jest, poison in jest; no offense i' th' world.   210

KING: What do you call the play?

HAMLET: "The Mousetrap." Marry, how? Tropically.° This play is the
image of a murder done in Vienna. Gonzago is the Duke's name; his
wife, Baptista. You shall see anon. 'Tis a knavish piece of work, but
what of that? Your Majesty, and we that have free° souls, it touches us   215
not. Let the gall'd jade° winch,° our withers° are unwrung.°

(Enter LUCIANUS.*)*

This is one Lucianus, nephew to the King.

OPHELIA: You are as good as a chorus,° my lord.

HAMLET: I could interpret between you and your love, if I could see the
puppets dallying.°   220

OPHELIA: You are keen, my lord, you are keen.

HAMLET: It would cost you a groaning to take off mine edge.

OPHELIA: Still better, and worse.°

HAMLET: So° you mistake° your husbands. Begin, murderer; leave thy damnable faces, and begin. Come, the croaking raven doth bellow for revenge.   225

LUCIANUS: Thoughts black, hands apt, drugs fit, and time agreeing,
Confederate season,° else no creature seeing,
Thou mixture rank, of midnight weeds collected,
With Hecate's ban° thrice blasted, thrice infected,
Thy natural magic and dire property   230
On wholesome life usurp immediately.

(Pours the poison into the sleeper's ears.)

---

209 *argument:* Plot. 212 *Tropically:* Figuratively. 215 *free:* Guiltless. 216 *gall'd jade:* Horse whose
hide is rubbed by saddle or harness; *winch:* Wince; *withers:* The part between the horse's shoulder
blades; *unwrung:* Not rubbed sore. 218 *chorus:* In many Elizabethan plays the forthcoming action
was explained by an actor known as the "chorus"; at a puppet show the actor who spoke the
dialogue was known as an "interpreter," as indicated by the lines following. 220 *dallying:* With
sexual suggestion, continued in *keen,* i.e., sexually aroused, *groaning,* i.e., moaning in pregnancy,
and *edge,* i.e., sexual desire or impetuosity. 223 *Still . . . worse:* More keen-witted and less deco-
rous. 224 *So:* even thus (in marriage); *mistake:* Mis-take, take erringly, falseheartedly. 227
Confederate season: The time and occasion conspiring (to assist the murderer). 229 *Hecate's ban:*
The curse of Hecate, the goddess of witchcraft.

HAMLET: 'A poisons him i' th' garden for his estate. His name's Gonzago. The story is extant, and written in very choice Italian. You shall see anon how the murderer gets the love of Gonzago's wife.

(CLAUDIUS rises.)

OPHELIA: The King rises.   235

HAMLET: What, frighted with false fire?°

QUEEN: How fares my lord?

POLONIUS: Give o'er the play.

KING: Give me some light. Away!

POLONIUS: Lights, lights, lights!   240

(Exeunt all but HAMLET and HORATIO.)

HAMLET: "Why, let the strucken deer go weep,
    The hart ungalled° play.
For some must watch,° while some must sleep;
    Thus runs the world away."°
Would not this,° sir, and a forest of feathers°—if the rest of my fortunes 245
turn Turk with° me—with two Provincial roses° on my raz'd° shoes,
get me a fellowship in a cry of players?°

HORATIO: Half a share.

HAMLET: A whole one, I.
    "For thou dost know, O Damon dear,   250
        This realm dismantled° was
    Of Jove himself, and now reigns here
        A very, very—pajock."°

HORATIO: You might have rhym'd.

HAMLET: O good Horatio, I'll take the ghost's word for a thousand pound. 255
Didst perceive?

HORATIO: Very well, my lord.

HAMLET: Upon the talk of pois'ning?

HORATIO: I did very well note him.

HAMLET: Ah, ha! Come, some music! Come, the recorders!°   260
    "For if the King like not the comedy,
    Why then, belike, he likes it not, perdy."°
Come, some music!

(Enter ROSENCRANTZ and GUILDENSTERN.)

236 *false fire:* The blank discharge of a gun loaded with powder but not shot.   242 *ungalled:* Unafflicted.   243 *watch:* Remain awake.   241–44 *Why . . . away:* Probably from an old ballad, with allusion to the popular belief that a wounded deer retires to weep and die.   245 *this:* The play; *feathers:* Allusion to the plumes which Elizabethan actors were fond of wearing.   246 *turn Turk with:* Turn renegade against, go back on; *Provincial roses:* Rosettes of ribbon like the roses of a part of France; *raz'd:* With ornamental slashing.   247 *fellowship . . . players:* Partnership in a theatrical company.   251 *dismantled:* Stripped, divested.   253 *pajock:* Peacock, a bird with a bad reputation (here substituted for the obvious rhyme-word *ass*).   260 *recorders:* Wind instruments like the flute.   262 *perdy:* A corruption of the French "par dieu," by God.

GUILDENSTERN: Good my lord, vouchsafe me a word with you.

HAMLET: Sir, a whole history. 265

GUILDENSTERN: The King, sir—

HAMLET: Ay, sir, what of him?

GUILDENSTERN: Is in his retirement marvelous distemp'red.

HAMLET: With drink, sir?

GUILDENSTERN: No, my lord, with choler.° 270

HAMLET: Your wisdom should show itself more richer to signify this to
the doctor, for for me to put him to his purgation would perhaps
plunge him into more choler.

GUILDENSTERN: Good my lord, put your discourse into some frame°
and start not so wildly from my affair. 275

HAMLET: I am tame, sir. Pronounce.

GUILDENSTERN: The Queen, your mother, in most great affliction of
spirit, hath sent me to you.

HAMLET: You are welcome.

GUILDENSTERN: Nay, good my lord, this courtesy is not of the right 280
breed. If it shall please you to make me a wholesome answer, I will do
your mother's commandment; if not, your pardon° and my return shall
be the end of my business.

HAMLET: Sir, I cannot.

ROSENCRANTZ: What, my lord? 285

HAMLET: Make you a wholesome answer; my wit's diseas'd. But, sir, such
answer as I can make, you shall command, or rather, as you say, my
mother. Therefore no more, but to the matter. My mother, you say—

ROSENCRANTZ: Then thus she says: your behavior hath struck her into
amazement and admiration.° 290

HAMLET: O wonderful son, that can so stonish a mother! But is there no
sequel at the heels of this mother's admiration? Impart.

ROSENCRANTZ: She desires to speak with you in her closet,° ere you go
to bed.

HAMLET: We shall obey, were she ten times our mother. Have you any 295
further trade with us?

ROSENCRANTZ: My lord, you once did love me.

HAMLET: And do still, by these pickers and stealers.°

ROSENCRANTZ: Good my lord, what is your cause of distemper? You
do surely bar the door upon your own liberty, if you deny your griefs 300
to your friend.

HAMLET: Sir, I lack advancement.

ROSENCRANTZ: How can that be, when you have the voice of the King
himself for your succession in Denmark?

---

270 *choler:* Anger. (But Hamlet takes the word in its more basic humors sense of "bilious disorder.")   274 *frame:* Order.   282 *pardon:* Permission to depart.   290 *admiration:* Wonder.   293 *closet:*
Private chamber.   298 *pickers and stealers:* Hands (so called from the catechism, "to keep my hands
from picking and stealing").

HAMLET: Ay, sir, but "While the grass grows"°—the proverb is something° 305
musty.

(Enter the PLAYERS *with recorders.)*

O, the recorders! Let me see one. *(He takes a recorder.)* To withdraw°
with you: why do you go about to recover the wind° of me, as if you
would drive me into a toil?°

GUILDENSTERN: O, my lord, if my duty be too bold, my love is too 310
unmannerly.°

HAMLET: I do not well understand that. Will you play upon this pipe?

GUILDENSTERN: My lord, I cannot.

HAMLET: I pray you.

GUILDENSTERN: Believe me, I cannot. 315

HAMLET: I do beseech you.

GUILDENSTERN: I know no touch of it, my lord.

HAMLET: It is as easy as lying. Govern these ventages° with your fingers
and thumb, give it breath with your mouth, and it will discourse most
eloquent music. Look you, these are the stops. 320

GUILDENSTERN: But these cannot I command to any utt'rance of harmony; I have not the skill.

HAMLET: Why, look you now, how unworthy a thing you make of me!
You would play upon me, you would seem to know my stops, you
would pluck out the heart of my mystery, you would sound me from 325
my lowest note to the top of my compass,° and there is much music,
excellent voice, in this little organ,° yet cannot you make it speak.
'Sblood, do you think I am easier to be play'd on than a pipe? Call me
what instrument you will, though you can fret° me, you cannot play
upon me. 330

(Enter POLONIUS.*)*

God bless you, sir!

POLONIUS: My lord, the Queen would speak with you, and presently.°

HAMLET: Do you see yonder cloud that's almost in shape of a camel?

POLONIUS: By th' mass, and 'tis like a camel, indeed.

HAMLET: Methinks it is like a weasel. 335

POLONIUS: It is back'd like a weasel.

HAMLET: Or like a whale?

POLONIUS: Very like a whale.

---

305 *While . . . grows:* The rest of the proverb is "the silly horse starves"; Hamlet may not live
long enough to succeed to the kingdom; *something:* Somewhat. 307 *withdraw:* Speak privately.
308 *recover the wind:* Get the windward side. 309 *toil:* Snare. 310–11 *if . . . unmannerly:* If I am
using an unmannerly boldness, it is my love which occasions it. 318 *ventages:* Stops of the
recorder. 326 *compass:* Range (of voice). 327 *organ:* Musical instrument. 329 *fret:* Irritate (with
a quibble on *fret* meaning the piece of wood, gut, or metal which regulates the fingering on an
instrument). 332 *presently:* At once.

HAMLET: Then I will come to my mother by and by.° *(Aside.)* They fool
    me° to the top of my bent.°—I will come by and by.   340
POLONIUS: I will say so.   *(Exit.)*
HAMLET: "By and by" is easily said. Leave me, friends.

                  (Exeunt all but HAMLET.*)*

    'Tis now the very witching time° of night,
    When churchyards yawn and hell itself breathes out
    Contagion to this world. Now could I drink hot blood,   345
    And do such bitter business as the day
    Would quake to look on. Soft, now to my mother.
    O heart, lose not thy nature! Let not ever
    The soul of Nero° enter this firm bosom.
    Let me be cruel, not unnatural;   350
    I will speak daggers to her, but use none.
    My tongue and soul in this be hypocrites:
    How in my words somever° she be shent,°
    To give them seals° never, my soul, consent!   *(Exit.)*

SCENE III°

(Enter KING, ROSENCRANTZ, *and* GUILDENSTERN.*)*

KING: I like him not, nor stands it safe with us
    To let his madness range. Therefore prepare you.
    I your commission will forthwith dispatch,°
    And he to England shall along with you.
    The terms° of our estate° may not endure   5
    Hazard so near 's as doth hourly grow
    Out of his brows.°
GUILDENSTERN: We will ourselves provide.
    Most holy and religious fear it is
    To keep those many many bodies safe
    That live and feed upon your Majesty.   10
ROSENCRANTZ: The single and peculiar° life is bound
    With all the strength and armor of the mind
    To keep itself from noyance,° but much more
    That spirit upon whose weal depends and rests
    The lives of many. The cess° of majesty   15

---

339 *by and by:* Immediately. 339–40 *fool me:* Make me play the fool. 340 *top of my bent:* Limit
of my ability or endurance (literally, the extent to which a bow may be bent). 343 *witching time:*
Time when spells are cast and evil is abroad. 349 *Nero:* Murderer of his mother, Agrippina. 353
How . . . somever: However much by my words; *shent:* Rebuked. 354 *give them seals:* Confirm
them with deeds. ACT III, SCENE III. *Location:* The castle. 3 *dispatch:* Prepare, cause to be
drawn up. 5 *terms:* Condition, circumstances; *our estate:* My royal position. 7 *brows:* Effronteries,
threatening frowns (?), brain (?). 11 *single and peculiar:* Individual and private. 13 *noyance:* Harm.
15 *cess:* Decease.

Dies not alone, but like a gulf° doth draw
What's near it with it; or it is a massy wheel
Fix'd on the summit of the highest mount,
To whose huge spokes ten thousand lesser things
Are mortis'd and adjoin'd, which, when it falls,   20
Each small annexment, petty consequence,
Attends° the boist'rous ruin. Never alone
Did the King sigh, but with a general groan.
KING: Arm° you, I pray you, to this speedy voyage,
For we will fetters put about this fear,   25
Which now goes too free-footed.
ROSENCRANTZ: We will haste us.

(Exeunt GENTLEMEN *[*ROSENCRANTZ *and* GUILDENSTERN*].)*

(Enter POLONIUS*.)*

POLONIUS: My lord, he's going to his mother's closet.
Behind the arras° I'll convey myself
To hear the process.° I'll warrant she'll tax him home,°
And, as you said, and wisely was it said,   30
'Tis meet that some more audience than a mother,
Since nature makes them partial, should o'erhear
The speech, of vantage.° Fare you well, my liege.
I'll call upon you ere you go to bed,
And tell you what I know.
KING: Thanks, dear my lord.   *(Exit* POLONIUS*.)* 35
O, my offense is rank, it smells to heaven;
It hath the primal eldest curse° upon 't,
A brother's murder. Pray can I not,
Though inclination be as sharp as will.°
My stronger guilt defeats my strong intent,   40
And, like a man to double business bound,
I stand in pause where I shall first begin,
And both neglect. What if this cursed hand
Were thicker than itself with brother's blood,
Is there not rain enough in the sweet heavens   45
To wash it white as snow? Whereto serves mercy
But to confront the visage of offense?°

---

16 *gulf:* Whirlpool. 22 *Attends:* Participates in. 24 *Arm:* Prepare. 28 *arras:* Screen of tapestry placed around the walls of household apartments. (On the Elizabethan stage, the arras was presumably over a door or discovery space in the tiring-house facade.) 29 *process:* Proceedings; *tax him home:* Reprove him severely. 33 *of vantage:* From an advantageous place. 37 *primal eldest curse:* The curse of Cain, the first murderer; he killed his brother, Abel. 39 *Though . . . will:* Though my desire is as strong as my determination. 46–47 *Whereto . . . offense:* For what function does mercy serve other than to undo the effects of sin?

And what's in prayer but this twofold force,
To be forestalled° ere we come to fall,
Or pardon'd being down? Then I'll look up;   50
My fault is past. But, O, what form of prayer
Can serve my turn? "Forgive me my foul murder"?
That cannot be, since I am still possess'd
Of those effects for which I did the murder,
My crown, mine own ambition, and my queen.   55
May one be pardon'd and retain th' offense?
In the corrupted currents° of this world
Offense's gilded hand° may shove by justice,
And oft 'tis seen the wicked prize° itself
Buys out the law. But 'tis not so above.   60
There is no shuffling,° there the action lies°
In his° true nature, and we ourselves compell'd,
Even to the teeth and forehead° of our faults,
To give in evidence. What then? What rests?°
Try what repentance can. What can it not?   65
Yet what can it, when one cannot repent?
O wretched state! O bosom black as death!
O limed° soul, that, struggling to be free,
Art more engag'd!° Help, angels! Make assay.°
Bow, stubborn knees, and heart with strings of steel,   70
Be soft as sinews of the new-born babe!
All may be well.   *(He kneels.)*

(Enter HAMLET *with sword drawn.)*

HAMLET: Now might I do it pat,° now 'a is a-praying;
And now I'll do 't. And so 'a goes to heaven;
And so am I reveng'd. That would be scann'd:°   75
A villain kills my father, and for that,
I, his sole son, do this same villain send
To heaven.
Why, this is hire and salary, not revenge.
'A took my father grossly,° full of bread,°   80
With all his crimes broad blown,° as flush° as May;
And how his audit° stands who knows save heaven?

---

49 *forestalled:* Prevented (from sinning). 57 *currents:* Courses. 58 *gilded hand:* Hand offering gold
as a bribe. 59 *wicked prize:* Prize won by wickedness. 61 *shuffling:* Escape by trickery; *the action
lies:* The accusation is made manifest, comes up for consideration (a legal metaphor). 62 *his:* Its.
63 *teeth and forehead:* Face to face, concealing nothing. 64 *rests:* Remains. 68 *limed:* Caught as
with birdlime, a sticky substance used to ensnare birds. 69 *engag'd:* Embedded; *assay:* Trial. 73
pat: Opportunely. 75 *would be scann'd:* Needs to be looked into. 80 *grossly:* Not spiritually
prepared; *full of bread:* Enjoying his worldly pleasures. (See Ezek. 16:49.) 81 *crimes broad blown:*
Sins in full bloom; *flush:* Lusty. 82 *audit:* Account.

But in our circumstance and course° of thought,
'Tis heavy with him. And am I then reveng'd,
To take him in the purging of his soul,   85
When he is fit and season'd for his passage?
No!
Up, sword, and know thou a more horrid hent.°   *(Puts up his sword.)*
When he is drunk asleep, or in his rage,
Or in th' incestuous pleasure of his bed,   90
At game a-swearing, or about some act
That has no relish of salvation in 't—
Then trip him, that his heels may kick at heaven,
And that his soul may be as damn'd and black
As hell, whereto it goes. My mother stays.   95
This physic° but prolongs thy sickly days.   *(Exit.)*
KING: My words fly up, my thoughts remain below.
Words without thoughts never to heaven go.   *(Exit.)*

SCENE IV°

(Enter QUEEN GERTRUDE *and* POLONIUS.*)*

POLONIUS: 'A will come straight. Look you lay° home to him.
Tell him his pranks have been too broad° to bear with,
And that your Grace hath screen'd and stood between
Much heat° and him. I'll sconce° me even here.
Pray you, be round° with him.   5
HAMLET *(within)*: Mother, mother, mother!
QUEEN: I'll warrant you, fear me not.
Withdraw, I hear him coming.   *(*POLONIUS *hides behind the arras.)*

(Enter HAMLET.*)*

HAMLET: Now, mother, what's the matter?
QUEEN: Hamlet, thou hast thy father° much offended.   10
HAMLET: Mother, you have my father much offended.
QUEEN: Come, come, you answer with an idle° tongue.
HAMLET: Go, go, you question with a wicked tongue.
QUEEN: Why, how now, Hamlet?
HAMLET: What's the matter now?
QUEEN: Have you forgot me?
HAMLET: No, by the rood,° not so: 15

---

83 *in . . . course:* As we see it in our mortal situation. 88 *know . . . hent:* Await to be grasped by
me on a more horrid occasion. 96 *physic:* Purging (by prayer). ACT III, SCENE IV. *Location:*
The Queen's private chamber. 1 *lay:* Thrust (i.e., reprove him soundly). 2 *broad:* Unrestrained.
4 *Much heat:* The King's anger; *sconce:* Ensconce, hide. 5 *round:* Blunt. 10 *thy father:* Your
stepfather, Claudius. 12 *idle:* Foolish. 15 *rood:* Cross.

You are the Queen, your husband's brother's wife,
And—would it were not so!—you are my mother.
QUEEN: Nay, then, I'll set those to you that can speak.
HAMLET: Come, come, and sit you down; you shall not budge.
You go not till I set you up a glass   20
Where you may see the inmost part of you.
QUEEN: What wilt thou do? Thou wilt not murder me?
Help, ho!
POLONIUS (behind): What, ho! Help!
HAMLET (drawing): How now? A rat? Dead, for a ducat, dead!   25
                            (Makes a pass through the arras.)
POLONIUS (behind): O, I am slain!   (Falls and dies.)
QUEEN: O me, what hast thou done?
HAMLET: Nay, I know not. Is it the King?
QUEEN: O, what a rash and bloody deed is this!
HAMLET: A bloody deed—almost as bad, good mother,
As kill a king, and marry with his brother.   30
QUEEN: As kill a king!
HAMLET: Ay, lady, it was my word.
                    (Parts the arras and discovers POLONIUS.)
Thou wretched, rash, intruding fool, farewell!
I took thee for thy better. Take thy fortune.
Thou find'st to be too busy is some danger.—
Leave wringing of your hands. Peace, sit you down,   35
And let me wring your heart, for so I shall,
If it be made of penetrable stuff,
If damned custom° have not braz'd° it so
That it be proof° and bulwark against sense.°
QUEEN: What have I done, that thou dar'st wag thy tongue   40
In noise so rude against me?
HAMLET: Such an art
That blurs the grace and blush of modesty,
Calls virtue hypocrite, takes off the rose
From the fair forehead of an innocent love
And sets a blister° there, makes marriage-vows   45
As false as dicers' oaths. O, such a deed
As from the body of contraction° plucks
The very soul, and sweet religion° makes
A rhapsody° of words. Heaven's face does glow
O'er this solidity and compound mass   50

---

38 *damned custom:* Habitual wickedness; *braz'd:* Brazened, hardened. 39 *proof:* Armor; *sense:*
Feeling. 45 *sets a blister:* Brands as a harlot. 47 *contraction:* The marriage contract. 48 *religion:*
Religious vows. 49 *rhapsody:* Senseless string.

With heated visage, as against the doom,
Is thought-sick at the act.
QUEEN: Ay me, what act,°
That roars so loud and thunders in the index?°
HAMLET: Look here, upon this picture, and on this,
The counterfeit presentment° of two brothers.   55

(Shows her two likenesses.)

See, what a grace was seated on this brow:
Hyperion's° curls, the front° of Jove himself,
An eye like Mars, to threaten and command,
A station° like the herald Mercury
New-lighted on a heaven-kissing hill—   60
A combination and a form indeed,
Where every god did seem to set his seal,
To give the world assurance of a man.
This was your husband. Look you now, what follows:
Here is your husband, like a mildew'd ear,°   65
Blasting his wholesome brother. Have you eyes?
Could you on this fair mountain leave to feed,
And batten° on this moor?° Ha, have you eyes?
You cannot call it love, for at your age
The heyday° in the blood is tame, it's humble,   70
And waits upon the judgment, and what judgment
Would step from this to this? Sense,° sure, you have,
Else could you not have motion, but sure that sense
Is apoplex'd,° for madness would not err,
Nor sense to ecstasy was ne'er so thrall'd   75
But it reserv'd some quantity of choice
To serve in such a difference. What devil was 't
That thus hath cozen'd° you at hoodman-blind?°
Eyes without feeling, feeling without sight,
Ears without hands or eyes, smelling sans° all,   80
Or but a sickly part of one true sense
Could not so mope.°

49–52 *Heaven's . . . act:* Heaven's face flushes with anger to look down upon this solid world, this compound mass, with hot face as though the day of doom were near, and is thought-sick at the deed (i.e., Gertrude's marriage). 53 *index:* Table of contents, prelude, or preface. 55 *counterfeit presentment:* Portrayed representation. 57 *Hyperion:* The sun god; *front:* Brow. 59 *station:* Manner of standing. 65 *ear:* I.e., of grain. 68 *batten:* Gorge; *moor:* Barren upland. 70 *heyday:* State of excitement. 72 *Sense:* Perception through the five senses (the functions of the middle or sensible soul). 74 *apoplex'd:* Paralyzed. (Hamlet goes on to explain that without such a paralysis of will, mere madness would not err, nor would the five senses so enthrall themselves to *ecstasy* or lunacy; even such deranged states of mind would be able to make the obvious choice between Hamlet Senior and Claudius.) 78 *cozen'd:* Cheated; *hoodman-blind:* Blindman's buff. 80 *sans:* Without. 82 *mope:* Be dazed, act aimlessly.

O shame, where is thy blush? Rebellious hell,
If thou canst mutine° in a matron's bones,
To flaming youth let virtue be as wax,   85
And melt in her own fire. Proclaim no shame
When the compulsive ardor gives the charge,
Since frost itself as actively doth burn,
And reason panders will.°

QUEEN: O Hamlet, speak no more!   90
Thou turn'st mine eyes into my very soul,
And there I see such black and grained° spots
As will not leave their tinct.°

HAMLET: Nay, but to live
In the rank sweat of an enseamed° bed,
Stew'd in corruption, honeying and making love   95
Over the nasty sty—

QUEEN: O, speak to me no more.
These words, like daggers, enter in my ears.
No more, sweet Hamlet!

HAMLET: A murderer and a villain,
A slave that is not twentieth part the tithe°   100
Of your precedent° lord, a vice° of kings,
A cutpurse of the empire and the rule,
That from a shelf the precious diadem stole,
And put it in his pocket!

QUEEN: No more!   105

(Enter GHOST in his nightgown.)

HAMLET: A king of shreds and patches°—
Save me, and hover o'er me with your wings,
You heavenly guards! What would your gracious figure?

QUEEN: Alas, he's mad!

HAMLET: Do you not come your tardy son to chide,   110
That, laps'd in time and passion,° lets go by
Th' important° acting of your dread command?
O, say!

GHOST: Do not forget. This visitation
Is but to whet thy almost blunted purpose.   115
But, look, amazement° on thy mother sits.

---

84 *mutine:* Mutiny. 86–89 *Proclaim . . . will:* Call it no shameful business when the compelling
ardor of youth delivers the attack, i.e., commits lechery, since the frost of advanced age burns
with as active a fire of lust and reason perverts itself by fomenting lust rather than restraining it.
92 *grained:* Dyed in grain, indelible. 93 *tinct:* Color. 94 *enseamed:* Laden with grease. 100 *tithe:*
Tenth part. 101 *precedent:* Former (i.e., the elder Hamlet); *vice:* Buffoon (a reference to the vice
of the morality plays). 106 *shreds and patches:* Motley, the traditional costume of the clown or
fool. 111 *laps'd . . . passion:* Having allowed time to lapse and passion to cool. 112 *important:*
Importunate, urgent. 116 *amazement:* Distraction.

O, step between her and her fighting soul!
Conceit° in weakest bodies strongest works.
Speak to her, Hamlet.

HAMLET: How is it with you, lady?

QUEEN: Alas, how is 't with you,   120
That you do bend your eye on vacancy,
And with th' incorporal° air do hold discourse?
Forth at your eyes your spirits wildly peep,
And, as the sleeping soldiers in th' alarm,
Your bedded° hair, like life in excrements,°   125
Start up and stand an° end. O gentle son,
Upon the heat and flame of thy distemper
Sprinkle cool patience. Whereon do you look?

HAMLET: On him, on him! Look you how pale he glares!
His form and cause conjoin'd,° preaching to stones,   130
Would make them capable.°—Do not look upon me,
Lest with this piteous action you convert
My stern effects.° Then what I have to do
Will want true color°—tears perchance for blood.

QUEEN: To whom do you speak this?   135

HAMLET: Do you see nothing there?

QUEEN: Nothing at all; yet all that is I see.

HAMLET: Nor did you nothing hear?

QUEEN: No, nothing but ourselves.

HAMLET: Why, look you there, look how it steals away!   140
My father, in his habit° as he lived!
Look, where he goes, even now, out at the portal!   *(Exit* GHOST.*)*

QUEEN: This is the very coinage of your brain.
This bodiless creation ecstasy°
Is very cunning in.   145

HAMLET: Ecstasy?
My pulse, as yours, doth temperately keep time,
And makes as healthful music. It is not madness
That I have utter'd. Bring me to the test,
And I the matter will reword, which madness   150
Would gambol° from. Mother, for love of grace,
Lay not that flattering unction° to your soul
That not your trespass but my madness speaks.
It will but skin and film the ulcerous place,

118 *Conceit:* Imagination. 122 *incorporal:* Immaterial. 125 *bedded:* Laid in smooth layers; *excrements:* Outgrowths. 126 *an:* On. 130 *His . . . conjoin'd:* His appearance joined to his cause for speaking. 131 *capable:* Receptive. 132–33 *convert . . . effects:* Divert me from my stern duty. 134 *want true color:* Lack plausibility so that (with a play on the normal sense of "color") I shall shed tears instead of blood. 141 *habit:* Dress. 144 *ecstasy:* Madness. 151 *gambol:* Skip away. 152 *unction:* Ointment.

Whiles rank corruption, mining° all within,   155
Infects unseen. Confess yourself to heaven,
Repent what's past, avoid what is to come,
And do not spread the compost° on the weeds
To make them ranker. Forgive me this my virtue;°
For in the fatness° of these pursy° times   160
Virtue itself of vice must pardon beg,
Yea, curb° and woo for leave° to do him good.

QUEEN: O Hamlet, thou hast cleft my heart in twain.

HAMLET: O, throw away the worser part of it,
And live the purer with the other half.   165
Good night. But go not to my uncle's bed;
Assume a virtue, if you have it not.
That monster, custom, who all sense doth eat,°
Of habits devil,° is angel yet in this,
That to the use of actions fair and good   170
He likewise gives a frock or livery°
That aptly is put on. Refrain tonight,
And that shall lend a kind of easiness
To the next abstinence; the next more easy;
For use° almost can change the stamp of nature,   175
And either° . . . the devil, or throw him out
With wondrous potency. Once more, good night;
And when you are desirous to be bless'd,°
I'll blessing beg of you. For this same lord,   *(Pointing to* POLONIUS.*)*
I do repent; but heaven hath pleas'd it so   180
To punish me with this, and this with me,
That I must be their scourge and minister.°
I will bestow° him, and will answer well
The death I gave him. So, again, good night.
I must be cruel only to be kind.   185
Thus bad begins and worse remains behind.°
One word more, good lady.

QUEEN: What shall I do?

HAMLET: Not this, by no means, that I bid you do:
Let the bloat° king tempt you again to bed,
Pinch wanton on your cheek, call you his mouse,   190

---

155 *mining:* Working under the surface. 158 *compost:* Manure. 159 *this my virtue:* My virtuous talk
in reproving you. 160 *fatness:* Grossness; *pursy:* Short-winded, corpulent. 162 *curb:* Bow, bend the
knee; *leave:* Permission. 168 *who . . . eat:* Who consumes all proper or natural feeling. 169 *Of habits
devil:* Devil-like in prompting evil habits. 171 *livery:* An outer appearance, a customary garb (and
hence a predisposition easily assumed in time of stress). 175 *use:* Habit. 176 *And either:* A defective
line usually emended by inserting the word "master" after "either." 178 *be bless'd:* Become blessed,
i.e., repentant. 182 *their scourge and minister:* Agent of heavenly retribution. (By *scourge,* Hamlet also
suggests that he himself will eventually suffer punishment in the process of fulfilling heaven's will.)
183 *bestow:* Stow, dispose of. 186 *behind:* To come. 189 *bloat:* Bloated.

And let him, for a pair of reechy° kisses,
Or paddling in your neck with his damn'd fingers,
Make you to ravel all this matter out,
That I essentially am not in madness,
But mad in craft. 'Twere good° you let him know,   195
For who that's but a queen, fair, sober, wise,
Would from a paddock,° from a bat, a gib,°
Such dear concernings° hide? Who would do so?
No, in despite of sense and secrecy,
Unpeg the basket° on the house's top,   200
Let the birds fly, and, like the famous ape,°
To try conclusions,° in the basket creep
And break your own neck down.
QUEEN: Be thou assur'd, if words be made of breath,
And breath of life, I have no life to breathe   205
What thou hast said to me.
HAMLET: I must to England; you know that?
QUEEN: Alack,
I had forgot. 'Tis so concluded on.
HAMLET: There's letters seal'd, and my two schoolfellows,
Whom I will trust as I will adders fang'd,   210
They bear the mandate; they must sweep my way,°
And marshal me to knavery. Let it work.
For 'tis the sport to have the enginer°
Hoist with° his own petar,° and 't shall go hard
But I will delve one yard below their mines,°   215
And blow them at the moon. O, 'tis most sweet,
When in one line two crafts° directly meet.
This man shall set me packing.°
I'll lug the guts into the neighbor room.
Mother, good night indeed. This counselor   220
Is now most still, most secret, and most grave,
Who was in life a foolish prating knave.
Come, sir, to draw toward an end° with you.
Good night, mother.
                    (Exeunt severally, HAMLET *dragging in* POLONIUS.*)*

191 *reechy:* Dirty, filthy. 195 *good:* Said ironically; also the following eight lines. 197 *paddock:* Toad;
gib: Tomcat. 198 *dear concernings:* Important affairs. 200 *Unpeg the basket:* Open the cage, i.e., let
out the secret. 201 *famous ape:* In a story now lost. 202 *conclusions:* Experiments (in which the ape
apparently enters a cage from which birds have been released and then tries to fly out of the cage
as they have done, falling to his death). 211 *sweep my way:* Go before me. 213 *enginer:* Constructor
of military contrivances. 214 *Hoist with:* Blown up by; *petar:* Petard, an explosive used to blow in
a door or make a breach. 215 *mines:* Tunnels used in warfare to undermine the enemy's emplace-
ments; Hamlet will countermine by going under their mines. 217 *crafts:* Acts of guile, plots. 218
set me packing: Set me to making schemes, and set me to lugging (him) and, also, send me off in a
hurry. 223 *draw . . . end:* Finish up (with a pun on "draw," pull).

ACT IV
SCENE I°

(Enter KING and QUEEN, with ROSENCRANTZ and
GUILDENSTERN.)

KING: There's matter in these sighs, these profound heaves
You must translate; 'tis fit we understand them.
Where is your son?
QUEEN: Bestow this place on us a little while.
             (Exeunt ROSENCRANTZ and GUILDENSTERN.)
Ah, mine own lord, what have I seen tonight!   5
KING: What, Gertrude? How does Hamlet?
QUEEN: Mad as the sea and wind when both contend
Which is the mightier. In his lawless fit,
Behind the arras hearing something stir,
Whips out his rapier, cries, "A rat, a rat!"   10
And, in this brainish apprehension,° kills
The unseen good old man.
KING: O heavy deed!
It had been so with us, had we been there.
His liberty is full of threats to all—
To you yourself, to us, to everyone.   15
Alas, how shall this bloody deed be answer'd?
It will be laid to us, whose providence°
Should have kept short,° restrain'd, and out of haunt°
This mad young man. But so much was our love
We would not understand what was most fit,   20
But, like the owner of a foul disease,
To keep it from divulging,° let it feed
Even on the pith of life. Where is he gone?
QUEEN: To draw apart the body he hath kill'd,
O'er whom his very madness, like some ore°   25
Among a mineral° of metals base,
Shows itself pure: 'a weeps for what is done.
KING: O Gertrude, come away!
The sun no sooner shall the mountains touch
But we will ship him hence; and this vile deed   30
We must, with all our majesty and skill,
Both countenance and excuse. Ho, Guildenstern!

(Enter ROSENCRANTZ and GUILDENSTERN.)

ACT IV, SCENE I. Location: The castle.   11 brainish apprehension: Headstrong conception.   17
providence: Foresight.   18 short: On a short tether; out of haunt: Secluded.   22 divulging: Becoming
evident.   25 ore: Vein of gold.   26 mineral: Mine.

Friends both, go join you with some further aid.
Hamlet in madness hath Polonius slain,
And from his mother's closet hath he dragg'd him.   35
Go seek him out; speak fair, and bring the body
Into the chapel. I pray you, haste in this.
       (Exeunt ROSENCRANTZ *and* GUILDENSTERN.*)*
Come, Gertrude, we'll call up our wisest friends
And let them know both what we mean to do
And what's untimely done°   40
Whose whisper o'er the world's diameter,°
As level° as the cannon to his blank,°
Transports his pois'ned shot, may miss our name,
And hit the woundless° air. O, come away!
My soul is full of discord and dismay.   *(Exeunt.)* 45

SCENE II°

(Enter HAMLET.*)*

HAMLET: Safely stow'd.
ROSENCRANTZ, GUILDENSTERN *(within)*: Hamlet! Lord Hamlet!
HAMLET: But soft, what noise? Who calls on Hamlet? O, here they come.

(Enter ROSENCRANTZ *and* GUILDENSTERN.*)*

ROSENCRANTZ: What have you done, my lord, with the dead body?
HAMLET: Compounded it with dust, whereto 'tis kin.   5
ROSENCRANTZ: Tell us where 'tis, that we may take it thence
    And bear it to the chapel.
HAMLET: Do not believe it.
ROSENCRANTZ: Believe what?
HAMLET: That I can keep your counsel and not mine own. Besides, to be   10
    demanded of° a sponge, what replication° should be made by the son
    of a king?
ROSENCRANTZ: Take you me for a sponge, my lord?
HAMLET: Ay, sir, that soaks up the King's countenance,° his rewards, his
    authorities. But such officers do the King best service in the end. He   15
    keeps them, like an ape an apple, in the corner of his jaw, first mouth'd,
    to be last swallow'd. When he needs what you have glean'd, it is but
    squeezing you, and, sponge, you shall be dry again.
ROSENCRANTZ: I understand you not, my lord.

---

40 *And . . . done:* A defective line. 41 *diameter:* Extent from side to side. 42 *As level:* With as direct aim; *blank:* White spot in the center of a target. 44 *woundless:* invulnerable. ACT IV, SCENE II. *Location:* The castle. 11 *demanded of:* Questioned by; *replication:* Reply. 14 *countenance:* Favor.

HAMLET: I am glad of it. A knavish speech sleeps in° a foolish ear.　　20
ROSENCRANTZ: My lord, you must tell us where the body is, and go
　　with us to the King.
HAMLET: The body is with the King, but the King is not with the body.°
　　The King is a thing—
GUILDENSTERN: A thing, my lord?　　25
HAMLET: Of nothing.° Bring me to him. Hide fox, and all after.°

　　　　　　　　　　　　　　　　　　　　　　　　　　(Exeunt.)

SCENE III°

　　(Enter KING, *and two or three.)*

KING: I have sent to seek him, and to find the body.
　　How dangerous is it that this man goes loose!
　　Yet must not we put the strong law on him.
　　He's lov'd of the distracted° multitude,
　　Who like not in their judgment, but their eyes,　　5
　　And where 'tis so, th' offender's scourge° is weigh'd,°
　　But never the offense. To bear° all smooth and even,
　　This sudden sending him away must seem
　　Deliberate pause.° Diseases desperate grown
　　By desperate appliance are reliev'd,　　10
　　Or not at all.

　　(Enter ROSENCRANTZ, GUILDENSTERN, *and all the rest.)*

　　　　　　　　　How now? What hath befall'n?
ROSENCRANTZ: Where the dead body is bestow'd, my lord,
　　We cannot get from him.
KING:　　　　　　　　　　But where is he?
ROSENCRANTZ: Without, my lord; guarded, to know your pleasure.
KING: Bring him before us.
ROSENCRANTZ:　　　　　　Ho! Bring in the lord.　　15

　　(They enter with HAMLET.*)*

KING: Now, Hamlet, where's Polonius?
HAMLET: At supper.
KING: At supper? Where?

---

20 *sleeps in:* Has no meaning to. 23 *The . . . body:* Perhaps alludes to the legal commonplace of "the king's two bodies," which drew a distinction between the sacred office of kingship and the particular mortal who possessed it at any given time. 26 *Of nothing:* Of no account; *Hide . . . after:* An old signal cry in the game of hide-and-seek, suggesting that Hamlet now runs away from them. ACT IV, SCENE III. *Location:* The castle. 4 *distracted:* Fickle, unstable. 6 *scourge:* Punishment; *weigh'd:* Taken into consideration. 7 *bear:* Manage. 9 *Deliberate pause:* Carefully considered action.

HAMLET: Not where he eats, but where 'a is eaten. A certain convocation
    of politic worms° are e'en at him. Your worm is your only emperor for   20
    diet.° We fat all creatures else to fat us, and we fat ourselves for mag-
    gots. Your fat king and your lean beggar is but variable service,° two
    dishes, but to one table—that's the end.

KING: Alas, alas!

HAMLET: A man may fish with the worm that hath eat° of a king, and eat   25
    of the fish that hath fed of that worm.

KING: What dost thou mean by this?

HAMLET: Nothing but to show you how a king may go a progress°
    through the guts of a beggar.

KING: Where is Polonius?   30

HAMLET: In heaven. Send thither to see. If your messenger find him not
    there, seek him i' th' other place yourself. But if indeed you find him
    not within this month, you shall nose him as you go up the stairs into
    the lobby.

KING *(to some* ATTENDANTS*)*: Go seek him there.   35

HAMLET: 'A will stay till you come.   *(Exit* ATTENDANTS*.)*

KING: Hamlet, this deed, for thine especial safety.—
    Which we do tender,° as we dearly° grieve
    For that which thou hast done—must send thee hence
    With fiery quickness. Therefore prepare thyself.   40
    The bark° is ready, and the wind at help,
    Th' associates tend,° and everything is bent°
    For England.

HAMLET: For England!

KING: Ay, Hamlet.   45

HAMLET: Good.

KING: So is it, if thou knew'st our purposes.

HAMLET: I see a cherub° that sees them. But, come, for England! Farewell,
    dear mother.

KING: Thy loving father, Hamlet.   50

HAMLET: My mother. Father and mother is man and wife, man and wife
    is one flesh, and so, my mother. Come, for England!   *(Exit.)*

KING: Follow him at foot;° tempt him with speed aboard.
    Delay it not; I'll have him hence tonight.
    Away! For everything is seal'd and done   55
    That else leans on° th' affair. Pray you, make haste.
                        (Exeunt all but the KING*.)*

---

20 *politic worms:* Crafty worms (suited to a master spy like Polonius). 21 *diet:* Food, eating (with
perhaps a punning reference to the Diet of Worms, a famous convocation held in 1521). 22
variable service: Different courses of a single meal. 25 *eat:* Eaten (pronounced "et"). 28 *progress:*
Royal journey of state. 38 *tender:* Regard, hold dear; *dearly:* Intensely. 41 *bark:* Sailing vessel.
42 *tend:* Wait; *bent:* In readiness. 48 *cherub:* Cherubim are angels of knowledge. 53 *at foot:* Close
behind, at heel. 56 *leans on:* Bears upon, is related to.

And, England,° if my love thou hold'st at aught—
As my great power thereof may give thee sense,
Since yet thy cicatrice° looks raw and red
After the Danish sword, and thy free awe°   60
Pays homage to us—thou mayst not coldly set°
Our sovereign process,° which imports at full,
By letters congruing° to that effect,
The present° death of Hamlet. Do it, England,
For like the hectic° in my blood he rages,   65
And thou must cure me. Till I know 'tis done,
Howe'er my haps,° my joys were ne'er begun.   *(Exit.)*

SCENE IV°

(Enter FORTINBRAS *with his* ARMY *over the stage.)*

FORTINBRAS: Go, captain, from me greet the Danish king.
Tell him that, by his license,° Fortinbras
Craves the conveyance° of a promis'd march
Over his kingdom. You know the rendezvous.
If that his Majesty would aught with us,   5
We shall express our duty in his eye;°
And let him know so.
CAPTAIN: I will do 't, my lord.
FORTINBRAS: Go softly° on.   *(Exeunt all but the* CAPTAIN.*)*

(Enter HAMLET, ROSENCRANTZ, GUILDENSTERN, *etc.)*

HAMLET: Good sir, whose powers° are these?
CAPTAIN: They are of Norway, sir.   10
HAMLET: How purposed, sir, I pray you?
CAPTAIN: Against some part of Poland.
HAMLET: Who commands them, sir?
CAPTAIN: The nephew to old Norway, Fortinbras.
HAMLET: Goes it against the main° of Poland, sir,   15
    Or for some frontier?
CAPTAIN: Truly to speak, and with no addition,°
    We go to gain a little patch of ground
    That hath in it no profit but the name.
    To pay° five ducats, five, I would not farm it;°   20
    Nor will it yield to Norway or the Pole
    A ranker° rate, should it be sold in fee.°

---

57 *England:* King of England. 59 *cicatrice:* Scar. 60 *free awe:* Voluntary show of respect. 61 *set:* Esteem. 62 *process:* Command. 63 *congruing:* Agreeing. 64 *present:* Immediate. 65 *hectic:* Persistent fever. 67 *haps:* Fortunes. ACT IV, SCENE IV. *Location:* The coast of Denmark. 2 *license:* Permission. 3 *conveyance:* Escort, convoy. 6 *eye:* Presence. 8 *softly:* Slowly. 9 *powers:* Forces. 15 *main:* Main part. 17 *addition:* Exaggeration. 20 *To pay:* I.e., for a yearly rental of; *farm it:* Take a lease of it. 22 *ranker:* Higher; *in fee:* Fee simple, outright.

HAMLET: Why, then the Polack never will defend it.
CAPTAIN: Yes, it is already garrison'd.
HAMLET: Two thousand souls and twenty thousand ducats   25
    Will not debate the question of this straw.°
    This is th' imposthume° of much wealth and peace,
    That inward breaks, and shows no cause without
    Why the man dies. I humbly thank you, sir.
CAPTAIN: God buy you, sir.   *(Exit.)*
ROSENCRANTZ: Will 't please you go, my lord?   30
HAMLET: I'll be with you straight. Go a little before.
                    (Exit all except HAMLET.*)*
    How all occasions do inform against° me,
    And spur my dull revenge! What is a man,
    If his chief good and market of° his time
    Be but to sleep and feed? A beast, no more.   35
    Sure he that made us with such large discourse,°
    Looking before and after, gave us not
    That capability and god-like reason
    To fust° in us unus'd. Now, whether it be
    Bestial oblivion,° or some craven scruple   40
    Of thinking too precisely on th' event°—
    A thought which, quarter'd, hath but one part wisdom
    And ever three parts coward—I do not know
    Why yet I live to say "This thing's to do,"
    Sith° I have cause and will and strength and means   45
    To do 't. Examples gross° as earth exhort me:
    Witness this army of such mass and charge°
    Led by a delicate and tender prince,
    Whose spirit, with divine ambition puff'd
    Makes mouths° at the invisible event,   50
    Exposing what is mortal and unsure
    To all that fortune, death, and danger dare,
    Even for an egg-shell. Rightly to be great
    Is not to stir without great argument,
    But greatly to find quarrel in a straw   55
    When honor's at the stake. How stand I then,
    That have a father kill'd, a mother stain'd,
    Excitements of° my reason and my blood,
    And let all sleep, while, to my shame, I see
    The imminent death of twenty thousand men,   60

---

26 *debate . . . straw:* Settle this trifling matter. 27 *imposthume:* Abscess. 32 *inform against:* Denounce, betray; take shape against. 34 *market of:* Profit of, compensation for. 36 *discourse:* Power of reasoning. 39 *fust:* Grow moldy. 40 *oblivion:* Forgetfulness. 41 *event:* Outcome. 45 *Sith:* Since. 46 *gross:* Obvious. 47 *charge:* Expense. 50 *Makes mouths:* Makes scornful faces. 58 *Excitements of:* Promptings by.

That, for a fantasy° and trick° of fame,
Go to their graves like beds, fight for a plot°
Whereon the numbers cannot try the cause°
Which is not tomb enough and continent°
To hide the slain? O, from this time forth,   65
My thoughts be bloody, or be nothing worth!   *(Exit.)*

SCENE V°

(Enter HORATIO, QUEEN GERTRUDE, *and a* GENTLEMAN.)

QUEEN: I will not speak with her.
GENTLEMAN: She is importunate, indeed distract.
    Her mood will needs be pitied.
QUEEN: What would she have?
GENTLEMAN: She speaks much of her father, says she hears
    There's tricks° i' th' world, and hems, and beats her heart°   5
    Spurns enviously at straws° speaks things in doubt°
    That carry but half sense. Her speech is nothing,
    Yet the unshaped use° of it doth move
    The hearers to collection;° they yawn° at it,
    And botch° the words up fit to their own thoughts,   10
    Which, as her winks and nods and gestures yield° them,
    Indeed would make one think there might be thought°
    Though nothing sure, yet much unhappily.
HORATIO: 'Twere good she were spoken with, for she may strew
    Dangerous conjectures in ill-breeding° minds.   15
QUEEN: Let her come in.   *(Exit* GENTLEMEN.)
    (Aside.) To my sick soul, as sin's true nature is,
    Each toy° seems prologue to some great amiss.°
    So full of artless jealousy is guilt,
    It spills itself in fearing to be spilt.°   20

(Enter OPHELIA *distracted.)*

OPHELIA: Where is the beauteous majesty of Denmark?
QUEEN: How now, Ophelia?
OPHELIA *(she sings):* "How should I your true love know

---

61 *fantasy:* Fanciful caprice; *trick:* Trifle. 62 *plot:* I.e., of ground. 63 *Whereon . . . cause:* On which there is insufficient room for the soldiers needed to engage in a military contest. 64 *continent:* Receptacle, container. ACT IV, SCENE V. *Location:* The castle. 5 *tricks:* Deceptions; *heart:* Breast. 6 *Spurns . . . straws:* Kicks spitefully, takes offense at trifles; *in doubt:* Obscurely. 8 *unshaped use:* Distracted manner. 9 *collection:* Inference, a guess at some sort of meaning; *yawn:* Wonder, grasp. 10 *botch:* Patch. 11 *yield:* Delivery, bring forth (her words). 12 *thought:* Conjectured. 15 *ill-breeding:* Prone to suspect the worst. 18 *toy:* Trifle; *amiss:* Calamity. 19–20 *So . . . spilt:* Guilt is so full of suspicion that it unskillfully betrays itself in fearing betrayal.

       From another one?
    By his cockle hat° and staff,   25
       And his sandal shoon."°
QUEEN: Alas, sweet lady, what imports this song?
OPHELIA: Say you? Nay, pray you, mark.
    "He is dead and gone, lady,   *(Song.)*
       He is dead and gone;   30
    At his head a grass-green turf,
       At his heels a stone."
    O, ho!
QUEEN: Nay, but Ophelia—
OPHELIA: Pray you mark.   35
    (Sings.) "What his shroud as the mountain snow"—

    (Enter KING.*)*

QUEEN: Alas, look here, my lord.
OPHELIA: "Larded° all with flowers   *(Song.)*
    Which bewept to the ground did not go
       With true-love showers."   40
KING: How do you, pretty lady?
OPHELIA: Well, God 'ild° you! They say the owl° was a baker's daughter.
    Lord, we know what we are, but know not what we may be. God be
    at your table!
KING: Conceit° upon her father.   45
OPHELIA: Pray let's have no words of this; but when they ask you what it
    means, say you this:
    "Tomorrow is Saint Valentine's° day.   *(Song.)*
       All in the morning betime,
    And I a maid at your window,   50
       To be your Valentine.
    Then up he rose, and donn'd his clo'es,
       And dupp'd° the chamber-door,
    Let in the maid, that out a maid
       Never departed more."   55
KING: Pretty Ophelia!
OPHELIA: Indeed, la, without an oath, I'll make an end on 't:
    (Sings.) "By Gis° and by Saint Charity,
       Alack, and fie for shame!
    Young men will do 't, if they come to 't;
       By Cock,° they are to blame.

---

25 *cockle hat:* Hat with cockleshell stuck in it as a sign that the wearer had been a pilgrim to the shrine of St. James of Compostella in Spain. 26 *shoon:* Shoes. 38 *Larded:* Decorated. 42 *God 'ild:* God yield or reward; *owl:* Refers to a legend about a baker's daughter who was turned into an owl for refusing Jesus bread. 45 *Conceit:* Brooding. 48 *Valentine's:* This song alludes to the belief that the first girl seen by a man on the morning of this day was his valentine or true love. 53 *dupp'd:* Opened. 58 *Gis:* Jesus. 61 *Cock:* A perversion of "God" in oaths.

> Quoth she, 'Before you tumbled me,
>> You promised me to wed.'"
> He answers:
> "'So would I ha' done, by yonder sun, 65
>> And thou hadst not come to my bed.'"

KING: How long hath she been thus?

OPHELIA: I hope all will be well. We must be patient, but I cannot choose but weep, to think they would lay him i' th' cold ground. My brother shall know of it; and so I thank you for your good counsel. Come, my 70 coach! Good night, ladies; good night, sweet ladies; good night, good night. *(Exit.)*

KING: Follow her close; give her good watch, I pray you.

(Exit HORATIO*.)*

> O, this is the poison of deep grief; it springs
> All from her father's death—and now behold!
> O Gertrude, Gertrude, 75
> When sorrows come, they come not single spies,°
> But in battalions. First, her father slain;
> Next, your son gone, and he most violent author
> Of his own just remove; the people muddied,° 80
> Thick and unwholesome in their thoughts and whispers,
> For good Polonius' death; and we have done but greenly,°
> In hugger-mugger° to inter him; poor Ophelia
> Divided from herself and her fair judgment,
> Without the which we are pictures, or mere beasts; 85
> Last, and as much containing as all these,
> Her brother is in secret come from France,
> Feeds on his wonder, keeps himself in clouds,°
> And wants° not buzzers° to infect his ear
> With pestilent speeches of his father's death, 90
> Wherein necessity, of matter beggar'd,°
> Will nothing stick our person to arraign
> In ear and ear.° O my dear Gertrude, this,
> Like to a murd'ring-piece° in many places
> Gives me superfluous death. *(A noise within.)* 95

QUEEN: Alack, what noise is this?

KING: Attend!

> Where are my Switzers?° Let them guard the door.

(Enter a MESSENGER*.)*

> What is the matter?

---

77 *spies:* Scouts sent in advance of the main force. 80 *muddied:* Stirred up, confused. 82 *greenly:* Imprudently, foolishly. 83 *hugger-mugger:* Secret haste. 88 *in clouds:* I.e., of suspicion and rumor. 89 *wants:* Lacks; *buzzers:* Gossipers, informers. 91 *of matter beggar'd:* Unprovided with facts. 92–93 *Will . . . and ear:* Will not hesitate to accuse my (royal) person in everybody's ears. 94 *murd'ring-piece:* Cannon loaded so as to scatter its shot. 98 *Switzers:* Swiss guards, mercenaries.

MESSENGER: Save yourself, my lord!
  The ocean, overpeering of his list,°   100
  Eats not the flats° with more impiteous° haste
  Than young Laertes, in a riotous head,°
  O'erbears your officers. The rabble call him lord,
  And, as° the world were now but to begin,
  Antiquity forgot, custom not known,   105
  The ratifiers and props° of every word,°
  They cry, "Choose we! Laertes shall be king!"
  Caps, hands, and tongues applaud it to the clouds,
  "Laertes shall be king, Laertes king!"   *(A noise within.)*
QUEEN: How cheerfully on the false trail they cry!   110
  O, this is counter,° you false Danish dogs!

(Enter LAERTES *with others.)*

KING: The doors are broke.
LAERTES: Where is this King? Sirs, stand you all without.
ALL: No, let's come in.
LAERTES: I pray you, give me leave.
ALL: We will, we will.   *(They retire without the door.)* 115
LAERTES: I thank you. Keep the door. O thou vile king,
  Give me my father!
QUEEN: Calmly, good Laertes.   *(She tries to hold him back.)*
LAERTES: That drop of blood that's calm proclaims me bastard,
  Cries cuckold to my father, brands the harlot
  Even here, between the chaste unsmirched brow   120
  Of my true mother.
KING: What is the cause, Laertes,
  That thy rebellion looks so giant-like?
  Let him go, Gertrude. Do not fear our° person.
  There's such divinity doth hedge a king
  That treason can but peep to what it would,°   125
  Acts little of his will.° Tell me, Laertes,
  Why thou art thus incens'd. Let him go, Gertrude.
  Speak, man.
LAERTES: Where is my father?
KING: Dead.
QUEEN: But not by him.
KING: Let him demand his fill.

---

100 *overpeering of his list:* Overflowing its shore. 101 *flats:* Flatlands near shore; *impiteous:* Pitiless.
102 *head:* Armed force. 104 *as:* As if. 106 *ratifiers and props:* Refer to *antiquity* and *custom; word:*
Promise. 111 *counter:* A hunting term meaning to follow the trail in a direction opposite to that
which the game has taken. 123 *fear our:* Fear for my. 125 *can . . . would:* Can only glance; as
from far off or through a barrier, at what it would intend. 126 *Acts . . . will:* (But) performs
little of what it intends.

LAERTES: How came he dead? I'll not be juggled with.   130
　　　　To hell, allegiance! Vows, to the blackest devil!
　　　　Conscience and grace, to the profoundest pit!
　　　　I dare damnation. To this point I stand,
　　　　That both the worlds I give to negligence,°
　　　　Let come what comes, only I'll be reveng'd   135
　　　　Most throughly° for my father.
KING: Who shall stay you?
LAERTES: My will, not all the world's.°
　　　　And for my means, I'll husband them so well,
　　　　They shall go far with little.
KING: Good Laertes,
　　　　If you desire to know the certainty   140
　　　　Of your dear father, is 't writ in your revenge
　　　　That, swoopstake,° you will draw both friend and foe,
　　　　Winner and loser?
LAERTES: None but his enemies.
KING: Will you know them then?
LAERTES: To his good friends thus wide I'll ope my arms,   145
　　　　And, like the kind life-rend'ring pelican,°
　　　　Repast° them with my blood.
KING: Why, now you speak
　　　　Like a good child and a true gentleman.
　　　　That I am guiltless of your father's death,
　　　　And am most sensibly° in grief for it,   150
　　　　It shall as level° to your judgment 'pear
　　　　As day does to your eye.
　　　　　　　　　　(A noise within:) "Let her come in."
LAERTES: How now? What noise is that?

(Enter OPHELIA.)

　　　　O heat, dry up my brains! Tears seven times salt
　　　　Burn out the sense and virtue° of mine eye!   155
　　　　By heaven, thy madness shall be paid with weight°
　　　　Till our scale turn the beam.° O rose of May!
　　　　Dear maid, kind sister, sweet Ophelia!
　　　　O heavens, is 't possible a young maid's wits
　　　　Should be as mortal as an old man's life?   160
　　　　Nature is fine in° love, and where 'tis fine,

---

134 *both . . . negligence:* Both this world and the next are of no consequence to me. 136 *throughly:* Thoroughly. 137 *My will . . . world's:* I'll stop *(stay)* when my will is accomplished, not for anyone else's. 142 *swoopstake:* Literally, taking all stakes on the gambling table at once, i.e., indiscriminately; "draw" is also a gambling term. 146 *pelican:* Refers to the belief that the female pelican fed its young with its own blood. 147 *Repast:* Feed. 150 *sensibly:* Feelingly. 151 *level:* Plain. 155 *virtue:* Faculty, power. 156 *paid with weight:* Repaid, avenged equally or more. 157 *beam:* Crossbar of a balance.

It sends some precious instance° of itself
After the thing it loves.°

OPHELIA: "They bore him barefac'd on the bier;   *(Song.)*
 Hey non nonny, nonny, hey nonny,   165
 And in his grave rain'd many a tear"—
 Fare you well, my dove!

LAERTES: Hadst thou thy wits, and didst persuade° revenge,
 It could not move thus.

OPHELIA: You must sing "A-down a-down,   170
 And you call him a-down-a."
 O, how the wheel° becomes it! It is the false steward° that stole his
 master's daughter.

LAERTES: This nothing's more than matter.°

OPHELIA: There's rosemary,° that's for remembrance; pray you, love, re-   175
 member. And there is pansies,° that's for thoughts.

LAERTES: A document° in madness, thoughts and remembrance fitted.

OPHELIA: There's fennel° for you, and columbines.° There's rue° for you,
 and here's some for me; we may call it herb of grace o' Sundays. You
 may wear your rue with a difference.° There's a daisy.° I would give   180
 you some violets,° but they wither'd all when my father died. They say
 'a made a good end—
 (Sings.) "For bonny sweet Robin is all my joy."

LAERTES: Thought° and affliction, passion, hell itself,
 She turns to favor° and to prettiness.   185

OPHELIA: "And will 'a not come again?   *(Song.)*
 And will 'a not come again?
  No, no, he is dead,
  Go to thy death-bed,
 He never will come again.   190

 "His beard was as white as snow,
 All flaxen was his poll.°
  He is gone, he is gone,
  And we cast away moan.
 God 'a' mercy on his soul!"   195
 And of all Christians' souls, I pray God. God buy you.   *(Exit.)*

---

161 *fine in:* Refined by. 162 *instance:* Token. 163 *After . . . loves:* Into the grave, along with Polonius. 168 *persuade:* Argue cogently for. 172 *wheel:* Spinning wheel as accompaniment to the song, or refrain; *false steward:* The story is unknown. 174 *This . . . matter:* This seeming nonsense is more meaningful than sane utterance. 175 *rosemary:* Used as a symbol of remembrance both at weddings and at funerals. 176 *pansies:* Emblems of love and courtship; perhaps from French "pensées," thoughts. 177 *document:* Instruction, lesson. 178 *fennel:* Emblem of flattery; *columbines:* Emblems of unchastity (?) or ingratitude (?); *rue:* Emblem of repentance; when mingled with holy water, it was known as "herb of grace." 180 *with a difference:* Suggests that Ophelia and the Queen have different causes of sorrow and repentance; perhaps with a play on "rue" in the sense of ruth, pity; *daisy:* Emblem of dissembling, faithlessness. 181 *violets:* Emblems of faithfulness. 184 *Thought:* Melancholy. 185 *favor:* Grace. 192 *poll:* Head.

LAERTES: Do you see this, O God?
KING: Laertes, I must commune with your grief,
    Or you deny me right. Go but apart,
    Make choice of whom your wisest friends you will,   200
    And they shall hear and judge 'twixt you and me.
    If by direct or by collateral° hand
    They find us touch'd,° we will our kingdom give,
    Our crown, our life, and all that we call ours,
    To you in satisfaction; but if not,   205
    Be you content to lend your patience to us,
    And we shall jointly labor with your soul
    To give it due content.
LAERTES: Let this be so.
    His means of death, his obscure funeral—
    No trophy,° sword, nor hatchment° o'er his bones,   210
    No noble rite nor formal ostentation°—
    Cry to be heard, as 'twere from heaven to earth,
    That I must call 't in question.
KING: So you shall;
    And where th' offense is, let the great ax fall.
    I pray you go with me.   *(Exeunt.)* 215

SCENE VI°

(Enter HORATIO *and others.)*

HORATIO: What are they that would speak with me?
GENTLEMAN: Seafaring men, sir. They say they have letters for you.
HORATIO: Let them come in.   *(Exit* GENTLEMAN.)
    I do not know from what part of the world
    I should be greeted, if not from lord Hamlet.   5

(Enter SAILORS.)

FIRST SAILOR: God bless you sir.
HORATIO: Let him bless thee too.
FIRST SAILOR: 'A shall, sir, an 't please him. There's a letter for you, sir—
    it came from th' ambassador that was bound for England—if your name
    be Horatio, as I am let to know it is.   *(Gives letter.)* 10
HORATIO *(reads):* "Horatio, when thou shalt have overlook'd this, give
    these fellows some means° to the King; they have letters for him. Ere
    we were two days old at sea, a pirate of very warlike appointment° gave

---

202 *collateral:* Indirect. 203 *us touch'd:* Me implicated. 210 *trophy:* Memorial; *hatchment:* Tablet displaying the armorial bearings of a deceased person. 211 *ostentation:* Ceremony. ACT IV, SCENE VI. *Location:* The castle. 12 *means:* Means of access. 13 *appointment:* Equipage.

us chase. Finding ourselves too slow of sail, we put on a compell'd
valor, and in the grapple I boarded them. On the instant they got clear   15
of our ship, so I alone became their prisoner. They have dealt with me
like thieves of mercy,° but they knew what they did: I am to do a good
turn for them. Let the King have the letters I have sent, and repair thou
to me with as much speed as thou wouldest fly death. I have words to
speak in thine ear will make thee dumb; yet are they much too light   20
for the bore° of the matter. These good fellows will bring thee where
I am. Rosencrantz and Guildenstern hold their course for England. Of
them I have much to tell thee. Farewell.

                                 He that thou knowest thine, Hamlet."
Come, I will give you way for these your letters,   25
And do 't the speedier that you may direct me
To him from whom you brought them.   *(Exeunt.)*

SCENE VII°

(Enter KING *and* LAERTES.)

KING: Now must your conscience my acquittance seal,°
     And you must put me in your heart for friend,
     Sith you have heard, and with a knowing ear,
     That he which hath your noble father slain
     Pursued my life.
LAERTES: It well appears. But tell me   5
     Why you proceeded not against these feats°
     So criminal and so capital° in nature,
     As by your safety, greatness, wisdom, all things else,
     You mainly° were stirr'd up.
KING: O, for two special reasons,
     Which may to you, perhaps, seem much unsinew'd,°   10
     But yet to me th' are strong. The Queen his mother
     Lives almost by his looks, and for myself—
     My virtue or my plague, be it either which—
     She's so conjunctive° to my life and soul
     That, as the star moves not but in his sphere,°   15
     I could not but by her. The other motive,
     Why to a public count° I might not go,
     Is the great love the general gender° bear him,
     Who, dipping all his faults in their affection,

17 *thieves of mercy:* Merciful thieves. 21 *bore:* Caliber, i.e., importance. ACT IV, SCENE VII.
Location: The castle. 1 *my acquittance seal:* Confirm or acknowledge my innocence. 6 *feats:* Acts.
7 *capital:* Punishable by death. 9 *mainly:* Greatly. 10 *unsinew'd:* Weak. 14 *conjunctive:* Closely
united. 15 *sphere:* The hollow sphere in which, according to Ptolemaic astronomy, the planets
moved. 17 *count:* Account, reckoning. 18 *general gender:* Common people.

Would, like the spring° that turneth wood to stone,   20
Convert his gyves° to graces, so that my arrows,
Too slightly timber'd° for so loud° a wind,
Would have reverted to my bow again
And not where I had aim'd them.
LAERTES: And so have I a noble father lost,   25
A sister driven into desp'rate terms,°
Whose worth, if praises may go back° again,
Stood challenger on mount° of all the age
For her perfections. But my revenge will come.
KING: Break not your sleeps for that. You must not think   30
That we are made of stuff so flat and dull
That we can let our beard be shook with danger
And think it pastime. You shortly shall hear more.
I lov'd your father, and we love ourself;
And that, I hope, will teach you to imagine—   35

(Enter a MESSENGER *with letters.)*

How now? What news?
MESSENGER: Letters, my lord, from Hamlet:
These to your Majesty, this to the Queen.   *(Gives letters.)*
KING: From Hamlet? Who brought them?
MESSENGER: Sailors, my lord, they say; I saw them not.
They were given me by Claudio. He receiv'd them   40
Of him that brought them.
KING: Laertes, you shall hear them.
Leave us.   *(Exit* MESSENGER.*)*
(Reads.) "High and mighty, you shall know I am set naked° on your
kingdom. Tomorrow shall I beg leave to see your kingly eyes, when I
shall, first asking your pardon° thereunto, recount the occasion of my   45
sudden and more strange return.   Hamlet." What should this mean?
Are all the rest come back? Or is it some abuse,° and no such thing?
LAERTES: Know you the hand?
KING: 'Tis Hamlet's character.° "Naked!"
And in a postscript here, he says "alone."
Can you devise° me?   50
LAERTES: I am lost in it, my lord. But let me come.
It warms the very sickness in my heart
That I shall live and tell him to his teeth,
"Thus didst thou."

---

20 *spring:* A spring with such a concentration of lime that it coats a piece of wood with limestone, in effect gilding it. 21 *gyves:* Fetters (which, gilded by the people's praise, would look like badges of honor). 22 *slightly timber'd:* Light; *loud:* Strong. 26 *terms:* State, condition. 27 *go back:* Recall Ophelia's former virtues. 28 *on mount:* On high. 43 *naked:* Destitute, unarmed, without following. 45 *pardon:* Permission. 47 *abuse:* Deceit. 48 *character:* Handwriting. 50 *devise:* Explain to.

KING: If it be so, Laertes—
    As how should it be so? How otherwise?°—   55
    Will you be ruled by me?
LAERTES: Ay, my lord,
    So° you will not o'errule me to a peace.
KING: To thine own peace. If he be now returned,
    As checking at° his voyage, and that he means
    No more to undertake it, I will work him   60
    To an exploit, now ripe in my device,
    Under the which he shall not choose but fall;
    And for his death no wind of blame shall breathe,
    But even his mother shall uncharge the practice°
    And call it accident.
LAERTES: My lord, I will be rul'd,   65
    The rather if you could devise it so
    That I might be the organ.°
KING: It falls right.
    You have been talk'd of since your travel much,
    And that in Hamlet's hearing, for a quality
    Wherein, they say, you shine. Your sum of parts°   70
    Did not together pluck such envy from him
    As did that one, and that, in my regard,
    Of the unworthiest siege.°
LAERTES: What part is that, my lord?
KING: A very riband in the cap of youth,   75
    Yet needful too, for youth no less becomes
    The light and careless livery that it wears
    Than settled age his sables° and his weeds,°
    Importing health° and graveness. Two months since
    Here was a gentleman of Normandy.   80
    I have seen myself, and serv'd against, the French,
    And they can well° on horseback, but this gallant
    Had witchcraft in 't; he grew unto his seat,
    And to such wondrous doing brought his horse
    As had he been incorps'd and demi-natured°   85
    With the brave beast. So far he topp'd° my thought
    That I, in forgery° of shapes and tricks,
    Come short of what he did.

---

55 *As . . . otherwise:* How can this (Hamlet's return) be true? Yet how otherwise than true (since we have the evidence of his letter). 57 *So:* Provided that. 59 *checking at:* Turning aside from (like a falcon leaving the quarry to fly at a chance bird). 64 *uncharge the practice:* Acquit the stratagem of being a plot. 67 *organ:* Agent, instrument. 70 *Your . . . parts:* All your other virtues. 73 *unworthiest siege:* Least important rank. 78 *sables:* Rich robes furred with sable; *weeds:* Garments. 79 *Importing health:* Indicating prosperity. 82 *can well:* Are skilled. 85 *incorps'd and demi-natur'd:* Of one body and nearly of one nature (like the centaur). 86 *topp'd:* Surpassed. 87 *forgery:* Invention.

LAERTES:　　　　　　　　　A Norman was 't?
KING:　A Norman.
LAERTES:　Upon my life, Lamord.
KING:　　　　　　　　　The very same.　　　　　　　　　　　90
LAERTES:　I know him well. He is the brooch° indeed
　　And gem of all the nation.
KING:　He made confession° of you,
　　And gave you such a masterly report
　　For art and exercise in your defense,　　　　　　　　95
　　And for your rapier most especial,
　　That he cried out, 'twould be a sight indeed,
　　If one could match you. The scrimers° of their nation,
　　He swore, had neither motion, guard, nor eye,
　　If you oppos'd them. Sir, this report of his　　　　　100
　　Did Hamlet so envenom with his envy
　　That he could nothing do but wish and beg
　　Your sudden coming o'er to play° with you.
　　Now, out of this—
LAERTES:　　　　　　　　What out of this, my lord?
KING:　Laertes, was your father dear to you?　　　　　105
　　Or are you like the painting of a sorrow,
　　A face without a heart?
LAERTES:　　　　　　　　Why ask you this?
KING:　Not that I think you did not love your father,
　　But that I know love is begun by time,°
　　And that I see, in passages of proof,°　　　　　　　110
　　Time qualifies° the spark and fire of it.
　　There lives within the very flame of love
　　A kind of wick or snuff° that will abate it,
　　And nothing is at a like goodness still,°
　　For goodness, growing to a plurisy,°　　　　　　　115
　　Dies in his own too much.° That° we would do,
　　We should do when we would; for this "would" changes
　　And hath abatements° and delays as many
　　As there are tongues, are hands, are accidents,°
　　And then this "should" is like a spendthrift's sigh,°　120
　　That hurts by easing.° But, to the quick o' th' ulcer;
　　Hamlet comes back. What would you undertake

---

91 *brooch:* Ornament.　93 *confession:* Admission of superiority.　98 *scrimers:* Fencers.　103 *play:* Fence.　109 *begun by time:* Subject to change.　110 *passages of proof:* Actual instances.　111 *qualifies:* Weakens.　113 *snuff:* The charred part of a candlewick.　114 *nothing . . . still:* Nothing remains at a constant level of perfection.　115 *plurisy:* Excess, plethora.　116 *in . . . much:* Of its own excess; *That:* That which.　118 *abatements:* Diminutions.　119 *accidents:* Occurrences, incidents. 120 *spendthrift's sigh:* An allusion to the belief that each sigh cost the heart a drop of blood.　121 *hurts by easing:* Costs the heart blood even while it affords emotional relief.

To show yourself your father's son in deed
More than in words?
LAERTES: To cut his throat i' th' church!
KING: No place, indeed, should murder sanctuarize;°   125
Revenge should have no bounds. But, good Laertes,
Will you do this,° keep close within your chamber.
Hamlet return'd shall know you are come home.
We'll put on those° shall praise your excellence
And set a double varnish on the fame   130
The Frenchman gave you, bring you in fine° together,
And wager on your heads. He, being remiss,°
Most generous,° and free from all contriving,
Will not peruse the foils, so that, with ease,
Or with a little shuffling, you may choose   135
A sword unbated,° and in a pass of practice°
Requite him for your father.
LAERTES: I will do 't.
And for that purpose I'll anoint my sword.
I bought an unction° of a mountebank°
So mortal that, but dip a knife in it,   140
Where it draws blood no cataplasm° so rare,
Collected from all simples° that have virtue
Under the moon, can save the thing from death
That is but scratch'd withal. I'll touch my point
With this contagion, that, if I gall° him slightly,   145
It may be death.
KING: Let's further think of this,
Weigh what convenience both of time and means
May fit us to our shape.° If this should fail,
And that our drift look through our bad performance,°
'Twere better not assay'd. Therefore this project   150
Should have a back or second, that might hold
If this did blast in proof.° Soft, let me see.
We'll make a solemn wager on your cunnings—
I ha 't!
When in your motion you are hot and dry—   155
As° make your bouts more violent to that end—
And that he calls for drink, I'll have prepar'd him

---

125 *sanctuarize:* Protect from punishment (alludes to the right of sanctuary with which certain religious places were invested).   127 *Will you do this:* If you wish to do this.   129 *put on those:* Instigate those who.   131 *in fine:* Finally.   132 *remiss:* Negligently unsuspicious.   133 *generous:* Noble-minded.   136 *unbated:* Not blunted, having no button; *pass of practice:* Treacherous thrust.   139 *unction:* Ointment; *mountebank:* Quack doctor.   141 *cataplasm:* Plaster or poultice.   142 *simples:* Herbs.   145 *gall:* Graze, wound.   148 *shape:* Part that we propose to act.   149 *drift . . . performance:* I.e., intention be disclosed by our bungling.   152 *blast in proof:* Burst in the test (like a cannon).   156 *As:* And you should.

A chalice for the nonce,° whereon but sipping,
If he by chance escape your venom'd stuck,°
Our purpose may hold there. *(A cry within.)* But stay, what noise?   160

(Enter QUEEN.*)*

QUEEN: One woe doth tread upon another's heel,
    So fast they follow. Your sister's drowned, Laertes.
LAERTES: Drown'd! O, where?
QUEEN: There is a willow grows askant° the brook,
    That shows his hoar° leaves in the glassy stream;   165
    Therewith fantastic garlands did she make
    Of crow-flowers, nettles, daisies, and long purples°
    That liberal° shepherds give a grosser name,
    But our cold° maids do dead men's fingers call them.
    There on the pendent boughs her crownet° weeds   170
    Clamb'ring to hang, an envious sliver° broke,
    When down her weedy° trophies and herself
    Fell in the weeping brook. Her clothes spread wide,
    And mermaid-like awhile they bore her up,
    Which time she chanted snatches of old lauds,°   175
    As one incapable° of her own distress,
    Or like a creature native and indued°
    Unto that element. But long it could not be
    Till that her garments, heavy with their drink,
    Pull'd the poor wretch from her melodious lay   180
    To muddy death.
LAERTES: Alas, then she is drown'd?
QUEEN: Drown'd, drown'd.
LAERTES: Too much of water hast thou, poor Ophelia,
    And therefore I forbid my tears. But yet
    It is our trick;° nature her custom holds,   185
    Let shame say what it will. *(He weeps.)* When these are gone,
    The woman will be out.° Adieu, my lord.
    I have a speech of fire, that fain would blaze,
    But that this folly drowns it.   *(Exit.)*
KING: Let's follow, Gertrude.
    How much I had to do to calm his rage!   190
    Now fear I this will give it start again;
    Therefore let's follow.   *(Exeunt.)*

---

158 *nonce:* Occasion. 159 *stuck:* Thrust (from "stoccado," a fencing term). 164 *askant:* Aslant.
165 *hoar:* White or gray. 167 *long purples:* Early purple orchids. 168 *liberal:* Free-spoken. 169
cold: Chaste. 170 *crownet:* Made into a chaplet or coronet. 171 *envious sliver:* Malicious branch.
172 *weedy:* I.e., of plants. 175 *lauds:* Hymns. 176 *incapable:* Lacking capacity to apprehend. 177
indued: Adapted by nature. 185 *It is our trick:* Weeping is our natural way (when sad). 186–87
When . . . out: When my tears are all shed, the woman in me will be expended, satisfied.

ACT V
SCENE I°

(Enter two CLOWNS° *with spades, etc.)*

FIRST CLOWN: Is she to be buried in Christian burial when she willfully
seeks her own salvation?

SECOND CLOWN: I tell thee she is; therefore make her grave straight.°
The crowner° hath sat on her, and finds it Christian burial.

FIRST CLOWN: How can that be, unless she drown'd herself in her own   5
defense?

SECOND CLOWN: Why, 'tis found so.

FIRST CLOWN: It must be "se offendendo";° it cannot be else. For here
lies the point: if I drown myself wittingly, it argues an act, and an act
hath three branches—it is to act, to do, and to perform. Argal,° she   10
drown'd herself wittingly.

SECOND CLOWN: Nay, but hear you, goodman delver—

FIRST CLOWN: Give me leave. Here lies the water; good. Here stands the
man; good. If the man go to this water, and drown himself, it is, will
he,° nill he, he goes, mark you that. But if the water come to him and   15
drown him, he drowns not himself. Argal, he that is not guilty of his
own death shortens not his own life.

SECOND CLOWN: But is this law?

FIRST CLOWN: Ay, marry, is 't—crowner's quest° law.

SECOND CLOWN: Will you ha' the truth on 't? If this had not been a   20
gentlewoman, she should have been buried out o' Christian burial.

FIRST CLOWN: Why, there thou say'st.° And the more pity that great folk
should have count'nance° in this world to drown or hang themselves,
more than their even-Christen.° Come, my spade. There is no ancient
gentlemen but gard'ners, ditchers, and grave-makers. They hold up   25
Adam's profession.

SECOND CLOWN: Was he a gentleman?

FIRST CLOWN: 'A was the first that ever bore arms.

SECOND CLOWN: Why, he had none.

FIRST CLOWN: What, art a heathen? How dost thou understand the   30
Scripture? The Scripture says "Adam digg'd." Could he dig without
arms? I'll put another question to thee. If thou answerest me not to the
purpose, confess thyself°—

SECOND CLOWN: Go to.

FIRST CLOWN: What is he that builds stronger than either the mason, the   35
shipwright, or the carpenter?

ACT V, SCENE I. *Location:* A churchyard. s.d. *Clowns:* Rustics. 3 *straight:* Straightway, immediately. 4 *crowner:* Coroner. 8 *se offendendo:* A comic mistake for "se defendendo," term used in
verdicts of justifiable homicide. 10 *Argal:* Corruption of "ergo," therefore. 14–15 *will he:* Will
he not. 19 *quest:* Inquest. 22 *there you say'st:* That's right. 23 *count'nance:* Privilege. 24 *even-
Christen:* Fellow Christian. 33 *confess thyself:* The saying continues, "and be hanged."

SECOND CLOWN: The gallows-maker, for that frame outlives a thousand tenants.

FIRST CLOWN: I like thy wit well, in good faith. The gallows does well; but how does it well? It does well to those that do ill. Now thou dost ill to say the gallows is built stronger than the church. Argal, the gallows may do well to thee. To 't again, come. 40

SECOND CLOWN: "Who builds stronger than a mason, a shipwright, or a carpenter?"

FIRST CLOWN: Ay, tell me that, and unyoke.° 45

SECOND CLOWN: Marry, now I can tell.

FIRST CLOWN: To 't.

SECOND CLOWN: Mass,° I cannot tell.

(Enter HAMLET *and* HORATIO *at a distance.)*

FIRST CLOWN: Cudgel thy brains no more about it, for your dull ass will not mend his pace with beating; and, when you are ask'd this question next, say "a grave-maker." The houses he makes lasts till doomsday. Go, get thee in, and fetch me a stoup° of liquor. 50

(Exit SECOND CLOWN. FIRST CLOWN *digs.)*

"In youth, when I did love, did love,° *(Song.)*
    Methought it was very sweet,
To contract—O—the time for—a—my behove,° 55
    O, methought there—a—was nothing—a—meet."°

HAMLET: Has this fellow no feeling of his business, that a sings at grave-making?

HORATIO: Custom hath made it in him a property of easiness.°

HAMLET: 'Tis e'en so. The hand of little employment hath the daintier sense.° 60

FIRST CLOWN: "But age, with his stealing steps, *(Song.)*
    Hath claw'd me in his clutch,
And hath shipped me into the land,°
    As if I had never been such." *(Throws up a skull.)* 65

HAMLET: That skull had a tongue in it, and could sing once. How the knave jowls° it to the ground, as if 'twere Cain's jaw-bone, that did the

---

45 *unyoke:* After this great effort you may unharness the team of your wits. 48 *Mass:* By the Mass. 52 *stoup:* Two-quart measure. 53 *In . . . love:* This and the two following stanzas, with nonsensical variations, are from a poem attributed to Lord Vaux and printed in *Tottel's Miscellany* (1557). The *O* and *a* (for "ah") seemingly are the grunts of the digger. 55 *To contract . . . behove:* To make a betrothal agreement for my benefit (?). 56 *meet:* Suitable, i.e., more suitable. 59 *property of easiness:* Something he can do easily and without thinking. 60–61 *daintier sense:* More delicate sense of feeling. 64 *into the land:* Toward my grave (?) (but note the lack of rhyme in *steps, land*). 67 *jowls:* Dashes.

first murder! This might be the pate of a politician,° which this ass now
o'erreaches,° one that would circumvent God, might it not?

HORATIO: It might, my lord.   70

HAMLET: Or of a courtier, which could say "Good morrow, sweet lord!
How dost thou, sweet lord?" This might be my Lord Such-a-one, that
prais'd my Lord Such-a-one's horse when 'a meant to beg it, might
it not?

HORATIO: Ay, my lord.   75

HAMLET: Why, e'en so, and now my Lady Worm's, chapless,° and knock'd
about the mazzard° with a sexton's spade. Here's fine revolution,° an°
we had the trick to see 't. Did these bones cost no more the breeding,°
but to play at loggats° with them? Mine ache to think on 't.

FIRST CLOWN: "A pick-axe, and a spade, a spade,   *(Song.)* 80
    For and° a shrouding sheet;
    O, a pit of clay for to be made
    For such a guest is meet."   *(Throws up another skull.)*

HAMLET: There's another. Why may not that be the skull of a lawyer?
Where be his quiddities° now, his quillities,° his cases, his tenures,° and   85
his tricks? Why does he suffer this mad knave now to knock him about
the sconce° with a dirty shovel, and will not tell him of his action of
battery? Hum! This fellow might be in 's time a great buyer of land,
with his statutes, his recognizances,° his fines, his double° vouchers,° his
recoveries.° Is this the fine of his fines, and the recovery of his recov-   90
eries, to have his fine pate full of fine dirt?° Will his vouchers vouch
him no more of his purchases, and double ones too, than the length
and breadth of a pair of indentures?° The very conveyances° of his lands
will scarcely lie in this box,° and must th' inheritor° himself have no
more, ha?   95

HORATIO: Not a jot more, my lord.

HAMLET: Is not parchment made of sheep-skins?

HORATIO: Ay, my lord, and of calf-skins too.

---

68 *politician:* Schemer, plotter. 69 *o'erreaches:* Circumvents, gets the better of (with a quibble on
the literal sense). 76 *chapless:* Having no lower jaw. 77 *mazzard:* Head (literally, a drinking
vessel); *revolution:* Change; *an:* If. 78 *the breeding:* In the breeding, raising. 79 *loggats:* A game in
which pieces of hardwood are thrown to lie as near as possible to a stake. 81 *For and:* And
moreover. 85 *quiddities:* Subtleties, quibbles (from Latin "quid," a thing); *quillities:* Verbal niceties,
subtle distinctions (variation of "quiddities"); *tenures:* The holding of a piece of property or
office, or the conditions or period of such holding. 87 *sconce:* Head. 89 *statutes, recognizances:*
Legal documents guaranteeing a debt by attaching land and property. 89–90 *fines, recoveries:* Ways
of converting entailed estates into "fee simple" or freehold. 89 *double:* Signed by two signatories;
vouchers: Guarantees of the legality of a title to real estate. 90–91 *fine of his fines . . . fine pate . .
. fine dirt:* End of his legal maneuvers . . . elegant head . . . minutely sifted dirt. 93 *pair of
indentures:* Legal document drawn up in duplicate on a single sheet and then cut apart on a zigzag
line so that each pair was uniquely matched (Hamlet may refer to two rows of teeth, or den-
tures.); *conveyances:* Deeds. 94 *this box:* The skull; *inheritor:* Possessor, owner.

HAMLET: They are sheep and calves which seek out assurance in that.° I
   will speak to this fellow.— Whose grave's this, sirrah?°   100
FIRST CLOWN: Mine, sir.
   (Sings.) "O, a pit of clay for to be made
   For such a guest is meet."
HAMLET: I think it be thine, indeed, for thou liest in 't.
FIRST CLOWN: You lie out on 't, sir, and therefore 'tis not yours. For my   105
   part, I do not lie in 't, yet it is mine.
HAMLET: Thou dost lie in 't, to be in 't and say it is thine. 'Tis for the
   dead, not for the quick;° therefore thou liest.
FIRST CLOWN: 'Tis a quick lie, sir; 'twill away again from me to you.
HAMLET: What man dost thou dig it for?   110
FIRST CLOWN: For no man, sir.
HAMLET: What woman, then?
FIRST CLOWN: For none, neither.
HAMLET: Who is to be buried in 't?
FIRST CLOWN: One that was a woman, sir, but, rest her soul, she's dead.   115
HAMLET: How absolute° the knave is! We must speak by the card,° or
   equivocation° will undo us. By the Lord, Horatio, this three years I
   have taken note of it: the age is grown so pick'd° that the toe of the
   peasant comes so near the heel of the courtier, he galls his kibe.° How
   long hast thou been a grave-maker?   120
FIRST CLOWN: Of all the days i' th' year, I came to 't that day that our
   last king Hamlet overcame Fortinbras.
HAMLET: How long is that since?
FIRST CLOWN: Cannot you tell that? Every fool can tell that. It was that
   very day that young Hamlet was born—he that is mad, and sent into   125
   England.
HAMLET: Ay, marry, why was he sent into England?
FIRST CLOWN: Why, because 'a was mad. 'A shall recover his wits there,
   or, if 'a do not, 'tis no great matter there.
HAMLET: Why?   130
FIRST CLOWN: 'Twill not be seen in him there. There the men are as
   mad as he.
HAMLET: How came he mad?
FIRST CLOWN: Very strangely, they say.
HAMLET: How strangely?   135
FIRST CLOWN: Faith, e'en with losing his wits.
HAMLET: Upon what ground?

---

99 *assurance in that:* Safety in legal parchments. 100 *sirrah:* Term of address to inferiors. 108
quick: Living. 116 *absolute:* Positive, decided; *by the card:* By the mariner's card on which the
points of the compass were marked, i.e., with precision. 117 *equivocation:* Ambiguity in the use
of terms. 118 *pick'd:* Refined, fastidious. 119 *galls his kibe:* Chafes the courtier's chilblain (a
swelling or sore caused by cold).

FIRST CLOWN: Why, here in Denmark. I have been sexton here, man
and boy, thirty years.

HAMLET: How long will a man lie i' th' earth ere he rot?   140

FIRST CLOWN: Faith, if 'a be not rotten before 'a die—as we have many
pocky° corses now-a-days, that will scarce hold the laying in—'a will
last you some eight year or nine year. A tanner will last you nine year.

HAMLET: Why he more than another?

FIRST CLOWN: Why, sir, his hide is so tann'd with his trade that 'a will   145
keep out water a great while, and your water is a sore decayer of your
whoreson dead body. *(Picks up a skull.)* Here's a skull now hath lain
you° i' th' earth three and twenty years.

HAMLET: Whose was it?

FIRST CLOWN: A whoreson mad fellow's it was. Whose do you think   150
it was?

HAMLET: Nay, I know not.

FIRST CLOWN: A pestilence on him for a mad rogue! 'A pour'd a flagon
of Rhenish° on my head once. This same skull, sir, was Yorick's skull,
the King's jester.   155

HAMLET: This?

FIRST CLOWN: E'en that.

HAMLET: Let me see. *(Takes the skull.)* Alas, poor Yorick! I knew him,
Horatio, a fellow of infinite jest, of most excellent fancy. He hath borne
me on his back a thousand times; and now, how abhorr'd in my imag-   160
ination it is! My gorge rises at it. Here hung those lips that I have kiss'd
I know not how oft. Where be your gibes now? Your gambols, your
songs, your flashes of merriment that were wont to set the table on a
roar? Not one now, to mock your own grinning? Quite chap-fall'n?°
Now get you to my lady's chamber, and tell her, let her paint an inch   165
thick, to this favor° she must come; make her laugh at that. Prithee,
Horatio, tell me one thing.

HORATIO: What's that, my lord?

HAMLET: Dost thou think Alexander look'd o' this fashion i' th' earth?

HORATIO: E'en so.   170

HAMLET: And smelt so? Pah! *(Puts down the skull.)*

HORATIO: E'en so, my lord.

HAMLET: To what base uses we may return, Horatio! Why may not imagination trace the noble dust of Alexander, till a' find it stopping a bung-
hole!   175

HORATIO: 'Twere to consider too curiously,° to consider so.

HAMLET: No, faith, not a jot, but to follow him thither with modesty°
enough, and likelihood to lead it. As thus: Alexander died, Alexander

---

142 *pocky:* Rotten, diseased (literally, with the pox, or syphilis). 147–48 *lain you:* Lain. 154
Rhenish: Rhine wine. 164 *chap-fall'n:* (1) Lacking the lower jaw, (2) dejected. 166 *favor:* Aspect,
appearance. 176 *curiously:* Minutely. 177 *modesty:* Moderation.

was buried, Alexander returneth to dust; the dust is earth; of earth we
make loam;° and why of that loam, whereto he was converted, might   180
they not stop a beer-barrel?
Imperious° Caesar, dead and turn'd to clay,
Might stop a hole to keep the wind away.
O, that that earth which kept the world in awe
Should patch a wall t' expel the winter's flaw!°   185
But soft, but soft awhile! Here comes the King.

(Enter KING, QUEEN, LAERTES, *and the Corse of* OPHELIA, *in
procession, with* PRIEST, LORDS *etc.)*

The Queen, the courtiers. Who is this they follow?
And with such maimed rites? This doth betoken
The corse they follow did with desp'rate hand
Fordo it° own life. 'Twas of some estate.°   190
Couch° we awhile, and mark.

> *(He and* HORATIO *conceal themselves.*
> OPHELIA'*s body is taken to the grave.)*

LAERTES: What ceremony else?
HAMLET *(to* HORATIO*)*: That is Laertes, a very noble youth. Mark.
LAERTES: What ceremony else?
PRIEST: Her obsequies have been as far enlarg'd   195
As we have warranty. Her death was doubtful,
And, but that great command o'ersways the order,
She should in ground unsanctified been lodg'd
Till the last trumpet. For° charitable prayers,
Shards,° flints, and pebbles should be thrown on her.   200
Yet here she is allow'd her virgin crants,°
Her maiden strewments,° and the bringing home
Of bell and burial.°
LAERTES: Must there no more be done?
PRIEST: No more be done.
We should profane the service of the dead   205
To sing a requiem and such rest to her
As to peace-parted souls.
LAERTES: Lay her i' th' earth,
And from her fair and unpolluted flesh
May violets° spring! I tell thee, churlish priest,

---

180 *loam:* Clay mixture for brickmaking or other clay use. 182 *Imperious:* Imperial. 185 *flaw:*
Gust of wind. 190 *Fordo it:* Destroy its; *estate:* Rank. 191 *Couch:* Hide, lurk. 199 *For:* In place
of. 200 *Shards:* Broken bits of pottery. 201 *crants:* Garland. 202 *strewments:* Traditional strewing
of flowers. 202–3 *bringing . . . burial:* Laying to rest of the body in consecrated ground, to the
sound of the bell. 209 *violets:* see IV.v.181 and note.

A minist'ring angel should my sister be   210
When thou liest howling!

HAMLET *(to* HORATIO*)*:   What, the fair Ophelia!

QUEEN *(scattering flowers)*: Sweets to the sweet! Farewell.
I hoped thou shouldst have been my Hamlet's wife.
I thought thy bride-bed to have deck'd, sweet maid,
And not have strew'd thy grave.

LAERTES: O, treble woe   215
Fall ten times treble on that cursed head
Whose wicked deed thy most ingenious sense°
Depriv'd thee of! Hold off the earth awhile,
Till I have caught her once more in mine arms.

                    (Leaps into the grave and embraces OPHELIA*.)*
Now pile your dust upon the quick and dead,   220
Till of this flat a mountain you have made
T 'o'ertop old Pelion,° or the skyish head
Of blue Olympus.°

HAMLET *(coming forward)*: What is he whose grief
Bears such an emphasis, whose phrase of sorrow   225
Conjures the wand'ring stars,° and makes them stand
Like wonder-wounded hearers? This is I,
Hamlet the Dane.°

LAERTES: The devil take thy soul!   *(Grappling with him.)*

HAMLET: Thou pray'st not well.
I prithee, take thy fingers from my throat;   230
For, though I am not splenitive° and rash,
Yet have I in me something dangerous,
Which let thy wisdom fear. Hold off thy hand.

KING: Pluck them asunder.

QUEEN: Hamlet, Hamlet!

ALL: Gentlemen!

HORATIO: Good my lord, be quiet.   235

                    *(*HAMLET *and* HORATIO *are parted.)*

HAMLET: Why, I will fight with him upon this theme
Until my eyelids will no longer wag.

QUEEN: O my son, what theme?

HAMLET: I lov'd Ophelia. Forty thousand brothers
Could not with all their quantity of love   240
Make up my sum. What wilt thou do for her?

KING: O, he is mad, Laertes.

QUEEN: For love of God, forbear him.

---

217 *ingenious sense:* Mind endowed with finest qualities. 222–23 *Pelion, Olympus:* Mountains in
the north of Thessaly; see also *Ossa* at line 253. 226 *wand'ring stars:* Planets. 228 *the Dane:* This
title normally signifies the King; see I.i.15 and note. 231 *splenitive:* Quick-tempered.

HAMLET: 'Swounds,° show me what thou't do.
    Woo 't° weep? Woo 't fight? Woo 't fast? Woo 't tear thyself?   245
    Woo 't drink up eisel?° Eat a crocodile?
    I'll do 't. Dost thou come here to whine?
    To outface me with leaping in her grave?
    Be buried quick° with her, and so will I.
    And, if thou prate of mountains, let them throw   250
    Millions of acres on us, till our ground,
    Singeing his pate° against the burning zone,°
    Make Ossa° like a wart! Nay, an thou 'lt mouth,°
    I'll rant as well as thou.
QUEEN: This is mere° madness,
    And thus a while the fit will work on him;   255
    Anon, as patient as the female dove
    When that her golden couplets° are disclos'd,°
    His silence will sit drooping.
HAMLET: Hear you, sir.
    What is the reason that you use me thus?
    I lov'd you ever. But it is no matter.   260
    Let Hercules himself do what he may,
    The cat will mew, and dog will have his day.°
KING: I pray thee, good Horatio, wait upon him.
                        (Exit HAMLET *and* HORATIO.*)*
    (To LAERTES.*)* Strengthen your patience in° our last night's speech;
    We'll put the matter to the present push.°—   265
    Good Gertrude, set some watch over your son.—
    This grave shall have a living° monument.
    An hour of quiet shortly shall we see;
    Till then, in patience our proceeding be.   *(Exeunt.)*

SCENE II°

(Enter HAMLET *and* HORATIO.*)*

HAMLET: So much for this, sir; now shall you see the other.°
    You do remember all the circumstance?
HORATIO: Remember it, my lord!

---

244 *'Swounds:* By His (Christ's) wounds. 245 *Woo 't:* Wilt thou. 246 *eisel:* Vinegar. 249 *quick:* Alive. 252 *his pate:* Its head, i.e., top; *burning zone:* Sun's orbit. 253 *Ossa:* Another mountain in Thessaly (In their war against the Olympian gods, the giants attempted to heap Ossa, Pelion, and Olympus on one another to scale heaven.); *mouth:* Rant. 254 *mere:* Utter. 257 *golden couplets:* Two baby pigeons, covered with yellow down; *disclos'd:* Hatched. 261–62 *Let . . . day:* Despite any blustering attempts at interference every person will sooner or later do what he must do. 264 *in:* By recalling. 265 *present push:* Immediate test. 267 *living:* Lasting; also refers (for Laertes' benefit) to the plot against Hamlet. ACT V, SCENE II. *Location:* The castle. 1 *see the other:* Hear the other news.

HAMLET: Sir, in my heart there was a kind of fighting
    That would not let me sleep. Methought I lay   5
    Worse than the mutines° in the bilboes.° Rashly,°
    And prais'd be rashness for it—let us know,°
    Our indiscretion sometime serves us well
    When our deep plots do pall,° and that should learn° us
    There's a divinity that shapes our ends,   10
    Rough-hew° them how we will—
HORATIO: That is most certain.
HAMLET: Up from my cabin,
    My sea-grown scarf'd about me, in the dark
    Grop'd I to find out them, had my desire,
    Finger'd° their packet, and in fine° withdrew   15
    To mine own room again, making so bold,
    My fears forgetting manners, to unseal
    Their grand commission; where I found, Horatio—
    Ah, royal knavery!—an exact command,
    Larded° with many several sorts of reasons   20
    Importing° Denmark's health and England's too,
    With, ho, such bugs° and goblins in my life,°
    That, on the supervise,° no leisure bated,°
    No, not to stay the grinding of the axe,
    My head should be struck off.
HORATIO: Is 't possible?   25
HAMLET: Here's the commission; read it at more leisure. *(Gives document.)*
    But wilt thou hear now how I did proceed?
HORATIO: I beseech you.
HAMLET: Being thus benetted round with villainies,
    Or I could make a prologue to my brains,   30
    They had begun the play.° I sat me down,
    Devis'd a new commission, wrote it fair.°
    I once did hold it, as our statists° do,
    A baseness° to write fair, and labor'd much
    How to forget that learning, but, sir, now   35
    It did me yeoman's° service. Wilt thou know
    Th' effect° of what I wrote?
HORATIO: Ay, good my lord.

---

6 *mutines:* Mutineers; *bilboes:* Shackles; *Rashly:* On impulse (this adverb goes with line 12ff.). 7 *know:* Acknowledge. 9 *pall:* Fail; *learn:* Teach. 11 *Rough-hew:* Shape roughly. 15 *Finger'd:* Pilfered, pinched; *in fine:* Finally, in conclusion. 20 *Larded:* Enriched. 21 *Importing:* Relating to. 22 *bugs:* Bugbears, hobgoblins; *in my life:* To be feared if I were allowed to live. 23 *supervise:* Reading; *leisure bated:* Delay allowed. 30–31 *Or . . . play:* Before I could consciously turn my brain to the matter, it had started working on a plan. (*Or* means ere.) 32 *fair:* In a clear hand. 33 *statists:* Statesmen. 34 *baseness:* Lower-class trait. 36 *yeoman's:* Substantial, workmanlike. 37 *effect:* Purport.

HAMLET: An earnest conjuration from the King,
    As England was his faithful tributary,
    As love between them like the palm might flourish,   40
    As peace should still her wheaten garland° wear
    And stand a comma° 'tween their amities,
    And many such-like as's° of great charge,°
    That, on the view and knowing of these contents,
    Without debatement further, more or less,   45
    He should those bearers put to sudden death,
    Not shriving time° allow'd.
HORATIO: How was this seal'd?
HAMLET: Why, even in that was heaven ordinant.°
    I had my father's signet° in my purse,
    Which was the model of that Danish seal;   50
    Folded the writ up in the form of th' other,
    Subscrib'd° it, gave 't th' impression,° plac'd it safely,
    The changeling° never known. Now, the next day
    Was our sea-fight, and what to this was sequent
    Thou knowest already.   55
HORATIO: So Guildenstern and Rosencrantz go to 't.
HAMLET: Why, man, they did make love to this employment.
    They are not near my conscience. Their defeat
    Does by their own insinuation° grow.
    'Tis dangerous when the baser nature comes   60
    Between the pass° and fell° incensed points
    Of mighty opposites.
HORATIO: Why, what a king is this!
HAMLET: Does it not, think thee, stand° me now upon—
    He that hath killed my king and whor'd my mother,
    Popp'd in between th' election° and my hopes,   65
    Thrown out his angle° for my proper° life,
    And with such coz'nage°—is 't not perfect conscience
    To quit° him with this arm? And is 't not to be damn'd
    To let this canker° of our nature come
    In further evil?   70
HORATIO: It must be shortly known to him from England
    What is the issue of the business there.

---

41 *wheaten garland:* Symbolic of fruitful agriculture, of peace. 42 *comma:* Indicating continuity, link. 43 *as's:* (1) The "whereases" of formal document, (2) asses; *charge:* (1) Import, (2) burden. 47 *shriving time:* Time for confession and absolution. 48 *ordinant:* Directing. 49 *signet:* Small seal. 52 *Subscrib'd:* Signed; *impression:* With a wax seal. 53 *changeling:* The substituted letter (literally, a fairy child substituted for a human one). 59 *insinuation:* Interference. 61 *pass:* Thrust; *fell:* Fierce. 63 *stand:* Become incumbent. 65 *election:* The Danish monarch was "elected" by a small number of high-ranking electors. 66 *angle:* Fishing line; *proper:* Very. 67 *coz'nage:* Trickery. 68 *quit:* Repay. 69 *canker:* Ulcer.

HAMLET: It will be short. The interim is mine,
And a man's life 's no more than to say "One."°
But I am very sorry, good Horatio,   75
That to Laertes I forgot myself,
For by the image of my cause I see
The portraiture of his. I'll court his favors.
But, sure, the bravery° of his grief did put me
Into a tow'ring passion.
HORATIO: Peace, who comes here?   80

(Enter a COURTIER *[*OSRIC*].)*

OSRIC: Your lordship is right welcome back to Denmark.
HAMLET: I humbly thank you, sir. *(To* HORATIO.*)* Dost know this
water-fly?
HORATIO: No, my good lord.
HAMLET: Thy state is the more gracious, for 'tis a vice to know him. He   85
hath much land, and fertile. Let a beast be lord of beasts, and his crib
shall stand at the King's mess.° 'Tis a chough,° but, as I say, spacious in
the possession of dirt.
OSRIC: Sweet lord, if your lordship were at leisure, I should impart a thing
to you from his Majesty.   90
HAMLET: I will receive it, sir, with all diligence of spirit. Put your bonnet
to his right use; 'tis for the head.
OSRIC: I thank your lordship, it is very hot.
HAMLET: No, believe me, 'tis very cold; the wind is northerly.
OSRIC: It is indifferent° cold, my lord, indeed.   95
HAMLET: But yet methinks it is very sultry and hot for my complexion.°
OSRIC: Exceedingly, my lord; it is very sultry, as 'twere—I cannot tell how.
My lord, his Majesty bade me signify to you that 'a has laid a great
wager on your head. Sir, this is the matter—
HAMLET: I beseech you, remember—   100
                    *(*HAMLET *moves him to put on his hat.)*
OSRIC: Nay, good my lord; for my ease,° in good faith. Sir, here is newly
come to court Laertes—believe me, an absolute gentleman, full of most
excellent differences,° of very soft society° and great showing.° Indeed,
to speak feelingly° of him, he is the card° or calendar° of gentry,° for you
shall find in him the continent of what part° a gentleman would see.   105

74 *a man's . . . "One":* To take a man's life requires no more than to count to one as one duels.
79 *bravery:* Bravado. 86–87 *Let . . . mess:* If a man, no matter how beastlike, is as rich in
possessions as Osric, he may eat at the King's table. 87 *chough:* Chattering jackdaw. 95 *indifferent:*
Somewhat. 96 *complexion:* Temperament. 101 *for my ease:* A conventional reply declining the
invitation to put his hat back on. 103 *differences:* Special qualities; *soft society:* Agreeable manners;
great showing: Distinguished appearance. 104 *feelingly:* With just perception; *card:* Chart, map;
calendar: Guide; *gentry:* Good breeding. 105 *the continent . . . part:* One who contains in him all
the qualities (a *continent* is that which contains).

HAMLET: Sir, his definement° suffers no perdition° in you, though, I
know, to divide him inventorially° would dozy° th' arithmetic of memory, and yet but yaw° neither° in respect of° his quick sail. But, in the
verity of extolment,° I take him to be a soul of great article,° and his
infusion° of such dearth and rareness,° as, to make true diction° of him,   110
his semblable° is his mirror, and who else would trace° him, his
umbrage,° nothing more.

OSRIC: Your lordship speaks most infallibly of him.

HAMLET: The concernancy,° sir? Why do we wrap the gentleman in our
more rawer breath?°   115

OSRIC: Sir?

HORATIO: Is 't not possible to understand in another tongue?° You will
do 't,° sir, really.

HAMLET: What imports the nomination° of this gentleman?

OSRIC: Of Laertes?   120

HORATIO *(to HAMLET)*: His purse is empty already; all 's golden words
are spent.

HAMLET: Of him, sir.

OSRIC: I know you are not ignorant—

HAMLET: I would you did, sir; yet, in faith, if you did, it would not much   125
approve° me. Well, sir?

OSRIC: You are not ignorant of what excellence Laertes is—

HAMLET: I dare not confess that, lest I should compare° with him in
excellence; but to know a man well were to know himself.°

OSRIC: I mean, sir, for his weapon; but in the imputation laid on him by   130
them,° in his meed° he's unfellow'd.°

HAMLET: What's his weapon?

OSRIC: Rapier and dagger.

HAMLET: That's two of his weapons—but well.

OSRIC: The King, sir, hath wager'd with him six Barbary horses, against   135
the which he has impawn'd,° as I take it, six French rapiers and pon-

---

106 *definement:* Definition. (Hamlet proceeds to mock Osric by using his lofty diction back at
him.); *perdition:* Loss, diminution.   107 *divide him inventorially:* Enumerate his graces; *dozy:* Dizzy.
108 *yaw:* To move unsteadily (said of a ship); *neither:* For all that; *in respect of:* In comparison
with.   108–9 *in . . . extolment:* In true praise (of him).   109 *article:* Moment or importance.   110
infusion: Essence, character imparted by nature; *dearth and rareness:* Rarity; *make true diction:* Speak
truly.   111 *semblable:* Only true likeness; *who . . . trace:* Any other person who would wish to
follow.   112 *umbrage:* Shadow.   114 *concernancy:* Import, relevance.   115 *breath:* Speech.   117 *to
understand . . . tongue:* For Osric to understand when someone else speaks in his manner. (Horatio
twits Osric for not being able to understand the kind of flowery speech he himself uses when
Hamlet speaks in such a vein.)   117–18 *You will do 't:* You can if you try.   119 *nomination:*
Naming.   126 *approve:* Commend.   128 *compare:* Seem to compete.   129 *but . . . himself:* For, to
recognize excellence in another man, one must know oneself.   130–31 *imputation . . . them:*
Reputation given him by others.   131 *meed:* Merit; *unfellow'd:* Unmatched.   136 *impawn'd:*
Staked, wagered.

iards, with their assigns,° as girdle, hangers,° and so. Three of the carriages,° in faith, are very dear to fancy,° very responsive° to the hilts,
most delicate° carriages, and of very liberal conceit.°

HAMLET: What call you the carriages? 140

HORATIO *(to* HAMLET*)*: I knew you must be edified by the margent° ere
you had done.

OSRIC: The carriages, sir, are the hangers.

HAMLET: The phrase would be more germane to the matter if we could
carry a cannon by our sides; I would it might be hangers till then. But, 145
on: six Barb'ry horses against six French swords, their assigns, and three
liberal-conceited carriages; that's the French bet against the Danish.
Why is this impawn'd, as you call it?

OSRIC: The King, sir, hath laid,° sir, that in a dozen passes° between yourself and him, he shall not exceed you three hits. He hath laid on twelve 150
for nine, and it would come to immediate trial, if your lordship would
vouchsafe the answer.

HAMLET: How if I answer no?

OSRIC: I mean, my lord, the opposition of your person in trial.

HAMLET: Sir, I will walk here in the hall. If it please his Majesty, it is the 155
breathing time° of day with me. Let the foils be brought, the gentleman
willing, and the King hold his purpose, I will win for him an I can; if
not, I will gain nothing but my shame and the odd hits.

OSRIC: Shall I deliver you so?

HAMLET: To this effect, sir—after what flourish your nature will. 160

OSRIC: I commend my duty to your lordship.

HAMLET: Yours, yours. *(Exit* OSRIC.*)* He does well to commend it himself; there are no tongues else for 's turn.

HORATIO: This lapwing° runs away with the shell on his head.

HAMLET: 'A did comply, sir, with his dug,° before 'a suck'd it. Thus has 165
he—and many more of the same breed that I know the drossy° age
dotes on—only got the tune° of the time and, out of an habit of
encounter,° a kind of yesty° collection,° which carries them through

137 *assigns:* Appurtenances; *hangers:* Straps on the sword belt (*girdle*) from which the sword hung.
137–38 *carriages:* An affected way of saying *hangers;* literally, gun-carriages. 138 *dear to fancy:*
Fancifully designed, tasteful; *responsive:* Corresponding closely, matching. 139 *delicate:* I.e., in
workmanship; *liberal conceit:* Elaborate design. 141 *margent:* Margin of a book, place for explanatory notes. 149 *laid:* Wagered; *passes:* Bouts. (The odds of the betting are hard to explain.
Possibly the King bets that Hamlet will win at least five out of twelve, at which point Laertes
raises the odds against himself by betting he will win nine.) 156 *breathing time:* Exercise period.
164 *lapwing:* A bird that draws intruders away from its nest and was thought to run about when
newly hatched with its head in the shell; a seeming reference to Osric's hat. 165 *comply . . . dug:*
Observe ceremonious formality toward his mother's teat. 166 *drossy:* Frivolous. 167 *tune:* Temper, mood, manner of speech. 167–68 *habit of encounter:* Demeanor of social intercourse. 168
yesty: Yeasty, frothy; *collection:* I.e., of current phrases.

and through the most fann'd and winnow'd° opinions; and do but blow
them to their trial, the bubbles are out.°   170

(Enter a LORD.)

LORD: My lord, his Majesty commended him to you by young Osric, who
    brings back to him that you attend him in the hall. He sends to know
    if your pleasure hold to play with Laertes, or that you will take longer
    time.
HAMLET: I am constant to my purposes; they follow the King's pleasure. If 175
    his fitness speaks,° mine is ready; now or whensoever, provided I be so
    able as now.
LORD: The King and Queen and all are coming down.
HAMLET: In happy time.°
LORD: The Queen desires you to use some gentle entertainment° to Laertes 180
    before you fall to play.
HAMLET: She well instructs me.   (Exit LORD.)
HORATIO: You will lose, my lord.
HAMLET: I do not think so. Since he went into France, I have been in
    continual practice; I shall win at the odds. But thou wouldst not think 185
    how ill all's here about my heart; but it is no matter.
HORATIO: Nay, good my lord—
HAMLET: It is but foolery, but it is such a kind of gain-giving,° as would
    perhaps trouble a woman.
HORATIO: If your mind dislike anything, obey it. I will forestall their 190
    repair hither, and say you are not fit.
HAMLET: Not a whit, we defy augury. There is special providence in the
    fall of a sparrow. If it be now, 'tis not to come; if it be not to come, it
    will be now; if it be not now; yet it will come. The readiness is all.
    Since no man of aught he leaves knows what is 't to leave betimes,° 195
    let be.

(A table prepar'd. Enter trumpets, drums, and OFFICERS with cushions;
KING, QUEEN, OSRIC, and all the State; foils, daggers, and wine borne
in; and LAERTES.)

KING: Come, Hamlet, come, and take this hand from me.
               (The KING puts LAERTES' hand into HAMLET's.)
HAMLET: Give me your pardon, sir. I have done you wrong,
    But pardon 't, as you are a gentleman.°
    This presence° knows,   200
    And you must needs have heard, how I am punish'd

---

169 fann'd and winnow'd: Select and refined. 169–70 blow . . . out: Put them to the test, and their
ignorance is exposed. 175–76 If . . . speaks: If his readiness answers to the time. 179 In happy
time: A phrase of courtesy indicating acceptance. 180 entertainment: Greeting. 188 gain-giving:
Misgiving. 195 what . . . betimes: What is the best time to leave it. 200 presence: Royal
assembly.

With a sore distraction. What I have done
That might your nature, honor, and exception°
Roughly awake, I here proclaim was madness.
Was 't Hamlet wrong'd Laertes? Never Hamlet.   205
If Hamlet from himself be ta'en away,
And when he's not himself does wrong Laertes,
Then Hamlet does it not, Hamlet denies it.
Who does it, then? His madness. If 't be so,
Hamlet is of the faction that is wrong'd;   210
His madness is poor Hamlet's enemy.
Sir, in this audience,
Let my disclaiming from a purpos'd evil
Free me so far in your most generous thoughts
That I have shot my arrow o'er the house   215
And hurt my brother.
LAERTES: I am satisfied in nature,°
Whose motive in this case should stir me most
To my revenge. But in my terms of honor
I stand aloof, and will no reconcilement
Till by some elder masters of known honor   220
I have a voice° and precedent of peace
To keep my name ungor'd. But till that time,
I do receive your offer'd love like love,
And will not wrong it.
HAMLET: I embrace it freely,
And will this brothers' wager frankly play.   225
Give us the foils. Come on.
LAERTES: Come, one for me.
HAMLET: I'll be your foil,° Laertes. In mine ignorance
Your skill shall, like a star i' th' darkest night,
Stick fiery off° indeed.
LAERTES: You mock me, sir.
HAMLET: No, by this hand.   230
KING: Give them the foils, young Osric. Cousin Hamlet,
You know the wager?
HAMLET: Very well, my lord.
Your Grace has laid the odds o' th' weaker side.
KING: I do not fear it; I have seen you both.
But since he is better'd,° we have therefore odds.   235
LAERTES: This is too heavy, let me see another.

(Exchanges his foil for another.)

203 *exception:* Disapproval. 216 *in nature:* As to my personal feelings. 221 *voice:* Authoritative pronouncement. 227 *foil:* Thin metal background which sets a jewel off (with pun on the blunted rapier for fencing). 229 *Stick fiery off:* Stand out brilliantly. 235 *is better'd:* Has improved; is the odds-on favorite.

HAMLET: This likes me well. These foils have all a length?

(They prepare to play.)

OSRIC: Ay, my good lord.

KING: Set me the stoups of wine upon that table.
If Hamlet give the first or second hit,   240
Or quit° in answer of the third exchange,
Let all the battlements their ordnance fire.
The King shall drink to Hamlet's better breath,
And in the cup an union° shall he throw,
Richer than that which four successive kings   245
In Denmark's crown have worn. Give me the cups,
And let the kettle° to the trumpet speak,
The trumpet to the cannoneer without,
The cannons to the heavens, the heaven to earth,
"Now the King drinks to Hamlet." Come, begin. *(Trumpets the while.)* 250
And you, the judges, bear a wary eye.

HAMLET: Come on sir.

LAERTES: Come, my lord.   *(They play.* HAMLET *scores a hit.)*

HAMLET: One.

LAERTES: No.   255

HAMLET: Judgment.

OSRIC: A hit, a very palpable hit.

(Drum, trumpets, and shot. Flourish. A piece goes off.)

LAERTES: Well, again.

KING: Stay, give me drink. Hamlet, this pearl is thine.

(He throws a pearl in HAMLET'*s cup and drinks.)*

Here's to thy health. Give him the cup.

HAMLET: I'll play this bout first; set it by awhile.   260
Come. *(They play.)* Another hit; what say you?

LAERTES: A touch, a touch, I do confess 't.

KING: Our son shall win.

QUEEN: He's fat,° and scant of breath.
Here, Hamlet, take my napkin,° rub thy brows.
The Queen carouses° to thy fortune, Hamlet.   265

HAMLET: Good madam!

KING: Gertrude, do not drink.

QUEEN: I will, my lord; I pray you pardon me.   *(Drinks.)*

KING *(aside):* It is the pois'ned cup. It is too late.

HAMLET: I dare not drink yet, madam; by and by.   270

QUEEN: Come, let me wipe thy face.

---

241 *quit:* Repay (with a hit).   244 *union:* Pearl (so called, according to Pliny's *Natural History,* IX, because pearls are *unique,* never identical).   247 *kettle:* Kettledrum.   263 *fat:* Not physically fit, out of training.   264 *napkin:* Handkerchief.   265 *carouses:* Drinks a toast.

LAERTES *(to* KING*)*: My lord, I'll hit him now.

KING: I do not think 't.

LAERTES *(aside)*: And yet it is almost against my conscience.

HAMLET: Come, for the third, Laertes. You do but dally.
  I pray you, pass with your best violence;   275
  I am afeard you make a wanton of me.°

LAERTES: Say you so? Come on.   *(They play.)*

OSRIC: Nothing, neither way.

LAERTES: Have at you now!

> *(*LAERTES *wounds* HAMLET; *then, in scuffling,*
> *they change rapiers,*° *and* HAMLET *wounds* LAERTES*.)*

KING: Part them! They are incens'd.

HAMLET: Nay, come, again.   *(The* QUEEN *falls.)*

OSRIC: Look to the Queen there, ho!   280

HORATIO: They bleed on both sides. How is it, my lord?

OSRIC: How is 't, Laertes?

LAERTES: Why, as a woodcock° to mine own springe,° Osric;
  I am justly kill'd with mine own treachery.

HAMLET: How does the Queen?

KING: She swoons to see them bleed.   285

QUEEN: No, no, the drink, the drink—O my dear Hamlet—
  The drink, the drink! I am pois'ned.   *(Dies.)*

HAMLET: O villainy! Ho, let the door be lock'd!
  Treachery! Seek it out.   *(*LAERTES *falls.)*

LAERTES: It is here, Hamlet. Hamlet, thou art slain.   290
  No med'cine in the world can do thee good;
  In thee there is not half an hour's life.
  The treacherous instrument is in thy hand,
  Unbated° and envenom'd. The foul practice
  Hath turn'd itself on me. Lo, here I lie,   295
  Never to rise again. Thy mother's pois'ned.
  I can no more. The King, the King's to blame.

HAMLET: The point envenom'd too? Then, venom, to thy work.
                                                  (Stabs the KING*.)*

ALL: Treason! Treason!

KING: O, yet defend me, friends; I am but hurt.   300

HAMLET: Here, thou incestuous, murd'rous, damned Dane,
                (He forces the KING *to drink the poisoned cup.)*

---

276 *make . . . me:* Treat me like a spoiled child, holding back to give me an advantage. 279 s.d.
in scuffling, they change rapiers: According to a widespread stage tradition, Hamlet receives a scratch,
realizes that Laertes' sword is unbated, and accordingly forces an exchange. 283 *woodcock:* A
bird, a type of stupidity or as a decoy; *springe:* Trap, snare. 294 *Unbated:* Not blunted with a
button.

Drink off this potion. Is thy union° here?
Follow my mother.   *(KING dies.)*

LAERTES: He is justly serv'd.
It is a poison temper'd° by himself.
Exchange forgiveness with me, noble Hamlet.   305
Mine and my father's death come not upon thee,
Nor thine on me!   *(Dies.)*

HAMLET: Heaven make thee free of it! I follow thee.
I am dead, Horatio. Wretched Queen, adieu!
You that look pale and tremble at this chance,   310
That are but mutes° or audience to this act,
Had I but time—as this fell° sergeant,° Death,
Is strict in his arrest—O, I could tell you—
But let it be. Horatio, I am dead;
Thou livest. Report me and my cause aright   315
To the unsatisfied.

HORATIO: Never believe it.
I am more an antique Roman° than a Dane.
Here's yet some liquor left.
        (He attempts to drink from the poisoned cup. HAMLET prevents him.)

HAMLET: As th' art a man,
Give me the cup! Let go! By heaven, I'll ha 't.
O God, Horatio, what a wounded name,   320
Things standing thus unknown, shall I leave behind me!
If thou didst ever hold me in thy heart,
Absent thee from felicity awhile,
And in this harsh world draw thy breath in pain
To tell my story.   *(A march afar off and a volley within.)*
        What warlike noise is this?   325

OSRIC: Young Fortinbras, with conquest come from Poland,
To the ambassadors of England gives
This warlike volley.

HAMLET: O, I die, Horatio!
The potent poison quite o'ercrows° my spirit.
I cannot live to hear the news from England,   330
But I do prophesy th' election lights
On Fortinbras. He has my dying voice.°
So tell him, with th' occurrents° more and less
Which have solicited°—the rest is silence.   *(Dies.)*

---

302 *union:* Pearl (see line 244; with grim puns on the word's other meanings: marriage, shared death[?]). 304 *temper'd:* Mixed. 311 *mutes:* Silent observers. 312 *fell:* Cruel; *sergeant:* Sheriff's officer. 317 *Roman:* It was the Roman custom to follow masters in death. 329 *o'ercrows:* Triumphs over. 332 *voice:* Vote. 333 *occurrents:* Events, incidents. 334 *solicited:* Moved, urged.

HORATIO: Now cracks a noble heart. Good night, sweet prince;   335
    And flights of angels sing thee to thy rest!   *(March within.)*
    Why does the drum come hither?

(Enter FORTINBRAS, *with the English* AMBASSADORS *with drum,
colors, and* ATTENDANTS.)

FORTINBRAS: Where is this sight?
HORATIO: What is it you would see?
    If aught of woe or wonder, cease your search.
FORTINBRAS: This quarry° cries on havoc.° O proud Death,   340
    What feast is toward° in thine eternal cell,
    That thou so many princes at a shot
    So bloodily hast struck?
FIRST AMBASSADOR: The sight is dismal;
    And our affairs from England come too late.
    The ears are senseless that should give us hearing,   345
    To tell him his commandment is fulfill'd,
    That Rosencrantz and Guildenstern are dead.
    Where should we have our thanks?
HORATIO: Not from his° mouth,
    Had it th' ability of life to thank you.
    He never gave commandment for their death.   350
    But since, so jump° upon this bloody question,°
    You from the Polack wars, and you from England,
    Are here arriv'd, give order that these bodies
    High on a stage° be placed to the view,
    And let me speak to th' yet unknowing world   355
    How these things came about. So shall you hear
    Of carnal, bloody, and unnatural acts,
    Of accidental judgments,° casual° slaughters,
    Of deaths put on° by cunning and forc'd cause,
    And, in this upshot, purposes mistook   360
    Fall'n on th' inventors' heads. All this can I
    Truly deliver.
FORTINBRAS: Let us haste to hear it,
    And call the noblest to the audience.
    For me, with sorrow I embrace my fortune.   365
    I have some rights of memory° in this kingdom,
    Which now to claim my vantage° doth invite me.

---

340 *quarry:* Heap of dead; *cries on havoc:* Proclaims a general slaughter. 341 *toward:* In preparation.
348 *his:* Claudius's. 351 *jump:* Precisely; *question:* Dispute. 354 *stage:* Platform. 358 *judgments:*
Retributions; *casual:* Occurring by chance. 359 *put on:* Instigated. 366 *of memory:* Traditional,
remembered. 367 *vantage:* Presence at this opportune moment.

HORATIO: Of that I shall have also cause to speak,
  And from his mouth whose voice will draw on more.°
  But let this same be presently° perform'd,   370
  Even while men's minds are wild, lest more mischance
  On° plots and errors happen.
FORTINBRAS: Let four captains
  Bear Hamlet, like a soldier, to the stage,
  For he was likely, had he been put on,°
  To have prov'd most royal; and, for his passage,°   375
  The soldiers' music and the rite of war
  Speak loudly for him.
  Take up the bodies. Such a sight as this
  Becomes the field,° but here shows much amiss.
  Go, bid the soldiers shoot.   380
      (Exeunt marching, bearing off the dead bodies; a peal of ordnance is shot off.)

369 *voice . . . more:* Vote will influence still others. 370 *presently:* Immediately. 372 *On:* On the basis of. 376 *put on:* Invested in royal office and so put to the test. 375 *passage:* Death. 379 *field:* I.e., of battle.

Considerations

1. Reread the "dram of eale (evil)" passage (I.iv.13ff.). In this speech, Hamlet suggests three possible ways of looking at the problem of evil. Explain each of these responses and then discuss how any (or all) of them might apply to the actions (or failure to act) of any of the play's characters.
2. Identify passages that show the change in Hamlet's character after his father's death. Consider not only what Hamlet himself says but also what other characters say and how they react to or interact with Hamlet.
3. Choose any one of Hamlet's soliloquies. Based on what he says, evaluate his ability to make reliable assessments of himself and of other characters' motivations and behaviors.
4. What do you think of Gertrude? Is she an innocent victim of Claudius's villainy? Or does she seem to have some complicity in her husband's death? Can you identify evidence suggesting that she did or did not know how King Hamlet met his death?
5. Evaluate Hamlet's relationship with Ophelia. Consider especially his behavior toward her after the "To be or not to be" soliloquy. To what extent would you hold Hamlet responsible for Ophelia's suicide?
6. How important is the Ghost's role in the play? Why does Hamlet first accept the "honesty" of the Ghost and then express deep doubts about the truth of the Ghost's message? How does Hamlet's reaction to and interaction with the Ghost suggest one of the play's major conflicts?

7. Consider any one of the play's minor characters: Fortinbras, Rosencrantz and Guildenstern, Horatio, or Polonius. What roles do these characters play? How do they contribute to the conflict or to the development of the major characters?

8. What motivates Hamlet to refrain from killing Claudius in Act III? Do you find his hesitation valid or simply a form of procrastination and rationalization? Explain.

9. Analyze the actions and reactions of the major characters during the "Mousetrap" (play within a play) scene. How does this scene contribute to developing the conflicts, themes, and characterizations of *Hamlet?*

10. What would be lost (or gained) if the gravedigger scene (V.I.1ff.) were omitted? As you respond to this question, consider whether the scene simply provides a moment of comic relief or whether it does more.

Commentary

SIGMUND FREUD

On Hamlet: from The Interpretation of Dreams

Another of the great creations of tragic poetry, Shakespeare's *Hamlet,* has its roots in the same soil as *Oedipus Rex.* But the changed treatment of the same material reveals the whole difference in the mental life of these two widely separated epochs of civilization: the secular advance of repression in the emotional life of mankind. In the *Oedipus* the child's wishful phantasy that underlies it is brought into the open and realized as it would be in a dream. In *Hamlet* it remains repressed; and—just as in the case of a neurosis— we only learn of its existence from its inhibiting consequences. Strangely enough, the overwhelming effect produced by the more modern tragedy has turned out to be compatible with the fact that people have remained completely in the dark as to the hero's character. The play is built up on Hamlet's hesitations over fulfilling the task of revenge that is assigned to him; but its text offers no reasons or motives for these hesitations and an immense variety of attempts at interpreting them have failed to produce a result. According to the view which was originated by Goethe and is still the prevailing one to-day, Hamlet represents the type of man whose power of direct action is paralysed by an excessive development of his intellect. (He is "sicklied o'er with the pale cast of thought.") According to another view, the dramatist has tried to portray a pathologically irresolute character which might be classed as neurasthenic. The plot of the drama shows us, however, that Hamlet is far from being represented as a person incapable of taking any action. We see him doing so on two occasions: first in a sudden outburst of temper, when he runs his sword through the eavesdropper behind the arras, and secondly in a premeditated and even crafty fashion, when, with all the callousness of a Renaissance prince, he sends the two courtiers to the death that had been planned for himself. What is it, then, that inhibits him in fulfilling the task set him by his father's ghost? The answer, once again, is that it is the peculiar nature of the task. Hamlet is able to do anything—except take vengeance on the man who did away with his father and took that father's place with his mother, the man who shows him the repressed wishes of his own childhood realized. Thus the loathing which should drive him on to revenge is replaced in him by self-reproaches, by scruples of conscience, which remind him that he himself is literally no better than the sinner whom he is to punish.

Commentary

LEONARD TENNENHOUSE
Power in Hamlet

Hamlet rehearses [the] dilemma of a state torn between two competitors, neither of whom can embody the mystical power of blood and land associated with the natural body. Hamlet's claim to power derives from his position as son in a patrilinear system as well as from "popular support." It is this support which Claudius consistently lacks and which, at the same time, prevents him from moving openly against Hamlet. Following the murder of Polonius, for example, Claudius says of Hamlet, "Yet must not we put the strong law on him. / He's lov'd of the distracted multitude . . ." (IV.iii.3–4). But this alone does not guarantee authority. Hamlet is not by nature capable of exercising force. To signal this lack, Shakespeare has given him the speech of Stoical writing, which shifts all action onto a mental plane where any show of force becomes self-inflicted aggression. We find this identification of force with self-assault made explicit in Hamlet's speeches on suicide as well as those in which he berates himself for his inability to act.

In contrast with Hamlet, Claudius's authority comes by way of his marriage to Gertrude. Where he would be second to Hamlet and Hamlet's line in a patrilineal system, the queen's husband and uncle of the king's son occupies the privileged male position in a matrilineal system. Like one of the successful figures from a history play, Claudius overthrew the reigning patriarch. Like one of the successful courtiers in a romantic comedy, he married into the aristocratic community. What is perhaps more important, he has taken the position through the effective use of force. Thus Shakespeare sets in opposition the two claims to authority—the exercise of force and the magic of blood—by means of these two members of the royal family. Because each has a claim, neither Hamlet nor Claudius achieves legitimate control over Denmark. Each one consequently assaults the aristocratic body in attempting to acquire the crown. It is to be expected that Claudius could not legally possess the crown, the matrilinear succession having the weaker claim on British political thinking. Thus the tragedy resides not in his failure but in the impossibility of Hamlet's rising according to Elizabethan strategies of state. This calls the relationship between the metaphysics of patriarchy and the force of law into question.

Commentary

CAROLYN HEILBRUN
The Character of Hamlet's Mother

The character of Hamlet's mother has not received the specific critical attention it deserves. Moreover, the traditional account of her personality as rendered by the critics will not stand up under close scrutiny of Shakespeare's play.

None of the critics of course has failed to see Gertrude as vital to the action of the play; not only is she the mother of the hero, the widow of the Ghost, and the wife of the current King of Denmark, but the fact of her hasty and, to the Elizabethans, incestuous marriage, the whole question of her "falling off," occupies a position of barely secondary importance in the mind of her son, and of the Ghost. Indeed, Freud and Jones see her, the object of Hamlet's Oedipus complex, as central to the motivation of the play.[1] But the critics, with no exception that I have been able to find, have accepted Hamlet's word "fraility" as applying to her whole personality, and have seen in her not one weakness, or passion in the Elizabethan sense, but a character of which weakness and lack of depth and vigorous intelligence are the entire explanation. Of her can it truly be said that carrying the "stamp of one defect," she did "in the general censure take corruption from that particular fault" (I.iv.35–36).

The critics are agreed that Gertrude was not a party to the late King's murder and indeed knew nothing of it, a point which on the clear evidence of the play, is indisputable. They have also discussed whether or not Gertrude, guilty of more than an "o'er-hasty marriage," had committed adultery with Claudius before her husband's death. I will return to this point later on. Beyond discussing these two points, those critics who have dealt specifically with the Queen have traditionally seen her as well-meaning but shallow and feminine, in the pejorative sense of the word: incapable of any sustained rational process, superficial and flighty. It is this tradition which a closer reading of the play will show to be erroneous.

Professor Bradley describes the traditional Gertrude thus:

> The Queen was not a bad-hearted woman, not at all the woman to think little of murder. But she had a soft animal nature and was very dull and very shallow. She loved to be happy, like a sheep in the sun, and to do her justice, it pleased her to see others happy, like more sheep in the sun. . . . It was pleasant to sit upon her throne and see smiling faces around her, and foolish and unkind in Hamlet to persist in grieving for his father instead of marrying Ophelia and making everything comfortable. . . . The belief at the bottom of her heart was that the world is a place constructed simply that people may be happy in it in a good-humored sensual fashion.[2]

Later on, Bradley says of her that when affliction comes to her "the good in her nature struggles to the surface through the heavy mass of sloth."

Granville-Barker is not quite so extreme. Shakespeare, he says,

> gives us in Gertrude the woman who does not mature, who clings to her youth and all that belongs to it, whose charm will not change but at last fade and wither, a pretty creature, as we see her, desperately refusing to grow old. . . . She is drawn for us with unemphatic strokes, and she has but a passive part in the play's action. She moves throughout in Claudius' shadow; he holds her as he won her, by the witchcraft of his wit.[3]

Elsewhere Granville-Barker says "Gertrude who will certainly never see forty-five again, might better be 'old.' [That is, portrayed by an older, mature actress.] But that would make her relations with Claudius—and *their* likelihood is vital to the play—quite incredible" (p. 226). Granville-Barker is saying here that a woman about forty-five years of age cannot feel any sexual passion nor arouse it. This is one of the mistakes which lie at the heart of the misunderstanding about Gertrude.

Professor Dover Wilson sees Gertrude as more forceful than either of these two critics will admit, but even he finds the Ghost's unwillingness to shock her with knowledge of his murder to be one of the basic motivations of the play, and he says of her "Gertrude is always hoping for the best."[4]

Now whether Claudius won Gertrude before or after her husband's death, it was certainly not, as Granville-Barker implies, with "the witchcraft of his wit" alone. Granville-Barker would have us believe that Claudius won her simply by the force of his persuasive tongue. "It is plain," he writes, that the Queen "does little except echo his [Claudius'] wishes; sometimes—as in the welcome to Rosencrantz and Guildenstern—she repeats his very words" (p. 227), though Wilson must admit later that Gertrude does not tell Claudius everything. Without dwelling here on the psychology of the Ghost, or the greater burden borne by the Elizabethan words "witchcraft" and "wit," we can plainly see, for the Ghost tells us, how Claudius won the Queen: the Ghost considers his brother to be garbage, and "lust," the Ghost says, "will sate itself in a celestial bed and prey on garbage" (I.v.54–55). "Lust"—in a woman of forty-five or more—is the key word here. Bradley, Granville-Barker, and to a lesser extent Professor Dover Wilson, misunderstand Gertrude largely because they are unable to see lust, the desire for sexual relations, as the passion, in the Elizabethan sense of the word, the flaw, the weakness which drives Gertrude to an incestuous marriage, appalls her son, and keeps him from the throne. Unable to explain her marriage to Claudius as the act of any but a weak-minded vacillating woman, they fail to see Gertrude for the strong-minded, intelligent, succinct, and, apart from this passion, sensible woman that she is.

To understand Gertrude properly, it is only necessary to examine the lines Shakespeare has chosen for her to say. She is, except for her description of Ophelia's death, concise and pithy in speech, with a talent for seeing the essence of every situation presented before her eyes. If she is not profound, she is certainly never silly. We first hear her asking Hamlet to stop wearing black, to stop walking about with his eyes downcast, and to realize that death is an inevitable part of life. She is, in short, asking him not to give way to the passion of grief, a passion of whose force and dangers the Elizabethans are aware, as Miss Campbell has shown.[5] Claudius echoes her with a well-reasoned argument against grief which was, in its philosophy if not in its language, a piece of commonplace Elizabethan lore. After Claudius' speech, Gertrude asks Hamlet to remain in Denmark, where he is rightly loved. Her speeches have been short, however warm and loving, and conciseness of statement is not the mark of a dull and shallow woman.

We next hear her, as Queen and gracious hostess, welcoming Rosencrantz and Guildenstern to the court, hoping, with the King, that they may cheer Hamlet and discover what is depressing him. Claudius then tells Gertrude, when they are alone, that Polonius believes he knows what is upsetting Hamlet. The Queen answers:

> I doubt it is no other than the main,
> His father's death and our o'er-hasty marriage. (II.ii.56–57)

This statement is concise, remarkably to the point, and not a little courageous. It is not the statement of a dull, slothful woman who can only echo her husband's words. Next, Polonius enters with his most unbrief apotheosis to brevity. The Queen interrupts him with five words: "More matter with less art" (II.ii.95). It would be difficult to find a phrase more applicable to Polonius. When this gentleman, in no way deterred from his loquacity, after purveying the startling news that he has a daughter, begins to read a letter, the Queen asks pointedly "Came this from Hamlet to her?" (II.ii.114).

We see Gertrude next in Act III, asking Rosencrantz and Guildenstern, with her usual directness, if Hamlet received them well, and if they were able to tempt him to any pastime. But before leaving the room, she stops for a word of kindness to Ophelia. It is a humane gesture, for she is unwilling to leave Ophelia, the unhappy tool of the King and Polonius, without some kindly and intelligent appreciation of her help:

> And for your part, Ophelia, I do wish
> That your good beauties be the happy cause
> Of Hamlet's wildness. So shall I hope your virtues
> Will bring him to his wonted way again,
> To both your honors. (III.i.38–42)

It is difficult to see in this speech, as Bradley apparently does, the gushing shallow wish of a sentimental woman that class distinctions shall not stand in the way of true love.

At the play, the Queen asks Hamlet to sit near her. She is clearly trying to make him feel he has a place in the court of Denmark. She does not speak again until Hamlet asks her how she likes the play. "The lady doth protest too much, methinks" (III.ii.240) is her immortal comment on the player queen. The scene gives her four more words: when Claudius leaps to his feet, she asks "How fares my Lord?" (III.ii.278).

I will for the moment pass over the scene in the Queen's closet, to follow her quickly through the remainder of the play. After the closet scene, the Queen comes to speak to Claudius. She tells him, as Hamlet has asked her to, that he, Hamlet, is mad, and has killed Polonius. She adds, however, that he now weeps for what he has done. She does not wish Claudius to know what she now knows, how wild and fearsome Hamlet has become. Later, she does not wish to see Ophelia, but hearing how distracted she is, consents. When Laertes bursts in ready to attack Claudius, she immediately steps between Claudius and Laertes to protect the King, and tells Laertes it is not Claudius who has killed his father. Laertes will of course soon learn this, but it is Gertrude who manages to tell him before he can do any meaningless damage. She leaves Laertes and the King together, and then returns to tell Laertes that his sister is drowned. She gives her news directly, realizing that suspense will increase the pain of it, but this is the one time in the play when her usual pointed conciseness would be the mark neither of intelligence nor kindness, and so, gently, and at some length, she tells Laertes of his sister's death, giving him time to recover from the shock of grief, and to absorb the meaning of her words. At Ophelia's funeral the Queen scatters flowers over the grave:

> Sweets to the sweet; farewell!
> I hop'd thou shouldst have been my Hamlet's wife.
> I thought thy bride-bed to have deck'd, sweet maid,
> And not t' have strew'd thy grave. (V.i.266–269)

She is the only one present decently mourning the death of someone young, and not heated in the fire of some personal passion.

At the match between Hamlet and Laertes, the Queen believes that Hamlet is out of training, but glad to see him at some sport, she gives him her handkerchief to wipe his brow, and drinks to his success. The drink is poisoned and she dies. But before she dies she does not waste time on vituperation; she warns Hamlet that the drink is poisoned to prevent his drinking it. They are her last words. Those critics who have thought her stupid admire her death; they call it uncharacteristic.

In Act III, when Hamlet goes to his mother in her closet his nerves are pitched at the very height of tension; he is on the edge of hysteria. The possibility of murdering his mother has in fact entered his mind, and he has just met and refused an opportunity to kill Claudius. His mother, meanwhile, waiting for him, has told Polonius not to fear for her, but she knows when she sees Hamlet that he may be violently mad. Hamlet quips with her, insults her, tells her he wishes she were not his mother, and when she, still retaining dignity, attempts to end the interview, Hamlet seizes her and she cries for help. The important thing to note is that the Queen's cry "Thou wilt not murder me" (III.iv.21) is not foolish. She has seen from Hamlet's demeanor that he is capable of murder, as indeed in the next instant he proves himself to be.

We next learn from the Queen's startled "As kill a king" (III.iv.30) that   15
she has no knowledge of the murder, though of course this is only confir-mation here of what we already know. Then the Queen asks Hamlet why he is so hysterical:

> What have I done, that thou dar'st wag thy tongue
> In noise so rude against me? (III.iv.39–40)

Hamlet tells her: it is her lust, the need of sexual passion, which has driven her from the arms and memory of her husband to the incomparably cruder charms of his brother. He cries out that she has not even the excuse of youth for her lust:

> O Shame! where is thy blush? Rebellious hell,
> If thou canst mutine in a matron's bones,
> To flaming youth let virtue be as wax
> And melt in her own fire. Proclaim no shame
> When the compulsive ardor gives the charge,
> Since frost itself as actively doth burn,
> And reason panders will. (III.iv.82–87)

This is not only a lust, but a lust which throws out of joint all the structure of human morality and relationships. And the Queen admits it. If there is one quality that has characterized, and will characterize, every speech of Gertrude's in the play, it is the ability to see reality clearly, and to express it. This talent is not lost when turned upon herself:

> O Hamlet, speak no more!
> Thou turn'st mine eyes into my very soul,
> And there I see such black and grained spots
> As will not leave their tinct. (III.iv.88–91)

She knows that lust has driven her, that this is her sin, and she admits it. Not that she wishes to linger in the contemplation of her sin. No more, she cries, no more. And then the Ghost appears to Hamlet. The Queen thinks him mad again—as well she might—but she promises Hamlet that she will not betray him—and she does not.

Where, in all that we have seen of Gertrude, is there the picture of "a soft animal nature, very dull and very shallow"? She may indeed be "animal" in the sense of "lustful." But it does not follow that because she wishes to continue a life of sexual experience, her brain is soft or her wit unperceptive.

Some critics, having accepted Gertrude as a weak and vacillating woman, see no reason to suppose that she did not fall victim to Claudius' charms before the death of her husband and commit adultery with him. These critics, Professor Bradley among them (p. 166), claim that the elder

Hamlet clearly tells his son that Gertrude has committed adultery with Claudius in the speech beginning "Ay that incestuous, that adulterate beast" (I.v.41ff). Professor Dover Wilson presents the argument:

> Is the Ghost speaking here of the o'er-hasty marriage of Claudius and Gertrude? Assuredly not. His "certain term" is drawing rapidly to an end, and he is already beginning to "scent the morning air." Hamlet knew of the marriage, and his whole soul was filled with nausea at the thought of the speedy hasting to "incestuous sheets." Why then should the Ghost waste precious moments in telling Hamlet what he was fully cognisant of before? . . . Moreover, though the word "incestuous" was applicable to the marriage, the rest of the passage is entirely inapplicable to it. Expressions like "witchcraft", "traitorous gifts", "seduce", "shameful lust", and "seeming virtuous" may be noted in passing. But the rest of the quotation leaves no doubt upon the matter. (p. 293)

Professor Dover Wilson and other critics have accepted the Ghost's word "adulterate" in its modern meaning. The Elizabethan word "adultery," however, was not restricted to its modern meaning, but was used to define any sexual relationship which could be called unchaste, including of course an incestuous one.[6] Certainly the elder Hamlet considered the marriage of Claudius and Gertrude to be unchaste and unseemly, and while his use of the word "adulterate" indicates his very strong feelings about the marriage, it would not to an Elizabethan audience necessarily mean that he believed Gertrude to have been false to him before his death. It is important to notice, too, that the Ghost does not apply the term "adulterate" to Gertrude, and he may well have considered the term a just description of Claudius' entire sexual life.

But even if the Ghost used the word "adulterate" in full awareness of its modern restricted meaning, it is not necessary to assume on the basis of this single speech (and it is the only shadow of evidence we have for such a conclusion) that Gertrude was unfaithful to him while he lived. It is quite probable that the elder Hamlet still considered himself married to Gertrude, and he is moreover revolted that her lust for him ("why she would hang on him as if increase of appetite had grown by what it fed on") should have so easily transferred itself to another. This is why he uses the expressions "seduce," "shameful lust," and others. Professor Dover Wilson has himself said "Hamlet knew of the marriage, and his whole soul was filled with nausea at the thought of the speedy hasting to incestuous sheets"; the soul of the elder Hamlet was undoubtedly filled with nausea too, and this could well explain his using such strong language, as well as his taking the time to mention the matter at all. It is not necessary to consider Gertrude an adulteress to account for the speech of the Ghost.

Gertrude's lust was, of course, more important to the plot than we may at first perceive. Charlton Lewis, among others, has shown how Shakespeare kept 20 many of the facts of the plots from which he borrowed without maintaining the structures which explained them. In the original Belleforest story, Gertrude (substituting Shakespeare's more familiar names) was daughter of the king; to become king, it was necessary to marry her. The elder Hamlet, in marrying Gertrude, ousted Claudius from the throne.[7] Shakespeare retained the shell of this in his play. When she no longer has a husband, the form of election would be followed to declare the next king, in this case undoubtedly her son Hamlet. By marrying Gertrude, Claudius "popp'd in between th' election and my hopes" (V.ii.65), that is, kept young Hamlet from the throne. Gertrude's flaw of lust made Claudius' ambition possible, for without taking advantage of the Queen's desire still to be married, he could not have been king.

But Gertrude, if she is lustful, is also intelligent, penetrating, and gifted with a remarkable talent for concise and pithy speech. In all the play, the person whose language hers most closely resembles is Horatio. "Sweets to the sweet," she has said at Ophelia's grave. "Good night sweet prince," Horatio says at the end. They are neither of them dull, or shallow, or slothful, though one of them is passion's slave.

ENDNOTES

1. William Shakespeare, *Hamlet,* with a psycholoanalytical study by Ernest Jones, M.D. (London: Vision Press, 1947), pp. 7–42.

2. A. C. Bradley, *Shakespearean Tragedy* (New York: Macmillan, 1949), p. 167.

3. Harley Granville-Barker, *Prefaces to Shakespeare* (Princeton: Princeton University Press, 1946), 1:227.

4. J. Dover Wilson, *What Happens in Hamlet* (Cambridge: Cambridge University Press, 1951), p. 125.

5. Lily B. Campbell, *Shakespeare's Tragic Heroes* (New York: Barnes & Noble, 1952), pp. 112–113.

6. See Bertram Joseph, *Conscience and the King* (London: Chatto and Windus, 1953), pp. 16–19.

7. Charlton M. Lewis, *The Genesis of Hamlet* (New York: Henry Holt, 1907), p. 36.

LANGSTON HUGHES (1902–1967)

Salvation

> Born in Joplin, Missouri, Langston Hughes graduated from Lincoln University
> in 1929 and gained an outstanding literary reputation as one of the key fig-
> ures of the Harlem Renaissance of the 1920s, a period which saw a rich
> proliferation of art, music, and literature that celebrated African-American
> heritage and experience in the United States. In addition to writing poetry,
> Hughes worked as a reporter for the Baltimore Afro-American and for the
> Chicago Defender. He wrote more than twenty-five plays and, in addition,
> created jazz scores to accompany many of his poems and dramas. "Salvation,"
> an autobiographical essay, first appeared in his collection The Big Sea (1940).

I was saved from sin when I was going on thirteen. But not really
saved. It happened like this. There was a big revival at my Auntie Reed's
church. Every night for weeks there had been much preaching, singing,
praying, and shouting, and some very hardened sinners had been brought to
Christ, and the membership of the church had grown by leaps and bounds.
Then just before the revival ended, they held a special meeting for children,
"to bring the young lambs to the fold." My aunt spoke of it for days ahead.
That night I was escorted to the front row and placed on the mourners'
bench with all the other young sinners, who had not yet been brought to Jesus.

My aunt told me that when you were saved you saw a light, and
something happened to you inside! And Jesus came into your life! And God
was with you from then on! She said you could see and hear and feel Jesus
in your soul. I believed her. I had heard a great many old people say the
same thing and it seemed to me they ought to know. So I sat there calmly in
the hot, crowded church, waiting for Jesus to come to me.

The preacher preached a wonderful rhythmical sermon, all moans and
shouts and lonely cries and dire pictures of hell, and then he sang a song
about the ninety and nine safe in the fold, but one little lamb was left out in
the cold. Then he said: "Won't you come? Won't you come to Jesus? Young
lambs, won't you come?" And he held out his arms to all us young sinners
there on the mourners' bench. And the little girls cried. And some of them
jumped up and went to Jesus right away. But most of us just sat there.

A great many old people came and knelt around us and prayed, old
women with jet-black faces and braided hair, old men with work-gnarled
hands. And the church sang a song about the lower lights are burning, some
poor sinners to be saved. And the whole building rocked with prayer and song.

Still I kept waiting to *see* Jesus.   5

Finally all the young people had gone to the altar and were saved, but
one boy and me. He was a rounder's son named Westley. Westley and I
were surrounded by sisters and deacons praying. It was very hot in the
church, and getting late now. Finally Westley said to me in a whisper: "God

damn! I'm tired o' sitting here. Let's get up and be saved." So he got up and was saved.

Then I was left all alone on the mourners' bench. My aunt came and knelt at my knees and cried, while prayers and song swirled all around me in the little church. The whole congregation prayed for me alone, in a mighty wail of moans and voices. And I kept waiting serenely for Jesus, waiting, waiting—but he didn't come. I wanted to see him, but nothing happened to me. Nothing! I wanted something to happen to me, but nothing happened.

I heard the songs and the minister saying: "Why don't you come? My dear child, why don't you come to Jesus? Jesus is waiting for you. He wants you. Why don't you come? Sister Reed, what is this child's name?"

"Langston," my aunt sobbed.

"Langston, why don't you come? Why don't you come and be saved?   10 Oh, Lamb of God! Why don't you come?"

Now it was really getting late. I began to be ashamed of myself, holding everything up so long. I began to wonder what God thought about Westley, who certainly hadn't seen Jesus either, but who was now sitting proudly on the platform, swinging his knickerbockered legs and grinning down at me, surrounded by deacons and old women on their knees praying. God had not struck Westley dead for taking his name in vain or for lying in the temple. So I decided that maybe to save further trouble, I'd better lie, too, and say that Jesus had come, and get up and be saved.

So I got up.

Suddenly the whole room broke into a sea of shouting, as they saw me rise. Waves of rejoicing swept the place. Women leaped in the air. My aunt threw her arms around me. The minister took me by the hand and led me to the platform.

When things quieted down, in a hushed silence, punctuated by a few ecstatic "Amens," all the new young lambs were blessed in the name of God. Then joyous singing filled the room.

That night, for the last time in my life but one—for I was a big boy   15 twelve years old—I cried. I cried, in bed alone, and couldn't stop. I buried my head under the quilts, but my aunt heard me. She woke up and told my uncle I was crying because the Holy Ghost had come into my life, and because I had seen Jesus. But I was really crying because I couldn't bear to tell her that I had lied, that I had deceived everybody in the church, that I hadn't seen Jesus, and that now I didn't believe there was a Jesus any more, since he didn't come to help me.

Considerations

1. Compare the narrator to Westley. Keep in mind the narrator's hopes, fears, and expectations and, using evidence provided by the words and actions of the two boys, speculate on how they might contrast with Westley's.

2. What is your definition of "salvation"? How many possible meanings of "salvation" are stated or implied in Hughes's memoir?

3. Evaluate Auntie Reed's motives and expectations. What does she want for the narrator? What does she want for herself?

4. Why does the narrator cry? Consider the reasons he states and speculate on other reasons (and on the implications of those reasons).

5. This essay describes a moment when a young man comes to doubt a strongly held belief. Notice that he recalls in detail the sights, sounds, and feelings of that moment. Think about a strongly held belief that you have come to question and describe an incident that led you to doubt that belief. Use Hughes's essay as an example; recreate for your readers the sights, sounds, and feelings of the moment you describe.

MAYA ANGELOU (1928–   )

Graduation in Stamps

Originally named Marguerite Johnson, Maya Angelou was born in St. Louis in 1928. From age three to eight, Angelou and her brother grew up in Stamps, Arkansas, under the watchful, loving eye of their grandmother, whom they called "Momma." Unfortunately, her grandmother's boundless energy and affection could not protect Angelou from the pain of poverty, segregated schools, and violence at the hands of both whites and blacks. At age eight, she went to stay with her mother. At her mother's home, she was raped by her mother's lover; subsequently, Angelou refused to talk for more than a year. Shortly after the rape, she returned to her grandmother's home, where she began to read voraciously, memorizing extensive passages from writers varying from Shakespeare to the poets of the Harlem Renaissance. The cadences and rhythms of her early love affair with poetry weave throughout her works. In 1972 her book of poems, Just Give Me a Cool Drink of Water 'fore I Die, *was nominated for a Pulitzer Prize. In 1993, as Poet Laureate of the United States, she wrote and read a poem for the inauguration of President Clinton.*

A champion of the narrative as complex, serious art, Angelou sees her work as "stemming from the slave narrative and developing into a new American literary form." This selection, a chapter from Angelou's highly praised autobiography, I Know Why the Caged Bird Sings *(1969), demonstrates her strong and hopeful vision of the African-American experience.*

The children in Stamps trembled visibly with anticipation. Some adults were excited too, but to be certain the whole young population had come down with graduation epidemic. Large classes were graduating from both the grammar school and the high school. Even those who were years removed from their own day of glorious release were anxious to help with preparations as a kind of dry run. The junior students who were moving into the vacating classes' chairs were tradition-bound to show their talents for leadership and management. They strutted through the school and around the campus exerting pressure on the lower grades. Their authority was so new that occasionally if they pressed a little too hard it had to be overlooked. After all, next term was coming, and it never hurt a sixth grader to have a play sister in the eighth grade, or a tenth-year student to be able to call a twelfth grader Bubba. So all was endured in a spirit of shared understanding. But the graduating classes themselves were the nobility. Like travelers with exotic destinations on their minds, the graduates were remarkably forgetful. They came to school without their books, or tablets or even pencils. Volunteers fell over themselves to secure replacements for the missing equipment. When accepted, the willing workers might or might not be thanked, and it was of no importance to the pre-graduation rites. Even teachers were respectful of the now quiet and aging seniors, and tended to speak to them, if not as equals, as beings only slightly lower than themselves. After tests were returned and grades given, the student body, which acted like an extended family, knew who did well, who excelled, and what piteous ones had failed.

Unlike the white high school, Lafayette County Training School distinguished itself by having neither lawn, nor hedges, nor tennis court, nor climbing ivy. Its two buildings (main classrooms, the grade school and home economics) were set on a dirt hill with no fence to limit either its boundaries or those of bordering farms. There was a large expanse to the left of the school which was used alternately as a baseball diamond or a basketball court. Rusty hoops on the swaying poles represented the permanent recreational equipment, although bats and balls could be borrowed from the P.E. teacher if the borrower was qualified and if the diamond wasn't occupied.

Over this rocky area relieved by a few shady tall persimmon trees the graduating class walked. The girls often held hands and no longer bothered to speak to the lower students. There was a sadness about them, as if this old world was not their home and they were bound for higher ground. The boys, on the other hand, had become more friendly, more outgoing. A decided change from the closed attitude they projected while studying for finals. Now they seemed not ready to give up the old school, the familiar paths and classrooms. Only a small percentage would be continuing on to college—one of the South's A & M (agricultural and mechanical) schools, which trained Negro youths to be carpenters, farmers, handymen, masons, maids, cooks and baby nurses. Their future rode heavily on their shoulders, and blinded them to the collective joy that had pervaded the lives of the boys and girls in the grammar school graduating class.

Parents who could afford it had ordered new shoes and ready-made clothes for themselves from Sears and Roebuck or Montgomery Ward. They also engaged the best seamstresses to make the floating graduating dresses and to cut down secondhand pants which would be pressed to a military slickness for the important event.

Oh, it was important, all right. Whitefolks would attend the ceremony, and two or three would speak of God and home, and the Southern way of life, and Mrs. Parsons, the principal's wife, would play the graduation march while the lower-grade graduates paraded down the aisles and took their seats below the platform. The high school seniors would wait in empty classrooms to make their dramatic entrance. 5

In the Store I was the person of the moment. The birthday girl. The center. Bailey had graduated the year before, although to do so he had had to forfeit all pleasures to make up for his time lost in Baton Rouge.

My class was wearing butter-yellow piqué dresses, and Momma launched out on mine. She smocked the yoke into tiny crisscrossing puckers, then shirred the rest of the bodice. Her dark fingers ducked in and out of the lemony cloth as she embroidered raised daisies around the hem. Before she considered herself finished she had added a crocheted cuff on the puff sleeves, and a pointy crocheted collar.

I was going to be lovely. A walking model of all the various styles of fine hand sewing and it didn't worry me that I was only twelve years old and merely graduating from the eighth grade. Besides, many teachers in Arkansas Negro schools had only that diploma and were licensed to impart wisdom.

The days had become longer and more noticeable. The faded beige of former times had been replaced with strong and sure colors. I began to see my classmates' clothes, their skin tones, and the dust that waved off pussy willows. Clouds that lazed across the sky were objects of great concern to me. Their shiftier shapes might have held a message that in my new happiness and with a little bit of time I'd soon decipher. During that period I looked at the arch of heaven so religiously my neck kept a steady ache. I had taken to smiling more often, and my jaws hurt from the unaccustomed activity. Between the two physical sore spots, I suppose I could have been uncomfortable, but that was not the case. As a member of the winning team (the graduating class of 1940) I had outdistanced unpleasant sensations by miles. I was headed for the freedom of open fields.

Youth and social approval allied themselves with me and we tram-   10
meled memories of slights and insults. The wind of our swift passage re-modeled my features. Lost tears were pounded to mud and then to dust. Years of withdrawal were brushed aside and left behind, as hanging ropes of parasitic moss.

My work alone had awarded me a top place and I was going to be one of the first called in the graduating ceremonies. On the classroom blackboard, as well as on the bulletin board in the auditorium, there were blue stars and white stars and red stars. No absences, no tardinesses, and my academic work was among the best of the year. I could say the preamble to the Constitution even faster than Bailey. We timed ourselves often: "Wethepeopleofthe-UnitedStatesinordertoformamoreperfectunion . . ." I had memorized the Presidents of the United States from Washington to Roosevelt in chronolog-ical as well as alphabetical order.

My hair pleased me too. Gradually the black mass had lengthened and thickened, so that it kept at last to its braided pattern, and I didn't have to yank my scalp off when I tried to comb it.

Louise and I had rehearsed the exercises until we tired out ourselves. Henry Reed was class valedictorian. He was a small, very black boy with hooded eyes, a long, broad nose and an oddly shaped head. I had admired him for years because each term he and I vied for the best grades in our class. Most often he bested me, but instead of being disappointed, I was pleased that we shared top places between us. Like many Southern black children, he lived with his grandmother, who was as strict as Momma and as kind as she knew how to be. He was courteous, respectful and soft-spoken to elders, but on the playground he chose to play the roughest games. I admired him. Anyone, I reckoned, sufficiently afraid or sufficiently dull could be polite. But to be able to operate at a top level with both adults and children was admirable.

His valedictory speech was entitled "To Be or Not to Be." The rigid tenth-grade teacher had helped him write it. He'd been working on the dramatic stresses for months.

The weeks until graduation were filled with heady activities. A group of small children were to be presented in a play about buttercups and daisies and bunny rabbits. They could be heard throughout the building practicing their hops and their little songs that sounded like silver bells. The older girls (non-graduates, of course) were assigned the task of making refreshments for the night's festivities. A tangy scent of ginger, cinnamon, nutmeg and chocolate wafted around the home economics building as the budding cooks made samples for themselves and their teachers.

In every corner of the workshop, axes and saws split fresh timber as the woodshop boys made sets and stage scenery. Only the graduates were left out of the general bustle. We were free to sit in the library at the back of the building or look in quite detachedly, naturally, on the measures being taken for our event.

Even the minister preached on graduation the Sunday before. His subject was, "Let your light so shine that men will see your good works and praise your Father, Who is in Heaven." Although the sermon was purported to be addressed to us, he used the occasion to speak to backsliders, gamblers and general ne'er-do-wells. But since he had called our names at the beginning of the service we were mollified.

Among Negros the tradition was to give presents to children going only from one grade to another. How much more important this was when the person was graduating at the top of the class. Uncle Willie and Momma had sent away for a Mickey Mouse watch like Bailey's. Louise gave me four embroidered handkerchiefs. (I gave her three crocheted doilies.) Mrs. Sneed, the minister's wife, made me an underskirt to wear for graduation, and nearly every customer gave me a nickel or maybe even a dime with the instruction "Keep on moving to higher ground," or some such encouragement.

Amazingly the great day finally dawned and I was out of bed before I knew it. I threw open the back door to see it more clearly, but Momma said, "Sister, come away from that door and put your robe on."

I hoped the memory of that morning would never leave me. Sunlight was itself still young, and the day had none of the insistence maturity would bring it in a few hours. In my robe and barefoot in the backyard, under cover of going to see about my new beans, I gave myself up to the gentle warmth and thanked God that no matter what evil I had done in my life He had allowed me to live to see this day. Somewhere in my fatalism I had expected to die, accidentally, and never have the chance to walk up the stairs in the auditorium and gracefully receive my hard-earned diploma. Out of God's merciful bosom I had won reprieve.

Bailey came out in his robe and gave me a box wrapped in Christmas paper. He said he had saved his money for months to pay for it. It felt like a box of chocolates, but I knew Bailey wouldn't save money to buy candy when we had all we could want under our noses.

He was as proud of the gift as I. It was a soft-leather-bound copy of a collection of poems by Edgar Allan Poe,° or, as Bailey and I called him, "Eap." I turned to "Annabel Lee" and we walked up and down the garden rows, the cool dirt between our toes, reciting the beautifully sad lines.

Momma made a Sunday breakfast although it was only Friday. After we finished the blessing, I opened my eyes to find the watch on my plate. It was a dream of a day. Everything went smoothly and to my credit. I didn't have to be reminded or scolded for anything. Near evening I was too jittery to attend to chores, so Bailey volunteered to do all before his bath.

Days before, we had made a sign for the Store, and as we turned out the lights Momma hung the cardboard over the doorknob. It read clearly: CLOSED: GRADUATION.

My dress fitted perfectly and everyone said that I looked like a sunbeam   25 in it. On the hill, going toward the school, Bailey walked behind with Uncle Willie, who muttered, "Go on, Ju." He wanted him to walk ahead with us because it embarrassed him to have to walk so slowly. Bailey said he'd let the ladies walk together, and the men would bring up the rear. We all laughed, nicely.

Little children dashed by out of the dark like fireflies. Their crepe paper dresses and butterfly wings were not made for running and we heard more than one rip, dryly, and the regretful "uh uh" that followed.

The school blazed without gaiety. The windows seemed cold and un-friendly from the lower hill. A sense of ill-fated timing crept over me, and if Momma hadn't reached for my hand I would have drifted back to Bailey and Uncle Willie, and possibly beyond. She made a few slow jokes about my feet getting cold, and tugged me along to the now-strange building.

Around the front steps, assurance came back. There were my fellow "greats," the graduating class. Hair brushed back, legs oiled, new dresses and pressed pleats, fresh pocket handkerchiefs and little handbags, all home-sewn. Oh, we were up to snuff, all right. I joined my comrades and didn't even see my family go in to find seats in the crowded auditorium.

The school band struck up a march and all classes filed in as had been rehearsed. We stood in front of our seats, as assigned, and on a signal from the choir director, we sat. No sooner had this been accomplished than the band started to play the national anthem. We rose again and sang the song, after which we recited the pledge of allegiance. We remained standing for a brief minute before the choir director and the principal signaled to us, rather desperately I thought, to take our seats. The command was so unusual that

---

Edgar Allan Poe: (1809–1849) American editor, critic, poet, and short-story writer. A brilliant, haunted man, Poe created poems and stories that combined the beautiful with the grotesque, the real with the fantastic.

our carefully rehearsed and smooth-running machine was thrown off. For a full minute we fumbled for our chairs and bumped into each other awkwardly. Habits change or solidify under pressure, so in our state of nervous tension we had been ready to follow our usual assembly pattern: the American national anthem, then the pledge of allegiance, then the song every Black person I knew called the Negro National Anthem. All done in the same key, with the same passion and most often standing on the same foot.

Finding my seat at last, I was overcome with a presentiment of worse   30
things to come. Something unrehearsed, unplanned, was going to happen, and we were going to be made to look bad. I distinctly remember being explicit in the choice of pronoun. It was "we," the graduating class, the unit, that concerned me then.

The principal welcomed "parents and friends" and asked the Baptist minister to lead us in prayer. His invocation was brief and punchy, and for a second I thought we were getting back on the high road to right action. When the principal came back to the dais, however, his voice had changed. Sounds always affected me profoundly and the principal's voice was one of my favorites. During assembly it melted and lowed weakly into the audience. It had not been in my plan to listen to him, but my curiosity was piqued and I straightened up to give him my attention.

He was talking about Booker T. Washington,° our "late great leader," who said we can be as close as the fingers on the hand, etc. . . . Then he said a few vague things about friendship and the friendship of kindly people to those less fortunate than themselves. With that his voice nearly faded, thin, away. Like a river diminishing to a stream and then to a trickle. But he cleared his throat and said, "Our speaker tonight, who is also our friend, came from Texarkana to deliver the commencement address, but due to the irregularity of the train schedule, he's going to, as they say, 'speak and run.' " He said that we understood and wanted the man to know that we were most grateful for the time he was able to give us and then something about how we were willing always to adjust to another's program; and without more ado—"I give you Mr. Edward Donleavy."

Not one but two white men came through the door offstage. The shorter one walked to the speaker's platform, and the tall one moved over to the center seat and sat down. But that was our principal's seat, and already occupied. The dislodged gentleman bounced around for a long breath or two before the Baptist minister gave him his chair, then with more dignity than the situation deserved, the minister walked off the stage.

Booker T. Washington: (1856–1915) African-American educator who founded Tuskegee Institute, a post–high school institution of learning for black students who were not, at that time, admitted to most colleges and universities. He was criticized by many African-American leaders because he argued that social equality could not be attained—and should not be a goal for African-Americans—until they had, on their own, attained economic independence.

Donleavy looked at the audience once (on reflection, I'm sure that he wanted only to reassure himself that we were really there), adjusted his glasses and began to read from a sheaf of papers.

He was glad "to be here and to see the work going on just as it was in   35 the other schools."

At the first "Amen" from the audience I willed the offender to immediate death by choking on the word. But Amens and Yes, sir's began to fall around the room like rain through a ragged umbrella.

He told us of the wonderful changes we children in Stamps had in store. The Central School (naturally, the white school was Central) had already been granted improvements that would be in use in the fall. A well-known artist was coming from Little Rock to teach art to them. They were going to have the newest microscopes and chemistry equipment for their laboratory. Mr. Donleavy didn't leave us long in the dark over who made these improvements available to Central High. Nor were we to be ignored in the general betterment scheme he had in mind.

He said that he had pointed out to people at a very high level that one of the first-line football tacklers at Arkansas Agricultural and Mechanical College had graduated from good old Lafayette County Training School. Here fewer Amen's were heard. Those few that did break through lay dully in the air with the heaviness of habit.

He went on to praise us. He went on to say how he had bragged that "one of the best basketball players at Fisk sank his first ball right here at Lafayette County Training School."

The white kids were going to have a chance to become Galileos° and   40 Madame Curies° and Edisons° and Gauguins,° and our boys (the girls weren't even in on it) would try to be Jesse Owenses° and Joe Louises.°

Owens and the Brown Bomber were great heroes in our world, but what school official in the white-goddom of Little Rock had the right to decide that those two men must be our only heroes? Who decided that for Henry Reed to become a scientist he had to work like George Washington

---

Galileo: (1564–1642) Italian astronomer and physicist. He discovered many physical laws, constructed the first telescope, and confirmed the theory that the earth moves around the sun. *Madame Curie:* (1867–1934) Polish-born French physicist. She won the Nobel Prize in 1911 for the discovery of metallic radium. *Thomas Alva Edison:* (1847–1931) One of the most productive American inventors. Among his significant inventions were the record player, the motion picture, the incandescent lamp, and a system for the distribution of electricity. *Paul Gauguin:* (1848–1903) French painter, associated with the impressionists, noted especially for rejecting traditional naturalism and, instead, using nature as an inspiration for abstract symbols and figures. *Jesse Owens:* (1913–1981) African-American track star who won four gold medals at the 1936 Olympics, which were held in Berlin. Owens made a mockery of Hitler's contention that "Aryan" athletes were superior to all others. *Joe Louis:* African-American boxer. Holder of the heavyweight title, Louis was known as the Brown Bomber.

Carver,° as a bootblack, to buy a lousy microscope? Bailey was obviously always going to be too small to be an athlete, so which concrete angel glued to what county seat had decided that if my brother wanted to become a lawyer he had to first pay penance for his skin by picking cotton and hoeing corn and studying correspondence books at night for twenty years?

The man's dead words fell like bricks around the auditorium and too many settled in my belly. Constrained by hard-learned manners I couldn't look behind me, but to my left and right the proud graduating class of 1940 had dropped their heads. Every girl in my row had found something new to do with her handkerchief. Some folded the tiny squares into love knots, some into triangles, but most were wadding them, then pressing them flat on their yellow laps.

On the dais, the ancient tragedy was being replayed. Professor Parsons sat, a sculptor's reject, rigid. His large, heavy body seemed devoid of will or willingness, and his eyes said he was no longer with us. The other teachers examined the flag (which was draped stage right) or their notes, or the windows which opened on our now-famous playing diamond.

Graduation, the hush-hush magic time of frills and gifts and congratulations and diplomas, was finished for me before my name was called. The accomplishment was nothing. The meticulous maps, drawn in three colors of ink, learning and spelling decasyllabic words, memorizing the whole of *The Rape of Lucrece*°—it was for nothing. Donleavy had exposed us.

We were maids and farmers, handymen and washerwomen, and any- 45
thing higher that we aspired to was farcical and presumptuous.

Then I wished that Gabriel Prosser° and Nat Turner° had killed all whitefolks in their beds and that Abraham Lincoln had been assassinated before the signing of the Emancipation Proclamation, and that Harriet Tubman° had been killed by that blow on her head and Christopher Columbus had drowned in the *Santa Maria*.

It was awful to be Negro and have no control over my life. It was brutal to be young and already trained to sit quietly and listen to charges brought against my color with no chance of defense. We should all be dead. I thought I should like to see us all dead, one on top of the other. A pyramid of flesh with the whitefolks on the bottom, as the broad base, then the Indians with

---

George Washington Carver: (1864–1943) African-American agricultural chemist. Born a slave, he later taught at Tuskegee Institute, where he carried out research that led to crop diversification in the South. He is particularly credited with discovering new uses for crops such as peanuts and soybeans. *The Rape of Lucrece:* A narrative poem, 1855 lines long, written by William Shakespeare. *Gabriel Prosser, Nat Turner:* Leaders of slave rebellions. In 1800, Prosser recruited several hundred slaves to attack Richmond. Before they could attack, they were betrayed, and the leaders of the rebellion were captured and executed. In 1831, Turner led a group of slaves who eventually killed 57 white men, women, and children as a protest against slavery. *Harriet Tubman* (1820–1913): An African-American abolitionist who escaped from slavery in 1849 and worked with the underground railroad, leading more than 300 slaves north to freedom.

their silly tomahawks and tepees and wigwams and treaties, the Negroes with their mops and recipes and cotton sacks and spirituals sticking out of their mouths. The Dutch children should all stumble in their wooden shoes and break their necks. The French should choke to death on the Louisiana Purchase (1803) while silkworms ate all the Chinese with their stupid pigtails. As a species, we were an abomination. All of us.

Donleavy was running for election, and assured our parents that if he won we could count on having the only colored paved playing field in that part of Arkansas. Also—he never looked up to acknowledge the grunts of acceptance—also, we were bound to get some new equipment for the home economics building and the workshop.

He finished, and since there was no need to give any more than the most perfunctory thank-you's, he nodded to the men on the stage, and the tall white man who was never introduced joined him at the door. They left with the attitude that now they were off to something really important. (The graduation ceremonies at Lafayette County Training School had been a mere preliminary.)

The ugliness they left was palpable. An uninvited guest who wouldn't leave. The choir was summoned and sang a modern arrangement of "Onward, Christian Soldiers," with new words pertaining to graduates seeking their place in the world. But it didn't work. Elouise, the daughter of the Baptist minister, recited "Invictus," and I could have cried at the impertinence of "I am the master of my fate, I am the captain of my soul." 50

My name had lost its ring of familiarity and I had to be nudged to go and receive my diploma. All my preparations had fled. I neither marched up to the stage like a conquering Amazon, nor did I look in the audience for Bailey's nod of approval. Marguerite Johnson, I heard the name again, my honors were read, there were noises in the audience of appreciation, and I took my place on the stage as rehearsed.

I thought about colors I hated: ecru, puce, lavender, beige and black.

There was shuffling and rustling around me, then Henry Reed was giving his valedictory address, "To Be or Not to Be." Hadn't he heard the whitefolks? We couldn't *be,* so the question was a waste of time. Henry's voice came clear and strong. I feared to look at him. Hadn't he got the message? There was no "nobler in the mind" for Negroes because the world didn't think we had minds, and they let us know it. "Outrageous fortune"? Now, that was a joke. When the ceremony was over I had to tell Henry Reed some things. That is, if I still cared. Not "rub," Henry, "erase." "Ah, there's the erase." Us.

Henry had been a good student in elocution. His voice rose on tides of promise and fell on waves of warnings. The English teacher had helped him to create a sermon winging through Hamlet's soliloquy. To be a man, a doer, a builder, a leader, or to be a tool, an unfunny joke, a crusher of funky toadstools. I marveled that Henry could go through the speech as if we had a choice.

I had been listening and silently rebutting each sentence with my eyes 55
closed; then there was a hush, which in an audience warns that something
unplanned is happening. I looked up and saw Henry Reed, the conservative,
the proper, the A student, turn his back to the audience and turn to us (the
proud graduating class of 1940) and sing, nearly speaking,

> Lift ev'ry voice and sing
> Till earth and heaven ring
> Ring with the harmonies of Liberty . . .*

It was the poem written by James Weldon Johnson. It was the music composed by J. Rosamond Johnson. It was the Negro national anthem. Out of
habit we were singing it.

Our mothers and fathers stood in the dark hall and joined the hymn of
encouragement. A kindergarten teacher led the small children onto the stage
and the buttercups and daisies and bunny rabbits marked time and tried to
follow:

> Stony the road we trod
> Bitter the chastening rod
> Felt in the days when hope, unborn, had died.
> Yet with a steady beat
> Have not our weary feet
> Come to the place for which our fathers sighed?

Every child I knew had learned that song with his ABC's and along
with "Jesus Loves Me This I Know." But I personally had never heard it
before. Never heard the words, despite the thousands of times I had sung
them. Never thought they had anything to do with me.

On the other hand, the words of Patrick Henry° had made such an
impression on me that I had been able to stretch myself tall and trembling
and say, "I know not what course others may take, but as for me, give me
liberty or give me death."

And now I heard, really for the first time:

> We have come over a way that with tears has been watered,
> We have come, treading our path through the blood of the slaughtered.

While echoes of the song shivered in the air, Henry Reed bowed his 60
head, said "Thank you," and returned to his place in the line. The tears that
slipped down many faces were not wiped away in shame.

---

*"Lift Ev'ry Voice and Sing"—words by James Weldon Johnson and music by
J. Rosamond Johnson. Copyright by Edward B. Marks Music Corporation. Used by
permission.

Patrick Henry: (1726–1799) A leader of the American Revolution who was admired for his skills
as a public speaker. The rallying cry "Give me liberty or give me death" is attributed to him.

We were on top again. As always, again. We survived. The depths had been icy and dark, but now a bright sun spoke to our souls. I was no longer simply a member of the proud graduating class of 1940; I was a proud member of the wonderful beautiful Negro race.

Considerations

1. Although the word "graduation" appears in the title, the first half of the work focuses on preparation for the event. What effect does Maya Angelou (pen name of Marguerite Johnson) create by describing in such detail the community's involvement in and anticipation of the ceremony? What—if anything—would be lost if the first half of the essay were abbreviated or omitted?

2. Describe the attitude of the white officials who attend the graduation. Provide details from the essay to explain your analysis of their actions, words, and responses.

3. Henry Reed's speech is titled "To Be or Not to Be." Using a dictionary of quotations, identify the allusion made by the title as well as by Angelou's comments on the title. Speculate on the irony suggested by the title and by Reed's speech as contrasted to Mr. Donleavy's speech.

4. Describe Marguerite Johnson's response when she is called to receive her diploma. How does the reality compare with the way she had imagined the moment? How can you explain this change and its implications?

5. Maya Angelou describes an incident related to her formal education that taught her lessons different from those she learned from books. Think of your own school experiences and describe an incident—apart from regular subject-matter study—that taught you something you consider valuable. As you write your essay, consider the strategies Angelou uses. For instance, notice her description of setting, her arrangement of events in chronological order, and her direct quotation of conversations and speeches.

CONNECTIONS: INNOCENCE AND EXPERIENCE

1. "The Circling Hand" and "Salvation" show children or young adults who become disillusioned through the words and actions of adults they have loved and trusted. Compare and comment on the experiences depicted in these works.

2. "Araby," "And the Soul Shall Dance," "When I was one-and-twenty," and "In the Orchard" relate to experiences with love. Comment on the changes experienced by the main characters in the short stories and the speakers in the poems.

3. Discuss the role of conflicts between parents and children as part of the passage from innocence to experience. Consider at least three of these

works: "The Circling Hand," *Hamlet,* "In the Counselor's Waiting Room," and "The Centaur."

4. What are the differences—if any—in the ways males and females move from innocence to experience? Consider any of the following works as you think about this question.

Works Relating to Males	Works Relating to Females
"Araby"	"And the Soul Shall Dance"
"The Red Convertible"	"The Circling Hand"
"Battle Royal"	"In the Counselor's Waiting Room"
"Salvation"	"The Centaur"
	"Graduation in Stamps"

5. Consider how prejudice affects young people as they grow and mature. You may include "Battle Royal," "Incident," and "Graduation in Stamps" as part of your consideration. Although these works focus on the prejudice of whites against blacks, you may include other forms of prejudice in your discussion.

6

Roots, Identity, and Culture

JAMES BALDWIN (1924–1987)

Sonny's Blues

> *Born to Emma Berdis, a single mother, James Baldwin became part of a large*
> *and complex family when his mother later married David Baldwin, with*
> *whom she subsequently had eight more children. James Baldwin often acted as*
> *a father figure to the younger children, and his fiction shows sensitivity to the*
> *complex relationships between parents and their sons and daughters. "Sonny's*
> *Blues," first published as part of his collection* Going to Meet the Man
> *(1965) demonstrates his concern with the theme of families, roots, and identity.*

I read about it in the paper, in the subway, on my way to work. I read
it, and I couldn't believe it, and I read it again. Then perhaps I just stared at
it, at the newsprint spelling out his name, spelling out the story. I stared at it
in the swinging lights of the subway car, and in the faces and bodies of the
people, and in my own face, trapped in the darkness which roared outside.

It was not to be believed and I kept telling myself that, as I walked from
the subway station to the high school. And at the same time I couldn't doubt
it. I was scared, scared for Sonny. He became real to me again. A great block
of ice got settled in my belly and kept melting there slowly all day long,
while I taught my classes algebra. It was a special kind of ice. It kept melting,
sending trickles of ice water all up and down my veins, but it never got less.
Sometimes it hardened and seemed to expand until I felt my guts were going
to come spilling out or that I was going to choke or scream. This would
always be at a moment when I was remembering some specific thing Sonny
had once said or done.

When he was about as old as the boys in my class his face had been
bright and open, there was a lot of copper in it; and he'd had wonderfully
direct brown eyes, and great gentleness and privacy. I wondered what he
looked like now. He had been picked up, the evening before, in a raid on an
apartment downtown, for peddling and using heroin.

I couldn't believe it: but what I mean by that is that I couldn't find any
room for it anywhere inside me. I had kept it outside me for a long time. I
hadn't wanted to know. I had had suspicions, but I didn't name them, I kept
putting them away. I told myself that Sonny was wild, but he wasn't crazy. And
he'd always been a good boy, he hadn't ever turned hard or evil or disrespectful,
the way kids can, so quick, so quick, especially in Harlem. I didn't want to
believe that I'd ever see my brother going down, coming to nothing, all that
light in his face gone out, in the condition I'd already seen so many others. Yet
it had happened and here I was, talking about algebra to a lot of boys who
might, every one of them for all I knew, be popping off needles every time they
went to the head. Maybe it did more for them than algebra could.

I was sure that the first time Sonny had ever had horse, he couldn't
have been much older than these boys were now. These boys, now, were

5

living as we'd been living then, they were growing up with a rush and their heads bumped abruptly against the low ceiling of their actual possibilities. They were filled with rage. All they really knew were two darknesses, the darkness of their lives, which was now closing in on them, and the darkness of the movies, which had blinded them to that other darkness, and in which they now, vindictively, dreamed, at once more together than they were at any other time, and more alone.

When the last bell rang, the last class ended, I let out my breath. It seemed I'd been holding it for all that time. My clothes were wet—I may have looked as though I'd been sitting in a steam bath, all dressed up, all afternoon. I sat alone in the classroom a long time. I listened to the boys outside, downstairs, shouting and cursing and laughing. Their laughter struck me for perhaps the first time. It was not the joyous laughter which —God knows why—one associates with children. It was mocking and insular, its intent was to denigrate. It was disenchanted, and in this, also, lay the authority of their curses. Perhaps I was listening to them because I was thinking about my brother and in them I heard my brother. And myself.

One boy was whistling a tune, at once very complicated and very simple, it seemed to be pouring out of him as though he were a bird, and it sounded very cool and moving through all that harsh, bright air, only just holding its own through all those other sounds.

I stood up and walked over to the window and looked down into the courtyard. It was the beginning of the spring and the sap was rising in the boys. A teacher passed through them every now and again, quickly, as though he or she couldn't wait to get out of that courtyard, to get those boys out of their sight and off their minds. I started collecting my stuff. I thought I'd better get home and talk to Isabel.

The courtyard was almost deserted by the time I got downstairs. I saw this boy standing in the shadow of a doorway, looking just like Sonny. I almost called his name. Then I saw that it wasn't Sonny, but somebody we used to know, a boy from around our block. He'd been Sonny's friend. He'd never been mine, having been too young for me, and, anyway, I'd never liked him. And now, even though he was a grown-up man, he still hung around that block, still spent hours on the street corners, was always high and raggy. I used to run into him from time to time and he'd often work around to asking me for a quarter or fifty cents. He always had some real good excuse, too, and I always gave it to him, I don't know why.

But now, abruptly, I hated him. I couldn't stand the way he looked at me, partly like a dog, partly like a cunning child. I wanted to ask him what the hell he was doing in the school courtyard.

He sort of shuffled over to me, and he said, "I see you got the papers. So you already know about it."

"You mean about Sonny? Yes, I already know about it. How come they didn't get you?"

He grinned. It made him repulsive and it also brought to mind what he'd looked like as a kid. "I wasn't there. I stay away from them people."

"Good for you." I offered him a cigarette and I watched him through the smoke. "You come all the way down here just to tell me about Sonny?"

"That's right." He was sort of shaking his head and his eyes looked   15 strange, as though they were about to cross. The bright sun deadened his damp dark brown skin and it made his eyes look yellow and showed up the dirt in his kinked hair. He smelled funky. I moved a little away from him and I said, "Well, thanks. But I already know about it and I got to get home."

"I'll walk you a little ways," he said. We started walking. There were a couple of kids still loitering in the courtyard and one of them said goodnight to me and looked strangely at the boy beside me.

"What're you going to do?" he asked me. "I mean, about Sonny?"

"Look. I haven't seen Sonny for over a year, I'm not sure I'm going to do anything. Anyway, what the hell *can* I do?"

"That's right," he said quickly, "ain't nothing you can do. Can't much help old Sonny no more, I guess."

It was what I was thinking and so it seemed to me he had no right to   20 say it.

"I'm surprised at Sonny, though," he went on—he had a funny way of talking, he looked straight ahead as though he were talking to himself—"I thought Sonny was a smart boy, I thought he was too smart to get hung."

"I guess he thought so too," I said sharply, "and that's how he got hung. And how about you? You're pretty goddamn smart, I bet."

Then he looked directly at me, just for a minute. "I ain't smart," he said. "If I was smart, I'd have reached for a pistol a long time ago."

"Look. Don't tell *me* your sad story, if it was up to me, I'd give you one." Then I felt guilty—guilty, probably, for never having supposed that the poor bastard *had* a story of his own, much less a sad one, and I asked, quickly, "What's going to happen to him now?"

He didn't answer this. He was off by himself some place. "Funny   25 thing," he said, and from his tone we might have been discussing the quickest way to get to Brooklyn, "when I saw the papers this morning, the first thing I asked myself was if I had anything to do with it. I felt sort of responsible."

I began to listen more carefully. The subway station was on the corner, just before us, and I stopped. He stopped, too. We were in front of a bar and he ducked slightly, peering in, but whoever he was looking for didn't seem to be there. The juke box was blasting away with something black and bouncy and I half watched the barmaid as she danced her way from the juke box to her place behind the bar. And I watched her face as she laughingly responded to something someone said to her, still keeping time to the music. When she smiled one saw the little girl, one sensed the doomed, still-struggling woman beneath the battered face of the semi-whore.

"I never *give* Sonny nothing," the boy said finally, "but a long time ago I come to school high and Sonny asked me how it felt." He paused, I couldn't bear to watch him, I watched the barmaid, and I listened to the music which seemed to be causing the pavement to shake. "I told him it felt great." The music stopped, the barmaid paused and watched the juke box until the music began again. "It did."

All this was carrying me some place I didn't want to go. I certainly didn't want to know how it felt. It filled everything, the people, the houses, the music, the dark, quicksilver barmaid, with menace; and this menace was their reality.

"What's going to happen to him now?" I asked again.

"They'll send him away some place and they'll try to cure him." He shook his head. "Maybe he'll even think he's kicked the habit. Then they'll let him loose"—he gestured, throwing his cigarette into the gutter. "That's all." *30*

"What do you mean, that's *all?*"

But I knew what he meant.

"I *mean,* that's *all.*" He turned his head and looked at me, pulling down the corners of his mouth. "Don't you know what I mean?" he asked, softly.

"How the hell *would* I know what you mean?" I almost whispered it, I don't know why.

"That's right," he said to the air, "how would *he* know what I mean?" *35* He turned toward me again, patient and calm, and yet I somehow felt him shaking, shaking as though he were going to fall apart. I felt that ice in my guts again, the dread I'd felt all afternoon; and again I watched the barmaid, moving about the bar, washing glasses, and singing. "Listen. They'll let him out and then it'll just start all over again. That's what I mean."

"You mean—they'll let him out. And then he'll just start working his way back in again. You mean he'll never kick the habit. Is that what you mean?"

"That's right," he said, cheerfully. "*You* see what I mean."

"Tell me," I said at last, "why does he want to die? He must want to die, he's killing himself, why does he want to die?"

He looked at me in surprise. He licked his lips. "He don't want to die. He wants to live. Don't nobody want to die, ever."

Then I wanted to ask him—too many things. He could not have *40* answered, or if he had, I could not have borne the answers. I started walking. "Well, I guess it's none of my business."

"It's going to be rough on old Sonny," he said. We reached the subway station. "This is your station?" he asked. I nodded. I took one step down. "Damn!" he said, suddenly. I looked up at him. He grinned again. "Damn it if I didn't leave all my money home. You ain't got a dollar on you, have you? Just for a couple of days, is all."

All at once something inside gave and threatened to come pouring out of me. I didn't hate him any more. I felt that in another moment I'd start crying like a child.

"Sure," I said. "Don't swear." I looked in my wallet and didn't have a dollar, I only had a five. "Here," I said. "That hold you?"

He didn't look at it—he didn't want to look at it. A terrible, closed look came over his face, as though he were keeping the number on the bill a secret from him and me. "Thanks," he said, and now he was dying to see me go. "Don't worry about Sonny. Maybe I'll write him or something."

"Sure," I said. "You do that. So long." 45

"Be seeing you," he said. I went down the steps.

And I didn't write Sonny or send him anything for a long time. When I finally did, it was just after my little girl died, he wrote me back a letter which made me feel like a bastard.

Here's what he said:

Dear Brother,

You don't know how much I needed to hear from you. I wanted to write you many a time but I dug how much I must have hurt you and so I didn't write. But now I feel like a man who's been trying to climb up out of some deep, real deep and funky hole and just saw the sun up there, outside. I got to get outside.

I can't tell you much about how I got here. I mean I don't know how to tell you. I guess I was afraid of something or I was trying to escape from something and you know I have never been very strong in the head (smile). I'm glad Mama and Daddy are dead and can't see what's happened to their son and I swear if I'd known what I was doing I would never have hurt you so, you and a lot of other fine people who were nice to me and who believed in me.

I don't want you to think it had anything to do with me being a 50 musician. It's more than that. Or maybe less than that. I can't get anything straight in my head down here and I try not to think about what's going to happen to me when I get outside again. Sometime I think I'm going to flip and *never* get outside and sometime I think I'll come straight back. I tell you one thing, though, I'd rather blow my brains out than go through this again. But that's what they all say, so they tell me. If I tell you when I'm coming to New York and if you could meet me, I sure would appreciate it. Give my love to Isabel and the kids and I was sure sorry to hear about little Gracie. I wish I could be like Mama and say the Lord's will be done, but I don't know it seems to me that trouble is the one thing that never does get stopped and I don't know what good it does to blame it on the Lord. But maybe it does some good if you believe it.

Your brother,
Sonny

Then I kept in constant touch with him and I sent him whatever I could and I went to meet him when he came back to New York. When I saw him many things I thought I had forgotten came flooding back to me. This was because I had begun, finally, to wonder about Sonny, about the life that Sonny lived inside. This life, whatever it was, had made him older and thinner and it had deepened the distant stillness in which he had always moved. He looked very unlike my baby brother. Yet, when he smiled, when we shook hands, the baby brother I'd never known looked out from the depths of his private life, like an animal waiting to be coaxed into the light.

"How you been keeping?" he asked me.

"All right. And you?"

"Just fine." He was smiling all over his face. "It's good to see you again."

"It's good to see you." 55

The seven years' difference in our ages lay between us like a chasm: I wondered if these years would ever operate between us as a bridge. I was remembering, and it made it hard to catch my breath, that I had been there when he was born; and I had heard the first words he had ever spoken. When he started to walk, he walked from our mother straight to me. I caught him just before he fell when he took the first steps he ever took in this world.

"How's Isabel?"

"Just fine. She's dying to see you."

"And the boys?"

"They're fine, too. They're anxious to see their uncle." 60

"Oh, come on. You know they don't remember me."

"Are you kidding? Of course they remember you."

He grinned again. We got into a taxi. We had a lot to say to each other, far too much to know how to begin.

As the taxi began to move, I asked, "You still want to go to India?"

He laughed. "You still remember that. Hell, no. This place is Indian 65 enough for me."

"It used to belong to them," I said.

And he laughed again. "They damn sure knew what they were doing when they got rid of it."

Years ago, when he was around fourteen, he'd been all hipped on the idea of going to India. He read books about people sitting on rocks, naked, in all kinds of weather, but mostly bad, naturally, and walking barefoot through hot coals and arriving at wisdom. I used to say that it sounded to me as though they were getting away from wisdom as fast as they could. I think he sort of looked down on me for that.

"Do you mind," he asked, "if we have the driver drive alongside the park? On the west side—I haven't seen the city in so long."

"Of course not," I said. I was afraid that I might sound as though I 70 were humoring him, but I hoped he wouldn't take it that way.

So we drove along, between the green of the park and the stony, lifeless elegance of hotels and apartment buildings, toward the vivid, killing streets of our childhood. These streets hadn't changed, though housing projects jutted up out of them now like rocks in the middle of a boiling sea. Most of the houses in which we had grown up had vanished, as had the stores from which we had stolen, the basements in which we had first tried sex, the rooftops from which we had hurled tin cans and bricks. But houses exactly like the houses of our past yet dominated the landscape, boys exactly like the boys we once had been found themselves smothering in these houses, came down into the streets for light and air and found themselves encircled by disaster. Some escaped the trap, most didn't. Those who got out always left something of themselves behind, as some animals amputate a leg and leave it in the trap. It might be said, perhaps, that I had escaped, after all, I was a school teacher; or that Sonny had, he hadn't lived in Harlem for years. Yet, as the cab moved uptown through streets which seemed, with a rush, to darken with dark people, and as I covertly studied Sonny's face, it came to me that what we were both seeking through our separate cab windows was that part of ourselves which had been left behind. It's always at the hour of trouble and confrontation that the missing member aches.

We hit 110th Street and started rolling up Lenox Avenue. And I'd known this avenue all my life, but it seemed to me again, as it had seemed on the day I'd first heard about Sonny's trouble, filled with a hidden menace which was its very breath of life.

"We almost there," said Sonny.

"Almost." We were both too nervous to say anything more.

We lived in a housing project. It hasn't been up long. A few days after it was up it seemed uninhabitably new, now, of course, it's already rundown. It looks like a parody of the good, clean, faceless life—God knows the people who live in it do their best to make it a parody. The beat-looking grass lying around isn't enough to make their lives green, the hedges will never hold out the streets, and they know it. The big windows fool no one, they aren't big enough to make space out of no space. They don't bother with the windows, they watch the TV screen instead. The playground is most popular with the children who don't play at jacks, or skip rope, or roller skate, or swing, and they can be found in it after dark. We moved in partly because it's not too far from where I teach, and partly for the kids; but it's really just like the houses in which Sonny and I grew up. The same things happen, they'll have the same things to remember. The moment Sonny and I started into the house I had the feeling that I was simply bringing him back into the danger he had almost died trying to escape.

Sonny has never been talkative. So I don't know why I was sure he'd be dying to talk to me when supper was over the first night. Everything went fine, the oldest boy remembered him, and the youngest boy liked him, and Sonny had remembered to bring something for each of them; and Isabel, who is really much nicer than I am, more open and giving, had gone to a lot of trouble about dinner and was genuinely glad to see him. And she's always been able to tease Sonny in a way that I haven't. It was nice to see her face so vivid again and to hear her laugh and watch her make Sonny laugh. She wasn't, or, anyway, she didn't seem to be, at all uneasy or embarrassed. She chatted as though there were no subject which had to be avoided

75

and she got Sonny past his first, faint stiffness. And thank God she was there, for I was filled with that icy dread again. Everything I did seemed awkward to me, and everything I said sounded freighted with hidden meaning. I was trying to remember everything I'd heard about dope addiction and I couldn't help watching Sonny for signs. I wasn't doing it out of malice. I was trying to find out something about my brother. I was dying to hear him tell me he was safe.

"Safe!" my father grunted, whenever Mama suggested trying to move to a neighborhood which might be safer for children. "Safe, hell! Ain't no place safe for kids, nor nobody."

He always went on like this, but he wasn't, ever, really as bad as he sounded, not even on weekends, when he got drunk. As a matter of fact, he was always on the lookout for "something a little better," but he died before he found it. He died suddenly, during a drunken weekend in the middle of the war, when Sonny was fifteen. He and Sonny hadn't ever got on too well. And this was partly because Sonny was the apple of his father's eye. It was because he loved Sonny so much and was frightened for him, that he was always fighting with him. It doesn't do any good to fight with Sonny. Sonny just moves back, inside himself, where he can't be reached. But the principal reason that they never hit it off is that they were so much alike. Daddy was big and rough and loud-talking, just the opposite of Sonny, but they both had—that same privacy.

Mama tried to tell me something about this, just after Daddy died. I was home on leave from the army.

This was the last time I ever saw my mother alive. Just the same, this picture gets all mixed up in my mind with pictures I had of her when she was younger. The way I always see her is the way she used to be on a Sunday afternoon, say, when the old folks were talking after the big Sunday dinner. I always see her wearing pale blue. She'd be sitting on the sofa. And my father would be sitting in the easy chair, not far from her. And the living room would be full of church folks and relatives. There they sit, in chairs all around the living room, and the night is creeping up outside, but nobody knows it yet. You can see the darkness growing against the windowpanes and you hear the street noises every now and again, or maybe the jangling beat of a tambourine from one of the churches close by, but it's real quiet in the room. For a moment nobody's talking, but every face looks darkening, like the sky outside. And my mother rocks a little from the waist, and my father's eyes are closed. Everyone is looking at something a child can't see. For a minute they've forgotten the children. Maybe a kid is lying on the rug, half asleep. Maybe somebody's got a kid in his lap and is absent-mindedly stroking the kid's head. Maybe there's a kid, quiet and big-eyed, curled up in a big chair in the corner. The silence, the darkness coming, and the darkness in the faces frightens the child obscurely. He hopes that the hand which strokes his forehead will never stop—will never die. He hopes that there will never come a time when the old folks won't be sitting around the living room, talking about where they've come from, and what they've seen, and what's happening to them and their kinfolk.

But something deep and watchful in the child knows that this is bound to end, is already ending. In a moment someone will get up and turn on the light. Then the old folks will remember the children and they won't talk any more that day. And when light fills the room, the child is filled with darkness. He knows that every time this happens he's moved just a little closer to that darkness outside. The darkness outside is what the old folks have been talking about. It's what they've come from. It's what they endure. The child knows that they won't talk any more because if he knows too much about what's happened to *them,* he'll know too much too soon, about what's going to happen to *him.*

The last time I talked to my mother, I remember I was restless. I wanted to get out and see Isabel. We weren't married then and we had a lot to straighten out between us.

There Mama sat, in black, by the window. She was humming an old church song, *Lord, you brought me from a long ways off.* Sonny was out somewhere. Mama kept watching the streets.

"I don't know," she said, "if I'll ever see you again, after you go off from here. But I hope you'll remember the things I tried to teach you."

"Don't talk like that," I said, and smiled. "You'll be here a long time yet."   85

She smiled, too, but she said nothing. She was quiet for a long time. And I said, "Mama, don't you worry about nothing. I'll be writing all the time, and you be getting the checks. . . ."

"I want to talk to you about your brother," she said, suddenly. "If anything happens to me he ain't going to have nobody to look out for him."

"Mama," I said, "ain't nothing going to happen to you *or* Sonny. Sonny's all right. He's a good boy and he's got good sense."

"It ain't a question of his being a good boy," Mama said, "nor of his having good sense. It ain't only the bad ones, nor yet the dumb ones that gets sucked under." She stopped, looking at me. "Your Daddy once had a brother," she said, and she smiled in a way that made me feel she was in pain. "You didn't never know that, did you?"

"No," I said, "I never knew that," and I watched her face.   90

"Oh, yes," she said, "your Daddy had a brother." She looked out of the window again. "I know you never saw your Daddy cry. But I did— many a time, through all these years."

I asked her, "What happened to his brother? How come nobody's ever talked about him?"

This was the first time I ever saw my mother look old.

"His brother got killed," she said, "when he was just a little younger than you are now. I knew him. He was a fine boy. He was maybe a little full of the devil, but he didn't mean nobody no harm."

Then she stopped and the room was silent, exactly as it had sometimes   95 been on those Sunday afternoons. Mama kept looking out into the streets.

"He used to have a job in the mill," she said, "and, like all young folks, he just liked to perform on Saturday nights. Saturday nights, him and your father would drift around to different places, go to dances and things like that, or just sit around with people they knew, and your father's brother would sing, he had a fine voice, and play along with himself on his guitar. Well, this particular Saturday night, him and your father was coming home from some place, and they were both a little drunk and there was a moon that night, it was bright like day. Your father's brother was feeling kind of good, and he was whistling to himself, and he had his guitar slung over his shoulder. They was coming down a hill and beneath them was a road that turned off from the highway. Well, your father's brother, being always kind of frisky, decided to run down this hill, and he did, with that guitar banging and clanging behind him, and he ran across the road, and he was making water behind a tree. And your father was sort of amused at him and he was still coming down the hill, kind of slow. Then he heard a car motor and that same minute his brother stepped from behind the tree, into the road, in the moonlight. And he started to cross the road. And your father started to run down the hill, he says he don't know why. This car was full of white men. They was all drunk, and when they seen your father's brother they let out a great whoop and holler and they aimed the car straight at him. They was having fun, they just wanted to scare him, the way they do sometimes, you know. But they was drunk. And I guess the boy, being drunk, too, and scared, kind of lost his head. By the time he jumped it was too late. Your father says he heard his brother scream when the car rolled over him, and he heard the wood of that guitar when it give, and he heard them strings go flying, and he heard them white men shouting, and the car kept on a going and it ain't stopped till this day. And, time your father got down the hill, his brother weren't nothing but blood and pulp."

Tears were gleaming on my mother's face. There wasn't anything I could say.

"He never mentioned it," she said, "because I never let him mention it before you children. Your Daddy was like a crazy man that night and for many a night thereafter. He says he never in his life seen anything as dark as that road after the lights of that car had gone away. Weren't nothing; weren't nobody on that road, just your Daddy and his brother and that busted guitar. Oh, yes. Your Daddy never did really get right again. Till the day he died he wasn't sure but that every white man he saw was the man that killed his brother."

She stopped and took out a handkerchief and dried her eyes and looked at me.

"I ain't telling you all this," she said, "to make you scared or bitter or to make you hate nobody. I'm telling you this because you got a brother. And the world ain't changed."

I guess I didn't want to believe this. I guess she saw this in my face. She turned away from me, toward the window again, searching those streets.

"But I praise my Redeemer," she said at last, "that He called your Daddy home before me. I ain't saying it to throw no flowers at myself, but, I declare, it keeps me from feeling too cast down to know I helped your father get safely through this world. Your father always acted like he was the roughest, strongest man on earth. And everybody took him to be like that. But if he hadn't had *me* there—to see his tears!"

She was crying again. Still, I couldn't move. I said, "Lord, Lord, Mama, I didn't know it was like that."

"Oh, honey," she said, "there's a lot that you don't know. But you are going to find out." She stood up from the window and came over to me. "You got to hold on to your brother," she said, "and don't let him fall, no matter what it looks like is happening to him and no matter how evil you gets with him. You going to be evil with him many a time. But don't you forget what I told you, you hear?"

"I won't forget," I said. "Don't you worry, I won't forget. I won't let nothing happen to Sonny." 105

My mother smiled as though she were amused at something she saw in my face. Then, "You may not be able to stop nothing from happening. But you got to let him know you's *there*."

Two days later I was married, and then I was gone. And I had a lot of things on my mind and I pretty well forgot my promise to Mama until I got shipped home on a special furlough for her funeral.

And, after the funeral, with just Sonny and me alone in the empty kitchen, I tried to find out something about him.

"What do you want to do?" I asked him.

"I'm going to be a musician," he said. 110

For he had graduated, in the time I had been away, from dancing to the juke box to finding out who was playing what, and what they were doing with it, and he had bought himself a set of drums.

"You mean, you want to be a drummer?" I somehow had the feeling that being a drummer might be all right for other people but not for my brother Sonny.

"I don't think," he said, looking at me very gravely, "that I'll ever be a good drummer. But I think I can play a piano."

I frowned. I'd never played the role of the older brother quite so seriously before, had scarcely ever, in fact, *asked* Sonny a damn thing. I sensed myself in the presence of something I didn't really know how to handle, didn't understand. So I made my frown a little deeper as I asked: "What kind of musician do you want to be?"

He grinned. "How many kinds do you think there are?" 115

"Be *serious*," I said.

He laughed, throwing his head back, and looked at me. "I *am* serious."

"Well, then, for Christ's sake, stop kidding around and answer a serious question. I mean, do you want to be a concert pianist, you want to play classical music and all that, or—or what?" Long before I finished he was laughing again. "For Christ's *sake,* Sonny!"

He sobered, but with difficulty. "I'm sorry. But you sound so—*scared!*" and he was off again.

"Well, you may think it's funny now, baby, but it's not going to   120 be so funny when you have to make your living at it, let me tell you *that.*" I was furious because I knew he was laughing at me and I didn't know why.

"No," he said, very sober now, and afraid, perhaps, that he'd hurt me, "I don't want to be a classical pianist. That isn't what interests me. I mean"—he paused, looking hard at me, as though his eyes would help me to understand, and then gestured helplessly, as though perhaps his hand would help—"I mean, I'll have a lot of studying to do, and I'll have to study *everything,* but, I mean, I want to play *with*—jazz musicians." He stopped. "I want to play jazz," he said.

Well, the word had never before sounded as heavy, as real, as it sounded that afternoon in Sonny's mouth. I just looked at him and I was probably frowning a real frown by this time. I simply couldn't see why on earth he'd want to spend his time hanging around nightclubs, clowning around on band stands, while people pushed each other around a dance floor. It seemed— beneath him, somehow. I had never thought about it before, had never been forced to, but I suppose I had always put jazz musicians in a class with what Daddy called "goodtime people."

"Are you *serious?*"

"Hell, *yes,* I'm serious."

He looked more helpless than ever, and annoyed, and deeply hurt.   125

I suggested, helpfully: "You mean—like Louis Armstrong?"

His face closed as though I'd struck him. "No. I'm not talking about none of that old-time, down home crap."

"Well, look, Sonny, I'm sorry, don't get mad. I just don't altogether get it, that's all. Name somebody—you know, a jazz musician you admire."

"Bird."

"Who?"   130

"Bird! Charlie Parker! Don't they teach you nothing in the goddamn army?"

I lit a cigarette. I was surprised and then a little amused to discover that I was trembling. "I've been out of touch," I said. "You'll have to be patient with me. Now. Who's this Parker character?"

"He's just one of the greatest jazz musicians alive," said Sonny, sullenly, his hands in his pockets, his back to me. "Maybe *the* greatest," he added, bitterly, "that's probably why *you* never heard of him."

"All right," I said, "I'm ignorant. I'm sorry. I'll go out and buy all the cat's records right away, all right?"

"It don't," said Sonny, with dignity, "make any difference to me. I don't   135 care what you listen to. Don't do me no favors."

I was beginning to realize that I'd never seen him so upset before. With another part of my mind I was thinking that this would probably turn out to be one of those things kids go through and that I shouldn't make it seem important by pushing it too hard. Still, I didn't think it would do any harm to ask: "Doesn't all this take a lot of time? Can you make a living at it?"

He turned back to me and half leaned, half sat, on the kitchen table. "Everything takes time," he said, "and—well, yes, sure, I can make a living at it. But what I don't seem to be able to make you understand is that it's the only thing I want to do."

"Well, Sonny," I said, gently, "you know people can't always do exactly what they *want* to do—"

"*No,* I don't know that," said Sonny, surprising me. "I think people *ought* to do what they want to do, what else are they alive for?"

"You getting to be a big boy," I said desperately, "it's time you started 140
thinking about your future."

"I'm thinking about my future," said Sonny, grimly. "I think about it all the time."

I gave up. I decided, if he didn't change his mind, that we could always talk about it later. "In the meantime," I said, "you got to finish school." We had already decided that he'd have to move in with Isabel and her folks. I knew this wasn't the ideal arrangement because Isabel's folks are inclined to be dicty and they hadn't especially wanted Isabel to marry me. But I didn't know what else to do. "And we have to get you fixed up at Isabel's."

There was a long silence. He moved from the kitchen table to the window. "That's a terrible idea. You know it yourself."

"Do you have a *better* idea?"

He just walked up and down the kitchen for a minute. He was as tall 145
as I was. He had started to shave. I suddenly had the feeling that I didn't know him at all.

He stopped at the kitchen table and picked up my cigarettes. Looking at me with a kind of mocking, amused defiance, he put one between his lips. "You mind?"

"You smoking already?"

He lit the cigarette and nodded, watching me through the smoke. "I just wanted to see if I'd have the courage to smoke in front of you." He grinned and blew a great cloud of smoke to the ceiling. "It was easy." He looked at my face. "Come on, now. I bet you was smoking at my age, tell the truth."

I didn't say anything but the truth was on my face, and he laughed. But now there was something very strained in his laugh. "Sure. And I bet that ain't all you was doing."

He was frightening me a little. "Cut the crap," I said. "We already 150
decided that you was going to go and live at Isabel's. Now what's got into you all of a sudden?"

"*You* decided it," he pointed out. "*I* didn't decide nothing." He stopped in front of me, leaning against the stove, arms loosely folded. "Look, brother.

I don't want to stay in Harlem no more, I really don't." He was very earnest. He looked at me, then over toward the kitchen window. There was something in his eyes I'd never seen before, some thoughtfulness, some worry all his own. He rubbed the muscle of one arm. "It's time I was getting out of here."

"Where do you want to go, Sonny?"

"I want to join the army. Or the navy, I don't care. If I say I'm old enough, they'll believe me."

Then I got mad. It was because I was so scared. "You must be crazy. You god-damn fool, what the hell do you want to go and join the *army* for?"

"I just told you. To get out of Harlem."   155

"Sonny, you haven't even finished *school*. And if you really want to be a musician, how do you expect to study if you're in the *army?*"

He looked at me, trapped, and in anguish. "There's ways. I might be able to work out some kind of deal. Anyway, I'll have the G.I. Bill when I come out."

"*If* you come out." We stared at each other. "Sonny, please. Be reasonable. I know the setup is far from perfect. But we got to do the best we can."

"I ain't learning nothing in school," he said. "Even when I go." He turned away from me and opened the window and threw his cigarette out into the narrow alley. I watched his back. "At least, I ain't learning nothing you'd want me to learn." He slammed the window so hard I thought the glass would fly out, and turned back to me. "And I'm sick of the stink of these garbage cans!"

"Sonny," I said, "I know how you feel. But if you don't finish school   160 now, you're going to be sorry later that you didn't." I grabbed him by the shoulders. "And you only got another year. It ain't so bad. And I'll come back and I swear I'll help you do *whatever* you want to do. Just try to put up with it till I come back. Will you please do that? For me?"

He didn't answer and he wouldn't look at me.

"Sonny. You hear me?"

He pulled away. "I hear you. But you never hear anything I say."

I didn't know what to say to that. He looked out of the window and then back at me. "OK," he said, and sighed. "I'll try."

Then I said, trying to cheer him up a little, "They got a piano at   165 Isabel's. You can practice on it."

And as a matter of fact, it did cheer him up for a minute. "That's right," he said to himself. "I forgot that." His face relaxed a little. But the worry, the thoughtfulness, played on it still, the way shadows play on a face which is staring into the fire.

But I thought I'd never hear the end of that piano. At first, Isabel would write me, saying how nice it was that Sonny was so serious about his music and how, as soon as he came in from school, or wherever he had been when he was supposed to be at school, he went straight to that piano and stayed there until suppertime. And, after supper, he went back to that piano and stayed there until everybody went to bed. He was at the piano all day Saturday and all day Sunday. Then he bought a record player and started playing records. He'd play one record over and over again, all day long sometimes, and he'd improvise along with it on the piano. Or he'd play one section of the record, one chord, one change, one progression, then he'd do it on the piano. Then back to the record. Then back to the piano.

Well, I really don't know how they stood it. Isabel finally confessed that it wasn't like living with a person at all, it was like living with sound. And the sound didn't make any sense to her, didn't make any sense to any of them—naturally. They began, in a way, to be afflicted by this presence that was living in their home. It was as though Sonny were some sort of god, or monster. He moved in an atmosphere which wasn't like theirs at all. They fed him and he ate, he washed himself, he walked in and out of their door; he certainly wasn't nasty or unpleasant or rude, Sonny isn't any of those things; but it was as though he were all wrapped up in some cloud, some fire, some vision all his own; and there wasn't any way to reach him.

At the same time, he wasn't really a man yet, he was still a child, and they had to watch out for him in all kinds of ways. They certainly couldn't throw him out. Neither did they dare to make a great scene about that piano because even they dimly sensed, as I sensed, from so many thousands of miles away, that Sonny was at that piano playing for his life.

But he hadn't been going to school. One day a letter came from the school board and Isabel's mother got it—there had, apparently, been other letters but Sonny had torn them up. This day, when Sonny came in, Isabel's mother showed him the letter and asked where he'd been spending his time. And she finally got it out of him that he'd been down in Greenwich Village, with musicians and other characters, in a white girl's apartment. And this scared her and she started to scream at him and what came up, once she began—though she denies it to this day—was what sacrifices they were making to give Sonny a decent home and how little he appreciated it.

Sonny didn't play the piano that day. By evening, Isabel's mother had calmed down but then there was the old man to deal with, and Isabel herself. Isabel says she did her best to be calm but she broke down and started crying. She says she just watched Sonny's face. She could tell, by watching him, what was happening with him. And what was happening was that they penetrated his cloud, they had reached him. Even if their fingers had been a thousand times more gentle than human fingers ever are, he could hardly help feeling that they had stripped him naked and were spitting on that nakedness. For he also had to see that his presence, that music, which was life or death to him, had been torture for them and that they had endured it, not at all for his sake, but only for mine. And Sonny couldn't take that. He can take it a little better today than he could then but he's still not very good at it and, frankly, I don't know anybody who is.

The silence of the next few days must have been louder than the sound of all the music ever played since time began. One morning, before she went to work, Isabel was in his room for something and she suddenly realized that all of his records were gone. And she knew for certain that he was gone. And

170

he was. He went as far as the navy would carry him. He finally sent me a postcard from some place in Greece and that was the first I knew that Sonny was still alive. I didn't see him any more until we were both back in New York and the war had long been over.

He was a man by then, of course, but I wasn't willing to see it. He came by the house from time to time, but we fought almost every time we met. I didn't like the way he carried himself, loose and dreamlike all the time, and I didn't like his friends, and his music seemed to be merely an excuse for the life he led. It sounded just that weird and disordered.

Then we had a fight, a pretty awful fight, and I didn't see him for months. By and by I looked him up, where he was living, in a furnished room in the Village, and I tried to make it up. But there were lots of other people in the room and Sonny just lay on his bed, and he wouldn't come downstairs with me, and he treated these other people as though they were his family and I weren't. So I got mad and then he got mad, and then I told him that he might just as well be dead as live the way he was living. Then he stood up and he told me not to worry about him any more in life, that he *was* dead as far as I was concerned. Then he pushed me to the door and the other people looked on as though nothing were happening, and he slammed the door behind me. I stood in the hallway, staring at the door. I heard somebody laugh in the room and then the tears came to my eyes. I started down the steps, whistling to keep from crying, I kept whistling to myself, *You going to need me, baby, one of these cold, rainy days.*

I read about Sonny's trouble in the spring. Little Grace died in the fall. She was a beautiful little girl. But she only lived a little over two years. She died of polio and she suffered. She had a slight fever for a couple of days, but it didn't seem like anything and we just kept her in bed. And we would certainly have called the doctor, but the fever dropped, she seemed to be all right. So we thought it had just been a cold. Then, one day, she was up, playing, Isabel was in the kitchen fixing lunch for the two boys when they'd come in from school, and she heard Grace fall down in the living room. When you have a lot of children you don't always start running when one of them falls, unless they start screaming or something. And, this time, Grace was quiet. Yet, Isabel says that when she heard that *thump* and then that silence, something happened in her to make her afraid. And she ran to the living room and there was little Grace on the floor, all twisted up, and the reason she hadn't screamed was that she couldn't get her breath. And when she did scream, it was the worst sound, Isabel says, that she'd ever heard in all her life, and she still hears it sometimes in her dreams. Isabel will sometimes wake me up with a low, moaning, strangled sound and I have to be quick to awaken her and hold her to me and where Isabel is weeping against me seems a mortal wound.

I think I may have written Sonny the very day that little Grace was buried. I was sitting in the living room in the dark, by myself, and I suddenly thought of Sonny. My trouble made his real.

One Saturday afternoon, when Sonny had been living with us, or, anyway, been in our house, for nearly two weeks, I found myself wandering aimlessly about the living room, drinking from a can of beer, and trying to work up the courage to search Sonny's room. He was out, he was usually out whenever I was home, and Isabel had taken the children to see their grandparents. Suddenly I was standing still in front of the living room window, watching Seventh Avenue. The idea of searching Sonny's room made me still. I scarcely dared to admit to myself what I'd be searching for. I didn't know what I'd do if I found it. Or if I didn't.

On the sidewalk across from me, near the entrance to a barbecue joint, some people were holding an old-fashioned revival meeting. The barbecue cook, wearing a dirty white apron, his conked hair reddish and metallic in the pale sun, and a cigarette between his lips, stood in the doorway, watching them. Kids and older people paused in their errands and stood there, along with some older men and a couple of very tough-looking women who watched everything that happened on the avenue, as though they owned it, or were maybe owned by it. Well, they were watching this, too. The revival was being carried on by three sisters in black, and a brother. All they had were their voices and their Bibles and a tambourine. The brother was testifying and while he testified two of the sisters stood together, seeming to say, amen, and the third sister walked around with the tambourine outstretched and a couple of people dropped coins into it. Then the brother's testimony ended and the sister who had been taking up the collection dumped the coins into her palm and transferred them to the pocket of her long black robe. Then she raised both hands, striking the tambourine against the air, and then against one hand, and she started to sing. And the two other sisters and the brother joined in.

It was strange, suddenly, to watch, though I had been seeing these street meetings all my life. So, of course, had everybody else down there. Yet, they paused and watched and listened and I stood still at the window. *"Tis the old ship of Zion,"* they sang, and the sister with the tambourine kept a steady, jangling beat, *"it has rescued many a thousand!"* Not a soul under the sound of their voices was hearing this song for the first time, not one of them had been rescued. Nor had they seen much in the way of rescue work being done around them. Neither did they especially believe in the holiness of the three sisters and the brother, they knew too much about them, knew where they lived, and how. The woman with the tambourine, whose voice dominated the air, whose face was bright with joy, was divided by very little from the woman who stood watching her, a cigarette between her heavy, chapped lips, her hair a cuckoo's nest, her face scarred and swollen from many beatings, and her black eyes glittering like coal. Perhaps they both knew this, which was why, when, as rarely, they addressed each other, they addressed each other as Sister. As the singing filled the air the watching, listening faces underwent a change, the eyes focusing on something within; the music seemed to soothe a poison out of them; and time seemed, nearly, to fall away from the sullen, belligerent, battered faces, as though they were fleeing back to their first condition, while dreaming of their last. The barbecue cook half shook his head and smiled, and dropped his cigarette and disappeared into his joint. A man fumbled in his pockets for change and stood holding it in his hand impatiently, as though he had just remembered a pressing appointment further up the avenue. He looked furious. Then I saw Sonny, standing on the edge of the crowd. He was carrying a wide, flat notebook with a green cover, and it made him look, from where I was standing, almost like a schoolboy. The coppery sun brought out the copper in his skin, he was very faintly smiling, standing very still. Then the singing stopped, the tambourine turned into a collection plate again. The furious man dropped in his coins and vanished, so did a couple of the women, and Sonny dropped some change in the plate, looking directly at the woman with a little smile. He started across the avenue, toward the house. He has a slow, loping walk, something like the way Harlem hipsters walk, only he's imposed on this his own half-beat. I had never really noticed it before.

Sonny's walk

    I stayed at the window, both relieved and apprehensive. As Sonny dis-   180
appeared from my sight, they began singing again. And they were still singing when his key turned in the lock.
    "Hey," he said.
    "Hey, yourself. You want some beer?"
    "No. Well, maybe." But he came up to the window and stood beside me, looking out. "What a warm voice," he said.
    They were singing *If I could only hear my mother pray again!*
    "Yes," I said, "and she can sure beat that tambourine."   185
    "But what a terrible song," he said, and laughed. He dropped his notebook on the sofa and disappeared into the kitchen. "Where's Isabel and the kids?"
    "I think they went to see their grandparents. You hungry?"
    "No." He came back into the living room with his can of beer. "You want to come some place with me tonight?"
    I sensed, I don't know how, that I couldn't possibly say no. "Sure. Where?"
    He sat down on the sofa and picked up his notebook and started leafing   190
through it. "I'm going to sit in with some fellows in a joint in the Village."
    "You mean, you're going to play, tonight?"
    "That's right." He took a swallow of his beer and moved back to the window. He gave me a sidelong look. "If you can stand it."
    "I'll try," I said.
    He smiled to himself and we both watched as the meeting across the way broke up. The three sisters and the brother, heads bowed, were singing *God be with you till we meet again.* The faces around them were very quiet. Then the song ended. The small crowd dispersed. We watched the three women and the lone man walk slowly up the avenue.

Heroin

    "When she was singing before," said Sonny, abruptly, "her voice re-   195
minded me for a minute of what heroin feels like sometimes—when it's in

your veins. It makes you feel sort of warm and cool at the same time. And distant. And—and sure." He sipped his beer, very deliberately not looking at me. I watched his face. "It makes you feel—in control. Sometimes you've got to have that feeling."

"Do you?" I sat down slowly in the easy chair.

"Sometimes." He went to the sofa and picked up his notebook again. "Some people do."

"In order," I asked, "to play?" And my voice was very ugly, full of contempt and anger.

"Well"—he looked at me with great, troubled eyes, as though, in fact, he hoped his eyes would tell me things he could never otherwise say—"they *think* so. And *if* they think so—!"

"And what do *you* think?" I asked.   200

He sat on the sofa and put his can of beer on the floor. "I don't know," he said, and I couldn't be sure if he were answering my question or pursuing his thoughts. His face didn't tell me. "It's not so much to *play*. It's to *stand* it, to be able to make it at all. On any level." He frowned and smiled: "In order to keep from shaking to pieces."

"But these friends of yours," I said, "they seem to shake themselves to pieces pretty goddamn fast."

"Maybe." He played with his notebook. And something told me that I should curb my tongue, that Sonny was doing his best to talk, that I should listen. "But of course you only know the ones that've gone to pieces. Some don't—or at least they haven't *yet* and that's just about all *any* of us can say." He paused. "And then there are some who just live, really, in hell, and they know it and they see what's happening and they go right on. I don't know." He sighed, dropped the notebook, folded his arms. "Some guys, you can tell from the way they play, they on something *all* the time. And you can see that, well, it makes something real for them. But of course," he picked up his beer from the floor and sipped it and put the can down again, "they *want* to, too, you've got to see that. Even some of them that say they don't—*some, not all.*"

"And what about you?" I asked—I couldn't help it. "What about you? Do *you* want to?"

He stood up and walked to the window and remained silent for a long   205 time. Then he sighed. "Me," he said. Then: "While I was downstairs before, on my way here, listening to that woman sing, it struck me all of a sudden how much suffering she must have had to go through—to sing like that. It's *repulsive* to think that you have to suffer that much."

I said: "But there's no way not to suffer—is there, Sonny?"

"I believe not," he said and smiled, "but that's never stopped anyone from trying." He looked at me. "Has it?" I realized, with this mocking look, that there stood between us, forever, beyond the power of time or forgiveness, the fact that I had held silence—so long!—when he had needed human speech to help him. He turned back to the window. "No, there's no way not to suffer. But you try all kinds of ways to keep from drowning in it, to keep on top of it, and to make it seem—well, like *you*. Like you did something, all right, and now you're suffering for it. You know?" I said nothing. "Well you know," he said, impatiently, "why *do* people suffer? Maybe it's better to do something to give it a reason, *any* reason."

"But we just agreed," I said, "that there's no way not to suffer. Isn't it better, then, just to—take it?"

"But nobody just takes it," Sonny cried, "that's what I'm telling you! *Everybody* tries not to. You're just hung up on the *way* some people try—it's not *your* way!"

The hair on my face began to itch, my face felt wet. "That's not true," I said, "that's not true. I don't give a damn what other people do, I don't even care how they suffer. I just care how *you* suffer." And he looked at me. "Please believe me," I said, "I don't want to see you—die—trying not to suffer."

"I won't," he said, flatly, "die trying not to suffer. At least, not any faster than anybody else."

"But there's no need," I said, trying to laugh, "is there? in killing yourself."

I wanted to say more, but I couldn't. I wanted to talk about will power and how life could be—well, beautiful. I wanted to say that it was all within; but was it? or, rather, wasn't that exactly the trouble? And I wanted to promise that I would never fail him again. But it would all have sounded—empty words and lies.

So I made the promise to myself and prayed that I would keep it.

"It's terrible sometimes, inside," he said, "that's what's the trouble. You walk these streets, black and funky and cold, and there's not really a living ass to talk to, and there's nothing shaking, and there's no way of getting it out—that storm inside. You can't talk it and you can't make love with it, and when you finally try to get with it and play it, you realize *nobody's* listening. So *you've* got to listen. You got to find a way to listen."

And then he walked away from the window and sat on the sofa again, as though all the wind had suddenly been knocked out of him. "Sometimes you'll do *anything* to play, even cut your mother's throat." He laughed and looked at me. "Or your brother's." Then he sobered. "Or your own." Then: "Don't worry. I'm all right now and I think I'll *be* all right. But I can't forget—where I've been. I don't mean just the physical place I've been, I mean where I've *been*. And *what* I've been."

"What have you been, Sonny?" I asked.

He smiled—but sat sideways on the sofa, his elbow resting on the back, his fingers playing with his mouth and chin, not looking at me. "I've been something I didn't recognize, didn't know I could be. Didn't know anybody could be." He stopped, looking inward, looking helplessly young, looking old. "I'm not talking about it now because I feel *guilty* or anything like that—maybe it would be better if I did, I don't know. Anyway, I can't really talk

210

215

about it. Not to you, not to anybody," and now he turned and faced me. "Sometimes, you know, and it was actually when I was most *out* of the world, I felt that I was in it, that I was *with* it, really, and I could play or I didn't really have to *play*, it just came out of me, it was there. And I don't know how I played, thinking about it now, but I know I did awful things, those times, sometimes, to people. Or it wasn't that I *did* anything to them—it was that they weren't real." He picked up the beer can; it was empty; he rolled it between his palms: "And other times—well, I needed a fix, I needed to find a place to lean, I needed to clear a space to *listen*—and I couldn't find it, and I—went crazy, I did terrible things to *me*, I was terrible *for* me." He began pressing the beer can between his hands, I watched the metal begin to give. It glittered, as he played with it, like a knife, and I was afraid he would cut himself, but I said nothing. "Oh well. I can never tell you. I was all by myself at the bottom of something, stinking and sweating and crying and shaking, and I smelled it, you know? *my* stink, and I thought I'd die if I couldn't get away from it and yet, all the same, I knew that everything I was doing was just locking me in with it. And I didn't know," he paused, still flattening the beer can, "I didn't know, I still *don't* know, something kept telling me that maybe it was good to smell your own stink, but I didn't think that *that* was what I'd been trying to do—and—who can stand it?" and he abruptly dropped the ruined beer can, looking at me with a small, still smile, and then rose, walking to the window as though it were the lodestone rock. I watched his face, he watched the avenue. "I couldn't tell you when Mama died—but the reason I wanted to leave Harlem so bad was to get away from drugs. And then, when I ran away, that's what I was running from—really. When I came back, nothing had changed, I hadn't changed, I was just—older." And he stopped, drumming with his fingers on the windowpane. The sun had vanished, soon darkness would fall. I watched his face. "It can come again," he said, almost as though speaking to himself. Then he turned to me. "It can come again," he repeated. "I just want you to know that."

"All right," I said, at last. "So it can come again. All right."

He smiled, but the smile was sorrowful. "I had to try to tell you," 220 he said.

"Yes," I said. "I understand that."

"You're my brother," he said, looking straight at me, and not smiling at all.

"Yes," I repeated, "yes. I understand that."

He turned back to the window, looking out. "All that hatred down there," he said, "all that hatred and misery and love. It's a wonder it doesn't blow the avenue apart."

We went to the only nightclub on a short, dark street, downtown. 225 We squeezed through the narrow, chattering, jam-packed bar to the entrance of the big room, where the bandstand was. And we stood there for a moment, for the lights were very dim in this room and we couldn't see. Then, "Hello, boy," said a voice and an enormous black man, much older than Sonny or myself, erupted out of all that atmospheric lighting and put an arm around Sonny's shoulder. "I been sitting right here," he said, "waiting for you."

He had a big voice, too, and heads in the darkness turned toward us.

Sonny grinned and pulled a little away, and said, "Creole, this is my brother. I told you about him."

Creole shook my hand. "I'm glad to meet you, son," he said, and it was clear that he was glad to meet me *there* for Sonny's sake. And he smiled, "You got a real musician in *your* family," and he took his arm from Sonny's shoulder and slapped him, lightly, affectionately, with the back of his hand.

"Well. Now I've heard it all," said a voice behind us. This was another musician, and a friend of Sonny's, a coal-black, cheerful-looking man, built close to the ground. He immediately began confiding to me, at the top of his lungs, the most terrible things about Sonny, his teeth gleaming like a lighthouse and his laugh coming up out of him like the beginning of an earthquake. And it turned out that everyone at the bar knew Sonny, or almost everyone; some were musicians, working there, or nearby, or not working, some were simply hangers-on, and some were there to hear Sonny play. I was introduced to all of them and they were all very polite to me. Yet, it was clear that, for them, I was only Sonny's brother. Here, I was in Sonny's world. Or, rather: his kingdom. Here, it was not even a question that his veins bore royal blood.

They were going to play soon and Creole installed me, by myself, at a 230 table in a dark corner. Then I watched them, Creole, and the little black man, and Sonny, and the others, while they horsed around, standing just below the bandstand. The light from the bandstand spilled just a little short of them and, watching them laughing and gesturing and moving about, I had the feeling that they, nevertheless, were being most careful not to step into that circle of light too suddenly: that if they moved into the light too suddenly, without thinking, they would perish in flame. Then, while I watched, one of them, the small, black man, moved into the light and crossed the bandstand and started fooling around with his drums. Then—being funny and being, also, extremely ceremonious—Creole took Sonny by the arm and led him to the piano. A woman's voice called Sonny's name and a few hands started clapping. And Sonny, also being funny and being ceremonious, and so touched, I think, that he could have cried, but neither hiding it nor showing it, riding it like a man, grinned, and put both hands to his heart and bowed from the waist.

Creole then went to the bass fiddle and a lean, very bright-skinned brown man jumped up on the bandstand and picked up his horn. So there they were, and the atmosphere on the bandstand and in the room began to change and tighten. Someone stepped up to the microphone and announced them. Then there were all kinds of murmurs. Some people at the bar shushed others. The waitress ran around, frantically getting in the last orders, guys and chicks got closer to each other, and the lights on the bandstand, on the quartet, turned to a kind of indigo. Then they all looked different there. Creole looked about him for the last time, as though he were making certain that all his chickens were in the coop, and then he—jumped and struck the fiddle. And there they were.

All I know about music is that not many people ever really hear it. And even then, on the rare occasions when something opens within, and the music enters, what we mainly hear, or hear corroborated, are personal, private, vanishing evocations. But the man who creates the music is hearing something else, is dealing with the roar rising from the void and imposing order on it as it hits the air. What is evoked in him, then, is of another order, more terrible because it has no words, and triumphant, too, for that same reason. And his triumph, when he triumphs, is ours. I just watched Sonny's face. His face was troubled, he was working hard, but he wasn't with it. And I had the feeling that, in a way, everyone on the bandstand was waiting for him, both waiting for him and pushing him along. But as I began to watch Creole, I realized that it was Creole who held them all back. He had them on a short rein. Up there, keeping the beat with his whole body, wailing on the fiddle, with his eyes half closed, he was listening to everything, but he was listening to Sonny. He was having a dialogue with Sonny. He wanted Sonny to leave the shoreline and strike out for the deep water. He was Sonny's witness that deep water and drowning were not the same thing—he had been there, and he knew. And he wanted Sonny to know. He was waiting for Sonny to do the things on the keys which would let Creole know that Sonny was in the water.

And, while Creole listened, Sonny moved, deep within, exactly like someone in torment. I had never before thought of how awful the relationship must be between the musician and his instrument. He has to fill it, this instrument, with the breath of life, his own. He has to make it do what he wants it to do. And a piano is just a piano. It's made out of so much wood and wires and little hammers and big ones, and ivory. While there's only so much you can do with it, the only way to find this out is to try; to try and make it do everything.

And Sonny hadn't been near a piano for over a year. And he wasn't on much better terms with his life, not the life that stretched before him now. He and the piano stammered, started one way, got scared, stopped; started another way, panicked, marked time, started again; then seemed to have found a direction, panicked again, got stuck. And the face I saw on Sonny I'd never seen before. Everything had been burned out of it, and, at the same time, things usually hidden were being burned in, by the fire and fury of the battle which was occurring in him up there.

Yet, watching Creole's face as they neared the end of the first set, I had the feeling that something had happened, something I hadn't heard. Then they finished, there was scattered applause, and then, without an instant's warning, Creole started into something else, it was almost sardonic, it was *Am I Blue*. And, as though he commanded, Sonny began to play. Something

235

began to happen. And Creole let out the reins. The dry, low, black man said something awful on the drums, Creole answered, and the drums talked back. Then the horn insisted, sweet and high, slightly detached perhaps, and Creole listened, commenting now and then, dry, and driving, beautiful and calm and old. Then they all came together again, and Sonny was part of the family again. I could tell this from his face. He seemed to have found, right there beneath his fingers, a damn brand-new piano. It seemed that he couldn't get over it. Then, for awhile, just being happy with Sonny, they seemed to be agreeing with him that brand-new pianos certainly were a gas.

Then Creole stepped forward to remind them that what they were playing was the blues. He hit something in all of them, he hit something in me, myself, and the music tightened and deepened, apprehension began to beat the air. Creole began to tell us what the blues were all about. They were not about anything very new. He and his boys up there were keeping it new, at the risk of ruin, destruction, madness, and death, in order to find new ways to make us listen. For, while the tale of how we suffer, and how we are delighted, and how we may triumph is never new, it always must be heard. There isn't any other tale to tell, it's the only light we've got in all this darkness.

And this tale, according to that face, that body, those strong hands on those strings, has another aspect in every country, and a new depth in every generation. Listen, Creole seemed to be saying, listen. Now these are Sonny's blues. He made the little black man on the drums know it, and the bright, brown man on the horn. Creole wasn't trying any longer to get Sonny in the water. He was wishing him Godspeed. Then he stepped back, very slowly, filling the air with the immense suggestion that Sonny speak for himself.

Then they all gathered around Sonny and Sonny played. Every now and again one of them seemed to say, amen. Sonny's fingers filled the air with life, his life. But that life contained so many others. And Sonny went all the way back, he really began with the spare, flat statement of the opening phrase of the song. Then he began to make it his. It was very beautiful because it wasn't hurried and it was no longer a lament. I seemed to hear with what burning he had made it his, with what burning we had yet to make it ours, how we could cease lamenting. Freedom lurked around us and I understood, at last, that he could help us to be free if we would listen, that he would never be free until we did. Yet, there was no battle in his face now. I heard what he had gone through, and would continue to go through until he came to rest in earth. He had made it his: that long line, of which we knew only Mama and Daddy. And he was giving it back, as everything must be given back, so that, passing through death, it can live forever. I saw my mother's face again, and felt, for the first time, how the stones of the road she had walked on must have bruised her feet. I saw the moonlit road where my father's brother died. And it brought something else back to me, and carried me past it, I saw my little girl again and felt Isabel's tears again, and I felt my own tears begin to rise. And I was yet aware that this was only a moment, that the world waited outside, as hungry as a tiger, and that trouble stretched above us, longer than the sky.

Then it was over. Creole and Sonny let out their breath, both soaking wet, and grinning. There was a lot of applause and some of it was real. In the dark, the girl came by and I asked her to take drinks to the bandstand. There was a long pause, while they talked up there in the indigo light and after awhile I saw the girl put a Scotch and milk on top of the piano for Sonny. He didn't seem to notice it, but just before they started playing again, he sipped from it and looked toward me, and nodded. Then he put it back on top of the piano. For me, then, as they began to play again, it glowed and shook above my brother's head like the very cup of trembling.

Considerations

1. How does the story's chronology affect your response? Consider, for example, how the story would change for you if the events were recounted as they occurred rather than retrospectively.
2. Describe the relationship between Sonny and his brother. Explain the changes they go through in the course of the story, and speculate on the reason for those changes.
3. How do the song lyrics that appear throughout the story relate to the conflict, action, and character?
4. How do the following forces relate to Sonny's search for identity: his parents, his neighborhood, his brother, and his music?
5. Compare and contrast Sonny's struggle with the struggles of the narrator in "Battle Royal" (page 169).

ALICE WALKER (1944–   )

Everyday Use
For Your Grandmama

As the youngest of eight children born in Eatonton, Georgia, to sharecroppers Minnie and Willie Lee Walker, Alice Walker was exposed to a number of contradictory forces that shaped her early life. On the one hand, she suffered from economic deprivation and the hardships imposed by segregation. On the other hand, she derived strength from her closely knit family and the extended black church congregation and community. She credits her mother with passing on the creativity she expressed through the flower gardens she nurtured and the stories she told. Walker describes the pivotal role her mother played in her life in the moving essay "In Search of Our Mothers' Gardens" (page 992), which traces the roots of current black women writers to the artistry of their mothers and grandmothers. This artistry often came to light through handwork such as quilting (as reflected in "Everyday Use") or, as in her own mother's case, through growing flowers to provide beauty and sustenance for the spirits of their families.

Walker has been widely acclaimed for her novel The Color Purple, *which was awarded both the Pulitzer Prize and the American Book Award in 1983 and was later made into a highly acclaimed film. Since then, she has published two more novels,* The Temple of My Familiar *(1989) and* Possessing the Secret of Joy *(1992). "Everyday Use" comes from the collection* In Love and In Trouble *(1967).*

I will wait for her in the yard that Maggie and I made so clean and wavy yesterday afternoon. A yard like this is more comfortable than most people know. It is not just a yard. It is like an extended living room. When the hard clay is swept clean as a floor and the fine sand around the edges lined with tiny, irregular grooves anyone can come and sit and look up into the elm tree and wait for the breezes that never come inside the house.

Maggie will be nervous until after her sister goes: she will stand hopelessly in corners homely and ashamed of the burn scars down her arms and legs, eyeing her sister with a mixture of envy and awe. She thinks her sister has held life always in the palm of one hand, that "no" is a word the world never learned to say to her.

You've no doubt seen those TV shows where the child who has "made it" is confronted, as a surprise, by her own mother and father, tottering in weakly from backstage. (A pleasant surprise, of course: What would they do if parent and child came on the show only to curse out and insult each other?) On TV mother and child embrace and smile into each other's faces. Sometimes the mother and father weep, the child wraps them in her arms and leans across the table to tell how she would not have made it without their help. I have seen these programs.

Sometimes I dream a dream in which Dee and I are suddenly brought together on a TV program of this sort. Out of a dark and soft-seated limousine I am ushered into a bright room filled with many people. There I meet a smiling, gray, sporty man like Johnny Carson who shakes my hand and tells me what a fine girl I have. Then we are on the stage and Dee is embracing me with tears in her eyes. She pins on my dress a large orchid, even though she has told me once that she thinks orchids are tacky flowers.

In real life I am a large, big-boned woman with rough, man-working 5 hands. In the winter I wear flannel nightgowns to bed and overalls during the day. I can kill and clean a hog as mercilessly as a man. My fat keeps me hot in zero weather. I can work outside all day, breaking ice to get water for washing; I can eat pork liver cooked over the open fire minutes after it comes steaming from the hog. One winter I knocked a bull calf straight in the brain between the eyes with a sledge hammer and had the meat hung up to chill before nightfall. But of course all this does not show on television. I am the way my daughter would want me to be: a hundred pounds lighter, my skin like an uncooked barley pancake. My hair glistens in the hot bright lights. Johnny Carson has much to do to keep up with my quick and witty tongue.

But that is a mistake. I know even before I wake up. Who ever knew a Johnson with a quick tongue? Who can even imagine me looking a strange white man in the eye? It seems to me I have talked to them always with one foot raised in flight, with my head turned in whichever way is farthest from them. Dee, though. She would always look anyone in the eye. Hesitation was no part of her nature.

"How do I look, Mama?" Maggie says, showing just enough of her thin body enveloped in pink skirt and red blouse for me to know she's there, almost hidden by the door.

"Come out into the yard," I say.

Have you ever seen a lame animal, perhaps a dog run over by some careless person rich enough to own a car, sidle up to someone who is ignorant enough to be kind to him? That is the way my Maggie walks. She has been like this, chin on chest, eyes on ground, feet in shuffle, ever since the fire that burned the other house to the ground.

Dee is lighter than Maggie, with nicer hair and a fuller figure. She's a 10 woman now, though sometimes I forget. How long ago was it that the other house burned? Ten, twelve years? Sometimes I can still hear the flames and feel Maggie's arms sticking to me, her hair smoking and her dress falling off her in little black papery flakes. Her eyes seemed stretched open, blazed open by the flames reflected in them. And Dee. I see her standing off under the sweet gum tree she used to dig gum out of; a look of concentration on her face as she watched the last dingy gray board of the house fall in toward the red-hot brick chimney. Why don't you do a dance around the ashes? I'd wanted to ask her. She had hated the house that much.

I used to think she hated Maggie, too. But that was before we raised the money, the church and me, to send her to Augusta to school. She used to read to us without pity; forcing words, lies, other folks' habits, whole lives upon us two, sitting trapped and ignorant underneath her voice. She washed us in a river of make-believe, burned us with a lot of knowledge we didn't necessarily need to know. Pressed us to her with the serious way she read, to shove us away at just the moment, like dimwits, we seemed about to understand.

Dee wanted nice things. A yellow organdy dress to wear to her graduation from high school; black pumps to match a green suit she'd made from an old suit somebody gave me. She was determined to stare down any disaster in her efforts. Her eyelids would not flicker for minutes at a time. Often I fought off the temptation to shake her. At sixteen she had a style of her own: and knew what style was.

I never had an education myself. After second grade the school was closed down. Don't ask me why: in 1927 colored asked fewer questions than they do now. Sometimes Maggie reads to me. She stumbles along good-naturedly but can't see well. She knows she is not bright. Like good looks and money, quickness passed her by. She will marry John Thomas (who has mossy teeth in an earnest face) and then I'll be free to sit here and I guess just sing church songs to myself. Although I never was a good singer. Never could carry a tune. I was always better at a man's job. I used to love to milk till I was hooked in the side in '49. Cows are soothing and slow and don't bother you, unless you try to milk them the wrong way.

I have deliberately turned my back on the house. It is three rooms, just like the one that burned, except the roof is tin; they don't make shingle roofs any more. There are no real windows, just some holes cut in the sides, like the portholes in a ship, but not round and not square, with rawhide holding the shutters up on the outside. This house is in a pasture, too, like the other one. No doubt when Dee sees it she will want to tear it down. She wrote me once that no matter where we "choose" to live, she will manage to come see us. But she will never bring her friends. Maggie and I thought about this and Maggie asked me, "Mama, when did Dee ever *have* any friends?"

She had a few. Furtive boys in pink shirts hanging about on washday   15 after school. Nervous girls who never laughed. Impressed with her they worshiped the well-turned phrase, the cute shape, the scalding humor that erupted like bubbles in lye. She read to them.

When she was courting Jimmy T she didn't have much time to pay to us, but turned all her faultfinding power on him. He *flew* to marry a cheap gal from a family of ignorant flashy people. She hardly had time to recompose herself.

When she comes I will meet—but there they are!

Maggie attempts to make a dash for the house, in her shuffling way, but I stay her with my hand. "Come back here," I say. And she stops and tries to dig a well in the sand with her toe.

It is hard to see them clearly through the strong sun. But even the first glimpse of leg out of the car tells me it is Dee. Her feet were always neat-looking, as if God himself had shaped them with a certain style. From the other side of the car comes a short, stocky man. Hair is all over his head a foot long and hanging from his chin like a kinky mule tail. I hear Maggie suck in her breath. "Uhnnnh," is what it sounds like. Like when you see the wriggling end of a snake just in front of your foot on the road. "Uhnnnh."

Dee next. A dress down to the ground, in this hot weather. A dress so 20 loud it hurts my eyes. There are yellows and oranges enough to throw back the light of the sun. I feel my whole face warming from the heat waves it throws out. Earrings gold, too, and hanging down to her shoulders. Bracelets dangling and making noises when she moves her arm up to shake the folds of the dress out of her armpits. The dress is loose and flows, and as she walks closer, I like it. I hear Maggie go "Uhnnnh" again. It is her sister's hair. It stands straight up like the wool on a sheep. It is black as night and around the edges are two long pigtails that rope about like small lizards disappearing behind her ears.

"Wa-su-zo-Tean-o!" she says, coming on in that gliding way the dress makes her move. The short stocky fellow with the hair to his navel is all grinning and he follows up with "Asalamalakim, my mother and sister!" He moves to hug Maggie but she falls back, right up against the back of my chair. I feel her trembling there and when I look up I see the perspiration falling off her chin.

"Don't get up," says Dee. Since I am stout it takes something of a push. You can see me trying to move a second or two before I make it. She turns, showing white heels through her sandals, and goes back to the car. Out she peeks next with a Polaroid. She stoops down quickly and lines up picture after picture of me sitting there in front of the house with Maggie cowering behind me. She never takes a shot without making sure the house is included. When a cow comes nibbling around the edge of the yard she snaps it and me and Maggie *and* the house. Then she puts the Polaroid in the back seat of the car, and comes up and kisses me on the forehead.

Meanwhile Asalamalakim is going through the motions with Maggie's hand. Maggie's hand is as limp as a fish, and probably as cold, despite the sweat, and she keeps trying to pull it back. It looks like Asalamalakim wants to shake hands but wants to do it fancy. Or maybe he don't know how people shake hands. Anyhow, he soon gives up on Maggie.

"Well," I say. "Dee."

"No, Mama," she says. "Not 'Dee,' Wangero Leewanika Kemanjo!" 25

"What happened to 'Dee'?" I wanted to know.

"She's dead," Wangero said. "I couldn't bear it any longer being named after the people who oppress me."

"You know as well as me you was named after your aunt Dicie," I said. Dicie is my sister. She named Dee. We called her "Big Dee" after Dee was born.

"But who was *she* named after?" asked Wangero.

"I guess after Grandma Dee," I said.   30

"And who was she named after?" asked Wangero.

"Her mother," I said, and saw Wangero was getting tired. "That's about as far back as I can trace it," I said. Though, in fact, I probably could have carried it back beyond the Civil War through the branches.

"Well," said Asalamalakim, "there you are."

"Uhnnnh," I heard Maggie say.

"There I was not," I said, "before 'Dicie' cropped up in our family, so   35
why should I try to trace it that far back?"

He just stood there grinning, looking down on me like somebody inspecting a Model A car. Every once in a while he and Wangero sent eye signals over my head.

"How do you pronounce this name?" I asked.

"You don't have to call me by it if you don't want to," said Wangero.

"Why shouldn't I?" I asked. "If that's what you want us to call you, we'll call you."

"I know it might sound awkward at first," said Wangero.   40

"I'll get used to it," I said. "Ream it out again."

Well, soon we got the name out of the way. Asalamalakim had a name twice as long and three times as hard. After I tripped over it two or three times he told me to just call him Hakim-a-barber. I wanted to ask him was he a barber, but I didn't really think he was, so I didn't ask.

"You must belong to those beef-cattle peoples down the road," I said. They said "Asalamalakim" when they met you, too, but they didn't shake hands. Always too busy: feeding the cattle, fixing the fences, putting up salt-lick shelters, throwing down hay. When the white folks poisoned some of the herd the men stayed up all night with rifles in their hands. I walked a mile and a half just to see the sight.

Hakim-a-barber said, "I accept some of their doctrines, but farming and raising cattle is not my style." (They didn't tell me, and I didn't ask, whether Wangero [Dee] had really gone and married him.)

We sat down to eat and right away he said he didn't eat collards and   45
pork was unclean. Wangero, though, went on through the chitlins and corn bread, the greens and everything else. She talked a blue streak over the sweet potatoes. Everything delighted her. Even the fact that we still used the benches her daddy made for the table when we couldn't afford to buy chairs.

"Oh, Mama!" she cried. Then turned to Hakim-a-barber. "I never knew how lovely these benches are. You can feel the rump prints," she said, running her hands underneath her and along the bench. Then she gave a sigh and her hand closed over Grandma Dee's butter dish. "That's it!" she said. "I knew there was something I wanted to ask you if I could have." She jumped up from the table and went over in the corner where the churn stood, the milk in it clabber by now. She looked at the churn and looked at it.

"This churn top is what I need," she said. "Didn't Uncle Buddy whittle it out of a tree you all used to have?"

"Yes," I said.

"Uh huh," she said happily. "And I want the dasher, too."

"Uncle Buddy whittle that, too?" asked the barber. 50

Dee (Wangero) looked up at me.

"Aunt Dee's first husband whittled the dash," said Maggie so low you almost couldn't hear her. "His name was Henry, but they called him Stash."

"Maggie's brain is like an elephant's," Wangero said, laughing. "I can use the churn top as a centerpiece for the alcove table," she said, sliding a plate over the churn, "and I'll think of something artistic to do with the dasher."

When she finished wrapping the dasher the handle stuck out. I took it for a moment in my hands. You didn't even have to look close to see where hands pushing the dasher up and down to make butter had left a kind of sink in the wood. In fact, there were a lot of small sinks; you could see where thumbs and fingers had sunk into the wood. It was beautiful light yellow wood, from a tree that grew in the yard where Big Dee and Stash had lived.

After dinner Dee (Wangero) went to the trunk at the foot of my bed 55
and started rifling through it. Maggie hung back in the kitchen over the dishpan. Out came Wangero with two quilts. They had been pieced by Grandma Dee and then Big Dee and me had hung them on the quilt frames on the front porch and quilted them. One was in the Lone Star pattern. The other was Walk Around the Mountain. In both of them were scraps of dresses Grandma Dee had worn fifty and more years ago. Bits and pieces of Grandpa Jarrell's paisley shirts. And one teeny faded blue piece, about the size of a penny matchbox, that was from Great Grandpa Ezra's uniform that he wore in the Civil War.

"Mama," Wangero said sweet as a bird. "Can I have these old quilts?"

I heard something fall in the kitchen, and a minute later the kitchen door slammed.

"Why don't you take one or two of the others?" I asked. "These old things was just done by me and Big Dee from some tops your grandma pieced before she died."

"No," said Wangero. "I don't want those. They are stitched around the borders by machine."

"That'll make them last better," I said. 60

"That's not the point," said Wangero. "These are all pieces of dresses Grandma used to wear. She did all this stitching by hand. Imagine!" She held the quilts securely in her arms, stroking them.

"Some of the pieces, like those lavender ones, come from old clothes her mother handed down to her," I said, moving up to touch the quilts. Dee (Wangero) moved back just enough so that I couldn't reach the quilts. They already belonged to her.

"Imagine!" she breathed again, clutching them closely to her bosom.

"The truth is," I said, "I promised to give them quilts to Maggie, for when she marries John Thomas."

She gasped like a bee had stung her.   65

"Maggie can't appreciate these quilts!" she said. "She'd probably be backward enough to put them to everyday use."

"I reckon she would," I said. "God knows I been saving 'em for long enough with nobody using 'em. I hope she will!" I didn't want to bring up how I had offered Dee (Wangero) a quilt when she went away to college. Then she had told me they were old-fashioned, out of style.

"But they're *priceless!*" she was saying now, furiously; for she has a temper. "Maggie would put them on the bed and in five years they'd be in rags. Less than that!"

"She can always make some more," I said. "Maggie knows how to quilt."

Dee (Wangero) looked at me with hatred. "You just will not under- 70
stand. The point is these quilts, *these* quilts!"

"Well," I said, stumped. "What would *you* do with them?"

"Hang them," she said. As if that was the only thing you *could* do with quilts.

Maggie by now was standing in the door. I could almost hear the sound her feet made as they scraped over each other.

"She can have them, Mama," she said, like somebody used to never winning anything, or having anything reserved for her. "I can 'member Grandma Dee without the quilts."

I looked at her hard. She had filled her bottom lip with checkerberry 75
snuff and it gave her face a kind of dopey, hangdog look. It was Grandma Dee and Big Dee who taught her how to quilt herself. She stood there with her scarred hands hidden in the folds of her skirt. She looked at her sister with something like fear but she wasn't mad at her. This was Maggie's portion. This was the way she knew God to work.

When I looked at her like that something hit me in the top of my head and ran down to the soles of my feet. Just like when I'm in church and the spirit of God touches me and I get happy and shout. I did something I never had done before: hugged Maggie to me, then dragged her on into the room, snatched the quilts out of Miss Wangero's hands and dumped them into Maggie's lap. Maggie just sat there on my bed with her mouth open.

"Take one or two of the others," I said to Dee.

But she turned without a word and went out to Hakim-a-barber.

"You just don't understand," she said, as Maggie and I came out to the car.

"What don't I understand?" I wanted to know.   80

"Your heritage," she said. And then she turned to Maggie, kissed her, and said, "You ought to try to make something of yourself, too, Maggie. It's really a new day for us. But from the way you and Mama still live you'd never know it."

She put on some sunglasses that hid everything above the tip of her nose and her chin.

Maggie smiled; maybe at the sunglasses. But a real smile, not scared. After we watched the car dust settle I asked Maggie to bring me a dip of snuff. And then the two of us sat there just enjoying, until it was time to go in the house and go to bed.

Considerations

1. Give a brief summary of the first four sections of the story, and discuss how they relate to the longer final section.
2. Discuss the significance of Dee's name change. How does her adoption of a new name relate to her search for roots?
3. Why does Walker subtitle her story "For Your Grandmama"? Whose grandmama is she talking about?
4. Speculate on Dee's motives for coming home with her friend even though she had told her mother that she would never bring friends to the family's house. What is it that she now values about her past? Why, for example, does she want the churn top and the quilts? What is it that Maggie and her mother value about their past and the objects that reflect their past?
5. Analyze the implications of the story's title. For example, consider Dee's statement that if Maggie got the quilts, "she'd probably be backward enough to put them to everyday use." If you were to arbitrate this disagreement, whose side would you be on? Should the quilts be put to everyday use? Why or why not?

RAYMOND CARVER (1939–1988)

Cathedral

> *Born in Clatskanie, a logging town in Oregon, Raymond Carver graduated*
> *from California State University at Humboldt. After a year in the Writer's*
> *Workshop at the University of Iowa, he taught writing at the University of*
> *California, the University of Texas, and Syracuse University. When he was*
> *not teaching, he held various jobs, including truck driver, custodian, and deliv-*
> *eryman, to support himself while he wrote poetry and fiction. "Cathedral"*
> *appears in the collection* Cathedral *(1982).*

This blind man, an old friend of my wife's, he was on his way to spend the night. His wife had died. So he was visiting the dead wife's relatives in Connecticut. He called my wife from his in-laws'. Arrangements were made. He would come by train, a five-hour trip, and my wife would meet him at the station. She hadn't seen him since she worked for him one summer in Seattle ten years ago. But she and the blind man had kept in touch. They made tapes and mailed them back and forth. I wasn't enthusiastic about his visit. He was no one I knew. And his being blind bothered me. My idea of blindness came from the movies. In the movies, the blind moved slowly and never laughed. Sometimes they were led by seeing-eye dogs. A blind man in my house was not something I looked forward to.

That summer in Seattle she had needed a job. She didn't have any money. The man she was going to marry at the end of the summer was in officers' training school. He didn't have any money, either. But she was in love with the guy, and he was in love with her, etc. She'd seen something in the paper: HELP WANTED—*Reading to Blind Man*, and a telephone number. She phoned and went over, was hired on the spot. She'd worked with this blind man all summer. She read stuff to him, case studies, reports, that sort of thing. She helped him organize his little office in the county social-service department. They'd become good friends, my wife and the blind man. How do I know these things? She told me. And she told me something else. On her last day in the office, the blind man asked if he could touch her face. She agreed to this. She told me he touched his fingers to every part of her face, her nose—even her neck! She never forgot it. She even tried to write a poem about it. She was always trying to write a poem. She wrote a poem or two every year, usually after something really important had happened to her.

When we first started going out together, she showed me the poem. In the poem, she recalled his fingers and the way they had moved around over her face. In the poem, she talked about what she had felt at the time, about what went through her mind when the blind man touched her nose and lips. I can remember I didn't think much of the poem. Of course, I didn't tell her that. Maybe I just don't understand poetry. I admit it's not the first thing I reach for when I pick up something to read.

Anyway, this man who'd first enjoyed her favors, the officer-to-be, he'd been her childhood sweetheart. So okay. I'm saying that at the end of the summer she let the blind man run his hands over her face, said goodbye to him, married her childhood etc., who was now a commissioned officer, and she moved away from Seattle. But they'd kept in touch, she and the blind man. She made the first contact after a year or so. She called him up one night from an Air Force base in Alabama. She wanted to talk. They talked. He asked her to send him a tape and tell him about her life. She did this. She sent the tape. On the tape, she told the blind man about her husband and about their life together in the military. She told the blind man she loved her husband but she didn't like it where they lived and she didn't like it that he was part of the military-industrial thing. She told the blind man she'd written a poem and he was in it. She told him that she was writing a poem about what it was like to be an Air Force officer's wife. The poem wasn't finished yet. She was still writing it. The blind man made a tape. He sent her the tape. She made a tape. This went on for years. My wife's officer was posted to one base and then another. She sent tapes from Moody AFB, McGuire, McConnell, and finally Travis, near Sacramento, where one night she got to feeling lonely and cut off from people she kept losing in that moving-around life. She got to feeling she couldn't go it another step. She went in and swallowed all the pills and capsules in the medicine chest and washed them down with a bottle of gin. Then she got into a hot bath and passed out.

But instead of dying, she got sick. She threw up. Her officer—why   5
should he have a name? he was the childhood sweetheart, and what more does he want?—came home from somewhere, found her, and called the ambulance. In time, she put it all on a tape and sent the tape to the blind man. Over the years, she put all kinds of stuff on tapes and sent the tapes off lickety-split. Next to writing a poem every year, I think it was her chief means of recreation. On one tape, she told the blind man she'd decided to live away from her officer for a time. On another tape, she told him about her divorce. She and I began going out, and of course she told her blind man about it. She told him everything, or so it seemed to me. Once she asked me if I'd like to hear the latest tape from the blind man. This was a year ago. I was on the tape, she said. So I said okay, I'd listen to it. I got us drinks and we settled down in the living room. We made ready to listen. First she inserted the tape into the player and adjusted a couple of dials. Then she pushed a lever. The tape squeaked and someone began to talk in this loud voice. She lowered the volume. After a few minutes of harmless chitchat, I heard my own name in the mouth of this stranger, this blind man I didn't even know! And then this: "From all you've said about him, I can only conclude—" But we were interrupted, a knock at the door, something, and we didn't ever get back to the tape. Maybe it was just as well. I'd heard all I wanted to.

Now this same blind man was coming to sleep in my house.

"Maybe I could take him bowling," I said to my wife. She was at the draining board doing scalloped potatoes. She put down the knife she was using and turned around.

"If you love me," she said, "you can do this for me. If you don't love me, okay. But if you had a friend, any friend, and the friend came to visit, I'd make him feel comfortable." She wiped her hands with the dish towel.

"I don't have any blind friends," I said.

"You don't have *any* friends," she said. "Period. Besides," she said, 10
"goddamn it, his wife's just died! Don't you understand that? The man's lost his wife!"

I didn't answer. She'd told me a little about the blind man's wife. Her name was Beulah. Beulah! That's a name for a colored woman.

"Was his wife a Negro?" I asked.

"Are you crazy?" my wife said. "Have you just flipped or something?" She picked up a potato. I saw it hit the floor, then roll under the stove. "What's wrong with you?" she said. "Are you drunk?"

"I'm just asking," I said.

Right then my wife filled me in with more detail than I cared to know. 15
I made a drink and sat at the kitchen table to listen. Pieces of the story began to fall into place.

Beulah had gone to work for the blind man the summer after my wife had stopped working for him. Pretty soon Beulah and the blind man had themselves a church wedding. It was a little wedding—who'd want to go to such a wedding in the first place?—just the two of them, plus the minister and the minister's wife. But it was a church wedding just the same. It was what Beulah had wanted, he'd said. But even then Beulah must have been carrying the cancer in her glands. After they had been inseparable for eight years— my wife's word, *inseparable*—Beulah's health went into rapid decline. She died in a Seattle hospital room, the blind man sitting beside the bed and holding on to her hand. They'd married, lived and worked together, slept together—had sex, sure—and then the blind man had to bury her. All this without his having ever seen what the goddamned woman looked like. It was beyond my understanding. Hearing this, I felt sorry for the blind man for a little bit. And then I found myself thinking what a pitiful life this woman must have led. Imagine a woman who could never see herself as she was seen in the eyes of her loved one. A woman who could go on day after day and never receive the smallest compliment from her beloved. A woman whose husband could never read the expression on her face, be it misery or something better. Someone who could wear makeup or not—what difference to him? She could, if she wanted, wear green eye-shadow around one eye, a straight pin in her nostril, yellow slacks and purple shoes, no matter. And then to slip off into death, the blind man's hand on her hand, his blind eyes streaming tears—I'm imagining now—her last thought maybe this: that he never even knew what she looked like, and she on an express to the grave. Robert was left with a small insurance policy and half of a twenty-peso

Mexican coin. The other half of the coin went into the box with her. Pathetic.

So when the time rolled around, my wife went to the depot to pick him up. With nothing to do but wait—sure, I blamed him for that—I was having a drink and watching the TV when I heard the car pull into the drive. I got up from the sofa with my drink and went to the window to have a look.

I saw my wife laughing as she parked the car. I saw her get out of the car and shut the door. She was still wearing a smile. Just amazing. She went around to the other side of the car to where the blind man was already starting to get out. This blind man, feature this, he was wearing a full beard! A beard on a blind man! Too much, I say. The blind man reached into the back seat and dragged out a suitcase. My wife took his arm, shut the car door, and, talking all the way, moved him down the drive and then up the steps to the front porch. I turned off the TV. I finished my drink, rinsed the glass, dried my hands. Then I went to the door.

My wife said, "I want you to meet Robert. Robert, this is my husband. I've told you all about him." She was beaming. She had this blind man by his coat sleeve.

The blind man let go of his suitcase and up came his hand. 20

I took it. He squeezed hard, held my hand, and then he let it go.

"I feel like we've already met," he boomed.

"Likewise," I said. I didn't know what else to say. Then I said, "Welcome. I've heard a lot about you." We began to move then, a little group, from the porch into the living room, my wife guiding him by the arm. The blind man was carrying his suitcase in his other hand. My wife said things like, "To your left here, Robert. That's right. Now watch it, there's a chair. That's it. Sit down right here. This is the sofa. We just bought this sofa two weeks ago."

I started to say something about the old sofa. I'd liked that old sofa. But I didn't say anything. Then I wanted to say something else, small-talk, about the scenic ride along the Hudson. How going *to* New York, you should sit on the right-hand side of the train, and coming *from* New York, the left-hand side.

"Did you have a good train ride?" I said. "Which side of the train did 25 you sit on, by the way?"

"What a question, which side!" my wife said. "What's it matter which side?" she said.

"I just asked," I said.

"Right side," the blind man said. "I hadn't been on a train in nearly forty years. Not since I was a kid. With my folks. That's been a long time. I'd nearly forgotten the sensation. I have winter in my beard now," he said. "So I've been told, anyway. Do I look distinguished, my dear?" the blind man said to my wife.

"You look distinguished, Robert," she said. "Robert," she said. "Robert, it's just so good to see you."

My wife finally took her eyes off the blind man and looked at me. I 30 had the feeling she didn't like what she saw. I shrugged.

I've never met, or personally known, anyone who was blind. This blind man was late forties, a heavy-set, balding man with stooped shoulders, as if he carried a great weight there. He wore brown slacks, brown shoes, a light-brown shirt, a tie, a sports coat. Spiffy. He also had this full beard. But he didn't use a cane and he didn't wear dark glasses. I'd always thought dark glasses were a must for the blind. Fact was, I wished he had a pair. At first glance, his eyes looked like anyone else's eyes. But if you looked close, there was something different about them. Too much white in the iris, for one thing, and the pupils seemed to move around in the sockets without his knowing it or being able to stop it. Creepy. As I stared at his face, I saw the left pupil turn in toward his nose while the other made an effort to keep in one place. But it was only an effort, for that eye was on the roam without his knowing it or wanting it to be.

I said, "Let me get you a drink. What's your pleasure? We have a little of everything. It's one of our pastimes."

"Bub, I'm a Scotch man myself," he said fast enough in this big voice.

"Right," I said. Bub! "Sure you are. I knew it."

He let his fingers touch his suitcase, which was sitting alongside the   35
sofa. He was taking his bearings. I didn't blame him for that.

"I'll move that up to your room," my wife said.

"No, that's fine," the blind man said loudly. "It can go up when I go up."

"A little water with the Scotch?" I said.

"Very little," he said.

"I knew it," I said.   40

He said, "Just a tad. The Irish actor, Barry Fitzgerald? I'm like that fellow. When I drink water, Fitzgerald said, I drink water. When I drink whiskey, I drink whiskey." My wife laughed. The blind man brought his hand up under his beard. He lifted his beard slowly and let it drop.

I did the drinks, three big glasses of Scotch with a splash of water in each. Then we made ourselves comfortable and talked about Robert's travels. First the long flight from the West Coast to Connecticut, we covered that. Then from Connecticut up here by train. We had another drink concerning that leg of the trip.

I remembered having read somewhere that the blind didn't smoke be-cause, as speculation had it, they couldn't see the smoke they exhaled. I thought I knew that much and that much only about blind people. But this blind man smoked his cigarette down to the nubbin and then lit another one. This blind man filled his ashtray and my wife emptied it.

When we sat down at the table for dinner, we had another drink. My wife heaped Robert's plate with cube steak, scalloped potatoes, green beans. I buttered him up two slices of bread. I said, "Here's bread and butter for you." I swallowed some of my drink. "Now let us pray," I said, and the blind man lowered his head. My wife looked at me, her mouth agape. "Pray the phone won't ring and the food doesn't get cold," I said.

We dug in. We ate everything there was to eat on the table. We ate   45
like there was no tomorrow. We didn't talk. We ate. We scarfed. We grazed

that table. We were into serious eating. The blind man had right away located his foods, he knew just where everything was on his plate. I watched with admiration as he used his knife and fork on the meat. He'd cut two pieces of meat, fork the meat into his mouth, and then go all out for the scalloped potatoes, the beans next, and then he'd tear off a hunk of buttered bread and eat that. He'd follow this up with a big drink of milk. It didn't seem to bother him to use his fingers once in a while, either.

We finished everything, including half a strawberry pie. For a few moments, we sat as if stunned. Sweat beaded on our faces. Finally, we got up from the table and left the dirty plates. We didn't look back. We took our-selves into the living room and sank into our places again. Robert and my wife sat on the sofa. I took the big chair. We had us two or three more drinks while they talked about the major things that had come to pass for them in the past ten years. For the most part, I just listened. Now and then I joined in. I didn't want him to think I'd left the room, and I didn't want her to think I was feeling left out. They talked of things that had happened to them—to them—these past ten years. I waited in vain to hear my name on my wife's sweet lips: "And then my dear husband came into my life"— something like that. But I heard nothing of the sort. More talk of Robert. Robert had done a little of everything, it seemed, a regular blind jack-of-all-trades. But most recently he and his wife had had an Amway distributorship, from which, I gathered, they'd earned their living, such as it was. The blind man was also a ham radio operator. He talked in his loud voice about con-versations he'd had with fellow operators in Guam, in the Philippines, in Alaska, and even in Tahiti. He said he'd have a lot of friends there if he ever wanted to go visit those places. From time to time, he'd turn his blind face toward me, put his hand under his beard, ask me something. How long had I been in my present position? (Three years.) Did I like my work? (I didn't.) Was I going to stay with it? (What were the options?) Finally, when I thought he was beginning to run down, I got up and turned on the TV.

My wife looked at me with irritation. She was heading toward a boil. Then she looked at the blind man and said, "Robert, do you have a TV?"

The blind man said, "My dear, I have two TVs. I have a color set and a black-and-white thing, an old relic. It's funny, but if I turn the TV on, and I'm always turning it on, I turn on the color set. It's funny, don't you think?"

I didn't know what to say to that. I had absolutely nothing to say to that. No opinion. So I watched the news program and tried to listen to what the announcer was saying.

"This is a color TV," the blind man said. "Don't ask me how, but I can tell." 50

"We traded up a while ago," I said.

The blind man had another taste of his drink. He lifted his beard, sniffed it, and let it fall. He leaned forward on the sofa. He positioned his ashtray on the coffee table, then put the lighter to his cigarette. He leaned back on the sofa and crossed his legs at the ankles.

My wife covered her mouth, and then she yawned. She stretched. She said, "I think I'll go upstairs and put on my robe. I think I'll change into something else. Robert, you make yourself comfortable," she said.

"I'm comfortable," the blind man said.

"I want you to feel comfortable in this house," she said.

"I am comfortable," the blind man said.

After she'd left the room, he and I listened to the weather report and then to the sports roundup. By that time, she'd been gone so long I didn't know if she was going to come back. I thought she might have gone to bed. I wished she'd come back downstairs. I didn't want to be left alone with a blind man. I asked him if he wanted another drink, and he said sure. Then I asked if he wanted to smoke some dope with me. I said I'd just rolled a number. I hadn't, but I planned to do so in about two shakes. "I'll try some with you," he said.

"Damn right," I said. "That's the stuff."

I got our drinks and sat down on the sofa with him. Then I roll us two fat numbers. I lit one and passed it. I brought it to his fingers. He took it and inhaled.

"Hold it as long as you can," I said. I could tell he didn't know the first thing.

My wife came back downstairs wearing her pink robe and her pink slippers.

"What do I smell?" she said.

"We thought we'd have us some cannabis," I said.

My wife gave me a savage look. Then she looked at the blind man and said, "Robert, I didn't know you smoked."

He said, "I do now, my dear. There's a first time for everything. But I don't feel anything yet."

"This stuff is pretty mellow," I said. "This stuff is mild. It's dope you can reason with," I said. "It doesn't mess you up."

"Not much it doesn't, bub," he said, and laughed.

My wife sat on the sofa between the blind man and me. I passed her the number. She took it and toked and then passed it back to me. "Which way is this going?" she said. Then she said, "I shouldn't be smoking this. I can hardly keep my eyes open as it is. That dinner did me in. I shouldn't have eaten so much."

"It was the strawberry pie," the blind man said. "That's what did it," he said, and he laughed his big laugh. Then he shook his head.

"There's more strawberry pie," I said.

"Do you want some more, Robert?" my wife said.

"Maybe in a little while," he said.

We gave our attention to the TV. My wife yawned again. She said, "Your bed is made up when you feel like going to bed, Robert. I know you must have had a long day. When you're ready to go to bed, say so." She pulled his arm. "Robert?"

He came to and said, "I've had a real nice time. This beats tapes, doesn't it?"

I said, "Coming at you," and I put the number between his fingers. He inhaled, held the smoke, and then let it go. It was like he'd been doing it since he was nine years old.

"Thanks, bub," he said. "But I think this is all for me. I think I'm beginning to feel it," he said. He held the burning roach out for my wife.

"Same here," she said. "Ditto. Me, too." She took the roach and passed it to me. "I may just sit here for a while between you two guys with my eyes closed. But don't let me bother you, okay? Either one of you. If it bothers you, say so. Otherwise, I may just sit here with my eyes closed until you're ready to go to bed," she said. "Your bed's made up, Robert, when you're ready. It's right next to our room at the top of the stairs. We'll show you up when you're ready. You wake me up now, you guys, if I fall asleep." She said that and then she closed her eyes and went to sleep.

The news program ended. I got up and changed the channel. I sat back down on the sofa. I wished my wife hadn't pooped out. Her head lay across the back of the sofa, her mouth open. She'd turned so that her robe had slipped away from her legs, exposing a juicy thigh. I reached to draw her robe back over her, and it was then that I glanced at the blind man. What the hell! I flipped the robe open again.

"You say when you want some strawberry pie," I said.

"I will," he said.

I said, "Are you tired? Do you want me to take you up to your bed? Are you ready to hit the hay?"

"Not yet," he said. "No, I'll stay up with you, bub. If that's all right. I'll stay up until you're ready to turn in. We haven't had a chance to talk. Know what I mean? I feel like me and her monopolized the evening." He lifted his beard and he let it fall. He picked up his cigarettes and his lighter.

"That's all right," I said. Then I said, "I'm glad for the company."

And I guess I was. Every night I smoked dope and stayed up as long as I could before I fell asleep. My wife and I hardly ever went to bed at the same time. When I did go to sleep, I had these dreams. Sometimes I'd wake up from one of them, my heart going crazy.

Something about the church and the Middle Ages was on the TV. Not your run-of-the-mill TV fare. I wanted to watch something else. I turned to the other channels. But there was nothing on them, either. So I turned back to the first channel and apologized.

"Bub, it's all right," the blind man said. "It's fine with me. Whatever you want to watch is okay. I'm always learning something. Learning never ends. It won't hurt me to learn something tonight. I got ears," he said.

We didn't say anything for a time. He was leaning forward with his head turned at me, his right ear aimed in the direction of the set. Very disconcerting. Now and then his eyelids drooped and then they snapped open again. Now and then he put his fingers into his beard and tugged, like he was thinking about something he was hearing on the television.

On the screen, a group of men wearing cowls was being set upon and tormented by men dressed in skeleton costumes and men dressed as devils. The men dressed as devils wore devil masks, horns, and long tails. This pageant was part of a procession. The Englishman who was narrating the thing said it took place in Spain once a year. I tried to explain to the blind man what was happening.

"Skeletons," he said. "I know about skeletons," he said, and he nodded.

The TV showed this one cathedral. Then there was a long, slow look   90 at another one. Finally, the picture switched to the famous one in Paris, with its flying buttresses and its spires reaching up to the clouds. The camera pulled away to show the whole of the cathedral rising above the skyline.

There were times when the Englishman who was telling the thing would shut up, would simply let the camera move around over the cathedrals. Or else the camera would tour the countryside, men in fields walking behind oxen. I waited as long as I could. Then I felt I had to say something. I said, "They're showing the outside of this cathedral now. Gargoyles. Little statues carved to look like monsters. Now I guess they're in Italy. Yeah, they're in Italy. There's paintings on the walls of this one church."

"Are those fresco paintings, bub?" he asked, and he sipped from his drink.

I reached for my glass. But it was empty. I tried to remember what I could remember. "You're asking me are those frescoes?" I said. "That's a good question. I don't know."

The camera moved to a cathedral outside Lisbon. The differences in the Portuguese cathedral compared with the French and Italian were not that great. But they were there. Mostly the interior stuff. Then something occurred to me, and I said, "Something has occurred to me. Do you have any idea what a cathedral is? What they look like, that is? Do you follow me? If somebody says cathedral to you, do you have any notion what they're talking about? Do you know the difference between that and a Baptist church, say?"

He let the smoke dribble from his mouth. "I know they took hundreds   95 of workers fifty or a thousand years to build," he said. "I just heard the man say that, of course. I know generations of the same families worked on a cathedral. I heard him say that, too. The men who began their life's work on them, they never lived to see the completion of their work. In that wise, bub, they're no different from the rest of us, right?" He laughed. Then his eyelids drooped again. His head nodded. He seemed to be snoozing. Maybe he was imagining himself in Portugal. The TV was showing another cathedral now. This one was in Germany. The Englishman's voice droned on. "Cathedrals," the blind man said. He sat up and rolled his head back and forth. "If you want the truth, bub, that's about all I know. What I just said.

What I heard him say. But maybe you could describe one to me? I wish you'd do it. I'd like that. If you want to know, I really don't have a good idea."

I stared hard at the shot of the cathedral on the TV. How could I even begin to describe it? But say my life depended on it. Say my life was being threatened by an insane guy who said I had to do it or else.

I stared some more at the cathedral before the picture flipped off into the countryside. There was no use. I turned to the blind man and said, "To begin with, they're very tall." I was looking around the room for clues. "They reach way up. Up and up. Toward the sky. They're so big, some of them, they have to have these supports. To help hold them up, so to speak. These supports are called buttresses. They remind me of viaducts, for some reason. But maybe you don't know viaducts, either? Sometimes the cathedrals have devils and such carved into the front. Sometimes lords and ladies. Don't ask me why this is," I said.

He was nodding. The whole upper part of his body seemed to be moving back and forth.

"I'm not doing so good, am I?" I said.

He stopped nodding and leaned forward on the edge of the sofa. As he   100
listened to me, he was running his fingers through his beard. I wasn't getting through to him, I could see that. But he waited for me to go on just the same. He nodded, like he was trying to encourage me. I tried to think what else to say. "They're really big," I said. "They're massive. They're built of stone. Marble, too, sometimes. In those olden days, when they built cathedrals, men wanted to be close to God. In those olden days, God was an important part of everyone's life. You could tell this from their cathedral-building. I'm sorry," I said, "but it looks like that's the best I can do for you. I'm just no good at it."

"That's all right, bub," the blind man said. "Hey, listen. I hope you don't mind my asking you. Can I ask you something? Let me ask you a simple question, yes or no. I'm just curious and there's no offense. You're my host. But let me ask if you are in any way religious? You don't mind my asking?"

I shook my head. He couldn't see that, though. A wink is the same as a nod to a blind man. "I guess I don't believe in it. In anything. Sometimes it's hard. You know what I'm saying?"

"Sure, I do," he said.

"Right," I said.

The Englishman was still holding forth. My wife sighed in her sleep.   105
She drew a long breath and went on with her sleeping.

"You'll have to forgive me," I said. "But I can't tell you what a cathedral looks like. It just isn't in me to do it. I can't do any more than I've done."

The blind man sat very still, his head down, as he listened to me.

I said, "The truth is, cathedrals don't mean anything special to me. Nothing. Cathedrals. They're something to look at on late-night TV. That's all they are."

It was then that the blind man cleared his throat. He brought something up. He took a handkerchief from his back pocket. Then he said, "I get it, bub. It's okay. It happens. Don't worry about it," he said. "Hey, listen to me. Will you do me a favor? I got an idea. Why don't you find us some heavy paper? And a pen. We'll do something. We'll draw one together. Get us a pen and some heavy paper. Go on, bub, get the stuff," he said.

So I went upstairs. My legs felt like they didn't have any strength in   110
them. They felt like they did after I'd done some running. In my wife's room, I looked around. I found some ballpoints in a little basket on her table. And then I tried to think where to look for the kind of paper he was talking about.

Downstairs, in the kitchen, I found a shopping bag with onion skins in the bottom of the bag. I emptied the bag and shook it. I brought it into the living room and sat down with it near his legs. I moved some things, smoothed the wrinkles from the bag, spread it out on the coffee table.

The blind man got down from the sofa and sat next to me on the carpet.

He ran his fingers over the paper. He went up and down the sides of the paper. The edges, even the edges. He fingered the corners.

"All right," he said. "All right, let's do her."

He found my hand, the hand with the pen. He closed his hand over   115
my hand. "Go ahead, bub, draw," he said. "Draw. You'll see. I'll follow along with you. It'll be okay. Just begin now like I'm telling you. You'll see. Draw," the blind man said.

So I began. First I drew a box that looked like a house. It could have been the house I lived in. Then I put a roof on it. At either end of the roof, I drew spires. Crazy.

"Swell," he said. "Terrific. You're doing fine," he said. "Never thought anything like this could happen in your lifetime, did you, bub? Well, it's a strange life, we all know that. Go on now. Keep it up."

I put in windows with arches. I drew flying buttresses. I hung great doors. I couldn't stop. The TV station went off the air. I put down the pen and closed and opened my fingers. The blind man felt around over the paper. He moved the tips of his fingers over the paper, all over what I had drawn, and he nodded.

"Doing fine," the blind man said.

I took up the pen again, and he found my hand. I kept at it. I'm no   120
artist. But I kept drawing just the same.

My wife opened her eyes and gazed at us. She sat up on the sofa, her robe hanging open. She said, "What are you doing? Tell me, I want to know."

I didn't answer her.

The blind man said, "We're drawing a cathedral. Me and him are working on it. Press hard," he said to me. "That's right. That's good," he said. "Sure, you got it, bub. I can tell. You didn't think you could. But you can, can't you? You're cooking with gas now. You know what I'm saying? We're going to really have us something here in a minute. How's the old arm?" he said. "Put some people in there now. What's a cathedral without people?"

My wife said, "What's going on? Robert, what are you doing? What's going on?"

"It's all right," he said to her. "Close your eyes now," the blind man   125
said to me.

I did it. I closed them just like he said.

"Are they closed?" he said. "Don't fudge."

"They're closed," I said.

"Keep them that way," he said. "Don't stop now. Draw."

So we kept on with it. His fingers rode my fingers as my hand went   130
over the paper. It was like nothing else in my life up to now.

Then he said, "I think that's it. I think you got it," he said. "Take a look. What do you think?"

But I had my eyes closed. I thought I'd keep them that way for a little longer. I thought it was something I ought to do.

"Well?" he said. "Are you looking?"

My eyes were still closed. I was in my house. I knew that. But I didn't feel like I was inside anything.

"It's really something," I said.   135

Considerations

1. Read the first part of the story (through paragraph 16, when Robert arrives at the narrator's house), then write a brief description of the narrator and your response to him.
2. In an article in *Studies in Short Fiction* (Summer 1986), Mark A. R. Facknitz suggests that what motivates one to continue reading this story, in spite of its unattractive narrator, is "a fear of the harm he may do to his wife and her blind friend." Do you agree with this observation? Explain.
3. In what ways do the narrator and Robert belong to different cultures? How are their identities related to these cultures?
4. What happens in the final scene? Why does Carver choose to have Robert and the narrator watch a television program about cathedrals rather than, for example, old schoolhouses or national monuments?
5. How does Robert contribute to the narrator's wife's search for identity? How does she contribute to Robert's sense of who he is?

ANNA LEE WALTERS (1946–   )

The Warriors

Anna Lee Walters was born in Oklahoma. A Pawnee/Otoe, she currently lives with the Navajo Nation and has served as an educational consultant and curriculum specialist at Navajo Community College and as an editor at Navajo Community College Press. She has written many poems and short stories, which have been anthologized in such collections as Voices of the Rainbow *(1975) and* The Remembered Earth *(1978). "The Warriors" comes from* The Sun Is Not Merciful *(1985).*

In our youth, we saw hobos come and go, sliding by our faded white house like wary cats who did not want us too close. Sister and I waved at the strange procession of passing men and women hobos. Just between ourselves, Sister and I talked of that hobo parade. We guessed at and imagined the places and towns we thought the hobos might have come from or had been. Mostly they were white or black people. But there were Indian hobos, too. It never occurred to Sister and me that this would be Uncle Ralph's end.

Sister and I were little, and Uncle Ralph came to visit us. He lifted us over his head and shook us around him like gourd rattles. He was Momma's younger brother, and he could have disciplined us if he so desired. That was part of our custom. But he never did. Instead, he taught us Pawnee words. "*Pari* is Pawnee and *pita* is man," he said. Between the words, he tapped out drumbeats with his fingers on the table top, ghost dance and round dance songs that he suddenly remembered and sang. His melodic voice lilted over us and hung around the corners of the house for days. His stories of life and death were fierce and gentle. Warriors dangled in delicate balance.

He told us his version of the story of Pahukatawa, a Skidi Pawnee warrior. He was killed by the Sioux, but the animals, feeling compassion for him, brought Pahukatawa to life again. "The Evening Star and the Morning Star bore children and some people say that these offspring are who we are," he often said. At times he pointed to those stars and greeted them by their Pawnee names. He liked to pray for Sister and me, for everyone and every tiny thing in the world, but we never heard him ask for anything for himself from *Atius,* the Father.

"For beauty is why we live," Uncle Ralph said when he talked of precious things only the Pawnees know. "We die for it, too." He called himself an ancient Pawnee warrior when he was quite young. He told us that warriors must brave all storms and odds and stand their ground. He knew intimate details of every battle the Pawnees ever fought since Pawnee time began, and Sister and I knew even then that Uncle Ralph had a great battlefield of his own.

As a child I thought that Uncle Ralph had been born into the wrong time. The Pawnees had been ravaged so often by then. The tribe of several thousand when it was at its peak over a century before were then a few hundred people who had been closely confined for more than a hundred years. The warrior life was gone. Uncle Ralph was trapped in a transparent bubble of a new time. The bubble bound him tight as it blew around us.

Uncle Ralph talked obsessively of warriors, painted proud warriors who shrieked poignant battle cries at the top of their lungs and died with honor. Sister and I were little then, lost from him in the world of children who saw everything with children's eyes. And though we saw with wide eyes the painted warriors that he fantasized and heard their fierce and haunting battle cries, we did not hear his. Now that we are old and Uncle Ralph has been gone for a long time, Sister and I know that when he died, he was tired and alone. But he was a warrior.

The hobos were always around in our youth. Sister and I were curious about them, and this curiosity claimed much of our time. They crept by the house at all hours of the day and night, dressed in rags and odd clothing. They wandered to us from the railroad tracks where they had leaped from slow-moving boxcars onto the flatland. They hid in high clumps of weeds and brush that ran along the fence near the tracks. The hobos usually traveled alone, but Sister and I saw them come together, like poor families, to share a can of beans or a tin of sardines that they ate with sticks or twigs. Uncle Ralph also watched them from a distance.

One early morning, Sister and I crossed the tracks on our way to school and collided with a tall, haggard white man. He wore a very old-fashioned pin-striped black jacket covered with lint and soot. There was fright in his eyes when they met ours. He scurried around us, quickening his pace. The pole over his shoulder where his possessions hung in a bundle at the end bounced as he nearly ran from us.

"Looks just like a scared jackrabbit," Sister said, watching him dart away.

That evening we told Momma about the scared man. She warned us about the dangers of hobos as our father threw us a stern look. Uncle Ralph was visiting but he didn't say anything. He stayed the night and Sister asked him, "Hey, Uncle Ralph, why do you suppose they's hobos?"

Uncle Ralph was a large man. He took Sister and put her on one knee. "You see, Sister," he said, "hobos are a different kind. They see things in a different way. Them hobos are kind of like us. We're not like other people in some ways and yet we are. It has to do with what you see and feel when you look at this old world."

His answer satisfied Sister for a while. He taught us some more Pawnee words that night.

Not long after Uncle Ralph's explanation, Sister and I surprised a black man with white whiskers and fuzzy hair. He was climbing through the barbed-wire fence that marked our property line. He wore faded blue overalls with pockets stuffed full of handkerchiefs. He wiped sweat from his face. When it dried, he looked up and saw us. I remembered what Uncle Ralph had said and wondered what the black man saw when he looked at us standing there.

"We might scare him," Sister said softly to me, remembering the white man who had scampered away.

Sister whispered, "Hi," to the black man. Her voice was barely audible.   15

"Boy, it's sure hot," he said. His voice was big and he smiled.

"Where are you going?" Sister asked.

"Me? Nowheres, I guess," he muttered.

"Then what you doing here?" Sister went on. She was bold for a seven-year-old kid. I was older but I was also quieter. "This here place is ours," she said.

He looked around and saw our house with its flowering mimosa trees   20 and rich green mowed lawn stretching out before him. Other houses sat around ours.

"I reckon I'm lost," he said.

Sister pointed to the weeds and brush further up the road. "That's where you want to go. That's where they all go, the hobos."

I tried to quiet Sister but she didn't hush. "The hobos stay up there," she said. "You a hobo?"

He ignored her question and asked his own. "Say, what is you all? You not black, you not white. What is you all?"

Sister looked at me. She put one hand on her chest and the other hand   25 on me. "We Indians!" Sister said.

He stared at us and smiled again. "Is that a fact?" he said.

"Know what kind of Indians we are?" Sister asked him.

He shook his fuzzy head. "Indians is Indians, I guess," he said.

Sister wrinkled her forehead and retorted, "Not us! We not like others. We see things different. We're Pawnees. We're warriors!"

I pushed my elbow into Sister's side. She quieted.   30

The man was looking down the road and he shuffled his feet. "I'd best go," he said.

Sister pointed to the brush and weeds one more time. "That way," she said.

He climbed back through the fence and brush as Sister yelled, "Bye now!" He waved a damp handkerchief.

Sister and I didn't tell Momma and Dad about the black man. But much later Sister told Uncle Ralph every word that had been exchanged with the black man. Uncle Ralph listened and smiled.

Months later when the warm weather had cooled and Uncle Ralph   35 came to stay with us for a couple of weeks, Sister and I went to the hobo place. We had planned it for a long time. That afternoon when we pushed away the weeds, not a hobo was in sight.

The ground was packed down tight in the clearing among the high weeds. We walked around the encircling brush and found folded cardboards stacked together. Burned cans in assorted sizes were stashed under the cardboards, and there were remains of old fires. Rags were tied to the brush, snapping in the hard wind.

Sister said, "Maybe they're all in the boxcars now. It's starting to get cold."

She was right. The November wind had a bite to it and the cold stung our hands and froze our breaths as we spoke.

"You want to go over to them boxcars?" she asked. We looked at the Railroad Crossing sign where the boxcars stood.

I was prepared to answer when a voice roared from somewhere be- 40 hind us.

"Now, you young ones, you git on home! Go on! Git!"

A man crawled out of the weeds and looked angrily at us. His eyes were red and his face was unshaven. He wore a red plaid shirt with striped gray and black pants too large for him. His face was swollen and bruised. An old woolen pink scarf hid some of the bruise marks around his neck, and his topcoat was splattered with mud.

Sister looked at him. She stood close to me and told him defiantly, "You can't tell us what to do! You don't know us!"

He didn't answer Sister but tried to stand. He couldn't. Sister ran to him and took his arm and pulled on it. "You need help?" she questioned.

He frowned at her but let us help him. He was tall. He seemed to be 45 embarrassed by our help.

"You Indian, ain't you?" I dared to ask him.

He didn't answer me but looked at his feet as if they could talk so he wouldn't have to. His feet were in big brown overshoes.

"Who's your people?" Sister asked. He looked to be about Uncle Ralph's age when he finally lifted his face and met mine. He didn't respond for a minute. Then he sighed. "I ain't got no people," he told us as he tenderly stroked his swollen jaw.

"Sure you got people. Our folks says a man's always got people," I said softly. The wind blew our clothes and covered the words.

But he heard. He exploded like a firecracker. "Well, I don't! I ain't got 50 no people! I ain't got nobody!"

"What you doing out here anyway?" Sister asked. "You hurt? You want to come over to our house?"

"Naw," he said. "Now you little ones, go on home. Don't be walking round out here. Didn't nobody tell you little girls ain't supposed to be going round by themselves? You might git hurt."

"We just wanted to talk to hobos," Sister said.

"Naw, you don't. Just go on home. Your folks is probably looking for you and worrying 'bout you."

I took Sister's arm and told her we were going home. Then we said 55 bye to the man. But Sister couldn't resist a few last words, "You Indian, ain't you?"

He nodded his head like it was a painful thing to do. "Yeah, I'm Indian."

"You ought to go on home yourself," Sister said. "Your folks probably looking for you and worrying 'bout you."

His voice rose again as Sister and I walked away from him. "I told you kids, I don't have no people!" There was exasperation in his voice.

Sister would not be outdone. She turned and yelled, "Oh yeah? You Indian ain't you? Ain't you?" she screamed. "We your people!"

His topcoat and pink scarf flapped in the wind as we turned away   60 from him.

We went home to Momma and Dad and Uncle Ralph then. Uncle Ralph met us at the front door. "Where you all been?" he asked looking toward the railroad tracks. Momma and Dad were talking in the kitchen.

"Just playing, Uncle," Sister and I said simultaneously.

Uncle Ralph grabbed both Sister and me by our hands and yanked us out the door. "*Awkuh!*" he said, using the Pawnee expression to show his dissatisfaction.

Outside, we sat on the cement porch. Uncle Ralph was quiet for a long time, and neither Sister nor I knew what to expect.

"I want to tell you all a story," he finally said. "Once, there were these   65 two rats who ran around everywhere and got into everything all the time. Everything they were told not to do, well they went right out and did. They'd get into one mess and then another. It seems that they never could learn."

At that point Uncle Ralph cleared his throat. He looked at me and said, "Sister, do you understand this story? Is it too hard for you? You're older."

I nodded my head up and down and said, "I understand."

Then Uncle Ralph looked at Sister. He said to her, "Sister, do I need to go on with this story?"

Sister shook her head from side to side. "Naw, Uncle Ralph," she said.

"So you both know how this story ends?" he said gruffly. Sister and I   70 bobbed our heads up and down again.

We followed at his heels the rest of the day. When he tightened the loose hide on top of his drum, we watched him and held it in place as he laced the wet hide down. He got his drumsticks down from the top shelf of the closet and began to pound the drum slowly.

"Where you going, Uncle Ralph?" I asked. Sister and I knew that when he took his drum out, he was always gone shortly after.

"I have to be a drummer at some doings tomorrow," he said.

"You a good singer, Uncle Ralph," Sister said. "You know all them old songs."

"The young people nowadays, it seems they don't care 'bout nothing   75 that's old. They just want to go to the Moon." He was drumming low as he spoke.

"We care, Uncle Ralph," Sister said.

"Why?" Uncle Ralph asked in a hard, challenging tone that he seldom used on us.

Sister thought for a moment and then said, "I guess because you care so much, Uncle Ralph."

His eyes softened as he said, "I'll sing you an *Eruska* song, a song for the warriors."

The song he sang was a war dance song. At first Sister and I listened attentively, but then Sister began to dance the men's dance. She had never danced before and tried to imitate what she had seen. Her chubby body whirled and jumped the way she'd seen the men dance. Her head tilted from side to side the way the men moved theirs. I laughed aloud at her clumsy effort, and Uncle Ralph laughed heartily, too. 80

Uncle Ralph went in and out of our lives after that. We heard that he sang at one place and then another, and people came to Momma to find him. They said that he was only one of a few who knew the old ways and the songs.

When he came to visit us, he always brought something to eat. The Pawnee custom was that the man, the warrior, should bring food, preferably meat. Then, whatever food was brought to the host was prepared and served to the man, the warrior, along with the host's family. Many times Momma and I, or Sister and I, came home to an empty house to find a sack of food on the table. Momma or I cooked it for the next meal, and Uncle Ralph showed up to eat.

As Sister and I grew older, our fascination with the hobos decreased. Other things took our time, and Uncle Ralph did not appear as frequently as he did before.

Once while I was home alone, I picked up Momma's old photo album. Inside was a gray photo of Uncle Ralph in an army uniform. Behind him were tents on a flat terrain. Other photos showed other poses but only in one picture did he smile. All the photos were written over in black ink in Momma's handwriting. "Ralphie in Korea," the writing said.

Other photos in the album showed our Pawnee relatives. Dad was from 85 another tribe. Momma's momma was in the album, a tiny gray-haired woman who no longer lived. And Momma's momma's dad was in the album; he wore old Pawnee leggings and the long feathers of a dark bird sat upon his head. I closed the album when Momma, Dad, and Sister came home.

Momma went into the kitchen to cook. She called me and Sister to help. As she put on a bibbed apron, she said, "We just came from town, and we saw someone from home there." She meant someone from her tribal community.

"This man told me that Ralphie's been drinking hard," she said sadly. "He used to do that quite a bit a long time ago, but we thought it had stopped. He seemed to be all right for a few years." We cooked and then ate in silence.

Washing the dishes, I asked Momma, "How come Uncle Ralph never did marry?"

Momma looked up at me but was not surprised by my question. She answered, "I don't know, Sister. It would have been better if he had. There was one woman who I thought he really loved. I think he still does. I think it had something to do with Mom. She wanted him to wait."

"Wait for what?" I asked.   90

"I don't know," Momma said, and sank into a chair.

After that we heard unsettling rumors of Uncle Ralph drinking here and there.

He finally came to the house once when only I happened to be home. He was haggard and tired. His appearance was much like that of the white man that Sister and I met on the railroad tracks years before.

I opened the door when he tapped on it. Uncle Ralph looked years older than his age. He brought food in his arms. "*Nowa,* Sister," he said in greeting. "Where's the other one?" He meant my sister.

"She's gone now, Uncle Ralph. School in Kansas," I answered. "Where   95 you been, Uncle Ralph? We been worrying about you."

He ignored my question and said, "I bring food. The warrior brings home food. To his family, to his people." His face was lined and had not been cleaned for days. He smelled of cheap wine.

I asked again, "Where you been, Uncle Ralph?"

He forced himself to smile. "Pumpkin Flower," he said, using the Pawnee name, "I've been out with my warriors all this time."

He put one arm around me as we went to the kitchen table with the food. "That's what your Pawnee name is. Now don't forget it."

"Did somebody bring you here, Uncle Ralph, or are you on foot?" I   100 asked him.

"I'm on foot," he answered. "Where's your Momma?"

I told him that she and Dad would be back soon. I started to prepare the food he brought.

Then I heard Uncle Ralph say, "Life is sure hard sometimes. Sometimes it seems I just can't go on."

"What's wrong, Uncle Ralph?" I asked.

Uncle Ralph let out a bitter little laugh. "What's wrong?" he repeated.   105 "What's wrong? All my life, I've tried to live what I've been taught, but Pumpkin Flower, some things are all wrong!"

He took a folded pack of Camel cigarettes from his coat pocket. His hand shook as he pulled one from the pack and lit the end. "Too much drink," he said sadly. "That stuff is bad for us."

"What are you trying to do, Uncle Ralph?" I asked him.

"Live," he said.

He puffed on the shaking cigarette a while and said, "The old people said to live beautifully with prayers and song. Some died for beauty, too."

"How do we do that, Uncle Ralph, live for beauty?" I asked.   110

"It's simple, Pumpkin Flower," he said. "Believe!"

"Believe what?" I asked.

He looked at me hard. "*Awkuh!*" he said. "That's one of the things that is wrong. Everyone questions. Everyone doubts. No one believes in the old ways anymore. They want to believe when it's convenient, when it doesn't cost them anything and they get something in return. There are no more believers. There are no more warriors. They are all gone. Those who are left only want to go to the Moon."

A car drove up outside. It was Momma and Dad. Uncle Ralph heard it too. He slumped in the chair, resigned to whatever Momma would say to him.

Momma came in first. Dad then greeted Uncle Ralph and disappeared 115 into the back of the house. Custom and etiquette required that Dad, who was not a member of Momma's tribe, allow Momma to handle her brother's problems.

She hugged Uncle Ralph. Her eyes filled with tears when she saw how thin he was and how his hands shook.

"Ralphie," she said, "you look awful, but I am glad to see you."

She then spoke to him of everyday things, how the car failed to start and the latest gossip. He was silent, tolerant of the passing of time in this way. His eyes sent me a pleading look while his hands shook and he tried to hold them still.

When supper was ready, Uncle Ralph went to wash himself for the meal. When he returned to the table, he was calm. His hands didn't shake so much.

At first he ate without many words, but in the course of the meal he 120 left the table twice. Each time he came back, he was more talkative than before, answering Momma's questions in Pawnee. He left the table a third time and Dad rose.

Dad said to Momma, "He's drinking again. Can't you tell?" Dad left the table and went outside.

Momma frowned. A determined look grew on her face.

When Uncle Ralph sat down to the table once more, Momma told him, "Ralphie, you're my brother but I want you to leave now. Come back when you're sober."

He held a tarnished spoon in mid-air and put it down slowly. He hadn't finished eating, but he didn't seem to mind leaving. He stood, looked at me with his red eyes, and went to the door. Momma followed him. In a low voice she said, "Ralphie, you've got to stop drinking and wandering—or don't come to see us again."

He pulled himself to his full height then. His frame filled the doorway. 125 He leaned over Momma and yelled, "Who are you? Are you God that you will say what will be or will not be?"

Momma met his angry eyes. She stood firm and did not back down.

His eyes finally dropped from her face to the linoleum floor. A cough came from deep in his throat.

"I'll leave here," he said. "But I'll get all my warriors and come back! I have thousands of warriors and they'll ride with me. We'll get our bows and arrows. Then we'll come back!" He staggered out the door.

In the years that followed, Uncle Ralph saw us only when he was sober. He visited less and less. When he did show up, he did a tapping ritual on our front door. We welcomed the rare visits. Occasionally he stayed at our house for a few days at a time when he was not drinking. He slept on the floor.

He did odd jobs for minimum pay but never complained about the   130
work or money. He'd acquired a vacant look in his eyes. It was the same look
that Sister and I had seen in the hobos when we were children. He wore a
similar careless array of clothing and carried no property with him at all.

The last time he came to the house, he called me by my English name
and asked if I remembered anything of all that he'd taught me. His hair had
turned pure white. He looked older than anyone I knew. I marveled at his
appearance and said, "I remember everything." That night I pointed out his
stars for him and told him how Pahukatawa lived and died and lived again
through another's dreams. I'd grown, and Uncle Ralph could not hold me
on his knee anymore. His arm circled my waist while we sat on the grass.

He was moved by my recitation and clutched my hand tightly. He said,
"It's more than this. It's more than just repeating words. You know that,
don't you?"

I nodded my head. "Yes, I know. The recitation is the easiest part but
it's more than this, Uncle Ralph."

He was quiet, but after a few minutes his hand touched my shoulder.
He said, "I couldn't make it work. I tried to fit the pieces."

"I know," I said.   135

"Now before I go," he said, "do you know who you are?"

The question took me by surprise. I thought very hard. I cleared my
throat and told him, "I know that I am fourteen. I know that it's too young."

"Do you know that you are a Pawnee?" he asked in a choked whisper.

"Yes, Uncle," I said.

"Good," he said with a long sigh that was swallowed by the night.   140
Then he stood and said, "Well, Sister, I have to go. Have to move on."

"Where are you going?" I asked. "Where all the warriors go?" I teased.

He managed a smile and a soft laugh. "Yeah, wherever the warriors are,
I'll find them."

I said to him, "Before you go, I want to ask you . . . Uncle Ralph, can
women be warriors too?"

He laughed again and hugged me merrily. "Don't tell me you want to   145
be one of the warriors too?"

"No, Uncle," I said. "Just one of yours." I hated to let him go because
I knew I would not see him again.

He pulled away. His last words were, "Don't forget what I've told you
all these years. It's the only chance not to become what everyone else is. Do
you understand?"

I nodded and he left.

I never saw him again.

The years passed quickly. I moved away from Momma and Dad and   150
married. Sister left before I did.

Years later in another town, hundreds of miles away, I awoke in a
terrible gloom, a sense that something was gone from the world the Pawnees
knew. The despair filled days, though the reason for the sense of loss went

unexplained. Finally, the telephone rang. Momma was on the line. She said, "Sister came home for a few days not too long ago. While she was here and alone, someone tapped on the door, like Ralphie always does. Sister yelled, 'Is that you, Uncle Ralphie? Come on in.' But no one entered."

Then I understood that Uncle Ralph was dead. Momma probably knew too. She wept softly into the phone.

Later Momma received an official call confirming Uncle Ralph's death. He had died from exposure in a hobo shanty, near the railroad tracks outside a tiny Oklahoma town. He'd been dead for several days and nobody knew but Momma, Sister, and me.

Momma reported to me that the funeral was well attended by the Pawnee people. Uncle Ralph and I had said our farewells years earlier. Momma told me that someone there had spoken well of Uncle Ralph before they put him in the ground. It was said that "Ralphie came from a fine family, an old line of warriors."

Ten years later, Sister and I visited briefly at Momma's and Dad's home.   155
We had been separated by hundreds of miles for all that time. As we sat under Momma's flowering mimosa trees, I made a confession to Sister. I said, "Sometimes I wish that Uncle Ralph were here. I'm a grown woman but I still miss him after all these years."

Sister nodded her head in agreement. I continued. "He knew so many things. He knew why the sun pours it liquid all over us and why it must do just that. He knew why babes and insects crawl. He knew that we must live beautifully or not live at all."

Sister's eyes were thoughtful, but she waited to speak while I went on. "To live beautifully from day to day is a battle all the way. The things that he knew are so beautiful. And to feel and know that kind of beauty is the reason that we should live at all. Uncle Ralph said so. But now, there is no one who knows what that beauty is or any of the other things that he knew."

Sister pushed back smoky gray wisps of her dark hair. "You do," she pronounced. "And I do, too."

"Why do you suppose he left us like that?" I asked.

"It couldn't be helped," Sister said. "There was a battle on."   160

"I wanted to be one of his warriors," I said with an embarrassed half-smile.

She leaned over and patted my hand. "You are," she said. Then she stood and placed one hand on her bosom and one hand on my arm. "We'll carry on," she said.

I touched her hand resting on my arm. I said, "Sister, tell me again. What is the battle for?"

She looked down toward the fence where a hobo was coming through. We waved at him.

"Beauty," she said to me. "Our battle is for beauty. It's what Uncle   165
Ralph fought for, too. He often said that everyone else just wanted to go to the Moon. But remember, Sister, you and I done been there. Don't forget, after all, we're children of the stars."

Considerations

1. How do Uncle Ralph's visits and his interactions with the narrator and her sister contribute to the way they identify with and see themselves as part of the Pawnee culture?

2. Uncle Ralph announces that he is leaving to become a warrior, but in fact he becomes a hobo. In what ways might the culture of the warrior and the culture of the hobo be related? Explain.

3. Describe the sisters' encounter with the black hobo. What issues are raised by their conversation? What is your response to this conversation?

4. Uncle Ralph says "young people nowadays . . . don't care 'bout nothing that's old" but "just want to go to the Moon" (page 395). What do you think he means? Try applying his comment to a culture to which you belong. Do you agree with him? Explain.

5. At the end of the story, Uncle Ralph asks the narrator, "Do you know who you are?" Write down her response, and then explain your reaction to what she says. What sort of future do you predict for her? Base your prediction on evidence from the story.

AMY TAN (1952–   )

Rules of the Game

Amy Tan was born two and a half years after her parents arrived from China to settle in Oakland, California, and grew up in an Asian-American household. As an adult, she visited China with her mother. After returning, Tan published her first novel, The Joy Luck Club *(1989), which was made into a critically acclaimed film in 1993. "Rules of the Game" appears as a chapter in* The Joy Luck Club.

I was six when my mother taught me the art of invisible strength. It was a strategy for winning arguments, respect from others, and eventually, though neither of us knew it at the time, chess games.

"Bite back your tongue," scolded my mother when I cried loudly, yanking her hand toward the store that sold bags of salted plums. At home, she said, "Wise guy, he not go against wind. In Chinese we say, Come from South, blow with wind—poom!—North will follow. Strongest wind cannot be seen."

The next week I bit back my tongue as we entered the store with the forbidden candies. When my mother finished her shopping, she quietly plucked a small bag of plums from the rack and put it on the counter with the rest of the items.

My mother imparted her daily truths so she could help my older brothers and me rise above our circumstances. We lived in San Francisco's Chinatown. Like most of the other Chinese children who played in the back alleys of restaurants and curio shops, I didn't think we were poor. My bowl was always full, three five-course meals every day, beginning with a soup full of mysterious things I didn't want to know the names of.

We lived on Waverly Place, in a warm, clean, two-bedroom flat that   5
sat above a small Chinese bakery specializing in steamed pastries and dim sum. In the early morning, when the alley was still quiet, I could smell fragrant red beans as they were cooked down to a pasty sweetness. By daybreak, our flat was heavy with the odor of fried sesame balls and sweet curried chicken crescents. From my bed, I would listen as my father got ready for work, then locked the door behind him, one-two-three clicks.

At the end of our two-block alley was a small sandlot playground with swings and slides well-shined down the middle with use. The play area was bordered by wood-slat benches where old-country people sat cracking roasted watermelon seeds with their golden teeth and scattering the husks to an impatient gathering of gurgling pigeons. The best playground, however, was the dark alley itself. It was crammed with daily mysteries and adventures. My brothers and I would peer into the medicinal herb shop, watching old Li dole out onto a stiff sheet of white paper the right amount of insect shells, saffron-colored seeds, and pungent leaves for his ailing customers. It was said that he once cured a woman dying of an ancestral curse that had eluded the best of American doctors. Next to the pharmacy was a printer who specialized in gold-embossed wedding invitations and festive red banners.

Farther down the street was Ping Yuen Fish Market. The front window displayed a tank crowded with doomed fish and turtles struggling to gain footing on the slimy green-tiled sides. A hand-written sign informed tourists, "Within this store, is all for food, not for pet." Inside, the butchers with their bloodstained white smocks deftly gutted the fish while customers cried out their orders and shouted, "Give me your freshest," to which the butchers always protested, "All are freshest." On less crowded market days, we would inspect the crates of live frogs and crabs which we were warned not to poke, boxes of dried cuttlefish, and row upon row of iced prawns, squid, and slippery fish. The sanddabs made me shiver each time; their eyes lay on one flattened side and reminded me of my mother's story of a careless girl who ran into a crowded street and was crushed by a cab. "Was smash flat," reported my mother.

At the corner of the alley was Hong Sing's, a four-table café with a recessed stairwell in front that led to a door marked "Tradesmen." My brothers and I believed the bad people emerged from this door at night. Tourists never went to Hong Sing's, since the menu was printed only in Chinese. A Caucasian man with a big camera once posed me and my playmates in front of the restaurant. He had us move to the side of the picture window so the photo would capture the roasted duck with its head dangling from a juice-covered rope. After he took the picture, I told him he should go into Hong Sing's and eat dinner. When he smiled and asked me what they served, I shouted, "Guts and duck's feet and octopus gizzards!" Then I ran off with my friends, shrieking with laughter as we scampered across the alley and hid in the entryway grotto of the China Gem Company, my heart pounding with hope that he would chase us.

My mother named me after the street that we lived on: Waverly Place Jong, my official name for important American documents. But my family called me Meimei, "Little Sister." I was the youngest, the only daughter. Each morning before school, my mother would twist and yank on my thick black hair until she had formed two tightly wound pigtails. One day, as she struggled to weave a hard-toothed comb through my disobedient hair, I had a sly thought.

I asked her, "Ma, what is Chinese torture?" My mother shook her head. A bobby pin was wedged between her lips. She wetted her palm and smoothed the hair above my ear, then pushed the pin in so that it nicked sharply against my scalp.

"Who say this word?" she asked without a trace of knowing how wicked I was being. I shrugged my shoulders and said, "Some boy in my class said Chinese people do Chinese torture."

"Chinese people do many things," she said simply. "Chinese people do business, do medicine, do painting. Not lazy like American people. We do torture. Best torture."

10

My older brother Vincent was the one who actually got the chess set. We had gone to the annual Christmas party held at the First Chinese Baptist Church at the end of the alley. The missionary ladies had put together a Santa bag of gifts donated by members of another church. None of the gifts had names on them. There were separate sacks for boys and girls of different ages.

One of the Chinese parishioners had donned a Santa Claus costume and a stiff paper beard with cotton balls glued to it. I think the only children who thought he was the real thing were too young to know that Santa Claus was not Chinese. When my turn came up, the Santa man asked me how old I was. I thought it was a trick question; I was seven according to the American formula and eight by the Chinese calendar. I said I was born on March 17, 1951. That seemed to satisfy him. He then solemnly asked if I had been a very, very good girl this year and did I believe in Jesus Christ and obey my parents. I knew the only answer to that. I nodded back with equal solemnity.

Having watched the other children opening their gifts, I already knew   15
that the big gifts were not necessarily the nicest ones. One girl my age got a large coloring book of biblical characters, while a less greedy girl who selected a smaller box received a glass vial of lavender toilet water. The sound of the box was also important. A ten-year-old boy had chosen a box that jangled when he shook it. It was a tin globe of the world with a slit for inserting money. He must have thought it was full of dimes and nickels, because when he saw that it had just ten pennies, his face fell with such undisguised disappointment that his mother slapped the side of his head and led him out of the church hall, apologizing to the crowd for her son who had such bad manners he couldn't appreciate such a fine gift.

As I peered into the sack, I quickly fingered the remaining presents, testing their weight, imagining what they contained. I chose a heavy, compact one that was wrapped in shiny silver foil and a red satin ribbon. It was a twelve-pack of Life Savers and I spent the rest of the party arranging and rearranging the candy tubes in the order of my favorites. My brother Winston chose wisely as well. His present turned out to be a box of intricate plastic parts; the instructions on the box proclaimed that when they were properly assembled he would have an authentic miniature replica of a World War II submarine.

Vincent got the chess set, which would have been a very decent present to get at a church Christmas party, except it was obviously used and, as we discovered later, it was missing a black pawn and a white knight. My mother graciously thanked the unknown benefactor, saying, "Too good. Cost too much." At which point, an old lady with fine white, wispy hair nodded toward our family and said with a whistling whisper, "Merry, merry Christmas."

When we got home, my mother told Vincent to throw the chess set away. "She not want it. We not want it," she said, tossing her head stiffly to the side with a tight, proud smile. My brothers had deaf ears. They were already lining up the chess pieces and reading from the dog-eared instruction book.

I watched Vincent and Winston play during Christmas week. The chessboard seemed to hold elaborate secrets waiting to be untangled. The chessmen were more powerful than old Li's magic herbs that cured ancestral curses. And my brothers wore such serious faces that I was sure something was at stake that was greater than avoiding the tradesmen's door to Hong Sing's.

"Let me! Let me!" I begged between games when one brother or the   20
other would sit back with a deep sigh of relief and victory, the other annoyed, unable to let go of the outcome. Vincent at first refused to let me play, but when I offered my Life Savers as replacements for the buttons that filled in for the missing pieces, he relented. He chose the flavors: wild cherry for the black pawn and peppermint for the white knight. Winner could eat both.

As our mother sprinkled flour and rolled out small doughy circles for the steamed dumplings that would be our dinner that night, Vincent explained the rules, pointing to each piece. "You have sixteen pieces and so do I. One king and queen, two bishops, two knights, two castles, and eight pawns. The pawns can only move forward one step, except on the first move. Then they can move two. But they can only take men by moving crossways like this, except in the beginning, when you can move ahead and take another pawn."

"Why?" I asked as I moved my pawn. "Why can't they move more steps?"

"Because they're pawns," he said.

"But why do they go crossways to take other men? Why aren't there any women and children?"

"Why is the sky blue? Why must you always ask stupid questions?"   25
asked Vincent. "This is a game. These are the rules. I didn't make them up. See. Here. In the book." He jabbed a page with a pawn in his hand. "Pawn. P-A-W-N. Pawn. Read it yourself."

My mother patted the flour off her hands. "Let me see book," she said quietly. She scanned the pages quickly, not reading the foreign English symbols, seeming to search deliberately for nothing in particular.

"This American rules," she concluded at last. "Every time people come out from foreign country, must know rules. You not know, judge say, Too bad, go back. They not telling you why so you can use their way go forward. They say, Don't know why, you find out yourself. But they knowing all the time. Better you take it, find out why yourself." She tossed her head back with a satisfied smile.

I found out about all the whys later. I read the rules and looked up all the big words in a dictionary. I borrowed books from the Chinatown library. I studied each chess piece, trying to absorb the power each contained.

I learned about opening moves and why it's important to control the center early on; the shortest distance between two points is straight down the middle. I learned about the middle game and why tactics between two adversaries are like clashing ideas; the one who plays better has the clearest plans for both attacking and getting out of traps. I learned why it is essential in the endgame to have foresight, a mathematical understanding of all possible moves, and patience; all weaknesses and advantages become evident to a strong adversary and are obscured to a tiring opponent. I discovered that for the whole game one must gather invisible strengths and see the endgame before the game begins.

I also found out why I should never reveal "why" to others. A little   30
knowledge withheld is a great advantage one should store for future use.
That is the power of chess. It is a game of secrets in which one must show
and never tell.

I loved the secrets I found within the sixty-four black and white
squares. I carefully drew a handmade chessboard and pinned it to the wall
next to my bed, where at night I would stare for hours at imaginary battles.
Soon I no longer lost any games or Life Savers, but I lost my adversaries.
Winston and Vincent decided they were more interested in roaming the
streets after school in their Hopalong Cassidy cowboy hats.

On a cold spring afternoon, while walking home from school, I detoured through the playground at the end of our alley. I saw a group of old men, two seated across a folding table playing a game of chess, others smoking pipes, eating peanuts, and watching. I ran home and grabbed Vincent's chess set, which was bound in a cardboard box with rubber bands. I also carefully selected two prized rolls of Life Savers. I came back to the park and approached a man who was observing the game.

"Want to play?" I asked him. His face widened with surprise and he grinned as he looked at the box under my arm.

"Little sister, been a long time since I play with dolls," he said, smiling benevolently. I quickly put the box down next to him on the bench and displayed my retort.

Lau Po, as he allowed me to call him, turned out to be a much better   35
player than my brothers. I lost many games and many Life Savers. But over the weeks, with each diminishing roll of candies, I added new secrets. Lau Po gave me the names. The Double Attack from the East and West Shores. Throwing Stones on the Drowning Man. The Sudden Meeting of the Clan. The Surprise from the Sleeping Guard. The Humble Servant Who Kills the King. Sand in the Eyes of Advancing Forces. A Double Killing Without Blood.

There were also the fine points of chess etiquette. Keep captured men in neat rows, as well-tended prisoners. Never announce "Check" with vanity, lest someone with an unseen sword slit your throat. Never hurl pieces into the sandbox after you have lost a game, because then you must find them again, by yourself, after apologizing to all around you. By the end of the summer, Lau Po had taught me all he knew, and I had become a better chess player.

A small weekend crowd of Chinese people and tourists would gather as I played and defeated my opponents one by one. My mother would join the crowds during these outdoor exhibition games. She sat proudly on the bench, telling my admirers with proper Chinese humility, "Is luck."

A man who watched me play in the park suggested that my mother allow me to play in local chess tournaments. My mother smiled graciously, an answer that meant nothing. I desperately wanted to go, but I bit back my tongue. I knew she would not let me play among strangers. So as we walked home I said in a small voice that I didn't want to play in the local tournament. They would have American rules. If I lost, I would bring shame on my family.

"Is shame you fall down nobody push you," said my mother.

During my first tournament, my mother sat with me in the front row 40 as I waited for my turn. I frequently bounced my legs to unstick them from the cold metal seat of the folding chair. When my name was called, I leapt up. My mother unwrapped something in her lap. It was her *chang,* a small tablet of red jade which held the sun's fire. "Is luck," she whispered, and tucked it into my dress pocket. I turned to my opponent, a fifteen-year-old boy from Oakland. He looked at me, wrinkling his nose.

As I began to play, the boy disappeared, the color ran out of the room, and I saw only my white pieces and his black ones waiting on the other side. A light wind began blowing past my ears. It whispered secrets only I could hear.

"Blow from the South," it murmured. "The wind leaves no trail." I saw a clear path, the traps to avoid. The crowd rustled. "Shhh! Shhh!" said the corners of the room. The wind blew stronger. "Throw sand from the East to distract him." The knight came forward ready for the sacrifice. The wind hissed, louder and louder. "Blow, blow, blow. He cannot see. He is blind now. Make him lean away from the wind so he is easier to knock down."

"Check," I said, as the wind roared with laughter. The wind died down to little puffs, my own breath.

My mother placed my first trophy next to a new plastic chess set that the neighborhood Tao society had given to me. As she wiped each piece with a soft cloth, she said, "Next time win more, lose less."

"Ma, it's not how many pieces you lose," I said. "Sometimes you need 45 to lose pieces to get ahead."

"Better to lose less, see if you really need."

At the next tournament, I won again, but it was my mother who wore the triumphant grin.

"Lost eight piece this time. Last time was eleven. What I tell you? Better off lose less!" I was annoyed, but I couldn't say anything.

I attended more tournaments, each one farther away from home. I won all games, in all divisions. The Chinese bakery downstairs from our flat displayed my growing collection of trophies in its window, amidst the dust-covered cakes that were never picked up. The day after I won an important regional tournament, the window encased a fresh sheet cake with whipped-cream frosting and red script saying "Congratulations, Waverly Jong, Chinatown Chess Champion." Soon after that, a flower shop, headstone engraver, and funeral parlor offered to sponsor me in national tournaments. That's when my mother decided I no longer had to do the dishes. Winston and Vincent had to do my chores.

"Why does she get to play and we do all the work," complained 50
Vincent.

"Is new American rules," said my mother. "Meimei play, squeeze all her brains out for win chess. You play, worth squeeze towel."

By my ninth birthday, I was a national chess champion. I was still some 429 points away from grand-master status, but I was touted as the Great American Hope, a child prodigy and a girl to boot. They ran a photo of me in *Life* magazine next to a quote in which Bobby Fischer said, "There will never be a woman grand master." "Your move, Bobby," said the caption.

The day they took the magazine picture I wore neatly plaited braids clipped with plastic barrettes trimmed with rhinestones. I was playing in a large high school auditorium that echoed with phlegmy coughs and the squeaky rubber knobs of chair legs sliding across freshly waxed wooden floors. Seated across from me was an American man, about the same age as Lau Po, maybe fifty. I remember that his sweaty brow seemed to weep at my every move. He wore a dark, malodorous suit. One of his pockets was stuffed with a great white kerchief on which he wiped his palm before sweeping his hand over the chosen chess piece with great flourish.

In my crisp pink-and-white dress with scratchy lace at the neck, one of two my mother had sewn for these special occasions, I would clasp my hands under my chin, the delicate points of my elbows poised lightly on the table in the manner my mother had shown me for posing for the press. I would swing my patent leather shoes back and forth like an impatient child riding on a school bus. Then I would pause, suck in my lips, twirl my chosen piece in midair as if undecided, and then firmly plant it in its new threatening place, with a triumphant smile thrown back at my opponent for good measure.

I no longer played in the alley of Waverly Place. I never visited the 55
playground where the pigeons and old men gathered. I went to school, then directly home to learn new chess secrets, cleverly concealed advantages, more escape routes.

But I found it difficult to concentrate at home. My mother had a habit of standing over me while I plotted out my games. I think she thought of herself as my protective ally. Her lips would be sealed tight, and after each move I made, a soft "Hmmmmph" would escape from her nose.

"Ma, I can't practice when you stand there like that," I said one day. She retreated to the kitchen and made loud noises with the pots and pans.

When the crashing stopped, I could see out of the corner of my eye that she was standing in the doorway. "Hmmmph!" Only this one came out of her tight throat.

My parents made many concessions to allow me to practice. One time I complained that the bedroom I shared was so noisy that I couldn't think. Thereafter, my brothers slept in a bed in the living room facing the street. I said I couldn't finish my rice; my head didn't work right when my stomach was too full. I left the table with half-finished bowls and nobody complained. But there was one duty I couldn't avoid. I had to accompany my mother on Saturday market days when I had no tournament to play. My mother would proudly walk with me, visiting many shops, buying very little. "This my daughter Wave-ly Jong," she said to whoever looked her way.

One day after we left a shop I said under my breath, "I wish you wouldn't do that, telling everybody I'm your daughter." My mother stopped walking. Crowds of people with heavy bags pushed past us on the sidewalk, bumping into first one shoulder, then another.

"Aiii-ya. So shame be with mother?" She grasped my hand even tighter   60
as she glared at me.

I looked down. "It's not that, it's just so obvious. It's just so embar-rassing."

"Embarrass you be my daughter?" Her voice was cracking with anger.

"That's not what I meant. That's not what I said."

"What you say?"

I knew it was a mistake to say anything more, but I heard my voice   65
speaking, "Why do you have to use me to show off? If you want to show off, then why don't you learn to play chess?"

My mother's eyes turned into dangerous black slits. She had no words for me, just sharp silence.

I felt the wind rushing around my hot ears. I jerked my hand out of my mother's tight grasp and spun around, knocking into an old woman. Her bag of groceries spilled to the ground.

"Aii-ya! Stupid girl!" my mother and the woman cried. Oranges and tin cans careened down the sidewalk. As my mother stooped to help the old woman pick up the escaping food, I took off.

I raced down the street, dashing between people, not looking back as my mother screamed shrilly, "Meimei! Meimei!" I fled down an alley, past dark, curtained shops and merchants washing the grime off their windows. I sped into the sunlight, into a large street crowded with tourists examining trinkets and souvenirs. I ducked into another dark alley, down another street, up another alley. I ran until it hurt and I realized I had nowhere to go, that I was not running from anything. The alleys contained no escape routes.

My breath came out like angry smoke. It was cold. I sat down on an   70
upturned plastic pail next to a stack of empty boxes, cupping my chin with my hands, thinking hard. I imagined my mother, first walking briskly down

one street or another looking for me, then giving up and returning home to await my arrival. After two hours, I stood up on creaking legs and slowly walked home.

The alley was quiet and I could see the yellow lights shining from our flat like two tiger's eyes in the night. I climbed the sixteen steps to the door, advancing quietly up each so as not to make any warning sounds. I turned the knob; the door was locked. I heard a chair moving, quick steps, the locks turning—click! click! click!—and then the door opened.

"About time you got home," said Vincent. "Boy, are you in trouble."

He slid back to the dinner table. On a platter were the remains of a large fish, its fleshy head still connected to bones swimming upstream in vain escape. Standing there waiting for my punishment, I heard my mother speak in a dry voice.

"We not concerning this girl. This girl not have concerning for us."

Nobody looked at me. Bone chopsticks clinked against the inside of 75 bowls being emptied into hungry mouths.

I walked into my room, closed the door, and lay down on my bed. The room was dark, the ceiling filled with shadows from the dinnertime lights of neighboring flats.

In my head, I saw a chessboard with sixty-four black and white squares. Opposite me was my opponent, two angry black slits. She wore a triumphant smile. "Strongest wind cannot be seen," she said.

Her black men advanced across the plane, slowly marching to each successive level as a single unit. My white pieces screamed as they scurried and fell off the board one by one. As her men drew closer to my edge, I felt myself growing light. I rose up into the air and flew out the window. Higher and higher, above the alley, over the tops of tiled roofs, where I was gathered up by the wind and pushed up toward the night sky until everything below me disappeared and I was alone.

I closed my eyes and pondered my next move.

Considerations

1. How does the game of chess relate to the identity that Waverly's mother dreams of for her daughter? Consider especially the first sentence of the story as you address this topic.
2. Describe the changes Waverly goes through as she becomes adept at chess. How do her relationships with her family, her friends, and her opponents evolve? Do you see these changes as positive or negative? Explain.
3. Consider the theme of competition as part of identity. How does Waverly react to competition? How does her mother react to competition? Do you see Waverly and her mother as mainly similar to or mainly different from each other? Explain.

4. Who is the opponent Waverly faces in the final, imagined chess game of the story? What does the opponent mean when she says, "Strongest wind cannot be seen"? How does her pronouncement relate to the themes of the story?
5. Compare Waverly's relationship with her mother to the relationship between the narrator and her mother in "The Circling Hand" (page 181). How do the relationships seem to reflect the different cultures of the two mother–daughter pairs? How do the relationships seem to be similar in ways that transcend the distinctions of culture?

WILLIAM WORDSWORTH (1770–1850)

The world is too much with us

> *William Wordsworth grew up in the Lake District of northern England and was educated at Cambridge University. His poems often demonstrate his complex understanding of human nature and his longing to shun anything that he saw as devaluing the relationship between humans and their natural environment.*

The world is too much with us; late and soon,
Getting and spending, we lay waste our powers;
Little we see in Nature that is ours;
We have given our hearts away, a sordid boon!
This Sea that bares her bosom to the moon,   5
The winds that will be howling at all hours,
And are up-gathered now like sleeping flowers,
For this, for everything, we are out of tune;
It moves us not.—Great God! I'd rather be
A Pagan suckled in a creed outworn;   10
So might I, standing on this pleasant lea,
Have glimpses that would make me less forlorn;
Have sight of Proteus° rising from the sea;
Or hear old Triton° blow his wreathéd horn.

13 *Proteus:* Sea god who could change his appearance. 14 *Triton:* Sea god with the upper body of a man and the lower body of a fish. He used a conch shell as a horn.

Considerations

1. What are the two cultures described by the speaker? What is his evaluation of each culture?

2. Paraphrase the first three lines of the poem. To what extent do you believe these lines ring true today?
3. The speaker in this poem envisions himself as part of a culture that is different from the one to which he belongs. He imagines himself more comfortable in this distant and ancient culture. Write a description in which you imagine yourself as part of a different culture that might bring you "glimpses that would make [you] less forlorn." Explain.

PAUL LAURENCE DUNBAR (1872–1906)

We wear the mask

Paul Laurence Dunbar was born in Dayton, Ohio, to parents who were for-mer slaves. His first collection of poetry, Oak and Ivy, *was published in 1893. Dunbar's poems often address the themes of culture and race, and his works include traditional rhythms and forms as well as experimental rhythms that incorporate black dialect.*

We wear the mask that grins and lies,
It hides our cheeks and shades our eyes—
This debt we pay to human guile;
With torn and bleeding hearts we smile,
And mouth with myriad subtleties.   5

Why should the world be over-wise,
In counting all our tears and sighs?
Nay, let them only see us, while
   We wear the mask.

We smile, but, O great Christ, our cries   10
To thee from tortured souls arise.
We sing, but oh the clay is vile
Beneath our feet, and long the mile;
But let the world dream otherwise,
   We wear the mask!   15

Considerations

1. The speaker suggests that we all wear masks and that these masks serve a purpose. Do you see this purpose as positive? Explain.
2. Do you agree that nearly everyone wears masks? If so, do you believe that you and other people wear the same mask throughout life or change them? Explain.

3. Do you think that the concept of wearing masks is related to one's cultural identity? Explain, using examples from the poem as well as from your own observations and experiences.

T. S. ELIOT (1888–1965)

Journey of the Magi

> Born in the United States, Thomas Stearns Eliot pursued graduate study in Paris and England and in 1927 became a naturalized British citizen. He believed strongly in the importance of understanding the traditions and myths that underlie one's culture.

'A cold coming we had of it,
Just the worst time of the year
For a journey, and such a long journey:
The ways deep and the weather sharp,
The very dead of winter.'   5
And the camels galled, sore-footed, refractory,
Lying down in the melting snow.
There were times we regretted
The summer palaces on slopes, the terraces,
And the silken girls bringing sherbet.   10
Then the camel men cursing and grumbling
And running away, and wanting their liquor and women,
And the night-fires going out, and the lack of shelters,
And the cities hostile and the towns unfriendly
And the villages dirty and charging high prices: 15
A hard time we had of it.
At the end we preferred to travel all night,
Sleeping in snatches,
With the voices singing in our ears, saying
That this was all folly.   20

Then at dawn we came down to a temperate valley,
Wet, below the snow line, smelling of vegetation;
With a running stream and a water-mill beating the darkness,
And three trees on the low sky,
And an old white horse galloped away in the meadow.   25
Then we came to a tavern with vine-leaves over the lintel,
Six hands at an open door dicing for pieces of silver,
And feet kicking the empty wine-skins.
But there was no information, and so we continued

And arrived at evening, not a moment too soon   30
Finding the place; it was (you may say) satisfactory.

All this was a long time ago, I remember,
And I would do it again, but set down
This set down
This: were we led all that way for   35
Birth or Death? There was a Birth, certainly,
We had evidence and no doubt. I had seen birth and death,
But had thought they were different; this Birth was
Hard and bitter agony for us, like Death, our death.
We returned to our places, these Kingdoms,   40
But no longer at ease here, in the old dispensation,
With an alien people clutching their gods.
I should be glad of another death.

Considerations

1. Read the account of Jesus' birth and the attendance of the Wise Men (the Magi) in the New Testament books of Matthew and Mark. How do these accounts compare with the view of that event suggested by "Journey of the Magi"?
2. Imagine yourself as one of the Magi. (Read biblical accounts of Jesus' birth for background information.) Write a memoir explaining your response to the events in Bethlehem.
3. How might readers from different religious cultures respond to this poem? Ask four people, two who are active members of Christian denominations and two who are active members of other religious cultures, to read this poem. Then interview them to learn their responses.

WILLIAM BUTLER YEATS (1865–1939)

The Lake Isle of Innisfree

> *Born and raised in Ireland, William Butler Yeats wrote many poems and plays that reflect his connection with the history and culture of his native country. Yeats's achievement as a poet was recognized in 1923, when he won the Nobel Prize for literature. "The Lake Isle of Innisfree" comes from the collection* The Rose, *which was published in 1893, when Yeats was not yet thirty.*

I will arise and go now, and go to Innisfree,
And a small cabin build there, of clay and wattles made:
Nine bean-rows will I have there, a hive for the honey-bee.
And live alone in the bee-loud glade.

And I shall have some peace there, for peace comes dropping slow   5
Dropping from the veils of the morning to where the cricket sings;
There midnight's all a glimmer, and noon a purple glow,
And evening full of the linnet's wings.

I will arise and go now, for always night and day
I hear lake water lapping with low sounds by the shore;   10
While I stand on the roadway, or on the pavements grey,
I hear it in the deep heart's core.

Considerations

1. List several images the speaker provides to describe his ideal refuge at Innisfree. What qualities of life do these images suggest?
2. Describe your own ideal refuge, the one you can imagine as solace when you "stand on the roadway" or "on the pavements grey."
3. How does love of a particular place relate to the understanding of one's roots, culture, and identity? Refer to your own observations and experiences as well as to those of the speaker in the poem.

WOLE SOYINKA (1934–   )

Telephone Conversation

> *Born in Nigeria and educated at Leeds College in England, Wole Soyinka integrates his tribal and European cultures in his works. A diverse writer, Soyinka is an acclaimed poet, novelist, playwright, translator, and essayist. "Telephone Conversation" was first published in 1960.*

The price seemed reasonable, location
Indifferent. The landlady swore she lived
Off premises. Nothing remained
But self-confession. 'Madam,' I warned,
'I hate a wasted journey—I am African.'   5
Silence. Silenced transmission of

Pressurized good-breeding. Voice, when it came,
Lipstick coated, long gold-rolled
Cigarette-holder pipped. Caught I was, foully.
'HOW DARK?' . . . I had not misheard. . . . 'ARE YOU LIGHT   10
OR VERY DARK?' Button B. Button A. Stench
Of rancid breath of public hide-and-speak.
Red booth. Red pillar-box. Red double-tiered
Omnibus squelching tar. It *was* real! Shamed
By ill-mannered silence, surrender   15
Pushed dumbfoundment to beg simplification.
Considerate she was, varying the emphasis—
'ARE YOU DARK? OR VERY LIGHT?' Revelation came.
'You mean—like plain or milk chocolate?'
Her assent was clinical, crushing in its light   20
Impersonality. Rapidly, wave-length adjusted.
I chose. 'West African sepia'—and as afterthought,
'Down in my passport.' Silence for spectroscopic
Flight of fancy, till truthfulness clanged her accent
Hard on the mouthpiece. 'WHAT'S THAT?' conceding   25
'DON'T KNOW WHAT THAT IS.' 'Like brunette.'
'THAT'S DARK, ISN'T IT?' 'Not altogether.
Facially, I am brunette, but madam, you should see
The rest of me. Palm of my hand, soles of my feet
Are a peroxide blonde. Friction, caused—   30
Foolishly madam—by sitting down, has turned
My bottom raven black—One moment madam!'—sensing
Her receiver rearing on the thunderclap
About my ears—'Madam,' I pleaded, 'wouldn't you rather
See for yourself?'   35

Considerations

1. What cultural expectations, both on the part of the speaker and on the part of the prospective landlady, does this telephone conversation suggest?
2. Write a dialogue (or monologue) in which the landlady describes this telephone encounter to a friend. What are her fears? What are her concerns? How does she explain and justify her responses?
3. How might this encounter have differed if the speaker had applied for the room in person? Write a dialogue describing this encounter, perhaps in poetic form, similar to Soyinka's original poem.

MARI EVANS (1923–   )

I Am a Black Woman

Born in Toledo, Ohio, Mari Evans is a professor at the University of Toledo, where she holds the title of Distinguished Writer-in-Residence. Deeply concerned with the public role of the poet, she has stated, "I understand that Black writers have a responsibility to use the language in the manner it is and always has been used by non-Black writers and by the State itself: as a political force."

I am a black woman
the music of my song
some sweet arpeggio of tears
is written in a minor key
and I   5
can be heard humming in the night
Can be heard
                humming
in the night

I saw my mate leap screaming to the sea   10
and I/with these hands/cupped the lifebreath
from my issue in the canebrake
I lost Nat's swinging body in a rain of tears
and heard my son scream all the way from Anzio
for Peace he never knew. . . . I   15
learned Da Nang and Pork Chop Hill
in anguish
Now my nostrils know the gas
and these trigger tire/d fingers
seek the softness in my warrior's beard   20

I
am a black woman
tall as a cypress
strong
beyond all definition still   25
defying place
and time
and circumstance
    assailed
        impervious   30
            indestructible
Look
    on me and be
renewed

CATHY SONG (1955–   )

The Youngest Daughter

> *Cathy Song was born in Honolulu, Hawaii, to a Chinese mother and Korean father. As "The Youngest Daughter" (from* Picture Bride, *1983) demonstrates, many of her poems balance themes of commitment to family and tradition with the theme of commitment to oneself.*

The sky has been dark
for many years.
My skin has become as damp
and pale as rice paper
and feels the way   5
mother's used to before the drying sun
parched it out there in the fields.

    Lately, when I touch my eyelids,
my hands react as if
I had just touched something   10
hot enough to burn.
My skin, aspirin colored,
tingles with migraine. Mother
has been massaging the left side of my face
especially in the evenings   15
when the pain flares up.

This morning
her breathing was graveled,
her voice gruff with affection
when I wheeled her into the bath.   20
She was in a good humor,
making jokes about her great breasts,
floating in the milky water
like two walruses,
flaccid and whiskered around the nipples.   25
I scrubbed them with a sour taste
in my mouth, thinking:
six children and an old man
have sucked from these brown nipples.

I was almost tender   30
when I came to the blue bruises
that freckle her body,
places where she has been injecting insulin

for thirty years. I soaped her slowly,
she sighed deeply, her eyes closed.   35
It seems it has always
been like this: the two of us
in this sunless room,
the splashing of the bathwater.

In the afternoons   40
when she has rested,
she prepares our ritual of tea and rice,
garnished with a shred of gingered fish,
a slice of pickled turnip,
a token for my white body.   45
We eat in the familiar silence.
She knows I am not to be trusted,
even now planning my escape.
As I toast to her health
with the tea she has poured,   50
a thousand cranes curtain the window,
fly up in a sudden breeze.

WENDY ROSE (1948–   )

I Expected My Skin and My Blood to Ripen

*Wendy Rose, a Hopi, was born in California. She has taught ethnic studies
and Native American studies and has served as the coordinator of the American Indian Studies Program at Fresno City College, California. Her poetry
often provides a connection between the ancient stories of her heritage and modern literary culture. "I Expected My Skin and My Blood to Ripen" comes
from* Academic Squaw: Reports to the World from the Ivory Tower"
(1977).

"When the blizzard subsided four days later (after the massacre), a
burial party was sent to Wounded Knee. A long trench was dug.
Many of the bodies were stripped by whites who went out in order
to get the ghost shirts and other accoutrements the Indians wore . . .
the frozen bodies were thrown into the trench stiff and naked . . .
only a handful of items remain in private hands . . . exposure to
snow has stiffened the leggings and moccasins, and all the objects
show the effects of age and long use. . . ." There follows: moccasins
at $140, hide scraper at $350, buckskin shirt at $1200, woman's
leggings at $275, bone breastplate at $1000.
                    Plains Indian Art: Sales Catalog by Kenneth Canfield, 1977

I expected my skin and my blood
to ripen
not be ripped from my bones;
like green fruit I am peeled
tasted, discarded; my seeds are stepped on   5
and crushed
as if there were no future. Now
there has been
no past.   My own body gave up the beads
my own arms handed the babies away   10
to be strung on bayonets, to be counted
one by one like rosary stones and then
to be tossed to each side of life
as if the pain of their borning
had never been.   15
My feet were frozen to the leather,
pried apart, left behind—bits of flesh
on the moccasins, bits of papery deerhide
on the bones. My back was stripped
of its cover, its quilling intact; was torn,   20
was taken away, was restored.
My leggings were taken like in a rape
and shriveled to the size of stick figures
like they had never felt
the push of my strong woman's body   25
walking in the hills.
It was my own baby whose cradleboard I held.
Would've put her in my mouth
like a snake
if I could, would've turned her   30
into a bush or old rock
if there'd been enough magic
to work such changes. Not enough magic
even to stop the bullets.
Not enough magic   35
to stop the scientists.
Not enough magic
to stop the collectors.

MEI-MEI BERSSENBRUGGE (1947–   )

Chronicle

Born in Peking, Mei-Mei Berssenbrugge now lives in New Mexico, where she works full time as a writer. "Chronicle" first appeared in Summits Move with the Tide *in* The Greenfield Review *(1974).*

I was born the year of the loon
in a great commotion. My mother—
who used to pack $500 cash
in the shoulders of her fur gambling coat,
who had always considered herself   5
the family's "First Son"—
took one look at me
and lit out again
for a vacation to Sumatra.
Her brother purchased my baby clothes;   10
I've seen them, little clown suits
of silk and color.

Each day
my Chinese grandmother bathed me
with elaboration in an iron tub;   15
amahs waiting in lines
with sterilized water and towels
clucked and smiled
and rushed about the tall stone room
in tiny slippers.   20

After my grandfather
accustomed himself
to this betrayal by First Son,
he would take me in his arms,
walk with me   25
by the plum trees, cherries, persimmons;
he showed me the stiff robes
of my ancestors and their drafty hall,
the long beards of his learned old friends,
and his crickets.   30

Grandfather talked to me, taught me.
At two months, my mother tells me,
I could sniff for flowers,
stab my small hand upwards to moon.

Even today I get proud   35
when I remember
this all took place in Chinese.

JUDITH ORTIZ COFER (1952–   )

Latin Women Pray

> Born in Puerto Rico, Judith Ortiz Cofer spent her early years moving from
> place to place in Puerto Rico and the mainland United States in accordance
> with the orders received by her father, a career officer in the United States
> Navy. Because of these moves, she attended school in many different cultural
> environments, eventually earning a master's degree in English from the Univer-
> sity of Florida and pursuing further graduate work at Oxford University in
> England. "Latin Women Pray" is from Triple Crown (1987).

Latin women pray
In incense sweet churches
They pray in Spanish to an Anglo God
With a Jewish heritage.
And this Great White Father   5
Imperturbable in his marble pedestal
Looks down upon his brown daughters
Votive candles shining like lust
In his all seeing eyes
Unmoved by their persistent prayers.   10

Yet year after year
Before his image they kneel
Margarita Josefina Maria and Isabel
All fervently hoping
That if not omnipotent   15
At least he be bilingual

SOPHOCLES (c. 496–406 B.C.)

Oedipus Rex

Born at Colonus, a village near Athens, Sophocles grew to be a handsome young man who was often chosen to lead the chorus at major festivals because of his attractive appearance and graceful dramatic performance. In the traditional Athenian spring drama competition in 468 B.C., Sophocles, at age 28, submitted a tragedy that triumphed over the play submitted by Aeschylus, the playwright favored to win. Sophocles' victory was attributed in part to his willingness to take risks and to break old conventions: until the 468 B.C. competition, tragedies were written so that no more than two actors appeared on stage at the same time; Sophocles, however, added a third. During his lifetime, Sophocles—who lived for nearly a century—saw the Greeks rise to power over the Persian Empire. Toward the end of his life, however, Athenian power declined. Sophocles, unlike his native country, maintained his power until the end of his life. He wrote more than 120 plays, including seven that remain today: Ajax, Antigone, Oedipus Rex, Electra, Philoctetes, The Trachinian Women, and his final play, Oedipus at Colonus, which was written when Sophocles was nearly 90.

Characters

OEDIPUS, *King of Thebes, supposed son of Polybos and Merope, King and*
   Queen of Corinth
IOKASTE, *wife of Oedipus and widow of the late King Laios*
KREON, *brother of Iokaste, a prince of Thebes*
TEIRESIAS, *a blind seer who serves Apollo*
PRIEST
MESSENGER, *from Corinth*
SHEPHERD, *former servant of Laios*
SECOND MESSENGER, *from the palace*
CHORUS OF THEBAN ELDERS
CHORAGOS, *leader of the Chorus*
ANTIGONE and ISMENE, *young daughters of Oedipus and Iokaste. They*
   appear in the Exodos but do not speak.
SUPPLIANTS, GUARDS, SERVANTS

Scene *Before the palace of Oedipus, King of Thebes. A central door and two lateral doors open onto a platform which runs the length of the facade. On the platform, right and left, are altars; and three steps lead down into the orchestra, or chorus-ground. At the beginning of the action these steps are crowded by suppliants who have brought branches and chaplets of olive leaves and who sit in various attitudes of despair. Oedipus enters.*

PROLOGUE

OEDIPUS: My children, generations of the living
　　　　In the line of Kadmos,° nursed at his ancient hearth:
　　　　Why have you strewn yourselves before these altars
　　　　In supplication, with your boughs and garlands?
　　　　The breath of incense rises from the city   5
　　　　With a sound of prayer and lamentation.
　　　　　　　　　　　　　　　　　　　　Children,
　　　　I would not have you speak through messengers,
　　　　And therefore I have come myself to hear you—
　　　　I, Oedipus, who bear the famous name.
　　　　(To a PRIEST.) You, there, since you are eldest in the company,   10
　　　　Speak for them all, tell me what preys upon you,
　　　　Whether you come in dread, or crave some blessing:
　　　　Tell me, and never doubt that I will help you
　　　　In every way I can; I should be heartless
　　　　Were I not moved to find you suppliant here.   15
PRIEST: Great Oedipus, O powerful king of Thebes!
　　　　You see how all the ages of our people
　　　　Cling to your altar steps: here are boys
　　　　Who can barely stand alone, and here are priests
　　　　By weight of age, as I am a priest of God,   20
　　　　And young men chosen from those yet unmarried;
　　　　As for the others, all that multitude,
　　　　They wait with olive chaplets in the squares,
　　　　At the two shrines of Pallas,° and where Apollo°
　　　　Speaks in the glowing embers.
　　　　　　　　　　　　　　　　　　Your own eyes   25
　　　　Must tell you: Thebes is tossed on a murdering sea
　　　　And can not lift her head from the death surge.
　　　　A rust consumes the buds and fruits of the earth;
　　　　The herds are sick; children die unborn,
　　　　And labor is vain. The god of plague and pyre   30
　　　　Raids like detestable lightning through the city,
　　　　And all the house of Kadmos is laid waste,
　　　　All emptied, and all darkened: Death alone
　　　　Battens upon the misery of Thebes.

　　　　You are not one of the immortal gods, we know;   35
　　　　Yet we have come to you to make our prayer

---

2 *Kadmos*: Founder of Thebes, according to legend. 24 *Pallas*: Pallas Athena, Zeus's daughter; goddess of wisdom; *Apollo*: Zeus's son, god of the sun, truth, and poetry.

As to the man surest in mortal ways
And wisest in the ways of God. You saved us
From the Sphinx,° that flinty singer, and the tribute
We paid to her so long; yet you were never   40
Better informed than we, nor could we teach you:
A god's touch, it seems, enabled you to help us.

Therefore, O mighty power, we turn to you:
Find us our safety, find us a remedy,
Whether by counsel of the gods or of men.   45
A king of wisdom tested in the past
Can act in a time of troubles, and act well.
Noblest of men, restore
Life to your city! Think how all men call you
Liberator for your boldness long ago;   50
Ah, when your years of kingship are remembered,
Let them not say *We rose, but later fell*—
Keep the State from going down in the storm!
Once, years ago, with happy augury,
You brought us fortune; be the same again!   55
No man questions your power to rule the land:
But rule over men, not over a dead city!
Ships are only hulls, high walls are nothing,
When no life moves in the empty passageways.

OEDIPUS: Poor children! You may be sure I know   60
All that you longed for in your coming here.
I know that you are deathly sick; and yet,
Sick as you are, not one is as sick as I.
Each of you suffers in himself alone
His anguish, not another's; but my spirit   65
Groans for the city, for myself, for you.

I was not sleeping, you are not waking me.
No, I have been in tears for a long while
And in my restless thought walked many ways.
In all my search I found one remedy,   70
And I have adopted it: I have sent Kreon,
Son of Menoikeus, brother of the queen,
To Delphi,° Apollo's place of revelation,
To learn there, if he can,

---

39 *Sphinx:* A monster with the body of a lion, the wings of a bird, and the face of a woman. The Sphinx had challenged Thebes with a riddle, killing those who failed to solve it. When Oedipus answered correctly, the Sphinx killed herself. 73 *Delphi:* Location of the prophetic oracle, regarded as the keeper of religious truth.

What act or pledge of mine may save the city.   75
I have counted the days, and now, this very day,
I am troubled, for he has overstayed his time.
What is he doing? He has been gone too long.
Yet whenever he comes back, I should do ill
Not to take any action the god orders.   80
PRIEST: It is a timely promise. At this instant
They tell me Kreon is here.
OEDIPUS: O Lord Apollo!
May his news be fair as his face is radiant!
PRIEST: Good news, I gather! he is crowned with bay,
The chaplet is thick with berries.
OEDIPUS: We shall soon know;   85
He is near enough to hear us now. *(Enter* KREON.*)* O prince:
Brother: son of Menoikeus:
What answer do you bring us from the god?
KREON: A strong one. I can tell you, great afflictions
Will turn out well, if they are taken well.   90
OEDIPUS: What was the oracle? These vague words
Leave me still hanging between hope and fear.
KREON: Is it your pleasure to hear me with all these
Gathered around us? I am prepared to speak,
But should we not go in?
OEDIPUS: Speak to them all,   95
It is for them I suffer, more than for myself.
KREON: Then I will tell you what I heard at Delphi.
In plain words
The god commands us to expel from the land of Thebes
An old defilement we are sheltering.   100
It is a deathly thing, beyond cure;
We must not let it feed upon us longer.
OEDIPUS: What defilement? How shall we rid ourselves of it?
KREON: By exile or death, blood for blood. It was
Murder that brought the plague-wind on the city.   105
OEDIPUS: Murder of whom? Surely the god has named him?
KREON: My Lord: Laios once ruled this land,
Before you came to govern us.
OEDIPUS: I know;
I learned of him from others; I never saw him.
KREON: He was murdered; and Apollo commands us now   110
To take revenge upon whoever killed him.
OEDIPUS: Upon whom? Where are they? Where shall we find a clue
To solve that crime, after so many years?
KREON: Here in this land, he said. Search reveals
Things that escape an inattentive man.   115
OEDIPUS: Tell me: Was Laios murdered in his house,

Or in the fields, or in some foreign country?
KREON: He said he planned to make a pilgrimage.
   He did not come home again.
OEDIPUS: And was there no one,
   No witness, no companion, to tell what happened?   120
KREON: They were all killed but one, and he got away
   So frightened that he could remember one thing only.
OEDIPUS: What was that one thing? One may be the key
   To everything, if we resolve to use it.
KREON: He said that a band of highwaymen attacked them,   125
   Outnumbered them, and overwhelmed the king.
OEDIPUS: Strange, that a highwayman should be so daring—
   Unless some faction here bribed him to do it.
KREON: We thought of that. But after Laios' death
   New troubles arose and we had no avenger.   130
OEDIPUS: What troubles could prevent your hunting down the killers?
KREON: The riddling Sphinx's song
   Made us deaf to all mysteries but her own.
OEDIPUS: Then once more I must bring what is dark to light.
   It is most fitting that Apollo shows,   135
   As you do, this compunction for the dead.
   You shall see how I stand by you, as I should,
   Avenging this country and the god as well,
   And not as though it were for some distant friend,
   But for my own sake, to be rid of evil.   140
   Whoever killed King Laios might—who knows?—
   Lay violent hands even on me—and soon.
   I act for the murdered king in my own interest.

   Come, then, my children: leave the altar steps,
   Lift up your olive boughs!
                              One of you go   145
   And summon the people of Kadmos to gather here.
   I will do all that I can; you may tell them that.   *(Exit a PAGE.)*
   So, with the help of God,
   We shall be saved—or else indeed we are lost.
PRIEST: Let us rise, children. It was for this we came,   150
   And now the king has promised it.
   Phoibos° has sent us an oracle; may he descend
   Himself to save us and drive out the plague.

   *(Exeunt° OEDIPUS and KREON into the palace by the central door. The
   PRIEST and the SUPPLIANTS disperse right and left. After a short pause
   the CHORUS enters the orchestra.)*

152 *Phoibos:* Apollo. *s.d. Exeunt:* Latin term meaning "they exit."

PARODOS
• Strophe 1

CHORUS: What is God singing in his profound
    Delphi of gold and shadow?
    What oracle for Thebes, the Sunwhipped city?
    Fear unjoints me, the roots of my heart tremble.
    Now I remember, O Healer, your power, and wonder: 5
    Will you send doom like a sudden cloud, or weave it
    Like nightfall of the past?
    Speak to me, tell me, O
    Child of golden Hope, immortal Voice.

Antistrophe 1

    Let me pray to Athene, the immortal daughter of Zeus,   10
    And to Artemis° her sister
    Who keeps her famous throne in the market ring,
    And to Apollo, archer from distant heaven—
    O gods, descend! Like three streams leap against
    The fires of our grief, the fires of darkness;   15
    Be swift to bring us rest!
    As in the old time from the brilliant house
    Of air you stepped to save us, come again!

Strophe 2

    Now our afflictions have no end,
    Now all our stricken host lies down   20
    And no man fights off death with his mind;
    The noble plowland bears no grain,
    And groaning mothers can not bear—
    See, how our lives like birds take wing,
    Like sparks that fly when a fire soars,   25
    To the shore of the god of evening.

Antistrophe 2

    The plague burns on, it is pitiless,
    Though pallid children laden with death
    Lie unwept in the stony ways,
    And old gray women by every path   30

---

11 *Artemis:* Goddess of the hunt.

Flock to the strand about the altars
There to strike their breasts and cry
Worship of Phoibos in wailing prayers:
Be kind, God's golden child!

Strophe 3

There are no swords in this attack by fire,   35
No shields, but we are ringed with cries.
Send the besieger plunging from our homes
Into the vast sea-room of the Atlantic
Or into the waves that foam eastward of Thrace—
For the day ravages what the night spares—   40
Destroy our enemy, lord of the thunder!
Let him be riven by lightning from heaven!

Antistrophe 3

Phoibos Apollo, stretch the sun's bowstring,
That golden cord, until it sing for us,
Flashing arrows in heaven!
                              Artemis, Huntress,   45
Race with flaring lights upon our mountains!
O scarlet god,° O golden-banded brow,
O Theban Bacchos in a storm of Maenads,°

(Enter OEDIPUS, *center.)*

Whirl upon Death, that all the Undying hate!
Come with blinding torches, come in joy!   50

SCENE 1

OEDIPUS: Is this your prayer? It may be answered. Come,
Listen to me, act as the crisis demands,
And you shall have relief from all these evils.

Until now I was a stranger to this tale,
As I had been a stranger to the crime.   5
Could I track down the murderer without a clue?
But now, friends,
As one who became a citizen after the murder,
I make this proclamation to all Thebans:

---

47 *scarlet god:* Bacchos, god of wine and revelry. 48 *Maenads:* Female attendants of Bacchos.

If any man knows by whose hand Laios, son of Labdakos,   10
Met his death, I direct that man to tell me everything,
No matter what he fears for having so long withheld it.
Let it stand as promised that no further trouble
Will come to him, but he may leave the land in safety.
Moreover: If anyone knows the murderer to be foreign,   15
Let him not keep silent: he shall have his reward from me.
However, if he does conceal it; if any man
Fearing for his friend or for himself disobeys this edict,
Hear what I propose to do:

I solemnly forbid the people of this country,   20
Where power and throne are mine, ever to receive that man
Or speak to him, no matter who he is, or let him
Join in sacrifice, lustration, or in prayer.
I decree that he be driven from every house,
Being, as he is, corruption itself to us: the Delphic   25
Voice of Apollo has pronounced this revelation.
Thus I associate myself with the oracle
And take the side of the murdered king.

As for the criminal, I pray to God—
Whether it be a lurking thief, or one of a number—   30
I pray that that man's life be consumed in evil and wretchedness.
And as for me, this curse applies no less
If it should turn out that the culprit is my guest here,
Sharing my hearth.
             You have heard the penalty.
I lay it on you now to attend to this   35
For my sake, for Apollo's, for the sick
Sterile city that heaven has abandoned.
Suppose the oracle had given you no command:
Should this defilement go uncleansed for ever?
You should have found the murderer: your king,   40
A noble king, had been destroyed!
             Now I,
Having the power that he held before me,
Having his bed, begetting children there
Upon his wife, as he would have, had he lived—
Their son would have been my children's brother,   45
If Laios had had luck in fatherhood!
(And now his bad fortune has struck him down)—
I say I take the son's part, just as though
I were his son, to press the fight for him
And see it won! I'll find the hand that brought   50

Death to Labdakos' and Polydoros' child,
Heir of Kadmos' and Agenor's line.°
And as for those who fail me,
May the gods deny them the fruit of the earth,
Fruit of the womb, and may they rot utterly!   55
Let them be wretched as we are wretched, and worse!

For you, for loyal Thebans, and for all
Who find my actions right, I pray the favor
Of justice, and of all the immortal gods.
CHORAGOS: Since I am under oath, my lord, I swear   60
I did not do the murder, I can not name
The murderer. Phoibos ordained the search;
Why did he not say who the culprit was?
OEDIPUS: An honest question. But no man in the world
Can make the gods do more than the gods will.   65
CHORAGOS: There is an alternative, I think—
OEDIPUS: Tell me.
Any or all, you must not fail to tell me.
CHORAGOS: A lord clairvoyant to the lord Apollo,
As we all know, is the skilled Teiresias.
One might learn much about this from him, Oedipus.   70
OEDIPUS: I am not wasting time:
Kreon spoke of this, and I have sent for him—
Twice, in fact; it is strange that he is not here.
CHORAGOS: The other matter—that old report—seems useless.
OEDIPUS: What was that? I am interested in all reports.   75
CHORAGOS: The king was said to have been killed by highwaymen.
OEDIPUS: I know. But we have no witnesses to that.
CHORAGOS: If the killer can feel a particle of dread,
Your curse will bring him out of hiding!
OEDIPUS: No.
The man who dared that act will fear no curse.   80

(Enter the blind seer TEIRESIAS, led by a PAGE.)

CHORAGOS: But there is one man who may detect the criminal.
This is Teiresias, this is the holy prophet
In whom, alone of all men, truth was born.
OEDIPUS: Teiresias: seer: student of mysteries,
Of all that's taught and all that no man tells,   85
Secrets of Heaven and secrets of the earth:
Blind though you are, you know the city lies

51–52 *Labdakos, Polydoros, Kadmos,* and *Agenor:* Ancestors of Laios.

Sick with plague; and from this plague, my lord,
We find that you alone can guard or save us.

Possibly you did not hear the messengers?   90
Apollo, when we sent to him,
Sent us back word that this great pestilence
Would lift, but only if we established clearly
The identity of those who murdered Laios.
They must be killed or exiled.
                                        Can you use   95
Birdflight° or any art of divination
To purify yourself, and Thebes, and me
From this contagion? We are in your hands.
There is no fairer duty
Than that of helping others in distress.   100

TEIRESIAS: How dreadful knowledge of the truth can be
When there's no help in truth! I knew this well,
But did not act on it; else I should not have come.

OEDIPUS: What is troubling you? Why are your eyes so cold?

TEIRESIAS: Let me go home. Bear your own fate, and I'll   105
Bear mine. It is better so: trust what I say.

OEDIPUS: What you say is ungracious and unhelpful
To your native country. Do not refuse to speak.

TEIRESIAS: When it comes to speech, your own is neither temperate
Nor opportune. I wish to be more prudent.   110

OEDIPUS: In God's name, we all beg you—

TEIRESIAS: You are all ignorant.
No; I will never tell you what I know.
Now it is my misery; then, it would be yours.

OEDIPUS: What! You do know something, and will not tell us?
You would betray us all and wreck the State?   115

TEIRESIAS: I do not intend to torture myself, or you.
Why persist in asking? You will not persuade me.

OEDIPUS: What a wicked old man you are! You'd try a stone's
Patience! Out with it! Have you no feeling at all?

TEIRESIAS: You call me unfeeling. If you could only see   120
The nature of your own feelings . . .

OEDIPUS: Why,
Who would not feel as I do? Who could endure
Your arrogance toward the city?

TEIRESIAS: What does it matter?
Whether I speak or not, it is bound to come.

---

96 *Birdflight:* The flight of birds was one sign used to predict the future.

OEDIPUS: Then, if "it" is bound to come, you are bound to tell me. 125
TEIRESIAS: No, I will not go on. Rage as you please.
OEDIPUS: Rage? Why not!
                    And I'll tell you what I think:
    You planned it, you had it done, you all but
    Killed him with your own hands: if you had eyes,
    I'd say the crime was yours, and yours alone. 130
TEIRESIAS: So? I charge you, then,
    Abide by the proclamation you have made:
    From this day forth
    Never speak again to these men or to me;
    You yourself are the pollution of this country. 135
OEDIPUS: You dare say that! Can you possibly think you have
    Some way of going free, after such insolence?
TEIRESIAS: I have gone free. It is the truth sustains me.
OEDIPUS: Who taught you shamelessness? It was not your craft.
TEIRESIAS: You did. You made me speak. I did not want to. 140
OEDIPUS: Speak what? Let me hear it again more clearly.
TEIRESIAS: Was it not clear before? Are you tempting me?
OEDIPUS: I did not understand it. Say it again.
TEIRESIAS: I say that you are the murderer whom you seek.
OEDIPUS: Now twice you have spat out infamy. You'll pay for it! 145
TEIRESIAS: Would you care for more? Do you wish to be really angry?
OEDIPUS: Say what you will. Whatever you say is worthless.
TEIRESIAS: I say you live in hideous shame with those
    Most dear to you. You can not see the evil.
OEDIPUS: Can you go on babbling like this for ever? 150
TEIRESIAS: I can, if there is power in truth.
OEDIPUS: There is:
    But not for you, not for you,
    You sightless, witless, senseless, mad old man!
TEIRESIAS: You are the madman. There is no one here
    Who will not curse you soon, as you curse me. 155
OEDIPUS: You child of total night! I would not touch you;
    Neither would any man who sees the sun.
TEIRESIAS: True: it is not from you my fate will come.
    That lies within Apollo's competence,
    As it is his concern.
OEDIPUS: Tell me, who made 160
    These fine discoveries? Kreon? or someone else?
TEIRESIAS: Kreon is no threat. You weave your own doom.
OEDIPUS: Wealth, power, craft of statemanship!
    Kingly position, everywhere admired!
    What savage envy is stored up against these, 165
    If Kreon, whom I trusted, Kreon my friend,

For this great office which the city once
Put in my hands unsought—if for this power
Kreon desires in secret to destroy me!

He has bought this decrepit fortune-teller, this   170
Collector of dirty pennies, this prophet fraud—
Why, he is no more clairvoyant than I am!
                                        Tell us:
Has your mystic mummery ever approached the truth?
When that hellcat the Sphinx was performing here,
What help were you to these people?   175
Her magic was not for the first man who came along:
It demanded a real exorcist. Your birds—
What good were they? or the gods, for the matter of that?
But I came by,
Oedipus, the simple man, who knows nothing—   180
I thought it out for myself, no birds helped me!
And this is the man you think you can destroy,
That you may be close to Kreon when he's king!
Well, you and your friend Kreon, it seems to me,
Will suffer most. If you were not an old man,   185
You would have paid already for your plot.
CHORAGOS: We can not see that his words or yours
Have been spoken except in anger, Oedipus,
And of anger we have no need. How to accomplish
The god's will best: that is what most concerns us.   190
TEIRESIAS: You are a king. But where argument's concerned
I am your man, as much a king as you.
I am not your servant, but Apollo's.
I have no need of Kreon or Kreon's name.

Listen to me. You mock my blindness, do you?   195
But I say that you, with both your eyes, are blind:
You can not see the wretchedness of your life,
Nor in whose house you live, no, nor with whom.
Who are your father and mother? Can you tell me?
You do not even know the blind wrongs   200
That you have done them, on earth and in the world below.
But the double lash of your parents' curse will whip you
Out of this land some day, with only night
Upon your precious eyes.
Your cries then—where will they not be heard?   205
What fastness of Kithairon° will not echo them?

---

206 *Kithairon:* Mountain where the infant Oedipus was left for dead.

And that bridal-descant of yours—you'll know it then,
The song they sang when you came here to Thebes
And found your misguided berthing.
All this, and more, that you can not guess at now,   210
Will bring you to yourself among your children.

Be angry, then. Curse Kreon. Curse my words.
I tell you, no man that walks upon the earth
Shall be rooted out more horribly than you.

OEDIPUS: Am I to bear this from him?—Damnation   215
    Take you! Out of this place! Out of my sight!

TEIRESIAS: I would not have come at all if you had not asked me.

OEDIPUS: Could I have told that you'd talk nonsense, that
    You'd come here to make a fool of yourself, and of me?

TEIRESIAS: A fool? Your parents thought me sane enough.   220

OEDIPUS: My parents again!—Wait: who were my parents?

TEIRESIAS: This day will give you a father, and break your heart.

OEDIPUS: Your infantile riddles! Your damned abracadabra!

TEIRESIAS: You were a great man once at solving riddles.

OEDIPUS: Mock me with that if you like; you will find it true.   225

TEIRESIAS: It was true enough. It brought about your ruin.

OEDIPUS: But if it saved this town?

TEIRESIAS *(to the* PAGE*)*:   Boy, give me your hand.

OEDIPUS: Yes, boy; lead him away.

                            —While you are here
    We can do nothing. Go; leave us in peace.

TEIRESIAS: I will go when I have said what I have to say.   230
    How can you hurt me? And I tell you again:
    The man you have been looking for all this time,
    The damned man, the murderer of Laios,
    That man is in Thebes. To your mind he is foreign-born,
    But it will soon be shown that he is a Theban,   235
    A revelation that will fail to please.
                            A blind man,
    Who has his eyes now; a penniless man, who is rich now;
    And he will go tapping the strange earth with his staff.
    To the children with whom he lives now he will be
    Brother and father—the very same; to her   240
    Who bore him, son and husband—the very same
    Who came to his father's bed, wet with his father's blood.
    Enough. Go think that over.
    If later you find error in what I have said,
    You may say that I have no skill in prophecy.   245

    (Exit TEIRESIAS, *led by his* PAGE. OEDIPUS *goes into the palace.)*

ODE 1 •
Strophe 1

CHORUS: The Delphic stone of prophecies
    Remembers ancient regicide
    And a still bloody hand.
    That killer's hour of flight has come.
    He must be stronger than riderless   5
    Coursers of untiring wind,
    For the son of Zeus° armed with his father's thunder
    Leaps in lightning after him;
    And the Furies° hold his track, the sad Furies.

Antistrophe 1

    Holy Parnassos'° peak of snow   10
    Flashes and blinds that secret man,
    That all shall hunt him down:
    Though he may roam the forest shade
    Like a bull gone wild from pasture
    To rage through glooms of stone.   15
    Doom comes down on him; flight will not avail him;
    For the world's heart calls him desolate,
    And the immortal voices follow, for ever follow.

Strophe 2

    But now a wilder thing is heard
    From the old man skilled at hearing Fate in the wing-beat of a bird.   20
    Bewildered as a blown bird, my soul hovers and can not find
    Foothold in this debate, or any reason or rest of mind.
    But no man ever brought—none can bring
    Proof of strife between Thebes' royal house,
    Labdakos' line, and the son of Polybos;°   25
    And never until now has any man brought word
    Of Laios' dark death staining Oedipus the King.

Antistrophe 2

    Divine Zeus and Apollo hold
    Perfect intelligence alone of all tales ever told;

---

7 *son of Zeus:* Apollo. 9 *Furies:* Female spirits who avenged evil deeds. 10 *Parnassos:* Holy
mountain, dwelling place of Zeus, king of the gods. 25 *Polybos:* Oedipus' adoptive father, king
of Corinth.

And well though this diviner works, he works in his own night;   30
No man can judge that rough unknown or trust in second sight,
For wisdom changes hands among the wise.
Shall I believe my great lord criminal
At a raging word that a blind old man let fall?
I saw him, when the carrion woman° faced him of old,   35
Prove his heroic mind. These evil words are lies.

SCENE 2

KREON: Men of Thebes:
I am told that heavy accusations
Have been brought against me by King Oedipus.

I am not the kind of man to bear this tamely.

If in these present difficulties   5
He holds me accountable for any harm to him
Through anything I have said or done—why, then,
I do not value life in this dishonor.
It is not as though this rumor touched upon
Some private indiscretion. The matter is grave.   10
The fact is that I am being called disloyal
To the State, to my fellow citizens, to my friends.
CHORAGOS: He may have spoken in anger, not from his mind.
KREON: But did you not hear him say I was the one
Who seduced the old prophet into lying?   15
CHORAGOS: The thing was said; I do not know how seriously.
KREON: But you were watching him! Were his eyes steady?
Did he look like a man in his right mind?
CHORAGOS: I do not know.
I can not judge the behavior of great men.
But here is the king himself.

(Enter OEDIPUS.*)*

OEDIPUS: So you dared come back.   20
Why? How brazen of you to come to my house,
You murderer!
            Do you think I do not know
That you plotted to kill me, plotted to steal my throne?
Tell me, in God's name: am I coward, a fool,
That you should dream you could accomplish this?   25

35 *woman:* The Sphinx.

A fool who could not see your slippery game?
A coward, not to fight back when I saw it?
You are the fool, Kreon, are you not? hoping
Without support or friends to get a throne?
Thrones may be won or bought: you could do neither.   30

KREON: Now listen to me. You have talked; let me talk, too.
    You can not judge unless you know the facts.

OEDIPUS: You speak well: there is one fact; but I find it hard
    To learn from the deadliest enemy I have.

KREON: That above all I must dispute with you.   35

OEDIPUS: That above all I will not hear you deny.

KREON: If you think there is anything good in being stubborn
    Against all reason, then I say you are wrong.

OEDIPUS: If you think a man can sin against his own kind
    And not be punished for it, I say you are mad.   40

KREON: I agree. But tell me: what have I done to you?

OEDIPUS: You advised me to send for that wizard, did you not?

KREON: I did. I should do it again.

OEDIPUS: Very well. Now tell me:
    How long has it been since Laios—

KREON: What of Laios?

OEDIPUS: Since he vanished in that onset by the road?   45

KREON: It was long ago, a long time.

OEDIPUS: And this prophet,
    Was he practicing here then?

KREON: He was; and with honor, as now.

OEDIPUS: Did he speak of me at that time?

KREON: He never did,
    At least, not when I was present.

OEDIPUS: But . . . the enquiry?
    I suppose you held one?

KREON: We did, but we learned nothing.   50

OEDIPUS: Why did the prophet not speak against me then?

KREON: I do not know; and I am the kind of man
    Who holds his tongue when he has no facts to go on.

OEDIPUS: There's one fact that you know, and you could tell it.

KREON: What fact is that? If I know it, you shall have it.   55

OEDIPUS: If he were not involved with you, he could not say
    That it was I who murdered Laios.

KREON: If he says that, you are the one that knows it!—
    But now it is my turn to question you.

OEDIPUS: Put your questions. I am no murderer.   60

KREON: First, then: You married my sister?

OEDIPUS: I married your sister.

KREON: And you rule the kingdom equally with her?

OEDIPUS: Everything that she wants she has from me.
KREON: And I am the third, equal to both of you?
OEDIPUS: That is why I call you a bad friend.   65
KREON: No. Reason it out, as I have done.
    Think of this first: would any sane man prefer
    Power, with all a king's anxieties,
    To that same power and the grace of sleep?
    Certainly not I.   70
    I have never longed for the king's power—only his rights.
    Would any wise man differ from me in this?
    As matters stand, I have my way in everything
    With your consent, and no responsibilities.
    If I were king, I should be a slave to policy.   75
    How could I desire a scepter more
    Than what is now mine—untroubled influence?
    No, I have not gone mad; I need no honors,
    Except those with the perquisites I have now.
    I am welcome everywhere; every man salutes me,   80
    And those who want your favor seek my ear,
    Since I know how to manage what they ask.
    Should I exchange this ease for that anxiety?
    Besides, no sober mind is treasonable.
    I hate anarchy   85
    And never would deal with any man who likes it.
    Test what I have said. Go to the priestess
    At Delphi, ask if I quoted her correctly.
    And as for this other thing: if I am found
    Guilty of treason with Teiresias,   90
    Then sentence me to death. You have my word
    It is a sentence I should cast my vote for—
    But not without evidence!
                        You do wrong
    When you take good men for bad, bad men for good.
    A true friend thrown aside—why, life itself   95
    Is not more precious!
                        In time you will know this well:
    For time, and time alone, will show the just man,
    Though scoundrels are discovered in a day.
CHORAGOS: This is well said, and a prudent man would ponder it.
    Judgments too quickly formed are dangerous.   100
OEDIPUS: But is he not quick in his duplicity?
    And shall I not be quick to parry him?
    Would you have me stand still, hold my peace, and let
    This man win everything, through my inaction?
KREON: And you want—what is it, then? To banish me?   105

OEDIPUS: No, not exile. It is your death I want,
So that all the world may see what treason means.
KREON: You will persist, then? You will not believe me?
OEDIPUS: How can I believe you?
KREON: Then you are a fool.
OEDIPUS: To save myself?
KREON: In justice, think of me.   110
OEDIPUS: You are evil incarnate.
KREON: But suppose that you are wrong?
OEDIPUS: Still I must rule.
KREON: But not if you rule badly.
OEDIPUS: O city, city!
KREON: It is my city, too!
CHORAGOS: Now, my lords, be still. I see the queen,
Iokaste, coming from her palace chambers;   115
And it is time she came, for the sake of you both.
This dreadful quarrel can be resolved through her.

(*Enter* IOKASTE.)

IOKASTE: Poor foolish men, what wicked din is this?
With Thebes sick to death, is it not shameful
That you should rake some private quarrel up?   120
(*To* OEDIPUS.) Come into the house.
                                    —And you, Kreon, go now:
Let us have no more of this tumult over nothing.
KREON: Nothing? No, sister: what your husband plans for me
Is one of two great evils: exile or death.
OEDIPUS: He is right.
                        Why, woman I have caught him squarely   125
Plotting against my life.
KREON: No! Let me die
Accurst if ever I have wished you harm!
IOKASTE: Ah, believe it, Oedipus!
In the name of the gods, respect this oath of his
For my sake, for the sake of these people here!   130

Strophe 1

CHORAGOS: Open your mind to her, my lord. Be ruled by her, I beg you!
OEDIPUS: What would you have me do?
CHORAGOS: Respect Kreon's word. He has never spoken like a fool,
And now he has sworn an oath.
OEDIPUS: You know what you ask?
CHORAGOS: I do.
OEDIPUS: Speak on, then.

CHORAGOS: A friend so sworn should not be baited so,   135
    In blind malice, and without final proof.
OEDIPUS: You are aware, I hope, that what you say
    Means death for me, or exile at the least.

Strophe 2

CHORAGOS: No, I swear by Helios, first in heaven!
    May I die friendless and accurst,   140
    The worst of deaths, if ever I meant that!
    It is the withering fields
      That hurt my sick heart:
    Must we bear all these ills,
    And now your bad blood as well?   145
OEDIPUS: Then let him go. And let me die, if I must,
    Or be driven by him in shame from the land of Thebes.
    It is your unhappiness, and not his talk,
    That touches me.
            As for him—
    Wherever he goes, hatred will follow him.   150
KREON: Ugly in yielding, as you were ugly in rage!
    Natures like yours chiefly torment themselves.
OEDIPUS: Can you not go? Can you not leave me?
KREON: I can.
    You do not know me; but the city knows me,
    And in its eyes I am just, if not in yours.   *(Exit* KREON.*)*   155

Antistrophe 1

CHORAGOS: Lady Iokaste, did you not ask the King to go to his chambers?
IOKASTE: First tell me what has happened.
CHORAGOS: There was suspicion without evidence; yet it rankled.
    As even false charges will.
IOKASTE: On both sides?
CHORAGOS: On both.
IOKASTE: But what was said?   160
CHORAGOS: Oh let it rest, let it be done with!
    Have we not suffered enough?
OEDIPUS: You see to what your decency has brought you:
    You have made difficulties where my heart saw none.

Antistrophe 2

CHORAGOS: Oedipus, it is not once only I have told you—   165
    You must know I should count myself unwise

To the point of madness, should I now forsake you—
    You, under whose hand,
      In the storm of another time,
    Our dear land sailed out free.   170
  But now stand fast at the helm!
IOKASTE: In God's name, Oedipus, inform your wife as well:
  Why are you so set in this hard anger?
OEDIPUS: I will tell you, for none of these men deserves
  My confidence as you do. It is Kreon's work,   175
  His treachery, his plotting against me.
IOKASTE: Go on, if you can make this clear to me.
OEDIPUS: He charges me with the murder of Laios.
IOKASTE: Has he some knowledge? Or does he speak from hearsay?
OEDIPUS: He would not commit himself to such a charge,   180
  But he has brought in that damnable soothsayer
  To tell his story.
IOKASTE: Set your mind at rest.
  If it is a question of soothsayers, I tell you
  That you will find no man whose craft gives knowledge
  Of the unknowable.
              Here is my proof: 185
  An oracle was reported to Laios once
  (I will not say from Phoibos himself, but from
  His appointed ministers, at any rate)
  That his doom would be death at the hands of his own son—
  His son, born of his flesh and of mine!   190

  Now, you remember the story: Laios was killed
  By marauding strangers where three highways meet;
  But his child had not been three days in this world
  Before the king had pierced the baby's ankles
  And left him to die on a lonely mountainside.   195

  Thus, Apollo never caused that child
  To kill his father, and it was not Laios' fate
  To die at the hands of his son, as he had feared.
  This is what prophets and prophecies are worth!
  Have no dread of them.
              It is God himself   200
  Who can show us what he wills, in his own way.
OEDIPUS: How strange a shadowy memory crossed my mind,
  Just now while you were speaking; it chilled my heart.
IOKASTE: What do you mean? What memory do you speak of?
OEDIPUS: If I understand you, Laios was killed   205
  At a place where three roads meet.

IOKASTE: So it was said;
    We have no later story.
OEDIPUS: Where did it happen?
IOKASTE: Phokis, it is called: at a place where the Theban Way
    Divides into the roads toward Delphi and Daulia.
OEDIPUS: When?
IOKASTE: We had the news not long before you came   210
    And proved the right to your succession here.
OEDIPUS: Ah, what net has God been weaving for me?
IOKASTE: Oedipus! Why does this trouble you?
OEDIPUS: Do not ask me yet.
    First, tell me how Laios looked, and tell me
    How old he was.
IOKASTE: He was tall, his hair just touched   215
    With white; his form was not unlike your own.
OEDIPUS: I think that I myself may be accurst
    By my own ignorant edict.
IOKASTE: You speak strangely.
    It makes me tremble to look at you, my king.
OEDIPUS: I am not sure that the blind man can not see.   220
    But I should know better if you were to tell me—
IOKASTE: Anything—though I dread to hear you ask it.
OEDIPUS: Was the king lightly escorted, or did he ride
    With a large company, as a ruler should?
IOKASTE: There were five men with him in all: one was a herald;   225
    And a single chariot, which he was driving.
OEDIPUS: Alas, that makes it plain enough!
                    But who—
    Who told you how it happened?
IOKASTE: A household servant,
    The only one to escape.
OEDIPUS: And is he still
    A servant of ours?
IOKASTE: No; for when he came back at last   230
    And found you enthroned in the place of the dead king,
    He came to me, touched my hand with his, and begged
    That I would send him away to the frontier district
    Where only the shepherds go—
    As far away from the city as I could send him.   235
    I granted his prayer; for although the man was a slave,
    He had earned more than this favor at my hands.
OEDIPUS: Can he be called back quickly?
IOKASTE: Easily.
    But why?
OEDIPUS: I have taken too much upon myself

Without enquiry; therefore I wish to consult him.   240
IOKASTE: Then he shall come.
                              But am I not one also
To whom you might confide these fears of yours?
OEDIPUS: That is your right; it will not be denied you,
Now least of all; for I have reached a pitch
Of wild foreboding. Is there anyone   245
To whom I should sooner speak?

Polybos of Corinth is my father.
My mother is a Dorian: Merope.
I grew up chief among the men of Corinth
Until a strange thing happened—   250
Not worth my passion, it may be, but strange.
At a feast, a drunken man maundering in his cups
Cries out that I am not my father's son!
I contained myself that night, though I felt anger
And a sinking heart. The next day I visited   255
My father and mother, and questioned them. They stormed,
Calling it all the slanderous rant of a fool;
And this relieved me. Yet the suspicion
Remained always aching in my mind;
I knew there was talk; I could not rest;   260
And finally, saying nothing to my parents,
I went to the shrine at Delphi.

The god dismissed my question without reply;
He spoke of other things.
                              Some were clear,
Full of wretchedness, dreadful, unbearable: 265
As, that I should lie with my own mother, breed
Children from whom all men would turn their eyes;
And that I should be my father's murderer.

I heard all this, and fled. And from that day
Corinth to me was only in the stars   270
Descending in that quarter of the sky,
As I wandered farther and farther on my way
To a land where I should never see the evil
Sung by the oracle. And I came to this country
Where, so you say, King Laios was killed.   275

I will tell you all that happened there, my lady.
There were three highways

Coming together at a place I passed;
And there a herald came towards me, and a chariot
Drawn by horses, with a man such as you describe   280
Seated in it. The groom leading the horses
Forced me off the road at his lord's command;
But as this charioteer lurched over towards me
I struck him in my rage. The old man saw me
And brought his double goad down upon my head   285
As I came abreast.
                        He was paid back, and more!
Swinging my club in this right hand I knocked him
Out of his car, and he rolled on the ground.
                                        I killed him.

I killed them all.
Now if that stranger and Laios were—kin,   290
Where is a man more miserable than I?
More hated by the gods? Citizen and alien alike
Must never shelter me or speak to me—
I must be shunned by all.
                        And I myself
Pronounced this malediction upon myself!   295

Think of it: I have touched you with these hands,
These hands that killed your husband. What defilement!

Am I all evil, then? It must be so,
Since I must flee from Thebes, yet never again
See my own countrymen, my own country,   300
For fear of joining my mother in marriage
And killing Polybos, my father.
                        Ah,
If I was created so, born to this fate,
Who could deny the savagery of God?

O holy majesty of heavenly powers!   305
May I never see that day! Never!
Rather let me vanish from the race of men
Than know the abomination destined me!
CHORAGOS: We too, my lord, have felt dismay at this.
But there is hope: you have yet to hear the shepherd.   310
OEDIPUS: Indeed, I fear no other hope is left me.
IOKASTE: What do you hope from him when he comes?
OEDIPUS: This much:
If his account of the murder tallies with yours,
Then I am cleared.

IOKASTE: What was it that I said
    Of such importance?
OEDIPUS: Why, "marauders," you said,   315
    Killed the king, according to this man's story.
    If he maintains that still, if there were several,
    Clearly the guilt is not mine: I was alone.
    But if he says one man, singlehanded, did it,
    Then the evidence all points to me.   320
IOKASTE: You may be sure that he said there were several;
    And can he call back that story now? He can not.
    The whole city heard it as plainly as I.
    But suppose he alters some detail of it:
    He can not ever show that Laios' death   325
    Fulfilled the oracle: for Apollo said
    My child was doomed to kill him; and my child—
    Poor baby!—it was my child that died first.

    No. From now on, where oracles are concerned,
    I would not waste a second thought on any.   330
OEDIPUS: You may be right.
                       But come: let someone go
    For the shepherd at once. This matter must be settled.
IOKASTE: I will send for him.
    I would not wish to cross you in anything,
    And surely not in this.—Let us go in.   *(Exeunt into the palace.)* 335

ODE 2 •

Strophe 1

CHORUS: Let me be reverent in the ways of right,
    Lowly the paths I journey on;
    Let all my words and actions keep
    The laws of the pure universe
    From highest Heaven handed down.   5
    For Heaven is their bright nurse,
    Those generations of the realms of light;
    Ah, never of mortal kind were they begot,
    Nor are they slaves of memory, lost in sleep:
    Their Father is greater than Time, and ages not.   10

Antistrophe 1

    The tyrant is a child of Pride
    Who drinks from his great sickening cup
    Recklessness and vanity,
    Until from his high crest headlong

He plummets to the dust of hope.   15
That strong man is not strong.
But let no fair ambition be denied;
May God protect the wrestler for the State
In government, in comely policy,
Who will fear God, and on his ordinance wait.   20

Strophe 2

Haughtiness and the high hand of disdain
Tempt and outrage God's holy law;
And any mortal who dares hold
No immortal Power in awe
Will be caught up in a net of pain: 25
The price for which his levity is sold.
Let each man take due earnings, then,
And keep his hands from holy things,
And from blasphemy stand apart—
Else the crackling blast of heaven   30
Blows on his head, and on his desperate heart.
Though fools will honor impious men,
In their cities no tragic poet sings.

Antistrophe 2

Shall we lose faith in Delphi's obscurities,
We who have heard the world's core   35
Discredited, and the sacred wood
Of Zeus at Elis praised no more?
The deeds and the strange prophecies
Must make a pattern yet to be understood.
Zeus, if indeed you are lord of all,   40
Throned in light over night and day,
Mirror this in your endless mind:
Our masters call the oracle
Words on the wind, and the Delphic vision blind!
Their hearts no longer know Apollo,   45
And reverence for the gods has died away.

SCENE 3

(Enter IOKASTE.*)*

IOKASTE: Princes of Thebes, it has occurred to me
To visit the altars of the gods, bearing
These branches as a suppliant, and this incense.

Our king is not himself: his noble soul
Is overwrought with fantasies of dread,   5
Else he would consider
The new prophecies in the light of the old.
He will listen to any voice that speaks disaster,
And my advice goes for nothing. *(She approaches the altar, right.)*
                                        To you, then, Apollo,
Lycean lord, since you are nearest, I turn in prayer   10
Receive these offerings, and grant us deliverance
From defilement. Our hearts are heavy with fear
When we see our leader distracted, as helpless sailors
Are terrified by the confusion of their helmsman.

(Enter MESSENGER.*)*

MESSENGER: Friends, no doubt you can direct me: 15
    Where shall I find the house of Oedipus,
    Or, better still, where is the king himself?
CHORAGOS: It is this very place, stranger; he is inside.
    This is his wife and mother of his children.
MESSENGER: I wish her happiness in a happy house,   20
    Blest in all the fulfillment of her marriage.
IOKASTE: I wish as much for you: your courtesy
    Deserves a like good fortune. But now, tell me:
    Why have you come? What have you to say to us?
MESSENGER: Good news, my lady, for your house and your husband.   25
IOKASTE: What news? Who sent you here?
MESSENGER: I am from Corinth.
    The news I bring ought to mean joy for you,
    Though it may be you will find some grief in it.
IOKASTE: What is it? How can it touch us in both ways?
MESSENGER: The word is that the people of the Isthmus   30
    Intend to call Oedipus to be their king.
IOKASTE: But old King Polybos—is he not reigning still?
MESSENGER: No. Death holds him in his sepulchre.
IOKASTE: What are you saying? Polybos is dead?
MESSENGER: If I am not telling the truth, may I die myself.   35
IOKASTE *(to a* MAIDSERVANT*)*: Go in, go quickly; tell this to your
    master.
    O riddlers of God's will, where are you now!
    This was the man whom Oedipus, long ago,
    Feared so, fled so, in dread of destroying him—
    But it was another fate by which he died.   40

(Enter OEDIPUS, *center.)*

OEDIPUS: Dearest Iokaste, why have you sent for me?
IOKASTE: Listen to what this man says, and then tell me
    What has become of the solemn prophecies.
OEDIPUS: Who is this man? What is his news for me?
IOKASTE: He has come from Corinth to announce your father's death!   45
OEDIPUS: Is it true, stranger? Tell me in your own words.
MESSENGER: I can not say it more clearly: the king is dead.
OEDIPUS: Was it by treason? Or by an attack of illness?
MESSENGER: A little thing brings old men to their rest.
OEDIPUS: It was sickness, then?
MESSENGER: Yes, and his many years.   50
OEDIPUS: Ah!
    Why should a man respect the Pythian hearth,° or
    Give heed to the birds that jangle above his head?
    They prophesied that I should kill Polybos,
    Kill my own father; but he is dead and buried,   55
    And I am here—I never touched him, never,
    Unless he died of grief for my departure,
    And thus, in a sense, through me. No. Polybos
    Has packed the oracles off with him underground.
    They are empty words.
IOKASTE: Had I not told you so?   60
OEDIPUS: You had; it was my faint heart that betrayed me.
IOKASTE: From now on never think of those things again.
OEDIPUS: And yet—must I not fear my mother's bed?
IOKASTE: Why should anyone in this world be afraid,
    Since Fate rules us and nothing can be foreseen?   65
    A man should live only for the present day.

    Have no more fear of sleeping with your mother:
    How many men, in dreams, have lain with their mothers!
    No reasonable man is troubled by such things.
OEDIPUS: That is true; only—   70
    If only my mother were not still alive!
    But she is alive. I can not help my dread.
IOKASTE: Yet this news of your father's death is wonderful.
OEDIPUS: Wonderful. But I fear the living woman.
MESSENGER: Tell me, who is this woman that you fear?   75
OEDIPUS: It is Merope, man; the wife of King Polybos.
MESSENGER: Merope? Why should you be afraid of her?
OEDIPUS: An oracle of the gods, a dreadful saying.

---

52 *Pythian hearth:* Delphi; the alternative name came from the dragon Python, which once
guarded Delphi until Apollo vanquished it.

MESSENGER: Can you tell me about it or are you sworn to silence?
OEDIPUS: I can tell you, and I will.   80
    Apollo said through his prophet that I was the man
    Who should marry his own mother, shed his father's blood
    With his own hands. And so, for all these years
    I have kept clear of Corinth, and no harm has come—
    Though it would have been sweet to see my parents again.   85
MESSENGER: And is this the fear that drove you out of Corinth?
OEDIPUS: Would you have me kill my father?
MESSENGER: As for that
    You must be reassured by the news I gave you.
OEDIPUS: If you could reassure me, I would reward you.
MESSENGER: I had that in mind, I will confess: I thought   90
    I could count on you when you returned to Corinth.
OEDIPUS: No: I will never go near my parents again.
MESSENGER: Ah, son, you still do not know what you are doing—
OEDIPUS: What do you mean? In the name of God tell me!
MESSENGER: —If these are your reasons for not going home.   95
OEDIPUS: I tell you, I fear the oracle may come true.
MESSENGER: And guilt may come upon you through your parents?
OEDIPUS: That is the dread that is always in my heart.
MESSENGER: Can you not see that all your fears are groundless?
OEDIPUS: Groundless? Am I not my parents' son?   100
MESSENGER: Polybos was not your father.
OEDIPUS: Not my father?
MESSENGER: No more your father than the man speaking to you.
OEDIPUS: But you are nothing to me!
MESSENGER: Neither was he.
OEDIPUS: Then why did he call me son?
MESSENGER: I will tell you:
    Long ago he had you from my hands, as a gift.   105
OEDIPUS: Then how could he love me so, if I was not his?
MESSENGER: He had no children, and his heart turned to you.
OEDIPUS: What of you? Did you buy me? Did you find me by chance?
MESSENGER: I came upon you in the woody vales of Kithairon.
OEDIPUS: And what were you doing there?
MESSENGER: Tending my flocks.   110
OEDIPUS: A wandering shepherd?
MESSENGER: But your savior, son, that day.
OEDIPUS: From what did you save me?
MESSENGER: Your ankles should tell you that.
OEDIPUS: Ah, stranger, why do you speak of that childhood pain?
MESSENGER: I pulled the skewer that pinned your feet together.
OEDIPUS: I have had the mark as long as I can remember.   115

MESSENGER: That was why you were given the name you bear.°
OEDIPUS: God! Was it my father or my mother who did it?
    Tell me!
MESSENGER: I do not know. The man who gave you to me
    Can tell you better than I.
OEDIPUS: It was not you that found me, but another?   120
MESSENGER: It was another shepherd gave you to me.
OEDIPUS: Who was he? Can you tell me who he was?
MESSENGER: I think he was said to be one of Laios' people.
OEDIPUS: You mean the Laios who was king here years ago?
MESSENGER: Yes; King Laios; and the man was one of his herdsmen.   125
OEDIPUS: Is he still alive? Can I see him?
MESSENGER: These men here
    Know best about such things.
OEDIPUS: Does anyone here
    Know this shepherd that he is talking about?
    Have you seen him in the fields, or in the town?
    If you have, tell me. It is time things were made plain.   130
CHORAGOS: I think the man he means is that same shepherd
    You have already asked to see. Iokaste perhaps
    Could tell you something.
OEDIPUS: Do you know anything
    About him, Lady? Is he the man we have summoned?
    Is that the man this shepherd means?
IOKASTE: Why think of him?   135
    Forget this herdsman. Forget it all.
    This talk is a waste of time.
OEDIPUS: How can you say that,
    When the clues to my true birth are in my hands?
IOKASTE: For God's love, let us have no more questioning!
    Is your life nothing to you?   140
    My own is pain enough for me to bear.
OEDIPUS: You need not worry. Suppose my mother a slave,
    And born of slaves: no baseness can touch you.
IOKASTE: Listen to me, I beg you: do not do this thing!
OEDIPUS: I will not listen; the truth must be made known.   145
IOKASTE: Everything that I say is for your own good!
OEDIPUS: My own good
    Snaps my patience, then; I want none of it.
IOKASTE: You are fatally wrong! May you never learn who you are!
OEDIPUS: Go, one of you, and bring the shepherd here.

---

116 *the name you bear:* "Oedipus" translates as "the one with a swollen foot."

Let us leave this woman to brag of her royal name.   150
IOKASTE: Ah, miserable!
    That is the only word I have for you now.
    That is the only word I can ever have.   *(Exit into the palace.)*
CHORAGOS: Why has she left us, Oedipus? Why has she gone
    In such a passion of sorrow? I fear this silence: 155
    Something dreadful may come of it.
OEDIPUS: Let it come!
    However base my birth, I must know about it.
    The Queen, like a woman, is perhaps ashamed
    To think of my low origin. But I
    Am a child of Luck; I can not be dishonored.   160
    Luck is my mother; the passing months, my brothers,
    Have seen me rich and poor.
                         If this is so,
    How could I wish that I were someone else?
    How could I not be glad to know my birth?

ODE 3 •

Strophe

CHORUS: If ever the coming time were known
    To my heart's pondering,
    Kithairon, now by Heaven I see the torches
    At the festival of the next full moon,
    And see the dance, and hear the choir sing   5
    A grace to your gentle shade:
    Mountain where Oedipus was found,
    O mountain guard of a noble race!
    May the god° who heals us lend his aid,
    And let that glory come to pass   10
    For our king's cradling-ground.

Antistrophe

    Of the nymphs that flower beyond the years,
    Who bore you,° royal child,
    To Pan° of the hills or the timberline Apollo,
    Cold in delight where the upland clears,   15

---

9 *god:* Apollo. 13 *Who bore you:* The Chorus wonders whether Oedipus might be the son of a
nymph and a god: Pan, Apollo, Hermes, or Dionysus. 14 *Pan:* God of nature; from the waist
up, he is human, from the waist down, a goat.

Or Hermes° for whom Kyllene's° heights are piled?
Or flushed as evening cloud,
Great Dionysos,° roamer of mountains,
He—was it he who found you there,
And caught you up in his own proud   20
Arms from the sweet god-ravisher
Who laughed by the Muses'° fountains?

SCENE 4

OEDIPUS: Sirs: though I do not know the man,
   I think I see him coming, this shepherd we want:
   He is old, like our friend here, and the men
   Bringing him seem to be servants of my house.
   But you can tell, if you have ever seen him.   5

   (Enter SHEPHERD *escorted by* SERVANTS.*)*

CHORAGOS: I know him, he was Laios' man. You can trust him.
OEDIPUS: Tell me first, you from Corinth: is this the shepherd
   We were discussing?
MESSENGER: This is the very man.
OEDIPUS *(to* SHEPHERD*)*: Come here. No, look at me. You must answer
   Everything I ask.—You belonged to Laios?   10
SHEPHERD: Yes: born his slave, brought up in his house.
OEDIPUS: Tell me: what kind of work did you do for him?
SHEPHERD: I was a shepherd of his, most of my life.
OEDIPUS: Where mainly did you go for pasturage?
SHEPHERD: Sometimes Kithairon, sometimes the hills near-by.   15
OEDIPUS: Do you remember ever seeing this man out there?
SHEPHERD: What would he be doing there? This man?
OEDIPUS: This man standing here. Have you ever seen him before?
SHEPHERD: No. At least, not to my recollection.
MESSENGER: And that is not strange, my lord. But I'll refresh   20
   His memory: he must remember when we two
   Spent three whole seasons together, March to September,
   On Kithairon or thereabouts. He had two flocks;
   I had one. Each autumn I'd drive mine home
   And he would go back with his to Laios' sheepfold.—   25
   Is this not true, just as I have described it?

---

16 *Hermes:* Zeus's son, messenger of the gods; *Kyllene:* Sacred mountain, the birthplace of Hermes. 18 *Dionysos:* (Dionysus) God of wine, sometimes called Bacchos. 22 *Muses:* Nine goddesses, sisters, who are the patronesses of poetry, music, art, and the sciences.

SHEPHERD: True, yes; but it was all so long ago.

MESSENGER: Well, then: do you remember, back in those days,
     That you gave me a baby boy to bring up as my own?

SHEPHERD: What if I did? What are you trying to say?   30

MESSENGER: King Oedipus was once that little child.

SHEPHERD: Damn you, hold your tongue!

OEDIPUS: No more of that!
     It is your tongue needs watching, not this man's.

SHEPHERD: My king, my master, what is it I have done wrong?

OEDIPUS: You have not answered his question about the boy.   35

SHEPHERD: He does not know . . . He is only making trouble . . .

OEDIPUS: Come, speak plainly, or it will go hard with you.

SHEPHERD: In God's name, do not torture an old man!

OEDIPUS: Come here, one of you; bind his arms behind him.

SHEPHERD: Unhappy king! What more do you wish to learn?   40

OEDIPUS: Did you give this man the child he speaks of?

SHEPHERD: I did.
     And I would to God I had died that very day.

OEDIPUS: You will die now unless you speak the truth.

SHEPHERD: Yet if I speak the truth, I am worse than dead.

OEDIPUS *(to* ATTENDANT*)*: He intends to draw it out, apparently—   45

SHEPHERD: No! I have told you already that I gave him the boy.

OEDIPUS: Where did you get him? From your house? From somewhere
     else?

SHEPHERD: Not from mine, no. A man gave him to me.

OEDIPUS: Is that man here? Whose house did he belong to?

SHEPHERD: For God's love, my king, do not ask me any more!   50

OEDIPUS: You are a dead man if I have to ask you again.

SHEPHERD: Then . . . Then the child was from the palace of Laios.

OEDIPUS: A slave child? or a child of his own line?

SHEPHERD: Ah, I am on the brink of dreadful speech!

OEDIPUS: And I of dreadful hearing. Yet I must hear.   55

SHEPHERD: If you must be told, then . . .
                              They said it was Laios' child;
     But it is your wife who can tell you about that.

OEDIPUS: My wife—Did she give it to you?

SHEPHERD: My lord, she did.

OEDIPUS: Do you know why?

SHEPHERD: I was told to get rid of it.

OEDIPUS: Oh heartless mother!

SHEPHERD: But in dread of prophecies . . .   60

OEDIPUS: Tell me.

SHEPHERD: It was said that the boy would kill his own father.

OEDIPUS: Then why did you give him over to this old man?

SHEPHERD: I pitied the baby, my king,
  And I thought that this man would take him far away
  To his own country.
                He saved him—but for what a fate!   65
  For if you are what this man says you are,
  No man living is more wretched than Oedipus.
OEDIPUS: Ah God!
  It was true!
            All the prophecies!
                      —Now,
  O Light, may I look on you for the last time!   70
  I, Oedipus,
  Oedipus, damned in his birth, in his marriage damned,
  Damned in the blood he shed with his own hand!

(He rushes into the palace.)

ODE 4 •
Strophe 1

CHORUS: Alas for the seed of men.
  What measure shall I give these generations
  That breathe on the void and are void
  And exist and do not exist?
  Who bears more weight of joy   5
  Than mass of sunlight shifting in images,
  Or who shall make his thought stay on
  That down time drifts away?
  Your splendor is all fallen.
  O naked brow of wrath and tears,   10
  O change of Oedipus!
  I who saw your days call no man blest—
  Your great days like ghosts gone.

Antistrophe 1

  That mind was a strong bow.
  Deep, how deep you drew it then, hard archer,   15
  At a dim fearful range,
  And brought dear glory down!
  You overcame the stranger°—
  The virgin with her hooking lion claws—

18 *stranger:* The Sphinx.

And though death sang, stood like a tower   20
To make pale Thebes take heart.
Fortress against our sorrow!
True king, giver of laws,
Majestic Oedipus!
No prince in Thebes had ever such renown,   25
No prince won such grace of power.

Strophe 2

And now of all men ever known
Most pitiful is this man's story:
His fortunes are most changed; his state
Fallen to a low slave's   30
Ground under bitter fate.
O Oedipus, most royal one!
The great door° that expelled you to the light
Gave at night—ah, gave night to your glory:
As to the father, to the fathering son.   35
All understood too late.
How could that queen whom Laios won,
The garden that he harrowed at his height,
Be silent when that act was done?

Antistrophe 2

But all eyes fail before time's eye,   40
All actions come to justice there.
Though never willed, though far down the deep past,
Your bed, your dread sirings,
Are brought to book at last.
Child by Laios doomed to die,   45
Then doomed to lose that fortunate little death,
Would God you never took breath in this air
That with my wailing lips I take to cry:
For I weep the world's outcast.
I was blind, and now I can tell why: 50
Asleep, for you had given ease of breath
To Thebes, while the false years went by.

---

33 *door:* Refers to the birth process.

EXODOS°

(Enter, from the palace, SECOND MESSENGER.*)*

SECOND MESSENGER: Elders of Thebes, most honored in this land,
What horrors are yours to see and hear, what weight
Of sorrow to be endured, if, true to your birth,
You venerate the line of Labdakos!
I think neither Istros nor Phasis, those great rivers,   5
Could purify this place of all the evil
It shelters now, or soon must bring to light—
Evil not done unconsciously, but willed.

The greatest griefs are those we cause ourselves.
CHORAGOS: Surely, friend, we have grief enough already;   10
What new sorrow do you mean?
SECOND MESSENGER: The queen is dead.
CHORAGOS: O miserable queen! But at whose hand?
SECOND MESSENGER: Her own.
The full horror of what happened you can not know,
For you did not see it; but I, who did, will tell you
As clearly as I can how she met her death.   15

When she had left us,
In passionate silence, passing through the court,
She ran to her apartment in the house,
Her hair clutched by the fingers of both hands.
She closed the doors behind her; then, by that bed   20
Where long ago the fatal son was conceived—
That son who should bring about his father's death—
We heard her call upon Laios, dead so many years,
And heard her wail for the double fruit of her marriage,
A husband by her husband, children by her child.   25
Exactly how she died I do not know:
For Oedipus burst in moaning and would not let us
Keep vigil to the end: it was by him
As he stormed about the room that our eyes were caught.
From one to another of us he went, begging a sword,   30
Hunting the wife who was not his wife, the mother
Whose womb had carried his own children and himself.
I do not know: it was none of us aided him,
But surely one of the gods was in control!
For with a dreadful cry   35

Exodos: Final scene.

He hurled his weight, as though wrenched out of himself,
    At the twin doors: the bolts gave, and he rushed in.
    And there we saw her hanging, her body swaying
    From the cruel cord she had noosed about her neck.
    A great sob broke from him, heartbreaking to hear,   40
    As he loosed the rope and lowered her to the ground.

I would blot out from my mind what happened next!
    For the king ripped from her gown the golden brooches
    That were her ornament, and raised them, and plunged them down
    Straight into his own eyeballs, crying, "No more,   45
    No more shall you look on the misery about me,
    The horrors of my own doing! Too long you have known
    The faces of those whom I should never have seen,
    Too long been blind to those for whom I was searching!
    From this hour, go in darkness!" And as he spoke,   50
    He struck at his eyes—not once, but many times;
    And the blood spattered his beard,
    Bursting from his ruined sockets like red hail.

So from the unhappiness of two this evil has sprung,
    A curse on the man and woman alike. The old   55
    Happiness of the house of Labdakos
    Was happiness enough: where is it today?
    It is all wailing and ruin, disgrace, death—all
    The misery of mankind that has a name—
    And it is wholly and for ever theirs.   60
CHORAGOS: Is he in agony still? Is there no rest for him?
SECOND MESSENGER: He is calling for someone to open the doors
    wide
    So that all the children of Kadmos may look upon
    His father's murderer, his mother's—no,
    I can not say it!
                And then he will leave Thebes,   65
    Self-exiled, in order that the curse
    Which he himself pronounced may depart from the house.
    He is weak, and there is none to lead him,
    So terrible is his suffering.
                But you will see:
    Look, the doors are opening; in a moment   70
    You will see a thing that would crush a heart of stone.

(The central door is opened; OEDIPUS, *blinded, is led in.)*

CHORAGOS: Dreadful indeed for men to see.
    Never have my own eyes

Looked on a sight so full of fear.

Oedipus!   75
What madness came upon you, what demon
Leaped on your life with heavier
Punishment than a mortal man can bear?
No: I can not even
Look at you, poor ruined one.   80
And I would speak, question, ponder,
If I were able. No.
You make me shudder.

OEDIPUS: God. God.
Is there a sorrow greater?   85
Where shall I find harbor in this world?
My voice is hurled far on a dark wind.
What has God done to me?

CHORAGOS: Too terrible to think of, or to see.

Strophe 1

OEDIPUS: O cloud of night,   90
Never to be turned away: night coming on,
I can not tell how: night like a shroud!
My fair winds brought me here.
                         O God. Again
The pain of the spikes where I had sight,
The flooding pain   95
Of memory, never to be gouged out.

CHORAGOS: This is not strange.
You suffer it all twice over, remorse in pain,
Pain in remorse.

Antistrophe 1

OEDIPUS: Ah dear friend   100
Are you faithful even yet, you alone?
Are you still standing near me, will you stay here,
Patient, to care for the blind?
                         The blind man!
Yet even blind I know who it is attends me,
By the voice's tone—   105
Though my new darkness hide the comforter.

CHORAGOS: Oh fearful act!
What god was it drove you to rake black
Night across your eyes?

Strophe 2

OEDIPUS: Apollo. Apollo. Dear   110
    Children, the god was Apollo.
    He brought my sick, sick fate upon me.
    But the blinding hand was my own!
    How could I bear to see
    When all my sight was horror everywhere?   115
CHORAGOS: Everywhere; that is true.
OEDIPUS: And now what is left?
    Images? Love? A greeting even,
    Sweet to the senses? Is there anything?
    Ah, no, friends: lead me away.   120
    Lead me away from Thebes.
                              Lead the great wreck
    And hell of Oedipus, whom the gods hate.
CHORAGOS: Your misery, you are not blind to that.
    Would God you had never found it out!

Antistrophe 2

OEDIPUS: Death take the man who unbound   125
    My feet on that hillside
    And delivered me from death to life! What life?
    If only I had died,
    This weight of monstrous doom
    Could not have dragged me and my darlings down.   130
CHORAGOS: I would have wished the same.
OEDIPUS: Oh never to have come here
    With my father's blood upon me! Never
    To have been the man they call his mother's husband!
    Oh accurst! Oh child of evil,   135
    To have entered that wretched bed—
                              the selfsame one!
    More primal than sin itself, this fell to me.
CHORAGOS: I do not know what words to offer you.
    You were better dead than alive and blind.
OEDIPUS: Do not counsel me any more. This punishment   140
    That I have laid upon myself is just.
    If I had eyes,
    I do not know how I could bear the sight
    Of my father, when I came to the house of Death,
    Or my mother: for I have sinned against them both   145
    So vilely that I could not make my peace

By strangling my own life.

     Or do you think my children,
Born as they were born, would be sweet to my eyes?
Ah never, never! Nor this town with its high walls,
Nor the holy images of the gods.

       For I,   150
Thrice miserable!—Oedipus, noblest of all the line
Of Kadmos, have condemned myself to enjoy
These things no more, by my own malediction
Expelling that man whom the gods declared
To be a defilement in the house of Laios.   155
After exposing the rankness of my own guilt,
How could I look men frankly in the eyes?
No, I swear it,
If I could have stifled my hearing at its source,
I would have done it and made all this body   160
A tight cell of misery, blank to light and sound:
So I should have been safe in my dark mind
Beyond external evil.

     Ah Kithairon!
Why did you shelter me? When I was cast upon you,
Why did I not die? Then I should never   165
Have shown the world my execrable birth.

Ah Polybos! Corinth, city that I believed
The ancient seat of my ancestors: how fair
I seemed, your child! And all the while this evil
Was cancerous within me!

      For I am sick   170
In my own being, sick in my origin.
O three roads, dark ravine, woodland and way
Where three roads met; you, drinking my father's blood,
My own blood, spilled by my own hand: can you remember
The unspeakable things I did there, and the things 175
I went on from there to do?

      O marriage, marriage!
The act that engendered me, and again the act
Performed by the son in the same bed—

        Ah, the net
Of incest, mingling fathers, brothers, sons,
With brides, wives, mothers: the last evil   180
That can be known by men: no tongue can say
How evil!

    No. For the love of God, conceal me

Somewhere far from Thebes; or kill me; or hurl me
Into the sea, away from men's eyes for ever.

Come, lead me. You need not fear to touch me.   185
Of all men, I alone can bear this guilt.

(Enter KREON.*)*

CHORAGOS: Kreon is here now. As to what you ask,
    He may decide the course to take. He only
    Is left to protect the city in your place.
OEDIPUS: Alas, how can I speak to him? What right have I   190
    To beg his courtesy whom I have deeply wronged?
KREON: I have not come to mock you, Oedipus,
    Or to reproach you, either.
    (To ATTENDANTS.*)*   —You, standing there:
    If you have lost all respect for man's dignity,
    At least respect the flame of Lord Helios: 195
    Do not allow this pollution to show itself
    Openly here, an affront to the earth
    And Heaven's rain and the light of day. No, take him
    Into the house as quickly as you can.
    For it is proper   200
    That only the close kindred see his grief.
OEDIPUS: I pray you in God's name, since your courtesy
    Ignores my dark expectation, visiting
    With mercy this man of all men most execrable:
    Give me what I ask—for your good, not for mine.   205
KREON: And what is it that you turn to me begging for?
OEDIPUS: Drive me out of this country as quickly as may be
    To a place where no human voice can ever greet me.
KREON: I should have done that before now—only,
    God's will had not been wholly revealed to me.   210
OEDIPUS: But his command is plain: the parricide
    Must be destroyed. I am that evil man.
KREON: That is the sense of it, yes; but as things are,
    We had best discover clearly what is to be done.
OEDIPUS: You would learn more about a man like me?   215
KREON: You are ready now to listen to the god.
OEDIPUS: I will listen. But it is to you
    That I must turn for help. I beg you, hear me.

    The woman is there—
    Give her whatever funeral you think proper: 220
    She is your sister.
               —But let me go, Kreon!

Let me purge my father's Thebes of the pollution
Of my living here, and go out to the wild hills,
To Kithairon, that has won such fame with me,
The tomb my mother and father appointed for me,   225
And let me die there, as they willed I should.
And yet I know
Death will not ever come to me through sickness
Or in any natural way: I have been preserved
For some unthinkable fate. But let that be.   230

As for my sons, you need not care for them.
They are men, they will find some way to live.
But my poor daughters, who have shared my table,
Who never before have been parted from their father—
Take care of them, Kreon; do this for me.   235

And will you let me touch them with my hands
A last time, and let us weep together?
Be kind, my lord,
Great prince, be kind!
                    Could I but touch them,
They would be mine again, as when I had my eyes.   240

(Enter ANTIGONE *and* ISMENE, *attended.)*

Ah, God!
Is it my dearest children I hear weeping?
Has Kreon pitied me and sent my daughters?
KREON: Yes, Oedipus: I knew that they were dear to you
    In the old days, and know you must love them still.   245
OEDIPUS: May God bless you for this—and be a friendlier
    Guardian to you than he has been to me!

Children, where are you?
Come quickly to my hands: they are your brother's—
Hands that have brought your father's once clear eyes   250
To this way of seeing—
                    Ah dearest ones,
I had neither sight nor knowledge then, your father
By the woman who was the source of his own life!
And I weep for you—having no strength to see you—,
I weep for you when I think of the bitterness   255
That men will visit upon you all your lives.
What homes, what festivals can you attend
Without being forced to depart again in tears?
And when you come to marriageable age,

Where is the man, my daughters, who would dare   260
Risk the bane that lies on all my children?
Is there any evil wanting? Your father killed
His father; sowed the womb of her who bore him;
Engendered you at the fount of his own existence!
That is what they will say of you.

                             Then, whom   265
Can you ever marry? There are no bridegrooms for you,
And your lives must wither away in sterile dreaming.

O Kreon, son of Menoikeus!
You are the only father my daughters have,
Since we, their parents, are both of us gone for ever.   270
They are your own blood: you will not let them
Fall into beggary and loneliness;
You will keep them from the miseries that are mine!
Take pity on them; see, they are only children,
Friendless except for you. Promise me this,   275
Great prince, and give me your hand in token of it.

(KREON *clasps his right hand.*)

Children:
I could say much, if you could understand me,
But as it is, I have only this prayer for you:
Live where you can, be as happy as you can—   280
Happier, please God, than God has made your father.
KREON: Enough. You have wept enough. Now go within.
OEDIPUS: I must; but it is hard.
KREON: Time eases all things.
OEDIPUS: You know my mind, then?
KREON: Say what you desire.
OEDIPUS: Send me from Thebes!
KREON: God grant that I may!   285
OEDIPUS: But since God hates me . . .
KREON: No, he will grant your wish.
OEDIPUS: You promise?
KREON: I can not speak beyond my knowledge.
OEDIPUS: Then lead me in.
KREON: Come now, and leave your children.
OEDIPUS: No! Do not take them from me!
KREON: Think no longer
That you are in command here, but rather think   290

How, when you were, you served your own destruction.

(Exeunt into the house all but the CHORUS; *the* CHORAGOS *chants directly to the audience.)*

CHORAGOS: Men of Thebes: look upon Oedipus.

This is the king who solved the famous riddle
And towered up, most powerful of men.
No mortal eyes but looked on him with envy,   295
Yet in the end ruin swept over him.

Let every man in mankind's frailty
Consider his last day; and let none
Presume on his good fortune until he find
Life, at his death, a memory without pain.   300

Considerations

1. Reread the Prologue, Scene I, and Ode I. Then list details that suggest the qualities of Oedipus's character. Write a description of Oedipus, incorporating these details where they are appropriate to support your observations about his strengths and weaknesses.
2. How do the references to light and darkness and seeing (vision) and blindness suggest the theme of the play? Consider especially the conflicts Oedipus faces and the way he resolves (or fails to resolve) these conflicts.
3. What are your responses toward the gods as you finish reading the play? Consider, for example, the havoc they have brought to the lives of the people of Thebes. Do you see these actions as justified or as random and cruel? In your response, consider also the attitudes of the play's characters toward the gods. Do these characters seem reverent or merely fearful as they talk about and act in reaction to the will of the gods?
4. How would you evaluate the character of Iokaste? To what extent, if any, does she contribute to Oedipus's tragic downfall? How would you defend Iokaste's actions and decisions to people who might view her as an unsympathetic character?
5. Sigmund Freud said of *Oedipus Rex* that "it is an immoral play; it sets aside the individual's responsibility to social law and displays divine forces ordaining the crime and rendering powerless the moral instincts of the human being which would guard him against the crime." With specific references to lines in the play, explain why you agree or disagree with Freud's statement.

AUGUST WILSON (1945–   )

Fences

> Born in Pittsburgh, Pennsylvania, August Wilson grew up in a neighborhood
> that almost certainly shared many similarities with the setting of Fences. Al-
> though he was an avid reader, he dropped out of high school and during the
> turbulent 1960s worked at various blue-collar jobs. Wilson became strongly
> committed to civil rights issues, particularly the fight against racism. In the late
> 1960s he began writing plays that challenge stereotypes of African Americans,
> especially African-American men. Wilson has said that his early years of grow-
> ing up, going to school, and working in Pittsburgh provided him with the
> characters, settings, and conflicts that appear in his plays. In addition, the
> speech patterns and rhythms (primarily blues) that flow through the dialogue
> of his plays reflect these early influences. Wilson's plays include Ma Rainey's
> Black Bottom *(1984) and* Joe Turner's Come and Gone *(1986).*
> Fences, *first performed at the Yale Repertory Theater in 1985, won the
> Pulitzer Prize for drama.*

Characters

TROY MAXSON

JIM BONO, *Troy's friend*

ROSE, *Troy's wife*

LYONS, *Troy's oldest son by previous marriage*

GABRIEL, *Troy's brother*

CORY, *Troy and Rose's son*

RAYNELL, *Troy's daughter*

Setting *The setting is the yard which fronts the only entrance to the Maxson household, an ancient two-story brick house set back off a small alley in a big-city neighborhood. The entrance to the house is gained by two or three steps leading to a wooden
porch badly in need of paint.*

*A relatively recent addition to the house and running its full width, the porch
lacks congruence. It is a sturdy porch with a flat roof. One or two chairs of dubious
value sit at one end where the kitchen window opens onto the porch. An old-fashioned
icebox stands silent guard at the opposite end.*

*The yard is a small dirt yard, partially fenced, except for the last scene, with a
wooden sawhorse, a pile of lumber, and other fence-building equipment set off to the
side. Opposite is a tree from which hangs a ball made of rags. A baseball bat leans
against the tree. Two oil drums serve as garbage receptacles and sit near the house at
right to complete the setting.*

The Play *Near the turn of the century, the destitute of Europe sprang on the city
with tenacious claws and an honest and solid dream. The city devoured them. They
swelled its belly until it burst into a thousand furnaces and sewing machines, a*

thousand butcher shops and bakers' ovens, a thousand churches and hospitals and funeral parlors and money-lenders. The city grew. It nourished itself and offered each man a partnership limited only by his talent, his guile, and his willingness and capacity for hard work. For the immigrants of Europe, a dream dared and won true.

The descendants of African slaves were offered no such welcome or participation. They came from places called the Carolinas and the Virginias, Georgia, Alabama, Mississippi, and Tennessee. They came strong, eager, searching. The city rejected them and they fled and settled along the riverbanks and under bridges in shallow, ramshackle houses made of sticks and tarpaper. They collected rags and wood. They sold the use of their muscles and their bodies. They cleaned houses and washed clothes, they shined shoes, and in quiet desperation and vengeful pride, they stole, and lived in pursuit of their own dream. That they could breathe free, finally, and stand to meet life with the force of dignity and whatever eloquence the heart could call upon.

By 1957, the hard-won victories of the European immigrants had solidified the industrial might of America. War had been confronted and won with new energies that used loyalty and patriotism as its fuel. Life was rich, full, and flourishing. The Milwaukee Braves won the World Series, and the hot winds of change that would make the sixties a turbulent, racing, dangerous, and provocative decade had not yet begun to blow full.

ACT I
SCENE I

It is 1957. TROY and BONO enter the yard, engaged in conversation. TROY is fifty-three years old, a large man with thick, heavy hands; it is this largeness that he strives to fill out and make an accommodation with. Together with his blackness, his largeness informs his sensibilities and the choices he has made in his life.

Of the two men, BONO is obviously the follower. His commitment to their friendship of thirty-odd years is rooted in his admiration of TROY's honesty, capacity for hard work, and his strength, which BONO seeks to emulate.

It is Friday night, payday, and the one night of the week the two men engage in a ritual of talk and drink. TROY is usually the most talkative and at times he can be crude and almost vulgar, though he is capable of rising to profound heights of expression. The men carry lunch buckets and wear or carry burlap aprons and are dressed in clothes suitable to their jobs as garbage collectors.

BONO: Troy, you ought to stop that lying!

TROY: I ain't lying! The nigger had a watermelon this big.

(He indicates with his hands.)

Talking about . . . "What watermelon, Mr. Rand?" I liked to fell out! "What watermelon, Mr. Rand?" . . . And it sitting there big as life.

BONO: What did Mr. Rand say?

TROY: Ain't said nothing. Figure if the nigger too dumb to know he carrying a watermelon, he wasn't gonna get much sense out of him.

Trying to hide that great big old watermelon under his coat. Afraid to let the white man see him carry it home.

BONO: I'm like you . . . I ain't got no time for them kind of people.

TROY: Now what he look like getting mad cause he see the man from the union talking to Mr. Rand?

BONO: He come to me talking about . . . "Maxson gonna get us fired." I told him to get away from me with that. He walked away from me calling you a troublemaker. What Mr. Rand say?

TROY: Ain't said nothing. He told me to go down the Commissioner's office next Friday. They called me down there to see them.

BONO: Well, as long as you got your complaint filed, they can't fire you. That's what one of them white fellows tell me.

TROY: I ain't worried about them firing me. They gonna fire me cause I asked a question? That's all I did. I went to Mr. Rand and asked him, "Why? Why you got the white mens driving and the colored lifting?" Told him, "What's the matter, don't I count? You think only white fellows got sense enough to drive a truck. That ain't no paper job! Hell, anybody can drive a truck. How come you got all whites driving and the colored lifting?" He told me "take it to the union." Well, hell, that's what I done! Now they wanna come up with this pack of lies.

BONO: I told Brownie if the man come and ask him any questions . . . just tell the truth! It ain't nothing but something they done trumped up on you cause you filed a complaint on them.

TROY: Brownie don't understand nothing. All I want them to do is change the job description. Give everybody a chance to drive the truck. Brownie can't see that. He ain't got that much sense.

BONO: How you figure he be making out with that gal be up at Taylors' all the time . . . that Alberta gal?

TROY: Same as you and me. Getting just as much as we is. Which is to say nothing.

BONO: It is, huh? I figure you doing a little better than me . . . and I ain't saying what I'm doing.

TROY: Aw, nigger, look here . . . I know you. If you had got anywhere near that gal, twenty minutes later you be looking to tell somebody. And the first one you gonna tell . . . that you gonna want to brag to . . . is gonna be me.

BONO: I ain't saying that. I see where you be eyeing her.

TROY: I eye all the women. I don't miss nothing. Don't never let nobody tell you Troy Maxson don't eye the women.

BONO: You been doing more than eyeing her. You done bought her a drink or two.

TROY: Hell yeah, I bought her a drink! What that mean? I bought you one, too. What that mean cause I buy her a drink? I'm just being polite.

BONO: It's all right to buy her one drink. That's what you call being polite. But when you wanna be buying two or three . . . that's what you call eyeing her.

TROY: Look here, as long as you known me . . . you ever known me to chase after women?

BONO: Hell yeah! Long as I done known you. You forgetting I knew you when.

TROY: Naw, I'm talking about since I been married to Rose?

BONO: Oh, not since you been married to Rose. Now, that's the truth, there. I can say that.

TROY: All right then! Case closed.

BONO: I see you be walking up around Alberta's house. You supposed to be at Taylors' and you be walking up around there.

TROY: What you watching where I'm walking for? I ain't watching after you.

BONO: I seen you walking around there more than once.

TROY: Hell, you liable to see me walking anywhere! That don't mean nothing cause you see me walking around there.

BONO: Where she come from anyway? She just kinda showed up one day.

TROY: Tallahassee. You can look at her and tell she one of them Florida gals. They got some big healthy women down there. Grow them right up out the ground. Got a little bit of Indian in her. Most of them niggers down in Florida got some Indian in them.

BONO: I don't know about that Indian part. But she damn sure big and healthy. Woman wear some big stockings. Got them great big old legs and hips as wide as the Mississippi River.

TROY: Legs don't mean nothing. You don't do nothing but push them out of the way. But them hips cushion the ride!

BONO: Troy, you ain't got no sense.

TROY: It's the truth! Like you riding on Goodyears!

(ROSE *enters from the house. She is ten years younger than* TROY, *her devotion to him stems from her recognition of the possibilities of her life without him: a succession of abusive men and their babies, a life of partying and running the streets, the Church, or aloneness with its attendant pain and frustration. She recognizes* TROY's *spirit as a fine and illuminating one and she either ignores or forgives his faults, only some of which she recognizes. Though she doesn't drink, her presence is an integral part of the Friday night rituals. She alternates between the porch and the kitchen, where supper preparations are under way.*)

ROSE: What you all out here getting into?

TROY: What you worried about what we getting into for? This is men talk, woman.

ROSE: What I care what you all talking about? Bono, you gonna stay for supper?

BONO: No, I thank you, Rose. But Lucille say she cooking up a pot of pigfeet.

TROY: Pigfeet! Hell, I'm going home with you! Might even stay the night if you got some pigfeet. You got something in there to top them pigfeet, Rose?

ROSE: I'm cooking up some chicken. I got some chicken and collard greens.

TROY: Well, go on back in the house and let me and Bono finish what we was talking about. This is men talk. I got some talk for you later. You know what kind of talk I mean. You go on and powder it up.

ROSE: Troy Maxson, don't you start that now!

TROY (*puts his arm around her*): Aw, woman . . . come here. Look here, Bono . . . when I met this woman . . . I got out that place, say, "Hitch up my pony, saddle up my mare . . . there's a woman out there for me somewhere. I looked here. Looked there. Saw Rose and latched on to her." I latched on to her and told her—I'm gonna tell you the truth— I told her, "Baby, I don't wanna marry, I just wanna be your man." Rose told me . . . tell him what you told me, Rose.

ROSE: I told him if he wasn't the marrying kind, then move out the way so the marrying kind could find me.

TROY: That's what she told me. "Nigger, you in my way. You blocking the view! Move out the way so I can find me a husband." I thought it over two or three days. Come back—

ROSE: Ain't no two or three days nothing. You was back the same night.

TROY: Come back, told her . . . "Okay, baby . . . but I'm gonna buy me a banty rooster and put him out there in the backyard . . . and when he see a stranger come, he'll flap his wings and crow . . ." Look here, Bono, I could watch the front door by myself . . . it was that back door I was worried about.

ROSE: Troy, you ought not talk like that. Troy ain't doing nothing but telling a lie.

TROY: Only thing is . . . when we first got married . . . forget the rooster . . . we ain't had no yard!

BONO: I hear you tell it. Me and Lucille was staying down there on Logan Street. Had two rooms with the outhouse in the back. I ain't mind the outhouse none. But when that goddamn wind blow through there in the winter . . . that's what I'm talking about! To this day I wonder why in the hell I ever stayed down there for six long years. But see, I didn't know I could do no better. I thought only white folks had inside toilets and things.

ROSE: There's a lot of people don't know they can do no better than they doing now. That's just something you got to learn. A lot of folks still shop at Bella's.

TROY: Ain't nothing wrong with shopping at Bella's. She got fresh food.

ROSE: I ain't said nothing about if she got fresh food. I'm talking about what she charge. She charge ten cents more than the A&P.

TROY: The A&P ain't never done nothing for me. I spends my money where I'm treated right. I go down to Bella, say, "I need a loaf of bread, I'll pay you Friday." She give it to me. What sense that make when I got money to go and spend it somewhere else and ignore the person who done right by me? That ain't in the Bible.

ROSE: We ain't talking about what's in the Bible. What sense it make to shop there when she overcharge?

TROY: You shop where you want to. I'll do my shopping where the people been good to me.

ROSE: Well, I don't think it's right for her to overcharge. That's all I was saying.

BONO: Look here . . . I got to get on. Lucille going be raising all kind of hell.

TROY: Where you going, nigger? We ain't finished this pint. Come here, finish this pint.

BONO: Well, hell, I am . . . if you ever turn the bottle loose.

TROY *(hands him the bottle):* The only thing I say about the A&P is I'm glad Cory got that job down there. Help him take care of his school clothes and things. Gabe done moved out and things getting tight around here. He got that job. . . . He can start to look out for himself.

ROSE: Cory done went and got recruited by a college football team.

TROY: I told that boy about that football stuff. The white man ain't gonna let him get nowhere with that football. I told him when he first come to me with it. Now you come telling me he done went and got more tied up in it. He ought to go and get recruited in how to fix cars or something where he can make a living.

ROSE: He ain't talking about making no living playing football. It's just something the boys in school do. They gonna send a recruiter by to talk to you. He'll tell you he ain't talking about making no living playing football. It's a honor to be recruited.

TROY: It ain't gonna get him nowhere. Bono'll tell you that.

BONO: If he be like you in the sports . . . he's gonna be all right. Ain't but two men ever played baseball as good as you. That's Babe Ruth and Josh Gibson.° Them's the only two men ever hit more home runs than you.

TROY: What it ever get me? Ain't got a pot to piss in or a window to throw it out of.

ROSE: Times have changed since you was playing baseball, Troy. That was before the war. Times have changed a lot since then.

Josh Gibson: (1911–1947), greatly admired black baseball player who played in the 1930s in the Negro leagues.

TROY: How in hell they done changed?

ROSE: They got lots of colored boys playing ball now. Baseball and football.

BONO: You right about that, Rose. Times have changed, Troy. You just come along too early.

TROY: There ought not never have been no time called too early! Now you take that fellow . . . what's that fellow they had playing right field for the Yankees back then? You know who I'm talking about, Bono. Used to play right field for the Yankees.

ROSE: Selkirk?

TROY: Selkirk! That's it! Man batting .269, understand? .269. What kind of sense that make? I was hitting .432 with thirty-seven home runs! Man batting .269 and playing right field for the Yankees! I saw Josh Gibson's daughter yesterday. She walking around with raggedy shoes on her feet. Now I bet you Selkirk's daughter ain't walking around with raggedy shoes on her feet! I bet you that!

ROSE: They got a lot of colored baseball players now. Jackie Robinson was the first. Folks had to wait for Jackie Robinson.

TROY: I done seen a hundred niggers play baseball better than Jackie Robinson. Hell, I know some teams Jackie Robinson couldn't even make! What you talking about Jackie Robinson. Jackie Robinson wasn't nobody. I'm talking about if you could play ball then they ought to have let you play. Don't care what color you were. Come telling me I come along too early. If you could play . . . then they ought to have let you play.

(TROY *takes a long drink from the bottle.*)

ROSE: You gonna drink yourself to death. You don't need to be drinking like that.

TROY: Death ain't nothing. I done seen him. Done wrassled with him. You can't tell me nothing about death. Death ain't nothing but a fastball on the outside corner. And you know what I'll do to that! Lookee here, Bono . . . am I lying? You get one of them fastballs, about waist high, over the outside corner of the plate where you can get the meat of the bat on it . . . and good god! You can kiss it goodbye. Now, am I lying?

BONO: Naw, you telling the truth there. I seen you do it.

TROY: If I'm lying . . . that 450 feet worth of lying!

(*Pause.*)

That's all death is to me. A fastball on the outside corner.

ROSE: I don't know why you want to get on talking about death.

TROY: Ain't nothing wrong with talking about death. That's part of life. Everybody gonna die. You gonna die, I'm gonna die. Bono's gonna die. Hell, we all gonna die.

ROSE: But you ain't got to talk about it. I don't like to talk about it.

TROY: You the one brought it up. Me and Bono was talking about base-ball . . . you tell me I'm gonna drink myself to death. Ain't that right, Bono? You know I don't drink this but one night out of the week. That's Friday night. I'm gonna drink just enough to where I can handle it. Then I cuts it loose. I leave it alone. So don't you worry about me drinking myself to death. 'Cause I ain't worried about Death. I done seen him. I done wrestled with him.

Look here, Bono . . . I looked up one day and Death was march-ing straight at me. Like Soldiers on Parade! The Army of Death was marching straight at me. The middle of July, 1941. It got real cold just like it be winter. It seem like Death himself reached out and touched me on the shoulder. He touch me just like I touch you. I got cold as ice and Death standing there grinning at me.

ROSE: Troy, why don't you hush that talk.

TROY: I say . . . What you want, Mr. Death? You be wanting me? You done brought your army to be getting me? I looked him dead in the eye. I wasn't fearing nothing. I was ready to tangle. Just like I'm ready to tangle now. The Bible say be ever vigilant. That's why I don't get but so drunk. I got to keep watch.

ROSE: Troy was right down there in Mercy Hospital. You remember he had pneumonia? Laying there with a fever talking plumb out of his head.

TROY: Death standing there staring at me . . . carrying that sickle in his hand. Finally he say, "You want bound over for another year?" See, just like that . . . "You want bound over for another year?" I told him, "Bound over hell! Let's settle this now!"

It seem like he kinda fell back when I said that, and all the cold went out of me. I reached down and grabbed that sickle and threw it just as far as I could throw it . . . and me and him commenced to wrestling.

We wrestled for three days and three nights. I can't say where I found the strength from. Every time it seemed like he was gonna get the best of me, I'd reach way down deep inside myself and find the strength to do him one better.

ROSE: Every time Troy tell that story he find different ways to tell it. Different things to make up about it.

TROY: I ain't making up nothing. I'm telling you the facts of what hap-pened. I wrestled with Death for three days and three nights and I'm standing here to tell you about it.

(Pause.)

All right. At the end of the third night we done weakened each other to where we can't hardly move. Death stood up, throwed on his robe . . . had him a white robe with a hood on it. He throwed on that robe and went off to look for his sickle. Say, "I'll be back." Just like that. "I'll be back." I told him, say, "Yeah, but . . . you gonna have to find me!" I wasn't no fool. I wan't going looking for him. Death ain't nothing to play with. And I know he's gonna get me. I know I got to join his army . . . his camp followers. But as long as I keep my strength and see him coming . . . as long as I keep up my vigilance . . . he's gonna have to fight to get me. I ain't going easy.

BONO: Well, look here, since you got to keep up your vigilance . . . let me have the bottle.

TROY: Aw hell, I shouldn't have told you that part. I should have left out that part.

ROSE: Troy be talking that stuff and half the time don't even know what he be talking about.

TROY: Bono know me better than that.

BONO: That's right. I know you. I know you got some Uncle Remus° in your blood. You got more stories than the devil got sinners.

TROY: Aw hell, I done seen him too! Done talked with the devil.

ROSE: Troy, don't nobody wanna be hearing all that stuff.

(LYONS *enters the yard from the street. Thirty-four years old,* TROY's *son by a previous marriage, he sports a neatly trimmed goatee, sport coat, white shirt, tieless and buttoned at the collar. Though he fancies himself a musician, he is more caught up in the rituals and "idea" of being a musician than in the actual practice of the music. He has come to borrow money from* TROY, *and while he knows he will be successful, he is uncertain as to what extent his lifestyle will be held up to scrutiny and ridicule.*)

LYONS: Hey, Pop.

TROY: What you come "Hey, Popping" me for?

LYONS: How you doing, Rose?

(*He kisses her.*)

Mr. Bono. How you doing?

BONO: Hey, Lyons . . . how you been?

TROY: He must have been doing all right. I ain't seen him around here last week.

ROSE: Troy, leave your boy alone. He come by to see you and you wanna start all that nonsense.

TROY: I ain't bothering Lyons.

(*Offers him the bottle.*)

Here . . . get you a drink. We got an understanding. I know why he come by to see me and he know I know.

Uncle Remus: The fictional narrator created by Joel Chandler Harris to tell traditional black stories.

LYONS: Come on, Pop . . . I just stopped by to say hi . . . see how you was doing.

TROY: You ain't stopped by yesterday.

ROSE: You gonna stay for supper, Lyons? I got some chicken cooking in the oven.

LYONS: No, Rose . . . thanks. I was just in the neighborhood and thought I'd stop by for a minute.

TROY: You was in the neighborhood all right, nigger. You telling the truth there. You was in the neighborhood cause it's my payday.

LYONS: Well, hell, since you mentioned it . . . let me have ten dollars.

TROY: I'll be damned! I'll die and go to hell and play blackjack with the devil before I give you ten dollars.

BONO: That's what I wanna know about . . . that devil you done seen.

LYONS: What . . . Pop done seen the devil? You too much, Pops.

TROY: Yeah, I done seen him. Talked to him too!

ROSE: You ain't seen no devil. I done told you that man ain't had nothing to do with the devil. Anything you can't understand, you want to call it the devil.

TROY: Look here, Bono . . . I went down to see Hertzberger about some furniture. Got three rooms for two-ninety-eight. That what it say on the radio. "Three rooms . . . two-ninety-eight." Even made up a little song about it. Go down there . . . man tell me I can't get no credit. I'm working every day and can't get no credit. What to do? I got an empty house with some raggedy furniture in it. Cory ain't got no bed. He's sleeping on a pile of rags on the floor. Working every day and can't get no credit. Come back here—Rose'll tell you—madder than hell. Sit down . . . try to figure what I'm gonna do. Come a knock on the door. Ain't been living here but three days. Who know I'm here? Open the door . . . devil standing there bigger than life. White fellow . . . got on good clothes and everything. Standing there with a clipboard in his hand. I ain't had to say nothing. First words come out of his mouth was . . . "I understand you need some furniture and can't get no credit." I liked to fell over. He say, "I'll give you all the credit you want, but you got to pay the interest on it." I told him, "Give me three rooms worth and charge whatever you want." Next day a truck pulled up here and two men unloaded them three rooms. Man what drove the truck give me a book. Say send ten dollars, first of every month to the address in the book and everything will be all right. Say if I miss a payment the devil was coming back and it'll be hell to pay. That was fifteen years ago. To this day . . . the first of the month I send my ten dollars, Rose'll tell you.

ROSE: Troy lying.

TROY: I ain't never seen that man since. Now you tell me who else that could have been but the devil? I ain't sold my soul or nothing like that, you understand. Naw, I wouldn't have truck with the devil about nothing like that. I got my furniture and pays my ten dollars the first of the month just like clockwork.

BONO: How long you say you been paying this ten dollars a month?

TROY: Fifteen years!

BONO: Hell, ain't you finished paying for it yet? How much the man done charged you.

TROY: Ah hell, I done paid for it. I done paid for it ten times over! The fact is I'm scared to stop paying it.

ROSE: Troy lying. We got that furniture from Mr. Glickman. He ain't paying no ten dollars a month to nobody.

TROY: Aw hell, woman. Bono know I ain't that big a fool.

LYONS: I was just getting ready to say ... I know where there's a bridge for sale.

TROY: Look here, I'll tell you this ... it don't matter to me if he was the devil. It don't matter if the devil give credit. Somebody has got to give it.

ROSE: It ought to matter. You going around talking about having truck with the devil ... God's the one you gonna have to answer to. He's the one gonna be at the Judgment.

LYONS: Yeah, well, look here, Pop ... let me have that ten dollars. I'll give it back to you. Bonnie got a job working at the hospital.

TROY: What I tell you, Bono? The only time I see this nigger is when he wants something. That's the only time I see him.

LYONS: Come on, Pop, Mr. Bono don't want to hear all that. Let me have the ten dollars. I told you Bonnie working.

TROY: What that mean to me? "Bonnie working." I don't care if she working. Go ask her for the ten dollars if she working. Talking about "Bonnie working." Why ain't you working?

LYONS: Aw, Pop, you know I can't find no decent job. Where am I gonna get a job at? You know I can't get no job.

TROY: I told you I know some people down there. I can get you on the rubbish if you want to work. I told you that the last time you came by here asking me for something.

LYONS: Naw, Pop ... thanks. That ain't for me. I don't wanna be carrying nobody's rubbish. I don't wanna be punching nobody's time clock.

TROY: What's the matter, you too good to carry people's rubbish? Where you think that ten dollars you talking about come from? I'm just supposed to haul people's rubbish and give my money to you cause you too lazy to work. You too lazy to work and wanna know why you ain't got what I got.

ROSE: What hospital Bonnie working at? Mercy?

LYONS: She's down at Passavant working in the laundry.

TROY: I ain't got nothing as it is. I give you that ten dollars and I got to eat beans the rest of the week. Naw ... you ain't getting no ten dollars here.

LYONS: You ain't got to be eating no beans. I don't know why you wanna say that.

TROY: I ain't got no extra money. Gabe done moved over to Miss Pearl's paying her the rent and things done got tight around here. I can't afford to be giving you every payday.

LYONS: I ain't asked you to give me nothing. I asked you to loan me ten dollars. I know you got ten dollars.

TROY: Yeah, I got it. You know why I got it? Cause I don't throw my money away out there in the streets. You living the fast life . . . wanna be a musician . . . running around in them clubs and things . . . then, you learn to take care of yourself. You ain't gonna find me going and asking nobody for nothing. I done spent too many years without.

LYONS: You and me is two different people, Pop.

TROY: I done learned my mistake and learned to do what's right by it. You still trying to get something for nothing. Life don't owe you nothing. You owe it to yourself. Ask Bono. He'll tell you I'm right.

LYONS: You got your way of dealing with the world . . . I got mine. The only thing that matters to me is the music.

TROY: Yeah, I can see that! It don't matter how you gonna eat . . . where your next dollar is coming from. You telling the truth there.

LYONS: I know I got to eat. But I got to live too. I need something that gonna help me to get out of the bed in the morning. Make me feel like I belong in the world. I don't bother nobody. I just stay with my music cause that's the only way I can find to live in the world. Otherwise there ain't no telling what I might do. Now I don't come criticizing you and how you live. I just come by to ask you for ten dollars. I don't wanna hear all that about how I live.

TROY: Boy, your mama did a hell of a job raising you.

LYONS: You can't change me, Pop. I'm thirty-four years old. If you wanted to change me, you should have been there when I was growing up. I come by to see you . . . ask for ten dollars and you want to talk about how I was raised. You don't know nothing about how I was raised.

ROSE: Let the boy have ten dollars, Troy.

TROY (to LYONS): What the hell you looking at me for? I ain't got no ten dollars. You know what I do with my money.

(To ROSE.)

Give him ten dollars if you want him to have it.

ROSE: I will. Just as soon as you turn it loose.

TROY (handing ROSE the money): There it is. Seventy-six dollars and forty-two cents. You see this, Bono? Now, I ain't gonna get but six of that back.

ROSE: You ought to stop telling that lie. Here, Lyons. (She hands him the money.)

LYONS: Thanks, Rose. Look . . . I got to run . . . I'll see you later.

TROY: Wait a minute. You gonna say, "thanks, Rose" and ain't gonna look to see where she got that ten dollars from? See how they do me, Bono?

LYONS: I know she got it from you, Pop. Thanks. I'll give it back to you.

TROY: There he go telling another lie. Time I see that ten dollars . . . he'll be owing me thirty more.

LYONS: See you, Mr. Bono.

BONO: Take care, Lyons!

LYONS: Thanks, Pop. I'll see you again.

(LYONS *exits the yard.*)

TROY: I don't know why he don't go and get him a decent job and take care of that woman he got.

BONO: He'll be all right, Troy. The boy is still young.

TROY: The *boy* is thirty-four years old.

ROSE: Let's not get off into all that.

BONO: Look here . . . I got to be going. I got to be getting on. Lucille gonna be waiting.

TROY (*puts his arm around* ROSE): See this woman, Bono? I love this woman. I love this woman so much it hurts. I love her so much . . . I done run out of ways of loving her. So I got to go back to basics. Don't you come by my house Monday morning talking about time to go to work . . . 'cause I'm still gonna be stroking!

ROSE: Troy! Stop it now!

BONO: I ain't paying him no mind, Rose. That ain't nothing but gin-talk. Go on, Troy. I'll see you Monday.

TROY: Don't you come by my house, nigger! I done told you what I'm gonna be doing.

(*The lights go down to black.*)

SCENE II

The lights come up on ROSE *hanging up clothes. She hums and sings softly to herself. It is the following morning.*

ROSE (*sings*): Jesus, be a fence all around me every day
Jesus, I want you to protect me as I travel on my way.
Jesus, be a fence all around me every day.

(TROY *enters from the house.*)

Jesus, I want you to protect me
As I travel on my way.
(*To* TROY.) 'Morning. You ready for breakfast? I can fix it soon as I finish hanging up these clothes?

TROY: I got the coffee on. That'll be all right. I'll just drink some of that this morning.

ROSE: That 651 hit yesterday. That's the second time this month. Miss Pearl hit for a dollar . . . seem like those that need the least always get lucky. Poor folks can't get nothing.

TROY: Them numbers don't know nobody. I don't know why you fool with them. You and Lyons both.

ROSE: It's something to do.

TROY: You ain't doing nothing but throwing your money away.

ROSE: Troy, you know I don't play foolishly. I just play a nickel here and a nickel there.

TROY: That's two nickels you done thrown away.

ROSE: Now I hit sometimes . . . that makes up for it. It always comes in handy when I do hit. I don't hear you complaining then.

TROY: I ain't complaining now. I just say it's foolish. Trying to guess out of six hundred ways which way the number gonna come. If I had all the money niggers, these Negroes, throw away on numbers for one week—just one week—I'd be a rich man.

ROSE: Well, you wishing and calling it foolish ain't gonna stop folks from playing numbers. That's one thing for sure. Besides . . . some good things come from playing numbers. Look where Pope done bought him that restaurant off of numbers.

TROY: I can't stand niggers like that. Man ain't had two dimes to rub to-gether. He walking around with his shoes all run over bumming money for cigarettes. All right. Got lucky there and hit the numbers . . .

ROSE: Troy, I know all about it.

TROY: Had good sense, I'll say that for him. He ain't throwed his money away. I seen niggers hit the numbers and go through two thousand dollars in four days. Man bought him that restaurant down there . . . fixed it up real nice . . . and then didn't want nobody to come in it! A Negro go in there and can't get no kind of service. I seen a white fellow come in there and order a bowl of stew. Pope picked all the meat out the pot for him. Man ain't had nothing but a bowl of meat! Negro come behind him and ain't got nothing but the potatoes and carrots. Talking about what numbers do for people, you picked a wrong example. Ain't done nothing but make a worser fool out of him than he was before.

ROSE: Troy, you ought to stop worrying about what happened at work yesterday.

TROY: I ain't worried. Just told me to be down there at the Commis-sioner's office on Friday. Everybody think they gonna fire me. I ain't worried about them firing me. You ain't got to worry about that.

(Pause.)

Where's Cory? Cory in the house? *(Calls.)* Cory?

ROSE: He gone out.

TROY: Out, huh? He gone out 'cause he know I want him to help me with this fence. I know how he is. That boy scared of work.

(GABRIEL enters. He comes halfway down the alley and, hearing TROY's voice, stops.)

TROY *(continues)*: He ain't done a lick of work in his life.

ROSE: He had to go to football practice. Coach wanted them to get in a little extra practice before the season start.

TROY: I got his practice . . . running out of here before he get his chores done.

ROSE: Troy, what is wrong with you this morning? Don't nothing set right with you. Go on back in there and go to bed . . . get up on the other side.

TROY: Why something got to be wrong with me? I ain't said nothing wrong with me.

ROSE: You got something to say about everything. First it's the numbers . . . then it's the way the man runs his restaurant . . . then you done got on Cory. What's it gonna be next? Take a look up there and see if the weather suits you . . . or is it gonna be how you gonna put up the fence with the clothes hanging in the yard.

TROY: You hit the nail on the head then.

ROSE: I know you like I know the back of my hand. Go on in there and get you some coffee . . . see if that straighten you up. 'Cause you ain't right this morning.

(TROY starts into the house and sees GABRIEL. GABRIEL starts singing. TROY's brother, he is seven years younger than TROY. Injured in World War II, he has a metal plate in his head. He carries an old trumpet tied around his waist and believes with every fiber of his being that he is the Archangel Gabriel. He carries a chipped basket with an assortment of discarded fruits and vegetables he has picked up in the strip district and which he attempts to sell.)

GABRIEL *(singing)*: Yes, ma'am, I got plums
You ask me how I sell them
Oh ten cents apiece
Three for a quarter
Come and buy now
'Cause I'm here today
And tomorrow I'll be gone

(GABRIEL enters.)

Hey, Rose!

ROSE: How you doing, Gabe?

GABRIEL: There's Troy . . . Hey, Troy!

TROY: Hey, Gabe.

(Exit into kitchen.)

ROSE *(to GABRIEL)*: What you got there?

GABRIEL: You know what I got, Rose. I got fruits and vegetables.

ROSE *(looking in basket)*: Where's all these plums you talking about?

GABRIEL: I ain't got no plums today, Rose. I was just singing that. Have some tomorrow. Put me in a big order for plums. Have enough plums tomorrow for St. Peter and everybody.

(TROY *reenters from kitchen, crosses to steps.*)
(*To* ROSE.)

Troy's mad at me.

TROY: I ain't mad at you. What I got to be mad at you about? You ain't done nothing to me.

GABRIEL: I just moved over to Miss Pearl's to keep out from in your way. I ain't mean no harm by it.

TROY: Who said anything about that? I ain't said anything about that.

GABRIEL: You ain't mad at me, is you?

TROY: Naw . . . I ain't mad at you, Gabe. If I was mad at you I'd tell you about it.

GABRIEL: Got me two rooms. In the basement. Got my own door too. Wanna see my key?

(*He holds up a key.*)

That's my own key! Ain't nobody else got a key like that. That's my key! My two rooms!

TROY: Well, that's good, Gabe. You got your own key . . . that's good.

ROSE: You hungry, Gabe? I was just fixing to cook Troy his breakfast.

GABRIEL: I'll take some biscuits. You got some biscuits? Did you know when I was in heaven . . . every morning me and St. Peter would sit down by the gate and eat some big fat biscuits? Oh, yeah! We had us a good time. We'd sit there and eat us them biscuits and then St. Peter would go off to sleep and tell me to wake him up when it's time to open the gates for the judgment.

ROSE: Well, come on . . . I'll make up a batch of biscuits.

(ROSE *exits into the house.*)

GABRIEL: Troy . . . St. Peter got your name in the book. I seen it. It say . . . Troy Maxson. I say . . . I know him! He got the same name like what I got. That's my brother!

TROY: How many times you gonna tell me that, Gabe?

GABRIEL: Ain't got my name in the book. Don't have to have my name. I done died and went to heaven. He got your name though. One morning St. Peter was looking at his book . . . marking it up for the judgment . . . and he let me see your name. Got it in there under M. Got Rose's name . . . I ain't seen it like I seen yours . . . but I know it's in there. He got a great big book. Got everybody's name what was ever been born. That's what he told me. But I seen your name. Seen it with my own eyes.

TROY: Go on in the house there. Rose going to fix you something to eat.

GABRIEL: Oh, I ain't hungry. I done had breakfast with Aunt Jemimah. She come by and cooked me up a whole mess of flapjacks. Remember how we used to eat them flapjacks?

TROY: Go on in the house and get you something to eat now.

GABRIEL: I got to go sell my plums. I done sold some tomatoes. Got me two quarters. Wanna see?

(He shows TROY *his quarters.)*

I'm gonna save them and buy me a new horn so St. Peter can hear me when it's time to open the gates.

(GABRIEL stops suddenly. Listens.)

Hear that? That's the hellhounds. I got to chase them out of here. Go on get out of here! Get out!

(GABRIEL exits singing.)

Better get ready for the judgment
Better get ready for the judgment
My Lord is coming down

(ROSE enters from the house.)

TROY: He gone off somewhere.

GABRIEL *(offstage)*: Better get ready for the judgment
Better get ready for the judgment morning
Better get ready for the judgment
My God is coming down

ROSE: He ain't eating right. Miss Pearl say she can't get him to eat nothing.

TROY: What you want me to do about it, Rose? I done did everything I can for the man. I can't make him get well. Man got half his head blown away . . . what you expect?

ROSE: Seem like something ought to be done to help him.

TROY: Man don't bother nobody. He just mixed up from that metal plate he got in his head. Ain't no sense for him to go back into the hospital.

ROSE: Least he be eating right. They can help him take care of himself.

TROY: Don't nobody wanna be locked up, Rose. What you wanna lock him up for? Man go over there and fight the war . . . messin' around with them Japs, get half his head blown off . . . and they give him a lousy three thousand dollars. And I had to swoop down on that.

ROSE: Is you fixing to go into that again?

TROY: That's the only way I got a roof over my head . . . cause of that metal plate.

ROSE: Ain't no sense you blaming yourself for nothing. Gabe wasn't in no condition to manage that money. You done what was right by him. Can't nobody say you ain't done what was right by him. Look how long you took care of him . . . till he wanted to have his own place and moved over there with Miss Pearl.

TROY: That ain't what I'm saying, woman! I'm just stating the facts. If my brother didn't have that metal plate in his head . . . I wouldn't have a pot to piss in or a window to throw it out of. And I'm fifty-three years old. Now see if you can understand that!

(TROY gets up from the porch and starts to exit the yard.)

ROSE: Where you going off to? You been running out of here every Saturday for weeks. I thought you was gonna work on this fence?

TROY: I'm gonna walk down to Taylors'. Listen to the ball game. I'll be back in a bit. I'll work on it when I get back.

(He exits the yard. The lights go to black.)

SCENE III

The lights come up on the yard. It is four hours later. ROSE *is taking down the clothes from the line.* CORY *enters carrying his football equipment.*

ROSE: Your daddy like to had a fit with you running out of here this morning without doing your chores.

CORY: I told you I had to go to practice.

ROSE: He say you were supposed to help him with this fence.

CORY: He been saying that the last four or five Saturdays, and then he don't never do nothing but go down to Taylors'. Did you tell him about the recruiter?

ROSE: Yeah, I told him.

CORY: What he say?

ROSE: He ain't said nothing too much. You get in there and get started on your chores before he gets back. Go on and scrub down them steps before he gets back here hollering and carrying on.

CORY: I'm hungry. What you got to eat, Mama?

ROSE: Go on and get started on your chores. I got some meat loaf in there. Go on and make you a sandwich . . . and don't leave no mess in there.

(CORY exits into the house. ROSE *continues to take down the clothes.* TROY *enters the yard and sneaks up and grabs her from behind.)*

Troy! Go on, now. You liked to scared me to death. What was the score of the game? Lucille had me on the phone and I couldn't keep up with it.

TROY: What I care about the game? Come here, woman. *(He tries to kiss her.)*

ROSE: I thought you went down Taylors' to listen to the game. Go on, Troy! You supposed to be putting up this fence.

TROY (*attempting to kiss her again*): I'll put it up when I finish with what is at hand.

ROSE: Go on, Troy. I ain't studying you.

TROY (*chasing after her*): I'm studying you . . . fixing to do my homework!

ROSE: Troy, you better leave me alone.

TROY: Where's Cory? That boy brought his butt home yet?

ROSE: He's in the house doing his chores.

TROY (*calling*): Cory! Get your butt out here, boy!

(ROSE *exits into the house with the laundry.* TROY *goes over to the pile of wood, picks up a board, and starts sawing.* CORY *enters from the house.*)

TROY: You just now coming in here from leaving this morning?

CORY: Yeah, I had to go to football practice.

TROY: Yeah, what?

CORY: Yessir.

TROY: I ain't but two seconds off you noway. The garbage sitting in there overflowing . . . you ain't done none of your chores . . . and you come in here talking about "Yeah."

CORY: I was just getting ready to do my chores now, Pop . . .

TROY: Your first chore is to help me with this fence on Saturday. Everything else come after that. Now get that saw and cut them boards.

(CORY *takes the saw and begins cutting the boards.* TROY *continues working. There is a long pause.*)

CORY: Hey, Pop . . . why don't you buy a TV?

TROY: What I want with a TV? What I want one of them for?

CORY: Everybody got one. Earl, Ba Bra . . . Jesse!

TROY: I ain't asked you who had one. I say what I want with one?

CORY: So you can watch it. They got lots of things on TV. Baseball games and everything. We could watch the World Series.

TROY: Yeah . . . and how much this TV cost?

CORY: I don't know. They got them on sale for around two hundred dollars.

TROY: Two hundred dollars, huh?

CORY: That ain't that much, Pop.

TROY: Naw, it's just two hundred dollars. See that roof you got over your head at night? Let me tell you something about that roof. It's been over ten years since that roof was last tarred. See now . . . the snow come this winter and sit up there on that roof like it is . . . and it's gonna seep inside. It's just gonna be a little bit . . . ain't gonna hardly notice it. Then the next thing you know, it's gonna be leaking all over the house. Then the wood rot from all that water and you gonna need a whole new roof. Now, how much you think it cost to get that roof tarred?

CORY: I don't know.

TROY: Two hundred and sixty-four dollars . . . cash money. While you thinking about a TV, I got to be thinking about the roof . . . and whatever else go wrong around here. Now if you had two hundred dollars, what would you do . . . fix the roof or buy a TV?

CORY: I'd buy a TV. Then when the roof started to leak . . . when it needed fixing . . . I'd fix it.

TROY: Where you gonna get the money from? You done spent it for a TV. You gonna sit up and watch the water run all over your brand new TV.

CORY: Aw, Pop. You got money. I know you do.

TROY: Where I got it at, huh?

CORY: You got it in the bank.

TROY: You wanna see my bankbook? You wanna see that seventy-three dollars and twenty-two cents I got sitting up in there.

CORY: You ain't got to pay for it all at one time. You can put a down payment on it and carry it on home with you.

TROY: Not me. I ain't gonna owe nobody nothing if I can help it. Miss a payment and they come and snatch it right out your house. Then what you got? Now, soon as I get two hundred dollars clear, then I'll buy a TV. Right now, as soon as I get two hundred and sixty-four dollars, I'm gonna have this roof tarred.

CORY: Aw . . . Pop!

TROY: You go on and get you two hundred dollars and buy one if ya want it. I got better things to do with my money.

CORY: I can't get no two hundred dollars. I ain't never seen two hundred dollars.

TROY: I'll tell you what . . . you get you a hundred dollars and I'll put the other hundred with it.

CORY: All right, I'm gonna show you.

TROY: You gonna show me how you can cut them boards right now.

(CORY *begins to cut the boards. There is a long pause.*)

CORY: The Pirates won today. That makes five in a row.

TROY: I ain't thinking about the Pirates. Got an all-white team. Got that boy . . . that Puerto Rican boy . . . Clemente. Don't even half-play him. That boy could be something if they give him a chance. Play him one day and sit him on the bench the next.

CORY: He gets a lot of chances to play.

TROY: I'm talking about playing regular. Playing every day so you can get your timing. That's what I'm talking about.

CORY: They got some white guys on the team that don't play every day. You can't play everybody at the same time.

TROY: If they got a white fellow sitting on the bench . . . you can bet your last dollar he can't play! The colored guy got to be twice as good before he get on the team. That's why I don't want you to get all tied up in

them sports. Man on the team and what it get him? They got colored
on the team and don't use them. Same as not having them. All them
teams the same.

CORY: The Braves got Hank Aaron and Wes Covington. Hank Aaron hit
two home runs today. That makes forty-three.

TROY: Hank Aaron ain't nobody. That's what you supposed to do. That's
how you supposed to play the game. Ain't nothing to it. It's just a
matter of timing . . . getting the right follow-through. Hell, I can hit
forty-three home runs right now!

CORY: Not off no major-league pitching, you couldn't.

TROY: We had better pitching in the Negro leagues. I hit seven home runs
off of Satchel Paige.° You can't get no better than that!

CORY: Sandy Koufax. He's leading the league in strikeouts.

TROY: I ain't thinking of no Sandy Koufax.

CORY: You got Warren Spahn and Lew Burdette. I bet you couldn't hit
no home runs off of Warren Spahn.

TROY: I'm through with it now. You go on and cut them boards.

(Pause.)

Your mama tell me you done got recruited by a college football team?
Is that right?

CORY: Yeah. Coach Zellman say the recruiter gonna be coming by to talk
to you. Get you to sign the permission papers.

TROY: I thought you supposed to be working down there at the A&P.
Ain't you suppose to be working down there after school?

CORY: Mr. Stawicki say he gonna hold my job for me until after the
football season. Say starting next week I can work weekends.

TROY: I thought we had an understanding about this football stuff? You
suppose to keep up with your chores and hold that job down at the
A&P. Ain't been around here all day on a Saturday. Ain't none of your
chores done . . . and now you telling me you done quit your job.

CORY: I'm gonna be working weekends.

TROY: You damn right you are! And ain't no need for nobody coming
around here to talk to me about signing nothing.

CORY: Hey, Pop . . . you can't do that. He's coming all the way from
North Carolina.

TROY: I don't care where he coming from. The white man ain't gonna let
you get nowhere with that football noway. You go on and get your
book-learning so you can work yourself up in that A&P or learn how
to fix cars or build houses or something, get you a trade. That way you
have something can't nobody take away from you. You go on and learn

---

Satchel Paige: (1906?–1982), greatly admired baseball player who pitched in the Negro leagues.

how to put your hands to some good use. Besides hauling people's garbage.

CORY: I get good grades, Pop. That's why the recruiter wants to talk with you. You got to keep up your grades to get recruited. This way I'll be going to college. I'll get a chance . . .

TROY: First you gonna get your butt down there to the A&P and get your job back.

CORY: Mr. Stawicki done already hired somebody else 'cause I told him I was playing football.

TROY: You a bigger fool than I thought . . . to let somebody take away your job so you can play some football. Where you gonna get your money to take out your girlfriend and whatnot? What kind of foolishness is that to let somebody take away your job?

CORY: I'm still gonna be working weekends.

TROY: Naw . . . naw. You getting your butt out of here and finding you another job.

CORY: Come on, Pop! I got to practice. I can't work after school and play football too. The team needs me. That's what Coach Zellman say . . .

TROY: I don't care what nobody else say. I'm the boss . . . you understand? I'm the boss around here. I do the only saying what counts.

CORY: Come on, Pop!

TROY: I asked you . . . did you understand?

CORY: Yeah . . .

TROY: What?!

CORY: Yessir.

TROY: You go on down there to that A&P and see if you can get your job back. If you can't do both . . . then you quit the football team. You've got to take the crookeds with the straights.

CORY: Yessir.

(Pause.)

Can I ask you a question?

TROY: What the hell you wanna ask me? Mr. Stawicki the one you got the questions for.

CORY: How come you ain't never liked me?

TROY: Liked you? Who the hell say I got to like you? What law is there say I got to like you? Wanna stand up in my face and ask a damn fool-ass question like that. Talking about liking somebody. Come here, boy, when I talk to you.

(CORY comes over to where TROY is working. He stands slouched over and TROY shoves him on his shoulder.)

Straighten up, goddammit! I asked you a question . . . what law is there say I got to like you?

CORY: None.

TROY: Well, all right then! Don't you eat every day?

(Pause.)

Answer me when I talk to you! Don't you eat every day?

CORY: Yeah.

TROY: Nigger, as long as you in my house, you put that sir on the end of it when you talk to me!

CORY: Yes . . . sir.

TROY: You eat every day.

CORY: Yessir!

TROY: Got a roof over your head.

CORY: Yessir!

TROY: Got clothes on your back.

CORY: Yessir.

TROY: Why you think that is?

CORY: Cause of you.

TROY: Ah, hell I know it's cause of me . . . but why do you think that is?

CORY *(hesitant)*: Cause you like me.

TROY: Like you? I go out of here every morning . . . bust my butt . . . putting up with them crackers° every day . . . cause I like you? You about the biggest fool I ever saw.

(Pause.)

It's my job. It's my responsibility! You understand that? A man got to take care of his family. You live in my house . . . sleep you behind on my bedclothes . . . fill you belly up with my food . . . cause you my son. You my flesh and blood. Not 'cause I like you! Cause it's my duty to take care of you. I owe a responsibility to you! Let's get this straight right here . . . before it go along any further . . . I ain't got to like you. Mr. Rand don't give me my money come payday cause he likes me. He gives me cause he owe me. I done give you everything I had to give you. I gave you your life! Me and your mama worked that out between us. And liking your black ass wasn't part of the bargain. Don't you try and go through life worrying about if somebody like you or not. You best be making sure they doing right by you. You understand what I'm saying, boy?

CORY: Yessir.

TROY: Then get the hell out of my face, and get on down to that A&P.

(ROSE has been standing behind the screen door for much of the scene. She enters as CORY exits.)

---

crackers: Derogatory slang, expression for white people.

ROSE: Why don't you let the boy go ahead and play football, Troy? Ain't no harm in that. He's just trying to be like you with the sports.

TROY: I don't want him to be like me! I want him to move as far away from my life as he can get. You the only decent thing that ever happened to me. I wish him that. But I don't wish him a thing else from my life. I decided seventeen years ago that boy wasn't getting involved in no sports. Not after what they did to me in the sports.

ROSE: Troy, why don't you admit you was too old to play in the major leagues? For once . . . why don't you admit that?

TROY: What do you mean too old? Don't come telling me I was too old. I just wasn't the right color. Hell, I'm fifty-three years old and can do better than Selkirk's .269 right now!

ROSE: How was you gonna play ball when you were over forty? Sometimes I can't get no sense out of you.

TROY: I got good sense, woman. I got sense enough not to let my boy get hurt over playing no sports. You been mothering that boy too much. Worried about if people like him.

ROSE: Everything that boy do . . . he do for you. He wants you to say "Good job, son." That's all.

TROY: Rose, I ain't got time for that. He's alive. He's healthy. He's got to make his own way. I made mine. Ain't nobody gonna hold his hand when he get out there in that world.

ROSE: Times have changed from when you was young, Troy. People change. The world's changing around you and you can't even see it.

TROY (*slow, methodical*): Woman . . . I do the best I can do. I come in here every Friday. I carry a sack of potatoes and a bucket of lard. You all line up at the door with your hands out. I give you the lint from my pockets. I give you my sweat and my blood. I ain't got no tears. I done spent them. We go upstairs in that room at night . . . and I fall down on you and try to blast a hole into forever. I get up Monday morning . . . find my lunch on the table. I go out. Make my way. Find my strength to carry me through to the next Friday.

(Pause.)

That's all I got, Rose. That's all I got to give. I can't give nothing else.

(TROY exits into the house. The lights go down to black.)

SCENE IV

It is Friday. Two weeks later. CORY *starts out of the house with his football equipment. The phone rings.*

CORY (*calling*): I got it!

(He answers the phone and stands in the screen door talking.)

Hello? Hey, Jesse. Naw . . . I was just getting ready to leave now.

ROSE *(calling):* Cory!

CORY: I told you, man, them spikes is all tore up. You can use them if you want, but they ain't no good. Earl got some spikes.

ROSE *(calling):* Cory!

CORY *(calling to* ROSE*):* Mam? I'm talking to Jesse.

(Into phone.)

When she say that? *(Pause.)* Aw, you lying, man. I'm gonna tell her you said that.

ROSE *(calling):* Cory, don't you go nowhere!

CORY: I got to go to the game, Ma!

(Into the phone.)

Yeah, hey, look, I'll talk to you later. Yeah, I'll meet you over Earl's house. Later. Bye, Ma.

(CORY exits the house and starts out the yard.)

ROSE: Cory, where you going off to? You got that stuff all pulled out and thrown all over your room.

CORY *(in the yard):* I was looking for my spikes. Jesse wanted to borrow my spikes.

ROSE: Get up there and get that cleaned up before your daddy get back in here.

CORY: I got to go to the game! I'll clean it up *when I get back.*

(CORY exits.)

ROSE: That's all he need to do is see that room all messed up.

(ROSE exits into the house. TROY and BONO enter the yard. TROY is dressed in clothes other than his work clothes.)

BONO: He told him the same thing he told you. Take it to the union.

TROY: Brownie ain't got that much sense. Man wasn't thinking about nothing. He wait until I confront them on it . . . then he wanna come crying seniority.

(Calls.)

Hey, Rose!

BONO: I wish I could have seen Mr. Rand's face when he told you.

TROY: He couldn't get it out of his mouth! Liked to bit his tongue! When they called me down there to the Commissioner's office . . . he thought they was gonna fire me. Like everybody else.

BONO: I didn't think they was gonna fire you. I thought they was gonna put you on the warning paper.

TROY: Hey, Rose!

(To BONO.*)*

Yeah, Mr. Rand like to bit his tongue.

*(*TROY *breaks the seal on the bottle, takes a drink, and hands it to* BONO.*)*

BONO: I see you run right down to Taylors' and told that Alberta gal.

TROY *(calling)*: Hey, Rose! *(To* BONO.*)* I told everybody. Hey, Rose! I went down there to cash my check.

ROSE *(entering from the house)*: Hush all that hollering, man! I know you out here. What they say down there at the Commissioner's office?

TROY: You supposed to come when I call you, woman. Bono'll tell you that.

(To BONO.*)*

Don't Lucille come when you call her?

ROSE: Man, hush your mouth. I ain't no dog . . . talk about "come when you call me."

TROY *(puts his arm around* ROSE*)*: You hear this, Bono? I had me an old dog used to get uppity like that. You say, "C'mere, Blue!" . . . and he just lay there and look at you. End up getting a stick and chasing him away trying to make him come.

ROSE: I ain't studying you and your dog. I remember you used to sing that old song.

TROY *(he sings)*: Hear it ring! Hear it ring! I had a dog his name was Blue.

ROSE: Don't nobody wanna hear you sing that old song.

TROY *(sings)*: You know Blue was mighty true.

ROSE: Used to have Cory running around here singing that song.

BONO: Hell, I remember that song myself.

TROY *(sings)*: You know Blue was a good old dog.
Blue treed a possum in a hollow log.
That was my daddy's song. My daddy made up that song.

ROSE: I don't care who made it up. Don't nobody wanna hear you sing it.

TROY *(makes a song like calling a dog)*: Come here, woman.

ROSE: You come in here carrying on, I reckon they ain't fired you. What they say down there at the Commissioner's office?

TROY: Look here, Rose . . . Mr. Rand called me into his office today when I got back from talking to them people down there . . . it come from up top . . . he called me in and told me they was making me a driver.

ROSE: Troy, you kidding!

TROY: No I ain't. Ask Bono.

ROSE: Well, that's great, Troy. Now you don't have to hassle them people no more.

*(*LYONS *enters from the street.)*

TROY: Aw hell, I wasn't looking to see you today. I thought you was in jail. Got it all over the front page of the *Courier* about them raiding Sefus' place . . . where you be hanging out with all them thugs.

LYONS: Hey, Pop . . . that ain't got nothing to do with me. I don't go down there gambling. I go down there to sit in with the band. I ain't got nothing to do with the gambling part. They got some good music down there.

TROY: They got some rogues . . . is what they got.

LYONS: How you been, Mr. Bono? Hi, Rose.

BONO: I see where you playing down at the Crawford Grill tonight.

ROSE: How come you ain't brought Bonnie like I told you. You should have brought Bonnie with you, she ain't been over in a month of Sundays.

LYONS: I was just in the neighborhood . . . thought I'd stop by.

TROY: Here he come . . .

BONO: Your daddy got a promotion on the rubbish. He's gonna be the first colored driver. Ain't got to do nothing but sit up there and read the paper like them white fellows.

LYONS: Hey, Pop . . . if you knew how to read you'd be all right.

BONO: Naw . . . naw . . . you mean if the nigger knew how to *drive* he'd be all right. Been fighting with them people about driving and ain't even got a license. Mr. Rand know you ain't got no driver's license?

TROY: Driving ain't nothing. All you do is point the truck where you want it to go. Driving ain't nothing.

BONO: Do Mr. Rand know you ain't got no driver's license? That's what I'm talking about. I ain't asked if driving was easy. I asked if Mr. Rand know you ain't got no driver's license.

TROY: He ain't got to know. The man ain't got to know my business. Time he find out, I have two or three driver's licenses.

LYONS (*going into his pocket*): Say, look here, Pop . . .

TROY: I knew it was coming. Didn't I tell you, Bono? I know what kind of "Look here, Pop" that was. The nigger fixing to ask me for some money. It's Friday night. It's my payday. All them rogues down there on the avenue . . . the ones that ain't in jail . . . and Lyons is hopping in his shoes to get down there with them.

LYONS: See, Pop . . . if you give somebody else a chance to talk sometime, you'd see that I was fixing to pay you back your ten dollars like I told you. Here . . . I told you I'd pay you when Bonnie got paid.

TROY: Naw . . . you go ahead and keep that ten dollars. Put it in the bank. The next time you feel like you wanna come by here and ask me for something . . . you go on down there and get that.

LYONS: Here's your ten dollars, Pop. I told you I don't want you to give me nothing. I just wanted to borrow ten dollars.

TROY: Naw . . . you go on and keep that for the next time you want to ask me.

LYONS: Come on, Pop . . . here go your ten dollars.

ROSE: Why don't you go on and let the boy pay you back, Troy?

LYONS: Here you go, Rose. If you don't take it I'm gonna have to hear about it for the next six months.

(He hands her the money.)

ROSE: You can hand yours over here too, Troy.

TROY: You see this, Bono. You see how they do me.

BONO: Yeah, Lucille do me the same way.

(GABRIEL is heard singing offstage. He enters.)

GABRIEL: Better get ready for the judgment! Better get ready for . . . Hey! . . . Hey! . . . There's Troy's boy!

LYONS: How are you doing, Uncle Gabe?

GABRIEL: Lyons . . . The King of the Jungle! Rose . . . hey, Rose. Got a flower for you.

(He takes a rose from his pocket.)

Picked it myself. That's the same rose like you is!

ROSE: That's right nice of you, Gabe.

LYONS: What you been doing, Uncle Gabe?

GABRIEL: Oh, I been chasing hellhounds and waiting on the time to tell St. Peter to open the gates.

LYONS: You been chasing hellhounds, huh? Well . . . you doing the right thing, Uncle Gabe. Somebody got to chase them.

GABRIEL: Oh, yeah . . . I know it. The devil's strong. The devil ain't no pushover. Hellhounds snipping at everybody's heels. But I got my trumpet waiting on the judgment time.

LYONS: Waiting on the Battle of Armageddon, huh?

GABRIEL: Ain't gonna be too much of a battle when God get to waving that Judgment sword. But the people's gonna have a hell of a time trying to get into heaven if them gates ain't open.

LYONS *(putting his arm around GABRIEL)*: You hear this, Pop. Uncle Gabe, you all right!

GABRIEL *(laughing with LYONS)*: Lyons! King of the Jungle.

ROSE: You gonna stay for supper, Gabe. Want me to fix you a plate?

GABRIEL: I'll take a sandwich, Rose. Don't want no plate. Just wanna eat with my hands. I'll take a sandwich.

ROSE: How about you, Lyons? You staying? Got some short ribs cooking.

LYONS: Naw, I won't eat nothing till after we finished playing.

(Pause.)

You ought to come down and listen to me play, Pop.

TROY: I don't like that Chinese music. All that noise.

ROSE: Go on in the house and wash up, Gabe . . . I'll fix you a sandwich.

GABRIEL *(to* LYONS, *as he exits)*: Troy's mad at me.

LYONS: What you mad at Uncle Gabe for, Pop.

ROSE: He thinks Troy's mad at him cause he moved over to Miss Pearl's.

TROY: I ain't mad at the man. He can live where he want to live at.

LYONS: What he move over there for? Miss Pearl don't like nobody.

ROSE: She don't mind him none. She treats him real nice. She just don't allow all that singing.

TROY: She don't mind that rent he be paying . . . that's what she don't mind.

ROSE: Troy, I ain't going through that with you no more. He's over there cause he want to have his own place. He can come and go as he please.

TROY: Hell, he could come and go as he please here. I wasn't stopping him. I ain't put no rules on him.

ROSE: It ain't the same thing, Troy. And you know it.

(GABRIEL comes to the door.)

Now, that's the last I wanna hear about that. I don't wanna hear nothing else about Gabe and Miss Pearl. And next week . . .

GABRIEL: I'm ready for my sandwich, Rose.

ROSE: And next week . . . when that recruiter come from that school . . . I want you to sign that paper and go on and let Cory play football. Then that'll be the last I have to hear about that.

TROY *(to* ROSE *as she exits into the house)*: I ain't thinking about Cory nothing.

LYONS: What . . . Cory got recruited? What school he going to?

TROY: That boy walking around here smelling his piss . . . thinking he's grown. Thinking he's gonna do what he want, irrespective of what I say. Look here, Bono . . . I left the Commissioner's office and went down to the A&P . . . that boy ain't working down there. He lying to me. Telling me he got his job back . . . telling me he working weekends . . . telling me he working after school . . . Mr. Stawicki tell me he ain't working down there at all!

LYONS: Cory just growing up. He's just busting at the seams trying to fill out your shoes.

TROY: I don't care what he's doing. When he get to the point where he wanna disobey me . . . then it's time for him to move on. Bono'll tell you that. I bet he ain't never disobeyed his daddy without paying the consequences.

BONO: I ain't never had a chance. My daddy came on through . . . but I ain't never knew him to see him . . . or what he had on his mind or where he went. Just moving on through. Searching out the New Land. That's what the old folks used to call it. See a fellow moving around from place to place . . . woman to woman . . . called it searching out the New Land. I can't say if he ever found it. I come along, didn't want no kids. Didn't know if I was gonna be in one place long enough to fix on them right as their daddy. I figured I was going searching too. As it turned out I been hooked up with Lucille near about as long as your daddy been with Rose. Going on sixteen years.

TROY: Sometimes I wish I hadn't known my daddy. He ain't cared nothing about no kids. A kid to him wasn't nothing. All he wanted was for you to learn how to walk so he could start you to working. When it come time for eating . . . he ate first. If there was anything left over, that's what you got. Man would sit down and eat two chickens and give you the wing.

LYONS: You ought to stop that, Pop. Everybody feed their kids. No matter how hard times is . . . everybody care about their kids. Make sure they have something to eat.

TROY: The only thing my daddy cared about was getting them bales of cotton in to Mr. Lubin. That's the only thing that mattered to him. Sometimes I used to wonder why he was living. Wonder why the devil hadn't come and got him. "Get them bales of cotton in to Mr. Lubin" and find out he owe him money . . .

LYONS: He should have just went on and left when he saw he couldn't get nowhere. That's what I would have done.

TROY: How he gonna leave with eleven kids? And where he gonna go? He ain't knew how to do nothing but farm. No, he was trapped and I think he knew it. But I'll say this for him . . . he felt a responsibility toward us. Maybe he ain't treated us the way I felt he should have . . . but without that responsibility he could have walked off and left us . . . made his own way.

BONO: A lot of them did. Back in those days what you talking about . . . they walk out their front door and just take on down one road or another and keep on walking.

LYONS: There you go! That's what I'm talking about.

BONO: Just keep on walking till you come to something else. Ain't you never heard of nobody having the walking blues? Well, that's what you call it when you just take off like that.

TROY: My daddy ain't had them walking blues! What you talking about? He stayed right there with his family. But he was just as evil as he could be. My mama couldn't stand him. Couldn't stand that evilness. She run off when I was about eight. She sneaked off one night after he had gone to sleep. Told me she was coming back for me. I ain't never seen her no more. All his women run off and left him. He wasn't good for nobody.

When my turn come to head out, I was fourteen and got to sniffing around Joe Canewell's daughter. Had us an old mule we called Greyboy. My daddy sent me out to do some plowing and I tied up Greyboy and went to fooling around with Joe Canewell's daughter. We done found us a nice little spot, got real cozy with each other. She about thirteen and we done figured we was grown anyway . . . so we down there enjoying ourselves . . . ain't thinking about nothing. We didn't know Greyboy had got loose and wandered back to the house and my daddy was looking for me. We down there by the creek enjoying ourselves when my daddy come up on us. Surprised us. He had them leather straps off the mule and commenced to whupping me like there was no tomorrow. I jumped up, mad and embarrassed. I was scared of my daddy. When he commenced to whupping on me . . . quite naturally I run to get out of the way.

(Pause.)

Now I thought he was mad cause I ain't done my work. But I see where he was chasing me off so he could have the gal for himself. When I see what the matter of it was, I lost all fear of my daddy. Right there is where I become a man . . . at fourteen years of age.

(Pause.)

Now it was my turn to run him off. I picked up them same reins that he had used on me. I picked up them reins and commenced to whupping on him. The gal jumped up and run off . . . and when my daddy turned to face me, I could see why the devil had never come to get him . . . cause he was the devil himself. I don't know what happened. When I woke up, I was laying right there by the creek, and Blue . . . this old dog we had . . . was licking my face. I thought I was blind. I couldn't see nothing. Both my eyes were swollen shut. I laid there and cried. I didn't know what I was gonna do. The only thing I knew was the time had come for me to leave my daddy's house. And right there the world suddenly got big. And it was a long time before I could cut it down to where I could handle it.

   Part of that cutting down was when I got to the place where I could feel him kicking in my blood and knew that the only thing that separated us was the matter of a few years.

(GABRIEL enters from the house with a sandwich.)

LYONS: What you got there, Uncle Gabe?

GABRIEL: Got me a ham sandwich. Rose gave me a ham sandwich.

TROY: I don't know what happened to him. I done lost touch with everybody except Gabriel. But I hope he's dead. I hope he found some peace.

LYONS: That's a heavy story, Pop. I didn't know you left home when you was fourteen.

TROY: And didn't know nothing. The only part of the world I knew was the forty-two acres of Mr. Lubin's land. That's all I knew about life.

LYONS: Fourteen's kinda young to be out on your own. *(Phone rings.)* I don't even think I was ready to be out on my own at fourteen. I don't know what I would have done.

TROY: I got up from the creek and walked on down to Mobile. I was through with farming. Figured I could do better in the city. So I walked the two hundred miles to Mobile.

LYONS: Wait a minute . . . you ain't walked no two hundred miles, Pop. Ain't nobody gonna walk no two hundred miles. You talking about some walking there.

BONO: That's the only way you got anywhere back in them days.

LYONS: Shhh. Damn if I wouldn't have hitched a ride with somebody!

TROY: Who you gonna hitch it with? They ain't had no cars and things like they got now. We talking about 1918.

ROSE *(entering)*: What you all out here getting into?

TROY *(to ROSE)*: I'm telling Lyons how good he got it. He don't know nothing about this I'm talking.

ROSE: Lyons, that was Bonnie on the phone. She say you supposed to pick her up.

LYONS: Yeah, okay, Rose.

TROY: I walked on down to Mobile and hitched up with some of them fellows that was heading this way. Got up here and found out . . . not only couldn't you get a job . . . you couldn't find no place to live. I thought I was in freedom. Shhh. Colored folks living down there on the riverbanks in whatever kind of shelter they could find for themselves. Right down there under the Brady Street Bridge. Living in shacks made of sticks and tarpaper. Messed around there and went from bad to worse. Started stealing. First it was food. Then I figured, hell, if I steal money I can buy me some food. Buy me some shoes too! One thing led to another. Met your mama. I was young and anxious to be a man. Met your mama and had you. What I do that for? Now I got to worry about feeding you and her. Got to steal three times as much. Went out one day looking for somebody to rob . . . that's what I was, a robber. I'll tell you the truth. I'm ashamed of it today. But it's the truth. Went to rob this fellow . . . pulled out my knife . . . and he pulled out a gun. Shot me in the chest. It felt just like somebody had taken a hot branding iron and laid it on me. When he shot me I jumped at him with my knife. They told me I killed him and they put me in the penitentiary and locked me up for fifteen years. That's where I met Bono. That's where I learned how to play baseball. Got out that place and your mama had taken you and went on to make life without me. Fifteen years was a long time for her to wait. But that fifteen years cured me of that robbing stuff. Rose'll tell you. She asked me when I met her if I had gotten all that foolishness out of my system. And I told her, "Baby, it's you and baseball all what count with me." You hear me, Bono? I meant it too. She say, "Which one comes first?" I told her, "Baby, ain't no doubt it's baseball . . . but you stick and get old with me and we'll both outlive this baseball." Am I right, Rose? And it's true.

ROSE: Man, hush your mouth. You ain't said no such thing. Talking about, "Baby, you know you'll always be number one with me." That's what you was talking.

TROY: You hear that, Bono. That's why I love her.

BONO: Rose'll keep you straight. You get off the track, she'll straighten you up.

ROSE: Lyons, you better get on up and get Bonnie. She waiting on you.

LYONS (gets up to go): Hey, Pop, why don't you come on down to the Grill and hear me play?

TROY: I ain't going down there. I'm too old to be sitting around in them clubs.

BONO: You got to be good to play down at the Grill.

LYONS: Come on, Pop . . .

TROY: I got to get up in the morning.

LYONS: You ain't got to stay long.

TROY: Naw, I'm gonna get my supper and go on to bed.

LYONS: Well, I got to go. I'll see you again.

TROY: Don't you come around my house on my payday.

ROSE: Pick up the phone and let somebody know you coming. And bring Bonnie with you. You know I'm always glad to see her.

LYONS: Yeah, I'll do that, Rose. You take care now. See you, Pop. See you, Mr. Bono. See you, Uncle Gabe.

GABRIEL: Lyons! King of the Jungle!

(LYONS exits.)

TROY: Is supper ready, woman? Me and you got some business to take care of. I'm gonna tear it up too.

ROSE: Troy, I done told you now!

TROY (puts his arm around BONO): Aw hell, woman . . . this is Bono. Bono like family. I done known this nigger since . . . how long I done know you?

BONO: It's been a long time.

TROY: I done known this nigger since Skippy was a pup. Me and him done been through some times.

BONO: You sure right about that.

TROY: Hell, I done know him longer than I known you. And we still standing shoulder to shoulder. Hey, look here, Bono . . . a man can't ask for no more than that.

(Drinks to him.)

I love you, nigger.

BONO: Hell, I love you too . . . but I got to get home see my woman. You got yours in hand. I got to go get mine.

(BONO starts to exit as CORY enters the yard, dressed in his football uniform. He gives TROY a hard, uncompromising look.)

CORY: What you do that for, Pop?

(He throws his helmet down in the direction of TROY.)

ROSE: What's the matter? Cory . . . what's the matter?

CORY: Papa done went up to the school and told Coach Zellman I can't play football no more. Wouldn't even let me play the game. Told him to tell the recruiter not to come.

ROSE: Troy . . .

TROY: What you Troying me for. Yeah, I did it. And the boy know why I did it.

CORY: Why you wanna do that to me? That was the one chance I had.

ROSE: Ain't nothing wrong with Cory playing football, Troy.

TROY: The boy lied to me. I told the nigger if he wanna play football . . . to keep up his chores and hold down that job at the A&P. That was the conditions. Stopped down there to see Mr. Stawicki . . .

CORY: I can't work after school during the football season, Pop! I tried to tell you that Mr. Stawicki's holding my job for me. You don't never want to listen to nobody. And then you wanna go and do this to me!

TROY: I ain't done nothing to you. You done it to yourself.

CORY: Just cause you didn't have a chance! You just scared I'm gonna be better than you, that's all.

TROY: Come here.

ROSE: Troy . . .

*(*CORY *reluctantly crosses over to* TROY.)

TROY: All right! See. You done made a mistake.

CORY: I didn't even do nothing!

TROY: I'm gonna tell you what your mistake was. See . . . you swung at the ball and didn't hit it. That's strike one. See, you in the batter's box now. You swung and you missed. That's strike one. Don't you strike out!

(Lights fade to black.)

ACT II
SCENE I

The following morning. CORY *is at the tree hitting the ball with the bat. He tries to mimic* TROY, *but his swing is awkward, less sure.* ROSE *enters from the house.*

ROSE: Cory, I want you to help me with this cupboard.

CORY: I ain't quitting the team. I don't care what Poppa say.

ROSE: I'll talk to him when he gets back. He had to go see about your Uncle Gabe. The police done arrested him. Say he was disturbing the peace. He'll be back directly. Come on in here and help me clean out the top of this cupboard.

(CORY *exits into the house.* ROSE *sees* TROY *and* BONO *coming down the alley.*)

Troy . . . what they say down there?

TROY: Ain't said nothing. I give them fifty dollars and they let him go. I'll talk to you about it. Where's Cory?

ROSE: He's in there helping me clean out these cupboards.

TROY: Tell him to get his butt out here.

(TROY *and* BONO *go over to the pile of wood.* BONO *picks up the saw and begins sawing.*)

TROY *(to* BONO*):* All they want is the money. That makes six or seven times I done went down there and got him. See me coming they stick out their *hands.*

BONO: Yeah. I know what you mean. That's all they care about . . . that money. They don't care about what's right.

(Pause.)

Nigger, why you got to go and get some hard wood? You ain't doing nothing but building a little old fence. Get you some soft pine wood. That's all you need.

TROY: I know what I'm doing. This is outside wood. You put pine wood inside the house. Pine wood is inside wood. This here is outside wood. Now you tell me where the fence is gonna be?

BONO: You don't need this wood. You can put it up with pine wood and it'll stand as long as you gonna be here looking at it.

TROY: How you know how long I'm gonna be here, nigger? Hell, I might just live forever. Live longer than old man Horsely.

BONO: That's what Magee used to say.

TROY: Magee's a damn fool. Now you tell me who you ever heard of gonna pull their own teeth with a pair of rusty pliers.

BONO: The old folks . . . my granddaddy used to pull his teeth with pliers. They ain't had no dentists for the colored folks back then.

TROY: Get clean pliers! You understand? Clean pliers! Sterilize them! Besides we ain't living back then. All Magee had to do was walk over to Doc Goldblum's.

BONO: I see where you and that Tallahassee gal . . . that Alberta . . . I see where you all done got tight.

TROY: What you mean "got tight"?

BONO: I see where you be laughing and joking with her all the time.

TROY: I laughs and jokes with all of them, Bono. You know me.

BONO: That ain't the kind of laughing and joking I'm talking about.

(CORY *enters from the house.*)

CORY: How you doing, Mr. Bono?

TROY: Cory? Get that saw from Bono and cut some wood. He talking about the wood's too hard to cut. Stand back there, Jim, and let that young boy show you how it's done.

BONO: He's sure welcome to it.

(CORY *takes the saw and begins to cut the wood.*)

Whew-e-e! Look at that. Big old strong boy. Look like Joe Louis. Hell, must be getting old the way I'm watching that boy whip through that wood.

CORY: I don't see why Mama want a fence around the yard noways.

TROY: Damn if I know either. What the hell she keeping out with it? She ain't got nothing nobody want.

BONO: Some people build fences to keep people out . . . and other people build fences to keep people in. Rose wants to hold on to you all. She loves you.

TROY: Hell, nigger, I don't need nobody to tell me my wife loves me. Cory . . . go on in the house and see if you can find that other saw.

CORY: Where's it at?

TROY: I said find it! Look for it till you find it!

(CORY *exits into the house.*)

What's that supposed to mean? Wanna keep us in?

BONO: Troy . . . I done known you seem like damn near my whole life. You and Rose both. I done know both of you all for a long time. I remember when you met Rose. When you was hitting them baseball out the park. A lot of them old gals was after you then. You had the pick of the litter. When you picked Rose, I was happy for you. That was the first time I knew you had any sense. I said . . . My man Troy knows what he's doing . . . I'm gonna follow this nigger . . . he might take me somewhere. I been following you too. I done learned a whole heap of things about life watching you. I done learned how to tell where the shit lies. How to tell it from the alfalfa. You done learned me a lot of things. You showed me how to not make the same mistakes . . . to take life as it comes along and keep putting one foot in front of the other.

(*Pause.*)

Rose a good woman, Troy.

TROY: Hell, nigger, I know she a good woman. I been married to her for eighteen years. What you got on your mind, Bono?

BONO: I just say she a good woman. Just like I say anything. I ain't got to have nothing on my mind.

TROY: You just gonna say she a good woman and leave it hanging out there like that? Why you telling me she a good woman?

BONO: She loves you, Troy. Rose loves you.

TROY: You saying I don't measure up. That's what you trying to say. I don't measure up cause I'm seeing this other gal. I know what you trying to say.

BONO: I know what Rose means to you, Troy. I'm just trying to say I don't want to see you mess up.

TROY: Yeah, I appreciate that, Bono. If you was messing around on Lucille I'd be telling you the same thing.

BONO: Well, that's all I got to say. I just say that because I love you both.

TROY: Hell, you know me . . . I wasn't out there looking for nothing. You can't find a better woman than Rose. I know that. But seems like this woman just stuck onto me where I can't shake her loose. I done wrestled with it, tried to throw her off me . . . but she just stuck on tighter. Now she's stuck on for good.

BONO: You's in control . . . that's what you tell me all the time. You responsible for what you do.

TROY: I ain't ducking the responsibility of it. As long as it sets right in my heart . . . then I'm okay. Cause that's all I listen to. It'll tell me right from wrong every time. And I ain't talking about doing Rose no bad turn. I love Rose. She done carried me a long ways and I love and respect her for that.

BONO: I know you do. That's why I don't want to see you hurt her. But what you gonna do when she find out? What you got then? If you try and juggle both of them . . . sooner or later you gonna drop one of them. That's common sense.

TROY: Yeah, I hear what you saying, Bono. I been trying to figure a way to work it out.

BONO: Work it out right, Troy. I don't want to be getting all up between you and Rose's business . . . but work it so it come out right.

TROY: Ah hell, I get all up between you and Lucille's business. When you gonna get that woman that refrigerator she been wanting? Don't tell me you ain't got no money now. I know who your banker is. Mellon don't need that money bad as Lucille want that refrigerator. I'll tell you that.

BONO: Tell you what I'll do . . . when you finish building this fence for Rose . . . I'll buy Lucille that refrigerator.

TROY: You done stuck your foot in your mouth now!

(TROY *grabs up a board and begins to saw.* BONO *starts to walk out the yard.*)

Hey, nigger . . . where you going?

BONO: I'm going home. I know you don't expect me to help you now. I'm protecting my money. I wanna see you put that fence up by yourself. That's what I want to see. You'll be here another six months without me.

TROY: Nigger, you ain't right.

BONO: When it comes to my money . . . I'm right as fireworks on the Fourth of July.

TROY: All right, we gonna see now. You better get out your bankbook.

(BONO exits, and TROY continues to work. ROSE enters from the house.)

ROSE: What they say down there? What's happening with Gabe?

TROY: I went down there and got him out. Cost me fifty dollars. Say he was disturbing the peace. Judge set up a hearing for him in three weeks. Say to show cause why he shouldn't be recommitted.

ROSE: What was he doing that cause them to arrest him?

TROY: Some kids was teasing him and he run them off home. Say he was howling and carrying on. Some folks seen him and called the police. That's all it was.

ROSE: Well, what'd you say? What'd you tell the judge?

TROY: Told him I'd look after him. It didn't make no sense to recommit the man. He stuck out his big greasy palm and told me to give him fifty dollars and take him on home.

ROSE: Where's he at now? Where'd he go off to?

TROY: He's gone on about his business. He don't need nobody to hold his hand.

ROSE: Well, I don't know. Seem like that would be the best place for him if they did put him into the hospital. I know what you're gonna say. But that's what I think would be best.

TROY: The man done had his life ruined fighting for what? And they wanna take and lock him up. Let him be free. He don't bother nobody.

ROSE: Well, everybody got their own way of looking at it I guess. Come on and get your lunch. I got a bowl of lima beans and some cornbread in the oven. Come on get something to eat. Ain't no sense you fretting over Gabe.

(ROSE turns to go into the house.)

TROY: Rose . . . got something to tell you.

ROSE: Well, come on . . . wait till I get this food on the table.

TROY: Rose!

(She stops and turns around.)

I don't know how to say this.

(Pause.)

I can't explain it none. It just sort of grows on you till it gets out of hand. It starts out like a little bush . . . and the next thing you know it's a whole forest.

ROSE: Troy . . . what is you talking about?

TROY: I'm talking, woman, let me talk. I'm trying to find a way to tell you . . . I'm gonna be a daddy. I'm gonna be somebody's daddy.

ROSE: Troy . . . you're not telling me this? You're gonna be . . . what?

TROY: Rose . . . now . . . see . . .

ROSE: You telling me you gonna be somebody's daddy? You telling your *wife* this?

(GABRIEL enters from the street. He carries a rose in his hand.)

GABRIEL: Hey, Troy! Hey, Rose!

ROSE: I have to wait eighteen years to hear something like this.

GABRIEL: Hey, Rose . . . I got a flower for you.

(He hands it to her.)

That's a rose. Same rose like you is.

ROSE: Thanks, Gabe.

GABRIEL: Troy, you ain't mad at me is you? Them bad mens come and put me away. You ain't mad at me is you?

TROY: Naw, Gabe, I ain't mad at you.

ROSE: Eighteen years and you wanna come with this.

GABRIEL *(takes a quarter out of his pocket)*: See what I got? Got a brand new quarter.

TROY: Rose . . . it's just . . .

ROSE: Ain't nothing you can say, Troy. Ain't no way of explaining that.

GABRIEL: Fellow that give me this quarter had a whole mess of them. I'm gonna keep this quarter till it stop shining.

ROSE: Gabe, go on in the house there. I got some watermelon in the frigidaire. Go on and get you a piece.

GABRIEL: Say, Rose . . . you know I was chasing hellhounds and them bad mens come and get me and take me away. Troy helped me. He come down there and told them they better let me go before he beat them up. Yeah, he did!

ROSE: You go on and get you a piece of watermelon, Gabe. Them bad mens is gone now.

GABRIEL: Okay, Rose . . . gonna get me some watermelon. The kind with the stripes on it.

(GABRIEL exits into the house.)

ROSE: Why, Troy? Why? After all these years to come dragging this in to me now. It don't make no sense at your age. I could have expected this ten or fifteen years ago, but not now.

TROY: Age ain't got nothing to do with it, Rose.

ROSE: I done tried to be everything a wife should be. Everything a wife could be. Been married eighteen years and I got to live to see the day you tell me you been seeing another woman and done fathered a child by her. And you know I ain't never wanted no half nothing in my family. My whole family is half. Everybody got different fathers and mothers . . . my two sisters and my brother. Can't hardly tell who's who. Can't never sit down and talk about Papa and Mama. It's your papa and your mama and my papa and my mama . . .

T R O Y : Rose . . . stop it now.

R O S E : I ain't never wanted that for none of my children. And now you wanna drag your behind in here and tell me something like this.

T R O Y : You ought to know. It's time for you to know.

R O S E : Well, I don't want to know, goddamn it!

T R O Y : I can't just make it go away. It's done now. I can't wish the circumstance of the thing away.

R O S E : And you don't want to either. Maybe you want to wish me and my boy away. Maybe that's what you want? Well, you can't wish us away. I've got eighteen years of my life invested in you. You ought to have stayed upstairs in my bed where you belong.

T R O Y : Rose . . . now listen to me . . . we can get a handle on this thing. We can talk this out . . . come to an understanding.

R O S E : All of a sudden it's "we." Where was "we" at when you was down there rolling around with some godforsaken woman? "We" should have come to an understanding before you started making a damn fool of yourself. You're a day late and a dollar short when it comes to an understanding with me.

T R O Y : It's just . . . She gives me a different idea . . . a different understanding about myself. I can step out of this house and get away from the pressures and problems . . . be a different man. I ain't got to wonder how I'm gonna pay the bills or get the roof fixed. I can just be a part of myself that I ain't never been.

R O S E : What I want to know . . . is do you plan to continue seeing her. That's all you can say to me.

T R O Y : I can sit up in her house and laugh. Do you understand what I'm saying. I can laugh out loud . . . and it feels good. It reaches all the way down to the bottom of my shoes.

(Pause.)

Rose, I can't give that up.

R O S E : Maybe you ought to go on and stay down there with her . . . if she's a better woman than me.

T R O Y : It ain't about nobody being a better woman or nothing. Rose, you ain't the blame. A man couldn't ask for no woman to be a better wife than you've been. I'm responsible for it. I done locked myself into a pattern trying to take care of you all that I forgot about myself.

R O S E : What the hell was I there for? That was my job, not somebody else's.

T R O Y : Rose, I done tried all my life to live decent . . . to live a clean . . . hard . . . useful life. I tried to be a good husband to you. In every way

I knew how. Maybe I come into the world backwards, I don't know. But . . . you born with two strikes on you before you come to the plate. You got to guard it closely . . . always looking for the curve ball on the inside corner. You can't afford to let none get past you. You can't afford a call strike. If you going down . . . you going down swinging. Everything lined up against you. What you gonna do. I fooled them, Rose. I bunted. When I found you and Cory and a halfway decent job . . . I was safe. Couldn't nothing touch me. I wasn't gonna strike out no more. I wasn't going back to the penitentiary. I wasn't gonna lay in the streets with a bottle of wine. I was safe. I had me a family. A job. I wasn't gonna get that last strike. I was on first looking for one of them boys to knock me in. To get me home.

ROSE: You should have stayed in my bed, Troy.

TROY: Then when I saw that gal . . . she firmed up my backbone. And I got to thinking that if I tried . . . I just might be able to steal second. Do you understand after eighteen years I wanted to steal second.

ROSE: You should have held me tight. You should have grabbed me and held on.

TROY: I stood on first base for eighteen years and I thought . . . well, goddamn it . . . go on for it!

ROSE: We're not talking about baseball! We're talking about you going off to lay in bed with another woman . . . and then bring it home to me. That's what we're talking about. We ain't talking about no baseball.

TROY: Rose, you're not listening to me. I'm trying the best I can to explain it to you. It's not easy for me to admit that I been standing in the same place for eighteen years.

ROSE: I been standing with you! I been right here with you, Troy. I got a life too. I gave eighteen years of my life to stand in the same spot with you. Don't you think I ever wanted other things? Don't you think I had dreams and hopes? What about my life? What about me. Don't you think it ever crossed my mind to want to know other men? That I wanted to lay up somewhere and forget about my responsibilities? That I wanted someone to make me laugh so I could feel good? You not the only one who's got wants and needs. But I held on to you, Troy. I took all my feelings, my wants and needs, my dreams . . . and I buried them inside you. I planted a seed and watched and prayed over it. I planted myself inside you and waited to bloom. And it didn't take me no eighteen years to find out the soil was hard and rocky and it wasn't never gonna bloom.

But I held on to you, Troy. I held you tighter. You was my husband. I owed you everything I had. Every part of me I could find to give you. And upstairs in that room . . . with the darkness falling in on me . . . I gave everything I had to try and erase the doubt that you wasn't the finest man in the world. And wherever you was going . . . I wanted to be there with you. Cause you was my husband. Cause that's the only way I was gonna survive as your wife. You always talking about what you give . . . and what you don't have to give. But you take too. You take . . . and don't even know nobody's giving!

(ROSE *turns to exit into the house;* TROY *grabs her arm.*)

TROY: You say I take and don't give!
ROSE: Troy! You're hurting me!
TROY: You say I take and don't give.
ROSE: Troy . . . you're hurting my arm! Let go!
TROY: I done give you everything I got. Don't you tell that lie on me.
ROSE: Troy!
TROY: Don't you tell that lie on me!

(CORY *enters from the house.*)

CORY: Mama!
ROSE: Troy. You're hurting me.
TROY: Don't you tell me about no taking and giving.

(CORY *comes up behind* TROY *and grabs him* TROY, *surprised, is thrown off balance just as* CORY *throws a glancing blow that catches him on the chest and knocks him down.* TROY *is stunned, as is* CORY.)

ROSE: Troy. Troy. No!

(TROY *gets to his feet and starts at* CORY.)

Troy . . . no. Please! Troy!

(ROSE *pulls on* TROY *to hold him back.* TROY *stops himself.*)

TROY *(to* CORY*):* All right. That's strike two. You stay away from around me, boy. Don't you strike out. You living with a full count. Don't you strike out.

(TROY *exits out the yard as the lights go down.*)

SCENE II

It is six months later, early afternoon. TROY *enters from the house and starts to exit the yard.* ROSE *enters from the house.*

ROSE: Troy, I want to talk to you.
TROY: All of a sudden, after all this time, you want to talk to me, huh? You ain't wanted to talk to me for months. You ain't wanted to talk to me last night. You ain't wanted no part of me then. What you wanna talk to me about now?
ROSE: Tomorrow's Friday.

TROY: I know what day tomorrow is. You think I don't know tomorrow's Friday? My whole life I ain't done nothing but look to see Friday coming and you got to tell me it's Friday.

ROSE: I want to know if you're coming home.

TROY: I always come home, Rose. You know that. There ain't never been a night I ain't come home.

ROSE: That ain't what I mean . . . and you know it. I want to know if you're coming straight home after work.

TROY: I figure I'd cash my check . . . hang out at Taylors' with the boys . . . maybe play a game of checkers . . .

ROSE: Troy, I can't live like this. I won't live like this. You livin' on borrowed time with me. It's been going on six months now you ain't been coming home.

TROY: I be here every night. Every night of the year. That's 365 days.

ROSE: I want you to come home tomorrow after work.

TROY: Rose . . . I don't mess up my pay. You know that now. I take my pay and I give it to you. I don't have no money but what you give me back. I just want to have a little time to myself . . . a little time to enjoy life.

ROSE: What about me? When's my time to enjoy life?

TROY: I don't know what to tell you, Rose. I'm doing the best I can.

ROSE: You ain't been home from work but time enough to change your clothes and run out . . . and you wanna call that the best you can do?

TROY: I'm going over to the hospital to see Alberta. She went into the hospital this afternoon. Look like she might have the baby early. I won't be gone long.

ROSE: Well, you ought to know. They went over to Miss Pearl's and got Gabe today. She said you told them to go ahead and lock him up.

TROY: I ain't said no such thing. Whoever told you that is telling a lie. Pearl ain't doing nothing but telling a big fat lie.

ROSE: She ain't had to tell me. I read it on the papers.

TROY: I ain't told them nothing of the kind.

ROSE: I saw it right there on the papers.

TROY: What it say, huh?

ROSE: It said you told them to take him.

TROY: Then they screwed that up, just the way they screw up everything. I ain't worried about what they got on the paper.

ROSE: Say the government send part of his check to the hospital and the other part to you.

TROY: I ain't got nothing to do with that if that's the way it works. I ain't made up the rules about how it work.

ROSE: You did Gabe just like you did Cory. You wouldn't sign the paper for Cory . . . but you signed for Gabe. You signed that paper.

(The telephone is heard ringing inside the house.)

TROY: I told you I ain't signed nothing, woman! The only thing I signed was the release form. Hell, I can't read, I don't know what they had on that paper! I ain't signed nothing about sending Gabe away.

ROSE: I said send him to the hospital . . . you said let him be free . . . now you done went down there and signed him to the hospital for half his money. You went back on yourself, Troy. You gonna have to answer for that.

TROY: See now . . . you been over there talking to Miss Pearl. She done got mad cause she ain't getting Gabe's rent money. That's all it is. She's liable to say anything.

ROSE: Troy, I seen where you signed the paper.

TROY: You ain't seen nothing I signed. What she doing got papers on my brother anyway? Miss Pearl telling a big fat lie. And I'm gonna tell her about it too! You ain't seen nothing I signed. Say . . . you ain't seen nothing I signed.

(ROSE *exits into the house to answer the telephone. Presently she returns.*)

ROSE: Troy . . . that was the hospital. Alberta had the baby.

TROY: What she have? What is it?

ROSE: It's a girl.

TROY: I better get on down to the hospital to see her.

ROSE: Troy . . .

TROY: Rose . . . I got to go see her now. That's only right . . . what's the matter . . . the baby's all right, ain't it?

ROSE: Alberta died having the baby.

TROY: Died . . . you say she's dead? Alberta's dead?

ROSE: They said they done all they could. They couldn't do nothing for her.

TROY: The baby? How's the baby?

ROSE: They say it's healthy. I wonder who's gonna bury her.

TROY: She had family, Rose. She wasn't living in the world by herself.

ROSE: I know she wasn't living in the world by herself.

TROY: Next thing you gonna want to know if she had any insurance.

ROSE: Troy, you ain't got to talk like that.

TROY: That's the first thing that jumped out your mouth. "Who's gonna bury her?" Like I'm fixing to take on that task for myself.

ROSE: I am your wife. Don't push me away.

TROY: I ain't pushing nobody away. Just give me some space. That's all. Just give me some room to breathe.

(ROSE *exits into the house.* TROY *walks about the yard.*)

TROY (*with a quiet rage that threatens to consume him*): All right . . . Mr. Death. See now . . . I'm gonna tell you what I'm gonna do. I'm gonna take and build me a fence around this yard. See? I'm gonna build me a fence around what belongs to me. And then I want you to stay on the other side. See? You stay over there until you're ready for me. Then you come on. Bring your army. Bring your sickle. Bring your wrestling clothes. I ain't gonna fall down on my vigilance this time. You ain't gonna sneak up on me no more. When you ready for me . . . when the top of your list say Troy Maxson . . . that's when you come around here. You come up and knock on the front door. Ain't nobody else got nothing to do with this. This is between you and me. Man to man. You stay on the other side of that fence until you ready for me. Then you come up and knock on the front door. Anytime you want. I'll be ready for you.

(The lights go down to black.)

SCENE III

The lights come up on the porch. It is late evening three days later. ROSE *sits listening to the ball game waiting for* TROY. *The final out of the game is made and* ROSE *switches off the radio.* TROY *enters the yard carrying an infant wrapped in blankets. He stands back from the house and calls.*

ROSE *enters and stands on the porch. There is a long, awkward silence, the weight of which grows heavier with each passing second.*

TROY: Rose . . . I'm standing here with my daughter in my arms. She ain't but a wee bittie little old thing. She don't know nothing about grown-ups' business. She innocent . . . and she ain't got no mama.

ROSE: What you telling me for, Troy?

(She turns and exits into the house.)

TROY: Well . . . I guess we'll just sit out here on the porch.

(He sits down on the porch. There is an awkward indelicateness about the way he handles the baby. His largeness engulfs and seems to swallow it. He speaks loud enough for ROSE *to hear.)*

A man's got to do what's right for him. I ain't sorry for nothing I done. It felt right in my heart.

(To the baby.)

What you smiling at? Your daddy's a big man. Got these great big old hands. But sometimes he's scared. And right now your daddy's scared cause we sitting out here and ain't got no home. Oh, I been homeless before. I ain't had no little baby with me. But I been homeless. You just be out on the road by your lonesome and you see one of them trains coming and you just kinda go like this . . .

(He sings as a lullaby.)

Please, Mr. Engineer let a man ride the line

Please, Mr. Engineer let a man ride the line
I ain't got no ticket please let me ride the blinds

(ROSE *enters from the house.* TROY, *hearing her steps behind him, stands
and faces her.*)

She's my daughter, Rose. My own flesh and blood. I can't deny her no
more than I can deny them boys.

(*Pause.*)

You and them boys is my family. You and them and this child is all I
got in the world. So I guess what I'm saying is . . . I'd appreciate it if
you'd help me take care of her.

ROSE: Okay, Troy . . . you're right. I'll take care of your baby for you . . .
cause . . . like you say . . . she's innocent . . . and you can't visit the sins
of the father upon the child. A motherless child has got a hard time.

(*She takes the baby from him.*)

From right now . . . this child got a mother. But you a womanless man.

(ROSE *turns and exits into the house with the baby. Lights go down to black.*)

SCENE IV

It is two months later. LYONS *enters from the street. He knocks on the door
and calls.*

LYONS: Hey, Rose! (*Pause.*) Rose!
ROSE (*from inside the house*): Stop that yelling. You gonna wake up Raynell.
I just got her to sleep.
LYONS: I just stopped by to pay Papa this twenty dollars I owe him.
Where's Papa at?
ROSE: He should be here in a minute. I'm getting ready to go down to the
church. Sit down and wait on him.
LYONS: I got to go pick up Bonnie over her mother's house.
ROSE: Well, sit it down there on the table. He'll get it.
LYONS (*enters the house and sets the money on the table*): Tell Papa I said
thanks. I'll see you again.
ROSE: All right, Lyons. We'll see you.

(LYONS *starts to exit as* CORY *enters.*)

CORY: Hey, Lyons.
LYONS: What's happening, Cory. Say man, I'm sorry I missed your grad-
uation. You know I had a gig and couldn't get away. Otherwise, I
would have been there, man. So what you doing?
CORY: I'm trying to find a job.
LYONS: Yeah I know how that go, man. It's rough out here. Jobs are scarce.

CORY: Yeah, I know.

LYONS: Look here, I got to run. Talk to Papa . . . he know some people. He'll be able to help get you a job. Talk to him . . . see what he say.

CORY: Yeah . . . all right, Lyons.

LYONS: You take care. I'll talk to you soon. We'll find some time to talk.

(LYONS exits the yard. CORY wanders over to the tree, picks up the bat, and assumes a batting stance. He studies an imaginary pitcher and swings. Dissatisfied with the result, he tries again. TROY enters. They eye each other for a beat. CORY puts the bat down and exits the yard. TROY starts into the house as ROSE exits with RAYNELL. She is carrying a cake.)

TROY: I'm coming in and everybody's going out.

ROSE: I'm taking this cake down to the church for the bake sale. Lyons was by to see you. He stopped by to pay you your twenty dollars. It's laying in there on the table.

TROY *(going into his pocket)*: Well . . . here go this money.

ROSE: Put it in there on the table, Troy. I'll get it.

TROY: What time you coming back?

ROSE: Ain't no use in you studying me. It don't matter what time I come back.

TROY: I just asked you a question, woman. What's the matter . . . can't I ask you a question?

ROSE: Troy, I don't want to go into it. Your dinner's in there on the stove. All you got to do is heat it up. And don't you be eating the rest of them cakes in there. I'm coming back for them. We having a bake sale at the church tomorrow.

(ROSE exits the yard. TROY sits down on the steps, takes a pint bottle from his pocket, opens it, and drinks. He begins to sing.)

TROY: Hear it ring! Hear it ring!
Had an old dog his name was Blue
You know Blue was mighty true
You know Blue was a good old dog
Blue trees a possum in a hollow log
You know from that he was a good old dog

(BONO enters the yard.)

BONO: Hey, Troy.

TROY: Hey, what's happening, Bono?

BONO: I just thought I'd stop by to see you.

TROY: What you stop by and see me for? You ain't stopped by in a month of Sundays. Hell, I must owe you money or something.

BONO: Since you got your promotion I can't keep up with you. Used to see you every day. Now I don't even know what route you working.

TROY: They keep switching me around. Got me out in Greentree now . . . hauling white folks' garbage.

BONO: Greentree, huh? You lucky, at least you ain't got to be lifting them barrels. Damn if they ain't getting heavier. I'm gonna put in my two years and call it quits.

TROY: I'm thinking about retiring myself.

BONO: You got it easy. You can *drive* for another five years.

TROY: It ain't the same, Bono. It ain't like working the back of the truck. Ain't got nobody to talk to . . . feel like you working by yourself. Naw, I'm thinking about retiring. How's Lucille?

BONO: She all right. Her arthritis get to acting up on her sometime. Saw Rose on my way in. She going down to the church, huh?

TROY: Yeah, she took up going down there. All them preachers looking for somebody to fatten their pockets.

(Pause.)

Got some gin here.

BONO: Naw, thanks. I just stopped by to say hello.

TROY: Hell, nigger . . . you can take a drink. I ain't never known you to say no to a drink. You ain't got to work tomorrow.

BONO: I just stopped by. I'm fixing to go over to Skinner's. We got us a domino game going over his house every Friday.

TROY: Nigger, you can't play no dominoes. I used to whup you four games out of five.

BONO: Well, that learned me. I'm getting better.

TROY: Yeah? Well, that's all right.

BONO: Look here . . . I got to be getting on. Stop by sometime, huh?

TROY: Yeah, I'll do that, Bono. Lucille told Rose you bought her a new refrigerator.

BONO: Yeah, Rose told Lucille you had finally built your fence . . . so I figured we'd call it even.

TROY: I knew you would.

BONO: Yeah . . . okay. I'll be talking to you.

TROY: Yeah, take care, Bono. Good to see you. I'm gonna stop over.

BONO: Yeah. Okay, Troy.

(BONO exits. TROY drinks from the bottle.)

TROY: Old Blue died and I dig his grave
Let him down with a golden chain
Every night when I hear old Blue bark
I know Blue treed a possum in Noah's Ark.
Hear it ring! Hear it ring!

(CORY enters the yard. They eye each other for a beat. TROY is sitting in the middle of the steps. CORY walks over.)

CORY: I got to get by.

TROY: Say what? What's you say?

CORY: You in my way. I got to get by.

TROY: You got to get by where? This is my house. Bought and paid for. In full. Took me fifteen years. And if you wanna go in my house and I'm sitting on the steps . . . you say excuse me. Like your mama taught you.

CORY: Come on, Pop . . . I got to get by.

(CORY *starts to maneuver his way past* TROY. TROY *grabs his leg and shoves him back.*)

TROY: You just gonna walk over top of me?

CORY: I live here too!

TROY (*advancing toward him*): You just gonna walk over top of me in my own house?

CORY: I ain't scared of you.

TROY: I ain't asked if you was scared of me. I asked you if you was fixing to walk over top of me in my own house? That's the question. You ain't gonna say excuse me? You just gonna walk over top of me?

CORY: If you wanna put it like that.

TROY: How else am I gonna put it?

CORY: I was walking by you to go into the house cause you sitting on the steps drunk, singing to yourself. You can put it like that.

TROY: Without saying excuse me???

(CORY *doesn't respond.*)

I asked you a question. Without saying excuse me???

CORY: I ain't got to say excuse me to you. You don't count around here no more.

TROY: Oh, I see . . . I don't count around here no more. You ain't got to say excuse me to your daddy. All of a sudden you done got so grown that your daddy don't count around here no more . . . Around here in his own house and yard that he done paid for with the sweat of his brow. You done got so grown to where you gonna take over. You gonna take over my house. Is that right? You gonna wear my pants. You gonna go in there and stretch out on my bed. You ain't got to say excuse me cause I don't count around here no more. Is that right?

CORY: That's right. You always talking this dumb stuff. Now, why don't you just get out my way.

TROY: I guess you got someplace to sleep and something to put in your belly. You got that, huh? You got that? That's what you need. You got that, huh?

CORY: You don't know what I got. You ain't got to worry about what I got.

TROY: You right! You one hundred percent right! I done spent the last seventeen years worrying about what you got. Now it's your turn, see? I'll tell you what to do. You grown . . . we done established that. You a man. Now, let's see you act like one. Turn your behind around and walk out this yard. And when you get out there in the alley . . . you can forget about this house. See? 'Cause this is my house. You go on and be a man and get your own house. You can forget about this. 'Cause this is mine. You go on and get yours 'cause I'm through with doing for you.

CORY: You talking about what you did for me . . . what'd you ever give me?

TROY: Them feet and bones! That pumping heart, nigger! I give you more than anybody else is ever gonna give you.

CORY: You ain't never gave me nothing! You ain't never done nothing but hold me back. Afraid I was gonna be better than you. All you ever did was try and make me scared of you. I used to tremble every time you called my name. Every time I heard your footsteps in the house. Wondering all the time . . . what's Papa gonna say if I do this? . . . What's he gonna say if I do that? . . . What's Papa gonna say if I turn on the radio? And Mama, too . . . she tries . . . but she's scared of you.

TROY: You leave your mama out of this. She ain't got nothing to do with this.

CORY: I don't know how she stand you . . . after what you did to her.

TROY: I told you to leave your mama out of this!

(He advances toward CORY.*)*

CORY: What you gonna do . . . give me a whupping? You can't whup me no more. You're too old. You just an old man.

TROY *(shoves him on his shoulder)*: Nigger! That's what you are. You just another nigger on the street to me!

CORY: You crazy! You know that?

TROY: Go on now! You got the devil in you. Get on away from me!

CORY: You just a crazy old man . . . talking about I got the devil in me.

TROY: Yeah, I'm crazy! If you don't get on the other side of that yard . . . I'm gonna show you how crazy I am! Go on . . . get the hell out of my yard.

CORY: It ain't your yard. You took Uncle Gabe's money he got from the army to buy this house and then you put him out.

TROY *(*TROY *advances on* CORY*)*: Get your black ass out of my yard!

*(*TROY's *advance backs* CORY *up against the tree.* CORY *grabs up the bat.)*

CORY: I ain't going nowhere! Come on . . . put me out! I ain't scared of you.

TROY: That's my bat!

CORY: Come on!

TROY: Put my bat down!

CORY: Come on, put me out.

(CORY swings at TROY, who backs across the yard.)

What's the matter? You so bad . . . put me out!

(TROY advances toward CORY.)

CORY *(backing up)*: Come on! Come on!

TROY: You're gonna have to use it! You wanna draw that bat back on me . . . you're gonna have to use it.

CORY: Come on! . . . Come on!

(CORY swings the bat at TROY a second time. He misses. TROY continues to advance toward him.)

TROY: You're gonna have to kill me! You wanna draw that bat back on me. You're gonna have to kill me.

(CORY, backed up against the tree, can go no farther. TROY taunts him. He sticks out his head and offers him a target.)

Come on! Come on!

(CORY is unable to swing the bat. TROY grabs it.)

TROY: Then I'll show you.

(CORY and TROY struggle over the bat. The struggle is fierce and fully engaged. TROY ultimately is the stronger and takes the bat from CORY and stands over him ready to swing. He stops himself.)

Go on and get away from around my house.

(CORY, stung by his defeat, picks himself up, walks slowly out of the yard and up the alley.)

CORY: Tell Mama I'll be back for my things.

TROY: They'll be on the other side of that fence.

(CORY exits.)

TROY: I can't taste nothing. Hallelujah! I can't taste nothing no more. *(TROY assumes a batting posture and begins to taunt Death, the fastball on the outside corner.)* Come on! It's between you and me now! Come on! Anytime you want! Come on! I be ready for you . . . but I ain't gonna be easy.

(The lights go down on the scene.)

SCENE V

The time is 1965. The lights come up in the yard. It is the morning of TROY'*s funeral. A funeral plaque with a light hangs beside the door. There is a small garden plot off to the side. There is noise and activity in the house as* ROSE, LYONS, *and* BONO *have gathered. The door opens and* RAYNELL, *seven years old, enters dressed in a flannel nightgown. She crosses to the garden and pokes around with a stick.* ROSE *calls from the house.*

ROSE: Raynell!
RAYNELL: Mam?
ROSE: What you doing out there?
RAYNELL: Nothing.

> (ROSE *comes to the door.*)

ROSE: Girl, get in here and get dressed. What you doing?
RAYNELL: Seeing if my garden growed.
ROSE: I told you it ain't gonna grow overnight. You got to wait.
RAYNELL: It don't look like it never gonna grow. Dag!
ROSE: I told you a watched pot never boils. Get in here and get dressed.
RAYNELL: This ain't even no pot, Mama.
ROSE: You just have to give it a chance. It'll grow. Now you come on and do what I told you. We got to be getting ready. This ain't no morning to be playing around. You hear me?
RAYNELL: Yes, mam.

> (ROSE *exits into the house.* RAYNELL *continues to poke at her garden with a stick.* CORY *enters. He is dressed in a Marine corporal's uniform, and carries a duffel bag. His posture is that of a military man, and his speech has a clipped sternness.*)

CORY (*to* RAYNELL): Hi.

> (*Pause.*)

I bet your name is Raynell.
RAYNELL: Uh huh.
CORY: Is your mama home?

> (RAYNELL *runs up on the porch and calls through the screen door.*)

RAYNELL: Mama . . . there's some man out here. Mama?

> (ROSE *comes to the door.*)

ROSE: Cory? Lord have mercy! Look here, you all!

> (ROSE *and* CORY *embrace in a tearful reunion as* BONO *and* LYONS *enter from the house dressed in funeral clothes.*)

BONO: Aw, looka here . . .

ROSE: Done got all grown up!

CORY: Don't cry, Mama. What you crying about?

ROSE: I'm just so glad you made it.

CORY: Hey Lyons. How you doing, Mr. Bono.

(LYONS *goes to embrace* CORY.)

LYONS: Look at you, man. Look at you. Don't he look good, Rose. Got them Corporal stripes.

ROSE: What took you so long.

CORY: You know how the Marines are, Mama. They got to get all their paperwork straight before they let you do anything.

ROSE: Well, I'm sure glad you made it. They let Lyons come. Your Uncle Gabe's still in the hospital. They don't know if they gonna let him out or not. I just talked to them a little while ago.

LYONS: A Corporal in the United States Marines.

BONO: Your daddy knew you had it in you. He used to tell me all the time.

LYONS: Don't he look good, Mr. Bono?

BONO: Yeah, he remind me of Troy when I first met him.

(Pause.)

Say, Rose, Lucille's down at the church with the choir. I'm gonna go down and get the pallbearers lined up. I'll be back to get you all.

ROSE: Thanks, Jim.

CORY: See you, Mr. Bono.

LYONS (*with his arm around* RAYNELL): Cory . . . look at Raynell. Ain't she precious? She gonna break a whole lot of hearts.

ROSE: Raynell, come and say hello to your brother. This is your brother, Cory. You remember Cory.

RAYNELL: No, Mam.

CORY: She don't remember me, Mama.

ROSE: Well, we talk about you. She heard us talk about you. (*To* RAYNELL.) This is your brother, Cory. Come on and say hello.

RAYNELL: Hi.

CORY: Hi. So you're Raynell. Mama told me a lot about you.

ROSE: You all come on into the house and let me fix you some breakfast. Keep up your strength.

CORY: I ain't hungry, Mama.

LYONS: You can fix me something, Rose. I'll be in there in a minute.

ROSE: Cory, you sure you don't want nothing. I know they ain't feeding you right.

CORY: No, Mama . . . thanks. I don't feel like eating. I'll get something later.

ROSE: Raynell . . . get on upstairs and get that dress on like I told you.

(ROSE and RAYNELL exit into the house.)

LYONS: So . . . I hear you thinking about getting married.

CORY: Yeah, I done found the right one, Lyons. It's about time.

LYONS: Me and Bonnie been split up about four years now. About the time Papa retired. I guess she just got tired of all them changes I was putting her through.

(Pause.)

I always knew you was gonna make something out yourself. Your head was always in the right direction. So . . . you gonna stay in . . . make it a career . . . put in your twenty years?

CORY: I don't know. I got six already, I think that's enough.

LYONS: Stick with Uncle Sam and retire early. Ain't nothing out here. I guess Rose told you what happened with me. They got me down the workhouse. I thought I was being slick cashing other people's checks.

CORY: How much time you doing?

LYONS: They give me three years. I got that beat now. I ain't got but nine more months. It ain't so bad. You learn to deal with it like anything else. You got to take the crookeds with the straights. That's what Papa used to say. He used to say that when he struck out. I seen him strike out three times in a row . . . and the next time up he hit the ball over the grandstand. Right out there in Homestead Field. He wasn't satisfied hitting in the seats . . . he want to hit it over everything! After the game he had two hundred people standing around waiting to shake his hand. You got to take the crookeds with the straights. Yeah, Papa was something else.

CORY: You still playing?

LYONS: Cory . . . you know I'm gonna do that. There's some fellows down there we got us a band . . . we gonna try and stay together when we get out . . . but yeah, I'm still playing. It still helps me to get out of bed in the morning. As long as it do that I'm gonna be right there playing and trying to make some sense out of it.

ROSE *(calling)*: Lyons, I got these eggs in the pan.

LYONS: Let me go on and get these eggs, man. Get ready to go bury Papa.

(Pause.)

How you doing? You doing all right?

(CORY nods. LYONS touches him on the shoulder and they share a moment of silent grief. LYONS exits into the house. CORY wanders about the yard. RAYNELL enters.)

RAYNELL: Hi.

CORY: Hi.

RAYNELL: Did you used to sleep in my room?

CORY: Yeah . . . that used to be my room.

RAYNELL: That's what Papa call it. "Cory's room." It got your football in the closet.

(ROSE *comes to the door.*)

ROSE: Raynell, get in there and get them good shoes on.

RAYNELL: Mama, can't I wear these. Them other one hurt my feet.

ROSE: Well, they just gonna have to hurt your feet for a while. You ain't said they hurt your feet when you went down to the store and got them.

RAYNELL: They didn't hurt then. My feet done got bigger.

ROSE: Don't you give me no backtalk now. You get in there and get them shoes on.

(RAYNELL *exits into the house.*)

Ain't too much changed. He still got that piece of rag tied to that tree. He was out there swinging that bat. I was just ready to go back in the house. He swung that bat and then he just fell over. Seem like he swung it and stood there with this grin on his face . . . and then he just fell over. They carried him on down to the hospital, but I knew there wasn't no need . . . why don't you come on in the house?

CORY: Mama . . . I got something to tell you. I don't know how to tell you this . . . but I've got to tell you . . . I'm not going to Papa's funeral.

ROSE: Boy, hush your mouth. That's your daddy you talking about. I don't want hear that kind of talk this morning. I done raised you to come to this? You standing there all healthy and grown talking about you ain't going to your daddy's funeral?

CORY: Mama . . . listen . . .

ROSE: I don't want to hear it, Cory. You just get that thought out of your head.

CORY: I can't drag Papa with me everywhere I go. I've got to say no to him. One time in my life I've got to say no.

ROSE: Don't nobody have to listen to nothing like that. I know you and your daddy ain't seen eye to eye, but I ain't got to listen to that kind of talk this morning. Whatever was between you and your daddy . . . the time has come to put it aside. Just take it and set it over there on the shelf and forget about it. Disrespecting your daddy ain't gonna make you a man, Cory. You got to find a way to come to that on your own. Not going to your daddy's funeral ain't gonna make you a man.

CORY: The whole time I was growing up . . . living in his house . . . Papa was like a shadow that followed you everywhere. It weighed on you and sunk into your flesh. It would wrap around you and lay there until you couldn't tell which one was you anymore. That shadow digging in your flesh. Trying to crawl in. Trying to live through you. Everywhere I looked, Troy Maxson was staring back at me . . . hiding under the bed . . . in the closet. I'm just saying I've got to find a way to get rid of that shadow, Mama.

ROSE: You just like him. You got him in you good.

CORY: Don't tell me that, Mama.

ROSE: You Troy Maxson all over again.

CORY: I don't want to be Troy Maxson. I want to be me.

ROSE: You can't be nobody but who you are, Cory. That shadow wasn't nothing but you growing into yourself. You either got to grow into it or cut it down to fit you. But that's all you got to make life with. That's all you got to measure yourself against that world out there. Your daddy wanted you to be everything he wasn't . . . and at the same time he tried to make you into everything he was. I don't know if he was right or wrong . . . but I do know he meant to do more good than he meant to do harm. He wasn't always right. Sometimes when he touched he bruised. And sometimes when he took me in his arms he cut.

When I first met your daddy I thought . . . Here is a man I can lay down with and make a baby. That's the first thing I thought when I seen him. I was thirty years old and had done seen my share of men. But when he walked up to me and said, "I can dance a waltz that'll make you dizzy," I thought, Rose Lee, here is a man that you can open yourself up to and be filled to bursting. Here is a man that can fill all them empty spaces you been tipping around the edges of. One of them empty spaces was being somebody's mother.

I married your daddy and settled down to cooking his supper and keeping clean sheets on the bed. When your daddy walked through the house he was so big he filled it up. That was my first mistake. Not to make him leave some room for me. For my part in the matter. But at that time I wanted that. I wanted a house that I could sing in. And that's what your daddy gave me. I didn't know to keep up his strength I had to give up little pieces of mine. I did that. I took on his life as mine and mixed up the pieces so that you couldn't hardly tell which was which anymore. It was my choice. It was my life and I didn't have to live it like that. But that's what life offered me in the way of being a woman and I took it. I grabbed hold of it with both hands.

By the time Raynell came into the house, me and your daddy had done lost touch with one another. I didn't want to make my blessing off of nobody's misfortune . . . but I took on to Raynell like she was all them babies I had wanted and never had.

(The phone rings.)

Like I'd been blessed to relive a part of my life. And if the Lord see fit to keep up my strength . . . I'm gonna do her just like your daddy did you . . . I'm gonna give her the best of what's in me.

RAYNELL *(entering, still with her old shoes)*: Mama . . . Reverend Tollivier on the phone.

(ROSE *exits into the house.*)

RAYNELL: Hi.

CORY: Hi.

RAYNELL: You in the Army or the Marines?

CORY: Marines.

RAYNELL: Papa said it was the Army. Did you know Blue?

CORY: Blue? Who's Blue?

RAYNELL: Papa's dog what he sing about all the time.

CORY *(singing)*: Hear it ring! Hear it ring!
    I had a dog his name was Blue
    You know Blue was mighty true
    You know Blue was a good old dog
    Blue treed a possum in a hollow log
    You know from that he was a good old dog
    Hear it ring! Hear it ring!

(RAYNELL *joins in singing.*)

CORY AND RAYNELL: Blue treed a possum out on a limb
    Blue looked at me and I looked at him
    Grabbed that possum and put him in a sack
    Blue stayed there till I came back
    Old Blue's feets was big and round
    Never allowed a possum to touch the ground.

    Old Blue died and I dug his grave
    I dug his grave with a silver spade
    Let him down with a golden chain
    And every night I call his name
    Go on Blue, you good dog you
    Go on Blue, you good dog you

RAYNELL: Blue laid down and died like a man
    Blue laid down and died . . .

BOTH: Blue laid down and died like a man
    Now he's treeing possums in the Promised Land
    I'm gonna tell you this to let you know
    Blue's gone where the good dogs go
    When I hear old Blue bark
    When I hear old Blue bark
    Blue treed a possum in Noah's Ark
    Blue treed a possum in Noah's Ark.

(ROSE *comes to the screen door.*)

ROSE: Cory, we gonna be ready to go in a minute.

CORY *(to* RAYNELL*)*: You go on in the house and change them shoes like
    Mama told you so we can go to Papa's funeral.

RAYNELL: Okay, I'll be back.

(*RAYNELL exits into the house. CORY gets up and crosses over to the tree. ROSE stands in the screen door watching him. GABRIEL enters from the alley.*)

GABRIEL *(calling)*: Hey, Rose!

ROSE: Gabe?

GABRIEL: I'm here, Rose. Hey Rose, I'm here!

(*ROSE enters from the house.*)

ROSE: Lord . . . Look here, Lyons!

LYONS: See, I told you, Rose . . . I told you they'd let him come.

CORY: How you doing, Uncle Gabe?

LYONS: How you doing, Uncle Gabe?

GABRIEL: Hey, Rose. It's time. It's time to tell St. Peter to open the gates. Troy, you ready? You ready, Troy. I'm gonna tell St. Peter to open the gates. You get ready now.

(*GABRIEL, with great fanfare, braces himself to blow. The trumpet is without a mouthpiece. He puts the end of it into his mouth and blows with great force, like a man who has been waiting some twenty-odd years for this single moment. No sound comes out of the trumpet. He braces himself and blows again with the same result. A third time he blows. There is a weight of impossible description that falls away and leaves him bare and exposed to a frightful realization. It is a trauma that a sane and normal mind would be unable to withstand. He begins to dance. A slow, strange dance, eerie and life-giving. A dance of atavistic signature and ritual. LYONS attempts to embrace him. GABRIEL pushes LYONS away. He begins to howl in what is an attempt at song, or perhaps a song turning back into itself in an attempt at speech. He finishes his dance and the gates of heaven stand open as wide as God's closet.*)

That's the way that go!

Considerations

1. Reread the stage directions at the beginning of the play carefully. Explain how they contribute to the reader's understanding of the culture and identity of the characters in the play.
2. Make brief notes describing the action in each scene in which Gabriel appears. How do the actions relate to Gabriel's biblical name and to his belief that he is an angel?
3. Describe and evaluate the values on which each of the main characters bases his or her life. Explain how these values support or conflict with one another.

4. How do "hopes and dreams" serve as a theme for the play? Consider especially how Troy uses baseball as a metaphor throughout the play.

5. Why is the play called *Fences* rather than *The Fence?* Explain the significance of fences to each of the main characters' lives in your response to this question.

Commentary

DAVID SAVRAN (1950–   )

Interview with August Wilson

SAVRAN: In reading *Fences,* I came to view Troy more and more critically as the play progressed, sharing Rose's point of view. We see that Troy has been crippled by his father. That's being replayed in Troy's relationship with Cory. Do you think there's a way out of that cycle?

WILSON: Surely. First of all, we're all like our parents. The things we are taught early in life, how to respond to the world, our sense of morality— everything, we get from them. Now you can take that legacy and do with it anything you want to do. It's in your hands. Cory is Troy's son. How can he be Troy's son without sharing Troy's values? I was trying to get at why Troy made the choices he made, how they have influenced his values and how he attempts to pass those along to his son. Each generation gives the succeeding generation what they think they need. One question in the play is "Are the tools we are given sufficient to compete in a world that is different from the one our parents knew?" I think they are—it's just that we have to do different things with the tools. That's all Troy has to give. Troy's flaw is that he does not recognize that the world was changing. That's because he spent fifteen years in a penitentiary.

As African-Americans, we should demand to participate in society as Africans. That's the way out of the vicious cycle of poverty and neglect that exists in 1987 in America, where you have a huge percentage of blacks living in the equivalent of South African townships, in housing projects. No one is inviting these people to participate in society. Look at the poverty levels— $8,500 for a family of four, if you have $8,501 you're not counted. Those statistics would go up enormously if we had an honest assessment of the cost of living in America. I don't know how anybody can support a family of four on $8,500. What I'm saying is that 85 or 90 percent of blacks in America are living in abject poverty and, for the most part, are crowded into what amount to concentration camps. The situation for blacks in America is worse than it was forty years ago. Some sociologists will tell you about the tremendous progress we've made. They didn't put me out when I walked in the door. And you can always point to someone who works on Wall Street, or is a doctor. But they don't count in the larger scheme of things.

SAVRAN: Do you have any idea how these political changes could take place?

WILSON: I'm not sure. I know that blacks must be allowed their cultural differences. I think the process of assimilation to white American society was a big mistake. We don't want to be like you. Blacks living in housing projects are isolated from the society, for the most part—living as

5

they choose, as Africans. Only they don't realize the value in what they're doing because they have accepted their victimization. They've marked themselves as victims. Once they recognize that, they can begin to move through society in a different manner, from a stronger position, and claim what is theirs.

SAVRAN: A project of yours is to point up what happens when oppression is internalized.

WILSON: Yes, transfer of aggression to the wrong target. I think it's interesting that the two roads open to blacks for "full participation" are entertainment and sports. *Ma Rainey* and *Fences,* and I didn't plan it that way. I don't think that they're the correct roads. I think Troy's right. Now with the benefit of historical perspective, I can say that the athletic scholarship was actually a way of exploiting. Now you've got two million kids who think they're going to play in the NBA. In the sixties the universities made a lot of money off of athletics. You had kids playing for free who, by and large, were not getting educated, were taking courses in basketweaving. Some of them could barely read.

SAVRAN: Troy may be right about that issue, but it seems that he has passed on certain destructive traits in spite of himself. Take the hostility between father and son.

WILSON: I think every generation says to the previous generation: you're in my way, I've got to get by. The father-son conflict is actually a normal generational conflict that happens all the time.

SAVRAN: So it's a healthy and a good thing?   10

WILSON: Oh, sure. Troy is seeing this boy walk around, smelling his piss. Two men cannot live in the same household. Troy would have been tremendously disappointed if Cory had not challenged him. Troy knows that this boy has to go out and do battle with that world: "So I had best prepare him because I know that's a harsh, cruel place out there. But that's going to be easy compared to what he's getting here. Ain't nobody gonna whip your ass like I'm gonna whip it." He has a tremendous love for the kid. But he's not going to say, "I love you," he's going to demonstrate it. He's carrying garbage for seventeen years just for the kid. The only world Troy knows is the one that he made. Cory's going to go on to find another one, he's going to arrive at the same place as Troy. I think one of the most important lines in the play is when Troy is talking about his father: "I got to the place where I could feel him kicking in my blood and knew that the only thing that separated us was the matter of a few years."

Hopefully, Cory will do things a bit differently with his son. For Troy, sports was not the way to go, the white man wouldn't let him get away with that. "Get you a job, with your hands, something that nobody can take away from you." The idea of school—he doesn't know what that is. That's for white folks. Very few blacks had paperwork jobs. But if you knew how to fix cars, you could always make some money. That's what Troy wants for Cory. There aren't many people who ever jumped up in Troy's face. So he's proud of the kid at the same time that he expresses a hurt that all men feel. You got to cut your kid loose at some point. There's that sense of loss and separation. You find out how Troy left his father's house and you see how Cory leaves his house. I suspect with Cory it will repeat with some differences and maybe, after five or six generations, they'll find a different way to do it.

SAVRAN: Where Cory ends up is very ambiguous, as a marine in 1965.

WILSON: Yes. For the average black kid on the street, that was an alternative. You went into the army because you could learn how to do something. I can remember my parents talking about the son of some friends: "He's in the navy. He *did* something"—as opposed to standing on the street corner, shooting drugs, drinking wine, and robbing stores. Lyons says to Cory, "I always knew you were going to make something out of yourself." It really wounds me. He's a corporal in the marines. For blacks, that is a sense of accomplishment. Therein lies one of the tragedies of blacks in America. Cory says, "I don't know. I put in six years. That's enough." Anyone who goes into the army and makes a career out of it is a loser. They sit there and are nurtured by the army and they don't have to confront life. Then they get out of the army and find there's nothing to do. They didn't learn any skills. And if they did, they can't find a job. Four months later, they're shooting dope. In the sixties a whole bunch of blacks went over, fought and died in the Vietnam War. The survivors came back to the same street corners and found out nothing had changed. They still couldn't get a job.

At the end of *Fences* every person, with the exception of Raynell, is institutionalized. Rose is in a church. Lyons is in a penitentiary. Gabriel's in a mental hospital and Cory's in the marines. The only free person is the girl, Troy's daughter, the hope for the future. That was conscious on my part because in '57 that's what I saw. Blacks have relied on institutions which are really foreign—except for the black church, which has been our saving grace. I have some problems with it but I recognize it as a central social organization and sometimes an economic organization for the black community. I would like to see blacks develop their own institutions that respond to their needs.

CHIEF SEATTLE (1786–1866)

My People

Chief of the Suquamish and leader of other tribes in what is now Washington State, Chief Seattle was born around 1786. In 1854, the governor of Washington Territories, Isaac Stevens, proposed to buy two million acres of land from the tribes Seattle led. This speech is Seattle's reply to the offer. His words offer a chilling prediction of the massacres and relocations that decimated Native American tribes beginning in the 1860s.

Yonder sky that has wept tears upon my people for centuries untold, and which to us appears changeless and eternal, may change. Today is fair. Tomorrow may be overcast with clouds. My words are like the stars that never change. Whatever Seattle says the great chief at Washington can rely upon with as much certainty as he can upon the return of the sun or the seasons. The White Chief says that Big Chief at Washington sends us greetings of friendship and goodwill. That is kind of him for we know he has little need of our friendship in return. His people are many. They are like the grass that covers vast prairies. My people are few. They resemble the scattering trees of a storm-swept plain. The great, and—I presume—good, White Chief sends us word that he wishes to buy our lands but is willing to allow us enough to live comfortably. This indeed appears just, even generous, for the Red Man no longer has rights that he need respect, and the offer may be wise also, as we are no longer in need of an extensive country. . . . I will not dwell on, nor mourn over, our untimely decay, nor reproach our paleface brothers with hastening it, as we too may have been somewhat to blame.

Youth is impulsive. When our young men grow angry at some real or imaginary wrong, and disfigure their faces with black paint, it denotes that their hearts are black, and then they are often cruel and relentless, and our old men and old women are unable to restrain them. Thus it has ever been. Thus it was when the white men first began to push our forefathers further westward. But let us hope that the hostilities between us may never return. We would have everything to lose and nothing to gain. Revenge by young men is considered gain, even at the cost of their own lives, but old men who stay at home in times of war, and mothers who have sons to lose, know better.

Our good father at Washington—for I presume he is now our father as well as yours, since King George has moved his boundaries further north— our great good father, I say, sends us word that if we do as he desires he will protect us. His brave warriors will be to us a bristling wall of strength, and his wonderful ships of war will fill our harbors so that our ancient enemies far to the northward—the Hydas and Tsimpsians—will cease to frighten our women, children, and old men. Then in reality will he be our father and we his children. But can that ever be? Your God is not our God! Your God loves your people and hates mine. He folds his strong and protecting arms lovingly about the paleface and leads him by the hand as a father leads his infant son—but He has forsaken His red children—if they really are his. Our God, the Great Spirit, seems also to have forsaken us. Your God makes your people wax strong every day. Soon they will fill the land. Our people are ebbing away like a rapidly receding tide that will never return. The white man's God cannot love our people or He would protect them. They seem to be orphans who can look nowhere for help. How then can we be brothers? How can your God become our God and renew our prosperity and awaken in us dreams of returning greatness? If we have a common heavenly father He must be partial—for He came to his paleface children. We never saw Him. He gave you laws but He had no word for His red children whose teeming multitudes once filled this vast continent as stars fill the firmament. No; we are two distinct races with separate origins and separate destinies. There is little in common between us.

To us the ashes of our ancestors are sacred and their resting place is hallowed ground. You wander far from the graves of your ancestors and seemingly without regret. Your religion was written upon tables of stone by the iron finger of your God so that you could not forget. The Red Man could never comprehend nor remember it. Our religion is the traditions of our ancestors—the dreams of our old men, given them in solemn hours of night by the Great Spirit; and the visions of our sachems°; and it is written in the hearts of our people.

Your dead cease to love you and the land of their nativity as soon as they pass the portals of the tomb and wander way beyond the stars. They are soon forgotten and never return. Our dead never forget the beautiful world that gave them being.   5

Day and night cannot dwell together. The Red Man has ever fled the approach of the White Man, as the morning mist flees before the morning sun. However, your proposition seems fair and I think that my people will accept it and will retire to the reservation you offer them. Then we will dwell apart in peace, for the words of the Great White Chief seem to be the words of nature speaking to my people out of dense darkness.

It matters little where we pass the remnant of our days. They will not be many. A few more moons; a few more winters—and not one of the descendants of the mighty hosts that once moved over this broad land or lived in happy homes, protected by the Great Spirit, will remain to mourn over the graves of a people once more powerful and hopeful than yours. But why should I mourn at the untimely fate of my people? Tribe follows tribe, and nation follows nation, like the waves of the sea. It is the order of nature, and regret is useless. Your time of decay may be distant, but it will surely come, for even the White Man whose God walked and talked with him as

sachems: Tribal chiefs.

friend with friend, cannot be exempt from the common destiny. We may be brothers after all. We will see.

We will ponder your proposition, and when we decide we will let you know. But should we accept it, I here and now make this condition that we will not be denied the privilege without molestation of visiting at any time the tombs of our ancestors, friends and children. Every part of this soil is sacred in the estimation of my people. Every hillside, every valley, every plain and grove, has been hallowed by some sad or happy event in days long vanished. . . . The very dust upon which you now stand responds more lovingly to their footsteps than to yours, because it is rich with the blood of our ancestors and our bare feet are conscious of the sympathetic touch. . . . Even the little children who lived here and rejoiced here for a brief season will love these somber solitudes and at eventide they greet shadowy returning spirits. And when the last Red Man shall have perished, and the memory of my tribe shall have become a myth among the White Men, these shores will swarm with the invisible dead of my tribe, and when your children's children think themselves alone in the field, the store, the shop, upon the highway, or in the silence of the pathless woods, they will not be alone. . . . At night when the streets of your cities and villages are silent and you think them deserted, they will throng with the returning hosts that once filled and still love this beautiful land. The White Man will never be alone.

Let him be just and deal kindly with my people, for the dead are not powerless. Dead, did I say? There is not death, only a change of worlds.

Considerations

1. Note the images and comparisons Chief Seattle chooses to express his ideas. What does his language suggest about his view of the world?
2. The tone of Seattle's message is complex. Identify and discuss specific passages that suggest his view of white people and of their offer to buy the lands where his tribe has lived.
3. This message was composed in 1853. To what extent has Seattle's prophecy been proved true? Consider particularly the vision he projects in the last part of paragraph 8.
4. Briefly describe the audience to whom Chief Seattle delivers his message. What tone does he take? Cite specific examples to argue either for or against the following proposition: Chief Seattle's speech is a masterpiece of diplomacy.
5. In paragraph 2, Chief Seattle describes the young men of his tribe in this way: "Youth is impulsive. When our young men grow angry at some real or imaginary wrong . . . then they are often cruel and relentless." What is his attitude toward this cruelty and relentlessness? Comment on the application of Seattle's observations to any of your own present-day actions or observations.

JEANNE WAKATSUKI HOUSTON (1935–   )
and JAMES D. HOUSTON (1933–   )

Arrival at Manzanar

Born in California in 1935, Jeanne Wakatsuki was among thousands of Americans of Japanese descent who were rounded up and sent to internment camps during World War II (following the Japanese attack on Pearl Harbor in December 1941). She remained at the camp from the age of seven to the age of eleven. Later, while studying journalism at San Jose State University, she met her future husband, novelist James D. Houston. Together, the Houstons wrote Farewell to Manzanar *to document her life there and to describe the impact of the internment on the Wakatsuki family as well as other families who spent the duration of the war at the camp.*

In December of 1941 Papa's disappearance didn't bother me nearly so much as the world I soon found myself in.

He had been a jack-of-all-trades. When I was born he was farming near Inglewood. Later, when he started fishing, we moved to Ocean Park, near Santa Monica, and until they picked him up, that's where we lived, in a big frame house with a brick fireplace, a block back from the beach. We were the only Japanese family in the neighborhood. Papa liked it that way. He didn't want to be labeled or grouped by anyone. But with him gone and no way of knowing what to expect, my mother moved all of us down to Terminal Island. Woody already lived there, and one of my older sisters had married a Terminal Island boy. Mama's first concern now was to keep the family together; and once the war began, she felt safer there than isolated racially in Ocean Park. But for me, at age seven, the island was a country as foreign as India or Arabia would have been. It was the first time I had lived among other Japanese, or gone to school with them, and I was terrified all the time.

This was partly Papa's fault. One of his threats to keep us younger kids in line was "I'm going to sell you to the Chinaman." When I had entered kindergarten two years earlier, I was the only Oriental in the class. They sat me next to a Caucasian girl who happened to have very slanted eyes. I looked at her and began to scream, certain Papa had sold me out at last. My fear of her ran so deep I could not speak of it, even to Mama, couldn't explain why I was screaming. For two weeks I had nightmares about this girl, until the teachers finally moved me to the other side of the room. And it was still with me, this fear of Oriental faces, when we moved to Terminal Island.

In those days it was a company town, a ghetto owned and controlled by the canneries. The men went after fish, and whenever the boats came back—day or night—the women would be called to process the catch while it was fresh. One in the afternoon or four in the morning, it made no difference. My mother had to go to work right after we moved there. I can still hear the whistle—two toots for French's, three for Van Camp's—and she and Chizu would be out of bed in the middle of the night, heading for the cannery.

The house we lived in was nothing more than a shack, a barracks with   5
single plank walls and rough wooden floors, like the cheapest kind of migrant workers' housing. The people around us were hard-working, boisterous, a little proud of their nickname, *yo-go-re,* which meant literally *uncouth one,* or roughneck, or dead-end kid. They not only spoke Japanese exclusively, they spoke a dialect peculiar to Kyushu, where their families had come from in Japan, a rough, fisherman's language, full of oaths and insults. Instead of saying *ba-ka-ta-re,* a common insult meaning *stupid,* Terminal Islanders would say *ba-ka-ya-ro,* a coarser and exclusively masculine use of the word, which implies gross stupidity. They would swagger and pick on outsiders and per-secute anyone who didn't speak as they did. That was what made my own time there so hateful. I had never spoken anything but English, and the other kids in the second grade despised me for it. They were tough and mean, like ghetto kids anywhere. Each day after school I dreaded their ambush. My brother Kiyo, three years older, would wait for me at the door, where we would decide whether to run straight home together, or split up, or try a new and unexpected route.

None of these kids ever actually attacked. It was the threat that fright-ened us, their fearful looks, and the noises they would make, like miniature Samurai, in a language we couldn't understand.

At the time it seemed we had been living under this reign of fear for years. In fact, we lived there about two months. Late in February the navy decided to clear Terminal Island completely. Even though most of us were American-born, it was dangerous having that many Orientals so close to the Long Beach Naval Station, on the opposite end of the island. We had known something like this was coming. But, like Papa's arrest, not much could be done ahead of time. There were four of us kids still young enough to be living with Mama, plus Granny, her mother, sixty-five then, speaking no English, and nearly blind. Mama didn't know where else she could get work, and we had nowhere else to move *to.* On February 25 the choice was made for us. We were given forty-eight hours to clear out.

The secondhand dealers had been prowling around for weeks, like wolves, offering humiliating prices for goods and furniture they knew many of us would have to sell sooner or later. Mama had left all but her most valuable possessions in Ocean Park, simply because she had nowhere to put them. She had brought along her pottery, her silver, heirlooms like the ki-monos Granny had brought from Japan, tea sets, lacquered tables, and one fine old set of china, blue and white porcelain, almost translucent. On the day we were leaving, Woody's car was so crammed with boxes and luggage and kids we had just run out of room. Mama had to sell this china.

One of the dealers offered her fifteen dollars for it. She said it was a full setting for twelve and worth at least two hundred. He said fifteen was his top price. Mama started to quiver. Her eyes blazed up at him. She had been packing all night and trying to calm down Granny, who didn't understand why we were moving again and what all the rush was about. Mama's nerves were shot, and now navy jeeps were patrolling the streets. She didn't say another word. She just glared at this man, all the rage and frustration channeled at him through her eyes.

He watched her for a moment and said he was sure he couldn't pay   10 more than seventeen fifty for that china. She reached into the red velvet case, took out a dinner plate and hurled it at the floor right in front of his feet.

The man leaped back shouting, "Hey! Hey, don't do that! Those are valuable dishes!"

Mama took out another dinner plate and hurled it at the floor, then another and another, never moving, never opening her mouth, just quivering and glaring at the retreating dealer, with tears streaming down her cheeks. He finally turned and scuttled out the door, heading for the next house. When he was gone she stood there smashing cups and bowls and platters until the whole set lay in scattered blue and white fragments across the wooden floor.

The name Manzanar meant nothing to us when we left Boyle Heights. We didn't know where it was or what it was. We went because the government ordered us to. And, in the case of my older brothers and sisters, we went with a certain amount of relief. They had all heard stories of Japanese homes being attacked, of beatings in the streets of California towns. They were as frightened of the Caucasians as Caucasians were of us. Moving, under what appeared to be government protection, to an area less directly threatened by the war seemed not such a bad idea at all. For some it actually sounded like a fine adventure.

Our pickup point was a Buddhist church in Los Angeles. It was very early, and misty, when we got there with our luggage. Mama had bought heavy coats for all of us. She grew up in eastern Washington and knew that anywhere inland in early April would be cold. I was proud of my new coat, and I remember sitting on a duffel bag trying to be friendly with the Greyhound driver. I smiled at him. He didn't smile back. He was befriending no one. Someone tied a numbered tag to my collar and to the duffel bag (each family was given a number, and that became our official designation until the camps were closed), someone else passed out box lunches for the trip, and we climbed aboard.

I had never been outside Los Angeles County, never traveled more than   15 ten miles from the coast, had never even ridden on a bus. I was full of excitement, the way any kid would be, and wanted to look out the window. But for the first few hours the shades were drawn. Around me other people played cards, read magazines, dozed, waiting. I settled back, waiting too, and finally fell asleep. The bus felt very secure to me. Almost half its passengers were immediate relatives. Mama and my older brothers had succeeded in keeping most of us together, on the same bus, headed for the same camp. I didn't realize until much later what a job that was. The strategy had been, first, to have everyone living in the same district when the evacuation began, and then to get all of us included under the same family number, even though names had been changed by marriage. Many families weren't as lucky as ours and suffered months of anguish while trying to arrange transfers from one camp to another.

We rode all day. By the time we reached our destination, the shades were up. It was late afternoon. The first thing I saw was a yellow swirl across a blurred, reddish setting sun. The bus was being pelted by what sounded like splattering rain. It wasn't rain. This was my first look at something I would soon know very well, a billowing flurry of dust and sand churned up by the wind through Owens Valley.

We drove past a barbed-wire fence, through a gate, and into an open space where trunks and sacks and packages had been dumped from the baggage trucks that drove out ahead of us. I could see a few tents set up, the first rows of black barracks, and beyond them, blurred by sand, rows of barracks that seemed to spread for miles across this plain. People were sitting on cartons or milling around, with their backs to the wind, waiting to see which friends or relatives might be on this bus. As we approached, they turned or stood up, and some moved toward us expectantly. But inside the bus no one stirred. No one waved or spoke. They just stared out the windows, ominously silent. I didn't understand this. Hadn't we finally arrived, our whole family intact? I opened a window, leaned out, and yelled happily. "Hey! This whole bus is full of Wakatsukis!"

Outside, the greeters smiled. Inside there was an explosion of laughter, hysterical, tension-breaking laughter that left my brothers choking and whacking each other across the shoulders.

We had pulled up just in time for dinner. The mess halls weren't completed yet. An outdoor chow line snaked around a half-finished building that broke a good part of the wind. They issued us army mess kits, the round metal kind that fold over, and plopped in scoops of canned Vienna sausage, canned string beans, steamed rice that had been cooked too long, and on top of the rice a serving of canned apricots. The Caucasian servers were thinking the fruit poured over rice would make a good dessert. Among the Japanese, of course, rice is never eaten with sweet foods, only with salty or savory foods. Few of us could eat such a mixture. But at this point no one dared protest. It would have been impolite. I was horrified when I saw the apricot syrup seeping through my little mound of rice. I opened my mouth to complain. My mother jabbed me in the back to keep quiet. We moved on through the line and joined the others squatting in the lee of half-raised walls, dabbing courteously at what was, for almost everyone there, an inedible concoction.

After dinner we were taken to Block 16, a cluster of fifteen barracks   20 that had just been finished a day or so earlier—although finished was hardly the word for it. The shacks were built of one thickness of pine planking covered with tarpaper. They sat on concrete footings, with about two feet of open space between the floorboards and the ground. Gaps showed between the planks, and as the weeks passed and the green wood dried out, the gaps widened. Knotholes gaped in the uncovered floor.

Each barracks was divided into six units, sixteen by twenty feet, about the size of a living room, with one bare bulb hanging from the ceiling and an oil stove for heat. We were assigned two of these for the twelve people in our family group; and our official family "number" was enlarged by three digits—16 plus the number of this barracks. We were issued steel army cots, two brown army blankets each, and some mattress covers, which my brothers stuffed with straw.

The first task was to divide up what space we had for sleeping. Bill and Woody contributed a blanket each and partitioned off the first room: one side for Bill and Tomi, one side for Woody and Chizu and their baby girl. Woody also got the stove, for heating formulas.

The people who had it hardest during the first few months were young couples like these, many of whom had married just before the evacuation began, in order not to be separated and sent to different camps. Our two rooms were crowded, but at least it was all in the family. My oldest sister and her husband were shoved into one of those sixteen-by-twenty-foot compartments with six people they had never seen before—two other couples, one recently married like themselves, the other with two teenage boys. Partitioning off a room like that wasn't easy. It was bitter cold when we arrived, and the wind did not abate. All they had to use for room dividers were those army blankets, two of which were barely enough to keep one person warm. They argued over whose blanket should be sacrificed and later argued about noise at night—the parents wanted their boys asleep by 9:00 P.M.—and they continued arguing over matters like that for six months, until my sister and her husband left to harvest sugar beets in Idaho. It was grueling work up there, and wages were pitiful, but when the call came through camp for workers to alleviate the wartime labor shortage, it sounded better than their life at Manzanar. They knew they'd have, if nothing else, a room, perhaps a cabin of their own.

That first night in Block 16, the rest of us squeezed into the second room—Granny, Lillian, age fourteen, Ray, thirteen, May, eleven, Kiyo, ten, Mama, and me. I didn't mind this at all at the time. Being youngest meant I got to sleep with Mama. And before we went to bed I had a great time jumping up and down on the mattress. The boys had stuffed so much straw into hers, we had to flatten it some so we wouldn't slide off. I slept with her every night after that until Papa came back.

Considerations

1. Describe Jeanne Wakatsuki's childhood view of other Asian people. Where did her views come from? What is your response to the way she reacts to the children she meets in school and at Terminal Island?

2. Cite details that indicate the values of the people who were involved in some way with the involuntary internment of the Wakatsukis and other American families of Japanese ancestry.

3. Do research to discover why only Japanese Americans were interned during World War II whereas German Americans and Italian Americans were not (even though both Germany and Italy were fighting against the Allies).

4. Consider Wakatsuki's portrayal of different members of her family. If they lived in your neighborhood today, do you think you and your family would become close friends with them? Good neighbors? Distant neighbors? Have no relationship with them? Would you prefer to be friends with some of the Wakatsuki family members and not with others? Explain.

5. Because of the essay's various lively anecdotes, the child's perspective shines through in this piece. How do you think the child's point of view affects the essay? How might it have been different if it had been written by a family member who was an adult at the time of the internment?

CONNECTIONS: ROOTS, IDENTITY, AND CULTURE

1. "Sonny's Blues," "Everyday Use," "We Wear the Mask," "Telephone Conversation," "I Am a Black Woman," and *Fences* all look at the experiences of African-American men and women living in a dominantly white culture. From reading these works, what observations can you make about the similarities and differences in these experiences?

2. "The Warriors," "I Expected My Skin and My Blood to Ripen," and "My People," are written by Native Americans. Imagine a dialogue between Chief Seattle, Wendy Rose, and any of the characters in "The Warriors." In the dialogue, consider what questions these individuals might ask each other as well as what advice they might offer.

3. Examine ways in which people's life choices are or are not controlled by their roots and culture. Consider any of the following works: "Sonny's Blues," "Everyday Use," "Rules of the Game," "Chronicle," "Latin Women Pray," *Fences,* or *Oedipus Rex.*

4. In "Cathedral," the narrator and Robert come from different cultures— one man is sighted, the other is blind. In the encounter between the two cultures, what do you think is gained? By whom? In what other works in this chapter do you see encounters between people of different cultures? What gains or losses do you observe as the result of these encounters? (Remember that "culture" need not refer only to race; gender, class, religion, occupation, and many other categories also serve to define the cultures of which we are a part.)

5. What role do family customs, values, and traditions play in the development of a person's identity? Consider any of the following works, as well as your own observations and experiences, in your response: "Sonny's Blues," "Everyday Use," "The Warriors," "Rules of the Game," "The Youngest Daughter," or *Fences*.

7

Work

WILLIAM CARLOS WILLIAMS (1883–1963)

The Use of Force

> It is no wonder that William Carlos Williams, who was born in New Jersey yet grew up speaking Spanish at home, considered himself quintessentially representative of the American immigrant experience: his mother was born in Puerto Rico to Basque and French-Dutch-Jewish parents, and his father was born in England but was raised in the West Indies. In 1906, Williams graduated from the University of Pennsylvania as a medical doctor and then studied pediatrics in Leipzig before returning to practice medicine in his hometown of Rutherford, New Jersey. His daily visits with patients often provided inspiration for his poetry and short stories. During the mid 1950s, Williams suffered a stroke that forced him to retire from the practice of medicine. Nevertheless, he continued to write and in 1963 won the Pulitzer Prize for literature.

They were new patients to me, all I had was the name, Olson. Please come down as soon as you can, my daughter is very sick.

When I arrived I was met by the mother, a big startled looking woman, very clean and apologetic who merely said, Is this the doctor? and let me in. In the back, she added. You must excuse us, doctor, we have her in the kitchen where it is warm. It is very damp here sometimes.

The child was fully dressed and sitting on her father's lap near the kitchen table. He tried to get up, but I motioned for him not to bother, took off my overcoat and started to look things over. I could see that they were all very nervous, eyeing me up and down distrustfully. As often, in such cases, they weren't telling me more than they had to, it was up to me to tell them; that's why they were spending three dollars on me.

The child was fairly eating me up with her cold, steady eyes, and no expression to her face whatever. She did not move and seemed, inwardly, quiet; an unusually attractive little thing, and as strong as a heifer in appearance. But her face was flushed, she was breathing rapidly, and I realized that she had a high fever. She had magnificent blonde hair, in profusion. One of those picture children often reproduced in advertising leaflets and the photogravure sections of the Sunday papers.

She's had a fever for three days, began the father, and we don't know what it comes from. My wife has given her things, you know, like people do, but it don't do no good. And there's been a lot of sickness around. So we tho't you'd better look her over and tell us what is the matter.

As doctors often do I took a trial shot at it as a point of departure. Has she had a sore throat?

Both parents answered me together, No . . . No, she says her throat don't hurt her.

Does your throat hurt you? added the mother to the child. But the little girl's expression didn't change, nor did she move her eyes from my face.

5

Have you looked?

I tried to, said the mother, but I couldn't see.   10

As it happens, we had been having a number of cases of diphtheria in the school to which this child went during that month and we were all, quite apparently, thinking of that, though no one had as yet spoken of the thing.

Well, I said, suppose we take a look at the throat first. I smiled in my best professional manner and asking for the child's first name I said, come on, Mathilda, open your mouth and let's take a look at your throat.

Nothing doing.

Aw, come on, I coaxed, just open your mouth wide and let me take a look. Look, I said opening both hands wide, I haven't anything in my hands. Just open up and let me see.

Such a nice man, put in the mother. Look how kind he is to you.   15
Come on, do what he tells you to. He won't hurt you.

At that I ground my teeth in disgust. If only they wouldn't use the word "hurt" I might be able to get somewhere. But I did not allow myself to be hurried or disturbed, but speaking quietly and slowly I approached the child again.

As I moved my chair a little nearer, suddenly with one catlike movement both her hands clawed instinctively for my eyes and she almost reached them too. In fact she knocked my glasses flying and they fell, though unbroken, several feet away from me on the kitchen floor.

Both the mother and father almost turned themselves inside out in embarrassment and apology. You bad girl, said the mother, taking her and shaking her by one arm. Look what you've done. The nice man. . . .

For heaven's sake, I broke in. Don't call me a nice man to her. I'm here to look at her throat on the chance that she might have diphtheria and possibly die of it. But that's nothing to her. Look here, I said to the child, we're going to look at your throat. You're old enough to understand what I'm saying. Will you open it now by yourself or shall we have to open it for you?

Not a move. Even her expression hadn't changed. Her breaths however   20
were coming faster and faster. Then the battle began. I had to do it. I had to have a throat culture for her own protection. But first I told the parents that it was entirely up to them. I explained the danger but said that I would not insist on a throat examination so long as they would take the responsibility.

If you don't do what the doctor says you'll have to go to the hospital, the mother admonished her severely.

Oh yeah? I had to smile to myself. After all, I had already fallen in love with the savage brat, the parents were contemptible to me. In the ensuing struggle they grew more and more abject, crushed, exhausted while she surely rose to magnificent heights of insane fury of effort bred of her terror of me.

The father tried his best, and he was a big man but the fact that she was his daughter, his shame at her behavior and his dread of hurting her made him release her just at the critical moment several times when I had almost achieved success, till I wanted to kill him. But his dread also that she might have diphtheria made him tell me to go on, go on though he himself was almost fainting, while the mother moved back and forth behind us raising and lowering her hands in an agony of apprehension.

Put her in front of you on your lap, I ordered, and hold both her wrists.

But as soon as he did the child let out a scream. Don't, you're hurting   25 me. Let go of my hands. Let them go I tell you. Then she shrieked terrifyingly, hysterically. Stop it! Stop it! You're killing me!

Do you think she can stand it, doctor! said the mother.

You get out, said the husband to his wife. Do you want her to die of diphtheria?

Come on now, hold her, I said.

Then I grasped the child's head with my left hand and tried to get the wooden tongue depressor between her teeth. She fought, with clenched teeth, desperately! But now I also had grown furious—at a child. I tried to hold myself down but I couldn't. I know how to expose a throat for inspection. And I did my best. When finally I got the wooden spatula behind the last teeth and just the point of it into the mouth cavity, she opened up for an instant but before I could see anything she came down again and gripping the wooden blade between her molars she reduced it to splinters before I could get it out again.

Aren't you ashamed, the mother yelled at her. Aren't you ashamed to   30 act like that in front of the doctor?

Get me a smooth-handled spoon of some sort, I told the mother. We're going through with this. The child's mouth was already bleeding. Her tongue was cut and she was screaming in wild hysterical shrieks. Perhaps I should have desisted and come back in an hour or more. No doubt it would have been better. But I have seen at least two children lying dead in bed of neglect in such cases, and feeling that I must get a diagnosis now or never I went at it again. But the worst of it was that I too had got beyond reason. I could have torn the child apart in my own fury and enjoyed it. It was a pleasure to attack her. My face was burning with it.

The damned little brat must be protected against her own idiocy, one says to one's self at such times. Others must be protected against her. It is social necessity. And all these things are true. But a blind fury, a feeling of adult shame, bred of a longing for muscular release are the operatives. One goes on to the end.

In a final unreasoning assault I overpowered the child's neck and jaws. I forced the heavy silver spoon back of her teeth and down her throat till she gagged. And there it was—both tonsils covered with membrane. She had fought valiantly to keep me from knowing her secret. She had been hiding that sore throat for three days at least and lying to her parents in order to escape just such an outcome as this.

Now truly she was furious. She had been on the defensive before but now she attacked. Tried to get off her father's lap and fly at me while tears of defeat blinded her eyes.

Considerations

1. What is your initial response to the characters in this story? Do you sympathize primarily with the doctor? With Mathilda? With the parents? Do your sympathies change throughout the story? Explain.
2. What is the doctor's attitude toward his work? What is his attitude toward his patient? Look closely at the words he uses to describe her. How does the tone of those words change as the story progresses?
3. List as many conflicts as you can find in "The Use of Force." Explain how these conflicts relate to each other and how they are resolved (or why they are left unresolved).
4. Argue for or against the following proposition: The doctor's use of force was necessary and justified.
5. Think about a conflict you have encountered at work. Using both dialogue and descriptive details, explain the situation and discuss your response to it.

SARAH ORNE JEWETT (1849–1909)

Tom's Husband

Sarah Orne Jewett was born, grew up, and died in the pre-Revolutionary house her prosperous shipbuilder father had bought. Her works often reflect the conservative values of her Yankee heritage, yet she also writes from a feminist viewpoint. In this story, based on an actual event in her hometown of South Berwick, Maine, Jewett daringly invited her nineteenth-century readers to imagine seriously a world where the definitions of men's work and women's work were challenged and carefully examined.

I shall not dwell long upon the circumstances that led to the marriage of my hero and heroine; though their courtship was to them, the only one that has ever noticeably approached the ideal, it had many aspects in which it was entirely commonplace in other people's eyes. While the world in general smiles at lovers with kindly approval and sympathy, it refuses to be aware of the unprecedented delight which is amazing to the lovers themselves.

But, as has been true in many other cases, when they were at last married, the most ideal of situations was found to have been changed to the most practical. Instead of having shared their original duties, and, as school-boys would say, going halves, they discovered that the cares of life had been doubled. This led to some distressing moments for both our friends; they understood suddenly that instead of dwelling in heaven they were still upon earth, and had made themselves slaves to new laws and limitations. Instead of being freer and happier than ever before, they had assumed new responsibilities; they had established a new household, and must fulfill in some way or another the obligations of it. They looked back with affection to their engagement; they had been longing to have each other to themselves, apart from the world, but it seemed that they never felt so keenly that they were still units in modern society. Since Adam and Eve were in Paradise, before the devil joined them, nobody has had a chance to imitate that unlucky couple. In some respects they told the truth when, twenty times a day, they said that life had never been so pleasant before; but there were mental reservations on either side which might have subjected them to the accusation of lying. Somehow, there was a little feeling of disappointment, and they caught themselves wondering—though they would have died sooner than confess it—whether they were quite so happy as they had expected. The truth was, they were much happier than people usually are, for they had an uncommon capacity for enjoyment. For a little while they were like a sail-boat that is beating and has to drift a few minutes before it can catch the wind and start off on the other tack. And they had the same feeling, too, that any one is likely to have who has been long pursuing some object of his ambition or desire. Whether it is a coin, or a picture, or a stray volume of some old edition of Shakespeare, or whether it is an office under government or a lover, when fairly in one's grasp there is a loss of the eagerness that was felt in pursuit. Satisfaction, even after one has dined well, is not so interesting and eager a feeling as hunger.

My hero and heroine were reasonably well established to begin with: they each had some money, though Mr. Wilson had most. His father had at one time been a rich man, but with the decline, a few years before, of manufacturing interests, he had become, mostly through the fault of others, somewhat involved; and at the time of his death his affairs were in such a condition that it was still a question whether a very large sum or a moderately large one would represent his estate. Mrs. Wilson, Tom's step-mother, was somewhat of an invalid; she suffered severely at times with asthma, but she was almost entirely relieved by living in another part of the country. While her husband lived, she had accepted her illness as inevitable, and rarely left home; but during the last few years she had lived in Philadelphia with her own people, making short and wheezing visits only from time to time, and had not undergone a voluntary period of suffering since the occasion of Tom's marriage, which she had entirely approved. She had a sufficient property of her own, and she and Tom were independent of each other in that way. Her only other step-child was a daughter, who had married a navy officer, and had at this time gone out to spend three years (or less) with her husband, who had been ordered to Japan.

It is not unfrequently noticed that in many marriages one of the persons who choose each other as partners for life is said to have thrown himself or herself away, and the relatives and friends look on with dismal forebodings and ill-concealed submission. In this case it was the wife who might have done so much better, according to public opinion. She did not think so herself, luckily, either before marriage or afterward, and I do not think it occurred to her to picture to herself the sort of career which would have been her alternative. She had been an only child, and had usually taken her own way. Some one once said that it was a great pity that she had not been obliged to work for her living, for she had inherited a most uncommon business talent, and, without being disreputably keen at a bargain, her insight into the practical working of affairs was very clear and far-reaching. Her father, who had also been a manufacturer, like Tom's, had often said it had been a mistake that she was a girl instead of a boy. Such executive ability as hers is often wasted in the more contracted sphere of women, and is apt to be more a disadvantage than a help. She was too independent and self-reliant for a wife; it would seem at first thought that she needed a wife herself more than she did a husband. Most men like best the women whose natures cling and appeal to theirs for protection. But Tom Wilson, while he did not wish to be protected himself, liked these very qualities in his wife which would have displeased some other men; to tell the truth, he was very much in love with his wife just as she was. He was a successful collector of almost everything but money, and during a great part of his life he had been an invalid, and he had grown, as he laughingly confessed, very old-womanish. He had been badly lamed, when a boy, by being caught in some machinery in his father's mill, near which he was idling one afternoon, and though he had almost entirely outgrown the effect of his injury, it had not been until after many years. He had been in college, but his eyes had given out there, and he had been obliged to leave in the middle of his junior year, though he had kept up a pleasant intercourse with the members of his class, with whom he had been a great favorite. He was a good deal of an idler in the world. I do not think his ambition, except in the case of securing Mary Dunn for his wife, had ever been distinct; he seemed to make the most he could of each day as it came, without making all his days' works tend toward some grand result, and go toward the upbuilding of some grand plan and purpose. He consequently gave no promise of being either distinguished or great. When his eyes would allow, he was an indefatigable reader; and although he would have said that he read only for amusement, yet he amused himself with books that were well worth the time he spent over them.

The house where he lived nominally belonged to his step-mother, but she had taken for granted that Tom would bring his wife home to it, and assured him that it should be to all intents and purposes his. Tom was deeply attached to the old place, which was altogether the pleasantest in town. He had kept bachelor's hall there most of the time since his father's death, and he had taken great pleasure, before his marriage, in refitting it to some extent, though it was already comfortable and furnished in remarkably good taste. People said of him that if it had not been for his illnesses, and if he had been a poor boy, he probably would have made something of himself. As it was, he was not very well known by the townspeople, being somewhat reserved, and not taking much interest in their every-day subjects of conversation. Nobody liked him so well as they liked his wife, yet there was no reason why he should be disliked enough to have much said about him.

After our friends had been married for some time, and had outlived the first strangeness of the new order of things, and had done their duty to their neighbors with so much apparent willingness and generosity that even Tom himself was liked a great deal better than he ever had been before, they were sitting together one stormy evening in the library, before the fire. Mrs. Wilson had been reading Tom the letters which had come to him by the night's mail. There was a long one from his sister in Nagasaki, which had been written with a good deal of ill-disguised reproach. She complained of the smallness of the income of her share in her father's estate, and said that she had been assured by American friends that the smaller mills were starting up everywhere, and beginning to do well again. Since so much of their money was invested in the factory, she had been surprised and sorry to find by Tom's last letters that he had seemed to have no idea of putting in a proper person as superintendent, and going to work again. Four per cent on her other property, which she had been told she must soon expect instead of eight, would make a great difference to her. A navy captain in a foreign port was obliged to entertain a great deal, and Tom must know that it cost them much more to live than it did him, and ought to think of their interests. She hoped he would talk over what was best to be done with their mother (who had been made executor, with Tom, of his father's will).

Tom laughed a little, but looked disturbed. His wife had said something to the same effect, and his mother had spoken once or twice in her letters of the prospect of starting the mill again. He was not a bit of a business man, and he did not feel certain, with the theories which he had arrived at of the state of the country, that it was safe yet to spend the money which would have to be spent in putting the mill in order. "They think that the minute it is going again we shall be making money hand over hand, just as father did when we were children," he said. "It is going to cost us no end of money before we can make anything. Before father died he meant to put in a good deal of new machinery, I remember. I don't know anything about the business myself, and I would have sold out long ago if I had had an offer that came anywhere near the value. The larger mills are the only ones that are good for anything now, and we should have to bring a crowd of French Canadians here; the day is past for the people who live in this part of the country to go into the factory again. Even the Irish all go West when they come into the country, and don't come to places like this any more."

"But there are a good many of the old work-people down in the village," said Mrs. Wilson. "Jack Towne asked me the other day if you weren't going to start up in the spring."

Tom moved uneasily in his chair, "I'll put you in for superintendent, if you like," he said, half angrily, whereupon Mary threw the newspaper at him; but by the time he had thrown it back he was in good humor again.

"Do you know, Tom," she said, with amazing seriousness, "that I believe I should like nothing in the world so much as to be the head of a large business? I hate keeping house,—I always did; and I never did so much of it in all my life put together as I have since I have been married. I suppose it isn't womanly to say so, but if I could escape from the whole thing I believe I should be perfectly happy. If you get rich when the mill is going again, I shall beg for a housekeeper, and shirk everything. I give you fair warning. I don't believe I keep this house half so well as you did before I came here."   10

Tom's eyes twinkled. "I am going to have that glory,—I don't think you do, Polly; but you can't say that I have not been forbearing. I certainly have not told you more than twice how we used to have things cooked. I'm not going to be your kitchen-colonel."

"Of course it seemed the proper thing to do," said his wife, meditatively; "but I think we should have been even happier than we have if I had been spared it. I have had some days of wretchedness that I shudder to think of. I never know what to have for breakfast; and I ought not to say it, but I don't mind the sight of dust. I look upon housekeeping as my life's great discipline"; and at this pathetic confession they both laughed heartily.

"I've a great mind to take it off your hands," said Tom. "I always rather liked it, to tell the truth, and I ought to be a better housekeeper,—I have been at it for five years; though housekeeping for one is different from what it is for two, and one of them a woman. You see you have brought a different element into my family. Luckily, the servants are pretty well drilled. I do think you upset them a good deal at first!"

Mary Wilson smiled as if she only half heard what he was saying. She drummed with her foot on the floor and looked intently at the fire, and presently gave it a vigorous poking. "Well?" said Tom, after he had waited patiently as long as he could.

"Tom! I'm going to propose something to you. I wish you would really 15 do as you said, and take all the home affairs under your care, and let me start the mill. I am certain I could manage it. Of course I should get people who understood the thing to teach me. I believe I was made for it; I should like it above all things. And this is what I will do: I will bear the cost of starting it, myself,—I think I have money enough, or can get it; and if I have not put affairs in the right trim at the end of a year I will stop, and you may make some other arrangement. If I have, you and your mother and sister can pay me back."

"So I am going to be the wife, and you the husband," said Tom, a little indignantly; "at least, that is what people will say. It's a regular Darby and Joan affair, and you think you can do more work in a day than I can do in three. Do you know that you must go to town to buy cotton? And do you know there are a thousand things about it that you don't know?"

"And never will?" said Mary, with perfect good humor. "Why, Tom, I can learn as well as you, and a good deal better, for I like business, and you don't. You forget that I was always father's right-hand man after I was a dozen years old, and that you have let me invest my money and some of your own, and I haven't made a blunder yet."

Tom thought that his wife had never looked so handsome or so happy. "I don't care. I should rather like the fun of knowing what people will say. It is a new departure, at any rate. Women think they can do everything better than men in these days, but I'm the first man, apparently, who has wished he were a woman."

"Of course people will laugh," said Mary, "but they will say that it's just like me, and think I am fortunate to have married a man who will let me do as I choose. I don't see why it isn't sensible: you will be living exactly as you were before you married, as to home affairs; and since it was a good thing for you to know something about housekeeping then, I can't imagine why you shouldn't go on with it now, since it makes me miserable, and I am wasting a fine business talent while I do it. What do we care for people's talking about it?"

"It seems to me that it is something like women's smoking: it isn't 20 wicked, but it isn't the custom of the country. And I don't like the idea of your going among business men. Of course I should be above going with you, and having people think I must be an idiot; they would say that you married a manufacturing interest, and I was thrown in. I can foresee that my pride is going to be humbled to the dust in every way," Tom declared in mournful tones, and began to shake with laughter. "It is one of your lovely castles in the air, dear Polly, but an old brick mill needs a better foundation than the clouds. No, I'll look around, and get an honest, experienced man for agent. I suppose it's the best thing we can do, for the machinery ought not to lie still any longer; but I mean to sell the factory as soon as I can. I devoutly wish it would take fire, for the insurance would be the best price we are likely to get. That is a famous letter from Alice! I am afraid the captain has been growling over his pay, or they have been giving too many little dinners on board ship. If we were rid of the mill, you and I might go out there this winter. It would be capital fun."

Mary smiled again in an absent-minded way. Tom had an uneasy feeling that he had not heard the end of it yet, but nothing more was said for a day or two. When Mrs. Tom Wilson announced, with no apparent thought of being contradicted, that she had entirely made up her mind, and she meant to see those men who had been overseers of the different departments, who still lived in the village, and have the mill put in order at once, Tom looked disturbed, but made no opposition; and soon after breakfast his wife formally presented him with a handful of keys, and told him there was some lamb in the house for dinner; and presently he heard the wheels of her little phaeton rattling off down the road. I should be untruthful if I tried to persuade any one that he was not provoked; he thought she would at least have waited for his formal permission, and at first he meant to take another horse, and chase her, and bring her back in disgrace, and put a stop to the whole thing. But something assured him that she knew what she was about, and he determined to let her have her own way. If she failed, it might do no harm, and this was the only ungallant thought he gave her. He was sure that she would do nothing unladylike, or be unmindful of his dignity; and he believed it would be looked upon as one of her odd, independent freaks, which always had won respect in the end, however much they had been laughed at in the beginning. "Susan," said he, as that estimable person went by the door with the dust-pan, "you may tell Catherine to come to me for orders about the house, and you may do so yourself. I am going to take charge again, as I did before I was married. It is no trouble to me, and Mrs. Wilson dislikes it. Besides, she is going into business, and will have a great deal else to think of."

"Yes, sir; very well, sir," said Susan, who was suddenly moved to ask so many questions that she was utterly silent. But her master looked very happy; there was evidently no disapproval of his wife; and she went on up the stairs, and began to sweep them down, knocking the dust-brush about excitedly, as if she were trying to kill a descending colony of insects.

Tom went out to the stable and mounted his horse, which had been waiting for him to take his customary after-breakfast ride to the post-office, and he galloped down the road in quest of the phaeton. He saw Mary talking with Jack Towne, who had been an overseer and a valued workman of his father's. He was looking much surprised and pleased.

"I wasn't caring so much about getting work, myself," he explained; "I've got what will carry me and my wife through; but it'll be better for the young folks about here to work near home. My nephews are wanting something to do; they were going to Lynn next week. I don't say but I should like to be to work in the old place again. I've sort of missed it, since we shut down."

"I'm sorry I was so long in overtaking you," said Tom, politely, to his wife. "Well, Jack, did Mrs. Wilson tell you she's going to start the mill? You must give her all the help you can." 25

"'Deed I will," said Mr. Towne, gallantly, without a bit of astonishment.

"I don't know much about the business yet," said Mrs. Wilson, who had been a little overcome at Jack Towne's lingo of the different rooms and machinery, and who felt an overpowering sense of having a great deal before her in the next few weeks. "By the time the mill is ready, I will be ready, too," she said, taking heart a little; and Tom, who was quick to understand her moods, could not help laughing, as he rode alongside. "We want a new barrel of flour, Tom, dear," she said, by way of punishment for his untimely mirth.

If she lost courage in the long delay, or was disheartened at the steady call for funds, she made no sign; and after a while the mill started up, and her cares were lightened, so that she told Tom that before next pay day she would like to go to Boston for a few days, and go to the theatre, and have a frolic and a rest. She really looked pale and thin, and she said she never worked so hard in all her life; but nobody knew how happy she was, and she was so glad she had married Tom, for some men would have laughed at it.

"I laughed at it," said Tom, meekly. "All is, if I don't cry by and by, because I am a beggar, I shall be lucky." But Mary looked fearlessly serene, and said that there was no danger at present.

It would have been ridiculous to expect a dividend the first year, though the Nagasaki people were pacified with difficulty. All the business letters came to Tom's address, and everybody who was not directly concerned thought that he was the motive power of the reawakened enterprise. Sometimes business people came to the mill, and were amazed at having to confer with Mrs. Wilson, but they soon had to respect her talents and her success. She was helped by the old clerk, who had been promptly recalled and reinstated, and she certainly did capitally well. She was laughed at, as she had expected to be, and people said they should think Tom would be ashamed of himself; but it soon appeared that he was not to blame, and what reproach was offered was on the score of his wife's oddity. There was nothing about the mill that she did not understand before very long, and at the end of the second year she declared a small dividend with great pride and triumph. And she was congratulated on her success, and every one thought of her project in a different way from the way they had thought of it in the beginning. She had singularly good fortune: at the end of the third year she was making money for herself and her friends faster than most people were, 30 and approving letters began to come from Nagasaki. The Ashtons had been ordered to stay in that region, and it was evident that they were continually being obliged to entertain more instead of less. Their children were growing fast, too, and constantly becoming more expensive. The captain and his wife had already begun to congratulate themselves secretly that their two sons would in all probability come into possession, one day, of their uncle Tom's handsome property.

For a good while Tom enjoyed life, and went on his quiet way serenely. He was anxious at first, for he thought that Mary was going to make ducks and drakes of his money and her own. And then he did not exactly like the looks of the thing, either; he feared that his wife was growing successful as a business person at the risk of losing her womanliness. But as time went on, and he found there was no fear of that, he accepted the situation philosophically. He gave up his collection of engravings, having become more interested in one of coins and medals, which took up most of his leisure time. He often went to the city in pursuit of such treasures, and gained much renown in certain quarters as a numismatologist of great skill and experience. But at last his house (which had almost kept itself, and had given him little to do beside ordering the dinners, while faithful old Catherine and her niece Susan were his aids) suddenly became a great care to him. Catherine, who had been the main-stay of the family for many years, died after a short illness, and Susan must needs choose that time, of all others, for being married to one of the second hands in the mill. There followed a long and dismal season of experimenting, and for a time there was a procession of incapable creatures going in at one kitchen door and out of the other. His wife would not have liked to say so, but it seemed to her that Tom was growing fussy about the house affairs, and took more notice of those minor details than he used. She wished more than once, when she was tired, that he would not talk so much about the housekeeping; he seemed sometimes to have no other thought.

In the early days of Mrs. Wilson's business life, she had made it a rule to consult her husband on every subject of importance; but it had speedily proved to be a formality. Tom tried manfully to show a deep interest which he did not feel, and his wife gave up, little by little, telling him much about her affairs. She said that she liked to drop business when she came home in the evening; and at last she fell into the habit of taking a nap on the library sofa, while Tom, who could not use his eyes much by lamp-light, sat smoking or in utter idleness before the fire. When they were first married his wife had made it a rule that she should always read him the evening papers, and afterward they had always gone on with some book of history or philosophy, in which they were both interested. These evenings of their early married life had been charming to both of them, and from time to time one would say to the other that they ought to take up again the habit of reading together. Mary was so unaffectedly tired in the evening that Tom never liked to propose a walk; for, though he was not a man of peculiarly social nature, he had always been accustomed to pay an occasional evening visit to his neighbors in the village. And though he had little interest in the business world, and still less knowledge of it, after a while he wished that his wife would have more to say about what she was planning and doing, or how things were getting on. He thought that her chief aid, old Mr. Jackson, was far more in her thoughts than he. She was forever quoting Jackson's opinions. He did not like to find that she took it for granted that he was not interested in the welfare of his own property; it made him feel like a sort of pensioner and dependent, though, when they had guests at the house, which was by no means seldom, there was nothing in her manner that would imply that she thought herself in any way the head of the family. It was hard work to find fault with his wife in any way, though, to give him his due, he rarely tried.

But, this being a wholly unnatural state of things, the reader must expect to hear of its change at last, and the first blow from the enemy was dealt by an old woman, who lived nearby, and who called to Tom one morning, as he was driving down to the village in a great hurry (to post a letter, which ordered his agent to secure a long-wished-for ancient copper coin, at any price), to ask him if they had made yeast that week, and if she could borrow a cupful, as her own had met with some misfortune. Tom was instantly in a rage, and he mentally condemned her to some undeserved fate, but told her aloud to go and see the cook. This slight delay, besides being killing to his dignity, caused him to lose the mail, and in the end his much-desired copper coin. It was a hard day for him, altogether; it was Wednesday, and the first days of the week having been stormy the washing was very late. And Mary came home to dinner provokingly good-natured. She had met an old schoolmate and her husband driving home from the mountains, and had first taken them over her factory, to their great amusement and delight, and then had brought them home to dinner. Tom greeted them cordially, and manifested his usual graceful hospitality; but the minute he saw his wife alone he said in a plaintive tone of rebuke, "I should think you might have remembered that the servants are unusually busy to-day. I do wish you would take a little interest in things at home. The women have been washing, and I'm sure I don't know what sort of a dinner we can give your friends. I wish you had thought to bring home some steak. I have been busy myself, and couldn't go down to the village. I thought we would only have a lunch."

Mary was hungry, but she said nothing, except that it would be all right,—she didn't mind; and perhaps they could have some canned soup.

She often went to town to buy or look at cotton, or to see some improvement in machinery, and she brought home beautiful bits of furniture and new pictures for the house, and showed a touching thoughtfulness in remembering Tom's fancies; but somehow he had an uneasy suspicion that she could get along pretty well without him when it came to the deeper wishes and hopes of her life, and that her most important concerns were all matters in which he had no share. He seemed to himself to have merged his life in his wife's; he lost his interest in things outside the house and grounds;

35

he felt himself fast growing rusty and behind the times, and to have somehow missed a good deal in life; he had a suspicion that he was a failure. One day the thought rushed over him that his had been almost exactly the experience of most women, and he wondered if it really was any more disappointing and ignominious to him than it was to women themselves. "Some of them may be contented with it," he said to himself, soberly. "People think women are designed for such careers by nature, but I don't know why I ever made such a fool of myself."

Having once seen his situation in life from such a standpoint, he felt it day by day to be more degrading, and he wondered what he should do about it; and once, drawn by a new, strange sympathy, he went to the little family burying-ground. It was one of the mild, dim days that come sometimes in early November, when the pale sunlight is like the pathetic smile of a sad face, and he sat for a long time on the limp, frost-bitten grass beside his mother's grave.

But when he went home in the twilight his step-mother, who just then was making them a little visit, mentioned that she had been looking through some boxes of hers that had been packed long before and stowed away in the garret. "Everything looks very nice up there," she said, in her wheezing voice (which, worse than usual that day, always made him nervous), and added, without any intentional slight to his feelings, "I do think you have always been a most excellent housekeeper."

"I'm tired of such nonsense!" he exclaimed, with surprising indignation. "Mary, I wish you to arrange your affairs so that you can leave them for six months at least. I am going to spend this winter in Europe."

"Why, Tom, dear!" said his wife, appealingly. "I couldn't leave my business any way in the"—

But she caught sight of a look on his usually placid countenance that   40
was something more than decision, and refrained from saying anything more.

And three weeks from that day they sailed.

Considerations

1. What are the qualities that led people to say of Mary "that it was a great pity that she had not been obliged to work for her living" and her father to observe that "it had been a mistake that she was a girl instead of a boy"? Do these comments reflect attitudes that have now been abandoned (the story was written in 1884), or are comments like these still made today? Give examples to support your response.
2. What conflicts arise in the Wilson's marriage? How are those conflicts related to the work each wants to do? To what extent are the conflicts related to community opinion?
3. Comment on the way each of the Wilsons views the importance of holding power within the marriage.

4. What critique of traditional "women's work" is implied by Tom's growing dissatisfaction? What is your response to this critique?
5. Discuss your response to a situation in which you decided (or were required) to act in a role that has not been traditionally defined as "appropriate" for your sex.

MARY E. WILKINS FREEMAN (1852–1930)

The Revolt of "Mother"

Mary Wilkins Freeman spent most of her life in Randolph, Massachusetts, and her finest short stories depict the lives of New England women who confront their circumstances in life with determination, strength, and independence. Wilkins herself was no stranger to making her way under difficult circumstances. Following her father's financial reverses and the subsequent death of both her parents, Wilkins found herself alone and impoverished at the age of 31. The only thing that saved her from destitution or the humiliation of accepting charity was her literary success. At first, her writing earned her only small sums, barely enough for survival; later, her work brought her both financial success and fame.

"Father!"

"What is it?"

"What are them men diggin' over there in the field for?"

There was a sudden dropping and enlarging of the lower part of the old man's face, as if some heavy weight had settled therein; he shut his mouth tight, and went on harnessing the great bay mare. He hustled the collar on to her neck with a jerk.

"Father!"   5

The old man slapped the saddle upon the mare's back.

"Look here, father, I want to know what them men are diggin' over in the field for, an' I'm goin' to know."

"I wish you'd go into the house, mother, an' 'tend to your own affairs," the old man said then. He ran his words together, and his speech was almost as inarticulate as a growl.

But the woman understood; it was her most native tongue. "I ain't goin' into the house till you tell me what them men are doin' over there in the field," said she.

Then she stood waiting. She was a small woman, short and straight-   10
waisted like a child in her brown cotton gown. Her forehead was mild and benevolent between the smooth curves of gray hair; there were meek downward lines about her nose and mouth; but her eyes, fixed upon the old man, looked as if the meekness had been the result of her own will, never of the will of another.

They were in the barn, standing before the wide open doors. The spring air, full of the smell of growing grass and unseen blossoms, came in their faces. The deep yard in front was littered with farm wagons and piles of wood; on the edges, close to the fence and the house, the grass was a vivid green, and there were some dandelions.

The old man glanced doggedly at his wife as he tightened the last buckles on the harness. She looked as immovable to him as one of the rocks in his pasture-land, bound to the earth with generations of blackberry vines. He slapped the reins over the horse, and started forth from the barn.

"*Father!*" said she.

The old man pulled up. "What is it?"

"I want to know what them men are diggin' over there in that field for." 15

"They're diggin' a cellar, I s'pose, if you've got to know."

"A cellar for what?"

"A barn."

"A barn? You ain't goin' to build a barn over there where we was goin' to have a house, father?"

The old man said not another word. He hurried the horse into the farm wagon, and clattered out of the yard, jouncing as sturdily on his seat as a boy. 20

The woman stood a moment looking after him, then she went out of the barn across a corner of the yard to the house. The house, standing at right angles with the great barn and a long reach of sheds and out-buildings, was infinitesimal compared with them. It was scarcely as commodious for people as the little boxes under the barn eaves were for doves.

A pretty girl's face, pink and delicate as a flower, was looking out of one of the house windows. She was watching three men who were digging over in the field which bounded the yard near the road line. She turned quietly when the woman entered.

"What are they digging for, mother?" said she. "Did he tell you?"

"They're diggin' for—a cellar for a new barn."

"Oh, mother, he ain't going to build another barn?" 25

"That's what he says."

A boy stood before the kitchen glass combing his hair. He combed slowly and painstakingly, arranging his brown hair in a smooth hillock over his forehead. He did not seem to pay any attention to the conversation.

"Sammy, did you know father was going to build a new barn?" asked the girl.

The boy combed assiduously.

"Sammy!" 30

He turned, and showed a face like his father's under his smooth crest of hair. "Yes, I s'pose I did," he said, reluctantly.

"How long have you known it?" asked his mother.

"'Bout three months, I guess."

"Why didn't you tell of it?"

"Didn't think 'twould do no good." 35

"I don't see what father wants another barn for," said the girl, in her sweet, slow voice. She turned again to the window, and stared out at the digging men in the field. Her tender, sweet face was full of a gentle distress. Her forehead was as bald and innocent as a baby's, with the light hair strained back from it in a row of curl-papers. She was quite large, but her soft curves did not look as if they covered muscles.

Her mother looked sternly at the boy. "Is he goin' to buy more cows?" said she.

The boy did not reply; he was tying his shoes.

"Sammy, I want you to tell me if he's goin' to buy more cows."

"I s'pose he is."   40

"How many?"

"Four, I guess."

His mother said nothing more. She went into the pantry, and there was a clatter of dishes. The boy got his cap from a nail behind the door, took an old arithmetic from the shelf, and started for school. He was lightly built, but clumsy. He went out of the yard with a curious spring in his hips, that made his loose home-made jacket tilt up in the rear.

The girl went to the sink, and began to wash the dishes that were piled up there. Her mother came promptly out of the pantry, and shoved her aside. "You wipe 'em," said she; "I'll wash. There's a good many this mornin'."

The mother plunged her hands vigorously into the water, the girl   45
wiped the plates slowly and dreamily. "Mother," said she, "don't you think it's too bad father's going to build that new barn, much as we need a decent house to live in?"

Her mother scrubbed a dish fiercely. "You ain't found out yet we're women-folks, Nanny Penn," said she. "You ain't seen enough of men-folks yet to. One of these days you'll find it out, an' then you'll know that we know only what men-folks think we do, so far as any use of it goes, an' how we'd ought to reckon men-folks in with Providence, an' not complain of what they do any more than we do of the weather."

"I don't care; I don't believe George is anything like that, anyhow," said Nanny. Her delicate face flushed pink, her lips pouted softly, as if she were going to cry.

"You wait an' see. I guess George Eastman ain't no better than other men. You hadn't ought to judge father, though. He can't help it, 'cause he don't look at things jest the way we do. An' we've been pretty comfortable here, after all. The roof don't leak—ain't never but once—that's one thing. Father's kept it shingled right up."

"I do wish we had a parlor."

"I guess it won't hurt George Eastman any to come to see you in a   50
nice clean kitchen. I guess a good many girls don't have as good a place as this. Nobody's ever heard me complain."

"I ain't complained either, mother."

"Well, I don't think you'd better, a good father an' a good home as you've got. S'pose your father made you go out an' work for your livin'? Lots of girls have to that ain't no stronger an' better able to than you be."

Sarah Penn washed the frying pan with a conclusive air. She scrubbed the outside of it as faithfully as the inside. She was a masterly keeper of her box of a house. Her one living room never seemed to have in it any of the dust which the friction of life with inanimate matter produces. She swept, and there seemed to be no dirt to go before the broom; she cleaned, and one could see no difference. She was like an artist so perfect that he has apparently no art. To-day she got out a mixing bowl and a board, and rolled some pies, and there was no more flour upon her than upon her daughter who was doing finer work. Nanny was to be married in the fall, and she was sewing on some white cambric and embroidery. She sewed industriously while her mother cooked, her soft milk-white hands and wrists showed whiter than her delicate work.

"We must have the stove moved out in the shed before long," said Mrs. Penn. "Talk about not havin' things, it's been a real blessin' to be able to put a stove up in that shed in hot weather. Father did one good thing when he fixed that stove-pipe out there."

Sarah Penn's face as she rolled her pies had that expression of meek vigor which might have characterized one of the New Testament saints. She was making mince-pies. Her husband, Adoniram Penn, liked them better than any other kind. She baked twice a week. Adoniram often liked a piece of pie between meals. She hurried this morning. It had been later than usual when she began, and she wanted to have a pie baked for dinner. However deep a resentment she might be forced to hold against her husband, she would never fail in sedulous attention to his wants. 55

Nobility of character manifests itself at loop-holes when it is not provided with large doors. Sarah Penn's showed itself to-day in flaky dishes of pastry. So she made the pies faithfully, while across the table she could see, when she glanced up from her work, the sight that rankled in her patient and steadfast soul—the digging of the cellar of the new barn in the place where Adoniram forty years ago had promised her their new house should stand.

The pies were done for dinner. Adoniram and Sammy were home a few minutes after twelve o'clock. The dinner was eaten with serious haste. There was never much conversation at the table in the Penn family. Adoniram asked a blessing, and they ate promptly, then rose up and went about their work.

Sammy went back to school, taking soft sly lopes out of the yard like a rabbit. He wanted a game of marbles before school, and feared his father would give him some chores to do. Adoniram hastened to the door and called after him, but he was out of sight.

"I don't see what you let him go for, mother," said he. "I wanted him to help me unload that wood."

Adoniram went to work out in the yard unloading wood from the wagon. Sarah put away the dinner dishes, while Nanny took down her curl-papers and changed her dress. She was going down to the store to buy some more embroidery and thread. 60

When Nanny was gone, Mrs. Penn went to the door. "Father!" she called.

"Well, what is it!"

"I want to see you jest a minute, father."

"I can't leave this wood nohow. I've got to git it unloaded an' go for a load of gravel afore two o'clock. Sammy had ought to helped me. You hadn't ought to let him go to school so early."

"I want to see you jest a minute." 65

"I tell ye I can't, nohow, mother."

"Father, you come here." Sarah Penn stood in the door like a queen; she held her head as if it bore a crown; there was that patience which makes authority royal in her voice. Adoniram went.

Mrs. Penn led the way into the kitchen, and pointed to a chair. "Sit down, father," said she: "I've got somethin' I want to say to you."

He sat down heavily; his face was quite stolid, but he looked at her with restive eyes. "Well, what is it, mother?"

"I want to know what you're buildin' that new barn for, father?" 70

"I ain't got nothin' to say about it."

"It can't be you think you need another barn?"

"I tell ye I ain't got nothin' to say about it, mother; an' I ain't goin' to say nothin'."

"Be you goin' to buy more cows?"

Adoniram did not reply; he shut his mouth tight. 75

"I know you be, as well as I want to. Now, father, look here"—Sarah Penn had not sat down; she stood before her husband in the humble fashion of a Scripture woman—"I'm goin' to talk real plain to you; I never have sence I married you, but I'm goin' to now. I ain't never complained, an' I ain't goin' to complain now, but I'm goin' to talk plain. You see this room here, father; you look at it well. You see there ain't no carpet on the floor, an' you see the paper is all dirty, an' droppin' off the walls. We ain't had no new paper on it for ten year, an' then I put it on myself, an' it didn't cost but ninepence a roll. You see this room, father; it's all the one I've had to work in an' eat in an' sit in sence we was married. There ain't another woman in the whole town whose husband ain't got half the means you have but what's got better. It's all the room Nanny's got to have her company in; an' there ain't one of her mates but what's got better, an' their fathers not so able as hers is. It's all the room she'll have to be married in. What would you have thought, father, if we had had our weddin' in a room no better than this? I was married in my mother's parlor, with a carpet on the floor, an' stuffed furniture, an' a mahogany card-table. An' this is all the room my daughter will have to be married in. Look here, father!"

Sarah Penn went across the room as though it were a tragic stage. She flung open a door and disclosed a tiny bedroom, only large enough for a bed and bureau, with a path between. "There, father," said she—"there's all the room I've had to sleep in forty year. All my children were born there—the two that died, an' the two that's livin'. I was sick with a fever there."

She stepped to another door and opened it. It led into the small, ill-lighted pantry. "Here," said she, "is all the buttery I've got—every place I've got for my dishes, to set away my victuals in, an' to keep my milk-pans in.

Father, I've been takin' care of the milk of six cows in this place, an' now you're goin' to build a new barn, an' keep more cows, an' give me more to do in it."

She threw open another door. A narrow crooked flight of stairs wound upward from it. "There, father," said she, "I want you to look at the stairs that go up to them two unfinished chambers that are all the places our son an' daughter have had to sleep in all their lives. There ain't a prettier girl in town nor a more ladylike one than Nanny, an' that's the place she has to sleep in. It ain't so good as your horse's stall; it ain't so warm an' tight."

Sarah Penn went back and stood before her husband. "Now, father," said she, "I want to know if you think you're doin' right an' accordin' to what you profess. Here, when we was married, forty year ago, you promised me faithful that we should have a new house built in that lot over in the field before the year was out. You said you had money enough, an' you wouldn't ask me to live in no such place as this. It is forty year now, an' you've been makin' more money, an' I've been savin' of it for you ever since, an' you ain't built no house yet. You've built sheds an' cowhouses an' one new barn, an' now you're goin' to build another. Father, I want to know if you think it's right. You're lodgin' your dumb beasts better than you are your own flesh an' blood. I want to know if you think it's right." 80

"I ain't got nothin' to say."

"You can't say nothin' without ownin' it ain't right, father. An' there's another thing—I ain't complained; I've got along forty year, an' I s'pose I should forty more, if it wa'n't for that—if we don't have another house. Nanny she can't live with us after she's married. She'll have to go somewheres else to live away from us, an' it don't seem as if I could have it so, noways, father. She wa'n't ever strong. She's got considerable color, but there wa'n't ever any backbone to her. I've always took the heft of everything off her, an' she ain't fit to keep house an' do everything herself. She'll be all worn out inside of a year. Think of her doin' all the washin' an' ironin' an' bakin' with them soft white hands an' arms, an' sweepin'! I can't have it so, noways, father."

Mrs. Penn's face was burning; her mild eyes gleamed. She had pleaded her little cause like a Webster; she had ranged from severity to pathos; but her opponent employed that obstinate silence which makes eloquence futile with mocking echoes. Adoniram arose clumsily.

"Father, ain't you got nothin' to say?" said Mrs. Penn.

"I've got to go off after that load of gravel. I can't stan' here talkin' all day." 85

"Father, won't you think it over, an' have a house built there instead of a barn?"

"I ain't got nothin' to say."

Adoniram shuffled out. Mrs. Penn went into her bedroom. When she came out, her eyes were red. She had a roll of unbleached cotton cloth. She spread it out on the kitchen table, and began cutting out some shirts for her husband. The men over in the field had a team to help them this afternoon; she could hear their halloos. She had a scanty pattern for the shirts; she had to plan and piece the sleeves.

Nanny came home with her embroidery, and sat down with her needlework. She had taken down her curl-papers, and there was a soft roll of fair hair like an aureole over her forehead; her face was as delicately fine and clear as porcelain. Suddenly she looked up, and the tender red flamed all over her face and neck. "Mother," said she.

"What say?"   90

"I've been thinking—I don't see how we're goin' to have any—wedding in this room. I'd be ashamed to have his folks come if we didn't have anybody else."

"Mebbe we can have some new paper before then; I can put it on. I guess you won't have no call to be ashamed of your belongin's."

"We might have the wedding in the new barn," said Nanny, with gentle pettishness. "Why, mother, what makes you look so?"

Mrs. Penn had started, and was staring at her with a curious expression. She turned again to her work, and spread out a pattern carefully on the cloth. "Nothin'," said she.

Presently Adoniram clattered out of the yard in his two-wheeled dump   95
cart, standing as proudly upright as a Roman charioteer. Mrs. Penn opened the door and stood there a minute looking out; the halloos of the men sounded louder.

It seemed to her all through the spring months that she heard nothing but the halloos and the noises of saws and hammers. The new barn grew fast. It was a fine edifice for this little village. Men came on pleasant Sundays, in their meeting suits and clean shirt bosoms, and stood around it admiringly. Mrs. Penn did not speak of it, and Adoniram did not mention it to her, although sometimes, upon a return from inspecting it, he bore himself with injured dignity.

"It's a strange thing how your mother feels about the new barn," he said, confidentially, to Sammy one day.

Sammy only grunted after an odd fashion for a boy; he had learned it from his father.

The barn was all completed ready for use by the third week in July. Adoniram had planned to move his stock in on Wednesday; on Tuesday he received a letter which changed his plans. He came in with it early in the morning. "Sammy's been to the post-office," said he, "an' I've got a letter from Hiram." Hiram was Mrs. Penn's brother, who lived in Vermont.

"Well," said Mrs. Penn, "what does he say about the folks?"   100

"I guess they're all right. He says he thinks if I come up country right off there's a chance to buy jest the kind of a horse I want." He stared reflectively out of the window at the new barn.

Mrs. Penn was making pies. She went on clapping the rolling-pin into the crust, although she was very pale, and her heart beat loudly.

"I dun' know but what I'd better go," said Adoniram. "I hate to go off just now, right in the midst of hayin', but the ten-acre lot's cut, an' I guess Rufus an' the others can git along without me three or four days. I can't get a horse round here to suit me, nohow, an' I've got to have another for all that wood-haulin' in the fall. I told Hiram to watch out, an' if he got wind of a good horse to let me know. I guess I'd better go."

"I'll get out your clean shirt an' collar," said Mrs. Penn calmly.

She laid out Adoniram's Sunday suit and his clean clothes on the bed   105
in the little bedroom. She got his shaving-water and razor ready. At last she buttoned on his collar and fastened his black cravat.

Adoniram never wore his collar and cravat except on extra occasions. He held his head high, with a rasped dignity. When he was all ready, with his coat and hat brushed, and a lunch of pie and cheese in a paper bag, he hesitated on the threshold of the door. He looked at his wife, and his manner was defiantly apologetic. "*If* them cows come to-day, Sammy can drive 'em into the new barn," said he; "an' when they bring the hay up, they can pitch it in there."

"Well," replied Mrs. Penn.

Adoniram set his shaven face ahead and started. When he had cleared the door-step, he turned and looked back with a kind of nervous solemnity. "I shall be back by Saturday if nothin' happens," said he.

"Do be careful, father," returned his wife.

She stood in the door with Nanny at her elbow and watched him out   110
of sight. Her eyes had a strange, doubtful expression in them; her peaceful forehead was contracted. She went in, and about her baking again. Nanny sat sewing. Her wedding-day was drawing nearer, and she was getting pale and thin with her steady sewing. Her mother kept glancing at her.

"Have you got that pain in your side this mornin'?" she asked.

"A little."

Mrs. Penn's face, as she worked, changed, her perplexed forehead smoothed, her eyes were steady, her lips firmly set. She formed a maxim for herself, although incoherently with her unlettered thoughts. "Unsolicited opportunities are the guide-posts of the Lord to the new roads of life," she repeated in effect and she made up her mind to her course of action.

"S'posin' I *had* wrote to Hiram," she muttered once, when she was in the pantry—"s'posin' I had wrote, an' asked him if he knew of any horse? But I didn't, an' father's goin' wa'n't none of my doin'. It looks like a providence." Her voice rang out quite loud at the last.

"What you talkin' about, mother?" called Nanny.   115

"Nothin'."

Mrs. Penn hurried her baking; at eleven o'clock it was all done. The load of hay from the west field came slowly down the cart track, and drew up at the new barn. Mrs. Penn ran out. "Stop!" she screamed—"stop!"

The men stopped and looked; Sammy upreared from the top of the load, and stared at his mother.

"Stop!" she cried out again. "Don't you put the hay in that barn; put it in the old one."

"Why, he said to put it in here," returned one of the hay-makers,   120 wonderingly. He was a young man, a neighbor's son, whom Adoniram hired by the year to help on the farm.

"Don't you put the hay in the new barn; there's room enough in the old one, ain't there?" said Mrs. Penn.

"Room enough," returned the hired man, in his thick, rustic tones. "Didn't need the new barn, nohow, far as room's concerned. Well, I s'pose he changed his mind." He took hold of the horses' bridles.

Mrs. Penn went back to the house. Soon the kitchen windows were darkened, and a fragrance like warm honey came into the room.

Nanny laid down her work. "I thought father wanted them to put the hay into the new barn?" she said, wonderingly.

"It's all right," replied her mother.   125

Sammy slid down from the load of hay, and came in to see if dinner was ready.

"I ain't goin' to get a regular dinner to-day, as long as father's gone," said his mother. "I've let the fire go out. You can have some bread an' milk an' pie. I thought we could get along." She set out some bowls of milk, some bread and a pie on the kitchen table. "You'd better eat your dinner now," said she. "You might jest as well get through with it. I want you to help me afterward."

Nanny and Sammy stared at each other. There was something strange in their mother's manner. Mrs. Penn did not eat anything herself. She went into the pantry, and they heard her moving dishes while they ate. Presently she came out with a pile of plates. She got the clothes-basket out of the shed, and packed them in it. Nanny and Sammy watched. She brought out cups and saucers, and put them in with the plates.

"What you goin' to do, mother?" inquired Nanny, in a timid voice. A sense of something unusual made her tremble, as if it were a ghost. Sammy rolled his eyes over his pie.

"You'll see what I'm goin' to do," replied Mrs. Penn. "If you're   130 through, Nanny, I want you to go up-stairs an' pack up your things; an' I want you, Sammy, to help me take down the bed in the bedroom."

"Oh, mother, what for?" gasped Nanny.

"You'll see."

During the next few hours a feat was performed by this simple, pious New England mother which was equal in its way to Wolfe's° storming of the Heights of Abraham. It took no more genius and audacity of bravery for Wolfe to cheer his wondering soldiers up those steep precipices, under the

---

Wolfe: James Wolfe, a British general, and his troops climbed the steep bluffs called the Heights of Abraham to win an important battle against Quebec during the Seven Years War (1756–1763).

sleeping eyes of the enemy, than for Sarah Penn, at the head of her children, to move all their little household goods into the new barn while her husband was away.

Nanny and Sammy followed their mother's instructions without a murmur; indeed, they were overawed. There is a certain uncannny and superhuman quality about all such purely original undertakings as their mother's was to them. Nanny went back and forth with her light loads, and Sammy tugged with sober energy.

At five o'clock in the afternoon the little house in which the Penns had lived for forty years had emptied itself into the new barn. 135

Every builder builds somewhat for unknown purposes, and is in a measure a prophet. The architect of Adoniram Penn's barn, while he designed it for the comfort of four-footed animals, had planned better than he knew for the comfort of humans. Sarah Penn saw at a glance its possibilities. These great box-stalls, with quilts hung before them, would make better bedrooms than the one she had occupied for forty years, and there was a tight carriage-room. The harness-room, with its chimney and shelves, would make a kitchen of her dreams. The great middle space would make a parlor, by-and-by, fit for a palace. Up-stairs there was as much room as down. With partitions and windows, what a house would there be! Sarah looked at the row of stanchions before the allotted space for cows, and reflected that she would have her front entry there.

At six o'clock the stove was up in the harness-room, the kettle was boiling, and the table set for tea. It looked almost as home-like as the abandoned house across the yard had ever done. The young hired man milked, and Sarah directed him calmly to bring the milk to the new barn. He came gaping, dropping little blots of foam from the brimming pails on the grass. Before the next morning he had spread the story of Adoniram Penn's wife moving into the new barn all over the little village. Men assembled in the store and talked it over, women with shawls over their heads scuttled into each other's houses before their work was done. Any deviation from the ordinary course of life in this quiet town was enough to stop all progress in it. Everybody paused to look at the staid, independent figure on the side track. There was a difference of opinion with regard to her. Some held her to be insane; some, of a lawless and rebellious spirit.

Friday the minister went to see her. It was in the forenoon, and she was at the barn door shelling pease for dinner. She looked up and returned his salutation with dignity, then she went on with her work. She did not invite him in. The saintly expression of her face remained fixed, but there was an angry flush over it.

The minister stood awkwardly before her, and talked. She handled the pease as if they were bullets. At last she looked up, and her eyes showed the spirit that her meek front had covered for a lifetime.

"There ain't no use talkin', Mr. Hersey," said she. "I've thought it all 140
over an' over, an' I believe I'm doin' what's right. I've made it the subject of

prayer, an' it's betwixt me an' the Lord an' Adoniram. There ain't no call for nobody else to worry about it."

"Well, of course, if you have brought it to the Lord in prayer, and feel satisfied that you are doing right, Mrs. Penn," said the minister, helplessly. His thin gray-bearded face was pathetic. He was a sickly man; his youthful confidence had cooled; he had to scourge himself up to some of his pastoral duties as relentlessly as a Catholic ascetic, and then he was prostrated by the smart.

"I think it's right jest as much as I think it was right for our forefathers to come over from the old country 'cause they didn't have what belonged to 'em," said Mrs. Penn. She arose. The barn threshold might have been Plymouth Rock from her bearing. "I don't doubt you mean well, Mr. Hersey," said she, "but there are things people hadn't ought to interfere with. I've been a member of the church for over forty year. I've got my own mind an' my own feet, an' I'm goin' to think my own thoughts an' go my own ways, an' nobody but the Lord is goin' to dictate to me unless I've a mind to have him. Won't you come in an' set down? How is Mis' Hersey?"

"She is well, I thank you," replied the minister. He added some more perplexed apologetic remarks; then he retreated.

He could expound the intricacies of every character study in the Scriptures, he was competent to grasp the Pilgrim Fathers and all historical innovators, but Sarah Penn was beyond him. He could deal with primal cases, but parallel ones worsted him. But, after all, although it was aside from his province, he wondered more how Adoniram Penn would deal with his wife than how the Lord would. Everybody shared the wonder. When Adoniram's four new cows arrived, Sarah ordered three to be put in the old barn, the other in the house shed where the cooking-stove had stood. That added to the excitement. It was whispered that all four cows were domiciled in the house.

Towards sunset on Saturday, when Adoniram was expected home, there 145 was a knot of men in the road near the new barn. The hired man had milked, but he still hung around the premises. Sarah Penn had supper all ready. There were brown bread and baked beans and a custard pie; it was the supper Adoniram loved on a Saturday night. She had a clean calico, and she bore herself imperturbably. Nanny and Sammy kept close at her heels. Their eyes were large, and Nanny was full of nervous tremors. Still there was to them more pleasant excitement than anything else. An inborn confidence in their mother over their father asserted itself.

Sammy looked out of the harness-room window. "There he is," he announced, in an awed whisper. He and Nanny peeped around the casing. Mrs. Penn kept on about her work. The children watched Adoniram leave the new horse standing in the drive while he went to the house door. It was fastened. Then he went around to the shed. That door was seldom locked, even when the family was away. The thought how her father would be confronted by the cow flashed upon Nanny. There was a hysterical sob in her throat. Adoniram emerged from the shed and stood looking about in a dazed fashion. His lips moved; he was saying something, but they could not hear what it was. The hired man was peeping around a corner of the old barn, but nobody saw him.

Adoniram took the new horse by the bridle and led him across the yard to the new barn. Nanny and Sammy slunk close to their mother. The barn doors rolled back, and there stood Adoniram, with the long mild face of the great Canadian farm horse looking over his shoulder.

Nanny kept behind her mother, but Sammy stepped suddenly forward, and stood in front of her.

Adoniram stared at the group. "What on airth you all down here for?" said he. "What's the matter over to the house?"

"We've come here to live, father," said Sammy. His shrill voice qua-   150
vered out bravely.

"What"—Adoniram sniffed—"what is it smells like cookin'?" said he. He stepped forward and looked in the open door of the harness-room. Then he turned to his wife. His old bristling face was pale and frightened. "What on airth does this mean, mother?" he gasped.

"You come in here, father," said Sarah. She led the way into the harness-room and shut the door. "Now, father," said she, "you needn't be scared. I ain't crazy. There ain't nothin' to be upset over. But we've come here to live, an' we're goin' to live here. We've got jest as good a right here as new horses an' cows. The house wa'n't fit for us to live in any longer, an' I made up my mind I wa'n't goin' to stay there. I've done my duty by you forty year, an' I'm goin' to do it now; but I'm goin' to live here. You've got to put in some windows and partitions; an' you'll have to buy some furniture."

"Why, mother!" the old man gasped.

"You'd better take your coat off an' get washed—there's the wash-basin—an' then we'll have supper."

"Why, mother!"   155

Sammy went past the window, leading the new horse to the old barn. The old man saw him, and shook his head speechlessly. He tried to take off his coat, but his arms seemed to lack the power. His wife helped him. She poured some water into the tin basin, and put in a piece of soap. She got the comb and brush, and smoothed his thin gray hair after he had washed. Then she put the beans, hot bread, and tea on the table. Sammy came in, and the family drew up. Adoniram sat looking dazedly at his plate, and they waited.

"Ain't you goin' to ask a blessin', father?" said Sarah.

And the old man bent his head and mumbled.

All through the meal he stopped eating at intervals, and stared furtively at his wife; but he ate well. The home food tasted good to him, and his old frame was too sturdily healthy to be affected by his mind. But after supper he went out, and sat down on the step of the smaller door at the right of the barn, through which he had meant his Jerseys to pass in stately file, but which Sarah designed for her front house door, and he leaned his head on his hands.

After the supper dishes were cleared away and the milk-pans washed, 160
Sarah went out to him. The twilight was deepening. There was a clear green
glow in the sky. Before them stretched the smooth level of field; in the
distance was a cluster of hay-stacks like the huts of a village; the air was very
cool and calm and sweet. The landscape might have been an ideal one of
peace.

Sarah bent over and touched her husband on one of his thin, sinewy
shoulders. "Father!"

The old man's shoulders heaved: he was weeping.

"Why, don't do so, father," said Sarah.

"I'll—put up the—partitions, an'—everything you—want, mother."

Sarah put her apron up to her face; she was overcome by her own 165
triumph.

Adoniram was like a fortress whose walls had no active resistance, and
went down the instant the right besieging tools were used. "Why, mother,"
he said, hoarsely, "I hadn't no idee you was so set on't as all this comes to."

Considerations

1. Characterize the relationship between Sarah Penn and her husband,
   Adoniram, at the beginning of the story. Pay attention not only to their
   conversations but also to their actions. How do these two people differ in
   the way they see their family, each other, and themselves?
2. Discuss the work Sarah Penn and Adoniram Penn do. What are the similarities and differences between their work? How do they see their work?
   How do others see their work?
3. Describe the changes that take place in the two main characters and in
   their children. Do you think the changes suggested by the resolution of
   the conflict over the house and barn will be permanent? Explain.
4. Choose any incident in the story and describe it from Adoniram's point
   of view. Try using the nineteenth-century New England dialect as you
   record his thoughts.
5. Do you see this story primarily as a depiction of a very different time in
   the history of the United States, or do you see its themes as relevant today?
   Can you imagine an updated version of "The Revolt of 'Mother'"?

JOSÉ ARMAS (1944–   )

El Tonto° del Barrio°

*José Armas is a publisher, writer, and community activist who in 1974 won a
fellowship associated with the Urban Planning Department at MIT. Armas
has taught at the University of New Mexico and at the University of Albu-
querque. In addition, he writes a column for* The Abuquerque Journal *on
issues of particular importance to the Hispanic community. In 1980, the National Endowment for the Arts granted him a writing fellowship. "El Tonto
del Barrio" was first published in 1982.*

Romero Estrado was called "El Cotoro"° because he was always whistling and singing. He made nice music even though his songs were sponta-
neous compositions made up of words with sounds that he liked but which
seldom made any sense. But that didn't seem to bother either Romero or
anyone else in the Golden Heights Centro where he lived. Not even the kids
made fun of him. It just was not permitted.

Romero had a ritual that he followed almost every day. After breakfast
he would get his broom and go up and down the main street of the Golden
Heights Centro whistling and singing and sweeping the sidewalks for all the
businesses. He would sweep in front of the Tortillería America, the XXX
Liquor Store, the Tres Milpas Bar run by Tino Gabaldon, Barelas' Barber
Shop, the used furniture store owned by Goldstein, El Centro Market of
the Avila family, the Model Cities Office, and Lourdes Printing Store.
Then, in the afternoons, he would come back and sit in Barelas' Barber
Shop and spend the day looking at magazines and watching and waving to
the passing people as he sang and composed his songs without a care in the
world.

When business was slow, Barelas would let him sit in the barber's chair.
Romero loved it. It was a routine that Romero kept every day except Sundays and Mondays when Barelas' Barber Shop was closed. After a period of
years, people in the barrio got used to seeing Romero do his little task of
sweeping the sidewalks and sitting in Barelas' Barber Shop. If he didn't show
up one day someone assumed the responsibility to go to his house to see if
he was ill. People would stop to say hello to Romero on the street and
although he never initiated a conversation while he was sober, he always
smiled and responded cheerfully to everyone. People passing the barber shop
in the afternoons made it a point to wave even though they couldn't see
him; they knew he was in there and was expecting some salutation.

When he was feeling real good, Romero would sweep in front of the
houses on both sides of the block also. He took his job seriously and took

---

El Tonto: Stupid one; *del Barrio:* Of the Spanish-speaking community. *El Cotoro:* The parrot or
magpie; chatterbox (slang).

great care to sweep cleanly, between the cracks and even between the sides
of the buildings. The dirt and small scraps went into the gutter. The bottles
and bigger pieces of litter were put carefully in cardboard boxes, ready for
the garbage man.

If he did it the way he wanted, the work took him the whole morning.   5
And always cheerful—always with some song.

Only once did someone call attention to his work. Frank Avila told
him in jest that Romero had forgotten to pick up an empty bottle of wine
from his door. Romero was so offended and made such a commotion that it
got around very quickly that no one should criticize his work. There was, in
fact, no reason to.

Although it had been long acknowledged that Romero was a little
"touched," he fit very well into the community. He was a respected citizen.

He could be found at the Tres Milpas Bar drinking his occasional beer
in the evenings. Romero had a rivalry going with the Ranchera songs on the
jukebox. He would try to outsing the songs using the same melody but
inserting his own selection of random words. Sometimes, like all people, he
would "bust out" and get drunk.

One could always tell when Romero was getting drunk because he
would begin telling everyone that he loved them.

"I looov youuu," he would sing to someone and offer to compose   10
them a song.

"Ta bueno, Romero. Ta bueno, ya bete,"° they would tell him.

Sometimes when he got too drunk he would crap in his pants and then
Tino would make him go home.

Romero received some money from Social Security but it wasn't much.
None of the merchants gave him any credit because he would always forget
to pay his bills. He didn't do it on purpose, he just forgot and spent his
money on something else. So instead, the businessmen preferred to do little
things for him occasionally. Barelas would trim his hair when things were
slow. The Tortillería America would give him menudo° and fresh-made
tortillas at noon when he was finished with his sweeping. El Centro Market
would give him the overripe fruit and broken boxes of food that no one else
would buy. Although it was unspoken and unwritten, there was an agreement that existed between Romero and the Golden Heights Centro. Romero
kept the sidewalks clean and the barrio looked after him. It was a contract
that worked well for a long time.

Then, when Seferino, Barelas' oldest son, graduated from high school
he went to work in the barber shop for the summer. Seferino was a conscientious and sensitive young man and it wasn't long before he took notice of
Romero and came to feel sorry for him.

One day when Romero was in the shop Seferino decided to act.   15

Ta bueno, ya bete: It's all right; go away now. *menudo:* Dish made with internal organs.

"Mira, Romero. Yo te doy 50 centavos por cada dia que me barres la banqueta.° Fifty cents for every day you sweep the sidewalk for us. Qué te parece?"°

Romero thought about it carefully.

"Hecho! Done!" he exclaimed. He started for home right away to get his broom.

"Why did you do that for, m'ijo?"° asked Barelas.

"It don't seem right, Dad. The man works and no one pays him for his 20
work. Everyone should get paid for what they do."

"He don't need no pay. Romero has everything he needs."

"It's not the same, Dad. How would you like to do what he does and be treated the same way? It's degrading the way he has to go around getting scraps and handouts."

"I'm not Romero. Besides you don't know about these things, m'ijo. Romero would be unhappy if his schedule was upset. Right now everyone likes him and takes care of him. He sweeps the sidewalks because he wants something to do, not because he wants money."

"I'll pay him out of my money, don't worry about it then."

"The money is not the point. The point is that money will not help 25
Romero. Don't you understand that?"

"Look, Dad. Just put yourself in his place. Would you do it? Would you cut hair for nothing?"

Barelas just knew his son was putting something over on him but he didn't know how to answer. It seemed to make sense the way Seferino explained it. But it still went against his "instinct." On the other hand, Seferino had gone and finished high school. He must know something. There were few kids who had finished high school in the barrio, and fewer who had gone to college. Barelas knew them all. He noted (with some pride) that Seferino was going to be enrolled at Harvard University this year. That must count for something, he thought. Barelas himself had never gone to school. So maybe his son had something there. On the other hand . . . it upset Barelas that he wasn't able to get Seferino to see the issue. How can we be so far apart on something so simple, he thought. But he decided not to say anything else about it.

Romero came back right away and swept the front of Barelas' shop again and put what little dirt he found into the curb. He swept up the gutter, put the trash in a shoe box and threw it in a garbage can.

Seferino watched with pride as Romero went about his job and when he was finished he went outside and shook Romero's hand. Seferino told him he had done a good job. Romero beamed.

Manolo was coming into the shop to get his hair cut as Seferino was 30
giving Romero his wages. He noticed Romero with his broom.

Mira, Romero. . . . la banqueta: Look here, Romero. I'll give you 50 cents for every day you sweep the sidewalk for me. *Qué te parece?:* How does that seem to you? *m'ijo:* My son.

"What's going on?" he asked. Barelas shrugged his shoulders. "Qué tiene Romero?° Is he sick or something?"

"No, he's not sick," explained Seferino, who had now come inside. He told Manolo the story.

"We're going to make Romero a businessman," said Seferino. "Do you realize how much money Romero would make if everyone paid him just fifty cents a day. Like my dad says, 'Everyone should be able to keep his dignity, no matter how poor.' And he does a job, you know."

"Well, it makes sense," said Manolo.

"Hey. Maybe I'll ask people to do that," said Seferino. "That way the   35 poor old man could make a decent wage. Do you want to help, Manolo? You can go with me to ask people to pay him."

"Well," said Manolo as he glanced at Barelas, "I'm not too good at asking people for money."

This did not discourage Seferino. He went out and contacted all the businesses on his own, but no one else wanted to contribute. This didn't discourage Seferino either. He went on giving Romero fifty cents a day.

After a while, Seferino heard that Romero had asked for credit at the grocery store. "See, Dad. What did I tell you? Things are getting better for him already. He's becoming his own man. And look. It's only been a couple of weeks." Barelas did not reply.

But then the next week Romero did not show up to sweep any sidewalks. He was around but he didn't do any work for anybody the entire week. He walked around Golden Heights Centro in his best gray work pants and his slouch hat, looking important and making it a point to walk right past the barber shop every little while.

Of course, the people in the Golden Heights Centro noticed the   40 change immediately, and since they saw Romero in the street, they knew he wasn't ill. But the change was clearly disturbing the community. They discussed him in the Tortillería America where people got together for coffee, and at the Tres Milpas Bar. Everywhere the topic of conversation was the great change that had come over Romero. Only Barelas did not talk about it.

The following week Romero came into the barber shop and asked to talk with Seferino in private. Barelas knew immediately something was wrong. Romero never initiated a conversation unless he was drunk.

They went into the back room where Barelas could not hear and then Romero informed Seferino, "I want a raise."

"What? What do you mean, a raise? You haven't been around for a week. You only worked a few weeks and now you want a raise?" Seferino was clearly angry but Romero was calm and insistent.

Romero correctly pointed out that he had been sweeping the sidewalks for a long time. Even before Seferino finished high school.

"I deserve a raise," he repeated after an eloquent presentation.   45

Seferino looked coldly at Romero. It was clearly a stand-off.

Qué tiene Romero?: What's Romero doing?

Then Seferino said, "Look, maybe we should forget the whole thing. I was just trying to help you out and look at what you do."

Romero held his ground. "I helped you out too. No one told me to do it and I did it anyway. I helped you many years."

"Well, let's forget about the whole thing then," said Seferino.

"I quit then," said Romero.   50

"Quit?" exclaimed Seferino as he laughed at Romero.

"Quit! I quit!" said Romero as he walked out the front of the shop past Barelas who was cutting a customer's hair.

Seferino came out shaking his head and laughing.

"Can you imagine that old guy?"

Barelas did not seem too amused. He felt he could have predicted that   55
something bad like this would happen.

Romero began sweeping the sidewalks again the next day with the exception that when he came to the barber shop he would go around it and continue sweeping the rest of the sidewalks. He did this for the rest of the week. And the following Tuesday he began sweeping the sidewalk all the way up to the shop and then pushing the trash to the sidewalk in front of the barber shop. Romero then stopped coming to the barber shop in the afternoon.

The barrio buzzed with fact and rumor about Romero. Tino commented that Romero was not singing anymore. Even if someone offered to buy him a beer he wouldn't sing. Frank Avila said the neighbors were complaining because he was leaving his TV on loud the whole day and night. He still greeted people but seldom smiled. He had run up a big bill at the liquor store and when the manager stopped his credit, he caught Romero stealing bottles of whiskey. He was also getting careless about his dress. He didn't shave and clean like he used to. Women complained that he walked around in soiled pants, that he smelled bad. Even one of the little kids complained that Romero had kicked his puppy, but that seemed hard to believe.

Barelas felt terrible. He felt responsible. But he couldn't convince Seferino that what he had done was wrong. Barelas himself stopped going to the Tres Milpas Bar after work to avoid hearing about Romero. Once he came across Romero on the street and Barelas said hello but with a sense of guilt. Romero responded, avoiding Barelas' eyes and moving past him awkwardly and quickly. Romero's behavior continued to get erratic and some people started talking about having Romero committed.

"You can't do that," said Barelas when he was presented with a petition.

"He's flipped," said Tino, who made up part of the delegation circulating   60
the petition. "No one likes Romero more than I do, you know that Barelas."

"But he's really crazy," said Frank Avila.

"He was crazy before. No one noticed," pleaded Barelas.

"But it was a crazy we could depend on. Now he just wants to sit on the curb and pull up the women's skirts. It's terrible. The women are going crazy. He's also running into the street stopping traffic. You see how he is. What choice do we have?"

"It's for his own good," put in one of the workers from the Model Cities Office. Barelas dismissed them as outsiders. Seferino was there and wanted to say something but a look from Barelas stopped him.

"We just can't do that," insisted Barelas. "Let's wait. Maybe he's just 65 going through a cycle. Look. We've had a full moon recently, qué no?° That must be it. You know how the moon affects people in his condition."

"I don't know," said Tino. "What if he hurts . . ."

"He's not going to hurt anyone," cut in Barelas.

"No, Barelas. I was going to say, what if he hurts himself. He has no one at home. I'd say, let him come home with me for a while but you know how stubborn he is. You can't even talk to him any more."

"He gives everyone the finger when they try to pull him out of the traffic," said Frank Avila. "The cops have missed him, but it won't be long before they see him doing some of his antics and arrest him. Then what? Then the poor guy is in real trouble."

"Well, look," said Barelas. "How many names you got on the list?" 70

Tino responded slowly, "Well, we sort of wanted you to start off the list."

"Let's wait a while longer," said Barelas. "I just know that Romero will come around. Let's wait just a while, okay?"

No one had the heart to fight the issue and so they postponed the petition.

There was no dramatic change in Romero even though the full moon had completed its cycle. Still, no one initiated the petition again and then in the middle of August Seferino left for Cambridge to look for housing and to register early for school. Suddenly everything began to change again. One day Romero began sweeping the entire sidewalk again. His spirits began to pick up and his strange antics began to disappear.

At the Tortillería America the original committee met for coffee and 75 the talk turned to Romero.

"He's going to be all right now," said a jubilant Barelas. "I guarantee it."

"Well, don't hold your breath yet," said Tino. "The full moon is coming up again."

"Yeah," said Frank Avila dejectedly.

When the next full moon was in force the group was together again drinking coffee and Tino asked, "Well, how's Romero doing?"

Barelas smiled and said, "Well. Singing songs like crazy." 80

qué no?: Haven't we?

Considerations

1. Is Romero Estrado "El Tonto del Barrio" (the stupid one of the neighborhood)? Is there another person or persons in the story to whom the title could be awarded? Explain.

2. Make a list of the qualities and characteristics you see in Barelas. Why do the other barrio dwellers cast him in the role of leader? Do you agree with their view of Barelas? Explain.

3. Barelas and his son Seferino argue about paying Romero for his work. Seferino thinks paying Romero will give him dignity. Do you agree that being paid for work generally grants the worker dignity that is not granted to unpaid labor? Explain.

4. Why do you think Romero reacts to the pay as he does? Write a monologue describing the thoughts that explain the changes he goes through after he is offered 50 cents a day to sweep the sidewalk.

5. What do you think of the story's ending? Are there any clear winners or losers? Explain.

CHARLOTTE PERKINS GILMAN (1860–1935)

The Yellow Wallpaper

Charlotte Perkins Gilman was born in Hartford, Connecticut. Her father left the family shortly after her birth, and she and her brother were raised by her mother. As a young adult, Gilman attended the Rhode Island School of Design, which provided the training she needed to work as an art teacher. In 1884, she married her first husband, Charles Walter Stetson. Following the birth of their first child, a daughter, Gilman suffered a severe breakdown. After she recovered, she moved with her mother and daughter to California, obtained a divorce, and finally sent her daughter back to Connecticut to live with her former husband and his new wife. Gilman remained in California, support-ing herself by lecturing, editing, writing, and teaching. In 1900, she married George Houghton Gilman, and the two were happily married for many years, during which Charlotte became a prominent lecturer and writer on feminism and the labor movement. "The Yellow Wallpaper" was first published in 1892 in the New England Magazine.

It is very seldom that mere ordinary people like John and myself secure ancestral halls for the summer.

A colonial mansion, a hereditary estate, I would say a haunted house and reach the height of romantic felicity—but that would be asking too much of fate!

Still I will proudly declare that there is something queer about it.

Else, why should it be let so cheaply? And why have stood so long untenanted?

John laughs at me, of course, but one expects that.   5

John is practical in the extreme. He has no patience with faith, an intense horror of superstition, and he scoffs openly at any talk of things not to be felt and seen and put down in figures.

John is a physician, and *perhaps*—(I would not say it to a living soul, of course, but this is dead paper and a great relief to my mind)—*perhaps* that is one reason I do not get well faster.

You see, he does not believe I am sick! And what can one do?

If a physician of high standing, and one's own husband, assures friends and relatives that there is really nothing the matter with one but temporary nervous depression—a slight hysterical tendency—what is one to do?

My brother is also a physician, and also of high standing, and he says   10
the same thing.

So I take phosphates or phosphites—whichever it is—and tonics, and air and exercise, and journeys, and am absolutely forbidden to "work" until I am well again.

Personally, I disagree with their ideas.

Personally, I believe that congenial work, with excitement and change, would do me good.

But what is one to do?

I did write for a while in spite of them; but it *does* exhaust me a good deal—having to be so sly about it, or else meet with heavy opposition.

I sometimes fancy that in my condition, if I had less opposition and more society and stimulus—but John says the very worst thing I can do is to think about my condition, and I confess it always makes me feel bad.

So I will let it alone and talk about the house.

The most beautiful place! It is quite alone, standing well back from the road, quite three miles from the village. It makes me think of English places that you read about, for there are hedges and walls and gates that lock, and lots of separate little houses for the gardeners and people.

There is a *delicious* garden! I never saw such a garden—large and shady, full of box-bordered paths, and lined with long grape-covered arbors with seats under them.

There were greenhouses, but they are all broken now.

There was some legal trouble, I believe, something about the heirs and co-heirs; anyhow, the place has been empty for years.

That spoils my ghostliness, I am afraid, but I don't care—there is something strange about the house—I can feel it.

I even said so to John one moonlight evening, but he said what I felt was a draught, and shut the window.

I get unreasonably angry with John sometimes. I'm sure I never used to be so sensitive. I think it is due to this nervous condition.

But John says if I feel so I shall neglect proper self-control; so I take pains to control myself—before him, at least, and that makes me very tired.

I don't like our room a bit. I wanted one downstairs that opened onto the piazza and had roses all over the window, and such pretty old-fashioned chintz hangings! But John would not hear of it.

He said there was only one window and not room for two beds, and no near room for him if he took another.

He is very careful and loving, and hardly lets me stir without special direction.

I have a schedule prescription for each hour in the day; he takes all care from me, and so I feel basely ungrateful not to value it more.

He said he came here solely on my account, that I was to have perfect rest and all the air I could get. "Your exercise depends on your strength, my dear," said he, "and your food somewhat on your appetite; but air you can absorb all the time." So we took the nursery at the top of the house.

It is a big, airy room, the whole floor nearly, with windows that look all ways, and air and sunshine galore. It was a nursery first, and then playroom and gymnasium, I should judge, for the windows are barred for little children, and there are rings and things in the walls.

The paint and paper look as if a boys' school had used it. It is stripped off—the paper—in great patches all around the head of my bed, about as far as I can reach, and in a great place on the other side of the room low down. I never saw a worse paper in my life. One of those sprawling, flamboyant patterns committing every artistic sin.

It is dull enough to confuse the eye in following, pronounced enough constantly to irritate and provoke study, and when you follow the lame uncertain curves for a little distance they suddenly commit suicide—plunge off at outrageous angles, destroy themselves in unheard-of contradictions.

The color is repellent, almost revolting: a smouldering unclean yellow, strangely faded by the slow-turning sunlight. It is a dull yet lurid orange in some places, a sickly sulphur tint in others.

No wonder the children hated it! I should hate it myself if I had to live   35 in this room long.

There comes John, and I must put this away—he hates to have me write a word.

We have been here two weeks, and I haven't felt like writing before, since that first day.

I am sitting by the window now, up in this atrocious nursery, and there is nothing to hinder my writing as much as I please, save lack of strength.

John is away all day, and even some nights when his cases are serious.

I'm glad my case is not serious!   40

But these nervous troubles are dreadfully depressing.

John does not know how much I really suffer. He knows there is no reason to suffer, and that satisfies him.

Of course it is only nervousness. It does weigh on me so not to do my duty in any way!

I meant to be such a help to John, such a real rest and comfort, and here I am a comparative burden already!

Nobody would believe what an effort it is to do what little I am able—   45 to dress and entertain, and order things.

It is fortunate Mary is so good with the baby. Such a dear baby!

And yet I *cannot* be with him, it makes me so nervous.

I suppose John never was nervous in his life. He laughs at me so about this wallpaper!

At first he meant to repaper the room, but afterward he said that I was letting it get the better of me, and that nothing was worse for a nervous patient than to give way to such fancies.

He said that after the wallpaper was changed it would be the heavy   50 bedstead, and then the barred windows, and then that gate at the head of the stairs, and so on.

"You know the place is doing you good," he said, "and really, dear, I don't care to renovate the house just for a three months' rental."

"Then do let us go downstairs," I said. "There are such pretty rooms there."

Then he took me in his arms and called me a blessed little goose, and said he would go down to the cellar, if I wished, and have it whitewashed into the bargain.

But he is right enough about the beds and windows and things

It is as airy and comfortable a room as anyone need wish, and, of course, I would not be so silly as to make him uncomfortable just for a whim. 55

I'm really getting quite fond of the big room, all but that horrid paper.

Out of one window I can see the garden—those mysterious deep-shaded arbors, the riotous old-fashioned flowers, and bushes and gnarly trees.

Out of another I get a lovely view of the bay and a little private wharf belonging to the estate. There is a beautiful shaded lane that runs down there from the house. I always fancy I see people walking in these numerous paths and arbors, but John has cautioned me not to give way to fancy in the least. He says that with my imaginative power and habit of story-making, a nervous weakness like mine is sure to lead to all manner of excited fancies, and that I ought to use my will and good sense to check the tendency. So I try.

I think sometimes that if I were only well enough to write a little it would relieve the press of ideas and rest me.

But I find I get pretty tired when I try. 60

It is so discouraging not to have any advice and companionship about my work. When I get really well, John says we will ask Cousin Henry and Julia down for a long visit; but he says he would as soon put fireworks in my pillow-case as to let me have those stimulating people about now.

I wish I could get well faster.

But I must not think about that. This paper looks to me as if it *knew* what a vicious influence it had!

There is a recurrent spot where the pattern lolls like a broken neck and two bulbous eyes stare at you upside down.

I get positively angry with the impertinence of it and the everlasting- 65 ness. Up and down and sideways they crawl, and those absurd unblinking eyes are everywhere. There is one place where two breadths didn't match, and the eyes go all up and down the line, one a little higher than the other.

I never saw so much expression in an inanimate thing before, and we all know how much expression they have! I used to lie awake as a child and get more entertainment and terror out of blank walls and plain furniture than most children could find in a toy-store.

I remember what a kindly wink the knobs of our big old bureau used to have, and there was one chair that always seemed like a strong friend.

I used to feel that if any of the other things looked too fierce I could always hop into that chair and be safe.

The furniture in this room is no worse than inharmonious, however, for we had to bring it all from downstairs. I suppose when this was used as a playroom they had to take the nursery things out, and no wonder! I never saw such ravages as the children have made here.

The wallpaper, as I said before, is torn off in spots, and it sticketh closer 70 than a brother—they must have had perseverance as well as hatred.

Then the floor is scratched and gouged and splintered, the plaster itself is dug out here and there, and this great heavy bed, which is all we found in the room, looks as if it had been through the wars.

But I don't mind it a bit—only the paper.

There comes John's sister. Such a dear girl as she is, and so careful of me! I must not let her find me writing.

She is a perfect and enthusiastic housekeeper, and hopes for no better profession. I verily believe she thinks it is the writing which made me sick!

But I can write when she is out, and see her a long way off from these 75 windows.

There is one that commands the road, a lovely shaded winding road, and one that just looks off over the country. A lovely country, too, full of great elms and velvet meadows.

This wallpaper has a kind of sub-pattern in a different shade, a particularly irritating one, for you can only see it in certain lights, and not clearly then.

But in the places where it isn't faded and where the sun is just so—I can see a strange, provoking, formless sort of figure that seems to skulk about behind that silly and conspicuous front design.

There's sister on the stairs!

Well, the Fourth of July is over! The people are all gone, and I am tired 80 out. John thought it might do me good to see a little company, so we just had Mother and Nellie and the children down for a week.

Of course I didn't do a thing. Jennie sees to everything now.

But it tired me all the same.

John says if I don't pick up faster he shall send me to Weir Mitchell in the fall.

But I don't want to go there at all. I had a friend who was in his hands once, and she says he is just like John and my brother, only more so!

Besides, it is such an undertaking to go so far. 85

I don't feel as if it was worthwhile to turn my hand over for anything, and I'm getting dreadfully fretful and querulous.

I cry at nothing, and cry most of the time.

Of course I don't when John is here, or anybody else, but when I am alone.

And I am alone a good deal just now. John is kept in town very often by serious cases, and Jennie is good and lets me alone when I want her to.

So I walk a little in the garden or down that lovely lane, sit on the 90 porch under the roses, and lie down up here a good deal.

I'm getting really fond of the room in spite of the wallpaper. Perhaps *because* of the wallpaper.

It dwells in my mind so!

I lie here on this great immovable bed—it is nailed down, I believe— and follow that pattern about by the hour. It is as good as gymnastics, I assure you. I start, we'll say, at the bottom, down in the corner over there where it has not been touched, and I determine for the thousandth time that I *will* follow that pointless pattern to some sort of a conclusion.

I know a little of the principle of design, and I know this thing was not arranged on any laws of radiation, or alternation, or repetition, or symmetry, or anything else that I ever heard of.

It is repeated, of course, by the breadths, but not otherwise.   95

Looked at in one way, each breadth stands alone; the bloated curves and flourishes—a kind of "debased Romanesque" with delirium tremens— go waddling up and down in isolated columns of fatuity.

But, on the other hand, they connect diagonally, and the sprawling outlines run off in great slanting waves of optic horror, like a lot of wallowing sea-weeds in full chase.

The whole thing goes horizontally, too, at least it seems so, and I exhaust myself trying to distinguish the order of its going in that direction.

They have used a horizontal breadth for a frieze, and that adds won- derfully to the confusion.

There is one end of the room where it is almost intact, and there, when   100 the crosslights fade and the low sun shines directly upon it, I can almost fancy radiation after all—the interminable grotesque seems to form around a com- mon center and rush off in headlong plunges of equal distraction.

It makes me tired to follow it. I will take a nap, I guess.

I don't know why I should write this.

I don't want to.

I don't feel able.

And I know John would think it absurd. But I *must* say what I feel and   105 think in some way—it is such a relief!

But the effort is getting to be greater than the relief.

Half the time now I am awfully lazy, and lie down ever so much. John says I musn't lose my strength, and has me take cod liver oil and lots of tonics and things, to say nothing of ale and wine and rare meat.

Dear John! He loves me very dearly, and hates to have me sick. I tried to have a real earnest reasonable talk with him the other day, and tell him how I wish he would let me go and make a visit to Cousin Henry and Julia.

But he said I wasn't able to go, nor able to stand it after I got there; and I did not make out a very good case for myself, for I was crying before I had finished.

It is getting to be a great effort for me to think straight. Just this nervous   110 weakness, I suppose.

And dear John gathered me up in his arms, and just carried me upstairs and laid me on the bed, and sat by me and read to me till it tired my head.

He said I was his darling and his comfort and all he had, and that I must take care of myself for his sake, and keep well.

He says no one but myself can help me out of it, that I must use my will and self-control and not let any silly fancies run away with me.

There's one comfort—the baby is well and happy, and does not have to occupy this nursery with the horrid wallpaper.

If we had not used it, that blessed child would have! What a fortunate 115 escape! Why, I wouldn't have a child of mine, an impressionable little thing, live in such a room for worlds.

I never thought of it before, but it is lucky that John kept me here after all; I can stand it so much easier than a baby, you see.

Of course I never mention it to them any more—I am too wise—but I keep watch for it all the same.

There are things in that wallpaper that nobody knows about but me, or ever will.

Behind that outside pattern the dim shapes get clearer every day.

It is always the same shape, only very numerous. 120

And it is like a woman stooping down and creeping about behind that pattern. I don't like it a bit. I wonder—I begin to think—I wish John would take me away from here!

It is so hard to talk with John about my case, because he is so wise, and because he loves me so.

But I tried it last night.

It was moonlight. The moon shines in all around just as the sun does.

I hate to see it sometimes, it creeps so slowly, and always comes in by 125 one window or another.

John was asleep and I hated to waken him, so I kept still and watched the moonlight on that undulating wallpaper till I felt creepy.

The faint figure behind seemed to shake the pattern, just as if she wanted to get out.

I got up softly and went to feel and see if the paper *did* move, and when I came back John was awake.

"What is it, little girl?" he said. "Don't go walking about like that— you'll get cold."

I thought it was a good time to talk, so I told him that I really was not 130 gaining here, and that I wished he would take me away.

"Why, darling!" said he. "Our lease will be up in three weeks, and I can't see how to leave before.

"The repairs are not done at home, and I cannot possibly leave town just now. Of course, if you were in any danger, I could and would, but you really are better, dear, whether you can see it or not. I am a doctor, dear, and I know. You are gaining flesh and color, your appetite is better, I feel really much easier about you."

"I don't weigh a bit more," said I, "nor as much; and my appetite may be better in the evening when you are here but it is worse in the morning when you are away!"

"Bless her little heart!" said he with a big hug. "She shall be as sick as she pleases! But now let's improve the shining hours by going to sleep, and talk about it in the morning!"

"And you won't go away?" I asked gloomily.   135

"Why, how can I, dear? It is only three weeks more and then we will take a nice little trip of a few days while Jennie is getting the house ready. Really, dear, you are better!"

"Better in body perhaps—" I began, and stopped short, for he sat up straight and looked at me with such a stern, reproachful look that I could not say another word.

"My darling," said he, "I beg of you, for my sake and for our child's sake, as well as for your own, that you will never for one instant let that idea enter your mind! There is nothing so dangerous, so fascinating, to a temperament like yours. It is a false and foolish fancy. Can you not trust me as a physician when I tell you so?"

So of course I said no more on that score, and we went to sleep before long. He thought I was asleep first, but I wasn't, and lay there for hours trying to decide whether that front pattern and the back pattern really did move together or separately.

On a pattern like this, by daylight, there is a lack of sequence, a defi-   140
ance of law, that is a constant irritant to a normal mind.

The color is hideous enough, and unreliable enough, and infuriating enough, but the pattern is torturing.

You think you have mastered it, but just as you get well under way in following, it turns a back-somersault and there you are. It slaps you in the face, knocks you down, and tramples upon you. It is like a bad dream.

The outside pattern is a florid arabesque, reminding one of a fungus. If you can imagine a toadstool in joints, an interminable string of toad-stools, budding and sprouting in endless convolutions—why, that is something like it.

That is, sometimes!

There is one marked peculiarity about this paper, a thing nobody seems   145
to notice but myself, and that is that it changes as the light changes.

When the sun shoots in through the east window—I always watch for that first long, straight ray—it changes so quickly that I never can quite believe it.

That is why I watch it always.

By moonlight—the moon shines in all night when there is a moon— I wouldn't know it was the same paper.

At night in any kind of light, in twilight, candlelight, lamplight, and worst of all by moonlight, it becomes bars! The outside pattern, I mean, and the woman behind it is as plain as can be.

I didn't realize for a long time what the thing was that showed behind, 150
that dim sub-pattern, but now I am quite sure it is a woman.

By daylight she is subdued, quiet. I fancy it is the pattern that keeps
her so still. It is so puzzling. It keeps me quiet by the hour.

I lie down ever so much now. John says it is good for me, and to sleep
all I can.

Indeed he started the habit by making me lie down for an hour after
each meal.

It is a very bad habit, I am convinced, for you see, I don't sleep.

And that cultivates deceit, for I don't tell them I'm awake—oh, no! 155

The fact is I am getting a little afraid of John.

He seems very queer sometimes, and even Jennie has an inexplicable
look.

It strikes me occasionally, just as a scientific hypothesis, that perhaps it
is the paper!

I have watched John when he did not know I was looking, and come
into the room suddenly on the most innocent excuses, and I've caught him
several times *looking at the paper!* And Jennie too. I caught Jennie with her
hand on it once.

She didn't know I was in the room, and when I asked her in a quiet, a 160
very quiet voice, with the most restrained manner possible, what she was
doing with the paper, she turned around as if she had been caught stealing,
and looked quite angry—asked me why I should frighten her so!

Then she said that the paper stained everything it touched, that she had
found yellow smooches on all my clothes and John's and she wished we
would be more careful!

Did not that sound innocent? But I know she was studying that pattern,
and I am determined that nobody shall find it out but myself!

Life is very much more exciting now than it used to be. You see, I
have something more to expect, to look forward to, to watch. I really do eat
better, and am more quiet than I was.

John is so pleased to see me improve! He laughed a little the other day,
and said I seemed to be flourishing in spite of my wallpaper.

I turned it off with a laugh. I had no intention of telling him it was 165
because of the wallpaper—he would make fun of me. He might even want to
take me away.

I don't want to leave now until I have found it out. There is a week
more, and I think that will be enough.

I'm feeling so much better!

I don't sleep much at night, for it is so interesting to watch developments; but I sleep a good deal during the daytime.

In the daytime it is tiresome and perplexing.

There are always new shoots on the fungus, and new shades of yellow 170
all over it. I cannot keep count of them, though I have tried conscientiously.

It is the strangest yellow, that wallpaper! It makes me think of all the yellow things I ever saw—not beautiful like buttercups, but old, foul, bad yellow things.

But there is something else about that paper—the smell! I noticed it the moment we came into the room, but with so much air and sun it was not bad. Now we have had a week of fog and rain, and whether the windows are open or not, the smell is here.

It creeps all over the house.

I find it hovering in the dining-room, skulking in the parlor, hiding in the hall, lying in wait for me on the stairs.

It gets into my hair. 175

Even when I go to ride, if I turn my head suddenly and surprise it— there is that smell!

Such a peculiar odor, too! I have spent hours in trying to analyze it, to find what it smelled like.

It is not bad—at first—and very gentle, but quite the subtlest, most enduring odor I ever met.

In this damp weather it is awful. I wake up in the night and find it hanging over me.

It used to disturb me at first. I thought seriously of burning the house— 180 to reach the smell.

But now I am used to it. The only thing I can think of that it is like is the *color* of the paper! A yellow smell.

There is a very funny mark on this wall, low down, near the mopboard. A streak that runs round the room. It goes behind every piece of furniture, except the bed, a long, straight, even *smooch,* as if it had been rubbed over and over.

I wonder how it was done and who did it, and what they did it for. Round and round and round—round and round and round—it makes me dizzy!

I really have discovered something at last.

Through watching so much at night, when it changes so, I have finally 185 found out.

The front pattern *does* move—and no wonder! The woman behind shakes it!

Sometimes I think there are a great many women behind, and sometimes only one, and she crawls around fast, and her crawling shakes it all over.

Then in the very bright spots she keeps still, and in the very shady spots she just takes hold of the bars and shakes them hard.

And she is all the time trying to climb through. But nobody could climb through that pattern—it strangles so; I think that is why it has so many heads.

They get through, and then the pattern strangles them off and turns 190 them upside down and makes their eyes white!

If those heads were covered or taken off it would not be half so bad.

I think that woman gets out in the daytime!
And I'll tell you why—privately—I've seen her!
I can see her out of every one of my windows!
It is the same woman, I know, for she is always creeping, and most 195
women do not creep by daylight.
I see her in that long shaded lane, creeping up and down. I see her in
those dark grape arbors, creeping all around the garden.
I see her on that long road under the trees, creeping along, and when
a carriage comes she hides under the blackberry vines.
I don't blame her a bit. It must be very humiliating to be caught
creeping by daylight!
I always lock the door when I creep by daylight. I can't do it at night,
for I know John would suspect something at once.
And John is so queer now that I don't want to irritate him. I wish he 200
would take another room! Besides, I don't want anybody to get that woman
out at night but myself.
I often wonder if I could see her out of all the windows at once.
But, turn as fast as I can, I can only see out of one at one time.
And though I always see her, she *may* be able to creep faster than I can
turn! I have watched her sometimes away off in the open country, creeping
as fast as a cloud shadow in a high wind.

If only that top pattern could be gotten off from the under one! I mean
to try it, little by little.
I have found out another funny thing, but I shan't tell it this time! It 205
does not do to trust people too much.
There are only two more days to get this paper off, and I believe John
is beginning to notice. I don't like the look in his eyes.
And I hear him ask Jennie a lot of professional questions about me. She
had a very good report to give.
She said I slept a good deal in the daytime.
John knows I don't sleep very well at night, for all I'm so quiet!
He asked me all sorts of questions, too, and pretended to be very loving 210
and kind.
As if I couldn't see through him!
Still, I don't wonder he acts so, sleeping under this paper for three
months.
It only interests me, but I feel sure John and Jennie are affected by it.

Hurrah! This is the last day, but it is enough. John is to stay in town
over night, and won't be out until this evening.
Jennie wanted to sleep with me—the sly thing; but I told her I should 215
undoubtedly rest better for a night all alone.

That was clever, for really I wasn't alone a bit! As soon as it was moon-light and that poor thing began to crawl and shake the pattern, I got up and ran to help her.

I pulled and she shook. I shook and she pulled, and before morning we had peeled off yards of that paper.

A strip about as high as my head and half around the room.

And then when the sun came and that awful pattern began to laugh at me, I declared I would finish it today!

We go away tomorrow, and they are moving all my furniture down 220 again to leave things as they were before.

Jennie looked at the wall in amazement, but I told her merrily that I did it out of pure spite at the vicious thing.

She laughed and said she wouldn't mind doing it herself, but I must not get tired.

How she betrayed herself that time!

But I am here, and no person touches this paper but Me—not *alive!*

She tried to get me out of the room—it was too patent! But I said it 225 was so quiet and empty and clean now that I believed I would lie down again and sleep all I could, and not to wake me even for dinner—I would call when I woke.

So now she is gone, and the servants are gone, and the things are gone, and there is nothing left but that great bedstead nailed down, with the canvas mattress we found on it.

We shall sleep downstairs tonight, and take the boat home tomorrow.

I quite enjoy the room, now it is bare again.

How those children did tear about here!

This bedstead is fairly gnawed! 230

But I must get to work.

I have locked the door and thrown the key down into the front path.

I don't want to go out, and I don't want to have anybody come in, till John comes.

I want to astonish him.

I've got a rope up here that even Jennie did not find. If that woman 235 does get out, and tries to get away, I can tie her!

But I forgot I could not reach far without anything to stand on!

This bed will *not* move!

I tried to lift and push it until I was lame, and then I got so angry I bit off a little piece at one corner—but it hurt my teeth.

Then I peeled off all the paper I could reach standing on the floor. It sticks horribly and the pattern just enjoys it! All those strangled heads and bulbous eyes and waddling fungus growths just shriek with derision!

I am getting angry enough to do something desperate. To jump out 240 of the window would be admirable exercise, but the bars are too strong even to try.

Besides I wouldn't do it. Of course not. I know well enough that a step like that is improper and might be misconstrued.

I don't like to *look* out of the windows even—there are so many of those creeping women, and they creep so fast.

I wonder if they all come out of that wallpaper as I did?

But I am securely fastened now by my well-hidden rope—you don't get *me* out in the road there!

I suppose I shall have to get back behind the pattern when it comes night, and that is hard! 245

It is so pleasant to be out in this great room and creep around as I please!

I don't want to go outside. I won't, even if Jennie asks me to.

For outside you have to creep on the ground, and everything is green instead of yellow.

But here I can creep smoothly on the floor, and my shoulder just fits in that long smooch around the wall, so I cannot lose my way.

Why, there's John at the door! 250

It is no use, young man, you can't open it!

How he does call and pound!

Now he's crying to Jennie for an axe.

It would be a shame to break down that beautiful door!

"John, dear!" said I in the gentlest voice. "The key is down by the front steps, under a plantain leaf!" 255

That silenced him for a few moments.

Then he said, very quietly indeed, "Open the door, my darling!"

"I can't," said I. "The key is down by the front door under a plantain leaf!" And then I said it again, several times, very gently and slowly, and said it so often that he had to go and see, and he got it of course, and came in. He stopped short by the door.

"What is the matter?" he cried. "For God's sake, what are you doing!"

I kept on creeping just the same, but I looked at him over my shoulder. 260

"I've got out at last," said I, "in spite of you and Jane. And I've pulled off most of the paper, so you can't put me back!"

Now why should that man have fainted? But he did, and right across my path by the wall, so that I had to creep over him every time!

Considerations

1. Describe the work of the narrator. How is her work significant to the conflicts and themes of the story?
2. Explain how John's profession relates to the development of the plot. How does the narrator regard John's work? How does he regard her work?
3. Make a list of details describing the room the narrator occupies. She interprets these details as indicators that the room was once a nursery. What other possibilities would fit the same details?
4. "The Yellow Wallpaper" has often been anthologized as a ghost story. Do you see the woman in the wallpaper as a supernatural element? What other possibilities can you suggest?

5. Read either or both of the following commentaries on "The Yellow Wallpaper." Then write a response to either or both, explaining how reading them has changed or confirmed your own views of the story.

Commentary

CHARLOTTE PERKINS GILMAN
Why I Wrote "The Yellow Wallpaper"

Many and many a reader has asked that. When the story first came out, in the *New England Magazine* about 1891, a Boston physician made protest in *The Transcript*. Such a story ought not to be written, he said; it was enough to drive anyone mad to read it.

Another physician, in Kansas I think, wrote to say that it was the best description of incipient insanity he had ever seen, and—begging my pardon—had I been there?

Now the story of the story is this:

For many years I suffered from a severe and continuous nervous breakdown tending to melancholia—and beyond. During about the third year of this trouble I went, in devout faith and some faint stir of hope, to a noted specialist in nervous diseases, the best known in the country.° This wise man put me to bed and applied the rest cure, to which a still-good physique responded so promptly that he concluded there was nothing much the matter with me, and sent me home with solemn advice to "live as domestic a life as far as possible," to "have but two hours' intellectual life a day," and "never to touch pen, brush, or pencil again" as long as I lived. This was in 1887.

I went home and obeyed those directions for some three months, and came so near the borderline of utter mental ruin that I could see over.   5

Then, using the remnants of intelligence that remained, and helped by a wise friend, I cast the noted specialist's advice to the winds and went to work again—work, the normal life of every human being; work, in which is joy and growth and service, without which one is a pauper and a parasite—ultimately recovering some measure of power.

Being naturally moved to rejoicing by this narrow escape, I wrote "The Yellow Wallpaper," with its embellishments and additions, to carry out the ideal (I never had hallucinations or objections to my mural decorations) and sent a copy to the physician who so nearly drove me mad. He never acknowledged it.

The little book is valued by alienists° and as a good specimen of one kind of literature. It has, to my knowledge, saved one woman from a similar fate—so terrifying her family that they let her out into normal activity and she recovered.

---

noted specialist . . . best known in the country: Dr. S. Weir Mitchell of Philadelphia, a famous "nerve specialist" of the time. Mitchell is mentioned by the narrator of "The Yellow Wallpaper." *alienist:* Nineteenth-century word for "psychiatrist."

But the best result is this. Many years later I was told that the great specialist had admitted to friends of his that he had altered his treatment of neurasthenia since reading "The Yellow Wallpaper."

It was not intended to drive people crazy, but to save people from being driven crazy, and it worked.

10

Commentary

JUDITH FETTERLEY

Reading about Reading: "The Yellow Wallpaper"

In her "Afterword" to the 1973 Feminist Press Edition of Charlotte Perkins Gilman's "The Yellow Wallpaper," Elaine Hedges claims that until recently "no one seems to have made the connection between the insanity and the sex, or sexual role, of the victim." Nevertheless, it seems likely, as she also suggests, that the content of the story has provided the reason for its negative reception, outright rejection, and eventual obliteration by a male-dominated literary establishment. Though not, I would argue, as determinedly instructive as [Susan Glaspell's] "A Jury of Her Peers,"° neither, I would equally propose, is "The Yellow Wallpaper" susceptible of a masculinist reading as, for example, is "The Murders in the Rue Morgue." That it has taken a generation of feminist critics to make Gilman's story a "classic" bears out the truth of Glaspell's thesis.

Gilman opens her story with language evocative of Poe: "It is very seldom that mere ordinary people like John and myself secure ancestral halls for the summer." Here we have echoes of the "scenes of mere household events" which the narrator of "The Black Cat" wishes "to place before the world, plainly, succinctly, and without comment." Poe's ancestral halls serve as image and symbol of the mind of his narrator, and they serve as analogue for the texts men write and read. These halls/texts are haunted by the ghosts of women buried alive within them, hacked to death to produce their effect, killed by and in the service of the necessities of male art: "The death, then, of a beautiful woman is, unquestionably, the most poetical topic in the world—and equally is it beyond doubt that the lips best suited for such topic are those of a bereaved lover." Die, then, women must so that men may sing. If such self-knowledge ultimately drives Roderick Usher mad, nevertheless as he goes down he takes self and text and sister with him; no other voice is heard, no alternate text remains. No doubt the madness of Poe's narrators reflects that masculine anxiety mentioned earlier, the fear that solipsism, annihilation, nothingness, will be the inevitable result of habitually silencing the other. Yet apparently such anxiety is preferable to the loss of power and control which would accompany giving voice to that other.

"A Jury of Her Peers": A short-story version of *Trifles* (see pages 608–19).

Gilman's narrator recognizes that she is in a haunted house, despite the protestations of her John, who is far less up-front than Poe's Roderick. Writing from the point of view of a character trapped in that male text—as if the black cat or Madeline Usher should actually find words and speak—Gilman's narrator shifts the center of attention away from the male mind that has produced the text and directs it instead to the consequences for women's lives of men's control of textuality. For it is precisely at this point that "The Yellow Wallpaper" enters this discussion of the connections between gender and reading. In this text we find the analysis of why who gets to tell the story and what story one is required, allowed, or encouraged to read matter so much, and therefore why in a sexist culture the practice of reading follows the theory proposed by Glaspell. Gilman's story makes clear the connection between male control of textuality and male dominance in other areas, and in it we feel the force behind what is usually passed off as a casual accident of personal preference or justified by invoking "absolute" standards of "universal" value: these are just books I happen to like and I want to share them with you; these are our great texts and you must read them if you want to be literate. As man, husband, and doctor, John controls the narrator's life. That he chooses to make such an issue out of what and how she reads tells us what we need to know about the politics of reading.

In "The Yellow Wallpaper," Gilman argues that male control of textuality constitutes one of the primary causes of women's madness in a patriarchal culture. Forced to read men's texts, women are forced to become characters in those texts. And since the stories men tell assert as fact what women know to be fiction, not only do women lose the power that comes from authoring; more significantly, they are forced to deny their own reality and to commit in effect a kind of psychic suicide. For Gilman works out in considerable detail the position implicit in "A Jury of Her Peers"—namely, that in a sexist culture the interests of men and women are antithetical, and, thus, the stories each has to tell are not simply alternate versions of reality, they are, rather, radically incompatible. The two stories cannot coexist; if one is accepted as true, then the other must be false, and vice versa. Thus, the struggle for control of textuality is nothing less than the struggle for control over the definition of reality and hence over the definition of sanity and madness. The nameless narrator of Gilman's story has two choices. She can accept her husband's definition of reality, the prime component of which is the proposition that for her to write her own text is "madness" and for her to read his text is "sanity"; that is, she can agree to become a character in his text, accept his definition of sanity, which is madness for her, and thus commit psychic suicide, killing herself into his text to serve his interests. Or she can refuse to read his text, refuse to become a character in it, and insist on writing her own, behavior for which John will define and treat her as mad. Though Gilman herself was able to choose a third alternative, that of writing "The Yellow Wallpaper," she implicitly recognizes that her escape from this dilemma is the exception, not the rule. Though the narrator chooses the second alternative, she does as a result go literally mad and, thus, ironically fulfills the script John has written for her. Nevertheless, in the process she manages to expose the fact of John's fiction and the implications of his insistence on asserting his fiction as fact. And she does, however briefly, force him to become a character in her text.

An appropriate title for the story the narrator writes, as distinct from the story Gilman writes, could well be "John Says." Though the narrator attempts to confide to "dead" paper her alternative view of reality, she is, at least initially, careful to present John's text as well. Thoroughly subject to his control, she writes with the distinct possibility of his discovering her text and consequently escalating her punishment for refusing to accept his text— punishment that includes, among other things, solitary confinement in an attic nursery. She rightly suspects that the treason of a resisting author is more serious than that of a resisting reader; for this reason, in part, she turns the wallpaper into her primary text: what she writes on this paper can not be read by John.

Gilman, however, structures the narrator's reporting of John's text so as to expose its madness. John's definition of sanity requires that his wife neither have nor tell her own story. Presumably the narrator would be released from her prison and even allowed to write again were John sure that she would tell only "true" stories and not "fancies"; "John has cautioned me not to give way to fancy in the least. He says that with my imaginative power and habit of story-making, a nervous weakness like mine is sure to lead to all manner of excited fancies, and that I ought to use my will and good sense to check the tendency. So I try." But, of course, what John labels "fancies" are the narrator's facts: "Still I will proudly declare that there is something queer about it. Else, why should it be let so cheaply? And why have stood so long untenanted? John laughs at me, of course, but one expects that. John is practical in the extreme"; "that spoils my ghostliness, I am afraid, but I don't care—there is something strange about the house—I can feel it." John's laughter, like that of the husbands in "A Jury of Her Peers," is designed to undermine the narrator's belief in the validity of her own perceptions and to prevent her from writing them down and thus claiming them as true. Indeed, John is "practical in the extreme."

Conversely, John's facts appear rather fanciful. In John's story, he "loves" his wife and everything he does is for her benefit: "He said we came here solely on my account, that I was to have perfect rest and all the air I could get." Yet he denies her request for a room on the first floor with access to the air outside, and confines her instead to the attic, where she can neither sleep nor rest. Later, when she asks to have the attic wallpaper changed, he "took me in his arms and called me a blessed little goose, and said he would go down to the cellar, if I wished, and have it whitewashed into the bargain." Yet while he may be willing to whitewash the cellar, he won't change the attic because "I don't care to renovate the house for a three months' rental."

For a three months' confinement, though, John has been willing to rearrange the furniture so as to make her prison ugly: "The furniture in this room is no worse than inharmonious, however, for we had to bring it all from downstairs." Though the narrator is under steady pressure to validate the fiction of John's concern for her—"He is very careful and loving . . . he takes all care from me, and so I feel basely ungrateful not to value it more"—she nevertheless intuits that his "love" is part of her problem: "It is so hard to talk with John about my case, because he is so wise, and because he loves me so." And, in fact her narrative reveals John to be her enemy whose "love" will destroy her.

John's definition of sanity for the narrator, however, includes more than the requirement that she accept his fiction as fact and reject her facts as fancy. In effect, it requires nothing less than she eliminate from herself the subjectivity capable of generating an alternate reality from his. Thus, "John says that the very worst thing I can do is think about my condition," and he designs a treatment calculated to pressure the narrator into concluding that her self not him is the enemy, and calculated also to force her to give her self up. She is denied activity, work, conversation, society, even the opportunity to observe the activity of others. She is to receive no stimulus that might lead to the development of subjectivity. Indeed, one might argue that the narrator overinterprets the wallpaper, the one stimulus in her immediate environment, as a reaction against this sensory deprivation. Nor is the narrator allowed access to her feelings: "I get unreasonably angry with John sometimes. . . . But John says if I feel so I shall neglect proper self control; so I take pains to control myself." By "proper self-control," John means control to the point of eliminating the self that tells a different story from his. If the narrator learns the exercise of this kind of self-control, John need no longer fear her writing.

The more the narrator "rests," the more exhausted she becomes. Her exhaustion testifies to the energy she devotes to repressing her subjectivity and to the resistance she offers to that effort. In this struggle, "dead" paper provides her with her only vital sign. It constitutes her sole link with her embattled self. Yet because she is imprisoned in John's house and text and because his text has infected her mind, she experiences anxiety, contradiction, and ambivalence in the act of writing. Forced to view her work from the perspective of his text, to see it not as *work* but "work"—the denigrating quotation marks reflecting John's point of view—she finds it increasingly difficult to put pen to paper. Blocked from expressing herself *on* paper, she seeks to express herself *through* paper. Literally, she converts the wall*paper* into her text. Initially the narrator identifies the wallpaper with her prison and reads the text as enemy. The wallpaper represents the condition she is not to think about as she is being driven into it. It is ugly, "one of those sprawling flamboyant patterns committing every artistic sin," disorderly, confusing, and full of contradictions. In struggling to organize the paper into a coherent text, the narrator establishes her artistic self and maintains her link with subjectivity and sanity. Yet the narrator at some level identifies with the wallpaper, as well. Just as she recognizes that John's definition of madness is her idea of sanity, so she recognizes in the wallpaper elements of her own resisting self. Sprawling, flamboyant, sinful, irritating, provoking, outrageous, unheard of—not only do these adjectives describe a female self intolerable to the patriarchy, they are also code words that reflect the masculinist response to the perception of female subjectivity per se. In identifying with the wallpaper and in seeing herself in it, the narrator lets herself out; increasingly, her behavior becomes flamboyant and outrageous. Getting out through the text of the wallpaper, she not surprisingly gets in to the subtext within the text that presents the story of a woman trying to get out.

Possessed by the need to impose order on the "impertinence" of row 10 after row of unmatched breadths and to retain, thus, a sense of the self as orderly and ordering, and at the same time identifying with the monstrously disruptive self implicit in the broken necks and bulbous eyes, the narrator continues to elaborate and revise her text. Her descriptions of the wallpaper become increasingly detailed and increasingly feminine, reflecting the intuition that her disintegration derives from the "condition" of being female: "Looked at in one way each breadth stands alone, the bloated curves and flourishes—a kind of 'debased Romanesque' with *delirium tremens*—go waddling up and down in isolated columns of fatuity." Yet the "delirium tremens" of "isolated columns of fatuity" can serve as a metaphor for the patterns conventionally assigned to women's lives and for the "sanity" conventionally prescribed for women. In the "pointless pattern," the narrator senses the patriarchal point. Thus, the narrator concentrates on her subtext, "a thing nobody seems to notice but myself," on the pattern behind the pattern, the woman who wants out.

At the end of "The Yellow Wallpaper," we witness a war between texts. The patriarchal text is a formidable foe; it has an enormous capacity for maintaining itself: "there are always new shoots on the fungus"; and its influence is pervasive: "I find it hovering in the dining-room, skulking in the parlor, hiding the hall, lying in wait for me on the stairs. It gets into my hair. . . . I thought seriously of burning the house—to reach the smell." Its repressive power is equally large: "But nobody could climb through that pattern—it strangles so." Nevertheless, the narrator is sure that her woman "gets out in the daytime." And she is prepared to help her: "I pulled and she shook, I shook and she pulled, and before morning we had peeled off yards of that paper."

Despite the narrator's final claim that she has, like the woman in the paper, "got out at last," she does not in fact escape the patriarchal text. Her choice of literal madness may be as good as or better than the "sanity" prescribed for her by John, but in going mad she fulfills his script and becomes a character in his text. Still, going mad gives the narrator temporary sanity. It enables her to articulate her perception of reality and, in particular, to cut through the fiction of John's love: "He asked me all sorts of questions, too, and pretended to be very loving and kind. As if I couldn't see through him!" It also enables her to contact her feelings, the heart of the subjectivity that John seeks to eliminate. She no longer needs to project her rage onto the imaginary children who occupied her prison before her, gouging the floor, ripping the paper, gnawing the bedstead, for she is now herself "angry enough to do something desperate." Angry, she is energized; she has gotten through to and found her work. If the effort to be sane has made her sick, her madness makes her feel "ever so much better."

This relief, however, is only temporary, for the narrator's solution finally validates John's fiction. In his text, female madness results from work that engages the mind and will; from the recognition and expression of feelings, and particularly of anger; in a word, from the existence of a subjectivity capable of generating a different version of reality from his own. And, indeed, the onset of the narrator's literal madness coincides precisely with her expression of these behaviors. More insidious still, through her madness the narrator does not simply become the character John already imagines her to be as part of his definition of feminine nature; she becomes a version of John himself. Mad, the narrator is manipulative, secretive, dishonest; she learns to lie, obscure, and distort. Further, she masters the art of sinister definition; she claims normalcy for herself, labels John "queer," and determines that he needs watching. This desire to duplicate John's text but with the roles reversed determines the narrator's choice of an ending. Wishing to drive John mad, she selects a denouement that will reduce him to a woman seized by a hysterical fainting fit. Temporary success, however, exacts an enormous price, for when John recovers from his faint, he will put her in a prison from which there will be no escape. John has now got his story, the story, embedded in a text like *Jane Eyre,* of the victimized and suffering husband with a mad wife in the attic. John will tell his story, and there will be no alternate text to expose him.

Gilman, however, has exposed John. And in analyzing how men drive women mad through the control of textuality, Gilman has escaped the fate of her narrator and created a text that can help the woman reader to effect a similar escape. The struggle recorded in the text has its analogue in the struggle around and about the text, for nothing less than our sanity and survival is at stake in the issue of what we read.

Note: In conceptualizing this essay, I have been enormously helped by the work of Annette Kolodny, in particular her "A Map for Rereading: Or, Gender and the Interpretation of Literary Texts" and of Jean E. Kennard in "Convention Coverage, or How to Read Your Own Life." In writing, revising, and rewriting, I owe a large debt to the following readers and writers: Judith Barlow, Susan Kress, Margorie Pryse, Joan Schulz, Patsy Schweickart.

MARGE PIERCY (1936–   )

To Be of Use

*Marge Piercy lives near Wellfleet, Cape Cod, in a communal household where
she writes poetry and novels dedicated to exploring themes of economic, racial,
and sexual inequality. Her best known novels include* Small Changes
(1973), Woman on the Edge of Time *(1976), and* Vida *(1979).*

The people I love the best
jump into work head first
without dallying in the shallows
and swim off with sure strokes almost out of sight.
They seem to become natives of that element,   5
the black sleek heads of seals
bouncing like half-submerged balls.

I love people who harness themselves, an ox to a heavy cart,
who pull like water buffalo, with massive patience,
who strain in the mud and the muck to move things forward,   10
who do what has to be done, again and again.

I want to be with people who submerge
in the task, who go into the fields to harvest
and work in a row and pass the bags along,
who stand in the line and haul in their places,   15
who are not parlor generals and field deserters
but move in a common rhythm
when the food must come in or the fire be put out.

The work of the world is common as mud.
Botched, it smears the hands, crumbles to dust.   20
But the thing worth doing well done
has a shape that satisfies, clean and evident.
Greek amphoras for wine or oil,
Hopi vases that held corn, are put in museums
but you know they were made to be used.   25
The pitcher cries for water to carry
and a person for work that is real.

Considerations

1. What kind of work and workers does the speaker say she admires? Consider the extended metaphor in the first stanza in your response.

2. How does the speaker relate her views on art to her views on work? Can creating art be viewed as work—even if the object has no practical use or application? Explain.
3. Does the definition of admired workers apply only to physical laborers? In what way might it apply to those who work with their minds rather than their hands?

P. K. PAGE (1916–   )

Typists

> *After working as a scriptwriter and following the publication of two volumes of poetry, P. K. Page traveled widely through Australia, Brazil, and Mexico. Her published works include* The Sun, the Moon and Other Fictions *(1973),* Poems Selected and New *(1974), and* Evening Dance of the Grey Flies *(1981). "Typists" was first published in 1943.*

They without message, having read
the running words on their machines,
know every letter as a stamp
cutting the stencils of their ears.
Deep in their hands, like pianists,   5
all longing gropes and moves, is trapped
behind the tensile gloves of skin.

Or blind, sit with their faces locked
away from work. Their varied eyes
are stiff as everlasting flowers.   10
While fingers on a different plane

perform the automatic act
as questions grope along the dark
and twisting corridors of brain.

Crowded together typists touch   15
softly as ducks and seem to sense
each other's anguish with the swift
sympathy of the deaf and dumb.

Considerations

1. Speculate on why the speaker describes the typists as being "without message." What are the implications of this phrase?

2. Explicate the image in the final stanza. Does the speaker seem sympathetic toward or critical of typists? Explain.
3. Imagine yourself as someone who has worked as a typist for many years. Write a letter to the poet, P. K. Page, explaining your response to the poem.

RICHARD WILBUR (1921–   )
The Writer

> *Richard Wilbur is noted for writing carefully crafted poetry, often using traditional forms such as sonnets and other formal patterns. He has published many volumes of poetry, and in 1957 he won the National Book Award and the Pulitzer Prize for* Things of This World. *"The Writer" first appeared in* The Mind Reader *(1970).*

In her room at the prow of the house
Where light breaks, and the windows are tossed with linden,
My daughter is writing a story.

I pause in the stairwell, hearing
From her shut door a commotion of typewriter-keys   5
Like a chain hauled over a gunwale.

Young as she is, the stuff
Of her life is a great cargo, and some of it heavy:
I wish her a lucky passage.

But now it is she who pauses,   10
As if to reject my thought and its easy figure.
A stillness greatens, in which

The whole house seems to be thinking,
And then she is at it again with a bunched clamor
Of strokes, and again is silent.   15

I remember the dazed starling
Which was trapped in that very room, two years ago;
How we stole in, lifted a sash

And retreated, not to affright it;
And how for a helpless hour, through the crack of the door,   20
We watched the sleek, wild, dark

And iridescent creature
Batter against the brilliance, drop like a glove
To the hard floor, or the desk-top,

And wait then, humped and bloody,   25
For the wits to try it again; and how our spirits
Rose when, suddenly sure,

It lifted off from a chair-back,
Beating a smooth course for the right window
And clearing the sill of the world.   30

It is always a matter, my darling,
Of life or death, as I had forgotten. I wish
What I wished you before, but harder.

Considerations

1. The subject of the poem is a young girl—probably a child. Do you
   consider a child engaged in writing to be "working"? Explain.
2. Comment on the relationship of the "dazed starling" (described in lines
   16–30) to the speaker's daughter.
3. Speculate on the significance of the final stanza. What is it that is "always
   a matter . . . / Of life or death"? And what is it that the speaker wished
   for his daughter (and now wishes even "harder")?

JUDY GRAHN (1940–   )

Ella, in a square apron, along Highway 80

> *Born and raised in New Mexico, Judy Grahn has worked at many jobs, in-
> cluding meat wrapper, secretary, domestic servant, and waitress. Her best-
> known poems are collected in* The Work of a Common Woman *(1978),
> in which "Ella, in a square apron, along Highway 80" appears.*

She's a copperheaded waitress,
tired and sharp-worded, she hides
her bad brown tooth behind a wicked
smile, and flicks her ass
out of habit, to fend off the pass   5
that passes for affection.
She keeps her mind the way men

keep a knife—keen to strip the game
down to her size. She has a thin spine,
swallows her eggs cold, and tells lies.   10
She slaps a wet rag at the truck drivers
if they should complain. She understands
the necessity for pain, turns away
the smaller tips, out of pride, and
keeps a flask under the counter. Once,   15
she shot a lover who misused her child.
Before she got out of jail, the courts had pounced
and given the child away. Like some isolated lake,
her flat blue eyes take care of their own stark
bottoms. Her hands are nervous, curled, ready   20
to scrape.
The common woman is as common
as a rattlesnake.

Considerations

1. Cite specific images in the poem that relate to the simile in the final two
   lines. What is your response to this comparison? Do you see Ella as
   admirable? Frightening? Comic? Dangerous? Explain.
2. Look for word play in the poem. What words have more than one meaning? How does the word play relate to the central comparison of the
   poem?
3. Describe one scene or incident suggested by the poem as Ella might have
   written about it in her journal.

KRAFT ROMPF (1948–   )

Waiting Table

> Kraft Rompf is a professor of English at Essex Community College in Balti-
> more. He studied writing at the State University of New York at Stony Brook
> and earned a master's degree from the Writing Seminar at Johns Hopkins
> University. "Waiting Table" first appeared in Five Fingers (1981).

To serve, I wait and pluck
the rose, brush crumbs, carry

madly trays of oysters and
Bloody Marys. Swinging through

doors, I hear them: mouths
open, eyes bugging, choking;   5

they beat a white clothed
table for caffeine piping

hot and sweet, sweet sugar.
Oh, I should pour it in   10

their eyes! And set their
tongues afire. How the chef

understands when I order
tartare and shout, "Let them

eat it raw!" Oh I would stuff   15
their noses with garlic

and the house pianist
could play the Hammer March

on their toes. But for a
tip—for a tip, for a tip—   20

I would work so very, very
hard, and so gladly let

them shine into my soul,
and bow to them and laugh

with them and sing. I would   25
gladly give them everything.

Considerations

1. Make a list of as many examples of repetition as you can find in the poem.
   How does the repetition relate to the tone the speaker uses to describe
   his work?
2. What images does the speaker use to describe the restaurant's customers?
   What do these images suggest about the way he sees himself and his work?
3. What is the speaker's primary motive for working? Explain your response
   to the values suggested by this motive.

RANICE HENDERSON CROSBY (1952–   )

Waitresses

> *Shortly after she wrote "Waitresses" (1975), Ranice Henderson Crosby quit her job as a waitress and went to work for the Feminist Press.*

I think they give us uniforms
so we remember who we are
that's what I think.

our faces are
one gigantic grin.   5
I don't think they even notice
when we show our teeth
and raise our hackles.
we're always smiling
and nodding   10
and pleasing.

as for me
my uniform feels like skin.

CHERRÍE MORAGA (1952–   )

The Welder

> *Born in Los Angeles, Cherríe Moraga has published two collections of her own writing,* Loving in the War Years: Lo que nunca paso por sus labios *(1983) and* Giving Up the Ghost *(1986). She teaches Chicano studies at the University of California at Berkeley. Many of her poems examine themes of cultural and personal identity. "The Welder" first appeared in* This Bridge Called My Back: Writings by Radical Women of Color *(1983).*

I am a welder.
Not an alchemist.
I am interested in the blend
of common elements to make
a common thing.   5

No magic here.
Only the heat of my desire to fuse
what I already know
exists. Is possible.

We plead to each other,   10
we all come from the same rock
we all come from the same rock
ignoring the fact that we bend
at different temperatures
that each of us is malleable   15
up to a point.

Yes, fusion *is* possible
but only if things get hot enough—
all else is temporary adhesion,
patching up.   20

It is the intimacy of steel melting
into steel, the fire of our individual
passion to take hold of ourselves
that makes sculpture of our lives,
builds buildings.   25

And I am not talking about skyscrapers,
merely structures that can support us
without fear
of trembling.

For too long a time   30
the heat of my heavy hands,
has been smoldering
in the pockets of other
people's business—
they need oxygen to make fire.   35

I am now
coming up for air.
Yes, I *am*
picking up the torch.

I am the welder.   40
I understand the capacity of heat
to change the shape of things.
I am suited to work
within the realm of sparks
out of control.   45

I am the welder.
I am taking the power
into my own hands.

W. H. AUDEN (1907–1973)

The Unknown Citizen

> *W. H. Auden was born in York, England, and was educated at Oxford University. He then taught at several universities in the United States and became a naturalized citizen in 1946. His collection of poems,* The Age of Anxiety, *a phrase he invented to describe his impression of the 1930s, won the Pulitzer Prize in 1948. "The Unknown Citizen" appeared in* W. H. Auden, Collected Poems *in 1940.*

(To JS/07/M/378
This Marble Monument Is Erected by the State)

He was found by the Bureau of Statistics to be
One against whom there was no official complaint,
And all the reports on his conduct agree
That, in the modern sense of an old-fashioned word, he was a saint,
For in everything he did he served the Greater Community.   5
Except for the War till the day he retired
He worked in a factory and never got fired
But satisfied his employers, Fudge Motors Inc.
Yet he wasn't a scab or odd in his views,
For his Union reports that he paid his dues,   10
(Our report on his Union shows it was sound)
And our Social Psychology workers found
That he was popular with his mates and liked a drink.
The Press are convinced that he bought a paper every day
And that his reactions to advertisements were normal in every way.   15
Policies taken out in his name prove that he was fully insured,
And his Health-card shows he was once in hospital but left it cured.
Both Producers Research and High-Grade Living declare
He was fully sensible to the advantages of the Installment Plan
And had everything necessary to the Modern Man,   20
A phonograph, a radio, a car and a frigidaire.
Our researchers into Public Opinion are content
That he held the proper opinions for the time of year;
When there was peace, he was for peace; when there was war, he went.
He was married and added five children to the population,   25
Which our Eugenist° says was the right number for a parent of his
    generation.

---

26 *Eugenist:* A person who studies the improvement of a species through the control of hereditary factors.

And our teachers report that he never interfered with their education.
Was he free? Was he happy? The question is absurd:
Had anything been wrong, we should certainly have heard.

ANA CASTILLO

Napa, California

Ana Castillo was born in Chicago. Her work has been published in many journals and, especially, in bilingual poetry magazines such as Maize *and* Revista Chicano-Riqueña, *in which "Napa, California" first appeared in 1976.*

Dedicado al Sr. Chávez, Sept. 1975°

We pick
    the bittersweet grapes
    at harvest
    one
      by   5
        one
    with leather worn hands
As they pick
    at our dignity
    and wipe our pride   10
    away
    like the sweat we wipe
    from our sun beaten brows
    at mid day
In fields   15
    so vast
    that our youth seems
    to pass before us
    and we have grown
    very   20
      very
        old
          by dark . . .

Sr. Chávez: Cesar Chávez, organizer of migrant worker groups and leader of boycotts and strikes for the rights of migrant workers.

(bueno pues ¿qué vamos hacer, Ambrosio?
bueno pues, ¡seguirle, compadre, seguirle!   25
¡Ay, Mamá!
Sí pues ¿qué vamos hacer, compadre?
¡Seguirle, Ambrosio, seguirle!)°

We pick
      with a desire   30
      that only survival
      inspires
While the end
      of each day only brings
      a tired night   35
      that waits for the sun
      and the land
      that in turn waits
      for us . . .

AI (PELORHANKHE OGAWA) (1947–   )

The Country Midwife: A Day

> Ai describes her heritage as follows: "My father was Japanese and my
> mother is black, Choctaw Indian, and Irish with some German coming
> from somewhere." Ai teaches at Wayne State University, and her poems have
> appeared in many journals, including Antaeus, Choice, and American
> Poetry Review. "A Country Midwife" first appeared in her collection
> Cruelty (1973).

I bend over the woman.
This is the third time between abortions.
I dip a towel into a bucket of hot water
and catch the first bit of blood,
as the blue-pink dome of a head breaks through.   5
A scraggy, red child comes out of her into my hands
like warehouse ice sliding down the chute.

24–28 (bueno . . . seguirle!):
So then, what are we going to do, Ambrosio?
So then, follow him, my good friend, follow him!
O, Mama!
If so, what are we going to do, good friend?
Follow him, Ambrosio, follow him!

It's done, the stink of birth, Old Grizzly
rears up on his hind legs in front of me
and I want to go outside,   10
but the air smells the same there too.
The woman's left eye twitches
and beneath her, a stain as orange as sunrise
spreads over the sheet.
I lift my short, blunt fingers to my face   15
and I let her bleed, Lord, I let her bleed.

SUSAN GLASPELL (1882–1948)
Trifles

*Born in Davenport, Iowa, Susan Glaspell was the daughter of an Irish immi-
grant mother; her father was a feed dealer. Following her graduation from
Drake University, she worked as a reporter and began to publish short stories
and novels. In 1911, she moved to New York City, where she met and
married George Cram Cook, who, ironically, also came from Davenport. She
worked in collaboration with her husband: Glaspell wrote plays, and her husband directed them. During the summer, they resided on Cape Cod, where
they helped to found the Playwrights' Theater and devoted their time to the
Provincetown Players, a theatrical group that performed Glaspell's plays as well
as those by other renowned playwrights, including Eugene O'Neill and Edna
St. Vincent Millay. In 1931, Glaspell won the Pulitzer Prize for drama for
Alison's House, a dramatization of the life of a poet, a character who was
thought to be based on Emily Dickinson. Trifles was published in 1916,
three years before women in the United States were granted the right to vote.*

Characters
GEORGE HENDERSON, *county attorney*
HENRY PETERS, *sheriff*
LEWIS HALE, *a neighboring farmer*
MRS. PETERS
MRS. HALE

Scene *The kitchen in the now abandoned farmhouse of John Wright, a gloomy
kitchen, and left without having been put in order—unwashed pans under the sink,
a loaf of bread outside the breadbox, a dish towel on the table—other signs of
incompleted work. At the rear the outer door opens and the* SHERIFF *comes in
followed by the* COUNTY ATTORNEY *and* HALE. *The* SHERIFF *and*
HALE *are men in middle life, the* COUNTY ATTORNEY *is a young man; all
are much bundled up and go at once to the stove. They are followed by two women—
the* SHERIFF's WIFE *first; she is a slight wiry woman, a thin nervous face.* MRS.
HALE *is larger and would ordinarily be called more comfortable looking, but she is
disturbed now and looks fearfully about as she enters. The women have come in slowly,
and stand close together near the door.*

COUNTY ATTORNEY *(rubbing his hands)*: This feels good. Come up to
the fire, ladies.
MRS. PETERS *(after taking a step forward)*: I'm not—cold.
SHERIFF *(unbuttoning his overcoat and stepping away from the stove as if to mark
the beginning of official business)*: Now, Mr. Hale, before we move things
about, you explain to Mr. Henderson just what you saw when you
came here yesterday morning.
COUNTY ATTORNEY: By the way, has anything been moved? Are
things just as you left them yesterday?

SHERIFF *(looking about)*: It's just the same. When it dropped below zero last night I thought I'd better send Frank out this morning to make a fire for us—no use getting pneumonia with a big case on, but I told him not to touch anything except the stove—and you know Frank.

COUNTY ATTORNEY: Somebody should have been left here yesterday.

SHERIFF: Oh—yesterday. When I had to send Frank to Morris Center for that man who went crazy—I want you to know I had my hands full yesterday, I knew you could get back from Omaha by today and as long as I went over everything here myself—

COUNTY ATTORNEY: Well, Mr. Hale, tell just what happened when you came here yesterday morning.

HALE: Harry and I had started to town with a load of potatoes. We came along the road from my place and as I got here I said, "I'm going to see if I can't get John Wright to go in with me on a party telephone." I spoke to Wright about it once before and he put me off, saying folks talked too much anyway, and all he asked was peace and quiet—I guess you know about how much he talked himself; but I thought maybe if I went to the house and talked about it before his wife, though I said to Harry that I didn't know as what his wife wanted made such differ-ence to John—

COUNTY ATTORNEY: Let's talk about that later, Mr. Hale. I do want to talk about that, but tell now just what happened when you got to the house.

HALE: I didn't hear or see anything; I knocked at the door, and still it was all quiet inside. I knew they must be up, it was past eight o'clock. So I knocked again, and I thought I heard somebody say, "Come in." I wasn't sure, I'm not sure yet, but I opened the door—this door *(indi-cating the door by which the two women are still standing)* and there in that rocker—*(pointing to it)* sat Mrs. Wright.

(They all look at the rocker.)

COUNTY ATTORNEY: What—was she doing?

HALE: She was rockin' back and forth. She had her apron in her hand and was kind of—pleating it.

COUNTY ATTORNEY: And how did she—look?

HALE: Well, she looked queer.

COUNTY ATTORNEY: How do you mean—queer?

HALE: Well, as if she didn't know what she was going to do next. And kind of done up.

COUNTY ATTORNEY: How did she seem to feel about your coming?

HALE: Why, I don't think she minded—one way or other. She didn't pay much attention. I said, "How do, Mrs. Wright, it's cold, ain't it?" And she said, "Is it?"—and went on kind of pleating at her apron. Well, I was surprised; she didn't ask me to come up to the stove, or to set down, but just sat there, not even looking at me, so I said, "I want to see John." And then she—laughed. I guess you would call it a laugh. I thought of Harry and the team outside, so I said a little sharp: "Can't I see John?" "No," she says, kind o' dull like. "Ain't he home?" says I. "Yes," says she, "he's home." "Then why can't I see him?" I asked her, out of patience. "'Cause he's dead," says she. "*Dead?*" says I. She just nodded her head, not getting a bit excited, but rockin' back and forth. "Why—where is he?" says I, not knowing what to say. She just pointed upstairs—like that *(himself pointing to the room above)*. I got up, with the idea of going up there. I walked from there to here—then I says, "Why, what did he die of?" "He died of a rope around his neck," says she, and just went on pleatin' at her apron. Well, I went out and called Harry. I thought I might—need help. We went upstairs and there he was lyin'—

COUNTY ATTORNEY: I think I'd rather have you go into that upstairs, where you can point it all out. Just go on now with the rest of the story.

HALE: Well, my first thought was to get that rope off. It looked . . . *(stops, his face twitches)* . . . but Harry, he went up to him, and he said, "No, he's dead all right, and we'd better not touch anything." So we went back down stairs. She was still sitting that same way. "Has anybody been notified?" I asked. "No," says she, unconcerned. "Who did this, Mrs. Wright?" said Harry. He said it businesslike—and she stopped pleatin' of her apron. "I don't know," she says. "You don't *know?*" says Harry. "No," says she. "Weren't you sleepin' in the bed with him?" says Harry. "Yes," says she, "but I was on the inside." "Somebody slipped a rope around his neck and strangled him and you didn't wake up?" says Harry. "I didn't wake up," she said after him. We must 'a looked as if we didn't see how that could be, for after a minute she said, "I sleep sound." Harry was going to ask her more questions but I said maybe we ought to let her tell her story first to the coroner, or the sheriff, so Harry went fast as he could to Rivers' place, where there's a telephone.

COUNTY ATTORNEY: And what did Mrs. Wright do when she knew that you had gone for the coroner?

HALE: She moved from that chair to this one over here *(pointing to a small chair in the corner)* and just sat there with her hands held together and looking down. I got a feeling that I ought to make some conversation, so I said I had come in to see if John wanted to put in a telephone, and at that she started to laugh, and then she stopped and looked at me— scared. *(The* COUNTY ATTORNEY, *who has had his notebook out, makes a note.)* I dunno, maybe it wasn't scared. I wouldn't like to say it was. Soon Harry got back, and then Dr. Lloyd came, and you, Mr. Peters, and so I guess that's all I know that you don't.

COUNTY ATTORNEY *(looking around)*: I guess we'll go upstairs first— and then out to the barn and around there. *(To the* SHERIFF.*)* You're convinced that there was nothing important here—nothing that would point to any motive.

SHERIFF: Nothing here but kitchen things.

(The COUNTY ATTORNEY, after again looking around the kitchen, opens the door of a cupboard closet. He gets up on a chair and looks on a shelf. Pulls his hand away, sticky.)

COUNTY ATTORNEY: Here's a nice mess.

(The women draw nearer.)

MRS. PETERS *(to the other woman)*: Oh, her fruit; it did freeze. *(To the COUNTY ATTORNEY.)* She worried about that when it turned so cold. She said the fire'd go out and her jars would break.

SHERIFF: Well, can you beat the women! Held for murder and worryin' about her preserves.

COUNTY ATTORNEY: I guess before we're through she may have something more serious than preserves to worry about.

HALE: Well, women are used to worrying over trifles.

(The two women move a little closer together.)

COUNTY ATTORNEY *(with the gallantry of a young politician)*: And yet, for all their worries, what would we do without the ladies? *(The women do not unbend. He goes to the sink, takes a dipperful of water from the pail and pouring it into a basin, washes his hands. Starts to wipe them on the roller towel, turns it for a cleaner place.)* Dirty towels! *(Kicks his foot against the pans under the sink.)* Not much of a housekeeper, would you say ladies?

MRS. HALE *(stiffly)*: There's a great deal of work to be done on a farm.

COUNTY ATTORNEY: To be sure. And yet *(with a little bow to her)* I know there are some Dickson county farmhouses which do not have such roller towels.

(He gives it a pull to expose its full length again.)

MRS. HALE: Those towels get dirty awful quick. Men's hands aren't always as clean as they might be.

COUNTY ATTORNEY: Ah, loyal to your sex, I see. But you and Mrs. Wright were neighbors. I suppose you were friends, too.

MRS. HALE *(shaking her head)*: I've not seen much of her of late years. I've not been in this house—it's more than a year.

COUNTY ATTORNEY: And why was that? You didn't like her?

MRS. HALE: I liked her all well enough. Farmers' wives have their hands full, Mr. Henderson. And then—

COUNTY ATTORNEY: Yes—?

MRS. HALE *(looking about)*: It never seemed a very cheerful place.

COUNTY ATTORNEY: No—it's not cheerful. I shouldn't say she had the homemaking instinct.

MRS. HALE: Well, I don't know as Wright had, either.

COUNTY ATTORNEY: You mean that they didn't get on very well?

MRS. HALE: No, I don't mean anything. But I don't think a place'd be any cheerfuller for John Wright's being in it.

COUNTY ATTORNEY: I'd like to talk more of that a little later. I want to get the lay of things upstairs now.

(He goes to the left, where three steps lead to a stair door.)

SHERIFF: I suppose anything Mrs. Peters does'll be all right. She was to take in some clothes for her, you know, and a few little things. We left in such a hurry yesterday.

COUNTY ATTORNEY: Yes, but I would like to see what you take, Mrs. Peters, and keep an eye out for anything that might be of use to us.

MRS. PETERS: Yes, Mr. Henderson.

(The women listen to the men's steps on the stairs, then look about the kitchen.)

MRS. HALE: I'd hate to have men coming into my kitchen, snooping around and criticising.

(She arranges the pans under sink which the COUNTY ATTORNEY had shoved out of place.)

MRS. PETERS: Of course it's no more than their duty.

MRS. HALE: Duty's all right, but I guess that deputy sheriff that came out to make the fire might have got a little of this on. *(Gives the roller towel a pull.)* Wish I'd thought of that sooner. Seems mean to talk about her for not having things slicked up when she had to come away in such a hurry.

MRS. PETERS *(who has gone to a small table in the left rear corner of the room, and lifted one end of a towel that covers a pan)*: She had bread set.

(Stands still.)

MRS. HALE *(Eyes fixed on a loaf of bread beside the breadbox, which is on a low shelf at the other side of the room. Moves slowly toward it.)*: She was going to put this in there. *(Picks up loaf, then abruptly drops it. In a manner of returning to familiar things.)* It's a shame about her fruit. I wonder if it's all gone. *(Gets up on the chair and looks.)* I think there's some here that's all right, Mrs. Peters. Yes—here; *(holding it toward the window)* this is cherries, too. *(Looking again.)* I declare I believe that's the only one. *(Gets down, bottle in her hand. Goes to the sink and wipes it off on the outside.)* She'll feel awful bad after all her hard work in the hot weather. I remember the afternoon I put up my cherries last summer.

(She puts the bottle on the big kitchen table, center of the room. With a sigh, is about to sit down in the rocking-chair. Before she is seated realizes what chair it is; with a slow look at it, steps back. The chair which she has touched rocks back and forth.)

MRS. PETERS: Well, I must get those things from the front room closet. *(She goes to the door at the right, but after looking into the other room, steps back.)* You coming with me, Mrs. Hale? You could help me carry them.

(They go in the other room; reappear, MRS. PETERS carrying a dress and skirt, MRS. HALE following with a pair of shoes.)

MRS. PETERS: My, it's cold in there.

(She puts the clothes on the big table, and hurries to the stove.)

MRS. HALE *(examining her skirt)*: Wright was close. I think maybe that's why she kept so much to herself. She didn't even belong to the Ladies Aid. I suppose she felt she couldn't do her part, and then you don't enjoy things when you feel shabby. She used to wear pretty clothes and be lively, when she was Minnie Foster, one of the town girls singing in the choir. But that—oh, that was thirty years ago. This all you was to take in?

MRS. PETERS: She said she wanted an apron. Funny thing to want, for there isn't much to get you dirty in jail, goodness knows. But I suppose just to make her feel more natural. She said they was in the top drawer in this cupboard. Yes, here. And then her little shawl that always hung behind the door. *(Opens stair door and looks.)* Yes, here it is.

(Quickly shuts door leading upstairs.)

MRS. HALE *(abruptly moving toward her)*: Mrs. Peters?

MRS. PETERS: Yes, Mrs. Hale?

MRS. HALE: Do you think she did it?

MRS. PETERS *(in a frightened voice)*: Oh, I don't know.

MRS. HALE: Well, I don't think she did. Asking for an apron and her little shawl. Worrying about her fruit.

MRS. PETERS *(Starts to speak, glances up, where footsteps are heard in the room above. In a low voice.)*: Mr. Peters says it looks bad for her. Mr. Henderson is awful sarcastic in a speech and he'll make fun of her sayin' she didn't wake up.

MRS. HALE: Well, I guess John Wright didn't wake when they was slipping that rope under his neck.

MRS. PETERS: No, it's strange. It must have been done awful crafty and still. They say it was such a—funny way to kill a man, rigging it all up like that.

MRS. HALE: That's just what Mr. Hale said. There was a gun in the house. He says that's what he can't understand.

MRS. PETERS: Mr. Henderson said coming out that what was needed for the case was a motive; something to show anger, or—sudden feeling.

MRS. HALE *(who is standing by the table)*: Well, I don't see any signs of anger around here. *(She puts her hand on the dish towel which lies on the table, stands looking down at table, one half of which is clean, the other half messy.)*

It's wiped to here. (*Makes a move as if to finish work, then turns and looks at loaf of bread outside the breadbox. Drops towel. In that voice of coming back to familiar things.*) Wonder how they are finding things upstairs. I hope she had it a little more red-up up there. You know, it seems kind of *sneaking.* Locking her up in town and then coming out here and trying to get her own house to turn against her!

MRS. PETERS: But Mrs. Hale, the law is the law.

MRS. HALE: I s'pose 'tis. (*Unbuttoning her coat.*) Better loosen up your things, Mrs. Peters. You won't feel them when you go out.

(MRS. PETERS *takes off her fur tippet, goes to hang it on hook at back of room, stands looking at the under part of the small corner table.*)

MRS. PETERS: She was piecing a quilt.

(*She brings the large sewing basket and they look at the bright pieces.*)

MRS. HALE: It's log cabin pattern. Pretty, isn't it? I wonder if she was goin' to quilt it or just knot it?

(*Footsteps have been heard coming down the stairs. The* SHERIFF *enters followed by* HALE *and the* COUNTY ATTORNEY.)

SHERIFF: They wonder if she was going to quilt it or just knot it!

(*The men laugh; the women look abashed.*)

COUNTY ATTORNEY (*rubbing his hands over the stove*): Frank's fire didn't do much up there, did it? Well, let's go out to the barn and get that cleared up.

(*The men go outside.*)

MRS. HALE (*resentfully*): I don't know as there's anything so strange, our takin' up our time with little things while we're waiting for them to get the evidence. (*She sits down at the big table smoothing out a block with decision.*) I don't see as it's anything to laugh about.

MRS. PETERS (*apologetically*): Of course they've got awful important things on their minds.

(*Pulls up a chair and joins* MRS. HALE *at the table.*)

MRS. HALE (*examining another block*): Mrs. Peters, look at this one. Here, this is the one she was working on, and look at the sewing! All the rest of it has been so nice and even. And look at this! It's all over the place! Why, it looks as if she didn't know what she was about!

(*After she has said this they look at each other, then start to glance back at the door. After an instant* MRS. HALE *has pulled at a knot and ripped the sewing.*)

MRS. PETERS: Oh, what are you doing, Mrs. Hale?

MRS. HALE (*mildly*): Just pulling out a stitch or two that's not sewed very good. (*Threading a needle.*) Bad sewing always made me fidgety.

MRS. PETERS (*nervously*): I don't think we ought to touch things.

MRS. HALE: I'll just finish up this end. (*Suddenly stopping and leaning forward.*) Mrs. Peters?

MRS. PETERS: Yes, Mrs. Hale?

MRS. HALE: What do you suppose she was so nervous about?

MRS. PETERS: Oh—I don't know. I don't know as she was nervous. I sometimes sew awful queer when I'm just tired. (MRS. HALE *starts to say something, looks at* MRS. PETERS, *then goes on sewing.*) Well, I must get these things wrapped up. They may be through sooner than we think. (*Putting apron and other things together.*) I wonder where I can find a piece of paper, and string.

MRS. HALE: In that cupboard, maybe.

MRS. PETERS (*looking in cupboard*): Why, here's a birdcage. (*Holds it up.*) Did she have a bird, Mrs. Hale?

MRS. HALE: Why, I don't know whether she did or not—I've not been here for so long. There was a man around last year selling canaries cheap, but I don't know as she took one; maybe she did. She used to sing real pretty herself.

MRS. PETERS (*glancing around*): Seems funny to think of a bird here. But she must have had one, or why would she have a cage? I wonder what happened to it.

MRS. HALE: I s'pose maybe the cat got it.

MRS. PETERS: No, she didn't have a cat. She's got that feeling some people have about cats—being afraid of them. My cat got in her room and she was real upset and asked me to take it out.

MRS. HALE: My sister Bessie was like that. Queer, ain't it?

MRS. PETERS (*examining the cage*): Why, look at this door. It's broke. One hinge is pulled apart.

MRS. HALE (*looking too*): Looks as if someone must have been rough with it.

MRS. PETERS: Why, yes.

(*She brings the cage forward and puts it on the table.*)

MRS. HALE: I wish if they're going to find any evidence they'd be about it. I don't like this place.

MRS. PETERS: But I'm awful glad you came with me, Mrs. Hale. It would be lonesome for me sitting here alone.

MRS. HALE: It would, wouldn't it? (*Dropping her sewing.*) But I tell you what I do wish, Mrs. Peters. I wish I had come over sometimes when *she* was here. I—(*looking around the room*)—wish I had.

MRS. PETERS: But of course you were awful busy, Mrs. Hale—your house and your children.

MRS. HALE: I could've come. I stayed away because it weren't cheerful—and that's why I ought to have come. I—I've never liked this place.

Maybe because it's down in a hollow and you don't see the road. I dunno what it is but it's a lonesome place and always was. I wish I had come over to see Minnie Foster sometimes. I can see now—

(Shakes her head.)

MRS. PETERS: Well, you mustn't reproach yourself, Mrs. Hale. Somehow we just don't see how it is with other folks until—something comes up.

MRS. HALE: Not having children makes less work—but it makes a quiet house, and Wright out to work all day, and no company when he did come in. Did you know John Wright, Mrs. Peters?

MRS. PETERS: Not to know him; I've seen him in town. They say he was a good man.

MRS. HALE: Yes—good; he didn't drink, and kept his word as well as most, I guess, and paid his debts. But he was a hard man, Mrs. Peters. Just to pass the time of day with him—*(Shivers.)* Like a raw wind that gets to the bone. *(Pauses, her eye falling on the cage.)* I should think she would 'a wanted a bird. But what do you suppose went with it?

MRS. PETERS: I don't know, unless it got sick and died.

(She reaches over and swings the broken door, swings it again. Both women watch it.)

MRS. HALE: You weren't raised round here, were you? *(MRS. PETERS shakes her head.)* You didn't know—her?

MRS. PETERS: Not till they brought her yesterday.

MRS. HALE: She—come to think of it, she was kind of like a bird herself— real sweet and pretty, but kind of timid and—fluttery. How—she— did—change. *(Silence; then as if struck by a happy thought and relieved to get back to everyday things.)* Tell you what, Mrs. Peters, why don't you take the quilt in with you? It might take up her mind.

MRS. PETERS: Why, I think that's a real nice idea, Mrs. Hale. There couldn't possibly be any objection to it, could there? Now, just what would I take? I wonder if her patches are in here—and her things.

(They look in the sewing basket.)

MRS. HALE: Here's some red. I expect this has got sewing things in it. *(Brings out a fancy box.)* What a pretty box. Looks like something somebody would give you. Maybe her scissors are in here. *(Opens box. Suddenly puts her hand to her nose.)* Why—*(MRS. PETERS bends nearer, then turns her face away.)* There's something wrapped up in this piece of silk.

MRS. PETERS: Why, this isn't her scissors.

MRS. HALE *(lifting the silk)*: Oh, Mrs. Peters—it's—

(MRS. PETERS bends closer.)

MRS. PETERS: It's the bird.

MRS. HALE (jumping up): But, Mrs. Peters—look at it! Its neck! Look at its neck! It's all—other side to.

MRS. PETERS: Somebody—wrung—its—neck.

(Their eyes meet. A look of growing comprehension, of horror. Steps are heard outside. MRS. HALE slips box under quilt pieces, and sinks into her chair. Enter SHERIFF and COUNTY ATTORNEY. MRS. PETERS rises.)

COUNTY ATTORNEY (as one turning from serious things to little pleasantries): Well, ladies, have you decided whether she was going to quilt it or knot it?

MRS. PETERS: We think she was going to—knot it.

COUNTY ATTORNEY: Well, that's interesting, I'm sure. (Seeing the bird-cage.) Has the bird flown?

MRS. HALE (putting more quilt pieces over the box): We think the—cat got it.

COUNTY ATTORNEY (preoccupied): Is there a cat?

(MRS. HALE glances in a quick covert way at MRS. PETERS.)

MRS. PETERS: Well, not now. They're superstitious, you know. They leave.

COUNTY ATTORNEY (to SHERIFF PETERS, continuing an interrupted conversation): No sign at all of anyone having come from the outside. Their own rope. Now let's go up again and go over it piece by piece. (They start upstairs.) It would have to have been someone who knew just the—

(MRS. PETERS sits down. The two women sit there not looking at one another, but as if peering into something and at the same time holding back. When they talk now it is in the manner of feeling their way over strange ground, as if afraid of what they are saying, but as if they can not help saying it.)

MRS. HALE: She liked the bird. She was going to bury it in that pretty box.

MRS. PETERS (in a whisper): When I was a girl—my kitten—there was a boy took a hatchet, and before my eyes—and before I could get there— (Covers her face an instant.) If they hadn't held me back I would have— (catches herself, looks upstairs where steps are heard, falters weakly)—hurt him.

MRS. HALE (with a slow look around her): I wonder how it would seem never to have had any children around. (Pause.) No, Wright wouldn't like the bird—a thing that sang. She used to sing. He killed that, too.

MRS. PETERS (moving uneasily): We don't know who killed the bird.

MRS. HALE: I knew John Wright.

MRS. PETERS: It was an awful thing was done in this house that night, Mrs. Hale. Killing a man while he slept, slipping a rope around his neck that choked the life out of him.

MRS. HALE: His neck. Choked the life out of him.

(Her hand goes out and rests on the birdcage.)

MRS. PETERS *(with rising voice)*: We don't know who killed him. We don't know.

MRS. HALE *(her own feeling not interrupted)*: If there'd been years and years of nothing, then a bird to sing to you, it would be awful—still, after the bird was still.

MRS. PETERS *(something within her speaking)*: I know what stillness is. When we homesteaded in Dakota, and my first baby died—after he was two years old, and me with no other then—

MRS. HALE *(moving)*: How soon do you suppose they'll be through, looking for the evidence?

MRS. PETERS: I know what stillness is. *(Pulling herself back.)* The law has got to punish crime, Mrs. Hale.

MRS. HALE *(not as if answering that)*: I wish you'd seen Minnie Foster when she wore a white dress with blue ribbons and stood up there in the choir and sang. *(A look around the room.)* Oh, I *wish* I'd come over here once in a while! That was a crime! That was a crime! Who's going to punish that?

MRS. PETERS *(looking upstairs)*: We mustn't—take on.

MRS. HALE: I might have known she needed help! I know how things can be—for women. I tell you, it's queer, Mrs. Peters. We live close together and we live far apart. We all go through the same things—it's all just a different kind of the same thing. *(Brushes her eyes; noticing the bottle of fruit, reaches out for it.)* If I was you I wouldn't tell her her fruit was gone. Tell her it *ain't*. Tell her it's all right. Take this in to prove it to her. She—she may never know whether it was broke or not.

MRS. PETERS *(Takes the bottle, looks about for something to wrap it in; takes petticoat from the clothes brought from the other room, very nervously begins winding this around the bottle. In a false voice.)*: My, it's a good thing the men couldn't hear us. Wouldn't they just laugh! Getting all stirred up over a little thing like a—dead canary. As if that could have anything to do with—with—wouldn't they *laugh!*

(The men are heard coming down stairs.)

MRS. HALE *(under her breath)*: Maybe they would—maybe they wouldn't.

COUNTY ATTORNEY: No, Peters, it's all perfectly clear except a reason for doing it. But you know juries when it comes to women. If there was some definite thing. Something to show—something to make a story about—a thing that would connect up with this strange way of doing it—

(The women's eyes meet for an instant. Enter HALE from outer door.)

HALE: Well, I've got the team around. Pretty cold out there.

COUNTY ATTORNEY: I'm going to stay here a while by myself. *(To the SHERIFF.)* You can send Frank out for me, can't you? I want to go over everything. I'm not satisfied that we can't do better.

SHERIFF: Do you want to see what Mrs. Peters is going to take in?

(The COUNTY ATTORNEY *goes to the table, picks up the apron, laughs.)*

COUNTY ATTORNEY: Oh, I guess they're not very dangerous things the ladies have picked out. *(Moves a few things about, disturbing the quilt pieces which cover the box. Steps back.)* No, Mrs. Peters doesn't need supervising. For that matter, a sheriff's wife is married to the law. Ever think of it that way, Mrs. Peters?

MRS. PETERS: Not—just that way.

SHERIFF *(chuckling)*: Married to the law. *(Moves toward the other room.)* I just want you to come in here a minute, George. We ought to take a look at these windows.

COUNTY ATTORNEY *(scoffingly)*: Oh, windows!

SHERIFF: We'll be right out, Mr. Hale.

*(*HALE *goes outside. The* SHERIFF *follows the* COUNTY ATTORNEY *into the other room. Then* MRS. HALE *rises, hands tight together, looking intensely at* MRS. PETERS, *whose eyes make a slow turn, finally meeting* MRS. HALE*'s. A moment* MRS. HALE *holds her, then her own eyes point the way to where the box is concealed. Suddenly* MRS. PETERS *throws back quilt pieces and tries to put the box in the bag she is wearing. It is too big. She opens box, starts to take bird out, cannot touch it, goes to pieces, stands there helpless. Sound of a knob turning in the other room.* MRS. HALE *snatches the box and puts it in the pocket of her big coat. Enter* COUNTY ATTORNEY *and* SHERIFF.*)*

COUNTY ATTORNEY *(facetiously)*: Well, Henry, at least we found out that she was not going to quilt it. She was going to—what is it you call it, ladies?

MRS. HALE *(her hand against her pocket)*: We call it—knot it, Mr. Henderson.

Considerations

1. Make a chronological list of the events that happened (or that you speculate might have happened) both before and during the action of the play. Begin with Mr. and Mrs. Wright sitting in their living room. How would the play be changed if Glaspell had chosen to show us the action that takes place before the investigation on which the drama focuses?

2. What work do the men in the play do? What work do the women do? Explain how the men and women view and value their own work and how they view and value the work of the opposite sex.

3. Susan Glaspell wrote a short story describing the same events and characters depicted in *Trifles*. The story is titled "A Jury of Her Peers." Discuss the significance of each title and explain which you prefer.

4. What is your response to the decision made by Mrs. Peters and Mrs. Hale to hide the dead bird from the men? What are their motives? What values do their actions imply?

5. Comment on the final line of the play. Suggest several possible meanings for Mrs. Hale's response to the county attorney's question.

VIRGINIA WOOLF (1882–1941)

Professions for Women

> *Born in England, Virginia Woolf was the daughter of Leslie Stephen, a well-known scholar. She was educated primarily at home and attributed her love of reading to the early and complete access she was given to her father's library. With her husband, Leonard Woolf, she founded the Hogarth Press and became known as a member of the Bloomsbury group of intellectuals, which included economist John Maynard Keynes, biographer Lytton Strachey, novelist E. M. Forster, and art historian Clive Bell. Although she was a central figure in London literary life, Woolf often saw herself as isolated from the mainstream because she was a woman. Her 1929 book* A Room of One's Own *documents her desire for women to take their rightful place in literary history. Woolf is best known for her experimental, modernist novels, including* Mrs. Dalloway *(1925) and* To the Lighthouse *(1927). "Professions for Women" is a paper that Woolf read to the Women's Service League, an organization for professional women in London.*

When your secretary invited me to come here, she told me that your Society is concerned with the employment of women and she suggested that I might tell you something about my own professional experiences. It is true I am a woman; it is true I am employed, but what professional experiences have I had? It is difficult to say. My profession is literature; and in that profession there are fewer experiences for women than in any other, with the exception of the stage—fewer, I mean, that are peculiar to women. For the road was cut many years ago—by Fanny Burney, by Aphra Behn, by Harriet Martineau, by Jane Austen, by George Eliot°—many famous women, and many more unknown and forgotten, have been before me, making the path smooth, and regulating my steps. Thus, when I came to write, there were very few material obstacles in my way. Writing was a reputable and harmless occupation. The family peace was not broken by the scratching of a pen. No demand was made upon the family purse. For ten and sixpence one can buy paper enough to write all the plays of Shakespeare—if one has a mind that way. Pianos and models, Paris, Vienna and Berlin, masters and mistresses, are not needed by a writer. The cheapness of writing paper is, of course, the reason why women have succeeded as writers before they have succeeded in the other professions.

But to tell you my story—it is a simple one. You have only got to figure to yourselves a girl in a bedroom with a pen in her hand. She had only to move that pen from left to right—from ten o'clock to one. Then it

---

Fanny Burney, Aphra Behn, Harriet Martineau, Jane Austen, and George Eliot (the pen name of Mary Ann Evans): All eighteenth- or nineteenth-century authors. These women often faced disapproval, ridicule, and lack of acceptance because they chose to write for publication.

occurred to her to do what is simple and cheap enough after all—to slip a few of those pages into an envelope, fix a penny stamp in the corner, and drop the envelope in the red box at the corner. It was thus that I became a journalist; and my effort was rewarded on the first day of the following month—a very glorious day it was for me—by a letter from an editor containing a check for one pound ten shillings and sixpence. But to show you how little I deserve to be called a professional woman, how little I know of the struggles and difficulties of such lives, I have to admit that instead of spending that sum upon bread and butter, rent, shoes and stockings, or butcher's bills, I went out and bought a cat—a beautiful cat, a Persian cat, which very soon involved me in bitter disputes with my neighbors.

What could be easier than to write articles and to buy Persian cats with the profits? But wait a moment. Articles have to be about something. Mine, I seem to remember, was about a novel by a famous man. And while I was writing this review, I discovered that if I were going to review books I should need to do battle with a certain phantom. And the phantom was a woman, and when I came to know her better I called her after the heroine of a famous poem, The Angel in the House. It was she who used to come between me and my paper when I was writing reviews. It was she who bothered me and wasted my time and so tormented me that at last I killed her. You who come of a younger and happier generation may not have heard of her—you may not know what I mean by the Angel in the House. I will describe her as shortly as I can. She was intensely sympathetic. She was immensely charming. She was utterly unselfish. She excelled in the difficult arts of family life. She sacrificed herself daily. If there was chicken, she took the leg; if there was a draught she sat in it—in short she was so constituted that she never had a mind or a wish of her own, but preferred to sympathize always with the minds and wishes of others. Above all—I need not say it— she was pure. Her purity was supposed to be her chief beauty—her blushes, her great grace. In those days—the last of Queen Victoria—every house had its Angel. And when I came to write I encountered her with the very first words. The shadow of her wings fell on my page; I heard the rustling of her skirts in the room. Directly, that is to say, I took my pen in hand to review that novel by a famous man, she slipped behind me and whispered: "My dear, you are a young woman. You are writing about a book that has been written by a man. Be sympathetic; be tender; flatter; deceive; use all the arts and wiles of our sex. Never let anybody guess that you have a mind of your own. Above all, be pure." And she made as if to guide my pen. I now record the one act for which I take some credit to myself, though the credit rightly belongs to some excellent ancestors of mine who left me a certain sum of money—shall we say five hundred pounds a year?—so that it was not necessary for me to depend solely on charm for my living. I turned upon her and caught her by the throat. I did my best to kill her. My excuse, if I were to be had up in a court of law, would be that I acted in self-defense. Had I not killed her she would have killed me. She would have plucked the heart out of my writing. For, as I found, directly I put pen to paper, you cannot review even a novel without having a mind of your own, without expressing what you think to be the truth about human relations, morality, sex. And all these questions, according to the Angel in the House, cannot be dealt with freely and openly by women; they must charm, they must conciliate, they must—to put it bluntly—tell lies if they are to succeed. Thus, whenever I felt the shadow of her wing or the radiance of her halo upon my page, I took up the inkpot and flung it at her. She died hard. Her fictitious nature was of great assistance to her. It is far harder to kill a phantom than a reality. She was always creeping back when I thought I had despatched her. Though I flatter myself that I killed her in the end, the struggle was severe; it took much time that I had better have spent upon learning Greek grammar, or in roaming the world in search of adventures. But it was a real experience; it was an experience that was bound to befall all women writers at that time: Killing the Angel in the House was part of the occupation of a woman writer.

But to continue my story. The Angel was dead; what then remained? You may say that what remained was a simple and common object—a young woman in a bedroom with an inkpot. In other words, now that she had rid herself of falsehood, that young woman had only to be herself. Ah, but what is "herself"? I mean, what is a woman? I assure you, I do not know. I do not believe that you know. I do not believe that anybody can know until she has expressed herself in all the arts and professions open to human skill. That indeed is one of the reasons why I have come here—out of respect for you, who are in process of showing us by your experiments what a woman is, who are in process of providing us, by your failures and successes, with that extremely important piece of information.

But to continue the story of my professional experiences. I made one pound ten and six by my first review; and I bought a Persian cat with the proceeds. Then I grew ambitious. A Persian cat is all very well, I said; but a Persian cat is not enough. I must have a motor car. And it was thus that I became a novelist—for it is a very strange thing that people will give you a motor car if you will tell them a story. It is a still stranger thing that there is nothing so delightful in the world as telling stories. It is far pleasanter than writing reviews of famous novels. And yet, if I am to obey your secretary and tell you my professional experiences as a novelist, I must tell you about a very strange experience that befell me as a novelist. And to understand it you must try first to imagine a novelist's state of mind. I hope I am not giving away professional secrets if I say that a novelist's chief desire is to be as unconscious as possible. He has to induce in himself a state of perpetual lethargy. He wants life to proceed with the utmost quiet and regularity. He wants to see the same faces, to read the same books, to do the same things day after day, month after month, while he is writing, so that nothing may break the illusion in which he is living—so that nothing may disturb or disquiet the mysterious nosings about, feelings round, darts, dashes and sudden

5

discoveries of that very shy and illusive spirit, the imagination. I suspect that this state is the same both for men and women. Be that as it may, I want you to imagine me writing a novel in a state of trance. I want you to figure to yourselves a girl sitting with a pen in her hand, which for minutes, and indeed for hours, she never dips into the inkpot. The image that comes to my mind when I think of this girl is the image of a fisherman lying sunk in dreams on the verge of a deep lake with a rod held out over the water. She was letting her imagination sweep unchecked round every rock and cranny of the world that lies submerged in the depths of our unconscious being. Now came the experience, the experience that I believe to be far commoner with women writers than with men. The line raced through the girl's fingers. Her imagination had rushed away. It had sought the pools, the depths, the dark places where the largest fish slumber. And then there was a smash. There was an explosion. There was foam and confusion. The imagination had dashed itself against something hard. The girl was roused from her dream. She was indeed in a state of the most acute and difficult distress. To speak without figure she had thought of something, something about the body, about the passions which it was unfitting for her as a woman to say. Men, her reason told her, would be shocked. The consciousness of what men will say of a woman who speaks the truth about her passions had roused her from her artist's state of unconsciousness. She could write no more. The trance was over. Her imagination could work no longer. This I believe to be a very common experience with women writers—they are impeded by the extreme conventionality of the other sex. For though men sensibly allow themselves great freedom in these respects, I doubt that they realize or can control the extreme severity with which they condemn such freedom in women.

These then were two very genuine experiences of my own. These were two of the adventures of my professional life. The first—killing the Angel in the House—I think I solved. She died. But the second, telling the truth about my own experiences as a body, I do not think I solved. I doubt that any woman has solved it yet. The obstacles against her are still immensely powerful—and yet they are very difficult to define. Outwardly, what is simpler than to write books? Outwardly, what obstacles are there for a woman rather than for a man? Inwardly, I think, the case is very different; she has still many ghosts to fight, many prejudices to overcome. Indeed it will be a long time still, I think, before a women can sit down to write a book without finding a phantom to be slain, a rock to be dashed against. And if this is so in literature, the freest of all professions for women, how is it in the new professions which you are now for the first time entering?

Those are the questions that I should like, had I time, to ask you. And indeed, if I have laid stress upon these professional experiences of mine, it is because I believe that they are, though in different forms, yours also. Even when the path is nominally open—when there is nothing to prevent a woman from being a doctor, a lawyer, a civil servant—there are many phantoms and obstacles, as I believe, looming in her way. To discuss and define them is I think of great value and importance; for thus only can the labor be shared, the difficulties be solved. But besides this, it is necessary also to discuss the ends and the aims for which we are fighting, for which we are doing battle with these formidable obstacles. Those aims cannot be taken for granted; they must be perpetually questioned and examined. The whole position, as I see it—here in this hall surrounded by women practicing for the first time in history I know not how many different professions—is one of extraordinary interest and importance. You have won rooms of your own in the house hitherto exclusively owned by men. You are able, though not without great labor and effort, to pay the rent. You are earning your five hundred pounds a year. But this freedom is only a beginning; the room is your own, but it is still bare. It has to be furnished; it has to be decorated; it has to be shared. How are you going to furnish it, how are you going to decorate it? With whom are you going to share it, and upon what terms? These, I think, are questions of the utmost importance and interest. For the first time in history you are able to ask them; for the first time you are able to decide for yourselves what the answers should be. Willingly would I stay and discuss those questions and answers—but not tonight. My time is up; and I must cease.

Considerations

1. What reasons does Woolf give for finding writing a comfortable profession for a woman to pursue? What do these reasons suggest about the relationship between women, their families, and the world of work?
2. What does Woolf mean when she says that she was hindered in writing reviews of men's writing by "The Angel in the House"? Who or what does the Angel represent?

   Make a list of the Angel's qualities and consider why Woolf believes those qualities to be dangerous to a writer.

   What does Woolf mean when she says she killed the Angel?
3. In paragraph 4, Woolf asks, "What is a woman?" Explain her response to this question and then work on your own definition.

   Try also to answer the question "What is a man?" How is your definition different from your definition of a woman? How do you explain the discrepancies?
4. What problems did Woolf encounter when she moved from writing reviews to writing novels? Explain the metaphor she uses in paragraph 5 to describe this problem.
5. Woolf ends her essay with a series of questions about the rooms women occupy (or will occupy) "in the house hitherto exclusively owned by men." She wrote "Professions for Women" in 1931; how would you answer her questions today, from the perspective of the 1990s?

DOUGLAS HARPER (1948–)
Willie

*During the fall of 1975, Douglas Harper took a position teaching sociology
at the State University of New York at Potsdam. As he was driving in the
countryside outside Potsdam, a small town on the Canadian border, his aging
Saab broke down. This event led to his meeting Willie, a mechanic whom he
later interviewed and wrote about in his book* Working Knowledge *(1987).
Harper has also spent time talking and living with people who spend their
lives hitching rides on America's railroads. His book* Good Company *(1982)
describes their values, hopes, goals, and thought processes.*

A person is many things—mate, parent, worker, entertainer, community
member. Self-consciousness, and sometimes self-deception, integrates the often contradictory demands of different roles. In traditional or preindustrial
societies there are relatively few of these personal role contradictions. Willie's
community, though tied to industrial society, is in this way a great deal like
the traditional world. Work is the well from which the other components of
self are drawn. The single source makes the different roles minor variations
rather than entirely different personae. In the following I study Willie's sense
of himself both in the immediate sphere of his work and in the context of
his community.

Willie finds himself in his work. To study Willie's attitude toward work,
then, is to study his attitudes toward his own being. This is best done in the
family and community contexts in which the work exists.

Willie's children have grown up knowing their father, in large part, by
helping him work. As I have watched Willie showing one of his children
how to do a job, a sequence from *Nanook of the North,* a 1922 documentary
of Eskimo life, has often come to mind. As Nanook teaches his young son
to shoot his miniature bow and arrow at a tiny snow polar bear—patient,
ever attentive, warming his son's hands with his own—the viewer is shown
that the Eskimo experiences the world directly and that the skills needed to
manage it are known by the father and taught to the children. Willie's children recognize his skill and understand its value because they see and participate in the work of the shop and overhear the conversations and stories that
are always going on. Willie's skill is also relevant to their personal worlds—it
is not only their bikes, their motor scooters, and eventually their automobiles
and houses that Willie helps them assemble or maintain. One day I was a bit
startled to find Willie bent over white lace fabric spread on the floor of his
house, making a dress (without a pattern) for the confirmation ceremony of
one of his daughters. The idea that his children know their father through
his work seems simple. But it is unusual in a society where most fathers work
away from home, doing things their children do not really know about and
that are in any case probably irrelevant to the children's own needs or prob-

lems. Willie's authority as a parent, then, is related to his children's recognition of his skills and the frequent relevance of those skills to their own lives.[1]

His relationship with his wife is also strongly rooted in his work. In a number of ways the shop represents the collective work of a family. Pauline often helps with jobs, shares the paperwork or the hassles that go with collecting on bad checks, and feeds people who are in her house because of their business with Willie. Although the work is collective, the division of labor is based on traditional male and female roles. Willie often makes it clear that though many people participate in the work of the shop, he is—at the center—the provider.

Finally, Willie's self-image exists in the context of the community. His status, born in his work world, extends into such varied roles as candidate for the office of highway supervisor, president of his bowling league, organizer of citizens band radio activities, and leader in public hearings over zoning legislation.

Willie's self-image comes, then, from the various human contexts he lives in. It also comes from the self-consciousness that arises from his working experience. This self-recognition has several elements. Overall, Willie's accounts reflect an understanding of the effect good work has upon a person. He typically discounts, with no false modesty, the specialness of his talents, yet he also identifies his work as unique and important to the community. Finally, he recognizes and uses the social power that comes from having knowledge and skill needed by others.

Willie discounts his skill by suggesting that the key to his method is patience and the willingness to do jobs others will not take on. Many mechanics do not accept the jobs Willie does because they are too ill defined, too time consuming, and even, one can say, too difficult. [A] blower repair . . . for example, came to Willie because "nobody else would fix it." Willie discounted the particular difficulties of the job with the statement that all the job required was patience. This is a common theme Willie sometimes plays with. Recently, for example, a new customer brought him a water-pump casing with three bolts broken off even with the surface. Willie began with a frown: "*Oh-oh—cast* and steel—*that's* trouble!" The man told Willie he'd been to a machine shop in town, but they couldn't fix his pump. I envisioned a long process of drilling out the studs, extracting the pieces, and rethreading the holes. Willie clamped the casing in his vise, brought out a small punch he had sharpened on one side, and picked up a tiny ball peen hammer. He carefully turned the broken pieces out of the casing by hammering ever so delicately with the beveled punch on the uneven surface of the broken studs.

[1]The idea that parental authority is traditionally rooted in family work systems, and that it has been largely displaced by industrial capitalism—that is, the creation of wage labor and the subsequent removal of the father from productive activity in the house—is a central theme in modern sociology. In *Middletown* (1924), Robert and Helen Lynd described the effect of these industrial processes one generation after they had taken place.

But when the customer hailed his accomplishment, Willie replied that the other machinist could easily have done the job; he just didn't want to be bothered with such stuff. It may or may not have been true, but in any case it was a characteristic disclaimer.

Willie does, however, understand that his patience is unusual and important to his own working method. "Oh, yes," Willie once replied, "you get stumped. But you've got to be a little calm, a little patient, and figure out *why*."

To succeed at repairs other mechanics either haven't wanted to attempt or could not manage certainly fosters a positive self-image. Part of Willie's satisfaction comes from his capacity to focus on each step of a task as equally important. And part of the satisfaction, one can assume, comes from the simple problem solving in his daily work. Willie put it this way:

> A lot of them that come in here are pretty impatient. If you rush through things, you can't enjoy them. And it's a challenge—no job's the same. If you had a thousand jobs in a year, not two of those thousand jobs would be the same. Even the ones that are supposed to be the same aren't. Things are broken or worn in different ways— they each have their own characteristics.

Although Willie often discounts his skill, he also recognizes its quality. 10 He tells some stories over and over, such as how he established his reputation with the owner of the local Saab dealership by fixing the first Saab transmission he'd ever seen in three hours less than shop time for the job. But usually when Willie tells these stories it is because he cannot believe others could not easily do as well. At times a story tells how he put an unusual material to use, such as when he made a head gasket for a tractor from a sheet of copper ("that was twenty years ago, and that tractor is still running—it's owned by the town of Louisville"), or relates his ability to save his customers money by solving their problems more simply than other mechanics thought possible.

Willie also sees himself as something of a visionary. He patiently explains his designs and their logic to customers and friends. It might be an electrical system, a solar heating design, or a novel approach to a mundane repair. If the listener cannot fully grasp what he is talking about, Willie approaches his subject from several directions until the listener is at least convinced that *Willie* knows what he is talking about. I once asked Willie when he had begun the designing and engineering that is now such an important part of his work. He told me about making a violin out of a cigar box as a school project for the county fair, winning twelve dollars and a blue ribbon. Then he pointed to a small wooden airplane that hung up by the ceiling, nearly hidden between the beams.

> That airplane was made back before many people thought airplanes should look that way. Everyone laughed at me when I was making it. A few years after that was made, airplanes started to look like that.

They were all double wingers before that. I made that in 1936. . . .
That took first prize in the fair, too. I whittled it out with a knife—
every bit of it. I was just a boy. I used shoe nails—cobbler nails they
call it—to put it together with. My father used to do all our shoe
work.

We take the airplane down to examine it more closely. I comment that
the joints are still tight.

Lost the wheels off it—the landing gear—that got broke off. . . .
My idea for that was out of Buck Rogers. I called it a Buck Rogers
plane at the time. Your five-passenger planes came out looking like
that. . . . I figured that was the safest place to hang it—up there out
of sight! You start looking at that and you start reminiscing, though,
about school days. I was about eleven years old when I carved that
out—ten or eleven, something like that. And I was fifteen or sixteen
when we made our first glider. Our gliders were built on the same
principle as this. But we rode in those.

The engineering, embedded as it is in the daily work of the shop,
cannot be separated from the continuing work of repair. Willie summed up
his attitude toward his whole range of mechanical skills:

It's like when I was taking aviation mechanics. The guy who taught
us says, "Some of you boys will go out of here mechanics, and some
of you will go out of here as parts exchangers—you'll never be a
mechanic." It's a type of knowledge that you can pick up and store
in your mind. Quite a difference between the two. And we've got
more parts exchangers around here than we've got mechanics. Fewer
people find out the reason something has broken and solve the problem as well as maybe changing the part.

Willie is, in his own eyes, a mechanic. That identity is reconfirmed
every time a job is completed.

Willie also recognizes the importance of his work to the community,   15
and this recognition contributes a significant part of his overall self-image.
He knows he is good at what he does and that his work is often crucial to
his neighbors. Although some of this work gets neighbors out of mechanical
jams, the primary responsibility Willie expresses is to the farmers he works for.
This responsibility is expressed indirectly toward the farmers and more
directly toward their work. During the peak periods in the farmers' schedules
Willie works long hours. It is not uncommon on a rainy day in the summer
to find five or six farmers at the shop, waiting their turns as Willie fixes and
mends others' equipment. This is one way he put his attitude toward this
work:

I've worked for the farmers around here for so long I can't turn
them away. Their work comes ahead of anything else. A guy's broke

down in the field—they've got to get fixed and get back working. Because weather has a lot to do with their work. I've been with these farmers twenty-seven years.

Perhaps the most telling example of his attitude toward work, and thus self, is his view of those his own age who live on disability payments. When I first began spending time at the shop I found the number of these men who stopped by or hung around to be surprisingly large. It appears to be a form of early retirement for many working-class men, some of whom look quite healthy. Many of the real health problems are the result of industrial accidents. Others are caused by diseases like arthritis, hypoglycemia, or, quite commonly, diabetes (called "sugar"). Willie himself suffers, often severely, from the effects of his industrial accident and from hypoglycemia, but he continues working. He spoke about the issue:

> You know the thing that gets me, though, on something like that— he's [a man who often came to the shop] more able to work than I am, and he's drawing disability. He claims he can't use his arms. *I* can't raise my one arm up and use it the way I'm supposed to, either. See, even when I scratch my head I use my other hand! [Scratches head.] Some of the ones on disability have lost it because they got sent to a different doctor when they went back to be reclassified, and the doctors found out there was nothing wrong with them. Some guys have artificial legs, or partial artificial legs—several of those. Some are wearing braces. I know guys that have worked every day of their lives who are that way.

I ask Willie why he didn't go on disability after his accident:

> They put me on [classified me as] full disability. I refused it, because I'd have to close the shop if I took it. With compensation disability—you don't work. You can't work at all, unless they give you percentage disability. If they'd given me percentage disability I'd be all right. But they gave me full disability.
> "In the ten years I've known you," I say, "you've had a lot of illness that seems to be connected with that old injury."
> Oh, yeah. Like right now I'm hurting in my shoulder. And this arm is just like a toothache. I didn't take my pain pills like I'm supposed to. Which I forget quite often. Intentionally, most of the time.

The decision not to stop working to gain disability payments is perhaps most important because it signals Willie's view of the proper role of work in a person's life. It is true that the net of social services, because of his low income and frequent illness owing to his old injury, has extended to Willie and his family in the form of assistance for medical bills, occasional surplus food, and so forth. These are seen by Willie, and others in his environment, as legitimate claims from a working person temporarily in need of help.

Considerations

1. How does Willie's work affect his relationship with his family, his friends, and the members of his community?

2. Describe Willie's attitude toward his work. Does his attitude seem similar to those of people you know who do work similar to his? Explain.

3. At the beginning of paragraph 2, Harper notes, "Willie finds himself in his work." Argue for or against the following proposition: It is a good thing to find one's identity primarily through one's chosen work in life.

4. In paragraph 10, Harper describes the stories Willie tells about his work and explains why he thinks Willie tells these stories. Interview someone you know about his or her work, asking for stories that might illustrate points this person is making. Then write down one or more of the stories and explain your response to them.

5. Paragraphs 15–18 explain Willie's attitude toward those who live on disability payments. Assume the identity of one of Willie's friends who lives on disability and tell your side of the story; explain why you think Willie should be more sympathetic to your point of view.

CONNECTIONS: WORK

1. How would you define ambition? Do you see ambition as positive or negative? Consider the following works as you formulate your definition:
   "The Use of Force"
   "The Revolt of 'Mother'"
   "Tom's Husband"
   "El Tonto del Barrio"
   "Willie"
   Which characters in these works seem ambitious? Which seem to lack ambition? Explain.

2. Discuss issues related to women and work as suggested by "Tom's Husband," "The Revolt of 'Mother,'" *Trifles,* and "Professions for Women."

3. Consider conflicts between workers and employers as suggested by "El Tonto del Barrio," "Typists," and "Napa, California."

4. Compare Marge Piercy's view of workers she admires ("To Be of Use") with the views expressed by Douglas Harper in "Willie." Would Piercy admire Willie?

5. Compare the waiter in Kraft Rompf's "Waiting Table" to the waitress in Judy Grahn's "Ella, in a square apron, along Highway 80" and to Ranice Henderson Crosby's waitresses.

8

Men and Women

NATHANIEL HAWTHORNE (1804–1864)

Young Goodman Brown

*After his father, a sea captain, died while on a journey, Nathaniel Hawthorne was raised mainly by his mother, living in various family households in Maine and Massachusetts. From his earliest years, Hawthorne was fascinated with his ancestor William Hathorne, a magistrate in early Salem, Massachusetts, and with William's son John, who was one of the three presiding judges at the witch trials of 1692. Many of his short stories, as well as two of his novels—*The Scarlet Letter *and* The House of Seven Gables*—explore the moral complexities related to life in Puritan America. "Young Goodman Brown" was first published in 1846.*

Young Goodman° Brown came forth, at sunset, into the street at Salem village; but put his head back, after crossing the threshold, to exchange a parting kiss with his young wife. And Faith, as the wife was aptly named, thrust her pretty head into the street, letting the wind play with the pink ribbons of her cap while she called to Goodman Brown.

"Dearest heart," whispered she, softly and rather sadly, when her lips were close to his ear, "prithee put off your journey until sunrise and sleep in your own bed to-night. A lone woman is troubled with such dreams and such thoughts that she's afeared of herself sometimes. Pray tarry with me this night, dear husband, of all nights in the year."

"My love and my Faith," replied young Goodman Brown, "of all nights in the year, this one night must I tarry away from thee. My journey, as thou callest it, forth and back again, must needs be done 'twixt now and sunrise. What, my sweet, pretty wife, dost thou doubt me already, and we but three months married?"

"Then God bless you!" said Faith, with the pink ribbons; "and may you find all well when you come back."

"Amen!" cried Goodman Brown. "Say thy prayers, dear Faith, and go to bed at dusk, and no harm will come to thee."   5

So they parted; and the young man pursued his way until, being about to turn the corner by the meeting-house, he looked back and saw the head of Faith still peeping after him with a melancholy air, in spite of her pink ribbons.

"Poor little Faith!" thought he, for his heart smote him. "What a wretch am I to leave her on such an errand! She talks of dreams, too. Methought as she spoke there was trouble in her face, as if a dream had warned her what work is to be done to-night. But no, no; 'twould kill her to think it. Well, she's a blessed angel on earth; and after this one night, I'll cling to her skirts and follow her to heaven."

Goodman: Polite term of address for a man who ranks below gentleman.

With this excellent resolve for the future, Goodman Brown felt himself justified in making more haste on his present evil purpose. He had taken a dreary road, darkened by all the gloomiest trees of the forest, which barely stood aside to let the narrow path creep through, and closed immediately behind. It was all as lonely as could be; and there is this peculiarity in such a solitude, that the traveller knows not who may be concealed by the innumerable trunks and the thick boughs overhead; so that with lonely footsteps he may yet be passing through an unseen multitude.

"There may be a devilish Indian behind every tree," said Goodman Brown, to himself and he glanced fearfully behind him as he added, "What if the devil himself should be at my very elbow!"

His head being turned back, he passed a crook of the road, and, looking   10 forward again, beheld the figure of a man, in grave and decent attire, seated at the foot of an old tree. He arose at Goodman Brown's approach and walked onward side by side with him.

"You are late, Goodman Brown," said he. "The clock of the Old South was striking as I came through Boston, and that is full fifteen minutes agone."

"Faith kept me back a while," replied the young man, with a tremor in his voice, caused by the sudden appearance of his companion, though not wholly unexpected.

It was now deep dusk in the forest, and deepest in that part of it where these two were journeying. As nearly as could be discerned, the second traveller was about fifty years old, apparently in the same rank of life as Goodman Brown, and bearing a considerable resemblance to him, though perhaps more in expression than features. Still they might have been taken for father and son. And yet, though the elder person was as simply clad as the younger, and as simple in manner too, he had an indescribable air of one who knew the world, and who would not have felt abashed at the governor's dinner table, or in King William's° court, were it possible that his affairs should call him thither. But the only thing about him that could be fixed upon as remarkable was his staff, which bore the likeness of a great black snake, so curiously wrought that it might almost be seen to twist and wriggle itself like a living serpent. This, of course, must have been an ocular deception, assisted by the uncertain light.

"Come, Goodman Brown," cried his fellow-traveller, "this is a dull pace for the beginning of a journey. Take my staff, if you are so soon weary."

"Friend," said the other, exchanging his slow pace for a full stop, "hav-   15 ing kept covenant by meeting thee here, it is my purpose now to return whence I came. I have scruples touching the matter thou wot'st° of."

"Sayest thou so?" replied he of the serpent, smiling apart. "Let us walk on, nevertheless, reasoning as we go; and if I convince thee not thou shalt turn back. We are but a little way in the forest yet."

King William: William III, king of England from 1689 to 1702. wot'st: knowest.

"Too far! too far!" exclaimed the goodman, unconsciously resuming his walk. "My father never went into the woods on such an errand, nor his father before him. We have been a race of honest men and good Christians since the days of the martyrs; and shall I be the first of the name of Brown that ever took this path and kept—"

"Such company, thou wouldst say," observed the elder person, interpreting his pause. "Well said, Goodman Brown! I have been as well acquainted with your family as with ever a one among the Puritans; and that's no trifle to say. I helped your grandfather, the constable, when he lashed the Quaker woman so smartly through the streets of Salem; and it was I that brought your father a pitch-pine knot, kindled at my own hearth, to set fire to an Indian village, in King Philip's war.° They were my good friends, both; and many a pleasant walk have we had along this path, and returned merrily after midnight. I would fain be friends with you for their sake."

"If it be as thou sayest," replied Goodman Brown, "I marvel they never spoke of these matters, or, verily, I marvel not, seeing that the least rumor of the sort would have driven them from New England. We are a people of prayer, and good works to boot, and abide no such wickedness."

"Wickedness or not," said the traveller with the twisted staff, "I have a   20
very general acquaintance here in New England. The deacons of many a church have drunk the communion wine with me; the selectmen of divers towns make me their chairman; and a majority of the Great and General Court are firm supporters of my interest. The governor and I, too—But these are state secrets."

"Can this be so!" cried Goodman Brown, with a stare of amazement at his undisturbed companion. "Howbeit, I have nothing to do with the governor and council; they have their own ways, and are no rule for a simple husbandman° like me. But, were I to go on with thee, how should I meet the eye of that good old man, our minister at, Salem village? Oh, his voice would make me tremble both Sabbath day and lecture day!"

Thus far the elder traveller had listened with due gravity; but now burst into a fit of irrepressible mirth, shaking himself so violently that his snake-life staff actually seemed to wriggle in sympathy.

"Ha! ha! ha!" shouted he again and again; then composing himself, "Well, go on, Goodman Brown, go on; but, prithee, don't kill me with laughing."

"Well, then, to end the matter at once," said Goodman Brown, considerably nettled, "there is my wife, Faith. It would break her dear little heart; and I'd rather break my own."

"Nay, if that be the case," answered the other, "e'en go thy ways,   25
Goodman Brown. I would not for twenty old women like the one hobbling before us that Faith should come to any harm."

King Philip's war: War waged between the Colonists (1675–1676) and the Wampanoag Indians, led by Metacomet, known as "King Philip."   *husbandman:* A common man; sometimes used specifically to denote a farmer.

As he spoke he pointed his staff at a female figure on the path, in whom Goodman Brown recognized a very pious and exemplary dame, who had taught him his catechism in youth, and was still his moral and spiritual adviser, jointly with the minister and Deacon Gookin.

"A marvel, truly, that Goody° Cloyse should be so far in the wilderness at night fall," said he. "But with your leave, friend, I shall take a cut through the woods until we have left this Christian woman behind. Being a stranger to you, she might ask whom I was consorting with and whither I was going."

"Be it so," said his fellow-traveller. "Betake you the woods, and let me keep the path."

Accordingly the young man turned aside, but took care to watch his companion, who advanced softly along the road until he had come within a staff's length of the old dame. She, meanwhile, was making the best of her way, with singular speed for so aged a woman, and mumbling some indistinct words—a prayer, doubtless—as she went. The traveller put forth his staff and touched her withered neck with what seemed the serpent's tail.

"The devil!" screamed the pious old lady.   30

"Then Goody Cloyse knows her old friend?" observed the traveller, confronting her and leaning on his writhing stick.

"Ah, forsooth, and is it your worship indeed?" cried the good dame. "Yea, truly is it, and in the very image of my old gossip, Goodman Brown, the grandfather of the silly fellow that now is. But—would your worship believe it?—my broomstick hath strangely disappeared, stolen, as I suspect, by that unhanged witch, Goody Cory, and that, too, when I was all anointed with the juice of smallage and cinquefoil and wolf's bane—"

"Mingled with fine wheat and the fat of a new-born babe," said the shape of old Goodman Brown.

"Ah, your worship knows the recipe," cried the old lady, cackling aloud. "So, as I was saying, being all ready for the meeting, and no horse to ride on, I made up my mind to foot it; for they tell me there is a nice young man to be taken into communion to-night. But now your good worship will lend me your arm, and we shall be there in a twinkling."

"That can hardly be," answered her friend. "I may not spare you my   35 arm, Goody Cloyse; but here is my staff, if you will."

So saying, he threw it down at her feet, where, perhaps, it assumed life, being one of the rods which its owner had formerly lent to the Egyptian magi. Of this fact, however, Goodman Brown could not take cognizance. He had cast up his eyes in astonishment, and, looking down again, beheld neither Goody Cloyse nor the serpentine staff but his fellow-traveller alone, who waited for him as calmly as if nothing had happened.

"That old woman taught me my catechism," said the young man; and there was a world of meaning in this simple comment.

Goody: Contraction of "Goodwife," a polite title for a married woman of humble rank.

They continued to walk onward, while the elder traveller exhorted his companion to make good speed and persevere in the path, discoursing so aptly that his arguments seemed rather to spring up in the bosom of his auditor than to be suggested by himself. As they went, he plucked a branch of maple to serve for a walking-stick, and began to strip it of the twigs and little boughs, which were wet with evening dew. The moment his fingers touched them they became strangely withered and dried up as with a week's sunshine. Thus the pair proceeded, at a good free pace, until suddenly, in a gloomy hollow of the road, Goodman Brown sat himself down on the stump of a tree and refused to go any farther.

"Friend," said he, stubbornly, "my mind is made up. Not another step will I budge on this errand. What if a wretched old woman do choose to go to the devil when I thought she was going to heaven: is that any reason why I should quit my dear Faith and go after her?"

"You will think better of this by and by," said his acquaintance, com- 40 posedly. "Sit here and rest yourself a while; and when you feel like moving again, there is my staff to help you along."

Without more words, he threw his companion the maple stick, and was as speedily out of sight as if he had vanished into the deepening gloom. The young man sat a few moments by the roadside, applauding himself greatly, and thinking with how clear a conscience he should meet the minister in his morning walk, nor shrink from the eye of good old Deacon Gookin. And what calm sleep would be his that very night, which was to have been spent so wickedly, but so purely and sweetly now, in the arms of Faith! Amidst these pleasant and praiseworthy meditations, Goodman Brown heard the tramp of horses along the road, and deemed it advisable to conceal himself within the verge of the forest, conscious of the guilty purpose that had brought him thither, though now so happily turned from it.

On came the hoof-tramps and the voices of the riders, two grave old voices, conversing soberly as they drew near. These mingled sounds appeared to pass along the road, within a few yards of the young man's hiding-place; but, owing doubtless to the depth of the gloom at that particular spot, neither the travellers nor their steeds were visible. Though their figures brushed the small boughs by the wayside, it could not be seen that they intercepted, even for a moment, the faint gleam from the strip of bright sky athwart which they must have passed. Goodman Brown alternately crouched and stood on tiptoe, pulling aside the branches and thrusting forth his head as far as he durst without discerning so much as a shadow. It vexed him the more, because he could have sworn, were such a thing possible, that he recognized the voices of the minister and Deacon Gookin, jogging along quietly, as they were wont to do, when bound to some ordination or ecclesiastical council. While yet within hearing, one of the riders stopped to pluck a switch.

"Of the two, reverend sir," said the voice like the deacon's, "I had rather miss an ordination dinner than to-night's meeting. They tell me that some of our community are to be here from Falmouth and beyond, and others from

Connecticut and Rhode Island, besides several of the Indian powwows, who, after their fashion, know almost as much deviltry as the best of us. Moreover, there is a goodly young woman to be taken into communion."

"Mighty well, Deacon Gookin!" replied the solemn old tones of the minister. "Spur up, or we shall be late. Nothing can be done, you know, until I get on the ground."

The hoofs clattered again; and the voices, talking so strangely in the empty air, passed on through the forest, where no church had ever been gathered or solitary Christian prayed. Whither, then, could these holy men be journeying so deep into the heathen wilderness? Young Goodman Brown caught hold of a tree for support, being ready to sink down on the ground, faint and overburdened with the heavy sickness of his heart. He looked up to the sky, doubting whether there really was a heaven above him. Yet, there was the blue arch, and the stars brightening in it. 45

"With heaven above, and Faith below, I will yet stand firm against the devil!" cried Goodman Brown.

While he still gazed upward into the deep arch of the firmament and had lifted his hands to pray, a cloud, though no wind was stirring, hurried across the zenith and hid the brightening stars. The blue sky was still visible, except directly overhead, where this black mass of cloud was sweeping swiftly northward. Aloft in the air, as if from the depths of the cloud, came a confused and doubtful sound of voices. Once the listener fancied that he could distinguish the accents of towns-people of his own, men and women, both pious and ungodly, many of whom he had met at the communion table, and had seen others rioting at the tavern. The next moment, so indistinct were the sounds, he doubted whether he had heard aught but the murmur of the old forest, whispering without a wind. Then came a stronger swell of those familiar tones, heard daily in the sunshine at Salem village, but never until now from a cloud of night. There was one voice, of a young woman, uttering lamentations, yet with an uncertain sorrow, and entreating for some favor, which, perhaps, it would grieve her to obtain; and all the unseen multitude, both saints and sinners, seemed to encourage her onward.

"Faith!" shouted Goodman Brown, in a voice of agony and desperation; and the echoes of the forest mocked him, crying, "Faith! Faith!" as if bewildered wretches were seeking her all through the wilderness.

The cry of grief, rage, and terror was yet piercing the night, when the unhappy husband held his breath for a response. There was a scream, drowned immediately in a louder murmur of voices, fading into far-off laughter, as the dark cloud swept away, leaving the clear and silent sky above Goodman Brown. But something fluttered lightly down through the air and caught on the branch of a tree. The young man seized it, and beheld a pink ribbon.

"My Faith is gone!" cried he, after one stupefied moment. "There is 50 no good on earth; and sin is but a name. Come, devil; for to thee is this world given."

And, maddened with despair, so that he laughed loud and long, did Goodman Brown grasp his staff and set forth again, at such a rate that he seemed to fly along the forest path, rather than to walk or run. The road grew wilder and drearier and more faintly traced, and vanished at length, leaving him in the heart of the dark wilderness, still rushing onward with the instinct that guides mortal man to evil. The whole forest was peopled with frightful sounds—the creaking of the trees, the howling of wild beasts, and the yell of Indians; while sometimes the wind tolled like a distant church bell, and sometimes gave a broad roar around the traveller, as if all Nature were laughing him to scorn. But he was himself the chief horror of the scene, and shrank not from its other horrors.

"Ha! ha! ha!" roared Goodman Brown when the wind laughed at him. "Let us hear which will laugh loudest! Think not to frighten me with your deviltry! Come witch, come wizard, come Indian powwow, come devil himself, and here comes Goodman Brown. You may as well fear him as he fear you!"

In truth, all through the haunted forest there could be nothing more frightful than the figure of Goodman Brown. On he flew among the black pines, brandishing his staff with frenzied gestures, now giving vent to an inspiration of horrid blasphemy, and now shouting forth such laughter as set all the echoes of the forest laughing like demons around him. The fiend in his own shape is less hideous than when he rages in the breast of man. Thus sped the demoniac on his course, until, quivering among the trees, he saw a red light before him, as when the felled trunks and branches of a clearing have been set on fire, and throw up their lurid blaze against the sky, at the hour of midnight. He paused, in a lull of the tempest that had driven him onward, and heard the swell of what seemed a hymn, rolling solemnly from a distance with the weight of many voices. He knew the tune; it was a familiar one in the choir of the village meeting-house. The verse died heavily away, and was lengthened by a chorus, not of human voices, but of all the sounds of the benighted wilderness pealing in awful harmony together. Goodman Brown cried out; and his cry was lost to his own ear by its unison with the cry of the desert.

In the interval of silence he stole forward until the light glared full upon his eyes. At one extremity of an open space, hemmed in by the dark wall of the forest, arose a rock, bearing some rude, natural resemblance either to an altar or a pulpit, and surrounded by four blazing pines, their tops aflame, their stems untouched, like candles at an evening meeting. The mass of foliage that had overgrown the summit of the rock was all on fire, blazing high into the night and fitfully illuminating the whole field. Each pendent twig and leafy festoon was in a blaze. As the red light arose and fell, a numerous congregation alternately shone forth, then disappeared in shadow, and again grew, as it were, out of the darkness, peopling the heart of the solitary woods at once.

"A grave and dark-clad company," quoth Goodman Brown.

55

In truth, they were such. Among them, quivering to-and-fro between gloom and splendor, appeared faces that would be seen next day at the council board of the province, and others which, Sabbath after Sabbath, looked devoutly heavenward, and benignantly over the crowded pews, from the holiest pulpits in the land. Some affirm that the lady of the governor was there. At least there were high dames well known to her, and wives of honored husbands, and widows, a great multitude, and ancient maidens, all of excellent repute, and fair young girls, who trembled lest their mothers should espy them. Either the sudden gleams of light flashing over the obscure field bedazzled Goodman Brown, or he recognized a score of the church-members of Salem village famous for their especial sanctity. Good old Deacon Gookin had arrived, and waited at the skirts of that venerable saint, his revered pastor. But, irreverently consorting with these grave, reputable, and pious people, these elders of the church, these chaste dames and dewy virgins, there were men of dissolute lives and women of spotted fame, wretches given over to all mean and filthy vice, and suspected even of horrid crimes. It was strange to see, that the good shrank not from the wicked, nor were the sinners abashed by the saints. Scattered also among their pale-faced enemies were the Indian priests, or powwows, who had often scared their native forest with more hideous incantations than any known to English witchcraft.

"But, where is Faith?" thought Goodman Brown; and, as hope came into his heart, he trembled.

Another verse of the hymn arose, a slow and mournful strain, such as the pious love, but joined to words which expressed all that our nature can conceive of sin, and darkly hinted at far more. Unfathomable to mere mortals is the lore of fiends. Verse after verse was sung; and still the chorus of the desert swelled between, like the deepest tone of a mighty organ; and, with the final peal of that dreadful anthem there came a sound, as if the roaring wind, the rushing streams, the howling beasts, and every other voice of the unconcerted wilderness were mingling and according with the voice of guilty man in homage to the prince of all. The four blazing pines threw up a loftier flame, and obscurely discovered shapes and visages of horror on the smoke wreaths above the impious assembly. At the same moment the fire on the rock shot redly forth and formed a glowing arch above its base, where now appeared a figure. With reverence be it spoken, the figure bore no slight similitude, both in garb and manner, to some grave divine of the New England churches.

"Bring forth the converts!" cried a voice that echoed through the field and rolled into the forest.

At the word, Goodman Brown stepped forth from the shadow of the trees and approached the congregation, with whom he felt a loathful brotherhood by the sympathy of all that was wicked in his heart. He could have well nigh sworn that the shape of his own dead father beckoned him to advance, looking downward from a smoke wreath, while a woman, with dim features of despair, threw out her hand to warn him back. Was it his mother?

60

But he had no power to retreat one step, nor to resist, even in thought, when the minister and good old Deacon Gookin seized his arms and led him to the blazing rock. Thither came also the slender form of a veiled female, led between Goody Cloyse, that pious teacher of the catechism, and Martha Carrier,° who had received the devil's promise to be queen of hell. A rampant hag was she. And there stood the proselytes beneath the canopy of fire.

"Welcome, my children," said the dark figure, "to the communion of your race. Ye have found thus young your nature and your destiny. My children, look behind you!"

They turned; and flashing forth, as it were, in a sheet of flame, the fiend worshippers were seen; the smile of welcome gleamed darkly on every visage.

"There," resumed the sable form, "are all whom ye have reverenced from youth. Ye deemed them holier than yourselves, and shrank from your own sin, contrasting it with their lives of righteousness and prayerful aspirations heavenward. Yet here are they all in my worshipping assembly. This night it shall be granted you to know their secret deeds: how hoary-bearded elders of the church have whispered wanton words to the young maids of their households; how many a woman, eager for widow's weeds, has given her husband a drink at bedtime, and let him sleep his last sleep in her bosom; how beardless youths have made haste to inherit their fathers' wealth; and how fair damsels—blush not, sweet ones—have dug little graves in the garden, and bidden me, the sole guest, to an infant's funeral. By the sympathy of your human hearts for sin ye shall scent out all the places—whether in church, bed-chamber, street, field, or forest—where crime has been committed, and shall exult to behold the whole earth one stain of guilt, one mighty blood spot. Far more than this. It shall be yours to penetrate, in every bosom, the deep mystery of sin, the fountain of all wicked arts, and which inexhaustibly supplies more evil impulses than human power—than my power at its utmost—can make manifest in deeds. And now, my children, look upon each other."

They did so; and, by the blaze of the hell-kindled torches, the wretched man beheld his Faith, and the wife her husband, trembling before that unhallowed altar.

"Lo, there ye stand, my children," said the figure, in a deep and solemn 65
tone, almost sad with its despairing awfulness, as if his once angelic nature could yet mourn for our miserable race. "Depending upon one another's hearts, ye had still hoped that virtue were not all a dream. Now are ye undeceived. Evil is the nature of mankind. Evil must be your only happiness. Welcome, again, my children, to the communion of your race."

"Welcome," repeated the fiend worshippers, in one cry of despair and triumph.

Martha Carrier: One of the women hanged for witchcraft in Salem in 1697.

And there they stood, the only pair, as it seemed, who were yet hesitating on the verge of wickedness in this dark world. A basin was hollowed, naturally, in the rock. Did it contain water, reddened by the lurid light? or was it blood? or, perchance, a liquid flame? Herein did the shape of evil dip his hand and prepare to lay the mark of baptism upon their foreheads, that they might be partakers of the mystery of sin, more conscious of the secret guilt of others, both in deed and thought, than they could now be of their own. The husband cast one look at his pale wife, and Faith at him. What polluted wretches would the next glance show them to each other, shuddering alike at what they disclosed and what they saw!

"Faith! Faith!" cried the husband, "look up to heaven, and resist the wicked one."

Whether Faith obeyed he knew not. Hardly had he spoken when he found himself amid calm night and solitude, listening to a roar of the wind which died heavily away through the forest. He staggered against the rock, and felt it chill and damp; while a hanging twig, that had been all on fire, besprinkled his cheek with the coldest dew.

The next morning young Goodman Brown came slowly into the street   70
of Salem village, staring around him like a bewildered man. The good old minister was taking a walk along the graveyard to get an appetite for breakfast and meditate his sermon, and bestowed a blessing, as he passed, on Goodman Brown. He shrank from the venerable saint as if to avoid an anathema. Old Deacon Gookin was at domestic worship, and the holy words of his prayer were heard through the open window. "What God doth the wizard pray to?" quoth Goodman Brown. Goody Cloyse, that excellent old Christian, stood in the early sunshine at her own lattice, catechizing a little girl who had brought her a pint of morning's milk. Goodman Brown snatched away the child as from the grasp of the fiend himself. Turning the corner by the meeting-house, he spied the head of Faith, with the pink ribbons, gazing anxiously forth, and bursting into such joy at sight of him that she skipped along the street and almost kissed her husband before the whole village. But Goodman Brown looked sternly and sadly into her face, and passed on without a greeting.

Had Goodman Brown fallen asleep in the forest and only dreamed a wild dream of a witch-meeting?

Be it so, if you will; but, alas! it was a dream of evil omen for young Goodman Brown. A stern, a sad, a darkly meditative, a distrustful, if not a desperate man did he become from the night of that fearful dream. On the Sabbath day, when the congregation were singing a holy psalm, he could not listen because an anthem of sin rushed loudly upon his ear and drowned all the blessed strain. When the minister spoke from the pulpit with power and fervid eloquence, and, with his hand on the open Bible, of the sacred truths of our religion, and of saint-like lives and triumphant deaths, and of future bliss or misery unutterable, then did Goodman Brown turn pale, dreading lest the roof should thunder down upon the gray blasphemer and his hearers.

Often, awakening suddenly at midnight, he shrank from the bosom of Faith; and at morning or eventide, when the family knelt down at prayer, he scowled and muttered to himself, and gazed sternly at his wife, and turned away. And when he had lived long, and was borne to his grave a hoary corpse, followed by Faith, an aged woman, and children and grandchildren, a goodly procession, besides neighbors, not a few, they carved no hopeful verse upon his tombstone, for his dying face was gloom.

Considerations

1. How is Faith's name significant to the story? What qualities does Faith represent to her husband? Contrast the way present-day readers might respond to her name with the way that Hawthorne's nineteenth-century audience—who were mostly middle- or upper-class, well-educated, white Protestants—might have responded.

2. How does Goodman Brown's journey into the forest relate to his relationship with his wife? How would you compare the second traveler to Faith? Who or what might the second traveler (who bears "a considerable resemblance" to Goodman Brown) represent?

3. Make a list of the other men and women whom Goodman Brown encounters. How does Hawthorne portray the men? The women? Do you see any significant similarities or differences?

4. Referring to evidence in the story, explain why you do or do not see the encounter in the forest as an actual event (as opposed to a dream or fantasy).

5. Read the final paragraph of the story carefully. Does Goodman Brown's lifelong depression seem justified? Or does the narrator seem critical of his response to his encounter with darkness? Explain.

CONNECTIONS: ART AND POETRY

Poets create with words, while artists work with a variety of media including paint, ink, paper, canvas, clay, and metal. Yet both poets and artists offer us pictures reflecting their responses to images, experiences, people, places, emotions—observed, remembered, or imagined.

On the pages that follow, you will find poems paired with works of art. In two instances, the artist responds to the poem (Demuth's *I Saw the Figure 5 in Gold* and Williams's "The Great Figure"; Hunt's and Tennyson's *The Lady of Shalott*). In one case, the artist (Motherwell) responds to the combination of art (Picasso's "The Old Guitarist") and poetry (Stevens's "The Man with the Blue Guitar") in his "Blue Air." In the other pairs, the poet writes in response to the artist's work. (You'll also find two poets responding to a single painting—Edward Hopper's *Nighthawks*.)

As you read the poems and look at the art work, notice the connections you see. Begin by considering these questions:
- What is your initial response to each work considered separately?
- Does your response change when you consider the two works together?
- Can each work be appreciated on its own or is one entirely dependent on the other?
- How are the works of art similar to the poems?
- How are they different?
  - What details appear in the poem, but not in the art work?
  - What details appear in the art work, but not in the poem?
  - If the poem responds to a work of art, what has the poet chosen to add or alter?
  - If the painting responds to a poem, what has the artist chosen to add or alter?
  - What similarities and differences do you see in the artist's style and the poet's style?
  - What similarities and differences do you see in the way the artist and the poet have chosen to organize and present the details of the work?
- What significance do you see in the similarities and differences you have observed?
- How do the similarities and differences you have observed affect your response either to the poem or to the work of art?

Albrecht Dürer. (German, 1471–1528). *Knight, Death, and the Devil*. 1513. Engraving. 250 x 191 mm. Courtesy of the Fogg Art Museum, Harvard University Art Museums, Cambridge, MA. Gift of William Gray from the Collection of Francis Calley Gray. G1111.

RANDALL JARRELL (1914–1965)

The Knight, Death, and the Devil

Cowhorn-crowned, shockheaded, cornshuck-bearded,
Death is a scarecrow—his death's-head a teetotum
That tilts up toward man confidentially
But trimmed with adders; ringlet-maned, rope-bridled,
The mare he rides crops herbs beside a skull.   5
He holds up, warning, the crossed cones of time:
Here, narrowing into now, the Past and Future
Are quicksand.
          A hoofed pikeman trots behind.
His pike's claw-hammer mocks—in duplicate, inverted—
The pocked, ribbed, soaring crescent of his horn.   10
A scapegoat aged into a steer; boar-snouted;
His great limp ears stuck sidelong out in air;
A dewlap bunched at his breast; a ram's-horn wound
Beneath each ear; a spur licked up and out
From the hide of his forehead; bat-winged, but in bone;   15
His eye a ring inside a ring inside a ring
That leers up, joyless, vile, in meek obscenity—
This is the devil. Flesh to flesh, he bleats
The herd back to the pit of being.

In fluted mail; upon his lance the bush   20
Of that old fox; a sheep-dog bounding at his stirrup,
In its eyes the cast of faithfulness (our help,
Our foolish help); his dun war-horse pacing
Beneath in strength, in ceremonious magnificence;
His castle—some man's castle—set on every crag: 25
So, companioned so, the knight moves through this world.
The fiend moos in amity, Death mouths, reminding:
He listens in assurance, has no glance
To spare for them, but looks past steadily
At—at—
          a man's look completes itself.   30

The death of his own flesh, set up outside him;
The flesh of his own soul, set up outside him—
Death and the devil, what are these to him?
His being accuses him—and yet his face is firm
In resolution, in absolute persistence;   35
The folds of smiling do for steadiness;
The face is its own fate—*a man does what he must*—
And the body underneath it says: *I am.*

Henri Matisse. (French, 1869–1954). *Two Girls, Red and Green Background*. 1947. Oil on canvas, 56.2 x 46.4 cm. The Baltimore Museum of Art: The Cone Collection, formed by Dr. Claribel Cone and Miss Etta Cone of Baltimore, MD. BMA 1950.264.

MOLLY PEACOCK (1947–   )

Matisse: Two Girls

I know who they are. That one's me,
the brunette on the right. The blond
in the yellow dress is you.

It's a picture without protection
like the snaps of us on our vacations   5
with the sun in our eyes. But here we are inside

a perfect summer house, like mine
when I was married and rich, with cool walls
and enormous windows flung open behind us

to the tops of old maples. They are not maples   10
in the *picture*—they are green clouds slashed
with brown stripes—but don't you like to look

at the places and faces in pictures to find out
where and which you are? I must be
the frightened one in blue, after my affair   15

with your husband. By the indictment of
your pointed nose, chin, elbows thrust
from that yellow dress, I know. Is yellow

the fiercer color? Or blue.
Well, the figure I chose as you—   20
her hair's too short, for one thing.

I thought it was you, since neither girl
will look at the other, but it is not us.
There is no wine, no cigarettes,

and the flowers on the table are too fresh.   25
I just cut them from my mother's garden,
having gotten up and dressed and almost

beaten my mother to the breakfast table.
But evidently she had eaten long before,
since there, in the picture,   30

the table's set only for one. The late one.
She has already watched the sunrise and has turned
away from the window to stare at the floor.

But her body sits toward me,
my arms stuck under my breasts, anticipating   35
the explosion—for having slept, for having cut . . .

for having what? A blue dress?
I wait for the hair to toss or
the figure to turn. It does not.

In fact, my mother turns to me quite often.   40
The blowsy head in the picture can't be her.
Look how young the girl in blue is,

how carefully she holds herself.
Her hair is parted so nicely,
as though she cared for it.   45

It is the color of the antlered branches
behind her, and her dress matches the sky.
What a burden she has to distinguish herself!

She must be a younger sister. Mine.
So the woman in yellow is me,   50
the pointed nose, the pointed chin,

the angularity in the summer room.
And my frightened younger sister,
newly married in this lovely summer house,

with such first luck at flowers   55
that she cannot be sure it is her talent,
has cut these roses to placate me,

because she cannot see my face
and watches only the points
seeming to pivot toward her.   60

But I am standing here,
and I do not mistake
where the rude lines originate.

Vincent van Gogh. (Dutch, 1853–1890.) *The Starry Night*. 1889. Oil on canvas. 29 x 36 ¹/₄″ (73.7 x 92.1 cm). The Museum of Modern Art, New York. Acquired through the Lillie P. Bliss Bequest. Photograph © 1995 The Museum of Modern Art, New York.

ANNE SEXTON (1928–1975)

The Starry Night

That does not keep me from having a terrible need of—shall I say the word—religion.
Then I go out at night to paint the stars.   Vincent van Gogh in a letter to his brother

The town does not exist
except where one black-haired tree slips
up like a drowned woman into the hot sky.
The town is silent. The night boils with eleven stars
Oh starry starry night! This is how   5
I want to die.

It moves. They are all alive.
Even the moon bulges in its orange irons
to push children, like a god, from its eye.
The old unseen serpent swallows up the stars.   10
Oh starry starry night! This is how
I want to die:

into that rushing beast of the night,
sucked up by that great dragon, to split
from my life with no flag,   15
no belly,
no cry.

William Holman Hunt. (English, 1827–1910.) *The Lady of Shalott*. 1886–1905. Oil on canvas.
Wadsworth Atheneum, Hartford. The Ella Gallup Sumner and Mary Catlin Sumner Collection
Fund. Accession number 1961.470.

ALFRED, LORD TENNYSON (1809–1892)

The Lady of Shalott

Part 2

There she weaves by night and day
A magic web with colors gay.
She has heard a whisper say,
A curse is on her if she stay
      To look down to Camelot.   5
She knows not what the curse may be,
And so she weaveth steadily,
And little other care hath she,
      The Lady of Shalott.

And moving through a mirror clear   10
That hangs before her all the year,
Shadows of the world appear.
There she sees the highway near
      Winding down to Camelot;
There the river eddy whirls,   15
And there the surly village churls,
And the red cloaks of market girls,
      Pass onward from Shalott.

Sometimes a troop of damsels glad,
An abbott on an ambling pad,   20
Sometimes a curly shepherd lad,
Or long-haired page in crimson clad,
      Goes by to towered Camelot;
And sometimes through the mirror blue
The knights come riding two and two: 25
She hath no loyal knight and true,
      The Lady of Shalott.

But in her web she still delights
To weave the mirror's magic sights,
For often through the silent nights   30
A funeral, with plumes and lights
      And music, went to Camelot;
Or when the moon was overhead,
Came two young lovers lately wed:
"I am half sick of shadows," said   35
      The Lady of Shalott.

Part 3

A bowshot from her bower eaves,
He rode between the barley sheaves,

The sun came dazzling through the leaves,
And flamed upon the brazen greaves 40
    Of bold Sir Lancelot.
A red-cross knight forever kneeled
To a lady in his shield,
That sparkled on the yellow field,
    Beside remote Shalott. 45

The gemmy bridle glittered free,
Like to some branch of stars we see
Hung in the golden Galaxy.
The bridle bells rang merrily
    As he rode down to Camelot; 50
And from his blazoned baldric slung
A mighty silver bugle hung,
And as he rode his armor rung,
    Beside remote Shalott.

All in the blue unclouded weather 55
Thick-jeweled shone the saddle leather,
The helmet and the helmet-feather
Burned like one burning flame together,
    As he rode down to Camelot;
As often through the purple night, 60
Below the starry clusters bright,
Some bearded meteor, trailing light,
    Moves over still Shalott.

His broad clear brow in sunlight glowed;
On burnished hooves his war horse trode; 65
From underneath his helmet flowed
His coal-black curls as on he rode,
    As he rode down to Camelot.
From the bank and from the river
He flashed into the crystal mirror, 70
"Tirra lirra," by the river
    Sang Sir Lancelot.

She left the web, she left the loom,
She made three paces through the room,
She saw the water lily bloom, 75
She saw the helmet and the plume,
    She looked down to Camelot.
Out flew the web and floated wide;
The mirror cracked from side to side;
"The curse is come upon me," cried 80
    The Lady of Shalott.

Pieter Breughel the Elder. (Dutch, 1520–1569.) *Peasants Dance (The Kermess)*. 1568. Kunsthistorisches Museum, Vienna, Austria. © Erich Lessing/Art Resource, NY.

WILLIAM CARLOS WILLIAMS (1883 1963)

The Dance

In Breughel's great picture, The Kermess,
the dancers go round, they go round and
around, the squeal and the blare and the
tweedle of bagpipes, a bugle and fiddles
tipping their bellies (round as the thick-   5
sided glasses whose wash they impound)
their hips and their bellies off balance
to turn them. Kicking and rolling about
the Fair Grounds, swinging their butts, those
shanks must be sound to bear up under such   10
rollicking measures, prance as they dance
in Breughel's great picture, The Kermess.

Charles Henry Demuth. (1883–1935). *I Saw the Figure 5 in Gold*. Oil on composition board.
H. 36 in. W. 29-3/4 in. (91.4 x 75.6 cm.). The Metropolitan Museum of Art, Alfred Stieglitz
Collection, 1949. 49.59.1.

WILLIAM CARLOS WILLIAMS (1883–1963)

The Great Figure

Among the rain
and lights
I saw the figure 5
in gold
on a red   5
fire truck
moving
tense
unheeded
to gong clangs   10
siren howls
and wheels rumbling
through the dark city

Pieter Brueghel the Elder. (Dutch, 1520–1569). *Landscape with the Fall of Icarus.* Musées Royaux des Beaux-Arts, Brussels, Belgium. © Scala/Art Resource, NY.

W. H. AUDEN (1907–1973)

Musée des Beaux Arts

About suffering they were never wrong,
The Old Masters: how well they understood
Its human position; how it takes place
While someone else is eating or opening a window or just walking dully along;
How, when the aged are reverently, passionately waiting   5
For the miraculous birth, there always must be
Children who did not specially want it to happen, skating
On a pond at the edge of the wood:
They never forgot
That even the dreadful martyrdom must run its course   10
Anyhow in a corner, some untidy spot
Where the dogs go on with their doggy life and the torturer's horse
Scratches its innocent behind on a tree.

In Brueghel's *Icarus,* for instance: how everything turns away
Quite leisurely from the disaster; the ploughman may   15
Have heard the splash, the forsaken cry,
But for him it was not an important failure; the sun shone
As it had to on the white legs disappearing into the green
Water; and the expensive delicate ship that must have seen
Something amazing, a boy falling out of the sky,   20
Had somewhere to get to and sailed calmly on.

Pieter Brueghel the Elder. (Dutch, 1520–1569). *Two Chained Monkeys*. 1562. Staatliche Museen zu Berlin. Preußischer Kulturbesitz Gemäldegalerie. Photographed by Jörg P. Anders.

WISLAWA SZYMBORSKA (1923–   )

Brueghel's Two Monkeys
(Translated from the Polish by Stanislaw Baranczak and Clare Cavanagh.)

This is what I see in my dream about final exams:
two monkeys, chained to the floor, sit on the windowsill,
the sky behind them flutters,
the sea is taking its bath.

The exam is History of Mankind.   5
I stammer and hedge.

One monkey stares and listens with mocking disdain,
the other seems to be dreaming away—
but when it's clear I don't know what to say
he prompts me with a gentle   10
clinking of his chain.

Jan Vermeer (Dutch, 1632–1675). *The Loveletter.* Oil on canvas. 44 x 38.5 cm. Collectie Rijksmuseum Amsterdam. Inv. nr. SK-A-1595.

SANDRA NELSON (1951–   )

When a Woman Holds a Letter

It is always from a man. Jan Vermeer
knows this as he paints the dark
note in Clarissa's right hand;
her left strangling the fretted neck coming
from the pear-shaped body of his   5
mandolin. Her upturned eyes may be tied
to a ferris wheel of sparrows' biting love.
Or she may feel the heavy curve of his instrument
against her stomach and her eyes
instinctively flip up to heaven to see   10
if anyone is watching. I am
probably wrong. There *is* another woman
behind her (a washerwoman whose head
is wrapped in a wimple to keep out the dirt).
Perhaps it is to her that Clarissa's eyes roll.   15

Pierre Bonnard. (French, 1867–1947). *The Breakfast Room.* c. 1930–31. Oil on canvas. 62 $^7/_8$ x 44 $^7/_8$″ (159.6 x 113.8 cm). The Museum of Modern Art, New York. Given anonymously. Photograph © 1995 The Museum of Modern Art, New York.

EAMON GRENNAN (1941–   )

Breakfast Room

1.
The words have stirred, always, a sudden
surge of light, an air of new beginnings, something
neat and simple, a space
both elemental and domestic—because, perhaps,
they bear a sort of innocent sheen   5
of privilege, a room so set apart
for an event so ordinary, a glimmer of ritual
where mostly we know only broken facts, bits and pieces
stumbling numbly into one another. Here
is a murmur of voices, discretion's homely music   10
of spoons on saucers, the decent movements
people make around each other—eager to
let themselves become themselves again
after the uncertain journeys of the night. Or it may be
the secret knowing smiles that lovers save, sitting   15
to face one another in their quaint conspiracy
of hope and saying, *Pass the milk, please,* but meaning
Nothing has ever pleased me more
than how your naked shoulders and the small of your back
lay on my spread hands; your earlobe, tongue, wide eyes   20
entering half frightened mine in the dark.

2.
And in Bonnard's "The Breakfast Room" you'll see
the impeccable ordinary order he finds in things: white,
slate blue, the tablecloth bears its own still-life
of teapot, cream pitcher, sugar bowl, china cup   25
and scalloped saucer, the half glass of raspberry juice,
bread in yellow napkins, that heaped dish
of purple figs and a peach. And, as if
accidental by the French windows—
through which morning light   30
passes its binding declarative sentence
on every detail—a woman stands
almost out of the picture, her back
against the patterned drapes, dressed to go out
and giving a last look back, her eyes and strict lips   35
asking directly, *You think this*
changes anything? Yet she too
is part of this stillness, this sense that things

are about to achieve
illumination. Beyond the window   40
a stone balustrade, and beyond that
nature's blue-green tangle tangles
with the light that's melting one thing
into another—blue, scrubbed green, straw gold,
a house with a white-and-lilac roof   45
at the dead end of a sun-streaked avenue
on which the trees are
blobs of turquoise. Inside and quite distinct, that woman
is held to her last look back, her
sudden pulse beat shaking   50
all the orderly arrangements
of the table. Through its ambivalence of light,
its double tongue of detail and the world at large,
we are brought into the picture, into a kingdom
we might find under our noses: morning's   55
nourishment and necessary peace; a pause
on the brink of something
always edging
into shape, about to happen.

Edward Hopper (American, 1882–1967). *Nighthawks.* 1942. Oil on canvas, 84.1 x 152.4 cm.
Friends of American Art Collection, 1942.51. Photograph © 1994, The Art Institute of Chicago. All
rights reserved.

DAVID RAY

A Midnight Diner by Edward Hopper

Your own greyhounds bark at your side.
It is you, dressed like a Siennese,
Galloping, ripping the gown as the fabled
White-skinned woman runs, seeking freedom.
Tiny points of birches rise from hills,   5
Spin like serrulate corkscrews toward the sky;
In other rooms it is your happiness
Flower petals fall for, your brocade
You rediscover, feel bloom upon your shoulder.

And freedom's what the gallery's for.   10
You roam in large rooms and choose your beauty.
Yet, Madman, it's your own life you turn back to:
In one postcard purchase you wipe out
Centuries of light and smiles, golden skin
And openness, forest babes and calves.   15
You forsake the sparkler breast
That makes the galaxies, you betray
The women who dance upon the water,

Daniel MacDonald. (1821–1853). *Bowling Match at Castlemary, Cloyne, 1847.* Crawford Municipal Art Gallery, Cork/Bridgeman Art Library, London. CAG73997.

GREG DELANTY

After Viewing The Bowling Match at Castlemary, Cloyne *(1847)*

I promised to show you the bowlers
    out the Blarney Road after Sunday mass,
you were so taken with that painting
    of the snazzy, top-hatted peasant class
        all agog at the bowler in full swing,   5
        down to his open shirt, in trousers
as indecently tight as a baseballer's.

You would relish each fling's span
    along blackberry boreens and delight
in a *dinger* of a curve throw   10
    as the bowl hurls out of sight,
        not to mention the earthy lingo
        & antics of gambling fans,
giving players thumbs-up or *down the banks.*

It's not just to witness such shenanigans   15
    for themselves, but to be relieved
from whatever lurks in our day's background,
    just as the picture's crowd is freed
        of famine & exile darkening the land,
        waiting to see where the bowl spins   20
off, a planet out of orbit, and who wins.

Jacopo Tintoretto. (Italian, 1518–1594). *Crucifixion*. Scuola Grande di S. Rocco, Venice, Italy. Erich Lessing/Art Resource, NY.

N. SCOTT MOMADAY (1934–   )

Before an Old Painting of the Crucifixion

The Mission Carmel,
June, 1960

I ponder how He died, despairing once.
I've heard the cry subside in vacant skies,
In clearings where no other was. Despair,
Which, in the vibrant wake of utterance,
Resides in desolate calm, preoccupies,   5
Though it is still. There is no solace there.

That calm inhabits wilderness, the sea,
And where no peace inheres but solitude;
Near death it most impends. It was for Him,
Absurd and public in His agony,   10
Inscrutably itself, nor misconstrued,
Nor metaphrased in art or pseudonym:

A vague contagion. Old, the mural fades . . .
Reminded of the fainter sea I scanned,
I recollect: How mute in constancy!   15
I could not leave the wall of palisades
Till cormorants returned my eyes on land.
The mural but implies eternity:

Not death, but silence after death is change.
Judean hills, the endless afternoon,   20
The farther groves and arbors seasonless
But fix the mind within the moment's range.
Where evening would obscure our sorrow soon,
There shines too much a sterile loveliness.

No imprecisions of commingled shade,   25
No shimmering deceptions of the sun,
Herein no semblances remark the cold
Unhindered swell of time, for time is stayed.
The Passion wanes into oblivion,
And time and timelessness confuse, I'm told.   30

These centuries removed from either fact
Have lain upon the critical expanse
And been of little consequence. The void
Is calendared in stone; the human act,
Outrageous, is in vain. The hours advance   35
Like flecks of foam borne landward and destroyed.

RICHARD WILBUR (1921–   )

Giacometti

Rock insults us, hard and so boldly browed
Its scorn needs not to focus, and with fists
Which still unstirring strike:
Collected it resists
Until its buried glare begets a like   5
Anger in us, and finds our hardness. Proud,

Then, and armed, and with a patient rage
We carve cliff, shear stone to blocks,
And down to the image of man
Batter and shape the rock's   10
Fierce composure, closing its veins within
That outside man, itself its captive cage.

So we can baffle rock, and in our will
Can clothe and keep it. But if our will, though locked
In stone it clutches, change,   15
Then are we much worse mocked
Than cliffs can do: then we ourselves are strange
To what we were, which lowers on us still.

High in the air those habitants of stone
Look heavenward, lean to a thought, or stride   20
Toward some concluded war,
While we on every side,
Random as shells the sea drops down ashore,
Are walking, walking, many and alone.

What stony shape could hold us now, what hard   25
Bent can we bulk in air, where shall our feet
Come to a common stand?
Follow along this street
(Where rock recovers carven eye and hand),
Open the gate, and cross the narrow yard   30

And look where Giacometti in a room
Dim as a cave of the sea, has built the man
We are, and made him walk:
Towering like a thin
Coral, out of a reef of plaster chalk,   35
This is the single form we can assume.

We are this man unspeakably alone
Yet stripped of the singular utterly, shaved and scraped
Of all but being there,
Whose fullness is escaped   40
Like a burst balloon's: no nakedness so bare
As flesh gone in inquiring of the bone.

He is pruned of every gesture, saving only
The habit of coming and going. Every pace
Shuffles a million feet.   45
The faces in this face
Are all forgotten faces of the street
Gathered to one anonymous and lonely.

No prince and no Leviathan, he is made
Of infinite farewells. Oh never more   50
Diminished, nonetheless
Embodied here, we are
This starless walker, one who cannot guess
His will, his keel his nose's bony blade.

And volumes hover round like future shades   55
This least of man, in whom we join and take
A pilgrim's step behind,
And in whose guise we make
Our grim departures now, walking to find
What railleries of rock, what palisades?   60

Alberto Giacometti. (Swiss, 1901–1966). *Walking Man II.*
1948. Bronze, 26$^{1}/_{2}$ x 4$^{1}/_{2}$ x 11$^{5}/_{8}$″ in. Hirshhorn Museum
and Sculpture Garden, Smithsonian Institution, Washington D.C.
Gift of Joseph H. Hirshhorn, 1966. Photograph by Lee
Stalsworth. Accession number 66.2028. © 1996 Artists Rights
Society (ARS), New York/ADAGP, Paris.

Pablo Picasso. (Spanish, 1881–1973). *The Old Guitarist*. 1903. Oil on panel. 122.9 x 82.6 cm.
Helen Birch Bartlett Memorial Collection. 1926.253. © 1996 Artists Rights Society (ARS), New
York/Spadem, Paris. Photograph © 1994, The Art Institute of Chicago. All rights reserved.

WALLACE STEVENS (1879–1955)

The Man with the Blue Guitar

I

The man bent over his guitar,
A shearsman of sorts. The day was green.

They said, "You have a blue guitar,
You do not play things as they are."

The man replied, "Things as they are   5
Are changed upon the blue guitar."

And they said then, "But play, you must,
A tune beyond us, yet ourselves,

A tune upon the blue guitar
Of things exactly as they are."   10

II

I cannot bring a world quite round,
Although I patch it as I can.

I sing a hero's head, large eye
And bearded bronze, but not a man,

Although I patch him as I can   15
And reach through him almost to man.

If to serenade almost to man
Is to miss, by that, things as they are,

Say that it is the serenade
Of a man that plays a blue guitar.   20

III

Ah, but to play man number one,
To drive the dagger in his heart,

To lay his brain upon the board
And pick the acrid colors out,

To nail his thought across the door,   25
Its wings spread wide to rain and snow,

To strike his living hi and ho,
To tick it, tock it, turn it true,

To bang it from a savage blue,
Jangling the metal of the strings . . .   30

IV

So that's life, then: things as they are?
It picks its way on the blue guitar.

A million people on one string?
And all their manner in the thing,

And all their manner, right or wrong,   35
And all their manner, weak and strong?

The feelings crazily, craftily call,
Life a buzzing of flies in autumn air,

And that's life, then: things as they are,
This buzzing of the blue guitar.   40

Robert Motherwell (American, 1915–1991). *Blue Air.* 1946. Oil and sand on paperboard. 41 x 27″. Hirshhorn Museum and Sculpture Garden, Smithsonian Institution, Washington, D.C. Gift of Joseph H. Hirshhorn, 1966. Photographed by Lee Stalsworth. Accession number 66.3671. © 1995 Dedalus Foundation/Licensed by VAGA, New York, NY. Among the more literary of the group of artists known as Abstract Expressionists, Motherwell created several artworks during his career that were based on Stevens's "The Man with the Blue Guitar."

KATE CHOPIN (1851–1904)

The Storm

After the death of her Irish immigrant father when she was four, Kate Chopin was raised by her French Creole mother. She was educated in Catholic schools and read widely in French literature. When she was nineteen, she married Oscar Chopin, a wealthy New Orleans cotton broker. In 1888, Oscar Chopin died, having lost his fortune a few years earlier. Thus, at the age of 37, Kate Chopin was left with six children and no money with which to raise them. She moved the family to St. Louis, where she began to write stories depicting the Creole life she knew so well. Many of the stories were published and eventually collected in two anthologies, Bayou Folk *(1894) and* A Night in Arcadie *(1899). When she published her novel* The Awakening *(1899), her public judged it immoral, and subsequently her work lost favor with readers. "The Storm," which remained unpublished in Chopin's lifetime, was written after* The Awakening *and also deals with a controversial theme.*

1

The leaves were so still that even Bibi thought it was going to rain. Bobinôt, who was accustomed to converse on terms of perfect equality with his little son, called the child's attention to certain sombre clouds that were rolling with sinister intention from the west, accompanied by a sullen, threatening roar. They were at Friedheimer's store and decided to remain there till the storm had passed. They sat within the door on two empty kegs. Bibi was four years old and looked very wise.

"Mama'll be 'fraid, yes," he suggested with blinking eyes.

"She'll shut the house. Maybe she got Sylvie helpin' her this evenin'," Bobinôt responded reassuringly.

"No; she ent got Sylvie. Sylvie was helpin' her yistiday," piped Bibi.

Bobinôt arose and going across to the counter purchased a can of shrimps, of which Calixta was very fond. Then he returned to his perch on the keg and sat stolidly holding the can of shrimps while the storm burst. It shook the wooden store and seemed to be ripping great furrows in the distant field. Bibi laid his little hand on his father's knee and was not afraid.

2

Calixta, at home, felt no uneasiness for their safety. She sat at a side window sewing furiously on a sewing machine. She was greatly occupied and did not notice the approaching storm. But she felt very warm and often stopped to mop her face on which the perspiration gathered in beads. She unfastened her white sacque at the throat. It began to grow dark, and suddenly realizing the situation she got up hurriedly and went about closing windows and doors.

Out on the small front gallery she had hung Bobinôt's Sunday clothes to air and she hastened out to gather them before the rain fell. As she stepped outside, Alcée Laballière rode in at the gate. She had not seen him very often since her marriage, and never alone. She stood there with Bobinôt's coat in her hands, and the big rain drops began to fall. Alcée rode his horse under the shelter of a side projection where the chickens had huddled and there were plows and a harrow piled up in the corner.

"May I come and wait on your gallery till the storm is over, Calixta?" he asked.

"Come 'long in, M'sieur Alcée."

His voice and her own startled her as if from a trance, and she seized   10
Bobinôt's vest. Alcée, mounting to the porch, grabbed the trousers and snatched Bibi's braided jacket that was about to be carried away by a sudden gust of wind. He expressed an intention to remain outside, but it was soon apparent that he might as well have been out in the open: the water beat in upon the boards in driving sheets, and he went inside, closing the door after him. It was even necessary to put something beneath the door to keep the water out.

"My! what a rain! It's good two years sence it rain' like that," exclaimed Calixta as she rolled up a piece of bagging and Alcée helped her to thrust it beneath the crack.

She was a little fuller of figure than five years before when she married; but she had lost nothing of her vivacity. Her blue eyes still retained their melting quality; and her yellow hair, dishevelled by the wind and rain, kinked more stubbornly than ever about her ears and temples.

The rain beat upon the low, shingled roof with a force and clatter that threatened to break an entrance and deluge them there. They were in the dining room—the sitting room—the general utility room. Adjoining was her bed room, with Bibi's couch along side her own. The door stood open, and the room with its white, monumental bed, its closed shutters, looked dim and mysterious.

Alcée flung himself into a rocker and Calixta nervously began to gather up from the floor the lengths of a cotton sheet which she had been sewing.

"If this keeps up, *Dieu sait*° if the levees goin' to stan' it!" she exclaimed.   15

"What have you got to do with the levees?"

"I got enough to do! An' there's Bobinôt with Bibi out in that storm— if he only didn' left Friedheimer's!"

"Let us hope, Calixta, that Bobinôt's got sense enough to come in out of a cyclone."

She went and stood at the window with a greatly disturbed look on her face. She wiped the frame that was clouded with moisture. It was stiflingly hot. Alcée got up and joined her at the window, looking over her shoulder. The rain was coming down in sheets obscuring the view of far-off cabins and enveloping the distant wood in a gray mist. The playing of the lightning was incessant. A bolt struck a tall chinaberry tree at the edge of the

---

Dieu sait: God knows.

field. It filled all visible space with a blinding glare and the crash seemed to invade the very boards they stood upon.

Calixta put her hands to her eyes, and with a cry, staggered backward.   20 Alcée's arm encircled her, and for an instant he drew her close and spasmodically to him.

"*Bonté!*"° she cried, releasing herself from his encircling arm and retreating from the window, "the house'll go next! If I only knew w'ere Bibi was!" She would not compose herself; she would not be seated. Alcée clasped her shoulders and looked into her face. The contact of her warm, palpitating body when he had unthinkingly drawn her into his arms, had aroused all the old-time infatuation and desire for her flesh.

"Calixta," he said, "don't be frightened. Nothing can happen. The house is too low to be struck, with so many tall trees standing about. There! aren't you going to be quiet? say, aren't you?" He pushed her hair back from her face that was warm and steaming. Her lips were as red and moist as pomegranate seed. Her white neck and a glimpse of her full, firm bosom disturbed him powerfully. As she glanced up at him the fear in her liquid blue eyes had given place to a drowsy gleam that unconsciously betrayed a sensuous desire. He looked down into her eyes and there was nothing for him to do but to gather her lips in a kiss. It reminded him of Assumption.

"Do you remember—in Assumption. Calixta?" he asked in a low voice broken by passion. Oh! she remembered; for in Assumption he had kissed her and kissed and kissed her; until his senses would well nigh fail, and to save her he would resort to a desperate flight. If she was not an immaculate dove in those days, she was still inviolate; a passionate creature whose very defenselessness had made her defense, against which his honor forbade him to prevail. Now—well, now—her lips seemed in a manner free to be tasted, as well as her round, white throat and her whiter breasts.

They did not heed the crashing torrents, and the roar of the elements made her laugh as she lay in his arms. She was a revelation in that dim, mysterious chamber; as white as the couch she lay upon. Her firm, elastic flesh that was knowing for the first time its birthright, was like a creamy lily that the sun invites to contribute its breath and perfume to the undying life of the world.

The generous abundance of her passion, without guile or trickery, was   25 like a white flame which penetrated and found response in depths of his own sensuous nature that had never yet been reached.

When he touched her breasts they gave themselves up in quivering ecstasy, inviting his lips. Her mouth was a fountain of delight. And when he possessed her, they seemed to swoon together at the very borderland of life's mystery.

He stayed cushioned upon her, breathless, dazed, enervated, with his heart beating like a hammer upon her. With one hand she clasped his head, her lips lightly touching his forehead. The other hand stroked with a soothing rhythm his muscular shoulders.

Bonté!: My goodness!

The growl of the thunder was distant and passing away. The rain beat softly upon the shingles, inviting them to drowsiness and sleep. But they dared not yield.

The rain was over; and the sun was turning the glistening green world into a palace of gems. Calixta, on the gallery, watched Alcée ride away. He turned and smiled at her with a beaming face; and she lifted her pretty chin in the air and laughed aloud.

3

Bobinôt and Bibi, trudging home, stopped without at the cistern to make themselves presentable.   30

"My! Bibi, w'at will yo' mama say! You ought to be ashame'. You oughtn' put on those good pants. Look at 'em! An' that mud on yo' collar! How you got that mud on yo' collar, Bibi? I never saw such a boy!" Bibi was the picture of pathetic resignation. Bobinôt was the embodiment of serious solicitude as he strove to remove from his own person and his son's the signs of their tramp over heavy roads and through wet fields. He scraped the mud off Bibi's bare legs and feet with a stick and carefully removed all traces from his heavy brogans. Then, prepared for the worst—the meeting with an over-scrupulous housewife, they entered cautiously at the back door.

Calixta was preparing supper. She had set the table and was dripping coffee at the hearth. She sprang up as they came in.

"Oh, Bobinôt! You back! My! but I was uneasy. W'ere you been during the rain? An' Bibi? he ain't wet? he ain't hurt?" She had clasped Bibi and was kissing him effusively. Bobinôt's explanations and apologies which he had been composing all along the way, died on his lips as Calixta felt him to see if he were dry, and seemed to express nothing but satisfaction at their safe return.

"I brought you some shrimps, Calixta," offered Bobinôt, hauling the can from his ample side pocket and laying it on the table.

"Shrimps! Oh, Bobinôt! you too good fo' anything!" and she gave him   35
a smacking kiss on the cheek that resounded. "*J'vous reponds,*° we'll have a feas' to-night! umph-umph!"

Bobinôt and Bibi began to relax and enjoy themselves, and when the three seated themselves at table they laughed much and so loud that anyone might have heard them as far away as Laballière's.

4

Alcée Laballière wrote to his wife, Clarisse, that night. It was a loving letter, full of tender solitude. He told her not to hurry back, but if she and the babies liked it at Biloxi, to stay a month longer. He was getting on nicely; and though he missed them, he was willing to bear the separation a while

J'vous reponds: I assure you.

longer—realizing that their health and pleasure were the first things to be considered.

5

As for Clarisse, she was charmed upon receiving her husband's letter. She and the babies were doing well. The society was agreeable; many of her old friends and acquaintances were at the bay. And the first free breath since her marriage seemed to restore the pleasant liberty of her maiden days. Devoted as she was to her husband, their intimate conjugal life was something which she was more than willing to forego for a while.

So the storm passed and everyone was happy.

Considerations

1. Analyze Calixta and Bobinôt's marriage, using details from the story to back up your analysis. Would you describe the marriage as "good" or "bad"—or would you use a different word? What are the positive elements of the marriage? Does anything seem to be missing?

2. Look carefully at the words Chopin chooses to describe the scenes between Calixta and Alcée. What do the words and images suggest about the author's attitude toward her characters? Does she sympathize? Is she judging them? Explain.

3. What differences do you notice between Calixta's and Alcée's speech patterns? What might these differences suggest about their social, economic, and educational background? Given this analysis, write a narrative describing their last evening together in Assumption. Why might they have decided to part rather than to marry?

4. What purpose is served by the opening and ending sections of the story? How would the story be changed (and how would your response change) if they were omitted and the second section stood as the whole story? Consider how your evaluation of characters, actions, and choices might be affected.

5. Write an argument defending or criticizing Calixta's and Alcée's actions. As you plan your argument, consider the final line of the story, "So the storm passed and everyone was happy." Do you agree?

MARÍA LUISA BOMBAL (1910–1980)

New Islands

Born in Chile, María Luisa Bombal was educated in France, where she ma-
jored in philosophy and literature at the Sorbonne. In 1934, while sharing an
apartment in Buenos Aires with the poet Pablo Neruda and his wife, Bombal
wrote her first novella, The Final Mist *(1935). This work received great*
critical acclaim and established her as an outstanding innovative writer of Latin
American literature. From 1937 to 1940 she wrote screenplays for Argentina's
Sonofilm, as well as many short stories. "New Islands" appears in the collec-
tion New Islands *(1982).*

TRANSLATED BY RICHARD AND LUCIA CUNNINGHAM

All night long a howling wind had raged across the pampa. Now and
then it would slip inside the house through cracks in the doors and window
frames, sending ripples through the mosquito netting. Each time this happened, Yolanda would turn on the light, which flickered, held for a moment,
and then faded out again. At dawn, when her brother Federico came into
the room, she lay on her left shoulder, breathing with difficulty, moaning in
her sleep.

"Yolanda! Yolanda!"

She sat up like a shot. In order to see Federico, she parted her long
black hair and tossed it over her shoulders.

"Were you dreaming?" he asked.

"Oh, yes—horrible dreams."   5

"Why must you always sleep in that position? It's bad for your heart."

"I know, I know. What time is it? And where are you off to so early in
all this wind?"

"The lakes. It seems another island has emerged. That makes four so
far. Some people from La Figura hacienda have come to see them. So we'll
be having guests later. I wanted to let you know before I left."

Without shifting her position, Yolanda regarded her brother: a thin,
white-haired man whose tightfitting riding boots lent him an air of youth.
Men—how absurd they were! Always in motion, forever willing to take an
interest in everything. Upon retiring for the night, they demand to be awakened at daybreak. If they go to a fireplace, they remain standing, ready to
run to the other end of the room—ready always to escape, to flee toward
the futile. And they cough and smoke, speak loud as if they feared silence—
indeed, as if tranquillity were a mortal enemy.

"It's all right, Federico."   10

"So long, then."

The door slams; Federico's spurs jingle on the tile floor in the corridor.
Yolanda closes her eyes once more and, delicately, using elaborate care, sinks

back onto the pillows on her left shoulder, curling herself as usual into that position which Federico claims is so damaging to one's heart. Breathing heavily, she sighs, falling suddenly into one of her disturbing dreams—dreams from which, morning after morning, she wakes pale and exhausted, as if she had been battling insomnia throughout the entire night.

The visitors from La Figura hacienda, meanwhile, had reached the grassy bank where the lakes began. Daylight was spreading across the water, unfurling over the landscape like a fire. Out there against the horizon, barely visible under the cloudy sky, were the new islands: still smoking from the fiery effort that had lifted them from who knows what stratified depths.

"Four, four new islands!" the people shouted.

The wind did not subside until nightfall, by which time the men were   15
returning from hunting.

Do, re, mi, fa, sol, la, ti, do . . . Do, re, mi, fa, sol, la, ti, do . . .

The notes rise and fall, rise and fall like round, limpid crystal bubbles carried on the wind from the house, now flattened in the distance, to burst over the hunters like solemn, regulated raindrops.

Do, re, mi, fa, sol, la, ti, do . . .

It's Yolanda practicing, Sylvester says to himself. He pauses a moment to shift the carbine slung on his left shoulder, his heavy body trembling slightly.

Among the bushes bordering the lawn there are white flowers that   20
appear touched by frost. Juan Manuel bends over to examine one.

"Don't touch them," Sylvester warns. "They turn yellow. They're Yolanda's camellias," he adds with a smile.

That humble smile which does not suit him, thinks Juan Manuel. As soon as he relaxes his proud countenance, you see how old he is.

The house is in total darkness, but the notes continue to flow regularly: Do, re, mi, fa, sol, la, ti, do . . . Do, re, mi, fa, sol, la, ti, do . . .

"Have you met my sister Yolanda, Juan Manuel?"

On Federico's question, the woman sitting in shadow at the piano gives   25
the stranger her hand, withdrawing it immediately. She then rises, so slowly that she seems to grow upright, uncoiling like a beautiful snake. Very tall, she is extremely slender. Juan Manuel follows her with his eyes as she quickly and quietly turns on the lamps.

She is exactly like her name, thinks Juan Manuel. Pale, angular, and a bit savage. And there is something odd about her that I cannot place. But of course, he realizes as she glides through the door and disappears—her feet are too small. How strange that she can support such a long body on such tiny feet.

How dull this dinner among men, Juan Manuel decides. Among ten hunters thwarted by the wind who gulp down their food without a single manly deed to boast about. And Yolanda, he reflects, why doesn't she preside over the table now that Federico's wife is in Buenos Aires? What an extraordinary figure she makes! Ugly? Pretty? Fragile, that's it, very fragile. And that dark and brilliant gaze of hers—aggressive yet hunted . . . Whom does she look like? What does she resemble?

Juan Manuel lifts his glass, staring at the wine. Across from him sits Sylvester, who is drinking heavily and talking and laughing in a loud voice. He seems desperate.

The hunters stir the coals with a scoop and tongs, scattering ashes over the multiple fiery eyes which refuse to close—this the final act in a long and boring evening.

And now suddenly the grass and the trees in the garden begin to shiver 30 in the cold night breeze. Large insects beat their wings against the lantern illuminating the long open corridor. Leaning on Juan Manuel, Sylvester staggers toward his room, his feet slipping on the tiles that shine with vapor as if they had just been washed. His footsteps send frogs scurrying off to hide timidly in dark corners.

The iron grilles slamming shut across the doors seem in the silence of the night to echo the useless volley of shots fired by the hunters. Sylvester throws his heavy body on the bed and buries his emaciated face in his hands. His sighs irritate Juan Manuel—he who always detested sharing a room with anyone, let alone with a drunkard who moans.

"Oh, Juan Manuel, Juan Manuel . . ."

"What's the matter, Don Sylvester? You don't feel well?"

"Oh, my boy—who could know, who could know! . . ."

"Know what, Don Sylvester?" 35

"This," said the old man, taking his wallet from his jacket and handing it to Juan Manuel. "Look for the letter. Read it. Yes, a letter. That one, yes. Read it and tell me if you understand it."

An elongated, wavering handwriting flows like smoke across the yellowed, wrinkled pages: *Sylvester, I cannot marry you. Believe me, I have thought it over at great length. It isn't possible, it just isn't. Nevertheless, I love you, Sylvester, I love you and I suffer. But I cannot. Forget me. In vain I ask myself what might save me. A son, perhaps, a child whose sweet weight I could feel inside me forever. Forever! Not to see him grow, separated from me! Myself attached forever to that tiny heart, possessed always by that presence! I weep, Sylvester, I weep; and I cannot explain myself.—Yolanda.*

"I don't understand," Juan Manuel whispers uneasily.

"I have been trying for thirty years to understand," said Sylvester. "I loved her. You cannot know how much I loved her. No one loves like that anymore, Juan Manuel . . . One night, two weeks before we were to be married, she sent me this letter. Afterwards she refused to offer any explanation, and I was never permitted to see her alone. I waited, telling myself that time would solve everything. I am still waiting."

Juan Manuel seemed confused. "Was it the mother, Don Sylvester? Was 40 she also named Yolanda?"

"What? I am speaking of the one and only Yolanda, who tonight has again rejected me. This evening when I saw her, I said to myself: Maybe now that so many years have passed, Yolanda will at long last give me an explanation. But, as usual, she left the room. Sometimes, you know, Federico tries to talk to her about all this. But she starts trembling and runs away, as always . . ."

The far-off chugging of a train can now be heard. The steady insistent clacking seems to increase Juan Manuel's uneasiness.

"Yolanda was your fiancée, Don Sylvester?"

"Yes, my fiancée . . . my fiancée . . ."

Juan Manuel stares coldly at Sylvester's disoriented gestures, his swollen, sixty-year-old body so disastrously preserved. Don Sylvester, his father's old friend, and Yolanda's fiancé.

"Then she is not a young girl, Don Sylvester?"

Sylvester laughs stupidly.

"How old is she?" Juan Manuel inquires.

Sylvester rubs his forehead, eyes closed, trying to count. "Let's see, at that time I was twenty . . . no, twenty-three . . ."

But Juan Manuel hardly listens, momentarily relieved by a consoling reflection: What does age matter when one is so prodigiously young!

"Therefore she must be . . ."

Sylvester's words dissolve in a hacking cough. And again Juan Manuel feels a resurgence of the anxiety that holds him attentive to the secret Sylvester is drunkenly unraveling. And that train in the distance, coming closer now, its regular rhythm as laden with suspense as a drum roll—like a threat not yet become reality. The muffled, monotonous pounding unnerves him, growing louder and louder until, like one seeking escape, he goes to the window, pushes it open, and bends into the night. The headlights of the express glare across the immense plain like malevolent eyes.

"Damned train!" he grumbles. "When will it pass?"

Sylvester comes over to lean beside him, breathing deep as he gestures toward the two shimmering lights.

"It just left Lobos," he explains. "It generally takes half an hour to go by here."

She is fragile and her feet are too small for her height.

"How old is she, Don Sylvester?"

"I don't remember. I'll tell you tomorrow."

But why? Juan Manuel asks himself. Why this preoccupation with a woman I have seen only once in my life? Do I desire her? The train. Oh, that monotonous hissing monster advancing slowly, inexorably across the pampa! What's wrong with me? It must be that I am tired, he thinks, closing the window.

Meanwhile, she is at one end of the garden, leaning against the fence overlooking the hill as if she were bending over the rail of a ship anchored on the prairie. In the sky, a single motionless star: a large red star that seems about to shake loose from its orbit and spin off into infinite space. Juan Manuel stands beside her at the fence, gazing, too, at the pampa now submerged in the dark saturnine twilight. He speaks. What does he say? He whispers words of destiny in her ear. And now he takes her in his arms. And now the arms around her waist tremble, slide lower, caressing her gently. And she tosses, struggles, gripping the wooden rail to better resist. And then she wakes to find herself clutching the sheets, sobbing deep in her throat.

For a long time she weeps without moving, listening to the house quaver. The mirror moves slightly. A withered camellia blossom falls from a vase, dropping on the carpet with the soft thick sound of ripe fruit.

She waits for the train to go by and then, listening to its receding sonic boom, she drifts back to sleep, lying on her left shoulder.

In the morning the wind has resumed its fierce race across the pampa. But this day the hunters are in no mood to waste their ammunition in a gale. Instead, they launch two boats, bound for those new islands afloat on the horizon, rising from a cloud of foam and wheeling birds.

They land proudly, boisterously, carbines on their shoulders as they leap to shore, only to discover an oppressive, foul-smelling atmosphere that stops them in their tracks. After a brief pause they advance, stepping in amazement on slimy weeds that seem to be oozing from the hot and shifting soil. They stagger on amid spirals of sea gulls that swoop around them, flashing by their faces and screeching as they dip and rise. At one point, Juan Manuel lurches as the edge of a wing flails his chest.

And still they advance, crushing under their boots frenzied silver fish 65
stranded by the tide. Farther on, they find more strange vegetation: low bushes of pink coral, which they struggle for some time to uproot, pulling and pulling until their hands bleed.

The sea gulls cluster round them in ever-tightening spirals. Low, running clouds skim by overhead, weaving a vertiginous pattern of shadows. The fumes rising from the earth grow more dense by the moment. Everything boils, shakes violently, trembles. The hunters cannot see; can hardly breathe. Disheartened and afraid, they flee to their boats, return in silence to the mainland.

All afternoon they sat around a bonfire, chatting with the peons who periodically fed the flames with eucalyptus branches, waiting for the wind to abate. But again, as if to exasperate them, the wind did not die down until dusk.

Do, re, mi, fa, sol, la, ti, do . . . Once again, that methodical scale drifts toward them from the house. Juan Manuel pricks up his ears.

Do, re, mi, fa, sol, la, ti, do . . . Do, re, mi, fa, sol, la, ti, do . . . Do, re, mi, fa . . . Do, re, mi, fa . . . —the piano insists. And those notes repeated over and over beat against Juan Manuel's heart, striking where the sea gull's wing had wounded him that morning. Without knowing why, he gets to his feet and starts walking toward that music chiming endlessly through the trees like a summons.

As he reaches the camellia bushes, the piano suddenly falls silent. He 70
enters the darkened drawing room almost at a run, sees logs burning in the fireplace, the piano open . . . But where is Yolanda?

At the far end of the garden she leans against the fence, as if resting on the rail of a ship anchored on the pampa. And now she trembles, hearing the rustle of the lowermost pine-tree branches being brushed aside by someone coming up cautiously behind her. If only it were Juan Manuel!

She slowly turns her head. It is him, in the flesh this time. Oh, his dark, golden complexion in the gray twilight! Golden as though he were enveloped by a sunray. Joining her at the fence, he, too, stares out across the pampa. Frogs begin to sing in the irrigation ditches; and it is as if night were being ushered in by thousands of crystal bells.

Now he looks at her and smiles. Oh, his fine white teeth! They must be cold and hard like tiny chips of ice. And that warm virile odor he gives off, piercing her with pleasure. How sad to resist such pleasure, to shun that circle formed by this strong, beautiful man and his shadow!

"Yolanda," he murmurs.

She feels upon hearing her name that a sudden intimacy exists between them. How marvelous that he called her by name! It would seem that now they are linked by a long and passionate past. Not sharing a past— that was what held them apart and inhibited them.

"All night long I dreamed of you, Juan Manuel, all night long . . ."

He embraces her; she does not reject him. But she obliges his arm to remain chastely around her waist.

"Someone is calling me," she says abruptly, moving out of his embrace and running off. The pine branches she hastily brushes aside rebound with a snap in Juan Manuel's face, scratching his cheek. Disconcerted by a woman for the first time in his life, he runs after her.

She is dressed in white. Only now, as she goes over to her brother to light his pipe—gravely and meticulously, as if performing a trifling daily ritual—only now does he notice that she is wearing a long gown. She has put it on to dine with them. Then Juan Manuel remembers the mud on his boots and rushes to his room to clean them.

On his return to the drawing room, he finds Yolanda seated on a sofa in front of the fireplace. The dancing flames alternately lighten and darken her black eyes. With her arms crossed behind her neck, she is long and slender like a sword, or like . . . like what? In vain Juan Manuel searches for the proper simile.

"Dinner is served," the maid announces.

As Yolanda rises, her flame-lightened pupils are suddenly extinguished. And going past Juan Manuel, she casts those opaque black eyes on him, the sheer tulle sleeve of her dress grazing his chest like a wing. And in that instant the simile comes to him.

"Now I know what you look like," he whispers. "A sea gull."

Uttering a strange, hoarse cry, Yolanda collapses on the carpet. Momentarily stunned, the others now rush to her side, pick her up, carry her unconscious form to the sofa. Federico sends the maid scurrying for water. Turning angrily to Juan Manuel, he asks: "What did you say to her? What did you *say?*"

"I told her . . ." Juan Manuel begins; then lapses into silence, feeling a   85
sudden stab of guilt—fearing, without knowing why, to reveal a secret which
is not his.

Yolanda, meanwhile, comes to. Sighing, she presses her heart with both
hands, as if recovering from a fright. She half sits up, then stretches out on
her left shoulder.

"No," Federico protests, "not on your heart. It's bad for you."

She gives him a weak smile, whispers as she waves him away: "I know,
I know. Now please leave me alone."

And there is such sad vehemence, such weariness in her gesture, that
everyone moves off into the next room without objecting—everyone except
Juan Manuel, who remains standing beside the fireplace.

Pale and motionless, Yolanda sleeps, or pretends to sleep, while Juan   90
Manuel, a silent sentinel, waits anxiously for a sign—be it to stay or go.

At daybreak on this third morning the hunters gather once more at the
edge of the lakes, which today at last are calm. Mute, they contemplate the
smooth surface of the water, shocked into silence by the vista on that distant
gray horizon.

For the new islands have vanished.

Again they launch boats, Juan Manuel setting off alone in a dinghy.
He rows determinedly, skirting the old islands, which teem with wildlife,
refusing to be tempted like his companions by the lashing sound of wings,
of cooing and small sharp cries—the old islands, where things rattle and
crack like rattan splitting, where the banks are covered with oozy moving
flowers spread out like a bed of slime. Soon Juan Manuel is lost in the
distance, a receding silhouette rowing a zigzagging course in search of the
exact spot where only yesterday they had landed to explore the four new
islands. Where was the first one? Here. No, there. No, rather, here. He
leans over the water to look for it, though he knows that his eyes could
never see the muddy bottom, where, after its vertiginous plunge, the island
sank into silt and algae.

Within the circle of a nearby whirlpool something soft and transparent
floats: a small jellyfish. Plucking it from the water in his handkerchief, Juan
Manuel ties the four corners of the cloth over it like a pouch.

The day is drawing to a close when Yolanda brings her horse to a halt   95
at the base of the hill and opens the gate for the returning hunters. Setting
off again, she rides on ahead to the house, the skirt of her tweed riding habit
brushing the bushes. And Juan Manuel notes that, though she is mounted in
the old-fashioned way, sitting genteelly sidesaddle, with her hair streaming
around her face she looks like an Amazon huntress. The light is fading fast,
giving way to a dusky bluish spectrum. A chorus of long-tailed magpies
croaks by overhead before fluttering down on the naked branches of the now
ashen forest.

Juan Manuel suddenly recalls a painting that still hangs in the corridor of his old hacienda in Adrogué: a tall, pensive Amazon equestrienne who, having surrendered to her horse's will, seems to wander lost and disheartened among dry leaves at dusk. The picture is entitled "Autumn," or "Sadness"— he does not remember which.

On the night table in his room he finds a letter from his mother. *Since you are not here, I will take the orchid for Elsa tomorrow,* she writes. Tomorrow. That is today, he realizes. Today, then, is the fifth anniversary of his wife's death. Five years already. Her name was Elsa. He had never grown accustomed to the fact that she had such a lovely name. "And your name is *Elsa,*" he would say as he embraced her, as if that alone were a miracle more breathtaking even than her fair beauty and placid smile. Elsa! The perfection of her features! Her translucent complexion, under which ran veins that seemed the fine blue strokes of a master watercolorist. So many years of love! And then that deadly disease. Like a piercing knife comes the memory of that night when, covering her face with her hands to ward off his kiss, she had cried: "I don't want you to see me like this, so ugly . . . not even after death. You must cover my face with orchids. You have to promise me . . ."

But Juan Manuel does not want to begin thinking of all that. Desolate, he tosses the letter on the night table without reading further.

The same serene twilight suffusing the pampa washes over Buenos Aires, inundating in steel blue the stones and the air and the mist-covered trees in Recoleta Square.

Juan Manuel's mother walks confidently through a labyrinth of narrow   100 streets. Never has she lost her way in this intricate city, for as a child her parents taught her how to find her bearings in any quarter. And here is their dwelling—the small cold crypt where parents, grandparents, and so many ancestors rest. So many in such a narrow chamber! If only it were true that each of them sleeps alone with his past and his present, isolated yet side by side! But no, that isn't possible. She lays her spray of orchids on the ground, rummaging through her purse for the key. Then, before the altar, she makes the sign of the cross and checks that the candelabra are well polished, that the white altar cloth is well starched. She sighs and descends into the crypt, holding nervously on to the bronze railing. An oil lamp hangs from the low ceiling, its flame mirrored in the black marble floor and shining on the bronze rings of the various compartments arranged sequentially by date. Here all is order and solemn indifference.

Outside, the drizzle starts up again. The raindrops rebound audibly on the concrete streets. But here everything seems remote: the rain, the city, the obligations that await her at home. And now she sighs again, going over to the smallest and newest compartment, and places the orchids at the head of the casket—where Elsa's face reposes. Poor Juan Manuel, she thinks.

She tries unsuccessfully to feel sadness for her daughter-in-law's fate. But that rancor she admits only to the priest persists in her heart, despite the dozens of rosaries and the multiple short prayers her confessor orders her to recite as penance.

She stares hard at the casket, wishing her eyes could pierce the metal liner, wanting to see, to know, to verify . . . Dead for five years! She was so fragile. Perhaps the plain gold ring has already slipped off her frivolous crumbling fingers, fallen into that dusty hole that was once her bosom. Maybe so. But is she dead? No. She has won in spite of everything. One never dies entirely, that is the truth. That strong dark little boy who continues their line, the grandson who has become her only reason for living, has the blue and candid eyes of Elsa.

At three o'clock in the morning Juan Manuel finally resolves to abandon the armchair beside the fireplace where, nearly stupefied by the heat of the flames, he has been smoking and drinking listlessly for hours. He hops over the dogs asleep in the doorway and starts down the long, open corridor. He feels lazy and tired, very tired. Last night Sylvester, he thinks, and tonight me. I am completely drunk.

Sylvester is asleep. He must have dropped off unexpectedly, because the   105
lamp on the night table is still lit.

His mother's letter lies where he left it, still half open. A long postscript scribbled by his son brings a brief smile to his lips. He tries to decipher the winding infantile handwriting through blurred eyes: *Papa. Grandma says I can write to you here. I have learned three more words from the new geography book you gave me. And I am going to write the words and the definitions from memory.*

Aerolite: Name given to pieces of minerals that fall from outer space to the earth's surface. Aerolites are planetary fragments that float in space and . . .

"Aiee!" Juan Manuel moans to himself, staggering as he shakes his head to blot out the definition, those evocative, dazzling words that blind him as though a thousand tiny suns were bursting in front of his eyes.

Hurricane: Violent swirling wind made up of various opposing air masses that form whirlwinds . . .

"That boy!" Juan Manuel groans. And he feels chilled to the bone,   110
while a tremendous roaring pounds his brain like icy waves pounding a beach.

Halo: Luminous circle that sometimes surrounds the moon.

A light mist seeping through the open window obscures his vision, a blue mist that enfolds him softly. "Halo," he murmurs. An immense tenderness comes over him. Yolanda! If only he could see her, talk to her!

If only he could stand at her bedroom door and listen to her breathing.

Everyone, everything is asleep. How many doors he had to open, some by force, as he crept across the east wing of that old hacienda, hooding the lamp flame with his cupped hand! How many empty, dusty rooms where furniture lay piled in the corners, and how many others in which, as he passed by, unrecognizable people sighed and turned under the sheets!

He had chosen the way of ghosts and murderers.   115

And now that he has his ear against Yolanda's door, all he can hear is the beating of his own heart.

A piece of furniture must, no doubt, block the door from the inside; a very light piece of furniture, since he shoves it aside with little effort. Who is moaning? Juan Manuel turns up the lamp; the room at first seems to spin, then becomes quiet and orderly as his eyes adjust.

He sees a narrow bed veiled by mosquito netting where Yolanda sleeps on her left side, her dark curly hair covering her face like a latticework of luxuriant vines. She moans, caught in some nightmare. Juan Manuel sets the lamp on the floor, parts the mosquito netting, and takes her hand. She clutches his fingers as he helps her to rise from the pillows, to escape from the dream and the weight of that monstrous hair which must have pinned her down in those dark regions of sleep.

She opens her eyes at last, sighs with relief, and whispers: "Thank you."

"Thank you," she repeats, fixing him with her somnambulant eyes. 120 "Oh, it was awful!" she explains. "I was in a horrible place. In a park I often visit in my sleep. A park. Giant plants. Ferns tall as trees. And silence . . . I don't know how to describe it . . . Silence as green as chloroform . . . and suddenly, beneath the silence, a low buzzing sound, growing louder, coming nearer . . . Death, it is death. And then I tried to escape, to wake up. Because if I did not wake up, if death ever found me in that park, I would be doomed to stay forever, don't you think?"

Juan Manuel makes no reply, fearing to shatter this intimacy with the sound of his voice.

Taking a deep breath, Yolanda continues. "They say that in sleep we return to those places where we lived in a prior existence. I, too, sometimes return to a certain Creole house. A room, a patio, a room, another patio with a fountain in the center. I go there and . . ."

She falls silent and looks at him.

The moment he feared so much has come. The moment when, lucid at last and free from terror, she asks herself how and why this man is sitting on the edge of her bed. He waits, resigned for the imperious "Out of here!" and that solemn gesture with which women are reported to show one the door in instances like this.

But no. Yolanda puts her head on his chest, pressing against his heart. 125

Astonished, Juan Manuel does not move. Oh, that delicate temple and the smell of flowering honeysuckle coming from those locks of hair pressed against his lips! He remains motionless for a long time. Motionless, tender, full of wonder—as if an unexpected and priceless treasure had fallen into his arms by accident.

Yolanda! His embrace tightens, pressing her to him. But she cries out—a brief, husky, strange cry—and grabs his arms. They struggle, Juan Manuel entangling himself in her thick, sweet-scented hair. He grapples until he is able to seize her by the neck, and then he brutally throws her down on her back.

Gasping, she tosses her head from side to side, weeping as Juan Manuel kisses her mouth and caresses one of her breasts, small and hard like the camellias she cultivates. So many tears. Running silently down her cheeks, so many tears. Falling on the pillow like hot watery pearls, dropping into the hollow of his hand still gripping her neck.

Ashamed, his passion ebbing, Juan Manuel relaxes his embrace.

"Do you hate me, Yolanda?"   130

She is silent, inert.

"Shall I stay?"

Closing her eyes, she whispers: "No, please go."

The wooden floorboards creak as he crosses to the lamp and goes to the door, leaving Yolanda submerged in shadow.

On the fourth day, a fine mist shrouds the pampa in a white cottony   135
silence that muffles and shortens the sound of the hunters' guns out on the islands and blinds the frightened storks planing in to seek sanctuary on the lake.

And Yolanda—what is she doing? Juan Manuel wonders. What is she doing while he drags his mudheavy boots through the reeds, killing birds without reason or passion? Maybe she is in the orchard looking for the last strawberries, or pulling up the first radishes: *One must grasp the leaves tight and take them with a single pull, tearing them out of the dark earth like tiny red hearts.* Or it may be that she is in the house, standing on a stool by an open cupboard, the maid handing her a stack of freshly ironed sheets which she will carefully arrange in even piles. And if she were waiting at the window for his return? Anything is possible with a woman like Yolanda, such a strange woman, one who resembles a . . . But he checks himself, afraid of hurting her in his thoughts.

Twilight again. The hunter gazes across the shadowy pampa, trying to locate the hill and the house. A distant light blinks on amid the fog, pointing the way like a miniature lighthouse.

He drags his boat up the bank and starts across the grassland toward the light. On the way he puts to flight a few head of grazing cattle, their hair twisted into curls by the damp breath of the fog. He leaps barbed-wire fences, the fog clinging to the points like fleece. He sidesteps the thick clumps of thistle that glisten silvery and phosphorescent in the darkness.

Reaching the gate, he crosses the park and goes past the camellias in the garden to a certain window, where he wipes the pane free of fog and then stands transfixed as before his eyes a fairy tale unfolds.

Yolanda is standing naked in the bathroom, absorbed in the contempla-   140
tion of her right shoulder.

Her right shoulder—on which something light and flexible looms, drooping down to cover a small portion of her back. A wing, or rather, the beginning of a wing. Or more exactly, the stump of a wing. A small atrophied member which she now strokes carefully, as if dreading the touch.

The rest of her body is exactly as he had imagined: slender, proud, and white.

A hallucination, Juan Manuel thinks to himself as he drives crazily, his hands shaking on the steering wheel, along the highway. The long walk, the fog, the weariness, and this state of anxiety I've been living in for the last few days have all combined to make me see what does not exist. Should I go back? But how would I explain my abrupt departure? Don't think about it until you get to Buenos Aires. That's the best thing to do.

By the time he reaches the suburbs of the city, a fine powdery mist coats the windshield. The windshield wipers click like nickel swords, tic-tac, tic-tac, back and forth with a regularity as implacable as his anguish.

He crosses Buenos Aires, dark and deserted in the light shower which   145
bursts into heavy rain as he opens the gate and starts up the walk to his house.

"What's the matter?" his mother asks. "Why have you come back at this hour?"

"My son?"

"Sleeping. It's eleven o'clock, Juan Manuel."

"I want to see him. Good night, Mother."

The old woman shrugs her shoulders and pads off to her room wrapped   150
in a long robe. No, she will never grow accustomed to her son's whims. He is very bright, a fine lawyer; but she would have preferred him less talented and more conventional, like everyone else's sons.

Juan Manuel goes into his son's bedroom and turns on the light. Curled up next to the wall, his head covered by the sheets, the boy resembles a ball of white twine. Uncovering him, Juan Manuel thinks: He sleeps like an untamed little animal. In spite of the fact that he is nine years old, and notwithstanding his meticulous grandmother.

"Billy, wake up."

The boy sits up in bed, blinks his eyes, and grants his father a sleepy smile.

"I brought you a gift, Billy."

The boy stretches out his hand. Searching through his pockets, Juan   155
Manuel takes out the handkerchief tied into a pouch and hands it to his son. Billy unties the knots and spreads the handkerchief open. Finding nothing, he looks up at his father with a trusting expression, waiting for an explanation.

"It was a kind of flower, Billy—a magnificent jellyfish, I swear. I fished it from the lake for you . . . and it has disappeared . . ."

The boy thinks for a moment and then cries triumphantly: "No, Papa, it didn't disappear; it *melted*. Because jellyfish are made out of water, just water. I learned it in the geography book you gave me."

Outside, the rain lashes the great leaves of the palm tree in the corner of their garden, its shiny-as-patent-leather branches thrashing against the walls.

"You're right, Billy. It melted."

"But . . . jellyfish live in the sea, Papa. How did they get to the lakes?" 160

"I don't know, son," says Juan Manuel, suddenly tired of the conversation, his mind whirling.

Maybe I should telephone Yolanda, he thinks. Everything might seem less vague, less dreadful if I could hear her voice—which, like all other voices under similar circumstances, would simply sound distant, a bit surprised by an unexpected call.

He covers Billy and arranges the pillows. Then he goes back down the solemn staircase in that huge house, so cold and ugly in the rain and lightning. The telephone hangs in the hall—another of his mother's inspirations. As he unhooks the small tube-like receiver, a flash of lightning illuminates the front windows from top to bottom. He asks the operator for a number, and while he waits, the deafening thunderclap rolls over the sleeping city like a train roaring through his living room.

And my call, he thinks, now races through the wires under the rain. Now it is passing through Rivadavia with its line of darkened streetlights, and now it is zooming by the suburbs with their muddy flooding pathways, taking now to the freeway and flying along that straight and lonely road until, by now surely, it reaches the vast pampa with its occasional small villages, going like a bullet now across provincial cities where the asphalt glistens like water under the moonlight, and now perhaps shooting out into open country, alone in the rain again, hurtling past a closed railway station, and then dashing across the pasture to the hill, along the poplar-lined drive to dive into the house. And now it rings insistently, echoing and reechoing in the large deserted drawing room, where the wooden floors creak and the roof leaks in one corner.

The ringing resounds for a long time, vibrating hoarsely in Juan Manuel's ear, echoing sharply in the empty drawing room while he waits anxiously. Then someone suddenly lifts the receiver at the other end. But before the voice can say a word, Juan Manuel slams the receiver onto its hook. 165

Thinking: If I had said, "I can't go through with it, Yolanda. I've thought it out, believe me. It just isn't possible." If I had at least confirmed my doubts about that horror. But I'm afraid to know the truth.

He climbs the staircase slowly.

There was something more cruel, more punishing than death, after all. And he had believed that death was the final mystery, the ultimate suffering!

Death—that blind alley!

While he grew older, Elsa would remain eternally young, preserved forever at age thirty-three as on the day she departed from this life. And the day would come when Billy would be older than his mother, when he would know more of the world than she. 170

Think of it: Elsa's hands become dust, yet her very gestures perpetuated in her letters, in the sweater she knitted for him; and those luminous irises of her now empty eyes still shining with life in her photographs . . . Elsa erased, fixed in the earth but yet living in their memory and still part of their everyday life as though her spirit kept growing and could react even to things she once ignored.

Nevertheless, Juan Manuel now knows that there is a condition far more cruel and incomprehensible than any of death's little corollaries, for he has perceived a new mystery: a suffering consisting of amazement and fear.

The light from Billy's bedroom throws a shaft into the dark corridor, inviting him to enter once more in hope of finding his son still awake. But Billy is asleep, and so Juan Manuel looks around the room for something to distract himself and thereby ease his anguish. He goes to Billy's desk and turns the pages of the new geography book. *History of the Earth . . . The Sidereal Phase of the Earth . . . Life in the Paleozoic Era . . .*

And then he reads: *How beautiful must this silent landscape have been in which giant lycopodiums and equisetums raised themselves to such a height, and where mammoth ferns swayed like trees in the humid air . . .*

What landscape is this? he wonders. I cannot have seen it before, surely.   175 Why, then, does it seem so familiar? He turns the page, reading at random: . . . *In any case, it is during the Carboniferous Period when swarms of flying insects appear over the now arborescent regions. During the Late Carboniferous there were insects which possessed three pairs of wings. The most remarkable insects of this Period were very large, similar in shape to our present-day dragonflies but much bigger, having a wingspan of sixty-five centimeters . . .*

Yolanda's dreams, he realizes. The sweet and terrible secret of her shoulder. Perhaps this was where the explanation of the mystery lay.

But Juan Manuel feels incapable of soaring into the intricate galleries of Nature in order to arrive at the mystery's origin. He fears losing his way in that wild world with its disorderly and poorly mapped pathways, strewn with an unsystematic confusion of clues; fears falling into some dark abyss that no amount of logic will lead him out of. And abandoning Yolanda once more, he closes the book, turns off the light, and leaves the room.

Considerations

1. The story is divided into twelve sections. Briefly summarize each section and explain the relationship of the sections to each other. How do they work together to present characters, conflicts, and themes?
2. In the first section, how does Yolanda characterize men? Do the actions in the story support this characterization? If Federico could know what his sister thought about men, how do you think he might respond to her?
3. How does the conversation between Juan Manuel and Don Sylvester in the second section of the story change the picture you have formed of Yolanda after reading the first section?

4. What details do you learn about the relationship between Juan Manuel and his mother? About the relationships among Juan Manuel, his mother, and his wife?

5. What is "the sweet and terrible secret of [Yolanda's] shoulder"? How does this secret relate to the story's themes and to its vision of the relationships between men and women?

BOBBIE ANN MASON (1940–   )

Shiloh

*Born and raised in rural western Kentucky, Bobbie Ann Mason graduated
from the University of Kentucky before pursuing graduate studies at the State
University of New York at Binghamton and the University of Connecticut,
where she earned a Ph.D. She has worked as a feature reporter for several
magazines and in 1975 published* The Girl Sleuth: A Guide to the
Bobbsey Twins, Nancy Drew, and Their Sisters. *Her stories, many of
which focus on the lives of people in rural Kentucky, have received wide praise.
She is also noted as the author of* In Country, *a novel addressing themes
related to the Vietnam War; this novel has been made into a film.* "Shiloh"
appears in Shiloh and Other Stories *(1982).*

Leroy Moffitt's wife, Norma Jean, is working on her pectorals. She lifts
three-pound dumbbells to warm up, then progresses to a twenty-pound barbell. Standing with her legs apart, she reminds Leroy of Wonder Woman.

"I'd give anything if I could just get these muscles to where they're real
hard," says Norma Jean. "Feel this arm. It's not as hard as the other one."

"That's 'cause you're right-handed," says Leroy, dodging as she swings
the barbell in an arc.

"Do you think so?"

"Sure."   5

Leroy is a truckdriver. He injured his leg in a highway accident four
months ago, and his physical therapy, which involves weights and a pulley,
prompted Norma Jean to try building herself up. Now she is attending a
body-building class. Leroy has been collecting temporary disability since his
tractor-trailer jackknifed in Missouri, badly twisting his left leg in its socket.
He has a steel pin in his hip. He will probably not be able to drive his rig
again. It sits in the backyard, like a gigantic bird that has flown home to
roost. Leroy has been home in Kentucky for three months, and his leg is
almost healed, but the accident frightened him and he does not want to drive
any more long hauls. He is not sure what to do next. In the meantime, he
makes things from craft kits. He started by building a miniature log cabin
from notched Popsicle sticks. He varnished it and placed it on the TV set,
where it remains. It reminds him of a rustic Nativity scene. Then he tried
string art (sailing ships on black velvet), a macramé owl kit, a snap-together
B-17 Flying Fortress, and a lamp made out of a model truck, with a light
fixture screwed in the top of the cab. At first the kits were diversions, something to kill time, but now he is thinking about building a full-scale log
house from a kit. It would be considerably cheaper than building a regular
house, and besides, Leroy has grown to appreciate how things are put together. He has begun to realize that in all the years he was on the road he
never took time to examine anything. He was always flying past scenery.

"They won't let you build a log cabin in any of the new subdivisions," Norma Jean tells him.

"They will if I tell them it's for you," he says, teasing her. Ever since they were married, he has promised Norma Jean he would build her a new home one day. They have always rented, and the house they live in is small and nondescript. It does not even feel like a home, Leroy realizes now.

Norma Jean works at the Rexall drugstore, and she has acquired an amazing amount of information about cosmetics. When she explains to Leroy the three stages of complexion care, involving creams, toners, and moisturizers, he thinks happily of other petroleum products—axle grease, diesel fuel. This is a connection between him and Norma Jean. Since he has been home, he has felt unusually tender about his wife and guilty over his long absences. But he can't tell what she feels about him. Norma Jean has never complained about his traveling; she has never made hurt remarks, like calling his truck a "widow-maker." He is reasonably certain she has been faithful to him, but he wishes she would celebrate his permanent homecoming more happily. Norma Jean is often startled to find Leroy at home, and he thinks she seems a little disappointed about it. Perhaps he reminds her too much of the early days of their marriage, before he went on the road. They had a child who died as an infant, years ago. They never speak about their memories of Randy, which have almost faded, but now that Leroy is home all the time, they sometimes feel awkward around each other, and Leroy wonders if one of them should mention the child. He has the feeling that they are waking up out of a dream together—that they must create a new marriage, start afresh. They are lucky they are still married. Leroy has read that for most people losing a child destroys the marriage—or else he heard this on *Donahue*. He can't always remember where he learns things anymore.

At Christmas, Leroy bought an electric organ for Norma Jean. She   10
used to play the piano when she was in high school. "It don't leave you," she told him once. "It's like riding a bicycle."

The new instrument had so many keys and buttons that she was bewildered by it at first. She touched the keys tentatively, pushed some buttons, then pecked out "Chopsticks." It came out in an amplified fox-trot rhythm, with marimba sounds.

"It's an orchestra!" she cried.

The organ had a pecan-look finish and eighteen preset chords, with optional flute, violin, trumpet, clarinet, and banjo accompaniments. Norma Jean mastered the organ almost immediately. At first she played Christmas songs. Then she bought *The Sixties Songbook* and learned every tune in it, adding variations to each with the rows of brightly colored buttons.

"I didn't like these old songs back then," she said. "But I have this crazy feeling I missed something."

"You didn't miss a thing," said Leroy.   15

Leroy likes to lie on the couch and smoke a joint and listen to Norma Jean play "Can't Take My Eyes Off You" and "I'll Be Back." He is back again. After fifteen years on the road, he is finally settling down with the woman he loves. She is still pretty. Her skin is flawless. Her frosted curls resemble pencil trimmings.

Now that Leroy has come home to stay, he notices how much the town has changed. Subdivisions are spreading across western Kentucky like an oil slick. The sign at the edge of town says "Pop: 11,500"—only seven hundred more than it said twenty years before. Leroy can't figure out who is living in all the new houses. The farmers who used to gather around the courthouse square on Saturday afternoons to play checkers and spit tobacco juice have gone. It has been years since Leroy has thought about the farmers, and they have disappeared without his noticing.

Leroy meets a kid named Stevie Hamilton in the parking lot at the new shopping center. While they pretend to be strangers meeting over a stalled car, Stevie tosses an ounce of marijuana under the front seat of Leroy's car. Stevie is wearing orange jogging shoes and a T-shirt that says CHATTAHOO-CHEE SUPER-RAT. His father is a prominent doctor who lives in one of the expensive subdivisions in a new white-columned brick house that looks like a funeral parlor. In the phone book under his name there is a separate number, with the listing "Teenagers."

"Where do you get this stuff?" asks Leroy. "From your pappy?"

"That's for me to know and you to find out," Stevie says. He is slit-   20
eyed and skinny.

"What else you got?"

"What you interested in?"

"Nothing special. Just wondered."

Leroy used to take speed on the road. Now he has to go slowly. He needs to be mellow. He leans back against the car and says, "I'm aiming to build me a log house, soon as I get time. My wife, though, I don't think she likes the idea."

"Well, let me know when you want me again," Stevie says. He has a   25
cigarette in his cupped palm, as though sheltering it from the wind. He takes a long drag, then stomps it on the asphalt and slouches away.

Stevie's father was two years ahead of Leroy in high school. Leroy is thirty-four. He married Norma Jean when they were both eighteen, and their child Randy was born a few months later, but he died at the age of four months and three days. He would be about Stevie's age now. Norma Jean and Leroy were at the drive-in, watching a double feature (*Dr. Strangelove* and *Lover Come Back*), and the baby was sleeping in the back seat. When the first movie ended, the baby was dead. It was the sudden infant death syndrome. Leroy remembers handing Randy to a nurse at the emergency room, as though he were offering her a large doll as a present. A dead baby feels like a sack of flour. "It just happens sometimes," said the doctor, in what Leroy always recalls as a nonchalant tone. Leroy can hardly remember the child anymore, but he still sees vividly a scene from *Dr. Strangelove* in which the

President of the United States was talking in a folksy voice on the hot line to the Soviet premier about the bomber accidentally headed toward Russia. He was in the War Room, and the world map was lit up. Leroy remembers Norma Jean standing catatonically beside him in the hospital and himself thinking: Who is this strange girl? He had forgotten who she was. Now scientists are saying that crib death is caused by a virus. Nobody knows anything, Leroy thinks. The answers are always changing.

When Leroy gets home from the shopping center, Norma Jean's mother, Mabel Beasley, is there. Until this year, Leroy has not realized how much time she spends with Norma Jean. When she visits, she inspects the closets and then the plants, informing Norma Jean when a plant is droopy or yellow. Mabel calls the plants "flowers," although there are never any blooms. She always notices if Norma Jean's laundry is piling up. Mabel is a short, overweight woman whose tight, brown-dyed curls look more like a wig than the actual wig she sometimes wears. Today she has brought Norma Jean an off-white dust ruffle she made for the bed; Mabel works in a custom-upholstery shop.

"This is the tenth one I made this year," Mabel says. "I got started and couldn't stop."

"It's real pretty," says Norma Jean.

"Now we can hide things under the bed," says Leroy, who gets along   30 with his mother-in-law primarily by joking with her. Mabel has never really forgiven him for disgracing her by getting Norma Jean pregnant. When the baby died, she said that fate was mocking her.

"What's that thing?" Mabel says to Leroy in a loud voice, pointing to a tangle of yarn on a piece of canvas.

Leroy holds it up for Mabel to see. "It's my needlepoint," he explains. "This is a *Star Trek* pillow cover."

"That's what a woman would do," says Mabel. "Great day in the morning!"

"All the big football players on TV do it," he says.

"Why, Leroy, you're always trying to fool me. I don't believe you for   35 one minute. You don't know what to do with yourself—that's the whole trouble. Sewing!"

"I'm aiming to build us a log house," says Leroy. "Soon as my plans come."

"Like *heck* you are," says Norma Jean. She takes Leroy's needlepoint and shoves it into a drawer. "You have to find a job first. Nobody can afford to build now anyway."

Mabel straightens her girdle and says, "I still think before you get tied down y'all ought to take a little run to Shiloh."

"One of these days, Mama," Norma Jean says impatiently.

Mabel is talking about Shiloh, Tennessee. For the past few years, she   40 has been urging Leroy and Norma Jean to visit the Civil War battleground there. Mabel went there on her honeymoon—the only real trip she ever took. Her husband died of a perforated ulcer when Norma Jean was ten, but

Mabel, who was accepted into the United Daughters of the Confederacy in 1975, is still preoccupied with going back to Shiloh.

"I've been to kingdom come and back in that truck out yonder," Leroy says to Mabel, "but we never yet set foot in that battleground. Ain't that something? How did I miss it?"

"It's not even that far," Mabel says.

After Mabel leaves, Norma Jean reads to Leroy from a list she has made. "Things you could do," she announces. "You could get a job as a guard at Union Carbide, where they'd let you set on a stool. You could get on at the lumberyard. You could do a little carpenter work, if you want to build so bad. You could—"

"I can't do something where I'd have to stand up all day."

"You ought to try standing up all day behind a cosmetics counter. It's   45 amazing that I have strong feet, coming from two parents that never had strong feet at all." At the moment Norma Jean is holding on to the kitchen counter, raising her knees one at a time as she talks. She is wearing two-pound ankle weights.

"Don't worry," says Leroy. "I'll do something."

"You could truck calves to slaughter for somebody. You wouldn't have to drive any big old truck for that."

"I'm going to build you this house," says Leroy. "I want to make you a real home."

"I don't want to live in any log cabin."

"It's not a cabin. It's a house."   50

"I don't care. It looks like a cabin."

"You and me together could lift those logs. It's just like lifting weights."

Norma Jean doesn't answer. Under her breath, she is counting. Now she is marching through the kitchen. She is doing goose steps.

Before his accident, when Leroy came home he used to stay in the house with Norma Jean, watching TV in bed and playing cards. She would cook fried chicken, picnic ham, chocolate pie—all his favorites. Now he is home alone much of the time. In the mornings, Norma Jean disappears, leaving a cooling place in the bed. She eats a cereal called Body Buddies, and she leaves the bowl on the table, with the soggy tan balls floating in a milk puddle. He sees things about Norma Jean that he never realized before. When she chops onions, she stares off into a corner, as if she can't bear to look. She puts on her house slippers almost precisely at nine o'clock every evening and nudges her jogging shoes under the couch. She saves bread heels for the birds. Leroy watches the birds at the feeder. He notices the peculiar way goldfinches fly past the window. They close their wings, then fall, then spread their wings to catch and lift themselves. He wonders if they close their eyes when they fall. Norma Jean closes her eyes when they are in bed. She wants the lights turned out. Even then, he is sure she closes her eyes.

He goes for long drives around town. He tends to drive a car rather   55
carelessly. Power steering and an automatic shift make a car feel so small and
inconsequential that his body is hardly involved in the driving process. His
injured leg stretches out comfortably. Once or twice he has almost hit something, but even the prospect of an accident seems minor in a car. He cruises
the new subdivisions, feeling like a criminal rehearsing for a robbery. Norma
Jean is probably right about a log house being inappropriate here in the new
subdivisions. All the houses look grand and complicated. They depress him.

One day when Leroy comes home from a drive he finds Norma Jean
in tears. She is in the kitchen making a potato and mushroom-soup casserole,
with grated-cheese topping. She is crying because her mother caught her
smoking.

"I didn't hear her coming. I was standing here puffing away pretty as
you please," Norma Jean says, wiping her eyes.

"I knew it would happen sooner or later," says Leroy, putting his arm
around her.

"She don't know the meaning of the word 'knock,'" says Norma Jean.
"It's a wonder she hadn't caught me years ago."

"Think of it this way," Leroy says. "What if she caught me with a   60
joint?"

"You better not let her!" Norma Jean shrieks. "I'm warning you, Leroy
Moffitt!"

"I'm just kidding. Here, play me a tune. That'll help you relax."

Norma Jean puts the casserole in the oven and sets the timer. Then she
plays a ragtime tune, with horns and banjo, as Leroy lights up a joint and lies
on the couch, laughing to himself about Mabel's catching him at it. He thinks
of Stevie Hamilton—a doctor's son pushing grass. Everything is funny. The
whole town seems crazy and small. He is reminded of Virgil Mathis, a
boastful policeman Leroy used to shoot pool with. Virgil recently led a drug
bust in a back room at a bowling alley, where he seized ten thousand dollars'
worth of marijuana. The newspaper had a picture of him holding up the
bags of grass and grinning widely. Right now, Leroy can imagine Virgil
breaking down the door and arresting him with a lungful of smoke. Virgil
would probably have been alerted to the scene because of all the racket
Norma Jean is making. Now she sounds like a hard-rock band. Norma Jean
is terrific. When she switches to a Latin-rhythm version of "Sunshine Super-
man," Leroy hums along. Norma Jean's foot goes up and down, up and
down.

"Well, what do you think?" Leroy says, when Norma Jean pauses to
search through her music.

"What do I think about what?"   65

His mind has gone blank. Then he says, "I'll sell my rig and build us a
house." That wasn't what he wanted to say. He wanted to know what she
thought—what she *really* thought—about them.

"Don't start in on that again," says Norma Jean. She begins playing
"Who'll Be the Next in Line?"

Leroy used to tell hitchhikers his whole life story—about his travels, his hometown, the baby. He would end with a question: "Well, what do you think?" It was just a rhetorical question. In time, he had the feeling that he'd been telling the same story over and over to the same hitchhikers. He quit talking to hitchhikers when he realized how his voice sounded—whining and self-pitying, like some teenage-tragedy song. Now Leroy has the sudden impulse to tell Norma Jean about himself, as if he had just met her. They have known each other so long they have forgotten a lot about each other. They could become reacquainted. But when the oven timer goes off and she runs to the kitchen, he forgets why he wants to do this.

The next day, Mabel drops by. It is Saturday and Norma Jean is cleaning. Leroy is studying the plans of his log house, which have finally come in the mail. He has them spread out on the table—big sheets of stiff blue paper, with diagrams and numbers printed in white. While Norma Jean runs the vacuum, Mabel drinks coffee. She sets her coffee cup on a blueprint.

"I'm just waiting for time to pass," she says to Leroy, drumming her   70
fingers on the table.

As soon as Norma Jean switches off the vacuum, Mabel says in a loud voice, "Did you hear about the datsun dog that killed the baby?"

Norma Jean says, "The word is 'dachshund.'"

"They put the dog on trial. It chewed the baby's legs off. The mother was in the next room all the time." She raises her voice. "They thought it was neglect."

Norma Jean is holding her ears. Leroy manages to open the refrigerator and get some Diet Pepsi to offer Mabel. Mabel still has some coffee and she waves away the Pepsi.

"Datsuns are like that," Mabel says. "They're jealous dogs. They'll tear   75
a place to pieces if you don't keep an eye on them."

"You better watch out what you're saying, Mabel," says Leroy.

"Well, facts is facts."

Leroy looks out the window at his rig. It is like a huge piece of furniture gathering dust in the backyard. Pretty soon it will be an antique. He hears the vacuum cleaner. Norma Jean seems to be cleaning the living room rug again.

Later, she says to Leroy, "She just said that about the baby because she caught me smoking. She's trying to pay me back."

"What are you talking about?" Leroy says, nervously shuffling blueprints.   80

"You know good and well," Norma Jean says. She is sitting in a kitchen chair with her feet up and her arms wrapped around her knees. She looks small and helpless. She says, "The very idea, her bringing up a subject like that! Saying it was neglect."

"She didn't mean that," Leroy says.

"She might not have *thought* she meant it. She always says things like that. You don't know how she goes on."

"But she didn't really mean it. She was just talking."

Leroy opens a king-sized bottle of beer and pours it into two glasses, 85 dividing it carefully. He hands a glass to Norma Jean and she takes it from him mechanically. For a long time, they sit by the kitchen window watching the birds at the feeder.

Something is happening. Norma Jean is going to night school. She has graduated from her six-week body-building course and now she is taking an adult-education course in composition at Paducah Community College. She spends her evenings outlining paragraphs.

"First you have a topic sentence," she explains to Leroy. "Then you divide it up. Your secondary topic has to be connected to your primary topic."

To Leroy, this sounds intimidating. "I never was any good in English," he says.

"It makes a lot of sense."

"What are you doing this for, anyhow?" 90

She shrugs. "It's something to do." She stands up and lifts her dumbbells a few times.

"Driving a rig, nobody cared about my English."

"I'm not criticizing your English."

Norma Jean used to say, "If I lose ten minutes' sleep, I just drag all day." Now she stays up late, writing compositions. She got a B on her first paper—a how-to theme on soup-based casseroles. Recently Norma Jean has been cooking unusual foods—tacos, lasagna, Bombay chicken. She doesn't play the organ anymore, though her second paper was called "Why Music Is Important to Me." She sits at the kitchen table, concentrating on her outlines, while Leroy plays with his log house plans, practicing with a set of Lincoln Logs. The thought of getting a truckload of notched, numbered logs scares him, and he wants to be prepared. As he and Norma Jean work together at the kitchen table, Leroy has the hopeful thought that they are sharing something, but he knows he is a fool to think this. Norma Jean is miles away. He knows he is going to lose her. Like Mabel, he is just waiting for time to pass.

One day, Mabel is there before Norma Jean gets home from work, and 95 Leroy finds himself confiding in her. Mabel, he realizes, must know Norma Jean better than he does.

"I don't know what's got into that girl," Mabel says. "She used to go to bed with the chickens. Now you say she's up all hours. Plus her a-smoking. I like to died."

"I want to make her this beautiful home," Leroy says, indicating the Lincoln Logs. "I don't think she even wants it. Maybe she was happier with me gone."

"She don't know what to make of you, coming home like this."

"Is that it?"

Mabel takes the roof off his Lincoln Log cabin. "You couldn't get *me* 100 in a log cabin," she says. "I was raised in one. It's no picnic, let me tell you."

"They're different now," says Leroy.

"I tell you what," Mabel says, smiling oddly at Leroy.

"What?"

"Take her on down to Shiloh. Y'all need to get out together, stir a little. Her brain's all balled up over them books."

Leroy can see traces of Norma Jean's features in her mother's face. 105 Mabel's worn face has the texture of crinkled cotton, but suddenly she looks pretty. It occurs to Leroy that Mabel has been hinting all along that she wants them to take her with them to Shiloh.

"Let's all go to Shiloh," he says. "You and me and her. Come Sunday."

Mabel throws up her hands in protest. "Oh, no, not me. Young folks want to be by theirselves."

When Norma Jean comes in with groceries, Leroy says excitedly, "Your mama here's been dying to go to Shiloh for thirty-five years. It's about time we went, don't you think?"

"I'm not going to butt in on anybody's second honeymoon," Mabel says.

"Who's going on a honeymoon, for Christ's sake?" Norma Jean says 110 loudly.

"I never raised no daughter of mine to talk that-a-way," Mabel says.

"You ain't seen nothing yet," says Norma Jean. She starts putting away boxes and cans, slamming cabinet doors.

"There's a log cabin at Shiloh," Mabel says. "It was there during the battle. There's bullet holes in it."

"When are you going to *shut up* about Shiloh, Mama?" asks Norma Jean.

"I always thought Shiloh was the prettiest place, so full of history," 115 Mabel goes on. "I just hoped y'all could see it once before I die, so you could tell me about it." Later, she whispers to Leroy, "You do what I said. A little change is what she needs."

"Your name means 'the king,'" Norma Jean says to Leroy that evening. He is trying to get her to go to Shiloh, and she is reading a book about another century.

"Well, I reckon I ought to be right proud."

"I guess so."

"Am I still king around here?"

Norma Jean flexes her biceps and feels them for hardness. "I'm not 120 fooling around with anybody, if that's what you mean," she says.

"Would you tell me if you were?"

"I don't know."

"What does *your* name mean?"

"It was Marilyn Monroe's real name."

"No kidding!" 125

"Norma comes from the Normans. They were invaders," she says. She closes her book and looks hard at Leroy. "I'll go to Shiloh with you if you'll stop staring at me."

On Sunday, Norma Jean packs a picnic and they go to Shiloh. To Leroy's relief, Mabel says she does not want to come with them. Norma Jean drives, and Leroy, sitting beside her, feels like some boring hitchhiker she has picked up. He tries some conversation, but she answers him in monosyllables. At Shiloh, she drives aimlessly through the park, past bluffs and trails and steep ravines. Shiloh is an immense place, and Leroy cannot see it as a battleground. It is not what he expected. He thought it would look like a golf course. Monuments are everywhere, showing through the thick clusters of trees. Norma Jean passes the log cabin Mabel mentioned. It is surrounded by tourists looking for bullet holes.

"That's not the kind of log house I've got in mind," says Leroy apologetically.

"I know *that*."

"This is a pretty place. Your mama was right."   130

"It's O.K.," says Norma Jean. "Well, we've seen it. I hope she's satisfied."

They burst out laughing together.

At the park museum, a movie on Shiloh is shown every half hour, but they decide that they don't want to see it. They buy a souvenir Confederate flag for Mabel, and then they find a picnic spot near the cemetery. Norma Jean has brought a picnic cooler, with pimiento sandwiches, soft drinks, and Yodels. Leroy eats a sandwich and then smokes a joint, hiding it behind the picnic cooler. Norma Jean has quit smoking altogether. She is picking cake crumbs from the cellophane wrapper, like a fussy bird.

Leroy says, "So the boys in gray ended up in Corinth. The Union soldiers zapped 'em finally. April 7, 1862."

They both know that he doesn't know any history. He is just talking   135 about some of the historical plaques they have read. He feels awkward, like a boy on a date with an older girl. They are still just making conversation.

"Corinth is where Mama eloped to," says Norma Jean.

They sit in silence and stare at the cemetery for the Union dead and, beyond, at a tall cluster of trees. Campers are parked nearby, bumper to bumper, and small children in bright clothing are cavorting and squealing. Norma Jean wads up the cake wrapper and squeezes it tightly in her hand. Without looking at Leroy, she says, "I want to leave you."

Leroy takes a bottle of Coke out of the cooler and flips off the cap. He holds the bottle poised near his mouth but cannot remember to take a drink. Finally he says, "No, you don't."

"Yes, I do."

"I won't let you."   140

"You can't stop me."

"Don't do me that way."

Leroy knows Norma Jean will have her own way. "Didn't I promise to be home from now on?" he says.

"In some ways, a woman prefers a man who wanders," says Norma Jean. "That sounds crazy, I know."

"You're not crazy." 145

Leroy remembers to drink from his Coke. Then he says, "Yes, you *are* crazy. You and me could start all over again. Right back at the beginning."

"We *have* started all over again," says Norma Jean. "And this is how it turned out."

"What did I do wrong?"

"Nothing."

"Is this one of those women's lib things?" Leroy asks. 150

"Don't be funny."

The cemetery, a green slope dotted with white markers, looks like a subdivision site. Leroy is trying to comprehend that his marriage is breaking up, but for some reason he is wondering about white slabs in a graveyard.

"Everything was fine till Mama caught me smoking," says Norma Jean, standing up. "That set something off."

"What are you talking about?"

"She won't leave me alone—*you* won't leave me alone." Norma Jean 155 seems to be crying, but she is looking away from him. "I feel eighteen again. I can't face that all over again." She starts walking away. "No, it *wasn't* fine. I don't know what I'm saying. Forget it."

Leroy takes a lungful of smoke and closes his eyes as Norma Jean's words sink in. He tries to focus on the fact that thirty-five hundred soldiers died on the grounds around him. He can only think of that war as a board game with plastic soldiers. Leroy almost smiles, as he compares the Confederates' daring attack on the Union camps and Virgil Mathis's raid on the bowling alley. General Grant, drunk and furious, shoved the Southerners back to Corinth, where Mabel and Jet Beasley were married years later, when Mabel was still thin and good-looking. The next day, Mabel and Jet visited the battleground, and then Norma Jean was born, and then she married Leroy and they had a baby, which they lost, and now Leroy and Norma Jean are here at the same battleground. Leroy knows he is leaving out a lot. He is leaving out the insides of history. History was always just names and dates to him. It occurs to him that building a house out of logs is similarly empty—too simple. And the real inner workings of a marriage, like most of history, have escaped him. Now he sees that building a log house is the dumbest idea he could have had. It was clumsy of him to think Norma Jean would want a log house. It was a crazy idea. He'll have to think of something else, quickly. He will wad the blueprints into tight balls and fling them into the lake. Then he'll get moving again. He opens his eyes. Norma Jean has moved away and is walking through the cemetery, following a serpentine brick path.

Leroy gets up to follow his wife, but his good leg is asleep and his bad leg still hurts him. Norma Jean is far away, walking rapidly toward the bluff by the river, and he tries to hobble toward her. Some children run past him, screaming noisily. Norma Jean has reached the bluff, and she is looking out over the Tennessee River. Now she turns toward Leroy and waves her arms. Is she beckoning to him? She seems to be doing an exercise for her chest muscles. The sky is unusually pale—the color of the dust ruffle Mabel made for their bed.

Considerations

1. The story's title, the site of a famous Civil War battle, raises expectations of conflict. List the various "battles" you see taking place, both between characters and within characters. What connections might there be between these battles?
2. History—particularly the history of the South—is extremely important to the characters in "Shiloh." Notice that Leroy develops his own definition of history—both public and private. Do you agree with his view? Explain.
3. Both Leroy and Norma Jean refuse to talk about the death of their infant son. In what way might Randy's death contribute to the conflicts you see in the story? To what extent do you think Leroy and Norma Jean have dealt successfully with this loss?
4. Leroy and Norma Jean pursue very different activities. How do these activities help to define the fears and hopes of each character?
5. Read the final paragraph of the story. Do you see it as hopeful? Ominous? Ambiguous? Or something else? What do you see as the future possibilities for Leroy and Norma Jean? Explain.

ALBERTO MORAVIA (1907–1990)

The Chase

After a childhood bout with tuberculosis left him in fragile health, Alberto Moravia, who was born in Rome, received most of his education at home. As a young adult, he had regained his strength and by 1929 had published his first novel, A Time of Indifference. *Following the novel's publication he traveled widely, working as a feature reporter for Italian newspapers and sending back articles from all over America and Europe. During World War II, he opposed the Fascist regime through his writings and was forced to leave Italy and seek asylum when the Germans occupied his country. After the war, he returned to Italy and wrote several novels and collections of short stories. "The Chase" appeared in* Una Cosa e Una Cosa *(1967).*

I have never been a sportsman—or, rather, I have been a sportsman only once, and that was the first and last time. I was a child, and one day, for some reason or other, I found myself together with my father, who was holding a gun in his hand, behind a bush, watching a bird that had perched on a branch not very far away. It was a large, gray bird—or perhaps it was brown—with a long—or perhaps a short—beak; I don't remember. I only remember what I felt at that moment as I looked at it. It was like watching an animal whose vitality was rendered more intense by the very fact of my watching it and of the animal's not knowing that I was watching it.

At that moment, I say, the notion of wildness entered my mind, never again to leave it: everything is wild which is autonomous and unpredictable and does not depend upon us. Then all of a sudden there was an explosion; I could no longer see the bird and I thought it had flown away. But my father was leading the way, walking in front of me through the undergrowth. Finally he stooped down, picked up something, and put it in my hand. I was aware of something warm and soft and I lowered my eyes: there was the bird in the palm of my hand, its dangling, shattered head crowned with a plume of already-thickening blood. I burst into tears and dropped the corpse on the ground, and that was the end of my shooting experience.

I thought again of this remote episode in my life this very day after watching my wife, for the first and also the last time, as she was walking through the streets of the city. But let us take things in order.

What had my wife been like; what was she like now? She once had been, to put it briefly, "wild"—that is, entirely autonomous and unpredictable; latterly she had become "tame"—that is, predictable and dependent. For a long time she had been like the bird that, on that far-off morning in my childhood, I had seen perching on the bough; latterly, I am sorry to say, she had become like a hen about which one knows everything in advance—how it moves, how it eats, how it lays eggs, how it sleeps, and so on.

Nevertheless I would not wish anyone to think that my wife's wild- 5 ness consisted of an uncouth, rough, rebellious character. Apart from being extremely beautiful, she is the gentlest, politest, most discreet person in the world. Rather her wildness consisted of the air of charming unpredictability, of independence in her way of living, with which during the first years of our marriage she acted in my presence, both at home and abroad. Wildness signified intimacy, privacy, secrecy. Yes, my wife as she sat in front of her dressing table, her eyes fixed on the looking glass, passing the hairbrush with a repeated motion over her long, loose hair, was just as wild as the solitary quail hopping forward along a sun-filled furrow or the furtive fox coming out into a clearing and stopping to look around before running on. She was wild because I, as I looked at her, could never manage to foresee when she would give a last stroke with the hairbrush and rise and come toward me; wild to such a degree that sometimes when I went into our bedroom the smell of her, floating in the air, would have something of the acrid quality of a wild beast's lair.

Gradually she became less wild, tamer. I had had a fox, a quail, in the house, as I have said; then one day I realized that I had a hen. What effect does a hen have on someone who watches it? It has the effect of being, so to speak, an automaton in the form of a bird; automatic are the brief, rapid steps with which it moves about; automatic its hard, terse pecking; automatic the glance of the round eyes in its head that nods and turns; automatic its ready crouching down under the cock; automatic the dropping of the egg wherever it may be and the cry with which it announces that the egg has been laid. Good-by to the fox; good-by to the quail. And her smell—this no longer brought to my mind, in any way, the innocent odor of a wild animal; rather I detected in it the chemical suavity of some ordinary French perfume.

Our flat is on the first floor of a big building in a modern quarter of town; our windows look out on a square in which there is a small public garden, the haunt of nurses and children and dogs. One day I was standing at the window, looking in a melancholy way at the garden. My wife, shortly before, had dressed to go out; and once again, watching her, I had noticed the irrevocable and, so to speak, invisible character of her gestures and personality: something which gave one the feeling of a thing already seen and already done and which therefore evaded even the most determined observation. And now, as I stood looking at the garden and at the same time wondering why the adorable wildness of former times had so completely disappeared, suddenly my wife came into my range of vision as she walked quickly across the garden in the direction of the bus stop. I watched her and then I almost jumped for joy; in a movement she was making to pull down a fold of her narrow skirt and smooth it over her thigh with the tips of her long, sharp nails, in this movement I recognized the wildness that in the past had made me love her. It was only an instant, but in that instant I said to myself: She's become wild again because she's convinced that I am not there and am not watching her. Then I left the window and rushed out.

But I did not join her at the bus stop; I felt that I must not allow myself to be seen. Instead I hurried to my car, which was standing nearby, got in, and waited. A bus came and she got in together with some other people; the bus started off again and I began following it. Then there came back to me the memory of that one shooting expedition in which I had taken part as a child, and I saw that the bus was the undergrowth with its bushes and trees, my wife the bird perching on the bough while I, unseen, watched it living before my eyes. And the whole town, during this pursuit, became, as though by magic, a fact of nature like the countryside: the houses were hills, the streets valleys, the vehicles hedges and woods, and even the passersby on the pavements had something unpredictable and autonomous—that is, wild— about them. And in my mouth, behind my clenched teeth, there was the acrid, metallic taste of gunfire; and my eyes, usually listless and wandering, had become sharp, watchful, attentive.

These eyes were fixed intently upon the exit door when the bus came to the end of its run. A number of people got out, and then I saw my wife getting out. Once again I recognized, in the manner in which she broke free of the crowd and started off toward a neighboring street, the wildness that pleased me so much. I jumped out of the car and started following her.

She was walking in front of me, ignorant of my presence, a tall woman   10 with an elegant figure, long-legged, narrow-hipped, broad-backed, her brown hair falling on her shoulders.

Men turned around as she went past; perhaps they were aware of what I myself was now sensing with an intensity that quickened the beating of my heart and took my breath away: the unrestricted, steadily increasing, irresistible character of her mysterious wildness.

She walked hurriedly, having evidently some purpose in view, and even the fact that she had a purpose of which I was ignorant added to her wildness; I did not know where she was going, just as on that far-off morning I had not known what the bird perching on the bough was about to do. Moreover I thought the gradual, steady increase in this quality of wildness came partly from the fact that as she drew nearer to the object of this mysterious walk there was an increase in her—how shall I express it?—of biological tension, of existential excitement, of vital effervescence. Then, unexpectedly, with the suddenness of a film, her purpose was revealed.

A fair-haired young man in a leather jacket and a pair of corduroy trousers was leaning against the wall of a house in that ancient, narrow street. He was idly smoking as he looked in front of him. But as my wife passed close to him, he threw away his cigarette with a decisive gesture, took a step forward, and seized her arm. I was expecting her to rebuff him, to move away from him, but nothing happened: evidently obeying the rules of some kind of erotic ritual, she went on walking beside the young man. Then after a few steps, with a movement that confirmed her own complicity, she put her arm around her companion's waist and he put his around her.

I understood then that this unknown man who took such liberties with my wife was also attracted by wildness. And so, instead of making a conventional appointment with her, instead of meeting in a café with a handshake, a falsely friendly and respectful welcome, he had preferred, by agreement with her, to take her by surprise—or, rather, to pretend to do so—while she was apparently taking a walk on her own account. All this I perceived by intuition, noticing that at the very moment when he stepped forward and took her arm her wildness had, so to speak, given an upward bound. It was years since I had seen my wife so alive, but alas, the source of this life could not be traced to me.

They walked on thus entwined and then, without any preliminaries,   15
just like two wild animals, they did an unexpected thing: they went into one of the dark doorways in order to kiss. I stopped and watched them from a distance, peering into the darkness of the entrance. My wife was turned away from me and was bending back with the pressure of his body, her hair hanging free. I looked at that long, thick mane of brown hair, which as she leaned back fell free of her shoulders, and I felt at that moment her vitality reached its diapason, just as happens with wild animals when they couple and their customary wildness is redoubled by the violence of love. I watched for a long time and then, since the kiss went on and on and in fact seemed to be prolonged beyond the limits of my power of endurance, I saw that I would have to intervene.

I would have to go forward, seize my wife by the arm—or actually by that hair, which hung down and conveyed so well the feeling of feminine passivity—then hurl myself with clenched fists upon the blond young man. After this encounter I would carry off my wife, weeping, mortified, ashamed, while I was raging and brokenhearted, upbraiding her and pouring scorn upon her.

But what else would this intervention amount to but the shot my father fired at that free, unknowing bird as it perched on the bough? The disorder and confusion, the mortification, the shame, that would follow would irreparably destroy the rare and precious moment of wildness that I was witnessing inside the dark doorway. It was true that this wildness was directed against me; but I had to remember that wildness, always and everywhere, is directed against everything and everybody. After the scene of my intervention it might be possible for me to regain control of my wife, but I should find her shattered and lifeless in my arms like the bird that my father placed in my hand so that I might throw it into the shooting bag.

The kiss went on and on: well, it was a kiss of passion—that could not be denied. I waited until they finished, until they came out of the doorway, until they walked on again still linked together. Then I turned back.

Considerations

1. Read the opening section carefully. How does this section suggest the way the narrator sees himself in relation to others? What role does he play in his world?
2. How well does the narrator think he knows his wife? How well does he actually know her? What do the discrepancies between these two views suggest about their relationship?
3. How does the narrator's wife apparently feel about the narrator's responses to her and about his actions? What effects does he seem to expect his actions to have on the marriage? What effects do you think his actions will have?
4. Describe the final incident—the meeting with the "fair-haired young man"—from the wife's point of view. Explain her feelings and motivations as she walks toward, meets, and embraces her lover.
5. What is the significance of the title? How does the image of the hunt—and the narrator's memories of his childhood hunting incident—suggest possible themes?

ANDREW MARVELL (1621–1678)

To His Coy Mistress

> *Born in Yorkshire, England, Andrew Marvell was educated at Cambridge and then traveled on the European continent for four years. Following his return to England, he supported the Puritans during the civil war, although he was not himself a member of the Puritan party. Just before the restoration of the monarchy in 1660, Marvell was elected to Parliament, where he continued to serve for the rest of his life. In addition to his love poems, for which he is best known today, Marvell also wrote and published many political satires.*

    Had we but world enough, and time,
This coyness, lady, were no crime.
We would sit down, and think which way
To walk, and pass our long love's day.
Thou by the Indian Ganges'° side   5
Shoudst rubies find; I by the tide
Of Humber° would complain. I would
Love you ten years before the flood,

---

5 *Ganges:* River in northern India. 7 *Humber:* Estuary in northern England formed by the Ouse and Trent rivers.

And you should, if you please, refuse
Till the conversion of the Jews.   10
My vegetable love should grow
Vaster than empires and more slow;
An hundred years should go to praise
Thine eyes, and on thy forehead gaze;
Two hundred to adore each breast,   15
But thirty thousand to the rest;
An age at least to every part,
And the last age should show your heart.
For, lady, you deserve this state,
Nor would I love at lower rate.   20
    But at my back I always hear
Time's wingèd chariot hurrying near;
And yonder all before us lie
Deserts of vast eternity.
Thy beauty shall no more be found;   25
Nor, in thy marble vault, shall sound
My echoing song; then worms shall try
That long-preserved virginity,
And your quaint honor turn to dust,
And into ashes all my lust: 30
The grave's a fine and private place,
But none, I think, do there embrace.
    Now therefore, while the youthful hue
Sits on thy skin like morning dew
And while thy willing soul transpires   35
At every pore with instant fires,
Now let us sport us while we may,
And now, like amorous birds of prey,
Rather at once our time devour
Than languish in his slow-chapped power.   40
Let us roll all our strength and all
Our sweetness up into one ball,
And tear our pleasures with rough strife
Thorough the iron gates of life:
Thus, though we cannot make our sun   45
Stand still, yet we will make him run.

Considerations

1. What subject—love or time—is the main theme of this poem? How do
   the images of the poem connect and relate the two?
2. Write a prose version of this argument, listing each new point separately.
   How convincing do you find the argument? Explain your reasons.

3. Imagine that you are the woman to whom this poem is addressed. Write a letter giving the speaker your answer. Consider each point of his argument in your response.

APHRA BEHN (1640–1689)

The Willing Mistress

> *In* A Room of One's Own, *Virginia Woolf said, "All women together ought to let flowers fall upon the tomb of Aphra Behn, for it was she who earned them the right to speak their minds." Woolf's tribute refers to Behn's unprecedented literary career. Widowed in 1666, she desperately needed a way to support herself. She turned first to working as a spy for King Charles II in Antwerp and then, in 1670, published her first play,* The Forced Marriage. *In doing so, she became the first woman in the history of England to earn her living by writing. In addition to her plays, for which she is best known, Behn also wrote poems such as "The Willing Mistress," first published in 1673.*

Amyntas led me to a grove,
   Where all the trees did shade us;
The sun itself, though it had strove,
   It could not have betrayed us.
The place secured from human eyes   5
   No other fear allows
But when the winds that gently rise
   Do kiss the yielding boughs.

Down there we sat upon the moss,
   And did begin to play   10
A thousand amorous tricks, to pass
   The heat of all the day.
A many kisses did he give
   And I returned the same,
Which made me willing to receive   15
   That which I dare not name.

His charming eyes no aid required
   To tell their softening tale;
On her that was already fired
   'Twas easy to prevail.   20
He did but kiss and clasp me round,
   Whilst those his thoughts expressed:

And laid me gently on the ground;
    Ah who can guess the rest?

Considerations

1. What does the language of the poem suggest about the speaker's attitude toward sexual love? Cite specific images to support your view.
2. Compare the view of women suggested by this poem to the view of women suggested by "To His Coy Mistress."
3. This poem is part of a play, where it is sung by a maidservant to her mistress. Create the scene that leads up to the maid's decision to reveal this love affair to the woman who employs her.

ALAN DUGAN (1923–   )

Love Song: I and Thou

> Born in Brooklyn, New York, Alan Dugan served in the United States Air Force during World War II. Following the war, he earned a bachelor of arts degree in English from Mexico City College. He has taught at Sarah Lawrence College and at the Fine Arts Work Center in Provincetown, Massachusetts. In 1962, he won the Pulitzer Prize for his collection Poems, in which "Love Song: I and Thou" appears.

Nothing is plumb, level or square:
    the studs are bowed, the joists
are shaky by nature, no piece fits
    any other piece without a gap
or pinch, and bent nails   5
    dance all over the surfacing
like maggots. By Christ
    I am no carpenter, I built
the roof for myself, the walls
    for myself, the floors   10
for myself, and got
    hung up in it myself. I
danced with a purple thumb
    at this house-warming, drunk
with my prime whiskey: rage.   15
    Oh I spat rage's nails
into the frame-up of my work:
    it held. It settled plumb,

level, solid, square and true
 for that great moment. Then   20
it screamed and went on through,
 skewing as wrong the other way.
God damned it. This is hell,
 but I planned it, I sawed it,
I nailed it, and I   25
 will live in it until it kills me.
I can nail my left palm
 to the left-hand cross-piece but
I can't do everything myself.
 I need a hand to nail the right,   30
a help, a love, a you, a wife.

Considerations

1. Describe the house suggested by the central image of the poem. What might the house represent? What meanings are suggested by the details relating to building the house?
2. Is the title ironic? In what way can this poem be considered a love song?
3. What role does the speaker suggest for the woman to whom this poem is addressed? How do you evaluate the implications of that role?

ANNE SEXTON (1928–1974)

For My Lover, Returning to His Wife

> *Often described as a "confessional" poet, Anne Sexton frequently used the details of her own life to serve as images for conveying themes she saw as relevant to the world in which she lived. Although she wrote prolifically and her work won many awards and honors, Sexton was a deeply troubled person who spent much of her life dealing with emotional problems that began during her childhood. In 1974 she committed suicide.*

She is all there.
She was melted carefully down for you
and cast up from your childhood,
cast up from your one hundred favorite aggies.

She has always been there, my darling.   5
She is, in fact, exquisite.
Fireworks in the dull middle of February
and as real as a cast-iron pot.

Let's face it, I have been momentary.
A luxury. A bright red sloop in the harbor.
My hair rising like smoke from the car window.
Littleneck clams out of season.

She is more than that. She is your have to have,
has grown you your practical your tropical growth.
This is not an experiment. She is all harmony.
She sees to oars and oarlocks for the dinghy,

has placed wild flowers at the window at breakfast,
sat by the potter's wheel at midday,
set forth three children under the moon,
three cherubs drawn by Michelangelo,

done this with her legs spread out
in the terrible months in the chapel.
If you glance up, the children are there
like delicate balloons resting on the ceiling.

She has also carried each one down the hall
after supper, their heads privately bent,
two legs protesting, person to person,
her face flushed with a song and their little sleep.

I give you back your heart.
I give you permission—

for the fuse inside her, throbbing
angrily in the dirt, for the bitch in her
and the burying of her wound—
for the burying of her small red wound alive—

for the pale flickering flare under her ribs,
for the drunken sailor who waits in her left pulse,
for the mother's knee, for the stockings,
for the garter belt, for the call—

the curious call
when you will burrow in arms and breasts
and tug at the orange ribbon in her hair
and answer the call, the curious call.

She is so naked and singular.
She is the sum of yourself and your dream.

Climb her like a monument, step after step.   45
She is solid.

As for me, I am a watercolor.
I wash off.

Considerations

1. List the images that the speaker uses in the first 30 lines to describe the
   wife as well as the images she uses to describe herself. What do these
   images suggest about the role she sees the wife and herself playing in her
   lover's life?
2. Discuss the reference in lines 19–24 to Michelangelo. How is the wife
   like this artist?
3. How do the images of the wife in lines 31–46 contrast with the images
   in earlier lines? Why might the speaker use both the earlier and later
   images in describing the wife to her lover?

KRISTINE BATEY (1951–   )

Lot's Wife

> *Kristine Batey, who decided at age six to be a writer, lives with her husband in
> Chicago, where she works as a researcher for a medical publisher. She describes
> "Lot's Wife," which was first published in 1978 and won a Pushcart Prize as
> one of the best poems appearing in a small press publication for that year, as
> follows: " 'Lot's Wife' is a poem about being a woman and, therefore, a
> human being."*

While Lot, the conscience of a nation,
struggles with the Lord,
she struggles with the housework.
The City of Sin is where
she raises the children.   5
Ba'al° or Adonai°—
Whoever is God—
the bread must still be made
and the doorsill swept.

---

6 *Ba'al:* Old Testament name for the chief god of the Canaanites, whose cult practiced prostitu-
tion and child sacrifice. This cult was denounced by Jewish prophets; *Adonai:* Hebrew term for
God.

The Lord may kill the children tomorrow,   10
but today they must be bathed and fed.
Well and good to condemn your neighbors' religion;
but weren't they there
when the baby was born,
and when the well collapsed?   15
While her husband communes with God
she tucks the children into bed.
In the morning, when he tells her of the judgment,
she puts down the lamp she is cleaning
and calmly begins to pack.   20
In between bundling up the children
and deciding what will go,
she runs for a moment
to say goodbye to the herd,
gently patting each soft head   25
with tears in her eyes for the animals that will not understand.
She smiles blindly to the woman
who held her hand at childbed.
It is easy for eyes that have always turned to heaven
not to look back;   30
those that have been—by necessity—drawn to earth
cannot forget that life is lived from day to day.
Good, to a God, and good in human terms
are two different things.
On the breast of the hill, she chooses to be human,   35
and turns, in farewell—
and never regrets
the sacrifice.

Considerations

1. Read the biblical story of Lot and his wife (Genesis 19:1–26), and compare that story with the account in the poem.
2. What values are suggested by the details that describe Lot? By the details that describe his wife? In the poem, it is suggested that these values conflict. Do you think such values still conflict today? Explain.
3. The poem mentions neighbors. Imagine yourself as one of the neighbors and write your description of Lot and of his wife.

AMY LOWELL (1874–1925)

Patterns

Born the daughter of a prominent Boston family, Amy Lowell was expected to lead the life of a proper young lady. Trying to please her family, Lowell engaged in the social and philanthropic activities prescribed by the society in which she lived. All the while, however, she suffered from serious emotional problems, including what today would probably be known as an eating disorder—periods of gorging followed by severe dieting. As a mature woman, she moved away from the society life of her parents and became a member of the community of writers that included Henry James, D. H. Lawrence, Robert Frost, and Hilda Doolittle. Her poetry was widely published and admired, and in 1925, following her death, her final volume of poems, What's O'Clock, *received the Pulitzer Prize.*

I walk down the garden paths,
And all the daffodils
Are blowing, and the bright blue squills.
I walk down the patterned garden paths
In my stiff, brocaded gown.   5
With my powdered hair and jewelled fan,
I too am a rare
Pattern. As I wander down
The garden paths.

My dress is richly figured,   10
And the train
Makes a pink and silver stain
On the gravel, and the thrift
Of the borders.
Just a plate of current fashion,   15
Tripping by in high-heeled, ribboned shoes.
Not a softness anywhere about me,
Only whalebone and brocade.
And I sink on a seat in the shade
Of a lime tree. For my passion   20
Wars against the stiff brocade.
The daffodils and squills
Flutter in the breeze
As they please.
And I weep;   25
For the lime-tree is in blossom
And one small flower has dropped upon my bosom.

And the plashing of waterdrops
In the marble fountain

Comes down the garden paths. 30
The dripping never stops.
Underneath my stiffened gown
Is the softness of a woman bathing in a marble basin,
A basin in the midst of hedges grown
So thick, she cannot see her lover hiding, 35
But she guesses he is near,
And the sliding of the water
Seems the stroking of a dear
Hand upon her.
What is Summer in a fine brocaded gown! 40
I should like to see it lying in a heap upon the ground.
All the pink and silver crumpled up on the ground.

I would be the pink and silver as I ran along the paths,
And he would stumble after,
Bewildered by my laughter.
I should see the sun flashing from his sword-hilt and the buckles on his shoes. 45
I would choose
To lead him in a maze along the patterned paths,
A bright and laughing maze for my heavy-booted lover.
Till he caught me in the shade. 50
And the buttons of his waistcoat bruised my body as he clasped me,
Aching, melting, unafraid.
With the shadows of the leaves and the sundrops,
And the plopping of the waterdrops,
All about us in the open afternoon— 55
I am very like to swoon
With the weight of this brocade,
For the sun sifts through the shade.

Underneath the fallen blossom
In my bosom,
Is a letter I have hid. 60
It was brought to me this morning by a rider from the Duke.
'Madam, we regret to inform you that Lord Hartwell
Died in action Thursday se'nnight.'
As I read it in the white, morning sunlight, 65
The letters squirmed like snakes.
'Any answer, Madam,' said my footman.
'No,' I told him.
'See that the messenger takes some refreshment.
No, no answer.' 70
And I walked into the garden,
Up and down the patterned paths,
In my stiff, correct brocade.

The blue and yellow flowers stood up proudly in the sun,
Each one.   75
I stood upright too,
Held rigid to the pattern
By the stiffness of my gown.
Up and down I walked,
Up and down.   80

In a month he would have been my husband.
In a month, here, underneath this lime,
We would have broke the pattern;
He for me, and I for him,
He as Colonel, I as Lady,   85
On this shady seat.
He had a whim
That sunlight carried blessing.
And I answered, 'It shall be as you have said.'
Now he is dead.   90

In Summer and in Winter I shall walk
Up and down
The patterned garden paths
In my stiff, brocaded gown.
The squills and daffodils   95
Will give place to pillared roses, and to asters, and to snow.
I shall go
Up and down,
In my gown.
Gorgeously arrayed,   100
Boned and stayed.
And the softness of my body will be guarded from embrace
By each button, hook, and lace.
For the man who should loose me is dead,
Fighting with the Duke in Flanders,   105
In a pattern called a war.
Christ! What are patterns for?

Considerations

1. Consider the many ways the characters and actions in the poem suggest
   and relate to the title.
2. How does the speaker respond to the patterns in her life?
3. What patterns do you see in modern life? Are today's patterns as clearly
   defined as the patterns suggested by Lowell's poem? Do people today still
   feel limited and restricted by the patterns of their lives? Explain.

SAPPHO (610 B.C.?–580 B.C.?)

To me he seems like a god

> *Although little is known of her life, Sappho is acknowledged as the finest woman poet of the ancient world. Born to an aristocratic Greek family, she wrote poetry that was extremely innovative for its time because of her use of common language rather than the formal diction used by conventional poets.*

To me he seems like a god
as he sits facing you and
hears you near as you speak
softly and laugh
in a sweet echo that jolts   5
the heart in my ribs. For now
as I look at you my voice
is empty and

can say nothing as my tongue
cracks and slender fire is quick   10
under my skin. My eyes are dead
to light, my ears

pound, and sweat pours over me.
I convulse, paler than grass,
and feel my mind slip as I   15
go close to death

[but must suffer all, being poor.]

TRANSLATED BY WILLIS BARNSTONE

CHRISTOPHER MARLOWE (1564–1593)

The Passionate Shepherd to His Love

> *Born in Canterbury, Christopher Marlowe attended Cambridge University intending to become a priest. His career as a writer led him to set aside this plan. In 1593, he was arrested for being an atheist, but he was murdered before he was brought to trial. Best known for his plays, Marlowe also wrote and published many poems.*

Come live with me and be my love,
And we will all the pleasures prove

That valleys, groves, hills, and fields,
Woods, or steepy mountain yields.

And we will sit upon the rocks,   5
Seeing the shepherds feed their flocks,
By shallow rivers to whose falls
Melodious birds sing madrigals.

And I will make thee beds of roses
And a thousand fragrant posies,   10
A cap of flowers, and a kirtle
Embroidered all with leaves of myrtle;

A gown made of the finest wool
Which from our pretty lambs we pull;
Fair lined slippers for the cold,   15
With buckles of the purest gold;

A belt of straw and ivy buds,
With coral clasps and amber studs:
And if these pleasures may thee move
Come live with me, and be my love.   20

The shepherds' swains shall dance and sing
For thy delight each May morning:
If these delights thy mind may move,
Then live with me and be my love.

SIR WALTER RALEIGH (1552?–1618)

The Nymph's Reply to the Shepherd

> *Best known as a key adviser who fell in and out of favor with Queen Elizabeth I and thus ended his life imprisoned in the Tower of London, Sir Walter Raleigh loved adventure and exploration. In addition to his poetry, he is also the author of* A History of the World *(1614), written while he was in prison.*

If all the world and love were young,
And truth in every shepherd's tongue,
These pretty pleasures might me move
To live with thee and be thy love.

Time drives the flocks from field to fold   5
When rivers rage and rocks grow cold,

And Philomel becometh dumb;
The rest complains of cares to come.

The flowers do fade, and wanton fields
To wayward winter reckoning yields;   10
A honey tongue, a heart of gall,
Is fancy's spring, but sorrow's fall.

Thy gowns, thy shoes, thy beds of roses,
Thy cap, thy kirtle, and thy posies
Soon break, soon wither, soon forgotten—   15
In folly ripe, in reason rotten.

Thy belt of straw and ivy buds,
Thy coral clasps and amber studs,
All these in me no means can move
To come to thee and be thy love.   20

But could youth last and love still breed,
Had joys no date nor age no need,
Then these delights my mind might move
To live with thee and be thy love.

WILLIAM SHAKESPEARE (1564–1616)

Let me not to the marriage of true minds

For biographical information about William Shakespeare, see page 209.

Let me not to the marriage of true minds
Admit impediments. Love is not love
Which alters when it alteration finds,
Or bends with the remover to remove:

Oh, no! it is an ever-fixéd mark,   5
That looks on tempests and is never shaken;
It is the star to every wandering bark,
Whose worth's unknown, although his height be taken.
Love's not Time's fool, though rosy lips and cheeks
Within his bending sickle's compass come;   10
Love alters not with his brief hours and weeks,
But bears it out even to the edge of doom.
    If this be error and upon me proved,
    I never writ, nor no man ever loved.

EDGAR ALLAN POE (1809–1849)

Annabel Lee

Born in Boston, Massachusetts, to itinerant actors, Edgar Allan Poe was orphaned at the age of three. He was adopted by a young merchant, John Allan, who lived with his family in Richmond, Virginia. After a stormy adolescence, Poe attended the University of Virginia, where, in spite of gambling sprees and bouts of heavy drinking, he did well in his studies. After his freshman year, however, his gambling debts led to a quarrel with his stepfather, who then refused to support him. Poe left school and served in the army from 1827 to 1829. Later he attended West Point, but he was expelled for failing to observe military discipline and academy policies. He then began a career as an editor, reporter, and reviewer while writing poetry and short stories on his own time. In 1836, he married Virginia Clemm, his thirteen-year-old cousin; the marriage ended tragically with her death from tuberculosis in 1837. Many scholars believe that "Annabel Lee" pays tribute to Poe's love for Virginia. Poe was known as the father of the American short story, and his works include "The Gold Bug," "The Murders in the Rue Morgue," "The Tell-Tale Heart," and "The Fall of the House of Usher." In 1849, he was found unconscious in a street in Philadelphia and died the next day.

It was many and many a year ago,
  In a kingdom by the sea
That a maiden there lived whom you may know.
  By the name of Annabel Lee;
And this maiden she lived with no other thought 5
  Than to love and be loved by me.

I was a child and *she* was a child,
  In this kingdom by the sea;
But we loved with a love that was more than love—
  I and my Annabel Lee— 10
With a love that the wingèd seraphs of heaven
  Coveted her and me.

And this was the reason that, long ago,
  In this kingdom by the sea,
A wind blew out of a cloud, chilling 15
  My beautiful Annabel Lee;
So that her highborn kinsmen came
  And bore her away from me,
To shut her up in a sepulchre
  In this kingdom by the sea. 20

The angels, not half so happy in heaven,
  Went envying her and me—

Yes!—that was the reason (as all men know,
    In this kingdom by the sea)
That the wind came out of the cloud by night,   25
    Chilling and killing my Annabel Lee.

But our love it was stronger by far than the love
    Of those who were older than we—
    Of many far wiser than we—
And neither the angels in heaven above,   30
    Nor the demons down under the sea,
Can ever dissever my soul from the soul
    Of the beautiful Annabel Lee:

For the moon never beams, without bringing me dreams
    Of the beautiful Annabel Lee;   35
And the stars never rise, but I feel the bright eyes
    Of the beautiful Annabel Lee:
And so, all the night tide, I lie down by the side
Of my darling—my darling—my life and my bride,
    In her sepulchre there by the sea—   40
    In her tomb by the sounding sea.

HENRIK IBSEN (1828–1906)

A Doll House

Henrik Ibsen was the son of a wealthy merchant in Norway. In 1836, how-ever, the elder Ibsen filed for bankruptcy. The family was forced to move to a small house, and Henrik had to leave his beloved private school to attend a public school, which he always believed left him with an inferior education. He left home as soon as he was old enough to become a druggist's apprentice. As a young man, Ibsen was both a social and political rebel, founding a radical club that worked to promote issues of personal and national freedom. He drank and gambled heavily, and at the age of 18 he became an unwed father. In 1850 he wrote his first play, and in 1857 he became the director of the Norwegian Theater in the city that is now Oslo. Following the bankruptcy of the Norwegian Theater, he and his family moved abroad. They lived primarily in Italy until 1891, and Ibsen wrote his major plays during this time: Peer Gynt *(1867),* A Doll House *(1879),* Ghosts *(1881), and* An Enemy of the People *(1882). Ibsen and his family returned to Norway in 1891, and in 1900 he suffered a stroke that left him an invalid until his death in 1906. Of this major pioneer in modern realistic theater, the playwright Luigi Piran-dello said, "After Shakespeare, I put Ibsen first."*

TRANSLATED BY ROLF FJELDE

Characters

TORVALD HELMER, *a lawyer*
NORA, *his wife*
DR. RANK
MRS. LINDE
NILS KROGSTAD, *a bank clerk*
THE HELMERS' THREE SMALL CHILDREN
ANNE-MARIE, *their nurse*
HELENE, *a maid*
A DELIVERY BOY

Scene *The action takes place in* HELMER's *residence.*

ACT I

Scene *A comfortable room, tastefully but not expensively furnished. A door to the right in the back wall leads to the entryway, another to the left leads to* HELMER's *study. Between these doors, a piano. Midway in the left-hand wall a door, and further back a window. Near the window a round table with an armchair and a small sofa. In the right-hand wall, toward the rear a door, and nearer the foreground a porcelain stove with two armchairs and a rocking chair beside it. Between the stove and the side* *door, a small table. Engravings on the walls. An étagère with china figures and other small art objects; a small bookcase with richly bound books; the floor carpeted; a fire burning in the stove. It is a winter day.*

A bell rings in the entryway; shortly after we hear the door being unlocked. NORA *comes into the room, humming happily to herself; she is wearing street clothes and carries an armload of packages, which she puts down on the table to the right. She has left the hall door open; and through it a* DELIVERY BOY *is seen, holding a Christmas tree and a basket which he gives to the* MAID *who let them in.*

NORA: Hide the tree well, Helene. The children mustn't get a glimpse of it till this evening, after it's trimmed. *(To the* DELIVERY BOY, *taking out her purse.)* How much?

DELIVERY BOY: Fifty, ma'am.

NORA: There's a crown. No, keep the change. *(The* BOY *thanks her and leaves.* NORA *shuts the door. She laughs softly to herself while taking off her street things. Drawing a bag of macaroons from her pocket, she eats a couple, then steals over and listens at her husband's study door.)* Yes, he's home. *(Hums again as she moves to the table, right.)*

HELMER *(from the study)*: Is that my little lark twittering out there?

NORA *(busy opening some packages)*: Yes, it is.

HELMER: Is that my squirrel rummaging around?

NORA: Yes!

HELMER: When did my squirrel get in?

NORA: Just now. *(Putting the macaroon bag in her pocket and wiping her mouth.)* Do come in, Torvald, and see what I've bought.

HELMER: Can't be disturbed. *(After a moment he opens the door and peers in, pen in hand.)* Bought, you say? All that there? Has the little spendthrift been out throwing money around again?

NORA: Oh, but Torvald, this year we really should let ourselves go a bit. It's the first Christmas we haven't had to economize.

HELMER: But you know we can't go squandering.

NORA: Oh yes, Torvald, we can squander a little now. Can't we? Just a tiny, wee bit. Now that you've got a big salary and are going to make piles and piles of money.

HELMER: Yes—starting New Year's. But then it's a full three months till the raise comes through.

NORA: Pooh! We can borrow that long.

HELMER: Nora! *(Goes over and playfully takes her by the ear.)* Are your scatterbrains off again? What if today I borrowed a thousand crowns, and you squandered them over Christmas week, and then on New Year's Eve a roof tile fell on my head, and I lay there—

NORA *(putting her hand on his mouth)*: Oh! Don't say such things!

HELMER: Yes, but what if it happened—then what?

NORA: If anything so awful happened, then it just wouldn't matter if I had debts or not.

HELMER: Well, but the people I'd borrowed from?

NORA: Them? Who cares about them! They're strangers.

HELMER: Nora, Nora, how like a woman! No, but seriously, Nora, you
know what I think about that. No debts! Never borrow! Something
of freedom's lost—and something of beauty, too—from a home that's
founded on borrowing and debt. We've made a brave stand up to
now, the two of us; and we'll go right on like that the little while we
have to.

NORA *(going toward the stove)*: Yes, whatever you say, Torvald.

HELMER *(following her)*: Now, now, the little lark's wings mustn't droop.
Come on, don't be a sulky squirrel. *(Taking out his wallet.)* Nora, guess
what I have here.

NORA *(turning quickly)*: Money!

HELMER: There, see. *(Hands her some notes.)* Good grief, I know how costs
go up in a house at Christmastime.

NORA: Ten—twenty—thirty—forty. Oh, thank you, Torvald; I can manage no end on this.

HELMER: You really will have to.

NORA: Oh yes, I promise I will! But come here so I can show you everything I bought. And so cheap! Look, new clothes for Ivar here—and a
sword. Here a horse and a trumpet for Bob. And a doll and a doll's bed
here for Emmy; they're nothing much, but she'll tear them to bits in
no time anyway. And here I have dress material and handkerchiefs for
the maids. Old Anne-Marie really deserves something more.

HELMER: And what's in that package there?

NORA *(with a cry)*: Torvald, no! You can't see that till tonight!

HELMER: I see. But tell me now, you little prodigal, what have you
thought of for yourself?

NORA: For myself? Oh, I don't want anything at all.

HELMER: Of course you do. Tell me just what—within reason—you'd
most like to have.

NORA: I honestly don't know. Oh, listen, Torvald—

HELMER: Well?

NORA *(fumbling at his coat buttons, without looking at him)*: If you want to
give me something, then maybe you could—you could—

HELMER: Come on, out with it.

NORA *(hurriedly)*: You could give me money, Torvald. No more than
you think you can spare, then one of these days I'll buy something
with it.

HELMER: But Nora—

NORA: Oh, please, Torvald darling, do that! I beg you, please. Then I could
hang the bills in pretty gilt paper on the Christmas tree. Wouldn't that
be fun?

HELMER: What are those little birds called that always fly through their
fortunes?

NORA: Oh yes, spendthrifts. I know all that. But let's do as I say, Torvald; then I'll have time to decide what I really need most. That's very sensible, isn't it?

HELMER *(smiling)*: Yes, very—that is, if you actually hung onto the money I give you, and you actually used it to buy yourself something. But it goes for the house and for all sorts of foolish things, and then I only have to lay out some more.

NORA: Oh, but Torvald—

HELMER: Don't deny it, my dear little Nora. *(Putting his arm around her waist.)* Spendthrifts are sweet, but they use up a frightful amount of money. It's incredible what it costs a man to feed such birds.

NORA: Oh, how can you say that! Really, I save everything I can.

HELMER *(laughing)*: Yes, that's the truth. Everything you can. But that's nothing at all.

NORA *(humming, with a smile of quiet satisfaction)*: Hm, if you only knew what expenses we larks and squirrels have, Torvald.

HELMER: You're an odd little one. Exactly the way your father was. You're never at a loss for scaring up money; but the moment you have it, it runs right out through your fingers; you never know what you've done with it. Well, one takes you as you are. It's deep in your blood. Yes, these things are hereditary, Nora.

NORA: Ah, I could wish I'd inherited many of Papa's qualities.

HELMER: And I couldn't wish you anything but just what you are, my sweet little lark. But wait; it seems to me you have a very—what should I call it?—a very suspicious look today—

NORA: I do?

HELMER: You certainly do. Look me straight in the eye.

NORA *(looking at him)*: Well?

HELMER *(shaking an admonitory finger)*: Surely my sweet tooth hasn't been running riot in town today, has she?

NORA: No. Why do you imagine that?

HELMER: My sweet tooth really didn't make a little detour through the confectioner's?

NORA: No, I assure you, Torvald—

HELMER: Hasn't nibbled some pastry?

NORA: No, not at all.

HELMER: Nor even munched a macaroon or two?

NORA: No, Torvald, I assure you, really—

HELMER: There, there now. Of course I'm only joking.

NORA *(going to the table, right)*: You know I could never think of going against you.

HELMER: No, I understand that; and you *have* given me your word. *(Going over to her.)* Well, you keep your little Christmas secrets to yourself, Nora darling. I expect they'll come to light this evening, when the tree is lit.

NORA: Did you remember to ask Dr. Rank?

HELMER: No. But there's no need for that; it's assumed he'll be dining with us. All the same, I'll ask him when he stops by here this morning. I've ordered some fine wine. Nora, you can't imagine how I'm looking forward to this evening.

NORA: So am I. And what fun for the children, Torvald!

HELMER: Ah, it's so gratifying to know that one's gotten a safe, secure job, and with a comfortable salary. It's a great satisfaction, isn't it?

NORA: Oh, it's wonderful!

HELMER: Remember last Christmas? Three whole weeks before, you shut yourself in every evening till long after midnight, making flowers for the Christmas tree, and all the other decorations to surprise us. Ugh, that was the dullest time I've ever lived through.

NORA: It wasn't at all dull for me.

HELMER *(smiling)*: But the outcome *was* pretty sorry, Nora.

NORA: Oh, don't tease me with that again. How could I help it that the cat came in and tore everything to shreds.

HELMER: No, poor thing, you certainly couldn't. You wanted so much to please us all, and that's what counts. But it's just as well that the hard times are past.

NORA: Yes, it's really wonderful.

HELMER: Now I don't have to sit here alone, boring myself, and you don't have to tire your precious eyes and your fair little delicate hands—

NORA *(clapping her hands)*: No, is it really true, Torvald, I don't have to? Oh, how wonderfully lovely to hear! *(Taking his arm.)* Now I'll tell you just how I've thought we should plan things. Right after Christmas— *(The doorbell rings.)* Oh, the bell. *(Straightening the room up a bit.)* Somebody would have to come. What a bore!

HELMER: I'm not at home to visitors, don't forget.

MAID *(from the hall doorway)*: Ma'am, a lady to see you—

NORA: All right, let her come in.

MAID *(to HELMER)*: And the doctor's just come too.

HELMER: Did he go right to my study?

MAID: Yes, he did.

(HELMER goes into his room. The MAID shows in MRS. LINDE, dressed in traveling clothes, and shuts the door after her.)

MRS. LINDE *(in a dispirited and somewhat hesitant voice)*: Hello, Nora.

NORA *(uncertain)*: Hello—

MRS. LINDE: You don't recognize me.

NORA: No, I don't know—but wait, I think—*(Exclaiming.)* What! Kristine! Is it really you?

MRS. LINDE: Yes, it's me.

NORA: Kristine! To think I didn't recognize you. But then, how could I? *(More quietly.)* How you've changed, Kristine!

MRS. LINDE: Yes, no doubt I have. In nine—ten long years.

NORA: Is it so long since we met! Yes, it's all of that. Oh, these last eight years have been a happy time, believe me. And so now you've come in to town, too. Made the long trip in the winter. That took courage.

MRS. LINDE: I just got here by ship this morning.

NORA: To enjoy yourself over Christmas, of course. Oh, how lovely! Yes, enjoy ourselves, we'll do that. But take your coat off. You're not still cold? *(Helping her.)* There now, let's get cozy here by the stove. No, the easy chair there! I'll take the rocker here. *(Seizing her hands.)* Yes, now you have your old look again; it was only in that first moment. You're a bit more pale, Kristine—and maybe a bit thinner.

MRS. LINDE: And much, much older, Nora.

NORA: Yes, perhaps, a bit older; a tiny, tiny bit; not much at all. *(Stopping short; suddenly serious.)* Oh, but thoughtless me, to sit here, chattering away. Sweet, good Kristine, can you forgive me?

MRS. LINDE: What do you mean, Nora?

NORA *(softly)*: Poor Kristine, you've become a widow.

MRS. LINDE: Yes, three years ago.

NORA: Oh, I knew it, of course; I read it in the papers. Oh Kristine, you must believe me; I often thought of writing you then, but I kept postponing it, and something always interfered.

MRS. LINDE: Nora dear, I understand completely.

NORA: No, it was awful of me, Kristine. You poor thing, how much you must have gone through. And he left you nothing?

MRS. LINDE: No.

NORA: And no children?

MRS. LINDE: No.

NORA: Nothing at all, then?

MRS. LINDE: Not even a sense of loss to feed on.

NORA *(looking incredulously at her)*: But Kristine, how could that be?

MRS. LINDE *(smiling wearily and smoothing her hair)*: Oh, sometimes it happens, Nora.

NORA: So completely alone. How terribly hard that must be for you. I have three lovely children. You can't see them now; they're out with the maid. But now you must tell me everything—

MRS. LINDE: No, no, no, tell me about yourself.

NORA: No, you begin. Today I don't want to be selfish. I want to think only of you today. But there *is* something I must tell you. Did you hear of the wonderful luck we had recently?

MRS. LINDE: No, what's that?

NORA: My husband's been made manager in the bank, just think!

MRS. LINDE: Your husband? How marvelous!

NORA: Isn't it? Being a lawyer is such an uncertain living, you know, especially if one won't touch any cases that aren't clean and decent. And of course Torvald would never do that, and I'm with him completely there. Oh, we're simply delighted, believe me! He'll join the bank right after New Year's and start getting a huge salary and lots of commissions. From now on we can live quite differently—just as we want. Oh, Kristine, I feel so light and happy! Won't it be lovely to have stacks of money and not a care in the world?

MRS. LINDE: Well, anyway, it would be lovely to have enough for necessities.

NORA: No, not just for necessities, but stacks and stacks of money!

MRS. LINDE (smiling): Nora, Nora, aren't you sensible yet? Back in school you were such a free spender.

NORA (with a quiet laugh): Yes, that's what Torvald still says. (Shaking her finger.) But "Nora, Nora" isn't as silly as you all think. Really, we've been in no position for me to go squandering. We've had to work, both of us.

MRS. LINDE: You too?

NORA: Yes, at odd jobs—needlework, crocheting, embroidery, and such— (casually) and other things too. You remember that Torvald left the department when we were married? There was no chance of promotion in his office, and of course he needed to earn more money. But that first year he drove himself terribly. He took on all kinds of extra work that kept him going morning and night. It wore him down, and then he fell deathly ill. The doctors said it was essential for him to travel south.

MRS. LINDE: Yes, didn't you spend a whole year in Italy?

NORA: That's right. It wasn't easy to get away, you know. Ivar had just been born. But of course we had to go. Oh, that was a beautiful trip, and it saved Torvald's life. But it cost a frightful sum, Kristine.

MRS. LINDE: I can well imagine.

NORA: Four thousand, eight hundred crowns it cost. That's really a lot of money.

MRS. LINDE: But it's lucky you had it when you needed it.

NORA: Well, as it was, we got it from Papa.

MRS. LINDE: I see. It was just about the time your father died.

NORA: Yes, just about then. And, you know, I couldn't make the trip out to nurse him. I had to stay here, expecting Ivar any moment, and with my poor sick Torvald to care for. Dearest Papa, I never saw him again, Kristine. Oh, that was the worst time I've known in all my marriage.

MRS. LINDE: I know how you loved him. And then you went off to Italy?

NORA: Yes. We had the means now, and the doctors urged us. So we left a month after.

MRS. LINDE: And your husband came back completely cured?

NORA: Sound as a drum!

MRS. LINDE: But—the doctor?

NORA: Who?

MRS. LINDE: I thought the maid said he was a doctor, the man who came in with me.

NORA: Yes, that was Dr. Rank—but he's not making a sick call. He's our closest friend, and he stops by at least once a day. No, Torvald hasn't had a sick moment since, and the children are fit and strong, and I am, too. *(Jumping up and clapping her hands.)* Oh, dear God, Kristine, what a lovely thing to live and be happy! But how disgusting of me—I'm talking of nothing but my own affairs. *(Sits on a stool close by* KRISTINE, *arms resting across her knees.)* Oh, don't be angry with me! Tell me, is it really true that you weren't in love with your husband? Why did you marry him, then?

MRS. LINDE: My mother was still alive, but bedridden and helpless—and I had two younger brothers to look after. In all conscience, I didn't think I could turn him down.

NORA: No, you were right there. But was he rich at the time?

MRS. LINDE: He was very well off, I'd say. But the business was shaky, Nora. When he died, it all fell apart, and nothing was left.

NORA: And then—?

MRS. LINDE: Yes, so I had to scrape up a living with a little shop and a little teaching and whatever else I could find. The last three years have been like one endless workday without a rest for me. Now it's over, Nora. My poor mother doesn't need me, for she's passed on. Nor the boys, either; they're working now and can take care of themselves.

NORA: How free you must feel—

MRS. LINDE: No—only unspeakably empty. Nothing to live for now. *(Standing up anxiously.)* That's why I couldn't take it any longer out in that desolate hole. Maybe here it'll be easier to find something to do and keep my mind occupied. If I could only be lucky enough to get a steady job, some office work—

NORA: Oh, but Kristine, that's so dreadfully tiring, and you already look so tired. It would be much better for you if you could go off to a bathing resort.

MRS. LINDE *(going toward the window)*: I have no father to give me travel money, Nora.

NORA *(rising)*: Oh, don't be angry with me.

MRS. LINDE *(going to her)*: Nora dear, don't you be angry with me. The worst of my kind of situation is all the bitterness that's stored away. No one to work for, and yet you're always having to snap up your opportunities. You have to live; and so you grow selfish. When you told me the happy change in your lot, do you know I was delighted less for your sakes than for mine?

NORA: How so? Oh, I see. You think maybe Torvald could do something for you.

MRS. LINDE: Yes, that's what I thought.

NORA: And he will, Kristine! Just leave it to me; I'll bring it up so delicately—find something attractive to humor him with. Oh, I'm so eager to help you.

MRS. LINDE: How very kind of you, Nora, to be so concerned over me
—doubly kind, considering you really know so little of life's burdens
yourself.

NORA: I—? I know so little—?

MRS. LINDE *(smiling)*: Well, my heavens—a little needlework and such—
Nora, you're just a child.

NORA *(tossing her head and pacing the floor)*: You don't have to act so superior.

MRS. LINDE: Oh?

NORA: You're just like the others. You all think I'm incapable of anything
serious—

MRS. LINDE: Come now—

NORA: That I've never had to face the raw world.

MRS. LINDE: Nora dear, you've just been telling me all your troubles.

NORA: Hm! Trivia! *(Quietly.)* I haven't told you the big thing.

MRS. LINDE: Big thing? What do you mean?

NORA: You look down on me so, Kristine, but you shouldn't. You're proud
that you worked so long and hard for your mother.

MRS. LINDE: I don't look down on a soul. But it is true; I'm proud—and
happy, too—to think it was given to me to make my mother's last days
almost free of care.

NORA: And you're also proud thinking of what you've done for your
brothers.

MRS. LINDE: I feel I've a right to be.

NORA: I agree. But listen to this, Kristine—I've also got something to be
proud and happy for.

MRS. LINDE: I don't doubt it. But whatever do you mean?

NORA: Not so loud. What if Torvald heard! He mustn't, not for anything
in the world. Nobody must know, Kristine. No one but you.

MRS. LINDE: But what is it, then?

NORA: Come here. *(Drawing her down beside her on the sofa.)* It's true—I've
also got something to be proud and happy for. I'm the one who saved
Torvald's life.

MRS. LINDE: Saved—? Saved how?

NORA: I told you about the trip to Italy. Torvald never would have lived if
he hadn't gone south—

MRS. LINDE: Of course, your father gave you the means—

NORA *(smiling)*: That's what Torvald and all the rest think, but—

MRS. LINDE: But—?

NORA: Papa didn't give us a pin. I was the one who raised the money.

MRS. LINDE: You? The whole amount?

NORA: Four thousand, eight hundred crowns. What do you say to that?

MRS. LINDE: But Nora, how was it possible? Did you win the lottery?

NORA *(disdainfully)*: The lottery? Pooh! No art to that.

MRS. LINDE: But where did you get it from then?

NORA *(humming, with a mysterious smile)*: Hmm, tra-la-la-la.

MRS. LINDE: Because you couldn't have borrowed it.

NORA: No? Why not?

MRS. LINDE: A wife can't borrow without her husband's consent.

NORA (*tossing her head*): Oh, but a wife with a little business sense, a wife who knows how to manage—

MRS. LINDE: Nora, I simply don't understand—

NORA: You don't have to. Whoever said I *borrowed* the money? I could have gotten it other ways. (*Throwing herself back on the sofa.*) I could have gotten it from some admirer or other. After all, a girl with my ravishing appeal—

MRS. LINDE: You lunatic.

NORA: I'll bet you're eaten up with curiosity, Kristine.

MRS. LINDE: Now listen here, Nora—you haven't done something indiscreet?

NORA (*sitting up again*): Is it indiscreet to save your husband's life?

MRS. LINDE: I think it's indiscreet that without his knowledge you—

NORA: But that's the point: he mustn't know! My Lord, can't you understand? He mustn't ever know the close call he had. It was to *me* the doctors came to say his life was in danger—that nothing could save him but a stay in the south. Didn't I try strategy then! I began talking about how lovely it would be for me to travel abroad like other young wives; I begged and I cried; I told him please to remember my condition, to be kind and indulge me; and then I dropped a hint that he could easily take out a loan. But at that, Kristine, he nearly exploded. He said I was frivolous, and it was his duty as man of the house not to indulge me in whims and fancies—as I think he called them. Aha, I thought, now you'll just have to be saved—and that's when I saw my chance.

MRS. LINDE: And your father never told Torvald the money wasn't from him?

NORA: No, never. Papa died right about then. I'd considered bringing him into my secret and begging him never to tell. But he was too sick at the time—and then, sadly, it didn't matter.

MRS. LINDE: And you've never confided in your husband since?

NORA: For heaven's sake, no! Are you serious? He's so strict on that subject. Besides—Torvald, with all his masculine pride—how painfully humiliating for him if he ever found out he was in debt to me. That would just ruin our relationship. Our beautiful happy home would never be the same.

MRS. LINDE: Won't you ever tell him?

NORA (*thoughtfully, half smiling*): Yes—maybe sometime, years from now, when I'm no longer so attractive. Don't laugh! I only mean when Torvald loves me less than now, when he stops enjoying my dancing and dressing up and reciting for him. Then it might be wise to have something in reserve—(*Breaking off.*) How ridiculous! That'll never happen—Well, Kristine, what do you think of my big secret? I'm capable of something too, hm? You can imagine, of course, how this thing hangs over me. It really hasn't been easy meeting the payments on time. In the business world there's what they call quarterly interest and what they call amortization, and these are always so terribly hard to manage. I've had to skimp a little here and there, wherever I could, you know. I could hardly spare anything from my house allowance, because Torvald has to live well. I couldn't let the children go poorly dressed; whatever I got for them, I felt I had to use up completely— the darlings!

MRS. LINDE: Poor Nora, so it had to come out of your own budget, then?

NORA: Yes, of course. But I was the one most responsible, too. Every time Torvald gave me money for new clothes and such, I never used more than half; always bought the simplest, cheapest outfits. It was a godsend that everything looks so well on me that Torvald never noticed. But it did weigh me down at times, Kristine. It *is* such a joy to wear fine things. You understand.

MRS. LINDE: Oh, of course.

NORA: And then I found other ways of making money. Last winter I was lucky enough to get a lot of copying to do. I locked myself in and sat writing every evening till late in the night. Ah, I was tired so often, dead tired. But still it was wonderful fun, sitting and working like that, earning money. It was almost like being a man.

MRS. LINDE: But how much have you paid off this way so far?

NORA: That's hard to say, exactly. These accounts, you know, aren't easy to figure. I only know that I've paid out all I could scrape together. Time and again I haven't known where to turn. (*Smiling.*) Then I'd sit here dreaming of a rich old gentleman who had fallen in love with me—

MRS. LINDE: What! Who is he?

NORA: Oh, really! And that he'd died, and when his will was opened, there in big letters it said, "All my fortune shall be paid over in cash, immediately, to that enchanting Mrs. Nora Helmer."

MRS. LINDE: But Nora dear—who *was* this gentleman?

NORA: Good grief, can't you understand? The old man never existed; that was only something I'd dream up time and again whenever I was at my wits' end for money. But it makes no difference now; the old fossil can go where he pleases for all I care; I don't need him or his will—because now I'm free. (*Jumping up.*) Oh, how lovely to think of that, Kristine! Carefree! To know you're carefree, utterly carefree, to be able to romp and play with the children, and to keep up a beautiful, charming home—everything just the way Torvald likes it! And think, spring is coming, with big blue skies. Maybe we can travel a little then. Maybe I'll see the ocean again. Oh yes, it *is* so marvelous to live and be happy!

(*The front doorbell rings.*)

MRS. LINDE (*rising*): There's the bell. It's probably best that I go.

NORA: No, stay. No one's expected. It must be for Torvald.

MAID *(from the hall doorway)*: Excuse me, ma'am—there's a gentleman here to see Mr. Helmer, but I didn't know—since the doctor's with him—

NORA: Who is the gentleman?

KROGSTAD *(from the doorway)*: It's me, Mrs. Helmer.

(MRS. LINDE starts and turns away toward the window.)

NORA *(stepping toward him, tense, her voice a whisper)*: You? What is it? Why do you want to speak to my husband?

KROGSTAD: Bank business—after a fashion. I have a small job in the investment bank, and I hear now your husband is going to be our chief—

NORA: In other words, it's—

KROGSTAD: Just dry business, Mrs. Helmer. Nothing but that.

NORA: Yes, then please be good enough to step into the study.

(She nods indifferently, as she sees him out by the hall door, then returns and begins stirring up the stove.)

MRS. LINDE: Nora—who was that man?

NORA: That was a Mr. Krogstad—a lawyer.

MRS. LINDE: Then it really was him.

NORA: Do you know that person?

MRS. LINDE: I did once—many years ago. For a time he was a law clerk in our town.

NORA: Yes, he's been that.

MRS. LINDE: How he's changed.

NORA: I understand he had a very unhappy marriage.

MRS. LINDE: He's a widower now.

NORA: With a number of children. There now, it's burning. *(She closes the stove door and moves the rocker a bit to one side.)*

MRS. LINDE: They say he has a hand in all kinds of business.

NORA: Oh? That may be true; I wouldn't know. But let's not think about business. It's so dull.

(DR. RANK enters from HELMER's study.)

RANK *(still in the doorway)*: No, no, really—I don't want to intrude, I'd just as soon talk a little while with your wife. *(Shuts the door, then notices MRS. LINDE.)* Oh, beg pardon, I'm intruding here too.

NORA: No, not at all. *(Introducing him.)* Dr. Rank, Mrs. Linde.

RANK: Well now, that's a name much heard in this house. I believe I passed the lady on the stairs as I came.

MRS. LINDE: Yes, I take the stairs very slowly. They're rather hard on me.

RANK: Uh-hm, some touch of internal weakness?

MRS. LINDE: More overexertion, I'd say.

RANK: Nothing else? Then you're probably here in town to rest up in a round of parties?

MRS. LINDE: I'm here to look for work.

RANK: Is that the best cure for overexertion?

MRS. LINDE: One has to live, Doctor.

RANK: Yes, there's a common prejudice to that effect.

NORA: Oh, come on, Dr. Rank—you really do want to live yourself.

RANK: Yes, I really do. Wretched as I am, I'll gladly prolong my torment indefinitely. All my patients feel like that. And it's quite the same, too, with the morally sick. Right at this moment there's one of those moral invalids in there with Helmer—

MRS. LINDE (softly): Ah!

NORA: Who do you mean?

RANK: Oh, it's a lawyer, Krogstad, a type you wouldn't know. His character is rotten to the root—but even he began chattering all-importantly about how he had to *live*.

NORA: Oh? What did he want to talk to Torvald about?

RANK: I really don't know. I only heard something about the bank.

NORA: I didn't know that Krog—that this man Krogstad had anything to do with the bank.

RANK: Yes, he's gotten some kind of berth down there. (To MRS. LINDE.) I don't know if you also have, in your neck of the woods, a type of person who scuttles about breathlessly, sniffing out hints of moral corruption, and then maneuvers his victim into some sort of key position where he can keep an eye on him. It's the healthy these days that are out in the cold.

MRS. LINDE: All the same, it's the sick who most need to be taken in.

RANK (with a shrug): Yes, there we have it. That's the concept that's turning society into a sanatorium.

(NORA, lost in her thoughts, breaks out into quiet laughter and claps her hands.)

RANK: Why do you laugh at that? Do you have any real idea of what society is?

NORA: What do I care about dreary old society? I was laughing at something quite different—something terribly funny. Tell me, Doctor—is everyone who works in the bank dependent now on Torvald?

RANK: Is that what you find so terribly funny?

NORA (smiling and humming): Never mind, never mind! (Pacing the floor.) Yes, that's really immensely amusing: that we—that Torvald has so much power now over all those people. (Taking the bag out of her pocket.) Dr. Rank, a little macaroon on that?

RANK: See here, macaroons! I thought they were contraband here.

NORA: Yes, but these are some that Kristine gave me.

MRS. LINDE: What? I—?

NORA: Now, now, don't be afraid. You couldn't possibly know that Torvald had forbidden them. You see, he's worried they'll ruin my teeth. But hmp! Just this once! Isn't that so, Dr. Rank? Help yourself! *(Puts a macaroon in his mouth.)* And you too, Kristine. And I'll also have one, only a little one—or two, at the most. *(Walking about again.)* Now I'm really tremendously happy. Now there's just one last thing in the world that I have an enormous desire to do.

RANK: Well! And what's that?

NORA: It's something I have such a consuming desire to say so Torvald could hear.

RANK: And why can't you say it?

NORA: I don't dare. It's quite shocking.

MRS. LINDE: Shocking?

RANK: Well, then it isn't advisable. But in front of us you certainly can. What do you have such a desire to say so Torvald could hear?

NORA: I have such a huge desire to say—to hell and be damned!

RANK: Are you crazy?

MRS. LINDE: My goodness, Nora!

RANK: Go on, say it. Here he is.

NORA *(hiding the macaroon bag)*: Shh, shh, shh!

(HELMER comes in from his study, hat in hand, overcoat over his arm.)

NORA *(going toward him)*: Well, Torvald dear, are you through with him?

HELMER: Yes, he just left.

NORA: Let me introduce you—this is Kristine, who's arrived here in town.

HELMER: Kristine—? I'm sorry, but I don't know—

NORA: Mrs. Linde, Torvald dear. Mrs. Kristine Linde.

HELMER: Of course. A childhood friend of my wife's, no doubt?

MRS. LINDE: Yes, we knew each other in those days.

NORA: And just think, she made the long trip down here in order to talk with you.

HELMER: What's this?

MRS. LINDE: Well, not exactly—

NORA: You see, Kristine is remarkably clever in office work, and so she's terribly eager to come under a capable man's supervision and add more to what she already knows—

HELMER: Very wise, Mrs. Linde.

NORA: And then when she heard that you'd become a bank manager— the story was wired out to the papers—then she came in as fast as she could and—Really, Torvald, for my sake you can do a little something for Kristine, can't you?

HELMER: Yes, it's not at all impossible. Mrs. Linde, I suppose you're a widow?

MRS. LINDE: Yes.

HELMER: Any experience in office work?

MRS. LINDE: Yes, a good deal.

HELMER: Well, it's quite likely that I can make an opening for you—

NORA (clapping her hands): You see, you see!

HELMER: You've come at a lucky moment, Mrs. Linde.

MRS. LINDE: Oh, how can I thank you?

HELMER: Not necessary. (Putting his overcoat on.) But today you'll have to excuse me—

RANK: Wait, I'll go with you. (He fetches his coat from the hall and warms it at the stove.)

NORA: Don't stay out long, dear.

HELMER: An hour; no more.

NORA: Are you going too, Kristine?

MRS. LINDE (putting on her winter garments): Yes, I have to see about a room now.

HELMER: Then perhaps we can all walk together.

NORA (helping her): What a shame we're so cramped here, but it's quite impossible for us to—

MRS. LINDE: Oh, don't even think of it! Good-bye, Nora dear, and thanks for everything.

NORA: Good-bye for now. Of course you'll be back again this evening. And you too, Dr. Rank. What? If you're well enough? Oh, you've got to be! Wrap up tight now.

(In a ripple of small talk the company moves out into the hall; children's voices are heard outside on the steps.)

NORA: There they are! There they are! (She runs to open the door. The children come in with their nurse, ANNE-MARIE.) Come in, come in! (Bends down and kisses them.) Oh, you darlings—! Look at them, Kristine. Aren't they lovely!

RANK: No loitering in the draft here.

HELMER: Come, Mrs. Linde—this place is unbearable now for anyone but mothers.

(DR. RANK, HELMER, and MRS. LINDE go down the stairs. ANNE-MARIE goes into the living room with the children. NORA follows, after closing the hall door.)

NORA: How fresh and strong you look. Oh, such red cheeks you have! Like apples and roses. (The children interrupt her throughout the following.) And it was so much fun? That's wonderful. Really? You pulled both Emmy and Bob on the sled? Imagine, all together! Yes, you're a clever boy, Ivar. Oh, let me hold her a bit, Anne-Marie. My sweet little doll baby! (Takes the smallest from the nurse and dances with her.) Yes, yes, Mama will dance with Bob as well. What? Did you throw snowballs? Oh, if I'd only been there! No, don't bother, Anne-Marie—I'll undress them myself. Oh yes, let me. It's such fun. Go in and rest; you look half frozen. There's hot coffee waiting for you on the stove. *(The nurse goes into the room to the left. Nora takes the children's winter things off, throwing them about, while the children talk to her all at once.)* Is that so? A big dog chased you? But it didn't bite? No, dogs never bite little, lovely doll babies. Don't peek in the packages, Ivar! What is it? Yes, wouldn't you like to know. No, no, it's an ugly something. Well? Shall we play? What shall we play? Hide-and-seek? Yes, let's play hide-and-seek. Bob must hide first. I must? Yes, let me hide first.

(Laughing and shouting, she and the children play in and out of the living room and the adjoining room to the right. At last NORA *hides under the table. The children come storming in, search, but cannot find her, then hear her muffled laughter, dash over to the table, lift the cloth and find her. Wild shouting. She creeps forward as if to scare them. More shouts. Meanwhile, a knock at the hall door; no one has noticed it. Now the door half opens, and* KROGSTAD *appears. He waits a moment; the game goes on.)*

KROGSTAD: Beg pardon, Mrs. Helmer—

NORA *(with a strangled cry, turning and scrambling to her knees)*: Oh! what do you want?

KROGSTAD: Excuse me. The outer door was ajar; it must be someone forgot to shut it—

NORA *(rising)*: My husband isn't home, Mr. Krogstad.

KROGSTAD: I know that.

NORA: Yes—then what do you want here?

KROGSTAD: A word with you.

NORA: With—? *(To the children, quietly.)* Go in to Anne-Marie. What? No, the strange man won't hurt Mama. When he's gone, we'll play some more. *(She leads the children into the room to the left and shuts the door after them. Then, tense and nervous.)* You want to speak to me?

KROGSTAD: Yes, I want to.

NORA: Today? But it's not yet the first of the month—

KROGSTAD: No, it's Christmas Eve. It's going to be up to you how merry a Christmas you have.

NORA: What is it you want? Today I absolutely can't—

KROGSTAD: We won't talk about that till later. This is something else. You do have a moment to spare, I suppose?

NORA: Oh yes, of course—I do, except—

KROGSTAD: Good. I was sitting over at Olsen's Restaurant when I saw your husband go down the street—

NORA: Yes?

KROGSTAD: With a lady.

NORA: Yes. So?

KROGSTAD: If you'll pardon my asking: wasn't that lady a Mrs. Linde?

NORA: Yes.

KROGSTAD: Just now come into town?

NORA: Yes, today.

KROGSTAD: She's a good friend of yours?

NORA: Yes, she is. But I don't see—

KROGSTAD: I also knew her once.

NORA: I'm aware of that.

KROGSTAD: Oh? You know all about it. I thought so. Well, then let me ask you short and sweet: is Mrs. Linde getting a job at the bank?

NORA: What makes you think you can cross-examine me, Mr. Krogstad— you, one of my husband's employees? But since you ask, you might as well know—yes, Mrs. Linde's going to be taken on at the bank. And I'm the one who spoke for her, Mr. Krogstad. Now you know.

KROGSTAD: So I guessed right.

NORA (pacing up and down): Oh, one does have a tiny bit of influence, I should hope. Just because I am a woman, don't think it means that— When one has a subordinate position, Mr. Krogstad, one really ought to be careful about pushing somebody who—hm—

KROGSTAD: Who has influence?

NORA: That's right.

KROGSTAD (in a different tone): Mrs. Helmer, would you be good enough to use your influence on my behalf?

NORA: What? What do you mean?

KROGSTAD: Would you please make sure that I keep my subordinate position in the bank?

NORA: What does that mean? Who's thinking of taking away your position?

KROGSTAD: Oh, don't play the innocent with me. I'm quite aware that your friend would hardly relish the chance of running into me again; and I'm also aware now whom I can thank for being turned out.

NORA: But I promise you—

KROGSTAD: Yes, yes, yes, to the point: there's still time, and I'm advising you to use your influence to prevent it.

NORA: But Mr. Krogstad, I have absolutely no influence.

KROGSTAD: You haven't? I thought you were just saying—

NORA: You shouldn't take me so literally. I! How can you believe that I have any such influence over my husband?

KROGSTAD: Oh, I've known your husband from our student days. I don't think the great bank manager's more steadfast than any other married man.

NORA: You speak insolently about my husband, and I'll show you the door.

KROGSTAD: The lady has spirit.

NORA: I'm not afraid of you any longer. After New Year's, I'll soon be done with the whole business.

KROGSTAD (restraining himself): Now listen to me, Mrs. Helmer. If necessary, I'll fight for my little job in the bank as if it were life itself.

NORA: Yes, so it seems.

KROGSTAD: It's not just a matter of income; that's the least of it. It's something else—All right, out with it! Look, this is the thing. You know, just like all the others, of course, that once, a good many years ago, I did something rather rash.

NORA: I've heard rumors to that effect.

KROGSTAD: The case never got into court; but all the same, every door was closed in my face from then on. So I took up those various activities you know about. I had to grab hold somewhere; and I dare say I haven't been among the worst. But now I want to drop all that. My boys are growing up. For their sakes, I'll have to win back as much respect as possible here in town. That job in the bank was like the first rung in my ladder. And now your husband wants to kick me right back down in the mud again.

NORA: But for heaven's sake, Mr. Krogstad, it's simply not in my power to help you.

KROGSTAD: That's because you haven't the will to—but I have the means to make you.

NORA: You certainly won't tell my husband that I owe you money?

KROGSTAD: Hm—what if I told him that?

NORA: That would be shameful of you. *(Nearly in tears.)* This secret—my joy and my pride—that he should learn it in such a crude and disgusting way—learn it from you. You'd expose me to the most horrible unpleasantness—

KROGSTAD: Only unpleasantness?

NORA *(vehemently)*: But go on and try. It'll turn out the worst for you, because then my husband will really see what a crook you are, and then you'll *never* be able to hold your job.

KROGSTAD: I asked if it was just domestic unpleasantness you were afraid of?

NORA: If my husband finds out, then of course he'll pay what I owe at once, and then we'd be through with you for good.

KROGSTAD *(a step closer)*: Listen, Mrs. Helmer—you've either got a very bad memory, or else no head at all for business. I'd better put you a little more in touch with the facts.

NORA: What do you mean?

KROGSTAD: When your husband was sick, you came to me for a loan of four thousand, eight hundred crowns.

NORA: Where else could I go?

KROGSTAD: I promised to get you that sum—

NORA: And you got it.

KROGSTAD: I promised to get you that sum, on certain conditions. You were so involved in your husband's illness, and so eager to finance your trip, that I guess you didn't think out all the details. It might just be a good idea to remind you. I promised you the money on the strength of a note I drew up.

NORA: Yes, and that I signed.

KROGSTAD: Right. But at the bottom I added some lines for your father to guarantee the loan. He was supposed to sign down there.

NORA: Supposed to? He did sign.

KROGSTAD: I left the date blank. In other words, your father would have dated his signature himself. Do you remember that?

NORA: Yes, I think—

KROGSTAD: Then I gave you the note for you to mail to your father. Isn't that so?

NORA: Yes.

KROGSTAD: And naturally you sent it at once—because only some five, six days later you brought me the note, properly signed. And with that, the money was yours.

NORA: Well, then; I've made my payments regularly, haven't I?

KROGSTAD: More or less. But—getting back to the point—those were hard times for you then, Mrs. Helmer.

NORA: Yes, they were.

KROGSTAD: Your father was very ill, I believe.

NORA: He was near the end.

KROGSTAD: He died soon after?

NORA: Yes.

KROGSTAD: Tell me, Mrs. Helmer, do you happen to recall the date of your father's death? The day of the month, I mean.

NORA: Papa died the twenty-ninth of September.

KROGSTAD: That's quite correct; I've already looked into that. And now we come to a curious thing —*(taking out a paper)* which I simply cannot comprehend.

NORA: Curious thing? I don't know—

KROGSTAD: This is the curious thing: that your father co-signed the note for your loan three days after his death.

NORA: How—? I don't understand.

KROGSTAD: Your father died the twenty-ninth of September. But look. Here your father dated his signature October second. Isn't that curious, Mrs. Helmer? *(NORA is silent.)* Can you explain it to me? *(NORA remains silent.)* It's also remarkable that the words "October second" and the year aren't written in your father's hand, but rather in one that I think I know. Well, it's easy to understand. Your father forgot perhaps to date his signature, and then someone or other added it, a bit sloppily, before anyone knew of his death. There's nothing wrong in that. It all comes down to the signature. And there's no question about *that,* Mrs. Helmer. It really *was* your father who signed his own name here, wasn't it?

NORA *(after a short silence, throwing her head back and looking squarely at him):* No, it wasn't. I signed Papa's name.

KROGSTAD: Wait, now—are you fully aware that this is a dangerous confession?

NORA: Why? You'll soon get your money.

KROGSTAD: Let me ask you a question—why didn't you send the paper to your father?

NORA: That was impossible. Papa was so sick. If I'd asked him for his signature, I also would have had to tell him what the money was for. But I couldn't tell him, sick as he was, that my husband's life was in danger. That was just impossible.

KROGSTAD: Then it would have been better if you'd given up the trip abroad.

NORA: I couldn't possibly. The trip was to save my husband's life. I couldn't give that up.

KROGSTAD: But didn't you ever consider that this was a fraud against me?

NORA: I couldn't let myself be bothered by that. You weren't any concern of mine. I couldn't stand you, with all those cold complications you made, even though you knew how badly off my husband was.

KROGSTAD: Mrs. Helmer, obviously you haven't the vaguest idea of what you've involved yourself in. But I can tell you this: it was nothing more and nothing worse than I once did—and it wrecked my whole reputation.

NORA: You? Do you expect me to believe that you ever acted bravely to save your wife's life?

KROGSTAD: Laws don't inquire into motives.

NORA: Then they must be very poor laws.

KROGSTAD: Poor or not—if I introduce this paper in court, you'll be judged according to law.

NORA: This I refuse to believe. A daughter hasn't a right to protect her dying father from anxiety and care? A wife hasn't a right to save her husband's life? I don't know much about laws, but I'm sure that somewhere in the books these things are allowed. And you don't know anything about it—you who practice the law? You must be an awful lawyer, Mr. Krogstad.

KROGSTAD: Could be. But business—the kind of business we two are mixed up in—don't you think I know about that? All right. Do what you want now. But I'm telling you *this:* if I get shoved down a second time, you're going to keep me company.

(He bows and goes out through the hall.)

NORA *(pensive for a moment, then tossing her head):* Oh, really! Trying to frighten me! I'm not so silly as all that. *(Begins gathering up the children's clothes, but soon stops.)* But—? No, but that's impossible! I did it out of love.

THE CHILDREN *(in the doorway, left):* Mama, that strange man's gone out the door.

NORA: Yes, yes, I know it. But don't tell anyone about the strange man. Do you hear. Not even Papa!

THE CHILDREN: No, Mama. But now will you play again?

NORA: No, not now.

THE CHILDREN: Oh, but Mama, you promised.

NORA: Yes, but I can't now. Go inside; I have too much to do. Go in, go in, my sweet darlings. *(She herds them gently back in the room and shuts the door after them. Settling on the sofa, she takes up a piece of embroidery and makes some stitches, but soon stops abruptly.)* No! *(Throws the work aside, rises, goes to the hall door and calls out.)* Helene! Let me have the tree in here. *(Goes to the table, left, opens the table drawer, and stops again.)* No, but that's utterly impossible!

MAID *(with the Christmas tree)*: Where should I put it, Ma'am?

NORA: There. The middle of the floor.

MAID: Should I bring anything else?

NORA: No, thanks. I have what I need.

(The MAID, who has set the tree down, goes out.)

NORA *(absorbed in trimming the tree)*: Candles here—and flowers here. That terrible creature! Talk, talk, talk! There's nothing to it at all. The tree's going to be lovely. I'll do anything to please you, Torvald. I'll sing for you, dance for you—

(HELMER comes in from the hall, with a sheaf of papers under his arm.)

NORA: Oh! You're back so soon?

HELMER: Yes. Has anyone been here?

NORA: Here? No.

HELMER: That's odd. I saw Krogstad leaving the front door.

NORA: So? Oh yes, that's true. Krogstad was here a moment.

HELMER: Nora, I can see by your face that he's been here, begging you to put in a good word for him.

NORA: Yes.

HELMER: And it was supposed to seem like your own idea? You were to hide it from me that he'd been here. He asked you that, too, didn't he?

NORA: Yes, Torvald, but—

HELMER: Nora, Nora, and you could fall for that? Talk with that sort of person and promise him anything? And then in the bargain, tell me an untruth.

NORA: An untruth—?

HELMER: Didn't you say that no one had been here? *(Wagging his finger.)* My little songbird must never do that again. A songbird needs a clean beak to warble with. No false notes. *(Putting his arm about her waist.)* That's the way it should be, isn't it? Yes, I'm sure of it. *(Releasing her.)* And so, enough of that. *(Sitting by the stove.)* Ah, how snug and cozy it is here. *(Leafing among his papers.)*

NORA *(busy with the tree, after a short pause)*: Torvald!

HELMER: Yes.

NORA: I'm so much looking forward to the Stenborgs' costume party, day after tomorrow.

HELMER: And I can't wait to see what you'll surprise me with.

NORA: Oh, that stupid business.

HELMER: What?

NORA: I can't find anything that's right. Everything seems so ridiculous, so inane.

HELMER: So my little Nora's come to *that* recognition?

NORA *(going behind his chair, her arms resting on its back)*: Are you very busy, Torvald?

HELMER: Oh—

NORA: What papers are those?

HELMER: Bank matters.

NORA: Already?

HELMER: I've gotten full authority from the retiring management to make all necessary changes in personnel and procedure. I'll need Christmas week for that. I want to have everything in order by New Year's.

NORA: So that was the reason this poor Krogstad—

HELMER: Hm.

NORA *(still leaning on the chair and slowly stroking the nape of his neck)*: If you weren't so very busy, I would have asked you an enormous favor, Torvald.

HELMER: Let's hear. What is it?

NORA: You know, there isn't anyone who has your good taste—and I want so much to look well at the costume party. Torvald, couldn't you take over and decide what I should be and plan my costume?

HELMER: Ah, is my stubborn little creature calling for a lifeguard?

NORA: Yes, Torvald, I can't get anywhere without your help.

HELMER: All right—I'll think it over. We'll hit on something.

NORA: Oh, how sweet of you. *(Goes to the tree again. Pause.)* Aren't the red flowers pretty—? But tell me, was it really such a crime that this Krogstad committed?

HELMER: Forgery. Do you have any idea what that means?

NORA: Couldn't he have done it out of need?

HELMER: Yes, or thoughtlessness, like so many others. I'm not so heartless that I'd condemn a man categorically for just one mistake.

NORA: No, of course not, Torvald!

HELMER: Plenty of men have redeemed themselves by openly confessing their crimes and taking their punishments.

NORA: Punishment—?

HELMER: But now Krogstad didn't go that way. He got himself out by sharp practices, and that's the real cause of his moral breakdown.

NORA: Do you really think that would—?

HELMER: Just imagine how a man with that sort of guilt in him has to lie and cheat and deceive on all sides, has to wear a mask even with the nearest and dearest he has, even with his own wife and children. And with the children, Nora—that's where it's most horrible.

NORA: Why?

HELMER: Because that kind of atmosphere of lies infects the whole life of a home. Every breath the children take in is filled with the terms of something degenerate.

NORA *(coming closer behind him)*: Are you sure of that?

HELMER: Oh, I've seen it often enough as a lawyer. Almost everyone who goes bad early in life has a mother who's a chronic liar.

NORA: Why just—the mother?

HELMER: It's usually the mother's influence that's dominant, but the father's works in the same way, of course. Every lawyer is quite familiar with it. And still this Krogstad's been going home year in, year out, poisoning his own children with lies and pretense; that's why I call him morally lost. *(Reaching his hands out toward her.)* So my sweet little Nora must promise me never to plead his cause. Your hand on it. Come, come, what's this? Give me your hand. There, now. All settled. I can tell you it'd be impossible for me to work alongside of him. I literally feel physically revolted when I'm anywhere near such a person.

NORA *(withdraws her hand and goes to the other side of the Christmas tree)*: How hot it is here! And I've got so much to do.

HELMER *(getting up and gathering his papers)*: Yes, and I have to think about getting some of these read through before dinner. I'll think about your costume, too. And something to hang on the tree in gilt paper, I may even see about that. *(Putting his hand on her head.)* Oh you, my darling little songbird.

(He goes into his study and closes the door after him.)

NORA *(softly, after a silence)*: Oh, really! It isn't so. It's impossible. It must be impossible.

ANNE-MARIE *(in the doorway, left)*: The children are begging so hard to come in to Mama.

NORA: No, no, no, don't let them in to me! You stay with them, Anne-Marie.

ANNE-MARIE: Of course, Ma'am. *(Closes the door.)*

NORA *(pale with terror)*: Hurt my children—! Poison my home? *(A moment's pause; then she tosses her head.)* That's not true. Never. Never in all the world.

ACT II

Scene *Same room. Beside the piano the Christmas tree now stands stripped of ornament, burned-down candle stubs on its ragged branches.* NORA's *street clothes lie on the sofa.* NORA, *alone in the room, moves restlessly about; at last she stops at the sofa and picks up her coat.*

NORA *(dropping the coat again)*: Someone's coming! *(Goes toward the door, listens.)* No—there's no one. Of course—nobody's coming today, Christmas Day—or tomorrow, either. But maybe—*(Opens the door and looks out.)* No, nothing in the mailbox. Quite empty. *(Coming forward.)* What nonsense! He won't do anything serious. Nothing terrible could happen. It's impossible. Why, I have three small children.

(ANNE-MARIE, with a large carton, comes in from the room to the left.)

ANNE-MARIE: Well, at last I found the box with the masquerade clothes.
NORA: Thanks. Put it on the table.
ANNE-MARIE *(does so)*: But they're all pretty much of a mess.
NORA: Ahh! I'd love to rip them in a million pieces!
ANNE-MARIE: Oh, mercy, they can be fixed right up. Just a little patience.
NORA: Yes, I'll go get Mrs. Linde to help me.
ANNE-MARIE: Out again now? In this nasty weather? Miss Nora will catch cold—get sick.
NORA: Oh, worse things could happen—How are the children?
ANNE-MARIE: The poor mites are playing with their Christmas presents, but—
NORA: Do they ask for me much?
ANNE-MARIE: They're so used to having Mama around, you know.
NORA: Yes, but Anne-Marie, I *can't* be together with them as much as I was.
ANNE-MARIE: Well, small children get used to anything.
NORA: You think so? Do you think they'd forget their mother if she was gone for good?
ANNE-MARIE: Oh, mercy—gone for good!
NORA: Wait, tell me, Anne-Marie—I've wondered so often—how could you ever have the heart to give your child over to strangers?
ANNE-MARIE: But I had to, you know, to become little Nora's nurse.
NORA: Yes, but how could you *do* it?
ANNE-MARIE: When I could get such a good place? A girl who's poor and who's gotten in trouble is glad enough for that. Because that slippery fish, he didn't do a thing for me, you know.
NORA: But your daughter's surely forgotten you.
ANNE-MARIE: Oh, she certainly has not. She's written to me, both when she was confirmed and when she was married.
NORA *(clasping her about the neck)*: You old Anne-Marie, you were a good mother for me when I was little.
ANNE-MARIE: Poor little Nora, with no other mother but me.
NORA: And if the babies didn't have one, then I know that you'd—What silly talk! *(Opening the carton.)* Go in to them. Now I'll have to— Tomorrow you can see how lovely I'll look.
ANNE-MARIE: Oh, there won't be anyone at the party as lovely as Miss Nora.

(She goes off into the room, left.)

NORA *(begins unpacking the box, but soon throws it aside)*: Oh, if I dared to go out. If only nobody would come. If only nothing would happen here while I'm out. What craziness—nobody's coming. Just don't think. This muff—needs a brushing. Beautiful gloves, beautiful gloves. Let it go. Let it go! One, two, three, four, five, six—*(With a cry.)* Oh, there they are! *(Poises to move toward the door, but remains irresolutely standing. MRS. LINDE enters from the hall, where she has removed her street clothes.)*

NORA: Oh, it's you, Kristine. There's no one else out there? How good that you've come.

MRS. LINDE: I hear you were up asking for me.

NORA: Yes, I just stopped by. There's something you really can help me with. Let's get settled on the sofa. Look, there's going to be a costume party tomorrow evening at the Stenborgs' right above us, and now Torvald wants me to go as a Neapolitan peasant girl and dance the tarantella that I learned in Capri.

MRS. LINDE: Really, you are giving a whole performance?

NORA: Torvald says yes, I should. See, here's the dress. Torvald had it made for me down there; but now it's all so tattered that I just don't know—

MRS. LINDE: Oh, we'll fix that up in no time. It's nothing more than the trimmings—they're a bit loose here and there. Needle and thread? Good, now we have what we need.

NORA: Oh, how sweet of you!

MRS. LINDE *(sewing)*: So you'll be in disguise tomorrow, Nora. You know what? I'll stop by then for a moment and have a look at you all dressed up. But listen, I've absolutely forgotten to thank you for that pleasant evening yesterday.

NORA *(getting up and walking about)*: I don't think it was as pleasant as usual yesterday. You should have come to town a bit sooner, Kristine—Yes, Torvald really knows how to give a home elegance and charm.

MRS. LINDE: And you do, too, if you ask me. You're not your father's daughter for nothing. But tell me, is Dr. Rank always so down in the mouth as yesterday?

NORA: No, that was quite an exception. But he goes around critically ill all the time—tuberculosis of the spine, poor man. You know, his father was a disgusting thing who kept mistresses and so on—and that's why the son's been sickly from birth.

MRS. LINDE *(lets her sewing fall to her lap)*: But my dearest Nora, how do you know about such things?

NORA *(walking more jauntily)*: Hmp! When you've had three children, then you've had a few visits from—women who know something of medicine, and they tell you this and that.

MRS. LINDE *(resumes sewing; a short pause)*: Does Dr. Rank come here every day?

NORA: Every blessed day. He's Torvald's best friend from childhood, and *my* good friend, too. Dr. Rank almost belongs to this house.

MRS. LINDE: But tell me—is he quite sincere? I mean, doesn't he rather enjoy flattering people?

NORA: Just the opposite. Why do you think that?

MRS. LINDE: When you introduced us yesterday, he was proclaiming that he'd often heard my name in this house; but later I noticed that your husband hadn't the slightest idea who I really was. So how could Dr. Rank—?

NORA: But it's all true, Kristine. You see, Torvald loves me beyond words, and, as he puts it, he'd like to keep me all to himself. For a long time he'd almost be jealous if I even mentioned any of my old friends back home. So of course I dropped that. But with Dr. Rank I talk a lot about such things, because he likes hearing about them.

MRS. LINDE: Now listen, Nora; in many ways you're still like a child. I'm a good deal older than you, with a little more experience. I'll tell you something; you ought to put an end to all this with Dr. Rank.

NORA: What should I put an end to?

MRS. LINDE: Both parts of it, I think. Yesterday you said something about a rich admirer who'd provide you with money—

NORA: Yes, one who doesn't exist—worse luck. So?

MRS. LINDE: Is Dr. Rank well off?

NORA: Yes, he is.

MRS. LINDE: With no dependents?

NORA: No, no one. But—

MRS. LINDE: And he's over here every day?

NORA: Yes, I told you that.

MRS. LINDE: How can a man of such refinement be so grasping?

NORA: I don't follow you at all.

MRS. LINDE: Now don't try to hide it, Nora. You think I can't guess who loaned you the forty-eight hundred crowns?

NORA: Are you out of your mind? How could you think of such a thing! A friend of ours, who comes here every single day. What an intolerable situation that would have been!

MRS. LINDE: Then it really wasn't him.

NORA: No, absolutely not. It never even crossed my mind for a moment— And he had nothing to lend in those days; his inheritance came later.

MRS. LINDE: Well, I think that was a stroke of luck for you, Nora dear.

NORA: No, it never would have occurred to me to ask Dr. Rank—Still, I'm quite sure that if I had asked him—

MRS. LINDE: Which you won't, of course.

NORA: No, of course not. I can't see that I'd ever need to. But I'm quite positive that if I talked to Dr. Rank—

MRS. LINDE: Behind your husband's back?

NORA: I've got to clear up this other thing: *that's* also behind his back. I've *got* to clear it all up.

MRS. LINDE: Yes, I was saying that yesterday, but—

NORA *(pacing up and down)*: A man handles these problems so much better than a woman—

MRS. LINDE: One's husband does, yes.

NORA: Nonsense. *(Stopping.)* When you pay everything you owe, then you get your note back, right?

MRS. LINDE: Yes, naturally.

NORA: And can rip it into a million pieces and burn it up—that filthy scrap of paper!

MRS. LINDE *(looking hard at her, laying her sewing aside, and rising slowly)*: Nora, you're hiding something from me.

NORA: You can see it in my face?

MRS. LINDE: Something's happened to you since yesterday morning. Nora, what is it?

NORA *(hurrying toward her)*: Kristine! *(Listening.)* Shh! Torvald's home. Look, go in with the children a while. Torvald can't bear all this snipping and stitching. Let Anne-Marie help you.

MRS. LINDE *(gathering up some of the things)*: All right, but I'm not leaving here until we've talked this out. *(She disappears into the room, left, as TORVALD enters from the hall.)*

NORA: Oh, how I've been waiting for you, Torvald dear.

HELMER: Was that the dressmaker?

NORA: No, that was Kristine. She's helping me fix up my costume. You know, it's going to be quite attractive.

HELMER: Yes, wasn't that a bright idea I had?

NORA: Brilliant! But then wasn't I good as well to give in to you?

HELMER: Good—because you give in to your husband's judgment? All right, you little goose, I know you didn't mean it like that. But I won't disturb you. You'll want to have a fitting, I suppose.

NORA: And you'll be working?

HELMER: Yes. *(Indicating a bundle of papers.)* See. I've been down to the bank. *(Starts toward his study.)*

NORA: Torvald.

HELMER *(stops)*: Yes.

NORA: If your little squirrel begged you, with all her heart and soul, for something—?

HELMER: What's that?

NORA: Then would you do it?

HELMER: First, naturally, I'd have to know what it was.

NORA: Your squirrel would scamper about and do tricks, if you'd only be sweet and give in.

HELMER: Out with it.

NORA: Your lark would be singing high and low in every room—

HELMER: Come on, she does that anyway.

NORA: I'd be a wood nymph and dance for you in the moonlight.

HELMER: Nora—don't tell me it's that same business from this morning?

NORA *(coming closer)*: Yes, Torvald, I beg you, please!

HELMER: And you actually have the nerve to drag that up again?

NORA: Yes, yes, you've got to give in to me; you have to let Krogstad keep his job in the bank.

HELMER: My dear Nora, I've slated his job for Mrs. Linde.

NORA: That's awfully kind of you. But you could just fire another clerk instead of Krogstad.

HELMER: This is the most incredible stubbornness! Because you go and give an impulsive promise to speak up for him, I'm expected to—

NORA: That's not the reason, Torvald. It's for your own sake. That man does writing for the worst papers; you said it yourself. He could do you any amount of harm. I'm scared to death of him—

HELMER: Ah, I understand. It's the old memories haunting you.

NORA: What do you mean by that?

HELMER: Of course, you're thinking about your father.

NORA: Yes, all right. Just remember how those nasty gossips wrote in the papers about Papa and slandered him so cruelly. I think they'd have had him dismissed if the department hadn't sent you up to investigate, and if you hadn't been so kind and open-minded toward him.

HELMER: My dear Nora, there's a notable difference between your father and me. Your father's official career was hardly above reproach. But mine is; and I hope it'll stay that way as long as I hold my position.

NORA: Oh, who can ever tell what vicious minds can invent? We could be so snug and happy now in our quiet, carefree home—you and I and the children, Torvald! That's why I'm pleading with you so—

HELMER: And just by pleading for him you make it impossible for me to keep him on. It's already known at the bank that I'm firing Krogstad. What if it's rumored around now that the new bank manager was vetoed by his wife—

NORA: Yes, what then—?

HELMER: Oh yes—as long as your little bundle of stubbornness gets her way—I should go and make myself ridiculous in front of the whole office—give people the idea I can be swayed by all kinds of outside pressure. Oh, you can bet I'd feel the effects of that soon enough! Besides—there's something that rules Krogstad right out at the bank as long as I'm the manager.

NORA: What's that?

HELMER: His moral failings I could maybe overlook if I had to—

NORA: Yes, Torvald, why not?

HELMER: And I hear he's quite efficient on the job. But he was a crony of mine back in my teens—one of those rash friendships that crop up again and again to embarrass you later in life. Well, I might as well say it straight out: we're on a first-name basis. And that tactless fool makes no effort at all to hide it in front of others. Quite the contrary—he thinks that entitles him to take a familiar air around me, and so every other second he comes booming out with his "Yes, Torvald!" and "Sure thing, Torvald!" I tell you, it's been excruciating for me. He's out to make my place in the bank unbearable.

NORA: Torvald, you can't be serious about all this.

HELMER: Oh no? Why not?

NORA: Because these are such petty considerations.

HELMER: What are you saying? Petty? You think I'm petty!

NORA: No, just the opposite, Torvald dear. That's exactly why—

HELMER: Never mind. You call my motives petty; then I might as well be just that. Petty! All right! We'll put a stop to this for good. *(Goes to the hall door and calls.)* Helene!

NORA: What do you want?

HELMER *(searching among his papers)*: A decision. *(The* MAID *comes in.)* Look here; take this letter, go out with it at once. Get hold of a messenger and have him deliver it. Quick now. It's already addressed. Wait, here's some money.

MAID: Yes, sir. *(She leaves with the letter.)*

HELMER *(straightening his papers)*: There, now, little Miss Willful.

NORA *(breathlessly)*: Torvald, what was that letter?

HELMER: Krogstad's notice.

NORA: Call it back, Torvald! There's still time. Oh Torvald, call it back! Do it for my sake—for your sake, for the children's sake! Do you hear, Torvald; do it! You don't know how this can harm us.

HELMER: Too late.

NORA: Yes, too late.

HELMER: Nora dear, I can forgive you this panic, even though basically you're insulting me. Yes, you are! Or isn't it an insult to think that I should be afraid of a courtroom hack's revenge? But I forgive you anyway, because this shows so beautifully how much you love me. *(Takes her in his arms.)* This is the way it should be, my darling Nora. Whatever comes, you'll see: when it really counts, I have strength and courage enough as a man to take on the whole weight myself.

NORA *(terrified)*: What do you mean by that?

HELMER: The whole weight, I said.

NORA *(resolutely)*: No, never in all the world.

HELMER: Good. So we'll share it, Nora, as man and wife. That's as it should be. *(Fondling her.)* Are you happy now? There, there, there—not these frightened dove's eyes. It's nothing at all but empty fantasies— Now you should run through your tarantella and practice your tambourine. I'll go to the inner office and shut both doors, so I won't hear a thing; you can make all the noise you like. *(Turning in the doorway.)* And when Rank comes, just tell him where he can find me. *(He nods to her and goes with his papers into the study, closing the door.)*

NORA *(standing as though rooted, dazed with fright, in a whisper)*: He really could do it. He will do it. He'll do it in spite of everything. No, not that, never, never! Anything but that! Escape! A way out—*(The doorbell rings.)* Dr. Rank! Anything but that! Anything, whatever it is! *(Her hands pass over her face, smoothing it; she pulls herself together, goes over and opens the hall door.* DR. RANK *stands outside, hanging his fur coat up. During the following scene, it begins getting dark.)*

NORA: Hello, Dr. Rank. I recognized your ring. But you mustn't go in to Torvald yet; I believe he's working.

RANK: And you?

NORA: For you, I always have an hour to spare—you know that.

(He has entered, and she shuts the door after him.)

RANK: Many thanks. I'll make use of these hours while I can.

NORA: What do you mean by that? While you can?

RANK: Does that disturb you?

NORA: Well, it's such an odd phrase. Is anything going to happen?

RANK: What's going to happen is what I've been expecting so long—but I honestly didn't think it would come so soon.

NORA *(gripping his arm)*: What is it you've found out? Dr. Rank, you have to tell me!

RANK *(sitting by the stove)*: It's all over with me. There's nothing to be done about it.

NORA *(breathing easier)*: Is it you—then—?

RANK: Who else? There's no point in lying to one's self. I'm the most miserable of all my patients, Mrs. Helmer. These past few days I've been auditing my internal accounts. Bankrupt! Within a month I'll probably be laid out and rotting in the churchyard.

NORA: Oh, what a horrible thing to say.

RANK: The thing itself is horrible. But the worst of it is all the other horror before it's over. There's only one final examination left; when I'm finished with that, I'll know about when my disintegration will begin. There's something I want to say. Helmer with his sensitivity has such a sharp distaste for anything ugly. I don't want him near my sickroom.

NORA: Oh, but Dr. Rank—

RANK: I won't have him in there. Under no condition. I'll lock my door to him—As soon as I'm completely sure of the worst, I'll send you my calling card marked with a black cross, and you'll know then the wreck has started to come apart.

NORA: No, today you're completely unreasonable. And I wanted you so much to be in a really good humor.

RANK: With death up my sleeve? And then to suffer this way for somebody else's sins. Is there any justice in that? And in every single family, in some way or another, this inevitable retribution of nature goes on—

NORA *(her hands pressed over her ears)*: Oh, stuff! Cheer up! Please—be gay!

RANK: Yes, I'd just as soon laugh at it all. My poor, innocent spine, serving time for my father's gay army days.

NORA *(by the table, left)*: He was so infatuated with asparagus tips and *pâté de foie gras,* wasn't that it?

RANK: Yes—and with truffles.

NORA: Truffles, yes. And then with oysters, I suppose?

RANK: Yes, tons of oysters, naturally.

NORA: And then the port and champagne to go with it. It's so sad that all these delectable things have to strike at our bones.

RANK: Especially when they strike at the unhappy bones that never shared in the fun.

NORA: Ah, that's the saddest of all.

RANK *(looks searchingly at her)*: Hm.

NORA *(after a moment)*: Why did you smile?

RANK: No, it was you who laughed.

NORA: No, it was you who smiled, Dr. Rank!

RANK *(getting up)*: You're even a bigger tease than I'd thought.

NORA: I'm full of wild ideas today.

RANK: That's obvious.

NORA *(putting both hands on his shoulders)*: Dear, dear Dr. Rank, you'll never die for Torvald and me.

RANK: Oh, that loss you'll easily get over. Those who go away are soon forgotten.

NORA *(looks fearfully at him)*: You believe that?

RANK: One makes new connections, and then—

NORA: Who makes new connections?

RANK: Both you and Torvald will when I'm gone. I'd say you're well under way already. What was that Mrs. Linde doing here last evening?

NORA: Oh, come—you can't be jealous of poor Kristine?

RANK: Oh yes, I am. She'll be my successor here in the house. When I'm down under, that woman will probably—

NORA: Shh! Not so loud. She's right in there.

RANK: Today as well. So you see.

NORA: Only to sew on my dress. Good gracious, how unreasonable you are. *(Sitting on the sofa.)* Be nice now, Dr. Rank. Tomorrow you'll see how beautifully I'll dance, and you can imagine then that I'm dancing only for you—yes, and of course for Torvald, too—that's understood. *(Takes various items out of the carton.)* Dr. Rank, sit over here and I'll show you something.

RANK *(sitting)*: What's that?

NORA: Look here. Look.

RANK: Silk stockings.

NORA: Flesh-colored. Aren't they lovely? Now it's so dark here, but tomorrow—No, no, no, just look at the feet. Oh well, you might as well look at the rest.

RANK: Hm—

NORA: Why do you look so critical? Don't you believe they'll fit?

RANK: I've never had any chance to form an opinion on that.

NORA *(glancing at him a moment)*:   Shame on you. *(Hits him lightly on the ear with the stockings.)* That's for you. *(Puts them away again.)*

RANK: And what other splendors am I going to see now?

NORA: Not the least bit more, because you've been naughty. *(She hums a little and rummages among her things.)*

RANK *(after a short silence)*:   When I sit here together with you like this, completely easy and open, then I don't know—I simply can't imagine —whatever would have become of me if I'd never come into this house.

NORA *(smiling)*:   Yes, I really think you feel completely at ease with us.

RANK *(more quietly, staring straight ahead)*:   And then to have to go away from it all—

NORA: Nonsense, you're not going away.

RANK *(his voice unchanged)*:   —and not even be able to leave some poor show of gratitude behind, scarcely a fleeting regret—no more than a vacant place that anyone can fill.

NORA: And if I asked you now for—? No—

RANK: For what?

NORA: For a great proof of your friendship—

RANK: Yes, yes?

NORA: No, I mean—for an exceptionally big favor—

RANK: Would you really, for once, make me so happy?

NORA: Oh, you haven't the vaguest idea what it is.

RANK: All right, then tell me.

NORA: No, but I can't, Dr. Rank—it's all out of reason. It's advice and help, too—and a favor—

RANK: So much the better. I can't fathom what you're hinting at. Just speak out. Don't you trust me?

NORA: Of course. More than anyone else. You're my best and truest friend, I'm sure. That's why I want to talk to you. All right, then, Dr. Rank: there's something you can help me prevent. You know how deeply, how inexpressibly dearly Torvald loves me; he'd never hesitate a second to give up his life for me.

RANK *(leaning close to her)*:   Nora—do you think he's the only one—

NORA *(with a slight start)*:   Who—?

RANK: Who'd gladly give up his life for you.

NORA *(heavily)*:   I see.

RANK: I swore to myself you should know this before I'm gone. I'll never find a better chance. Yes, Nora, now you know. And also you know now that you can trust me beyond anyone else.

NORA *(rising, natural and calm)*:   Let me by.

RANK *(making room for her, but still sitting)*:   Nora—

NORA *(in the hall doorway)*:   Helene, bring the lamp in. *(Goes over to the stove.)* Ah, dear Dr. Rank, that was really mean of you.

RANK (*getting up*): That I've loved you just as deeply as somebody else? Was *that* mean?

NORA: No, but that you came out and told me. That was quite unnecessary—

RANK: What do you mean? Have you known—?

(*The* MAID *comes in with the lamp, sets it on the table, and goes out again.*)

RANK: Nora—Mrs. Helmer—I'm asking you: have you known about it?

NORA: Oh, how can I tell what I know or don't know? Really, I don't know what to say—Why did you have to be so clumsy, Dr. Rank! Everything was so good.

RANK: Well, in any case, you now have the knowledge that my body and soul are at your command. So won't you speak out?

NORA (*looking at him*): After that?

RANK: Please, just let me know what it is.

NORA: You can't know anything now.

RANK: I have to. You mustn't punish me like this. Give me the chance to do whatever is humanly possible for you.

NORA: Now there's nothing you can do for me. Besides, actually, I don't need any help. You'll see—it's only my fantasies. That's what it is. Of course! (*Sits in the rocker, looks at him, and smiles.*) What a nice one you are, Dr. Rank. Aren't you a little bit ashamed, now that the lamp is here?

RANK: No, not exactly. But perhaps I'd better go—for good?

NORA: No, you certainly can't do that. You must come here just as you always have. You know Torvald can't do without you.

RANK: Yes, but *you?*

NORA: You know how much I enjoy it when you're here.

RANK: That's precisely what threw me off. You're a mystery to me. So many times I've felt you'd almost rather be with me than with Helmer.

NORA: Yes—you see, there are some people that one loves most and other people that one would almost prefer being with.

RANK: Yes, there's something to that.

NORA: When I was back home, of course I loved Papa most. But I always thought it was so much fun when I could sneak down to the maids' quarters, because they never tried to improve me, and it was always so amusing, the way they talked to each other.

RANK: Aha, so it's *their* place that I've filled.

NORA (*jumping up and going to him*): Oh, dear sweet Dr. Rank, that's not what I meant at all. But you can understand that with Torvald it's just the same as with Papa—

(*The* MAID *enters from the hall.*)

MAID: Ma'am—please! (*She whispers to* NORA *and hands her a calling card.*)

NORA (*glancing at the card*): Ah! (*Slips it into her pocket.*)

RANK: Anything wrong?

NORA: No, no, not at all. It's only some—it's my new dress—

RANK: Really? But—there's your dress.

NORA: Oh, that. But this is another one—I ordered it—Torvald mustn't know—

RANK: Ah, now we have the big secret.

NORA: That's right. Just go in with him—he's back in the inner study. Keep him there as long as—

RANK: Don't worry. He won't get away.   *(Goes into the study.)*

NORA *(to the MAID)*: And he's standing waiting in the kitchen.

MAID: Yes, he came up by the back stairs.

NORA: But didn't you tell him somebody was here?

MAID: Yes, but that didn't do any good.

NORA: He won't leave?

MAID: No, he won't go till he's talked with you, ma'am.

NORA: Let him come in, then—but quietly. Helene, don't breathe a word about this. It's a surprise for my husband.

MAID: Yes, yes, I understand—   *(Goes out.)*

NORA: This horror—it's going to happen. No, no, no, it can't happen, it mustn't. *(She goes and bolts HELMER's door. The MAID opens the hall door for KROGSTAD and shuts it behind him. He is dressed for travel in a fur coat, boots and a fur cap.)*

NORA *(going toward him)*: Talk softly. My husband's home.

KROGSTAD: Well, good for him.

NORA: What do you want?

KROGSTAD: Some information.

NORA: Hurry up, then. What is it?

KROGSTAD: You know, of course, that I got my notice.

NORA: I couldn't prevent it, Mr. Krogstad. I fought for you to the bitter end, but nothing worked.

KROGSTAD: Does your husband's love for you run so thin? He knows everything I can expose you to, and all the same he dares to—

NORA: How can you imagine he knows anything about this?

KROGSTAD: Ah, no—I can't imagine it either, now. It's not at all like my fine Torvald Helmer to have so much guts—

NORA: Mr. Krogstad, I demand respect for my husband!

KROGSTAD: Why, of course—all due respect. But since the lady's keeping it so carefully hidden, may I presume to ask if you're also a bit better informed than yesterday about what you've actually done?

NORA: More than you ever could teach me.

KROGSTAD: Yes, I *am* such an awful lawyer.

NORA: What is it you want from me?

KROGSTAD: Just a glimpse of how you are, Mrs. Helmer. I've been thinking about you all day long. A cashier, a night-court scribbler, a—well, a type like me also has a little of what they call a heart, you know.

NORA: Then show it. Think of my children.

KROGSTAD: Did you or your husband ever think of mine? But never mind. I simply wanted to tell you that you don't need to take this thing too seriously. For the present, I'm not proceeding with any action.

NORA: Oh no, really! Well—I knew that.

KROGSTAD: Everything can be settled in a friendly spirit. It doesn't have to get around town at all; it can stay just among us three.

NORA: My husband may never know anything of this.

KROGSTAD: How can you manage that? Perhaps you can pay me the balance?

NORA: No, not right now.

KROGSTAD: Or you know some way of raising the money in a day or two?

NORA: No way that I'm willing to use.

KROGSTAD: Well, it wouldn't have done you any good, anyway. If you stood in front of me with a fistful of bills, you still couldn't buy your signature back.

NORA: Then tell me what you're going to do with it.

KROGSTAD: I'll just hold onto it—keep it on file. There's no outsider who'll even get wind of it. So if you've been thinking of taking some desperate step—

NORA: I have!

KROGSTAD: Been thinking of running away from home—

NORA: I have!

KROGSTAD: Or even of something worse—

NORA: How could you guess that?

KROGSTAD: You can drop those thoughts.

NORA: How could you guess I was thinking of *that?*

KROGSTAD: Most of us think about *that* at first. I thought about it too, but I discovered I hadn't the courage—

NORA *(lifelessly)*: I don't either.

KROGSTAD *(relieved)*: That's true, you haven't the courage? You too?

NORA: I don't have it—I don't have it.

KROGSTAD: It would be terribly stupid, anyway. After that first storm at home blows out, why, then—I have here in my pocket a letter for your husband—

NORA: Telling everything?

KROGSTAD: As charitably as possible.

NORA *(quickly)*: He mustn't ever get that letter. Tear it up. I'll find some way to get money.

KROGSTAD: Beg pardon, Mrs. Helmer, but I think I just told you—

NORA: Oh, I don't mean the money I owe you. Let me know how much you want from my husband, and I'll manage it.

KROGSTAD: I don't want any money from your husband.

NORA: What do you want, then?

KROGSTAD: I'll tell you what. I want to recoup, Mrs. Helmer; I want to get on in the world—and there's where your husband can help me. For a year and a half I've kept myself clean of anything disreputable—all that time struggling with the worst conditions; but I was satisfied, working my way up step by step. Now I've been written right off, and I'm just not in the mood to come crawling back. I tell you, I want to move on. I want to get back in the bank—in a better position. Your husband can set up a job for me—

NORA: He'll never do that!

KROGSTAD: He'll do it. I know him. He won't dare breathe a word of protest. And once I'm in there together with him, you just wait and see! Inside of a year, I'll be the manager's right-hand man. It'll be Nils Krogstad, not Torvald Helmer, who runs the bank.

NORA: You'll never see the day!

KROGSTAD: Maybe you think you can—

NORA: I have the courage now—for *that*.

KROGSTAD: Oh, you don't scare me. A smart, spoiled lady like you—

NORA: You'll see; you'll see!

KROGSTAD: Under the ice, maybe? Down in the freezing, coal-black water? There, till you float up in the spring, ugly, unrecognizable, with your hair falling out—

NORA: You don't frighten me.

KROGSTAD: Nor do you frighten me. One doesn't do these things, Mrs. Helmer. Besides, what good would it be? I'd still have him safe in my pocket.

NORA: Afterwards? When I'm no longer—?

KROGSTAD: Are you forgetting that *I'll* be in control then over your final reputation? *(NORA stands speechless, staring at him.)* Good; now I've warned you. Don't do anything stupid. When Helmer's read my letter, I'll be waiting for his reply. And bear in mind that it's your husband himself who's forced me back to my old ways. I'll never forgive him for that. Good-bye, Mrs. Helmer.

(He goes out through the hall.)

NORA *(goes to the hall door, opens it a crack, and listens)*: He's gone. Didn't leave the letter. Oh no, no, that's impossible too! *(Opening the door more and more.)* What's that? He's standing outside—not going downstairs. He's thinking it over? Maybe he'll—? *(A letter falls in the mailbox; then* KROGSTAD's *footsteps are heard, dying away down a flight of stairs.* NORA *gives a muffled cry and runs over toward the sofa table. A short pause.)* In the mailbox. *(Slips warily over to the hall door.)* It's lying there. Torvald, Torvald—now we're lost!

MRS. LINDE *(entering with the costume from the room, left)*: There now, I can't see anything else to mend. Perhaps you'd like to try—

NORA *(in a hoarse whisper)*: Kristine, come here.

MRS. LINDE *(tossing the dress on the sofa)*: What's wrong? You look upset.

NORA: Come here. See that letter? *There!* Look—through the glass in the mailbox.

MRS. LINDE: Yes, yes, I see it.

NORA: That letter's from Krogstad—

MRS. LINDE: Nora—it's Krogstad who loaned you the money!

NORA: Yes, and now Torvald will find out everything.

MRS. LINDE: Believe me, Nora, it's best for both of you.

NORA: There's more you don't know. I forged a name.

MRS. LINDE: But for heaven's sake—?

NORA: I only want to tell you that, Kristine, so that you can be my witness.

MRS. LINDE: Witness? Why should I—?

NORA: If I should go out of my mind—it could easily happen—

MRS. LINDE: Nora!

NORA: Or anything else occurred—so I couldn't be present here—

MRS. LINDE: Nora, Nora, you aren't yourself at all!

NORA: And someone should try to take on the whole weight, all of the guilt, you follow me—

MRS. LINDE: Yes, of course, but why do you think—?

NORA: Then you're the witness that it isn't true, Kristine. I'm very much myself; my mind right now is perfectly clear; and I'm telling you: nobody else has known about this; I alone did everything. Remember that.

MRS. LINDE: I will. But I don't understand all this.

NORA: Oh, how could you ever understand it? It's the miracle now that's going to take place.

MRS. LINDE: The miracle?

NORA: Yes, the miracle. But it's so awful, Kristine. It mustn't take place, not for anything in the world.

MRS. LINDE: I'm going right over and talk with Krogstad.

NORA: Don't go near him; he'll do you some terrible harm!

MRS. LINDE: There was a time once when he'd gladly have done anything for me.

NORA: He?

MRS. LINDE: Where does he live?

NORA: Oh, how do I know? Yes. *(Searches in her pocket.)* Here's his card. But the letter, the letter—!

HELMER *(from the study, knocking on the door)*: Nora!

NORA *(with a cry of fear)*: Oh! What is it? What do you want?

HELMER: Now, now, don't be so frightened. We're not coming in. You locked the door—are you trying on the dress?

NORA: Yes, I'm trying it. I'll look just beautiful, Torvald.

MRS. LINDE *(who has read the card)*: He's living right around the corner.

NORA: Yes, but what's the use? We're lost. The letter's in the box.

MRS. LINDE: And your husband has the key?

NORA: Yes, always.

MRS. LINDE: Krogstad can ask for his letter back unread; he can find some excuse—

NORA: But it's just this time that Torvald usually—

MRS. LINDE: Stall him. Keep him in there. I'll be back as quick as I can. *(She hurries out through the hall entrance.)*

NORA *(goes to* HELMER'*s door, opens it, and peers in)*: Torvald!

HELMER *(from the inner study)*: Well—does one dare set foot in one's own living room at last? Come on, Rank, now we'll get a look—*(In the doorway.)* But what's this?

NORA: What, Torvald dear?

HELMER: Rank had me expecting some grand masquerade.

RANK *(in the doorway)*: That was my impression, but I must have been wrong.

NORA: No one can admire me in my splendor—not until tomorrow.

HELMER: But Nora dear, you look so exhausted. Have you practiced too hard?

NORA: No, I haven't practiced at all yet.

HELMER: You know, it's necessary—

NORA: Oh, it's absolutely necessary, Torvald. But I can't get anywhere without your help. I've forgotten the whole thing completely.

HELMER: Ah, we'll soon take care of that.

NORA: Yes, take care of me, Torvald, please! Promise me that? Oh, I'm so nervous. That big party—You must give up everything this evening for me. No business—don't even touch your pen. Yes? Dear Torvald, promise?

HELMER: It's a promise. Tonight I'm totally at your service—you little helpless thing. Hm—but first there's one thing I want to—*(Goes toward the hall door.)*

NORA: What are you looking for?

HELMER: Just to see if there's any mail.

NORA: No, no, don't do that, Torvald!

HELMER: Now what?

NORA: Torvald, please. There isn't any.

HELMER: Let me look, though. *(Starts out.* NORA, *at the piano, strikes the first notes of the tarantella.* HELMER, *at the door, stops.)* Aha!

NORA: I can't dance tomorrow if I don't practice with you.

HELMER *(going over to her)*: Nora dear, are you really so frightened?

NORA: Yes, so terribly frightened. Let me practice right now; there's still time before dinner. Oh, sit down and play for me, Torvald. Direct me. Teach me, the way you always have.

HELMER: Gladly, if it's what you want. *(Sits at the piano.)*

NORA *(snatches the tambourine up from the box, then a long, varicolored shawl, which she throws around herself, whereupon she springs forward and cries out)*: Play for me now! Now I'll dance!

(HELMER *plays and* NORA *dances.* RANK *stands behind* HELMER *at the piano and looks on.*)

HELMER (*as he plays*): Slower. Slow down.

NORA: Can't change it.

HELMER: Not so violent, Nora!

NORA: Has to be just like this.

HELMER (*stopping*): No, no, that won't do at all.

NORA (*laughing and swinging her tambourine*): Isn't that what I told you?

RANK: Let me play for her.

HELMER (*getting up*): Yes, go on, I can teach her more easily then.

(RANK *sits at the piano and plays;* NORA *dances more and more wildly.* HELMER *has stationed himself by the stove and repeatedly gives her directions; she seems not to hear them; her hair loosens and falls over her shoulders; she does not notice, but goes on dancing.* MRS. LINDE *enters.*)

MRS. LINDE (*standing dumbfounded at the door*): Ah—!

NORA (*still dancing*): See what fun, Kristine!

HELMER: But Nora darling, you dance as if your life were at stake.

NORA: And it is.

HELMER: Rank, stop! This is pure madness. Stop it, I say!

(RANK *breaks off playing, and* NORA *halts abruptly.*)

HELMER (*going over to her*): I never would have believed it. You've forgotten everything I taught you.

NORA (*throwing away the tambourine*): You see for yourself.

HELMER: Well, there's certainly room for instruction here.

NORA: Yes, you see how important it is. You've got to teach me to the very last minute. Promise me that, Torvald?

HELMER: You can bet on it.

NORA: You mustn't, either today or tomorrow, think about anything else but me; you mustn't open any letters—or the mailbox—

HELMER: Ah, it's still the fear of that man—

NORA: Oh yes, yes, that too.

HELMER: Nora, it's written all over you—there's already a letter from him out there.

NORA: I don't know. I guess so. But you mustn't read such things now; there mustn't be anything ugly between us before it's all over.

RANK (*quietly to* HELMER): You shouldn't deny her.

HELMER (*putting his arm around her*): The child can have her way. But tomorrow night, after you've danced—

NORA: Then you'll be free.

MAID (*in the doorway, right*): Ma'am, dinner is served.

NORA: We'll be wanting champagne, Helene.

MAID: Very good, ma'am.   (*Goes out.*)

HELMER: So—a regular banquet, hm?

NORA: Yes, a banquet—champagne till daybreak! *(Calling out.)* And some macaroons, Helene. Heaps of them—just this once.

HELMER *(taking her hands)*: Now, now, now—no hysterics. Be my own little lark again.

NORA: Oh, I will soon enough. But go on in—and you, Dr. Rank. Kristine, help me put up my hair.

RANK *(whispering, as they go)*: There's nothing wrong—really wrong, is there?

HELMER: Oh, of course not. It's nothing more than this childish anxiety I was telling you about.   *(They go out, right.)*

NORA: Well?

MRS. LINDE: Left town.

NORA: I could see by your face.

MRS. LINDE: He'll be home tomorrow evening. I wrote him a note.

NORA: You shouldn't have. Don't try to stop anything now. After all, it's a wonderful joy, this waiting here for the miracle.

MRS. LINDE: What is it you're waiting for?

NORA: Oh, you can't understand that. Go in to them, I'll be along in a moment.

(MRS. LINDE goes into the dining room. NORA stands a short while as if composing herself; then she looks at her watch.)

NORA: Five. Seven hours to midnight. Twenty-four hours to the midnight after, and then the tarantella's done. Seven and twenty-four? Thirty-one hours to live.

HELMER *(in the doorway, right)*: What's become of the little lark?

NORA *(going toward him with open arms)*: Here's your lark!

ACT III

Scene *Same scene. The table, with chairs around it, has been moved to the center of the room. A lamp on the table is lit. The hall door stands open. Dance music drifts down from the floor above.* MRS. LINDE *sits at the table, absently paging through a book, trying to read, but apparently unable to focus her thoughts. Once or twice she pauses, tensely listening for a sound at the outer entrance.*

MRS. LINDE *(glancing at her watch)*: Not yet—and there's hardly any time left. If only he's not—*(Listening again.)* Ah, there he is. *(She goes out in the hall and cautiously opens the outer door. Quiet footsteps are heard on the stairs. She whispers.)* Come in. Nobody's here.

KROGSTAD *(in the doorway)*: I found a note from you at home. What's back of all this?

MRS. LINDE: I just *had* to talk to you.

KROGSTAD: Oh? And it just *had* to be here in this house?

MRS. LINDE: At my place it was impossible; my room hasn't a private entrance. Come in; we're all alone. The maid's asleep, and the Helmers are at the dance upstairs.

KROGSTAD (*entering the room*): Well, well, the Helmers are dancing tonight? Really?

MRS. LINDE: Yes, why not?

KROGSTAD: How true—why not?

MRS. LINDE: All right, Krogstad, let's talk.

KROGSTAD: Do we two have anything more to talk about?

MRS. LINDE: We have a great deal to talk about.

KROGSTAD: I wouldn't have thought so.

MRS. LINDE: No, because you've never understood me, really.

KROGSTAD: Was there anything more to understand—except what's all too common in life? A calculating woman throws over a man the moment a better catch comes by.

MRS. LINDE: You think I'm so thoroughly calculating? You think I broke it off lightly?

KROGSTAD: Didn't you?

MRS. LINDE: Nils—is that what you really thought?

KROGSTAD: If you cared, then why did you write me the way you did?

MRS. LINDE: What else could I do? If I had to break off with you, then it was my job as well to root out everything you felt for me.

KROGSTAD (*wringing his hands*): So that was it. And this—all this, simply for money!

MRS. LINDE: Don't forget I had a helpless mother and two small brothers. We couldn't wait for you, Nils; you had such a long road ahead of you then.

KROGSTAD: That may be; but you still hadn't the right to abandon me for somebody else's sake.

MRS. LINDE: Yes—I don't know. So many, many times I've asked myself if I did have that right.

KROGSTAD (*more softly*): When I lost you, it was as if all the solid ground dissolved from under my feet. Look at me; I'm a half-drowned man now, hanging onto a wreck.

MRS. LINDE: Help may be near.

KROGSTAD: It was near—but then you came and blocked it off.

MRS. LINDE: Without my knowing it, Nils. Today for the first time I learned that it's you I'm replacing at the bank.

KROGSTAD: All right—I believe you. But now that you know, will you step aside?

MRS. LINDE: No, because that wouldn't benefit you in the slightest.

KROGSTAD: Not "benefit" me, hm! I'd step aside anyway.

MRS. LINDE: I've learned to be realistic. Life and hard, bitter necessity have taught me that.

KROGSTAD: And life's taught me never to trust fine phrases.

MRS. LINDE: Then life's taught you a very sound thing. But you do have
to trust in actions, don't you?

KROGSTAD: What does that mean?

MRS. LINDE: You said you were hanging on like a half-drowned man to
a wreck.

KROGSTAD: I've good reason to say that.

MRS. LINDE: I'm also like a half-drowned woman on a wreck. No one to
suffer with; no one to care for.

KROGSTAD: You made your choice.

MRS. LINDE: There wasn't any choice then.

KROGSTAD: So—what of it?

MRS. LINDE: Nils, if only we two shipwrecked people could reach across
to each other.

KROGSTAD: What are you saying?

MRS. LINDE: Two on one wreck are at least better off than each on his own.

KROGSTAD: Kristine!

MRS. LINDE: Why do you think I came into town?

KROGSTAD: Did you really have some thought of me?

MRS. LINDE: I have to work to go on living. All my born days, as long as
I can remember, I've worked, and it's been my best and my only joy.
But now I'm completely alone in the world; it frightens me to be so
empty and lost. To work for yourself—there's no joy in that. Nils, give
me something—someone to work for.

KROGSTAD: I don't believe all this. It's just some hysterical feminine urge
to go out and make a noble sacrifice.

MRS. LINDE: Have you ever found me to be hysterical?

KROGSTAD: Can you honestly mean this? Tell me—do you know everything about my past?

MRS. LINDE: Yes.

KROGSTAD: And you know what they think I'm worth around here.

MRS. LINDE: From what you were saying before, it would seem that with
me you could have been another person.

KROGSTAD: I'm positive of that.

MRS. LINDE: Couldn't it happen still?

KROGSTAD: Kristine—you're saying this in all seriousness? Yes, you are! I
can see it in you. And do you really have the courage, then—?

MRS. LINDE: I need to have someone to care for; and your children need
a mother. We both need each other. Nils, I have faith that you're good
at heart—I'll risk everything together with you.

KROGSTAD (gripping her hands): Kristine, thank you, thank you—Now I
know I can win back a place in their eyes. Yes—but I forgot—

MRS. LINDE (listening): Shh! The tarantella. Go now! Go on!

KROGSTAD: Why? What is it?

MRS. LINDE: Hear the dance up there? When that's over, they'll be coming down.

KROGSTAD: Oh, then I'll go. But—it's all pointless. Of course, you don't know the move I made against the Helmers.

MRS. LINDE: Yes, Nils, I know.

KROGSTAD: And all the same, you have the courage to—?

MRS. LINDE: I know how far despair can drive a man like you.

KROGSTAD: Oh, if I only could take it all back.

MRS. LINDE: You easily could—your letter's still lying in the mailbox.

KROGSTAD: Are you sure of that?

MRS. LINDE: Positive. But—

KROGSTAD (looks at her searchingly): Is that the meaning of it, then? You'll have your friend at any price. Tell me straight out. Is that it?

MRS. LINDE: Nils—anyone who's sold herself for somebody else once isn't going to do it again.

KROGSTAD: I'll demand my letter back.

MRS. LINDE: No, no.

KROGSTAD: Yes, of course. I'll stay here till Helmer comes down; I'll tell him to give me my letter again—that it only involves my dismissal—that he shouldn't read it—

MRS. LINDE: No, Nils, don't call the letter back.

KROGSTAD: But wasn't that exactly why you wrote me to come here?

MRS. LINDE: Yes, in that first panic. But it's been a whole day and night since then, and in that time I've seen such incredible things in this house. Helmer's got to learn everything; this dreadful secret has to be aired; those two have to come to a full understanding; all these lies and evasions can't go on.

KROGSTAD: Well, then, if you want to chance it. But at least there's one thing I can do, and do right away—

MRS. LINDE (listening): Go now, go quick! The dance is over. We're not safe another second.

KROGSTAD: I'll wait for you downstairs.

MRS. LINDE: Yes, please do; take me home.

KROGSTAD: I can't believe it; I've never been so happy. (He leaves by way of the outer door; the door between the room and the hall stays open.)

MRS. LINDE (straightening up a bit and getting together her street clothes): How different now! How different! Someone to work for, to live for—a home to build. Well, it is worth the try! Oh, if they'd only come! (Listening.) Ah, there they are. Bundle up. (She picks up her hat and coat. NORA's and HELMER's voices can be heard outside; a key turns in the lock, and HELMER brings NORA into the hall almost by force. She is wearing the Italian costume with a large black shawl about her; he has on evening dress, with a black domino° open over it.)

---

domino: Long, hooded cloak.

NORA *(struggling in the doorway)*: No, no, no, not inside! I'm going up again. I don't want to leave so soon.

HELMER: But Nora dear—

NORA: Oh, I beg you, please, Torvald. From the bottom of my heart, *please*—only an hour more!

HELMER: Not a single minute, Nora darling. You know our agreement. Come on, in we go; you'll catch cold out here. *(In spite of her resistance, he gently draws her into the room.)*

MRS. LINDE: Good evening.

NORA: Kristine!

HELMER: Why, Mrs. Linde—are you here so late?

MRS. LINDE: Yes, I'm sorry, but I did want to see Nora in costume.

NORA: Have you been sitting here, waiting for me?

MRS. LINDE: Yes. I didn't come early enough; you were all upstairs; and then I thought I really couldn't leave without seeing you.

HELMER *(removing* NORA'*s shawl.)*: Yes, take a good look. She's worth looking at, I can tell you that, Mrs. Linde. Isn't she lovely?

MRS. LINDE: Yes, I should say—

HELMER: A dream of loveliness, isn't she? That's what everyone thought at the party, too. But she's horribly stubborn—this sweet little thing. What's to be done with her? Can you imagine, I almost had to use force to pry her away.

NORA: Oh, Torvald, you're going to regret you didn't indulge me, even for just a half hour more.

HELMER: There, you see. She danced her tarantella and got a tumultuous hand—which was well earned, although the performance may have been a bit too naturalistic—I mean it rather overstepped the proprieties of art. But never mind—what's important is, she made a success, an overwhelming success. You think I could let her stay on after that and spoil the effect? Oh no; I took my lovely little Capri girl—my capricious little Capri girl, I should say—took her under my arm; one quick tour of the ballroom, a curtsy to every side, and then—as they say in novels—the beautiful vision disappeared. An exit should always be effective, Mrs. Linde, but that's what I can't get Nora to grasp. Phew, it's hot in here. *(Flings the domino on a chair and opens the door to his room.)* Why's it dark in here? Oh yes, of course. Excuse me. *(He goes in and lights a couple of candles.)*

NORA *(in a sharp, breathless whisper)*: So?

MRS. LINDE *(quietly)*: I talked with him.

NORA: And—?

MRS. LINDE: Nora—you must tell your husband everything.

NORA *(dully)*: I knew it.

MRS. LINDE: You've got nothing to fear from Krogstad, but you have to speak out.

NORA: I won't tell.

MRS. LINDE: Then the letter will.

NORA: Thanks, Kristine. I know now what's to be done. Shh!

HELMER *(reentering)*: Well, then, Mrs. Linde—have you admired her?

MRS. LINDE: Yes, and now I'll say good night.

HELMER: Oh, come, so soon? Is this yours, this knitting?

MRS. LINDE: Yes, thanks. I nearly forgot it.

HELMER: Do you knit, then?

MRS. LINDE: Oh yes.

HELMER: You know what? You should embroider instead.

MRS. LINDE: Really? Why?

HELMER: Yes, because it's a lot prettier. See here, one holds the embroidery so, in the left hand, and then one guides the needle with the right—so—in an easy, sweeping curve—right?

MRS. LINDE: Yes, I guess that's—

HELMER: But, on the other hand, knitting—it can never be anything but ugly. Look, see here, the arms tucked in, the knitting needles going up and down—there's something Chinese about it. Ah, that was really a glorious champagne they served.

MRS. LINDE: Yes, good night, Nora, and don't be stubborn anymore.

HELMER: Well put, Mrs. Linde!

MRS. LINDE: Good night, Mr. Helmer.

HELMER *(accompanying her to the door)*: Good night, good night. I hope you get home all right. I'd be very happy to—but you don't have far to go. Good night, good night. *(She leaves. He shuts the door after her and returns.)* There, now, at last we got her out the door. She's a deadly bore, that creature.

NORA: Aren't you pretty tired, Torvald?

HELMER: No, not a bit.

NORA: You're not sleepy?

HELMER: Not at all. On the contrary, I'm feeling quite exhilarated. But you? Yes, you really look tired and sleepy.

NORA: Yes, I'm very tired. Soon now I'll sleep.

HELMER: See! You see! I was right all along that we shouldn't stay longer.

NORA: Whatever you do is always right.

HELMER *(kissing her brow)*: Now my little lark talks sense. Say, did you notice what a time Rank was having tonight?

NORA: Oh, was he? I didn't get to speak with him.

HELMER: I scarcely did either, but it's a long time since I've seen him in such high spirits. *(Gazes at her a moment, then comes nearer her.)* Hm—it's marvelous, though, to be back home again—to be completely alone with you. Oh, you bewitchingly lovely young woman!

NORA: Torvald, don't look at me like that!

HELMER: Can't I look at my richest treasure? At all that beauty that's mine, mine alone—completely and utterly.

NORA *(moving around to the other side of the table)*: You mustn't talk to me that way tonight.

HELMER *(following her)*: The tarantella is still in your blood, I can see— and it makes you even more enticing. Listen. The guests are beginning to go. *(Dropping his voice.)* Nora—it'll soon be quiet through this whole house.

NORA: Yes, I hope so.

HELMER: You do, don't you, my love? Do you realize—when I'm out at a party like this with you—do you know why I talk to you so little, and keep such a distance away; just send you a stolen look now and then—you know why I do it? It's because I'm imagining then that you're my secret darling, my secret young bride-to-be, and that no one suspects there's anything between us.

NORA: Yes, yes; oh, yes, I know you're always thinking of me.

HELMER: And then when we leave and I place the shawl over those fine young rounded shoulders—over that wonderful curving neck—then I pretend that you're my young bride, that we're just coming from the wedding, that for the first time I'm bringing you into my house—that for the first time I'm alone with you—completely alone with you, your trembling young beauty! All this evening I've longed for nothing but you. When I saw you turn and sway in the tarantella—my blood was pounding till I couldn't stand it—that's why I brought you down here so early—

NORA: Go away, Torvald! Leave me alone. I don't want all this.

HELMER: What do you mean? Nora, you're teasing me. You will, won't you? Aren't I your husband—?

(A knock at the outside door.)

NORA *(startled)*: What's that?

HELMER *(going toward the hall)*: Who is it?

RANK *(outside)*: It's me. May I come in a moment?

HELMER *(with quiet irritation)*: Oh, what does he want now? *(Aloud.)* Hold on. *(Goes and opens the door.)* Oh, how nice that you didn't just pass us by!

RANK: I thought I heard your voice, and then I wanted so badly to have a look in. *(Lightly glancing about.)* Ah, me, these old familiar haunts. You have it snug and cozy in here, you two.

HELMER: You seemed to be having it pretty cozy upstairs, too.

RANK: Absolutely. Why shouldn't I? Why not take in everything in life? As much as you can, anyway, and as long as you can. The wine was superb—

HELMER: The champagne especially.

RANK: You noticed that too? It's amazing how much I could guzzle down.

NORA: Torvald also drank a lot of champagne this evening.

RANK: Oh?

NORA: Yes, and that always makes him so entertaining.

RANK: Well, why shouldn't one have a pleasant evening after a well-spent day?

HELMER: Well spent? I'm afraid I can't claim that.

RANK *(slapping him on the back)*: But I can, you see!

NORA: Dr. Rank, you must have done some scientific research today.

RANK: Quite so.

HELMER: Come now—little Nora talking about scientific research!

NORA: And can I congratulate you on the results?

RANK: Indeed you may.

NORA: Then they were good?

RANK: The best possible for both doctor and patient—certainty.

NORA *(quickly and searchingly)*: Certainty?

RANK: Complete certainty. So don't I owe myself a gay evening afterwards?

NORA: Yes, you're right, Dr. Rank.

HELMER: I'm with you—just so long as you don't have to suffer for it in the morning.

RANK: Well, one never gets something for nothing in life.

NORA: Dr. Rank—are you very fond of masquerade parties?

RANK: Yes, if there's a good array of odd disguises—

NORA: Tell me, what should we two go as at the next masquerade?

HELMER: You little feather head—already thinking of the next!

RANK: We two? I'll tell you what: you must go as Charmed Life—

HELMER: Yes, but find a costume for *that!*

RANK: Your wife can appear just as she looks every day.

HELMER: That was nicely put. But don't you know what you're going to be?

RANK: Yes, Helmer, I've made up my mind.

HELMER: Well?

RANK: At the next masquerade I'm going to be invisible.

HELMER: That's a funny idea.

RANK: They say there's a hat—black, huge—have you never heard of the hat that makes you invisible? You put it on, and then no one on earth can see you.

HELMER *(suppressing a smile)*: Ah, of course.

RANK: But I'm quite forgetting what I came for. Helmer, give me a cigar, one of the dark Havanas.

HELMER: With the greatest pleasure. *(Holds out his case.)*

RANK: Thanks. *(Takes one and cuts off the tip.)*

NORA *(striking a match)*: Let me give you a light.

RANK: Thank you. *(She holds the match for him; he lights the cigar.)* And now good-bye.

HELMER: Good-bye, good-bye, old friend.

NORA: Sleep well, Doctor.

RANK: Thanks for that wish.

NORA: Wish me the same.

RANK: You? All right, if you like—Sleep well. And thanks for the light.

(He nods to them both and leaves.)

HELMER *(his voice subdued)*: He's been drinking heavily.

NORA *(absently)*: Could be. *(HELMER takes his keys from his pocket and goes out in the hall.)* Torvald—what are you after?

HELMER: Got to empty the mailbox; it's nearly full. There won't be room for the morning papers.

NORA: Are you working tonight?

HELMER: You know I'm not. Why—what's this? Someone's been at the lock.

NORA: At the lock—?

HELMER: Yes, I'm positive. What do you suppose—? I can't imagine one of the maids—? Here's a broken hairpin. Nora, it's yours—

NORA *(quickly)*: Then it must be the children.

HELMER: You'd better break them of that. Hm, hm—well, opened it after all. *(Takes the contents out and calls into the kitchen.)* Helene! Helene, would you put out the lamp in the hall. *(He returns to the room, shutting the hall door, then displays the handful of mail.)* Look how it's piled up. *(Sorting through them.)* Now what's this?

NORA *(at the window)*: The letter! Oh, Torvald, no!

HELMER: Two calling cards—from Rank.

NORA: From Dr. Rank?

HELMER *(examining them)*: "Dr. Rank, Consulting Physician." They were on top. He must have dropped them as he left.

NORA: Is there anything on them?

HELMER: There's a black cross over the name. See? That's a gruesome notion. He could almost be announcing his own death.

NORA: That's just what he's doing.

HELMER: What! You've heard something? Something he's told you?

NORA: Yes. That when those cards came, he'd be taking his leave of us. He'll shut himself in now and die.

HELMER: Ah, my poor friend! Of course I knew he wouldn't be here much longer. But so soon—And then to hide himself away like a wounded animal.

NORA: If it has to happen, then it's best it happens in silence—don't you think so, Torvald?

HELMER *(pacing up and down)*: He's grown right into our lives. I simply can't imagine him gone. He with his suffering and loneliness—like a dark cloud setting off our sunlit happiness. Well, maybe it's best this way. For him, at least. *(Standing still.)* And maybe for us too, Nora. Now we're thrown back on each other completely. *(Embracing her.)* Oh you, my darling wife, how can I hold you close enough? You know what, Nora—time and again I've wished you were in some terrible danger, just so I could stake my life and soul and everything, for your sake.

NORA *(tearing herself away, her voice firm and decisive)*: Now you must read your mail, Torvald.

HELMER: No, no, not tonight. I want to stay with you, dearest.

NORA: With a dying friend on your mind?

HELMER: You're right. We've both had a shock. There's ugliness between us—these thoughts of death and corruption. We'll have to get free of them first. Until then—we'll stay apart.

NORA *(clinging about his neck)*: Torvald—good night! Good night!

HELMER *(kissing her on the cheek)*: Good night, little songbird. Sleep well, Nora. I'll be reading my mail now.

(He takes the letters into his room and shuts the door after him.)

NORA *(with bewildered glances, groping about, seizing HELMER's domino, throwing it around her, and speaking in short, hoarse, broken whispers)*: Never see him again. Never, never. *(Putting her shawl over her head.)* Never see the children either—them, too. Never, never. Oh, the freezing black water! The depths—down—Oh, I wish it were over—He has it now; he's reading it—now. Oh no, no, not yet. Torvald, good-bye, you and the children—*(She starts for the hall; as she does, HELMER throws open his door and stands with an open letter in his hand.)*

HELMER: Nora!

NORA *(screams)*: Oh—!

HELMER: What is this? You know what's in this letter?

NORA: Yes, I know. Let me go! Let me out!

HELMER *(holding her back)*: Where are you going?

NORA *(struggling to break loose)*: You can't save me, Torvald!

HELMER *(slumping back)*: True! Then it's true what he writes? How horrible! No, no, it's impossible—it can't be true.

NORA: It *is* true. I've loved you more than all this world.

HELMER: Ah, none of your slippery tricks.

NORA *(taking one step toward him)*: Torvald—!

HELMER: What *is* this you've blundered into!

NORA: Just let me loose. You're not going to suffer for my sake. You're not going to take on my guilt.

HELMER: No more playacting. *(Locks the hall door.)* You stay right here and give me a reckoning. You understand what you've done? Answer! You understand?

NORA *(looking squarely at him, her face hardening)*: Yes. I'm beginning to understand everything now.

HELMER *(striding about)*: Oh, what an awful awakening! In all these eight years—she who was my pride and joy—a hypocrite, a liar—worse, worse—a criminal! How infinitely disgusting it all is! The shame! *(NORA says nothing and goes on looking straight at him. He stops in front of her.)* I should have suspected something of the kind. I should have known. All your father's flimsy values—Be still! All your father's flimsy values have come out in you. No religion, no morals, no sense of duty—Oh, how I'm punished for letting him off! I did it for your sake, and you repay me like this.

NORA: Yes, like this.

HELMER: Now you've wrecked all my happiness—ruined my whole future. Oh, it's awful to think of. I'm in a cheap little grafter's hands; he can do anything he wants with me, ask for anything, play with me like a puppet—and I can't breathe a word. I'll be swept down miserably into the depths on account of a featherbrained woman.

NORA: When I'm gone from this world, you'll be free.

HELMER: Oh, quit posing. Your father had a mess of those speeches too. What good would that ever do me if you were gone from this world, as you say? Not the slightest. He can still make the whole thing known; and if he does, I could be falsely suspected as your accomplice. They might even think that I was behind it—that I put you up to it. And all that I can thank you for—you that I've coddled the whole of our marriage. Can you see now what you've done to me?

NORA (icily calm): Yes.

HELMER: It's so incredible, I just can't grasp it. But we'll have to patch up whatever we can. Take off the shawl. I said, take it off! I've got to appease him somehow or other. The thing has to be hushed up at any cost. And as for you and me, it's got to seem like everything between us is just as it was—to the outside world, that is. You'll go right on living in this house, of course. But you can't be allowed to bring up the children; I don't dare trust you with them—Oh, to have to say this to someone I've loved so much! Well, that's done with. From now on happiness doesn't matter; all that matters is saving the bits and pieces, the appearance—(The doorbell rings. HELMER starts.) What's that? And so late. Maybe the worst—? You think he'd—? Hide, Nora! Say you're sick. (NORA remains standing motionless. HELMER goes and opens the door.)

MAID (half dressed, in the hall): A letter for Mrs. Helmer.

HELMER: I'll take it. (Snatches the letter and shuts the door.) Yes, it's from him. You don't get it; I'm reading it myself.

NORA: Then read it.

HELMER (by the lamp): I hardly dare. We may be ruined, you and I. But—I've got to know. (Rips open the letter, skims through a few lines, glances at an enclosure, then cries out joyfully.) Nora! (NORA looks inquiringly at him.) Nora! Wait—better check it again—Yes, yes, it's true. I'm saved. Nora, I'm saved!

NORA: And I?

HELMER: You too, of course. We're both saved, both of us. Look. He's sent back your note. He says he's sorry and ashamed—that a happy development in his life—oh, who cares what he says! Nora, we're saved! No one can hurt you. Oh, Nora, Nora—but first, this ugliness all has to go. Let me see—*(Takes a look at the note.)* No, I don't want to see it; I want the whole thing to fade like a dream. *(Tears the note and both letters to pieces, throws them into the stove and watches them burn.)* There—now there's nothing left—He wrote that since Christmas Eve you—Oh, they must have been three terrible days for you, Nora.

NORA: I fought a hard fight.

HELMER: And suffered pain and saw no escape but—No, we're not going to dwell on anything unpleasant. We'll just be grateful and keep on repeating, it's over now, it's over! You hear me, Nora? You don't seem to realize—it's over. What's it mean—that frozen look? Oh, poor little Nora, I understand. You can't believe I've forgiven you. But I have, Nora; I swear I have. I know that what you did, you did out of love for me.

NORA: That's true.

HELMER: You love me the way a wife ought to love her husband. It's simply the means that you couldn't judge. But you think I love you any the less for not knowing how to handle your affairs? No, no—just lean on me: I'll guide you and teach you. I wouldn't be a man if this feminine helplessness didn't make you twice as attractive to me. You mustn't mind those sharp words I said—that was all in the first confusion of thinking my world had collapsed. I've forgiven you, Nora; I swear I've forgiven you.

NORA: My thanks for your forgiveness. *(She goes out through the door, right.)*

HELMER: No, wait—*(Peers in.)* What are you doing in there?

NORA *(inside)*: Getting out of my costume.

HELMER *(by the open door)*: Yes, do that. Try to calm yourself and collect your thoughts again, my frightened little songbird. You can rest easy now; I've got wide wings to shelter you with. *(Walking about close by the door.)* How snug and nice our home is, Nora. You're safe here; I'll keep you like a hunted dove I've rescued out of a hawk's claws. I'll bring peace to your poor, shuddering heart. Gradually it'll happen, Nora; you'll see. Tomorrow all this will look different to you; then everything will be as it was. I won't have to go on repeating I forgive you; you'll feel it for yourself. How can you imagine I'd ever conceivably want to disown you—or even blame you in any way? Ah, you don't know a man's heart, Nora. For a man there's something indescribably sweet and satisfying in knowing he's forgiven his wife—and forgiven her out of a full and open heart. It's as if she belongs to him in two ways now: in a sense he's given her fresh into the world again, and she's become his wife and his child as well. From now on that's what you'll be to me—you little bewildered, helpless thing. Don't be afraid of anything, Nora; just open your heart to me, and I'll be conscience and will to you both—*(NORA enters in her regular clothes.)* What's this? Not in bed? You've changed your dress?

NORA: Yes, Torvald, I've changed my dress.

HELMER: But why now, so late?

NORA: Tonight I'm not sleeping.

HELMER: But Nora dear—

NORA *(looking at her watch)*: It's still not so very late. Sit down, Torvald; we have a lot to talk over. *(She sits at one side of the table.)*

HELMER: Nora—what is this? That hard expression—

NORA: Sit down. This'll take some time. I have a lot to say.

HELMER *(sitting at the table directly opposite her)*: You worry me, Nora. And I don't understand you.

NORA: No, that's exactly it. You don't understand me. And I've never understood you either—until tonight. No, don't interrupt. You can just listen to what I say. We're closing out accounts, Torvald.

HELMER: How do you mean that?

NORA *(after a short pause)*: Doesn't anything strike you about our sitting here like this?

HELMER: What's that?

NORA: We've been married now eight years. Doesn't it occur to you that this is the first time we two, you and I, man and wife, have ever talked seriously together?

HELMER: What do you mean—seriously?

NORA: In eight whole years—longer even—right from our first acquaintance, we've never exchanged a serious word on any serious thing.

HELMER: You mean I should constantly go and involve you in problems you couldn't possibly help me with?

NORA: I'm not talking of problems, I'm saying that we've never sat down seriously together and tried to get to the bottom of anything.

HELMER: But dearest, what good would that ever do you?

NORA: That's the point right there: you've never understood me. I've been wronged greatly, Torvald—first by Papa, and then by you.

HELMER: What! By us—the two people who've loved you more than anyone else?

NORA *(shaking her head)*: You never loved me. You've thought it fun to be in love with me, that's all.

HELMER: Nora, what a thing to say!

NORA: Yes, it's true now, Torvald. When I lived at home with Papa, he told me all his opinions, so I had the same ones too; or if they were different I hid them, since he wouldn't have cared for that. He used to call me his doll-child, and he played with me the way I played with my dolls. Then I came into your house—

HELMER: How can you speak of our marriage like that?

NORA *(unperturbed)*: I mean, then I went from Papa's hands into yours. You arranged everything to your own taste, and so I got the same taste as you—or I pretended to; I can't remember. I guess a little of both, first one, then the other. Now when I look back, it seems as if I'd lived here like a beggar—just from hand to mouth. I've lived by doing tricks for you, Torvald. But that's the way you wanted it. It's a great sin what you and Papa did to me. You're to blame that nothing's become of me.

HELMER: Nora, how unfair and ungrateful you are! Haven't you been happy here?

NORA: No, never. I thought so—but I never have.

HELMER: Not—not happy!

NORA: No, only lighthearted. And you've always been so kind to me. But our home's been nothing but a playpen. I've been your doll-wife here, just as at home I was Papa's doll-child. And in turn the children have been my dolls. I thought it was fun when you played with me, just as they thought it fun when I played with them. That's been our marriage, Torvald.

HELMER: There's some truth in what you're saying—under all the raving exaggeration. But it'll all be different after this. Playtime's over; now for the schooling.

NORA: Whose schooling—mine or the children's?

HELMER: Both yours and the children's, dearest.

NORA: Oh, Torvald, you're not the man to teach me to be a good wife to you.

HELMER: And you can say that?

NORA: And I—how am I equipped to bring up children?

HELMER: Nora!

NORA: Didn't you say a moment ago that that was no job to trust me with?

HELMER: In a flare of temper! Why fasten on that?

NORA: Yes, but you were so very right. I'm not up to the job. There's another job I have to do first. I have to try to educate myself. You can't help me with that. I've got to do it alone. And that's why I'm leaving you now.

HELMER (jumping up): What's that?

NORA: I have to stand completely alone, if I'm ever going to discover myself and the world out there. So I can't go on living with you.

HELMER: Nora, Nora!

NORA: I want to leave right away. Kristine should put me up for the night—

HELMER: You're insane! You've no right! I forbid you!

NORA: From here on, there's no use forbidding me anything. I'll take with me whatever is mine. I don't want a thing from you, either now or later.

HELMER: What kind of madness is this!

NORA: Tomorrow I'm going home—I mean, home where I came from. It'll be easier up there to find something to do.

HELMER: Oh, you blind, incompetent child!

NORA: I must learn to be competent, Torvald.

HELMER: Abandon your home, your husband, your children! And you're not even thinking what people will say.

NORA: I can't be concerned about that. I only know how essential this is.

HELMER: Oh, it's outrageous. So you'll run out like this on your most sacred vows.

NORA: What do you think are my most sacred vows?

HELMER: And I have to tell you that! Aren't they your duties to your husband and children?

NORA: I have other duties equally sacred.

HELMER: That isn't true. What duties are they?

NORA: Duties to myself.

HELMER: Before all else, you're a wife and a mother.

NORA: I don't believe in that anymore. I believe that, before all else, I'm a human being, no less than you—or anyway, I ought to try to become one. I know the majority thinks you're right, Torvald, and plenty of books agree with you, too. But I can't go on believing what the majority says, or what's written in books. I have to think over these things myself and try to understand them.

HELMER: Why can't you understand your place in your own home? On a point like that, isn't there one everlasting guide you can turn to? Where's your religion?

NORA: Oh, Torvald, I'm really not sure what religion is.

HELMER: What—?

NORA: I only know what the minister said when I was confirmed. He told me religion was this thing and that. When I get clear and away by myself, I'll go into that problem too. I'll see if what the minister said was right, or, in any case, if it's right for me.

HELMER: A young woman your age shouldn't talk like that. If religion can't move you, I can try to rouse your conscience. You do have some moral feeling? Or, tell me—has that gone too?

NORA: It's not easy to answer that, Torvald. I simply don't know. I'm all confused about these things. I just know I see them so differently from you. I find out, for one thing, that the law's not at all what I'd thought—but I can't get it through my head that the law is fair. A woman hasn't a right to protect her dying father or save her husband's life! I can't believe that.

HELMER: You talk like a child. You don't know anything of the world you live in.

NORA: No, I don't. But now I'll begin to learn for myself. I'll try to discover who's right, the world or I.

HELMER: Nora, you're sick; you've got a fever. I almost think you're out of your head.

NORA: I've never felt more clearheaded and sure in my life.

HELMER: And—clearheaded and sure—you're leaving your husband and children?

NORA: Yes.

HELMER: Then there's only one possible reason.

NORA: What?

HELMER: You no longer love me.

NORA: No. That's exactly it.

HELMER: Nora! You can't be serious!

NORA: Oh, this is so hard, Torvald—you've been so kind to me always. But I can't help it. I don't love you anymore.

HELMER *(struggling for composure)*: Are you also clearheaded and sure about that?

NORA: Yes, completely. That's why I can't go on staying here.

HELMER: Can you tell me what I did to lose your love?

NORA: Yes, I can tell you. It was this evening when the miraculous thing didn't come—then I knew you weren't the man I'd imagined.

HELMER: Be more explicit; I don't follow you.

NORA: I've waited now so patiently eight long years—for, my Lord, I know miracles don't come every day. Then this crisis broke over me, and such a certainty filled me: *now* the miraculous event would occur. While Krogstad's letter was lying out there, I never for an instant dreamed that you could give in to his terms. I was so utterly sure you'd say to him: go on, tell your tale to the whole wide world. And when he'd done that—

HELMER: Yes, what then? When I'd delivered my own wife into shame and disgrace—!

NORA: When he'd done that, I was so utterly sure that you'd step forward, take the blame on yourself and say: I am the guilty one.

HELMER: Nora—!

NORA: You're thinking I'd never accept such a sacrifice from you? No, of course not. But what good would my protests be against you? That was the miracle I was waiting for, in terror and hope. And to stave that off, I would have taken my life.

HELMER: I'd gladly work for you day and night, Nora—and take on pain and deprivation. But there's no one who gives up honor for love.

NORA: Millions of women have done just that.

HELMER: Oh, you think and talk like a silly child.

NORA: Perhaps. But you neither think nor talk like the man I could join myself to. When your big fright was over—and it wasn't from any threat against me, only for what might damage you—when all the danger was past, for you it was just as if nothing had happened. I was exactly the same, your little lark, your doll, that you'd have to handle with double care now that I'd turned out so brittle and frail. *(Gets up.)* Torvald—in that instant it dawned on me that for eight years I've been

living here with a stranger, and that I'd even conceived three children—
oh, I can't stand the thought of it! I could tear myself to bits.

HELMER *(heavily)*: I see. There's a gulf that's opened between us—that's
clear. Oh, but Nora, can't we bridge it somehow?

NORA: The way I am now, I'm no wife for you.

HELMER: I have the strength to make myself over.

NORA: Maybe—if your doll gets taken away.

HELMER: But to part! To part from you! No, Nora, no—I can't imagine it.

NORA *(going out, right)*: All the more reason why it has to be. *(She reenters
with her coat and a small overnight bag, which she puts on a chair by the table.)*

HELMER: Nora, Nora, not now! Wait till tomorrow.

NORA: I can't spend the night in a strange man's room.

HELMER: But couldn't we live here like brother and sister—

NORA: You know very well how long that would last. *(Throws her shawl
about her.)* Good-bye, Torvald. I won't look in on the children. I know
they're in better hands than mine. The way I am now, I'm no use to
them.

HELMER: But someday, Nora—someday—?

NORA: How can I tell? I haven't the least idea what'll become of me.

HELMER: But you're my wife, now and wherever you go.

NORA: Listen, Torvald—I've heard that when a wife deserts her husband's
house just as I'm doing, then the law frees him from all responsibility.
In any case, I'm freeing you from being responsible. Don't feel yourself
bound, any more than I will. There has to be absolute freedom for us
both. Here, take your ring back. Give me mine.

HELMER: That too?

NORA: That too.

HELMER: There it is.

NORA: Good. Well, now it's all over. I'm putting the keys here. The maids
know all about keeping up the house—better than I do. Tomorrow,
after I've left town, Kristine will stop by to pack up everything that's
mine from home. I'd like those things shipped to me.

HELMER: Over! All over! Nora, won't you ever think about me?

NORA: I'm sure I'll think of you often, and about the children and the
house here.

HELMER: May I write you?

NORA: No—never. You're not to do that.

HELMER: Oh, but let me send you—

NORA: Nothing. Nothing.

HELMER: Or help if you need it.

NORA: No. I accept nothing from strangers.

HELMER: Nora—can I never be more than a stranger to you?

NORA *(picking up the overnight bag)*: Ah, Torvald—it would take the greatest
miracle of all—

HELMER: Tell me the greatest miracle!

NORA: You and I both would have to transform ourselves to the point that—Oh, Torvald, I've stopped believing in miracles.

HELMER: But I'll believe. Tell me! Transform ourselves to the point that—?

NORA: That our living together could be a true marriage.

(She goes out down the hall.)

HELMER *(sinks down on a chair by the door, face buried in his hands)*: Nora! Nora! *(Looking about and rising.)* Empty. She's gone. *(A sudden hope leaps in him.)* The greatest miracle—?

(From below, the sound of a door slamming shut.)

Considerations

1. How does Nora change from the beginning of the play to the end? Do you find her changes convincing? Explain.
2. Describe the relationships Nora has with each of the male characters. Do you believe she relates to any of these men as an equal? Does she relate to any of them as an inferior? As someone who is superior?
3. Comment on Torvald's values. What does he consider to be most important in life? Does he remain consistent throughout the play, or do you see him as having changed by the play's end?
4. Describe the setting, noting both time and place. How do the details of setting change throughout the play? Do these changes reflect the development of plot, conflict, and character?
5. Describe the values of each of the female characters in the play. Do you admire one character's values more than those of the others? Explain.

Commentary

WALTER KERR
Staging of A Doll's House

REVIEW OF THE PLAYHOUSE PRODUCTION, NEW YORK, 1971

The difficulty with Ibsen today is that we must try to take two separate things seriously, the playwright's ideas and the playwright's playwriting. The ideas, of course, present no particular problem. One has only to listen to Claire Bloom's last long speech in the current—and very sleek—revival of "A Doll's House," which will soon be alternating with "Hedda Gabler" at the Playhouse, or to glance at the brief excerpts from Ibsen's "Notes for a Modern Tragedy" that have been included in the program to know that the ideas were sound, advanced, on target. "A woman cannot be herself in modern society," the notes read: "It is an exclusively male society, with laws made by men and with prosecutors and judges who assess female conduct from a male standpoint." Kate Millett sounds old-fashioned beside that.

But how, how, how do you take the playwriting seriously? From what vantage point, what perch or roost or perspective in time, can you attend, without doubling up, to the spectacle of a woman so determined to keep a secret from her husband that she promptly spills it, virtually within his hearing, to the very first acquaintance who walks in the door? Add to that the fact that she hasn't seen the acquaintance in years, and doesn't even recognize her when they do meet, and you've got a rather peculiar secret-keeper on your hands.

Peculiar things are going to keep happening, peculiar and predictable. Ibsen did work by notebook, which means that he jotted down most logically all the little twists and turns of motivation he was going to need and then clipped them together to make a scene whether they precisely flowed or not. If they didn't flow, he forced them ("Tell me, is it true you didn't love your husband?").

The terrible danger in this shuffled-note method is that you are going to hear the papers rustling, the clips slipping on. You can't *help* hearing them. And so you know, infallibly, that the moment the child-wife Nora exclaims "Oh, God, it's good to be alive and happy!," a doorbell will ring and a furtive fellow will slip in who's going to bring down her doll's house in ruins. Just as you know, with a certainty close to hilarity, that when Nora's fatuous lord and master, Torvald, exclaims "I often wish you were threatened with some impending disaster so that I could risk everything!," disaster is not only impending but here. Torvald has only to go to the mailbox ("I'm going to see if there's any mail"), slit open the first letter to hand, and the fat is in the fire. (In the current production, the fat is not only in the fire, Nora is on the floor, having been hurled there by a vigorous spouse who, it turns out, is willing to risk nothing.)

The underpinnings are all transparent, line by line and blow by blow,   5 and we must struggle to induce in ourselves a state of mind that holds humor at bay in honor of the social proposition being so implausibly stated. It's a real battle, one that is often lost; Ibsen believed in his mechanics as well as in his creed, and we cannot. The effort isn't exacerbating, especially; we needn't come away exhausted from it. It is possible to look at the foolishness and feel fond, if not doting, as we wait for the message that is going to come of it all. But it's nip and tuck the whole way, and the thin ice of the situation poses extremely thorny problems for actors.

It's not only a matter of how the good lady doing Nora is going to try to stitch together the two parts of the role, the giddy, fawning creature who is willing to leap up and down like a puppy dog snatching at proffered bones for two acts and the serene, stern woman who lays down the new law in Act 3, having matured wonderfully during intermission. It's a matter of how everyone onstage, pompous husband, long-lost confidante, sniveling black-mailer, dying Dr. Rank who is willing to offer Nora his love with his next-to-last breath, is going to get us past the preposterous and into the ringing preachment. Do they try to steal home, eliding all that is awkward as quietly as possible? Do they rush it, pouncing upon line two before we have quite noticed line one? Do they stylize it, lifting themselves into daguerreotype postures that plainly have little to do with reality?

The present company, under Patrick Garland's direction, has tried taking it by storm, with a bit of the daguerreotype thrown in. Donald Madden, a Torvald who might well see Dr. Rank about hypertension, glides across the highly lacquered floor (this Nora has such difficulty getting money out of her husband that you feel he won't even allow the lady carpeting) to exchange his wife's swift kisses for quickly palmed coins as though the two were Harlequins giving a summer-park performance in a high wind. Robert Gerringer, the forger who has come to accuse Nora of forgery (motives do get piggy-backed in this odd way), keeps his mouth open and working so that no matter who is talking his teeth will show.

All work at a high pitch and in some fever, as though a Racinian *tirade* might spin off into space at any moment. (If you have never seen "A Doll's House," and I was stunned to discover how many first-nighters never had, this is a crystal-clear reading of it, laid out like silverware.) And there are some genuine successes within the near-stylization. Roy Shuman's Dr. Rank, for instance, is highly mannered: head thrown back, hands always on the point of clapping, eyes darting this way and that as he bluntly, briskly mocks himself and his approaching death. The effect is perfect, that of a man already halfway to the horizon waving farewell with his thumb to his nose. I have never seen the part more robustly or more persuasively played. Patricia Elliott's Kristine, so quickly privy to Nora's secrets, speaks vast amounts of exposition exquisitely, then zeroes in fiercely upon the play's point as she grips her shawl severely and remembers that her only happiness has lain in work.

But what of Nora? Claire Bloom has made, I think, an admirable choice, though a choice with a canker to it. Most Noras won't sacrifice the opportunity to charm, to be bird-like and winsome and if possible adorable, during the first two acts. And you can't entirely blame *them*. Nora is, as written in these acts, a ninny underneath, a girl who really can't feel any sympathy for creditors because, after all, they're "strangers," a girl who, though her secret debt is much on her mind, hasn't the faintest notion of how much of it she's paid off. She subsists, it would seem, on macaroons. But actresses who go for charm and a pretty mindlessness are stuck with the last act. How does one turn an enchanting child into a dominating adult, especially when the transition is missing?

Miss Bloom tries to create the transition from the beginning, which is   10 surely an intelligent thing to do. Even as her Nora is nestling her pretty head against her husband's waistcoat while she seduces him with quick flattery into giving her old friend a job, there is a strain about the eyes, an indication of an intelligence withheld, that adds initial dimension to the role. Where most Noras seem to have an instinct for being playful, fluttering as to the cocoon born, Miss Bloom's playfulness is plainly put on, a trick she has learned, a device that does not wholly engage her.

She is constantly listening to herself make the sounds a pompous husband expects, aware of their insincerity and worried about the gulf between what she is doing and what she might be feeling. Faintly alienated from the outset, she has given us a base for the play's ending. The reserve that we felt in her was the conscience that might have been awakened at any time but is not in fact awakened until it is time to make that speech and slam that door.

The catch to doing it this way, because the part is split in the writing, is a curious sense of heartlessness that overtakes Nora en route. Being to a degree disengaged, she seems not only indifferent to her children and extremely obtuse about her friend Kristine's personal problems but horrendously cold-blooded about the devoted Dr. Rank. He announces his impending death and she scarcely looks up from her sewing. He makes a gesture of love toward her, a gesture that has to be disinterested because he will never see her again, and she recoils as though he had proposed, perhaps, another forgery. Clipping the butterfly's wings leaves us with something of a dragonfly. Or are we merely being given a bit of "Hedda" ahead of time?

Miss Bloom works honorably, looks well, arrives at her last scene logically, and doesn't seem anyone you'd care to trust your heart with (I'm not thinking of Torvald, who is an oaf, but, say, of Dr. Rank, who is not). Miss Bloom has cooled Nora to make the way for the ultimate avalanche; the move does take away anything that was ever very appealing about her.

Good try. The problem, which persists, lies in the play. Ibsen simply could not, or did not, get his meaning and his method to match up. When he speaks of "laws made by men" and "judges who assess female conduct from a male standpoint," we know exactly what he is talking about. We also know that he is right. But the technical illustration in the play proper runs like this. Nora has forged her father's signature to get money to help her ailing husband, who must not know he is being helped. Why didn't she have her father sign the document? Because he, too, was ailing; she didn't want to trouble him. Thus there are two kinds of law: male law (don't forge) and female law (don't bother father). Serious as the point is, the illustration can only make us smile.

The actors must try to make us contain the smile, which, in this revival, 15 they occasionally do.

PAULA GUNN ALLEN (1939–   )

Where I Come from Is Like This

Paula Gunn Allen's roots include both the Laguna Pueblo and Sioux cultures. An acclaimed essayist, poet, and fiction writer, Allen is also the author of The Woman Who Owned the Shadows *(1983), her best-known novel. Currently she teaches at the University of California at Berkeley, where she is a professor of Native American and ethnic studies. This selection comes from her collection of nonfiction essays,* The Sacred Hoop *(1986).*

I

Modern American Indian women, like their non-Indian sisters, are deeply engaged in the struggle to redefine themselves. In their struggle they must reconcile traditional tribal definitions of women with industrial and postindustrial non-Indian definitions. Yet while these definitions seem to be more or less mutually exclusive, Indian women must somehow harmonize and integrate both in their own lives.

An American Indian woman is primarily defined by her tribal identity. In her eyes, her destiny is necessarily that of her people, and her sense of herself as a woman is first and foremost prescribed by her tribe. The definitions of woman's roles are as diverse as tribal cultures in the Americas. In some she is devalued, in others she wields considerable power. In some she is a familial/clan adjunct, in some she is as close to autonomous as her economic circumstances and psychological traits permit. But in no tribal definitions is she perceived in the same way as are women in western industrial and postindustrial cultures.

In the west, few images of women form part of the cultural mythos, and these are largely sexually charged. Among Christians, the madonna is the female prototype, and she is portrayed as essentially passive: her contribution is simply that of birthing. Little else is attributed to her and she certainly possesses few of the characteristics that are attributed to mythic figures among Indian tribes. This image is countered (rather than balanced) by the witch-goddess/whore characteristics designed to reinforce cultural beliefs about women, as well as western adversarial and dualistic perceptions of reality.

The tribes see women variously, but they do not question the power of femininity. Sometimes they see women as fearful, sometimes peaceful, sometimes omnipotent and omniscient, but they never portray women as mindless, helpless, simple, or oppressed. And while the women in a given tribe, clan, or band may be all these things, the individual woman is provided with a variety of images of women from the interconnected supernatural, natural, and social worlds she lives in.

As a half-breed American Indian woman, I cast about in my mind for   5 negative images of Indian women, and I find none that are directed to Indian women alone. The negative images I do have are of Indians in general and in fact are more often of males than of females. All these images come to me from non-Indian sources, and they are always balanced by a positive image. My ideas of womanhood, passed on largely by my mother and grandmothers, Laguna Pueblo women, are about practicality, strength, reasonableness, intelligence, wit, and competence. I also remember vividly the women who came to my father's store, the women who held me and sang to me, the women at Feast Day, at Grab Days,° the women in the kitchen of my Cubero home, the women I grew up with; none of them appeared weak or helpless, none of them presented herself tentatively. I remember a certain reserve on those lovely brown faces; I remember the direct gaze of eyes framed by bright-colored shawls draped over their heads and cascading down their backs. I remember the clean cotton dresses and carefully pressed hand-embroidered aprons they always wore; I remember laughter and good food, especially the sweet bread and the oven bread they gave us. Nowhere in my mind is there a foolish woman, a dumb woman, a vain woman, or a plastic woman, though the Indian women I have known have shown a wide range of personal style and demeanor.

My memory includes the Navajo woman who was badly beaten by her Sioux husband; but I also remember that my grandmother abandoned her Sioux husband long ago. I recall the stories about the Laguna woman beaten regularly by her husband in the presence of her children so that the children would not believe in the strength and power of femininity. And I remember the women who drank, who got into fights with other women and with the men, and who often won those battles. I have memories of tired women, partying women, stubborn women, sullen women, amicable women, selfish women, shy women, and aggressive women. Most of all I remember the women who laugh and scold and sit uncomplaining in the long sun on feast days and who cook wonderful food on wood stoves, in beehive mud ovens, and over open fires outdoors.

Among the images of women that come to me from various tribes as well as my own are White Buffalo Woman, who came to the Lakota long ago and brought them the religion of the Sacred Pipe which they still practice; Tinotzin the goddess who came to Juan Diego to remind him that she still walked the hills of her people and sent him with her message, her demand and her proof to the Catholic bishop in the city nearby. And from Laguna I take the images of Yellow Woman, Coyote Woman, Grandmother Spider (Spider Old Woman), who brought the light, who gave us weaving and medicine, who gave us life. Among the Keres she is known as Thought Woman who created us all and who keeps us in creation even now. I remember Iyatiku, Earth Woman, Corn Woman, who guides and counsels the people to peace and who welcomes us home when we cast off this coil of

---

Grab Days: Ritual of Laguna Pueblos during which women throw food and other small gifts to those attending the festival.

flesh as huskers cast off the leaves that wrap the corn. I remember Iyatiku's sister, Sun Woman, who held metals and cattle, pigs and sheep, highways and engines and so many things in her bundle, who went away to the east saying that one day she would return.

II

Since the coming of the Anglo-Europeans beginning in the fifteenth century, the fragile web of identity that long held tribal people secure has gradually been weakened and torn. But the oral tradition has prevented the complete destruction of the web, the ultimate disruption of tribal ways. The oral tradition is vital; it heals itself and the tribal web by adapting to the flow of the present while never relinquishing its connection to the past. Its adaptability has always been required, as many generations have experienced. Certainly the modern American Indian woman bears slight resemblance to her forebears—at least on superficial examination—but she is still a tribal woman in her deepest being. Her tribal sense of relationship to all that is continues to flourish. And though she is at times beset by her knowledge of the enormous gap between the life she lives and the life she was raised to live, and while she adapts her mind and being to the circumstances of her present life, she does so in tribal ways, mending the tears in the web of being from which she takes her existence as she goes.

My mother told me stories all the time, though I often did not recognize them as that. My mother told me stories about cooking and childbearing; she told me stories about menstruation and pregnancy; she told me stories about gods and heroes, about fairies and elves, about goddesses and spirits; she told me stories about the land and the sky, about cats and dogs, about snakes and spiders; she told me stories about climbing trees and exploring the mesas; she told me stories about going to dances and getting married; she told me stories about dressing and undressing, about sleeping and waking; she told me stories about herself, about her mother, about her grandmother. She told me stories about grieving and laughing, about thinking and doing; she told me stories about school and about people; about darning and mending; she told me stories about turquoise and about gold; she told me European stories and Laguna stories; she told me Catholic stories and Presbyterian stories; she told me city stories and country stories; she told me political stories and religious stories. She told me stories about living and stories about dying. And in all of those stories she told me who I was, who I was supposed to be, whom I came from, and who would follow me. In this way she taught me the meaning of the words she said, that all life is a circle and everything has a place within it. That's what she said and what she showed me in the things she did and the way she lives.

Of course, through my formal, white, Christian education, I discovered 10 that other people had stories of their own—about women, about Indians, about fact, about reality—and I was amazed by a number of startling suppositions that others made about tribal customs and beliefs. According to the un-Indian, non-

Indian view, for instance, Indians barred menstruating women from ceremonies and indeed segregated them from the rest of the people, consigning them to some space specially designed for them. This showed that Indians considered menstruating women unclean and not fit to enjoy the company of decent (nonmenstruating) people, that is, men. I was surprised and confused to hear this because my mother had taught me that white people had strange attitudes toward menstruation: they thought something was bad about it, that it meant you were sick, cursed, sinful, and weak and that you had to be very careful during that time. She taught me that menstruation was a normal occurrence, that I could go swimming or hiking or whatever else I wanted to do during my period. She actively scorned women who took to their beds, who were incapacitated by cramps, who "got the blues."

As I struggled to reconcile these very contradictory interpretations of American Indians' traditional beliefs concerning menstruation, I realized that the menstrual taboos were about power, not about sin or filth. My conclusion was later borne out by some tribes' own explanations, which, as you may well imagine, came as quite a relief to me.

The truth of the matter as many Indians see it is that women who are at the peak of their fecundity are believed to possess power that throws male power totally out of kilter. They emit such force that, in their presence, any male-owned or -dominated ritual or sacred object cannot do its usual task. For instance, the Lakota say that a menstruating woman anywhere near a yuwipi man, who is a special sort of psychic, spirit-empowered healer, for a day or so before he is to do his ceremony will effectively disempower him. Conversely, among many if not most tribes, important ceremonies cannot be held without the presence of women. Sometimes the ritual woman who empowers the ceremony must be unmarried and virginal so that the power she channels is unalloyed, unweakened by sexual arousal and penetration by a male. Other ceremonies require tumescent women, others the presence of mature women who have borne children, and still others depend for empowerment on post-menopausal women. Women may be segregated from the company of the whole band or village on certain occasions, but on certain occasions men are also segregated. In short, each ritual depends on a certain balance of power, and the positions of women within the phases of womanhood are used by tribal people to empower certain rites. This does not derive from a male-dominant view; it is not a ritual observance imposed on women by men. It derives from a tribal view of reality that distinguishes tribal people from feudal and industrial people.

Among the tribes, the occult power of women, inextricably bound to our hormonal life, is thought to be very great; many hold that we possess innately the blood-given power to kill—with a glance, with a step, or with a judicious mixing of menstrual blood into somebody's soup. Medicine women among the Pomo of California cannot practice until they are sufficiently mature; when they are immature, their power is diffuse and is likely to interfere with their practice until time and experience have it under control. So women of the tribes are not especially inclined to see themselves as poor helpless victims of male domination. Even in those tribes where something akin to male domination was present, women are perceived as powerful, socially, physically, and metaphysically. In times past, as in times present, women carried enormous burdens with aplomb. We were far indeed from the "weaker sex," the designation that white aristocratic sisters unhappily earned for us all.

I remember my mother moving furniture all over the house when she wanted it changed. She didn't wait for my father to come home and help— she just went ahead and moved the piano, a huge upright from the old days, the couch, the refrigerator. Nobody had told her she was too weak to do such things. In imitation of her, I would delight in loading trucks at my father's store with cases of pop or fifty-pound sacks of flour. Even when I was quite small I could do it, and it gave me a belief in my own physical strength that advancing middle age can't quite erase. My mother used to tell me about the Acoma Pueblo women she had seen as a child carrying huge ollas (water pots) on their heads as they wound their way up the tortuous stairwell carved into the face of the "Sky City" mesa, a feat I tried to imitate with books and tin buckets. ("Sky City" is the term used by the Chamber of Commerce for the mother village of Acoma, which is situated atop a high sandstone table mountain.) I was never very successful, but even the attempt reminded me that I was supposed to be strong and balanced to be a proper girl.

Of course, my mother's Laguna people are Keres Indian, reputed to be   15
the last extreme mother-right people on earth. So it is no wonder that I got notably nonwhite notions about the natural strength and prowess of women. Indeed, it is only when I am trying to get non-Indian approval, recognition, or acknowledgment that my "weak sister" emotional and intellectual ploys get the better of my tribal woman's good sense. At such times I forget that I just moved the piano or just wrote a competent paper or just completed a financial transaction satisfactorily or have supported myself and my children for most of my adult life.

Nor is my contradictory behavior atypical. Most Indian women I know are in the same bicultural bind: we vacillate between being dependent and strong, self-reliant and powerless, strongly motivated and hopelessly insecure. We resolve the dilemma in various ways: some of us party all the time; some of us drink to excess; some of us travel and move around a lot; some of us land good jobs and then quit them; some of us engage in violent exchanges; some of us blow our brains out. We act in these destructive ways because we suffer from the societal conflicts caused by having to identify with two hopelessly opposed cultural definitions of women. Through this destructive dissonance we are unhappy prey to the self-disparagement common to, indeed demanded of, Indians living in the United States today. Our situation is caused by the exigencies of a history of invasion, conquest, and colonization whose searing marks are probably ineradicable. A popular bumper sticker on many Indian cars proclaims: "If You're Indian You're In," to which I always find myself adding under my breath, "Trouble."

III

No Indian can grow to any age without being informed that her people were "savages" who interfered with the march of progress pursued by respectable, loving, civilized white people. We are the villains of the scenario when we are mentioned at all. We are absent from much of white history except when we are calmly, rationally, succinctly, and systematically dehumanized. On the few occasions we are noticed in any way other than as howling, bloodthirsty beings, we are acclaimed for our noble quaintness. In this definition, we are exotic curios. Our ancient arts and customs are used to draw tourist money to state coffers, into the pocketbooks and bank accounts of scholars, and into support of the American-in-Disneyland promoters' dream.

As a Roman Catholic child I was treated to bloody tales of how the savage Indians martyred the hapless priests and missionaries who went among them in an attempt to lead them to the one true path. By the time I was through high school I had the idea that Indians were people who had benefited mightily from the advanced knowledge and superior morality of the Anglo-Europeans. At least I had, perforce, that idea to lay beside the other one that derived from my daily experience of Indian life, an idea less dehumanizing and more accurate because it came from my mother and the other Indian people who raised me. That idea was that Indians are a people who don't tell lies, who care for their children and their old people. You never see an Indian orphan, they said. You always know when you're old that someone will take care of you—one of your children will. Then they'd list the old folks who were being taken care of by this child or that. No child is ever considered illegitimate among the Indians, they said. If a girl gets pregnant, the baby is still part of the family, and the mother is too. That's what they said, and they showed me real people who lived according to those principles.

Of course the ravages of colonization have taken their toll; there are orphans in Indian country now, and abandoned, brutalized old folks; there are even illegitimate children, though the very concept still strikes me as absurd. There are battered children and neglected children, and there are battered wives and women who have been raped by Indian men. Proximity to the "civilizing" effects of white Christians has not improved the moral quality of life in Indian country, though each group, Indian and white, explains the situation differently. Nor is there much yet in the oral tradition that can enable us to adapt to these inhuman changes. But a force is growing in that direction, and it is helping Indian women reclaim their lives. Their power, their sense of direction and of self will soon be visible. It is the force of the women who speak and work and write, and it is formidable.

Through all the centuries of war and death and cultural and psychic   20
destruction have endured the women who raise the children and tend the
fires, who pass along the tales and the traditions, who weep and bury the
dead, who are the dead, and who never forget. There are always the women,
who make pots and weave baskets, who fashion clothes and cheer their
children on at powwow, who make fry bread and piki bread, and corn soup
and chili stew, who dance and sing and remember and hold within their
hearts the dream of their ancient peoples—that one day the woman who
thinks will speak to us again, and everywhere there will be peace. Meanwhile
we tell the stories and write the books and trade tales of anger and woe and
stories of fun and scandal and laugh over all manner of things that happen
every day. We watch and we wait.

My great-grandmother told my mother: Never forget you are Indian.
And my mother told me the same thing. This, then, is how I have gone
about remembering, so that my children will remember too.

Considerations

1. How does the view of women suggested by this essay compare with the
   view of women held in your community?
2. What does Allen mean when she speaks of the "bicultural bind" faced by
   Native American women? How does this relate to the struggle of Native
   American women "to redefine themselves"?
3. How are Native American men portrayed in this essay? What roles do
   they play in the lives of the women described? What is the men's relationship to the current struggle of the women for new identity?
4. In what ways are stories significant to the author? How does she see
   stories and story-telling as particularly important in the lives of Native
   American women?
5. How does Allen's essay address and challenge the stereotypes of Native
   Americans? Cite examples and explanations she uses to refute specific
   negative images.

PAUL THEROUX (1941–   )
Being a Man

> *A novelist and travel writer, Paul Theroux has taught English in Uganda and Singapore. His novels often investigate social and psychological themes, and he is particularly interested in the effects of colonization on Third World nations. His novels include* Saint Jack *(1973),* The Consul's File *(1977),* Mosquito Coast *(1982), and* O'Zone *(1986).*

There is a pathetic sentence in the chapter "Fetishism" in Dr. Norman Cameron's book *Personality Development and Psychopathology.* It goes, "Fetishists are nearly always men; and their commonest fetish is a woman's shoe." I cannot read that sentence without thinking that it is just one more awful thing about being a man—and perhaps it is an important thing to know about us.

I have always disliked being a man. The whole idea of manhood in America is pitiful, in my opinion. This version of masculinity is a little like having to wear an ill-fitting coat for one's entire life (by contrast, I imagine femininity to be an oppressive sense of nakedness). Even the expression "Be a man!" strikes me as insulting and abusive. It means: Be stupid, be unfeeling, obedient, soldierly and stop thinking. Man means "manly"—how can one think about men without considering the terrible ambition of manliness? And yet it is part of every man's life. It is a hideous and crippling lie; it not only insists on difference and connives at superiority, it is also by its very nature destructive—emotionally damaging and socially harmful.

The youth who is subverted, as most are, into believing in the masculine idea is effectively separated from women and he spends the rest of his life finding women a riddle and a nuisance. Of course, there is a female version of this male affliction. It begins with mothers encouraging little girls to say (to other adults) "Do you like my new dress?" In a sense, little girls are traditionally urged to please adults with a kind of coquettishness, while boys are enjoined to behave like monkeys toward each other. The nine-year-old coquette proceeds to become womanish in a subtle power game in which she learns to be sexually indispensable, socially decorative and always alert to a man's sense of inadequacy.

Femininity—being lady-like—implies needing a man as witness and seducer; but masculinity celebrates the exclusive company of men. That is why it is so grotesque; and that is also why there is no manliness without inadequacy—because it denies men the natural friendship of women.

It is very hard to imagine any concept of manliness that does not belittle   5
women, and it begins very early. At an age when I wanted to meet girls—let's say the treacherous years of thirteen to sixteen—I was told to take up a sport, get more fresh air, join the Boy Scouts, and I was urged not to read so much. It was the 1950s and if you asked too many questions about sex you were sent to

camp—boy's camp, of course: the nightmare. Nothing is more unnatural or prison-like than a boy's camp, but if it were not for them we would have no Elks' Lodges, no pool rooms, no boxing matches, no Marines.

And perhaps no sports as we know them. Everyone is aware of how few in number are the athletes who behave like gentlemen. Just as high school basketball teaches you how to be a poor loser, the manly attitude towards sports seems to be little more than a recipe for creating bad marriages, social misfits, moral degenerates, sadists, latent rapists and just plain louts. I regard high school sports as a drug far worse than marijuana, and it is the reason that the average tennis champion, say, is a pathetic oaf.

Any objective study would find the quest for manliness essentially right-wing, puritanical, cowardly, neurotic and fueled largely by a fear of women. It is also certainly philistine. There is no book-hater like a Little League coach. But indeed all the creative arts are obnoxious to the manly ideal, because at their best the arts are pursued by uncompetitive and essentially solitary people. It makes it very hard for a creative youngster, for any boy who expresses the desire to be alone seems to be saying that there is something wrong with him.

It ought to be clear by now that I have something of an objection to the way we turn boys into men. It does not surprise me that when the President of the United States has his customary weekend off he dresses like a cowboy—it is both a measure of his insecurity and his willingness to please. In many ways, American culture does little more for a man than prepare him for modeling clothes in the L. L. Bean catalogue. I take this as a personal insult because for many years I found it impossible to admit to myself that I wanted to be a writer. It was my guilty secret, because being a writer was incompatible with being a man.

There are people who might deny this, but that is because the American writer, typically, has been so at pains to prove his manliness that we have come to see literariness and manliness as mingled qualities. But first there was a fear that writing was not a manly profession—indeed, not a profession at all. (The paradox in American letters is that it has always been easier for a woman to write and for a man to be published.) Growing up, I had thought of sports as wasteful and humiliating, and the idea of manliness was a bore. My wanting to become a writer was not a flight from that oppressive role-playing, but I quickly saw that it was at odds with it. Everything in stereotyped manliness goes against the life of the mind. The Hemingway personality is too tedious to go into here, and in any case his exertions are well-known, but certainly it was not until this aberrant behavior was examined by feminists in the 1960s that any male writer dared question the pugnacity in Hemingway's fiction. All the bullfighting and arm wrestling and elephant shooting diminished Hemingway as a writer, but it is consistent with a prevailing attitude in American writing: one cannot be a male writer without first proving that one is a man.

It is normal in America for a man to be dismissive or even somewhat apologetic about being a writer. Various factors make it easier. There is a   10 heartiness about journalism that makes it acceptable—journalism is the manliest form of American writing and, therefore, the profession the most independent-minded women seek (yes, it is an illusion, but that is my point). Fiction-writing is equated with a kind of dispirited failure and is only manly when it produces wealth—money is masculinity. So is drinking. Being a drunkard is another assertion, if misplaced, of manliness. The American male writer is traditionally proud of his heavy drinking. But we are also a very literal-minded people. A man proves his manhood in America in old-fashioned ways. He kills lions, like Hemingway; or he hunts ducks, like Nathanael West; or he makes pronouncements like, "A man should carry enough knife to defend himself with," as James Jones once said to a *Life* interviewer. Or he says he can drink you under the table. But even tiny drunken William Faulkner loved to mount a horse and go fox hunting, and Jack Kerouac roistered up and down Manhattan in a lumberjack shirt (and spent every night of *The Subterraneans* with his mother in Queens). And we are familiar with the lengths to which Norman Mailer is prepared, in his endearing way, to prove that he is just as much a monster as the next man.

When the novelist John Irving was revealed as a wrestler, people took him to be a very serious writer; and even a bubble reputation like Eric (*Love Story*) Segal's was enhanced by the news that he ran the marathon in a respectable time. How surprised we would be if Joyce Carol Oates were revealed as a sumo wrestler or Joan Didion active in pumping iron. "Lives in New York City with her three children" is the typical woman writer's biographical note, for just as the male writer must prove he has achieved a sort of muscular manhood, the woman writer—or rather her publicists—must prove her motherhood.

There would be no point in saying any of this if it were not generally accepted that to be a man is somehow—even now in feminist-influenced America—a privilege. It is on the contrary an unmerciful and punishing burden. Being a man is bad enough; being manly is appalling (in this sense, women's lib has done much more for men than for women). It is the sinister silliness of men's fashions, and a clubby attitude in the arts. It is the subversion of good students. It is the so-called "Dress Code" of the Ritz-Carlton Hotel in Boston, and it is the institutionalized cheating in college sports. It is the most primitive insecurity.

And this is also why men often object to feminism but are afraid to explain why: of course women have a justified grievance, but most men believe—and with reason—that their lives are just as bad.

Considerations

1. What is your response to the example in the opening paragraph? Speculate on the reasons why Theroux chose to begin with this example rather than with the second paragraph, where he explains the central idea of the essay.

2. In paragraph 3, Theroux suggests that the current American view of "manliness" encourages boys to feel distinctly apart from women and, therefore, "separated from women" for "the rest of . . . life." Such a man finds "women a riddle and nuisance." Do you agree with this observation? Support your view with specific examples from your observations, experiences, or reading.

3. Summarize Theroux's view of high school sports. Respond to his view, using specific examples that support or challenge his points.

4. Much of Theroux's essay discusses the attitude he believes Americans hold toward men who choose to be writers. What is your attitude toward writing as a profession for men? What have you observed the attitudes of others to be?

5. Compare Theroux's discussion of writing as a profession for men with Virginia Woolf's discussion of writing as a profession for women ("Professions for Women," page 621).

CONNECTIONS: MEN AND WOMEN

1. Compare the views of male and female sexuality as suggested by these works: "The Storm," "The Chase," "To His Coy Mistress," and "The Willing Mistress."

2. Compare the way roles of men and women are defined by the cultures represented in "The Chase," "New Islands," *A Doll House,* "Where I Come From Is Like This," and "Being a Man."

3. Consider how economic issues affect relationships between men and women in "Shiloh" and *A Doll House.*

4. Consider the theme of fidelity (and infidelity) in marriage in "Young Goodman Brown," "The Storm," "The Chase," and "For My Lover, Returning to His Wife."

5. "Young Goodman Brown," "Shiloh," "For My Lover, Returning to His Wife," and *A Doll House* all depict relationships that are failing for one reason or another. Compare the roles played by the men and women and the way those roles relate to the failure of the relationships.

9

Parents and Children

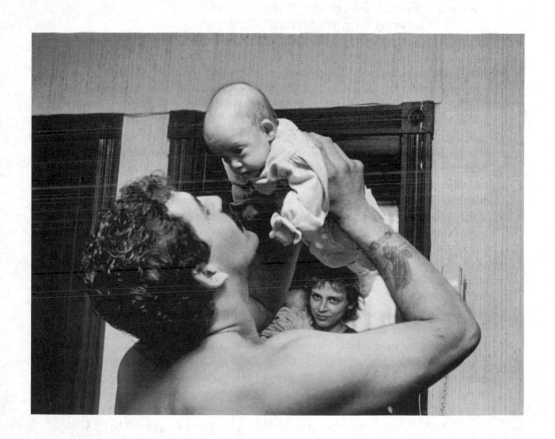

PHILIP ROTH (1933—   )

The Conversion of the Jews

Born in Newark, New Jersey, Philip Roth received the National Book Award at age 26 for Goodbye, Columbus, *from which "The Conversion of the Jews" is taken. This early work establishes his main theme, which recurs throughout most of his subsequent novels and short stories: a satiric view of the American Jew's striving to reconcile traditional culture with the values of mainstream society. When* Portnoy's Complaint *was published in 1969, it was regarded as highly controversial because of the title character's rejection of his Jewish heritage. Some critics maintain that Roth perpetuates Jewish stereotypes, and from time to time he has written essays defending his unflattering portrayal of Jewish characters.*

"You're a real one for opening your mouth in the first place," Itzie said. "What do you open your mouth all the time for?"

"I didn't bring it up, Itz, I didn't," Ozzie said.

"What do you care about Jesus Christ for anyway?"

"I didn't bring up Jesus Christ. He did. I didn't even know what he was talking about. Jesus is historical, he kept saying. Jesus is historical." Ozzie mimicked the monumental voice of Rabbi Binder.

"Jesus was a person that lived like you and me," Ozzie continued. 5
"That's what Binder said—"

"Yeah? . . . So what! What do I give two cents whether he lived or not. And what do you gotta open your mouth!" Itzie Lieberman favored closed-mouthedness, especially when it came to Ozzie Freedman's questions. Mrs. Freedman had to see Rabbi Binder twice before about Ozzie's questions and this Wednesday at four-thirty would be the third time. Itzie preferred to keep *his* mother in the kitchen; he settled for behind-the-back subtleties such as gestures, faces, snarls and other less delicate barnyard noises.

"He was a real person, Jesus, but he wasn't like God, and we don't believe he is God." Slowly, Ozzie was explaining Rabbi Binder's position to Itzie, who had been absent from Hebrew School the previous afternoon.

"The Catholics," Itzie said helpfully, "they believe in Jesus Christ, that he's God." Itzie Lieberman used "the Catholics" in its broadest sense—to include the Protestants.

Ozzie received Itzie's remark with a tiny head bob, as though it were a footnote, and went on. "His mother was Mary, and his father probably was Joseph," Ozzie said. "But the New Testament says his real father was God."

"His *real* father?" 10

"Yeah," Ozzie said, "that's the big thing, his father's supposed to be God."

"Bull."

"That's what Rabbi Binder says, that it's impossible—"

"Sure it's impossible. That stuff's all bull. To have a baby you gotta get laid," Itzie theologized. "Mary hadda get laid."

"That's what Binder says: 'The only way a woman can have a baby is   15
to have intercourse with a man.'"

"He said *that,* Ozz?" For a moment it appeared that Itzie had put the theological question aside. "He said that, intercourse?" A little curled smile shaped itself in the lower half of Itzie's face like a pink mustache. "What you guys do, Ozz, you laugh or something?"

"I raised my hand."

"Yeah? Whatja say?"

"That's when I asked the question."

Itzie's face lit up. "Whatja ask about—intercourse?"   20

"No, I asked the question about God, how if He could create the heaven and earth in six days, and make all the animals and the fish and the light in six days—the light especially, that's what always gets me, that He could make the light. Making fish and animals, that's pretty good—"

"That's damn good." Itzie's appreciation was honest but unimaginative: it was as though God had just pitched a one-hitter.

"But making light . . . I mean when you think about it, it's really something," Ozzie said. "Anyway, I asked Binder if He could make all that in six days, and He could *pick* the six days he wanted right out of nowhere, why couldn't He let a woman have a baby without having intercourse."

"You said intercourse, Ozz, to Binder?"

"Yeah."   25

"Right in class?"

"Yeah."

Itzie smacked the side of his head.

"I mean, no kidding around," Ozzie said, "that'd really be nothing. After all that other stuff, that'd practically be nothing."

Itzie considered a moment. "What'd Binder say?"   30

"He started all over again explaining how Jesus was historical and how he lived like you and me but he wasn't God. So I said I under*stood* that. What I wanted to know was different."

What Ozzie wanted to know was always different. The first time he had wanted to know how Rabbi Binder could call the Jews "The Chosen People" if the Declaration of Independence claimed all men to be created equal. Rabbi Binder tried to distinguish for him between political equality and spiritual legitimacy, but what Ozzie wanted to know, he insisted vehemently, was different. That was the first time his mother had to come.

Then there was the plane crash. Fifty-eight people had been killed in a plane crash at La Guardia. In studying a casualty list in the newspaper his mother had discovered among the list of those dead eight Jewish names (his grandmother had nine but she counted Miller as a Jewish name); because of the eight she said the plane crash was "a tragedy." During free-discussion time on Wednesday Ozzie had brought to Rabbi Binder's attention this matter of "some of his relations" always picking out the Jewish names. Rabbi Binder had begun to explain cultural unity and some other things when Ozzie stood up at his seat and said that what he wanted to know was different. Rabbi Binder insisted that he sit down and it was then that Ozzie shouted that he wished all fifty-eight were Jews. That was the second time his mother came.

"And he kept explaining about Jesus being historical, and so I kept asking him. No kidding, Itz, he was trying to make me look stupid."

"So what he finally do?" 35

"Finally he starts screaming that I was deliberately simple-minded and a wise guy, and that my mother had to come, and this was the last time. And that I'd never get bar-mitzvahed if he could help it. Then, Itz, then he starts talking in that voice like a statue, real slow and deep, and he says that I better think over what I said about the Lord. He told me to go to his office and think it over." Ozzie leaned his body towards Itzie. "Itz, I thought it over for a solid hour, and now I'm convinced God could do it."

Ozzie had planned to confess his latest transgression to his mother as soon as she came home from work. But it was a Friday night in November and already dark, and when Mrs. Freedman came through the door she tossed off her coat, kissed Ozzie quickly on the face, and went to the kitchen table to light the three yellow candles, two for the Sabbath and one for Ozzie's father.

When his mother lit the candles she would move her two arms slowly towards her, dragging them through the air, as though persuading people whose minds were half made up. And her eyes would get glassy with tears. Even when his father was alive Ozzie remembered that her eyes had gotten glassy, so it didn't have anything to do with his dying. It had something to do with lighting the candles.

As she touched the flaming match to the unlit wick of a Sabbath candle, the phone rang, and Ozzie, standing only a foot from it, plucked it off the receiver and held it muffled to his chest. When his mother lit candles Ozzie felt there should be no noise; even breathing if you could manage it, should be softened. Ozzie pressed the phone to his breast and watched his mother dragging whatever she was dragging, and he felt his own eyes get glassy. His mother was a round, tired, gray-haired penguin of a woman whose gray skin had begun to feel the tug of gravity and the weight of her own history. Even when she was dressed up she didn't look like a chosen person. But when she lit candles she looked like something better; like a woman who knew momentarily that God could do anything.

After a few mysterious minutes she was finished. Ozzie hung up the 40
phone and walked to the kitchen table where she was beginning to lay the two places for the four-course Sabbath meal. He told her that she would have to see Rabbi Binder next Wednesday at four-thirty, and then he told her why. For the first time in their life together she hit Ozzie across the face with her hand.

All through the chopped liver and chicken soup part of the dinner Ozzie cried; he didn't have any appetite for the rest.

On Wednesday, in the largest of the three basement classrooms of the synagogue, Rabbi Marvin Binder, a tall, handsome, broad-shouldered man of thirty with thick strong-fibered black hair, removed his watch from his pocket and saw that it was four o'clock. At the rear of the room Yakov Blotnik, the seventy-one-year-old custodian, slowly polished the large window, mumbling to himself, unaware that it was four o'clock or six o'clock, Monday or Wednesday. To most of the students Yakov Blotnik's mumbling, along with his brown curly beard, scythe nose, and two heel-trailing black cats, made of him an object of wonder, a foreigner, a relic, towards whom they were alternately fearful and disrespectful. To Ozzie the mumbling had always seemed a monotonous, curious prayer; what made it curious was that old Blotnik had been mumbling so steadily for so many years, Ozzie suspected he had memorized the prayers and forgotten all about God.

"It is now free-discussion time," Rabbi Binder said. "Feel free to talk about any Jewish matter at all—religion, family, politics, sports—"

There was silence. It was a gusty, clouded November afternoon and it did not seem as though there ever was or could be a thing called baseball. So nobody this week said a word about that hero from the past, Hank Greenberg—which limited free discussion considerably.

And the soul-battering Ozzie Freedman had just received from Rabbi   45
Binder had imposed its limitation. When it was Ozzie's turn to read aloud from the Hebrew book the rabbi had asked him petulantly why he didn't read more rapidly. He was showing no progress. Ozzie said he could read faster but that if he did he was sure not to understand what he was reading. Nevertheless, at the rabbi's repeated suggestion Ozzie tried, and showed a great talent, but in the midst of a long passage he stopped short and said he didn't understand a word he was reading, and started in again at a drag-footed pace. Then came the soul-battering.

Consequently when free-discussion time rolled around none of the students felt too free. The rabbi's invitation was answered only by the mumbling of feeble old Blotnik.

"Isn't there anything at all you would like to discuss?" Rabbi Binder asked again, looking at his watch. "No questions or comments?"

There was a small grumble from the third row. The rabbi requested that Ozzie rise and give the rest of the class the advantage of his thought.

Ozzie rose. "I forget it now," he said, and sat down in his place.

Rabbi Binder advanced a seat towards Ozzie and poised himself on the   50
edge of the desk. It was Itzie's desk and the rabbi's frame only a dagger's-length away from his face snapped him to sitting attention.

"Stand up again, Oscar," Rabbi Binder said calmly, "and try to assemble your thoughts."

Ozzie stood up. All his classmates turned in their seats and watched as he gave an unconvincing scratch to his forehead.

"I can't assemble any," he announced, and plunked himself down.

"Stand up!" Rabbi Binder advanced from Itzie's desk to the one directly in front of Ozzie; when the rabbinical back was turned Itzie gave it five-fingers off the tip of his nose, causing a small titter in the room. Rabbi Binder was too absorbed in squelching Ozzie's nonsense once and for all to bother with titters. "Stand up, Oscar. What's your question about?"

Ozzie pulled a word out of the air. It was the handiest word. "Religion." 55

"Oh, now you remember?"

"Yes."

"What is it?"

Trapped, Ozzie blurted the first thing that came to him. "Why can't He make anything He wants to make!"

As Rabbi Binder prepared an answer, a final answer, Itzie, ten feet 60 behind him, raised one finger on his left hand, gestured it meaningfully towards the rabbi's back, and brought the house down.

Binder twisted quickly to see what had happened and in the midst of the commotion Ozzie shouted into the rabbi's back what he couldn't have shouted to his face. It was a loud, toneless sound that had the timbre of something stored inside for about six days.

"You don't know! You don't know anything about God!"

The rabbi spun back towards Ozzie. "What?"

"You don't know—you don't—"

"Apologize, Oscar, apologize!" It was a threat. 65

"You don't—"

Rabbi Binder's hand flicked out at Ozzie's cheek. Perhaps it had only been meant to clamp the boy's mouth shut, but Ozzie ducked and the palm caught him squarely on the nose.

The blood came in a short, red spurt on to Ozzie's shirt front.

The next moment was all confusion. Ozzie screamed, "You bastard, you bastard!" and broke for the classroom door. Rabbi Binder lurched a step backwards, as though his own blood had started flowing violently in the opposite direction, then gave a clumsy lurch forward and bolted out the door after Ozzie. The class followed after the rabbi's huge blue-suited back, and before old Blotnik could turn from his window, the room was empty and everyone was headed full speed up the three flights leading to the roof.

If one should compare the light of day to the life of man: sunrise to 70 birth; sunset—the dropping down over the edge—to death; then as Ozzie Freedman wiggled through the trapdoor of the synagogue roof, his feet kicking backwards bronco-style at Rabbi Binder's outstretched arms—at that moment the day was fifty years old. As a rule fifty or fifty-five reflects accurately the age of late afternoons in November, for it is in that month, during those hours, that one's awareness of light seems no longer a matter of seeing, but of hearing: light begins clicking away. In fact, as Ozzie locked shut the trapdoor in the rabbi's face, the sharp click of the bolt into the lock might momentarily have been mistaken for the sound of the heavier gray that had just throbbed through the sky.

With all his weight Ozzie kneeled on the locked door; any instant he was certain that Rabbi Binder's shoulder would fling it open, splintering the wood into shrapnel and catapulting his body into the sky. But the door did not move and below him he heard only the rumble of feet, first loud then dim, like thunder rolling away.

A question shot through his brain. "Can this be *me?*" For a thirteen-year-old who had just labeled his religious leader a bastard, twice, it was not an improper question. Louder and louder the question came to him—"Is it me? Is it me?"—until he discovered himself no longer kneeling, but racing crazily towards the edge of the roof, his eyes crying, his throat screaming, and his arms flying everywhichway as though not his own.

"Is it me? Is it me Me Me Me Me! It has to be me—but is it!"

It is the question a thief must ask himself the night he jimmies open his first window, and it is said to be the question with which bridegrooms quiz themselves before the altar.

In the few wild seconds it took Ozzie's body to propel him to the edge of the roof, his self-examination began to grow fuzzy. Gazing down at the street, he became confused as to the problem beneath the question: was it, is-it-me-who-called-Binder-a-bastard? or, is-it-me-prancing-around-on-the-roof? However, the scene below settled all, for there is an instant in any action when whether it is you or somebody else is academic. The thief crams the money in his pockets and scoots out the window. The bridegroom signs the hotel register for two. And the boy on the roof finds a streetful of people gaping at him, necks stretched backwards, faces up, as though he were the ceiling of the Hayden Planetarium. Suddenly you know it's you.

"Oscar! Oscar Freedman!" A voice rose from the center of the crowd, a voice that, could it have been seen, would have looked like the writing on a scroll. "Oscar Freedman, get down from there. Immediately!" Rabbi Binder was pointing one arm stiffly up at him; and at the end of that arm, one finger aimed menacingly. It was the attitude of a dictator, but one—the eyes confessed all—whose personal valet had spit neatly in his face.

Ozzie didn't answer. Only for a blink's length did he look towards Rabbi Binder. Instead his eyes began to fit together the world beneath him, to sort out people from places, friends from enemies, participants from spectators. In little jagged starlike clusters his friends stood around Rabbi Binder, who was still pointing. The topmost point on a star compounded not of angels but of five adolescent boys was Itzie. What a world it was, with those stars below, Rabbi Binder below . . . Ozzie, who a moment earlier hadn't been able to control his own body, started to feel the meaning of the word control: he felt Peace and he felt Power.

"Oscar Freedman, I'll give you three to come down."

Few dictators give their subjects three to do anything; but, as always, Rabbi Binder only looked dictatorial.

"Are you ready, Oscar?"   80

Ozzie nodded his head yes, although he had no intention in the world— the lower one or the celestial one he'd just entered—of coming down even if Rabbi Binder should give him a million.

"All right then," said Rabbi Binder. He ran a hand through his black Samson hair as though it were the gesture prescribed for uttering the first digit. Then, with his other hand cutting a circle out of the small piece of sky around him, he spoke. "One!"

There was no thunder. On the contrary, at that moment, as though "one" was the cue for which he had been waiting, the world's least thunderous person appeared on the synagogue steps. He did not so much come out the synagogue door as lean out, onto the darkening air. He clutched at the doorknob with one hand and looked up at the roof.

"Oy!"

Yakov Blotnik's old mind hobbled slowly, as if on crutches, and though   85 he couldn't decide precisely what the boy was doing on the roof, he knew it wasn't good—that is, it wasn't-good-for-the-Jews. For Yakov Blotnik life had fractionated itself simply: things were either good-for-the-Jews or no-good-for-the-Jews.

He smacked his free hand to his in-sucked cheek, gently. "Oy. Gut!" And then quickly as he was able, he jacked down his head and surveyed the street. There was Rabbi Binder (like a man at an auction with only three dollars in his pocket, he had just delivered a shaky "Two!"); there were the students, and that was all. So far it-wasn't-so-bad-for-the-Jews. But the boy had to come down immediately, before anybody saw. The problem: how to get the boy off the roof?

Anybody who has ever had a cat on the roof knows how to get him down. You call the fire department. Or first you call the operator and you ask her for the fire department. And the next thing there is great jamming of brakes and clanging of bells and shouting of instructions. And then the cat is off the roof. You do the same thing to get a boy off the roof.

That is, you do the same thing if you are Yakov Blotnik and you once had a cat on the roof.

When the engines, all four of them, arrived, Rabbi Binder had four times given Ozzie the count of three. The big hook-and-ladder swung around the corner and one of the firemen leaped from it, plunging headlong towards the yellow fire hydrant in front of the synagogue. With a huge wrench he began to unscrew the top nozzle. Rabbi Binder raced over to him and pulled at his shoulder.

"There's no fire . . ."   90

The fireman mumbled back over his shoulder and, heatedly, continued working at the nozzle.

"But there's no fire, there's no fire . . ." Binder shouted. When the fireman mumbled again, the rabbi grasped his face with both his hands and pointed it up at the roof.

To Ozzie it looked as though Rabbi Binder was trying to tug the fireman's head out of his body, like a cork from a bottle. He had to giggle at the picture they made: it was a family portrait—rabbi in black skullcap, fireman in red fire hat, and the little yellow hydrant squatting beside like a kid brother, bareheaded. From the edge of the roof Ozzie waved at the portrait, a one-handed, flapping, mocking wave; in doing it his right foot slipped from under him. Rabbi Binder covered his eyes with his hands.

Firemen work fast. Before Ozzie had even regained his balance, a big, round, yellowed net was being held on the synagogue lawn. The firemen who held it looked up at Ozzie with stern, feelingless faces.

One of the firemen turned his head towards Rabbi Binder. "What, is the kid nuts or something?"   95

Rabbi Binder unpeeled his hands from his eyes, slowly, painfully, as if they were tape. Then he checked: nothing on the sidewalk, no dents in the net.

"Is he gonna jump, or what?" the fireman shouted.

In a voice not at all like a statue, Rabbi Binder finally answered. "Yes, yes, I think so . . . He's been threatening to . . ."

Threatening to? Why, the reason he was on the roof, Ozzie remembered, was to get away; he hadn't even thought about jumping. He had just run to get away, and the truth was that he hadn't really headed for the roof as much as he'd been chased there.

"What's his name, the kid?"   100

"Freedman," Rabbi Binder answered. "Oscar Freedman."

The fireman looked up at Ozzie. "What is it with you, Oscar? You gonna jump, or what?"

Ozzie did not answer. Frankly, the question had just arisen.

"Look, Oscar, if you're gonna jump, jump—and if you're not gonna jump, don't jump. But don't waste our time, willya?"

Ozzie looked at the fireman and then at Rabbi Binder. He wanted to see Rabbi Binder cover his eyes one more time.   105

"I'm going to jump."

And then he scampered around the edge of the roof to the corner, where there was no net below, and he flapped his arms at his sides, swishing the air and smacking his palms to his trousers on the downbeat. He began screaming like some kind of engine, "Wheeeee . . . wheeeeee," and leaning way out over the edge with the upper half of his body. The firemen whipped around to cover the ground with the net. Rabbi Binder mumbled a few words to Somebody and covered his eyes. Everything happened quickly, jerkily, as in a silent movie. The crowd, which had arrived with the fire engines, gave out a long, Fourth-of-July fireworks oooh-aahhh. In the excitement no one had paid the crowd much heed, except, of course, Yakov Blotnik, who swung from the doorknob counting heads. "Fier und tsvantsik . . . finf und tsvantsik . . . Oy, Gut!" It wasn't like this with the cat.

Rabbi Binder peeked through his fingers, checked the sidewalk and net. Empty. But there was Ozzie racing to the other corner. The firemen raced with him but were unable to keep up. Whenever Ozzie wanted to he might jump and splatter himself upon the sidewalk, and by the time the firemen scooted to the spot all they could do with their net would be to cover the mess.

"Wheeeee . . . wheeeee . . ."

"Hey, Oscar," the winded fireman yelled, "What the hell is this, a game   110 or something?"

"Wheeeee . . . wheeeee . . ."

"Hey, Oscar—"

But he was off now to the other corner, flapping his wings fiercely. Rabbi Binder couldn't take it any longer—the fire engines from nowhere, the screaming suicidal boy, the net. He fell to his knees, exhausted, and with his hands curled together in front of his chest like a little dome, he pleaded, "Oscar, stop it, Oscar. Don't jump, Oscar. Please come down . . . Please don't jump."

And further back in the crowd a single voice, a single young voice, shouted a lone word to the boy on the roof.

"Jump!"   115

It was Itzie. Ozzie momentarily stopped flapping.

"Go ahead, Ozz—jump!" Itzie broke off his point of the star and courageously, with the inspiration not of a wise-guy but of a disciple, stood alone. "Jump, Ozz, jump!"

Still on his knees, his hands still curled, Rabbi Binder twisted his body back. He looked at Itzie, then, agonizingly, back to Ozzie.

"OSCAR, DON'T JUMP! PLEASE, DON'T JUMP . . . please please . . ."

"Jump!" This time it wasn't Itzie but another point of the star. By the   120 time Mrs. Freedman arrived to keep her four-thirty appointment with Rabbi Binder, the whole little upside down heaven was shouting and pleading for Ozzie to jump, and Rabbi Binder no longer was pleading with him not to jump, but was crying into the dome of his hands.

Understandably Mrs. Freedman couldn't figure out what her son was doing on the roof. So she asked.

"Ozzie, my Ozzie, what are you doing? My Ozzie, what is it?"

Ozzie stopped wheeeeeing and slowed his arms down to a cruising flap, the kind birds use in soft winds, but he did not answer. He stood against the low, clouded, darkening sky—light clicked down swiftly now, as on a small gear—flapping softly and gazing down at the small bundle of a woman who was his mother.

"What are you doing, Ozzie?" She turned towards the kneeling Rabbi Binder and rushed so close that only a paper-thickness of dusk lay between her stomach and his shoulders.

"What is my baby doing?" 125

Rabbi Binder gaped up at her but he too was mute. All that moved was the dome of his hands; it shook back and forth like a weak pulse.

"Rabbi, get him down! He'll kill himself. Get him down, my only baby . . ."

"I can't," Rabbi Binder said, "I can't . . ." and he turned his handsome head towards the crowd of boys behind him. "It's them. Listen to them."

And for the first time Mrs. Freedman saw the crowd of boys, and she heard what they were yelling.

"He's doing it for them. He won't listen to me. It's them." Rabbi 130 Binder spoke like one in a trance.

"For them?"

"Yes."

"Why for them?"

"They want him to . . ."

Mrs. Freedman raised her two arms upward as though she were con- 135 ducting the sky. "For them he's doing it!" And then in a gesture older than pyramids, older than prophets and floods, her arms came slapping down to her sides. "A martyr I have. Look!" She tilted her head to the roof. Ozzie was still flapping softly. "My martyr."

"Oscar, come down, *please*," Rabbi Binder groaned.

In a startlingly even voice Mrs. Freedman called to the boy on the roof. "Ozzie, come down, Ozzie. Don't be a martyr, my baby."

As though it were a litany, Rabbi Binder repeated her words, "Don't be a martyr, my baby. Don't be a martyr."

"Gawhead, Ozz—*be* a Martin!" It was Itzie. "Be a Martin, be a Martin," and all the voices joined in singing for Martindom, whatever *it* was. "Be a Martin, be a Martin . . ."

Somehow when you're on a roof the darker it gets the less you can 140 hear. All Ozzie knew was that two groups wanted two new things: his friends were spirited and musical about what they wanted; his mother and the rabbi were even-toned, chanting, about what they didn't want. The rabbi's voice was without tears now and so was his mother's.

The big net stared up at Ozzie like a sightless eye. The big, clouded sky pushed down. From beneath it looked like a gray corrugated board. Suddenly, looking up into that unsympathetic sky, Ozzie realized all the strangeness of what these people, his friends, were asking: they wanted him to jump, to kill himself; they were singing about it now—it made them that happy. And there was an even greater strangeness: Rabbi Binder was on his knees, trembling. If there was a question to be asked now it was not "Is it me?" but rather "Is it us? . . . Is it us?"

Being on the roof, it turned out, was a serious thing. If he jumped would the singing become dancing? Would it? What would jumping stop? Yearningly, Ozzie wished he could rip open the sky, plunge his hands through, and pull out the sun; and on the sun, like a coin, would be stamped JUMP or DON'T JUMP.

Ozzie's knees rocked and sagged a little under him as though they were setting him for a dive. His arms tightened, stiffened, froze, from shoulders to fingernails. He felt as if each part of his body were going to vote as to whether he should kill himself or not—and each part as though it were independent of *him*.

The light took an unexpected click down and the new darkness, like a gag, hushed the friends singing for this and the mother and rabbi chanting for that.

Ozzie stopped counting votes, and in a curiously high voice, like one who wasn't prepared for speech, he spoke.   145

"Mamma?"

"Yes, Oscar."

"Mamma, get down on your knees, like Rabbi Binder."

"Oscar—"

"Get down on your knees," he said, "or I'll jump."   150

Ozzie heard a whimper, then a quick rustling, and when he looked down where his mother had stood he saw the top of a head and beneath that a circle of dress. She was kneeling beside Rabbi Binder.

He spoke again. "Everybody kneel." There was the sound of everybody kneeling.

Ozzie looked around. With one hand he pointed towards the synagogue entrance. "Make *him* kneel."

There was a noise, not of kneeling, but of body-and-cloth stretching. Ozzie could hear Rabbi Binder saying in a gruff whisper, ". . . or he'll *kill* himself," and when next he looked there was Yakov Blotnik off the doorknob and for the first time in his life upon his knees in the Gentile posture of prayer.

As for the firemen—it is not as difficult as one might imagine to hold a net taut while you are kneeling.   155

Ozzie looked around again; and then he called to Rabbi Binder.

"Rabbi?"

"Yes, Oscar."

"Rabbi Binder, do you believe in God?"

"Yes."   160

"Do you believe God can do Anything?" Ozzie leaned his head out into the darkness. "Anything?"

"Oscar, I think—"

"Tell me you believe God can do Anything."

There was a second's hesitation. Then: "God can do Anything."

"Tell me you believe God can make a child without intercourse."   165

"He can."

"Tell me!"

"God," Rabbi Binder admitted, "can make a child without intercourse."

"Mamma, you tell me."

"God can make a child without intercourse," his mother said.   170

"Make *him* tell me." There was no doubt who *him* was.

In a few moments Ozzie heard an old comical voice say something to the increasing darkness about God.

Next, Ozzie made everybody say it. And then he made them all say they believed in Jesus Christ—first one at a time, then all together.

When the catechizing was through it was the beginning of evening. From the street it sounded as if the boy on the roof might have sighed.

"Ozzie?" A woman's voice dared to speak. "You'll come down now?"   175

There was no answer, but the woman waited, and when a voice finally did speak it was thin and crying, and exhausted as that of an old man who has just finished pulling the bells.

"Mamma, don't you see—you shouldn't hit me. He shouldn't hit me. You shouldn't hit me about God, Mamma. You should never hit anybody about God—"

"Ozzie, please come down now."

"Promise me, promise me you'll never hit anybody about God."

He had asked only his mother, but for some reason everyone kneeling   180
in the street promised he would never hit anybody about God.

Once again there was silence.

"I can come down now, Mamma," the boy on the roof finally said. He turned his head both ways as though checking the traffic lights. "Now I can come down . . ."

And he did, right into the center of the yellow net that glowed in the evening's edge like an overgrown halo.

Considerations

1. Yakov Blotnik sees life in absolutes: "things were either good-for-the-Jews or no-good-for-the-Jews." As you read "The Conversion of the Jews," ask yourself how you think Blotnik would categorize the story, and explain whether you would agree or disagree with his assessment.

2. Do you find Ozzie an entirely sympathetic character? Are there any other characters whose values, views, and actions gain your support? Explain.

3. What do humor and irony contribute to the story's theme? Consider, for example, the characters' names as well as the irony of the central conflict.

4. What roles are played by Ozzie's mother, Yakov Blotnik, and Itzie? How would the story be changed if any one of them were not part of the action?

5. Choose one episode in the story, and tell it from the point of view of any of the other characters.

DORIS LESSING (1919–   )

Through the Tunnel

At the age of five, Doris Lessing accompanied her British parents in their move from Iran to southern Rhodesia (now Zimbabwe), where she lived for several years. In 1949, she moved to England and wrote her first novel, The Grass Is Singing *(1950), a book that details the repression and evil of apartheid. Her best-known work,* The Golden Notebook, *has received wide acclaim as a quintessential modern feminist novel. Because of her political activism, Lessing was barred from her early childhood home for twenty-five years but was allowed to return in 1979, when Zimbabwe, ruled by a black majority, became an independent state.* African Lands *(1992) describes her impressions of Zimbabwe, including problems related to the high incidence of AIDS, environmental pollution, and political corruption. "Through the Tunnel" appears in* The Habit of Loving *(1955).*

Going to the shore on the first morning of the holiday, the young English boy stopped at a turning of the path and looked down at a wild and rocky bay, and then over to the crowded beach he knew so well from other years. His mother walked on in front of him, carrying a bright-striped bag in one hand. Her other arm, swinging loose, was very white in the sun. The boy watched that white, naked arm, and turned his eyes, which had a frown behind them, toward the bay and back again to his mother. When she felt he was not with her, she swung around. "Oh, there you are, Jerry!" she said. She looked impatient, then smiled. "Why, darling, would you rather not come with me? Would you rather—" She frowned, conscientiously worrying over what amusements he might secretly be longing for which she had been too busy or too careless to imagine. He was very familiar with that anxious, apologetic smile. Contrition sent him running after her. And yet, as he ran, he looked back over his shoulder at the wild bay; and all morning, as he played on the safe beach, he was thinking of it.

Next morning, when it was time for the routine of swimming and sunbathing, his mother said, "Are you tired of the usual beach, Jerry? Would you like to go somewhere else?"

"Oh, no!" he said quickly, smiling at her out of that unfailing impulse of contrition—a sort of chivalry. Yet, walking down the path with her, he blurted out, "I'd like to go and have a look at those rocks down there."

She gave the idea her attention. It was a wild-looking place, and there was no one there, but she said, "Of course, Jerry. When you've had enough, come to the big beach. Or just go straight back to the villa, if you like." She walked away, that bare arm, now slightly reddened from yesterday's sun, swinging. And he almost ran after her again, feeling it unbearable that she should go by herself, but he did not.

She was thinking, Of course he's old enough to be safe without me. 5
Have I been keeping him too close? He mustn't feel he ought to be with
me. I must be careful.

He was an only child, eleven years old. She was a widow. She was
determined to be neither possessive nor lacking in devotion. She went worrying off to her beach.

As for Jerry, once he saw that his mother had gained her beach, he
began the steep descent to the bay. From where he was, high up among red-
brown rocks, it was a scoop of moving bluish green fringed with white. As
he went lower, he saw that it spread among small promontories and inlets of
rough, sharp rock, and the crisping, lapping surface showed stains of purple
and darker blue. Finally, as he ran sliding and scraping down the last few
yards, he saw an edge of white surf, and the shallow, luminous movement of
water over white sand, and, beyond that, a solid, heavy blue.

He ran straight into the water and began swimming. He was a good
swimmer. He went out fast over the gleaming sand, over a middle region
where rocks lay like discoloured monsters under the surface, and then he was
in the real sea—a warm sea where irregular cold currents from the deep
water shocked his limbs.

When he was so far out that he could look back not only on the little
bay but past the promontory that was between it and the big beach, he floated
on the buoyant surface and looked for his mother. There she was, a speck of
yellow under an umbrella that looked like a slice of orange peel. He swam
back to shore, relieved at being sure she was there, but all at once very lonely.

On the edge of a small cape that marked the side of the bay away from 10
the promontory was a loose scatter of rocks. Above them, some boys were
stripping off their clothes. They came running, naked, down to the rocks.
The English boy swam towards them, and kept his distance at a stone's throw.
They were of that coast, all of them burned smooth dark brown, and speaking a language he did not understand. To be with them, of them, was a
craving that filled his whole body. He swam a little closer; they turned and
watched him with narrowed, alert dark eyes. Then one smiled and waved. It
was enough. In a minute, he had swum in and was on the rocks beside them,
smiling with a desperate, nervous supplication. They shouted cheerful greetings at him, and then, as he preserved his nervous, uncomprehending smile,
they understood that he was a foreigner strayed from his own beach, and
they proceeded to forget him. But he was happy. He was with them.

They began diving again and again from a high point into a well of
blue sea between rough, pointed rocks. After they had dived and come up,
they swam around, hauled themselves up, and waited their turn to dive again.
They were big boys—men to Jerry. He dived, and they watched him, and
when he swam around to take his place, they made way for him. He felt he
was accepted, and he dived again, carefully, proud of himself.

Soon the biggest of the boys poised himself, shot down into the water,
and did not come up. The others stood about, watching. Jerry, after waiting

for the sleek brown head to appear, let out a yell of warning; they looked at him idly and turned their eyes back towards the water. After a long time, the boy came up on the other side of a big dark rock, letting the air out of his lungs in a sputtering gasp and a shout of triumph. Immediately, the rest of them dived in. One moment, the morning seemed full of chattering boys; the next, the air and the surface of the water were empty. But through the heavy blue, dark shapes could be seen moving and groping.

Jerry dived, shot past the school of underwater swimmers, saw a black wall of rock looming at him, touched it, and bobbed up at once to the surface, where the wall was a low barrier he could see across. There was no one visible; under him, in the water, the dim shapes of the swimmers had disappeared. Then one, and then another of the boys came up on the far side of the barrier of rock, and he understood that they had swum through some gap or hole in it. He plunged down again. He could see nothing through the stinging salt water but the blank rock. When he came up, the boys were all on the diving rock, preparing to attempt the feat again. And now, in a panic of failure, he yelled up, in English, "Look at me! Look!" and he began splashing and kicking in the water like a foolish dog.

They looked down gravely, frowning. He knew the frown. At moments of failure, when he clowned to claim his mother's attention, it was with just this grave, embarrassed inspection that she rewarded him. Through his hot shame, feeling the pleading grin on his face like a scar that he could never remove, he looked up at the group of big brown boys on the rock and shouted, "*Bonjour! Merci! Au revoir! Monsieur, monsieur!*" while he hooked his fingers round his ears and waggled them.

Water surged into his mouth; he choked, sank, came up. The rock, lately weighted with boys, seemed to rear up out of the water as their weight was removed. They were flying down past him, now, into the water; the air was full of falling bodies. Then the rock was empty in the hot sunlight. He counted one, two, three. . . .   15

At fifty, he was terrified. They must all be drowning beneath him, in the watery caves of the rock! At a hundred, he stared around him at the empty hillside, wondering if he should yell for help. He counted faster, faster, to hurry them up, to bring them to the surface quickly, to drown them quickly—anything rather than the terror of counting on and on into the blue emptiness of the morning. And then, at a hundred and sixty, the water beyond the rock was full of boys blowing like brown whales. They swam back to the shore without a look at him.

He climbed back to the diving rock and sat down, feeling the hot roughness of it under his thighs. The boys were gathering up their bits of clothing and running off along the shore to another promontory. They were leaving to get away from him. He cried openly, fists in his eyes. There was no one to see him, and he cried himself out.

It seemed to him that a long time had passed, and he swam out to where he could see his mother. Yes, she was still there, a yellow spot under an orange umbrella. He swam back to the big rock, climbed up, and dived into the blue pool among the fanged and angry boulders. Down he went, until he touched the wall of rock again. But the salt was so painful in his eyes that he could not see.

He came to the surface, swam to shore and went back to the villa to wait for his mother. Soon she walked slowly up the path, swinging her striped bag, the flushed, naked arm dangling beside her. "I want some swimming goggles," he panted, defiant and beseeching.

She gave him a patient, inquisitive look as she said casually, "Well, of course, darling."   20

But now, now, now! He must have them this minute, and no other time. He nagged and pestered until she went with him to a shop. As soon as she had bought the goggles, he grabbed them from her hand as if she were going to claim them for herself, and was off, running down the steep path to the bay.

Jerry swam out to the big barrier rock, adjusted the goggles, and dived. The impact of the water broke the rubber-enclosed vacuum, and the goggles came loose. He understood that he must swim down to the base of the rock from the surface of the water. He fixed the goggles tight and firm, filled his lungs, and floated, face down, on the water. Now he could see. It was as if he had eyes of a different kind—fish-eyes that showed everything clear and delicate and wavering in the bright water.

Under him, six or seven feet down, was a floor of perfectly clean, shining white sand, rippled firm and hard by the tides. Two greyish shapes steered there, like long, rounded pieces of wood or slate. They were fish. He saw them nose towards each other, poise motionless, make a dart forward, swerve off, and come around again. It was like a water dance. A few inches above them, the water sparkled as if sequins were dropping through it. Fish again—myriads of minute fish, the length of his fingernail, were drifting through the water, and in a moment he could feel the innumerable tiny touches of them against his limbs. It was like swimming in flaked silver. The great rock the big boys had swum through rose sheer out of the white sand, black, tufted lightly with greenish weed. He could see no gap in it. He swam down to its base.

Again and again he rose, took a big chestful of air, and went down. Again and again he groped over the surface of the rock, feeling it, almost hugging it in the desperate need to find the entrance. And then, once, while he was clinging to the black wall, his knees came up and he shot his feet out forward and they met no obstacle. He had found the hole.

He gained the surface, clambered about the stones that littered the   25 barrier rock until he found a big one, and, with this in his arms, let himself down over the side of the rock. He dropped, with the weight, straight to the sandy floor. Clinging tight to the anchor of stone, he lay on his side and looked in under the dark shelf at the place where his feet had gone. He could see the hole. It was an irregular, dark gap, but he could not see deep into it.

He let go of his anchor, clung with his hands to the edges of the hole, and tried to push himself in.

He got his head in, found his shoulders jammed, moved them in side-wise, and was inside as far as his waist. He could see nothing ahead. Something soft and clammy touched his mouth, he saw a dark frond moving against the greyish rock, and panic filled him. He thought of octopuses, of clinging weed. He pushed himself out backward and caught a glimpse, as he retreated, of a harmless tentacle of seaweed drifting in the mouth of the tunnel. But it was enough. He reached the sunlight, swam to shore, and lay on the diving rock. He looked down into the blue well of water. He knew he must find his way through that cave, or hole, or tunnel, and out the other side.

First, he thought, he must learn to control his breathing. He let himself down into the water with another big stone in his arms, so that he could lie effortlessly on the bottom of the sea. He counted. One, two, three. He counted steadily. He could hear the movement of blood in his chest. Fifty-one, fifty-two. . . . His chest was hurting. He let go of the rock and went up into the air. He saw that the sun was low. He rushed to the villa and found his mother at her supper. She said only "Did you enjoy yourself?" and he said "Yes."

All night, the boy dreamed of the water-filled cave in the rock, and as soon as breakfast was over he went to the bay.

That night, his nose bled badly. For hours he had been underwater, learning to hold his breath, and now he felt weak and dizzy. His mother said, "I shouldn't overdo things, darling, if I were you."

That day and the next, Jerry exercised his lungs as if everything, the whole of his life, all that he would become, depended upon it. And again his nose bled at night, and his mother insisted on his coming with her the next day. It was a torment to him to waste a day of his careful self-training, but he stayed with her on that other beach, which now seemed a place for small children, a place where his mother might lie safe in the sun. It was not his beach. 30

He did not ask for permission, on the following day, to go to his beach. He went, before his mother could consider the complicated rights and wrongs of the matter. A day's rest, he discovered, had improved his count by ten. The big boys had made the passage while he counted a hundred and sixty. He had been counting fast, in his fright. Probably now, if he tried, he could get through that long tunnel, but he was not going to try yet. A curious, most unchildlike persistence, a controlled impatience, made him wait. In the meantime, he lay underwater on the white sand, littered now by stones he had brought down from the upper air, and studied the entrance to the tunnel. He knew every jut and corner of it, as far as it was possible to see. It was as if he already felt its sharpness about his shoulders.

He sat by the clock in the villa, when his mother was not near, and checked his time. He was incredulous and then proud to find he could hold his breath without strain for two minutes. The words "two minutes," authorized by the clock, brought the adventure that was so necessary to him close.

In another four days, his mother said, casually one morning, they must go home. On the day before they left, he would do it. He would do it if it killed him, he said defiantly to himself. But two days before they were to leave—a day of triumph when he increased his count by fifteen—his nose bled so badly that he turned dizzy and had to lie limply over the big rock like a bit of seaweed, watching the thick red blood flow on to the rock and trickle slowly down to the sea. He was frightened. Supposing he turned dizzy in the tunnel? Supposing he died there, trapped? Supposing—his head went around, in the hot sun, and he almost gave up. He thought he would return to the house and lie down, and next summer, perhaps, when he had another year's growth in him—*then* he would go through the hole.

But even after he had made the decision, or thought he had, he found himself sitting up on the rock and looking down into the water, and he knew that now, this moment, when his nose had only just stopped bleeding, when his head was still sore and throbbing—this was the moment when he would try. If he did not do it now, he never would. He was trembling with fear that he would not go, and he was trembling with horror at that long, long tunnel under the rock, under the sea. Even in the open sunlight, the barrier rock seemed very wide and very heavy; tons of rock pressed down on where he would go. If he died there, he would lie until one day—perhaps not before next year—those big boys would swim into it and find it blocked.

He put on his goggles, fitted them tight, tested the vacuum. His hands   35
were shaking. Then he chose the biggest stone he could carry and slipped over the edge of the rock until half of him was in the cool, enclosing water and half in the hot sun. He looked up once at the empty sky, filled his lungs once, twice, and then sank fast to the bottom with the stone. He let it go and began to count. He took the edges of the hole in his hands and drew himself into it, wriggling his shoulders in sidewise as he remembered he must, kicking himself along with his feet.

Soon he was clear inside. He was in a small rock-bound hole filled with yellowish-grey water. The water was pushing him up against the roof. The roof was sharp and pained his back. He pulled himself along with his hands—fast, fast—and used his legs as levers. His head knocked against something; a sharp pain dizzied him. Fifty, fifty-one, fifty-two. . . . He was without light, and the water seemed to press upon him with the weight of rock. Seventy-one, seventy-two. . . . There was no strain on his lungs. He felt like an inflated balloon, his lungs were so light and easy, but his head was pulsing.

He was being continually pressed against the sharp roof, which felt slimy as well as sharp. Again he thought of octopuses, and wondered if the tunnel might be filled with weed that could tangle him. He gave himself a panicky, convulsive kick forward, ducked his head, and swam. His feet and hands moved freely, as if in open water. The hole must have widened out.

He thought he must be swimming fast, and he was frightened of banging his head if the tunnel narrowed.

A hundred, a hundred and one. . . . The water paled. Victory filled him. His lungs were beginning to hurt. A few more strokes and he would be out. He was counting wildly; he said a hundred and fifteen, and then, a long time later, a hundred and fifteen again. The water was a clear jewel-green all around him. Then he saw, above his head, a crack running up through the rock. Sunlight was falling through it, showing the clean dark rock of the tunnel, a single mussel shell, and darkness ahead.

He was at the end of what he could do. He looked up at the crack as if it were filled with air and not water, as if he could put his mouth to it to draw in air. A hundred and fifteen, he heard himself say inside his head— but he had said that long ago. He must go on into the blackness ahead, or he would drown. His head was swelling, his lungs cracking. A hundred and fifteen, a hundred and fifteen pounded through his head, and he feebly clutched at rocks in the dark, pulling himself forward, leaving the brief space of sunlit water behind. He felt he was dying. He was no longer quite conscious. He struggled on in the darkness between lapses into unconsciousness. An immense, swelling pain filled his head, and then the darkness cracked with an explosion of green light. His hands, groping forward, met nothing, and his feet, kicking back, propelled him out into the open sea.

He drifted to the surface, his face turned up to the air. He was gasping   40
like a fish. He felt he would sink now and drown; he could not swim the few feet back to the rock. Then he was clutching it and pulling himself up on to it. He lay face down, gasping. He could see nothing but a red-veined, clotted dark. His eyes must have burst, he thought; they were full of blood. He tore off his goggles and a gout of blood went into the sea. His nose was bleeding, and the blood had filled the goggles.

He scooped up handfuls of water from the cool, salty sea, to splash on his face, and did not know whether it was blood or salt water he tasted. After a time, his heart quieted, his eyes cleared, and he sat up. He could see the local boys diving and playing half a mile away. He did not want them. He wanted nothing but to get back home and lie down.

In a short while, Jerry swam to shore and climbed slowly up the path to the villa. He flung himself on his bed and slept, waking at the sound of feet on the path outside. His mother was coming back. He rushed to the bathroom, thinking she must not see his face with bloodstains, or tearstains, on it. He came out of the bathroom and met her as she walked into the villa, smiling, her eyes lighting up.

"Have a nice morning?" she asked, laying her hand on his warm brown shoulder a moment.

"Oh, yes, thank you," he said.

"You look a bit pale." And then, sharp and anxious, "How did you   45
bang your head?"

"Oh, just banged it," he told her.

She looked at him closely. He was strained. His eyes were glazed-looking. She was worried. And then she said to herself, "Oh, don't fuss! Nothing can happen. He can swim like a fish."

They sat down to lunch together.

"Mummy," he said. "I can stay under water for two minutes—three minutes, at least." It came bursting out of him.

"Can you, darling?" she said. "Well, I shouldn't overdo it. I don't think   50 you ought to swim any more today."

She was ready for a battle of wills, but he gave in at once. It was no longer of the least importance to go to the bay.

Considerations

1. List several details from the opening section of the story that indicate the relationship between Jerry and his mother. Then, using these details as evidence, evaluate the relationship.
2. What comparison does Jerry make between his relationship with his mother and his relationship to the boys who dive from the rocks? Speculate on the ways this comparison might contribute to his decision to find and swim through the tunnel.
3. Trace the changes in Jerry's attitude toward his mother—and in her attitude toward him—throughout the story. Consider not only words and thoughts but also gestures and other actions.
4. What motivates Jerry's swim through the tunnel? When you were reading about the swim, did you think he might drown, or were you quite certain he would live? What details in the story led you to either prediction?
5. Describe a risk (physical, emotional, or intellectual) that you have taken. Explain your motives as well as the results of the risk-taking.

TILLIE OLSEN (1913–   )

I Stand Here Ironing

Born in Nebraska, Tillie Olsen left high school after her junior year, educating herself through wide reading in public libraries. In the 1930s she published many poems and prose writings. Her next published work was Tell Me a Riddle, *a 1956 short story collection that includes "I Stand Here Ironing." The years from the late 1930s until the late 1950s were filled with the work of raising a family. Her 1978 book* Silences *examines the forces that often keep women writers from their work, referring frequently to Olsen's own twenty-year hiatus. She has received the O. Henry Award and has taught at Amherst College, Stanford University, and MIT.*

I stand here ironing, and what you asked me moves tormented back and forth with the iron.

"I wish you would manage the time to come in and talk with me about your daughter. I'm sure you can help me understand her. She's a youngster who needs help and whom I'm deeply interested in helping."

"Who needs help." . . . Even if I came, what good would it do? You think because I am her mother I have a key, or that in some way you could use me as a key? She has lived for nineteen years. There is all that life that has happened outside of me, beyond me.

And when is there time to remember, to sift, to weigh, to estimate, to total? I will start and there will be an interruption and I will have to gather it all together again. Or I will become engulfed with all I did or did not do, with what should have been and what cannot be helped.

She was a beautiful baby. The first and only one of our five that was beautiful at birth. You do not guess how new and uneasy her tenancy in her now-loveliness. You did not know her all those years she was thought homely, or see her poring over her baby pictures, making me tell her over and over how beautiful she had been—and would be, I would tell her—and was now, to the seeing eye. But the seeing eyes were few or nonexistent. Including mine.

I nursed her. They feel that's important nowadays. I nursed all the children, but with her, with all the fierce rigidity of first motherhood, I did like the books then said. Though her cries battered me to trembling and my breasts ached with swollenness, I waited till the clock decreed.

Why do I put that first? I do not even know if it matters, or if it explains anything.

She was a beautiful baby. She blew shining bubbles of sound. She loved motion, loved light, loved color and music and textures. She would lie on the floor in her blue overalls patting the surface so hard in ecstasy her hands and feet would blur. She was a miracle to me, but when she was eight months old I had to leave her daytimes with the woman downstairs to whom she was no miracle at all, for I worked or looked for work and for Emily's father, who "could no longer endure" (he wrote in his good-bye note) "sharing want with us."

I was nineteen. It was the pre-relief, pre-WPA world of the depression. I would start running as soon as I got off the streetcar, running up the stairs, the place smelling sour, and awake or asleep to startle awake, when she saw me she would break into a clogged weeping that could not be comforted, a weeping I can hear yet.

After a while I found a job hashing at night so I could be with her   10
days, and it was better. But it came to where I had to bring her to his family and leave her.

It took a long time to raise the money for her fare back. Then she got chicken pox and I had to wait longer. When she finally came, I hardly knew her, walking quick and nervous like her father, looking like her father, thin, and dressed in a shoddy red that yellowed her skin and glared at the pock-marks. All the baby loveliness gone.

She was two. Old enough for nursery school they said, and I did not know then what I know now—the fatigue of the long day, and the lacerations of group life in the kinds of nurseries that are only parking places for children.

Except that it would have made no difference if I had known. It was the only place there was. It was the only way we could be together, the only way I could hold a job.

And even without knowing, I knew. I knew the teacher that was evil because all these years it has curdled into my memory, the little boy hunched in the corner, her rasp, "why aren't you outside, because Alvin hits you? that's no reason, go out, scaredy." I knew Emily hated it even if she did not clutch and implore "don't go Mommy" like the other children, mornings.

She always had a reason why we should stay home. Momma, you look   15
sick. Momma, I feel sick. Momma, the teachers aren't there today, they're sick. Momma, we can't go, there was a fire there last night. Momma, it's a holiday today, no school, they told me.

But never a direct protest, never rebellion. I think of our others in their three-, four-year-oldness—the explosions, the tempers, the denunciations, the demands—and I feel suddenly ill. I put the iron down. What in me demanded that goodness in her? And what was the cost, the cost to her of such goodness?

The old man living in the back once said in his gentle way: "You should smile at Emily more when you look at her." What *was* in my face when I looked at her? I loved her. There were all the acts of love.

It was only with the others I remembered what he said, and it was the face of joy, and not of care or tightness or worry I turned to them—too late for Emily. She does not smile easily, let alone almost always as her brothers and sisters do. Her face is closed and sombre, but when she wants, how fluid. You must have seen it in her pantomimes, you spoke of her rare gift for comedy on the stage that rouses a laughter out of the audience so dear they applaud and applaud and do not want to let her go.

Where does it come from, that comedy? There was none of it in her when she came back to me that second time, after I had had to send her away again. She had a new daddy now to learn to love, and I think perhaps it was a better time.

Except when we left her alone nights, telling ourselves she was old 20 enough.

"Can't you go some other time, Mommy, like tomorrow?" she would ask. "Will it be just a little while you'll be gone? Do you promise?"

The time we came back, the front door open, the clock on the floor in the hall. She rigid awake. "It wasn't just a little while. I didn't cry. Three times I called you, just three times, and then I ran downstairs to open the door so you could come faster. The clock talked loud. I threw it away, it scared me what it talked."

She said the clock talked loud again that night I went to the hospital to have Susan. She was delirious with the fever that comes before red measles, but she was fully conscious all the week I was gone and the week after we were home when she could not come near the new baby or me.

She did not get well. She stayed skeleton thin, not wanting to eat, and night after night she had nightmares. She would call for me, and I would rouse from exhaustion to sleepily call back: "You're all right, darling, go to sleep, it's just a dream," and if she still called, in a sterner voice, "now go to sleep, Emily, there's nothing to hurt you." Twice, only twice, when I had to get up for Susan anyhow, I went in to sit with her.

Now when it is too late (as if she would let me hold and comfort her 25 like I do the others) I get up and go to her at once at her moan or restless stirring. "Are you awake, Emily? Can I get you something?" And the answer is always the same: "No, I'm all right, go back to sleep, Mother."

They persuaded me at the clinic to send her away to a convalescent home in the country where "she can have the kind of food and care you can't manage for her, and you'll be free to concentrate on the new baby." They still send children to that place. I see pictures on the society page of sleek young women planning affairs to raise money for it, or dancing at the affairs, or decorating Easter eggs or filling Christmas stockings for the children.

They never have a picture of the children so I do not know if the girls still wear those gigantic red bows and the ravaged looks on the every other Sunday when the parents can come to visit "unless otherwise notified"—as we were notified the first six weeks.

Oh it is a handsome place, green lawns and tall trees and fluted flower beds. High up on the balconies of each cottage the children stand, the girls in their red bows and white dresses, the boys in white suits and giant red ties. The parents stand below shrieking up to be heard and the children shriek down to be heard, and between them the invisible wall "Not To Be Contaminated by Parental Germs or Physical Affection."

There was a tiny girl who always stood hand in hand with Emily. Her parents never came. One visit she was gone. "They moved her to Rose Cottage" Emily shouted in explanation. "They don't like you to love anybody here."

She wrote once a week, the labored writing of a seven-year-old. "I am   30 fine. How is the baby. If I write my leter nicely I will have a star. Love." There never was a star. We wrote every other day, letters she could never hold or keep but only hear read—once. "We simply do not have room for children to keep any personal possessions," they patiently explained when we pieced one Sunday's shrieking together to plead how much it would mean to Emily, who loved so to keep things, to be allowed to keep her letters and cards.

Each visit she looked frailer. "She isn't eating," they told us.

(They had runny eggs for breakfast or mush with lumps, Emily said later, I'd hold it in my mouth and not swallow. Nothing ever tasted good, just when they had chicken.)

It took us eight months to get her released home, and only the fact that she gained back so little of her seven lost pounds convinced the social worker.

I used to try to hold and love her after she came back, but her body would stay stiff, and after a while she'd push away. She ate little. Food sickened her, and I think much of life too. Oh she had physical lightness and brightness, twinkling by on skates, bouncing like a ball up and down up and down over the jump rope, skimming over the hill; but these were momentary.

She fretted about her appearance, thin and dark and foreign-looking at   35 a time when every little girl was supposed to look or thought she should look a chubby blonde replica of Shirley Temple. The doorbell sometimes rang for her, but no one seemed to come and play in the house or be a best friend. Maybe because we moved so much.

There was a boy she loved painfully through two school semesters. Months later she told me how she had taken pennies from my purse to buy him candy. "Licorice was his favorite and I brought him some every day, but he still liked Jennifer better'n me. Why, Mommy?" The kind of question for which there is no answer.

School was a worry to her. She was not glib or quick in a world where glibness and quickness were easily confused with ability to learn. To her overworked and exasperated teachers she was an overconscientious "slow learner" who kept trying to catch up and was absent entirely too often.

I let her be absent, though sometimes the illness was imaginary. How different from my now-strictness about attendance with the others. I wasn't working. We had a new baby, I was home anyhow. Sometimes, after Susan grew old enough, I would keep her home from school, too, to have them all together.

Mostly Emily had asthma, and her breathing, harsh and labored, would fill the house with a curiously tranquil sound. I would bring the two old dresser mirrors and her boxes of collections to her bed. She would select beads and single earrings, bottle tops and shells, dried flowers and pebbles, old postcards and scraps, all sorts of oddments; then she and Susan would play Kingdom, setting up landscapes and furniture, peopling them with action.

Those were the only times of peaceful companionship between her and Susan. I have edged away from it, that poisonous feeling between them, that terrible balancing of hurts and needs I had to do between the two, and did so badly, those earlier years.

Oh there are conflicts between the others too, each one human, needing, demanding, hurting, taking—but only between Emily and Susan, no, Emily toward Susan that corroding resentment. It seems so obvious on the surface, yet it is not obvious. Susan, the second child, Susan, golden- and curly-haired and chubby, quick and articulate and assured, everything in appearance and manner Emily was not; Susan, not able to resist Emily's precious things, losing or sometimes clumsily breaking them; Susan telling jokes and riddles to company for applause while Emily sat silent (to say to me later; that was *my* riddle, Mother, I told it to Susan); Susan, who for all the five years' difference in age was just a year behind Emily in developing physically.

I am glad for that slow physical development that widened the difference between her and her contemporaries, though she suffered over it. She was too vulnerable for that terrible world of youthful competition, of preening and parading, of constant measuring of yourself against every other, of envy, "If I had that copper hair," "If I had that skin. . . ." She tormented herself enough about not looking like the others, there was enough of the unsureness, the having to be conscious of words before you speak, the constant caring—what are they thinking of me? without having it all magnified by the merciless physical drives.

Ronnie is calling. He is wet and I change him. It is rare there is such a cry now. That time of motherhood is almost behind me when the ear is not one's own but must always be racked and listening for the child cry, the child call. We sit for a while and I hold him, looking out over the city spread in charcoal with its soft aisles of light. "*Shoogily,*" he breathes and curls closer. I carry him back to bed, asleep. *Shoogily.* A funny word, a family word, inherited from Emily, invented by her to say: *comfort.*

In this and other ways she leaves her seal, I say aloud. And startle at my saying it. What do I mean? What did I start to gather together, to try and make coherent? I was at the terrible, growing years. War years. I do not remember them well. I was working, there were four smaller ones now, there was not time for her. She had to help be a mother, and housekeeper, and shopper. She had to set her seal. Mornings of crisis and near hysteria trying to get lunches packed, hair combed, coats and shoes found, everyone to school or Child Care on time, the baby ready for transportation. And always the paper scribbled on by a smaller one, the book looked at by Susan then mislaid, the homework not done. Running out to that huge school where she was one, she was lost, she was a drop; suffering over the unpreparedness, stammering and unsure in her classes.

There was so little time left at night after the kids were bedded down.   45
She would struggle over books, always eating (it was in those years she developed her enormous appetite that is legendary in our family) and I would be ironing, or preparing food for the next day, or writing V-mail to Bill, or tending the baby. Sometimes, to make me laugh, or out of her despair, she would imitate happenings or types at school.

I think I said once: "Why don't you do something like this in the school amateur show?" One morning she phoned me at work, hardly understandable through the weeping: "Mother, I did it. I won, I won; they gave me first prize; they clapped and clapped and wouldn't let me go."

Now suddenly she was Somebody, and as imprisoned in her difference as she had been in anonymity.

She began to be asked to perform at other high schools, even in colleges, then at city and statewide affairs. The first one we went to, I only recognized her that first moment when thin, shy, she almost drowned herself into the curtains. Then: Was this Emily? The control, the command, the convulsing and deadly clowning, the spell, then the roaring, stamping audience, unwilling to let this rare and precious laughter out of their lives.

Afterwards: You ought to do something about her with a gift like that— but without money or knowing how, what does one do? We have left it all to her, and the gift has as often eddied inside, clogged and clotted, as been used and growing.

She is coming. She runs up the stairs two at a time with her light   50
graceful step, and I know she is happy tonight. Whatever it was that occasioned your call did not happen today.

"Aren't you ever going to finish the ironing, Mother? Whistler painted his mother in a rocker. I'd have to paint mine standing over an ironing board." This is one of her communicative nights and she tells me everything and nothing as she fixes herself a plate of food out of the icebox.

She is so lovely. Why did you want me to come in at all? Why were you concerned? She will find her way.

She starts up the stairs to bed. "Don't get me up with the rest in the morning." "But I thought you were having midterms." "Oh, those," she comes back in, kisses me, and says quite lightly, "in a couple of years when we'll all be atom-dead they won't matter a bit."

She has said it before. She *believes* it. But because I have been dredging the past, and all that compounds a human being is so heavy and meaningful in me, I cannot endure it tonight.

I will never total it all. I will never come in to say: She was a child   55
seldom smiled at. Her father left me before she was a year old. I had to work her first six years when there was work, or I sent her home and to his relatives. There were years she had care she hated. She was dark and thin and foreign-looking in a world where the prestige went to blondeness and curly

hair and dimples, she was slow where glibness was prized. She was a child of anxious, not proud, love. We were poor and could not afford for her the soil of easy growth. I was a young mother, I was a distracted mother. There were the other children pushing up, demanding. Her younger sister seemed all that she was not. There were years she did not want me to touch her. She kept too much in herself, her life was such she had to keep too much in herself. My wisdom came too late. She has much to her and probably little will come of it. She is a child of her age, of depression, of war, of fear.

Let her be. So all that is in her will not bloom—but in how many does it? There is still enough left to live by. Only help her to know—help make it so there is cause for her to know—that she is more than this dress on the ironing board, helpless before the iron.

Considerations

1. What incident prompts the mother's long meditation as she stands at the ironing board? How does this incident suggest the relationship between the mother, her daughter, and the authority figures who have, to one degree or another, controlled the lives of both mother and daughter?
2. Make a list of the circumstances the mother sees as having prevented her from taking care of her children as she would have liked. To what extent do you find her explanations valid? To what extent do you find her explanations to be rationalizations?
3. The act of ironing is mentioned in the title, in the opening section, and in the conclusion. How does ironing serve as a metaphor for the mother's life? How does the mother use ironing as a metaphor to suggest the hopes she holds for her daughter's life?
4. How has Emily been affected by the circumstances of her life? Have the effects of these circumstances been entirely negative? Entirely positive?
5. Imagine that you are Emily and you have come across "I Stand Here Ironing" written as a meditation in the diary your mother has left open on the dining room table. Write a response to the feelings and ideas she has expressed.

EUDORA WELTY (1909–   )

A Worn Path

Eudora Welty was born in Jackson, Mississippi, and has spent nearly her whole life in the South. In her mid-twenties, she began to publish stories in the Southern Review *and the* Atlantic Monthly, *and during World War II she was a staff member of the* New York Times Book Review. *She has written many collections of short fiction, and her novel* The Optimist's Daughter *won the Pulitzer Prize in 1972. In the preface to her collected stories, published in 1980, Welty said, "I have been told, both in approval and in accusation, that I seem to love all my characters. What I do in writing of any character is to try to enter into the mind, heart, and skin of a human being who is not myself. Whether this happens to be a man or a woman, old or young, with skin black or white, the primary challenge lies in making the jump itself. It is the act of a writer's imagination that I set most high." "A Worn Path" was first published in 1941.*

It was December—a bright frozen day in the early morning. Far out in the country there was an old Negro woman with her head tied in a red rag, coming along a path through the pinewoods. Her name was Phoenix Jackson. She was very old and small and she walked slowly in the dark pine shadows, moving a little from side to side in her steps, with the balanced heaviness and lightness of a pendulum in a grandfather clock. She carried a thin, small cane made from an umbrella, and with this she kept tapping the frozen earth in front of her. This made a grave and persistent noise in the still air, that seemed meditative like the chirping of a solitary little bird.

She wore a dark striped dress reaching down to her shoetops, and an equally long apron of bleached sugar sacks, with a full pocket; all neat and tidy, but every time she took a step she might have fallen over her shoelaces, which dragged from her unlaced shoes. She looked straight ahead. Her eyes were blue with age. Her skin had a pattern all its own of numberless branching wrinkles and as though a whole little tree stood in the middle of her forehead, but a golden color ran underneath, and the two knobs of her cheeks were illuminated by a yellow burning under the dark. Under the red rag her hair came down on her neck in the frailest of ringlets, still black, and with an odor like copper.

Now and then there was a quivering in the thicket. Old Phoenix said, "Out of my way, all you foxes, owls, beetles, jack rabbits, coons, and wild animals! . . . Keep out from under these feet, little bobwhites. . . . Keep the big wild hogs out of my path. Don't let none of those come running my direction. I got a long way." Under her small black-freckled hand her cane, limber as a buggy whip, would switch at the brush as if to rouse up any hiding things.

On she went. The woods were deep and still. The sun made the pine needles almost too bright to look at, up where the wind rocked. The cones dropped as light as feathers. Down in the hollow was the mourning dove— it was not too late for him.

The path ran up a hill. "Seems like there is chains about my feet, time 5
I get this far," she said, in the voice of argument old people keep to use with themselves. "Something always take a hold on this hill—pleads I should stay."

After she got to the top she turned and gave a full, severe look behind her where she had come. "Up through pines," she said at length. "Now down through oaks."

Her eyes opened their widest and she started down gently. But before she got to the bottom of the hill a bush caught her dress.

Her fingers were busy and intent, but her skirts were full and long, so that before she could pull them free in one place they were caught in another. It was not possible to allow the dress to tear. "I in the thorny bush," she said. "Thorns, you doing your appointed work. Never want to let folks pass—no sir. Old eyes thought you was a pretty little green bush."

Finally, trembling all over, she stood free, and after a moment dared to stoop for her cane.

"Sun so high!" she cried, leaning back and looking, while the thick 10
tears went over her eyes. "The time getting all gone here."

At the foot of this hill was a place where a log was laid across the creek.

"Now comes the trial," said Phoenix.

Putting her right foot out, she mounted the log and shut her eyes. Lifting her skirt, levelling her cane fiercely before her, like a festival figure in some parade, she began to march across. Then she opened her eyes and she was safe on the other side.

"I wasn't as old as I thought," she said.

But she sat down to rest. She spread her skirts on the bank around her 15
and folded her hands over her knees. Up above her was a tree in a pearly cloud of mistletoe. She did not dare to close her eyes, and when a little boy brought her a little plate with a slice of marble-cake on it she spoke to him. "That would be acceptable," she said. But when she went to take it there was just her own hand in the air.

So she left that tree, and had to go through a barbed-wire fence. There she had to creep and crawl, spreading her knees and stretching her fingers like a baby trying to climb the steps. But she talked loudly to herself: she could not let her dress be torn now, so late in the day, and she could not pay for having her arm or her leg sawed off if she got caught fast where she was.

At last she was safe through the fence and risen up out in the clearing. Big dead trees, like black men with one arm, were standing in the purple stalks of the withered cotton field. There sat a buzzard.

"Who you watching?"

In the burrow she made her way along.

"Glad this not the season for bulls," she said, looking sideways, "and   20
the good Lord made his snakes to curl up and sleep in the winter. A pleasure
I don't see no two-headed snake coming around that tree, where it come
once. It took a while to get by him, back in the summer."

She passed through the old cotton and went into a field of dead corn.
It whispered and shook, and was taller than her head. "Through the maze
now," she said, for there was no path.

Then there was something tall, black, and skinny there, moving before her.

At first she took it for a man. It could have been a man dancing in the
field. But she stood still and listened, and it did not make a sound. It was as
silent as a ghost.

"Ghost," she said sharply, "who be you the ghost of? For I have heard
of nary death close by."

But there was no answer, only the ragged dancing in the wind.   25

She shut her eyes, reached out her hand, and touched a sleeve. She
found a coat and inside that an emptiness, cold as ice.

"You scarecrow," she said. Her face lighted. "I ought to be shut up
for good," she said with laughter. "My senses is gone. I too old. I the oldest people I ever know. Dance, old scarecrow," she said, "while I dancing
with you."

She kicked her foot over the furrow, and with mouth drawn down
shook her head once or twice in a little strutting way. Some husks blew
down and whirled in streamers about her skirts.

Then she went on, parting her way from side to side with the cane,
through the whispering field. At last she came to the end, to a wagon track,
where the silver grass blew between the red ruts. The quail were walking
around like pullets, seeming all dainty and unseen.

"Walk pretty," she said. "This the easy place. This the easy going."   30

She followed the track, swaying through the quiet bare fields, through
the little strings of trees silver in their dead leaves, past cabins silver from
weather, with the doors and windows boarded shut, all like old women
under a spell sitting there. "I walking in their sleep," she said, nodding her
head vigorously.

In a ravine she went where a spring was silently flowing through a
hollow log. Old Phoenix bent and drank. "Sweetgum makes the water
sweet," she said, and drank more. "Nobody knows who made this well, for
it was here when I was born."

The track crossed a swampy part where the moss hung as white as lace
from every limb. "Sleep on, alligators, and blow your bubbles." Then the
track went into the road.

Deep, deep the road went down between the high green-colored
banks. Overhead the live-oaks met, and it was as dark as a cave.

A black dog with a lolling tongue came up out of the weeds by the   35
ditch. She was meditating, and not ready, and when he came at her she only

hit him a little with her cane. Over she went in the ditch, like a little puff of milk–weed.

Down there, her senses drifted away. A dream visited her, and she reached her hand up, but nothing reached down and gave her a pull. So she lay there and presently went to talking. "Old woman," she said to herself, "that black dog came up out of the weeds to stall you off, and now there he sitting on his fine tail, smiling at you."

A white man finally came along and found her—a hunter, a young man, with his dog on a chain.

"Well, Granny!" he laughed. "What are you doing there?"

"Lying on my back like a June-bug waiting to be turned over, mister," she said, reaching up her hand.

He lifted her up, gave her a swing in the air, and set her down, "Any-   40 thing broken, Granny?"

"No sir, them old dead weeds is springy enough," said Phoenix, when she had got her breath. "I thank you for your trouble."

"Where do you live, Granny?" he asked, while the two dogs were growling at each other.

"Away back yonder, sir, behind the ridge. You can't even see it from here."

"On your way home?"

"No, sir, I going to town."   45

"Why, that's too far! That's as far as I walk when I come out myself, and I get something for my trouble." He patted the stuffed bag he carried, and there hung down a little closed claw. It was one of the bobwhites, with its beak hooked bitterly to show it was dead. "Now you go on home, Granny!"

"I bound to go to town, mister," said Phoenix. "The time come around."

He gave another laugh, filling the whole landscape. "I know you colored people! Wouldn't miss going to town to see Santa Claus!"

But something held Old Phoenix very still. The deep lines in her face went into a fierce and different radiation. Without warning she had seen with her own eyes a flashing nickel fall out of the man's pocket on to the ground.

"How old are you, Granny?" he was saying.   50

"There is no telling, mister," she said, "no telling."

Then she gave a little cry and clapped her hands, and said, "Git on away from here, dog! Look at that dog!" She laughed as if in admiration. "He ain't scared of nobody. He a big black dog." She whispered, "Sick him!"

"Watch me get rid of that cur," said the man. "Sick him, Pete! Sick him!"

Phoenix heard the dogs fighting and heard the man running and throwing sticks. She even heard a gunshot. But she was slowly bending forward by that time, further and further forward, the lids stretched down over her eyes, as if she were doing this in her sleep. Her chin was lowered almost to her knees. The yellow palm of her hand came out from the fold of her apron. Her fingers slid down and along the ground under the piece of money with the grace and care they would have in lifting an egg from under a sitting hen. Then she slowly straightened up, she stood erect, and the nickel was in her apron pocket. A bird flew by. Her lips moved. "God watching me the whole time. I come to stealing."

The man came back, and his own dog panted about them. "Well, I   55
scared him off that time," he said, and then he laughed and lifted his gun and pointed it at Phoenix.

She stood straight and faced him.

"Doesn't the gun scare you?" he said, still pointing it.

"No, sir, I seen plenty go off closer by, in my day, and for less than what I done," she said, holding utterly still.

He smiled, and shouldered the gun. "Well, Granny," he said, "you must be a hundred years old and scared of nothing. I'd give you a dime if I had any money with me. But you take my advice and stay home, and nothing will happen to you."

"I bound to go on my way, mister," said Phoenix. She inclined her   60
head in the red rag. Then they went in different directions, but she could hear the gun shooting again and again over the hill.

She walked on. The shadows hung from the oak trees to the road like curtains. Then she smelled wood-smoke, and smelled the river, and she saw a steeple and the cabins on their steep steps. Dozens of little black children whirled around her. There ahead was Natchez shining. Bells were ringing. She walked on.

In the paved city it was Christmas time. There were red and green electric lights strung and crisscrossed everywhere, and all turned on in the daytime. Old Phoenix would have been lost if she had not distrusted her eyesight and depended on her feet to know where to take her.

She paused quietly on the sidewalk, where people were passing by. A lady came along in the crowd, carrying an armful of red-, green-, and silver-wrapped presents; she gave off perfume like the red roses in hot summer, and Phoenix stopped her.

"Please, missy, will you lace up my shoe?" She held up her foot.

"What do you want, Grandma?"   65

"See my shoe," said Phoenix. "Do all right for out in the country, but wouldn't look right to go in a big building."

"Stand still then, Grandma," said the lady. She put her packages down carefully on the sidewalk beside her and laced and tied both shoes tightly.

"Can't lace 'em with a cane," said Phoenix. "Thank you, missy. I doesn't mind asking a nice lady to tie up my shoe when I gets out on the street."

Moving slowly and from side to side, she went into the stone building and into a tower of steps, where she walked up and around and around until her feet knew to stop.

She entered a door, and there she saw nailed up on the wall the docu‑   70
ment that had been stamped with the gold seal and framed in the gold frame
which matched the dream that was hung up in her head.

"Here I be," she said. There was a fixed and ceremonial stiffness over
her body.

"A charity case, I suppose," said an attendant who sat at the desk be‑
fore her.

But Phoenix only looked above her head. There was sweat on her face;
the wrinkles shone like a bright net.

"Speak up, Grandma," the woman said. "What's your name? We must
have your history, you know. Have you been here before? What seems to be
the trouble with you?"

Old Phoenix only gave a twitch to her face as if a fly were bothering her.   75

"Are you deaf?" cried the attendant.

But then the nurse came in.

"Oh, that's just old Aunt Phoenix," she said. "She doesn't come for
herself—she has a little grandson. She makes these trips just as regular as
clockwork. She lives away back off the Old Natchez Trace." She bent down.
"Well, Aunt Phoenix, why don't you just take a seat? We won't keep you
standing after your long trip." She pointed.

The old woman sat down, bolt upright in the chair.

"Now, how is the boy?" asked the nurse.   80

Old Phoenix did not speak.

"I said, how is the boy?"

But Phoenix only waited and stared straight ahead, her face very sol‑
emn and withdrawn into rigidity.

"Is his throat any better?" asked the nurse. "Aunt Phoenix, don't you
hear me? Is your grandson's throat any better since the last time you came
for the medicine?"

With her hand on her knees, the old woman waited, silent, erect and   85
motionless, just as if she were in armor.

"You mustn't take up our time this way, Aunt Phoenix," the nurse said.
"Tell us quickly about your grandson, and get it over. He isn't dead, is he?"

At last there came a flicker and then a flame of comprehension across
her face, and she spoke.

"My grandson. It was my memory had left me. There I sat and forgot
why I made my long trip."

"Forgot?" The nurse frowned. "After you came so far?"

Then Phoenix was like an old woman begging a dignified forgiveness   90
for waking up frightened in the night. "I never did go to school—I was too
old at the Surrender," she said in a soft voice. "I'm an old woman without
an education. It was my memory fail me. My little grandson, he is just the
same, and I forgot it in the coming."

"Throat never heals, does it?" said the nurse, speaking in a loud, sure
voice to Old Phoenix. By now she had a card with something written on it,

a little list. "Yes. Swallowed lye. When was it—January—two—three years ago—"

Phoenix spoke unasked now. "No, missy, he not dead, he just the same. Every little while his throat begin to close up again, and he not able to swallow. He not get his breath. He not able to help himself. So the time come around, and I go on another trip for the soothing-medicine."

"All right. The doctor said as long as you came to get it you could have it," said the nurse. "But it's an obstinate case."

"My little grandson, he sit up there in the house all wrapped up, waiting by himself," Phoenix went on. "We is the only two left in the world. He suffer and it don't seem to put him back at all. He got a sweet look. He going to last. He wear a little patch quilt and peep out, holding his mouth open like a little bird. I remembers so plain now. I not going to forget him again, no, the whole enduring time. I could tell him from all the others in creation."

"All right." The nurse was trying to hush her now. She brought her a   95
bottle of medicine. "Charity," she said, making a check mark in a book.

Old Phoenix held the bottle close to her eyes and then carefully put it into her pocket.

"I thank you," she said.

"It's Christmas time, Grandma," said the attendant. "Could I give you a few pennies out of my purse?"

"Five pennies is a nickel," said Phoenix stiffly.

"Here's a nickel," said the attendant.   100

Phoenix rose carefully and held out her hand. She received the nickel and then fished the other nickel out of her pocket and laid it beside the new one. She stared at her palm closely, with her head on one side.

Then she gave a tap with her cane on the floor.

"This is what come to me to do," she said. "I going to the store and buy my child a little windmill they sells, made out of paper. He going to find it hard to believe there such a thing in the world. I'll march myself back where he waiting, holding it straight up in this hand."

She lifted her free hand, gave a little nod, turned round, and walked out of the doctor's office. Then her slow step began on the stairs, going down.

Considerations

1. Discuss the significance of the title. Welty labels the path "worn," yet it often seems overgrown and difficult to pass through.
2. Describe Phoenix's responses to the white people she encounters on her journey. What do these brief meetings suggest about her? About the people she meets?
3. Describe Phoenix from the point of view of the hunter or the nurse at the clinic.

4. Research Phoenix's name, and discuss the relationship between the legend of the phoenix and the journey described in the story.
5. Comment on the story's ending. How is it related to the rest of the story? Consider especially any possible irony in the setting and action.

FLANNERY O'CONNOR (1925–1964)

A Good Man Is Hard to Find

Flannery O'Connor was raised in a devout Catholic family, living in Savannah, Georgia, an area whose population was mainly Protestant. Georgia and its rural population provide the focus of her thirty-one stories and two novels. The conflict that her characters most often face is their struggle to find connection with spirituality in the midst of a society dominated by a secular, materialistic culture. In 1951, O'Connor became seriously ill with lupus, yet she continued to write and publish until her untimely death at the age of 39. "A Good Man Is Hard to Find" was the title story in a volume of short fiction published in 1955.

The grandmother didn't want to go to Florida. She wanted to visit some of her connections in east Tennessee and she was seizing at every chance to change Bailey's mind. Bailey was the son she lived with, her only boy. He was sitting on the edge of his chair at the table, bent over the orange sports section of the *Journal.* "Now look here, Bailey," she said, "see here, read this," and she stood with one hand on her thin hip and the other rattling the newspaper at his bald head. "Here this fellow that calls himself The Misfit is aloose from the Federal Pen and headed toward Florida and you read here what it says he did to these people. Just you read it. I wouldn't take my children in any direction with a criminal like that aloose in it. I couldn't answer to my conscience if I did."

Bailey didn't look up from his reading so she wheeled around then and faced the children's mother, a young woman in slacks, whose face was as broad and innocent as a cabbage and was tied around with a green headkerchief that had two points on the top like rabbit's ears. She was sitting on the sofa, feeding the baby his apricots out of a jar. "The children have been to Florida before," the old lady said. "You all ought to take them somewhere else for a change so they would see different parts of the world and be broad. They never have been to east Tennessee."

The children's mother didn't seem to hear her but the eight-year-old boy, John Wesley, a stocky child with glasses, said, "If you don't want to go to Florida, why dontcha stay at home?" He and the little girl, June Star, were reading the funny papers on the floor.

"She wouldn't stay at home to be queen for a day," June Star said without raising her yellow head.

"Yes and what would you do if this fellow, The Misfit, caught you?" the grandmother asked.   5

"I'd smack his face," John Wesley said.

"She wouldn't stay at home for a million bucks," June Star said. "Afraid she'd miss something. She has to go everywhere we go."

"All right, Miss," the grandmother said. "Just remember that the next time you want me to curl your hair."

June Star said her hair was naturally curly.

The next morning the grandmother was the first one in the car, ready   10
to go. She had her big black valise that looked like the head of a hippopotamus in one corner, and underneath it she was hiding a basket with Pitty Sing, the cat, in it. She didn't intend for the cat to be left alone in the house for three days because he would miss her too much and she was afraid he might brush against one of her gas burners and accidentally asphyxiate himself. Her son, Bailey, didn't like to arrive at a motel with a cat.

She sat in the middle of the back seat with John Wesley and June Star on either side of her. Bailey and the children's mother and the baby sat in front and they left Atlanta at eight forty-five with the mileage on the car at 55890. The grandmother wrote this down because she thought it would be interesting to say how many miles they had been when they got back. It took them twenty minutes to reach the outskirts of the city.

The old lady settled herself comfortably, removing her white cotton gloves and putting them up with her purse on the shelf in front of the back window. The children's mother still had on slacks and still had her head tied up in a green kerchief, but the grandmother had on a navy blue straw sailor hat with a bunch of white violets on the brim and a navy blue dress with a small white dot in the print. Her collars and cuffs were white organdy trimmed with lace and at her neckline she had pinned a purple spray of cloth violets containing a sachet. In case of an accident, anyone seeing her dead on the highway would know at once that she was a lady.

She said she thought it was going to be a good day for driving, neither too hot nor too cold, and she cautioned Bailey that the speed limit was fifty-five miles an hour and that the patrolmen hid themselves behind billboards and small clumps of trees and sped out after you before you had a chance to slow down. She pointed out interesting details of the scenery: Stone Mountain; the blue granite that in some places came up to both sides of the highway; the brilliant red clay banks slightly streaked with purple; and the various crops that made rows of green lace-work on the ground. The trees were full of silver-white sunlight and the meanest of them sparkled. The children were reading comic magazines and their mother had gone back to sleep.

"Let's go through Georgia fast so we won't have to look at it much," John Wesley said.

"If I were a little boy," said the grandmother, "I wouldn't talk about   15
my native state that way. Tennessee has the mountains and Georgia has the hills."

"Tennessee is just a hillbilly dumping ground," John Wesley said, "and Georgia is a lousy state too."

"You said it," June Star said.

"In my time," said the grandmother, folding her thin veined fingers, "children were more respectful of their native states and their parents and everything else. People did right then. Oh look at the cute little pickaninny!"

she said and pointed to a Negro child standing in the door of a shack. "Wouldn't that make a picture, now?" she asked and they all turned and looked at the little Negro out of the back window. He waved.

"He didn't have any britches on," June Star said.

"He probably didn't have any," the grandmother explained. "Little nig- 20 gers in the country don't have things like we do. If I could paint, I'd paint that picture," she said.

The children exchanged comic books.

The grandmother offered to hold the baby and the children's mother passed him over the front seat to her. She set him on her knee and bounced him and told him about the things they were passing. She rolled her eyes and screwed up her mouth and stuck her leathery thin face into his smooth bland one. Occasionally he gave her a faraway smile. They passed a large cotton field with five or six graves fenced in the middle of it, like a small island. "Look at the graveyard!" the grandmother said, pointing it out. "That was the old family burying ground. That belonged to the plantation."

"Where's the plantation?" John Wesley asked.

"Gone With the Wind," said the grandmother. "Ha. Ha."

When the children finished all the comic books they had brought, they 25 opened the lunch and ate it. The grandmother ate a peanut butter sandwich and an olive and would not let the children throw the box and the paper napkins out the window. When there was nothing else to do they played a game by choosing a cloud and making the other two guess what shape it suggested. John Wesley took one the shape of a cow and June Star guessed a cow and John Wesley said, no, an automobile, and June Star said he didn't play fair, and they began to slap each other over the grandmother.

The grandmother said she would tell them a story if they would keep quiet. When she told a story, she rolled her eyes and waved her head and was very dramatic. She said once when she was a maiden lady she had been courted by a Mr. Edgar Atkins Teagarden from Jasper, Georgia. She said he was a very good-looking man and a gentleman and that he brought her a watermelon every Saturday afternoon with his initials cut in it, E. A. T. Well, one Saturday, she said, Mr. Teagarden brought the watermelon and there was nobody at home and he left it on the front porch and returned in his buggy to Jasper, but she never got the watermelon, she said, because a nigger boy ate it when he saw the initials, E.A.T.! This story tickled John Wesley's funny bone and he giggled and giggled but June Star didn't think it was any good. She said she wouldn't marry a man that just brought her a watermelon on Saturday. The grandmother said she would have done well to marry Mr. Teagarden because he was a gentleman and had bought Coca-Cola stock when it first came out and that he had died only a few years ago, a very wealthy man.

They stopped at The Tower for barbecued sandwiches. The Tower was a part stucco and part wood filling station and dance hall set in a clearing outside of Timothy. A fat man named Red Sammy Butts ran it and there

were signs stuck here and there on the building and for miles up and down the
highway saying, TRY RED SAMMY'S FAMOUS BARBECUE. NONE
LIKE FAMOUS RED SAMMY'S! RED SAM! THE FAT BOY WITH
THE HAPPY LAUGH. A VETERAN! RED SAMMY'S YOUR MAN!

Red Sammy was lying on the bare ground outside The Tower with his
head under a truck while a gray monkey about a foot high, chained to a
small chinaberry tree, chattered nearby. The monkey sprang back into the
tree and got on the highest limb as soon as he saw the children jump out of
the car and run toward him.

Inside, The Tower was a long dark room with a counter at one end
and tables at the other and dancing space in the middle. They all sat down at
a board table next to the nickelodeon and Red Sam's wife, a tall burnt-brown
woman with hair and eyes lighter than her skin, came and took their order.
The children's mother put a dime in the machine and played "The Tennessee
Waltz," and the grandmother said that tune always made her want to dance.
She asked Bailey if he would like to dance but he only glared at her. He
didn't have a naturally sunny disposition like she did and trips made him
nervous. The grandmother's brown eyes were very bright. She swayed her
head from side to side and pretended she was dancing in her chair. June Star
said play something she could tap to so the children's mother put in another
dime and played a fast number and June Star stepped out onto the dance
floor and did her tap routine.

"Ain't she cute?" Red Sam's wife said, leaning over the counter. "Would   30
you like to come be my little girl?"

"No I certainly wouldn't," June Star said. "I wouldn't live in a broken-
down place like this for a million bucks!" and she ran back to the table.

"Ain't she cute?" the woman repeated, stretching her mouth politely.

"Aren't you ashamed?" hissed the grandmother.

Red Sam came in and told his wife to quit lounging on the counter
and hurry up with these people's order. His khaki trousers reached just to his
hip bones and his stomach hung over them like a sack of meal swaying under
his shirt. He came over and sat down at a table nearby and let out a combination sigh and yodel. "You can't win," he said. "You can't win," and he
wiped his sweating red face off with a gray handkerchief. "These days you
don't know who to trust," he said. "Ain't that the truth?"

"People are certainly not nice like they used to be," said the grand-   35
mother.

"Two fellers come in here last week," Red Sammy said, "driving a
Chrysler. It was a old beat-up car but it was a good one and these boys
looked all right to me. Said they worked at the mill and you know I let them
fellers charge the gas they bought? Now why did I do that?"

"Because you're a good man!" the grandmother said at once.

"Yes'm, I suppose so," Red Sam said as if he were struck with this
answer.

His wife brought the orders, carrying the five plates all at once without a tray, two in each hand and one balanced on her arm. "It isn't a soul in this green world of God's that you can trust," she said. "And I don't count nobody out of that, not nobody," she repeated, looking at Red Sammy.

"Did you read about that criminal, The Misfit, that's escaped?" asked 40 the grandmother.

"I wouldn't be a bit surprised if he didn't attact this place right here," said the woman. "If he hears about it being here, I wouldn't be none surprised to see him. If he hears it's two cent in the cash register, I wouldn't be a tall surprised if he . . ."

"That'll do," Red Sam said. "Go bring these people their Co'-Colas," and the woman went off to get the rest of the order.

"A good man is hard to find," Red Sammy said. "Everything is getting terrible. I remember the day you could go off and leave your screen door unlatched. Not no more."

He and the grandmother discussed better times. The old lady said that in her opinion Europe was entirely to blame for the way things were now. She said the way Europe acted you would think we were made of money and Red Sam said it was no use talking about it, she was exactly right. The children ran outside into the white sunlight and looked at the monkey in the lacy chinaberry tree. He was busy catching fleas on himself and biting each one carefully between his teeth as if it were a delicacy.

They drove off again into the hot afternoon. The grandmother took 45 cat naps and woke up every few minutes with her own snoring. Outside of Toombsboro she woke up and recalled an old plantation that she had visited in this neighborhood once when she was a young lady. She said the house had six white columns across the front and that there was an avenue of oaks leading up to it and two little wooden trellis arbors on either side in front where you sat down with your suitor after a stroll in the garden. She recalled exactly which road to turn off to get to it. She knew that Bailey would not be willing to lose any time looking at an old house, but the more she talked about it, the more she wanted to see it once again and find out if the little twin arbors were still standing. "There was a secret panel in this house," she said craftily, not telling the truth but wishing that she were, "and the story went that all the family silver was hidden in it when Sherman came through but it was never found . . ."

"Hey!" John Wesley said. "Let's go see it! We'll find it! We'll poke all the woodwork and find it! Who lives there? Where do you turn off at? Hey Pop, can't we turn off there?"

"We never have seen a house with a secret panel!" June Star shrieked. "Let's go to the house with the secret panel! Hey Pop, can't we go see the house with the secret panel!"

"It's not far from here, I know," the grandmother said. "It wouldn't take over twenty minutes."

Bailey was looking straight ahead. His jaw was as rigid as a horseshoe. "No," he said.

The children began to yell and scream that they wanted to see the 50
house with the secret panel. John Wesley kicked the back of the front seat and June Star hung over her mother's shoulder and whined desperately into her ear that they never had any fun even on their vacation, that they could never do what THEY wanted to do. The baby began to scream and John Wesley kicked the back of the seat so hard that his father could feel the blows in his kidney.

"All right!" he shouted and drew the car to a stop at the side of the road. "Will you all shut up? Will you all just shut up for one second? If you don't shut up, we won't go anywhere."

"It would be very educational for them," the grandmother murmured.

"All right," Bailey said, "but get this: this is the only time we're going to stop for anything like this. This is the one and only time."

"The dirt road that you have to turn down is about a mile back," the grandmother directed. "I marked it when we passed."

"A dirt road," Bailey groaned. 55

After they had turned around and were headed toward the dirt road, the grandmother recalled other points about the house, the beautiful glass over the front doorway and the candle-lamp in the hall. John Wesley said that the secret panel was probably in the fireplace.

"You can't go inside this house," Bailey said. "You don't know who lives there."

"While you all talk to the people in front, I'll run around behind and get in a window," John Wesley suggested.

"We'll all stay in the car," his mother said.

They turned onto the dirt road and the car raced roughly along in a 60
swirl of pink dust. The grandmother recalled the times when there were no paved roads and thirty miles was a day's journey. The dirt road was hilly and there were sudden washes in it and sharp curves on dangerous embankments. All at once they would be on a hill, looking down over the blue tops of trees for miles around, then the next minute, they would be in a red depression with the dust-coated trees looking down on them.

"This place had better turn up in a minute," Bailey said, "or I'm going to turn around."

The road looked as if no one had traveled on it in months.

"It's not much farther," the grandmother said and just as she said it, a horrible thought came to her. The thought was so embarrassing that she turned red in the face and her eyes dilated and her feet jumped up, upsetting her valise in the corner. The instant the valise moved, the newspaper top she had over the basket under it rose with a snarl and Pitty Sing, the cat, sprang onto Bailey's shoulder.

The children were thrown to the floor and their mother, clutching the baby, was thrown out the door onto the ground; the old lady was thrown into the front seat. The car turned over once and landed right-side-up in a gulch off the side of the road. Bailey remained in the driver's seat with the cat—gray-striped with a broad white face and an orange nose—clinging to his neck like a caterpillar.

As soon as the children saw they could move their arms and legs, they scrambled out of the car, shouting, "We've had an ACCIDENT!" The grandmother was curled up under the dashboard, hoping she was injured so that Bailey's wrath would not come down on her all at once. The horrible thought she had had before the accident was that the house she had remembered so vividly was not in Georgia but in Tennessee.

Bailey removed the cat from his neck with both hands and flung it out the window against the side of a pine tree. Then he got out of the car and started looking for the children's mother. She was sitting against the side of the red gutted ditch, holding the screaming baby, but she only had a cut down her face and a broken shoulder. "We've had an ACCIDENT!" the children screamed in a frenzy of delight.

"But nobody's killed," June Star said with disappointment as the grandmother limped out of the car, her hat still pinned to her head but the broken front brim standing up at a jaunty angle and the violet spray hanging off the side. They all sat down in the ditch, except the children, to recover from the shock. They were all shaking.

"Maybe a car will come along," said the children's mother hoarsely.

"I believe I have injured an organ," said the grandmother, pressing her side, but no one answered her. Bailey's teeth were clattering. He had on a yellow sport shirt with bright blue parrots designed in it and his face was as yellow as the shirt. The grandmother decided that she would not mention that the house was in Tennessee.

The road was about ten feet above and they could see only the tops of the trees on the other side of it. Behind the ditch they were sitting in there were more woods, tall and dark and deep. In a few minutes they saw a car some distance away on top of a hill, coming slowly as if the occupants were watching them. The grandmother stood up and waved both arms dramatically to attract their attention. The car continued to come on slowly, disappeared around a bend and appeared again, moving even slower, on top of the hill they had gone over. It was a big black battered hearse-like automobile. There were three men in it.

It came to a stop just over them and for some minutes, the driver looked down with a steady expressionless gaze to where they were sitting, and didn't speak. Then he turned his head and muttered something to the other two and they got out. One was a fat boy in black trousers and a red sweat shirt with a silver stallion embossed on the front of it. He moved around on the right side of them and stood staring, his mouth partly open in a kind of loose grin. The other had on khaki pants and a blue striped coat and a gray hat pulled down very low, hiding most of his face. He came around slowly on the left side. Neither spoke.

The driver got out of the car and stood by the side of it, looking down at them. He was an older man than the other two. His hair was just beginning to gray and he wore silver-rimmed spectacles that gave him a scholarly look. He had a long creased face and didn't have on any shirt or undershirt. He had on blue jeans that were too tight for him and was holding a black hat and a gun. The two boys also had guns.

"We've had an ACCIDENT!" the children screamed.

The grandmother had the peculiar feeling that the bespectacled man was someone she knew. His face was as familiar to her as if she had known him all her life but she could not recall who he was. He moved away from the car and began to come down the embankment, placing his feet carefully so that he wouldn't slip. He had on tan and white shoes and no socks, and his ankles were red and thin. "Good afternoon," he said. "I see you all had you a little spill."

"We turned over twice!" said the grandmother.   75

"Oncet," he corrected. "We seen it happen. Try their car and see will it run, Hiram," he said quietly to the boy with the gray hat.

"What you got that gun for?" John Wesley asked. "Whatcha gonna do with that gun?"

"Lady," the man said to the children's mother, "would you mind calling them children to sit down by you? Children make me nervous. I want all you all to sit down right together there where you're at."

"What are you telling US what to do for?" June Star asked.

Behind them the line of woods gaped like a dark open mouth. "Come   80
here," said their mother.

"Look here now," Bailey began suddenly, "we're in a predicament! We're in . . ."

The grandmother shrieked. She scrambled to her feet and stood staring. "You're The Misfit!" she said. "I recognized you at once!"

"Yes'm," the man said, smiling slightly as if he were pleased in spite of himself to be known, "but it would have been better for all of you, lady, if you hadn't of reckernized me."

Bailey turned his head sharply and said something to his mother that shocked even the children. The old lady began to cry and The Misfit reddened.

"Lady," he said, "don't you get upset. Sometimes a man says things he   85
don't mean. I don't reckon he meant to talk to you thataway."

"You wouldn't shoot a lady, would you?" the grandmother said and removed a clean handkerchief from her cuff and began to slap at her eyes with it.

The Misfit pointed the toe of his shoe into the ground and made a little hole and then covered it up again. "I would hate to have to," he said.

"Listen," the grandmother almost screamed, "I know you're a good man. You don't look a bit like you have common blood. I know you must come from nice people!"

"Yes mam," he said, "finest people in the world." When he smiled he showed a row of strong white teeth. "God never made a finer woman than my mother and my daddy's heart was pure gold," he said. The boy with the red sweat shirt had come around behind them and was standing with his gun at his hip. The Misfit squatted down on the ground. "Watch them children, Bobby Lee," he said. "You know they make me nervous." He looked at the six of them huddled together in front of him and he seemed to be embarrassed as if he couldn't think of anything to say. "Ain't a cloud in the sky," he remarked, looking up at it. "Don't see no sun but don't see no cloud neither."

"Yes, it's a beautiful day," said the grandmother. "Listen," she said, "you   90
shouldn't call yourself The Misfit because I know you're a good man at heart. I can just look at you and tell."

"Hush!" Bailey yelled. "Hush! Everybody shut up and let me handle this!" He was squatting in the position of a runner about to sprint forward but he didn't move.

"I pre-chate that, lady," The Misfit said and drew a little circle in the ground with the butt of his gun.

"It'll take a half a hour to fix this here car," Hiram called, looking over the raised hood of it.

"Well, first you and Bobby Lee get him and that little boy to step over yonder with you," The Misfit said, pointing to Bailey and John Wesley. "The boys want to ast you something," he said to Bailey. "Would you mind stepping back in them woods there with them?"

"Listen," Bailey began, "we're in a terrible predicament! Nobody real-   95
izes what this is," and his voice cracked. His eyes were as blue and intense as the parrots in his shirt and he remained perfectly still.

The grandmother reached up to adjust her hat brim as if she were going to the woods with him but it came off in her hand. She stood staring at it and after a second she let it fall on the ground. Hiram pulled Bailey up by the arm as if he were assisting an old man. John Wesley caught hold of his father's hand and Bobby Lee followed. They went off toward the woods and just as they reached the dark edge, Bailey turned and supporting himself against a gray naked pine trunk, he shouted, "I'll be back in a minute, Mamma, wait on me!"

"Come back this instant!" his mother shrilled but they all disappeared into the woods.

"Bailey Boy!" the grandmother called in a tragic voice but she found she was looking at The Misfit squatting on the ground in front of her. "I just know you're a good man," she said desperately. "You're not a bit common!"

"Nome, I ain't a good man," The Misfit said after a second as if he had considered her statement carefully, "but I ain't the worst in the world neither. My daddy said I was a different breed of dog from my brothers and sisters. 'You know,' Daddy said, 'it's some that can live their whole life out without asking about it and it's others has to know why it is, and this boy is one of the latters. He's going to be into everything!'" He put on his black hat and looked up suddenly and then away deep into the woods as if he were embarrassed again. "I'm sorry I don't have on a shirt before you ladies," he said, hunching his shoulders slightly. "We buried our clothes that we had on when we escaped and we're just making do until we can get better. We borrowed these from some folks we met," he explained.

"That's perfectly all right," the grandmother said. "Maybe Bailey has 100 an extra shirt in his suitcase."

"I'll look and see terrectly," The Misfit said.

"Where are they taking him?" the children's mother screamed.

"Daddy was a card himself," The Misfit said. "You couldn't put anything over on him. He never got in trouble with the Authorities though. Just had the knack of handling them."

"You could be honest too if you'd only try," said the grandmother. "Think how wonderful it would be to settle down and live a comfortable life and not have to think about somebody chasing you all the time."

The Misfit kept scratching in the ground with the butt of his gun as if 105 he were thinking about it. "Yes'm, somebody is always after you," he murmured.

The grandmother noticed how thin his shoulder blades were just behind his hat because she was standing up looking down on him. "Do you ever pray?" she asked.

He shook his head. All she saw was the black hat wiggle between his shoulder blades. "Nome," he said.

There was a pistol shot from the woods, followed closely by another. Then silence. The old lady's head jerked around. She could hear the wind move through the tree tops like a long satisfied insuck of breath. "Bailey Boy!" she called.

"I was a gospel singer for a while," The Misfit said. "I been most everything. Been in the arm service, both land and sea, at home and abroad, been twict married, been an undertaker, been with the railroads, plowed Mother Earth, been in a tornado, seen a man burnt alive oncet," and he looked up at the children's mother and the little girl who were sitting close together, their faces white and their eyes glassy; "I even seen a woman flogged," he said.

"Pray, pray," the grandmother began, "pray, pray . . ." 110

"I never was a bad boy that I remember of," The Misfit said in an almost dreamy voice, "but somewheres along the line I done something wrong and got sent to the penitentiary. I was buried alive," and he looked up and held her attention to him by a steady stare.

"That's when you should have started to pray," she said. "What did you do to get sent to the penitentiary that first time?"

"Turn to the right, it was a wall," The Misfit said, looking up again at the cloudless sky. "Turn to the left, it was a wall. Look up it was a ceiling, look down it was a floor. I forget what I done, lady. I set there and set there, trying to remember what it was I done and I ain't recalled it to this day. Oncet in a while, I would think it was coming to me, but it never come."

"Maybe they put you in by mistake," the old lady said vaguely.

"Nome," he said. "It wasn't no mistake. They had the papers on me."   115

"You must have stolen something," she said.

The Misfit sneered slightly. "Nobody had nothing I wanted," he said. "It was a head-doctor at the penitentiary said what I had done was kill my daddy but I known that for a lie. My daddy died in nineteen ought nineteen of the epidemic flu and I never had a thing to do with it. He was buried in the Mount Hopewell Baptist churchyard and you can go there and see for yourself."

"If you would pray," the old lady said, "Jesus would help you."

"That's right," The Misfit said.

"Well then, why don't you pray?" she asked trembling with delight   120
suddenly.

"I don't want no hep," he said. "I'm doing all right by myself."

Bobby Lee and Hiram came ambling back from the woods. Bobby Lee was dragging a yellow shirt with bright blue parrots in it.

"Thow me that shirt, Bobby Lee," The Misfit said. The shirt came flying at him and landed on his shoulder and he put it on. The grandmother couldn't name what the shirt reminded her of. "No, lady," The Misfit said while he was buttoning it up, "I found out the crime don't matter. You can do one thing or you can do another, kill a man or take a tire off his car, because sooner or later you're going to forget what it was you done and just be punished for it."

The children's mother had begun to make heaving noises as if she couldn't get her breath. "Lady," he asked, "would you and that little girl like to step off yonder with Bobby Lee and Hiram and join your husband?"

"Yes, thank you," the mother said faintly. Her left arm dangled help-   125
lessly and she was holding the baby, who had gone to sleep, in the other. "Hep that lady up, Hiram," The Misfit said as she struggled to climb out of the ditch, "and Bobby Lee, you hold onto that little girl's hand."

"I don't want to hold hands with him," June Star said. "He reminds me of a pig."

The fat boy blushed and laughed and caught her by the arm and pulled her off into the woods after Hiram and her mother.

Alone with The Misfit, the grandmother found that she had lost her voice. There was not a cloud in the sky nor any sun. There was nothing around her but woods. She wanted to tell him that he must pray. She opened and closed her mouth several times before anything came out. Finally she found herself saying, "Jesus. Jesus," meaning, Jesus will help you, but the way she was saying it, it sounded as if she might be cursing.

"Yes'm," The Misfit said as if he agreed. "Jesus thown everything off balance. It was the same case with Him as with me except He hadn't committed any crime and they could prove I had committed one because they had the papers on me. Of course," he said, "they never shown me my papers. That's why I sign myself now. I said long ago, you get you a signature and sign everything you do and keep a copy of it. Then you'll know what you done and you can hold up the crime to the punishment and see do they match and in the end you'll have something to prove you ain't been treated right. I call myself The Misfit," he said, "because I can't make what all I done wrong fit what all I gone through in punishment."

There was a piercing scream from the woods, followed closely by a 130 pistol report. "Does it seem right to you, lady, that one is punished a heap and another ain't punished at all?"

"Jesus!" the old lady cried. "You've got good blood! I know you wouldn't shoot a lady! I know you come from nice people! Pray! Jesus, you ought not to shoot a lady. I'll give you all the money I've got!"

"Lady," The Misfit said, looking beyond her far into the woods, "there never was a body that give the undertaker a tip."

There were two more pistol reports and the grandmother raised her head like a parched old turkey hen crying for water and called, "Bailey Boy, Bailey Boy!" as if her heart would break.

"Jesus was the only One that ever raised the dead," The Misfit contin- ued, "and He shouldn't have done it. He thown everything off balance. If He did what He said, then it's nothing for you to do but thow away every- thing and follow Him, and if He didn't, then it's nothing for you to do but enjoy the few minutes you got left the best way you can—by killing some- body or burning down his house or doing some other meanness to him. No pleasure but meanness," he said and his voice had become almost a snarl.

"Maybe He didn't raise the dead," the old lady mumbled, not knowing 135 what she was saying and feeling so dizzy that she sank down in the ditch with her legs twisted under her.

"I wasn't there so I can't say He didn't," The Misfit said. "I wisht I had of been there," he said, hitting the ground with his fist. "It ain't right I wasn't there because if I had of been there I would of known. Listen lady," he said in a high voice, "if I had of been there I would of known and I wouldn't be like I am now." His voice seemed about to crack and the grandmother's head cleared for an instant. She saw the man's face twisted close to her own as if he were going to cry and she murmured, "Why you're one of my babies. You're one of my own children!" She reached out and touched him on the shoulder. The Misfit sprang back as if a snake had bitten him and shot her three times through the chest. Then he put his gun down on the ground and took off his glasses and began to clean them.

Hiram and Bobby Lee returned from the woods and stood over the ditch, looking down at the grandmother who half sat and half lay in a puddle of blood with her legs crossed under her like a child's and her face smiling up at the cloudless sky.

Without his glasses, The Misfit's eyes were red-rimmed and pale and defenseless-looking. "Take her off and thow her where you thown the oth- ers," he said, picking up the cat that was rubbing itself against his leg.

"She was a talker, wasn't she?" Bobby Lee said, sliding down the ditch with a yodel.

"She would of been a good woman," The Misfit said, "if it had been   140
somebody there to shoot her every minute of her life."

"Some fun!" Bobby Lee said.

"Shut up, Bobby Lee," The Misfit said. "It's no real pleasure in life."

Considerations

1. Describe the relationship between Bailey and his mother. Do you see any positive aspects, or do you think it is an entirely negative relationship?

2. Describe the relationship between June Star, John Wesley, and their parents. Then compare that relationship with the relationship between the children and their grandmother. Explain the significance you see in any similarities or differences.

3. What is the significance of the title? Are there any "good men" in the story? Explain.

4. Although the story has a tragic outcome, humor and irony dominate most of the episodes. Explain your response to the juxtaposition of the comic and tragic elements of this story.

5. What do you make of the final paragraphs of the story? Consider especially the grandmother's statement to The Misfit: "Why you're one of my babies. You're one of my own children!" and The Misfit's final observation: "It's no real pleasure in life."

6. Read either or both of the following commentaries on "A Good Man Is Hard to Find." Then explain how reading the commentary changed or reinforced your own responses to the story.

Commentary

FLANNERY O'CONNOR
A Reasonable Use of the Unreasonable

Last fall° I received a letter from a student who said she would be "graciously appreciative" if I would tell her "just what enlightenment" I expected her to get from each of my stories. I suspect she had a paper to write. I wrote her back to forget about the enlightenment and just try to enjoy them. I knew that was the most unsatisfactory answer I could have given because, of course, she didn't want to enjoy them, she just wanted to figure them out.

In most English classes the short story has become a kind of literary specimen to be dissected. Every time a story of mine appears in a Freshman anthology, I have a vision of it, with its little organs laid open, like a frog in a bottle.

I realize that a certain amount of this what-is-the-significance has to go on, but I think something has gone wrong in the process when, for so many students, the story becomes simply a problem to be solved, something which you evaporate to get Instant Enlightenment.

A story really isn't any good unless it successfully resists paraphrase, unless it hangs on and expands in the mind. Properly, you analyze to enjoy, but it's equally true that to analyze with any discrimination, you have to have enjoyed already, and I think that the best reason to hear a story read is that it should stimulate that primary enjoyment.

I don't have any pretensions to being an Aeschylus or Sophocles and providing you in this story with a cathartic experience out of your mythic background, though this story I'm going to read certainly calls up a good deal of the South's mythic background, and it should elicit from you a degree of pity and terror, even though its way of being serious is a comic one. I do think, though, that like the Greeks, you should know what is going to happen in this story so that any element of suspense in it will be transferred from its surface to its interior.

I would be most happy if you had already read it, happier still if you knew it well, but since experience has taught me to keep my expectations along these lines modest, I'll tell you that this is the story of a family of six which, on its way driving to Florida, gets wiped out by an escaped convict who calls himself the Misfit. The family is made up of the Grandmother and her son, Bailey, and his children, John Wesley and June Star and the baby,

5

Last fall: Refers to fall 1962. This commentary was made by Flannery O'Connor at Hollins College, Virginia, to introduce a reading of her story, "A Good Man Is Hard to Find," on October 14, 1963.

and there is also the cat and the children's mother. The cat is named Pitty Sing, and the Grandmother is taking him with them, hidden in a basket.

Now I think it behooves me to try to establish with you the basis on which reason operates in this story. Much of my fiction takes its character from a reasonable use of the unreasonable, though the reasonableness of my use of it may not always be apparent. The assumptions that underlie this use of it, however, are those of the central Christian mysteries. These are assumptions to which a large part of the modern audience takes exception. About this I can only say that there are perhaps other ways than my own in which this story could be read, but none other by which it could have been written. Belief, in my own case anyway, is the engine that makes perception operate.

The heroine of this story, the Grandmother, is in the most significant position life offers the Christian. She is facing death. And to all appearances she, like the rest of us, is not too well prepared for it. She would like to see the event postponed. Indefinitely.

I've talked to a number of teachers who use this story in class and who tell their students that the Grandmother is evil, that in fact, she's a witch, even down to the cat. One of these teachers told me that his students, and particularly his Southern students, resisted this interpretation with a certain bemused vigor, and he didn't understand why. I had to tell him that they resisted it because they all had grandmothers or great-aunts just like her at home, and they knew, from personal experience, that the old lady lacked comprehension, but that she had a good heart. The Southerner is usually tolerant of those weaknesses that proceed from innocence, and he knows that a taste for self-preservation can be readily combined with the missionary spirit.

The same teacher was telling his students that morally the Misfit was several cuts above the Grandmother. He had a really sentimental attachment to the Misfit. But then a prophet gone wrong is almost always more interesting than your grandmother, and you have to let people take their pleasures where they find them.

It is true that the old lady is a hypocritical old soul; her wits are no match for the Misfit's, nor is her capacity for grace equal to his; yet I think the unprejudiced reader will feel that the Grandmother has a special kind of triumph in this story which instinctively we do not allow to someone altogether bad.

I often ask myself what makes a story work, and what makes it hold up as a story, and I have decided that it is probably some action, some gesture of a character that is unlike any other in the story, one which indicates where the real heart of the story lies. This would have to be an action or a gesture which was both totally right and totally unexpected; it would have to be one that was both in character and beyond character; it would have to suggest both the world and eternity. The action or gesture I'm talking about would have to be on the anagogical level, that is, the level which has to do with the

10

Divine life and our participation in it. It would be a gesture that transcended any neat allegory that might have been intended or any pat moral categories a reader could make. It would be a gesture which somehow made contact with mystery.

There is a point in this story where such a gesture occurs. The Grandmother is at last alone, facing the Misfit. Her head clears for an instant and she realizes, even in her limited way, that she is responsible for the man before her and joined to him by ties of kinship which have their roots deep in the mystery she has been merely prattling about so far. And at this point, she does the right thing, she makes the right gesture.

I find that students are often puzzled by what she says and does here, but I think myself that if I took out this gesture and what she says with it, I would have no story. What was left would not be worth your attention. Our age not only does not have a very sharp eye for the almost imperceptible intrusions of grace, it no longer has much feeling for the nature of the violences which precede and follow them. The devil's greatest wile, Baudelaire has said, is to convince us that he does not exist.

I suppose the reasons for the use of so much violence in modern fiction will differ with each writer who uses it, but in my own stories I have found that violence is strangely capable of returning my characters to reality and preparing them to accept their moment of grace. Their heads are so hard that almost nothing else will do the work. This idea, that reality is something to which we must be returned at considerable cost, is one which is seldom understood by the casual reader, but it is one which is implicit in the Christian view of the world. 15

I don't want to equate the Misfit with the devil. I prefer to think that, however unlikely this may seem, the old lady's gesture, like the mustard-seed, will grow to be a great crow-filled tree in the Misfit's heart, and will be enough of a pain to him there to turn him into the prophet he was meant to become. But that's another story.

This story has been called grotesque, but I prefer to call it literal. A good story is literal in the same sense that a child's drawing is literal. When a child draws, he doesn't intend to distort but to set down exactly what he sees, and as his gaze is direct, he sees the lines that create motion. Now the lines of motion that interest the writer are usually invisible. They are lines of spiritual motion. And in this story you should be on the lookout for such things as the action of grace in the Grandmother's soul, and not for the dead bodies.

We hear many complaints about the prevalence of violence in modern fiction, and it is always assumed that this violence is a bad thing and meant to be an end in itself. With the serious writer, violence is never an end in itself. It is the extreme situation that best reveals what we are essentially, and I believe these are times when writers are more interested in what we are essentially than in the tenor of our daily lives. Violence is a force which can be used for good or evil, and among other things taken by it is the kingdom of heaven. But regardless of what can be taken by it, the man in the violent situation reveals those qualities least dispensable in his personality, those qualities which are all he will have to take into eternity with him; and since the characters in this story are all on the verge of eternity, it is appropriate to think of what they take with them. In any case, I hope that if you consider these points in connection with the story, you will come to see it as something more than an account of a family murdered on the way to Florida.

Commentary

HALLMAN B. BRYANT
Reading the Map in "A Good Man Is Hard to Find"

Flannery O'Connor, remarking on her most famous short story, "A Good Man Is Hard to Find," issues several caveats to critics. She allows that "a certain amount of what is the significance of this" kind of investigation has to go on in teaching and in literary analysis, but she cautions against reducing a story to "a problem to be solved" so that it becomes "something which you evaporate to get Instant Enlightenment."

Without evaporating too much I will try to shed light on the significance of some small details in "A Good Man Is Hard to Find." Although I do not think an analysis of O'Connor's use of place names in the story will create instant enlightenment, I believe that the towns alluded to along the route which the family travels were chosen for two reasons: first, and most obviously, to foreshadow; and second, to augment the theme of the story. Furthermore, because the numerous places mentioned in the story can actually be found on the map, with only one important exception, it is thus possible to estimate within a few miles the physical distance that the family travels.

The first thing one notices about "A Good Man Is Hard to Find" is that it is set in a real place—in the state of Georgia. The opening scene describes an Atlanta family quarreling about their vacation plans. The grandmother is opposed to going to Florida ostensibly because a convict "that calls himself The Misfit is aloose from the Federal pen and headed toward Florida." (Apparently the Federal penitentiary from which The Misfit has escaped is the one in Atlanta, although it is not specified in the story.) Regardless of the threat posed by The Misfit, the family heads south for Florida instead of east Tennessee where the grandmother had tried to persuade them to take her. We are told that the family left Atlanta at 8:35 in the morning with the mileage on the car at 55,890, a fact recorded by the grandmother because she "thought it would be interesting to say how many miles they had been when they got back." From this point on one can literally follow the journey of the family with a road map and take the mileage they put on their car before the wreck and the subsequent meeting with The Misfit and his henchmen.

One odd fact about their route emerges immediately to anyone familiar with Atlanta and its environs. Although the family lives in Atlanta and is headed south, we are told that they pass Stone Mountain along the way. This natural phenomenon and tourist attraction is about fifteen or sixteen miles from Atlanta on the northeast side of the city. At the time the story was written, one had to follow U.S. 78 North to get to Stone Mountain, a highly unlikely road to take out of Atlanta if one is going to Florida.[1]

Although one of the children urges his father to "go through Georgia fast so we won't have to look at it much," there nevertheless are some interesting details of scenery along the roadside, and the grandmother tells us about many of the things they pass by. She notices "a cute little pickaninny" standing in the door of a shanty that she fancies would make a nice study for a sentimental painting, but the same subject disgusts her granddaughter June Star, who comments acidly, "He didn't have any britches on." More significantly, the grandmother points out a graveyard with five or six graves fenced off in the middle of a large cotton field, which is a rather obvious foreshadowing of the fate that will befall the family.

When the grandmother can no longer hold the children's attention with roadside attractions, she tells them a story of one of her girlhood suitors, Mr. Edgar Atkins Teagarden, who was from Jasper, Georgia, a small north Georgia town located in Pickens County and approximately fifty or sixty miles from the Tennessee state line. Although we are not told just where the grandmother is from, only that she has "connections in east Tennessee," it seems that to be consistent with her tale of Mr. Teagarden's courtship, she would have to have lived somewhere near Jasper, since he drove to her house by buggy every Saturday and gave her a watermelon monogrammed with his initials, E. A. T.

The family's journey is interrupted by a stop for a lunch of barbecued sandwiches at a café called The Tower which is located in "a clearing outside of Timothy." For comic effect this is one of the great scenes in all of Flannery O'Connor's fiction; yet, here one cannot plot the location of the place on the map for there is no town of Timothy in Georgia. (If there is, it is such a small community it is not listed in the state atlas.) Since the other references to places in the story are to actual localities in the state, why does she create a fictitious name at this point? My theory is that in this scene, which has strong moral intention, O'Connor selected the name Timothy for the ironic effect it would produce. The allusion here is not geographical but Biblical, and the Timothy alluded to is almost certainly the book in the New Testament which bears the same name. Usually referred to as the Pastoral Letters, this gospel purports to be letters from Paul addressed to his disciples and through them to the Christian community at large. More than any other writing in the New Testament, the letters to Timothy are concerned with Christian orthodoxy. In this gospel Paul deals essentially with three topics: the opposition of false doctrine; the organization of the church and establishment of ecclesiastical regulations; and exhortations which indicate how to be a good citizen and Christian.

It seems to me that the concerns expressed by Paul in his letter to Timothy are very germane to the concerns expressed by Flannery O'Connor in "A Good Man Is Hard to Find," especially the concern with heretics and the advice on how to be a good Christian. One has only to set the family of six from Atlanta and Red Sammy and his wife (as well as The Misfit)—all of whom Flannery O'Connor considers heretics—against certain passages from Timothy to see that O'Connor's allusion ironically tells us just where these modern-day people are in error. For example, these verses seem to apply especially to Bailey. "He [the husband] must manage his own family well and see that his children obey him with proper respect" (I Tim. 3:4–5).

Also the author of the epistle commands good Christians to keep the faith and avoid "vain discussions" and concern with trivial matters and endless wrangling about genealogies (I Tim. 6:3–10). Further, he admonishes women "to dress modestly, with decency and propriety" and "to learn in quietness and full submission . . . and be silent" (I Tim. 2:9–12). This instruction seems to bear most directly on the grandmother, who is vain about her Old South heritage and certainly conscious of her social standing and what is required to be a lady. This is best brought out in her selection of attire for the trip. She is turned out in white gloves, black purse, a navy blue straw sailor hat with white violets on the brim, a navy blue polka dot dress with collar and cuffs of white organdy trimmed with lace, and on her neck she has pinned a purple spray of cloth violets containing a sachet. Her costume has been prepared so that, in the event of an accident, "anyone seeing her dead on the highway would know at once that she was a lady."

The grandmother's superficial conception of values is ironically underscored in the vain discussions with her grandchildren about what kind of conduct was once expected from children and her trivial remarks about plantation days and old suitors. Nowhere are her ideas more tellingly satirized than in her conversation with Red Sammy in the café where both complain of misplaced trust in their fellow man, which the grandmother sees as an indication of the general lack of manners in the modern world. She tells Red Sammy, "People are certainly not nice like they used to be." Of course, both Red Sammy and the grandmother are conceited enough to think that they are just as good as they ought to be. When Red Sammy complains of a recent theft of some gasoline by men driving a Chrysler and asks in a puzzled way why he had trusted them, he is quickly told by the grandmother that it was "because you're a good man," to which he candidly assents, "Yes'm, I suppose so." 10

The grandmother's inability to "learn in quietness" is tragically the cause of the deaths of the entire family. Shortly after Bailey overturns the car in a ditch, they are approached by a bespectacled man who the grandmother feels is "someone she knew" and soon she recognizes the stranger as The Misfit whose picture she has seen, and she blurts out this fact, saying, "You're The Misfit . . . I recognized you at once," to which he replies, "but it would have been better for all of you, lady, if you hadn't of reckernized me."

It is generally agreed that in the traumatic moments that follow in which the grandmother witnesses the deaths of her family and anticipates her own she does learn a lesson she has not heeded previously during her life. This lesson is the central message which Paul attempts to convey to Christians through Timothy and that is, "There is one God and one mediator between God and men, the Lord Jesus Christ, who gave himself to save mankind" (I Tim. 2:5). The evidence for assuming that she has come to a belated awareness that her faith has been misplaced in the pursuit of social graces and a concern with manners is limited to The Misfit's remark, "She would have been a good woman . . . if it had been somebody there to shoot her every minute of her life." Furthermore, in death she appears like a child, and her face is "smiling up at the cloudless sky," suggesting that she has found grace at last.

Another passage from Timothy seems especially applicable at this point: "The Spirit clearly says that in later times some will abandon the faith and follow deceiving spirits and things taught by demons. Such teachings come through hypocritical liars, whose consciences have been seared as with hot iron" (I Tim. 4:1–12). Although the whole cast of characters in the story has abandoned the faith and followed the wrong paths, the indictment of these lines would apply most forcibly to The Misfit who wears glasses and has a scholarly look. He has indeed been taught by demons, and from the Christian point of view that O'Connor takes in "A Good Man Is Hard to Find" he is a hypocritical liar who has no faith in a moral purpose in the universe and teaches that "it's nothing for you to do but enjoy the few minutes you got left the best way you can—by killing somebody or burning down his house or doing some other meanness to him." Thus, according to the ethics of this teacher, goodness is a matter of sadistic gratification. "No pleasure but meanness," he says, indicating how completely his conscience has been seared and his vision warped by his hedonistic atheism.

The numerous ways in which the content of this book of the New Testament dovetails with the characters and the theme of "A Good Man Is Hard to Find" could not be a complete accident. It cannot be demonstrated that Flannery O'Connor conceived of the moral of her story in terms of this specific book, but she made no bones about the fact that she wrote "from the standpoint of Christian orthodoxy;"[2] and there is no doubt that Paul wrote from a similar standpoint, and his letter to Timothy has the same hortatory, moralizing tone that we find just below the surface in "A Good Man Is Hard to Find." Thus, it seems likely that she put the town of Timothy on the map because she wanted the reader to pick up the allusion and perhaps refresh himself on the contents of the New Testament, but more probably she saw the parallel between her modern-day characters who have left the main road of Christian faith and Paul's warning to the church when he feared it was in danger off into the byways of heresy.

Just as the name of the town where the family stops for lunch is care- 15
fully chosen, so is the name of Red Sammy's café. In Christian iconography

towers are ambivalent symbols, that is, they speak *in bono* or *in malo,* to use the vocabulary of medieval exegetes, and can represent either good or evil qualities. For example, the Tower of Babel is symbolic of man's pride and stands for misbegotten human enterprises. The fate of the tower and its architects shows the consequences of overconfidence in the pursuit of fanciful ideas. (Interestingly enough, Nimrod, who began the construction of the tower, was also a mighty hunter, and like Red Sammy, a keeper of wild game, if Red Sammy's monkey can be called wild.)

As well as its nugatory meaning, the tower is a traditional symbol of the Virgin Mary and is a token of her purity and powers of transformation. Mary as the "refuge of sinners" according to Catholic doctrine is appropriately represented by the tower, a place associated with safety and sanctuary.

Outside of its Christian meaning the tower in arcane lore is a portent of disaster. In the sixteenth enigma of the Tarot pack of cards, catastrophe is indicated by the image of a tower struck by lightning. Whether O'Connor knew this fact about the meaning of the tower is uncertain, but she could not have been unaware of the former implications of the tower as a symbol, versed as she was in Biblical and church lore. It is appropriate that the conceited owner of this barbecue palace should have called it The Tower; it is ironic that this tower has no capacity to transform or give refuge.

Leaving Timothy and The Tower behind, both in the Biblical and geographical sense, the family resumes their trip and we are told that just beyond Toombsboro, Georgia, the grandmother awakens from a nap with the recollection, mistaken as it turns out, that there is an old plantation nearby which she had visited as a girl; she even thinks she remembers the road to take to get there and tells Bailey, "It's not far from here, I know. . . . It wouldn't take over twenty minutes." As it so happens there is a Toombsboro (spelled without the "b") on the map and it is only twenty-three miles south of Milledgeville, Flannery O'Connor's home. She surely knew the place and chose to mention it because the name has an ominous ring, and it also would have been a logical terminus for the family's trip in terms of the time and distance they have traveled since leaving Atlanta in the morning. In fact, if one follows the usual route from Atlanta to Milledgeville (Georgia Highway 212), the distance is 93 miles, and if one adds to this the 23 miles further to Toombsboro, plus the estimated 15 or so miles that the detour to the plantation takes, then it can be calculated that the family has come a total of 130 miles. Considering the conditions of Georgia roads in the late 1940s, one had to drive under 50 m.p.h. to keep from knocking the wheels out of line from the numerous potholes that Governor Talmadge's highway people never patched. Thus, if one assumes that Bailey has averaged around 45 m.p.h. and takes account of the lunch stop, they have been on the road four or five hours and their meeting with The Misfit occurs in the early afternoon of a cloudless day with the mileage on the car standing at about 56,020 on the meter. Sadly enough, the grandmother will be forever unaware of this "interesting fact," but we as readers should have a better understanding of how carefully O'Connor has used realistic detail for symbolic effects.

In the course of this story, the family's trip takes them from their complacent and smug living room to a confrontation with ultimate evil and ultimate reality as well. They are not prepared for the meeting because, like the heretics who concerned Paul in his epistle to Timothy, they have been occupied with the trivial things and involved in quarrels; and, like the builders of the Tower of Babel, they are preoccupied with vain enterprises.

Flannery O'Connor saw herself as a prophetic writer and her authorial strategy was to shock; her fiction is intended as a rebuke to rationalistic, materialistic and humanistic thought—the heresies of the twentieth century. She believed that people in the modern world were not following the true path and had to be made to see their condition for what it was—a wandering by the wayside. In "A Good Man Is Hard to Find" the family's wayward lives are given direction in their final moments, and from O'Connor's point of view they are at last on the right road.

20

NOTES

1. The detour by Stone Mountain was probably due to O'Connor's uncertainty about its exact location; she simply found it a convenient allusion since Stone Mountain was for years Georgia's most famous tourist attraction, but perhaps there is more than meets the eye. In 1915 a project was begun by the United Daughters of the Confederacy which called for Robert E. Lee and his lieutenants to be carved in heroic scale on the vertical face of the mountain. Ironically, the artist commissioned for the job was a Yankee sculptor named Gutzon Borglum who blasted and chiseled on the mountain until 1928 when funds and patience ran out. After expenditure of hundreds of thousands of dollars in a vain effort to impose the heroes of the "Lost Cause" on the side of the mountain, the project was dropped. The scarred carvings, empty catwalks and scaffolds were reminders of a long series of errors and frustrations of the U.D.C. ladies who dreamed of keeping the past alive with a memorial that would be "the perpetuation of a vision." (See *The Story of Stone Mountain* by Willard Neal [Atlanta: Neal and Rogers, 1963], pp. 23–33). Flannery O'Connor was amused by the quixotic qualities of the U.D.C., and Stone Mountain would evoke for Georgians of O'Connor's generation the folly of a sentimental project—a project almost as futile as the grandmother's in the story, whose fascination with past grandeur is congruent with that of the U.D.C.'s and has equally unfortunate results.

2. *The Habit of Being: Letters of Flannery O'Connor,* ed. Sally Fitzgerald (New York: Farrar, Straus and Giroux, 1979), 196.

THEODORE ROETHKE (1903–1963)

My Papa's Waltz

Born in Saginaw, Michigan, Theodore Roethke was the son of a greenhouse owner. After completing graduate study at Harvard, Roethke taught at several universities and was known as both a great teacher and a great poet. His collection The Waking: Poems 1933–1953 *won the Pulitzer Prize in 1954. "My Papa's Waltz" was first published in 1942.*

The whiskey on your breath
Could make a small boy dizzy;
But I hung on like death
Such waltzing was not easy.

We romped until the pans   5
Slid from the kitchen shelf;
My mother's countenance
Could not unfrown itself.

The hand that held my wrist
Was battered on one knuckle;   10
At every step you missed
My right ear scraped a buckle.

You beat time on my head
With a palm caked hard by dirt,
Then waltzed me off to bed   15
Still clinging to your shirt.

Considerations

1. List the images describing the father and his bedtime dance with his son. Do these words suggest the experience was positive? Negative? A mix? Explain.
2. Why is the mother frowning? Speculate on her reasons for refusing to join in the kitchen romp.
3. Rewrite this poem as a prose description of the same scene. Evaluate the changes that you make and comment on the way these changes alter the view of the experience described in the poem.

MAXINE KUMIN (1925–   )

Making the Jam without You

Maxine Kumin was born in Philadelphia, Pennsylvania, and currently lives on a farm in New Hampshire with her husband, the father of her three chil-dren. In 1973, her collection of poetry Up Country *won the Pulitzer Prize. "Making the Jam without You" appeared in* Our Ground Time Here Will Be Brief *(1970).*

for Judy

Old daughter, small traveler
asleep in a German featherbed
under the eaves in a postcard town
of turrets and towers,
I am putting a dream in your head.   5

Listen! Here it is afternoon.
The rain comes down like bullets.
I stand in the kitchen,
that harem of good smells
where we have bumped hips and   10
cracked the cupboards with our talk
while the stove top danced with pots
and it was not clear who did
the mothering. Now I am
crushing blackberries   15
to make the annual jam
in a white cocoon of steam.

Take it, my sleeper. Redo it
in any of your three
languages and nineteen years.   20
Change the geography.
Let there be a mountain,
the fat cows on it belled
like a cathedral. Let
there be someone beside you   ·25
as you come upon the ruins
of a schloss°, all overgrown   castle
with a glorious thicket,
its brambles soft as wool.
Let him bring the buckets   30

crooked on his angel arms
and may the berries, vaster
than any forage in
the mild hills of New Hampshire,
drop in your pail, plum size,   35
heavy as the eyes
of an honest dog
and may you bear them
home together to a square
white unreconstructed kitchen   40
not unlike this one.

Now may your two heads
touch over the kettle,
over the blood of the berries
that drink up sugar and sun,   45
over that tar-thick boil
love cannot stir down.
More plainly than
the bric-a-brac of shelves
filling with jelly glasses,   50
more surely than
the light driving through them
trite as rubies, I see him
as pale as paraffin beside you.
I see you cutting   55
fresh baked bread to spread it
with the bright royal fur.

At this time
I lift the flap of your dream
and slip out thinner than a sliver   60
as your two mouths open
for the sweet stain of purple.

Considerations

1. What do the details of this poem tell you about the mother? About the
   daughter? How old would you guess each of these women is?
2. Write a brief summary of the dream the mother builds for her daughter.
   Why does she choose to leave that dream?
3. How might making jam serve as a metaphor for the relationship between
   this mother and her daughter?

JUDITH ORTIZ COFER (1952–   )

My Father in the Navy: A Childhood Memory

"My Father in the Navy: A Childhood Memory" first appeared in Triple Crown, *1987. For biographical information about Judith Ortiz Cofer, see page 422.*

Stiff and immaculate
in the white cloth of his uniform
and a round cap on his head like a halo,
he was an apparition on leave from a shadow-world
and only flesh and blood when he rose from below   5
the waterline where he kept watch over the engines
and dials making sure the ship parted the waters
on a straight course.
Mother, brother and I kept vigil
on the nights and dawns of his arrivals,   10
watching the corner beyond the neon sign of a quasar
for the flash of white our father like an angel
heralding a new day.
His homecomings were the verses
we composed over the years making up   15
the siren's song that kept him coming back
from the bellies of iron whales
and into our nights
like the evening prayer.

Considerations

1. Make a list of the images describing the father. Then make a list of the images describing the way the speaker, her mother, and brother waited for the father's return. Evaluate the speaker's view of her father and her view of the relationship between him and the rest of the family.
2. Imagine that you are the mother in the poem. Write a journal entry describing the emotions you experience and the thoughts you have as you wait for your husband's return from sea duty.

ROBERT MEZEY (1935–   )

My Mother

Born in Philadelphia, Pennsylvania, Robert Mezey earned his bachelor of arts from the University of Iowa in 1959. Since then, he has worked at a variety of jobs, including advertising copywriter, probation officer, and social worker. He has taught at Case Western Reserve University, Franklin and Marshall College, California State University at Fresno, the University of Utah, and Pomona College. His most recent collection of poems is Evening Wind (1987).

My mother writes from Trenton,
a comedian to the bone
but underneath, serious
and all heart. "Honey," she says,
"be a mensch and Mary too,   5
it's no good to worry, you
are doing the best you can
your Dad and everyone
thinks you turned out very well
as long as you pay your bills   10
nobody can say a word
you can tell them to drop dead
so save a dollar it can't
hurt—remember Frank you went
to highschool with? he still lives   15
with his wife's mother, his wife
works while he writes his books and
did he ever sell a one
the four kids run around naked
36 and he's never had,   20
you'll forgive my expression
even a pot to piss in
or a window to throw it,
such a smart boy he couldn't
read the footprints on the wall   25
honey you think you know all
the answers you don't, please try
to put some money away
believe me it wouldn't hurt
artist shmartist life's too short   30
for that kind of, forgive me,
horseshit, I know what you want
better than you, all that counts
is to make a good living

and the best of everything,   35
as Sholem Aleichem said
he was a great writer did
you ever read his books dear,
you should make what he makes a year
anyway he says some place   40
Poverty is no disgrace
but it's no honor either
that's what I say,
love,
Mother"   45

Considerations

1. How do you respond to the mother in the poem? How does your response compare with her son's response (as suggested by his description of her)?
2. List several phrases from the poem that describe the mother. Then write a paragraph explaining what you can infer from those details.
3. What is the mother in this poem trying to convince her son to do? What strategies does she use to persuade her son to accept her point of view? How convincing do you find her argument?

ELLEN WOLFE (1940–   )

Amniocentesis°

> *Ellen Wolfe frequently draws on her own experiences, including becoming a mother late in life, as subjects for her poetry. Her work has been published in many small press magazines. "Amniocentesis" was first published in 1982.*

for Yona

Lie up under the umbrella of my ribs
my new island
Sleep while the thin throat
samples your lake
First planting in my old body   5
they worry about you

Amniocentesis: Surgical procedure performed on a pregnant woman to determine the presence of disease or genetic defects in the fetus.

These people who fear monsters
will be looking for monsters
They will be looking for the skewed pattern
the aberrant piece   10
of your chromosome puzzle
Love
they will be listening
Sing for them
your perfect song   15

Considerations

1. Whom is the speaker addressing? What is her message?
2. Who are the "people who fear monsters"? What is the attitude of the speaker toward these people? What is your response toward this attitude?
3. Discuss the hopes and fears implied by the images and theme of this poem.

ANONYMOUS

Lord Randal

> *"Lord Randal" is an old English ballad. A ballad is a poetic form that arose in the Middle Ages and was usually composed by and sung for common people. Once sung, a ballad might become popular and circulate from place to place and from generation to generation. Any ballad singer felt free to introduce changes, and it is impossible to identify the originator of any particular ballad. The form continues to be used today.*

"O where ha' you been, Lord Randal, my son?
And where ha' you been, my handsome young man?"
"I ha' been at the greenwood; mother, mak my bed soon,
For I'm wearied wi' hunting, and fain wad° lie down."   *would*

"An wha' met ye there, Lord Randal, my son?   5
An wha' met you there, my handsome young man?"
"O I met wi' my true-love; mother, mak my bed soon,
For I'm wearied wi' huntin', and fain wad lie down."

"And what did she give you, Lord Randal, my son?
And what did she give you, my handsome young man?"   10
"Eels fried in a pan; mother, mak my bed soon,
For I'm wearied wi' huntin', and fain wad lie down."

"And wha' gat your leavins, Lord Randal, my son?
And wha' gat your leavins, my handsome young man?"
"My hawks and my hounds; mother, mak my bed soon,   15
For I'm wearied wi' hunting, and fain wad lie down."

"And what becam of them, Lord Randal, my son?
And what becam of them, my handsome young man?"
"They stretched their legs out and died; mother, mak my bed soon,
For I'm wearied wi' huntin', and fain wad lie down."   20

"O I fear you are poisoned, Lord Randal, my son!
I fear you are poisoned, my handsome young man!"
"O yes, I am poisoned; mother, mak my bed soon,
For I'm sick at the heart, and I fain wad lie down."

"What d'ye leave to your mother, Lord Randal, my son?   25
What d'ye leave to your mother, my handsome young man?"
"Four and twenty milk kye°; mother, mak my bed soon,   _cows_
For I'm sick at the heart, and I fain wad lie down."

"What d'ye leave to your sister, Lord Randal, my son?
What d'ye leave to your sister, my handsome young man?"   30
"My gold and my silver; mother, mak my bed soon,
For I'm sick at the heart, and I fain wad lie down."

"What d'ye leave to your brother, Lord Randal, my son?
What d'ye leave to your brother, my handsome young man?"
"My houses and my lands; mother, mak my bed soon,   35
For I'm sick at the heart, and I fain wad lie down."

"What d'ye leave to your true-love, Lord Randal, my son?
What d'ye leave to your true-love, my handsome young man?"
"I leave her hell and fire; mother, make my bed soon,
For I'm sick at the heart, and I fain wad lie down."   40

MARGARET ATWOOD (1939–   )

Today

*Margaret Atwood, who was born in Ottawa, is one of Canada's foremost
writers. She has received many awards and fellowships, including Canada's
Molson Prize and a Guggenheim Fellowship in 1981. Atwood has won*

*international acclaim for her critical writing and fiction and has published many
novels, including* The Handmaid's Tale *(1986), which has been made into
a film.*

Today the lawn holds
my daughter like a hostage
where she walks, not as high
as the wrecked picnic table,
through the scant grass, burdock leaves   5
made ragged by the mower,
tripping, stopping
to pick up and put down.

(Watch the slope, hard clay with bladed
stones, posing   10
innocuous as daisies:
it leads down to the pond,
where the ducks beckon, eleven
of them, they are saying:
    feathers.   feathers.)   15

The lure of eleven birds
on water, the glitter
and true shine, how can I tell her
that white, that bluegreen gold
is treachery?   20

Each of these rescues
costs me something,
a loss, a dulling
of this bluegold eye.

Later she will learn   25
about edges. Or better, find
by luck or a longer journey
the shadow of that liquid
gold place, which can be
so single and clear for her   30
only now, when it means danger
only to me.

SYLVIA PLATH (1932–1963)
Metaphors

> Born in Boston, Sylvia Plath graduated summa cum laude from Smith College in 1955. She then became a Fulbright scholar and studied in England, where she met and married poet Ted Hughes in 1956. An extremely prolific poet, Plath also wrote one novel, The Bell Jar, an autobiographical novel that describes her battle with depression. This novel was published in 1963, the year Plath committed suicide.

I'm a riddle in nine syllables,
An elephant, a ponderous house,
A melon strolling on two tendrils.
O red fruit, ivory, fine timbers!
This loaf's big with its yeasty rising.   5
Money's new-minted in this fat purse.
I'm a means, a stage, a cow in calf.
I've eaten a bag of green apples,
Boarded the train there's no getting off.

DONALD HALL (1928–   )
My son, my executioner

> Donald Hall was born and grew up in New Haven, Connecticut. He now lives in New Hampshire on a farm that was once owned by his grandparents. Hall is widely respected as a teacher, poet, and essayist, and his book The One Day: A Poem in Three Parts (1988) won the National Book Critics Circle Award.

My son, my executioner,
    I take you in my arms,
Quiet and small and just astir,
    And whom my body warms.

Sweet death, small son, our instrument   5
    Of immortality,
Your cries and hungers document
    Our bodily decay.

We twenty-five and twenty-two,
    Who seemed to live forever,   10
Observe enduring life in you
    And start to die together.

JAMES MASAO MITSUI (1940–   )

Allowance

> James Masao Mitsui is a second-generation Japanese American who was born
> in Skykomish, Washington. A high school teacher, Mitsui has received a fel-
> lowship from the National Endowment for the Arts and has published three
> collections of poetry, Journal of the Sun *(1974),* Crossing the Phantom
> River *(1978), and* After the Long Train *(1986).*

I am ten.
My mother sits in a black
rocking chair in the parlor
and tells stories of a country school
surrounded by ricefields   5
and no roads.

I stand in the kerosene light
behind her,
earning my allowance.
A penny   10
for each white hair I pull.

SEAMUS HEANEY (1939–   )

Digging

> For biographical information about Seamus Heaney, see page 203.

Between my finger and my thumb
The squat pen rests; snug as a gun.

Under my window, a clean rasping sound
When the spade sinks into gravelly ground:
My father, digging. I look down   5

Till his straining rump among the flowerbeds
Bends low, comes up twenty years away
Stooping in rhythm through potato drills
Where he was digging.

The coarse boot nestled on the lug, the shaft   10
Against the inside knee was levered firmly.
He rooted out tall tops, buried the bright edge deep

To scatter new potatoes that we picked
Loving their cool hardness in our hands.

By God, the old man could handle a spade.   15
Just like his old man.

My grandfather cut more turf in a day
Than any other man on Toner's bog.
Once I carried him milk in a bottle
Corked sloppily with paper. He straightened up   20
To drink it, then fell to right away
Nicking and slicing neatly, heaving sods
Over his shoulder, going down and down
For the good turf. Digging.

The cold smell of potato mould, the squelch and slap   25
Of soggy peat, the curt cuts of an edge
Through living roots awaken in my head.
But I've no spade to follow men like them.

Between my finger and my thumb
The squat pen rests.   30
I'll dig with it.

TINA HOWE (1938–   )

Painting Churches

Born in New York City, Tina Howe received her bachelor of arts from Sarah Lawrence College and then pursued graduate studies at the Sorbonne in Paris, Columbia Teachers College in New York, and Chicago Teachers College. Her plays include Museum *(1976),* The Art of Dining *(1979), and* Coastal Disturbances *(1986), which was nominated for a Tony. Howe lives with her husband and children in Manhattan and teaches at New York University.* Painting Churches *won the 1983 Obie (Off-Broadway) Award for distinguished playwrighting.*

Characters

FANNY SEDGWICK CHURCH, *a Bostonian from a fine old family, in her sixties*

GARDNER CHURCH, *her husband, an eminent New England poet from a finer family, in his seventies*

MARGARET CHURCH (MAGS), *their daughter, a painter, in her early thirties*

During the scene changes, the opening measures of the following Chopin waltzes are played:

As the house lights dim, the Waltz in A Minor, opus posthumous

Setting up Act I, Scene 2, the Waltz in E Minor, opus posthumous

Setting up Act I, Scene 3, the Waltz in E Major, opus posthumous

To close Act I, the final notes of the Waltz in B Minor, opus 69, no. 2. As the house lights dim for Act II, the Waltz in A flat Major, opus 64, no. 3

Setting up Act II, Scene 2, repeat the Waltz in A Minor, opus posthumous

To accompany the final moments of GARDNER's *and* FANNY's *dance, the Waltz in D flat Major, opus 70, no. 3*

ACT 1
SCENE 1

TIME: *Several years ago.*

PLACE: *The living room of the Churches' townhouse on Beacon Hill one week before everything will be moved to Cape Cod. Empty packing cartons line the room and all the furniture has been tagged with brightly colored markers. At first glance it looks like any discreet Boston interior, but on closer scrutiny one notices a certain flamboyance. Oddities from secondhand stores are mixed in with the fine old furniture, and exotic handmade curios vie with tasteful family objets d'art. What makes the room remarkable, though, is the play of light that pours through three soaring arched windows. At one hour it's hard edged and brilliant; the next, it's dappled and yielding.*

It transforms whatever it touches, giving the room a distinct feeling of unreality. It's several years ago, a bright spring morning.

FANNY *is sitting on the sofa, wrapping a valuable old silver coffee service. She's wearing a worn bathrobe and fashionable hat. As she works, she makes a list of everything on a yellow legal pad.* GARDNER *can be heard typing in his study down the hall.*

FANNY: *(She picks up a coffee pot.)* God, this is good-looking! I'd forgotten how handsome Mama's old silver was! It's probably worth a fortune. It certainly weighs enough! *(Calling out.)* GARRRRRRRRRRRRRRRRRRD-NERRRRRRRRRRR? . . . Well, it should bring us a pretty penny, that's for sure. *(Wraps it, places it in a carton, and then picks up the tray that goes with it. She holds it up like a mirror and adjusts her hat. Louder in another register.)* OH, GARRRRRRRRRRRRRRRRDNERRRRR? . . .

(He continues typing.)

FANNY: *(She then reaches for a small box and opens it with reverence.)* Grandma's Paul Revere teaspoons! . . . *(She takes out several and fondles them.)* I don't care how desperate things get, these will never go! One has to maintain some standards! *(She writes on her list.)* "Grandma's Paul Revere teaspoons, Cotuit!" . . . WASN'T IT THE AMERICAN WING OF THE METROPOLITAN MUSEUM OF ART THAT WANTED GRANDMA'S PAUL REVERE TEASPOONS SO BADLY? . . . *(She looks at her reflection in the tray again.)* This is a very good-looking hat, if I do say so. I was awfully smart to grab it up.

(Silence.)

DON'T YOU REMEMBER A DISTINGUISHED-LOOKING MAN COMING TO THE HOUSE AND OFFERING US FIFTY THOUSAND DOLLARS FOR GRANDMA'S PAUL REVERE TEASPOONS? . . . HE HAD ON THESE MARVELOUS SHOES! THEY WERE SO POINTED AT THE ENDS WE COULDN'T IMAGINE HOW HE EVER GOT THEM ON AND THEY WERE SHINED TO WITHIN AN INCH OF THEIR LIVES AND I REMEMBER HIM SAYING HE CAME FROM THE . . . AMERICAN WING OF THE METROPOLITAN MUSEUM OF ART! . . . HELLO? . . . GARDNER? . . . ARE YOU THERE!

(The typing stops.)

FANNY: YOO-HOOOOOOO . . . *(Like a fog horn.)* GARRRRRRR-RRRRDNERRRRRRR? . . .

GARDNER: *(Offstage; from his study.)* YES, DEAR . . . IS THAT YOU? . . .

FANNY: OF COURSE IT'S ME! WHO ELSE COULD IT POSSIBLY BE? . . . DARLING, PLEASE COME HERE FOR A MINUTE.

(The typing resumes.)

FANNY: FOR GOD'S SAKE, WILL YOU STOP THAT DREADFUL TYPING BEFORE YOU SEND ME STRAIGHT TO THE NUT HOUSE? . . . *(In a new register.)* GARRRRRRRRRRRRRD-NERRRRRR? . . .

(He stops.)

GARDNER: *(Offstage.)* WHAT'S THAT? MAGS IS BACK FROM THE NUT HOUSE? . . .

FANNY: I SAID . . . Lord, I hate this yelling . . . PLEASE . . . COME . . . HERE!

(Brief silence.)

GARDNER: *(Offstage.)* I'LL BE WITH YOU IN A MO-MENT, I DIDN'T HEAR HER RING. *(Starts singing.)* "Nothing Could be Finer Than to Be in Carolina."

FANNY: It's a wonder I'm not in a strait jacket already. Actually, it might be rather nice for a change . . . peaceful. DAR-LING . . . I WANT TO SHOW YOU MY NEW HAT!

(Silence. GARDNER enters, still singing. He's wearing mismatched tweeds and is holding a stack of papers which keep drifting to the floor.)

GARDNER: Oh, don't you look nice! Very attractive, very attractive!

FANNY: But I'm still in my bathrobe.

GARDNER: *(Looking around the room, leaking more papers.)* Well, where's Mags?

FANNY: Darling, you're dropping your papers all over the floor.

GARDNER: *(Spies the silver tray.)* I remember this! Aunt Alice gave it to us, didn't she? *(He picks it up.)* Good Lord, it's heavy. What's it made of? Lead?!

FANNY: No, Aunt Alice did *not* give it to us. It was Mama's.

GARDNER: Oh, yes . . .

(He starts to exit with it.)

FANNY: Could I have it back, please?

GARDNER: *(Hands it to her, dropping more papers.)* Oh, sure thing. . . . Where's Mags? I thought you said she was here.

FANNY: I didn't say Mags was here, I asked *you* to come here.

GARDNER: *(Papers spilling.)* Damned papers keep falling. . . .

FANNY: I wanted to show you my new hat. I bought it in honor of Mags' visit. Isn't it marvelous?

GARDNER: *(Picking up the papers as more drop.)* Yes, yes, very nice . . .

FANNY: Gardner, you're not even looking at it!

GARDNER: Very becoming . . .

FANNY: You don't think it's too bright, do you? I don't want to look like a traffic light. Guess how much it cost?

GARDER: *(A whole sheaf of papers slides to the floor; he dives for them.)* OH, SHIT!

FANNY: *(Gets to them first.)* It's all right, I've got them, I've got them. *(She hands them to him.)*

GARDNER: You'd think they had wings on them. . . .

FANNY: Here you go . . .   GARDNER: . . . damned things
                                                                won't hold still!

FANNY: Gar? . . .

GARDNER: *(Has become engrossed in one of the pages.)* Mmmmm?

FANNY: HELLO?

GARDNER: *(Startled.)* What's that?

FANNY: *(In a whisper.)* My hat. Guess how much it cost.

GARDNER: Oh, yes. Let's see . . . ten dollars?

FANNY: Ten dollars . . . IS THAT ALL? . . .

GARDNER: Twenty?

FANNY: GARDNER, THIS HAPPENS TO BE A DESIGNER HAT! DESIGNER HATS START AT FIFTY DOLLARS . . . SEVENTY-FIVE!

GARDNER: *(Jumps.)* Was that the door bell?

FANNY: No, it wasn't the door bell. Though it's high time Mags were here. She was probably in a train wreck!

GARDNER: *(Looking through his papers.)* I'm beginning to get fond of Wallace Stevens again.

FANNY: This damned move is going to kill me! Send me straight to my grave!

GARDNER: *(Reading from a page.)*
"The mules that angels ride come slowly down
The blazing passes, from beyond the sun.
Descensions of their tinkling bells arrive.
These muleteers are dainty of their way . . ."
(Pause.) Don't you love that! "These muleteers are *dainty* of their way"!? . . .

FANNY: Gar, the hat. How much?

(GARDNER sighs.)

FANNY: Darling? . . .

GARDNER: Oh, yes. Let's see . . . fifty dollars? Seventy-five?

FANNY: It's French.

GARDNER: Three hundred!

FANNY: *(Triumphant.)* No, eighty-five cents.

GARDNER: Eighty-five cents! . . . I thought you said . . .

FANNY: That's right . . . eighty . . . five . . . *cents!*

GARDNER: Well, you sure had me fooled!

FANNY: I found it at the thrift shop.

GARDNER: I thought it cost at least fifty dollars or seventy-five. You know, designer hats are very expensive!

FANNY: It was on the mark-down table. *(She takes it off and shows him the label.)* See that! Lily Daché! When I saw that label, I nearly keeled over right into the fur coats!

GARDNER: *(Handling it.)* Well, what do you know, that's the same label that's in my bathrobe.

FANNY: Darling, Lily Daché designed hats, not men's bathrobes!

GARDNER: Yup . . . Lily Daché . . . same name . . .

FANNY: If you look again, I'm sure you'll see . . .

GARDNER: . . . same script, same color, same size. I'll show you.

(He exits.)

FANNY: Poor lamb can't keep anything straight anymore. *(Looks at herself in the tray again.)* God, this is a good-looking hat!

GARDNER: *(Returns with a nondescript bathrobe. He points to the label.)* See that? . . . What does it say?

FANNY: *(Refusing to look at it.)* Lily Daché was a *hat* designer! She designed ladies' *hats!*

GARDNER: What . . . does . . . it . . . say?

FANNY: Gardner, you're being ridiculous.

GARDNER: *(Forcing it on her.)* Read . . . the label!

FANNY: Lily Daché did *not* design this bathrobe, I don't care what the label says!

GARDNER: READ! *(FANNY reads it.)* ALL RIGHT, NOW WHAT DOES IT SAY? . . .

FANNY: *(Chagrined.)* Lily Daché.

GARDNER: I told you!

FANNY: Wait a minute, let me look at that again. *(She does; then throws the robe at him in disgust.)* Gar, Lily Daché never designed a bathrobe in her life! Someone obviously ripped the label off one of her hats and then sewed it into the robe.

GARDNER: *(Puts it on over his jacket.)* It's damned good-looking. I've always loved this robe. I think you gave it to me. . . . Well, I've got to get back to work.

(He abruptly exits.)

FANNY: Where did you get that robe anyway? . . . I didn't give it to you, did I? . . .

(Silence. GARDNER resumes typing.)

FANNY: *(Holding the tray up again and admiring herself.)* You know, I think I *did* give it to him. I remember how excited I was when I found it at the thrift shop . . . fifty cents and never worn! *I* couldn't have sewn

that label in it to impress him, could I? . . . I can't be that far gone! . . .
The poor lamb wouldn't even notice it, let alone understand its ca-
chet. . . . Uuuuuuh, this damned tray is even heavier than the coffee
pot. They must have been amazons in the old days! *(Writes on her pad.)*
"Empire tray, Parke-Bernet Galleries," and good riddance! *(She wraps it
and drops it into the carton with the coffee pot.)* Where *is* that wretched
Mags? It would be just like her to get into a train wreck! She was
supposed to be here hours ago. Well, if she doesn't show up soon,
I'm going to drop dead of exhaustion. God, wouldn't that be wonderful? . . . Then they could just cart me off into storage with all the old
chandeliers and china . . .

(The doorbell rings.)

FANNY: IT'S MAGS, IT'S
MAGS! *(A pause. Dashing
out of the room, colliding into
GARDNER.)* GOOD GOD,
LOOK AT ME! I'M STILL
IN MY BATHROBE!

GARDNER: *(Offstage.)* COMING,
COMING . . . I'VE GOT
IT . . . COMING! *(Dashing
into the room, colliding into
FANNY.)* I'VE GOT IT . . .
HOLD ON . . . COM-
ING . . . COMING . . .

FANNY: *(Offstage.)* MAGS IS HERE! IT'S MAGS. . . . SHE'S FINALLY
HERE!

*(GARDNER exits to open the front door. MAGS comes staggering in carrying
a suitcase and an enormous duffle bag. She wears wonderfully distinctive
clothes and has very much her own look. She's extremely out of breath and too
wrought up to drop her heavy bags.)*

MAGS: I'm sorry . . . I'm sorry I'm so late. . . . Everything went wrong!
A passenger had a heart attack outside of New London and we had
to stop. . . . It was terrifying! All these medics and policemen came
swarming onto the train and the conductor kept running up and down
the aisles telling everyone not to leave their seats under any circumstances. . . . Then the New London fire department came screeching
down to the tracks, sirens blaring, lights whirling, and all these men in
black rubber suits starting pouring through the doors. . . . *That* took
two hours. . . .

FANNY: DARLING . . . DARLING . . . WHERE ARE YOU? . . .

MAGS: *Then,* I couldn't get a cab at the station. There just weren't any! I
must have circled the block fifteen times. Finally I just stepped out into
the traffic with my thumb out, but no one would pick me up . . . so I
walked. . . .

FANNY: *(Offstage.)* Damned zipper's stuck. . . .

GARDNER: You walked all the way from the South Station?

MAGS: Well actually, I ran. . . .

GARDNER: You had poor Mum scared to death.

MAGS: *(Finally puts the bags down with a deep sigh.)* I'm sorry. . . . I'm really sorry. It was a nightmare.

FANNY: *(Reenters the room, her dress over her head. The zipper's stuck; she staggers around blindly.)* Damned zipper! Gar, will you please help me with this?

MAGS: I sprinted all the way up Beacon Hill.

GARDNER: *(Opening his arms wide.)* Well, come here and let's get a look at you. *(He hugs her.)* Mags! . . .

MAGS: *(Squeezing him tight.)* Oh, Daddy . . . Daddy!

GARDNER: My Mags!

MAGS: I never thought I'd get here! . . . Oh, you look wonderful!

GARDNER: Well, you don't look so bad yourself!

MAGS: I love your hair. It's gotten so . . . white!

FANNY: *(Still lost in her dress, struggling with the zipper.)* This is *so* typical . . . just as Mags arrives, my zipper has to break! *(FANNY grunts and struggles.)*

MAGS: *(Waves at her.)* Hi, Mum. . . .

FANNY: Just a minute, dear, my zipper's . . .

GARDNER: *(Picks up MAGS' bags.)* Well, sit down and take a load off your feet. . . .

MAGS: I was so afraid I'd never make it. . . .

GARDNER: *(Staggering under the weight of her bags.)* What have you got in here? Lead weights?

MAGS: I can't believe you're finally letting me do you.

FANNY: *(Flings her arms around MAGS, practically knocking her over.)* OH, DARLING . . . MY PRECIOUS MAGS, YOU'RE HERE AT LAST.

GARDNER: *(Lurching around in circles.)* Now let's see . . . where should I put these? . . .

FANNY: I was sure your train had derailed and you were lying dead in some ditch!

MAGS: *(Pulls away from FANNY to come to GARDNER's rescue.)* Daddy, please, let me . . . these are much too heavy.

FANNY: *(Finally noticing MAGS.)* GOOD LORD, WHAT HAVE YOU DONE TO YOUR HAIR?!

MAGS: *(Struggling to take the bags from GARDNER.)* Come on, give them to me . . . please? *(She sets them down by the sofa.)*

FANNY: *(As her dress starts to slide off one shoulder.)* Oh, not again! . . . Gar, would you give me a hand and see what's wrong with this zipper. One minute it's stuck, the next it's falling to pieces. *(GARDNER goes to her and starts fussing with it.)*

MAGS: *(Pacing.)* I don't know, it's been crazy all week. Monday, I forgot to keep an appointment I'd made with a new model. . . . Tuesday, I overslept and stood up my advanced painting students. . . . Wednesday, the day of my meeting with Max Zoll, I forgot to put on my underpants. . . .

FANNY: GOD DAMNIT, GAR, CAN'T YOU DO ANYTHING ABOUT THIS ZIPPER?!

MAGS: I mean, there I was, racing down Broome Street in this gauzy Tibetan skirt when I tripped and fell right at his feet . . . SPLATTT! My skirt goes flying over my head and there I am . . . everything staring him in the face . . .

FANNY: COME ON, GAR, USE A LITTLE MUSCLE!

MAGS: *(Laughing.)* Oh, well, all that matters is that I finally got here. . . . I mean . . . there you are. . . .

GARDNER: *(Struggling with the zipper.)* I can't see it, it's too small!

FANNY: *(Whirls away from* GARDNER*, pulling her dress off altogether.)* OH, FORGET IT! JUST FORGET IT! . . . The trolley's probably missing half its teeth, just like someone else I know. *(To* MAGS.*)* I grind my teeth in my sleep now, I've worn them all down to stubs. Look at that! *(She flings open her mouth and points.)* Nothing left but the gums!

GARDNER: I never hear you grind your teeth. . . .

FANNY: That's because I'm snoring so loud. How could you hear anything through all that racket? It even wakes me up. It's no wonder poor Daddy has to sleep downstairs.

MAGS: *(Looking around.)* Jeez, look at the place! So, you're finally doing it . . . selling the house and moving to Cotuit year round. I don't believe it. I just don't believe it!

GARDNER: Well, how about a drink to celebrate Mags' arrival?

MAGS: You've been here so long. Why move now?

FANNY: Gardner, what are you wearing that bathrobe for? . . .

MAGS: You can't move. I won't let you!

FANNY: *(Softly to* GARDNER.*)* Really, darling, you ought to pay more attention to your appearance.

MAGS: You love this house. *I* love this house . . . this room . . . the light.

GARDNER: So, Mags, how about a little . . . *(he drinks from an imaginary glass)* to wet your whistle?

FANNY: We can't start drinking now, it isn't even noon yet!

MAGS: I'm starving. I've got to get something to eat before I collapse!

(She exits toward the kitchen.)

FANNY: What *have* you done to your hair, dear? The color's so queer and all your nice curl is gone.

GARDNER: It looks to me as if she dyed it.

FANNY: Yes, that's it. You're absolutely right! It's a completely different color. She dyed it bright red!

(MAGS can be heard thumping and thudding through the icebox.)

FANNY: NOW, MAGS, I DON'T WANT YOU FILLING UP ON SNACKS. . . . I'VE MADE A PERFECTLY BEAUTIFUL LEG OF LAMB FOR LUNCH! . . . HELLO? . . . DO YOU HEAR ME? . . . *(To* GARDNER.*)* No one in our family has *ever* had red hair, it's so common looking.

GARDNER: I like it. It brings out her eyes.

FANNY: WHY ON EARTH DID YOU DYE YOUR HAIR *RED,* OF ALL COLORS?! . . .

MAGS: *(Returns, eating Saltines out of the box.)* I didn't dye my hair, I just added some highlight.

FANNY: I suppose that's what your arty friends in New York do . . . dye their hair all the colors of the rainbow!

GARDNER: Well, it's damned attractive if you ask me . . . damned attractive!

*(*MAGS *unzips her duffle bag and rummages around in it while eating the Saltines.)*

FANNY: Darling, I told you not to bring a lot of stuff with you. We're trying to get rid of things.

MAGS: *(Pulls out a folding easel and starts setting it up.)* AAAAAHHHHHH, here it is. Isn't it a beauty? I bought it just for you!

FANNY: Please don't get crumbs all over the floor. Crystal was just here yesterday. It was her last time before we move.

MAGS: *(At her easel.)* God, I can hardly wait! I can't believe you're finally letting me do you.

FANNY: *"Do"* us? . . . What *are* you talking about?

GARDNER: *(Reaching for the Saltines.)* Hey, Mags, could I have a couple of those?

MAGS: *(Tosses him the box.)* Sure! *(To* FANNY.*)* Your portrait.

GARDNER: Thanks. *(He starts munching on a handful.)*

FANNY: You're planning to paint our portrait now? While we're trying to move? . . .

GARDNER: *(Sputtering Saltines.)* Mmmmm, I'd forgotten just how delicious Saltines are!

MAGS: It's a perfect opportunity. There'll be no distractions; you'll be completely at my mercy. Also, you promised.

FANNY: I did?

MAGS: Yes, you did.

FANNY: Well, I must have been off my rocker.

MAGS: No, you said, "You can paint us, you can dip us in concrete, you can do anything you want with us, just so long as you help us get out of here!"

GARDNER: *(Offering the box of Saltines to* FANNY.*)* You really ought to try some of these, Fan, they're absolutely delicious!

FANNY: *(Taking a few.)* Why, thank you.

MAGS: I figure we'll pack in the morning and you'll pose in the afternoons. It'll be a nice diversion.

FANNY: These *are* good!

GARDNER: Here, dig in . . . take some more.

MAGS: I have some wonderful news . . . amazing news! I wanted to wait 'til I got here to tell you.

(They eat their Saltines, passing the box back and forth as MAGS *speaks.)*

MAGS: You'll die! Just fall over into the packing cartons and die! Are you ready? . . . BRACE YOURSELVES. . . . OK, HERE GOES. . . . I'm being given a one woman show at one of the most important galleries in New York this fall. Me, Margaret Church, exhibited at Castelli's, 420 West Broadway. . . . Can you believe it? . . . MY PORTRAITS HANGING IN THE SAME ROOMS THAT HAVE SHOWN RAUSCHENBERG, JOHNS, WARHOL, KELLY, LICHTEN-STEIN, STELLA, SERRA, ALL THE HEAVIES. . . . It's incredible, beyond belief . . . I mean, at my age. . . . Do you know how good you have to be to get in there? It's a miracle . . . an honest-to-God, star-spangled miracle!

(Pause.)

FANNY: *(Mouth full.)* Oh, darling, that's wonderful. We're so happy for you!

GARDNER: *(His mouth full.)* No one deserves it more, no one deserves it more!

MAGS: Through some fluke, some of Castelli's people showed up at our last faculty show at Pratt and were knocked out. . . .

FANNY: *(Reaching for the box of Saltines.)* More, more . . .

MAGS: They said they hadn't seen anyone handle light like me since the French Impressionists. They said I was this weird blend of Pierre Bonnard, Mary Cassatt and David Hockney. . . .

GARDNER: *(Swallowing his own mouthful.)* I told you they were good.

MAGS: Also, no one's doing portraits these days. They're considered passé. I'm so out of it, I'm in.

GARDNER: Well, you're loaded with talent and always have been.

FANNY: She gets it all from Mama, you know. Her miniature of Henry James is still one of the main attractions at the Atheneum. Of course no woman of breeding could be a professional artist in her day. It simply wasn't done. But talk about talent . . . that woman had talent to burn!

MAGS: I want to do one of you for the show.

FANNY: Oh, do Daddy, he's the famous one.

MAGS: No, I want to do you both. I've always wanted to do you and now I've finally got a good excuse.

FANNY: It's high time somebody painted Daddy again! I'm sick to death of that dreadful portrait of him in the National Gallery they keep reproducing. He looks like an undertaker!

GARDNER: Well, I think you should just do Mum. She's never looked handsomer.

FANNY: Oh, come on, I'm a perfect fright and you know it.

MAGS: I want to do you both. Side by side. In this room. Something really classy. You look so great. Mum with her crazy hats and everything and you with that face. If I could just get you to hold still long enough and actually pose.

GARDNER: *(Walking around, distracted.)* Where are those papers I just had? God damnit, Fanny. . . .

MAGS: I have the feeling it's either now or never.

GARDNER: I can't hold on to anything around here. *(He exits to his study.)*

MAGS: I've always wanted to do you. It would be such a challenge.

FANNY: *(Pulling MAGS next to her onto the sofa.)* I'm so glad you're finally here, Mags. I'm very worried about Daddy.

MAGS: Mummy, please. I just got here.

FANNY: He's getting quite gaga.

MAGS: Mummy! . . .

FANNY: You haven't seen him in almost a year. Two weeks ago he walked through the front door of the Codmans' house, kissed Emily on the cheek and settled down in the maid's room, thinking he was home!

MAGS: Oh, come on, you're exaggerating.

FANNY: He's as mad as a hatter and getting worse every day! It's this damned new book of his. He works on it around the clock. I've read some of it, and it doesn't make one word of sense, it's all at sixes and sevens. . . .

GARDNER: *(Poking his head back in the room, spies some of his papers on a table and grabs them.)* Ahhh, here they are.

(He exits.)

FANNY: *(Voice lowered.)* Ever since this dry spell with his poetry, he's been frantic, absolutely . . . frantic!

MAGS: I hate it when you do this.

FANNY: I'm just trying to get you to face the facts around here.

MAGS: There's nothing wrong with him! He's just as sane as the next man. Even saner, if you ask me.

FANNY: You know what he's doing now? You couldn't guess in a million years! . . . He's writing criticism! Daddy! *(She laughs.)* Can you believe it? The man doesn't have one analytic bone in his body. His mind is a complete jumble and always has been! *(There's a loud crash from GARD-NER's study.)*

GARDNER: *(Offstage.)* SHIT!

MAGS: He's abstracted. . . . That's the way he is.

FANNY: He doesn't spend any time with me anymore. He just holes up in that filthy study with Toots. God, I hate that bird! Though actually they're quite cunning together. Daddy's teaching him Gray's Elegy. You ought to see him in there, Toots perched on top of Daddy's head, spouting out verse after verse . . . Daddy, tap-tap-tapping away on his typewriter. They're quite a pair.

GARDNER: (Pokes his head back in.) Have you seen that Stevens poem I was reading before?

FANNY: (Long suffering.) NO, I HAVEN'T SEEN THAT STEVENS POEM YOU WERE READING BEFORE! . . . Things are getting very tight around here, in case you haven't noticed. Daddy's last Pulitzer didn't even cover our real estate tax, and now that he's too doddery to give readings anymore, that income is gone. . . . (Suddenly handing MAGS the sugar bowl she'd been wrapping.) Mags, do take this sugar bowl. You can use it to serve tea to your students at that wretched art school of yours. . . .

MAGS: It's called Pratt! The Pratt Institute.

FANNY: Pratt, Splatt, whatever . . .

MAGS: And I don't serve tea to my students, I teach them how to paint.

FANNY: Well, I'm sure none of them has ever seen a sugar bowl as handsome as this before.

GARDNER: (Reappearing again.) You're sure you haven't seen it? . . .

FANNY: (Loud and angry.) YES, I'M SURE I HAVEN'T SEEN IT! I JUST TOLD YOU I HAVEN'T SEEN IT!

GARDNER: (Retreating.) Right you are, right you are.

(He exits.)

FANNY: God!

(Silence.)

MAGS: What do you have to yell at him like that for?

FANNY: Because the poor thing's as deaf as an adder!

(MAGS sighs deeply; silence.)

FANNY: (Suddenly exuberant, leads her over to a lamp.) Come, I want to show you something.

MAGS: (Looking at it.) What is it?

FANNY: Something I made. (MAGS is about to turn it on.) WAIT, DON'T TURN IT ON YET! It's got to be dark to get the full effect. (She rushes to the windows and pulls down the shades.)

MAGS: What are you doing? . . .

FANNY: Hold your horses a minute. You'll see. . . . (As the room gets darker and darker.) Poor me, you wouldn't believe the lengths I go to to amuse myself these days. . . .

MAGS: (Touching the lamp shade.) What is this? It looks like a scene of some sort.

FANNY: It's an invention I made . . . a kind of magic lantern.

MAGS: Gee . . . it's amazing. . . .

FANNY: What I did was buy an old engraving of the Grand Canal. . . .

MAGS: You made this?

FANNY: . . . and then color it in with crayons. Next, I got out my sewing scissors and cut out all the street lamps and windows . . . anything that light would shine through. Then I pasted it over a plain lampshade, put the shade on this old horror of a lamp, turned on the switch and . . . *(She turns it on.)* VOILÀ . . . VENICE TWINKLING AT DUSK! It's quite effective, don't you think? . . .

MAGS: *(Walking around it.)* Jeeez . . .

FANNY: And see, I poked out all the little lights on the gondolas with a straight pin.

MAGS: Where on earth did you get the idea?

FANNY: Well you know, idle minds . . .

(FANNY spins the shade, making the lights whirl.)

MAGS: It's really amazing. I mean, you could sell this in a store!

GARDNER: *(Enters.)* HERE IT IS. IT WAS RIGHT ON TOP OF MY DESK THE WHOLE TIME. *(He crashes into a table.)* OOOOOWWWWW!

FANNY: LOOK OUT, LOOK OUT!

MAGS: *(Rushes over to him.)* Oh, Daddy, are you all right?

FANNY: WATCH WHERE YOU'RE GOING, WATCH WHERE YOU'RE GOING!

GARDNER: *(Hopping up and down on one leg.)* GOD DAMNIT! . . . I HIT MY SHIN.

FANNY: I was just showing Mags my lamp. . . .

GARDNER: *(Limping over to it.)* Oh, yes, isn't that something? Mum is awfully clever with that kind of thing. . . . It was all her idea. Buying the engraving, coloring it in, cutting out all those little dots.

FANNY: Not "dots" . . . lights and windows, lights and windows!

GARDNER: Right, right . . . lights and windows.

FANNY: Well, we'd better get some light back in here before someone breaks their neck. *(She zaps the shades back up.)*

GARDNER: *(Puts his arm around MAGS.)* Gee, it's good to have you back.

MAGS: It's good to be back.

GARDNER: And I like that new red hair of yours. It's very becoming.

MAGS: But I told you, I hardly touched it. . . .

GARDNER: Well, something's different. You've got a glow. So . . . how do you want us to pose for this grand portrait of yours? . . .

(He poses self-consciously.)

MAGS: Oh, Daddy, setting up a portrait takes a lot of time and thought. You've got to figure out the background, the lighting, what to wear, the sort of mood you want to . . .

FANNY: OOOOH, LET'S DRESS UP, LET'S DRESS UP! *(She grabs a packing blanket, drapes it around herself and links arms with* GARDNER, *striking an elegant pose.)* This is going to be fun. She was absolutely right! Come on, Gar, look distinguished!

MAGS: Mummy, please, it's not a game!

FANNY: *(More and more excited.)* You still have your tuxedo, don't you? And I'll wear my marvelous long black dress that makes me look like the fascinating woman in the Sargent painting! *(She strikes the famous profile pose.)*

MAGS: MUMMY?! . . .

FANNY: I'm sorry, we'll behave, just tell us what to do.

(They settle down next to each other.)

GARDNER: That's right, you're the boss.

FANNY: Yes, you're the boss.

MAGS: But I'm not ready yet; I haven't set anything up.

FANNY: Relax, darling, we just want to get the hang of it. . . .

(They stare straight ahead, trying to look like suitable subjects, but they can't hold still. They keep making faces, lifting an eyebrow, wriggling a nose, twitching a lip. Nothing big and grotesque, just flickering changes; a half-smile here, a self-important frown there. They steal glances at each other every so often.)

GARDNER: How am I doing, Fan?

FANNY: Brilliantly, absolutely brilliantly!

MAGS: But you're making faces.

FANNY: *I'm* not making faces. *(Turning to* GARDNER *and making a face.)* Are *you* making faces, Gar?

GARDNER: *(Instantly making one.)* Certainly not! I'm the picture of restraint!

(Without meaning to, they get sillier and sillier. They start giggling, then laughing.)

MAGS: *(Can't help but join in.)* You two are impossible . . . completely impossible! I was crazy to think I could ever pull this off! *(Laughing away.)* Look at you . . . just . . . look at you!

BLACKOUT

SCENE 2

Scene *Two days later, around five in the afternoon. Half of the Church household has been dragged into the living room for packing. Overflowing cartons are everywhere. They're filled with pots and pans, dishes and glasses, and the entire contents of two linen closets.* MAGS *has placed a stepladder under one of the windows. A pile of* *tablecloths and curtains is flung beneath it. Two side chairs are in readiness for the eventual pose.*

MAGS: *(Has just pulled a large crimson tablecloth out of a carton. She unfurls it with one shimmering toss.)* PERFECT . . . PERFECT! . . .

FANNY: *(Seated on the sofa, clutches an old pair of galoshes to her chest.)* Look at these old horrors; half the rubber is rotted away and the fasteners are falling to pieces. . . . GARDNER? . . . OH, GARRRRRRRRRRDNERRRRR? . . .

MAGS: *(Rippling out the tablecloth with shorter snapping motions.)* Have you ever seen such a color? . . .

FANNY: I'VE FOUND YOUR OLD SLEDDING GALOSHES IN WITH THE POTS AND PANS. DO YOU STILL WANT THEM?

MAGS: It's like something out of a Rubens! . . . *(She slings it over a chair and then sits on a footstool to finish the Sara Lee banana cake she started. As she eats, she looks at the tablecloth making happy grunting sounds.)*

FANNY: *(Lovingly puts the galoshes on over her shoes and wiggles her feet.)* God, these bring back memories! There were real snowstorms in the old days. Not these pathetic little two-inch droppings we have now. After a particularly heavy one, Daddy and I used to go sledding on the Common. This was way before you were born. . . . God, it was a hundred years ago! . . . Daddy would stop writing early, put on these galoshes and come looking for me, jingling the fasteners like castanets. It was a kind of mating call, almost. . . . *(She jingles them.)* The Common was always deserted after a storm; we had the whole place to ourselves. It was so romantic. . . . We'd haul the sled up Beacon Street, stop under the State House, and aim it straight down to the Park Street Church, which was much further away in those days. . . . Then Daddy would lie down on the sled, I'd lower myself on top of him, we'd rock back and forth a few times to gain momentum and then . . . WHOOOOOOOOSSSSSSSHHHHH . . . down we'd plunge like a pair of eagles locked in a spasm of lovemaking. God, it was wonderful! . . . The city whizzing past us at ninety miles an hour . . . the cold . . . the darkness . . . Daddy's hair in my mouth . . . GAR . . . REMEMBER HOW WE USED TO GO SLEDDING IN THE OLD DAYS? . . . Sometimes he'd lie on top of me. That was fun. I liked that even more. *(In her foghorn voice.)* GARRRRRRRRRRRDNERRRRR? . . .

MAGS: Didn't he say he was going out this afternoon?

FANNY: Why, so he did! I completely forgot. *(She takes off the galoshes.)* I'm getting just as bad as him. *(She drops them into a different carton—wistful.)* Gar's galoshes, Cotuit.

(A pause.)

MAGS: *(Picks up the tablecloth again; holds it high over her head.)* Isn't this fabulous? . . . *(She then wraps* FANNY *in it.)* It's the perfect backdrop. Look what it does to your skin.

FANNY: Mags, what *are* you doing?

MAGS: It makes you glow like a pomegranate. . . . *(She whips it off her.)* Now all I need is a hammer and nails. . . . *(She finds them.)* YES! *(She climbs up the stepladder and starts hammering a corner of the cloth into the moulding of one of the windows.)* This is going to look so great! . . . I've never seen such color!

FANNY: Darling, what is going on? . . .

MAGS: Rembrandt, eat your heart out! You seventeenth-century Dutch has-been, you. *(She hammers more furiously.)*

FANNY: MARGARET, THIS IS NOT A CONSTRUCTION SITE. . . . PLEASE . . . STOP IT. . . . YOOHOOOOO . . . DO YOU HEAR ME? . . .

(GARDNER suddenly appears, dressed in a raincoat.)

GARDNER: YES, DEAR, HERE I AM. I JUST STEPPED OUT FOR A WALK DOWN CHESTNUT STREET. BEAUTIFUL AFTERNOON, ABSOLUTELY BEAUTIFUL!

FANNY: *(To MAGS.)* YOU'RE GOING TO RUIN THE WALLS TO SAY NOTHING OF MAMA'S BEST TABLECLOTH. . . . MAGS, DO YOU HEAR ME? . . . YOO-HOO! . . .

GARDNER: WHY, THAT LOOKS VERY NICE, MAGS, very nice indeed. . . .

FANNY: DARLING, I MUST INSIST you stop that dreadful . . .

MAGS: *(Steps down; stands back and looks at it.)* That's it. That's IT!

FANNY: *(To GARDNER, worried.)* Where have *you* been? *(MAGS kisses her fingers at the backdrop and settles back into her banana cake.)*

GARDNER: *(To FANNY.)* You'll never guess who I ran into on Chestnut Street . . . Pate Baldwin!

(He takes his coat off and drops it on the floor. He then sits in one of the posing chairs.)

MAGS: *(Mouth full of cake.)* Oh, Daddy, I'm nowhere near ready for you yet.

FANNY: *(Picks up his coat and hands it to him.)* Darling, coats do *not* go on the floor.

GARDNER: *(Rises, but forgets where he's supposed to go.)* He was in terrible shape. I hardly recognized him. Well, it's the Parkinson's disease. . . .

FANNY: You mean, Hodgkin's disease. . . .

GARDNER: Hodgkin's disease? . . .

MAGS: *(Leaves her cake and returns to the tablecloth.)* Now to figure out exactly how to use this gorgeous light. . . .

FANNY: Yes, Pate has Hodgkin's disease, not Parkinson's disease. Sammy Bishop has Parkinson's disease. In the closet . . . your coat goes . . . in the closet!

GARDNER: You're absolutely right! Pate has Hodgkin's disease. *(He stands motionless, the coat over his arm.)*

FANNY: . . . and Goat Davis has Addison's disease.

GARDNER: I always get them confused.

FANNY: *(Pointing towards the closet.)* That way. . . . *(GARDNER exits to the closet;* FANNY *calls after him.)* Grace Phelps has it too. I think. Or, it might be Hodgkin's, like Pate. I can't remember.

GARDNER: *(Returns with a hanger.)* Doesn't the Goat have Parkinson's disease?

FANNY: No, that's Sammy Bishop.

GARDNER: God, I haven't seen the Goat in ages! *(The coat still over his arm, he hands* FANNY *the hanger.)*

FANNY: He hasn't been well.

GARDNER: Didn't Heppy . . . *die?!*

FANNY: What are you giving me this for? . . . Oh, Heppy's been dead for years. She died on the same day as Luster Bright, don't you remember?

GARDNER: I always liked her.

FANNY: *(Gives him back the hanger.)* Here, I don't want this.

GARDNER: She was awfully attractive.

FANNY: Who?

GARDNER: Heppy!

FANNY: Oh, yes, Heppy had real charm.

MAGS: *(Keeps adjusting the tablecloth.)* Better . . . better . . .

GARDNER: . . . which is something the Goat is short on, if you ask me. He has Hodgkin's disease, doesn't he?

(Puts his raincoat back on and sits down.)

FANNY: Darling, what *are* you doing? I thought you wanted to hang up your coat!

GARDNER: *(After a pause.)* OH, YES, THAT'S RIGHT! *(He goes back to the closet; a pause.)*

FANNY: Where were we?

GARDNER: *(Returns with yet another hanger.)* Let's see. . . .

FANNY: *(Takes both hangers from him.)* FOR GOD'S SAKE, GAR, PAY ATTENTION!

GARDNER: It was something about the Goat. . . .

FANNY: *(Takes the coat from GARDNER.)* HERE, LET ME DO IT! . . . *(Under her breath to MAGS.)* See what I mean about him? You don't know the half of it! *(She hangs it up in the closet.)* . . . Not the half.

MAGS: *(Still tinkering with the backdrop.)* Almost . . . almost . . .

GARDNER: *(Sitting back down in one of the posing chairs.)* Oh, Fan, did I tell you, I ran into Pate Baldwin just now. I'm afraid he's not long for this world.

FANNY: *(Returning.)* Well, it's that Hodgkin's disease. . . . *(She sits on the posing chair next to him.)*

GARDNER: God, I hate to see him go. He's one of the great editors of our times. I couldn't have done it without him. He gave me everything, everything!

MAGS: *(Makes a final adjustment.)* Yes, that's it! *(She stands back and gazes at them.)* You look wonderful! . . .

FANNY: Isn't it getting to be . . . *(she taps at an imaginary watch on her wrist and drains an imaginary glass)* cocktail time?!

GARDNER: *(Looks at his watch.)* On the button, on the button! *(He rises.)*

FANNY: I'll have the usual, please. Do join us, Mags! Daddy bought some Dubonnet especially for you!

MAGS: Hey. I was just getting some ideas.

GARDNER: *(To MAGS, as he exits for the bar.)* How about a little . . . *Dubonnet* to wet your whistle?

FANNY: Oh, Mags, it's like old times having you back with us like this!

GARDNER: *(Offstage.)* THE USUAL FOR YOU, FAN?

FANNY: I wish we saw more of you. . . . PLEASE! . . . Isn't he darling? Have you ever known anyone more darling than Daddy? . . .

GARDNER: *(Offstage. Hums Jolson's "You Made Me Love You.")* MAGS, HOW ABOUT YOU? . . . A LITTLE . . . DUBONNET? . . .

FANNY: Oh, *do* join us!   MAGS: *(To GARDNER.)* No, nothing, thanks.

FANNY: Well, what do you think of your aged parents picking up and moving to Cotuit year round? Pretty crazy, eh what? . . . Nothing but the gulls, oysters and us!

GARDNER: *(Returns with FANNY's drink.)* Here you go. . . .

FANNY: Why thank you, Gar. *(To MAGS.)* You sure you won't join us?

GARDNER: *(Lifts his glass towards FANNY and MAGS.)* Cheers!

(GARDNER and FANNY take that first life-saving gulp.)

FANNY: Aaaaahhhhh!   GARDNER: Hits the spot, hits the spot!

MAGS: Well, I certainly can't do you like that!

FANNY: Why not? I think we look very . . . *comme il faut!*

(She slouches into a rummy pose; GARDNER joins her.)

WAIT . . . I'VE GOT IT! I'VE GOT IT!

(She whispers excitedly to GARDNER.)

MAGS: Come on, let's not start this again!

GARDNER: What's that? . . . Oh, yes . . . yes, yes . . . I know the one you mean. Yes, right, right . . . of course.

(A pause.)

FANNY: How's . . . *this?!* . . . *(FANNY grabs a large serving fork and they fly into an imitation of Grant Wood's* American Gothic.)

MAGS: . . . and I wonder why it's taken me all these years to get you to pose for me. You just don't take me seriously! Poor old Mags and her ridiculous portraits . . .

FANNY: Oh, darling, your portraits aren't *ridiculous!* They may not be all that one *hopes* for, but they're certainly not . . .

MAGS: Remember how you behaved at my first group show in Soho? . . . Oh, come on, you remember. It was a real circus! Think back. . . . It was about six years ago. . . . Daddy had just been awarded some presidential medal of achievement and you insisted he wear it around his neck on a bright red ribbon, and you wore this . . . *huge* feathered hat to match! I'll never forget it! It was the size of a giant pizza with twenty-inch red turkey feathers shooting straight up into the air. . . . Oh, come on, you remember, don't you? . . .

FANNY: *(Leaping to her feet.)* HOLD EVERYTHING! THIS IS IT! THIS IS REALLY IT! Forgive me for interrupting, Mags darling, it'll just take a minute. *(She whispers excitedly to* GARDNER.*)*

MAGS: I had about eight portraits in the show, mostly of friends of mine, except for this old one I'd done of Mrs. Crowninshield.

GARDNER: All right, all right . . . let's give it a whirl.

(A pause; then they mime Michelangelo's Pietà with GARDNER *lying across* FANNY*'s lap as the dead Christ.)*

MAGS: *(Depressed.)* The *Pietà.* Terrific!

FANNY: *(Jabbing* GARDNER *in the ribs.)* Hey, we're getting good at this.

GARDNER: Of course it would help if we didn't have all these modern clothes on.

MAGS: AS I WAS SAYING . . .

FANNY: Sorry, Mags . . . sorry . . .

(Huffing and creaking with the physical exertion of it all, they return to their seats.)

MAGS: . . . As soon as you stepped foot in the gallery you spotted it and cried out, "MY GOD, WHAT'S MILLICENT CROWNINSHIELD DOING HERE?" Everyone looked up what with Daddy's clanking medal and your amazing hat which I was sure would take off and start flying around the room. A crowd gathered. . . . Through some utter fluke, you latched on to *the* most important critic in the city, I mean . . . Mr. Modern Art himself, and you hauled him over to the painting, trumpeting out for all to hear, "THAT'S MILLICENT CROWNIN-SHIELD! I GREW UP WITH HER. SHE LIVES RIGHT DOWN THE STREET FROM US IN BOSTON. BUT IT'S A VERY POOR LIKENESS, IF YOU ASK ME! HER NOSE ISN'T NEARLY THAT LARGE AND SHE DOESN'T HAVE SOME-THING QUEER GROWING OUT OF HER CHIN! THE CROWNINSHIELDS ARE REALLY QUITE GOOD-LOOKING, STUFFY, BUT GOOD-LOOKING NONETHELESS!"

GARDNER: *(Suddenly jumps up, ablaze.)* WAIT, WAIT . . . IF IT'S MI-CHELANGELO YOU WANT . . . I'm sorry, Mags. . . . One more . . . just one more . . . please?

MAGS: Sure, why not? Be my guest.

GARDNER: *Fanny, prepare yourself!*

(More whispering.)

FANNY: But I think *you* should be God.

GARDNER: Me? . . . Really?

FANNY: Yes, it's much more appropriate.

GARDNER: Well, if you say so . . . *(FANNY and GARDNER ease down to the floor with some difficulty and lie on their sides, FANNY as Adam, GARDNER as God, their fingers inching closer and closer in the attitude of Michelangelo's* The Creation. *Finally they touch.)*

MAGS: *(Cheers, whistles, applauds.)* THREE CHEERS . . . VERY GOOD . . . NICELY DONE, NICELY DONE! *(They hold the pose a moment more, flushed with pleasure; then rise, dust themselves off and grope back to their chairs.)* So, there we were. . . .

FANNY: Yes, *do* go on! . . .

MAGS: . . . huddled around Millicent Crowninshield, when you whipped into your pocketbook and suddenly announced, "HOLD EVERY-THING! I'VE GOT A PHOTOGRAPH OF HER RIGHT HERE, THEN YOU CAN SEE WHAT SHE REALLY LOOKS LIKE!" . . . You then proceeded to crouch down to the floor and dump everything out of your bag, and I mean . . . *everything!* . . . leaking packets of sequins and gummed stars, sea shells, odd pieces of fur, crochet hooks, a monarch butterfly embedded in plastic, dental floss, antique glass buttons, small jingling bells, lace . . . I thought I'd die! Just sink to the floor and quietly die! . . . You couldn't find it, you see. I mean, you spent the rest of the afternoon on your hands and knees crawling through this ocean of junk, muttering, "It's *got* to be here somewhere; I know I had it with me!" . . . Then Daddy pulled me into the thick of it all and said, "By the way, have you met our daughter Mags yet? She's the one who did all these pictures . . . paintings . . . portraits . . . whatever you call them." *(She drops to her hands and knees and begins crawling out of the room.)* By this time, Mum had somehow crawled out of the gallery and was lost on another floor. She began calling for me . . . "YOO-HOO, MAGS . . . WHERE ARE YOU? . . . OH, MAGS, DARLING . . . HELLO? . . . ARE YOU THERE? . . ." *(She reenters and faces them.)* This was at my *first* show.

BLACKOUT

SCENE 3

Scene *Twenty-four hours later. The impact of the impending move has struck with hurricane force.* FANNY *has lugged all their clothing into the room and dumped* *it in various cartons. There are coats, jackets, shoes, skirts, suits, hats, sweaters, dresses, the works. She and* GARDNER *are seated on the sofa, going through it all.*

FANNY: *(Wearing a different hat and dress, holds up a ratty overcoat.)* What about this gruesome old thing?

GARDNER: *(Is wearing several sweaters and vests, a Hawaiian holiday shirt, and a variety of scarves and ties around his neck. He holds up a pair of shoes.)* God . . . remember these shoes? Pound gave them to me when he came back from Italy. I remember it vividly.

FANNY: *Do* let me give it to the thrift shop! *(She stuffs the coat into the appropriate carton.)*

GARDNER: He bought them for me in Rome. Said he couldn't resist; bought himself a pair too since we both wore the same size. God, I miss him! *(Pause.)* HEY, WHAT ARE YOU DOING WITH MY OVERCOAT?!

FANNY: Darling, it's threadbare!

GARDNER: But that's my overcoat! *(He grabs it out of the carton.)* I've been wearing it every day for the past thirty-five years!

FANNY: That's just my point: It's had it.

GARDNER: *(Puts it on over everything else.)* There's nothing wrong with this coat!

FANNY: I trust you remember that the cottage is an eighth the size of this place and you simply won't have room for half this stuff! *(She holds up a sports jacket.)* This dreary old jacket, for instance. You've had it since Hector was a pup!

GARDNER: *(Grabs it and puts it on over his coat.)* Oh, no, you don't. . . .

FANNY: . . . and this God-awful hat . . .

GARDNER: Let me see that.

(He stands next to her and they fall into a lovely tableau.)

MAGS: *(Suddenly pops out from behind a wardrobe carton with a flash camera and takes a picture of them.)* PERFECT!

FANNY: *(Hands flying to her face.)* GARDNER: *(Hands flying to his*
GOOD GOD, WHAT WAS   *heart.)* JESUS CHRIST, I'VE
THAT? . . .   BEEN SHOT!

MAGS: *(Walks to the center of the room, advancing the film.)* That was terrific. See if you can do it again.

FANNY: What *are* you doing? . . .

GARDNER: *(Feeling his chest.)* Is there blood?

FANNY: I see lace everywhere. . . .

MAGS: It's all right, I was just taking a picture of you. I often use a Polaroid at this stage.

FANNY: *(Rubbing her eyes.)* Really, Mags, you might have given us some warning!

MAGS: But that's the whole point: to catch you unawares!

GARDNER: *(Rubbing his eyes.)* It's the damndest thing. . . . I see lace everywhere.

FANNY: Yes, so do I. . . .

GARDNER: It's rather nice, actually. It looks as if you're wearing a veil.

FANNY: I *am* wearing a veil!

(The camera spits out the photograph.)

MAGS: OH GOODY, HERE COMES THE PICTURE!

FANNY: *(Grabs the partially developed print out of her hands.)* Let me see, let me see. . . .

GARDNER: Yes, let's have a look.

(They have another quiet moment together looking at the photograph.)

MAGS: *(Tiptoes away from them and takes another picture.)* YES!

FANNY: NOT AGAIN! PLEASE,   GARDNER: WHAT WAS THAT?
DARLING!   . . . WHAT HAPPENED? . . .

(They stagger towards each other.)

MAGS: I'm sorry, I just couldn't resist. You looked so . . .

FANNY: WHAT ARE YOU TRYING TO DO . . . *BLIND* US?!

GARDNER: Really, Mags, enough is enough. . . .

(GARDNER and FANNY keep stumbling about kiddingly.)

FANNY: Are you still there, Gar?

GARDNER: Right as rain, right as rain!

MAGS: I'm sorry; I didn't mean to scare you. It's just a photograph can show you things you weren't aware of. Here, have a look. *(She gives them to FANNY.)* Well, I'm going out to the kitchen to get something to eat. Anybody want anything?

(She exits.)

FANNY: *(Looking at the photos, half-amused, half-horrified.)* Oh, Gardner, have you ever? . . .

GARDNER: *(Looks at them and laughs.)* Good grief . . .

MAGS: *(Offstage; from the kitchen.)* IS IT ALL RIGHT IF I TAKE THE REST OF THIS TAPIOCA FROM LAST NIGHT?

FANNY: IT'S ALL RIGHT WITH ME. How about you, Gar?

GARDNER: Sure, go right ahead. I've never been that crazy about tapioca.

FANNY: What are you talking about, tapioca is one of your favorites.

MAGS: *(Enters, slurping from a large bowl.)* Mmmmmmmm . . .

FANNY: Really, Mags, I've never seen anyone eat as much as you.

MAGS: *(Takes the photos back.)* It's strange. I only do this when I come home.

FANNY: What's the matter, don't I feed you enough?

GARDNER: Gee, it's hot in here!

(Starts taking off his coat.)

FANNY: God knows, you didn't eat anything as a child! I've never seen such a fussy eater. Gar, what *are* you doing?

GARDNER: Taking off some of these clothes. It's hotter than Tofit in here!

(Shedding clothes to the floor.)

MAGS: *(Looking at her photos.)* Yes, I like you looking at each other like that. . . .

FANNY: *(To GARDNER.)* Please watch where you're dropping things; I'm trying to keep some order around here.

GARDNER: *(Picks up what he dropped, dropping even more in the process.)* Right, right. . . .

MAGS: Now all I've got to do is figure out what you should wear.

FANNY: Well, I'm going to wear my long black dress, and you'd be a fool not to do Daddy in his tuxedo. He looks so distinguished in it, just like a banker!

MAGS: I haven't really decided yet.

FANNY: Just because you walk around looking like something the cat dragged in, doesn't mean Daddy and I want to, do we, Gar?

(GARDNER is making a worse and worse tangle of his clothes.)

FANNY: HELLO? . . .

GARDNER: *(Looks up at FANNY.)* Oh, yes, awfully attractive, awfully attractive!

FANNY: *(To MAGS.)* If you don't mind me saying so, I've never seen you looking so forlorn. You'll never catch a husband looking that way. Those peculiar clothes, that God-awful hair . . . really, Mags, it's very distressing!

MAGS: I don't think my hair's so bad, not that it's terrific or anything . . .

FANNY: Well, I don't see other girls walking around like you. I mean, girls from your background. What would Lyman Wigglesworth think if he saw you in the street?

MAGS: Lyman Wigglesworth?! . . . Uuuuuuughhhhhhh!

(She shudders.)

FANNY: All right then, that brilliant Cabot boy . . . what *is* his name?

GARDNER: Sammy.

FANNY: No, not Sammy . . .

GARDNER: Stephen . . . Stanley . . . Stuart . . . Sheldon . . . Sherlock . . . Sherlock! It's *Sherlock!*

MAGS: Spence!

FANNY: SPENCE, THAT'S IT! GARDNER: THAT'S IT . . .
HIS NAME IS SPENCE! SPENCE! SPENCE
 CABOT!

FANNY: Spence Cabot was first in his class at Harvard.

MAGS: Mum, he has no facial hair.

FANNY: He has his own law firm on Arlington Street.

MAGS: Spence Cabot has six fingers on his right hand!

FANNY: So, he isn't the best–looking thing in the world. Looks isn't everything. He can't help it if he has extra fingers. Have a little sympathy!

MAGS: But the extra one has this weird nail on it that looks like a talon. . . .
It's long and black and . . . *(She shudders.)*

FANNY: No one's perfect, darling. He has lovely handwriting and an absolutely saintly mother. Also, he's as rich as Croesus! He's a lot more
promising than some of those creatures you've dragged home. What
was the name of that dreadful Frenchman who smelled like sweaty
socks? . . . Jean Duke of Scripto?

MAGS: *(Laughing.)* Jean–Luc Zichot!

FANNY: . . . and that peculiar little Oriental fellow with all the teeth! Really, Mags, he could have been put on display at the circus!

MAGS: Oh, yes, Tsu Chin. He was strange, but very sexy. . . .

FANNY: *(Shudders.)* He had such tiny . . . feet! Really, Mags, you've got to
bear down. You're not getting any younger. Before you know it, all the
nice young men will be taken and then where will you be? . . . All by
yourself in that grim little apartment of yours with those peculiar
clothes and that bright red hair . . .

MAGS: MY HAIR IS NOT BRIGHT RED!

FANNY: I only want what's best for you, you know that. You seem to go
out of your way to look wanting. I don't understand it. . . . Gar, what
are you putting your coat on for? . . . You look like some derelict out
on the street. We don't wear coats in the house. *(She helps him out of it.)*
That's the way. . . . I'll just put this in the carton along with everything
else. . . . *(She drops it into the carton, then pauses.)* Isn't it about time for . . .
cocktails!

GARDNER: What's that?

(FANNY taps her wrist and mimes drinking.)

GARDNER: *(Looks at his watch.)* Right you are, right you are! *(Exits to the
bar.)* THE USUAL? . . .

FANNY: *Please!*

GARDNER: *(Offstage.)* HOW ABOUT SOMETHING FOR YOU,
MAGS?

MAGS: SURE, WHY NOT? . . . LET 'ER RIP!

GARDNER: *(Offstage.)* WHAT'S THAT? . . .

FANNY: SHE SAID YES. SHE   MAGS: I'LL HAVE SOME
SAID YES!   DUBONNET!

GARDNER: *(Poking his head back in.)* How about a little Dubonnet?

FANNY: That's just what she said. . . . She'd like some . . . Dubonnet!

GARDNER: *(Goes back to the bar and hums another Jolson tune.)* GEE, IT'S
GREAT HAVING YOU BACK LIKE THIS, MAGS. . . . IT'S JUST
GREAT! *(More singing.)*

FANNY: *(Leaning closer to* MAGS.*)* You have such *potential,* darling! It breaks my heart to see how you've let yourself go. If Lyman Wigglesworth . . .

MAGS: Amazing as it may seem, I don't *care* about Lyman Wigglesworth!

FANNY: From what I've heard, he's quite a lady killer!

MAGS: But with whom? . . . Don't think I haven't heard about his fling with . . . Hopie Stonewall!

FANNY: *(Begins to laugh.)* Oh, God, let's not get started on Hopie Stonewall again . . . ten feet tall with spots on her neck. . . . *(To* GARDNER.*)* OH, DARLING, DO HURRY BACK! WE'RE TALKING ABOUT PATHETIC HOPIE STONEWALL!

MAGS: It's not so much her incredible height and spotted skin; it's those tiny pointed teeth and the size eleven shoes!

FANNY: I love it when you're like this!

(MAGS starts clomping around the room making tiny pointed teeth nibbling sounds.)

FANNY: GARDNER . . . YOU'RE MISSING EVERYTHING! *(Still laughing.)* Why is it Boston girls are always so . . . tall?

MAGS: Hopie Stonewall isn't a Boston girl; she's a giraffe. *(She prances around the room with an imaginary dwarf-sized Lyman.)* She's perfect for Lyman Wigglesworth!

GARDNER: *(Returns with* FANNY*'s drink, which he hands her.)* Now, where were we? . . .

FANNY: *(Trying not to laugh.)* HOPIE STONEWALL! . . .

GARDNER: Oh, yes, she's the very tall one, isn't she?

(FANNY and MAGS burst into gales.)

MAGS: The only hope for us . . . "Boston girls" is to get as far away from our kind as possible.

FANNY: She always asks after you, darling. She's very fond of you, you know.

MAGS: Please, I don't want to hear!

FANNY: Your old friends are *always* asking after you.

MAGS: It's not so much how creepy they all are, as how much they remind me of myself!

FANNY: But you're not "creepy," darling . . . just . . . shabby!

MAGS: I mean, give me a few more inches and some brown splotches here and there, and Hopie and I could be sisters!

FANNY: *(In a whisper to* GARDNER.*)* Don't you love it when Mags is like this? I could listen to her forever!

MAGS: I mean . . . look at me!

FANNY: *(Gasping.)* Don't stop, don't stop!

MAGS: Awkward . . . plain . . . I don't know how to dress, I don't know how to talk. When people find out Daddy's my father, they're always amazed. . . . "Gardner Church is YOUR father?! Aw, come on, you're kidding?!"

FANNY: *(In a whisper.)* Isn't she divine? . . .

MAGS: Sometimes I don't even tell them. I pretend I grew up in the Midwest somewhere . . . farming people . . . we work with our hands.

GARDNER: *(To MAGS.)* Well, how about a little refill? . . .

MAGS: No, no more thanks.

(Pause.)

FANNY: What did you have to go and interrupt her for? She was just getting up a head of steam. . . .

MAGS: *(Walking over to her easel.)* The great thing about being a portrait painter, you see, is it's the *other* guy that's exposed; you're safely hidden behind the canvas and easel. *(Standing behind it.)* You can be as plain as a pitchfork, as inarticulate as mud, but it doesn't matter because you're completely concealed: your body, your face, your intentions. Just as you make your most intimate move, throw open your soul . . . they stretch and yawn, remembering the dog has to be let out at five. . . . To be so invisible while so enthralled . . . it takes your breath away!

GARDNER: Well put, Mags. Awfully well put!

MAGS: That's why I've always wanted to paint you, to see if I'm up to it. It's quite a risk. Remember what I went through as a child with my great masterpiece? . . .

FANNY: You painted a masterpiece when you were a child? . . .

MAGS: Well, it was a masterpiece to me.

FANNY: I had no idea you were precocious as a child. Gardner, do you remember Mags painting a masterpiece as a child?

MAGS: I didn't paint it. It was something I made!

FANNY: Well, this is all news to me! Gar, *do* get me another drink! I haven't had this much fun in years! *(She hands him her glass and reaches for MAGS'.)* Come on, darling, join me. . . .

MAGS: No, no more, thanks. I don't really like the taste.

FANNY: Oh, come on, kick up your heels for once!

MAGS: No, nothing . . . really.

FANNY: Please? Pretty please? . . . To keep me company?!

MAGS: *(Hands GARDNER her glass.)* Oh, all right, what the hell . . .

FANNY: That's a good girl!   GARDNER: *(Exiting.)* Coming right up, coming right up!

FANNY: *(Yelling after him.)* DON'T GIVE ME TOO MUCH NOW. THE LAST ONE WAS AWFULLY STRONG . . . AND HURRY BACK SO YOU DON'T MISS ANYTHING! . . . Daddy's so cunning, I don't know what I'd do without him. If anything should happen to him, I'd just . . .

MAGS: Mummy, nothing's going to happen to him! . . .

FANNY: Well, wait 'til you're our age, it's no garden party. Now . . . where were we? . . .

MAGS: My first masterpiece . . .

FANNY: Oh, yes, but *do* wait 'til Daddy gets back so he can hear it too.... YOO-HOO ... GARRRRRRDNERRRRRR? ... ARE YOU COMING? ... *(Silence.)* Go and check on him, will you?

GARDNER: *(Enters with both drinks. He's very shaken.)* I couldn't find the ice.

FANNY: Well, *finally!*

GARDNER: It just up and disappeared.... *(Hands FANNY her drink.)* There you go.

(FANNY kisses her fingers and takes a hefty swig.)

GARDNER: Mags.

(He hands MAGS her drink.)

MAGS: Thanks, Daddy.

GARDNER: Sorry about the ice.

MAGS: No problem, no problem.

(GARDNER sits down; silence.)

FANNY: *(To MAGS.)* Well, drink up, drink up! *(MAGS downs it in one gulp.)* GOOD GIRL! ... Now, what's all this about a masterpiece? ...

MAGS: I did it during that winter you sent me away from the dinner table. I was about nine years old.

FANNY: We sent you from the dinner table?

MAGS: I was banished for six months.

FANNY: You *were?* ... How extraordinary!

MAGS: Yes, it *was* rather extraordinary!

FANNY: But why?

MAGS: Because I played with my food.

FANNY: You did?

MAGS: I used to squirt it out between my front teeth.

FANNY: Oh, I remember that! God, it used to drive me crazy, absolutely ... crazy! *(Pause.)* "MARGARET, STOP THAT OOZING RIGHT THIS MINUTE, YOU ARE *NOT* A TUBE OF TOOTHPASTE!"

GARDNER: Oh, yes ...

FANNY: It was perfectly disgusting!

GARDNER: I remember. She used to lean over her plate and squirt it out in long runny ribbons. ...

FANNY: That's enough, dear.

GARDNER: They were quite colorful, actually; decorative almost. She made the most intricate designs. They looked rather like small, moist Oriental rugs. ...

FANNY: *(To MAGS.)* But why, darling? What on earth possessed you to do it?

MAGS: I couldn't swallow anything. My throat just closed up. I don't know, I must have been afraid of choking or something.

GARDNER: I remember one in particular. We'd had chicken fricassee and spinach. . . . She made the most extraordinary . . .

FANNY: *(To* GARDNER.*)* WILL YOU PLEASE SHUT UP?! *(Pause.)* Mags, what *are* you talking about? You never choked in your entire life! This is the most distressing conversation I've ever had. Don't you think it's distressing, Gar?

GARDNER: Well, that's not quite the word I'd use.

FANNY: What word *would* you use, then?

GARDNER: I don't know right off the bat, I'd have to think about it.

FANNY: THEN, THINK ABOUT IT!

(Silence.)

MAGS: I guess I was afraid of making a mess. I don't know; you were awfully strict about table manners. I was always afraid of losing control. What if I started to choke and began spitting up over everything? . . .

FANNY: All right, dear, that's enough.

MAGS: No, I was really terrified about making a mess; you always got so mad whenever I spilled. If I just got rid of everything in neat little curlicues beforehand, you see . . .

FANNY: I SAID: THAT'S ENOUGH!

(Silence.)

MAGS: *I* thought it was quite ingenious, but you didn't see it that way. You finally sent me from the table with, "When you're ready to eat like a human being, you can come back and join us!" . . . So, it was off to my room with a tray. But I couldn't seem to eat there either. I mean, it was so strange settling down to dinner in my *bedroom.* . . . So I just flushed everything down the toilet and sat on my bed listening to you: clinkity-clink, clatter clatter, slurp, slurp . . . but that got pretty boring after a while, so I looked around for something to do. It was winter-time, because I noticed I'd left some crayons on top of my radiator and they'd melted down into these beautiful shimmering globs, like spilled jello, trembling and pulsating. . . .

(Overlapping.)

GARDNER: *(Eyes closed.)* "This luscious and impeccable fruit of life
Falls, it appears, of its own weight to earth. . . ."

MAGS: Naturally, I wanted to try it myself, so I grabbed a red one and pressed it down against the hissing lid. It oozed and bubbled like rasp-berry jam!

GARDNER: "When you were Eve, its acrid juice was sweet,
Untasted, in its heavenly, orchard air. . . ."

MAGS: I mean, that radiator was really hot! It took incredible will power not to let go, but I held on, whispering, "Mags, if you let go of this crayon, you'll be run over by a truck on Newberry Street, so help you

God!" . . . So I pressed down harder, my fingers steaming and blistering. . . .

FANNY: I had no idea about any of this, did you, Gar?

MAGS: Once I'd melted one, I was hooked! I finished off my entire supply in one night, mixing color over color until my head swam! . . . The heat, the smell, the brilliance that sank and rose . . . I'd never felt such exhilaration! . . . Every week I spent my allowance on crayons. I must have cleared out every box of Crayolas in the city!

GARDNER: *(Gazing at MAGS.)* You know, I don't think I've ever seen you looking prettier! You're awfully attractive when you get going!

FANNY: Why, what a lovely thing to say.

MAGS: AFTER THREE MONTHS THAT RADIATOR WAS . . . SPECTACULAR! I MEAN, IT LOOKED LIKE SOME COLOSSAL FRUIT CAKE, FIVE FEET TALL! . . .

FANNY: It sounds perfectly hideous.

MAGS: It was a knockout; shimmering with pinks and blues, lavenders and maroons, turquoise and golds, oranges and creams. . . . For every color, I imagined a taste . . . YELLOW: lemon curls dipped in sugar . . . RED: glazed cherries laced with rum . . . GREEN: tiny peppermint leaves veined with chocolate . . . PURPLE: . . .

FANNY: That's quite enough!

MAGS: And then the frosting . . . ahhh, the frosting! A satiny mix of white and silver . . . I kept it hidden under blankets during the day. . . . My huge . . . *(she starts laughing)* looming . . . teetering sweet . . .

FANNY: I ASKED YOU TO STOP! GARDNER, WILL YOU PLEASE GET HER TO STOP!

GARDNER: See here, Mags, Mum asked you to . . .

MAGS: I was so . . . *hungry* . . . losing weight every week. I looked like a scarecrow what with the bags under my eyes and bits of crayon wrapper leaking out of my clothes. It's a wonder you didn't notice. But finally you came to my rescue . . . if you could call what happened a rescue. It was more like a rout!

FANNY: Darling . . . *Please!*   GARDNER: Now, look, young
                                                   lady . . .

MAGS: The winter was almost over. . . . It was very late at night. . . . I must have been having a nightmare because suddenly you and Daddy were at my bed, shaking me. . . . I quickly glanced towards the radiator to see if it was covered. . . . *It wasn't!* It glittered and towered in the moonlight like some . . . gigantic Viennese pastry! You followed my gaze and saw it. Mummy screamed . . . "WHAT HAVE YOU GOT IN HERE? . . . MAGS, WHAT HAVE YOU BEEN DOING?" . . . She crept forward and touched it, and then jumped back. "IT'S FOOD!" she cried . . . "IT'S ALL THE FOOD SHE'S BEEN SPITTING OUT! OH, GARDNER, IT'S A MOUNTAIN OF ROTTING GARBAGE!"

FANNY: *(Softly.)* Yes . . . it's coming back . . . it's coming back. . . .

MAGS: Daddy exited as usual; left the premises. He fainted, just keeled over onto the floor. . . .

GARDNER: Gosh, I don't remember any of this. . . .

MAGS: My heart stopped! I mean, I knew it was all over. My lovely creation didn't have a chance. Sure enough . . . out came the blow torch. Well, it couldn't have *really* been a blow torch, I mean, where would you have ever gotten a blow torch? . . . I just have this very strong memory of you standing over my bed, your hair streaming around your face, aiming this . . . flame thrower at my confection . . . my cake . . . my tart . . . my strudel. . . . "IT'S GOT TO BE DESTROYED IMMEDIATELY! THE THING'S ALIVE WITH VERMIN! . . . JUST LOOK AT IT! . . . IT'S PRACTICALLY CRAWLING ACROSS THE ROOM!" . . . Of course in a sense you were right. It *was* a monument of my cast-off dinners, only I hadn't built it with food. . . . I found my own materials. I was languishing with hunger, but oh, dear Mother . . . I FOUND MY OWN MATERIALS! . . .

FANNY: Darling . . . *please?!*

MAGS: I tried to stop you, but you wouldn't listen. . . . OUT SHOT THE FLAME! . . . I remember these waves of wax rolling across the room and Daddy coming to, wondering what on earth was going on. . . . Well, what did you know about my abilities? . . . You see, I had . . . I mean, I *have* abilities. . . . *(Struggling to say it.)* I have abilities. I have . . . strong abilities. I have . . . very strong abilities. They are very strong . . . very, very strong. . . .

(She rises and runs out of the room overcome as FANNY *and* GARDNER *watch, speechless.)*

THE CURTAIN FALLS

ACT II
SCENE 1

Scene *Three days later. Miracles have been accomplished. Almost all of the Churches' furniture has been moved out, and the cartons of dishes and clothing are gone. All that remains are odds and ends.* MAGS' *tableau looms, impregnable.* FANNY *and* GARDNER *are dressed in their formal evening clothes, frozen in their pose. They hold absolutely still.* MAGS *stands at her easel, her hands covering her eyes.*

FANNY: All right, you can look now.

MAGS: *(Removes her hands.)* Yes! . . . I told you you could trust me on the pose.

FANNY: Well, thank God you let us dress up. It makes all the difference. Now we really look like something.

MAGS: *(Starts to sketch them.)* I'll say. . . .

(A silence as she sketches.)

GARDNER: *(Recites Yeats's "The Song of Wandering Aengus" in a wonderfully resonant voice as they pose.)*
"I went out to the hazel wood,
Because a fire was in my head,
And cut and peeled a hazel wand,
And hooked a berry to a thread,
And when white moths were on the wing,
And moth-like stars were flickering out,
I dropped the berry in a stream
And caught a little silver trout.

When I had laid it on the floor
I went to blow the fire aflame,
But something rustled on the floor,
And someone called me by my name:
It had become a glimmering girl
With apple blossoms in her hair
Who called me by my name and ran
And faded through the brightening air.

Though I am old with wandering
Through hollow lands and hilly lands,
I will find out where she has gone,
And kiss her lips and take her hands;
And walk among long dappled grass,
And pluck till time and times are done,
The silver apples of the moon,
The golden apples of the sun."

FANNY: That's lovely, dear. Just lovely. Is it one of yours?

GARDNER: No, no, it's Yeats. I'm using it in my book.

FANNY: Well, you recited it beautifully, but then you've always recited beautifully. That's how you wooed me, in case you've forgotten. . . . You must have memorized every love poem in the English language! There was no stopping you when you got going . . . your Shakespeare, Byron, and Shelley . . . you were shameless . . . *shameless!*

GARDNER: *(Eyes closed.)* "I will find out where she has gone, And kiss her lips and take her hands . . ."

FANNY: And then there was your own poetry to do battle with; your sonnets and quatrains. When you got going with them, there was nothing left of me! You could have had your pick of any girl in Boston! Why you chose me, I'll never understand. I had no looks to speak of and nothing much in the brains department. . . . Well, what did you know about women and the world? . . . What did any of us know? . . . *(Silence.)* GOD, MAGS, HOW LONG ARE WE SUPPOSED TO SIT LIKE THIS? . . . IT'S AGONY!

MAGS: *(Working away.)* You're doing fine . . . just fine. . . .

FANNY: *(Breaking her pose.)* It's so . . . boring!

MAGS: Come on, don't move. You can have a break soon.

FANNY: I had no idea it would be so boring!

GARDNER: Gee, I'm enjoying it.

FANNY: You would! . . .

> *(A pause.)*

GARDNER: *(Begins reciting more Yeats, almost singing it.)*
"He stood among a crowd at Drumahair;
His heart hung all upon a silken dress,
And he had known at last some tenderness,
Before earth made of him her sleepy care;
But when a man poured fish into a pile,
It seemed they raised their little silver heads . . ."

FANNY: Gar . . . PLEASE! *(She lurches out of her seat.)* God, I can't take this anymore!

MAGS: *(Keeps sketching GARDNER.)* I know it's tedious at first, but it gets easier. . . .

FANNY: It's like a Chinese water torture! . . . *(Crosses to MAGS and looks at GARDNER posing.)* Oh, darling, you look marvelous, absolutely marvelous! Why don't you just do Daddy!?

MAGS: Because you look marvelous too. I want to do you both!

FANNY: Please! . . . I have one foot in the grave and you know it! Also, we're way behind in our packing. There's still one room left which everyone seems to have forgotten about!

GARDNER: Which one is that?

FANNY: You know perfectly well which one it is!

GARDNER: I do? . . .

FANNY: Yes, you do!

GARDNER: Well, it's news to me.

FANNY: I'll give you a hint. It's in . . . *that* direction. *(She points.)*

GARDNER: The dining room?

FANNY: No.

GARDNER: The bedroom?

FANNY: No.

GARDNER: Mags' room?

FANNY: No.

GARDNER: The kitchen?

FANNY: *Gar?!* . . .

GARDNER: The guest room?

FANNY: Your God-awful study!

GARDNER: Oh, shit!

FANNY: That's right, "Oh, shit!" It's books and papers up to the ceiling! If you ask me, we should just forget it's there and quietly tiptoe away. . . .

GARDNER: My study! . . .

FANNY: Let the new owners dispose of everything. . . .

GARDNER: *(Gets out of his posing chair.)* Now, just one minute. . . .

FANNY: You never look at half the stuff in there!

GARDNER: I don't want you touching those books! They're mine!

FANNY: Darling, we're moving to a cottage the size of a handkerchief! Where, pray tell, is there room for all your books?

GARDNER: I don't know. We'll just have to make room!

MAGS: *(Sketching away.)* RATS!

FANNY: I don't know what we're doing fooling around with Mags like this when there's still so much to do. . . .

GARDNER: *(Sits back down, overwhelmed.)* My study! . . .

FANNY: You can stay with her if you'd like, but one of us has got to tackle those books!

(She exits to his study.)

GARDNER: I'm not up to this.

MAGS: Oh, good, you're staying!

GARDNER: There's a lifetime of work in there. . . .

MAGS: Don't worry, I'll help. Mum and I will be able to pack everything up in no time.

GARDNER: God. . . .

MAGS: It won't be so bad. . . .

GARDNER: I'm just not up to it.

MAGS: We'll all pitch in. . . .

(GARDNER sighs, speechless. A silence as FANNY comes staggering in with an armload of books which she drops to the floor with a crash.)

GARDNER: WHAT WAS   MAGS: GOOD GRIEF!
    THAT?! . . .

FANNY: *(Sheepish.)* Sorry, sorry. . . .

(She exits for more.)

GARDNER: I don't know if I can take this. . . .

MAGS: Moving is awful . . . I know. . . .

GARDNER: *(Settling back into his pose.)* Ever since Mum began tearing the house apart, I've been having these dreams. . . . I'm a child again back at Sixteen Louisberg Square . . . and this stream of moving men is carrying furniture into our house . . . van after van of tables and chairs, sofas and love seats, desks and bureaus . . . rugs, bathtubs, mirrors, chiming clocks, pianos, iceboxes, china cabinets . . . but what's amazing is that all of it is familiar. . . . *(FANNY comes in with another load which she drops on the floor. She exits for more.)* No matter how many items appear, I've seen every one of them before. Since my mother is standing in the midst of it directing traffic, I ask her where it's all coming from, but she doesn't hear me because of the racket . . . so finally I just scream out . . . "WHERE IS ALL THIS FURNITURE COMING FROM?" . . . Just as a moving man is carrying Toots into the room, she looks at me and says, "Why, from the land of Skye!" . . . The next thing I know, *people* are being carried along with it. . . . *(FANNY enters with her next load; drops it and exits.)* People I've never seen before are sitting around our dining-room table. A group of foreigners is going through my books, chattering in a language I've never heard before. A man is playing a Chopin polonaise on Aunt Alice's piano. Several children are taking baths in our tubs from Cotuit. . . .

MAGS: It sounds marvelous.

GARDNER: Well, it isn't marvelous at all because all of these perfect strangers have taken over our things. . . .

(FANNY enters, hurls down another load and exits.)

MAGS: How odd. . . .

GARDNER: Well, it *is* odd, but then something even odder happens. . . .

MAGS: *(Sketching away.)* Tell me, tell me!

GARDNER: Well, our beds are carried in. They're all made up with sheets and everything, but instead of all these strange people in them, *we're* in them! . . .

MAGS: What's so odd about that? . . .

GARDNER: Well, you and Mum are brought in, both sleeping like angels . . . Mum snoring away to beat the band. . . .

MAGS: Yes . . .

(FANNY enters with another load; lets it fall.)

GARDNER: But there's no one in mine. It's completely empty, never even been slept in! It's as if I were dead or had never even existed. . . . *(FANNY exits.)* "HEY . . . WAIT UP!" I yell to the moving men . . . "THAT'S MY BED YOU'VE GOT THERE!" But they don't stop; they don't even acknowledge me. . . . "HEY, COME BACK HERE . . . I WANT TO GET INTO MY BED!" I cry again and I start running after them . . . down the hall, through the dining room, past the library. . . . Finally I catch up to them and hurl myself right into the center of the pillow. Just as I'm about to land, the bed suddenly vanishes and I go crashing down to the floor like some insect that's been hit by a fly swatter!

FANNY: *(Staggers in with her final load; drops it with a crash and then collapses in her posing chair.)* THAT'S IT FOR ME! I'M DEAD! *(Silence.)* Come on, Mags, how about you doing a little work around here.

MAGS: That's all I've been doing! This is the first free moment you've given me!

FANNY: You should see all the books in there . . . and papers! There are enough loose papers to sink a ship!

GARDNER: Why is it we're moving, again? . . .

FANNY: Because life is getting too complicated here.

GARDNER: *(Remembering.)* Oh, yes . . .

FANNY: And we can't afford it anymore.

GARDNER: That's right, that's right. . . .

FANNY: We don't have the . . . *income* we used to!

GARDNER: Oh, yes . . . *income!*

FANNY: *(Assuming her pose again.)* Of course, we have our savings and various trust funds, but I wouldn't dream of touching those!

GARDNER: No, no, you must never dip into capital!

FANNY: I told Daddy I'd be perfectly happy to buy a gun and put a bullet through our heads so we could avoid all this, but he wouldn't hear of it!

MAGS: *(Sketching away.)* No, I shouldn't think so.

(Pause.)

FANNY: I've always admired people who kill themselves when they get to our stage of life. Well, no one can touch my Uncle Edmond in that department. . . .

MAGS: I know, I know. . . .

FANNY: The day before his seventieth birthday he climbed to the top of the Old North Church and hurled himself facedown into Salem Street! They had to scrape him up with a spatula! God, he was a remarkable man . . . state senator, president of Harvard. . . .

GARDNER: *(Rises and wanders over to his books.)* Well, I guess I'm going to have to do something about all of these. . . .

FANNY: Come on, Mags, help Daddy! Why don't you start bringing in his papers. . . .

(GARDNER sits on the floor; picks up a book and soon is engrossed in it. MAGS keeps sketching, oblivious; silence.)

FANNY: *(To MAGS.)* Darling? . . . HELLO? . . . God, you two are impossible! Just look at you . . . heads in the clouds! No one would ever know we've got to be out of here in two days. If it weren't for me, nothing would get done around here. . . . *(She starts stacking GARDNER's books into piles.)* There! That's all the maroon ones!

GARDNER: *(Looks up.)* What do you mean, *maroon* ones?! . . .

FANNY: All your books that are maroon are in *this* pile . . . and your books that are green in *that* pile! . . . I'm trying to bring some order into your life for once. This will make unpacking so much easier.

GARDNER: But, my dear Fanny, it's not the color of a book that distinguishes it, but what's *inside* it!

FANNY: This will be a great help, you'll see. Now what about this awful striped thing? *(She picks up a slim, aged volume.)* Can't it go? . . .

GARDNER: No!

FANNY: But it's as queer as Dick's hat band! There are no others like it.

GARDNER: Open it and read. Go on . . . open it!

FANNY: We'll get nowhere at this rate.

GARDNER: I said . . . READ!

FANNY: Really, Gar, I . . .

GARDNER: Read the dedication!

FANNY: *(Opens and reads.)* "To Gardner Church, you led the way. With gratitude and affection, Robert Frost."

(She closes it and hands it to him.)

GARDNER: It was published the same year as my *Salem Gardens.*

FANNY: *(Picking up a very worn book.)* Well, what about this dreadful thing? It's filthy. *(She blows off a cloud of dust.)*

GARDNER: Please . . . *please?!*

FANNY: *(Looking through it.)* It's all in French.

GARDNER: *(Snatching it away from her.)* André Malraux gave me that! . . .

FANNY: I'm just trying to help.

GARDNER: It's a first edition of Baudelaire's *Fleurs du Mal.*

FANNY: *(Giving it back.)* Well, pardon me for living!

GARDNER: Why do you have to drag everything in here in the first place? . . .

FANNY: Because there's no room in your study. You ought to see the mess in there! . . . WAKE UP, MAGS, ARE YOU GOING TO PITCH IN OR NOT?! . . .

GARDNER: I'm not up to this.

FANNY: Well, you'd better be unless you want to be left behind!

MAGS: *(Stops her sketching.)* All right, all right . . . I just hope you'll give me some more time later this evening.

FANNY: *(To MAGS.)* Since you're young and in the best shape, why don't you bring in the books and I'll cope with the papers. *(She exits to the study.)*

GARDNER: Now just a minute. . . .

FANNY: *(Offstage.)* WE NEED A STEAM SHOVEL FOR THIS!

MAGS: OK, what do you want me to do?

GARDNER: Look, I don't want you messing around with my . . .

(FANNY enters with an armful of papers which she drops into an empty carton.)

GARDNER: HEY, WHAT'S GOING ON HERE?! . . .

FANNY: I'm packing up your papers. COME ON, MAGS, LET'S GET CRACKING!

(She exits for more papers.)

GARDNER: *(Plucks several papers out of the carton.)* What is this? . . .

MAGS: *(Exits into his study.)* GOOD LORD, WHAT HAVE YOU DONE IN HERE?! . . .

GARDNER: *(Reading.)* This is my manuscript.

(FANNY enters with another batch which she tosses on top of the others.)

GARDNER: What *are* you doing?! . . .

FANNY: Packing, darling . . . PACKING!

(She exits for more.)

GARDNER: SEE HERE, YOU CAN'T MANHANDLE MY THINGS THIS WAY! *(MAGS enters, staggering under a load of books which she sets down on the floor.)* I PACK MY MANUSCRIPT! I KNOW WHERE EVERYTHING IS!

FANNY: *(Offstage.)* IF IT WERE UP TO YOU, WE'D NEVER GET OUT OF HERE! WE'RE UNDER A TIME LIMIT, GARDNER. KITTY'S PICKING US UP IN TWO DAYS . . . TWO . . . DAYS!

(She enters with a larger batch of papers and heads for the carton.)

GARDNER: *(Grabbing FANNY's wrist.)* NOW, HOLD IT! . . . JUST . . . HOLD IT RIGHT THERE! . . .

FANNY: OOOOOWWWWWWWW!

GARDNER: *I* PACK MY THINGS! . . .

FANNY: LET GO, YOU'RE HURTING ME!

GARDNER: THAT'S MY MANUSCRIPT! GIVE IT TO ME!

FANNY: *(Lifting the papers high over her head.)* I'M IN CHARGE OF THIS MOVE, GARDNER! WE'VE GOT TO GET CRACKING!

GARDNER: I said . . . GIVE IT TO ME!

MAGS: Come on, Mum, let him have it.

(They struggle.)

GARDNER: *(Finally wrenches the pages from her.)* LET . . . ME . . . HAVE IT! . . . THAT'S MORE LIKE IT! . . .

FANNY: *(Soft and weepy.)* You see what he's like? . . . I try and help with his packing and what does he do? . . .

GARDNER: *(Rescues the rest of his papers from the carton.)* YOU DON'T JUST THROW EVERYTHING INTO A BOX LIKE A PILE OF GARBAGE! THIS IS A BOOK, FANNY. SOMETHING I'VE BEEN WORKING ON FOR TWO YEARS! . . . *(Trying to assemble his papers, but only making things worse, dropping them all over the place.)* You show a little respect for my things. . . . You don't just throw them around every which way. . . . It's tricky trying to make sense of poetry;

it's much easier to write the stuff . . . that is, if you've still got it in you. . . .

MAGS: Here, let me help. . . . *(Taking some of the papers.)*

GARDNER: Criticism is tough sledding. You can't just dash off a few images here, a few rhymes there. . . .

MAGS: Do you have these pages numbered in any way?

FANNY: *(Returning to her posing chair.)* HA!

GARDNER: This is just the introduction.

MAGS: I don't see any numbers on these.

GARDNER: *(Exiting to his study.)* The important stuff is in my study. . . .

FANNY: *(To MAGS.)* You don't know the half of it . . . *not the half!* . . .

GARDNER: *(Offstage; thumping around.)* HAVE YOU SEEN THOSE YEATS POEMS I JUST HAD? . . .

MAGS: *(Reading over several pages.)* What is this? . . . It doesn't make sense. It's just fragments . . . pieces of poems.

FANNY: That's it, honey! That's his book. His great critical study! Now that he can't write his own poetry, he's trying to explain other people's. The only problem is, he can't get beyond typing them out. The poor lamb doesn't have the stamina to get beyond the opening stanzas, let alone trying to make sense of them.

GARDNER: *(Thundering back with more papers which keep falling.)* GOD DAMNIT, FANNY, WHAT DID YOU DO IN THERE? I CAN'T FIND ANYTHING!

FANNY: I just took the papers that were on your desk.

GARDNER: Well, the entire beginning is gone.

(He exits.)

FANNY: I'M TRYING TO HELP YOU, DARLING!

GARDNER: *(Returns with another armload.)* SEE THAT? . . . NO SIGN OF CHAPTER ONE OR TWO. . . . *(He flings it all down to the floor.)*

FANNY: Gardner . . . PLEASE?!

GARDNER: *(Kicking through the mess.)* I TURN MY BACK FOR ONE MINUTE AND WHAT HAPPENS? . . . MY ENTIRE STUDY IS TORN APART!

(He exits.)

MAGS: Oh, Daddy . . . don't . . . please . . . Daddy . . . *please?!*

GARDNER: *(Returns with a new batch of papers which he tosses up into the air.)* THROWN OUT! . . . THE BEST PART IS THROWN OUT! . . . LOST. . . .

(He starts to exit again.)

MAGS: *(Reads one of the fragments to steady herself.)*
"I have known the inexorable sadness of pencils,
Neat in their boxes, dolor of pad and paperweight,

All the misery of manilla folders and mucilage . . ."
    They're beautiful . . . just beautiful.
GARDNER: *(Stops.)* Hey, what's that you've got there?
FANNY: It's your manuscript, darling. You see, it's right where you left it.
GARDNER: *(To MAGS.)* Read that again.
MAGS: "I have known the inexorable sadness of pencils,
    Neat in their boxes, dolor of pad and paperweight,
    All the misery of manilla folders and mucilage . . ."
GARDNER: Well, well, what do you know. . . .
FANNY: *(Hands him several random papers.)* You see . . . no one lost anything.
    Everything's here, still intact.
GARDNER: *(Reads.)* "I knew a woman, lovely in her bones,
    When small birds sighed, she would sigh back at them;
    Ah, when she moved, she moved more ways than one:
    The shapes a bright container can contain! . . ."
FANNY: *(Hands him another.)* And . . .
GARDNER: *(Reads.)* Ahh . . . Frost . . .
    "Some say the world will end in fire,
    Some say ice.
    From what I've tasted of desire
    I hold with those who favor fire."
FANNY: *(Under her breath to MAGS.)* He can't give up the words. It's the
    best he can do. *(Handing him another.)* Here you go, here's more.
GARDNER:
    "Farm boys wild to couple
    With anything   with soft wooded trees
    With mounds of earth   mounds
    Of pinestraw   will keep themselves off
    Animals by legends of their own . . ."
MAGS: *(Eyes shut.)* Oh, Daddy, I can't bear it . . . I . . .
FANNY: Of course no one will ever publish this.
GARDNER: Oh, here's a marvelous one. Listen to this!
    "There came a Wind like a Bugle—
    It quivered through the Grass
    And a Green Chill upon the Heat
    So ominous did pass
    We barred the Windows and the Doors
    As from an Emerald Ghost—
    The Doom's electric Moccasin . . ."
    SHIT, WHERE DID THE REST OF IT GO? . . .
FANNY: Well, don't ask *me.*
GARDNER: It just stopped in mid-air!
FANNY: Then go look for the original.
GARDNER: Good idea, good idea!

(He exits to his study.)

FANNY: *(To MAGS.)* He's incontinent now, too. He wets his pants, in case you haven't noticed. *(She starts laughing.)* You're not laughing. Don't you think it's funny? Daddy needs diapers . . . I don't know about you, but I could use a drink! GAR . . . WILL YOU GET ME A SPLASH WHILE YOU'RE OUT THERE? . . .

MAGS: STOP IT!

FANNY: It means we can't go out anymore. I mean, what would people say? . . .

MAGS: Stop it. Just stop it.

FANNY: My poet laureate can't hold it in! *(She laughs harder.)*

MAGS: That's enough . . . STOP IT . . . Mummy . . . I beg of you . . . *please stop it!*

GARDNER: *(Enters with a book and indeed a large stain has blossomed on his trousers. He plucks it away from his leg.)* Here we go . . . I found it. . . .

FANNY: *(Pointing at it.)* See that? See? . . . He just did it again! *(Goes off into a shower of laughter.)*

MAGS: *(Looks, turns away.)* SHUT . . . UP! . . . *(Building to a howl.)* WILL YOU PLEASE JUST . . . SHUT . . . UP!

FANNY: *(To GARDNER.)* Hey, what about that drink?

GARDNER: Oh, yes . . . sorry, sorry . . .

(He heads towards the bar.)

FANNY: Never mind, I'll get it, I'll get it. *(She exits, convulsed; silence.)*

GARDNER: Well, where were we? . . .

MAGS: *(Near tears.)* Your poem.

GARDNER: Oh, yes . . . the Dickinson. *(He shuts his eyes, reciting from memory, holding the book against his chest.)*
"There came a Wind like a Bugle—
It quivered through the Grass
And a Green Chill upon the Heat
So ominous did pass
We barred the Windows and the Doors
As from an Emerald Ghost—"
(Opens the book and starts riffling through it.) Let's see now, where's the rest? . . . *(He finally finds it.)* Ahhh, here we go! . . .

FANNY: *(Reenters, drink in hand.)* I'm back! *(Takes one look at GARDNER and bursts out laughing again.)*

MAGS: I don't believe you! How can you laugh at him?! . . .

FANNY: I'm sorry, I wish I could stop, but there's really nothing else to do. Look at him . . . just . . . look at him . . . !

(This is all simultaneous as MAGS gets angrier and angrier.)

MAGS: It's so cruel. . . . You're so . . . incredibly cruel to him. . . . I mean, YOUR DISDAIN REALLY TAKES MY BREATH AWAY! YOU'RE IN A CLASS BY YOURSELF WHEN IT COMES TO HUMILIATION! . . .

GARDNER: *(Reading.)*
"The Doom's electric Moccasin
That very instant passed—
On a strange Mob of panting Trees
And Fences fled away
And Rivers where the Houses ran
Those looked that lived—that Day—
The Bell within the steeple wild
The flying tidings told—
How much can come
And much can go,
And yet abide the World!"
(He shuts the book with a bang, pauses and looks around the room, confused.)
Now, where was I? . . .

FANNY: Safe and sound in the middle of the living room with Mags and me.

GARDNER: But I was looking for something, wasn't I? . . .

FANNY: Your manuscript.

GARDNER: THAT'S RIGHT! MY MANUSCRIPT! My manuscript!

FANNY: And here it is all over the floor. See, you're standing on it.

GARDNER: *(Picks up a few pages and looks at them.)* Why, so I am . . .

FANNY: Now all we have to do is get it up off the floor and packed neatly into these cartons!

GARDNER: Yes, yes, that's right. Into the cartons.

FANNY: *(Kicks a carton over to him.)* Here, you use this one and I'll start over here. . . . *(She starts dropping papers into a carton nearby.)* BOMBS AWAY! . . . Hey . . . this is fun! . . .

GARDNER: *(Picks up his own pile, lifts it high over his head and flings it down into the carton.)* BOMBS AWAY . . . This *is* fun! . . .

FANNY: I told you! The whole thing is to figure out a system!

GARDNER: I don't know what I'd do without you, Fan. I thought I'd lost everything.

FANNY: *(Makes dive-bomber noises and machine-gun explosions as she wheels more and more papers into the carton.)* TAKE THAT AND THAT AND THAT! . . .

GARDNER: *(Joins in the fun, outdoing her with dips, dives and blastings of his own.)* BLAM BLAM BLAM BLAM! . . . ZZZZZZZZRAAAAAA FOOM! . . . BLATTY-DE-BLATTY-DE-BLATTY-DE-KA-BOOOOOOOOM! . . . WHAAAAAAA . . . DA-DAT-DAT-DAT . . . WHEEEEEEEE AAAAAAAAAAAA . . . FOOOOOO . . .

(They get louder and louder as papers fly every which way.)

FANNY: *(Mimes getting hit with a bomb.)* AEEEEEEIIIIIIIIIIIII! YOU GOT ME RIGHT IN THE GIZZARD! *(She collapses on the floor and starts going through death throes, having an absolute ball.)*

GARDNER: TAKE THAT AND THAT AND THAT AND THAT ... *(A series of explosions follows.)*

MAGS: *(Furious.)* This is how you help him? ... THIS IS HOW YOU PACK HIS THINGS? ...

FANNY: I keep him company. I get involved ... which is a hell of a lot more than you do!

MAGS: *(Wild with rage.)* BUT YOU'RE MAKING A MOCKERY OF HIM ... YOU TREAT HIM LIKE A CHILD OR SOME DIM-WITTED SERVING BOY. HE'S JUST AN AMUSEMENT TO YOU! ...

FANNY: *(Fatigue has finally overtaken her. She's calm, almost serene.)* ... And to you who see him once a year, if that ... What is he to *you?* ... I mean, what do you give him from yourself that costs you something? ... Hmmmmmm? ... *(Imitating her.)* "Oh, hi Daddy, it's great to see you again. How have you been? ... Gee, I love your hair. It's gotten so ... *white!*" ... What color do you expect it to get when he's this age? ... I mean, if you care so much how he looks, why don't you come and see him once in a while? ... But oh, no ... you have your paintings to do and your shows to put on. You just come and see us when the whim strikes. *(Imitating her.)* "Hey, you know what would be really great? ... To do a portrait of you! I've always wanted to paint you, you're such great subjects!" ... *Paint* us?! ... What about opening your eyes and really *seeing* us? ... Noticing what's going on around here for a change! It's all over for Daddy and me. This is it! "Finita la commedia!" ... All I'm trying to do is exit with a little flourish; have some fun.... What's so terrible about that? ... It can get pretty grim around here, in case you haven't noticed ... Daddy, tap-tap-tapping out his nonsense all day; me traipsing around to the thrift shops trying to amuse myself ... He never keeps me company anymore; never takes me out anywhere.... I'd put a bullet through my head in a minute, but then who'd look after him? ... What do you think we're moving to the cottage for? ... So I can watch him like a hawk and make sure he doesn't get lost. Do you think that's anything to look forward to? ... Being Daddy's nursemaid out in the middle of nowhere? I'd much rather stay here in Boston with the few friends I have left, but you can't always do what you want in this world! "L'homme propose, Dieu dispose!" ... If you want to paint us so badly, you ought to paint us as we really are. There's your picture! ... *(She points to* GARDNER *who's quietly playing with a paper glide.)* Daddy spread out on the floor with all his toys and me hovering over him to make sure

he doesn't hurt himself! *(She goes over to him.)* YOO-HOO . . .
   GAR? . . . HELLO? . . .
GARDNER: *(Looks up at her.)* Oh, hi there, Fan. What's up?
FANNY: How's the packing coming? . . .
GARDNER: Packing? . . .
FANNY: Yes, you were packing your manuscript, remember? *(She lifts up a
   page and lets it fall into a carton.)*
GARDNER: Oh, yes. . . .
FANNY: Here's your picture, Mags. Face over this way . . . turn your easel
   over here. . . . *(She lets a few more papers fall.)* Up, up . . . and away. . . .

BLACKOUT

SCENE 2

Scene *The last day. All the books and boxes are gone. The room is completely empty
except for* MAGS' *backdrop. Late afternoon light dapples the walls; it changes from
pale peach to deeper violet. The finished portrait sits on the easel, covered with a cloth.*
MAGS *is taking down the backdrop.*

FANNY: *(Offstage; to* GARDNER.*)* DON'T FORGET TOOTS!
GARDNER: *(Offstage; from another part of the house.)* WHAT'S THAT? . . .
FANNY: *(Offstage.)* I SAID: DON'T FORGET TOOTS! HIS CAGE IS
   SITTING IN THE MIDDLE OF YOUR STUDY! *(Silence.)*
FANNY: *(Offstage.)* HELLO? . . .   GARDNER: *(Offstage.)* I'LL BE
   ARE YOU THERE? . . .   RIGHT WITH YOU; I'M
                                 GETTING TOOTS!
GARDNER: *(Offstage.)* WHAT'S THAT? I CAN'T HEAR YOU!
FANNY: *(Offstage.)* I'M GOING THROUGH THE ROOMS ONE
   MORE TIME TO MAKE SURE WE DIDN'T FORGET ANY-
   THING. . . . KITTY'S PICKING US UP IN FIFTEEN MINUTES,
   SO PLEASE BE READY. . . . SHE'S DROPPING MAGS OFF AT
   THE STATION AND THEN IT'S OUT TO ROUTE 3 AND THE
   CAPE HIGHWAY. . . .
GARDNER: *(Enters, carrying* TOOTS *in his cage.)* Well, this is it. The big
   moment has finally come, eh what, Toots? *(He sees* MAGS.*)* Oh, hi
   there, Mags, I didn't see you. . . .
MAGS: Oh, hi, Daddy, I'm just taking this down. . . . *(She does and walks
   over to* TOOTS.*)* Oh, Toots, I'll miss you. *(She makes little chattering
   noises into his cage.)*
GARDNER: Come on, recite a little Gray's Elegy for Mags before we go.
MAGS: Yes, Mum said he was really good at it now.
GARDNER: Well, the whole thing is to keep at it every day. *(Slowly to
   TOOTS.)*
   "The curfew tolls the knell of parting day,

The lowing herd wind slowly o'er the lea . . ."
Come on, show Mags your stuff!

(Slower.)

"The curfew tolls the knell of the parting day,
The lowing herd wind slowly o'er the lea . . ."

(Silence; GARDNER *makes little chattering sounds.)*

Come on, Toots, old boy. . . .
MAGS: How does it go?
GARDNER: *(To* MAGS.) "The curfew tolls the knell of parting day,
The lowing herd wind slowly o'er the lea . . ."
MAGS: *(Slowly to* TOOTS.) "The curfew tolls for you and me,
As quietly the herd winds down . . ."
GARDNER: No, no, it's, "The curfew tolls the knell of parting *day* . . ."!
MAGS: *(Repeating after him.)* "The curfew tolls the knell of parting day . . ."
GARDNER: "The lowing herd wind slowly o'er the lea . . ."
MAGS: *(With a deep breath.)* "The curfew tolls at parting day,
The herd low slowly down the lea . . . no, *knell!*
They come winding down the *knell! . . .*"
GARDNER: Listen, Mags . . . *listen!*

(A pause.)

TOOTS: *(Loud and clear with* GARDNER's *inflection.)*
"The curfew tolls the knell of parting day,
The lowing herd wind slowly o'er the lea,
The ploughman homeward plods his weary way,
And leaves the world to darkness and to me."
MAGS: HE SAID IT. . . . HE SAID IT! . . . AND IN YOUR VOICE! . . .
OH, DADDY, THAT'S AMAZING!
GARDNER: Well, Toots is very smart, which is more than I can say for a
lot of people I know. . . .
MAGS: *(To* TOOTS.) Polly want a cracker? Polly want a cracker?
GARDNER: You can teach a parakeet to say anything; all you need is
patience. . . .
MAGS: But *poetry* . . . that's so hard. . . .
FANNY: *(Enters carrying a suitcase and* GARDNER's *typewriter in its case. She's
dressed in her traveling suit, wearing a hat to match.)* WELL, THERE YOU
ARE! I THOUGHT YOU'D DIED!
MAGS: *(To* FANNY.) HE SAID IT! I FINALLY HEARD TOOTS RE-
CITE GRAY'S ELEGY. *(She makes silly clucking sounds into the cage.)*
FANNY: Isn't it uncanny how much he sounds like Daddy? Sometimes
when I'm alone here with him, I've actually thought he *was* Daddy and

started talking to him. Oh, yes, Toots and I have had quite a few meaty conversations together!

(FANNY *wolf-whistles into the cage; then draws back.* GARDNER *covers the cage with a traveling cloth. Silence.*)

FANNY: *(Looking around the room.)* God, the place looks so bare.

MAGS: I still can't believe it . . . Cotuit, year round. I wonder if there'll be any phosphorus when you get there?

FANNY: What on earth are you talking about? *(She carries the discarded backdrop out into the hall.)*

MAGS: Remember that summer when the ocean was full of phosphorus?

GARDNER: *(Taking* TOOTS *out into the hall.)* Oh, yes. . . .

MAGS: It was a great mystery where it came from or why it settled in Cotuit. But one evening when Daddy and I were taking a swim, suddenly it was there!

GARDNER: *(Returns.)* I remember.

MAGS: I don't know where Mum was. . . .

FANNY: *(Reentering.)* Probably doing the dishes!

MAGS: *(To* GARDNER.) As you dove into the water, this shower of silvery green sparks erupted all around you. It was incredible! I thought you were turning into a saint or something; but then you told me to jump in too and the same thing happened to me. . . .

GARDNER: Oh, yes, I remember that . . . the water smelled all queer.

MAGS: What *is* phosphorus, anyway?

GARDNER: Chemicals, chemicals . . .

FANNY: No, it isn't. Phosphorus is a green liquid inside insects. Fireflies have it. When you see sparks in the water it means insects are swimming around. . . .

GARDNER: Where on earth did you get that idea?

FANNY: If you're bitten by one of them, it's fatal!

MAGS: . . . and the next morning it was still there. . . .

GARDNER: It was the damndest stuff to get off! We'd have to stay in the shower a good ten minutes. It comes from chemical waste, you see. . . .

MAGS: Our bodies looked like mercury as we swam around. . . .

GARDNER: It stained all the towels a strange yellow green.

MAGS: I was in heaven, and so were you for that matter. You'd finished your day's poetry and would turn somersaults like some happy dolphin. . . .

FANNY: Damned dishes . . . why didn't I see any of this?! . . .

MAGS: I remember one night in particular. . . . We sensed the phosphorus was about to desert us; blow off to another town. We were chasing each other under water. At one point I lost you, the brilliance was so intense . . . but finally your foot appeared . . . then your leg. I grabbed it! . . . I remember wishing the moment would hold forever; that we could just be fixed there, laughing and iridescent. . . . Then I began to get panicky because I knew it would pass; it was passing already. You were slipping from my grasp. The summer was almost over. I'd be going back to art school; you'd be going back to Boston. . . . Even as I was reaching for you, you were gone. We'd never be like that again.

(Silence.)

FANNY: *(Spies MAGS' portrait covered on the easel.)* What's that over there? Don't tell me we forgot something!

MAGS: It's your portrait. I finished it.

FANNY: You finished it? How on earth did you manage that?

MAGS: I stayed up all night.

FANNY: You did? . . . *I* didn't hear you, did you hear her, Gar? . . .

GARDNER: Not a peep, not a peep!

MAGS: Well, I wanted to get it done before you left. You know, see what you thought. It's not bad, considering . . . I mean, I did it almost completely from memory. The light was terrible and I was trying to be quiet so I wouldn't wake you. It was hardly an ideal situation. . . . I mean, you weren't the most cooperative models. . . . *(She suddenly panics and snatches the painting off the easel. She hugs it to her chest and starts dancing around the room with it.)* Oh, God, you're going to hate it! You're going to hate it! How did I ever get into this? . . . Listen, you don't really want to see it . . . it's nothing . . . just a few dabs here and there. . . . It was awfully late when I finished it. The light was really impossible and my eyes were hurting like crazy. . . . Look, why don't we just go out to the sidewalk and wait for Kitty so she doesn't have to honk. . . .

GARDNER: *(Snatches the painting out from under her.)* WOULD YOU JUST SHUT UP A MINUTE AND LET US SEE IT? . . .

MAGS: *(Laughing and crying.)* But it's nothing, Daddy . . . *really!* . . . I've done better with my eyes closed! It was so late I could hardly see anything and then I spilled a whole bottle of thinner into my palette. . . .

GARDNER: *(Sets it down on the easel and stands back to look at it.)* THERE!

MAGS: *(Dancing around them in a panic.)* Listen, it's just a quick sketch. . . . It's still wet. . . . I didn't have enough time. . . . It takes at least forty hours to do a decent portrait. . . .

(Suddenly it's very quiet as FANNY and GARDNER stand back to look at it.)

MAGS: *(More and more beside herself, keeps leaping around the room wrapping her arms around herself, making little whimpering sounds.)* Please don't . . . no . . . don't . . . oh, please! . . . Come on, don't look. . . . Oh, God, don't . . . please. . . .

(An eternity passes as FANNY and GARDNER gaze at it.)

GARDNER: Well . . .

FANNY: Well . . . *(More silence.)*

FANNY: I think it's perfectly dreadful! GARDNER: Awfully clever, awfully clever!

FANNY: What on earth did you do to my face? . . .

GARDNER: I particularly like Mum!

FANNY: Since when do I have purple skin?! . . .

MAGS: I told you it was nothing, just a silly . . .

GARDNER: She looks like a million dollars!

FANNY: AND WILL YOU LOOK AT MY HAIR . . . IT'S BRIGHT ORANGE!

GARDNER: *(Views it from another angle.)* It's really very good!

FANNY: *(Pointing.)* That doesn't look anything like me!

GARDNER: . . . first rate!

FANNY: Since when do I have purple skin and bright orange hair?! . . .

MAGS: *(Trying to snatch it off the easel.)* Listen, you don't have to worry about my feelings . . . really . . . I . . .

GARDNER: *(Blocking her way.)* NOT SO FAST . . .

FANNY: . . . and look at how I'm sitting! I've never sat like that in my life!

GARDNER: *(Moving closer to it.)* Yes, yes, it's awfully clever . . .

FANNY: I HAVE NO FEET!

GARDNER: The whole thing is quite remarkable!

FANNY: And what happened to my legs, pray tell? . . . They just vanish below the knees! . . . At least my dress is presentable. I've always loved that dress.

GARDNER: It sparkles somehow. . . .

FANNY: *(To GARDNER.)* Don't you think it's becoming?

GARDNER: Yes, very becoming, awfully becoming . . .

FANNY: *(Examining it at closer range.)* Yes, she got the dress very well, how it shows off what's left of my figure. . . . My smile is nice too.

GARDNER: Good and wide. . . .

FANNY: I love how the corners of my mouth turn up. . . .

GARDNER: It's very clever. . . .

FANNY: They're almost quivering. . . .

GARDNER: Good lighting effects!

FANNY: Actually, I look quite . . . *young,* don't you think?

GARDNER: *(To MAGS.)* You're awfully good with those highlights.

FANNY: *(Looking at it from different angles.)* And *you* look darling! . . .

GARDNER: Well, I don't know about that. . . .

FANNY: No, you look absolutely darling. Good enough to eat!

MAGS: *(In a whisper.)* They like it. . . . They like it!

(A silence as FANNY *and* GARDNER *keep gazing at it.)*

FANNY: You know what it is? The wispy brush strokes make us look like a couple in a French Impressionist painting.

GARDNER: Yes, I see what you mean. . . .

FANNY: . . . a Manet or Renoir . . .

GARDNER: It's very evocative.

FANNY: There's something about the light. . . . *(They back up to survey it from a distance.)*

FANNY: You know those Renoir café scenes? . . .

GARDNER: She doesn't lay on the paint with a trowel; it's just touches here and there. . . .

MAGS: They *like* it! . . .

FANNY: You know the one with the couple dancing? . . . Not that we're dancing. There's just something similar in the mood . . . a kind of gaiety, almost. . . . The man has his back to you and he's swinging the woman around. . . . OH, GAR, YOU'VE SEEN IT A MILLION TIMES! IT'S HANGING IN THE MUSEUM OF FINE ARTS! . . . They're dancing like this. . . .

(She goes up to him and puts an arm on his shoulders.)

MAGS: They like it. . . . They like it!

FANNY: She's got on this wonderful flowered dress with ruffles at the neck and he's holding her like this. . . . That's right . . . and she's got the most rhapsodic expression on her face. . . .

GARDNER: *(Getting into the spirit of it, takes* FANNY *in his arms and slowly begins to dance around the room.)* Oh, yes . . . I know the one you mean. . . . They're in a sort of haze . . . and isn't there a little band playing off to one side? . . .

FANNY: Yes, that's it!

(Kitty's horn honks outside.)

MAGS: *(Is the only one who hears it.)* There's Kitty! *(She's torn and keeps looking toward the door, but finally gives in to their stolen moment.)*

FANNY: . . . and there's a man in a dark suit playing the violin and someone's conducting, I think. . . . And aren't Japanese lanterns strung up? . . .

(They pick up speed, dipping and whirling around the room. Strains of a faraway Chopin waltz are heard.)

GARDNER: Oh, yes! There are all these little lights twinkling in the trees. . . .

FANNY: . . . and doesn't the woman have a hat on? . . . A big red hat? . . .

GARDNER: . . . and lights all over the dancers, too. Everything shimmers with this marvelous glow. Yes, yes . . . I can see it perfectly! The whole thing is absolutely extraordinary!

(The lights become dreamy and dappled as they dance around the room. MAGS *watches them, moved to tears as . . .)*

SLOWLY THE CURTAIN FALLS

Considerations

1. Reread the author's description of the stage setting. What do the details suggest about the characters who will play out their conflicts in this setting? What predictions related to plot and theme can you make, based on the images Howe creates with her stage setting?
2. Write a brief description of each character's response to portraits and to the painting of portraits. How are the differences and similarities you have observed significant?
3. Consider the scenes that focus on food. How does food serve as a symbol of the relationship between Mags and her parents? Why does she always eat so voraciously when she is at her parents' home?
4. Consider carefully the two major actions in the play: the Churches' moving and the painting of the portrait. How are these actions related? How do they work together to define family conflicts and family solidarity?
5. Briefly summarize the two childhood memories Mags discusses. Then explain why each was particularly significant to the way she saw (and sees) herself in relation to her parents. Explain also any connections you see between the two memories.

AGNES G. HERMAN (1922–   )

A Parent's Journey Out of the Closet

Born in New York City, Agnes G. Herman earned a bachelor of arts from the University of Michigan and a master's degree in social work from Columbia University. A retired social worker, she works for the Union of American Hebrew Congregations Program on the Changing Jewish Family and the Synagogue. She is currently serving on its Committee on AIDS.

When we agreed to adopt seven-month-old Jeff, we knew that his life as a member of a Jewish family would begin the moment we brought him to our home. We celebrated that joyous homecoming with appropriate religious ritual, with blessings recited by Jeff's rabbi father as our gurgling, happy baby teethed on his infant kiddush cup° and enjoyed his challah°. There, in the warmth of our extended family circle of grandparents, an aunt, an uncle, and the Temple Board, our small son passed comfortably through his bris°, his initial Jewish milestone. There would be many more.

By the time he was two, Jeff ate an ice cream cone without spilling a drop; his face came out of the sticky encounter clean. At five, he watched other kids play ball in the alley, standing aside because he had been told not to play there. Besides, he seemed more comfortable playing with the little girl next door. There were awkward moments as he began to grow up, such as the times when the baseball bat, which his father insisted upon, was not comfortable in his hands, but the rolling pin, which his father decried, was. His grandmother, whom he adored, remarked, "Jeff is too good."

I knew she was right, and privately I felt a nagging fear I could hardly express to myself. Was Jeff a "sissy"? That archaic term was the only one I dared whisper to myself. "Gay" only meant "lively and fun-loving"; "homosexual" was a label not to be used in polite society and certainly never to be mentioned in the same sentence with a child's name. Such a term would certainly stigmatize a youngster and humiliate a family.

Jeff continued to be an eager volunteer in the kitchen and a reluctant participant on the ballfield. We fought the former and pressed to correct the latter, frustrating our son while we all grew tense. As to our silent fears, we repressed them.

Jeff developed reading problems in school. We worried, but accepted   5
the inappropriate assurance offered by his teacher. "He is such a good boy—don't confuse him with counseling." We bought it, for a while. As the reading problems continued, Jeff did enter therapy and was helped to become less anxious and learn how to read all over again. At our final parental consultation with the psychiatrist, I hesitantly asked, "Doctor, I often worry that

---

kiddush cup: Cup used as part of a Jewish ritual; *challah:* Braided bread, often part of Jewish holiday meals. *bris:* The ritual circumcision of male Jewish babies.

Jeff is effeminate. What do you think?" I held my breath while he offered his reassurance: "There is nothing wrong with your son. He is a sensitive boy—not aggressive or competitive. So he likes girls! In a few years you will be worrying about that for other reasons."

Jeff looked forward eagerly to religious school. He accompanied his dad, helped around the temple, and received many kudos. He was quick, efficient, and willingly took instructions. In later years, even after his father was no longer in the pulpit, Jeff continued his role as a temple volunteer. He moved chairs and carried books; later, he changed fuses, focused spotlights, and handled sound equipment. Jeff was comfortable; it was "his" temple. Other children there shared his interests and became his friends, later forming the temple youth group.

Bar mitzvah class, however, was a difficult obstacle. When Hebrew became a daily family battle, we withdrew him from Hebrew school to be tutored instead by his father. He spent a substantial amount of time, which otherwise was not available, with his dad. As a result, a potential failure was transformed into another family milestone. Jeff yawned his way through formal bar mitzvah training, but when his big day arrived, he was prepared, and pleased even himself.

During confirmation and youth group years, Jeff seemed to be struggling to be like his peers. Temple became the center of his life. He worked and played there, dated, went steady, and attended meetings and dances. He shared with no one—not his parents, his friends, or his rabbi—his own feelings of being "different."

When Jeff was sixteen, we moved from New Rochelle to Los Angeles. It was a difficult move for him, cutting off relationships and sources of recognition and acceptance. As we settled into our new home, Jeff began to explore the San Fernando Valley, enrolled in high school, and tried to make new friends. At our insistence, he attended one meeting of the local temple youth group, but felt rejected by the youngsters there. That marked the unfortunate beginning of Jeff's disenchantment with synagogues and withdrawal from family religious observances and celebrations.

Jeff gradually acclimated to his new environment. He took Amy, a Jewish girl his own age, to the senior prom; he cruised Van Nuys Boulevard on Wednesdays with Ann. He was always on the move—coming home to eat, shower, change clothes, and zip out again. We blamed it on the fast pace of California and the novelty of having his own "wheels": first a motorcycle, and then a car. There were several accidents—none serious, thank heavens! Again, in retrospect, the furious struggle with his identity must have played a part in his fast-paced behavior. At the time, though, we buried our heads in the sand, believing that Jeff was merely behaving like every other teenager.

After high school, the pace seemed to slow down a bit. So when Jeff was nineteen and we decided to leave him in charge for the six months of our sabbatical world tour, we had no hesitation. Conscientious and cautious, he could handle the cars and the checkbook. He would continue in college

10

and be available to his sister Judi, also attending college. We flew off to Europe and Israel, confident and secure.

When an overseas call came three months later in Jerusalem, my heart beat fast, and my sense of well-being faltered slightly. "Everything is fine, no problem. I have quit college. Now don't get excited . . . I want to go to business school and study interior design. Jobs are plentiful; I know a guy who will hire me the minute I graduate."

Jeff had always shown a creative flair for color and design. He constantly rearranged our furniture, changing one room after another. All this raced through my mind as I held the phone, separated from him by 9000 miles. Erv and I looked at each other, wished Jeff luck, and told him to write the check for his tuition.

When we finally returned home, Jeff was obviously depressed. His answers to our questions were surly, clipped, and evasive. Behaving unlike his usual loving self, he ran in and out of the house silently, furtively, always in a hurry. He seemed uninterested in our trip and was clearly trying to avoid us.

One day during Passover, Erv was searching for a favorite cantorial   15
record that Jeff often appropriated. He checked Jeff's record collection and poked about among the torn jeans. Speechless and ashen, Erv returned to the breakfast room and dropped a book into my lap: *Homosexuality in Modern Society.* "This was hidden in Jeff's room." My heart raced and skipped. Confrontation was finally at hand, not only with Jeff, but with my own fears as well.

Then our son came through the front door on the run: "I'm late . . . can't stop . . . talk to you later."

The tone of our response and expressions on our faces stopped him midflight. "Son, stand still! Something is going on, you are not yourself! Are you in trouble? Drugs, maybe? Is one of your girlfriends pregnant? Or, are you, is it possible that you are . . . homosexual?"

I waited, trembling. The faces of my beloveds were creased with anger and worry. I could barely breathe.

"Yes, I am gay." A simple sentence, yet I did not understand. Nothing was "gay"!

We asked in unison, "What does that mean?"   20

"I am homosexual," he explained. After long minutes of uncomfortable conversation, we sent Jeff on his way with "we'll talk later." I ran from the room to what was to become my comfort zone, the cool tile of the bathroom floor, and I cried my eyes out. I guess Erv went to work. All we can recall now is that neither of us could face the reality right then.

That evening and the next, we did an enormous amount of soul-searching. What did I, a social worker, know about homosexuality? What did my husband, the rabbi, know? Our academic credentials were impressive— professionally we were both well-trained to help other people in pain. But in our personal distress, we felt helpless.

Everything I had ever heard about homosexuality destroyed all my dreams about our son's future. He would never marry and have children. His warmth, caring, good looks, and so many other wonderful traits would not be passed along to a son or daughter, a grandchild. We wondered whether we could keep him in our family circle, or would we lose him to "that other world" of homosexuality, a world that was foreign to us.

We wracked ourselves with self-blame—what did we do wrong? I accepted all the myths about homosexuality. First, the myth of the strong mother—I was a strong mother, but what mother doesn't overexert her influence on her children? Second, the myth of the absent father—Erv spent so much time crisscrossing the country, berating himself for not being at home enough. Third was the myth of seduction—had someone lured Jeff into this awful lifestyle? And then, finally, I believed the myth of "the cure"— that the right therapist could change Jeff's sexual orientation.

We did seek help from a therapist. He was patient, caring, and ac-   25
cepting of Jeff and his lifestyle. He helped us begin to sort out myth from reality and guided us through a tangled web of grief, pain, and disappointment. He gently destroyed our unrealistic hope of "changing" Jeff. Our abiding love for our son was, of course, the key to this difficult yet hopeful journey.

I did not like Jeff's lifestyle at that time, but that did not interfere with my love for him. Understanding and acceptance gradually grew, but the path to real comfort continued to be bumpy.

Jeff sought help, too. At nineteen, he admitted that there was much that he wanted to know about himself. During that time, he offered a comment that we gratefully accepted: "Please stop blaming yourselves. It is not your fault that I have grown up gay." With those words, Jeff erased our most devastating, yet unspoken, anxiety.

Time moved along for all of us. We grieved the loss of deeply held expectations for our son's life. We experienced inner turmoil. Jeff struggled to make peace with himself. We learned to support one another.

Over time, we came to understand that a child who is homosexual needs no less understanding, support, and acceptance than one who is heterosexual. Clearly, our gay son has the same human needs that his straight sister has: for empathy and patience, for security and success, for caring and love. Rejection is difficult for both our children, yet perhaps more so for our gay child. Society has taught him that he will experience less validation and more unnecessary pain. He, and all of us who love him, are vulnerable to that pain.

It became clear that Jeff's sexual orientation was only one part of his   30
life. There remained the ordinary concerns and controversies intrinsic to raising any child. Jeff rode the roller coaster of financial and vocational problems. We provided advice, which he sometimes accepted, and loans, which he often repaid. Jeff's married sister behaved in much the same manner.

Jeff became ill and required the usual chicken soup and tender care in his apartment. He preferred receiving that attention from friends, but also expected Mother and Dad to stop by regularly with reassurance and love. His sister behaved the same way when she broke her leg and was living alone.

When a love affair went sour, Jeff became depressed and sad. We worried and tried to be especially sensitive to his pain. The same support was called for when his sister faced divorce with sadness and depression. We were happier when Jeff was living with a friend who cared about him and about whom he cared, and we felt the same way about his sister, now happily remarried.

During all this time, it never occurred to us to turn to the Jewish community for support, though we knew its resources well. We kept our concerns about Jeff's lifestyle to ourselves: We were in the closet. A child's homosexuality was not something one discussed in 1969 and throughout the 1970s. And sharing intimacies with others was not our way—these were matters we had to work out ourselves. We had decided alone, together, to marry each other; we decided alone, together, to have children. And we decided alone, together, to tough out our son's homosexuality, confront it, embrace him, and then face the world together.

I recall sitting with close friends one evening. Naturally, the conversation turned to our kids. At one point, someone said, "I think we have something in common." We all agreed, but even then, none of us could articulate it. In fact, on the way home, Erv asked, "Are you sure their oldest son is gay?"

Finally we came "halfway out," sharing only with family. We found almost unanimous acceptance; affection for Jeff did not falter. But it was seventeen long years before we went public in the Jewish community. Even during the years when my husband was deeply involved in supporting the establishment of a gay outreach synagogue in Los Angeles, when he was busy teaching others that Judaism must not turn its back on any of its children, we did not share our son's homosexuality with the Jewish public.   35

I "came out" for us, with Jeff's permission, in 1986, with an article in *The Reconstructionist,* a national Jewish magazine. The response was overwhelming. Support from rabbis, lay leaders, and friends poured in from around the country. Even at that late date, comfortable as we had become with Jeff's lifestyle, we found those messages heartwarming and reassuring.

Some of our friends were angry that we had not shared our pain with them. Perhaps we did not trust people to practice compassion and acceptance. Perhaps we did not trust them to understand that we are not failures as parents. We did not want our son to suffer rejection from those we loved. We did not want to be rejected by those we loved!

The pressure was greater on Jeff. Because he is a rabbi's child, he felt, correctly, that the expectations of him were high. Jeff was not alone in fearing the expectations of others; he had learned that sensitivity from us. Every family feels a need to be without flaws: a nonsensical, impossible attitude, but it is real. Among rabbis' families it is often exaggerated.

Should we have trusted our friends and colleagues from the beginning? Could we have dared to test the support of the synagogue leaders with whom Erv worked daily? Should we have risked our own self-image and left the closet earlier? Would any of that have made our son more comfortable at our seder table or at services? I do not have the answers. I believe we came out only when we were ready; getting ready took a long time.

There are Jewish parents who shut out their gay and lesbian children   40 and erect a wall of alienation. There is little solace in that course of action, or in believing that their child can be "changed" to heterosexuality. Those who reject the person rather than accept the reality, or who chase fantasies rather than learning facts, deserve our compassion and understanding. It is difficult to face the disappointment, grief, and guilt that often precede true acceptance. Parents need to be helped to mourn broken dreams, to keep communication open, and to prevent love and parental devotion from being overwhelmed by pain and confusion.

Some parents actually chant Kaddish° for their "wayward" children. For us, our Jewish dedication to family left no room for such behavior. Disappointment hurts, but is curable. Alienation, on the other hand, can kill relationships, love, and family. Thank God, our love—and our religious faith—did not falter.

We Jewish parents love our offspring, sometimes desperately. We can survive the shock of learning that a son is gay, or a daughter is lesbian. Eventually we can find that love will crumble the walls of alienation and that time is an ally. Our children, too, can learn to be patient with us as we grow.

Would we have done anything differently? Yes. We would have paid heed to the "flashing lights," the warnings of parenthood. We would have helped our son as early as possible to like himself and to make peace with himself. And when he did break the news to us in 1969, I wish we would have been wise enough to hug our beloved son and say, "We love you very much. Let's talk about it."

When strangers ask me today if our son is married, I do not hesitate to explain, "He is not. He is gay." We are out of the closet. It has been a long road, but well worth it.

Kaddish: A prayer for the dead.

Considerations

1. Several people describe Jeff as "good" or "too good," and this "goodness" worries his mother. Why would parents worry about a child being "good"? Would the examples of "good" behavior have been equally worrisome if the child involved were a girl?
2. Explain your response to the parents' reactions when they discover the book on homosexuality in Jeff's room.

3. Agnes Herman makes several comparisons between her married daughter and her son Jeff. What differences do you see between Jeff's circumstances and his sister's? To what extent does Agnes Herman seem to recognize and accept those differences?

4. Compare the Hermans' responses to Jeff's homosexuality to the responses Marian describes when she learns that her husband has left her for a male lover in Harvey Fierstein's *On Tidy Endings*, page 1174.

5. Write a letter to Agnes Herman explaining your response to her and her husband's decision to "come out" to their community.

HARRY DOLAN (1927–   )

I Remember Papa

In this essay, which first appeared in From the Ashes: Voices of Watts, *edited by Budd Schulberg, Harry Dolan shows the pitfalls his parents faced as they struggled with poverty, illness, and negative racial stereotypes. By explaining his father's life, Dolan urges readers to examine and perhaps reconsider their own views of families like his and, particularly, of the choices made by the men who are the fathers of those families.*

The other night after attending a gratifying function which had been initiated to help the black man, specifically to help build a nursery for children of working mothers, and after seeing and hearing white people make speeches professing their understanding and desire to go to any length to help, I found myself suddenly cornered and forced to defend the fabled laziness of the black man.

What was especially surprising was the fact that I assumed this white acquaintance—since he had paid thirty dollars to attend this dinner held for the purpose of helping the black man—did, at least in part, have some sympathy with what his, the white people, had tried to accomplish.

As I stood there watching his eyes I became suspect of my own sincerity, for I stood attentively nodding my head and smiling. I lit a cigarette, raised an eyebrow, performed all of the white man's laws of etiquette, and all the while I knew if it had been others of my black brothers, they would have cursed him for his smugness and invited him outside to test his theory of black man's courage and laziness. Of course I did none of these things. I grinned as he indicated in no uncertain terms that as soon as the black man got off his lazy butt and took advantage of all the blessings that had been offered him for the last two hundred years, then he, the white man, would indeed be willing to help.

I could have answered him—and was tempted to, for he was obviously sincere. Instead, I found an excuse to slip away and let a white man fight my battle, a friend, even a close friend. I went to a far corner and blindly played a game of pool by myself as the voices of this man and my friend dissected me. I stacked the pool balls, leaned over the table, and remembered a black man I had known.

It was said of him later in his life that he had let his family down. He'd   5
been lazy, no-account, a troublemaker. Maybe so, maybe so, but I can't help remembering nights of his pacing the squeaking floor muttering to himself, coming back across the floor, sitting down, his legs trembling as he listened to the woman plead for him not to do anything bad.

"I'll go to hell first before I'll let you and the children starve." God, how many times had I heard him say that! How many other men standing bunched in helpless stagnation have I heard vow to take a gun and get some food for their children! Yes, they were planning to commit a crime; yes, they were potential criminals. Then. They are usually black too—another crime, it seems.

I remember that man, but more I remember his woman, my mother. Curiously though, I never remember her dancing, running, playing; always lying down, the smell of disinfectant strong, the deep continuous coughing, the brown paper bag filled with the toilet paper red with bubbly spit and blood, lying half concealed under the bed.

I never remember her eating food such as bread, meat, potatoes; only apples and only Delicious apples. In those days five cents apiece. She was a small woman, barely five foot.

"Junior," she would say softly. She never spoke above a whisper. "Go to the store and get me an apple." The thin trembling hand would reverse itself and slide up and under the covers and under the pillow and then return as though of its own volition, the weight almost too much, and as I'd start out the door, she would always smile and say, "Hurry, Junior."

I'd nod, and always, always there seemed to be a need to hurry. Those   10
trips were always made with a feeling of breathless fear. I didn't know why then, only that for some reason I must always come back as soon as possible.

I was returning with an especially large apple, walking along, tempted to bite just a tiny piece, when I turned the corner and saw the black police ambulance standing in front of my door. Suddenly I had to go to the bathroom so bad I couldn't move. I stood watching as two uniformed men came out with the stretcher, and then the sound of my mother's shrill voice hit me.

"Mama, Mama," she was screaming. I could see her twisting and swinging at the lady next door as she was held back. I stood there feeling the hot piss run down my trembling legs, feeling cold chills spatter through my body, causing frozen limbs to spasmodically begin to move. I forced myself toward the police wagon as the men opened the doors and slid the stretcher along the bare metal. I saw my mother's head bounce on the floor.

"Wait," I moaned, "don't hurt her." Then I was running, screaming, "Please don't hurt her."

I looked down at her pain-filled face, and she smiled, even then she smiled. I showed her the apple. The effort to nod seemed a terrible effort but she did, her eyes so very bright, so very shiny.

"You eat it, Junior, you and sis."   15

"What's wrong, Mama?" I asked softly. "You really, really sick now?"

She nodded.

"Your father will be home soon. Tell him I'm at the General Hospital. Tell him to—to hurry."

"I'll tell him, Mama," I promised. "I'll tell him to hurry, Mama." She nodded sadly and puckered her lips as she always did since we weren't allowed to kiss her.

That was the last time I saw my mother except at the grave. My father   20
came to the funeral with two white men who stood on each side of him all

the time. There were people crying all around us. My grandmother kept squeezing me and moaning. I saw my father try to cover his face but one of the men said something and he stood up stiffly after that. I didn't cry, because my mother seemed to look happier, more rested than I had ever seen her. For some reason, I was glad she was dead. I think maybe, except for us, she was too.

I was nine, my sister five. It was not until ten years later that I saw my father again.

We sat on opposite sides of a screen and talked into telephones. I had come there to tell him that in spite of my beginning, I had made it. I was nineteen, and a radioman in the U.S. Coast Guard, ready to fight and die for my country. There had been something mysterious about his smile.

"I'm proud of you, boy," he said. "You're a real man. You know I volunteered for the front lines too, but they turned me down."

We don't want you, I thought, we're not criminals, we're honest, strong. Then I looked again at this thief, this "Loaf-of-bread gunman" as the papers had tagged him. He had taken five loaves of bread, along with twelve dollars. Suddenly I could not stay there condemning this man, my father. It seemed such a waste, this magnificently strong man sitting there, his tremendous chest barely moving, hands resting quietly, talking to me, his whole being showering torrents of words about me.

"Be careful, boy, there are so many ways to fail, the pitfall sometimes   25 seems to be the easiest way out. Beware of my future, for you must continue, you must live. You must, for in you are all the dreams of my nights, all the ambitions of my days."

A bell rang and we stood up and a man pointed me toward a heavy door. I looked back, and saw him standing easy, hands at his side, so very calm, yet my mind filled to overflowing with the many things he had not said. It was to be ten years before he walked again as a free man, that is, as a physically free man.

I remember an earlier time, an earlier chapter of my growing up. I remember the first time my mother said we were taking lunch to my father's job. We had been down to the welfare line and I had stood with her, our feet burning against the hot pavement, and slowly moved forward in the sun. Years later I stood in chow lines over half of the world, but no desert, no burning deck was as hot as that day.

At last we reached the man sitting at the desk and my mother handed him the book of stamps. She smiled, a weak almost timid smile, as he checked her name and thumbed her to the food line.

As we headed home, my wagon was loaded with cans of corned beef, powdered milk, powdered eggs, and white margarine that she would later color yellow to look like butter.

At home we made sandwiches and off we went to my father's job, to   30 take him his lunch. I pulled my sister along in my wagon, a Red Flyer.

It was to be a picnic, a celebration really, my father's new job.

I remember the wagon did not have a tongue or handle but only a rope with which I pulled it wobbling along. We were excited, my sister and I, as we left our district of dirt streets and unpaved sidewalks and began to make our way along roads called boulevards and malls we had never had occasion to travel. The streets themselves were fascinating, so different. They were twice as wide, and there were exotic trees along the sidewalks and lo and behold trees down the center of the street as far as I could see and then we turned the corner and before us stretched an overwhelming sight. An overhead highway was being built. Columns rose to staggering heights, bulldozers thrust what seemed to me mountains of dirt before them, and hundreds, no thousands of men seemed to be crawling like ants hurrying from one point to another. Cranes lifted nets of steel and laid them in rows on the crushed rock.

I stared in awe at important-looking white men in metal hats, carrying rolls of papers which they intermittently studied, then pointing into space at what to me seemed only emptiness.

And then I saw my father. He sat among fifty other black men, all surrounded by great boulders marked with red paint. They all held steel chisels with which they cut along the marked lines. They would strike a certain point and the boulder would split into smaller pieces and as we approached there was a silence around them except for the pinging of the hammer against the chisel. In all the noise it was a lonely sound, futile, lost, oppressive. My father seemed to be concentrating, his tremendous arm whipping the air. He was stripped to the waist, black muscles popping sweat, goggled eyes for the metal and stone only. We stood there, the three of us, my mother, my sister, and I, and watched my father work for us, and as he conquered the huge boulder my chest filled with pride. Each stroke shouted for all the world to hear: This is my family and I love them! No one can tell me this was the act of a lazy man.

Suddenly a white man walked up and blew a whistle and the black   35
men all looked up and stopped working. My father glanced over at me, grinned and winked. He was glistening with sweat, the smell strong and powerful. He dropped his big hand on my shoulder and guided me to a large boulder.

"Hey, boy, you see me beat that thing to bits? This one's next," he said, indicating the one that shaded us from the sun. "I'll pound it to gravel by nightfall." It was a challenge he expected, he welcomed. That was my lazy, shiftless father.

And then one day they brought him home, his thumb, index, and middle finger gone from his left hand. They sat him in the kitchen chair and mumbled something about carelessness. He sat there for two hours before he answered our pleadings.

"Chain broke, I—I was guiding boulder. I couldn't, I just couldn't get my hand out from under in time—I, goddam it, Jean, they took my fingers off. I layed right there, my hand under the rock, and they nipped them like butchering a hog. Look at my goddam hand."

My mother held him in her arms and talked to him. She spoke softly, so softly my sister and I, standing in the corner, couldn't hear the words, only the soothing softness of her voice.

"Joe, Joe, we can." And then he began to cry like—like I sometimes 40 did when I was hurt deep inside and couldn't do anything about it.

After that there was a change in him. My father had been a fighter. He had feared no man white or black. I remember the time we were sitting on a streetcar and a woman had forgotten her fare—or maybe she never had any in the first place. Anyway, the driver slammed the doors on her and held her squeezed between them.

My father jumped up, snatched the driver out of the seat, and let the woman out. He and the driver had words that led to battle and Pop knocked the driver down just as a patrolman arrived. The patrolman didn't listen to any of the people that tried to explain what had happened. He just began to swing his night stick at my father's head. It was a mistake. My father hit him once and even today I can see all the people laughing at the funny look on the policeman's face as he staggered back all the way across the street and up against a building, slowly sagging down.

The police wagon arrived with four other policemen and one told him they were going to beat his brains in when they got him down town.

My pop had laughed then and backed against the building.

"I guess ain't no sense me going peaceable then." 45

They knocked out all his upper front teeth that day, but as he said later, "Them four white boys will think of me every time they shave."

They finally overpowered him and dragged him, still struggling, to the wagon. One of them kept muttering, "He's one fighting son of a black bitch, he's a fighting son of a bitch."

All the time I hadn't said a word or cried or yelled as they stomped and kicked him. I had shut my eyes and held my lips tightly pressed together and I had done just as he'd always told me.

"You stay out of it, boy, stay real quiet, and when that wagon leaves, you run behind and keep it in sight. If they lose you, you ask someone where the closest police station is—that's where I'll be. You go home and tell your mother."

That's the way he had been before losing his left hand. Afterwards, 50 well, it took a lot from him. He told me one day, laughing and shaking the nub as he called it, "If I'd only had the thumb, just the lousy thumb, I'd have it made."

Gradually he lost the ability to see humor in the nub. I think the whole thing came to a head the night I killed the kitten.

We hadn't had meat or potatoes for over two weeks. Even the grease drippings were gone and my mother was too sick to raise her head from the pillow. So I had gotten the skillet and put it in the open grate. We had two cups of flour so I mixed water with it and poured it into the greasy skillet. I can still recall the coldness of the room on my back and the warmth from the grate on my face as my sister and I knelt and hungrily watched the flour brown.

You know, today my wife marvels at how, no matter what she puts before me, I eat with relish. My children say that I eat very fast. I pray to God they never have to experience the causes of my obsession. But back to the story—the flour finally hardened and I broke a piece for my sister and a piece for my mother and left mine in the skillet on the table.

I took my mother's piece over to the bed and put it in her hand. She didn't move so I raised her hand to her mouth and she began to suck on it. Then I heard my sister scream, "Topsy is eating your food, Junior, Topsy's eating your food!" I turned around to see the cat tearing at my tiny piece of hard dough. I went wild. I leaped across the room and grabbed the kitten by the tail and began slamming her against the wall.

"That's my food," I kept yelling, "my food!" At last I heard my sister   55
screaming, "She's bleeding, you're killing Topsy. Here, here, eat my bread. Please don't kill her."

I stopped, horrified, staring at the limp nothing I now held. It was two weeks later that they got me to speak and that same night my father left the house for the last time. I don't say that what he did was right. No, it most assuredly was wrong. But what I do ask is, what else could he have done? I need an answer quickly now, today, right away, for I tell you this, my children will not starve, not here, not in this time of millions to foreign countries and fountains to throw tons of water upward to the sky, and nothing to the hungry, thirsty multitudes a stone's throw away.

Considerations

1. Consider carefully the advice Dolan's father gives him (paragraph 25). Comment on that advice by referring to your own observations and experiences.
2. Describe the father's attitude when he first begins the job splitting boulders. Why and how does that attitude change? Evaluate the effect this change has on Dolan.
3. Make a list of details Dolan uses to describe his mother. What can you infer about her and about Dolan's feelings for her?
4. What is Dolan's response when he first visits his father in prison? How does his view of his father change later in life? What significance can you see in these changes?
5. Dolan emphasizes poverty as a motivation for crime. To what extent does he use this evaluation to justify his father's choices and actions? Explain why (and to what extent) you agree or disagree with Dolan.

CONNECTIONS: PARENTS AND CHILDREN

1. In this section, many of the selections deal in some way with children who are separated from (or are becoming separate from) their parents. Consider issues relating to separation as part of the parent-child relationship. In what ways do you see separation as harmful? As necessary? Important for growth?

2. Consider the role played by outside authorities in the parent-child relationship. To what extent do you see outside help and intervention as helpful? To what extent as detrimental? Refer to your own experiences and observations as well as to any of these works: "The Conversion of the Jews," "I Stand Here Ironing," "A Worn Path," "Amniocentesis," "A Parent's Journey Out of the Closet," and "I Remember Papa."

3. The works in this section focus on many different relationships among parents and children. Consider, for example, the following classifications:

Mother–daughter relationships:	"I Stand Here Ironing" "Making the Jam without You" *Painting Churches*
Mother–son relationships:	"The Conversion of the Jews" "Through the Tunnel" "My Mother" "A Parent's Journey Out of the Closet" "A Good Man Is Hard to Find"
Father–daughter relationships:	"My Father in the Navy" *Painting Churches*
Father–son relationships:	"My Papa's Waltz" "My son, my executioner" "I Remember Papa"

   Examining these relationships, can you see any significant similarities or differences within the groups? Among the groups? Explain.

4. Consider the impact of economic circumstances on the parent-child relationship as suggested by "I Stand Here Ironing," "A Worn Path," "Allowance," and "I Remember Papa."

5. What is your concept of the ideal mother, father, son, or daughter? Use characters, incidents, conflicts, and decisions from any of the works (either as positive or negative examples) to develop your definition.

10

Learning and Teaching

DONALD BARTHELME (1931–1989)

Me and Miss Mandible

> *Born in Philadelphia, Donald Barthelme was raised in Houston, Texas, where he became interested in writing at an early age. He won many awards in high school and went on to study writing at the University of Houston. Later he worked as a reporter and published many short stories in magazines such as the* New Yorker. *His fiction is highly experimental, combining dark humor with stylistic innovations. In addition to writing fiction for adults, Barthelme has also written* The Slightly Irregular Fire Engine, *which won the 1971 National Book Award for children's literature. His collection of short fiction* Sixty Stories *(1981), in which "Me and Miss Mandible" appears, won widespread critical acclaim.*

13 September

Miss Mandible wants to make love to me but she hesitates because I am officially a child; I am, according to the records, according to the grade-book on her desk, according to the card index in the principal's office, eleven years old. There is a misconception here, one that I haven't quite managed to get cleared up yet. I am in fact thirty-five, I've been in the Army, I am six feet one, I have hair in the appropriate places, my voice is a baritone, I know very well what to do with Miss Mandible if she ever makes up her mind.

In the meantime we are studying common fractions. I could, of course, answer all the questions, or at least most of them (there are things I don't remember). But I prefer to sit in this too-small seat with the desktop cramping my thighs and examine the life around me. There are thirty-two in the class, which is launched every morning with the pledge of allegiance to the flag. My own allegiance, at the moment, is divided between Miss Mandible and Sue Ann Brownly, who sits across the aisle from me all day long and is, like Miss Mandible, a fool for love. Of the two I prefer, today, Sue Ann; although between eleven and eleven and a half (she refuses to reveal her exact age) she is clearly a woman, with a woman's disguised aggression and a woman's peculiar contradictions.

15 September

Happily our geography text, which contains maps of all the principal land-masses of the world, is large enough to conceal my clandestine journal-keeping, accomplished in an ordinary black composition book. Every day I must wait until Geography to put down such thoughts as I may have had during the morning about my situation and my fellows. I have tried writing at other times and it does not work. Either the teacher is walking up and down the aisles (during this period, luckily, she sticks close to the map rack in the front of the room) or Bobby Vanderbilt, who sits behind me, is punching me in the kidneys and wanting to know what I am doing. Vanderbilt, I have found out from certain desultory conversations on the playground, is hung up on sports cars, a veteran consumer of *Road & Track*. This explains the continual roaring sounds which seem to emanate from his desk; he is reproducing a record album called *Sounds of Sebring*.°

19 September

Only I, at times (only at times), understand that somehow a mistake has been made, that I am in a place where I don't belong. It may be that Miss Mandible also knows this, at some level, but for reasons not fully understood by me she is going along with the game. When I was first assigned to this room I wanted to protest, the error seemed obvious, the stupidest principal could have seen it; but I have come to believe it was deliberate, that I have been betrayed again.

Now it seems to make little difference. This life-role is as interesting as   5 my former life-role, which was that of a claims adjuster for the Great Northern Insurance Company, a position which compelled me to spend my time amid the debris of our civilization: rumpled fenders, roofless sheds, gutted warehouses, smashed arms and legs. After ten years of this one has a tendency to see the world as a vast junkyard, looking at a man and seeing only his (potentially) mangled parts, entering a house only to trace the path of the inevitable fire. Therefore when I was installed here, although I knew an error had been made, I countenanced it, I was shrewd; I was aware that there might well be some kind of advantage to be gained from what seemed a disaster. The role of The Adjuster teaches one much.

22 September

I am being solicited for the volleyball team. I decline, refusing to take unfair profit from my height.

23 September

Every morning the roll is called: Bestvina, Bokenfohr, Broan, Brownly, Cone, Coyle, Crecelius, Darin, Durbin, Geiger, Guiswite, Heckler, Jacobs, Kleinschmidt, Lay, Logan, Masei, Mitgang, Pfeilsticker. It is like the litany chanted in the dim miserable dawns of Texas by the cadre sergeant of our basic training company.

In the Army, too, I was ever so slightly awry. It took me a fantastically long time to realize what the others grasped almost at once: that much of what we were doing was absolutely pointless, to no purpose. I kept wondering why. Then something happened that proposed a new question. One day we were commanded to whitewash, from the ground to the topmost leaves,

---

Sounds of Sebring: Recording of race-car track sounds.

all of the trees in our training area. The corporal who relayed the order was nervous and apologetic. Later an off-duty captain sauntered by and watched us, white-splashed and totally weary, strung out among the freakish shapes we had created. He walked away swearing. I understood the principle (orders are orders), but I wondered: Who decides?

29 September

Sue Ann is a wonder. Yesterday she viciously kicked my ankle for not paying attention when she was attempting to pass me a note during History. It is swollen still. But Miss Mandible was watching me, there was nothing I could do. Oddly enough Sue Ann reminds me of the wife I had in my former role, while Miss Mandible seems to be a child. She watches me constantly, trying to keep sexual significance out of her look; I am afraid the other children have noticed. I have already heard, on that ghostly frequency that is the medium of classroom communication, the words *"Teacher's pet!"*

2 October

Sometimes I speculate on the exact nature of the conspiracy which   10 brought me here. At times I believe it was instigated by my wife of former days, whose name was . . . I am only pretending to forget. I know her name very well, as well as I know the name of my former motor oil (Quaker State) or my old Army serial number (US 54109268). Her name was Brenda.

7 October

Today I tiptoed up to Miss Mandible's desk (when there was no one else in the room) and examined its surface. Miss Mandible is a clean-desk teacher, I discovered. There was nothing except her gradebook (the one in which I exist as a sixth-grader) and a text, which was open at a page headed *Making the Processes Meaningful.* I read: "Many pupils enjoy working fractions when they understand what they are doing. They have confidence in their ability to take the right steps and to obtain correct answers. However, to give the subject full social significance, it is necessary that many realistic situations requiring the processes be found. Many interesting and lifelike problems involving the use of fractions should be solved . . ."

8 October

I am not irritated by the feeling of having been through all this before. Things are done differently now. The children, moreover, are in some ways different from those who accompanied me on my first voyage through the elementary schools: *"They have confidence in their ability to take the right steps and to obtain correct answers."* This is surely true. When Bobby Vanderbilt, who sits behind me and has the great tactical advantage of being able to maneuver in my disproportionate shadow, wishes to bust a classmate in the mouth he first asks Miss Mandible to lower the blind, saying that the sun hurts his eyes.

When she does so, *bip!* My generation would never have been able to con authority so easily.

13 October

I misread a clue. Do not misunderstand me: it was a tragedy only from the point of view of the authorities. I conceived that it was my duty to obtain satisfaction for the injured, for an elderly lady (not even one of our policyholders, but a claimant against Big Ben Transfer & Storage, Inc.) from the company. The settlement was $165,000; the claim, I still believe, was just. But without my encouragement Mrs. Bichek would never have had the self-love to prize her injury so highly. The company paid, but its faith in me, in my efficacy in the role, was broken. Henry Goodykind, the district manager, expressed this thought in a few not altogether unsympathetic words, and told me at the same time that I was to have a new role. The next thing I knew I was here, at Horace Greeley Elementary, under the lubricious eye of Miss Mandible.

17 October

Today we are to have a fire drill. I know this because I am a Fire Marshal, not only for our room but for the entire right wing of the second floor. This distinction, which was awarded shortly after my arrival, is interpreted by some as another mark of my somewhat dubious relations with our teacher. My armband, which is red and decorated with white felt letters reading FIRE, sits on the little shelf under my desk, next to the brown bag containing the lunch I carefully make for myself each morning. One of the advantages of packing my own lunch (I have no one to pack it for me) is that I am able to fill it with things I enjoy. The peanut butter sandwiches that my mother made in my former existence, many years ago, have been banished in favor of ham and cheese. I have found that my diet has mysteriously adjusted to my new situation; I no longer drink, for instance, and when I smoke, it is in the boys' john, like everybody else. When school is out I hardly smoke at all. It is only in the matter of sex that I feel my own true age; this is apparently something that, once learned, can never be forgotten. I live in fear that Miss Mandible will one day keep me after school, and when we are alone, create a compromising situation. To avoid this I have become a model pupil: another reason for the pronounced dislike I have encountered in certain quarters. But I cannot deny that I am singed by those long glances from the vicinity of the chalkboard; Miss Mandible is in many ways, notably about the bust, a very tasty piece.

24 October

There are isolated challenges to my largeness, to my dimly realized   15
position in the class as Gulliver.° Most of my classmates are polite about this

---

Gulliver: The hero of Jonathan Swift's fantasy tale *Gulliver's Travels,* who in the Land of Lilliput was a giant.

matter, as they would be if I had only one eye, or wasted, metal-wrapped legs. I am viewed as a mutation of some sort but essentially a peer. However Harry Broan, whose father has made himself rich manufacturing the Broan Bathroom Vent (with which Harry is frequently reproached; he is always being asked how things are in Ventsville), today inquired if I wanted to fight. An interested group of his followers had gathered to observe this suicidal undertaking. I replied that I didn't feel quite up to it, for which he was obviously grateful. We are now friends forever. He has given me to understand privately that he can get me all the bathroom vents I will ever need, at a ridiculously modest figure.

25 October

"Many interesting and lifelike problems involving the use of fractions should be solved . . ." The theorists fail to realize that everything that is either interesting or lifelike in the classroom proceeds from what they would probably call interpersonal relations: Sue Ann Brownly kicking me in the ankle. How lifelike, how womanlike, is her tender solicitude after the deed! Her pride in my newly acquired limp is transparent; everyone knows that she has set her mark upon me, that it is a victory in her unequal struggle with Miss Mandible for my great, overgrown heart. Even Miss Mandible knows, and counters in perhaps the only way she can, with sarcasm. "Are you wounded, Joseph?" Conflagrations smolder behind her eyelids, yearning for the Fire Marshal clouds her eyes. I mumble that I have bumped my leg.

30 October

I return again and again to the problem of my future.

4 November

The underground circulating library has brought me a copy of *Movie-TV Secrets,* the multicolor cover blazoned with the headline "Debbie's Date Insults Liz!" It is a gift from Frankie Randolph, a rather plain girl who until today has had not one word for me, passed on via Bobby Vanderbilt. I nod and smile over my shoulder in acknowledgment; Frankie hides her head under her desk. I have seen these magazines being passed around among the girls (sometimes one of the boys will condescend to inspect a particularly lurid cover). Miss Mandible confiscates them whenever she finds one. I leaf through *Movie-TV Secrets* and get an eyeful. "The exclusive picture on these pages isn't what it seems. We know how it looks and we know what the gossipers will do. So in the interests of a nice guy, we're publishing the facts first. Here's what really happened!" The picture shows a rising young movie idol in bed, pajama-ed and bleary-eyed, while an equally blowzy young woman looks startled beside him. I am happy to know that the picture is not really what it seems; it seems to be nothing less than divorce evidence.

What do these hipless eleven-year-olds think when they come across, in the same magazine, the full-page ad for Maurice de Paree, which features "Hip Helpers" or what appear to be padded rumps? ("A real undercover agent that adds appeal to those hips and derriere, both!") If they cannot decipher the language the illustrations leave nothing to the imagination. "Drive him frantic . . ." the copy continues. Perhaps this explains Bobby Vanderbilt's preoccupation with Lancias and Maseratis; it is a defense against being driven frantic.

Sue Ann has observed Frankie Randolph's overture, and catching my   20
eye, she pulls from her satchel no less than seventeen of these magazines, thrusting them at me as if to prove that anything any of her rivals has to offer, she can top. I shuffle through them quickly, noting the broad editorial perspective:

"Debbie's Kids Are Crying"°
"Eddie Asks Debbie: Will You . . . ?"
"The Nightmares Liz Has About Eddie!"
"The Things Debbie Can Tell About Eddie"
"The Private Life of Eddie and Liz"
"Debbie Gets Her Man Back?"
"A New Life for Liz"
"Love Is a Tricky Affair"
"Eddie's Taylor-Made Love Nest"
"How Liz Made a Man of Eddie"
"Are They Planning to Live Together?"
"Isn't It Time to Stop Kicking Debbie Around?"
"Debbie's Dilemma"
"Eddie Becomes a Father Again"
"Is Debbie Planning to Re-wed?"
"Can Liz Fulfill Herself?"
"Why Debbie Is Sick of Hollywood"

Who are these people, Debbie, Eddie, Liz, and how did they get themselves in such a terrible predicament? Sue Ann knows, I am sure; it is obvious that she has been studying their history as a guide to what she may expect when she is suddenly freed from this drab, flat classroom.

I am angry and I shove the magazines back at her with not even a whisper of thanks.

5 November

The sixth grade at Horace Greeley Elementary is a furnace of love, love, love. Today it is raining, but inside the air is heavy and tense with

Debbie, Eddie, Liz: Actress Debbie Reynolds, singer Eddie Fisher, and actress Elizabeth Taylor, who were involved in a scandalous love triangle in the 1950s and 1960s.

passion. Sue Ann is absent; I suspect that yesterday's exchange has driven her to her bed. Guilt hangs about me. She is not responsible, I know, for what she reads, for the models proposed to her by a venal publishing industry; I should not have been so harsh. Perhaps it is only the flu.

Nowhere have I encountered an atmosphere as charged with aborted sexuality as this. Miss Mandible is helpless; nothing goes right today. Amos Darin has been found drawing a dirty picture in the cloakroom. Sad and inaccurate, it was offered not as a sign of something else but as an act of love in itself. It has excited even those who have not seen it, even those who saw but understood only that it was dirty. The room buzzes with imperfectly comprehended titillation. Amos stands by the door, waiting to be taken to the principal's office. He wavers between fear and enjoyment of his temporary celebrity. From time to time Miss Mandible looks at me reproachfully, as if blaming me for the uproar. But I did not create this atmosphere, I am caught in it like all the others.

8 November

Everything is promised my classmates and me, most of all the future.   25
We accept the outrageous assurances without blinking.

9 November

I have finally found the nerve to petition for a larger desk. At recess I can hardly walk; my legs do not wish to uncoil themselves. Miss Mandible says she will take it up with the custodian. She is worried about the excellence of my themes. Have I, she asks, been receiving help? For an instant I am on the brink of telling her my story. Something, however, warns me not to attempt it. Here I am safe, I have a place; I do not wish to entrust myself once more to the whimsy of authority. I resolve to make my themes less excellent in the future.

11 November

A ruined marriage, a ruined adjusting career, a grim interlude in the Army when I was almost not a person. This is the sum of my existence to date, a dismal total. Small wonder that re-education seemed my only hope. It is clear even to me that I need reworking in some fundamental way. How efficient is the society that provides thus for the salvage of its clinkers!

14 November

The distinction between children and adults, while probably useful for some purposes, is at bottom a specious one, I feel. There are only individual egos, crazy for love.

15 November

The custodian has informed Miss Mandible that our desks are all the correct size for sixth-graders, as specified by the Board of Estimate and furnished the schools by the Nu-Art Educational Supply Corporation of Englewood, California. He has pointed out that if the desk size is correct, then the pupil size must be incorrect. Miss Mandible, who has already arrived at this conclusion, refuses to press the matter further. I think I know why. An appeal to the administration might result in my removal from the class, in a transfer to some sort of setup for "exceptional children." This would be a disaster of the first magnitude. To sit in a room with child geniuses (or, more likely, children who are "retarded") would shrivel me in a week. Let my experience here be that of the common run, I say; let me be, please God, typical.

20 November

We read signs as promises. Miss Mandible understands by my great height, by my resonant vowels, that I will one day carry her off to bed. Sue Ann interprets these same signs to mean that I am unique among her male acquaintances, therefore most desirable, therefore her special property as is everything that is Most Desirable. If neither of these propositions works out then life has broken faith with them.

I myself, in my former existence, read the company motto ("Here to Help in Time of Need") as a description of the duty of the adjuster, drastically mislocating the company's deepest concerns. I believed that because I had obtained a wife who was made up of wife-signs (beauty, charm, softness, perfume, cookery) I had found love. Brenda, reading the same signs that have now misled Miss Mandible and Sue Ann Brownly, felt she had been promised that she would never be bored again. All of us, Miss Mandible, Sue Ann, myself, Brenda, Mr. Goodykind, still believe that the American flag betokens a kind of general righteousness.

But I say, looking about me in this incubator of future citizens, that signs are signs, and some of them are lies.

23 November

It may be that my experience as a child will save me after all. If only I can remain quietly in this classroom, making my notes while Napoleon plods through Russia in the droning voice of Harry Broan, reading aloud from our History text. All of the mysteries that perplexed me as an adult have their origins here. But Miss Mandible will not permit me to remain ungrown. Her hands rest on my shoulders too warmly, and for too long.

7 December

It is the pledges that this place makes to me, pledges that cannot be redeemed, that will confuse me later and make me feel I am not *getting anywhere.* Everything is presented as the result of some knowable process; if I wish to arrive at four I get there by way of two and two. If I wish to burn Moscow the route I must travel has already been marked out by another visitor. If, like Bobby Vanderbilt, I yearn for the wheel of the Lancia 2.4-liter coupé, I have only to go through the appropriate process, that is, get the money. And if it is money itself that I desire, I have only to *make* it. All of these goals are equally beautiful in the sight of the Board of Estimate; the proof is all around us, in the no-nonsense ugliness of this steel and glass building, in the straightline matter-of-factness with which Miss Mandible handles some of our less reputable wars. Who points out that arrangements sometimes slip, that errors are made, that signs are misread? *"They have confidence in their ability to take the right steps and to obtain correct answers."*

8 December

My enlightenment is proceeding wonderfully.   35

9 December

Disaster once again. Tomorrow I am to be sent to a doctor, for observation. Sue Ann Brownly caught Miss Mandible and me in the cloakroom, during recess, Miss Mandible's naked legs in a scissors around my waist. For a moment I thought Sue Ann was going to choke. She ran out of the room weeping, straight for the principal's office, certain now which of us was Debbie, which Eddie, which Liz. I am sorry to be the cause of her disillusionment, but I know that she will recover. Miss Mandible is ruined but fulfilled. Although she will be charged with contributing to the delinquency of a minor, she seems at peace, *her* promise has been kept. She knows now that everything she has been told about life, about America, is true.

I have tried to convince the school authorities that I am a minor only in a very special sense, that I am in fact mostly to blame—but it does no good. They are as dense as ever. My contemporaries are astounded that I present myself as anything other than an innocent victim. Like the Old Guard marching through the Russian drifts, the class marches to the conclusion that truth is punishment.

Bobby Vanderbilt has given me his copy of *Sounds of Sebring,* in farewell.

_____

Considerations

1. What does "mandible" mean? How does this teacher's name suggest the way the narrator sees her relationship with her students?
2. What implied comparisons does the narrator make between the world of work, the world of the army, and the world of elementary school? (See journal entries for September 19 and 23.) Do these comparisons

seem completely absurd to you, or do you see significant similarities? Explain.

3. What differences does the narrator see between sixth grade in "his day" and sixth grade as he is currently experiencing it? Does he seem to find one superior to the other? Explain.

4. The narrator claims to be an adult male, yet he seems to be a victim of nearly everyone in the story—Sue Ann, Harry Broan, and Miss Mandible, for example. How can you account for his sense of helplessness and powerlessness?

5. Read the final four journal entries. To what extent do you read the December 8 entry as ironic? Can it be read as literally accurate? Explain.

TONI CADE BAMBARA (1939–   )

The Lesson

Toni Cade Bambara grew up in Harlem and Bedford-Stuyvesant, New York. After earning a bachelor of arts from Queens College and a master of arts from the City College of New York and studying in Italy and Paris, she took a position as a social worker with the New York State Department of Welfare. In addition, she has worked as a youth counselor, a community organizer, and a freelance writer. Many of her stories focus on the lives of African-American women and their varied experiences in relationship to their families, their professional lives, and their communities. "The Lesson" appeared in her collection of short fiction Gorilla, My Love *(1972).*

Back in the days when everyone was old and stupid or young and foolish and me and Sugar were the only ones just right, this lady moved on our block with nappy hair and proper speech and no makeup. And quite naturally we laughed at her, laughed the way we did at the junk man who went about his business like he was some big-time president and his sorry-ass horse his secretary. And we kinda hated her too, hated the way we did the winos who cluttered up our parks and pissed on our handball walls and stank up our hallways and stairs so you couldn't halfway play hide-and-seek without a goddamn gas mask. Miss Moore was her name. The only woman on the block with no first name. And she was black as hell, cept for her feet, which were fish-white and spooky. And she was always planning these boring-ass things for us to do, us being my cousin, mostly, who lived on the block cause we all moved North the same time and to the same apartment then spread out gradual to breathe. And our parents would yank our heads into some kinda shape and crisp up our clothes so we'd be presentable for travel with Miss Moore, who always looked like she was going to church, though she never did. Which is just one of the things the grownups talked about when they talked behind her back like a dog. But when she came calling with some sachet she'd sewed up or some gingerbread she'd made or some book, why then they'd all be too embarrassed to turn her down and we'd get handed over all spruced up. She'd been to college and said it was only right that she should take responsibility for the young ones' education, and she not even related by marriage or blood. So they'd go for it. Specially Aunt Gretchen. She was the main gofer in the family. You got some ole dumb shit foolishness you want somebody to go for, you send for Aunt Gretchen. She been screwed into the go-along for so long, it's a blood-deep natural thing with her. Which is how she got saddled with me and Sugar and Junior in the first place while our mothers were in a la-de-da apartment up the block having a good ole time.

So this one day Miss Moore rounds us all up at the mailbox and it's puredee hot and she's knockin herself out about arithmetic. And school suppose to let up in summer I heard, but she don't never let up. And the starch in my pinafore scratching the shit outta me and I'm really hating this nappy-head bitch and her goddamn college degree. I'd much rather go to the pool or to the show where it's cool. So me and Sugar leaning on the mailbox being surly, which is a Miss Moore word. And Flyboy checking out what everybody brought for lunch. And Fat Butt already wasting his peanut-butter-and-jelly sandwich like the pig he is. And Junebug punchin on Q.T.'s arm for potato chips. And Rosie Giraffe shifting from one hip to the other waiting for somebody to step on her foot or ask her if she from Georgia so she can kick ass, preferably Mercedes'. And Miss Moore asking us do we know what money is, like we a bunch of retards. I mean real money, she say, like it's only poker chips or monopoly papers we lay on the grocer. So right away I'm tired of this and say so. And would much rather snatch Sugar and go to the Sunset and terrorize the West Indian kids and take their hair ribbons and their money too. And Miss Moore files that remark away for next week's lesson on brotherhood, I can tell. And finally I say we oughta get to the subway cause it's cooler and besides we might meet some cute boys. Sugar done swiped her mama's lipstick, so we ready.

So we heading down the street and she's boring us silly about what things cost and what our parents make and how much goes for rent and how money ain't divided up right in this country. And then she gets to the part about we all poor and live in the slums, which I don't feature. And I'm ready to speak on that, but she steps out in the street and hails two cabs just like that. Then she hustles half the crew in with her and hands me a five-dollar bill and tells me to calculate 10 percent tip for the driver. And we're off. Me and Sugar and Junebug and Flyboy hangin out the window and hollering to everybody, putting lipstick on each other cause Flyboy a faggot anyway, and making farts with our sweaty armpits. But I'm mostly trying to figure how to spend this money. But they all fascinated with the meter ticking and Junebug starts laying bets as to how much it'll read when Flyboy can't hold his breath no more. Then Sugar lays bets as to how much it'll be when we get there. So I'm stuck. Don't nobody want to go for my plan, which is to jump out at the next light and run off to the first bar-b-que we can find. Then the driver tells us to get the hell out cause we there already. And the meter reads eighty-five cents. And I'm stalling to figure out the tip and Sugar say give him a dime. And I decide he don't need it bad as I do, so later for him. But then he tries to take off with Junebug foot still in the door so we talk about his mama something ferocious. Then we check out that we on Fifth Avenue and everybody dressed up in stockings. One lady in a fur coat, hot as it is. White folks crazy.

"This is the place," Miss Moore say, presenting it to us in the voice she uses at the museum. "Let's look in the windows before we go in."

"Can we steal?" Sugar asks very serious like she's getting the ground rules squared away before she plays. "I beg your pardon," say Miss Moore, and we fall out. So she leads us around the windows of the toy store and me

5

and Sugar screamin, "This is mine, that's mine, I gotta have that, that was made for me, I was born for that," till Big Butt drowns us out.

"Hey, I'm going to buy that there."

"That there? You don't even know what it is, stupid."

"I do so," he say punchin on Rosie Giraffe. "It's a microscope."

"Whatcha gonna do with a microscope, fool?"

"Look at things." 10

"Like what, Ronald?" ask Miss Moore. And Big Butt ain't got the first notion. So here go Miss Moore gabbing about the thousands of bacteria in a drop of water and the somethinorother in a speck of blood and the million and one living things in the air around us is invisible to the naked eye. And what she say that for? Junebug go to town on that "naked" and we rolling. Then Miss Moore ask what it cost. So we all jam into the window smudgin it up and the price tag say $300. So then she ask how long'd take for Big Butt and Junebug to save up their allowances. "Too long," I say. "Yeh," adds Sugar, "outgrown it by that time." And Miss Moore say no, you never outgrow learning instruments. "Why, even medical students and interns and," blah, blah, blah. And we ready to choke Big Butt for bringing it up in the first damn place.

"This here costs four hundred eighty dollars," say Rosie Giraffe. So we pile up all over her to see what she pointin out. My eyes tells me it's a chunk of glass cracked with something heavy, and different-color inks dripped into the splits, then the whole thing put into a oven or something. But for $480 it don't make sense.

"That's a paperweight made of semi-precious stones fused together under tremendous pressure," she explains slowly, with her hands doing the mining and all the factory work.

"So what's a paperweight?" asks Rosie Giraffe.

"To weigh paper with, dumbbell," say Flyboy, the wise man from 15 the East.

"Not exactly," say Miss Moore, which is what she say when you warm or way off too. "It's to weigh paper down so it won't scatter and make your desk untidy." So right away me and Sugar curtsy to each other and then to Mercedes who is more the tidy type.

"We don't keep paper on top of the desk in my class," say Junebug, figuring Miss Moore crazy or lyin one.

"At home, then," she say. "Don't you have a calendar and a pencil case and a blotter and a letter-opener on your desk at home where you do your homework?" And she know damn well what our homes look like cause she nosys around in them every chance she gets.

"I don't even have a desk," say Junebug. "Do we?"

"No. And I don't get no homework neither," says Big Butt. 20

"And I don't even have a home," say Flyboy like he do at school to keep the white folks off his back and sorry for him. Send this poor kid to camp posters, is his specialty.

"I do," says Mercedes. "I have a box of stationery on my desk and a picture of my cat. My godmother bought the stationery and the desk. There's a big rose on each sheet and the envelopes smell like roses."

"Who wants to know about your smelly-ass stationery," say Rosie Giraffe fore I can get my two cents in.

"It's important to have a work area all your own so that . . . "

"Will you look at this sailboat, please," say Flyboy, cuttin her off and pointin to the thing like it was his. So once again we tumble all over each other to gaze at this magnificent thing in the toy store which is just big enough to maybe sail two kittens across the pond if you strap them to the posts tight. We all start reciting the price tag like we in assembly. "Hand-crafted sailboat of fiberglass at one thousand one hundred ninety-five dollars."

"Unbelievable," I hear myself say and am really stunned. I read it again for myself just in case the group recitation put me in a trance. Same thing. For some reason this pisses me off. We look at Miss Moore and she lookin at us, waiting for I dunno what.

"Who'd pay all that when you can buy a sailboat set for a quarter at Pop's, a tube of glue for a dime, and a ball of string for eight cents? It must have a motor and a whole lot else besides," I say. "My sailboat cost me about fifty cents."

"But will it take water?" say Mercedes with her smart ass.

"Took mine to Alley Pond Park once," say Flyboy. "String broke. Lost it. Pity."

"Sailed mine in Central Park and it keeled over and sank. Had to ask my father for another dollar."

"And you got the strap," laugh Big Butt. "The jerk didn't even have a string on it. My old man wailed on his behind."

Little Q.T. was staring hard at the sailboat and you could see he wanted it bad. But he too little and somebody'd just take it from him. So what the hell. "This boat for kids, Miss Moore?"

"Parents silly to buy something like that just to get all broke up," say Rosie Giraffe.

"That much money it should last forever," I figure.

"My father'd buy it for me if I wanted it."

"Your father, my ass," say Rosie Giraffe getting a chance to finally push Mercedes.

"Must be rich people shop here," say Q.T.

"You are a very bright boy," say Flyboy. "What was your first clue?" And he rap him on the head with the back of his knuckles, since Q.T. the only one he could get away with. Though Q.T. liable to come up behind you years later and get his licks in when you half expect it.

"What I want to know is," I says to Miss Moore though I never talk to her, I wouldn't give the bitch that satisfaction, "is how much a real boat costs? I figure a thousand'd get you a yacht any day."

25

30

35

"Why don't you check that out," she says, "and report back to the   40
group?" Which really pains my ass. If you gonna mess up a perfectly good
swim day least you could do is have some answers. "Let's go in," she say like
she got something up her sleeve. Only she don't lead the way. So me and
Sugar turn the corner to where the entrance is, but when we get there I
kinda hang back. Not that I'm scared, what's there to be afraid of, just a toy
store. But I feel funny, shame. But what I got to be shamed about? Got as
much right to go in as anybody. But somehow I can't seem to get hold of
the door, so I step away for Sugar to lead. But she hangs back too. And I
look at her and she looks at me and this is ridiculous. I mean, damn, I have
never ever been shy about doing nothing or going nowhere. But then Mercedes steps up and then Rosie Giraffe and Big Butt crowd in behind and
shove, and next thing we all stuffed into the doorway with only Mercedes
squeezing past us, smoothing out her jumper and walking right down the
aisle. Then the rest of us tumble in like a glued-together jigsaw done all
wrong. And people lookin at us. And it's like the time me and Sugar crashed
into the Catholic church on a dare. But once we got in there and everything
so hushed and holy and the candles and the bowin and the handkerchiefs on
all the drooping heads, I just couldn't go through with the plan. Which was
for me to run up to the altar and do a tap dance while Sugar played the nose
flute and messed around in the holy water. And Sugar kept givin me the
elbow. Then later teased me so bad I tied her up in the shower and turned it
on and locked her in. And she'd be there till this day if Aunt Gretchen hadn't
finally figured I was lyin about the boarder takin a shower.

Same thing in the store. We all walkin on tiptoe and hardly touchin
the games and puzzles and things. And I watched Miss Moore who is steady
watchin us like she waitin for a sign. Like Mama Drewery watches the sky
and sniffs the air and takes note of just how much slant is in the bird formation. Then me and Sugar bump smack into each other, so busy gazing at the
toys, 'specially the sailboat. But we don't laugh and go into our fat-lady
bump-stomach routine. We just stare at that price tag. Then Sugar run a
finger over the whole boat. And I'm jealous and want to hit her. Maybe not
her, but I sure want to punch somebody in the mouth.

"Watcha bring us here for, Miss Moore?"

"You sound angry, Sylvia. Are you mad about something?" Givin me
one of them grins like she tellin a grown-up joke that never turns out to be
funny. And she's lookin very closely at me like maybe she plannin to do my
portrait from memory. I'm mad, but I won't give her that satisfaction. So I
slouch around the store bein very bored and say, "Let's go."

Me and Sugar at the back of the train watchin the tracks whizzin by
large then small then gettin gobbled up in the dark. I'm thinkin about this
tricky toy I saw in the store. A clown that somersaults on a bar then does
chin-ups just cause you yank lightly at his leg. Cost $35. I could see me askin
my mother for a $35 birthday clown. "You wanna who that costs what?"
she'd say, cocking her head to the side to get a better view of the hole in my

head. Thirty-five dollars could buy new bunk beds for Junior and Gretchen's boy. Thirty-five dollars and the whole household could go visit Granddaddy Nelson in the country. Thirty-five dollars would pay for the rent and the piano bill too. Who are these people that spend that much for performing clowns and $1000 for toy sailboats? What kinda work they do and how they live and how come we ain't in on it? Where we are is who we are, Miss Moore always pointin out. But it don't necessarily have to be that way, she always adds then waits for somebody to say that poor people have to wake up and demand their share of the pie and don't none of us know what kind of pie she talking about in the first damn place. But she ain't so smart cause I still got her four dollars from the taxi and she sure ain't gettin it. Messin up my day with this shit. Sugar nudges me in my pocket and winks.

Miss Moore lines us up in front of the mailbox where we started from,   45
seem like years ago, and I got a headache for thinkin so hard. And we lean all over each other so we can hold up under the draggy-ass lecture she always finishes us off with at the end before we thank her for borin us to tears. But she just looks at us like she readin tea leaves. Finally she say, "Well, what did you think of F.A.O. Schwartz?"

Rosie Giraffe mumbles, "White folks crazy."

"I'd like to go there again when I get my birthday money," says Mercedes, and we shove her out the pack so she has to lean on the mailbox by herself.

"I'd like a shower. Tiring day," say Flyboy.

Then Sugar surprises me by sayin, "You know, Miss Moore, I don't think all of us here put together eat in a year what that sailboat costs." And Miss Moore lights up like somebody goosed her. "And?" she say, urging Sugar on. Only I'm standin on her foot so she don't continue.

"Imagine for a minute what kind of society it is in which some people   50
can spend on a toy what it would cost to feed a family of six or seven. What do you think?"

"I think," say Sugar pushing me off her feet like she never done before, cause I whip her ass in a minute, "that this is not much of a democracy if you ask me. Equal chance to pursue happiness means an equal crack at the dough, don't it?" Miss Moore is beside herself and I am disgusted with Sugar's treachery. So I stand on her foot one more time to see if she'll shove me. She shuts up, and Miss Moore looks at me, sorrowfully I'm thinkin. And somethin weird is goin on, I can feel it in my chest.

"Anybody else learn anything today?" lookin dead at me. I walk away and Sugar has to run to catch up and don't even seem to notice when I shrug her arm off my shoulder.

"Well, we got four dollars anyway," she says.

"Uh hunh."

"We could go to Hascombs and get half a chocolate layer and then go   55
to the Sunset and still have plenty money for potato chips and ice cream sodas."

"Uh hunh."

"Race you to Hascombs," she say.

We start down the block and she gets ahead which is O.K. by me cause I'm going to the West End and then over to the Drive to think this day through. She can run if she want to and even run faster. But ain't nobody gonna beat me at nuthin.

Considerations

1. Although Miss Moore does not teach Sugar, Sylvia, and their friends in a traditional classroom, in what ways does she fit the stereotype of an elementary schoolteacher? In what ways does she challenge or escape the stereotype?

2. Explain Miss Moore's attitude toward the children she teaches and toward their parents. How is her attitude reflected by her teaching methods?

3. What do you see as Miss Moore's purpose for bringing Sugar, Sylvia, and their friends to F.A.O. Schwartz? What speculations do the children make about the trip and its purpose?

4. Identify and discuss some of the comic elements in the story. Do you find these elements distracting, or do they in some way contribute to the theme(s) you see?

5. Sugar and Sylvia react differently to the trip to F.A.O. Schwartz. What do you think each learns? Based on their different reactions to Miss Moore's lesson, what future can you predict for each girl?

GRACE PALEY (1922–   )

The Loudest Voice

Born into a family of socialist Russian Jews in 1922, Grace Paley spent hours listening to the tales of her parents, uncles, and aunts. These stories, told alternately in Russian, English, and Yiddish, inspired Paley, as she explained in an interview with Shenandoah *magazine (1981). When she first began writing, she found herself too focused on "me—me—me." To get beyond this point, she started listening carefully to "other people's voices" and integrating them into her work by "writing with an accent." "The Loudest Voice" comes from Paley's collection of short fiction* The Little Disturbances of Man *(1959).*

There is a certain place where dumb-waiters boom, doors slam, dishes crash; every window is a mother's mouth bidding the street shut up, go skate somewhere else, come home. My voice is the loudest.

There, my own mother is still as full of breathing as me and the grocer stands up to speak to her. "Mrs. Abramowitz," he says, "people should not be afraid of their children."

"Ah, Mr. Bialik," my mother replies, "if you say to her or her father 'Ssh,' they say, 'In the grave it will be quiet.'"

"From Coney Island to the cemetery," says my papa. "It's the same subway; it's the same fare."

I am right next to the pickle barrel. My pinky is making tiny whirl-pools in the brine. I stop a moment to announce: "Campbell's Tomato Soup. Campbell's Vegetable Beef Soup. Campbell's S-c-otch Broth . . ." 5

"Be quiet," the grocer says, "the labels are coming off."

"Please, Shirley, be a little quiet," my mother begs me.

In that place the whole street groans: Be quiet! Be quiet! but steals from the happy chorus of my inside self not a tittle or a jot.

There, too, but just around the corner, is a red brick building that has been old for many years. Every morning the children stand before it in double lines which must be straight. They are not insulted. They are waiting anyway.

I am usually among them. I am, in fact, the first, since I begin with 10 "A."

One cold morning the monitor tapped me on the shoulder. "Go to Room 409, Shirley Abramowitz," he said. I did as I was told. I went in a hurry up a down staircase to Room 409, which contained sixth-graders. I had to wait at the desk without wiggling until Mr. Hilton, their teacher, had time to speak.

After five minutes he said, "Shirley?"

"What?" I whispered.

He said, "My! My! Shirley Abramowitz! They told me you had a particularly loud, clear voice and read with lots of expression. Could that be true?"

"Oh yes," I whispered.   15

"In that case, don't be silly; I might very well be your teacher someday. Speak up, speak up."

"Yes," I shouted.

"More like it," he said. "Now, Shirley, can you put a ribbon in your hair or a bobby pin? It's too messy."

"Yes!" I bawled.

"Now, now, calm down." He turned to the class. "Children, not a   20
sound. Open at page 39. Read till 52. When you finish, start again." He looked me over once more. "Now, Shirley, you know, I suppose, that Christmas is coming. We are preparing a beautiful play. Most of the parts have been given out. But I still need a child with a strong voice, lots of stamina. Do you know what stamina is? You do? Smart kid. You know, I heard you read 'The Lord is my shepherd' in Assembly yesterday. I was very impressed. Wonderful delivery. Mrs. Jordan, your teacher, speaks highly of you. Now listen to me, Shirley Abramowitz, if you want to take the part and be in the play repeat after me, 'I swear to work harder than I ever did before.'"

I looked to heaven and said at once, "Oh, I swear." I kissed my pinky and looked at God.

"That is an actor's life, my dear," he explained. "Like a soldier's, never tardy or disobedient to his general, the director. Everything," he said, "absolutely everything will depend on you."

That afternoon, all over the building, children scraped and scrubbed the turkeys and the sheaves of corn off the schoolroom windows. Goodbye Thanksgiving. The next morning a monitor brought red paper and green paper from the office. We made new shapes and hung them on the walls and glued them to the doors.

The teachers became happier and happier. Their heads were ringing like the bells of childhood. My best friend Evie was prone to evil, but she did not get a single demerit for whispering. We learned "Holy Night" without an error. "How wonderful!" said Miss Glacé, the student teacher. "To think that some of you don't even speak the language!" We learned "Deck the Halls" and "Hark! The Herald Angels." . . . They weren't ashamed and we weren't embarrassed.

Oh, but when my mother heard about it all, she said to my father: 25
"Misha, you don't know what's going on there. Cramer is the head of the Tickets Committee."

"Who?" asked my father. "Cramer? Oh yes, an active woman."

"Active? Active has to have a reason. Listen," she said sadly, "I'm surprised to see my neighbors making tra-la-la for Christmas."

My father couldn't think of what to say to that. Then he decided: "You're in America! Clara, you wanted to come here. In Palestine the Arabs would be eating you alive. Europe you had pogroms. Argentina is full of Indians. Here you got Christmas. . . . Some joke, ha?"

"Very funny, Misha. What is becoming of you? If we came to a new country a long time ago to run away from tyrants, and instead we fall into a creeping pogrom, that our children learn a lot of lies, so what's the joke? Ach, Misha, your idealism is going away."

"So is your sense of humor."   30

"That I never had, but idealism you had a lot of."

"I'm the same Misha Abramowitz, I didn't change an iota. Ask anyone."

"Only ask me," says my mama, may she rest in peace. "I got the answer."

Meanwhile the neighbors had to think of what to say too.

Marty's father said: "You know, he has a very important part, my boy."   35

"Mine also," said Mr. Sauerfeld.

"Not my boy!" said Mrs. Klieg. "I said to him no. The answer is no. When I say no! I mean no!"

The rabbi's wife said, "It's disgusting!" But no one listened to her. Under the narrow sky of God's great wisdom she wore a strawberry-blond wig.

Every day was noisy and full of experience. I was Right-hand Man. Mr. Hilton said: "How could I get along without you, Shirley?"

He said: "Your mother and father ought to get down on their knees   40
every night and thank God for giving them a child like you."

He also said: "You're absolutely a pleasure to work with, my dear, dear child."

Sometimes he said: "For God's sakes, what did I do with the script? Shirley! Shirley! Find it."

Then I answered quietly: "Here it is, Mr. Hilton."

Once in a while, when he was very tired, he would cry out: "Shirley, I'm just tired of screaming at those kids. Will you tell Ira Pushkov not to come in till Lester points to that star the second time?"

Then I roared: "Ira Pushkov, what's the matter with you? Dope! Mr.   45
Hilton told you five times already, don't come in till Lester points to that star the second time."

"Ach, Clara," my father asked, "what does she do there till six o'clock she can't even put the plates on the table?"

"Christmas," said my mother coldly.

"Ho! Ho!" my father said. "Christmas. What's the harm? After all, history teaches everyone. We learn from reading this is a holiday from pagan times also, candles, lights, even Chanukah. So we learn it's not altogether Christian. So if they think it's a private holiday, they're only ignorant, not patriotic. What belongs to history, belongs to all men. You want to go back to the Middle Ages? Is it better to shave your head with a secondhand razor? Does it hurt Shirley to learn to speak up? It does not. So maybe someday she won't live between the kitchen and the shop. She's not a fool."

I thank you, Papa, for your kindness. It is true about me to this day. I am foolish but I am not a fool.

That night my father kissed me and said with great interest in my   50
career, "Shirley, tomorrow's your big day. Congrats."

"Save it," my mother said. Then she shut all the windows in order to prevent tonsillitis.

In the morning it snowed. On the street corner a tree had been decorated for us by a kind city administration. In order to miss its chilly shadow our neighbors walked three blocks east to buy a loaf of bread. The butcher pulled down black window shades to keep the colored lights from shining on his chickens. Oh, not me. On the way to school, with both hands I tossed it a kiss of tolerance. Poor thing, it was a stranger in Egypt.

I walked straight into the auditorium past the staring children. "Go ahead, Shirley!" said the monitors. Four boys, big for their age, had already started work as propmen and stagehands.

Mr. Hilton was very nervous. He was not even happy. Whatever he started to say ended in a sideward look of sadness. He sat slumped in the middle of the first row and asked me to help Miss Glacé. I did this, although she thought my voice too resonant and said, "Showoff!"

Parents began to arrive long before we were ready. They wanted to   55
make a good impression. From among the yards of drapes I peeked out at the audience. I saw my embarrassed mother.

Ira, Lester, and Meyer were pasted to their beards by Miss Glacé. She almost forgot to thread the star on its wire, but I reminded her. I coughed a few times to clear my throat. Miss Glacé looked around and saw that everyone was in costume and on line waiting to play his part. She whispered, "All right . . ." Then:

Jackie Sauerfeld, the prettiest boy in first grade, parted the curtains with his skinny elbow and in a high voice sang out:

Parents dear
We are here
To make a Christmas play in time.
It we give
In narrative
And illustrate with pantomime.

He disappeared.

My voice burst immediately from the wings to the great shock of Ira, Lester, and Meyer, who were waiting for it but were surprised all the same.

"I remember, I remember, the house were I was born . . ."   60

Miss Glacé yanked the curtain open and there it was, the house— an old hayloft, where Celia Kornbluh lay in the straw with Cindy Lou, her favorite doll. Ira, Lester, and Meyer moved slowly from the wings toward her, sometimes pointing to a moving star and sometimes ahead to Cindy Lou.

It was a long story and it was a sad story. I carefully pronounced all the words about my lonesome childhood, while little Eddie Braunstein wandered upstage and down with his shepherd's stick, looking for sheep. I brought up lonesomeness again, and not being understood at all except by some women everybody hated. Eddie was too small for that and Marty Groff took his place, wearing his father's prayer shawl. I announced twelve friends, and half the boys in the fourth grade gathered round Marty, who stood on an orange crate while my voiced harangued. Sorrowful and loud, I declaimed about love and God and Man, but because of the terrible deceit of Abie Stock we came suddenly to a famous moment. Marty, whose remembering tongue I was, waited at the foot of the cross. He stared desperately at the audience. I groaned, "My God, my God why hast thou forsaken me?" The soldiers who were sheiks grabbed poor Marty to pin him up to die, but he wrenched free, turned again to the audience, and spread his arms aloft to show despair and the end. I murmured at the top of my voice, "The rest is silence, but as everyone in this room, in this city—in this world—now knows, I shall have life eternal."

That night Mrs. Kornbluh visited our kitchen for a glass of tea.

"How's the virgin?" asked my father with a look of concern.

"For a man with a daughter, you got a fresh mouth, Abramovitch." 65

"Here," said my father kindly, "have some lemon, it'll sweeten your disposition."

They debated a little in Yiddish, then fell in a puddle of Russian and Polish. What I understood next was my father, who said, "Still and all, it was certainly a beautiful affair, you have to admit, introducing us to the beliefs of a different culture."

"Well, yes," said Mrs. Kornbluh. "The only thing . . . you know Charlie Turner—that cute boy in Celia's class—a couple others? They got very small parts or no part at all. In very bad taste, it seemed to me. After all, it's their religion."

"Ach," explained my mother, "what could Mr. Hilton do? They got very small voices; after all, why should they holler? The English language they know from the beginning by heart. They're blond like angels. You think it's so important they should get in the play? Christmas . . . the whole piece of goods . . . they own it."

I listened and listened until I couldn't listen any more. Too sleepy, I 70 climbed out of bed and kneeled. I made a little church of my hands and said, "Hear, O Israel . . ." Then I called out in Yiddish, "Please, good night, good night. Ssh." My father said, "Ssh yourself," and slammed the kitchen door.

I was happy. I fell asleep at once. I had prayed for everybody: my talking family, cousins far away, passersby, and all the lonesome Christians. I expected to be heard. My voice was certainly the loudest.

Considerations

1. What differences do you see between the mother's and father's views on raising their daughter? What does each apparently want Shirley to learn?
2. What qualities does Mr. Hilton value in Shirley? What kind of advice does he give her? What do you think Shirley learns from her experiences with Mr. Hilton?
3. Consider the comments of Miss Glacé. What attitude does she have toward her students and their cultural background? To what extent do you see the Miss Glacés of this world as positive educators? To what extent do you see them as negative?
4. Why do some people object to Shirley's loud voice? What does Shirley, herself, think about her loud voice? How does the concept of a "loud voice" serve as a metaphor for the relationships and circumstances Shirley may face in real life rather than on the stage?
5. What does Shirley mean when she says she is "foolish but not a fool"? Do you agree with her evaluation? Explain.

CLARK BLAISE (1941–   )

A Class of New Canadians

Clark Blaise was born in North Dakota and educated at Denison University and the University of Iowa. He has won several fellowships and prizes for his writing, including a Guggenheim Fellowship. He has taught at schools in Montreal and Toronto, as well as at Skidmore College and the Iowa Writers' Workshop. His most recently published novel is Lusts. *"A Class of New Canadians" appears in his collection of short fiction* A North American Education *(1973).*

Norman Dyer hurried down Sherbrooke Street, collar turned against the snow. "Superb!" he muttered, passing a basement gallery next to a French bookstore. Bleached and tanned women in furs dashed from hotel lobbies into waiting cabs. Even the neon clutter of the side streets and the honks of slithering taxis seemed remote tonight through the peaceful snow. *Superb,* he thought again, waiting for a light and backing from a slushy curb: a word reserved for wines, cigars, and delicate sauces; he was feeling superb this evening. After eighteen months in Montreal, he still found himself freshly impressed by everything he saw. He was proud of himself for having steered his life north, even for jobs that were menial by standards he could have demanded. Great just being here no matter what they paid, looking at these buildings, these faces, and hearing all the languages. He was learning to be insulted by simple bad taste, wherever he encountered it.

Since leaving graduate school and coming to Montreal, he had sampled every ethnic restaurant downtown and in the old city, plus a few Levantine places out in Outremont. He had worked on conversational French and mastered much of the local dialect, done reviews for local papers, translated French-Canadian poets for Toronto quarterlies, and tweaked his colleagues for not sympathizing enough with Quebec separatism. He attended French performances of plays he had ignored in English, and kept a small but elegant apartment near a colony of *émigré* Russians just off Park Avenue. Since coming to Montreal he'd witnessed a hold-up, watched a murder, and seen several riots. When stopped on the street for directions, he would answer in French or accented English. To live this well and travel each long academic summer, he held two jobs. He had no intention of returning to the States. In fact, he had begun to think of himself as a semi-permanent, semi-political exile.

Now, stopped again a few blocks farther, he studied the window of Holt-Renfrew's exclusive men's shop. Incredible, he thought, the authority of simple good taste. Double-breasted chalk-striped suits he would never dare to buy. Knitted sweaters, and fifty-dollar shoes. One tanned mannequin was decked out in a brash checkered sportscoat with a burgundy vest and dashing ascot. Not a price tag under three hundred dollars. Unlike food, drink, cinema, and literature, clothing had never really involved him. Someday, he now realized, it would. Dyer's clothes, thus far, had all been bought in a chain department store. He was a walking violation of American law, clad shoes to scarf in Egyptian cottons, Polish leathers, and woolens from the People's Republic of China.

He had no time for dinner tonight; this was Wednesday, a day of lectures at one university, and then an evening course in English as a Foreign Language at McGill, beginning at six. He would eat afterwards.

Besides the money, he had kept this second job because it flattered him. 5 There was to Dyer something fiercely elemental, almost existential, about teaching both his language and his literature in a foreign country—like Joyce in Trieste, Isherwood and Nabokov in Berlin, Beckett in Paris. Also it was necessary for his students. It was the first time in his life that he had done something socially useful. What difference did it make that the job was beneath him, a recent Ph.D., while most of his colleagues in the evening school at McGill were idle housewives and bachelor civil servants? It didn't matter, even, that this job was a perversion of all the sentiments he held as a progressive young teacher. He was a god two evenings a week, sometimes suffering and fatigued, but nevertheless an omniscient, benevolent god. His students were silent, ignorant, and dedicated to learning English. No discussions, no demonstrations, no dialogue.

I love them, he thought. They need me.

He entered the room, pocketed his cap and ear muffs, and dropped his briefcase on the podium. Two girls smiled good evening.

They love me, he thought, taking off his boots and hanging up his coat; I'm not like their English-speaking bosses.

I love myself, he thought with amazement even while conducting a drill on word order. I love myself for tramping down Sherbrooke Street in zero weather just to help them with noun clauses. I love myself standing behind this podium and showing Gilles Carrier and Claude Veilleux the difference between the past continuous and the simple past; or the sultry Armenian girl with the bewitching half-glasses that "put on" is not the same as "take on"; or telling the dashing Mr. Miguel Mayor, late of Madrid, that simple futurity can be expressed in four different ways, at least.

This is what mastery is like, he thought. Being superb in one's chosen 10 field, not merely in one's mother tongue. A respected performer in the lecture halls of the major universities, equipped by twenty years' research in the remotest libraries, and slowly giving it back to those who must have it. Dishing it out suavely, even wittily. Being a legend. Being loved and a little feared.

"Yes, Mrs. David?"

A *sabra:* freckled, reddish hair, looking like a British model, speaks with a nifty British accent, and loves me.

"No," he smiled, "*I were* is not correct except in the present subjunctive, which you haven't studied yet."

The first hour's bell rang. The students closed their books for the intermission. Dyer put his away, then noticed a page of his Faulkner lecture from the afternoon class. *Absalom, Absalom!* his favorite.

"Can anyone here tell me what the *impregnable citadel of his passive*   15
rectitude means?"

"What, sir?" asked Mr. Vassilopoulos, ready to copy.

"What about *the presbyterian and lugubrious effluvium of his passive vindictiveness?*" A few girls giggled. "O.K.," said Dyer, "take your break."

In the halls of McGill they broke into the usual groups. French-Canadians and South Americans into two large circles, then the Greeks, Germans, Spanish, and French into smaller groups. The patterns interested Dyer. Madrid Spaniards and Parisian French always spoke English with their New World co-linguals. The Middle Europeans spoke German together, not Russian, preferring one occupier to the other. Two Israeli men went off alone. Dyer decided to join them for the break.

Not *sabras,* Dyer concluded, not like Mrs. David. The shorter one, dark and wavy-haired, held his cigarette like a violin bow. The other, Mr. Weinrot, was tall and pot-bellied, with a ruddy face and thick stubby fingers. Something about him suggested truck-driving, perhaps of beer, maybe in Germany. Neither one, he decided, could supply the name of a good Israeli restaurant.

"This is really hard, you know?" said Weinrot.   20

"Why?"

"I think it's because I'm not speaking much of English at my job."

"French?" asked Dyer.

"French? Pah! All the time Hebrew, sometimes German, sometimes little Polish. Crazy thing, eh? How long you think they let me speak Hebrew if I'm working in America?"

"Depends on where you're working," he said.   25

"Hell, I'm working for the Canadian government, what you think? Plant I work in—I'm engineer, see—makes boilers for the turbines going up North. Look. When I'm leaving Israel I go first to Italy. Right away— bamm I'm working in Italy I'm speaking Italian like a native. Passing for a native."

"A native Jew," said his dark-haired friend.

"Listen to him. So in Rome they think I'm from Tyrol—that's still native, eh? So I speak Russian and German and Italian like a Jew. My Hebrew is bad, I admit it, but it's a lousy language anyway. Nobody likes it. French I understand but English I'm talking like a bum. Arabic I know five dialects. Danish fluent. So what's the matter I can't learn English?'

"It'll come, don't worry," Dyer smiled. *Don't worry, my son;* he wanted to pat him on the arm. "Anyway, that's what makes Canada so appealing. Here they don't force you."

"What's this *appealing?* Means nice? Look, my friend, keep it, eh? Two   30
years in a country I don't learn the language means it isn't a country."

"Come on," said Dyer. "Neither does forcing you."

"Let me tell you a story why I come to Canada. Then you tell me if I
was wrong, O.K.?"

"Certainly," said Dyer, flattered.

In Italy, Weinrot told him, he had lost his job to a Communist union.
He left Italy for Denmark and opened up an Israeli restaurant with five other
friends. Then the six Israelis decided to rent a bigger apartment downtown
near the restaurant. They found a perfect nine-room place for two thousand
kroner a month, not bad shared six ways. Next day the landlord told them
the deal was off. "You tell me why," Weinrot demanded.

No Jews? Dyer wondered. "He wanted more rent," he finally said.   35

"More—you kidding? More we expected. *Less* we didn't expect. A
couple with eight kids is showing up after we're gone and the law in Denmark says a man has a right to a room for each kid plus a hundred kroner
knocked off the rent for each kid. What you think of that? So a guy who
comes in *after* us gets a nine-room place for a thousand kroner *less.* Law says
no way a bachelor can get a place ahead of a family, and bachelors pay twice
as much."

Dyer waited, then asked, "So?"

"So, I make up my mind the world is full of communisms, just like
Israel. So I take out applications next day for Australia, South Africa, U.S.A.,
and Canada. Canada says come right away, so I go. Should have waited for
South Africa."

"How could you?" Dyer cried. "What's wrong with you anyway?
South Africa is fascist. Australia is racist."

The bell rang, and the Israelis, with Dyer, began walking to the room.   40

"What I was wondering, then," said Mr. Weinrot, ignoring Dyer's outburst, "was if my English is good enough to be working in the United States.
You're American, aren't you?"

It was a question Dyer had often avoided in Europe, but had rarely
been asked in Montreal. "Yes," he admitted, "your English is probably
good enough for the States or South Africa, whichever one wants you
first."

He hurried ahead to the room, feeling that he had let Montreal down.
He wanted to turn and shout to Weinrot and to all the others that Montreal
was the greatest city on the continent, if only they knew it as well as he did.
If they'd just break out of their little ghettos.

At the door, the Armenian girl with the half-glasses caught his arm. She
was standing with Mrs. David and Miss Parizeau, a jolly French-Canadian girl
that Dyer had been thinking of asking out.

"Please, sir," she said, looking at him over the tops of her tiny glasses,   45
"what I was asking earlier—*put on*—I heard on the television. A man said

You are putting me on and everybody laughed. I think it was supposed to be
funny but *put on* we learned means get dressed, no?"

"Ah—*don't put me on,*" Dyer laughed.

"I yaven't erd it neither," said Miss Parizeau.

"To put some*body* on means to make a fool of him. To put some*thing*
on is to wear it. O.K.?" He gave examples.

"Ah, now I know," said Miss Parizeau. "Like bullshitting somebody. Is
it the same?"

"Ah, yes," he said, smiling. French-Canadians were like children learn-   50
ing the language. "Your example isn't considered polite. 'Put on' is very
common now in the States."

"Then maybe," said Miss Parizeau, "we'll ave it ere in twenty years."
The Armenian giggled.

"No—I've heard it here just as often," Dyer protested, but the girls had
already entered the room.

He began the second hour with a smile which slowly soured as he thought
of the Israelis. America's anticommunism was bad enough, but it was worse
hearing it echoed by immigrants, by Jews, here in Montreal. Wasn't there a
psychological type who chose Canada over South Africa? Or was it just a matter
of visas and slow adjustment? Did Johannesburg lose its Greeks, and Melbourne
its Italians, the way Dyer's students were always leaving Montreal?

And after class when Dyer was again feeling content and thinking of
approaching one of the Israelis for a restaurant tip, there came the flood of
small requests: should Mrs. Papadopoulos go into a more advanced course;
could Mr. Percz miss a week for an interview in Toronto; could Mr. Giguère,
who spoke English perfectly, have a harder book; Mr. Coté an easier one?

Then as he packed his briefcase in the empty room, Miguel Mayor, the   55
vain and impeccable Spaniard, came forward from the hallway.

"Sir," he began, walking stiffly, ready to bow or salute. He wore a loud
gray checkered sportscoat this evening, blue shirt, and matching ascot-
handkerchief, slightly mauve. He must have shaved just before class, Dyer
noticed, for two fresh daubs of antiseptic cream stood out on his jaw, just
under his earlobe.

"I have been wanting to ask *you* something, as a matter of fact," said
Dyer. "Do you know any good Spanish restaurants I might try tonight?"

"There are not any good Spanish restaurants in Montreal," he said. He
stepped closer. "Sir?"

"What's on your mind, then?"

"Please—have you the time to look on a letter for me?"   60

He laid the letter on the podium.

"Look *over* a letter," said Dyer. "What is it for?"

"I have applied," he began, stopping to emphasize the present perfect
construction, "for a job in Cleveland, Ohio, and I want to know if my letter
will be good. Will an American, I mean—"

"Why are you going there?"

"It is a good job." 65

"But Cleveland—"

"They have a blackman mayor, I have read. But the job is not in Cleveland."

"Let me see it."

Most honourable Sir: I humbly beg consideration for a position in your grand company . . .

"Who are you writing this to?" 70

"The president," said Miguel Mayor.

I am once a student of Dr. Ramiro Gutierrez of the Hydraulic Institute of Sevilla, Spain . . .

"Does the president know this Ramiro Gutierrez?"

"Oh, everybody is knowing him," Miguel Mayor assured, "he is the most famous expert in all Spain."

"Did he recommend this company to you?" 75

"No—I have said in my letter, if you look—"

An ancient student of Dr. Gutierrez, Salvador del Este, is actually a boiler expert who is being employed like supervisor is formerly a friend of mine . . .

"Is he still your friend?"

Whenever you say come to my city Miguel Mayor for talking I will be coming. I am working in Montreal since two years and am now wanting more money than I am getting here now . . .

"Well . . ." Dyer sighed. 80

"Sir—what I want from you is knowing in good English how to inter-view me by this man. The letters in Spanish are not the same to English ones, you know?"

I remain humbly at your orders . . .

"Why do you want to leave Montreal?"

"It's time for a change."

"Have you ever been to Cleveland?" 85

"I am one summer in California. Very beautiful there and hot like my country. Montreal is big port like Barcelona. Everybody mixed together and having no money. It is just a place to land, no?"

"Montreal? Don't be silly."

"I thought I come here and learn good English but where I work I get by in Spanish and French. It's hard, you know?" he smiled. Then he took a few steps back and gave his cuffs a gentle tug, exposing a set of jade cufflinks.

Dyer looked at the letter again and calculated how long he would be correcting it, then up at his student. How old is he? My age? Thirty? Is he married? Where do the Spanish live in Montreal? He looks so prosperous, so confident, like a male model off a page of *Playboy.* For an instant Dyer felt that his student was mocking him, somehow pitting his astounding confidence and wardrobe, sharp chin and matador's bearing against Dyer's command of English and mastery of the side streets, bistros, and ethnic restaurants. Mayor's letter was painful, yet he remained somehow competent. He would pass his interview, if he got one. What would he care about America, and the odiousness he'd soon be supporting? It was as though a superstructure of exploitation had been revealed, and Dyer felt himself abused by the very people he wanted so much to help. It had to end someplace.

He scratched out the second "humbly" from the letter, then folded the   90
sheet of foolscap. "Get it typed right away," he said. "Good luck."

"Thank you, sir," said his student, with a bow. Dyer watched the letter disappear in the inner pocket of the checkered sportscoat. Then the folding of the cashmere scarf, the draping of the camel's hair coat about the shoulders, the easing of the fur hat down to the rims of his ears. The meticulous filling of the pigskin gloves. Mayor's patent leather galoshes glistened.

"Good evening, sir," he said.

"*Buenas noches,*" Dyer replied.

He hurried now, back down Sherbrooke Street to his daytime office where he could deposit his books. Montreal on a winter night was still mysterious, still magical. Snow blurred the arc lights. The wind was dying. Every second car was now a taxi, crowned with an orange crescent. Slushy curbs had hardened. The window of Holt-Renfrew's was still attractive. The legless dummies invited a final stare. He stood longer than he had earlier, in front of the sporty mannequin with a burgundy waistcoat, the mauve and blue ensemble, the jade cufflinks.

Good evening, sir, he could almost hear. The ascot, the shirt, the com-   95
plete outfit, had leaped off the back of Miguel Mayor. He pictured how he must have entered the store with three hundred dollars and a prepared speech, and walked out again with everything off the torso's back.

I want that.

What, sir?

That.

The coat, sir?

Yes.   100

Very well, sir.

And *that.*

Which, sir?

All that.

"Absurd man!" Dyer whispered. There had been a moment of fear, as   105
though the naked body would leap from the window, and legless, chase him down Sherbrooke Street. But the moment was passing. Dyer realized now that it was comic, even touching. Miguel Mayor had simply tried too hard, too fast, and it would be good for him to stay in Montreal until he deserved those clothes, that touching vanity and confidence. With one last look at the window, he turned sharply, before the clothes could speak again.

Considerations

1. Make a list of details concerning Norman Dyer's life before the story takes place. What is his attitude toward the United States? Toward Montreal? How does he respond to his students' desire to leave Montreal?
2. Norman Dyer is a teacher. What would you say that he teaches in the story? What does he learn—particularly about himself?
3. Is Dyer presented as a sympathetic character? Does the author of the story seem to share Dyer's view of the cultural differences between Canada and the United States? Explain.
4. What does Miguel Mayor contribute to the story? Consider particularly the ending of the story and Mayor's conversation with Dyer.
5. Imagine that you are a student in one of Dyer's classes and that you must respond to the following question on the end-of-term evaluation form: Would you or would you not recommend this teacher and this course to another student like yourself? Explain your reasons.

DANNY SANTIAGO
Famous All Over Town

> Danny Santiago grew up in the Chicano barrio of Los Angeles. He has published many short stories reflecting his observations and experiences during those years. The following chapter comes from his first novel, Famous All Over Town *(1983), which the* New York Times Book Review *cited as "a classic of the Chicano urban experience."*

Next day I woke up before the alarm clock. Daylight Savings was almost over, the sun was tardy and the house was black but I woke up happy because today I would turn over my New Leaf. I was disgusted with the old one.

What about that zip gun, man? you might be wondering. Did it go off in my pocket? Did I get caught with it, or what? No is the answer. Did I get rid of it in the nearest trash barrel? And throw away a valuable piece of Shamrock hardware? And be a traitor to Boxer that trusted me? No, señor, I lived through two periods with it burning up my pocket and even carried it home, which won me merit badges with the Jesters even if it costed me two years' growth.

So anyway, I ate breakfast in the dark and went out back. The yard looked very different and misterioso at that time of day. A crouching leopard chilled my blood, which turned into an up-ended washtub. The moon hung low over City Hall. My neighbors were all asleep and I was temporary King of Shamrock Street, till I heard my father talking with the chickens. He was always the early bird of the family and preached for us to do the same but when he spotted me in the moonlight he seemed quite cranky that anybody should trespass on his private time of day.

"Qué milagro!"° he growled and went in the toledo.

Shamrock mostly walks to school by Broadway to show our face to the   5
public and because the chicks go that way too, for window-shopping, but today I went by the S.P. tracks which was the shortest road and safest from the Sierra. A steady little breeze blew on my back to help me on my way, which was a hopeful sign. The rails by now were turning pink, night was behind my back and day in front of me and my feet wanted to run. The railroad ties were spaced just right to land on every third one and I ran and ran as if I could run forever, and jumped up in the air and happy little yells and screeches came out of my mouth. Lucky for me, nobody was around to hear. Possibly my father was right, this was the best time of day after all and all my life I had been missing out on it.

It was 6:30 when I got to Audubon. The gates were still locked but I got in through Administration where the custodian was mopping halls. Out

---

Qué milagro!: What a miracle!

back the picnic tables were new-washed and the ground too. The place looked naked, not a single candy paper or Dixie Cup in sight. I dropped a crumpled page out of my notebook to dress it up, then sat down and waited for my tutor.

Who could quite possibly turn out to be some chick. They got better grades than the guys. It might even be some Paddy 9th-grader with blue eyes and stately shape, why not? which would be a new learning experience for me and may be just what I needed to straighten me out. Besides, they claim blondies often get quite interested in dark-skin Latins like myself, though I never quite saw it happen at Audubon Junior High. Whatever, I couldn't afford to show myself a dummy so I opened up my English assignment which slipped my mind last night.

Our text was supposed to be about a certain Mexican kid named Pancho which his father worked for the railroad and his sister María cleaned house for rich old ladies. The story started out in New Mexico where this Pancho specialized mostly in killing rattlesnakes under the baby's crib. They seemed to follow the guy around like a dog, but now Santa Fe has moved the family to Elmsville, Kansas. It's Pancho's first day in his new school but the blondie kids discriminate him and won't let him play on their ball teams so there he is, sitting on the bench. Except Miss Brewster proves very understanding the way teachers are in books and in the ninth inning with bases loaded she gets the bright idea to send him in to pitch. That's where our assignment began so I started reading:

> As Pancho advanced to the "mound," a howl of disapproval arose from his teammates. "Who ever heard of a Mexican pitcher?" the shortstop grumbled. "I quit." "He doesn't even have a baseball mitt," exclaimed the catcher. "Then someone can lend him his," Miss Brewster retorted. "Thank you, Miss Brewster," said Pancho, "I'd rather do without."
>
> Billy Jasper stepped into the batter's "box." He was the best hitter on his team. Pancho hurled his pitch. Billy swung his famous home run swing. But lo and behold, the ball twisted around his bat like a corkscrew.
>
> "Steerike one!" roared Miss Brewster in tones a Big League umpire well might envy. New hope came to Pancho's teammates.
>
> "Oh boy," cried one of them. "Did you see that "sinker?"
>
> Pancho pitched again. A sharp crack like a pistol shot was heard. It would be a "three-bagger" at least. But Pancho leaped high in the air and caught the ball bare-handed. He then ran nimbly to third base. It was a double play unassisted. The game was over.
>
> "Three cheers for Pancho," his teammates cried. Pancho's "strangeness" was now just a memory. Miss Brewster beamed. "This should be a lesson to us all," she remarked. But Pancho had no time to enjoy

his triumph. He had promised his sister María to help her clean house for rich Mrs. Murdock.

The sturdy lad ran all the way up Maple Street and down Persimmon Place and into the banker's spacious driveway. Scarcely noticing the presence of Sheriff Trotter's car parked before the towering white columns, he hurried to the kitchen door. Little did he suspect the painful situation into which he was about to stumble.

That ended our chapter and I wasn't sorry. Like always, they then asked ten questions. Number 1 was, "Can you find a good example of foreshadowing in the pages you have just read?" I went looking for one but before I could find it, here comes my tutor. It was no blondie chick, to my disgust, but only Eddie Velasquez from Milflores Street. Eddie was no friend of mine, but in one way you had to give him credit. He was a big success at Audubon, president of this, secretary of that and a straight-A student with horn-rim specs to prove it, but not even Eddie could find any of that foreshadowing my book told me to look out for.

"Tell you what, Rudy," he said. "Get up there in class and ask your   10
teacher what the question means."

"Ask her shit," I said.

"Hold it right there, guy." Eddie waved his finger back and forth in front of my eyes. "How dumb can you get? Ask a question and there's a question you won't have to answer. And teachers love it, Bontempo especially."

We all know the type that asks that kind of question, but why start an argument? So I sat on the bench and Eddie stood with one foot on it and told me the Secrets of Success at School. First, look neat and well-combed and always sit up straight and don't stare out the window. Have pencil and paper on you so you don't have to borrow. Put your hand up every chance you get and give your teacher a pleasant smile when convenient.

"Attitude," Eddie instructed me, "cooperation, guy, that's what gets you grades in English and Social Studies and all those bullshit courses. So let's look at your next question."

"What important lesson does this chapter teach us?" it asked.   15

"Learn to catch barehanded," I suggested.

"Wrong," he told me frankly. "They expect something way bigger, like Attitude to Life."

Eddie studied the air.

"Here you go," he said. "That chapter teaches us you can't keep a good man down irregardless of his race, how's that? So don't holler if they discriminate you, just be patient and your time will come. Can you remember that? Okay, tell it to Bontempo and there's an A for you every time."

I could remember, but how could I recite it with Pelón in the classroom?   20

"I know a lot of you guys call me a kiss-up," Eddie went on, "but give me ten years, then come up to my office and we'll see who's kissing whose! CPA, Rudy, Certified Public Accountant, that's where I'm heading. And how'm I going to get up there? Grades, buddy, grades. And school activities don't hurt you any when they're passing out those college scholarships. Like for instance, I'm making service points for tutoring you right now."

"Thanks anyway," I said.

"Take one tip from me," he said. "Cut loose from the Jesters. You'll never get nowhere with them guys, except dead or jailed."

I hated to admit it but it made you think. Shamrock had more than its share of early corpses and half our Veteranos ended up in the wrong class of college. Like old San Quentin U. On the other side, there was Eddie. The teachers loved him and right now he was running for Student Body president and had a good chance of winning, it was said, and some blondie chick would be his secretary.

The chainlink gates were open now. The yard was filling up with voters.   25

"Figure out those other questions on your own," Eddie told me. "I got to go associate. And hey, since I'm doing you a favor, do me one. Line up the Shamrock vote for me, I could do you guys a lot of favors if I get elected. See you tomorrow, Rudy, same place, same time."

And away went Eddie Velasquez, not walking cool and casual like us, more on the order of a diesel locomotive pounding down the track, one Mexican who was going places and I only wondered if I could go that road too. Yesterday I had done my bit for Shamrock. Today I would do it for me, myself and I, and Miss Bontempo's English class was my testing ground.

I'd hoped to be the first student there, to prove my Attitude but of course two Oriental guys were in their seats ahead of me. Possibly they spent the night in there. Miss Bontempo was at the blackboard writing down our Words-We-Live-With. Today they were solid ITES and IGHTS such as right and write, sight, night and kite. She omitted fight, I noticed, and was in a big hurry to finish her list before the class showed up. She never cared to turn her back on us for fear things might go flying.

Miss Bontempo was Italian and around twenty-six years old or twenty-four and not too bad-looking when she smiled. The only trouble was, her smile stayed glued on there too long. It got to looking more like a scream. She was fresh out of teacher college and how that lady had changed since the first day of school. She started out preaching Democracy in the Classroom and Everybody Express Yourself, which was a big change for Audubon after all those Don't-drop-a-pin-or-else teachers we were accustomed to. Then one day somebody stole $11 from Miss Bontempo's purse during Nutrition and a couple of windows got broken by mistake. She still talked Democratic ways but as soon as the discussion got interesting she suddenly turned cop on you.

So anyway, I sat down very studious to copy out my word list and   30
when I caught Bontempo's eye, I flashed her a grade-A smile. It gave her such a scare she dropped the chalk. When the tardy bell rang, the usual

stampede came through the door. Books banged down on desks. A guy from
Sierra yanked all the windows open. A Shamrock banged them shut. Then
came the usual parade of pencil and paper borrowers till finally something
more or less like quiet settled in.

"Good morning, people," Miss Bontempo started off. "And how many
of you bothered to read today's assignment?"

Half the hands went up, my own included, though I could see Miss
Bontempo serious doubted me.

"Very good. Excellent. Now tell me, class, is reading just some old-
fashioned subject we teachers assign to make your lives miserable?" I heard
some yesses but my teacher didn't. "Why is it we really need to read well
and easily? Can I see hands?"

A few went up, not mine. I hate that kind of question but all the
Oriental hands were flying.

"We read so we can get to college and make money."   35

"Very good, Wah, excellent. Are there any other reasons? Yes, Gloria?"

"How could we buy stuff at the store if we can't read the cans?"

"Like street signs too, man, not to get lost."

"My grandma can read Spanish even!"

"That's very nice, Linda," Miss Bontempo said, "and I only wish I   40
could too. Those are all good answers. Excellent, but we read for pleasure
too, do we not?"

Nobody passed any comments.

"A good book can whisk us off to India or deep into past ages, can it
not? Reading takes us out of our little lives and opens whole worlds for us to
roam in. Then too, there is another kind of book which gives us insights
into our own daily problems and helps us solve them. Our text for instance.
Young Pancho and his sister María, are they so very different from the boys
and girls seated in this room?"

Slapsy Annie of the Sierra spoke up. "María's working and I wish I
was!"

"What I mean is," Miss Bontempo said, "they're both Mexican-Amer-
ican young people like so many of us here. We can identify with them, can
we not? And learn from their experience. For instance, from Pancho we can
see how patience is rewarded when he proves himself. Isn't that the best way
for us to deal with Discrimination? And far better than just sulking or shouting our heads off?"

She had just killed Eddie's fine speech which I was all primed with. I   45
had to work fast and up went my hand.

"Yes, Rudy?" Miss Bontempo sighed.

"I don't get that first question," I told her. "What's all this 'foreshadowing' they ask you for?"

"Why, that's a very good question, Rudy. Excellent."

Pelón gave the back of his hand a fat juicy kiss. My face burned.

"I was hoping someone would ask that question," Miss Bontempo said.   50
"This is the first time we've met that useful word. Foreshadowing, can anyone tell me what it means? Class?"

Wah said it meant like sunset when it throws your shadow in front of
you like walking up Broadway.

"Almost," Miss Bontempo agreed. "But here it means that our author
is giving us a little hint that something very exciting is about to happen. He
FORESHADOWS it. Open your texts to page forty-seven. Do you see the
line, 'Little did Pancho suspect . . .'? That's how our author leads us on into
the next chapter."

"He don't lead me on," Pelón said. "He turns me off, man."

"Yes, Richard," which was Pelón's other name. "We all know how
hard you are to please."

"Oh, indubitably."   55

"You see," Miss Bontempo went on, "the writer is telling us to expect
trouble ahead, though none of us can guess just what it will be."

My hand was up. I was following Eddie to the letter.

"I could guess," I proudly said.

Possibly it was the wrong thing to say because I was told to stand up
and give the whole class the benefit of my wisdom.

"Well, that rich old lady, I bet she's lost her diamond bracelet so of   60
course she claims María stole it and calls the cops on her."

Miss Bontempo's smile left her for far-off places.

"Rudy, I'm afraid you read the next chapter." I denied it. "Rudy," she
sang my name, "you're not being very honest with us, and you're spoiling
the story. Nobody could possibly guess that from the text."

I got quite hot. "Then how come the sheriff's car is in the driveway,
huh?" I asked. "And how come in that other chapter Mrs. Murdock bragged
about her bracelet unless somebody's gonna steal it? Anybody can guess what
happens in these dumb books, where on the television—"

"You may be seated, Rudy."

Pelón was happy to take over. "Chato's right," he hollered. "And you   65
know something else? Sturdy old Pancho goes and finds that bracelet right
where the old lady lost it. In the toledo."

A big scream went up from the girls.

"In the what?" Miss Bontempo was stupid enough to ask.

"The toledo, Oheedo," said Pelón.

"Eeee, send him to the Vice, Miss, he's talking dirty about the rest-
room," Slapsy Annie screamed.

"Shut your big mouth," Boxer suggested.   70

Various others had other suggestions.

"Quiet! Class, settle down! I won't stand for this!"

"Look at Pelón, Miss," Annie yelled. "He just called me THAT
WORD!"

"I did not."

"He made it with his lips. I seen him."   75
"Your mother!"
"La tuya!"°

Annie was off in Spanish. Pelón said several things in both languages.
The Sierra backed up Annie. We backed our buddy. A pencil flew. Somebody tossed a book. Miss Bontempo hammered on her desk to establish
some kind of Law and Order.

"He found it in the toledo," Pelón repeated, "tucked away in a big old
raggedy—"

Scream scream went the girls.   80
"—roll of toledo paper."

"Out!" said Miss Bontempo.

"Who? Me?" Pelón asked innocently. "Out where?"

"How come?" I asked. "He was only guessing."

"You too. Out!"   85

"You're discriminating, lady," Pelón told her. "I'm gonna phone the
Mexican consul on you."

"Vice-principal!" was Miss Bontempo's answer.

She scratched angry words on pink slips and dealt them out to us.
The trip was nothing new for Pelón, but believe it or not, this was my first
time.

"You really set that Bontempo up," Pelón told me in the hall. "Little
brother, you done it perfect."

I felt quite proud of myself but as we passed by Mr. Pilger's office it   90
bothered me the way my new leaf had withered.

"Mr. Beaver is busy," the Vice's secretary informed us. "Wait in the
hall."

The happy sound of the paddle could be heard. We waited on the
mourner's bench.

"He'll give you a choice," Pelón advised me. "Either the paddle or else
he'll send home a note. Take the swats. Beaver has a heavy hand but your
father's hand is heavier."

Pelón popped one of his uncle Ruben's famous pills.

"Care for one?" he asked.   95

"Why not?"

"Did you hear the news?" he asked me. "We're gonna have it out with
Sierra after school. Fat Manuel's gonna meet us across the bridge. He'll have
the arsenal in the back of his car. Are we gonna slaughter them? Oh,
indubitably."

Pelón's pill hopped around in my stomach like a frog. I coughed and
almost threw it up.

"What's with you, guy?" Pelón inquired. "Did you swallow wrong?"

La tuya!: Yours!

Considerations

1. Rudy assumes that his success or failure in school will greatly affect what happens to him in his later life. Do the details of the story suggest that he is correct or incorrect in this assumption? Explain.
2. Explain the role Rudy's tutor, Eddie, plays in his life. What does each boy stand to gain from the tutoring experience? Does either stand to lose anything? Explain.
3. How would you evaluate Miss Bontempo's responses to her students? To what extent does she seem to rely on racial stereotypes in making judgments and in formulating her actions in the classroom?
4. What attitude do the students in this story seem to have toward authority figures? Does this attitude reflect a bias on their part, or does it seem a logical response to the behavior of the authority figures they have encountered?
5. In what ways has Danny's conflict with Miss Bontempo affected him? Write a description of Danny five years from the end of the story in which you suggest how this incident has affected him.

HENRY REED (1914–   )

Naming of Parts

> Born in Birmingham, England, Henry Reed served in the British Army from 1941 to 1942. His early poetry deals primarily with political and social issues; "Naming of Parts" was written as an ironic response to his experiences in basic training. In 1947, Reed began writing radio plays, mainly for BBC radio.

Today we have naming of parts. Yesterday,
We had daily cleaning. And tomorrow morning,
We shall have what to do after firing. But today,
Today we have naming of parts. Japonica
Glistens like coral in all of the neighboring gardens,   5
    And today we have naming of parts.

This is the lower sling swivel. And this
Is the upper sling swivel, whose use you will see,
When you are given your slings. And this is the piling swivel,
Which in your case you have not got. The branches   10
Hold in the gardens their silent, eloquent gestures,
    Which in our case we have not got.

This is the safety-catch, which is always released
With an easy flick of the thumb. And please do not let me
See anyone using his finger. You can do it quite easy   15
If you have any strength in your thumb. The blossoms
Are fragile and motionless, never letting anyone see
        Any of them using their finger.

And this you can see is the bolt. The purpose of this
Is to open the breech, as you see. We can slide it   20
Rapidly backwards and forwards: we call this
Easing the spring. And rapidly backwards and forwards
The early bees are assaulting and fumbling the flowers:
        They call it easing the Spring.

They call it easing the Spring: it is perfectly easy   25
If you have any strength in your thumb: like the bolt,
And the breech, and the cocking-piece, and the point of balance,
Which in our case we have not got; and the almond-blossom
Silent in all of the gardens and the bees going backwards and forwards,
        For today we have naming of parts.   30

Considerations

1. Identify the two distinct voices in this poem. Which voice is trying to teach? What is he teaching?
2. What is the contrast between what the teacher says and what the learner hears and thinks? What significance do you see in this contrast?
3. Read the final stanza, in which the two voices mix. What is the effect of this merging?

WALT WHITMAN (1819–1892)

There Was a Child Went Forth

Born on Long Island, New York, Walt Whitman grew up in Brooklyn in a blue-collar neighborhood where his father worked as a carpenter. After five years of public school, Whitman left to become a printer's assistant. Later he worked as a newspaper editor and as a volunteer nurse during the Civil War. Following the war he wrote his long poem Leaves of Grass, *which, mainly because of its highly controversial erotic imagery, was not published until many years after it was written.*

There was a child went forth every day,
And the first object he looked upon, that object he became,
And that object became part of him for the day or a certain part of the day,
Or for many years or stretching cycles of years.

The early lilacs became part of this child,   5
And grass and white and red morning-glories, and white and red clover,
    and the song of the phoebe-bird,
And the Third-month lambs and the sow's pink-faint litter, and the mare's
    foal and the cow's calf,
And the noisy brood of the barnyard or by the mire of the pond-side,
And the fish suspending themselves so curiously below there, and the
    beautiful curious liquid,
And the water-plants with their graceful flat heads, all became part of him.   10

The field-sprouts of Fourth-month and Fifth-month became part of him,
Winter-grain sprouts and those of the light-yellow corn, and the esculent
    roots of the garden,
And the apple-trees covered with blossoms and the fruit afterward, and the
    wood-berries, and the commonest weeds by the road,
And the old drunkard staggering home from the outhouse of the tavern
    whence he had lately risen,
And the schoolmistress that passed on her way to the school,   15
And the friendly boys that passed, and the quarrelsome boys,
And the tidy and fresh-cheeked girls, and the barefoot negro boy and girl,
And all the changes of city and country wherever he went.

His own parents, he that had fathered him and she that had conceived him
    in her womb and birthed him,
They gave this child more of themselves than that,   20
They gave him afterward every day, they became part of him.

The mother at home quietly placing the dishes on the supper-table,
The mother with mild words, clean her cap and gown, a wholesome odor
    falling off her person and clothes as she walks by,
The father, strong, self-sufficient, manly, mean, angered, unjust,
The blow, the quick loud word, the tight bargain, the crafty lure,   25
The family usages, the language, the company, the furniture, the yearning
    and swelling heart,
Affection that will not be gainsayed, the sense of what is real, the thought if
    after all it should prove unreal,
The doubts of day-time and the doubts of night-time, the curious whether
    and how,
Whether that which appears so is so, or is it all flashes and specks?
Men and women crowding fast in the streets, if they are not flashes and   30
    specks, what are they?

The streets themselves and the façades of houses, and goods in the
    windows,
Vehicles, teams, the heavy-planked wharves, the huge crossing at the ferries,
The village on the highland seen from afar at sunset, the river between,
Shadows, aureola and mist, the light falling on roofs and gables of white or
    brown two miles off,
The schooner near by sleepily dropping down the tide, the little boat slack-   35
    towed astern,
The hurrying tumbling waves, quick-broken crests, slapping,
The strata of colored clouds, the long bar of maroon-tint away solitary by
    itself, the spread of purity it lies motionless in,
The horizon's edge, the flying sea-crow, the fragrance of salt marsh and
    shore mud,
These became part of that child who went forth every day, and who now   40
    goes, and will always go forth every day.

Considerations

1. Discuss the poem's first stanza. In what ways do children—or any of
   us—"become" the objects that we "look upon"? When, how, and why
   do those objects sometimes become part of us for days, weeks, or years?
   How does this stanza relate to the final line of the poem?
2. This child has learned lessons both from his mother and father. Contrast
   those lessons. Comment on the significance of this contrast.
3. Make a list of significant "objects" that you can remember seeing as you
   "went forth" during your own childhood. Write a response to one or
   more of those "objects" from your current, adult perspective.

MARIANNE MOORE (1887–1972)

The Student

*Born near St. Louis, Missouri, Marianne Moore grew up in Pennsylvania and
graduated from Bryn Mawr College. After graduation, she traveled widely in
Europe, and by 1915 her poetry was appearing in journals on both sides of
the Atlantic. Moore's later years brought her many honors, including the Pulitzer Prize in 1951 and the Bollingen Prize in 1953. "The Student" appeared in her collection* What Are Years? *(1941).*

"In America," began
the lecturer, "everyone must have a
degree. The French do not think that
all can have it, they don't say everyone
    must go to college." We   5

incline to feel, here,
       that although it may be unnecessary

to know fifteen languages,
one degree is not too much. With us, a
school—like the singing tree of which   10
the leaves were mouths that sang in concert—
       is both a tree of knowledge
and of liberty,—
       seen in the unanimity of college

mottoes, *lux et veritas,*°   15
Christo et ecclesiae,° *sapiet*
felici.° It may be that we
have not knowledge, just opinions, that we
       are undergraduates,
not students; we know   20
       we have been told with smiles, by expatriates

of whom we had asked "When will
your experiment be finished?" "Science
is never finished." Secluded
from domestic strife, Jack Bookworm led a   25
       college life, says Goldsmith;°
and here also as
       in France or Oxford, study is beset with

dangers—with bookworms, mildews,
and complaisancies. But someone in New   30
England has known enough to say
that the student is patience personified,
       a variety
of hero, "patient
       of neglect and of reproach,"—who can "hold by   35

himself." You can't beat hens to
make them lay. Wolf's wool is the best of wool,
but it cannot be sheared, because
the wolf will not comply. With knowledge as
       with wolves' surliness,   40
the student studies
       voluntarily, refusing to be less

15 *lux et veritas:* Light and truth. 16 *Christo et ecclesiae:* Christ and the Church; *sapiet / felici:*
Knowledge makes one happy. 26 *Oliver Goldsmith:* (1730?–1774) Anglo-Irish poet, essayist, and
playwright.

than individual. He
    "gives his opinion and then rests upon it";
he renders service when there is   45
no reward, and is too reclusive for
    some things to seem to touch
him; not because he
    has no feeling but because he has so much.

Considerations

1. The lecturer contrasts America with other cultures, claiming that in America it is assumed that everyone should have a college degree. Do you agree with this observation? Should everyone be given the opportunity for higher education? Can everyone benefit from higher education? Defend your point of view with specific examples.
2. What is your response to the "someone in New / England" who says that "the student is patience personified, / a variety / of hero." Why must a student be patient? Does that make a student a "variety / of hero"? Explain. (Consider here your definition of "hero.")
3. Explain the paradox (apparent contradiction) implied by the final four lines of the poem.

LOUISE GLÜCK (1943–   )

The School Children

> *Born in New York City, Louise Glück attended Sarah Lawrence College and Columbia University. Currently she lives in Vermont, where she writes and teaches. She has been the recipient of both Rockefeller and Guggenheim fellowships. Her collections of poetry include* Firstborn *(1968),* Descending Figure *(1980), and* The House on Marshland *(1971), from which "The School Children" is taken.*

The children go forward with their little satchels.
And all morning the mothers have labored
to gather the late apples, red and gold,
like words of another language.

And on the other shore   5
are those who wait behind great desks
to receive these offerings.

How orderly they are—the nails
on which the children hang
their overcoats of blue or yellow wool.   10

And the teachers shall instruct them in silence
and the mothers shall scour the orchards for a way out,
drawing to themselves the gray limbs of the fruit trees
bearing so little ammunition.

Considerations

1. Look carefully at the language of the poem. What does it imply about the distance between the homes of these children and the schools the children attend? Speculate on how many kinds of "distance" might be implied.
2. What does the poem suggest the mothers are doing in the orchards? Suggest possible motives for their actions.
3. Does the poem give you a negative, positive, or neutral image of the school the children attend? Refer to specific images from the poem as you respond.

ANNA LEE WALTERS (1946–   )

A Teacher Taught Me

"A Teacher Taught Me" appears in Voices of the Rainbow, *edited by Kenneth Rosen (1975). For biographical information about Anna Lee Walters, see page 391.*

I

a teacher taught me
more than she knew
patting me on the head
putting words in my hand
—"pretty little *Indian* girl!"   5
saving them—
going to give them
back to her one day . . .
show them around too
cousins and friends   10
laugh and say—"aye"

II

binding by sincerity
hating that kindness
eight years' worth
third graders heard her   15
putting words in my hand
—"we should bow our heads
in shame for what we did
to the American Indian"
saving them—   20
going to give them

III

in jr. hi
a boy no color
transparent skin
except sprinkled freckles
followed me around   30
putting words in my hand
—"squaw, squaw, squaw"
(not that it mattered,
hell, man, I didn't know
what squaw meant . . .)   35
saving them—
going to give them
back to him one day . . .
show them around too
cousins and friends   40
laugh and say—"aye"

back to her one day . . .
show them around too
cousins and friends
laugh and say—"aye"   25

IV

slapping open handed
transparent boy
across freckled face
knocking glasses down   45
he finally sees
recollect a red
handprint over minutes
faded from others
he wears it still   50
putting words in my hand
—"sorry, so sorry"
saving them—
going to give them
back to him one day   55
show them around too
cousins and friends
laugh and say—"aye"

LINDA PASTAN (1932–   )

Ethics

> *Linda Pastan lives in Potomac, Maryland. She has published five volumes of poetry. Her poems have appeared in the* Atlantic Monthly, *the* New Republic, *and the* American Poetry Review. *She has received the Dylan Thomas Award, the diCastagnola Award, and a fellowship from the National Endowment for the Arts.*

In ethics class so many years ago
our teacher asked this question every fall:
if there were a fire in a museum
which would you save, a Rembrandt painting
or an old woman who hadn't many   5

years left anyhow? Restless on hard chairs
caring little for pictures or old age
we'd opt one year for life, the next for art
and always half-heartedly. Sometimes
the woman borrowed my grandmother's face   10
leaving her usual kitchen to wander
some drafty, half-imagined museum.
One year, feeling clever, I replied
why not let the woman decide herself?
Linda, the teacher would report, eschews   15
the burdens of responsibility.
This fall in a real museum I stand
before a real Rembrandt, old woman,
or nearly so, myself. The colors
within this frame are darker than autumn,   20
darker even than winter—the browns of earth,
though earth's most radiant elements burn
through the canvas. I know now that woman
and painting and season are almost one
and all beyond saving by children.   25

GARY GILDNER (1938–   )

First Practice

> Gary Gildner teaches creative writing at the University of Iowa. He has pub-
> lished several volumes of poetry, including First Practice (1970), from which
> this poem is taken. Following a year of teaching American literature in Poland
> while on a Fulbright Scholarship, Gildner wrote his latest novel, The War-
> saw Sparks (1990).

After the doctor checked to see
we weren't ruptured,
the man with the short cigar took us
under the grade school,
where we went in case of attack   5
or storm, and said
he was Clifford Hill, he was
a man who believed dogs
ate dogs, he had once killed
for his country, and if   10
there were any girls present
for them to leave now.
                    No one

left. OK, he said, he said I take
that to mean you are hungry
men who hate to lose as much   15
as I do. OK. Then
he made two lines of us
facing each other,
and across the way, he said,
is the man you hate most   20
in the world,
and if we are to win
that title I want to see how.
But I don't want to see
any marks when you're dressed,   25
he said. He said, *Now.*

TOM ROMANO

The Teacher

Tom Romano is a professor of English and a poet who lives in New Hampshire. "The Teacher" first appeared in The English Journal *of March 1982.*

Why do I forget question marks.
I am notorious for it.
My students scoff at me,
"How can you teach English when
you don't punctuate proper?"   5

I don't teach you anyway, I think,
just lead you like a scout master
and hope you'll dip your hand
into the brook—cold like no
tap water you've ever felt,   10
let you marvel, a little frightened,
at a snake, mouth agape,
before it darts between rocks,
an image you'll carry for years,
spur you to anger when I won't   15
stop to let you rest,
even hope you catch poison ivy,
and, as we race up the hill,
urge you on when
you leave me behind,   20
gasping,

a seeming spear
wedged between my ribs.

Of the absent question mark, I say,
"An innocent, harmless error,"   25
And those of you who aren't smug
point out that I should
extend to you
the same courteous understanding.
I uncap my canteen,   30
drop to the grass, and,
before I take a long swig,
say, "Why not."

FRANCES E. W. HARPER (1825–1911)

Learning to Read

> Born in Baltimore, Maryland, to free African-American parents, Frances Wat-
> kins attended school until she was thirteen and then supported herself at vari-
> ous jobs, including teacher, seamstress, and nursemaid. During the early 1850s
> she became active as a speaker for abolitionist groups. She published her first
> volume of poems, Forest Leaves, in 1845. Her book Iola Leroy, or
> Shadows Uplifted (1892) was acclaimed as the first novel by an African-
> American to describe the Reconstruction. "Learning to Read" was first pub-
> lished in 1872.

Very soon the Yankee teachers
   Came down and set up school;
But, oh! how the Rebs did hate it,—
   It was agin' their rule.

Our masters always tried to hide   5
   Book learning from our eyes;
Knowledge didn't agree with slavery—
   'Twould make us all too wise.

But some of us would try to steal
   A little from the book,   10
And put the words together,
   And learn by hook or crook.

I remember Uncle Caldwell,
   Who took pot liquor fat
And greased the pages of his book,   15
   And hid it in his hat.

And had his master ever seen
   The leaves upon his head,
He'd have thought them greasy papers,
   But nothing to be read.   20

And there was Mr. Turner's Ben,
   Who heard the children spell,
And picked the words right up by heart,
   And learned to read 'em well.

Well, the Northern folks kept sending   25
   The Yankee teachers down;
And they stood right up and helped us,
   Though Rebs did sneer and frown.

And, I longed to read my Bible,
   For precious words it said;   30
But when I begun to learn it,
   Folks just shook their heads,

And said there is no use trying,
   Oh! Chloe, you're too late;
But as I was rising sixty,   35
   I had no time to wait.

So I got a pair of glasses,
   And straight to work I went,
And never stopped till I could read
   The hymns and Testament.   40

Then I got a little cabin
   A place to call my own—
And I felt as independent
   As the queen upon her throne.

ANTLER (1946–   )

Raising My Hand

> *Antler thinks of himself as "a Great Lakes Bioregion poet." His collection of
> poetry* Factory *won the 1985 Walt Whitman Award from the Academy of
> American Poets. "Raising My Hand" comes from his 1986 collection,* Last Words.

One of the first things we learn in school is
   if we know the answer to a question
We must raise our hand and be called on
   before we can speak.

How strange it seemed to me then,
    raising my hand to be called on,   5
How at first I just blurted out,
    but that was not permitted.

How often I knew the answer
And the teacher (knowing I knew)   10
Called on others I knew (and she knew)
    had it wrong!
How I'd stretch my arm
    as if it would break free
    and shoot through the roof   15
    like a rocket!
How I'd wave and groan and sigh,
Even hold up my aching arm
    with my other hand
Begging to be called on,   20
Please, *me,* I know the answer!
Almost leaping from my seat
    hoping to hear my name.

Twenty-nine now, alone in the wilds,
Seated on some rocky outcrop   25
    under all the stars,
I find myself raising my hand
    as I did in first grade
Mimicking the excitement
    and expectancy felt then,   30
No one calls on me
    but the wind.

DAVID MAMET (1947–   )

Oleanna

Often described as one of the most important and highly regarded playwrights in the United States today, David Mamet has written the acclaimed plays American Buffalo, Speed-the-Plow, *and* Glengarry Glen Ross, *which won the Pulitzer Prize for drama in 1984. Mamet has also written screenplays for such films as* Homicide, House of Games, *and* The Verdict, *which received an Oscar nomination. Mamet's works frequently develop complex characters whose points of view clash, sometimes violently. Critics Trevor R. Griffiths and Carole Woddis have applauded his works for addressing "the multiplicity of human instincts [which] too few playwrights address with Mamet's courage" (*The Back Stage Theatre Guide*). He has also published three collections of essays and a volume of poetry.*

to be in *Oleanna,*
That's where I would rather be.
Than be bound in Norway
And drag the chains of slavery."

—folk song

Characters

CAROL, *a woman of twenty*
JOHN, *a man in his forties*

Scene *The play takes place in* JOHN's *office.*

ACT ONE

JOHN *is talking on the phone.* CAROL *is seated across the desk from him.*

JOHN *(on phone)*: And what about the land. *(Pause)* The land. And what about the land? *(Pause)* What about it? *(Pause)* No. I don't understand. Well, yes, I'm I'm . . . no, I'm *sure* it's signif . . . I'm sure it's significant. *(Pause)* Because it's significant to mmmmmm . . . did you call Jerry? *(Pause)* Because . . . no, no, no, no, no. What did they say . . . ? Did you speak to the *real* estate . . . where *is* she . . . ? Well, well, all right. Where are her notes? Where are the notes we took with her? *(Pause)* I thought you were? No. No, I'm sorry, I didn't mean that, I just thought that I saw you, when we were there . . . what . . . ? I thought I saw you with a *pencil.* WHY NOW? is what I'm say . . . well, that's why I say "call Jerry." Well, I can't right now, be . . . no, I *didn't* schedule any . . . Grace: I *didn't* . . . I'm well aware . . . Look: Look. Did you call Jerry? Will you call Jerry . . . ? Because I can't now. I'll be there, I'm sure I'll be there in fifteen, in twenty. I intend to. No, we aren't *going* to lose the, we aren't *going* to lose the house. Look: Look, I'm not minimizing it. The "easement." did she say "easement"? *(Pause)* What did she *say; is* it a "term of art," are we *bound* by it . . . I'm sorry . . . *(Pause)* are: we: yes. *Bound* by . . . Look: *(He checks his watch.)* before the other side *goes home,* all right? "a term of art." Because: that's right *(Pause)* The yard for the boy. Well, that's the whole . . . Look: I'm going to meet you there . . . *(He checks his watch.)* Is the realtor there? All right, tell her to show you the basement again. Look at the *this* because . . . Bec . . . I'm leaving in, I'm leaving in ten or fifteen . . . Yes. No, no, I'll meet you at the new . . . That's a good. If he thinks it's necc . . . you tell Jerry to meet . . . All right? We *aren't* going to lose the deposit. All right? I'm sure it's going to be . . . *(Pause)* I hope so. *(Pause)* I love you, too. *(Pause)* I love you, too. As soon as . . . I will.

    (He hangs up.) (He bends over the desk and makes a note.) (He looks up.) (To CAROL:*)* I'm sorry . . .

CAROL: *(Pause)* What is a "term of art"?

JOHN: *(Pause)* I'm sorry . . . ?

CAROL: *(Pause)* What is a "term of art"?

JOHN: Is that what you want to talk about?

CAROL: . . . to talk about . . . ?

JOHN: Let's take the mysticism out of it, shall we? Carol? *(Pause)* Don't you think? I'll tell you: when you have some "thing." Which must be broached. *(Pause)* Don't you think . . . ? *(Pause)*

CAROL: . . . don't I think . . . ?

JOHN: Mmm?

CAROL: . . . did I . . . ?

JOHN: . . . what?

CAROL: Did . . . did I . . . did I say something wr . . .

JOHN: *(Pause)* No. I'm sorry. No. You're right. I'm very sorry. I'm some-what rushed. As you see. I'm sorry. You're right. *(Pause)* What is a "term of art"? It seems to mean a *term,* which has come, through its use, to mean something *more specific* than the words would, to someone *not acquainted* with them . . . indicate. That, I believe, is what a "term of art" would mean. *(Pause)*

CAROL: You don't know what it means . . . ?

JOHN: I'm not sure that I know what it means. It's one of those things, perhaps you've had them, that, you look them up, or have someone explain them to you, and you say "aha," and, you immediately *forget* what . . .

CAROL: You don't do that.

JOHN: . . . I . . . ?

CAROL: You don't do . . .

JOHN: . . . I don't, what . . . ?

CAROL: . . . for . . .

JOHN: . . . I don't for . . .

CAROL: . . . no . . .

JOHN: . . . forget things? Everybody does that.

CAROL: No, they don't.

JOHN: They don't . . .

CAROL: No.

JOHN: *(Pause)* No. Everybody does that.

CAROL: Why would they do that . . . ?

JOHN: Because. I don't know. Because it doesn't interest them.

CAROL: No.

JOHN: I think so, though. *(Pause)* I'm sorry that I was distracted.

CAROL: You don't have to say that to me.

JOHN: You paid me the compliment, or the "obeisance"—all right—of coming in here . . . All right. *Carol.* I find that I am at a *standstill.* I find that I . . .

CAROL: . . . what . . .

JOHN: . . . one moment. In regard to your . . . to your . . .

CAROL: Oh, oh. You're buying a new house!

JOHN: No, let's get on with it.

CAROL: "get on"? *(Pause)*

JOHN: I know how . . . *believe* me. I know how . . . potentially *humiliating* these . . . I have no desire to . . . I have no desire other than to help you. But: *(He picks up some papers on his desk.)* I won't even say "but." I'll say that as I go back over the . . .

CAROL: I'm just, I'm just trying to . . .

JOHN: . . . no, it will not do.

CAROL: . . . what? What will . . . ?

JOHN: No. I see, I see what you, it . . . *(He gestures to the papers.)* but your work . . .

CAROL: I'm just: I sit in class I . . . *(She holds up her notebook.)* I take notes . . .

JOHN *(simultaneously with* "notes"*)*: Yes. I understand. What I am trying to *tell* you is that some, some basic . . .

CAROL: . . . I . . .

JOHN: . . . one moment: some basic missed communi . . .

CAROL: I'm doing what I'm told. I bought your book, I read your . . .

JOHN: No, I'm sure you . . .

CAROL: No, no, no. I'm doing what I'm told. It's *difficult* for me. It's *difficult* . . .

JOHN: . . . but . . .

CAROL: I don't . . . lots of the *language* . . .

JOHN: . . . please . . .

CAROL: The *language,* the "things" that you say . . .

JOHN: I'm sorry. No. I don't think that that's true.

CAROL: It *is* true. I . . .

JOHN: I think . . .

CAROL: It *is* true.

JOHN: . . . I . . .

CAROL: Why would I . . . ?

JOHN: I'll tell you why: you're an incredibly bright girl.

CAROL: . . . I . . .

JOHN: You're an incredibly . . . you have no problem with the . . . Who's kidding who?

CAROL: . . . I . . .

JOHN: No. No. I'll tell you why. I'll tell. . . . I think you're *angry,* I . . .

CAROL: . . . why would I . . .

JOHN: . . . wait one moment. I . . .

CAROL: It *is* true. I have *problems* . . .

JOHN: . . . every . . .

CAROL: . . . I come from a different *social* . . .

JOHN: . . . ev . . .

CAROL: a different economic . . .

JOHN: . . . Look:

CAROL: No. I: when I *came* to this school:

JOHN: Yes. Quite . . . *(Pause)*

CAROL: . . . does that mean nothing . . . ?

JOHN: . . . but look: look . . .

CAROL: . . . I . . .

JOHN: *(Picks up paper.)* Here: Please: Sit down. *(Pause)* Sit down. *(Reads from her paper.)* "I think that the ideas contained in this work express the author's feelings in a way that he intended, based on his results." What can that mean? Do you see? What . . .

CAROL: I, the best that I . . .

JOHN: I'm saying, that perhaps this course . . .

CAROL: No, no, no, you can't, you can't . . . I have to . . .

JOHN: . . . how . . .

CAROL: . . . I have to pass it . . .

JOHN: Carol, I:

CAROL: I *have* to pass this course, I . . .

JOHN: Well.

CAROL: . . . don't you . . .

JOHN: Either the . . .

CAROL: . . . I . . .

JOHN: . . . either the, I . . . either the *criteria* for judging progress in the class are . . .

CAROL: No, no, no, no, I have to pass it.

JOHN: Now, look: I'm a human being, I . . .

CAROL: I did what you told me. I did, I did everything that, I read your *book,* you told me to buy your book and read it. Everything you *say* I . . . *(She gestures to her notebook.)* *(The phone rings.)* I do. . . . Ev . . .

JOHN: . . . look:

CAROL: . . . everything I'm told . . .

JOHN: Look. Look. I'm not your *father*. *(Pause)*

CAROL: What?

JOHN: I'm.

CAROL: Did I say you were my father?

JOHN: . . . no . . .

CAROL: Why did you say that . . . ?

JOHN: I . . .

CAROL: . . . why . . . ?

JOHN: . . . in class I . . . *(He picks up the phone.) (Into phone:)* Hello. I can't talk now. Jerry? Yes? I underst . . . I can't talk now. I know . . . I know . . . Jerry. I can't *talk* now. Yes, I. Call me back in . . . Thank you. *(He hangs up.) (To* CAROL:*)* What do you want me to do? We are two people, all right? Both of whom have subscribed to . . .

CAROL: No, no . . .

JOHN: . . . certain arbitrary . . .

CAROL: No. You have to help me.

JOHN: Certain institutional . . . you tell me what you want me to do. . . . You tell me what you want me to . . .

CAROL: How can I go back and tell them the *grades* that I . . .

JOHN: . . . what can I do . . . ?

CAROL: *Teach* me. *Teach* me.

JOHN: . . . I'm trying to teach you.

CAROL: I read your book. I read it. I don't under . . .

JOHN: . . . you don't understand it.

CAROL: No.

JOHN: Well, perhaps it's not well *written* . . .

CAROL *(simultaneously with* "written"*)*: No. No. No. I want to *understand* it.

JOHN: What don't you understand? *(Pause)*

CAROL: *Any* of it. What you're trying to say. When you talk about . . .

JOHN: . . . yes . . . ? *(She consults her notes.)*

CAROL: "Virtual warehousing of the young" . . .

JOHN: "Virtual warehousing of the young." If we artificially prolong adolescence . . .

CAROL: . . . and about "The Curse of Modern Education."

JOHN: . . . well . . .

CAROL: I don't . . .

JOHN: Look. It's just a *course*, it's just a *book*, it's just a . . .

CAROL: No. No. There are *people* out there. People who came *here*. To know something they didn't *know*. Who *came* here. To be *helped*. To be *helped*. So someone would *help* them. To *do* something. To *know* something. To get, what do they say? "To get on in the world." How can I do that if I don't, if I fail? But I don't *understand*. I don't *understand*. I don't understand what anything means . . . and I walk around. From morning 'til night: with this one thought in my head. I'm *stupid*.

JOHN: No one thinks you're stupid.

CAROL: No? What am I . . . ?

JOHN: I . . .

CAROL: . . . what am I, then?

JOHN: I think you're angry. Many people are. I have a *telephone* call that I have to make. And an *appointment,* which is rather *pressing;* though I sympathize with your concerns, and though I wish I had the time, this was not a previously scheduled meeting and I . . .

CAROL: . . . you think I'm nothing . . .

JOHN: . . . have an appointment with a *realtor,* and with my wife and . . .

CAROL: You think that I'm stupid.

JOHN: No. I certainly don't.

CAROL: You said it.

JOHN: No. I did not.

CAROL: You did.

JOHN: When?

CAROL: . . . you . . .

JOHN: No. I never did, or never would say that to a student, and . . .

CAROL: You said, "What can that mean?" *(Pause)* "What can that mean?" . . . *(Pause)*

JOHN: . . . and what did that mean to you . . . ?

CAROL: That meant I'm stupid. And I'll never learn. That's what that meant. And you're right.

JOHN: . . . I . . .

CAROL: But then. But then, what am I doing here . . . ?

JOHN: . . . if you thought that I . . .

CAROL: . . . when nobody wants me, and . . .

JOHN: . . . if you interpreted . . .

CAROL: Nobody *tells* me anything. And I *sit* there . . . in the *corner.* In the *back.* And everybody's talking about "this" all the time. And "concepts," and "precepts" and, and, and, and, and, WHAT IN THE WORLD ARE YOU *TALKING* ABOUT? And I read your book. And they said, "Fine, go in that class." Because you talked about responsibility to the young. I DON'T KNOW WHAT IT MEANS AND I'M *FAILING* . . .

JOHN: May . . .

CAROL: No, you're right. "Oh, hell." I failed. Flunk me out of it. It's garbage. Everything I do. "The ideas contained in this work express the author's feelings." That's right. That's right. I know I'm stupid. I know what I am. *(Pause)* I know what I am, Professor. You don't have to tell me. *(Pause)* It's pathetic. Isn't it?

JOHN: . . . Aha . . . *(Pause)* Sit down. Sit down. Please. *(Pause)* Please sit down.

CAROL: Why?

JOHN: I want to talk to you.

CAROL: Why?

JOHN: Just sit down. *(Pause)* Please. Sit down. Will you, please . . . ? *(Pause. She does so.)* Thank you.

CAROL: What?

JOHN: I want to tell you something.

CAROL: *(Pause)* What?

JOHN: Well, I know what you're talking about.

CAROL: No. You don't.

JOHN: I think I do. *(Pause)*

CAROL: How can you?

JOHN: I'll tell you a story about myself. *(Pause)* Do you mind? *(Pause)* I was raised to think myself stupid. That's what I want to tell you. *(Pause)*

CAROL: What do you mean?

JOHN: Just what I said. I was brought up, and my earliest, and most persistent memories are of being told that I was stupid. "You have such *intelligence*. Why must you behave so *stupidly?*" Or, "Can't you *understand?* Can't you *understand?*" And I could *not* understand. I could *not* understand.

CAROL: What?

JOHN: The simplest problem. Was beyond me. It was a mystery.

CAROL: What was a mystery?

JOHN: How people learn. How *I* could learn. Which is what I've been speaking of in class. And of *course* you can't hear it. Carol. Of *course* you can't. *(Pause)* I used to speak of "real people," and wonder what the *real* people did. The *real* people. Who were they? *They* were the people other than myself. The *good* people. The *capable* people. The people who could do the things *I* could not do: learn, study, retain . . . all that *garbage*—which is what I have been talking of in class, and that's *exactly* what I have been talking of—If you are told. . . . Listen to this. If the young child is told he cannot understand. Then he takes it as a *description* of himself. What am I? I am *that which can not understand.* And I saw you out there, when we were speaking of the concepts of . . .

CAROL: I can't understand any of them.

JOHN: Well, then, that's *my* fault. That's not your fault. And that is not verbiage. That's what I firmly hold to be the truth. And I am sorry, and I owe you an apology.

CAROL: Why?

JOHN: And I suppose that I have had some *things* on my mind. . . . We're buying a *house,* and . . .

CAROL: People said that you were stupid . . . ?

JOHN: Yes.

CAROL: When?

JOHN: I'll tell you when. Through my life. In my childhood; and, perhaps, they stopped. But I heard them continue.

CAROL: And what did they say?

JOHN: They said I was incompetent. Do you see? And when I'm tested the, the, the *feelings* of my youth about the *very subject of learning* come up. And I . . . I become, I feel "unworthy," and "unprepared." . . .

CAROL: . . . yes.

JOHN: . . . eh?

CAROL: . . . yes.

JOHN: And I feel that I must fail. *(Pause)*

CAROL: . . . but then you *do* fail. *(Pause)* You have to. *(Pause)* Don't you?

JOHN: A *pilot.* Flying a plane. The pilot is flying the plane. He thinks: Oh, my *God,* my mind's been drifting! Oh, my God! What kind of a cursed imbecile am I, that I, with this so precious cargo of *Life* in my charge, would allow my attention to wander? Why was I born? How deluded are those who put their trust in me, . . . et cetera, so on, and he crashes the plane.

CAROL: *(Pause)* He could just . . .

JOHN: That's right.

CAROL: He could say:

JOHN: My attention *wandered* for a moment . . .

CAROL: . . . uh huh . . .

JOHN: I had a *thought* I did not like . . . but now:

CAROL: . . . but now it's . . .

JOHN: That's what I'm telling you. It's time to put my attention . . . see: it is not: this is what I learned. It is Not Magic. Yes. Yes. *You.* You are going to be frightened. When faced with what may or may not be but which you are going to perceive as a test. You will become frightened. And you will say: "I am incapable of . . ." and everything *in* you will think these two things. "I must. But I can't." And you will think: Why was I born to be the laughingstock of a world in which everyone is better than I? In which I am entitled to nothing. Where I can not learn.

(Pause)

CAROL: Is that . . . *(Pause)* Is that what I have . . . ?

JOHN: Well. I don't know if I'd put it that way. Listen: I'm talking to you as I'd talk to my son. Because that's what I'd like him to have that I never had. I'm talking to you the way I wish that someone had talked to me. I don't know how to do it, other than to be *personal,* . . . but . . .

CAROL: Why would you want to be personal with me?

JOHN: Well, you see? That's what I'm saying. We can only interpret the behavior of others through the screen we . . . *(The phone rings.)* Through . . . *(To phone:)* Hello . . . ? *(To* CAROL:*)* Through the screen we create. *(To phone:)* Hello. *(To* CAROL:*)* Excuse me a moment. *(To phone:)* Hello? No, I can't talk nnn . . . I know I did. In a few . . .

I'm . . . is he coming to the . . . yes. I talked to him. We'll meet you at the No, because I'm with a *student.* It's going to be fff . . . This is important, too. I'm with a *student,* Jerry's going to . . . Listen: the sooner I get off, the sooner I'll be down, all right. I love you. Listen, listen, I said "I love you," it's going to work *out* with the, because I feel that it is, I'll be right down. All right? Well, then it's going to take as long as it takes. *(He hangs up.)* *(To* CAROL:*)* I'm sorry.

CAROL: What was that?

JOHN: There are some problems, as there usually are, about the final agreements for the new house.

CAROL: You're buying a new house.

JOHN: That's right.

CAROL: Because of your promotion.

JOHN: Well, I suppose that that's right.

CAROL: Why did you stay here with me?

JOHN: Stay here.

CAROL: Yes. When you should have gone.

JOHN: Because I like you.

CAROL: You like me.

JOHN: Yes.

CAROL: Why?

JOHN: Why? Well? Perhaps we're similar. *(Pause)* Yes. *(Pause)*

CAROL: You said "everyone has problems."

JOHN: Everyone has problems.

CAROL: Do they?

JOHN: Certainly.

CAROL: You do?

JOHN: Yes.

CAROL: What are they?

JOHN: Well. *(Pause)* Well, you're perfectly right. *(Pause)* If we're going to take off the Artificial *Stricture,* of "Teacher," and "Student," why should *my* problems be any more a mystery than your own? Of *course* I have problems. As you saw.

CAROL: . . . with what?

JOHN: With my *wife* . . . with *work* . . .

CAROL: With work?

JOHN: Yes. And, and, perhaps my problems are, do you see? *Similar* to yours.

CAROL: Would you tell me?

JOHN: All right. *(Pause)* I came *late* to teaching. And I found it Artificial. The notion of "I know and you do not"; and I saw an *exploitation* in the education process. I told you. I hated school, I hated teachers. I hated everyone who was in the position of a "boss" because I *knew*—I didn't *think,* mind you, I *knew* I was going to fail. Because I was a fuckup. I was just no goddamned good. When I . . . late in life . . .

(Pause) When I *got out from under* . . . when I worked my way out of
the need to fail. When I . . .

CAROL: How do you do that? *(Pause)*

JOHN: You have to look at what you are, and what you feel, and how you
act. And, finally, you have to look at how you act. And say: If that's
what I *did,* that must be how I think of myself.

CAROL: I don't understand.

JOHN: If I fail all the time, it must be that I think of myself as a failure. If I
do not want to think of myself as a failure, perhaps I should begin by
succeeding now and again. Look. The tests, you see, which you encounter, in school, in college, in life, were designed, in the most part, for
idiots. *By* idiots. There is no need to fail at them. They are not a test
of your worth. They are a test of your ability to retain and spout back
misinformation. Of *course* you fail them. They're *nonsense.* And I . . .

CAROL: . . . no . . .

JOHN: Yes. They're *garbage.* They're a *joke.* Look at me. Look at me. The
Tenure Committee. The Tenure Committee. Come to judge me. The
Bad Tenure Committee.

The "Test." Do you see? They put me to the test. Why, they had
people voting on me I wouldn't employ to wax my car. And yet, I go
before the Great Tenure Committee, and I have an urge, to *vomit,* to,
to, to puke my *badness* on the table, to show them: "I'm no good. Why
would you pick *me?*"

CAROL: They granted you tenure.

JOHN: Oh no, they announced it, but they haven't *signed.* Do you see? "At
any moment . . ."

CAROL: . . . mmm . . .

JOHN: "They might not *sign*" . . . I might not . . . the *house* might not go
through . . . Eh? Eh? They'll find out my "dark secret." *(Pause)*

CAROL: . . . what is it . . . ?

JOHN: There *isn't* one. But *they* will find an index of my badness . . .

CAROL: Index?

JOHN: A " . . . pointer." A "Pointer." You see? Do you see? I *understand*
you. I. Know. That. Feeling. Am I entitled to my job, and my nice
home, and my *wife,* and my *family,* and so on. This is what I'm saying:
That theory of education which, that *theory:*

CAROL: I . . . I . . . *(Pause)*

JOHN: What?

CAROL: I . . .

JOHN: What?

CAROL: I want to know about my grade. *(Long pause)*

JOHN: Of course you do.

CAROL: Is that bad?

JOHN: No.

CAROL: Is it bad that I asked you that?

JOHN: No.

CAROL: Did I upset you?

JOHN: No. And I apologize. Of *course* you want to know about your grade. And, of course, you can't concentrate on anyth . . . *(The telephone starts to ring.)* Wait a moment.

CAROL: I should go.

JOHN: I'll make you a deal.

CAROL: No, you have to . . .

JOHN: Let it ring. I'll make you a deal. You stay here. We'll start the whole course over. I'm going to say it was not you, it was I who was not paying attention. We'll start the whole course over. Your grade is an "A." Your final grade is an "A." *(The phone stops ringing.)*

CAROL: But the class is only half over . . .

JOHN *(simultaneously with "over")*: Your grade for the whole term is an "A." If you will come back and meet with me. A few more times. Your grade's an "A." Forget about the paper. You didn't like it, you didn't like writing it. It's not important. What's important is that I awake your interest, if I can, and that I answer your questions. Let's start over. *(Pause)*

CAROL: Over. With what?

JOHN: Say this is the beginning.

CAROL: The beginning.

JOHN: Yes.

CAROL: Of what?

JOHN: Of the class.

CAROL: But we can't start over.

JOHN: I say we can. *(Pause)* I say we can.

CAROL: But I don't believe it.

JOHN: Yes, I know that. But it's true. What is The Class but you and me? *(Pause)*

CAROL: There are rules.

JOHN: Well. We'll break them.

CAROL: How can we?

JOHN: We won't tell anybody.

CAROL: Is that all right?

JOHN: I say that it's fine.

CAROL: Why would you do this for me?

JOHN: I like you. Is that so difficult for you to . . .

CAROL: Um . . .

JOHN: There's no one here but you and me. *(Pause)*

CAROL: All right. I did not understand. When you referred . . .

JOHN: All right, yes?

CAROL: When you referred to hazing.

JOHN: Hazing.

CAROL: You wrote, in your book. About the comparative . . . the comparative . . . *(She checks her notes.)*

JOHN: Are you checking your notes . . . ?

CAROL: Yes.

JOHN: Tell me in your own . . .

CAROL: I want to make sure that I have it right.

JOHN: No. Of course. You want to be exact.

CAROL: I want to know everything that went on.

JOHN: . . . that's good.

CAROL: . . . so I . . .

JOHN: That's very good. But I was suggesting, many times, that that which we wish to retain is retained oftentimes, I think, *better* with less expenditure of effort.

CAROL *(of notes)*: Here it is: you wrote of *hazing.*

JOHN: . . . that's correct. Now: I said "hazing." It means ritualized annoyance. We shove this book at you, we say read it. Now, you say you've read it? I think that you're *lying.* I'll *grill* you, and when I find you've lied, you'll be disgraced, and your life will be ruined. It's a sick game. Why do we do it? Does it educate? In no sense. Well, then, what is higher education? It is something-other-than-useful.

CAROL: What is "something-other-than-useful"?

JOHN: It has become a ritual, it has become an article of faith. That all must be subjected to, or to put it differently, that all are entitled to Higher Education. And my point . . .

CAROL: You disagree with that?

JOHN: Well, let's address that. What do you think?

CAROL: I don't know.

JOHN: What do you think, though? *(Pause)*

CAROL: I don't know.

JOHN: I spoke of it in class. Do you remember my example?

CAROL: Justice.

JOHN: Yes. Can you repeat it to me? *(She looks down at her notebook.)* Without your notes? I ask you as a favor to me, so that I can see if my idea was interesting.

CAROL: You said "justice" . . .

JOHN: Yes?

CAROL: . . . that all are entitled . . . *(Pause)* I . . . I . . . I . . .

JOHN: Yes. To a speedy trial. To a fair trial. But they needn't be given a trial *at all* unless they stand accused. Eh? Justice is their right, should they choose to avail themselves of it, they should have a fair trial. It does not follow, of necessity, a person's life is incomplete without a trial in it. Do you see?

My point is a confusion between equity and *utility* arose. So we confound the *usefulness* of higher education with our, granted, right to

equal access to the same. We, in effect, create a *prejudice* toward it, completely
 independent of . . .

CAROL: . . . that it is prejudice that we should go to school?

JOHN: Exactly. *(Pause)*

CAROL: How can you say that? How . . .

JOHN: Good. Good. *Good.* That's right! Speak up! What is a prejudice? An
 unreasoned belief. We are all subject to it. None of us is not. When it
 is threatened, or opposed, we feel anger, and feel, do we not? As you
 do now. Do you not? Good.

CAROL: . . . but how can you . . .

JOHN: . . . let us examine. Good.

CAROL: How . . .

JOHN: Good. Good. When . . .

CAROL: I'M SPEAKING . . . *(Pause)*

JOHN: I'm sorry.

CAROL: How can you . . .

JOHN: . . . I beg your pardon.

CAROL: That's all right.

JOHN: I beg your pardon.

CAROL: That's all right.

JOHN: I'm sorry I interrupted you.

CAROL: That's all right.

JOHN: You were saying?

CAROL: I was saying . . . I was saying . . . *(She checks her notes.)* How can you
 say in a class. Say in a college class, that college education is prejudice?

JOHN: I said that our predilection for it . . .

CAROL: Predilection . . .

JOHN: . . . you know what that means.

CAROL: Does it mean "liking"?

JOHN: Yes.

CAROL: But how can you say that? That College . . .

JOHN: . . . that's my *job,* don't you know.

CAROL: What is?

JOHN: To provoke you.

CAROL: No.

JOHN: Oh. Yes, though.

CAROL: To provoke me?

JOHN: That's right.

CAROL: To make me mad?

JOHN: That's right. To force you . . .

CAROL: . . . to make me mad is your job?

JOHN: To force you to . . . listen: *(Pause)* Ah. *(Pause)* When I was young
 somebody told me, are you ready, the rich copulate less often than the
 poor. But when they do, they take more of their clothes off. Years.

Years, mind you, I would compare experiences of my own to this dictum, saying, aha, this fits the norm, or ah, this is a variation from it. What did it mean? Nothing. It was some jerk thing, some school kid told me that took up room inside my head. *(Pause)*

Somebody told *you,* and you hold it as an article of faith, that higher education is an unassailable good. This notion is so dear to you that when I question it you become angry. Good. Good, I say. Are not those the very things which we should question? I say college education, since the war, has become so a matter of course, and such a fashionable necessity, for those either of or aspiring *to* to the new vast middle class, that we *espouse* it, as a matter of right, and have ceased to ask, "What is it good for?" *(Pause)*

What might be some reasons for pursuit of higher education?
One: A love of learning.
Two: The wish for mastery of a skill.
Three: For economic betterment.

(Stops. Makes a note.)

CAROL: I'm keeping you.
JOHN: One moment. I have to make a note . . .
CAROL: It's something that I said?
JOHN: No, we're buying a house.
CAROL: You're buying the new house.
JOHN: To go with the tenure. That's right. Nice *house,* close to the *private school* . . . *(He continues making his note.)* . . . We were talking of economic *betterment* (CAROL *writes in her notebook.*) . . . I was thinking of the School Tax. *(He continues writing.) (To himself:)* . . . *where is it written that I have to send my child to public school.* . . . Is it a law that I have to improve the City Schools at the expense of my own interest? And, is this not simply *The White Man's Burden?* Good. And *(Looks up to* CAROL*)* . . . does this interest you?
CAROL: No. I'm taking notes . . .
JOHN: You don't have to take notes, you know, you can just listen.
CAROL: I want to make sure I remember it. *(Pause)*
JOHN: I'm not lecturing you, I'm just trying to tell you some things I think.
CAROL: What do you think?
JOHN: Should all kids go to college? *Why* . . .
CAROL: *(Pause)* To learn.
JOHN: But if he does not learn.
CAROL: If the child does not learn?
JOHN: Then why is he in college? Because he was told it was his "right"?
CAROL: Some might find college instructive.
JOHN: I would hope so.

CAROL: But how do they feel? Being told they are wasting their time?

JOHN: I don't think I'm telling them that.

CAROL: You said that education was "prolonged and systematic hazing."

JOHN: Yes. It can be so.

CAROL: ... if education is so *bad,* why do you do it?

JOHN: I do it because I love it. *(Pause)* Let's. ... I suggest you look at the demographics, wage-earning capacity, college- and non-college-educated men and women, 1855 to 1980, and let's see if we can wring some worth from the statistics. Eh? And ...

CAROL: No.

JOHN: What?

CAROL: I can't understand them.

JOHN: ... you ... ?

CAROL: ... the "charts." The *Concepts,* the ...

JOHN: "Charts" are simply ...

CAROL: When I leave here ...

JOHN: Charts, do you see ...

CAROL: No, I can't ...

JOHN: You can, though.

CAROL: NO, NO—I DON'T UNDERSTAND. DO YOU SEE??? I DON'T *UNDERSTAND* ...

JOHN: What?

CAROL: *Any* of it. *Any* of it. I'm *smiling* in class, I'm *smiling,* the whole time. What are you *talking* about? What is everyone *talking* about? I don't *understand.* I don't know what it *means.* I don't know what it means to *be* here ... you tell me I'm intelligent, and then you tell me I should not be *here,* what do you *want* with me? What does it *mean?* Who should I *listen* to ... I ...

> *(He goes over to her and puts his arm around her shoulder.)*
> NO! *(She walks away from him.)*

JOHN: Sshhhh.

CAROL: No, I don't under ...

JOHN: Sshhhhh.

CAROL: I don't know what you're *saying* ...

JOHN: Sshhhhh. It's all right.

CAROL: ... I have no ...

JOHN: Sshhhhh. Sshhhhh. Let it go a moment. *(Pause)* Sshhhhh ... let it go. *(Pause)* Just let it go. *(Pause)* Just let it go. It's all right. *(Pause)* Sshhhhh. *(Pause)* I understand ... *(Pause)* What do you feel?

CAROL: I feel bad.

JOHN: I know. It's all right.

CAROL: I ... *(Pause)*

JOHN: What?

CAROL: I ...

JOHN: What? Tell me.

CAROL: I don't understand you.

JOHN: I know. It's all right.

CAROL: I . . .

JOHN: What? *(Pause)* What? *Tell* me.

CAROL: I can't tell you.

JOHN: No, you must.

CAROL: I can't.

JOHN: No. Tell me. *(Pause)*

CAROL: I'm bad. *(Pause)* Oh, God. *(Pause)*

JOHN: It's all right.

CAROL: I'm . . .

JOHN: It's all right.

CAROL: I can't talk about this.

JOHN: It's all right. Tell me.

CAROL: Why do you want to know this?

JOHN: I don't want to know. I want to know whatever you . . .

CAROL: I always . . .

JOHN: . . . good . . .

CAROL: I always . . . all my life . . . I have never told anyone this . . .

JOHN: Yes. Go on. *(Pause)* Go on.

CAROL: All of my life . . . *(The phone rings.)* *(Pause. JOHN goes to the phone and picks it up.)*

JOHN *(into phone)*: I can't talk now. *(Pause)* What? *(Pause)* Hmm. *(Pause)* All right, I . . . I. Can't. Talk. Now. No, no, no, I *Know* I did, but . . . . What? Hello. What? She *what?* She *can't,* she said the agreement is void? How, how is the agreement *void?* That's Our House.

I have the *paper;* when we come down, next week, with the payment, and the paper, that house is . . . wait, wait, wait, wait, wait, wait, wait: Did Jerry . . . is Jerry there? *(Pause)* Is *she* there . . . ? Does she have a *lawyer* . . . ? How the *hell,* how the *Hell.* That is . . . it's a question, you said, of the *easement.* I don't underst . . . it's not the *whole agreement.* It's just the *easement,* why would she? Put, put, put, *Jerry* on. *(Pause)* Jer, *Jerry:* What the *Hell* . . . that's my *house.* That's . . . Well, I'm, no, no, no, I'm *not* coming ddd . . . List, *Listen, screw* her. You *tell* her. You, listen: I want you to take *Grace,* you take Grace, and get out of that house. You *leave* her there. Her and her lawyer, and you *tell* them, we'll see them in court next . . . no. No. Leave her there, leave her to *stew* in it: You tell her, we're *getting* that house, and we are going to . . . No. I'm *not* coming down. I'll be damned if I'll sit in the same rrr . . . the next, you tell her the next time I *see* her is in court . . . I . . . *(Pause)* What? *(Pause)* What? I don't understand. *(Pause)* Well, what about the house? *(Pause)* There isn't any problem with the hhh . . . *(Pause)* No, no, no, that's all right. All ri . . . All right . . . *(Pause)* Of course. Tha . . . Thank you. No, I will. Right away. *(He hangs up.)* *(Pause)*

CAROL: What is it? *(Pause)*

JOHN: It's a surprise party.

CAROL: It is.

JOHN: Yes.

CAROL: A party for you.

JOHN: Yes.

CAROL: Is it your birthday?

JOHN: No.

CAROL: What is it?

JOHN: The tenure announcement.

CAROL: The tenure announcement.

JOHN: They're throwing a party for us in our new house.

CAROL: Your new house.

JOHN: The house that we're buying.

CAROL: You have to go.

JOHN: It seems that I do.

CAROL: *(Pause)* They're proud of you.

JOHN: Well, there are those who would say it's a form of aggression.

CAROL: What is?

JOHN: A surprise.

ACT TWO

JOHN *and* CAROL *seated across the desk from each other.*

JOHN: You see, *(Pause)* I love to teach. And flatter myself I am *skilled* at it. And I love the, the aspect of *performance.* I think I must confess that.

When I found I loved to teach I swore that I would not become that cold, rigid automaton of an instructor which I had encountered as a child.

Now, I was not unconscious that it was given me to err upon the other side. And, so, I asked and *ask* myself if I engaged in heterodoxy, I will not say "gratuitously" for I do not care to posit orthodoxy as a given good—but, "to the detriment of, of my students." *(Pause)*

As I said. When the possibility of tenure opened, and, of course, I'd long pursued it, I was, of course *happy,* and *covetous* of it.

I asked myself if I was wrong to covet it. And thought about it long, and, I hope, truthfully, and saw in myself several things in, I think, no particular order. *(Pause)*

That I *would* pursue it. That I *desired* it, that I was not pure of longing for security, and that that, perhaps, was not reprehensible in me. That I had duties *beyond* the school, and that my duty to my home, for instance, was, or should be, if it were not, of an equal weight. That tenure, and security, and yes, and *comfort,* were not, of themselves, to be scorned; and were even worthy of honorable pursuit. And that it was given me. Here, in this place, which I enjoy, and in which I find comfort, to assure myself of—as far as it rests in The Material—a continuation of that joy and comfort. In exchange for what? Teaching. Which I love.

What was the price of this security? To obtain *tenure.* Which tenure the committee is in the process of granting me. And on the basis of which I contracted to purchase a house. Now, as you don't have your own family, at this point, you may not know what that means. But to me it is important. A home. A Good Home. To raise my family. Now: The Tenure Committee will meet. This is the process, and a *good* process. Under which the school has functioned for quite a long time. They will meet, and hear your complaint—which you have the right to make; and they will dismiss it. They will *dismiss* your complaint; and, in the intervening period, I will lose my house. I will not be able to close on my house. I will lose my *deposit,* and the home I'd picked out for my wife and son will go by the boards. Now: I see I have angered you. I understand your anger at teachers. I was angry with mine. I felt hurt and humiliated by them. Which is one of the reasons that I went into education.

CAROL: What do you want of me?

JOHN: *(Pause)* I was hurt. When I received the report. Of the tenure committee. I was shocked. And I was hurt. No, I don't mean to subject you to my weak sensibilities. All right. Finally, I didn't understand. Then I thought: is it not always at those points at which we reckon ourselves unassailable that we are most vulnerable and . . . *(Pause)* Yes. All right. You find me pedantic. Yes. I am. By nature, by *birth,* by profession, I don't know . . . I'm always looking for a *paradigm* for . . .

CAROL: I don't know what a paradigm is.

JOHN: It's a model.

CAROL: Then why can't you use that word? *(Pause)*

JOHN: If it is important to you. Yes, all right. I was looking for a model. To continue: I feel that one point . . .

CAROL: I . . .

JOHN: One second . . . upon which I am unassailable is my unflinching concern for my students' dignity. I asked you here to . . . in the spirit of *investigation,* to ask you . . . to ask . . . *(Pause)* What have I done to you? *(Pause)* And, and, I suppose, how I can make amends. Can we not settle this now? It's pointless, really, and I want to know.

CAROL: What you can do to force me to retract?

JOHN: That is not what I meant at all.

CAROL: To bribe me, to convince me . . .

JOHN: . . . No.

CAROL: To retract . . .

JOHN: That is not what I meant at all. I think that you know it is not.

CAROL: That is not what I know. I *wish* I . . .

JOHN: I do not want to . . . you wish what?

CAROL: No, you said what amends can you make. To force me to retract.

JOHN: That is not what I said.

CAROL: I have my notes.

JOHN: Look. Look. The Stoics say . . .

CAROL: The Stoics?

JOHN: The Stoical Philosophers say if you remove the phrase "I have been injured," you have removed the injury. Now: Think: I know that you're upset. Just tell me. Literally. Literally: what wrong have I done you?

CAROL: Whatever you have done to me—to the extent that you've done it to *me,* do you know, rather than to me as a *student,* and, so, to the student body, is contained in my report. To the tenure committee.

JOHN: Well, all right. *(Pause)* Let's see. *(He reads.)* I find that I am sexist. That I am *elitist.* I'm not sure I know what that means, other than it's a derogatory word, meaning "bad." That I . . . That I insist on wasting time, in nonprescribed, in self-aggrandizing and theatrical *diversions* from the prescribed *text* . . . that these have taken both sexist and pornographic forms . . . here we find listed . . . *(Pause)* Here we find listed . . . instances ". . . closeted with a student" . . . "Told a rambling, sexually explicit story, in which the frequency and attitudes of fornication of the poor and rich are, it would seem, the central point . . . moved to *embrace* said student and . . . all part of a pattern . . ." *(Pause)*

    (He reads.) That I used the phrase "The White Man's Burden" . . . that I told you how I'd asked you to my room because I quote like you. *(Pause)*

    (He reads.) "He said he 'liked' me. That he 'liked being with me.' He'd let me write my examination paper over, if I could come back oftener to see him in his office." *(Pause) (To* CAROL:*)* It's *ludicrous.* Don't you know that? It's not *necessary.* It's going to *humiliate* you, and it's going to cost me my *house,* and . . .

CAROL: It's *"ludicrous . . ."*?

*(*JOHN *picks up the report and reads again.)*

JOHN: "He told me he had problems with his wife; and that he wanted to take off the artificial stricture of Teacher and Student. He put his arm around me . . ."

CAROL: Do you deny it? Can you deny it . . . ? Do you see? *(Pause)* Don't you see? You don't see, do you?

JOHN: I don't see . . .

CAROL: You think, you think you can deny that these things happened; or, if they *did,* if they *did,* that they meant what you *said* they meant.

Don't you see? You drag me in here, you drag us, to listen to you "go on";
and "go on" about this, or that, or we don't "express" ourselves very
well. We don't say what we mean. Don't we? Don't we? We *do* say
what we mean. And you say that "I don't understand you . . .": Then
you . . . (Points.)

JOHN: "Consult the Report"?

CAROL: . . . that's right.

JOHN: You see. You see. Can't you . . . . You see what I'm saying? Can't
you tell me in your own words?

CAROL: Those are my own words. *(Pause)*

JOHN: *(He reads.)* "He told me that if I would stay alone with him in his
office, he would change my grade to an A." *(To* CAROL:*)* What have
I done to you? Oh. My God, are you so hurt?

CAROL: What I "feel" is irrelevant. *(Pause)*

JOHN: Do you know that I tried to help you?

CAROL: What I know I have reported.

JOHN: I would like to help you now. I would. Before this escalates.

CAROL *(simultaneously with* "escalates"*)*: You see. I don't think that I need
your help. I don't think I need anything you have.

JOHN: I feel . . .

CAROL: I don't *care* what you feel. Do you see? DO YOU SEE? You can't
do that anymore. You. Do. Not. Have. The. Power. Did you misuse it?
Someone did. Are you part of that group? *Yes. Yes.* You Are. You've *done*
these things. And to say, and to say, "Oh. Let me help you with your
problem . . ."

JOHN: Yes. I understand. I understand. You're *hurt.* You're *angry.* Yes. I
think your *anger* is *betraying* you. Down a path which helps no one.

CAROL: I don't *care* what you think.

JOHN: You don't? *(Pause)* But you talk of *rights.* Don't you see? *I* have rights
too. Do you see? I have a *house* . . . part of the *real* world; and The
Tenure Committee, Good Men and True . . .

CAROL: . . . Professor . . .

JOHN: . . . Please: *Also* part of that world: you understand? This is my *life.*
I'm not a *bogeyman.* I don't "stand" for something, I . . .

CAROL: . . . Professor . . .

JOHN: . . . I . . .

CAROL: Professor. I came here as a *favor.* At your personal request. Perhaps I should not have done so. But I did. On my behalf, and on
behalf of my group. And you speak of the tenure committee, one of
whose members is a woman, as you know. And though you might
call it Good Fun, or An Historical Phrase, or An Oversight, or,
All of the Above, to refer to the committee as Good Men and True,
it is a demeaning remark. It is a sexist remark, and to overlook it
is to countenance continuation of that method of thought. It's a
remark . . .

JOHN: OH COME ON. Come on. . . . Sufficient to deprive a family of . . .

CAROL: Sufficient? Sufficient? Sufficient? Yes. It is a *fact* . . . and that story, which I quote, is *vile* and *classist,* and *manipulative* and *pornographic.* It . . .

JOHN: . . . it's pornographic . . . ?

CAROL: What gives you the *right.* Yes. To speak to a *woman* in your private . . . Yes. Yes. I'm sorry. I'm sorry. You feel yourself empowered . . . you say so yourself. To *strut.* To *posture.* To "perform." To "Call me in here . . ." Eh? You say that higher education is a joke. And treat it as such, you *treat* it as such. And *confess* to a taste to play the *Patriarch* in your class. To grant *this.* To deny *that.* To embrace your students.

JOHN: How can you assert. How can you stand there and . . .

CAROL: How can you *deny* it. You did it to me. *Here.* You *did* . . . . You *confess.* You love the Power. To *deviate.* To *invent,* to transgress . . . to *transgress* whatever norms have been established for us. And you think it's charming to "question" in yourself this taste to mock and destroy. But you should question it, Professor. And you pick those things which you feel *advance* you: publication, *tenure,* and the steps to get them you call "harmless rituals." And you perform those steps. Although you say it is hypocrisy. But to the aspirations of your students. Of *hardworking students,* who come here, who *slave* to come here—you have no idea what it cost me to come to this school—you *mock* us. You call education "hazing," and from your so-protected, so-elitist seat you hold our confusion as a *joke,* and our hopes and efforts with it. Then you sit there and say "what have I done?" And ask me to understand that *you* have aspirations too. But I tell you. I tell you. That you are vile. And that you are exploitative. And if you possess one ounce of that inner honesty you describe in your book, you can look in yourself and see those things that I see. And you can find revulsion equal to my own. Good day. *(She prepares to leave the room.)*

JOHN: Wait a second, will you, just one moment. *(Pause)* Nice day today.

CAROL: What?

JOHN: You said "Good day." I think that it is a nice day today.

CAROL: *Is* it?

JOHN: Yes, I think it is.

CAROL: And why is that important?

JOHN: Because it is the essence of all human communication. I say something conventional, you respond, and the information we exchange is not about the "weather," but that we both agree to converse. In effect, we agree that we are both human. *(Pause)*

I'm not a . . . "exploiter," and you're not a . . . "deranged," what? *Revolutionary* . . . that we may, that we may have . . . positions, and that we may have . . . desires, which are in *conflict,* but that we're just human. *(Pause)* That means that sometimes we're *imperfect.* *(Pause)* Often we're in conflict . . . *(Pause)* *Much* of what we do, you're right, in the name of "principles" is *self-serving* . . . much of what we do is *conventional*. *(Pause)* You're right. *(Pause)* You said you came in the class because you wanted to learn about *education*. I don't know that I can teach you about education. But I know that I can tell you what I *think* about education, and then *you* decide. And you don't have to fight with me. *I'm* not the subject. *(Pause)* And where I'm *wrong* . . . perhaps it's not your job to "fix" me. I don't want to fix *you*. I would like to tell you what I *think,* because that *is* my job, conventional as it is, and flawed as I may be. And then, if you can show me some better *form,* then we can proceed from there. But, just like "nice day, isn't it . . . ?" I don't think we can proceed until we accept that each of us is human. *(Pause)* And we still can have difficulties. We *will* have them . . . that's all right too. *(Pause)* Now:

CAROL: . . . wait . . .

JOHN: Yes. I want to hear it.

CAROL: . . . the . . .

JOHN: Yes. Tell me frankly.

CAROL: . . . my position . . .

JOHN: I want to hear it. In your own words. What you want. And what you feel.

CAROL: . . . I . . .

JOHN: . . . yes . . .

CAROL: My Group.

JOHN: Your "Group" . . . ? *(Pause)*

CAROL: The people I've been talking to . . .

JOHN: There's no shame in that. Everybody needs advisers. Everyone needs to expose themselves. To various points of view. It's not wrong. It's essential. Good. Good. Now: You and I . . . *(The phone rings.)*

You and I . . .

(He hesitates for a moment, and then picks it up.) (Into phone:) Hello. *(Pause)* Um . . . no, I know they do. *(Pause)* I know she does. Tell her that I . . . can I call you back? . . . Then tell her that I think it's going to be fine. *(Pause)* Tell her just, just hold on, I'll . . . can I get back to you? . . . Well . . . no, no, no, we're *taking* the house . . . we're . . . no, no, nn . . . no, she will nnn, it's not a *question* of refunding the dep . . . no . . . it's not a *question* of the deposit . . . will you call Jerry? Babe, baby, will you just call Jerry? Tell him, nnn . . . tell him they, well, they're to keep the deposit, because the deal, be . . . because the deal is going to go *through* . . . because I know . . . be . . . will you please? Just *trust* me. Be . . . well, I'm dealing with the complaint. Yes. Right *Now.* Which is why I . . . yes, no, no, it's really, I can't *talk* about it now. Call Jerry, and I can't talk now. Ff . . . fine. Gg . . . good-bye. *(Hangs up.)* *(Pause)* I'm sorry we were interrupted.

CAROL: No . . .

JOHN: I . . . I was saying:

CAROL: You said that we should agree to talk about my complaint.

JOHN: That's correct.

CAROL: But we *are* talking about it.

JOHN: Well, that's correct too. You see? This is the *gist* of education.

CAROL: No, no. I mean, we're talking about it at the Tenure Committee Hearing. *(Pause)*

JOHN: Yes, but I'm saying: we can talk about it *now,* as easily as . . .

CAROL: No. I think that we should stick to the process . . .

JOHN: . . . wait a . . .

CAROL: . . . the "conventional" process. As you said. *(She gets up.)* And you're right, I'm sorry if I was, um, if I was "discourteous" to you. You're right.

JOHN: Wait, wait a . . .

CAROL: I really should go.

JOHN: Now, look, granted. I have an interest. In the status quo. All right? Everyone does. But what I'm saying is that the *committee* . . .

CAROL: Professor, you're right. Just don't impinge on me. We'll take our differences, and . . .

JOHN: You're going to make a . . . look, look, look, you're going to . . .

CAROL: I shouldn't have come here. They told me . . .

JOHN: One moment. No. No. There are *norms,* here, and there's no reason. Look: I'm trying to *save* you . . .

CAROL: No one *asked* you to . . . you're trying to save *me?* Do me the courtesy to . . .

JOHN: I *am* doing you the courtesy. I'm talking *straight* to you. We can settle this *now.* And I want you to sit *down* and . . .

CAROL: You must excuse me . . . *(She starts to leave the room.)*

JOHN: Sit down, it seems we each have a . . . . Wait one moment. Wait one moment . . . just do me the courtesy to . . .

(He restrains her from leaving.)

CAROL: LET ME GO.

JOHN: I have no desire to *hold* you, I just want to *talk* to you . . .

CAROL: LET ME GO. LET ME GO. WOULD SOMEBODY *HELP* ME? WOULD SOMEBODY *HELP* ME PLEASE . . . ?

ACT THREE

At rise, CAROL *and* JOHN *are seated.*

JOHN: I have asked you here. *(Pause)* I have asked you here against, against my . . .

CAROL: I was most surprised you asked me.

JOHN: . . . against my better *judgment,* against . . .

CAROL: I was most surprised . . .

JOHN: . . . against the . . . yes. I'm sure.

CAROL: . . . If you would like me to leave, I'll leave. I'll go right now . . . *(She rises.)*

JOHN: Let us begin *correctly,* may we? I feel . . .

CAROL: That is what I wished to do. That's why I came here, but now . . .

JOHN: . . . I feel . . .

CAROL: But now perhaps you'd like me to leave . . .

JOHN: I don't want you to leave. I asked you to come . . .

CAROL: I didn't have to come here.

JOHN: No. *(Pause)* Thank you.

CAROL: All right. *(Pause) (She sits down.)*

JOHN: Although I feel that it *profits,* it would *profit* you something, to . . .

CAROL: . . . what I . . .

JOHN: If you would hear me out, if you would hear me out.

CAROL: I came here to, the court officers told me not to come.

JOHN: . . . the "court" officers . . . ?

CAROL: I was shocked that you asked.

JOHN: . . . wait . . .

CAROL: Yes. But I did *not* come here to hear what it "profits" me.

JOHN: The "court" officers . . .

CAROL: . . . no, no, perhaps I should leave . . . *(She gets up.)*

JOHN: Wait.

CAROL: No. I shouldn't have . . .

JOHN: . . . wait. Wait. Wait a moment.

CAROL: Yes? What is it you want? *(Pause)* What is it you want?

JOHN: I'd like you to stay.

CAROL: You want me to stay.

JOHN: Yes.

CAROL: You do.

JOHN: Yes. *(Pause)* Yes. I would like to have you hear me out. If you would. *(Pause)* Would you please? If you would do that I would be in your debt. *(Pause) (She sits.)* Thank You. *(Pause)*

CAROL: What is it you wish to tell me?

JOHN: All right. I cannot . . . *(Pause)* I cannot help but feel you are owed an apology. *(Pause) (Of papers in his hands)* I have read. *(Pause)* And reread these accusations.

CAROL: What "accusations"?

JOHN: The, the tenure comm . . . what other accusations . . . ?

CAROL: The tenure committee . . . ?

JOHN: Yes.

CAROL: Excuse me, but those are not accusations. They have been *proved.* They are facts.

JOHN: . . . I . . .

CAROL: No. Those are not "accusations."

JOHN: . . . those?

CAROL: . . . the committee *(The phone starts to ring.)* the committee has . . .

JOHN: . . . All right . . .

CAROL: . . . those are not accusations. The Tenure Committee.

JOHN: ALL RIGHT. ALL RIGHT. ALL RIGHT. *(He picks up the phone.)* Hello. Yes. No. I'm here. Tell Mister . . . No, I can't talk to him now . . . I'm sure he has, but I'm fff . . . I know . . . No, I have no time t . . . tell Mister . . . tell Mist . . . tell Jerry that I'm *fine* and that I'll call him right aw . . . *(Pause)* My wife . . . Yes. I'm sure she has. Yes, thank you. Yes, I'll call her too. I cannot talk to you now. *(He hangs up.) (Pause)* All right. It was good of you to come. Thank you. I have studied. I have spent some time studying the indictment.

CAROL: You will have to explain that word to me.

JOHN: An "indictment" . . .

CAROL: Yes.

JOHN: Is a "bill of particulars." A . . .

CAROL: All right. Yes.

JOHN: In which is alleged . . .

CAROL: No. I cannot allow that. I cannot allow that. Nothing is alleged. Everything is proved . . .

JOHN: Please, wait a sec . . .

CAROL: I cannot *come* to allow . . .

JOHN: If I may . . . If I may, from whatever you feel is "established," by . . .

CAROL: The issue here is not what I "feel." It is not my "feelings," but the feelings of women. And men. Your superiors, who've been "polled," do you see? To whom *evidence* has been presented, who have *ruled,* do you see? Who have weighed the testimony and the evidence, and have *ruled,* do you see? That you are *negligent.* That you are *guilty,* that you are found *wanting,* and in *error;* and are *not,* for the reasons so-told, to be given tenure. That you are to be disciplined. For facts. For *facts.* Not "alleged," what is the word? But *proved.* Do you see? *By your own actions.*

       That is what the tenure committee has said. That is what my lawyer said. For what you did in class. For what you did *in this office.*

JOHN: They're going to discharge me.

CAROL: As full well they should. You don't understand? You're angry? What has *led* you to this place? Not your sex. Not your race. Not your class. YOUR OWN ACTIONS. And you're *angry.* You *ask* me here. What *do* you want? You want to "charm" me. You want to "convince" me. You want me to recant. I will *not* recant. Why should I . . . ? What I say is right. You tell me, you are going to tell me that you have a wife and child. You are going to say that you have a career and that you've worked for twenty years for this. Do you know what you've *worked* for? *Power.* For *power.* Do you understand? And you sit there, and you tell me *stories.* About your *house,* about all the private *schools,* and about *privilege,* and how you are entitled. To *buy,* to *spend,* to *mock,* to *summon.*

All your stories. All your silly weak *guilt,* it's all about *privilege;* and you won't know it. Don't you see? You worked twenty years for the right to *insult* me. And you feel entitled to be *paid* for it. Your Home. Your Wife . . . Your sweet "deposit" on your house . . .

JOHN: Don't you have feelings?

CAROL: That's my point. You see? Don't you have feelings? Your final argument. What is it that has no feelings. *Animals.* I don't take your side, you question if I'm Human.

JOHN: Don't you have feelings?

CAROL: I have a responsibility. I . . .

JOHN: . . . to . . . ?

CAROL: To? This institution. To the *students.* To my *group.*

JOHN: . . . your "group." . . .

CAROL: Because I speak, yes, not for myself. But for the group; for those who suffer what I suffer. On behalf of whom, even if I, were, inclined, to what, forgive? Forget? What? Overlook your . . .

JOHN: . . . my behavior?

CAROL: . . . it would be wrong.

JOHN: Even if you were inclined to "forgive" me.

CAROL: It would be wrong.

JOHN: And what would transpire.

CAROL: Transpire?

JOHN: Yes.

CAROL: "Happen?"

JOHN: Yes.

CAROL: Then *say* it. For Christ's sake. Who the *hell* do you think that you are? You want a post. You want unlimited power. To do and to say what you want. As it pleases you—Testing, Questioning, Flirting . . .

JOHN: I never . . .

CAROL: Excuse me, one moment, will you?

> *(She reads from her notes.)*
>
> The twelfth: "Have a good day, dear."
>
> The fifteenth: "Now, don't *you* look fetching . . ."

April seventeenth: "If you girls would come over here . . ." I saw you. I saw you, Professor. For two semesters sit there, stand there and exploit our, as you thought, "paternal prerogative," and what is that but rape; I swear to God. You asked me in here to explain something to me, as a child, that I did not understand. But I came to explain something to you. You Are Not God. You ask me why I came? I came here to instruct you.

> *(She produces his book.)*

And your book? You think you're going to show me some "light"? You "*maverick.*" Outside of tradition. No, no, *(She reads from the book's liner notes.)* "*of* that fine tradition of *inquiry.* Of Polite *skepti-*

cism" . . . and you say you believe in free intellectual discourse. YOU BELIEVE IN NOTHING. YOU BELIEVE IN NOTHING AT ALL.

JOHN: I believe in freedom of thought.

CAROL: Isn't that fine. *Do* you?

JOHN: Yes. I do.

CAROL: Then why do you question, for one moment, the committee's decision refusing your tenure? Why do you question your suspension? You believe in what *you call* freedom of thought. Then, fine. *You* believe in freedom-of-thought *and* a home, and, *and* prerogatives for your kid, *and* tenure. And I'm going to tell you. You believe *not* in "freedom of thought," but in an elitist, in, in a protected hierarchy which rewards you. And for whom you are the clown. And you mock and exploit the system which pays your rent. You're wrong. I'm not wrong. You're wrong. You think that I'm full of hatred. I know what you think I am.

JOHN: Do you?

CAROL: You think I'm a, of course I do. You think I am a frightened, repressed, confused, I don't know, abandoned young thing of some doubtful sexuality, who wants, power and revenge. *(Pause) Don't* you? *(Pause)*

JOHN: Yes. I do. *(Pause)*

CAROL: Isn't that better? And I feel that that is the first moment which you've treated me with respect. For you told me the truth. *(Pause)* I did not come here, as you are assured, to gloat. Why would I want to gloat? I've profited nothing from your, your, as you say, your "misfortune." I came here, as you did me the honor to *ask* me here, I came here to *tell* you something.

   (Pause) That I think . . . that I think you've been wrong. That I think you've been terribly wrong. Do you hate me now? *(Pause)*

JOHN: Yes.

CAROL: Why do you hate me? Because you think me wrong? No. Because I have, you think, *power* over you. Listen to me. Listen to me, Professor. *(Pause)* It is the power that you hate. So deeply that, that any atmosphere of free discussion is impossible. It's not "unlikely." It's *impossible.* Isn't it?

JOHN: Yes.

CAROL: *Isn't* it . . . ?

JOHN: Yes. I suppose.

CAROL: Now. The thing which you find so cruel is the selfsame process of selection I, and my group, go through *every day of our lives.* In admittance to school. In our tests, in our class rankings. . . . Is it unfair? I can't tell you. But, if it is fair. Or even if it is "unfortunate but necessary" for us, then, by God, so must it be for you. *(Pause)* You write of your "responsibility to the young." Treat us with respect, and that will *show* you your responsibility. You write that education is just hazing.

(Pause) But we worked to get to this school. *(Pause)* And some of us. *(Pause)* Overcame prejudices. Economic, sexual, you cannot begin to imagine. And endured humiliations I *pray* that you and those you love never will encounter. *(Pause)* To gain admittance here. To pursue that same dream of security *you* pursue. We, who, who are, at any moment, in danger of being deprived of it. By . . .

JOHN: . . . by . . . ?

CAROL: By the administration. By the teachers. By *you.* By, say, one low grade, that keeps us out of graduate school; by one, say, one capricious or inventive answer on our parts, which, perhaps, you don't find amusing. Now you *know,* do you see? What it is to be subject to that power. *(Pause)*

JOHN: I don't understand. *(Pause)*

CAROL: My charges are not trivial. You see that in the haste, I think, with which they were accepted. A *joke* you have told, with a sexist tinge. The language you use, a verbal or physical caress, yes, yes, I know, you say that it is meaningless. I understand. I differ from you. To lay a hand on someone's shoulder.

JOHN: It was devoid of sexual content.

CAROL: I say it was not. I SAY IT WAS NOT. Don't you begin to *see* . . . ? Don't you begin to understand? IT'S NOT FOR YOU TO SAY.

JOHN: I take your point, and I see there is much good in what you refer to.

CAROL: . . . do you think so . . . ?

JOHN: . . . but, and this is not to say that I cannot change, in those things in which I am deficient . . . But, the . . .

CAROL: Do you hold yourself harmless from the charge of sexual exploitativeness . . . ? *(Pause)*

JOHN: Well, I . . . I . . . I . . . You know I, as I said. I . . . think I am not too old to *learn,* and I *can* learn, I . . .

CAROL: Do you hold yourself innocent of the charge of . . .

JOHN: . . . wait, wait, wait . . . All right, let's go back to . . .

CAROL: YOU FOOL. Who do you think I am? To come here and be taken in by a *smile.* You little yapping fool. You think I want "revenge." I don't want revenge. I WANT UNDERSTANDING.

JOHN: . . . *do* you?

CAROL: I do. *(Pause)*

JOHN: What's the use. It's over.

CAROL: Is it? What is?

JOHN: My job.

CAROL: Oh. Your job. That's what you want to talk about. *(Pause) (She starts to leave the room. She stops and turns back to him.)* All right. *(Pause)* What if it were possible that my Group withdraws its complaint. *(Pause)*

JOHN: What?

CAROL: That's right. *(Pause)*

JOHN: Why.

CAROL: Well, let's say as an act of friendship.

JOHN: An act of friendship.

CAROL: Yes. *(Pause)*

JOHN: In exchange for what.

CAROL: Yes. But I don't think, "exchange." Not "in exchange." For what do we derive from it? *(Pause)*

JOHN: "Derive."

CAROL: Yes.

JOHN: *(Pause)* Nothing. *(Pause)*

CAROL: That's right. We derive nothing. *(Pause)* Do you see that?

JOHN: Yes.

CAROL: That is a little word, Professor. "Yes." "I see that." But you will.

JOHN: And you might speak to the committee . . . ?

CAROL: To the committee?

JOHN: Yes.

CAROL: Well. Of course. That's on your mind. We might.

JOHN: "If" what?

CAROL: "Given" what. Perhaps. I think that that is more friendly.

JOHN: GIVEN WHAT?

CAROL: And, believe me, I understand your rage. It is not that I don't feel it. But I do not see that it is deserved, so I do not resent it. . . . All right. I have a list.

JOHN: . . . a list.

CAROL: Here is a list of books, which we . . .

JOHN: . . . a list of books . . . ?

CAROL: That's right. Which we find questionable.

JOHN: What?

CAROL: Is this so bizarre . . . ?

JOHN: I can't believe . . .

CAROL: It's not necessary you believe it.

JOHN: Academic freedom . . .

CAROL: Someone chooses the books. If you can choose them, others can. What are you, "God"?

JOHN: . . . no, no, the "dangerous." . . .

CAROL: You have an agenda, we have an agenda. I am not interested in your feelings or your motivation, but your actions. If you would like me to speak to the Tenure Committee, here is my list. You are a Free Person, you decide. *(Pause)*

JOHN: Give me the list. *(She does so. He reads.)*

CAROL: I think you'll find . . .

JOHN: I'm capable of reading it. Thank you.

CAROL: We have a number of *texts* we need re . . .

JOHN: I see that.

CAROL: We're amenable to . . .

JOHN: Aha. Well, let me look over the . . . *(He reads.)*

CAROL: I think that . . .

JOHN: LOOK. I'm reading your demands. All right?! *(He reads.) (Pause)* You want to ban my book?

CAROL: We do not . . .

JOHN *(of list)*: It says here . . .

CAROL: . . . We want it removed from inclusion as a representative example of the university.

JOHN: Get out of here.

CAROL: If you put aside the issues of personalities.

JOHN: Get the fuck out of my office.

CAROL: No, I think I would reconsider.

JOHN: . . . you think you can.

CAROL: We can and we *will*. Do you want our support? That is the only quest . . .

JOHN: . . . to ban my *book* . . . ?

CAROL: . . . that is correct . . .

JOHN: . . . this . . . this is a *university* . . . we . . .

CAROL: . . . and we have a statement . . . which we need you to . . . *(She hands him a sheet of paper.)*

JOHN: No, no. It's out of the question. I'm sorry. I don't know what I was thinking of. I want to tell you something. I'm a teacher. I am a teacher. Eh? It's my *name* on the door, and *I* teach the class, and that's what I do. I've got a book with my name on it. And my son will *see* that *book* someday. And I have a respon . . . No, I'm sorry I have a *responsibility* . . . to *myself,* to my *son,* to my *profession.* . . . I haven't been *home* for two days, do you know that? Thinking this out.

CAROL: . . . you haven't?

JOHN: I've been, no. If it's of interest to you. I've been in a *hotel. Thinking. (The phone starts ringing.) Thinking* . . .

CAROL: . . . you haven't been home?

JOHN: . . . *thinking,* do you see.

CAROL: Oh.

JOHN: And, and, I owe you a debt, I see that now. *(Pause)* You're *dangerous,* you're *wrong* and it's my *job* . . . to say no to you. That's my job. You are absolutely right. You want to ban my book? Go to *hell,* and they can do whatever they want to me.

CAROL: . . . you haven't been home in two days . . .

JOHN: I think I told you that.

CAROL: . . . you'd better get that phone. *(Pause)* I think that you should pick up the phone. *(Pause)*

(JOHN picks up the phone.)

JOHN *(on phone)*: Yes. *(Pause)* Yes. Wh . . . I. I. I had to be away. All ri . . . did they wor . . . did they worry ab . . . No. I'm all right, now, Jerry. I'm f . . . I got a little turned *around,* but I'm *sitting* here and . . . I've got it figured out. I'm fine. I'm fine don't worry about me. I got a little bit mixed up. But I am not sure that it's not a blessing. It cost me my job? Fine. Then the job was not worth having. Tell Grace that I'm coming home and everything is fff . . . *(Pause)* What? *(Pause)* What? *(Pause)* What do you *mean?* WHAT? Jerry . . . Jerry. They . . . Who, who, what can they do . . . ? *(Pause)* NO. *(Pause)* NO. They can't do th . . . What do you mean? *(Pause)* But how . . . *(Pause)* She's, she's, she's *here* with me. To . . . Jerry. I don't underst . . . *(Pause)* *(He hangs up.)* *(To* CAROL:*)* What does this mean?

CAROL: I thought you knew.

JOHN: What. *(Pause)* What does it mean. *(Pause)*

CAROL: You tried to rape me. *(Pause)* According to the law. *(Pause)*

JOHN: . . . what . . . ?

CAROL: You tried to rape me. I was leaving this office, you "pressed" yourself into me. You "pressed" your body into me.

JOHN: . . . I . . .

CAROL: My Group has told your lawyer that we may pursue criminal charges.

JOHN: . . . no . . .

CAROL: . . . under the statute. I am told. It was battery.

JOHN: . . . no . . .

CAROL: Yes. And attempted rape. That's right. *(Pause)*

JOHN: I think that you should go.

CAROL: Of course. I thought you knew.

JOHN: I have to talk to my lawyer.

CAROL: Yes. Perhaps you should.

(The phone rings again.) (Pause)

JOHN: *(Picks up phone. Into phone:)* Hello? I . . . Hello . . . ? I . . . Yes, he just called. No . . . I. I can't talk to you now, Baby. *(To* CAROL:*)* Get out.

CAROL: . . . your wife . . . ?

JOHN: . . . who it is is no concern of yours. Get out. *(To phone:)* No, no, it's going to be all right. I. I can't talk now, Baby. *(To* CAROL:*)* Get out of here.

CAROL: I'm going.

JOHN: Good.

CAROL *(exiting)*: . . . and don't call your wife "baby."

JOHN: What?

CAROL: Don't call your wife baby. You heard what I said.

*(*CAROL *starts to leave the room.* JOHN *grabs her and begins to beat her.)*

JOHN: You vicious little bitch. You think you can come in here with your political correctness and destroy my life?

(He knocks her to the floor.)

After how I treated you . . . ? You should be . . . *Rape you* . . . ? Are you kidding me . . . ?

(He picks up a chair, raises it above his head, and advances on her.)

I wouldn't touch you with a ten-foot pole. You little *cunt* . . .

(She cowers on the floor below him. Pause. He looks down at her. He lowers the chair. He moves to his desk, and arranges the papers on it. Pause. He looks over at her.)

. . . well . . .

(Pause. She looks at him.)

CAROL: Yes. That's right.

(She looks away from him, and lowers her head. To herself:) . . . yes. That's right.

END

Considerations

1. The printed text of the play begins with a folk song that refers to "Oleanna," the name of a utopian community in Norway that failed to flourish because its inhabitants could not (or did not) live up to their high ideals. The word "Oleanna," then, came to signify a fallen Eden. Given this information, do you think the title of the play is accurate—does the setting seem to be a fool's paradise? Explain.
2. Describe your responses to Carol and John after Act I. Explain how and why your responses change after Act II and Act III.
3. Identify several points in the play where Carol and John use (or understand) words differently. How do these moments of lost communication contribute to the play's conflicts and their resolution (or lack of resolution)?
4. A review in the *Village Voice* noted: "*Oleanna* is a tragedy built as a series of audience traps; the minute you get suckered into thinking it says one thing, you're likely to find it saying the opposite." Do you agree with this reviewer? Indicate specific incidents and speeches in the play to explain your response.
5. Write a defense of either Carol or John. Then, assume the opposite point of view and defend the other character. Finally—after having written the best defense possible for each character—explain whom you find the more sympathetic and why.

FREDERICK DOUGLASS (1817?–1895)

Learning to Read and Write

Born a slave in Talbot County, Maryland, in 1818, Frederick Douglass grew up on a plantation and was later sent to Baltimore to live with and work for the Auld family. During this period of his life, Douglass became aware of the essential relationship between literacy and independence. Although the Auld family thwarted him whenever they could, he discovered innovative ways of learning to read and write. He describes this phase of his education in the following excerpt from his autobiography, The Narrative of the Life of Frederick Douglass, an American Slave, Written by Himself *(1845).*

I lived in Master Hugh's family about seven years. During this time, I succeeded in learning to read and write. In accomplishing this, I was compelled to resort to various stratagems. I had no regular teacher. My mistress, who had kindly commenced to instruct me, had, in compliance with the advice and direction of her husband, not only ceased to instruct, but had set her face against my being instructed by any one else. It is due, however, to my mistress to say of her, that she did not adopt this course of treatment immediately. She at first lacked the depravity indispensable to shutting me up in mental darkness. It was at least necessary for her to have some training in the exercise of irresponsible power, to make her equal to the task of treating me as though I were a brute.

My mistress was, as I have said, a kind and tender-hearted woman; and in the simplicity of her soul she commenced, when I first went to live with her, to treat me as she supposed one human being ought to treat another. In entering upon the duties of a slaveholder, she did not seem to perceive that I sustained to her the relation of a mere chattel, and that for her to treat me as a human being was not only wrong, but dangerously so. Slavery proved as injurious to her as it did to me. When I went there, she was a pious, warm, and tender-hearted woman. There was no sorrow or suffering for which she had not a tear. She had bread for the hungry, clothes for the naked, and comfort for every mourner that came within her reach. Slavery soon proved its ability to divest her of these heavenly qualities. Under its influence, the tender heart became stone, and the lamblike disposition gave way to one of tiger-like fierceness. The first step in her downward course was in her ceasing to instruct me. She now commenced to practise her husband's precepts. She finally became even more violent in her opposition than her husband himself. She was not satisfied with simply doing as well as he had commanded; she seemed anxious to do better. Nothing seemed to make her more angry than to see me with a newspaper. She seemed to think that here lay the danger. I have had her rush at me with a face made all up of fury, and snatch from me a newspaper, in a manner that fully revealed her apprehension. She was an apt woman; and a little experience soon demonstrated, to her satisfaction, that education and slavery were incompatible with each other.

From this time I was most narrowly watched. If I was in a separate room any considerable length of time, I was sure to be suspected of having a book, and was at once called to give an account of myself. All this, however, was too late. The first step had been taken. Mistress, in teaching me the alphabet, had given me the *inch,* and no precaution could prevent me from taking the *ell.*

The plan which I adopted, and the one by which I was most successful, was that of making friends of all the little white boys whom I met in the street. As many of these as I could, I converted into teachers. With their kindly aid, obtained at different times and in different places, I finally succeeded in learning to read. When I was sent on errands, I always took my book with me, and by doing one part of my errand quickly, I found time to get a lesson before my return. I used also to carry bread with me, enough of which was always in the house, and to which I was always welcome; for I was much better off in this regard than many of the poor white children in our neighborhood. This bread I used to bestow upon the hungry little urchins, who, in return, would give me that more valuable bread of knowledge. I am strongly tempted to give the names of two or three of those little boys, as a testimonial of the gratitude and affection I bear them; but prudence forbids;—not that it would injure me, but it might embarrass them; for it is almost an unpardonable offence to teach slaves to read in this Christian country. It is enough to say of the dear little fellows, that they lived on Philpot Street, very near Durgin and Bailey's ship-yard. I used to talk this matter of slavery over with them. I would sometimes say to them, I wished I could be as free as they would be when they got to be men. "You will be free as soon as you are twenty-one, *but I am a slave for life!* Have not I as good a right to be free as you have?" These words used to trouble them; they would express for me the liveliest sympathy, and console me with the hope that something would occur by which I might be free.

I was now about twelve years old, and the thought of being *a slave for life* began to bear heavily upon my heart. Just about this time, I got hold of a book entitled "The Columbian Orator." Every opportunity I got, I used to read this book. Among much of other interesting matter, I found in it a dialogue between a master and his slave. The slave was represented as having run away from his master three times. The dialogue represented the conversation which took place between them, when the slave was retaken the third time. In this dialogue, the whole argument in behalf of slavery was brought forward by the master, all of which was disposed of by the slave. The slave was made to say some very smart as well as impressive things in reply to his master—things which had the desired though unexpected effect; for the conversation resulted in the voluntary emancipation of the slave on the part of the master.

In the same book, I met with one of Sheridan's mighty speeches on and in behalf of Catholic emancipation. These were choice documents to me. I read them over and over again with unabated interest. They gave

5

tongue to interesting thoughts of my own soul, which had frequently flashed through my mind, and died away for want of utterance. The moral which I gained from the dialogue was the power of truth over the conscience of even a slaveholder. What I got from Sheridan was a bold denunciation of slavery, and a powerful vindication of human rights. The reading of these documents enabled me to utter my thoughts, and to meet the arguments brought forward to sustain slavery; but while they relieved me of one difficulty, they brought on another even more painful than the one of which I was relieved. The more I read, the more I was led to abhor and detest my enslavers. I could regard them in no other light than a band of successful robbers, who had left their homes, and gone to Africa, and stolen us from our homes, and in a strange land reduced us to slavery. I loathed them as being the meanest as well as the most wicked of men. As I read and contemplated the subject, behold! that very discontentment which Master Hugh had predicted would follow my learning to read had already come, to torment and sting my soul to unutterable anguish. As I writhed under it, I would at times feel that learning to read had been a curse rather than a blessing. It had given me a view of my wretched condition, without the remedy. It opened my eyes to the horrible pit, but to no ladder upon which to get out. In moments of agony, I envied my fellow-slaves for their stupidity. I have often wished myself a beast. I preferred the condition of the meanest reptile to my own. Any thing, no matter what, to get rid of thinking! It was this everlasting thinking of my condition that tormented me. There was no getting rid of it. It was pressed upon me by every object within sight or hearing, animate or inanimate. The silver trump of freedom had roused my soul to eternal wakefulness. Freedom now appeared, to disappear no more forever. It was heard in every sound, and seen in every thing. It was ever present to torment me with a sense of my wretched condition. I saw nothing without seeing it, I heard nothing without hearing it, and felt nothing without feeling it. It looked from every star, it smiled in every calm, breathed in every wind, and moved in every storm.

I often found myself regretting my own existence, and wishing myself dead; and but for the hope of being free, I have no doubt but that I should have killed myself, or done something for which I should have been killed. While in this state of mind, I was eager to hear any one speak of slavery. I was a ready listener. Every little while, I could hear something about the abolitionists. It was some time before I found what the word meant. It was always used in such connections as to make it an interesting word to me. If a slave ran away and succeeded in getting clear, or if a slave killed his master, set fire to a barn, or did any thing very wrong in the mind of a slaveholder, it was spoken of as the fruit of *abolition*. Hearing the word in this connection very often, I set about learning what it meant. The dictionary afforded me little or no help. I found it was "the act of abolishing"; but then I did not know what was to be abolished. Here I was perplexed. I did not dare to ask any one about its meaning, for I was satisfied that it was something they wanted me to know very little about. After a patient waiting, I got one of our city papers, containing an account of the number of petitions from the north, praying for the abolition of slavery in the District of Columbia, and of the slave trade between the States. From this time I understood the words *abolition* and *abolitionist,* and always drew near when that word was spoken, expecting to hear something of importance to myself and fellow-slaves. The light broke in upon me by degrees. I went one day down on the wharf of Mr. Waters; and seeing two Irishmen unloading a scow of stone, I went, unasked, and helped them. When we had finished, one of them came to me and asked me if I were a slave. I told him I was. He asked, "Are ye a slave for life?" I told him that I was. The good Irishman seemed to be deeply affected by the statement. He said to the other that it was a pity so fine a little fellow as myself should be a slave for life. He said it was a shame to hold me. They both advised me to run away to the north; that I should find friends there, and that I should be free. I pretended not to be interested in what they said, and treated them as if I did not understand them; for I feared they might be treacherous. White men have been known to encourage slaves to escape, and then, to get the reward, catch them and return them to their masters. I was afraid that these seemingly good men might use me so; but I nevertheless remembered their advice, and from that time I resolved to run away. I looked forward to a time at which it would be safe for me to escape. I was too young to think of doing so immediately; besides, I wished to learn how to write, as I might have occasion to write my own pass. I consoled myself with the hope that I should one day find a good chance. Meanwhile, I would learn to write.

The idea as to how I might learn to write was suggested to me by being in Durgin and Bailey's ship-yard, and frequently seeing the ship carpenters, after hewing, and getting a piece of timber ready to use, write on the timber the name of that part of the ship for which it was intended. When a piece of timber was intended for the larboard side, it would be marked thus— "L." When a piece was for the starboard side, it would be marked thus—"S." A piece for the larboard side forward, would be marked thus—"L. F." When a piece was for starboard side forward, it would be marked thus—"S. F." For larboard aft, it would be marked thus—"L. A." For starboard aft, it would be marked thus—"S. A." I soon learned the names of these letters, and for what they were intended when placed upon a piece of timber in the ship-yard. I immediately commenced copying them, and in a short time was able to make the four letters named. After that, when I met with any boy who I knew could write, I would tell him I could write as well as he. The next word would be, "I don't believe you. Let me see you try it." I would then make the letters which I had been so fortunate as to learn, and ask him to beat that. In this way I got a good many lessons in writing, which it is quite possible I should never have gotten in any other way. During this time, my copy-book was the board fence, brick wall, and pavement; my pen and ink was a lump of chalk. With these, I learned mainly how to write. I then commenced and continued copying the Italics in Webster's Spelling Book, until I could make them all without looking on the book. By this time, my little Master Thomas had gone to school, and learned how to write, and had written over a number of copy-books. These had been brought home, and shown to some of our near neighbors, and then laid aside. My mistress used to go to class meeting at the Wilk Street meetinghouse every Monday afternoon, and leave me to take care of the house. When left thus, I used to spend the time in writing in the spaces left in Master Thomas's copy-book, copying what he had written. I continued to do this until I could write a hand very similar to that of Master Thomas. Thus, after a long, tedious effort for years, I finally succeeded in learning how to write.

Considerations

1. Douglass chooses to report certain incidents in his process of learning to read and write and to show other incidents by dramatizing them. Summarize one of these dramatized incidents and discuss why you think this episode might have been particularly significant to Douglass.
2. Although this selection, a chapter from Douglass's book *The Narrative of the Life of Frederick Douglass: An American Slave* (1845), is primarily told in story form, it also makes a profound argument against slavery. Explain how Douglass develops this argument and evaluate the evidence he uses to support his contentions.
3. Douglass compares the circumstances of slaves to the circumstances of Irish Catholics. Locate and list every mention of the Irish or of Catholicism in this selection and explain how Douglass uses this comparison to argue his case persuasively.
4. Discuss the role of Master Hugh's wife. What might her motives have been as she first sets out to educate Douglass and then becomes almost fanatic in her attempts to keep him away from books?
5. Put yourself in the place of one of the people who chooses to help Douglass. Describe the circumstances of your decision from that person's point of view. Keep in mind that it was against the law to educate slaves.

ALICE WALKER (1944–   )

In Search of Our Mothers' Gardens

"In Search of Our Mothers' Gardens" was first published in 1974 in a collection of essays with the same title. For biographical information about Alice Walker, see page 371.

I described her own nature and temperament. Told how they
needed a larger life for their expression. . . . I pointed out
that in lieu of proper channels, her emotions had overflowed
into paths that dissipated them. I talked, beautifully I
thought, about an art that would be born, an art that would
open the way for women the likes of her. I asked her to hope,
and build up an inner life against the coming of that day. . . .
I sang, with a strange quiver in my voice, a promise song.

> "Avey," Jean Toomer, *Cane*
> *The poet speaking to a prostitute who falls*
> *asleep while he's talking*

When the poet Jean Toomer walked through the South in the early twenties, he discovered a curious thing: black women whose spirituality was so intense, so deep, so *unconscious,* they were themselves unaware of the richness they held. They stumbled blindly through their lives: creatures so abused and mutilated in body, so dimmed and confused by pain, that they considered themselves unworthy even of hope. In the selfless abstractions their bodies became to the men who used them, they became more than "sexual objects," more even than mere women: they became "Saints." Instead of being perceived as whole persons, their bodies became shrines: what was thought to be their minds became temples suitable for worship. These crazy Saints stared out at the world, wildly, like lunatics—or quietly, like suicides; and the "God" that was in their gaze was as mute as a great stone.

Who were these Saints? These crazy, loony, pitiful women?

Some of them, without a doubt, were our mothers and grandmothers.

In the still heat of the post-Reconstruction South, this is how they seemed to Jean Toomer: exquisite butterflies trapped in an evil honey, toiling away their lives in an era, a century, that did not acknowledge them, except as "the *mule* of the world." They dreamed dreams that no one knew—not even themselves, in any coherent fashion—and saw visions no one could understand. They wandered or sat about the countryside crooning lullabies to ghosts, and drawing the mother of Christ in charcoal on courthouse walls.

They forced their minds to desert their bodies and their striving spirits   5
sought to rise, like frail whirlwinds from the hard red clay. And when those frail whirlwinds fell, in scattered particles, upon the ground, no one mourned.

Instead, men lit candles to celebrate the emptiness that remained, as people do who enter a beautiful but vacant space to resurrect a God.

Our mothers and grandmothers, some of them: moving to music not yet written. And they waited.

They waited for a day when the unknown thing that was in them would be made known; but guessed, somehow in their darkness, that on the day of their revelation they would be long dead. Therefore to Toomer they walked, and even ran, in slow motion. For they were going nowhere immediate, and the future was not yet within their grasp. And men took our mothers and grandmothers, "but got no pleasure from it." So complex was their passion and their calm.

To Toomer, they lay vacant and fallow as autumn fields, with harvest time never in sight: and he saw them enter loveless marriages, without joy; and become prostitutes, without resistance; and become mothers of children, without fulfillment.

For these grandmothers and mothers of ours were not Saints, but Artists; driven to a numb and bleeding madness by the springs of creativity in them for which there was no release. They were Creators, who lived lives of spiritual waste, because they were so rich in spirituality—which is the basis of Art—that the strain of enduring their unused and unwanted talent drove them insane. Throwing away this spirituality was their pathetic attempt to lighten the soul to a weight their work-worn, sexually abused bodies could bear.

What did it mean for a black woman to be an artist in our grandmothers' time? In our great-grandmothers' day? It is a question with an answer cruel enough to stop the blood.

10

Did you have a genius of a great-great grandmother who died under some ignorant and depraved white overseer's lash? Or was she required to bake biscuits for a lazy backwater tramp, when she cried out in her soul to paint watercolors of sunsets, or the rain falling on the green and peaceful pasturelands? Or was her body broken and forced to bear children (who were more often than not sold away from her)—eight, ten, fifteen, twenty children—when her one joy was the thought of modeling heroic figures of rebellion, in stone or clay?

How was the creativity of the black woman kept alive, year after year and century after century, when for most of the years black people have been in America, it was a punishable crime for a black person to read or write? And the freedom to paint, to sculpt, to expand the mind with action did not exist. Consider, if you can bear to imagine it, what might have been the result if singing, too, had been forbidden by law. Listen to the voices of Bessie Smith, Billie Holiday, Nina Simone, Roberta Flack, and Aretha Franklin, among others, and imagine those voices muzzled for life. Then you may begin to comprehend the lives of our "crazy," "Sainted" mothers and grandmothers. The agony of the lives of women who might have been Poets, Novelists, Essayists, and Short-Story Writers (over a period of centuries), who died with their real gifts stifled within them.

And, if this were the end of the story, we would have cause to cry out in my paraphrase of Okot p'Bitek's great poem:

> O, my clanswomen
> Let us all cry together!
> Come,
> Let us mourn the death of our mother,
> The death of a Queen
> The ash that was produced
> By a great fire!
> O, this homestead is utterly dead
> Close the gates
> With *lacari* thorns,
> For our mother
> The creator of the Stool is lost!
> And all the young men
> Have perished in the wilderness!

But this is not the end of the story, for all the young women—our mothers and grandmothers, *ourselves*—have not perished in the wilderness. And if we ask ourselves why, and search for and find the answer, we will know beyond all efforts to erase it from our minds, just exactly who, and of what, we black American women are.

One example, perhaps the most pathetic, most misunderstood one, can provide a backdrop for our mothers' work: Phillis Wheatley, a slave in the 1700s. 15

Virginia Woolf, in her book *A Room of One's Own,* wrote that in order for a woman to write fiction she must have two things, certainly: a room of her own (with key and lock) and enough money to support herself.

What then are we to make of Phillis Wheatley, a slave, who owned not even herself? This sickly, frail black girl who required a servant of her own at times—her health was so precarious—and who, had she been white, would have been easily considered the intellectual superior of all the women and most of the men in the society of her day.

Virginia Woolf wrote further, speaking of course not of our Phillis, that "any woman born with a great gift in the sixteenth century [insert "eighteenth century," insert "black woman," insert "born or made a slave"] would certainly have gone crazed, shot herself, or ended her days in some lonely cottage outside the village, half witch, half wizard [insert "Saint"], feared and mocked at. For it needs little skill and psychology to be sure that a highly gifted girl who had tried to use her gift of poetry would have been so thwarted and hindered by contrary instincts [add "chains, guns, the lash, the ownership of one's body by someone else, submission to an alien religion"], that she must have lost her health and sanity to a certainty."

The key words, as they relate to Phillis, are "contrary instincts." For when we read the poetry of Phillis Wheatley—as when we read the novels of Nella Larsen or the oddly false-sounding autobiography of that freest of all black women writers, Zora Hurston—evidence of "contrary instincts" is everywhere. Her loyalties were completely divided, as was, without question, her mind.

But how could this be otherwise? Captured at seven, a slave of wealthy, doting whites who instilled in her the "savagery" of the Africa they "rescued" her from . . . one wonders if she was even able to remember her homeland as she had known it, or as it really was.

Yet, because she did try to use her gift for poetry in a world that made her a slave, she was "so thwarted and hindered by . . . contrary instincts, that she . . . lost her health. . . ." In the last years of her brief life, burdened not only with the need to express her gift but also with a penniless, friendless "freedom" and several small children for whom she was forced to do strenuous work to feed, she lost her health, certainly. Suffering from malnutrition and neglect and who knows what mental agonies, Phillis Wheatley died.

So torn by "contrary instincts" was black, kidnapped, enslaved Phillis that her description of "the Goddess"—as she poetically called the Liberty she did not have—is ironically, cruelly humorous. And, in fact, has held Phillis up to ridicule for more than a century. It is usually read prior to hanging Phillis's memory as that of a fool. She wrote:

> The Goddess comes, she moves divinely fair,
> Olive and laurel binds her *golden* hair.
> Wherever shines this native of the skies,
> Unnumber'd charms and recent graces rise. [My italics]

It is obvious that Phillis, the slave, combed the "Goddess's" hair every morning; prior, perhaps, to bringing in the milk, or fixing her mistress's lunch. She took her imagery from the one thing she saw elevated above all others.

With the benefit of hindsight we ask, "How could she?"

But at last, Phillis, we understand. No more snickering when your stiff, struggling, ambivalent lines are forced on us. We know now that you were not an idiot or a traitor; only a sickly little black girl, snatched from your home and country and made a slave; a woman who still struggled to sing the song that was your gift, although in a land of barbarians who praised you for your bewildered tongue. It is not so much what you sang, as that you kept alive, in so many of our ancestors, *the notion of song.*

Black women are called, in the folklore that so aptly identifies one's status in society, "the *mule* of the world," because we have been handed the burdens that everyone else—*everyone* else—refused to carry. We have also been called "Matriarchs," "Superwomen," and "Mean and Evil Bitches." Not to mention "Castraters" and "Sapphire's Mama." When we have pleaded for understanding, our character has been distorted; when we have asked for simple caring, we have been handed empty inspirational appellations, then stuck in the farthest corner. When we have asked for love, we have been given children. In short, even our plainer gifts, our labors of fidelity and love, have been knocked down our throats. To be an artist and a black woman, even today, lowers our status in many respects, rather than raises it: and yet, artists we will be.

Therefore we must fearlessly pull out of ourselves and look at and identify with our lives the living creativity some of our great-grandmothers were not allowed to know. I stress *some* of them because it is well known that the majority of our great-grandmothers knew, even without "knowing" it, the reality of their spirituality, even if they didn't recognize it beyond what happened in the singing at church—and they never had any intention of giving it up.

How they did it—those millions of black women who were not Phillis Wheatley, or Lucy Terry or Frances Harper or Zora Hurston or Nella Larsen or Bessie Smith; or Elizabeth Catlett, or Katherine Dunham, either—brings me to the title of this essay, "In Search of Our Mothers' Gardens," which is a personal account that is yet shared, in its theme and its meaning, by all of us. I found, while thinking about the far-reaching world of the creative black woman, that often the truest answer to a question that really matters can be found very close.

In the late 1920s my mother ran away from home to marry my father. Marriage, if not running away, was expected of seventeen-year-old girls. By the time she was twenty, she had two children and was pregnant with a third. Five children later, I was born. And this is how I came to know my mother: she seemed a large, soft, loving-eyed woman who was rarely impatient in our home. Her quick, violent temper was on view only a few times a year, when she battled with the white landlord who had the misfortune to suggest to her that her children did not need to go to school.

She made all the clothes we wore, even my brothers' overalls. She made all the towels and sheets we used. She spent the summers canning vegetables and fruits. She spent the winter evenings making quilts enough to cover all our beds. 30

During the "working" day, she labored beside—not behind—my father in the fields. Her day began before sunup, and did not end until late at night. There was never a moment for her to sit down, undisturbed, to unravel her own private thoughts; never a time free from interruption—by work or the noisy inquiries of her many children. And yet, it is to my mother—and all our mothers who were not famous—that I went in search of the secret of what has fed that muzzled and often mutilated, but vibrant, creative spirit that the black woman has inherited, and that pops out in wild and unlikely places to this day.

But when, you will ask, did my overworked mother have time to know or care about feeding the creative spirit?

The answer is so simple that many of us have spent years discovering it. We have constantly looked high, when we should have looked high—and low.

For example: in the Smithsonian Institution in Washington, D.C., there hangs a quilt unlike any other in the world. In fanciful, inspired, and yet simple and identifiable figures, it portrays the story of the Crucifixion. It is considered rare, beyond price. Though it follows no known pattern of quilt-making, and though it is made of bits and pieces of worthless rags, it is obviously the work of a person of powerful imagination and deep spiritual feeling. Below this quilt I saw a note that says it was made by "an anonymous Black woman in Alabama, a hundred years ago."

If we could locate this "anonymous" black woman from Alabama, she   35
would turn out to be one of our grandmothers—an artist who left her mark in the only materials she could afford, and in the only medium her position in society allowed her to use.

As Virginia Woolf wrote further, in *A Room of One's Own:*

> Yet genius of a sort must have existed among women as it must have
> existed among the working class. [Change this to "slaves" and "the
> wives and daughters of sharecroppers."] Now and again an Emily
> Brontë or a Robert Burns [change this to "a Zora Hurston or a
> Richard Wright"] blazes out and proves its presence. But certainly it
> never got itself on to paper. When, however, one reads of a witch
> being ducked, of a woman possessed by devils [or "Sainthood"], of
> a wise woman selling herbs [our root workers], or even a very re-
> markable man who had a mother, then I think we are on the track
> of a lost novelist, a suppressed poet, or some mute and inglorious
> Jane Austen. . . . Indeed, I would venture to guess that Anon, who
> wrote so many poems without signing them, was often a woman. . . .

And so our mothers and grandmothers have, more often than not anonymously, handed on the creative spark, the seed of the flower they themselves never hoped to see: or like a sealed letter they could not plainly read.

And so it is, certainly, with my own mother. Unlike "Ma" Rainey's songs, which retained their creator's name even while blasting forth from Bessie Smith's mouth, no song or poem will bear my mother's name. Yet so many of the stories that I write, that we all write, are my mother's stories. Only recently did I fully realize this: that through years of listening to my mother's stories of her life, I have absorbed not only the stories themselves, but something of the manner in which she spoke, something of the urgency that involves the knowledge that her stories—like her life—must be re-corded. It is probably for this reason that so much of what I have written is about characters whose counterparts in real life are so much older than I am.

But the telling of these stories, which came from my mother's lips as naturally as breathing, was not the only way my mother showed herself as an artist. For stories, too, were subject to being distracted, to dying without conclusion. Dinners must be started, and cotton must be gathered before the big rains. The artist that was and is my mother showed itself to me only after many years. This is what I finally noticed:

Like Mem, a character in *The Third Life of Grange Copeland,* my mother 40 adorned with flowers whatever shabby house we were forced to live in. And not just your typical straggly country stand of zinnias, either. She planted ambitious gardens—and still does—with over fifty different varieties of plants that bloom profusely from early March until late November. Before she left home for the fields, she watered her flowers, chopped up the grass, and laid out new beds. When she returned from the fields she might divide clumps of bulbs, dig a cold pit, uproot and replant roses, or prune branches from her taller bushes or trees—until night came and it was too dark to see.

Whatever she planted grew as if by magic, and her fame as a grower of flowers spread over three counties. Because of her creativity with her flowers, even my memories of poverty are seen through a screen of blooms—sunflowers, petunias, roses, dahlias, forsythia, spirea, delphiniums, verbena . . . and on and on.

And I remember people coming to my mother's yard to be given cuttings from her flowers; I hear again the praise showered on her because whatever rocky soil she landed on, she turned into a garden. A garden so brilliant with colors, so original in its design, so magnificent with life and creativity, that to this day people drive by our house in Georgia—perfect strangers and imperfect strangers—and ask to stand or walk among my mother's art.

I notice that it is only when my mother is working in her flowers that she is radiant, almost to the point of being invisible—except as Creator: hand and eye. She is involved in work her soul must have. Ordering the universe in the image of her personal conception of Beauty.

Her face, as she prepares the Art that is her gift, is a legacy of respect she leaves to me, for all that illuminates and cherishes life. She has handed down respect for the possibilities—and the will to grasp them.

For her, so hindered and intruded upon in so many ways, being an 45 artist has still been a daily part of her life. This ability to hold on, even in very simple ways, is work black women have done for a very long time.

This poem is not enough, but it is something, for the woman who literally covered the holes in our walls with sunflowers:

> They were women then
> My mama's generation
> Husky of voice—Stout of
> Step
> With fists as well as
> Hands
> How they battered down

Doors
And ironed
Starched white
Shirts
How they led
Armies
Headragged Generals
Across mined
Fields
Booby-trapped
Kitchens
To discover books
Desks
A place for us
How they knew what we
Must know
Without knowing a page
Of it
Themselves.

Guided by my heritage of a love of beauty and a respect for strength—in search of my mother's garden, I found my own.

And perhaps in Africa over two hundred years ago, there was just such a mother; perhaps she painted vivid and daring decorations in oranges and yellows and greens on the walls of her hut; perhaps she sang—in a voice like Roberta Flack's—*sweetly* over the compounds of her village; perhaps she wove the most stunning mats or told the most ingenious stories of all the village storytellers. Perhaps she was herself a poet—though only her daughter's name is signed to the poems that we know.

Perhaps Phillis Wheatley's mother was also an artist.

Perhaps in more than Phillis Wheatley's biological life is her mother's   50
signature made clear.

Considerations

1. Identify the main sections of this essay, and suggest how the sections are related.
2. Consider carefully the epigraph by Jean Toomer that introduces the essay and the poems Walker quotes. Suggest a relationship between one of these quotations and the ideas Walker explores in her essay.
3. Explain the connection Walker sees between the current generation of African-American women who are artists, writers, and poets, and their mothers and grandmothers. In what ways are the mothers and grandmothers teachers?

4. Reread Alice Walker's short story "Everyday Use" (page 371), and identify similarities and differences between that story and "In Search of Our Mothers' Gardens." What significance do you see in these similarities and differences?

5. Read the following commentary, "The Black Woman as Wayward," and explain how it changes or contributes to your response to either "Everyday Use" (page 371) or "In Search of Our Mothers' Gardens."

Commentary

BARBARA CHRISTIAN
Alice Walker: The Black Woman as Wayward

Walker is drawn to the integral and economical process of quilt making as a model for her own craft, for through it, one can create out of seemingly disparate, everyday materials patterns of clarity, imagination, and beauty. Two of her works especially emphasize the idea of this process: her classic essay "In Search of Our Mothers' Gardens" and her short story "Everyday Use." Each piece complements the other and articulates the precise meaning of the quilt as idea and process for this writer.

In "In Search of Our Mothers' Gardens," Walker directly asks the question that every writer must: From whence do I, as a writer, come? What is my tradition? In pursuing the question she focuses most intensely on her female heritage, in itself a point of departure from the route most writers have taken. Walker traces the images of black women in the literature as well as those few who were able to be writers. However, as significant as the tracing of that literary history is, Walker's major insight in the essay is her illumination of the creative legacy of "ordinary" black women of the South, a focus that complements but finally transcends literary history. In her insistence on honesty, on examining the roots of *her own* creativity, she invokes not so much the literature of black women, which was probably unknown to her as a budding child writer, but the creativity of her mother, her grandmother, the women around her.

What did some slave women or black women of this century do with the creativity that might have, in a less restrictive society, expressed itself in paint, words, clay? Walker reflects on a truth so obvious it is seldom acknowledged: They used the few media left them by a society that labeled them lowly, menial. Some, like Walker's mother, expressed it in the growing of magnificent gardens; some in cooking; others in quilts of imagination and passion like the one Walker saw at the Smithsonian Institution. Walker's description of that quilt's impact on her brings together essential elements of her more recent work: the theme of the black woman's creativity, her transformation, despite opposition, of the bits and pieces allowed her by society into a work of functional beauty.

But Walker does not merely acknowledge quilts (or the art black women created out of "low" media) as high art, a tendency now fostered by many women who have discovered the works of their maternal ancestors. She is also impressed by their *functional* beauty and by the process that produced them. Her short story "Everyday Use" is in some ways a conclusion in fiction to her essay. Just as she juxtaposed the history of black women writers with the creative legacy of ordinary black women, so she complemented her own essay, a search for the roots of her own creativity, with a story that embodies the idea itself.

In "Everyday Use," Walker again scrutinized a popular premise of the   5
times. The story, which is dedicated to "your grandmama," is about the use and misuse of the concept of heritage. The mother of two daughters, one selfish and stylish, the other scarred and caring, passes on to us its true definition. Dee, the sister who has always despised the backward ways of her southern rural family, comes back to visit her old home. She has returned to her black roots because now they are fashionable. So she glibly delights in the artifacts of her heritage: the rough benches her father made, the hand-made butter churn that she intends to use for a decorative centerpiece, the quilts made by her grandma Dee after whom she was named—the *things* that have been passed on. Ironically, in keeping with the times, Dee has changed her name to Wangero, denying the existence of her namesake, even as she covets the quilts she made.

On the other hand, her sister Maggie is not aware of the word *heritage*. But she loves her grandma and cherishes her memory in the quilts she made. Maggie has accepted the *spirit* that was passed on to her. The contrast be-tween the two sisters is aptly summarized in Dee's focal line in the story: "'Maggie can't appreciate these quilts!' she said. 'She'd probably be backward enough to put them to everyday use.'" Which her mother counters with: "She can always make some more. Maggie knows how to quilt."

The mother affirms the functional nature of their heritage and insists that it must continually be renewed rather than fixed in the past. The moth-er's succinct phrasing of the meaning of *heritage* is underscored by Dee's lack of knowledge about the bits and pieces that make up these quilts, the process of quilting that Maggie knows. For Maggie appreciates the people who made them, while Dee can only possess the "priceless" products. Dee's final words, ironically, exemplify her misuse of the concept of heritage, of what is passed on:

> "What don't I understand?" I wanted to know.
> "Your heritage," she said. And then she turned to Maggie, kissed her, and said, "You ought to try to make something of yourself, too, Maggie. It's really a new day for us. But from the way you and mama still live you'd never know it."

In critically analyzing the uses of the concept of heritage, Walker ar-rived at important distinctions. As an abstraction rather than a living idea, its misuse can subordinate people to artifact, can elevate culture above the com-munity. And because she used, as the artifact, quilts that were made by southern black women, she focused attention on those supposedly backward folk who never heard the word heritage but fashioned a functional tradition out of little matter and much spirit.

In "Everyday Use," the mother, seemingly in a fit of contrariness, snatches the beautiful quilts out of the hands of the "black" Wangero and gives them to the "backward" Maggie. This story is one of eleven in Walker's first collection of short stories, *In Love and Trouble.* Though written over a period of some five years, the volume is unified by two of Walker's most persistent characteristics: her use of a southern black woman character as the protagonist, and that character's insistence on challenging convention, on being herself, sometimes in spite of herself. . . .

CONNECTIONS: LEARNING AND TEACHING

1. Compare and contrast the problems, hopes, and possibilities that minority children, both now and in the past, have faced as they become educated. Consider the following works: "The Lesson," "The Loudest Voice," "Famous All Over Town," "A Teacher Taught Me," "Learning to Read and Write."

2. Consider the role teachers play in our lives. Use examples from any or all of the following works: "Me and Miss Mandible," "The Lesson," "A Class of New Canadians," "Naming of Parts," "Raising My Hand."

3. Discuss how we can learn—and the importance of what we learn—outside of school. Consider any of the following works: "The Lesson," "Famous All Over Town," "There Was a Child Went Forth," "First Practice," "Learning to Read and Write."

4. Define "education." Refer to any of the works in this section as you develop and explain your definition.

5. Mark Twain once said, "Never let school get in the way of your education." Respond to this quotation, referring to any of the following works: "The Lesson," "The Loudest Voice," "The School Children," "Ethics," "Learning to Read and Write."

11

War and Power

ELIZABETH GORDON (1964–   )

On the Other Side of the War: A Story

Born in Saigon (Ho Chi Minh City) to a Vietnamese mother and American father, Elizabeth Gordon grew up in Tennessee. Early in life she discovered that she wanted to be a writer and studied writing both as an undergraduate and as a graduate student at Brown University, where she earned a master of fine arts degree in creative writing. Currently, she lives in Providence, Rhode Island, and works as a freelance writer. Commenting on her cultural background, Gordon noted, "I've found there's a certain built-in tension in having a mixed heritage. All kinds of questions arise from it: questions of identity, of belonging, of home" (Home to Stay 1990).

I. The Way We Came to America

The way we came to America was this: My father, who was in the Army, made an overseas call to his mom and dad in West Virginia.

"Listen," he said, "I've decided to adopt this poor little Vietnamese baby and bring her to America. What do you think?"

Now, both Grandma and Grandpa were true hillbillies in their lineage, habits, and mental faculties—which means they were as broke, as stubborn, and as sharp as folks can be. Not that my father's story required much genius to be seen right through. A twenty-four-year-old enlisted man wanting to bring home some mysterious oriental infant? They hadn't brought him up *that* good.

"It's all right, Skip," they told him. "You can get married, if you love her, and bring 'em both. Bring 'em both on home."

II. No One Had Expected

No one had expected anything like that to happen, least of all the   5
people it happened to.

My father had been quite prepared to meet and marry a sweet girl with a name like Layuna or Ginny Lee. A girl who hailed from one of the good neighboring towns of Beckley or Rainelle. A girl with a daddy, like his, who liked to work on cars, who'd every once in a while hit the booze and start cursing about black lung. There'd been no Nguyen Ngoc Huong from Saigon in *his* crystal ball.

And my mother never dreamed she'd live in an aluminum house on wheels, or see shaved ice swirling down from the sky. Her kitchen window looked out onto a pasture of cows, who stood utterly still with the weather piling up around their legs. It was a difficult thing for her to understand.

So while my father was out climbing telephone poles for Ma Bell, my mother was in the trailer with me, crying and crying for the cows who had not a plank against the cold.

III. Things Got Mixed Up

Things got mixed up sometimes between them. Though it was my father's unshakable belief that Common Sense prevailed in all circumstances, he seemed to forget that Common Sense is commonly rendered senseless whenever it crosses a few time zones.

For example, my mother would constantly confuse "hamburger" with "pancake," presumably because both were round, flat, and fried in a pan. So my father, after asking for his favorite breakfast, would soon smell the juicy aroma of sizzling ground beef coming from the kitchen. Other times, he'd find a stack of well-buttered flapjacks, along with a cold bottle of Coca-Cola, waiting for him at the dinner table.

One morning, before my father left for work, he asked my mother to make corn bread and pinto beans for supper. The result of this request was that my mother spent the remainder of the day peeling, one by one, an entire pound of pinto beans. How could she have known any better?

When my father returned home that night, he found her with ten sore fingers and a pot full of mush. He didn't know whether to laugh or cry, but he kissed her because there was nothing he could say.

IV. The Photograph

The photograph, circa 1965, is somewhat unusual. In the background there is a row of neat, nearly identical frame houses. The street in front of the houses is spacious and clean, as wholesome and as decent as sunshine.

Up a little closer, there is a car. It's a two-tone Chevy with curvaceous fenders, gleaming as though it's just been washed and waxed by hand. The weather looks like Sunday.

In the foreground not unexpectedly, a woman with a small child. The woman is a wife because she wears a gold ring. She is also a mother because of the way she holds her child.

The woman has a slim, dainty figure. Her smile is wide and loose, as though she is close to laughter. Maybe her husband, who is taking her picture, is telling a joke or making a silly face. It seems quite natural that the photographer is the husband. Who else would it be?

But something in the photograph seems not quite right. Strangers often tilt their heads when looking at it, as if it is uncomfortable to view straight up and down. Possibly, it's the incomparable blackness of the woman's hair, or the way it seems forced into a wave it can barely hold. Or maybe it has something to do with the baby's eyes which, though blue, are shaped exactly like the woman's: round at the center, narrow at the corners, and heavy-lidded.

What are eyes like that doing among frame houses and a shiny Chevrolet? It seems a reasonable thing to ask.

V. When I Started School

When I started school there were numerous forms to be filled out. Some of the questions were so simple, I could have answered them myself.

The task belonged to my mother, though. She handled most of the questions with ease, and I liked to watch the way she filled all those boxes and blanks with her pretty handwriting.

There was one question, however, that gave my mother a lot of trouble. Even though it was multiple choice, none of the answers seemed to fit. She decided to ask my father what to do.

He didn't have an answer right away, and for some reason that made him angry. The problem was, I was supposed to be in a race, but he couldn't figure out which one.

Finally, he told my mother to put an "H" in that blank. "For *human* race," he said.

I didn't understand what that meant, back then. But it sounded like a good race to me.

Considerations

1. Briefly summarize each section of the story, and evaluate the author's organization of her narrative. Do the sections seem entirely disconnected and unrelated, or do you see connections?
2. How appropriate is this story's title? How do you see the events, characters, and actions in the story as related or unrelated to war?
3. Using section IV as a model, describe and respond to a photograph (perhaps of your family or friends) that seems to you "somewhat unusual."
4. Discuss the issues raised by the dilemma that the narrator's parents face in section V. What are the implications of the questions on the forms they must fill out? Explain your response to the father's answer to the question about race. In what other ways might he have responded? How do you respond to such questions when you encounter them on forms you must complete?
5. Compare this story to any of the following: Patricia Grace's "Butterflies" (page 12), Jamaica Kincaid's "The Circling Hand" (page 181), Tillie Olsen's "I Stand Here Ironing" (page 790), or Grace Paley's "The Loudest Voice" (page 921).

LUISA VALENZUELA (1938–   )

I'm Your Horse in the Night

> *Born in Buenos Aires to a family that encouraged literary ventures, Luisa Valenzuela published her first short story at age 18. She grew up in Argentina and has lived and worked in New York City for many years. In addition to working as a journalist, Valenzuela commits much time and energy to political action through her membership in Amnesty International, the Freedom to Write Committee of PEN International, and the Americas Watch. She is particularly concerned with freedom of expression, and many of her works address this theme. She has published five collections of short stories and four novels, including* Hay que sonreir *(1966),* El gato eficaz *(1972), and* Cola de lagartija *(1983).*

TRANSLATED BY DEBORAH BONNER

The doorbell rang: three short rings and one long one. That was the signal, and I got up, annoyed and a little frightened; it could be them, and then again, maybe not; at these ungodly hours of the night it could be a trap. I opened the door expecting anything except him, face to face, at last.

He came in quickly and locked the door behind him before embracing me. So much in character, so cautious, first and foremost checking his— our—rear guard. Then he took me in his arms without saying a word, not even holding me too tight but letting all the emotions of our new encounter overflow, telling me so much by merely holding me in his arms and kissing me slowly. I think he never had much faith in words, and there he was, as silent as ever, sending me messages in the form of caresses.

We finally stepped back to look at one another from head to foot, not eye to eye, out of focus. And I was able to say Hello showing scarcely any surprise despite all those months when I had no idea where he could have been, and I was able to say

I thought you were fighting up north
I thought you'd been caught
I thought you were in hiding
I thought you'd been tortured and killed
I thought you were theorizing about the revolution in another country

Just one of many ways to tell him I'd been thinking of him, I hadn't stopped thinking of him or felt as if I'd been betrayed. And there he was, always so god-damn cautious, so much the master of his actions.

"Quiet, Chiquita. You're much better off not knowing what I've been up to."   5

Then he pulled out his treasures, potential clues that at the time eluded me: a bottle of cachça and a Gal Costa record. What had he been up to in

Brazil? What was he planning to do next? What had brought him back, risking his life, knowing they were after him? Then I stopped asking myself questions (quiet, Chiquita, he'd say). Come here, Chiquita, he was saying, and I chose to let myself sink into the joy of having him back again, trying not to worry. What would happen to us tomorrow, and the days that followed?

Cachça's a good drink. It goes down and up and down all the right tracks, and then stops to warm up the corners that need it most. Gal Costa's voice is hot, she envelops us in its sound and half-dancing, half-floating, we reach the bed. We lie down and keep on staring deep into each other's eyes, continue caressing each other without allowing ourselves to give into the pure senses just yet. We continue recognizing, rediscovering each other.

Beto, I say, looking at him. I know that isn't his real name, but it's the only one I can call him out loud. He replies:

"We'll make it someday, Chiquita, but let's not talk now."

It's better that way. Better if he doesn't start talking about how we'll   10
make it someday and ruin the wonder of what we're about to attain right now, the two of us, all alone.

"A noite eu so teu cavalo," Gal Costa suddenly sings from the record player.

"I'm your horse in the night," I translate slowly. And so as to bind him in a spell and stop him from thinking about other things:

"It's a saint's song, like in the *macumba*. Someone who's in a trance says she's the horse of the spirit who's riding her, she's his mount."

"Chiquita, you're always getting carried away with esoteric meanings and witchcraft. You know perfectly well that she isn't talking about spirits. If you're my horse in the night it's because I ride you, like this, see? . . . Like this . . . That's all."

It was so long, so deep and so insistent, so charged with affection that   15
we ended up exhausted. I fell asleep with him still on top of me.

I'm your horse in the night.

The goddamn phone pulled me out in waves from a deep well. Making an enormous effort to wake up, I walked over to the receiver, thinking it could be Beto, sure, who was no longer by my side, sure, following his inveterate habit of running away while I'm asleep without a word about where he's gone. To protect me, he says.

From the other end of the line, a voice I thought belonged to Andrés— the one we call Andrés—began to tell me:

"They found Beto dead, floating down the river near the other bank. It looks as if they threw him alive out of a chopper. He's all bloated and decomposed after six days in the water, but I'm almost sure it's him."

"No, it can't be Beto," I shouted carelessly. Suddenly the voice no   20
longer sounded like Andrés: it felt foreign, impersonal.

"You think so?"

"Who is this?" Only then did I think to ask. But that very moment they hung up.

Ten, fifteen minutes? How long must I have stayed there staring at the phone like an idiot until the police arrived? I didn't expect them. But, then again, how could I not? Their hands feeling me, their voices insulting and threatening, the house searched, turned inside out. But I already knew. So what did I care if they broke every breakable object and tore apart my dresser?

They wouldn't find a thing. My only real possession was a dream and they can't deprive me of my dreams just like that. My dream the night before, when Beto was there with me and we loved each other. I'd dreamed it, dreamed every bit of it, I was deeply convinced that I'd dreamed it all in the richest detail, even in full color. And dreams are none of the cops' business.

They want reality, tangible facts, the kind I couldn't even begin to 25 give them.

Where is he, you saw him, he was here with you, where did he go? Speak up, or you'll be sorry. Let's hear you sing, bitch, we know he came to see you, where is he, where is he holed up? He's in the city, come on, spill it, we know he came to get you.

I haven't heard a word from him in months. He abandoned me, I haven't heard from him in months. He ran away, went underground. What do I know, he ran off with someone else, he's in another country. What do I know, he abandoned me, I hate him, I know nothing.

(Go ahead, burn me with your cigarettes, kick me all you wish, threaten, go ahead, stick a mouse in me so it'll eat my insides out, pull my nails out, do as you please. Would I make something up for that? Would I tell you he was here when a thousand years ago he left me forever?)

I'm not about to tell them my dreams. Why should they care? I haven't seen that so-called Beto in more than six months, and I loved him. The man simply vanished. I only run into him in my dreams, and they're bad dreams that often become nightmares.

Beto, you know now, if it's true that they killed you, or wherever you 30 may be, Beto, I'm your horse in the night and you can inhabit me whenever you wish, even if I'm behind bars. Beto, now that I'm in jail I know that I dreamed you that night; it was just a dream. And if by some wild chance there's a Gal Costa record and a half-empty bottle of cachça in my house, I hope they'll forgive me: I will them out of existence.

Considerations

1. After reading the first six paragraphs, how would you describe the situations of the two people? What is their relationship? What does each of them seem to think of and expect from the other?
2. After reading the whole story, does the impression you gained from reading the first six paragraphs change or remain the same? Explain.
3. How do the title of the story and the song that bears the same title suggest possible themes, conflicts, and characterizations?

4. What evidence can you offer that the narrator's encounter with Beto was only a dream? What evidence can you offer that Beto really does come to her apartment?
5. How important is war to this story? Is it love or war that dominates the story's theme? Explain your response.

———————

FRANK O'CONNOR (1903–1966)

Guests of the Nation

Frank O'Connor is the pen name of Michael O'Donovan, who was born in County Cork, Ireland. Because of his family's poverty, he attended school only through the fourth grade, yet he developed a burning interest in reading and writing. Years later, after his brief service in the Irish Republican Army (IRA) during the Irish fight for independence from Great Britain, this interest in literature led him to work as a librarian. He later became director of the Abbey Theatre in Dublin. After moving to the United States in the 1950s, he enjoyed a brief stint as a Sunday morning television personality telling Irish stories. In addition, O'Connor taught creative writing at such renowned institutions as Harvard University and Northwestern University. In addition to his many volumes of short stories and translations of traditional Gaelic poems and tales, O'Connor also published The Mirror in the Roadway *(1956), a critical study of the novel, and* The Lonely Voice *(1963), a critical study of the short story.*

"Guests of the Nation," which was O'Connor's first published short story, first appeared in the Atlantic Monthly *in 1931.*

I

At dusk the big Englishman, Belcher, would shift his long legs out of the ashes and say "Well, chums, what about it?" and Noble or me would say "All right, chum" (for we had picked up some of their curious expressions), and the little Englishman, Hawkins, would light the lamp and bring out the cards. Sometimes Jeremiah Donovan would come up and supervise the game and get excited over Hawkins's cards, which he always played badly, and shout at him as if he was one of our own "Ah, you divil, you, why didn't you play the trey?"

But ordinarily Jeremiah was a sober and contented poor devil like the big Englishman, Belcher, and was looked up to only because he was a fair hand at documents, though he was slow enough even with them. He wore a small cloth hat and big gaiters over his long pants, and you seldom saw him with his hands out of his pockets. He reddened when you talked to him, tilting from toe to heel and back, and looking down all the time at his big farmer's feet. Noble and me used to make fun of his broad accent, because we were from the town.

I couldn't at the time see the point of me and Noble guarding Belcher and Hawkins at all, for it was my belief that you could have planted that pair down anywhere from this to Claregalway and they'd have taken root there like a native weed. I never in my short experience seen two men to take to the country as they did.

They were handed on to us by the Second Battalion when the search for them became too hot, and Noble and myself, being young, took over with a natural feeling of responsibility, but Hawkins made us look like fools when he showed that he knew the country better than we did.

"You're the bloke they calls Bonaparte," he says to me. "Mary Brigid 5 O'Connell told me to ask you what you done with the pair of her brother's socks you borrowed."

For it seemed, as they explained it, that the Second used to have little evenings, and some of the girls of the neighbourhood turned in, and, seeing they were such decent chaps, our fellows couldn't leave the two Englishmen out of them. Hawkins learned to dance "The Walls of Limerick," "The Siege of Ennis," and "The Waves of Tory" as well as any of them, though, naturally, he couldn't return the compliment, because our lads at that time did not dance foreign dances on principle.

So whatever privileges Belcher and Hawkins had with the Second they just naturally took with us, and after the first day or two we gave up all pretence of keeping a close eye on them. Not that they could have got far, for they had accents you could cut with a knife and wore khaki tunics and overcoats with civilian pants and boots. But it's my belief that they never had any idea of escaping and were quite content to be where they were.

It was a treat to see how Belcher got off with the old woman of the house where we were staying. She was a great warrant to scold, and cranky even with us, but before ever she had a chance of giving our guests, as I may call them, a lick of her tongue, Belcher had made her his friend for life. She was breaking sticks, and Belcher, who hadn't been more than ten minutes in the house, jumped up from his seat and went over to her.

"Allow me, madam," he says, smiling his queer little smile, "please allow me"; and he takes the bloody hatchet. She was struck too paralytic to speak, and after that, Belcher would be at her heels, carrying a bucket, a basket, or a load of turf, as the case might be. As Noble said, he got into looking before she leapt, and hot water, or any little thing she wanted, Belcher would have it ready for her. For such a huge man (and though I am five foot ten myself I had to look up at him) he had an uncommon shortness—or should I say lack?—of speech. It took us some time to get used to him, walking in and out, like a ghost, without a word. Especially because Hawkins talked enough for a platoon, it was strange to hear big Belcher with his toes in the ashes come out with a solitary "Excuse me, chum," or "That's right, chum." His one and only passion was cards, and I will say for him that he was a good card-player. He could have fleeced myself and Noble, but whatever we lost to him Hawkins lost to us, and Hawkins played with the money Belcher gave him.

Hawkins lost to us because he had too much old gab, and we probably 10 lost to Belcher for the same reason. Hawkins and Noble would spit at one another about religion into the early hours of the morning, and Hawkins worried the soul out of Noble, whose brother was a priest, with a string of questions that would puzzle a cardinal. To make it worse even in treating of holy subjects, Hawkins had a deplorable tongue. I never in all my career met a man who could mix such a variety of cursing and bad language into an argument. He was a terrible man, and a fright to argue. He never did a stroke of work, and when he had no one else to talk to, he got stuck in the old woman.

He met his match in her, for one day when he tried to get her to complain profanely of the drought, she gave him a great come-down by blaming it entirely on Jupiter Pluvius (a deity neither Hawkins nor I had ever heard of, though Noble said that among the pagans it was believed that he had something to do with the rain). Another day he was swearing at the capitalists for starting the German war° when the old lady laid down her iron, puckered up her little crab's mouth, and said: "Mr. Hawkins, you can say what you like about the war, and think you'll deceive me because I'm only a simple poor countrywoman, but I know what started the war. It was the Italian Count that stole the heathen divinity out of the temple in Japan. Believe me, Mr. Hawkins, nothing but sorrow and want can follow the people that disturb the hidden powers."

A queer old girl, all right.

II

We had our tea one evening, and Hawkins lit the lamp and we all sat into cards. Jeremiah Donovan came in too, and sat down and watched us for a while, and it suddenly struck me that he had no great love for the two Englishmen. It came as a great surprise to me, because I hadn't noticed anything about him before.

Late in the evening a really terrible argument blew up between Hawkins and Noble, about capitalists and priests and love of your country.

"The capitalists," says Hawkins with an angry gulp, "pays the priests to   15 tell you about the next world so as you won't notice what the bastards are up to in this."

"Nonsense, man!" says Noble, losing his temper. "Before ever a capitalist was thought of, people believed in the next world."

Hawkins stood up as though he was preaching a sermon.

"Oh, they did, did they?" he says with a sneer. "They believed all the things you believe, isn't that what you mean? And you believe that God created Adam, and Adam created Shem, and Shem created Jehoshophat. You believe all that silly old fairytale about Eve and Eden and the apple. Well, listen to me, chum. If you're entitled to hold a silly belief like that, I'm entitled to hold my silly belief—which is that the first thing your God created was a bleeding capitalist, with morality and Rolls-Royce complete. Am I right, chum?" he says to Belcher.

"You're right, chum," says Belcher with his amused smile, and got up from the table to stretch his long legs into the fire and stroke his moustache.

German war: World War I.

So, seeing that Jeremiah Donovan was going, and that there was no knowing
when the argument about religion would be over, I went out with him. We
strolled down to the village together, and then he stopped and started blushing and mumbling and saying I ought to be behind, keeping guard on the
prisoners. I didn't like the tone he took with me, and anyway I was bored
with life in the cottage, so I replied by asking him what the hell we wanted
guarding them at all for. I told him I'd talked it over with Noble, and that
we'd both rather be out with a fighting column.

"What use are those fellows to us?" says I.   20

He looked at me in surprise and said: "I thought you knew we were
keeping them as hostages."

"Hostages?" I said.

"The enemy have prisoners belonging to us," he says, "and now they're
talking of shooting them. If they shoot our prisoners, we'll shoot theirs."

"Shoot them?" I said.

"What else did you think we were keeping them for?" he says.   25

"Wasn't it very unforeseen of you not to warn Noble and myself of
that in the beginning?" I said.

"How was it?" says he. "You might have known it."

"We couldn't know it, Jeremiah Donovan," says I. "How could we
when they were on our hands so long?"

"The enemy have our prisoners as long and longer," says he.

"That's not the same thing at all," says I.   30

"What difference is there?" says he.

I couldn't tell him, because I knew he wouldn't understand. If it was
only an old dog that was going to the vet's, you'd try and not get too fond
of him, but Jeremiah Donovan wasn't a man that would ever be in danger
of that.

"And when is this thing going to be decided?" says I.

"We might hear tonight," he says. "Or tomorrow or the next day at
latest. So if it's only hanging round here that's a trouble to you, you'll be free
soon enough."

It wasn't the hanging round that was a trouble to me at all by this time.   35
I had worse things to worry about. When I got back to the cottage the
argument was still on. Hawkins was holding forth in his best style, maintaining that there was no next world, and Noble was maintaining that there was;
but I could see that Hawkins had had the best of it.

"Do you know what, chum?" he was saying with a saucy smile. "I
think you're just as big a bleeding unbeliever as I am. You say you believe in
the next world, and you know just as much about the next world as I do,
which is sweet damn-all. What's heaven? You don't know. Where's heaven?
You don't know. You know sweet damn-all! I ask you again, do they wear
wings?"

"Very well, then," says Noble, "they do. Is that enough for you? They
do wear wings."

"Where do they get them, then? Who makes them? Have they a factory for wings? Have they a sort of store where you hands in your chit and takes your bleeding wings?"

"You're an impossible man to argue with," says Noble. "Now, listen to me—" And they were off again.

It was long after midnight when we locked up and went to bed. As I   40
blew out the candle I told Noble what Jeremiah Donovan was after telling me. Noble took it very quietly. When we'd been in bed about an hour he asked me did I think we ought to tell the Englishmen. I didn't think we should, because it was more than likely that the English wouldn't shoot our men, and even if they did, the brigade officers, who were always up and down with the Second Battalion and knew the Englishmen well, wouldn't be likely to want them plugged. "I think so too," says Noble. "It would be great cruelty to put the wind up them now."

"It was very unforeseen of Jeremiah Donovan anyhow," says I.

It was next morning that we found it so hard to face Belcher and Hawkins. We went about the house all day scarcely saying a word. Belcher didn't seem to notice; he was stretched into the ashes as usual, with his usual look of waiting in quietness for something unforeseen to happen, but Hawkins noticed and put it down to Noble's being beaten in the argument of the night before.

"Why can't you take a discussion in the proper spirit?" he says severely. "You and your Adam and Eve! I'm a Communist, that's what I am. Communist or anarchist, it all comes to much the same thing." And for hours he went round the house, muttering when the fit took him. "Adam and Eve! Adam and Eve! Nothing better to do with their time than picking bleeding apples!"

III

I don't know how we got through that day, but I was very glad when it was over, the tea things were cleared away, and Belcher said in his peaceable way: "Well, chums, what about it?" We sat round the table and Hawkins took out the cards, and just then I heard Jeremiah Donovan's footstep on the path and a dark presentiment crossed my mind. I rose from the table and caught him before he reached the door.

"What do you want?" I asked.   45

"I want those two soldier friends of yours," he says, getting red.

"Is that the way, Jeremiah Donovan?" I asked.

"That's the way. There were four of our lads shot this morning, one of them a boy of sixteen."

"That's bad," I said.

At that moment Noble followed me out, and the three of us walked   50
down the path together, talking in whispers. Feeney, the local intelligence officer, was standing by the gate.

"What are you going to do about it?" I asked Jeremiah Donovan.

"I want you and Noble to get them out; tell them they're being shifted again; that'll be the quietest way."

"Leave me out of that," says Noble under his breath.

Jeremiah Donovan looks at him hard.

"All right," he says. "You and Feeney get a few tools from the shed and dig a hole by the far end of the bog. Bonaparte and myself will be after you. Don't let anyone see you with the tools. I wouldn't like it to go beyond ourselves." 55

We saw Feeney and Noble go round to the shed and went in ourselves. I left Jeremiah Donovan to do the explanations. He told them that he had orders to send them back to the Second Battalion. Hawkins let out a mouthful of curses, and you could see that though Belcher didn't say anything, he was a bit upset too. The old woman was for having them stay in spite of us, and she didn't stop advising them until Jeremiah Donovan lost his temper and turned on her. He had a nasty temper, I noticed. It was pitch-dark in the cottage by this time, but no one thought of lighting the lamp, and in the darkness the two Englishmen fetched their topcoats and said good-bye to the old woman.

"Just as a man makes a home of a bleeding place, some bastard at headquarters thinks you're too cushy and shunts you off," says Hawkins, shaking her hand.

"A thousand thanks, madam," says Belcher. "A thousand thanks for everything"—as though he'd made it up.

We went round to the back of the house and down towards the bog. It was only then that Jeremiah Donovan told them. He was shaking with excitement.

"There were four of our fellows shot in Cork this morning and now you're to be shot as a reprisal." 60

"What are you talking about?" snaps Hawkins. "It's bad enough being mucked about as we are without having to put up with your funny jokes."

"It isn't a joke," says Donovan. "I'm sorry, Hawkins, but it's true," and begins on the usual rigmarole about duty and how unpleasant it is.

I never noticed that people who talk a lot about duty find it much of a trouble to them.

"Oh, cut it out!" says Hawkins.

"Ask Bonaparte," says Donovan, seeing that Hawkins isn't taking him seriously. "Isn't it true, Bonaparte?" 65

"It is," I say, and Hawkins stops.

"Ah, for Christ's sake, chum!"

"I mean it, chum," I say.

"You don't sound as if you meant it."

"If he doesn't mean it, I do," says Donovan, working himself up. 70

"What have you against me, Jeremiah Donovan?"

"I never said I had anything against you. But why did your people take out four of our prisoners and shoot them in cold blood?"

He took Hawkins by the arm and dragged him on, but it was impossible to make him understand that we were in earnest. I had the Smith and Wesson in my pocket and I kept fingering it and wondering what I'd do if they put up a fight for it or ran, and wishing to God they'd do one or the other. I knew if they did run for it, that I'd never fire on them. Hawkins wanted to know was Noble in it, and when we said yes, he asked us why Noble wanted to plug him. Why did any of us want to plug him? What had he done to us? Weren't we all chums? Didn't we understand him and didn't he understand us? Did we imagine for an instant that he'd shoot us for all the so-and-so officers in the so-and-so British Army?

By this time we'd reached the bog, and I was so sick I couldn't even answer him. We walked along the edge of it in the darkness, and every now and then Hawkins would call a halt and begin all over again, as if he was wound up, about our being chums, and I knew that nothing but the sight of the grave would convince him that we had to do it. And all the time I was hoping that something would happen; that they'd run for it or that Noble would take over the responsibility from me. I had the feeling that it was worse on Noble than on me.

IV

At last we saw the lantern in the distance and made towards it. Noble   75
was carrying it, and Feeney was standing somewhere in the darkness behind him, and the picture of them so still and silent in the bogland brought it home to me that we were in earnest, and banished the last bit of hope I had.

Belcher, on recognizing Noble, said: "Hallo, chum," in his quiet way, but Hawkins flew at him at once, and the argument began all over again, only this time Noble had nothing to say for himself and stood with his head down, holding the lantern between his legs.

It was Jeremiah Donovan who did the answering. For the twentieth time, as though it was haunting his mind, Hawkins asked if anybody thought he'd shoot Noble.

"Yes, you would," says Jeremiah Donovan.

"No, I wouldn't, damn you!"

"You would, because you'd know you'd be shot for not doing it."   80

"I wouldn't, not if I was to be shot twenty times over. I wouldn't shoot a pal. And Belcher wouldn't—isn't that right, Belcher?"

"That's right, chum," Belcher said, but more by way of answering the question than of joining in the argument. Belcher sounded as though whatever unforeseen thing he'd always been waiting for had come at last.

"Anyway, who says Noble would be shot if I wasn't? What do you think I'd do if I was in his place, out in the middle of a blasted bog?"

"What would you do?" asks Donovan.

"I'd go with him wherever he was going, of course. Share my last bob   85
with him and stick by him through thick and thin. No one can ever say of me that I let down a pal."

"We had enough of this," says Jeremiah Donovan, cocking his revolver. "Is there any message you want to send?"

"No, there isn't."

"Do you want to say your prayers?"

Hawkins came out with a cold-blooded remark that even shocked me and turned on Noble again.

"Listen to me, Noble," he says. "You and me are chums. You can't come over to my side, so I'll come over to your side. That show you I mean what I say? Give me a rifle and I'll go along with you and the other lads." 90

Nobody answered him. We knew that was no way out.

"Hear what I'm saying?" he says. "I'm through with it. I'm a deserter or anything else you like. I don't believe in your stuff, but it's no worse than mine. That satisfy you?"

Noble raised his head, but Donovan began to speak and he lowered it again without replying.

"For the last time, have you any messages to send?" says Donovan in a cold, excited sort of voice.

"Shut up, Donovan! You don't understand me, but these lads do. They're not the sort to make a pal and kill a pal. They're not the tools of any capitalist." 95

I alone of the crowd saw Donovan raise his Webley to the back of Hawkins's neck, and as he did so I shut my eyes and tried to pray. Hawkins had begun to say something else when Donovan fired, and as I opened my eyes at the bang, I saw Hawkins stagger at the knees and lie out flat at Noble's feet, slowly and as quiet as a kid falling asleep, with the lantern-light on his lean legs and bright farmer's boots. We all stood very still, watching him settle out in the last agony.

Then Belcher took out a handkerchief and began to tie it about his own eyes (in our excitement we'd forgotten to do the same for Hawkins), and, seeing it wasn't big enough, turned and asked for the loan of mine. I gave it to him and he knotted the two together and pointed with his foot at Hawkins.

"He's not quite dead," he says. "Better give him another."

Sure enough, Hawkins's left knee is beginning to rise. I bend down and put my gun to his head; then, recollecting myself, I get up again. Belcher understands what's in my mind.

"Give him his first," he says. "I don't mind. Poor bastard, we don't know what's happening to him now." 100

I knelt and fired. By this time I didn't seem to know what I was doing. Belcher, who was fumbling a bit awkwardly with the handkerchiefs, came out with a laugh as he heard the shot. It was the first time I heard him laugh and it sent a shudder down my back; it sounded so unnatural.

"Poor bugger!" he said quietly. "And last night he was so curious about it all. It's very queer, chums, I always think. Now he knows as much about it as they'll ever let him know, and last night he was all in the dark."

Donovan helped him to tie the handkerchiefs about his eyes. "Thanks, chum," he said. Donovan asked if there were any messages he wanted sent.

"No, chum," he says. "Not for me. If any of you would like to write to Hawkins's mother, you'll find a letter from her in his pocket. He and his mother were great chums. But my missus left me eight years ago. Went away with another fellow and took the kid with her. I like the feeling of a home, as you may have noticed, but I couldn't start again after that."

It was an extraordinary thing, but in those few minutes Belcher said   105
more than in all the weeks before. It was just as if the sound of the shot had started a flood of talk in him and he could go on the whole night like that, quite happily, talking about himself. We stood round like fools now that he couldn't see us any longer. Donovan looked at Noble, and Noble shook his head. Then Donovan raised his Webley, and at that moment Belcher gives his queer laugh again. He may have thought we were talking about him, or perhaps he noticed the same thing I'd noticed and couldn't understand it.

"Excuse me, chums," he says. "I feel I'm talking the hell of a lot, and so silly, about my being so handy about a house and things like that. But this thing came on me suddenly. You'll forgive me, I'm sure."

"You don't want to say a prayer?" asks Donovan.

"No, chum," he says. "I don't think it would help. I'm ready, and you boys want to get it over."

"You understand that we're only doing our duty?" says Donovan.

Belcher's head was raised like a blind man's, so that you could only see   110
his chin and the tip of his nose in the lantern-light.

"I never could make out what duty was myself," he said. "I think you're all good lads, if that's what you mean. I'm not complaining."

Noble, just as if he couldn't bear any more of it, raised his fist at Donovan, and in a flash Donovan raised his gun and fired. The big man went over like a sack of meal, and this time there was no need of a second shot.

I don't remember much about the burying, but that it was worse than all the rest because we had to carry them to the grave. It was all mad lonely with nothing but a patch of lantern-light between ourselves and the dark, and birds hooting and screeching all round, disturbed by the guns. Noble went through Hawkins's belongings to find the letter from his mother, and then joined his hands together. He did the same with Belcher. Then, when we'd filled in the grave, we separated from Jeremiah Donovan and Feeny and took our tools back to the shed. All the way we didn't speak a word. The kitchen was dark and cold as we'd left it, and the old woman was sitting over the hearth, saying her beads. We walked past her into the room, and Noble struck a match to light the lamp. She rose quietly and came to the doorway with all her cantankerousness gone.

"What did ye do with them?" she asked in a whisper, and Noble started so that the match went out in his hand.

"What's that?" he asked without turning round.   115

"I heard ye," she said.

"What did you hear?" asked Noble.

"I heard ye. Do ye think I didn't hear ye, putting the spade back in the houseen?"

Noble struck another match and this time the lamp lit for him.

"Was that what ye did to them?" she asked.

120

Then, by God, in the very doorway, she fell on her knees and began praying, and after looking at her for a minute or two Noble did the same by the fireplace. I pushed my way out past her and left them at it. I stood at the door, watching the stars and listening to the shrieking of the birds dying out over the bogs. It is so strange what you feel at times like that you can't describe it. Noble says he saw everything ten times the size, as though there were nothing in the whole world but that little patch of bog with the two Englishmen stiffening into it, but with me it was as if the patch of bog where the Englishmen were was a million miles away, and even Noble and the old woman, mumbling behind me, and the birds and the bloody stars were all far away, and I was somehow very small and very lost and lonely like a child astray in the snow. And anything that happened to me afterwards, I never felt the same about again.

Considerations

1. List the details that suggest the setting (both time and place) of this story. How important is this specific setting to the story's action and theme? Might a story like this take place in a different time and location? Explain.

2. The four major characters demonstrate striking similarities and differences. How do these suggest the story's theme(s)?

3. What roles do the minor characters—the old woman and Donovan—play? How would the story be different if these characters were absent (or different)?

4. Throughout the story, several characters talk about "duty." What possible definitions of the word does the story suggest? How would you define the term? Consider, for example, different kinds of duty and evaluate whether one kind should take precedence over another.

5. Reread the details of the executions (part IV). What effect does O'Connor achieve—and what questions does he raise—by including the gory description of the prisoners' agonizing deaths as well as Belcher's and Hawkins's responses to the executions?

TIM O'BRIEN (1947–   )

The Things They Carried

> *Tim O'Brien was born in Austin, Minnesota. He was drafted in 1968 at age 21 and subsequently served in the infantry in Vietnam. In response to his experiences as a reluctant soldier (he has stated that he had briefly considered dodging the draft), O'Brien has written a collection of short stories,* The Things They Carried *(1990); a memoir,* If I Die in a Combat Zone *(1973); and three novels,* Northern Lights *(1975),* Going after Cacciato *(1979), which won the National Book Award, and* The Nuclear Age *(1994). O'Brien, who currently lives in Cambridge, Massachusetts, has received writing fellowships from the Guggenheim Foundation, the National Endowment for the Arts, and the Massachusetts Arts and Humanities Foundation.*

First Lieutenant Jimmy Cross carried letters from a girl named Martha, a junior at Mount Sebastian College in New Jersey. They were not love letters, but Lieutenant Cross was hoping, so he kept them folded in plastic at the bottom of his rucksack. In the late afternoon, after a day's march, he would dig his foxhole, wash his hands under a canteen, unwrap the letters, hold them with the tips of his fingers, and spend the last hour of light pretending. He would imagine romantic camping trips into the White Mountains in New Hampshire. He would sometimes taste the envelope flaps, knowing her tongue had been there. More than anything, he wanted Martha to love him as he loved her, but the letters were mostly chatty, elusive on the matter of love. She was a virgin, he was almost sure. She was an English major at Mount Sebastian, and she wrote beautifully about her professors and roommates and midterm exams, about her respect for Chaucer and her great affection for Virginia Woolf. She often quoted lines of poetry; she never mentioned the war, except to say, Jimmy, take care of yourself. The letters weighed ten ounces. They were signed "Love, Martha," but Lieutenant Cross understood that "Love" was only a way of signing and did not mean what he sometimes pretended it meant. At dusk, he would carefully return the letters to his rucksack. Slowly, a bit distracted, he would get up and move among his men, checking the perimeter, then at full dark he would return to his hole and watch the night and wonder if Martha was a virgin.

The things they carried were largely determined by necessity. Among the necessities or near necessities were P-38 can openers, pocket knives, heat tabs, wrist watches, dog tags, mosquito repellent, chewing gum, candy, cigarettes, salt tablets, packets of Kool-Aid, lighters, matches, sewing kits, Military Payment Certificates, C rations, and two or three canteens of water. Together, these items weighed between fifteen and twenty pounds, depending upon a man's habits or rate of metabolism. Henry Dobbins, who was a big man, carried extra rations; he was especially fond of canned peaches in heavy syrup over pound cake. Dave Jensen, who practiced field hygiene, carried a toothbrush, dental floss, and several hotel-size bars of soap he'd stolen on R&R° in Sydney, Australia. Ted Lavender, who was scared, carried tranquilizers until he was shot in the head outside the village of Than Khe in mid-April. By necessity, and because it was SOP,° they all carried steel helmets that weighed five pounds including the liner and camouflage cover. They carried the standard fatigue jackets and trousers. Very few carried underwear. On their feet they carried jungle boots—2.1 pounds—and Dave Jensen carried three pairs of socks and a can of Dr. Scholl's foot powder as a precaution against trench foot. Until he was shot, Ted Lavender carried six or seven ounces of premium dope, which for him was a necessity. Mitchell Sanders, the RTO, carried condoms. Norman Bowker carried a diary. Rat Kiley carried comic books. Kiowa, a devout Baptist, carried an illustrated New Testament that had been presented to him by his father, who taught Sunday school in Oklahoma City, Oklahoma. As a hedge against bad times, however, Kiowa also carried his grandmother's distrust of the white man, his grandfather's old hunting hatchet. Necessity dictated. Because the land was mined and booby-trapped, it was SOP for each man to carry a steel-centered, nylon-covered flak jacket, which weighed 6.7 pounds, but which on hot days seemed much heavier. Because you could die so quickly, each man carried at least one large compress bandage, usually in the helmet band for easy access. Because the nights were cold, and because the monsoons were wet, each carried a green plastic poncho that could be used as a raincoat or ground sheet or makeshift tent. With its quilted liner, the poncho weighed almost two pounds, but it was worth every ounce. In April, for instance, when Ted Lavender was shot, they used his poncho to wrap him up, then to carry him across the paddy, then to lift him into the chopper that took him away.

They were called legs or grunts.

To carry something was to "hump" it, as when Lieutenant Jimmy Cross humped his love for Martha up the hills and through the swamps. In its intransitive form, "to hump" meant "to walk," or "to march," but it implied burdens far beyond the intransitive.

Almost everyone humped photographs. In his wallet, Lieutenant Cross carried two photographs of Martha. The first was a Kodachrome snapshot signed "Love," though he knew better. She stood against a brick wall. Her eyes were gray and neutral, her lips slightly open as she stared straight-on at the camera. At night, sometimes, Lieutenant Cross wondered who had taken the picture, because he knew she had boyfriends, because he loved her so much, and because he could see the shadow of the picture taker spreading out against the brick wall. The second photograph had been clipped from

5

_____

R&R: Rest and recreation.   SOP: Standard operating procedure.

the 1968 Mount Sebastian yearbook. It was an action shot—women's volleyball—and Martha was bent horizontal to the floor, reaching, the palms of her hands in sharp focus, the tongue taut, the expression frank and competitive. There was no visible sweat. She wore white gym shorts. Her legs, he thought, were almost certainly the legs of a virgin, dry and without hair, the left knee cocked and carrying her entire weight, which was just over one hundred pounds. Lieutenant Cross remembered touching that left knee. A dark theater, he remembered, and the movie was *Bonnie and Clyde,* and Martha wore a tweed skirt, and during the final scene, when he touched her knee, she turned and looked at him in a sad, sober way that made him pull his hand back, but he would always remember the feel of the tweed skirt and the knee beneath it and the sound of the gunfire that killed Bonnie and Clyde, how embarrassing it was, how slow and oppressive. He remembered kissing her good night at the dorm door. Right then, he thought, he should've done something brave. He should've carried her up the stairs to her room and tied her to the bed and touched that left knee all night long. He should've risked it. Whenever he looked at the photographs, he thought of new things he should've done.

What they carried was partly a function of rank, partly of field specialty.

As a first lieutenant and platoon leader, Jimmy Cross carried a compass, maps, code books, binoculars, and a .45-caliber pistol that weighed 2.9 pounds fully loaded. He carried a strobe light and the responsibility for the lives of his men.

As an RTO, Mitchell Sanders carried the PRC-25 radio, a killer, twenty-six pounds with its battery.

As a medic, Rat Kiley carried a canvas satchel filled with morphine and plasma and malaria tablets and surgical tape and comic books and all the things a medic must carry, including M&M's for especially bad wounds, for a total weight of nearly twenty pounds.

As a big man, therefore a machine gunner, Henry Dobbins carried the   10
M-60, which weighed twenty-three pounds unloaded, but which was almost always loaded. In addition, Dobbins carried between ten and fifteen pounds of ammunition draped in belts across his chest and shoulders.

As PFCs or Spec 4s, most of them were common grunts and carried the standard M-16 gas-operated assault rifle. The weapon weighed 7.5 pounds unloaded, 8.2 pounds with its full twenty-round magazine. Depending on numerous factors, such as topography and psychology, the riflemen carried anywhere from twelve to twenty magazines, usually in cloth bandoliers, adding on another 8.4 pounds at minimum, fourteen pounds at maximum. When it was available, they also carried M-16 maintenance gear—rods and steel brushes and swabs and tubes of LSA oil—all of which weighed about a pound. Among the grunts, some carried the M-79 grenade launcher, 5.9 pounds unloaded, a reasonably light weapon except for the ammunition, which was heavy. A single round weighed ten ounces. The typical load was twenty-five rounds. But Ted Lavender, who was scared, carried thirty-four rounds when he was shot and killed outside Than Khe, and he went down under an exceptional burden, more than twenty pounds of ammunition, plus the flak jacket and helmet and rations and water and toilet paper and tranquilizers and all the rest, plus the unweighed fear. He was dead weight. There was no twitching or flopping. Kiowa, who saw it happen, said it was like watching a rock fall, or a big sandbag or something—just boom, then down— not like the movies where the dead guy rolls around and does fancy spins and goes ass over teakettle—not like that, Kiowa said, the poor bastard just flat-fuck fell. Boom. Down. Nothing else. It was a bright morning in mid-April. Lieutenant Cross felt the pain. He blamed himself. They stripped off Lavender's canteens and ammo, all the heavy things, and Rat Kiley said the obvious, the guy's dead, and Mitchell Sanders used his radio to report one U.S. KIA and to request a chopper. Then they wrapped Lavender in his poncho. They carried him out to a dry paddy, established security, and sat smoking the dead man's dope until the chopper came. Lieutenant Cross kept to himself. He pictured Martha's smooth young face, thinking he loved her more than anything, more than his men, and now Ted Lavender was dead because he loved her so much and could not stop thinking about her. When the dust-off arrived, they carried Lavender aboard. Afterward they burned Than Khe. They marched until dusk, then dug their holes, and that night Kiowa kept explaining how you had to be there, how fast it was, how the poor guy just dropped like so much concrete. Boom-down, he said. Like cement.

In addition to the three standard weapons—the M-60, M-16, and M-79—they carried whatever presented itself, or whatever seemed appropriate as a means of killing or staying alive. They carried catch-as-catch-can. At various times, in various situations, they carried M-14s and CAR-15s and Swedish Ks and grease guns and captured AK-47s and Chi-Coms and RPGs and Simonov carbines and black-market Uzis and .38-caliber Smith & Wesson handguns and 66 mm LAWs and shotguns and silencers and blackjacks and bayonets and C-4 plastic explosives. Lee Strunk carried a slingshot; a weapon of last resort, he called it. Mitchell Sanders carried brass knuckles. Kiowa carried his grandfather's feathered hatchet. Every third or fourth man carried a Claymore antipersonnel mine—3.5 pounds with its firing device. They all carried fragmentation grenades—fourteen ounces each. They all carried at least one M-18 colored smoke grenade—twenty-four ounces. Some carried CS or tear gas grenades. Some carried white-phosphorus grenades. They carried all they could bear, and then some, including a silent awe for the terrible power of the things they carried.

In the first week of April, before Lavender died, Lieutenant Jimmy Cross received a good-luck charm from Martha. It was a simple pebble, an ounce at most. Smooth to the touch, it was a milky-white color with flecks of orange and violet, oval-shaped, like a miniature egg. In the accompanying letter, Martha wrote that she had found the pebble on the Jersey shoreline, precisely where the land touched water at high tide, where things came together but also separated. It was this separate-but-together quality, she wrote, that had inspired her to pick up the pebble and to carry it in her breast pocket for several days, where it seemed weightless, and then to send it through the mail, by air, as a token of her truest feelings for him. Lieutenant Cross found this romantic. But he wondered what her truest feelings were, exactly, and what she meant by separate-but-together. He wondered how the tides and waves had come into play on that afternoon along the Jersey shoreline when Martha saw the pebble and bent down to rescue it from geology. He imagined bare feet. Martha was a poet, with the poet's sensibilities, and her feet would be brown and bare, the toenails unpainted, the eyes chilly and somber like the ocean in March, and though it was painful, he wondered who had been with her that afternoon. He imagined a pair of shadows moving along the strip of sand where things came together but also separated. It was phantom jealousy, he knew, but he couldn't help himself. He loved her so much. On the march, through the hot days of early April, he carried the pebble in his mouth, turning it with his tongue, tasting sea salts and moisture. His mind wandered. He had difficulty keeping his attention on the war. On occasion he would yell at his men to spread out the column, to keep their eyes open, but then he would slip away into daydreams, just pretending, walking barefoot along the Jersey shore, with Martha, carrying nothing. He would feel himself rising. Sun and waves and gentle winds, all love and lightness.

What they carried varied by mission.

When a mission took them to the mountains, they carried mosquito netting, machetes, canvas tarps, and extra bug juice.   15

If a mission seemed especially hazardous, or if it involved a place they knew to be bad, they carried everything they could. In certain heavily mined AOs, where the land was dense with Toe Poppers and Bouncing Betties, they took turns humping a twenty-eight-pound mine detector. With its headphones and big sensing plate, the equipment was a stress on the lower back and shoulders, awkward to handle, often useless because of the shrapnel in the earth, but they carried it anyway, partly for safety, partly for the illusion of safety.

On ambush, or other night missions, they carried peculiar little odds and ends. Kiowa always took along his New Testament and a pair of moccasins for silence. Dave Jensen carried night-sight vitamins high in carotin. Lee Strunk carried his slingshot; ammo, he claimed, would never be a problem. Rat Kiley carried brandy and M&M's. Until he was shot, Ted Lavender carried the starlight scope, which weighed 6.3 pounds with its aluminum carrying case. Henry Dobbins carried his girlfriend's pantyhose wrapped around his neck as a comforter. They all carried ghosts. When dark came, they would move out single file across the meadows and paddies to their ambush coordinates, where they would quietly set up the Claymores and lie down and spend the night waiting.

Other missions were more complicated and required special equipment. In mid-April, it was their mission to search out and destroy the elaborate tunnel complexes in the Than Khe area south of Chu Lai. To blow the tunnels, they carried one-pound blocks of pentrite high explosives, four blocks to a man, sixty-eight pounds in all. They carried wiring, detonators, and battery-powered clackers. Dave Jensen carried earplugs. Most often, before blowing the tunnels, they were ordered by higher command to search them, which was considered bad news, but by and large they just shrugged and carried out orders. Because he was a big man, Henry Dobbins was excused from tunnel duty. The others would draw numbers. Before Lavender died there were seventeen men in the platoon, and whoever drew the number seventeen would strip off his gear and crawl in head first with a flashlight and Lieutenant Cross's .45-caliber pistol. The rest of them would fan out as security. They would sit down or kneel, not facing the hole, listening to the ground beneath them, imagining cobwebs and ghosts, whatever was down there—the tunnel walls squeezing in—how the flashlight seemed impossibly heavy in the hand and how it was tunnel vision in the very strictest sense, compression in all ways, even time, and how you had to wiggle in—ass and elbows—a swallowed-up feeling—and how you found yourself worrying about odd things—will your flashlight go dead? Do rats carry rabies? If you screamed, how far would the sound carry? Would your buddies hear it? Would they have the courage to drag you out? In some respects, though not many, the waiting was worse than the tunnel itself. Imagination was a killer.

On April 16, when Lee Strunk drew the number seventeen, he laughed and muttered something and went down quickly. The morning was hot and very still. Not good, Kiowa said. He looked at the tunnel opening, then out across a dry paddy toward the village of Than Khe. Nothing moved. No clouds or birds or people. As they waited, the men smoked and drank Kool-Aid, not talking much, feeling sympathy for Lee Strunk but also feeling the luck of the draw. You win some, you lose some, said Mitchell Sanders, and sometimes you settle for a rain check. It was a tired line and no one laughed.

Henry Dobbins ate a tropical chocolate bar. Ted Lavender popped a   20
tranquilizer and went off to pee.

After five minutes, Lieutenant Jimmy Cross moved to the tunnel, leaned down, and examined the darkness. Trouble, he thought—a cave-in maybe. And then suddenly, without willing it, he was thinking about Martha. The stresses and fractures, the quick collapse, the two of them buried alive under all that weight. Dense, crushing love. Kneeling, watching the hole, he tried to concentrate on Lee Strunk and the war, all the dangers, but his love was too much for him, he felt paralyzed, he wanted to sleep inside her lungs and breathe her blood and be smothered. He wanted her to be a virgin and not a virgin, all at once. He wanted to know her. Intimate secrets—why poetry? Why so sad? Why that grayness in her eyes? Why so alone? Not lonely, just alone—riding her bike across campus or sitting off by herself in the cafeteria. Even dancing, she danced alone—and it was the aloneness that filled him with love. He remembered telling her that one evening. How she nodded and looked away. And how, later, when he kissed her, she received the kiss without returning it, her eyes wide open, not afraid, not a virgin's eyes, just flat and uninvolved.

Lieutenant Cross gazed at the tunnel. But he was not there. He was buried with Martha under the white sand at the Jersey shore. They were pressed together, and the pebble in his mouth was her tongue. He was smiling. Vaguely, he was aware of how quiet the day was, the sullen paddies, yet he could not bring himself to worry about matters of security. He was beyond that. He was just a kid at war, in love. He was twenty-two years old. He couldn't help it.

A few moments later Lee Strunk crawled out of the tunnel. He came up grinning, filthy but alive. Lieutenant Cross nodded and closed his eyes while the others clapped Strunk on the back and made jokes about rising from the dead.

Worms, Rat Kiley said. Right out of the grave. Fuckin' zombie.

The men laughed. They all felt great relief.   25

Spook City, said Mitchell Sanders.

Lee Strunk made a funny ghost sound, a kind of moaning, yet very happy, and right then, when Strunk made that high happy moaning sound, when he went *Ahhooooo*, right then Ted Lavender was shot in the head on his way back from peeing. He lay with his mouth open. The teeth were broken. There was a swollen black bruise under his left eye. The cheekbone was gone. Oh shit, Rat Kiley said, the guy's dead. The guy's dead, he kept saying, which seemed profound—the guy's dead. I mean really.

The things they carried were determined to some extent by superstition. Lieutenant Cross carried his good-luck pebble. Dave Jensen carried a rabbit's foot. Norman Bowker, otherwise a very gentle person, carried a thumb that had been presented to him as a gift by Mitchell Sanders. The thumb was dark brown, rubbery to the touch, and weighed four ounces at most. It had been cut from a VC° corpse, a boy of fifteen or sixteen. They'd found him at the bottom of an irrigation ditch, badly burned, flies in his mouth and eyes. The boy wore black shorts and sandals. At the time of his death he had been carrying a pouch of rice, a rifle, and three magazines of ammunition.

You want my opinion, Mitchell Sanders said, there's a definite moral here.

He put his hand on the dead boy's wrist. He was quiet for a time, as if   30
counting a pulse, then he patted the stomach, almost affectionately, and used Kiowa's hunting hatchet to remove the thumb.

VC: Viet Cong.

Henry Dobbins asked what the moral was.

Moral?

You know. *Moral.*

Sanders wrapped the thumb in toilet paper and handed it across to Norman Bowker. There was no blood. Smiling, he kicked the boy's head, watched the flies scatter, and said, It's like with that old TV show—Paladin. Have gun, will travel.

Henry Dobbins thought about it.   35

Yeah, well, he finally said. I don't see no moral.

There it *is,* man.

Fuck off.

They carried USO stationery and pencils and pens. They carried Sterno, safety pins, trip flares, signal flares, spools of wire, razor blades, chewing tobacco, liberated joss sticks and statuettes of the smiling Buddha, candles, grease pencils, *The Stars and Stripes,*° fingernail clippers, Psy Ops leaflets, bush hats, bolos, and much more. Twice a week, when the resupply choppers came in, they carried hot chow in green Mermite cans and large canvas bags filled with iced beer and soda pop. They carried plastic water containers, each with a two-gallon capacity. Mitchell Sanders carried a set of starched tiger fatigues for special occasions. Henry Dobbins carried Black Flag insecticide. Dave Jensen carried empty sandbags that could be filled at night for added protection. Lee Strunk carried tanning lotion. Some things they carried in common. Taking turns, they carried the big PRC-77 scrambler radio, which weighed thirty pounds with its battery. They shared the weight of memory. They took up what others could no longer bear. Often, they carried each other, the wounded or weak. They carried infections. They carried chess sets, basketballs, Vietnamese-English dictionaries, insignia of rank, Bronze Stars and Purple Hearts, plastic cards imprinted with the Code of Conduct. They carried diseases, among them malaria and dysentery. They carried lice and ringworm and leeches and paddy algae and various rots and molds. They carried the land itself—Vietnam, the place, the soil—a powdery orange-red dust that covered their boots and fatigues and faces. They carried the sky. The whole atmosphere, they carried it, the humidity, the monsoons, the stink of fungus and decay, all of it, they carried gravity. They moved like mules. By daylight they took sniper fire, at night they were mortared, but it was not battle, it was just the endless march, village to village, without purpose, nothing won or lost. They marched for the sake of the march. They plodded along slowly, dumbly, leaning forward against the heat, unthinking, all blood and bone, simple grunts, soldiering with their legs, toiling up the hills and down into the paddies and across the rivers and up again and down, just humping, one step and then the next and then another, but no volition, no will, because it was automatic, it was anatomy, and the war was entirely a matter of posture and carriage, the hump was everything,

Stars and Stripes: The military's officially sanctioned overseas newspaper.

a kind of inertia, a kind of emptiness, a dullness of desire and intellect and conscience and hope and human sensibility. Their principles were in their feet. Their calculations were biological. They had no sense of strategy or mission. They searched the villages without knowing what to look for, not caring, kicking over jars of rice, frisking children and old men, blowing tunnels, sometimes setting fires and sometimes not, then forming up and moving on to the next village, then other villages, where it would always be the same. They carried their own lives. The pressures were enormous. In the heat of early afternoon, they would remove their helmets and flak jackets, walking bare, which was dangerous but which helped ease the strain. They would often discard things along the route of march. Purely for comfort, they would throw away rations, blow their Claymores and grenades, no matter, because by nightfall the resupply choppers would arrive with more of the same, then a day or two later still more, fresh watermelons and crates of ammunition and sunglasses and woolen sweaters—the resources were stunning—sparklers for the Fourth of July, colored eggs for Easter. It was the great American war chest—the fruits of science, the smokestacks, the canneries, the arsenals at Hartford, the Minnesota forests, the machine shops, the vast fields of corn and wheat—they carried like freight trains; they carried it on their backs and shoulders—and for all the ambiguities of Vietnam, all the mysteries and unknowns, there was at least the single abiding certainty that they would never be at a loss for things to carry.

After the chopper took Lavender away, Lieutenant Jimmy Cross led his   40
men into the village of Than Khe. They burned everything. They shot chickens and dogs, they trashed the village well, they called in artillery and watched the wreckage, then they marched for several hours through the hot afternoon, and then at dusk, while Kiowa explained how Lavender died, Lieutenant Cross found himself trembling.

He tried not to cry. With his entrenching tool, which weighed five pounds, he began digging a hole in the earth.

He felt shame. He hated himself. He had loved Martha more than his men, and as a consequence Lavender was now dead, and this was something he would have to carry like a stone in his stomach for the rest of the war.

All he could do was dig. He used his entrenching tool like an ax, slashing, feeling both love and hate, and then later, when it was full dark, he sat at the bottom of his foxhole and wept. It went on for a long while. In part, he was grieving for Ted Lavender, but mostly it was for Martha, and for himself, because she belonged to another world, which was not quite real, and because she was a junior at Mount Sebastian College in New Jersey, a poet and a virgin and uninvolved, and because he realized she did not love him and never would.

Like cement, Kiowa whispered in the dark. I swear to God—boom-down. Not a word.

I've heard this, said Norman Bowker.   45

A pisser, you know? Still zipping himself up. Zapped while zipping.

All right, fine. That's enough.

Yeah, but you had to see it, the guy just—

I *heard,* man. Cement. So why not shut the fuck *up?*

Kiowa shook his head sadly and glanced over at the hole where Lieu-tenant Jimmy Cross sat watching the night. The air was thick and wet. A warm, dense fog had settled over the paddies and there was the stillness that precedes rain.

After a time Kiowa sighed.

One thing for sure, he said. The Lieutenant's in some deep hurt. I mean that crying jag—the way he was carrying on—it wasn't fake or any-thing, it was real heavy-duty hurt. The man cares.

Sure, Norman Bowker said.

Say what you want, the man does care.

We all got problems.

Not Lavender.

No, I guess not, Bowker said. Do me a favor, though.

Shut up?

That's a smart Indian. Shut up.

Shrugging, Kiowa pulled off his boots. He wanted to say more, just to lighten up his sleep, but instead he opened his New Testament and arranged it beneath his head as a pillow. The fog made things seem hollow and unat-tached. He tried not to think about Ted Lavender, but then he was thinking how fast it was, no drama, down and dead, and how it was hard to feel anything except surprise. It seemed un-Christian. He wished he could find some great sadness, or even anger, but the emotion wasn't there and he couldn't make it happen. Mostly he felt pleased to be alive. He liked the smell of the New Testament under his cheek, the leather and ink and paper and glue, whatever the chemicals were. He liked hearing the sounds of night. Even his fatigue, it felt fine, the stiff muscles and the prickly awareness of his own body, a floating feeling. He enjoyed not being dead. Lying there, Kiowa admired Lieutenant Jimmy Cross's capacity for grief. He wanted to share the man's pain, he wanted to care as Jimmy Cross cared. And yet when he closed his eyes, all he could think was Boom-down, and all he could feel was the pleasure of having his boots off and the fog curling in around him and the damp soil and the Bible smells and the plush comfort of night.

After a moment Norman Bowker sat up in the dark.

What the hell, he said. You want to talk, *talk.* Tell it to me.

Forget it.

No, man, go on. One thing I hate, it's a silent Indian.

For the most part they carried themselves with poise, a kind of dignity. Now and then, however, there were times of panic, when they squealed or wanted to squeal but couldn't, when they twitched and made moaning sounds and covered their heads and said Dear Jesus and flopped around on the earth and fired their weapons blindly and cringed and sobbed and begged for the noise to stop and went wild and made stupid promises to themselves and to God and to their mothers and fathers, hoping not to die. In different ways, it happened to all of them. Afterward, when the firing ended, they would blink and peek up. They would touch their bodies, feeling shame, then quickly hiding it. They would force themselves to stand. As if in slow motion, frame by frame, the world would take on the old logic—absolute silence, then the wind, then sunlight, then voices. It was the burden of being alive. Awkwardly, the men would reassemble themselves, first in private, then in groups, becoming soldiers again. They would repair the leaks in their eyes. They would check for casualties, call in dust-offs, light cigarettes, try to smile, clear their throats and spit and begin cleaning their weapons. After a time someone would shake his head and say, No lie, I almost shit my pants, and someone else would laugh, which meant it was bad, yes, but the guy had obviously not shit his pants, it wasn't that bad, and in any case nobody would ever do such a thing and then go ahead and talk about it. They would squint into the dense, oppressive sunlight. For a few moments, perhaps, they would fall silent, lighting a joint and tracking its passage from man to man, inhaling, holding in the humiliation. Scary stuff, one of them might say. But then someone else would grin or flick his eyebrows and say, Roger-dodger, almost cut me a new asshole, *almost.*

There were numerous such poses. Some carried themselves with a sort of wistful resignation, others with pride or stiff soldierly discipline or good humor or macho zeal. They were afraid of dying but they were even more afraid to show it.

They found jokes to tell.

They used a hard vocabulary to contain the terrible softness. *Greased,* they'd say. *Offed, lit up, zapped while zipping.* It wasn't cruelty, just stage presence. They were actors and the war came at them in 3-D. When someone died, it wasn't quite dying, because in a curious way it seemed scripted, and because they had their lines mostly memorized, irony mixed with tragedy, and because they called it by other names, as if to encyst and destroy the reality of death itself. They kicked corpses. They cut off thumbs. They talked grunt lingo. They told stories about Ted Lavender's supply of tranquilizers, how the poor guy didn't feel a thing, how incredibly tranquil he was.

There's a moral here, said Mitchell Sanders.

They were waiting for Lavender's chopper, smoking the dead man's dope. 70

The moral's pretty obvious, Sanders said, and winked. Stay away from drugs. No joke, they'll ruin your day every time.

Cute, said Henry Dobbins.

Mind-blower, get it? Talk about wiggy—nothing left, just blood and brains.

They made themselves laugh.

There it is, they'd say, over and over, as if the repetition itself were an 75 act of poise, a balance between crazy and almost crazy, knowing without going. There it is, which meant be cool, let it ride, because oh yeah, man, you can't change what can't be changed, there it is, there it absolutely and positively and fucking well *is*.

They were tough.

They carried all the emotional baggage of men who might die. Grief, terror, love, longing—these were intangibles, but the intangibles had their own mass and specific gravity, they had tangible weight. They carried shameful memories. They carried the common secret of cowardice barely restrained, the instinct to run or freeze or hide, and in many respects this was the heaviest burden of all, for it could never be put down, it required perfect balance and perfect posture. They carried their reputations. They carried the soldier's greatest fear, which was the fear of blushing. Men killed, and died, because they were embarrassed not to. It was what had brought them to the war in the first place, nothing positive, no dreams of glory or honor, just to avoid the blush of dishonor. They died so as not to die of embarrassment. They crawled into tunnels and walked point and advanced under fire. Each morning, despite the unknowns, they made their legs move. They endured. They kept humping. They did not submit to the obvious alternative, which was simply to close the eyes and fall. So easy, really. Go limp and tumble to the ground and let the muscles unwind and not speak and not budge until your buddies picked you up and lifted you into the chopper that would roar and dip its nose and carry you off to the world. A mere matter of falling, yet no one ever fell. It was not courage, exactly; the object was not valor. Rather, they were too frightened to be cowards.

By and large they carried these things inside, maintaining the masks of composure. They sneered at sick call. They spoke bitterly about guys who had found release by shooting off their own toes or fingers. Pussies, they'd say. Candyasses. It was fierce, mocking talk, with only a trace of envy or awe, but even so, the image played itself out behind their eyes.

They imagined the muzzle against flesh. They imagined the quick, sweet pain, then the evacuation to Japan, then a hospital with warm beds and cute geisha nurses.

They dreamed of freedom birds.

At night, on guard, staring into the dark, they were carried away by jumbo jets. They felt the rush of takeoff. *Gone!* they yelled. And then velocity, wings and engines, a smiling stewardess—but it was more than a plane, it was a real bird, a big sleek silver bird with feathers and talons and high screeching. They were flying. The weights fell off, there was nothing to bear. They laughed and held on tight, feeling the cold slap of wind and altitude, soaring, thinking *It's over, I'm gone!*—they were naked, they were light and free—it was all lightness, bright and fast and buoyant, light as light, a helium buzz in the brain, a giddy bubbling in the lungs as they were taken up over the clouds and the war, beyond duty, beyond gravity and mortification and global entanglements—*Sin loi!* they yelled, *I'm sorry, motherfuckers, but I'm out of it, I'm goofed, I'm on a space cruise, I'm gone!*—and it was a restful, disencum-

80

bered sensation, just riding the light waves, sailing that big silver freedom bird over the mountains and oceans, over America, over the farms and great sleeping cities and cemeteries and highways and the golden arches of Mc-Donald's. It was flight, a kind of fleeing, a kind of falling, falling higher and higher, spinning off the edge of the earth and beyond the sun and through the vast, silent vacuum where there were no burdens and where everything weighed exactly nothing. *Gone!* they screamed, *I'm sorry but I'm gone!* And so at night, not quite dreaming, they gave themselves over to lightness, they were carried, they were purely borne.

On the morning after Ted Lavender died, First Lieutenant Jimmy Cross crouched at the bottom of his foxhole and burned Martha's letters. Then he burned the two photographs. There was a steady rain falling, which made it difficult, but he used heat tabs and Sterno to build a small fire, screening it with his body, holding the photographs over the tight blue flame with the tips of his fingers.

He realized it was only a gesture. Stupid, he thought. Sentimental, too, but mostly just stupid.

Lavender was dead. You couldn't burn the blame.

Besides, the letters were in his head. And even now, without photo-   85 graphs, Lieutenant Cross could see Martha playing volleyball in her white gym shorts and yellow T-shirt. He could see her moving in the rain.

When the fire died out, Lieutenant Cross pulled his poncho over his shoulders and ate breakfast from a can.

There was no great mystery, he decided.

In those burned letters Martha had never mentioned the war, except to say, Jimmy, take care of yourself. She wasn't involved. She signed the letters "Love," but it wasn't love, and all the fine lines and technicalities did not matter.

The morning came up wet and blurry. Everything seemed part of everything else, the fog and Martha and the deepening rain.

It was a war, after all.   90

Half smiling, Lieutenant Jimmy Cross took out his maps. He shook his head hard, as if to clear it, then bent forward and began planning the day's march. In ten minutes, or maybe twenty, he would rouse the men and they would pack up and head west, where the maps showed the country to be green and inviting. They would do what they had always done. The rain might add some weight, but otherwise it would be one more day layered upon all the other days.

He was realistic about it. There was that new hardness in his stomach.

No more fantasies, he told himself.

Henceforth, when he thought about Martha, it would be only to think that she belonged elsewhere. He would shut down the daydreams. This was not Mount Sebastian, it was another world, where there were no pretty poems or midterm exams, a place where men died because of carelessness and gross stupidity. Kiowa was right. Boom down, and you were dead, never partly dead.

Briefly, in the rain, Lieutenant Cross saw Martha's gray eyes gazing   95
back at him.

He understood.

It was very sad, he thought. The things men carried inside. The things men did or felt they had to do.

He almost nodded at her, but didn't.

Instead he went back to his maps. He was now determined to perform his duties firmly and without negligence. It wouldn't help Lavender, he knew that, but from this point on he would comport himself as a soldier. He would dispose of his good-luck pebble. Swallow it, maybe, or use Lee Strunk's slingshot, or just drop it along the trail. On the march he would impose strict field discipline. He would be careful to send out flank security, to prevent straggling or bunching up, to keep his troops moving at the proper pace and at the proper interval. He would insist on clean weapons. He would confiscate the remainder of Lavender's dope. Later in the day, perhaps, he would call the men together and speak to them plainly. He would accept the blame for what had happened to Ted Lavender. He would be a man about it. He would look them in the eyes, keeping his chin level, and he would issue the new SOPs in a calm, impersonal tone of voice, an officer's voice, leaving no room for argument or discussion. Commencing immediately, he'd tell them, they would no longer abandon equipment along the route of march. They would police up their acts. They would get their shit together, and keep it together, and maintain it neatly and in good working order.

He would not tolerate laxity. He would show strength, distancing   100
himself.

Among the men there would be grumbling, of course, and maybe worse, because their days would seem longer and their loads heavier, but Lieutenant Cross reminded himself that his obligation was not to be loved but to lead. He would dispense with love; it was not now a factor. And if anyone quarreled or complained, he would simply tighten his lips and arrange his shoulders in the correct command posture. He might give a curt little nod. Or he might not. He might just shrug and say Carry on, then they would saddle up and form into a column and move out toward the villages of Than Khe.

Considerations

1. List the "things" carried by the men as they move through the Vietnamese countryside. Write a brief response to several of these "things," discussing what the men's choices suggest about their hopes, their fears, and their values.

2. To what extent is Lieutenant Cross responsible for Ted Lavender's death? Why does he think he is responsible? How does his response to Lavender's death change his attitude toward his command?
3. Evaluate the responses of the men to Lavender's death.
4. Mitchell Sanders says, "There's a moral here." Do you see any moral to the story of Lavender's death? To the story of the others' responses to his death?
5. How do Lieutenant Cross's fantasies about Martha change throughout the story? What significance do you see in these changes? Do you see them as negative? Positive? Or something else?

JANICE MIRIKITANI (1942–)

Spoils of War

*Born shortly after the United States entered World War II, Janice Mirikitani
is a third-generation Japanese American who, along with her family, was held
in an internment camp by the United States government during the war. Mirikitani lives and works in San Francisco and recently received her master of arts
degree in creative writing from San Francisco State University. In addition to
writing fiction and poetry, Mirikitani works as a dancer and teacher. She is
also an activist, advocating social and political justice in the communities where
she lives. She is currently the program director and president of the Corporation
at Glide Church/Urban Center. Mirikitani has served as editor for the following publications:* Aion, Third World Women, Time to Greesz!, Incantations from the Third World, *and* AYUMI, A Japanese American
Anthology. *Her published anthologies include* Awake in the River *and*
Shedding Silence: Poetry and Prose *(1987).*

Violet ran up the familiar path of Telman Park determined today to
make five miles. She knew the exact spot of her destination, through the
eucalyptus, past the emergency telephone box, up to the twin boulders where
she would sit triumphantly and rest in the warm sun.

He watched her from his green Volkswagen van. Her black hair bouncing at her shoulder blades, her sturdy thighs and sleek runner's calves. Her
small breasts jousled with each step under the sweatshirt that read, "Lotus
Blossom Doesn't Live Here."

Spirit of the bayonet.
red/march
white/hup
blue/eyes front
square your piece
left/right
kill 'em
thrust/jab
jab
jab/kill 'em,
"hey mamasan,
joto mate ichiban"
poontang one/two
poontang three/four
when we're done
we'll kill some more.

Of all the joggers he saw, this was the one he wanted. He would park and watch the several who, at the same time each day, would run the path up into the wooded hills of the park.

Violet started running after she had met Josh. In fact, she started doing a lot of things. All her life she had been introverted, studious, conscientious, shy. During her last graduate year, life revolted around her. There were so many demonstrations on campus against the Vietnam war, she didn't pay attention to the noises—the speeches, doomsday messages from wild-eyed street preachers and twitching panhandlers. So when the police stormed the gathered protestors, Violet did not move out of the way in time as the sweep of billyclubs and helmets picked her up like a wave. Violet hit the cement with her elbow, and curled up reflexively to protect her head from the stampede of legs and feet. Josh had stumbled over her and scrambling up, lifted her with him.

In the months of their new relationship, the world she had pulled around herself like a narrow corridor began to swell and pulse as they talked of civil rights, the war, military tycoonism, racism that had many faces. They saw and touched their common wounds.

Josh talked about his war. He who escaped the draft, his mother's endless work to help him through college, his father whose heart was crushed by the humiliation of worklessness. His father's death gave him life, the circumstance for exemption from the military, and the freedom to revolt, protest.

Violet talked about her war. The sheets of silence that covered history from the moment the gates slammed her parents into concentration camps in Arkansas. Her mother distant and forgetful. Her father demanding, critical. It didn't seem to matter what Violet achieved. They kept their silence like blades beneath their tongues.

Violet passed the old eucalyptus, branching high, its constant falling leaves and shedding bark making the air smell pungent. She noticed the green van, dismissed it in the glaring light of afternoon.

He crouched lower behind the wheel as she passed, seeing her closer, the dark sloping eyes, her olive skin browned by the sun, her delicate mouth and bones above her cheek. The beads of sweat popping around her brow.

They all had Vietnamese women.
None like mine.
She was bamboo thin,
her fingers clutching

the hem of her sleeve
like a child.
I felt red flame
licking the nape of my neck burning
deeper than napalm.
She was quiet,
her eyes, darker than night
helped me forget my My Lais.
Her beautiful body
curling around me,
flesh cocooned me against the
jungle where eyes were like rain,
Her arms like ivory bracelets
encircling my pain.
Flesh whole, sensual, shining
amidst the stench of rotting wounds
that fed the fat flies.
The insatiable flies of Vietnam.

Violet felt her anger draining with each step. The pounds shed, the   10
tightening of her thighs, the new curves at her hips, and the thoughts of
leaving home soon. Free as the wind in her face. Free from the jagged
silences of her mother, the brooding disapproval of her father. Violet had
informed them that she would be moving in with Josh. Perhaps they would
live in Oregon where he was interviewing for a job at the University. She
smiled, thinking of Josh's return, his sardonic grin when she told him of her
parents' reaction. Josh who encouraged her to run, to strengthen herself, to
speak her mind, to open her body, so long wrapped in years of suffocation.
Her body that she had felt pitifully shapeless, small, powerless, burdened with
blame and fault. If only he had not died. He was not due for another month.
Her mother's face, pinched in pain as water and blood ran from her, rushed
to the hospital. Her mother's body, wracked, gray, heaving and bellowing.
The child tearing to exit too soon. She could still hear the screams from her
mother's bones. The son, born dead. She remembered feeling alone. The
weight of their grief, the sense of regret that she remained alive, on her small
shoulders. All these years, the weight like boulders, the weight now shedding
with each step.

The sun was a hot hand on her back as Violet ran through the threaded
leaves, cracking beneath her steady feet.

He could feel the drugs wearing off. His skin twitching. He imagined
the sores popping anew, the smell from jungle rot seeping from his pale flesh,
tinted blue. He knew he would vomit.

She never withheld her warm thighs,
even when gorged with woman blood,
hot blood

sucking me deeper into her.
All the blood that would fill
a river.
Those jungles, villages like
a body split, slit, gouged
Blood on me.
Swelling within her,
my blade, gleaming in the moonlight
exits flesh, flashes in her eyes.
She licks the blood from the shaft.
Deep, I thrust it past her teeth.
She took it all
her throat tightening on it
blood bubbling from the edges
of her lips.
Her arms circling my hips,
her hands moving in my groin
with grenade.
My blade cuts the arm away,
splits her womb
that spumes hot blood.

Violet noticed the day emptier, the sun hotter. No wind. She would reach her boulders today. Her mouth opened slightly as she pushed her breath. The path became clearer, the trees very still. Like entering a strange new place. She remembered her corridor where she withdrew, compressed by whispers of guilt, mother's unhappiness, father's loneliness. Her narrow corridor, airless. Dark. Her flesh lined the walls. Josh's hands touching, warming her surfaces, expanding. His long runner's body entering her corners. Breathing. She discovers sensation. Muscles moving, sinews of desire. Nerve endings alive.

Violet stood before her parents and shouted. Her mother threatened to kill herself. Her father informed her she could never bring Josh into his house. It was bad enough to marry outside her race, but to live in sin with someone especially *that* color is endless disgrace. Violet's fury unleashed like exploding walls. She would leave this week. Run free of them. Lift it all from her like the wind picking up leaves and spinning them to the sky.

The son, blue and breathless, wrinkled like a raisin. Mother gave up   15
back then, switched off her eyes. Her dull face all these years never saw her daughter's pain. Well, Violet didn't want to take it on anymore. Can't bring him back to life. Can't trade places, can't be what they want, no matter what she did. Had he lived, he'd be in college or a soldier drafted, maybe dead anyway in Southeast Asia.

Violet running faster. She'd live her own life. She could see the boulders now.

He, crouching behind the trees, watched her lengthening shadow climbing the boulder where she lay down, stretched her bare arms and legs glistening with sweat. Her body lifted by her panting breath.

He pulls her by both legs onto the ground. She is surprised, not knowing how she fell. He pulls her to him, hand over her mouth and drags her into the trees. Her legs are strong, digging into the soft earth, resisting, thrashing. He reveals the long knife unsheathed, whispers that he will cut her throat if she screams. Violet retreats into her corridor, breathing quietly through her nose. He leads her far from the path, under brush and thicket of trees. He commands her to kneel in the leaves. Violet, terror exploding, screams, her fists beating against his pressing body, suffocating, scarred, distorted flesh. He falls upon her like a rock. His fists beat her again, brutally again, until she is unconscious. He pulls her shorts off, and gently. Gently. Caressing, kisses her slightly open mouth, her neck, her still arms. Inserts his blade in her womb and makes her bleed.

After, he carefully dresses himself. With a wide arched swing of his sharp knife, he severs her arm above the elbow.

Wiping the blood from his blade, gently he wraps the arm in his flak   20
jacket. Carries it like a child to his van and leaves.

The wind is still, the sun falling, casting long shadows from the boulders, the trees. In the thicket, the faint hum of flies gathering.

> Spirit of the bayonet.
> red/march
> white/hup
> blue/eyes front
> Square your piece
> left/right
> kill 'em
> thrust/jab
> jab
> jab/kill 'em
> "hey mamasan
> joto mate ichiban"
> poontang one/two
> poontang three/four
> when we're done
> we'll kill some more.

Considerations

1. Who is the man in the green Volkswagen? List as many details as you can, referring both to prose descriptions and to the poems that run through his head.
2. How does Violet characterize her parents? What does she consider the most important events in her parents' lives? How does she believe these

events have affected their relationship with her and the way they view the world?

3. How does Violet's relationship with Josh contrast with the relationship between the man in the Volkswagen and the woman he knew in Vietnam?

4. What does the motto on Violet's sweatshirt, "Lotus Blossom Doesn't Live Here," suggest about the way she wants others to see her? How do the stereotypes addressed by this motto relate to the story's conflicts?

5. Consider the story's title. What is the literal meaning of the phrase "spoils of war"? How does this phrase relate to the characters in this story? In your response, include all characters, including those in the thoughts of Violet and the man.

JORGE LUIS BORGES (1899–1986)
The End of the Duel

> *Jorge Luis Borges was born in Buenos Aires and grew up in a household*
> *where his father, a professor of psychology, frequently challenged him with com-*
> *plex philosophical puzzles. As an adult, Borges continued to explore these*
> *puzzles in his writing. After completing university studies in Spain, he joined*
> *a group of writers whose work is described as* Ultráisme: *writing that empha-*
> *sizes figures of speech—symbols, metaphors, and images—more than the ele-*
> *ments of character, conflict, action, or theme. After returning to Buenos Aires*
> *in 1921, Borges developed a writing style that drew on the antirealism of*
> *Ultráisme, but he no longer restricted himself to the boundaries of this move-*
> *ment. Among his best known works are* Fictions *(1944),* Labyrinths
> *(1962),* The Aleph and Other Stories *(1970), and* Doctor Brodie's
> Report *(1972).*

It's a good many years ago now that Carlos Reyles, the son of the
Uruguayan novelist, told me the story one summer evening out in Adrogué.
In my memory, after all this time, the long chronicle of a feud and its grim
ending are mixed up with the medicinal smell of the eucalyptus trees and the
babbling voices of birds.

We sat talking, as usual, of the tangled history of our two countries,
Uruguay and the Argentine. Reyles said that probably I'd heard of Juan
Patricio Nolan, who had won quite a reputation as a brave man, a practical
joker, and a rogue. Lying, I answered yes. Though Nolan had died back in
the nineties, people still thought of him as a friend. As always happens,
however, he had his enemies as well. Reyles gave me an account of one of
Nolan's many pranks. The thing had happened a short time before the battle
of Manantiales; two gauchos from Cerro Largo, Manuel Cardoso and Carmen Silveira, were the leading characters.

How and why did they begin hating each other? How, after a century,
can one unearth the long-forgotten story of two men whose only claim to
being remembered is their last duel? A foreman of Reyles' father, whose
name was Laderecha and "who had the whiskers of a tiger," had collected
from oral accounts certain details that I transcribe now with a good deal of
misgiving, since both forgetfulness and memory are apt to be inventive.

Manuel Cardoso and Carmen Silveira had a few acres of land that
bordered each other. Like the roots of other passions, those of hatred are
mysterious, but there was talk of a quarrel over some unbranded cattle or a
free-for-all horse race in which Silveira, who was the stronger of the two,
had run Cardoso's horse off the edge of the course. Months afterward, a long
two-handed game of *truco*° of thirty points was to take place in the local

---

truco: A card game.

saloon. Following almost every hand, Silveira congratulated his opponent on his skill, but in the end left him without a cent. When he tucked his winnings away in his money belt, Silveira thanked Cardoso for the lesson he had been given. It was then, I believe, that they were at the point of having it out. The game had had its ups and downs. In those rough places and in that day, man squared off against man and steel against steel. But the onlookers, who were quite a few, separated them. A peculiar twist of the story is that Manuel Cardoso and Carmen Silveira must have run across each other out in the hills on more than one occasion at sundown or at dawn, but they never actually faced each other until the very end. Maybe their poor and monotonous lives held nothing else for them than their hatred, and that was why they nursed it. In the long run, without suspecting it, each of the two became a slave to the other.

I no longer know whether the events I am about to relate are effects   5 or causes. Cardoso, less out of love than out of boredom, took up with a neighbor girl, La Serviliana. That was all Silveira had to find out, and, after his manner, he began courting her and brought her to his shack. A few months later, finding her in the way, he threw her out. Full of spite, the woman tried to seek shelter at Cardoso's. Cardoso spent one night with her, and by the next noon packed her off. He did not want the other man's leavings.

It was around that same time, just before or just after La Serviliana, that the incident of Silveira's sheepdog took place. Silveira was very fond of the animal, and had named him Treinta y Tres, after Uruguay's thirty-three founding fathers. When the dog was found dead in a ditch, Silveira was quick to suspect who had given it poison.

Sometime during the winter of 1870, a civil war broke out between the Colorados, or Reds, who were in power, and Aparicio's Blancos, or Whites. The revolution found Silveira and Cardoso in the same crossroads saloon where they had played their game of cards. A Brazilian half-breed, at the head of a detachment of gaucho militiamen, harangued all those present, telling them that the country needed them and that the government oppression was unbearable. He handed around white badges to mark them as Blancos, and at the end of his speech, which nobody understood, everyone in the place was rounded up. They were not allowed even to say goodbye to their families.

Manuel Cardoso and Carmen Silveira accepted their fate; a soldier's life was no harder than a gaucho's. Sleeping in the open on their sheepskin saddle blankets was something to which they were already hardened, and as for killing men, that held no difficulty for hands already in the habit of killing cattle. The clinking of stirrups and weapons is one of the things always heard when cavalry enter into action. The man who is not wounded at the outset thinks himself invulnerable. A lack of imagination freed Cardoso and Silveira from fear and from pity, although once in a while, heading a charge, fear brushed them. They were never homesick. The idea of patriotism was alien to them, and, in spite of the badges they wore on their hats, one party was to them the same as the other. During the course of marches and counter-marches, they learned what a man could do with a spear, and they found out that being companions allowed them to go on being enemies. They fought shoulder to shoulder and, for all we know, did not exchange a single word.

It was in the sultry fall of 1871 that their end was to come. The fight, which would not last an hour, happened in a place whose name they never knew. (Such places are later named by historians.) On the eve of battle, Cardoso crept on all fours into his officer's tent and asked him sheepishly would he save him one of the Reds if the Whites won the next day, because up till then he had not cut anyone's throat and he wanted to know what it was like. His superior promised him that if he handled himself like a man he would be granted that favor.

The Whites outnumbered the enemy, but the Reds were better equipped and cut them down from the crown of a hill. After two unsuccessful charges that never reached the summit, the Whites' commanding officer, badly wounded, surrendered. On the very spot, at his own request, he was put to death by the knife.

The men laid down their arms. Captain Juan Patricio Nolan, who commanded the Reds, arranged the expected execution of the prisoners down to the last detail. He was from Cerro Largo himself, and knew all about the old rivalry between Silveira and Cardoso. He sent for the pair and told them, "I already know you two can't stand the sight of each other, and that for some time now you've been looking for a chance to have it out. I have good news for you. Before sundown, the two of you are going to have that chance to show who's the better man. I'm going to stand you up and have your throats cut, and then you'll run a race. God knows who'll win." The soldier who had brought them took them away.

It was not long before the news spread throughout the camp. Nolan had made up his mind that the race would close the proceedings, but the prisoners sent him a representative to tell him that they, too, wanted to be spectators and to place wagers on the outcome. Nolan, who was an understanding man, let himself be convinced. The bets were laid down—money, riding gear, spears, sabers, and horses. In due time they would be handed over to the widows and next of kin. The heat was unusual. So that no one would miss his siesta, things were delayed until four o'clock. Nolan, in the South American style, kept them waiting another hour. He was probably discussing the campaign with his officers, his aide shuttling in and out with the maté° kettle.

Both sides of the dirt road in front of the tents were lined with prisoners, who, to make things easier, squatted on the ground with their hands tied behind their backs. A few of them relieved their feelings in a torrent of swearwords, one went over and over the beginning of the Lord's Prayer,

10

---

maté: A strong tea-like drink made from the South American yerba plant.

almost all were stunned. Of course, they would not smoke. They no longer cared about the race now, but they all watched.

"They'll be cutting my throat on me, too," one of them said, showing his envy.

"Sure, but along with the mob," said his neighbor.   15

"Same as you," the first man snapped back.

With his saber, a sergeant drew a line in the dust across the road. Silveira's and Cardoso's wrists had been untied so that they could run freely. A space of some five yards was between them. Each man toed the mark. A couple of the officers asked the two not to let them down because everyone had placed great faith in them, and the sums they had bet on them came to quite a pile.

It fell to Silveira's lot to draw as executioner the mulatto Nolan, whose forefathers had no doubt been slaves of the captain's family and therefore bore his name. Cardoso drew the Reds' official cutthroat, a man from Corrientes well along in years, who, to comfort a condemned man, would pat him on the shoulder and tell him, "Take heart, friend. Women go through far worse when they give birth."

Their torsos bent forward, the two eager men did not look at each other. Nolan gave the signal.

The mulatto, swelling with pride to be at the center of attention, over-   20
did his job and opened a showy slash that ran from ear to ear; the man from Corrientes did his with a narrow slit. Spurts of blood gushed from the men's throats. They dashed forward a number of steps before tumbling face down. Cardoso, as he fell, stretched out his arms. Perhaps never aware of it, he had won.

Considerations

1. In the first paragraph, the narrator notes that "the long chronicle of a feud and its grim ending are mixed up with the medicinal smell of the eucalyptus trees and the babbling voices of birds." Think about a memory of an unforgettable incident that someone described to you. Describe the memory, including both the incident and the images (sights, sounds, tastes, smells, sensation) that you associate with hearing the anecdote.

2. In paragraph 4, the narrator says that the roots of hatred are mysterious. Do you agree? Argue for or against this statement, providing evidence from your own observations and experiences to support your ideas.

3. According to the narrator, Cardoso and Silveira never experienced fear or pity because of "a lack of imagination." How might imagination be necessary for a person to feel fear or pity? Explain your response by citing examples from the story as well as from your own experiences and observations.

4. In what ways might the following elements be related: (1) the original feud between Cardoso and Silveira, (2) the war between the Reds and the Whites, and (3) the final duel between Cardoso and Silveira?

5. Read Borges's comments in "The Meaning and Form of 'The End of the Duel'" (page 1049). Then reread the story. Explain how learning Borges's views affected your response to the story.

Commentary

JORGE LUIS BORGES (1899–1986)
The Meaning and Form of "The End of the Duel"°

DI GIOVANNI: *Spurts of blood gushed from the men's throats. They dashed forward a number of steps before tumbling face down. Cardoso, as he fell, stretched out his arms. Perhaps never aware of it, he had won.*

BORGES: This is what always happens: We never know whether we are victors or whether we are defeated.

DI GIOVANNI: Borges, how long did you carry this story around in your head before you set it down?

BORGES: I must have carried it some twenty-five or thirty years. When I first heard it, I thought it was striking. The man who told it to me published it in *La Nación* under the title "*Crepusculo rojo*"—"Reddish Twilight"—but as he wrote it in a style full of purple patches, I felt I could hardly compete with him. After his death I wrote it down in as straightforward a way as possible. In between times, I carried it around in my memory for years, boring my friends with it. . . .

DI GIOVANNI: But can you say something about how you sift the   5
material and take only what you want? For instance, can you remember any facts that you didn't use from the anecdote you were told?

BORGES: No, because I was told it in a very bare way, and then Reyles wrote it down in a way full of purple patches and fine writing—the kind of thing I do my best to avoid. I can't write like that; I only went in for what might be called circumstantial invention. For example, I had to make them play *truco,* and I invented the episode about the sheep dog, and I gave him the right name—Treinta y Tres—because that's the kind of name a dog might have, although they are generally called Jazmín.

MACSHANE: Do you sometimes take one factual episode and combine it with another to make something new—a new story from two completely disconnected and different sources?

BORGES: Yes. In this story, for example, I witnessed the *truco* game not in Uruguay, but in the old Northside of Buenos Aires. . . .

Setting: In 1971, Jorge Luis Borges was a guest lecturer at a series of meetings for graduate students in the writing program at Columbia University. The commentary that follows is a portion of a transcript made during one of those meetings, in which translator Norman Thomas di Giovanni read sections of the story aloud. From time to time, Borges stopped the reading to offer comments and to invite questions from those who were present. The queries labeled "Question" came from graduate students, while those labeled "MacShane" came from Columbia professor Frank MacShane, who, with Norman Thomas di Giovanni and Frank Halpern, later edited a book, *Borges on Writing* (1973), which included the transcript of the entire series.

QUESTION: I believe that in one of your essays you wrote that a short story can be centered either on the characters or on the situation. In this story, characterization is at a minimum . . .

BORGES: It had to be minimal because the two characters are more or less the same character. They are two gauchos, but they could be two hundred or two thousand. They are not Hamlets or Raskolnikovs or Lord Jims.° They are just gauchos.

QUESTION: Then the situation is what counts?

BORGES: Yes, in this case. And generally speaking, what I think is most important in a short story is the plot or situation, while in a novel what's important are the characters. You may think of *Don Quixote* as being written with incidents, but what is really important are the two characters, Don Quixote and Sancho Panza. In the Sherlock Holmes saga, also, what is really important is the friendship between a very intelligent man and a rather dumb fellow like Dr. Watson. Therefore—if I may be allowed a sweeping statement—in writing a novel, you should know all about the characters, and any plot will do, while in a short story it is the situation that counts. That would be true for Henry James,° for example, or for Chesterton.°

QUESTION: Do you find some special vision of life in the anecdotes you use?

BORGES: I find that most of my stories come from anecdotes, although I distort or change them. Some, of course, come from characters, from people I know. In the short story, I think an anecdote may serve as a beginning point.

QUESTION: Do you think the changes you make are inherent in the anecdote?

BORGES: Well, that's a hard nut to crack. I don't know if they're inherent in the anecdote or not, but I know that I need them. If I told a story swiftly and curtly, it wouldn't be effective at all. I have tried to make this one effective by slowing it down. I couldn't begin by saying, "Two gauchos hated each other," because nobody would believe it. I had to make the hatred seem real. . . .

MACSHANE: Do you think [political and social issues] should be dealt with in fiction?

BORGES: In this story, there was nothing of the kind.

DI GIOVANNI: But there is.

BORGES: There may have been, for all I know, but I wasn't concerned about that. I was concerned with the idea of the two men running a race with their throats cut and of the whole thing's being thought of as a

---

Raskolnikovs . . . Lord Jims: Raskolnikov is the main character in *Crime and Punishment,* a novel by Russian author Fyodor Dostoevsky (1821–1881). Lord Jim is a character in a novel by Joseph Conrad. *Henry James:* American novelist and short story writer. *Chesterton:* English scholar and author G. K. Chesterton (1874–1936), who, like Borges and James, wrote stories that focused on out-of-the-ordinary meetings between characters.

joke or prank. Naturally, this story is wound up with the history of Argentina and of Uruguay and of the gauchos. It has associations with the whole of South American history, the wars of liberation, and so on. But I wasn't concerned about that. I was merely trying to tell my story in a convincing way. That was all I was concerned about, although you can link it to anything you like.

DI GIOVANNI: And in spite of your aims, it's a hell of a statement about politics at that time and in that place. It should satisfy anybody.

BORGES: And perhaps it's about the politics of any time or any place, I don't know. Of course, these politics are a bit picturesque.

QUESTION: How do you think the artist should relate to his own time?

BORGES: Oscar Wilde said that modernity of treatment and subject should be carefully avoided by the modern artist. Of course, he was being witty, but what he was saying was based on an obvious truth. Homer, for example, wrote several centuries after the Trojan war. The idea that a writer should be contemporaneous is itself modern, but I should say it belongs more to journalism than to literature. No real writer ever tried to be contemporary.

THOMAS HARDY (1840–1928)
The Man He Killed

> *Thomas Hardy was born and grew up in southeastern England, a region that he later fictionalized as "Wessex" in many of his novels. As a young man, he worked for several years as an apprentice to an ecclesiastical architect, but in 1861 he moved to London, seeking an education. He practiced architecture while attending King's College in the evenings. After completing his studies in 1867, he devoted all his time to writing poetry and fiction. His best known novels include* Tess of the d'Urbervilles *(1891) and* Jude the Obscure *(1896).*

    Had he and I but met
      By some old ancient inn,
We should have sat us down to wet
      Right many a nipperkin!

    But ranged as infantry,   5
      And staring face to face,
I shot at him as he at me,
      And killed him in his place.

    I shot him dead because—
      Because he was my foe.   10

Just so: my foe of course he was;
   That's clear enough; although

He thought he'd list, perhaps,
   Off-hand like—just as I—
Was out of work—had sold his traps—
   No other reason why.

                                                 15

Yes; quaint and curious war is!
   You shoot a fellow down
You'd treat, if met where any bar is,
   Or help to half-a-crown.

                                               20

Considerations

1. Describe the speaker. What kind of man is he? What kind of work does he do? What does he enjoy in his free time? What are his values?
2. Reread lines 9 and 10. What is the effect of the repeated word "because"? How would the meaning change if one "because" were omitted?
3. What questions does the poem raise about war? Does it suggest any answers to those questions? Explain.

WILFRED OWEN (1893–1918)

Dulce et Decorum Est°

> After growing up in the peaceful countryside of his native Shropshire, Wilfred Owen attended London University. A few years later, after teaching in England and France, he enlisted in the British Army. While serving in World War I, he wrote letters home, kept a journal, and composed poems describing and analyzing the horror he encountered every day. In 1917, he was wounded, but he returned to action only to be killed in 1918, a few days before the Armistice was signed.

Bent double, like old beggars under sacks,
Knock-kneed, coughing like hags, we cursed through sludge,
Till on the haunting flares we turned our backs
And towards our distant rest began to trudge.

Dulce et Decorum Est: "It is sweet and fitting." The words come from Horace's *Odes,* II.ii.13. The full quotation, given in the poem's final line, means, "It is sweet and fitting to die for one's country."

Men marched asleep. Many had lost their boots   5
But limped on, blood-shod. All went lame; all blind;
Drunk with fatigue; deaf even to the hoots
Of tired, outstripped Five-Nines° that dropped behind.

Gas! GAS! Quick, boys!—An ecstasy of fumbling,
Fitting the clumsy helmets just in time;   10
But someone still was yelling out and stumbling
And flound'ring like a man in fire or lime° . . .
Dim, through the misty panes and thick green light,
As under a green sea, I saw him drowning.

In all my dreams, before my helpless sight,   15
He plunges at me, guttering, choking, drowning.

If in some smothering dreams you too could pace
Behind the wagon that we flung him in,
And watch the white eyes writhing in his face,
His hanging face, like a devil's sick of sin;   20
If you could hear, at every jolt, the blood
Come gargling from the froth-corrupted lungs,
Obscene as cancer, bitter as the cud

Of vile, incurable sores on innocent tongues,—
My friend, you would not tell with such high zest   25
To children ardent for some desperate glory,
The old Lie: *Dulce et decorum est*
Pro patria mori.

8 *Five-Nines:* Gas bombs used by Germans in World War I. 12 *lime:* Quick-lime, a chemical that dissolves flesh and bones.

Considerations

1. Who are the people described in the opening stanza? What do the images Owen chooses suggest about their response to the circumstances they must face?
2. What purpose is served by the graphic details of the gas attack and, particularly, of the death of the soldier?
3. The Latin sentence, *Dulce et decorum est pro patria mori,* means "It is sweet and fitting to die for one's country." Owen, along with other British schoolchildren, would have learned this motto in his Latin classes. Do children today receive similar messages in school? Explain.

KARL SHAPIRO (1913–   )

The Conscientious Objector

Born in Baltimore, Karl Shapiro served in World War II. During this time, he wrote several volumes of poetry, including V-Letter and Other Poems *(1944), for which he won the Pulitzer Prize. His later collections of poetry include* Poems of a Jew *(1958) and* Collected Poems *(1978). In addition, he has won acclaim for his works of literary criticism, such as* Beyond Criticism *(1953) and* The Poetry Wreck *(1975).*

The gates clanged and they walked you into jail
More tense than felons but relieved to find
The hostile world shut out, flags that dripped
From every mother's windowpane, obscene
The bloodlust sweating from the public heart,   5
The dog authority slavering at your throat.
A sense of quiet, of pulling down the blind
Possessed you. Punishment you felt was clean.

The decks, the catwalks, and the narrow light
Composed a ship. This was a mutinous crew   10
Troubling the captains for plain decencies,
A *Mayflower* brim with pilgrims headed out
To establish new theocracies to west,
A Noah's ark coasting the topmost seas
Ten miles above the sodomites and fish.   15
These inmates loved the only living doves.

Like all men hunted from the world you made
A good community, voyaging the storm
To no safe Plymouth or green Ararat;°
Trouble or calm, the men with Bibles prayed,   20
The gaunt politicals construed our hate.
The opposite of all armies, you were best
Opposing uniformity and yourselves;
Prison and personality were your fate.

You suffered not so physically but knew   25
Maltreatment, hunger, ennui of the mind.
Well might the soldier kissing the hot beach
Erupting in his face damn all your kind.
Yet you who saved neither yourselves nor us

19 *Ararat:* The highest peak in Turkey, the landing place of Noah's ark.

Are equally with those who shed the blood   30
The heroes of our cause. Your conscience is
What we come back to in the armistice.

Considerations

1. Why have the men in this poem been imprisoned? What are their different responses to that imprisonment?
2. Who is the speaker in the poem? What is his attitude toward the conscientious objector he describes?
3. What is your response to the comparisons of the prison, filled with conscientious objectors, to Noah's ark and to the *Mayflower?*

CAROLYN FORCHÉ (1950–   )

The Colonel

> *Born to a working-class family in Detroit, Michigan, Carolyn Forché attended Catholic school during grades 1 through 12. She credits her school experiences with the "profound religious morality" that is an integral part of her writing. From January 1978 to March 1980, working for Amnesty International, she traveled to El Salvador to gather and verify information relating to human rights violations. Her book* The Country Between Us *(1982), from which "The Colonel" is excerpted, documents her experiences in El Salvador. Forché's other published works include* Flowers from the Volcano, *which is a volume of translations of the poetry of Claribel Alegría (1982), and* El Salvador: Work of Thirty Photographers *(1983).*

What you have heard is true. I was in his house. His wife carried a tray of coffee and sugar. His daughter filed her nails, his son went out for the night. There were daily papers, pet dogs, a pistol on the cushion beside him. The moon swung bare on its black cord over the house. On the television was a cop show. It was in English. Broken bottles were embedded in the walls around the house to scoop the kneecaps from a man's legs or cut his hands to lace. On the windows there were gratings like those in liquor stores. We had dinner, rack of lamb, good wine, a gold bell was on the table for calling the maid. The maid brought green mangoes, salt, a type of bread. I was asked how I enjoyed the country. There was a brief commercial in Spanish. His wife took everything away. There was some talk then of how difficult it had become to govern. The parrot said hello on the terrace. The colonel told it to shut up, and pushed himself from the table. My friend said to me with his eyes: say nothing. The colonel returned with a sack used to bring groceries home. He spilled many human ears on the table. They were like dried peach halves. There is no other way to say this. He took one of them in his hands, shook it in our faces, dropped it into a water glass. It came alive there. I am tired of fooling around he said. As for the rights of anyone, tell your people they can go fuck themselves. He swept the ears to the floor with his arm and held the last of his wine in the air. Something for your poetry, no? he said. Some of the ears on the floor caught this scrap of his voice. Some of the ears on the floor were pressed to the ground.

ELIZABETH BARRETT BROWNING (1806–1861)

Mother and Poet°
(Turin, After News from Gaeta, 1861)

> *Until the age of thirty-nine, Elizabeth Barrett lived in her father's house where, as a semi-invalid, she wrote poetry that was widely published and praised by the Victorian public. Although she preferred seclusion, she did occasionally receive visitors and, shortly before her fortieth birthday, she accepted a call from the poet Robert Browning. The two fell in love and, in defiance of Barrett's father, secretly married and eloped to Italy. The Brownings remained in Italy for many years, where they raised their son, Pen, and became deeply committed to the Italian nationalist cause.*

1

DEAD! One of them shot by the sea in the east,
　And one of them shot in the west by the sea.
Dead! both my boys! When you sit at the feast
　And are wanting a great song for Italy free,
　　Let none look at *me!*　　　　　　　　　　5

2

Yet I was a poetess only last year,
　And good at my art, for a woman, men said;
But *this* woman, *this,* who is agonised here,
　—The east sea and west sea rhyme on in her head
　　For ever instead.　　　　　　　　　　10

3

What art can a woman be good at? Oh, vain!
　What art *is* she good at, but hurting her breast

Mother and Poet: The persona in this poem is Laura Savio, Italian poet and patriot. Her sons were both killed in the battle over the unification of Italy in 1861.

With the milk-teeth of babes, and a smile at the pain?
  Ah boys, how you hurt! you were strong as you pressed,
    And I proud, by that test.   15

4

What art's for a woman? To hold on her knees
  Both darlings! to feel all their arms round her throat,
Cling, strangle a little! to sew by degrees
  And 'broider the long-clothes and neat little coat;
    To dream and to doat.   20

5

To teach them . . . It stings there! *I* made them indeed
  Speak plain the word *country*. *I* taught them, no doubt,
That a country's a thing men should die for at need.
  I prated of liberty, rights, and about
    The tyrant cast out.   25

6

And when their eyes flashed . . . Oh my beautiful eyes! . . .
  I exulted; nay, let them go forth at the wheels
Of the guns, and denied not. But then the surprise
  When one sits quite alone! Then one weeps, then one kneels!
    God, how the house feels!   30

7

At first, happy news came, in gay letters moiled
  With my kisses,—of camp-life and glory, and how
They both loved me; and, soon coming home to be spoiled
  In return would fan off every fly from my brow
    With their green laurel-bough.   35

8

Then was triumph at Turin: "Ancona was free!"
  And some one came out of the cheers in the street,
With a face pale as stone, to say something to me.
  My Guido was dead! I fell down at his feet,
    While they cheered in the street.   40

9

I bore it; friends soothed me; my grief looked sublime
  As the ransom of Italy. One boy remained
To be leant on and walked with, recalling the time
  When the first grew immortal, while both of us strained
    To the height he had gained.   45

10

And letters still came, shorter, sadder, more strong,
  Writ now but in one hand, "I was not to faint,—
One loved me for two—would be with me ere long:
  And *Viva l'Italia!*°—he died for, our saint,
    Who forbids our complaint."

50

11

My Nanni would add, "he was safe, and aware
  Of a presence that turned off the balls,—was imprest
It was Guido himself, who knew what I could bear,
  And how 'twas impossible, quite dispossessed
    To live on for the rest."

55

12

On which, without pause, up the telegraph line
  Swept smoothly the next news from Gaeta:—*Shot.*
Tell his mother. Ah, ah, "his," "their" mother,—not "mine,"
  No voice says "*My* mother" again to me. What!
    You think Guido forgot?

60

13

Are souls straight so happy that, dizzy with Heaven,
  They drop earth's affections, conceive not of woe?
I think not. Themselves were too lately forgiven
  Through THAT Love and Sorrow which reconciled so
    The Above and Below.

65

14

O Christ of the five wounds, who look'dst through the dark
  To the face of thy mother! consider, I pray,
How we common mothers stand desolate, mark,
  Whose sons, not being Christs, die with eyes turned away
    And no last word to say!

70

15

Both boys dead? but that's out of nature. We all
  Have been patriots, yet each house must always keep one.
'Twere imbecile, hewing out roads to a wall;
  And, when Italy's made, for what end is it done
    If we have not a son?

75

49 *Viva l'Italia!*: Long live (united) Italy!

16

Ah, ah, ah! when Gaeta's taken, what then?
    When the fair wicked queen° sits no more at her sport
Of the fire-balls of death crashing souls out of men?
    When the guns of Cavalli° with final retort
        Have cut the game short?   80

17

When Venice and Rome keep their new jubilee°
    When your flag takes all heaven for its white, green, and red,
When *you* have your country from mountain to sea,
    When King Victor has Italy's crown on his head,
        (And *I* have my Dead)—   85

18

What then? Do not mock me. Ah, ring your bells low,
    And burn your lights faintly! *My* country is *there,*
Above the star pricked by the last peak of snow:
    My Italy's THERE, with my brave civic Pair,
        To disfranchise despair!   90

19

Forgive me. Some women bear children in strength,
    And bite back the cry of their pain in self-scorn;
But the birth-pangs of nations will wring us at length
    Into wail such as this—and we sit on forlorn
        When the man-child is born.   95

20

Dead! One of them shot by the sea in the east,
    And one of them shot in the west by the sea.
Both! both my boys! If in keeping the feast
    You want a great song for your Italy free,
        Let none look at *me!*   100

77 *fair wicked queen:* Maria, wife of Frances II, the last king of the Neapolitan government, a force that opposed unification.   79 *Cavalli:* General who commanded the siege of Gaeta, where Nanni, Laura Savio's second son, was killed.   81 *new jubilee:* In 1861, when the poem was written, Venice and Rome were still not part of united Italy.

Considerations

1. In this poem, the speaker is the Italian poet and patriot Laura Savio, whose two sons died fighting in the war for the unification of Italy. One son was killed in the attack on the fortress at Ancona and the other at the

siege of Gaeta. How does knowing this historical background affect your
response to the poem? Or do you find your response unchanged? Explain.

2. What is the speaker's initial attitude toward the war? How and why does
her attitude change?

3. What is your response toward the mother's changing position? Are you
sympathetic? Critical? Something else? Explain.

ARIEL DORFMAN (1942–   )

Hope

*A native of Argentina, Ariel Dorfman later emigrated to Chile, where he
became involved in protests against the military dictatorship that took over the
government after the assassination of Salvador Allende. Dorfman's activism led
to his expulsion from Chile, and he now lives in the United States. His works
include the play* Death and the Maiden *(1992),* Last Waltz in Santiago
(1988), and My House Is on Fire: Short Stories *(1991).*

My son has been
missing
since May 8
of last year.

They took him   5
just for a few hours
they said
just for some routine
questioning.

After the car left,   10
the car with no license plate,
we couldn't

find out

anything else
about him.   15
But now things have changed.
We heard from a compañero
who just got out
that five months later
they were torturing him   20

in Villa Grimaldi,
at the end of September
they were questioning him
in the red house
that belonged to the Grimaldis.   25

    They say they recognized
    his voice his screams
    they say.

Somebody tell me frankly
what times are these   30
what kind of world
what country?
What I'm asking is
how can it be
that a father's   35
joy
a mother's
joy
is knowing
that they   40
that they are still
torturing
their son?
Which means
that he was alive   45
five months later
and our greatest
hope
will be to find out
next year   50
that they're still torturing him
eight months later

and he may   might   could
still be alive.

WALT WHITMAN (1819–1892)

The Dying Veteran
(A Long Island incident—early part of the nineteenth century)

For biographical information on Walt Whitman, see page 943.

Amid these days of order, ease, prosperity,
Amid the current songs of beauty, peace, decorum,
I cast a reminiscence—(likely 'twill offend you,
I heard it in my boyhood;)—More than a generation since,
A queer old savage man, a fighter under Washington himself, 5
(Large, brave, cleanly, hot-blooded, no talker, rather spiritualistic,
Had fought in the ranks—fought well—had been all through the
    Revolutionary war,)
Lay dying—sons, daughters, church-deacons, lovingly tending him,
Sharping their sense, their ears, towards his murmuring, half-caught words:
"Let me return again to my war-days, 10
To the sights and scenes—to forming the line of battle,
To the scouts ahead reconnoitering,
To the cannons, the grim artillery,
To the galloping aids, carrying orders,
To the wounded, the fallen, the heat, the suspense, 15
The perfume strong, the smoke, the deafening noise;
Away with your life of peace!—your joys of peace!
Give me my old wild battle-life again!"

DENISE LEVERTOV (1923–   )

What Were They Like?
(Questions and Answers)

*Born and raised in England, Denise Levertov first became exposed to war
during World War II, when she worked as a nurse at a British hospital in
Paris. She married Mitchell Goodman, an American writer, and emigrated to
the United States in 1948. Her writing career led her to serve as poet-in-
residence at several universities, including the Massachusetts Institute of Technology and Tufts University. A political activist, Levertov has been deeply
involved in antiwar protests and the antinuclear movement. Her works include*
The Sorrow Dance *(1967)*, Relearning the Alphabet *(1970), and Candles in Babylon *(1982).*

1) Did the people of Viet Nam
   use lanterns of stone?
2) Did they hold ceremonies
   to reverence the opening of buds?
3) Were they inclined to rippling laughter?   5
4) Did they use bone and ivory,
   jade and silver, for ornament?
5) Had they an epic poem?
6) Did they distinguish between speech and singing?

1) Sir, their light hearts turned to stone.   10
   It is not remembered whether in gardens
   stone lanterns illumined pleasant ways.
2) Perhaps they gathered once to delight in blossom,
   but after the children were killed
   there were no more buds.   15
3) Sir, laughter is bitter to the burned mouth.
4) A dream ago, perhaps. Ornament is for joy.
   All the bones were charred.
5) It is not remembered. Remember,
   most were peasants; their life   20
   was in rice and bamboo.
   When peaceful clouds were reflected in the paddies
   and the water-buffalo stepped surely along terraces,
   maybe fathers told their sons old tales.
   When bombs smashed the mirrors   25
   there was time only to scream.
6) There is an echo yet, it is said,
   of their speech which was like a song.
   It is reported their singing resembled
   the flight of moths in moonlight.   30
   Who can say? It is silent now.

RANDALL JARRELL (1914–1965)

Gunner

*Randall Jarrell was born in Nashville, Tennessee, and served as a navigation
tower operator in the United States Air Force during World War II. Following
the war, he taught at Sarah Lawrence College, Kenyon College, and the
Women's College of the University of North Carolina. He has published a
novel,* Pictures from an Institution *(1954), as well as several volumes of
poetry, including* Little Friend, Little Friend *(1945),* Losses *(1948), and*
The Lost World *(1965).*

Did they send me away from my cat and my wife
To a doctor who poked me and counted my teeth,
To a line on a plain, to a stove in a tent?
Did I nod in the flies of the schools?

And the fighters rolled into the tracer like rabbits,   5
The blood froze over my splints like a scab—
Did I snore, all still and grey in the turret,
Till the palms rose out of the sea with my death?

And the world ends here, in the sand of a grave,
All my wars over? . . . It was easy as that!   10
Has my wife a pension of so many mice?
Did the medals go home to my cat?

FERNANDO ARRABAL (1932–   )

Picnic on the Battlefield

> *Born in Spanish Morocco, Fernando Arrabal grew up in Madrid. At the age of only fourteen, Arrabal wrote* Picnic on the Battlefield, *a work that reflects the dark vision of his early years, a vision that was perhaps the result of his poor health and his growing frustration with political oppression. As a young man, he continued to experience many health problems, including bouts with tuberculosis. In 1955, he moved to Paris to escape both family problems and government censorship in Spain. Surgery in 1957 greatly improved his health, and he subsequently went on to write more plays, many of which were initially staged in Paris theaters.*

Characters

ZAPO, *a soldier*
MONSIEUR TÉPAN, *the soldier's father*
MADAME TÉPAN, *the soldier's mother*
ZÉPO, *an enemy soldier*
FIRST STRETCHER BEARER
SECOND STRETCHER BEARER

Scene   *A battlefield. The stage is covered with barbed wire and sandbags. The battle is at its height. Rifle shots, exploding bombs and machine guns can be heard.*

ZAPO is alone on the stage; flat on his stomach, hidden among the sandbags. He is very frightened. The sound of the fighting stops. Silence.

ZAPO takes a ball of wool and some needles out of a canvas workbag and starts knitting a pullover, which is already quite far advanced. The field telephone, which is by his side, suddenly starts ringing.

ZAPO: Hallo, hallo . . . yes, Captain . . . yes, I'm the sentry of sector 47 . . . Nothing new, Captain . . . Excuse me, Captain, but when's the fighting going to start again? And what am I supposed to do with the hand-grenades? Do I chuck them in front of me or behind me? . . . Don't get me wrong. I didn't mean to annoy you . . . Captain, I really feel terribly lonely, couldn't you send me someone to keep me company? . . . even if it's only a nanny-goat? *(The* CAPTAIN *is obviously severely reprimanding him.)* Whatever you say, Captain, whatever you say. *(*ZAPO *hangs up. He mutters to himself. Silence. Enter* MONSIEUR *and* MADAME TÉPAN *carrying baskets as if they were going on a picnic. They address their son, who has his back turned and doesn't see them come in.)*

MONS. T. *(ceremoniously)*: Stand up, my son, and kiss your mother on the brow. *(*ZAPO, *surprised, gets up and kisses his mother very respectfully on the forehead. He is about to speak, but his father doesn't give him a chance.)* And now, kiss *me.*

ZAPO: But, dear Father and dear Mother, how did you dare to come all this way, to such a dangerous place? You must leave at once.

MONS. T.: So you think you've got something to teach your father about war and danger, do you? All this is just a game to me. How many times—to take the first example that comes to mind—have I got off an underground train while it was still moving.

MME. T.: We thought you must be bored, so we came to pay you a little visit. This war must be a bit tedious, after all.

ZAPO: It all depends.

MONS. T.: I know exactly what happens. To start with you're attracted by the novelty of it all. It's fun to kill people, and throw hand-grenades about, and wear uniforms—you feel smart, but in the end you get bored stiff. You'd have found it much more interesting in my day. Wars were much more lively, much more highly colored. And then, the best thing was that there were horses, plenty of horses. It was a real pleasure; if the Captain ordered us to attack, there we all were immediately, on horseback, in our red uniforms. It was a sight to be seen. And then there were the charges at the gallop, sword in hand, and suddenly you found yourself face to face with the enemy, and he was equal to the occasion too—with his horses—there were always horses, lots of horses, with their well-rounded rumps—in his highly-polished boots, and his green uniform.

MME. T.: No, no, the enemy uniform wasn't green. It was blue. I remember distinctly that it was blue.

MONS. T.: I tell you it was green.

MME. T.: When I was little, how many times did I go out to the balcony to watch the battle and say to the neighbour's little boy: 'I bet you a gum-drop the blues win.' And the blues were our enemies.

MONS. T.: Oh, well, you must be right, then.

MME. T.: I've always liked battles. As a child I always said that when I grew up I wanted to be a Colonel of dragoons. But my mother wouldn't hear of it, you know how she will stick to her principles at all costs.

MONS. T.: Your mother's just a half-wit.

ZAPO: I'm sorry, but you really must go. You can't come into a war unless you're a soldier.

MONS. T.: I don't give a damn, we came here to have a picnic with you in the country and to enjoy our Sunday.

MME. T.: And I've prepared an excellent meal, too. Sausage, hard-boiled eggs—you know how you like them!—ham sandwiches, red wine, salad, and cakes.

ZAPO: All right, let's have it your way. But if the Captain comes he'll be absolutely furious. Because he isn't at all keen on us having visits when we're at the front. He never stops telling us: "Discipline and hand-grenades are what's wanted in war, not visits."

MONS. T.: Don't worry, I'll have a few words to say to your Captain.

ZAPO: And what if we have to start fighting again?

MONS. T.: You needn't think that'll frighten me, it won't be the first fighting I've seen. Now if only it was battles on horseback! Times have changed, you can't understand. *(Pause.)* We came by motor bike. No one said a word to us.

ZAPO: They must have thought you were the referees.

MONS. T.: We had enough trouble getting through, though. What with all the tanks and jeeps.

MME. T.: And do you remember the bottle-neck that cannon caused, just when we got here?

MONS. T.: You mustn't be surprised at anything in wartime, everyone knows that.

MME. T.: Good, let's start our meal.

MONS. T.: You're quite right, I feel as hungry as a hunter. It's the smell of gunpowder.

MME. T.: We'll sit on the rug while we're eating.

ZAPO: Can I bring my rifle with me?

MME. T.: You leave your rifle alone. It's not good manners to bring your rifle to table with you. *(Pause.)* But you're absolutely filthy, my boy. How on earth did you get into such a state? Let's have a look at your hands.

ZAPO *(ashamed, holding out his hands.)*: I had to crawl about on the ground during the manoeuvres.

MME. T.: And what about your ears?

ZAPO: I washed them this morning.

MME. T.: Well that's all right, then. And your teeth? *(He shows them.)* Very good. Who's going to give her little boy a great big kiss for cleaning his teeth so nicely? *(To her husband.)* Well, go on, kiss your son for cleaning his teeth so nicely. (M. TÉPAN *kisses his son.)* Because, you know, there's one thing I *will* not have, and that's making fighting a war an excuse for not washing.

ZAPO: Yes, mother. *(They eat.)*

MONS. T.: Well, my boy, did you make a good score?

ZAPO: When?

MONS. T.: In the last few days, of course.

ZAPO: Where?

MONS. T.: At the moment, since you're fighting a war.

ZAPO: No, nothing much. I didn't make a good score. Hardly ever scored a bull.

MONS. T.: Which are you best at shooting, enemy horses or soldiers?

ZAPO: No, not horses, there aren't any horses any more.

MONS. T.: Well, soldiers then?

ZAPO: Could be.

MONS. T.: Could be? Aren't you sure?

ZAPO: Well you see . . . I shoot without taking aim, *(pause)* and at the same time I say a Pater Noster for the chap I've shot.

MONS. T.: You must be braver than that. Like your father.

MME. T.: I'm going to put a record on. *(She puts a record on the gramophone—a pasodoble.° All three are sitting on the ground, listening.)*

MONS. T.: That really *is* music. Yes indeed, ole! *(The music continues. Enter an enemy soldier: ZÉPO. He is dressed like ZAPO. The only difference is the colour of their uniforms. ZÉPO is in green and ZAPO is in grey. ZÉPO listens to the music openmouthed. He is behind the family so they can't see him. The record ends. As he gets up ZAPO discovers ZÉPO. Both put their hands up. M. and MME. TÉPAN look at them in surprise.)* What's going on? *(ZAPO reacts—he hesitates. Finally, looking as if he's made up his mind, he points his rifle at ZÉPO.)*

ZAPO: Hands up! *(ZÉPO puts his hands up even higher, looking even more terrified. ZAPO doesn't know what to do. Suddenly he goes over quickly to ZÉPO and touches him gently on the shoulder, like a child playing a game of "tag.")* Got you! *(To his father, very pleased.)* There we are! A prisoner!

MONS. T.: Fine. And now what're you going to do with him?

ZAPO: I don't know, but, well, could be—they might make me a corporal.

MONS. T.: In the meantime, you'd better tie him up.

ZAPO: Tie him up? Why?

MONS. T.: Prisoners always get tied up!

ZAPO: How?

MONS. T.: Tie up his hands.

MME. T.: Yes, there's no doubt about it, you must tie up his hands, I've always seen them do that.

ZAPO: Right. *(To his prisoner.)* Put your hands together, if you please.

ZÉPO: Don't hurt me too much.

ZAPO: I won't.

ZÉPO: Ow! You're hurting me.

MONS. T.: Now, now, don't maltreat your prisoner.

MME. T.: Is that the way I brought you up? How many times have I told you that we must be considerate of our fellow-men?

ZAPO: I didn't do it on purpose. *(To ZÉPO.)* And like that, does it hurt?

ZÉPO: No, it's all right like that.

MONS. T.: Tell him straight out, say what you mean, don't mind us.

ZÉPO: It's all right like that.

MONS. T.: Now his feet.

ZAPO: His feet as well, whatever next?

MONS. T.: Didn't they teach you the rules?

ZAPO: Yes.

MONS. T.: Well then!

ZAPO *(very politely, to ZÉPO)*: Would you be good enough to sit on the ground, please?

---

pasodoble: A lively dance.

ZÉPO: Yes, but don't hurt me.

MME. T.: You'll see, he'll take a dislike to you.

ZAPO: No he won't, no he won't. I'm not hurting you, am I?

ZÉPO: No, that's perfect.

ZAPO: Papa, why don't you take a photo of the prisoner on the ground and me with my foot on his stomach?

MONS. T.: Oh, yes that'd look good.

ZÉPO: Oh no, not that!

MME. T.: Say yes, don't be obstinate.

ZÉPO: No, I said no, and no it is.

MME. T.: But just a little teeny weeny photo, what harm could that do you? And we could put it in the dining room, next to the life-saving certificate my husband won thirteen years ago.

ZÉPO: No—you won't shift me.

ZAPO: But why won't you let us?

ZÉPO: I'm engaged. And if she sees the photo one day, she'll say I don't know how to fight a war properly.

ZAPO: No she won't, all you'll need to say is that it isn't you, it's a panther.

MME. T.: Come on, do say yes.

ZÉPO: All right then. But only to please you.

ZAPO: Lie down flat. *(ZÉPO lies down. ZAPO puts a foot on his stomach and grabs his rifle with a martial air.)*

MME. T.: Stick your chest out a bit further.

ZAPO: Like this?

MME. T.: Yes like that, and don't breathe.

MONS. T.: Try to look like a hero.

ZAPO: What d'you mean, like a hero?

MONS. T.: It's quite simple; try and look like the butcher does when he's boasting about his successes with the girls.

ZAPO: Like this?

MONS. T.: Yes, like that.

MME. T.: The most important thing is to puff your chest out and not breathe.

ZÉPO: Have you nearly finished?

MONS. T.: Just be patient a moment. One . . . two . . . three.

ZAPO: I hope I'll come out well.

MME. T.: Yes, you looked very martial.

MONS. T.: You were fine.

MME. T.: It makes me want to have my photo taken with you.

MONS. T.: Now there's a good idea.

ZAPO: Right. I'll take it if you like.

MME. T.: Give me your helmet to make me look like a soldier.

ZÉPO: I don't want any more photos. Even one's far too many.

ZAPO: Don't take it like that. After all, what harm can it do you?

ZÉPO: It's my last word.

MONS. T. *(to his wife)*: Don't press the point, prisoners are always very sensitive. If we go on he'll get cross and spoil our fun.

ZAPO: Right, what're we going to do with him, then?

MME. T.: We could invite him to lunch. What do you say?

MONS. T.: I don't see why not.

ZAPO *(to* ZÉPO*)*: Well, will you have lunch with us, then?

ZÉPO: Er . . .

MONS. T.: We brought a good bottle with us.

ZÉPO: Oh well, all right then.

MME. T.: Make yourself at home, don't be afraid to ask for anything you want.

ZÉPO: All right.

MONS. T.: And what about you, did you make a good score?

ZÉPO: When?

MONS. T.: In the last few days, of course.

ZÉPO: Where?

MONS. T.: At the moment, since you're fighting a war.

ZÉPO: No, nothing much. I didn't make a good score, hardly ever scored a bull.

MONS. T.: Which are you best at shooting? Enemy horses or soldiers?

ZÉPO: No, not horses, there aren't any horses any more.

MONS. T.: Well, soldiers, then?

ZÉPO: Could be.

MONS. T.: Could be? Aren't you sure?

ZÉPO: Well you see . . . I shoot without taking aim, *(pause)* and at the same time I say an Ave Maria for the chap I've shot.

ZAPO: An Ave Maria? I'd have thought you'd have said a Pater Noster.

ZÉPO: No, always an Ave Maria. *(Pause.)* It's shorter.

MONS. T.: Come come, my dear fellow, you must be brave.

MME. T. *(to* ZÉPO*)*: We can untie you if you like.

ZÉPO: No, don't bother, it doesn't matter.

MONS. T.: Don't start getting stand-offish with us now. If you'd like us to untie you, say so.

MME. T.: Make yourself comfortable.

ZÉPO: Well, if that's how you feel, you can untie my feet, but it's only to please you.

MONS. T.: Zapo, untie him. *(*ZAPO *unties him.)*

MME. T.: Well, do you feel better?

ZÉPO: Yes, of course. I really am putting you to a lot of inconvenience.

MONS. T.: Not at all, just make yourself at home. And if you'd like us to untie your hands you only have to say so.

ZÉPO: No, not my hands, I don't want to impose upon you.

MONS. T.: No no, my dear chap, no no. I tell you, it's no trouble at all.

ZÉPO: Right . . . Well then, untie my hands too. But only for lunch, eh? I
   don't want you to think that you give me an inch and I take an ell.°

MONS. T.: Untie his hands, son.

MME. T.: Well, since our distinguished prisoner is so charming, we're going to have a marvelous day in the country.

ZÉPO: Don't call me your distinguished prisoner; just call me your prisoner.

MME. T.: Won't that embarrass you?

ZÉPO: No, no, not at all.

MONS. T.: Well, I must say you're modest. *(Noise of aeroplanes.)*

ZAPO: Aeroplanes. They're sure to be coming to bomb us. *(ZAPO and
   ZÉPO throw themselves on the sandbags and hide.) (To his parents.) Take
   cover. The bombs will fall on you. (The noise of the aeroplanes overpowers
   all the other noises. Bombs immediately start to fall. Shells explode very near
   the stage but not on it. A deafening noise. ZAPO and ZÉPO are cowering
   down between the sandbags. M. TÉPAN goes on talking calmly to his wife,
   and she answers in the same unruffled way. We can't hear what they are saying
   because of the bombing. MME. TÉPAN goes over to one of the baskets and
   takes an umbrella out of it. She opens it. M. and MME. TÉPAN shelter under
   it as if it were raining. They are standing up. They shift rhythmically from one
   foot to the other and talk about their personal affairs. The bombing continues.
   Finally the aeroplanes go away. Silence. M. TÉPAN stretches an arm outside
   the umbrella to make sure that nothing more is falling from the heavens.)*

MONS. T. *(to his wife)*: You can shut your umbrella. *(MME. TÉPAN does so.
   They both go over to their son and tap him lightly on the behind with the
   umbrella.)* Come on, out you come. The bombing's over. *(ZAPO and
   ZÉPO come out of their hiding place.)*

ZAPO: Didn't you get hit?

MONS. T.: What d'you think could happen to your father? *(Proudly.)* Little
   bombs like that! Don't make me laugh! *(Enter, left, two Red Cross Soldiers. They are carrying a stretcher.)*

1ST STRETCHER BEARER: Any dead here?

ZAPO: No, no one around these parts.

1ST STRETCHER BEARER: Are you sure you've looked properly?

ZAPO: Sure.

1ST STRETCHER BEARER: And there isn't a single person dead?

ZAPO: I've already told you there isn't.

1ST STRETCHER BEARER: No one wounded, even?

ZAPO: Not even that.

2ND STRETCHER BEARER *(to the 1ST S. B.)*: Well, now we're in a
   mess! *(To ZAPO persuasively.)* Just look again, search everywhere, and
   see if you can't find us a stiff.

---

ell: A unit of measure equalling 45 inches.

1ST STRETCHER BEARER: Don't keep on about it, they've told you quite clearly there aren't any.

2ND STRETCHER BEARER: What a lousy trick!

ZAPO: I'm terribly sorry. I promise you I didn't do it on purpose.

2ND STRETCHER BEARER: That's what they all say. That no one's dead and that they didn't do it on purpose.

1ST STRETCHER BEARER: Oh, let the chap alone!

MONS. T. *(obligingly)*: We should be only too pleased to help you. At your service.

2ND STRETCHER BEARER: Well, really, if things go on like this I don't know what the Captain will say to us.

MONS. T.: But what's it all about?

2ND STRETCHER BEARER: Quite simply that the others' wrists are aching with carting so many corpses and wounded men about, and that we haven't found any yet. And it's not because we haven't looked!

MONS. T.: Well, yes, that really is annoying. *(To* ZAPO.*)* Are you quite sure no one's dead?

ZAPO: Obviously, Papa.

MONS. T.: Have you looked under all the sandbags?

ZAPO: Yes, Papa.

MONS. T. *(angrily)*: Well then, you might as well say straight out that you don't want to lift a finger to help these gentlemen, when they're so nice, too!

1ST STRETCHER BEARER: Don't be angry with him. Let him be. We must just hope we'll have more luck in another trench and that all the lot'll be dead.

MONS. T.: I should be delighted.

MME. T.: Me too. There's nothing I like more than people who put their hearts into their work.

MONS. T. *(indignantly, addressing his remarks to the wings)*: Then is no one going to do anything for these gentlemen?

ZAPO: If it only rested with me, it'd already be done.

ZÉPO: I can say the same.

MONS. T.: But look here, is neither of you even wounded?

ZAPO *(ashamed)*: No, not me.

MONS. T. *(to* ZÉPO*)*: What about you?

ZÉPO *(ashamed)*: Me neither. I never have any luck.

MME. T. *(pleased)*: Now I remember! This morning, when I was peeling the onions, I cut my finger. Will that do you?

MONS. T.: Of course it will! *(Enthusiastically.)* They'll take you off at once!

1ST STRETCHER BEARER: No, that won't work. With ladies it doesn't work.

MONS. T.: We're no further advanced, then.

1ST STRETCHER BEARER: Never mind.

2ND STRETCHER BEARER: We may be able to make up for it in the other trenches. *(They start to go off.)*

MONS. T.: Don't worry! If we find a dead man we'll keep him for you! No fear of us giving him to anyone else!

2ND STRETCHER BEARER: Thank you very much, sir.

MONS. T.: Quite all right, old chap, think nothing of it. *(The two stretcher bearers say goodbye. All four answer them. The stretcher bearers go out.)*

MME. T.: That's what's so pleasant about spending a Sunday in the country. You always meet such nice people.

MONS. T. *(pause):* But why are you enemies?

MME. T.: Your father is the only one who's capable of thinking such ideas; don't forget he's a former student of the Ecole Normale, *and* a philatelist.°

ZÉPO: I don't know, I'm not very well educated.

MME. T.: Was it by birth, or did you become enemies afterwards?

ZÉPO: I don't know, I don't know anything about it.

MONS. T.: Well then, how did you come to be in the war?

ZÉPO: One day, at home, I was just mending my mother's iron, a man came and asked me: "Are you Zépo?" "Yes." "Right, you must come to the war." And so I asked him: "But what war?" and he said: "Don't you read the papers then? You're just a peasant!" I told him I did read the papers but not the war bits. . . .

ZAPO: Just how it was with me—exactly how it was with me.

MONS. T.: Yes, they came to fetch you too.

MME. T.: No, it wasn't quite the same; that day you weren't mending an iron, you were mending the car.

MONS. T.: I was talking about the rest of it. *(To ZÉPO.)* Go on, what happened then?

ZÉPO: Then I told him I had a fiancée and that if I didn't take her to the pictures on Sundays she wouldn't like it. He said that wasn't the least bit important.

ZAPO: Just how it was with me—exactly how it was with me.

ZÉPO: And then my father came down, and he said I couldn't go to the war because I didn't have a horse.

ZAPO: Just what my father said.

ZÉPO: The man said you didn't need a horse any more, and I asked him if I could take my fiancée with me. He said no. Then I asked whether I could take my aunt with me so that she could make me one of her custards on Thursdays; I'm very fond of them.

MME. T. *(realizing that she'd forgotten it):* Oh! The custard!

ZÉPO: He said no again.

ZAPO: Same as with me.

Ecole Normale . . . philatelist: Student of the Teacher's College and a stamp collector.

ZÉPO: And ever since then I've been alone in the trench nearly all the time.

MME. T.: I think you and your distinguished prisoner might play together this afternoon, as you're as close to each other and so bored.

ZAPO: Oh no, Mother, I'm too afraid, he's an enemy.

MONS. T.: Now now, you mustn't be afraid.

ZAPO: If you only knew what the General was saying about the enemy!

MME. T.: What did he say?

ZAPO: He said the enemy are very nasty people. When they take prisoners they put little stones in their shoes so that it hurts them to walk.

MME. T.: How awful! What barbarians!

MONS. T. *(indignantly, to* ZÉPO*)*: And aren't you ashamed to belong to an army of criminals?

ZÉPO: I haven't done anything. I don't do anybody any harm.

MME. T.: He was trying to take us in, pretending to be such a little saint!

MONS. T.: We oughtn't to have untied him. You never know, we only need to turn our backs and he'll be putting a stone in our shoes.

ZÉPO: Don't be so nasty to me.

MONS. T.: What'd you think we *should* be, then? I'm indignant. I know what I'll do. I'll go and find the Captain and ask him to let me fight in the war.

ZAPO: He won't let you, you're too old.

MONS. T.: Then I'll buy myself a horse and a sword and come and fight on my own account.

MME. T.: Bravo! If I were a man I'd do the same.

ZÉPO: Don't be like that with me, Madame. Anyway I'll tell you something—our General told us the same thing about you.

MME. T.: How could he dare tell such a lie!

ZAPO: No—but the same thing really?

ZÉPO: Yes, the same thing.

MONS. T.: Perhaps it was the same man who talked to you both?

MME. T.: Well if it was the same man he might at least have said something different. That's a fine thing—saying the same thing to everyone!

MONS. T. *(to* ZÉPO *in a different tone of voice)*: Another little drink?

MME. T.: I hope you liked our lunch?

MONS. T.: In any case, it was better than last Sunday.

ZÉPO: What happened?

MONS. T.: Well, we went to the country and we put the food on the rug. While we'd got our backs turned a cow ate up all our lunch, and the napkins as well.

ZÉPO: What a greedy cow!

MONS. T.: Yes, but afterwards, to get our own back, we ate the cow. *(They laugh.)*

ZAPO *(to* ZÉPO*)*: They couldn't have been very hungry after that!

MONS. T.: Cheers! *(They all drink.)*

MME. T. *(to* ZÉPO*)*: And what do you do to amuse yourself in the trench?

ZÉPO: I spend my time making flowers out of rags, to amuse myself. I get terribly bored.

MME. T.: And what do you do with the flowers?

ZÉPO: At the beginning I used to send them to my fiancée, but one day she told me that the greenhouse and the cellar were already full of them and that she didn't know what to do with them any more, and she asked me, if I didn't mind, to send her something else.

MME. T.: And what did you do?

ZÉPO: I go on making rag flowers to pass the time.

MME. T.: Do you throw them away afterwards, then?

ZÉPO: No, I've found a way to use them now. I give one flower for each pal who dies. That way I know that even if I make an awful lot there'll never be enough.

MONS. T.: That's a good solution you've hit on.

ZÉPO (shyly): Yes.

ZAPO: Well, what I do is knit, so as not to get bored.

MME. T.: But tell me, are all the soldiers as bored as you?

ZÉPO: It all depends on what they do to amuse themselves.

ZAPO: It's the same on our side.

MONS. T.: Then let's stop the war.

ZÉPO: How?

MONS. T.: It's very simple. (To ZAPO.) You just tell your pals that the enemy soldiers don't want to fight a war, and you (to ZÉPO) say the same to your comrades. And then everyone goes home.

ZAPO: Marvellous!

MME. T.: And then you'll be able to finish mending the iron.

ZAPO: How is it that no one thought of such a good idea before?

MME. T.: Your father is the only one who's capable of thinking such ideas; don't forget he's a former student of the Ecole Normale, *and* a philatelist.

ZÉPO: But what will the sergeant-majors and corporals do?

MONS. T.: We'll give them some guitars and castanets to keep them quiet!

ZÉPO: Very good idea.

MONS. T.: You see how easy it is. Everything's fixed.

ZÉPO: We shall have a tremendous success.

ZAPO: My pals will be terribly pleased.

MME. T.: What d'you say to putting on the pasodoble we were playing just now, to celebrate?

ZÉPO: Perfect.

ZAPO: Yes, put the record on, Mother. (MME. TÉPAN *puts a record on. She turns the handle. She waits. Nothing can be heard.*)

MONS. T.: I can't hear a thing.

MME. T.: Oh, how silly of me! Instead of putting a record on I put on a beret. (*She puts the record on. A gay pasodoble is heard.* ZAPO *dances with* ZÉPO *and* MME. TÉPAN *with her husband. They are all very gay. The field telephone rings. None of the four hears it. They go on dancing busily. The telephone rings again. The dance continues.*

The battle starts up again with a terrific din of bombs, shots and bursts of machine-gun fire. None of the four has seen anything and they go on dancing merrily. A burst of machine-gun fire mows them all down. They fall to the ground, stone dead. A shot must have grazed the gramophone; the record keeps repeating the same thing, like a scratched record. The music of the scratched record can be heard till the end of the play. The two STRETCHER BEAR-ERS *enter left. They are carrying the empty stretcher.)*

SUDDEN CURTAIN

Considerations

1. How would you describe the relationship between Zapo and his mother and father? In your response, focus on the way each of these people views the war.
2. Explain the values you see represented by Zapo's actions toward Zépo. Does Zépo seem to share these values? Explain.
3. Arrabal calls his work "panic theater," which he sees as related to theater of the absurd. After reading the definition of "theater of the absurd" (page 66), explain whether you agree or disagree with Arrabal's assessment of his own work.
4. Argue for or against the following proposition: "*Picnic on the Battlefield* should be required reading for men and women who are training to be military officers." Explain your reasons through direct reference to the play.
5. Imagine a different ending for this play. Perhaps Zépo and Zapo do return to their units, carrying the message described by Monsieur Tépan. Write the scenes in which these exchanges take place.

SOPHOCLES (c. 496–406 B.C.)

Antigone

For biographical information on Sophocles, see page 423.

Characters

ANTIGONE ⎫
⎬ *daughters of Oedipus*
ISMENE ⎭
EURYDICE, *wife of Kreon*
KREON, *King of Thebes*
HAIMON, *son of Kreon*
TEIRESIAS, *a blind seer*
A SENTRY
A MESSENGER
CHORUS

Scene *Before the palace of* KREON, *King of Thebes. A central double door, and two lateral doors. A platform extends the length of the facade, and from this platform three steps lead down into the orchestra, or chorus-ground.*

Time *Dawn of the day after the repulse of the Argive army from the assault on Thebes.*

Prologue° (ANTIGONE *and* ISMENE *enter from the central door of the palace.*)

ANTIGONE: Ismene, dear sister,
    You would think that we had already suffered enough
    For the curse on Oedipus.°
    I cannot imagine any grief
    That you and I have not gone through. And now—   5
    Have they told you of the new decree of our King Kreon?
ISMENE: I have heard nothing: I know
    That two sisters lost two brothers, a double death
    In a single hour; and I know that the Argive army
    Fled in the night; but beyond this, nothing.   10
ANTIGONE: I thought so. And that is why I wanted you
    To come out here with me. There is something we must do.
ISMENE: Why do you speak so strangely?
ANTIGONE: Listen, Ismene:

Prologue: Section of the play that explains the background and current action. *3 curse on Oedipus:* Ismene's and Antigone's father, Oedipus, was formerly King of Thebes. As an infant, Oedipus was ordered to be killed when an Oracle predicted that he would one day kill his father and marry his mother. Rescued and raised by a shepherd and his wife, Oedipus later returns to Thebes, where, unaware, he fulfills the prophecy by killing King Laios (his father) and marrying Jocasta (his mother). When Oedipus and Jocasta discover the truth, Jocasta kills herself and Oedipus blinds himself and leaves Thebes. His sons, Eteocles and Polyneices, later kill each other in battle. Kreon, Oedipus's uncle and now King of Thebes, orders Eteocles to be buried but commands that Polyneices, who has attacked Thebes, remain unburied.

Kreon buried our brother Eteocles 15
With military honors, gave him a soldier's funeral,
And it was right that he should; but Polyneices,
Who fought as bravely and died as miserably,—
They say that Kreon has sworn
No one shall bury him, no one mourn for him, 20
But his body must lie in the fields, a sweet treasure
For carrion birds to find as they search for food.
That is what they say, and our good Kreon is coming here
To announce it publicly; and the penalty—
Stoning to death in the public square! 25
                              There it is,
And now you can prove what you are:
A true sister, or a traitor to your family.
ISMENE: Antigone, you are mad! What could I possibly do?
ANTIGONE: You must decide whether you will help me or not.
ISMENE: I do not understand you. Help you in what? 30
ANTIGONE: Ismene, I am going to bury him. Will you come?
ISMENE: Bury him! You have just said the new law forbids it.
ANTIGONE: He is my brother. And he is your brother, too.
ISMENE: But think of the danger! Think what Kreon will do!
ANTIGONE: Kreon is not strong enough to stand in my way. 35
ISMENE: Ah sister!
Oedipus died, everyone hating him
For what his own search brought to light, his eyes
Ripped out by his own hand; and Iocaste died,
His mother and wife at once: she twisted the cords 40
That strangled her life; and our two brothers died,
Each killed by the other's sword. And we are left:
But oh, Antigone,
Think how much more terrible than these
Our own death would be if we should go against Kreon 45
And do what he has forbidden! We are only women,
We cannot fight with men, Antigone!
The law is strong, we must give in to the law
In this thing, and in worse. I beg the Dead
To forgive me, but I am helpless: I must yield 50
To those in authority. And I think it is dangerous business
To be always meddling.
ANTIGONE: If that is what you think,
I should not want you, even if you asked to come.
You have made your choice, you can be what you want to be.
But I will bury him; and if I must die, 55
I say that this crime is holy: I shall lie down
With him in death, and I shall be as dear

To him as he is to me.
                              It is the dead,
Not the living, who make the longest demands:
We die for ever . . .
                              You may do as you like,   60
Since apparently the laws of the gods mean nothing to you.
ISMENE: They mean a great deal to me; but I have no strength
     To break laws that were made for the public good.
ANTIGONE: That must be your excuse, I suppose. But as for me,
     I will bury the brother I love.
ISMENE: Antigone,   65
     I am so afraid for you!
ANTIGONE: You need not be:
     You have yourself to consider, after all.
ISMENE: But no one must hear of this, you must tell no one!
     I will keep it a secret, I promise!
ANTIGONE: O tell it! Tell everyone!
     Think how they'll hate you when it all comes out   70
     If they learn that you knew about it all the time!
ISMENE: So fiery! You should be cold with fear.
ANTIGONE: Perhaps. But I am doing only what I must.
ISMENE: But can you do it? I say that you cannot.
ANTIGONE: Very well: when my strength gives out,   75
     I shall do no more.
ISMENE: Impossible things should not be tried at all.
ANTIGONE: Go away, Ismene:
     I shall be hating you soon, and the dead will too,
     For your words are hateful. Leave me my foolish plan: 80
     I am not afraid of the danger; if it means death,
     It will not be the worst of deaths—death without honor.
ISMENE: Go then, if you feel that you must.
     You are unwise,
     But a loyal friend indeed to those who love you.   85

(Exit into the palace. ANTIGONE *goes off, left. Enter the* CHORUS.*)*

PARODOS° • Strophe° 1

CHORUS: Now the long blade of the sun, lying
     Level east to west, touches with glory
     Thebes of the Seven Gates. Open, unlidded
     Eye of golden day! O marching light

Parodos: Chant sung by Chorus as they enter; *Strophe:* Chant sung by Chorus as they move from
stage right to stage left.

Across the eddy and rush of Dirce's stream,°   5
Striking the white shields of the enemy
Thrown headlong backward from the blaze of morning!
CHORAGOS:° Polyneices their commander
    Roused them with windy phrases,
    He the wild eagle screaming   10
    Insults above our land,
    His wings their shields of snow,
    His crest their marshalled helms.

Antistrophe° 1

CHORUS: Against our seven gates in a yawning ring
    The famished spears came onward in the night;   15
    But before his jaws were sated with our blood,
    Or pinefire took the garland of our towers,
    He was thrown back, and as he turned, great Thebes—
    No tender victim for his noisy power—
    Rose like a dragon behind him, shouting war.   20
CHORAGOS: For God hates utterly
    The bray of bragging tongues;
    And when he beheld their smiling,
    Their swagger of golden helms,
    The frown of his thunder blasted   25
    Their first man from our walls.

Strophe 2

CHORUS: We heard his shout of triumph high in the air
    Turn to a scream; far out in a flaming arc
    He fell with his windy torch, and the earth struck him.
    And others storming in fury no less than his   30
    Found shock of death in the dusty joy of battle.
CHORAGOS: Seven captains at seven gates
    Yielded their clanging arms to the god
    That bends the battle-line and breaks it.
    These two only, brothers in blood,   35
    Face to face in matchless rage,
    Mirroring each the other's death,
    Clashed in long combat.

5 *Dirce's stream:* River near Thebes. 8 *Choragos:* Leader of chorus. *Antistrophe:* Chant sung by
Chorus as they move from stage left to stage right.

Antistrophe 2

CHORUS: But now in the beautiful morning of victory
    Let Thebes of the many chariots sing for joy!   40
    With hearts for dancing we'll take leave of war:
    Our temples shall be sweet with hymns of praise,
    And the long nights shall echo with our chorus.

SCENE 1

CHORAGOS: But now at last our new King is coming:
    Kreon of Thebes, Menoikeus' son.
    In this auspicious dawn of his reign
    What are the new complexities
    That shifting Fate has woven for him?   5
    What is his counsel? Why has he summoned
    The old men to hear him?

(Enter KREON *from the palace, center. He addresses the* CHORUS *from the top step.)*

KREON: Gentlemen: I have the honor to inform you that our Ship of State, which recent storms have threatened to destroy, has come safely to harbor at last, guided by the merciful wisdom of Heaven. I have sum-   10
moned you here this morning because I know that I can depend upon you: your devotion to King Laios was absolute; you never hesitated in your duty to our late ruler Oedipus; and when Oedipus died, your loyalty was transferred to his children. Unfortunately, as you know, his two sons, the princes Eteocles and Polyneices, have killed each   15
other in battle; and I, as the next in blood, have succeeded to the full power of the throne.

    I am aware, of course, that no Ruler can expect complete loyalty from his subjects until he has been tested in office. Nevertheless, I say to you at the very outset that I have nothing but contempt for the kind   20
of Governor who is afraid, for whatever reason, to follow the course that he knows is best for the State; and as for the man who sets private friendship above the public welfare,—I have no use for him, either. I call God to witness that if I saw my country headed for ruin, I should not be afraid to speak out plainly; and I need hardly remind you that I   25
would never have any dealings with an enemy of the people. No one values friendship more highly than I; but we must remember that friends made at the risk of wrecking our Ship are not real friends at all.

These are my principles, at any rate, and that is why I have made the following decision concerning the sons of Oedipus: Eteocles, who   30
died as a man should die, fighting for his country, is to be buried with full military honors, with all the ceremony that is usual when the

greatest heroes die; but his brother Polyneices, who broke his exile to
come back with fire and sword against his native city and the shrines
of his fathers' gods, whose one idea was to spill the blood of his blood   35
and sell his own people into slavery—Polyneices, I say, is to have no
burial: no man is to touch him or say the least prayer for him; he shall
lie on the plain, unburied; and the birds and the scavenging dogs can
do with him whatever they like.

      This is my command, and you can see the wisdom behind it. As   40
long as I am King, no traitor is going to be honored with the loyal
man. But whoever shows by word and deed that he is on the side of
the State,—he shall have my respect while he is living and my reverence when he is dead.

CHORAGOS: If that is your will, Kreon son of Menoikeus,   45
    You have the right to enforce it: we are yours.
KREON: That is my will. Take care that you do your part.
CHORAGOS: We are old men: let the younger ones carry it out.
KREON: I do not mean that: the sentries have been appointed.
CHORAGOS: Then what is it that you would have us do?   50
KREON: You will give no support to whoever breaks this law.
CHORAGOS: Only a crazy man is in love with death!
KREON: And death it is; yet money talks, and the wisest
    Have sometimes been known to count a few coins too many.

    (Enter SENTRY *from left.)*

SENTRY: I'll not say that I'm out of breath from running, King, because   55
every time I stopped to think about what I have to tell you, I felt like
going back. And all the time a voice kept saying, "You fool, don't you
know you're walking straight into trouble?"; and then another voice:
"Yes, but if you let somebody else get the news to Kreon first, it will
be even worse than that for you!" But good sense won out, at least I   60
hope it was good sense, and here I am with a story that makes no sense
at all; but I'll tell it anyhow, because, as they say, what's going to
happen's going to happen and—
KREON: Come to the point. What have you to say?
SENTRY: I did not do it. I did not see who did it. You must not punish me   65
    for what someone else has done.
KREON: A comprehensive defense! More effective, perhaps,
    If I knew its purpose. Come: what is it?
SENTRY: A dreadful thing . . . I don't know how to put it—
KREON: Out with it!
SENTRY: Well, then;   70
    The dead man—
        Polyneices—

    (Pause. The SENTRY *is overcome, fumbles for words.* KREON *waits*
impassively.)

out there—

someone,—

New dust on the slimy flesh!

(Pause. No sign from KREON.*)*

Someone has given it burial that way, and
Gone . . .

(Long pause. KREON *finally speaks with deadly control.)*

KREON: And the man who dared do this?
SENTRY: I swear I   75
Do not know! You must believe me!

Listen:
The ground was dry, not a sign of digging, no,
Not a wheeltrack in the dust, no trace of anyone.
It was when they relieved us this morning: and one of them,
The corporal, pointed to it.

There it was,   80
The strangest—

Look:
The body, just mounded over with light dust: you see?
Not buried really, but as if they'd covered it
Just enough for the ghost's peace. And no sign
Of dogs or any wild animal that had been there.   85

And then what a scene there was! Every man of us
Accusing the other: we all proved the other man did it,
We all had proof that we could not have done it.
We were ready to take hot iron in our hands,
Walk through fire, swear by all the gods,   90
It was not I!
I do not know who it was, but it was not I!

*(*KREON*'s rage has been mounting steadily, but the* SENTRY *is too intent
upon his story to notice it.)*

And then, when this came to nothing, someone said
A thing that silenced us and made us stare
Down at the ground: you had to be told the news,   95
And one of us had to do it! We threw the dice,
And the bad luck fell to me. So here I am,
No happier to be here than you are to have me:
Nobody likes the man who brings bad news.
CHORAGOS: I have been wondering, King: can it be that the gods have
done this?   100
KREON *(furiously)*: Stop!
Must you doddering wrecks

Go out of your heads entirely? "The gods"!
Intolerable!
The gods favor this corpse? Why? How had he served them?   105
Tried to loot their temples, burn their images,
Yes, and the whole State, and its laws with it!
Is it your senile opinion that the gods love to honor bad men?
A pious thought!—
                              No, from the very beginning
There have been those who have whispered together,   110
Stiff-necked anarchists, putting their heads together,
Scheming against me in alleys. These are the men,
And they have bribed my own guard to do this thing.
(Sententiously.) Money!
There's nothing in the world so demoralizing as money.   115
Down go your cities,
Homes gone, men gone, honest hearts corrupted,
Crookedness of all kinds, and all for money!
(To SENTRY*.)*   But you—
I swear by God and by the throne of God,
The man who has done this thing shall pay for it!   120
Find that man, bring him here to me, or your death
Will be the least of your problems: I'll string you up
Alive, and there will be certain ways to make you
Discover your employer before you die;
And the process may teach you a lesson you seem to have missed: 125
The dearest profit is sometimes all too dear:
That depends on the source. Do you understand me?
A fortune won is often misfortune.

SENTRY: King, may I speak?
KREON: Your very voice distresses me.
SENTRY: Are you sure that it is my voice, and not your conscience?   130
KREON: By God, he wants to analyze me now!
SENTRY: It is not what I say, but what has been done, that hurts you.
KREON: You talk too much.
SENTRY: Maybe; but I've done nothing.
KREON: Sold your soul for some silver: that's all you've done.
SENTRY: How dreadful it is when the right judge judges wrong!   135
KREON: Your figures of speech
    May entertain you now; but unless you bring me the man,
    You will get little profit from them in the end.
                              (Exit KREON *into the palace.)*
SENTRY: "Bring me the man"—!
    I'd like nothing better than bringing him the man!   140
    But bring him or not, you have seen the last of me here.
    At any rate, I am safe!   *(Exit* SENTRY*.)*

ODE° 1 • Strophe 1

CHORUS: Numberless are the world's wonders, but none
    More wonderful than man; the stormgray sea
    Yields to his prows, the huge crests bear him high;
    Earth, holy and inexhaustible, is graven
    With shining furrows where his plows have gone   5
    Year after year, the timeless labor of stallions.

Antistrophe 1

    The lightboned birds and beasts that cling to cover,
    The lithe fish lighting their reaches of dim water,
    All are taken, tamed in the net of his mind;
    The lion on the hill, the wild horse windy-maned,   10
    Resign to him; and his blunt yoke has broken
    The sultry shoulders of the mountain bull.

Strophe 2

    Words also, and thought as rapid as air,
    He fashions to his good use; statecraft is his,
    And his the skill that deflects the arrows of snow,   15
    The spears of winter rain: from every wind
    He has made himself secure—from all but one:
    In the late wind of death he cannot stand.

Antistrophe 2

    O clear intelligence, force beyond all measure!
    O fate of man, working both good and evil!   20
    When the laws are kept, how proudly his city stands!
    When the laws are broken, what of his city then?
    Never may the anarchic man find rest at my hearth,
    Never be it said that my thoughts are his thoughts.

SCENE 2

(Reenter SENTRY *leading* ANTIGONE.*)*

CHORAGOS: What does this mean? Surely this captive woman
    Is the Princess, Antigone. Why should she be taken?
SENTRY: Here is the one who did it! We caught her
    In the very act of burying him.—Where is Kreon?
CHORAGOS: Just coming from the house.

    (Enter KREON, *center.)*

Ode: Chant sung by the Chorus.

KREON: What has happened?   5
    Why have you come back so soon?
SENTRY *(expansively)*:   O King,
    A man should never be too sure of anything:
    I would have sworn
    That you'd not see me here again: your anger
    Frightened me so, and the things you threatened me with;   10
    But how could I tell then
    That I'd be able to solve the case so soon?
    No dice-throwing this time: I was only too glad to come!
    Here is this woman. She is the guilty one:
    We found her trying to bury him.   15
    Take her, then; question her; judge her as you will.
    I am through with the whole thing now, and glad of it.
KREON: But this is Antigone! Why have you brought her here?
SENTRY: She was burying him, I tell you!
KREON *(severely)*:   Is this the truth?
SENTRY: I saw her with my own eyes. Can I say more?   20
KREON: The details: come, tell me quickly!
SENTRY: It was like this:
    After those terrible threats of yours, King,
    We went back and brushed the dust away from the body.
    The flesh was soft by now, and stinking,
    So we sat on a hill to windward and kept guard.   25
    No napping this time! We kept each other awake.
    But nothing happened until the white round sun
    Whirled in the center of the round sky over us:
    Then, suddenly,
    A storm of dust roared up from the earth, and the sky   30
    Went out, the plain vanished with all its trees
    In the stinging dark. We closed our eyes and endured it.
    The whirlwind lasted a long time, but it passed;
    And then we looked, and there was Antigone!
    I have seen   35
    A mother bird come back to a stripped nest, heard
    Her crying bitterly a broken note or two
    For the young ones stolen. Just so, when this girl
    Found the bare corpse, and all her love's work wasted,
    She wept, and cried on heaven to damn the hands   40
    That had done this thing.
                        And then she brought more dust
    And sprinkled wine three times for her brother's ghost.

    We ran and took her at once. She was not afraid,
    Not even when we charged her with what she had done.
    She denied nothing.

And this was a comfort to me,   45
And some uneasiness: for it is a good thing
To escape from death, but it is no great pleasure
To bring death to a friend.
                              Yet I always say
There is nothing so comfortable as your own safe skin!
KREON *(slowly, dangerously)*: And you, Antigone,   50
    You with your head hanging,—do you confess this thing?
ANTIGONE: I do. I deny nothing.
KREON *(to* SENTRY*)*:   You may go.

                                          (Exit SENTRY*.)*

(To ANTIGONE*.)* Tell me, tell me briefly:
Had you heard my proclamation touching this matter?
ANTIGONE: It was public. Could I help hearing it?   55
KREON: And yet you dared defy the law.
ANTIGONE: I dared.
    It was not God's proclamation. That final Justice
    That rules the world below makes no such laws.

    Your edict, King, was strong,
    But all your strength is weakness itself against   60
    The immortal unrecorded laws of God.
    They are not merely now: they were, and shall be,
    Operative for ever, beyond man utterly.

    I knew I must die, even without your decree:
    I am only mortal. And if I must die   65
    Now, before it is my time to die,
    Surely this is no hardship: can anyone
    Living, as I live, with evil all about me,
    Think Death less than a friend? This death of mine
    Is of no importance; but if I had left my brother   70
    Lying in death unburied, I should have suffered.
    Now I do not.
                  You smile at me. Ah Kreon,
    Think me a fool, if you like; but it may well be
    That a fool convicts me of folly.
CHORAGOS: Like father, like daughter: both headstrong, deaf to reason! 75
    She has never learned to yield:
KREON: She has much to learn.
    The inflexible heart breaks first, the toughest iron
    Cracks first, and the wildest horses bend their necks
    At the pull of the smallest curb.
                                      Pride? In a slave?
    This girl is guilty of a double insolence,   80
    Breaking the given laws and boasting of it.

Who is the man here,
She or I, if this crime goes unpunished?
Sister's child, or more than sister's child,
Or closer yet in blood—she and her sister   85
Win bitter death for this!
(To Servants.)   Go, some of you,
Arrest Ismene. I accuse her equally.
Bring her: you will find her sniffling in the house there.

Her mind's a traitor: crimes kept in the dark
Cry for light, and the guardian brain shudders;   90
But how much worse than this
Is brazen boasting of barefaced anarchy!
ANTIGONE: Kreon, what more do you want than my death?
KREON: Nothing.
    That gives me everything.
ANTIGONE: Then I beg you: kill me.
    This talking is a great weariness: your words   95
    Are distasteful to me, and I am sure that mine
    Seem so to you. And yet they should not seem so:
    I should have praise and honor for what I have done.
    All these men here would praise me
    Were their lips not frozen shut with fear of you.   100
    (Bitterly.) Ah the good fortune of kings,
    Licensed to say and do whatever they please!
KREON: You are alone here in that opinion.
ANTIGONE: No, they are with me. But they keep their tongues in leash.
KREON: Maybe. But you are guilty, and they are not.   105
ANTIGONE: There is no guilt in reverence for the dead.
KREON: But Eteocles—was he not your brother too?
ANTIGONE: My brother too.
KREON: And you insult his memory?
ANTIGONE (softly): The dead man would not say that I insult it.
KREON: He would: for you honor a traitor as much as him.   110
ANTIGONE: His own brother, traitor or not, and equal in blood.
KREON: He made war on his country. Eteocles defended it.
ANTIGONE: Nevertheless, there are honors due all the dead.
KREON: But not the same for the wicked as for the just.
ANTIGONE: Ah Kreon, Kreon,   115
    Which of us can say what the gods hold wicked?
KREON: An enemy is an enemy, even dead.
ANTIGONE: It is my nature to join in love, not hate.
KREON (finally losing patience): Go join them then; if you must have
    your love,
    Find it in hell!   120

CHORAGOS: But see, Ismene comes:

(*Enter* ISMENE, *guarded.*)

    Those tears are sisterly, the cloud
    That shadows her eyes rains down gentle sorrow.
KREON: You too, Ismene,
    Snake in my ordered house, sucking my blood   125
    Stealthily—and all the time I never knew
    That these two sisters were aiming at my throne!
                              Ismene,
    Do you confess your share in this crime, or deny it?
    Answer me.
ISMENE: Yes, if she will let me say so. I am guilty.   130
ANTIGONE (*coldly*): No, Ismene. You have no right to say so.
    You would not help me, and I will not have you help me.
ISMENE: But now I know what you meant: and I am here
    To join you, to take my share of punishment.
ANTIGONE: The dead man and the gods who rule the dead   135
    Know whose act this was. Words are not friends.
ISMENE: Do you refuse me, Antigone? I want to die with you:
    I too have a duty that I must discharge to the dead.
ANTIGONE: You shall not lessen my death by sharing it.
ISMENE: What do I care for life when you are dead?   140
ANTIGONE: Ask Kreon. You're always hanging on his opinions.
ISMENE: You are laughing at me. Why, Antigone?
ANTIGONE: It's a joyless laughter, Ismene.
ISMENE: But can I do nothing?
ANTIGONE: Yes. Save yourself. I shall not envy you.
    There are those who will praise you; I shall have honor, too.   145
ISMENE: But we are equally guilty!
ANTIGONE: No more, Ismene.
    You are alive, but I belong to Death.
KREON (*to the* CHORUS): Gentlemen, I beg you to observe these girls:
    One has just now lost her mind; the other,
    It seems, has never had a mind at all.   150
ISMENE: Grief teaches the steadiest minds to waver, King.
KREON: Yours certainly did, when you assumed guilt with the guilty!
ISMENE: But how could I go on living without her?
KREON: You are.
    She is already dead.
ISMENE: But your own son's bride!
KREON: There are places enough for him to push his plow.   155
    I want no wicked women for my sons!
ISMENE: O dearest Haimon, how your father wrongs you!
KREON: I've had enough of your childish talk of marriage!

CHORAGOS: Do you really intend to steal this girl from your son?
KREON: No; Death will do that for me.
CHORAGOS: Then she must die?   160
KREON (*ironically*): You dazzle me.
                              —But enough of this talk!
    (*To Guards.*) You, there, take them away and guard them well:
    For they are but women, and even brave men run
    When they see Death coming.
                    (*Exeunt*° ISMENE, ANTIGONE, *and Guards.*)

ODE 2 • Strophe 1

CHORUS: Fortunate is the man who has never tasted God's vengeance!
    Where once the anger of heaven has struck, that house is shaken
    For ever: damnation rises behind each child
    Like a wave cresting out of the black northeast,
    When the long darkness under sea roars up   5
    And bursts drumming death upon the windwhipped sand.

Antistrophe 1

    I have seen this gathering sorrow from time long past
    Loom upon Oedipus' children: generation from generation
    Takes the compulsive rage of the enemy god.
    So lately this last flower of Oedipus' line   10
    Drank the sunlight! but now a passionate word
    And a handful of dust have closed up all its beauty.

Strophe 2

    What mortal arrogance
    Transcends the wrath of Zeus?
    Sleep cannot lull him nor the effortless long months   15
    Of the timeless gods: but he is young for ever,
    And his house is the shining day of high Olympos.
    All that is and shall be,
    And all the past, is his.
    No pride on earth is free of the curse of heaven.   20

Antistrophe 2

    The straying dreams of men
    May bring them ghosts of joy:

Exeunt: Latin for "they exit."

But as they drowse, the waking embers burn them;
Or they walk with fixed eyes, as blind men walk.
But the ancient wisdom speaks for our own time: 25
Fate works most for woe
With Folly's fairest show.
Man's little pleasure is the spring of sorrow.

SCENE 3

CHORAGOS: But here is Haimon, King, the last of all your sons.
Is it grief for Antigone that brings him here,
And bitterness at being robbed of his bride?

(Enter HAIMON.*)*

KREON: We shall soon see, and no need of diviners.
                                            —Son,
You have heard my final judgment on that girl: 5
Have you come here hating me, or have you come
With deference and with love, whatever I do?
HAIMON: I am your son, father. You are my guide.
You make things clear for me, and I obey you.
No marriage means more to me than your continuing wisdom.   10
KREON: Good. That is the way to behave: subordinate
Everything else, my son, to your father's will.
This is what a man prays for, that he may get
Sons attentive and dutiful in his house,
Each one hating his father's enemies,   15
Honoring his father's friends. But if his sons
Fail him, if they turn out unprofitably,
What has he fathered but trouble for himself
And amusement for the malicious?
                                So you are right
Not to lose your head over this woman.   20
Your pleasure with her would soon grow cold, Haimon,
And then you'd have a hellcat in bed and elsewhere.
Let her find her husband in Hell!
Of all the people in this city, only she
Has had contempt for my law and broken it.   25

Do you want me to show myself weak before the people?
Or to break my sworn word? No, and I will not.
The woman dies.
I suppose she'll plead "family ties." Well, let her.
If I permit my own family to rebel,   30
How shall I earn the world's obedience?

Show me the man who keeps his house in hand,
He's fit for public authority.
                              I'll have no dealings
With lawbreakers, critics of the government:
Whoever is chosen to govern should be obeyed—   35
Must be obeyed, in all things, great and small,
Just and unjust! O Haimon,
The man who knows how to obey, and that man only,
Knows how to give commands when the time comes.
You can depend on him, no matter how fast   40
The spears come: he's a good soldier, he'll stick it out.
Anarchy, anarchy! Show me a greater evil!
This is why cities tumble and the great houses rain down,
This is what scatters armies!
No, no: good lives are made so by discipline.   45
We keep the laws then, and the lawmakers,
And no woman shall seduce us. If we must lose,
Let's lose to a man, at least! Is a woman stronger than we?
CHORAGOS: Unless time has rusted my wits,
     What you say, King, is said with point and dignity.   50
HAIMON *(boyishly earnest)*: Father:
     Reason is God's crowning gift to man, and you are right
To warn me against losing mine. I cannot say—
I hope that I shall never want to say!—that you
Have reasoned badly. Yet there are other men   55
Who can reason, too; and their opinions might be helpful.
You are not in a position to know everything
That people say or do, or what they feel:
Your temper terrifies—everyone
Will tell you only what you like to hear.   60
But I, at any rate, can listen; and I have heard them
Muttering and whispering in the dark about this girl.
They say no woman has ever, so unreasonably,
Died so shameful a death for a generous act:
"She covered her brother's body. Is this indecent?   65
She kept him from dogs and vultures. Is this a crime?
Death?—She should have all the honor that we can give her!"

This is the way they talk out there in the city.

You must believe me:
Nothing is closer to me than your happiness.   70
What could be closer? Must not any son
Value his father's fortune as his father does his?

I beg you, do not be unchangeable:
Do not believe that you alone can be right.
The man who thinks that,   75
The man who maintains that only he has the power
To reason correctly, the gift to speak, the soul—
A man like that, when you know him, turns out empty.
It is not reason never to yield to reason!

In flood time you can see how some trees bend,   80
And because they bend, even their twigs are safe,
While stubborn trees are torn up, roots and all.
And the same thing happens in sailing:
Make your sheet fast, never slacken,—and over you go,
Head over heels and under: and there's your voyage.   85
Forget you are angry! Let yourself be moved!
I know I am young; but please let me say this:
The ideal condition
Would be, I admit, that men should be right by instinct;
But since we are all too likely to go astray,   90
The reasonable thing is to learn from those who can teach.
CHORAGOS: You will do well to listen to him, King,
　　If what he says is sensible. And you, Haimon,
　　Must listen to your father.—Both speak well.
KREON: You consider it right for a man of my years and experience   95
　　To go to school to a boy?
HAIMON:　　　　　　　　　　It is not right
　　If I am wrong. But if I am young, and right,
　　What does my age matter?
KREON: You think it is right to stand up for an anarchist?
HAIMON: Not at all. I pay no respect to criminals.   100
KREON: Then she is not a criminal?
HAIMON: The City would deny it, to a man.
KREON: And the City proposes to teach me how to rule?
HAIMON: Ah. Who is it that's talking like a boy now?
KREON: My voice is the one voice giving orders in this City!   105
HAIMON: It is no City if it takes orders from one voice.
KREON: The State is the King!
HAIMON:　　　　　　　　　　Yes, if the State is a desert.

　　(Pause.)

KREON: This boy, it seems, has sold out to a woman.
HAIMON: If you are a woman: my concern is only for you.
KREON: So? Your "concern"! In a public brawl with your father!   110
HAIMON: How about you, in a public brawl with justice?
KREON: With justice, when all that I do is within my rights?

HAIMON: You have no right to trample on God's right.

KREON (*completely out of control*): Fool, adolescent fool! Taken in by a
    woman!

HAIMON: You'll never see me taken in by anything vile.   115

KREON: Every word you say is for her!

HAIMON (*quietly, darkly*):   And for you.
    And for me. And for the gods under the earth.

KREON: You'll never marry her while she lives.

HAIMON: Then she must die.—But her death will cause another.

KREON: Another?   120
    Have you lost your senses? Is this an open threat?

HAIMON: There is no threat in speaking to emptiness.

KREON: I swear you'll regret this superior tone of yours!
    You are the empty one!

HAIMON: If you were not my father,
    I'd say you were perverse.   125

KREON: You girl-struck fool, don't play at words with me!

HAIMON: I am sorry. You prefer silence.

KREON: Now, by God—
    I swear, by all the gods in heaven above us,
    You'll watch it, I swear you shall!
    (*To the Servants.*)   Bring her out!
    Bring the woman out! Let her die before his eyes!   130
    Here, this instant, with her bridegroom beside her!

HAIMON: Not here, no; she will not die here, King.
    And you will never see my face again.
    Go on raving as long as you've a friend to endure you.

                            (*Exit* HAIMON.)

CHORAGOS: Gone, gone.   135
    Kreon, a young man in a rage is dangerous!

KREON: Let him do, or dream to do, more than a man can.
    He shall not save these girls from death.

CHORAGOS: These girls?
    You have sentenced them both?

KREON: No, you are right.
    I will not kill the one whose hands are clean.   140

CHORAGOS: But Antigone?

KREON (*somberly*):   I will carry her far away
    Out there in the wilderness, and lock her
    Living in a vault of stone. She shall have food,
    As the custom is, to absolve the State of her death.
    And there let her pray to the gods of hell: 145
    They are her only gods:
    Perhaps they will show her an escape from death,
    Or she may learn,

though late,
That piety shown the dead is pity in vain.

(Exit KREON.*)*

ODE 3 • Strophe

CHORUS: Love, unconquerable
　　　Waster of rich men, keeper
　　　Of warm lights and all-night vigil
　　　In the soft face of a girl:
　　　Sea-wanderer, forest-visitor!　　　　　　　　　　　　5
　　　Even the pure Immortals cannot escape you,
　　　And mortal man, in his one day's dusk,
　　　Trembles before your glory.

Antistrophe

　　　Surely you swerve upon ruin
　　　The just man's consenting heart,　　　　　　　　　10
　　　As here you have made bright anger
　　　Strike between father and son—
　　　And none has conquered but Love!
　　　A girl's glance working the will of heaven:
　　　Pleasure to her alone who mocks us,　　　　　　　15
　　　Merciless Aphrodite.°

SCENE 4

CHORAGOS *(as* ANTIGONE *enters guarded)*: But I can no longer stand in
　　　awe of this,
　　　Nor, seeing what I see, keep back my tears.
　　　Here is Antigone, passing to that chamber
　　　Where all find sleep at last.

Strophe 1

ANTIGONE: Look upon me, friends, and pity me　　　　　5
　　　Turning back at the night's edge to say
　　　Good-by to the sun that shines for me no longer;
　　　Now sleepy Death
　　　Summons me down to Acheron,° that cold shore:
　　　There is no bridesong there, nor any music.　　　　10

---

16 *Aphrodite:* Goddess of beauty and love. 9 *Acheron:* River in the underworld, the domain of
the dead.

CHORUS: Yet not unpraised, not without a kind of honor,
  You walk at last into the underworld;
  Untouched by sickness, broken by no sword.
  What woman has ever found your way to death?

Antistrophe 1

ANTIGONE: How often I have heard the story of Niobe,°   15
  Tantalos' wretched daughter, how the stone
  Clung fast about her, ivy-close: and they say
  The rain falls endlessly
  And sifting soft snow; her tears are never done.
  I feel the loneliness of her death in mine.   20
CHORUS: But she was born of heaven, and you
  Are woman, woman-born. If her death is yours,
  A mortal woman's, is this not for you
  Glory in our world and in the world beyond?

Strophe 2

ANTIGONE: You laugh at me. Ah, friends, friends,   25
  Can you not wait until I am dead? O Thebes,
  O men many-charioted, in love with Fortune,
  Dear springs of Dirce, sacred Theban grove,
  Be witnesses for me, denied all pity,
  Unjustly judged! and think a word of love   30
  For her whose path turns
  Under dark earth, where there are no more tears.
CHORUS: You have passed beyond human daring and come at last
  Into a place of stone where Justice sits.
  I cannot tell   35
  What shape of your father's guilt appears in this.

Antistrophe 2

ANTIGONE: You have touched it at last: that bridal bed
  Unspeakable, horror of son and mother mingling:
  Their crime, infection of all our family!
  O Oedipus, father and brother!   40
  Your marriage strikes from the grave to murder mine.
  I have been a stranger here in my own land:

15 *Niobe:* Mythological figure whose children were killed as punishment for her boastfulness. She was turned into a stone, and her tears became rushing streams that coursed down the mountainside.

All my life
The blasphemy of my birth has followed me.
CHORUS: Reverence is a virtue, but strength   45
Lives in established law: that must prevail.
You have made your choice,
Your death is the doing of your conscious hand.

Epode°

ANTIGONE: Then let me go, since all your words are bitter,
And the very light of the sun is cold to me.   50
Lead me to my vigil, where I must have
Neither love nor lamentation; no song, but silence.

(KREON interrupts impatiently.)

KREON: If dirges and planned lamentations could put off death,
Men would be singing for ever.
(To the Servants.)   Take her, go!
You know your orders: take her to the vault   55
And leave her alone there. And if she lives or dies,
That's her affair, not ours: our hands are clean.
ANTIGONE: O tomb, vaulted bride-bed in eternal rock,
Soon I shall be with my own again
Where Persephone° welcomes the thin ghosts underground: 60
And I shall see my father again, and you, mother,
And dearest Polyncices—
                    dearest indeed
To me, since it was my hand
That washed him clean and poured the ritual wine:
And my reward is death before my time!   65

And yet, as men's hearts know, I have done no wrong,
I have not sinned before God. Or if I have,
I shall know the truth in death. But if the guilt
Lies upon Kreon who judged me, then, I pray,
May his punishment equal my own.
CHORAGOS: O passionate heart,   70
Unyielding, tormented still by the same winds!
KREON: Her guards shall have good cause to regret their delaying.
ANTIGONE: Ah! That voice is like the voice of death!
KREON: I can give you no reason to think you are mistaken.
ANTIGONE: Thebes, and you my fathers' gods,   75

Epode: Chant sung by the Chorus following the strophe and antistrophe. 60 *Persephone:* Kidnapped by Pluto, god of the underworld, to be his wife and queen.

And rulers of Thebes, you see me now, the last
Unhappy daughter of a line of kings,
Your kings, led away to death. You will remember
What things I suffer, and at what men's hands,
Because I would not transgress the laws of heaven.   80
(To the Guards, simply.) Come: let us wait no longer.

                              (Exit ANTIGONE, *left, guarded.)*

ODE 4 • Strophe 1

CHORUS: All Danae's° beauty was locked away
         In a brazen cell where the sunlight could not come:
         A small room still as any grave, enclosed her.
         Yet she was a princess too,
         And Zeus in a rain of gold poured love upon her.   5
         O child, child,
         No power in wealth or war
         Or tough sea-blackened ships
         Can prevail against untiring Destiny!

Antistrophe 1

         And Dryas' son° also, that furious king,   10
         Bore the god's prisoning anger for his pride:
         Sealed up by Dionysos in deaf stone,
         His madness died among echoes.
         So at the last he learned what dreadful power
         His tongue had mocked: 15
         For he had profaned the revels,
         And fired the wrath of the nine
         Implacable Sisters° that love the sound of the flute.

Strophe 2

         And old men tell a half-remembered tale
         Of horror where a dark ledge splits the sea   20
         And a double surf beats on the gray shores:
         How a king's new woman,° sick

---

1 *Danae:* She was hidden away because of a prophecy that she would bear a son who would kill
her father. In spite of this precaution, she became pregnant when Zeus came to her in a shower
of gold. Her son later killed her father. 10 *Dryas' son:* King Lycurgas of Thrace, who had been
made insane by the god of wine and revelry, Dionysius. 18 *Implacable Sisters:* The muses. 22
king's new woman: Eidothea, the second wife of King Phineas, who blinded his sons after he had
imprisoned their mother, Cleopatra, in a cave.

With hatred for the queen he had imprisoned,
Ripped out his two sons' eyes with her bloody hands
While grinning Ares° watched the shuttle plunge   25
Four times: four blind wounds crying for revenge.

Antistrophe 2

Crying, tears and blood mingled.—Piteously born,
Those sons whose mother was of heavenly birth!
Her father was the god of the North Wind
And she was cradled by gales,   30
She raced with young colts on the glittering hills
And walked untrammeled in the open light:
But in her marriage deathless Fate found means
To build a tomb like yours for all her joy.

SCENE 5

(Enter blind TEIRESIAS, *led by a boy. The opening speeches of*
TEIRESIAS *should be in singsong contrast to the realistic lines of* KREON.*)*

TEIRESIAS: This is the way the blind man comes, Princes, Princes,
    Lockstep, two heads lit by the eyes of one.
KREON: What new thing have you to tell us, old Teiresias?
TEIRESIAS: I have much to tell you: listen to the prophet, Kreon.
KREON: I am not aware that I have ever failed to listen.   5
TEIRESIAS: Then you have done wisely, King, and ruled well.
KREON: I admit my debt to you. But what have you to say?
TEIRESIAS: This, Kreon: you stand once more on the edge of fate.
KREON: What do you mean? Your words are a kind of dread.
TEIRESIAS: Listen, Kreon: 10
    I was sitting in my chair of augury, at the place
    Where the birds gather about me. They were all a-chatter,
    As is their habit, when suddenly I heard
    A strange note in their jangling, a scream, a
    Whirring fury; I knew that they were fighting,   ·15
    Tearing each other, dying
    In a whirlwind of wings clashing. And I was afraid.
    I began the rites of burnt-offering at the altar,
    But Hephaistos° failed me: instead of bright flame,
    There was only the sputtering slime of the fat thigh-flesh   20
    Melting: the entrails dissolved in gray smoke,
    The bare bone burst from the welter. And no blaze!

25 *Ares:* God of war. 19 *Hephaistos:* God of fire.

This was a sign from heaven. My boy described it,
Seeing for me as I see for others.
I tell you, Kreon, you yourself have brought   25
This new calamity upon us. Our hearths and altars
Are stained with the corruption of dogs and carrion birds
That glut themselves on the corpse of Oedipus' son.
The gods are deaf when we pray to them, their fire
Recoils from our offering, their birds of omen   30
Have no cry of comfort, for they are gorged
With the thick blood of the dead.
                                    O my son,
These are no trifles! Think: all men make mistakes,
But a good man yields when he knows his course is wrong,
And repairs the evil. The only crime is pride.   35

Give in to the dead man, then: do not fight with a corpse—
What glory is it to kill a man who is dead?
Think, I beg you:
It is for your own good that I speak as I do.
You should be able to yield for your own good.   40
KREON: It seems that prophets have made me their especial province.
All my life long
I have been a kind of butt for the dull arrows
Of doddering fortune-tellers!
                            No, Teiresias:
If your birds—if the great eagles of God himself   45
Should carry him stinking bit by bit to heaven,
I would not yield. I am not afraid of pollution:
No man can defile the gods.
                            Do what you will,
Go into business, make money, speculate
In India gold or that synthetic gold from Sardis,   50
Get rich otherwise than by my consent to bury him.
Teiresias, it is a sorry thing when a wise man
Sells his wisdom, lets out his words for hire!
TEIRESIAS: Ah Kreon! Is there no man left in the world—
KREON: To do what?—Come, let's have the aphorism!   55
TEIRESIAS: No man who knows that wisdom outweighs any wealth?
KREON: As surely as bribes are baser than any baseness.
TEIRESIAS: You are sick, Kreon! You are deathly sick!
KREON: As you say: it is not my place to challenge a prophet.
TEIRESIAS: Yet you have said my prophecy is for sale.   60
KREON: The generation of prophets has always loved gold.
TEIRESIAS: The generation of kings has always loved brass.
KREON: You forget yourself! You are speaking to your King.

TEIRESIAS: I know it. You are a king because of me.
KREON: You have a certain skill; but you have sold out.   65
TEIRESIAS: King, you will drive me to words that—
KREON: Say them, say them!
     Only remember: I will not pay you for them.
TEIRESIAS: No, you will find them too costly.
KREON: No doubt. Speak:
     Whatever you say, you will not change my will.
TEIRESIAS: Then take this, and take it to heart!   70
     The time is not far off when you shall pay back
     Corpse for corpse, flesh of your own flesh.
     You have thrust the child of this world into living night,
     You have kept from the gods below the child that is theirs:
     The one in a grave before her death, the other,   75
     Dead, denied the grave. This is your crime:
     And the Furies° and the dark gods of Hell
     Are swift with terrible punishment for you.

     Do you want to buy me now, Kreon?

                              Not many days,
     And your house will be full of men and women weeping,   80
     And curses will be hurled at you from far
     Cities grieving for sons unburied, left to rot
     Before the walls of Thebes.

     These are my arrows, Kreon: they are all for you.

     (*To Boy.*) But come, child: lead me home.   85
     Let him waste his fine anger upon younger men.
     Maybe he will learn at last
     To control a wiser tongue in a better head.
                                   (*Exit* TEIRESIAS.)
CHORAGOS: The old man has gone, King, but his words
     Remain to plague us. I am old, too,   90
     But I cannot remember that he was ever false.
KREON: That is true. . . . It troubles me.
     Oh it is hard to give in! but it is worse
     To risk everything for stubborn pride.
CHORAGOS: Kreon: take my advice.
KREON: What shall I do?   95

---

77 *Furies:* Supernatural beings called upon to avenge crimes, especially those against relatives.

CHORAGOS: Go quickly: free Antigone from her vault
　　　And build a tomb for the body of Polyneices.
KREON: You would have me do this!
CHORAGOS:　　　　　　　　　　　　Kreon, yes!
　　　And it must be done at once: God moves
　　　Swiftly to cancel the folly of stubborn men.　　　　　　　　　100
KREON: It is hard to deny the heart! But I
　　　Will do it: I will not fight with destiny.
CHORAGOS: You must go yourself, you cannot leave it to others.
KREON: I will go.
　　　　　　　　—Bring axes, servants:
　　　Come with me to the tomb. I buried her, I　　　　　　　　　105
　　　Will set her free.
　　　　　　　　　　Oh, quickly!
　　　My mind misgives—
　　　The laws of the gods are mighty, and a man must serve them
　　　To the last day of his life!　　　　　　　　　(Exit KREON.)

PAEAN° • Strophe 1

CHORAGOS: God of many names
CHORUS:　　　　　　　　　　　O Iacchos°
　　　　　　　　　　　　　　　　son
　　　of Kadmeian Semele°
　　　　　　　　　O born of the Thunder!
　　　Guardian of the West
　　　　　　　　　　　Regent
　　　of Eleusis' plain
　　　　　　　　　　O Prince of maenad° Thebes
　　　and the Dragon Field by rippling Ismenos:°　　　　　　　　5

Antistrophe 1

CHORAGOS: God of many names
CHORUS:　　　　　　　　　　　　　the flame of torches
　　　flares on our hills
　　　　　　　　　　the nymphs of Iacchos
　　　dance at the spring of Castalia:°
　　　from the vine-close mountain
　　　　　　　　　　　　　come ah come in ivy:
　　　Evohe evohe!° sings through the streets of Thebes.　　　　　　10

Paean: A prayer, hymn, or song of praise. 1 Iacchos: Bacchus or Dionysius, god of wine. 2
Semele: Iacchos's mother; consort of Zeus. 4 maenad: Woman who worshipped Iacchos. 5
Ismenos: River near Thebes, where dragon's teeth were planted and the original residents of
Thebes sprang forth. 8 Castalia: Spring on Mount Parnassus, used by priestesses of Dionysius in
purification rites. 10 Evohe, evohe!: "Come forth, come forth!" The maenads' call to Dionysius.

Strophe 2

CHORAGOS: God of many names

CHORUS: Iacchos of Thebes
    heavenly Child
           of Semele bride of the Thunderer!
    The shadow of plague is upon us:
                   come
    with clement feet
           oh come from Parnasos
    down the long slopes
             across the lamenting water   15

Antistrophe 2

CHORAGOS: Io° Fire! Chorister of the throbbing stars!
    O purest among the voices of the night!
    Thou son of God, blaze for us!
CHORUS: Come with choric rapture of circling Maenads
    Who cry *Io Iacche!*
             God of many names!   20

EXODOS°

(Enter MESSENGER *from left.)*

MESSENGER: Men of the line of Kadmos,° you who live
    Near Amphion's citadel,°
               I cannot say
Of any condition of human life "This is fixed,
This is clearly good, or bad." Fate raises up,
And Fate casts down the happy and unhappy alike: 5
No man can foretell his Fate.
               Take the case of Kreon:
Kreon was happy once, as I count happiness:
Victorious in battle, sole governor of the land,
Fortunate father of children nobly born.
And now it has all gone from him! Who can say   10
That a man is still alive when his life's joy fails?
He is a walking dead man. Grant him rich,
Let him live like a king in his great house:
If his pleasure is gone, I would not give
So much as the shadow of smoke for all he owns.   15

---

16 *Io:* "Hail!" *Exodos:* Concluding scene. 1 *Kadmos:* Planted dragon's teeth from which grew the founders of Thebes. 2 *Amphion's citadel:* Thebes.

CHORAGOS: Your words hint at sorrow: what is your news for us?

MESSENGER: They are dead. The living are guilty of their death.

CHORAGOS: Who is guilty? Who is dead? Speak!

MESSENGER: Haimon.
Haimon is dead; and the hand that killed him
Is his own hand.

CHORAGOS: His father's? or his own?   20

MESSENGER: His own, driven mad by the murder his father had done.

CHORAGOS: Teiresias, Teiresias, how clearly you saw it all!

MESSENGER: This is my news: you must draw what conclusions you can
from it.

CHORAGOS: But look: Eurydice, our Queen:
Has she overheard us?   25

(Enter EURYDICE *from the palace, center.)*

EURYDICE: I have heard something, friends:
As I was unlocking the gate of Pallas'° shrine,
For I needed her help today, I heard a voice
Telling of some new sorrow. And I fainted
There at the temple with all my maidens about me.   30
But speak again: whatever it is, I can bear it:
Grief and I are no strangers.

MESSENGER: Dearest Lady,
I will tell you plainly all that I have seen.
I shall not try to comfort you: what is the use,
Since comfort could lie only in what is not true?   35
The truth is always best.
                              I went with Kreon
To the outer plain where Polyneices was lying,
No friend to pity him, his body shredded by dogs.
We made our prayers in that place to Hecate
And Pluto,° that they would be merciful. And we bathed   40
The corpse with holy water, and we brought
Fresh-broken branches to burn what was left of it,
And upon the urn we heaped up a towering barrow
Of the earth of his own land.
                              When we were done, we ran
To the vault where Antigone lay on her couch of stone.   45
One of the servants had gone ahead,
And while he was yet far off he heard a voice
Grieving within the chamber, and he came back

---

27 *Pallas:* Pallas Athene, goddess of wisdom. 39–40 *Hecate and Pluto:* Goddess of witchcraft and
sorcery and King of Hades, the underworld, realm of the dead.

And told Kreon. And as the King went closer,
The air was full of wailing, the words lost,   50
And he begged us to make all haste. "Am I a prophet?"
He said, weeping, "And must I walk this road,
The saddest of all that I have gone before?
My son's voice calls me on. Oh quickly, quickly!
Look through the crevice there, and tell me   55
If it is Haimon, or some deception of the gods!"

We obeyed; and in the cavern's farthest corner
We saw her lying:
She had made a noose of her fine linen veil
And hanged herself. Haimon lay beside her,   60
His arms about her waist, lamenting her,
His love lost under ground, crying out
That his father had stolen her away from him.

When Kreon saw him the tears rushed to his eyes
And he called to him: "What have you done, child? speak to me.   65
What are you thinking that makes your eyes so strange?
O my son, my son, I come to you on my knees!"
But Haimon spat in his face. He said not a word,
Staring—
            And suddenly drew his sword
And lunged. Kreon shrank back, the blade missed; and the boy,   70
Desperate against himself, drove it half its length
Into his own side, and fell. And as he died
He gathered Antigone close in his arms again,
Choking, his blood bright red on her white cheek.
And now he lies dead with the dead, and she is his   75
At last, his bride in the house of the dead.

                              (*Exit* EURYDICE *into the palace.*)
CHORAGOS: She has left us without a word. What can this mean?
MESSENGER: It troubles me, too; yet she knows what is best,
    Her grief is too great for public lamentation,
    And doubtless she has gone to her chamber to weep   80
    For her dead son, leading her maidens in his dirge.

    (*Pause*)

CHORAGOS: It may be so: but I fear this deep silence.
MESSENGER: I will see what she is doing. I will go in.
                              (*Exit* MESSENGER *into the palace.*)

(*Enter* KREON *with attendants, bearing* HAIMON's *body.*)

CHORAGOS: But here is the king himself: oh look at him,

Bearing his own damnation in his arms.   85
KREON: Nothing you say can touch me any more.
    My own blind heart has brought me
    From darkness to final darkness. Here you see
    The father murdering, the murdered son—
    And all my civic wisdom!   90

    Haimon my son, so young, so young to die,
    I was the fool, not you; and you died for me.
CHORAGOS: That is the truth; but you were late in learning it.
KREON: This truth is hard to bear. Surely a god
    Has crushed me beneath the hugest weight of heaven,   95
    And driven me headlong a barbaric way
    To trample out the thing I held most dear.

    The pains that men will take to come to pain!

(Enter MESSENGER *from the palace.)*

MESSENGER: The burden you carry in your hands is heavy,
    But it is not all: you will find more in your house.   100
KREON: What burden worse than this shall I find there?
MESSENGER: The Queen is dead.
KREON: O port of death, deaf world,
    Is there no pity for me? And you, Angel of evil,
    I was dead, and your words are death again.   105
    Is it true, boy? Can it be true?
    Is my wife dead? Has death bred death?
MESSENGER: You can see for yourself.

(The doors are opened and the body of EURYDICE *is disclosed within.)*

KREON: Oh pity!
    All true, all true, and more than I can bear!   110
    O my wife, my son!
MESSENGER: She stood before the altar, and her heart
    Welcomed the knife her own hand guided,
    And a great cry burst from her lips for Megareus° dead,
    And for Haimon dead, her sons; and her last breath   115
    Was a curse for their father, the murderer of her sons.
    And she fell, and the dark flowed in through her closing eyes.
KREON: O God, I am sick with fear.
    Are there no swords here? Has no one a blow for me?
MESSENGER: Her curse is upon you for the deaths of both.   120
KREON: It is right that it should be. I alone am guilty.

---

114 *Megareus:* Haimon's brother, son of Kreon. He believed his death would save Thebes and so
sacrificed himself in the unsuccessful attack on the city.

I know it, and I say it. Lead me in,
Quickly, friends.
I have neither life nor substance. Lead me in.
CHORAGOS: You are right, if there can be right in so much wrong. 125
The briefest way is best in a world of sorrow.
KREON: Let it come,
Let death come quickly, and be kind to me.
I would not ever see the sun again.
CHORAGOS: All that will come when it will; but we, meanwhile, 130
Have much to do. Leave the future to itself.
KREON: All my heart was in that prayer!
CHORAGOS: Then do not pray any more: the sky is deaf.
KREON: Lead me away. I have been rash and foolish.
I have killed my son and my wife. 135
I look for comfort; my comfort lies here dead.
Whatever my hands have touched has come to nothing.
Fate has brought all my pride to a thought of dust.

(As KREON *is being led into the house, the* CHORAGOS *advances and
speaks directly to the audience.)*

CHORAGOS: There is no happiness where there is no wisdom;
No wisdom but in submission to the gods. 140
Big words are always punished,
And proud men in old age learn to be wise.

Considerations

1. Summarize briefly the sections of the play, identifying significant action, conflict, or character development.
2. Explain the problem Antigone faces. How do her beliefs and values conflict with Kreon's? What arguments can you make for and against each character's views?
3. Sophocles titled this drama *Antigone,* yet much of the action focuses on Kreon and his conflicts with his advisors and with his son Haimon. How do these conflicts relate to his struggle with Antigone?
4. From reading the opening dialogue between Ismene and Antigone, what inferences can you make about their relationship, about the character and values of each woman, and about the role of women in ancient Greece?
5. Choose a scene you find particularly significant, and describe the way you would stage it if you were directing the play. As you plan the scene, consider the way the actors will move on the stage, where they will sit or stand, and what gestures and facial expressions you'll have them use. Do not feel obligated to conform to the limits of traditional Greek theater, as described in Chapter 3. Feel free to use modern technology as you envision the lighting, scenery, props, and costumes.

DONALD HALL (1928–   )

War Cards, Purpose, and Blame

Born in New Haven, Connecticut, Donald Hall was educated at Harvard Col-
lege and Oxford University. Following his graduation, he worked for the Paris
Review *as poetry editor and became a professor of English at the University of*
Michigan. In 1975, he left teaching to become a full-time writer. Married to
poet Jane Kenyon, Hall lives in an ancient farm house in New Hampshire that
has been in his family for many generations. He is best known for his poetry,
and anthologies of his works include A Blue Tit Tilts at the Edge of the
Sea: Selected Poems 1964–1974 *(1975) and* Kicking the Leaves *(1979).*
War Cards, Purpose, and Blame *was first published in 1989.*

My father was too young for the Great War, not fifteen when it ended,
and both of my grandfathers were too old. Their fathers fought in the Civil
War—archaic blue figures stiff-bearded in photographs—but in 1937, when
I was eight, Gettysburg might have been Agincourt or Marathon. As the
new war came closer, I understood that my father felt guilty about missing
the Great War, but I understood that he wanted to miss the new one as well.
Everyone was nervous, the Depression hanging on and war approaching. I
was an only child, alert to my parents' anxiety. My mother was thin and
attentive. She came to Connecticut from a remote farm in New Hampshire;
and as I grew up, I became aware that she felt lonely in the suburbs. She paid
more attention to her child, in her displacement, than she would have done
if she had stayed up north with her sisters.

Sometimes she took me on excursions to New Haven—Saturdays during the schoolyear, weekdays in summer. We walked up Ardmore Street to
Whitney Avenue and waited for the bus that came every ten minutes to roll
us four miles down Whitney and drop us at Church and Chapel outside
Liggett's across from New Haven's Green. While I tagged along, she shopped
at Shartenberg's and Malley's. When we had done shopping we ate lunch at
a place where I ordered beans and franks—two grilled hotdogs and a tiny
crock of pea-beans dark with molasses; dessert was jello with real whipped
cream or dry yellow cake with white frosting; lunch cost thirty-nine cents.

Then we went to the movies. We saw a first-run film, a B-movie, one
or two shorts, previews of coming attractions, and a newsreel. I remember
for certain only one film that I saw in 1937, but I'm almost sure that I
watched Spencer Tracy in *Captains Courageous;* maybe Paul Muni in *The Life
of Emile Zola* and *The Good Earth;* probably *Lost Horizon* and *A Star Is Born,*
maybe *One Hundred Men and a Girl.* The only movie I remember for certain,
after fifty-some years, is *The Last Train from Madrid.* After we took the bus
home to Ardmore Street, I stopped playing at war with my friends.

In 1937 we boys wore long woolen stockings that tucked over the
bottoms of corduroy knickers as we walked to Spring Glen Grammar School.

There were no schoolbuses. Children from my neighborhood took several different routes to school—for variety, or to avoid a bully or an old best friend who had become an enemy—but we always passed the Glendower Drug Store because it was only two short blocks from school. If we had change in our pockets, we spent it there. For a nickel, we bought big candybars. For one penny, we bought flat pieces of gum creased into five sticks, pink as a dog's tongue, that came with cards illustrating our different obsessions: Of course there were baseball cards, and I seem to remember cards for football as well; I remember G-Man cards, each of which illustrated a triumph of law and order as J. Edgar Hoover's agents flushed out Dillinger—shooting him in the alley outside a movie theatre—or Pretty Boy Floyd. Although G-Man cards were violent, they resembled the Society of Friends alongside another series that we bought and collected. We called them War Cards, and they thrived in the bellicose air of 1937.

For then the war in Spain shrieked from the front pages of newspapers   5
along with the Japanese invasion of China. In 1937 Stalin kept discovering to his astonishment that old colleagues had betrayed him; he shot seven of his best generals that year, doubtless a great advantage when Hitler invaded. In 1937 Trotsky found his way to Mexico, Amelia Earhart disappeared into the Pacific, the UAW invented the sit-down strike, Neville Chamberlain asked Hitler's cooperation in the interest of peace, the *Hindenburg* exploded and burned in New Jersey, Pierce-Arrow shut down, George Gershwin died, Orson Welles and Joseph Cotten appeared on Broadway in *Julius Caesar,* and thousands of American progressives joined the Lincoln Brigade to fight Fascism in Spain. Half of them never returned.

Even in the fourth grade we knew about Hitler, whose troops and planes fought with Franco against the Loyalists, aided by Stalin's troops and planes. Germany was the continuous enemy, less than twenty years after the Armistice of 1918. We were good, brave, loyal, outnumbered, and victorious against all odds; they were evil, cruel, cowardly, vicious, dumb, shrewd, and doomed. *We knew who was right and who was wrong.* (My father's mother's family had emigrated from Germany to New Haven in the last century, which was confusing.) In 1937 all of us—parents, teachers, even children—understood that there would be another war and that America would join it sooner this time. Isolationists and pacifists campaigned against war, but everyone knew that war was inevitable—whether it was or wasn't. A phenomenon like War Cards, as I remember them, makes it seem as if we were being prepared; as if *they* made sure that we grew up expecting to become soldiers, accepting the guns and the bombing.

At least no one—so soon after the Great War—had the temerity to present war as a Cub Scout expedition. When we went to the movies, we saw a newsreel and sometimes even the March of Time. The late 1930s was endless parades in black and white, soldiers marching, weapons rolling past reviewing stands; I remember refugees panicked on the narrow roads, all their possessions piled on donkeys, ancient trucks, or small bent backs. I remember the bombing and strafing of refugees. Ominous deep voices doom-spoke while the screen showed airplanes in formation, or artillery pieces recoiling with little puffs emerging from muzzles like speech-balloons in comic strips. I remember Hitler addressing rallies, immense crowds of identical figures sieg-heiling—robots of outrage and blood that jerked with a single will.

War Cards used a lot of red ink. On the back a short text described a notorious occasion and on the front an artist illustrated what happened. I remember one card which showed a Japanese bomb hitting a crowded Chinese bus, maybe in Shanghai: Bodies coming apart hurtled through the air, intestines stretching between the separated parts of a human figure, headless bodies littering the ground. I don't believe that these cards were clearly ideological; in the United States, there were two ideas about war in Europe—get in or stay out—and these cards seemed neither isolationist or interventionist. (As I recollect the cards carried a line that claimed them to be educational, because they illustrated the Horrors of War.) Of course, it occurred to me later, there wouldn't be much blood for us if we stayed out. Blood was the whole matter; blood was the food on which our boyish deathlove fed itself.

We loved our War Cards, chewing gum as we walked home to add a new one to our collections. If it was a duplicate we could swap, maybe the exploded bus for a card that showed the shelling of a boat. We collected War Cards as we collected ourselves for war. I loved airplanes in 1937 and read pulp stories about dogfights over the trenches. I loved the pilot-heroes of the 1930s—Wiley Post, Amelia Earhart, later Wrong-Way Corrigan. When I imagined myself going to war I joined the Lafayette Espadrille, flew Spads, and shot down Fokker Triplanes. I remember visiting the New Haven airport—later, it must have been—and seeing camouflaged fighter planes and bombers, including the mighty B-17 or Flying Fortress, which in retrospect resembles an ultralight. I remember watching parades on Memorial Day or the Fourth of July: tiny tanks clanking, soldiers marching with Springfield rifles and wearing Great War helmets.

Then I saw *The Last Train from Madrid*. Did it really change my life? 10 The phrase sounds exaggerated, melodramatic. I never registered as a CO. (Nor did I serve in the military.) Although I worked in Ann Arbor with the movement against the Vietnam War, I was never a leader; neither did I spell the country Amerika. It was war-horror that filled my chest, not political commitment: A horror is not an idea, as a shudder is not a conviction. My horror, I think, started with this film. Certain scenes of war retain the power to burst me into tears, especially the random slaughter of civilians. It is hard now to remember the outrage people felt over Guernica—after the bombings of London, Dresden, and Hiroshima—but Picasso's painting registers the shock and incredulity of 1937. I remember, in late adolescence after the war, trying to read an essay that told how French mothers struggled, dreading air raids in 1939, to fix their gas masks onto the tiny heads of their babies. I couldn't finish the page.

In September of 1990 I saw *The Last Train from Madrid* again, fifty-three years after I watched it as an eight-year-old in the Paramount Theater in New Haven. Over the years, I had thought of the film often, and assumed that it was anti-Fascist or Popular Front. It is no such thing; the film that I watched in 1990 is astonishingly without political ideology: Its single import is the randomness of war-horror. Cliches and stereotypes provide a plot, impossible to take seriously. As contemporary reviewers mentioned, the film is derivative—"Grand Hotel" on wheels—and its romantic framework hurries into irrelevance, leaving behind an expressive, almost expressionist, music of nightmare. I do not mean to say that *The Last Train from Madrid* is a good film; it is bad, bad art: The plot is improbable and the motivation incredible; the writing is ghastly, from clumsy exposition to the flattest cliches of dialogue. Yet it terrified me once; it retained much terror fifty-three years later.

The film begins with loud scare sounds and the hurtling image of a locomotive and train. A radio newscast tells us that tonight the last train will leave Madrid, after which—we understand—the city will be overrun by the nameless army that besieges it. The army lacks not only name but idea, and its only purpose is killing. As characters speak of the train's terminus in Valencia, on the other hand, Valencia becomes pure symbol: The destination is Arcadian peace in a countryside antithetic to the city of panic, chaos, and violent death. Naturally, everyone wants a seat on the train. The plot of the movie turns on separate and intermingled stories of people seeking passage on the train—their stratagems, their failures and successes. At the end the train steams out of Madrid carrying some of our people and leaving others behind—not only behind but dead; in the film's emotional terms, *behind* means *dead*.

As the film begins, a noble young officer (noble because he is handsome and stands straight; noble because he is Anthony Quinn) listens to impassioned pleas for passes and in his dutiful nobility refuses them. We dwell on an old lady, well-played, who begs and is refused. Most of our central figures are couples, two-by-two like the ark's animals: the romantic interest, which I doubtless ignored in 1937. It remains easy to ignore in 1990: None of it feels authentic, only partly because Dorothy Lamour (beloved of two leading men) plays her part with the expressiveness of a Malley's manikin. Lew Ayres is in love with Olympe Bradna, Robert Cummings with Helen Mack—and none of it matters. There is no genuine feeling between men and women. Love between two men matters more—Anthony Quinn and Gilbert Roland—who swore blood brotherhood as soldiers in Africa years before. This male loyalty is stereotypical—*Beau Geste* stuff—but it provides the strongest human bond in the film, its power only less than the forces of panic and dread. Quinn will betray any government or any commanding officer to remain loyal to his blood brother. In all of *Last Train,* we find no economic or political or social ideology; instead, we find the exaltation of private affection and a dream of pastoral peace in the midst of history's nightmare. Doubtless such dreams are conservative; they are not Fascist.

A slaphappy American journalist (Lew Ayres) picks up a girl (Olympe Bradna) who wants to get to Madrid to see her father before the firing squad executes him. (Naturally they fall in love; this pair makes it to the train.) She sees her father, he is executed—and we never receive an inkling, not a *notion* of what he did or stood for that led to his killing, by its nature dreadful because it is in cold blood. His death feels wholly arbitrary because no motive is supplied or suggested. In this film's eerie political emptiness, execution by firing squad becomes merely *ordinary*—a repetitive daily event like sunrise or the six o'clock news. In real life, the execution would have appeared unjust to some observers, and proper to others; it would have been a purposeful political act. The execution as presented occurs without purpose or meaning.

One soldier in the firing squad is tenderhearted and will not pull the trigger: Robert Cummings. For his compassion he will be sent to the front. He runs away and falls in love, and the plot of this falling-in-love is astonishing. It begins as we see two strangers parting, a man and a woman whom we have not met. We understand that they have just made love, and that she is a prostitute; they seem fond of each other, happy, making plans for their next encounter, and as the man walks into the street we spy his shape down the sight of a rifle—as a sniper shoots him dead. Although we must assume that the sniper waited for this particular man, no detail supports the assumption; we know nothing of this man or his killer or why anyone would want to kill him; we know nothing about the shooting except the fact. Like the execution, this street-killing—erotic idyll ended by bullet—presents itself as wholly random or arbitrary.

It is this young woman with whom Cummings falls in love—and she with him: immediately. After Mack and Cummings drag her dead lover's body into her flat, they talk; Cummings wants the dead man's pass for the last train. Soon enough, they scheme a double escape. During their brief courtship, these characters in their dialogue establish the farm-in-Valencia to which the train will deliver them—erecting the Arcadian alternative to Madrid. The dialogue is typically hackneyed. "This war can't go on forever," says Helen Mack as her lover stiffens in the adjacent room. (She has just said: "A moment ago he was so happy.") Toward the end of the film, as Mack and Cummings ride a wagon toward the train, it becomes her random turn to die. This time there is a hint of purpose; the killers want to hijack the wagon to get to the train themselves. However, it is arbitrary that Mack is the one to die—unless, under another agenda, she dies because she is not a virgin. (She should die for her dialogue.) Cummings makes it to the train alone.

In fact, there are few deaths in *Last Train from Madrid*. Channelsurfing today's television, happening upon a Chuck Norris special, you will see more carnage before you can switch channels than you'll observe in eighty minutes of this film. I remembered one more death from 1937. While the train remains in the station—only people with passes admitted on board—guards move through the cars rechecking passes. As they demand papers from

15

everyone, our anxiety mounts because they approach a vulnerable protagonist. Suddenly, looking at one man's pass—a stranger to us—the guards ask him to step outside. He looks nervous; he tries to run—and they shoot him down. They kill him *on purpose,* aiming their guns, yet they kill him *for no reason* that we understand.

Murderous paradox drives the film: Malignity exists everywhere, yet most of the time it appears motiveless. To the psyche, all these deaths are as arbitrary as death by bombs from the sky. One air raid takes its place at the center of the film, a riot of civilian panic, people running and frightened. The soundtrack plays fear music, camera shots are quick and angular, and in one quick shot nervous pigeons scurry.

In Robert Frost's "Design," he writes about the malign coincidence of an invisible spider haply arranged to kill a fly; the poet asks what could have caused this coming-together except for "design of darkness to appall." Then he qualifies the question in a further line: "If design govern in a thing so small." In *The Last Train from Madrid* we are surrounded by fear of imminent death, but, horribly, we lack design. As humans we wish or need to understand the cause or to place blame—on an enemy, on politicians who betrayed us, on the cupidity or moral squalor of a person or a class of people—because blame implies purpose, and it is our nature to wish to understand causes for our misfortunes. We search for anything that we may hold responsible for our fate: God, our political leaders, the Devil, the planets in conjunction at our births, the sins of our fathers, Muslims, biorhythms, Queen Elizabeth II, or a witch's curse. The film suggests that design may not govern in a thing so small as human life and death.

Print at the beginning of *Last Train from Madrid* scrolls its neutrality; 20 this movie will not uphold or defend either side of this war. This neutrality becomes vacancy, motiveless horror. When we read of battles in old histories, we study the motives of each side although the cause may mean little to us. "The river ran red with blood for seven days," we may remember—not, "Thus Centerville retained its passage to the Danube"—but always we understand that there appeared to be reasons for blood. By omitting ideology, *Last Train* purifies war from its historical context into pointless anonymous suffering. The film scrolls war's utter panic and sorrow. Oh, sorrow, sorrow, sorrow—the ripe life cut by hate without purpose, by anger lacking reason, by murder without blame.

How did my mother happen to take an eight-year-old to such a movie? Microfilm of the *New Haven Register* explains: The newspaper printed paragraphs of studio puffery that wholly misrepresented the film: "With but two pictures to her credit, both of which were outstanding successes, Dorothy Lamour, the glamorous brunette, one of the season's most sensational 'finds,' moves into the ranks of the screen's charming leading ladies. The event takes place in 'The Last Train from Madrid,' the romance laid in war-torn Spain." I find it breathtaking to read this notice of the film that horrified me. "In this story Miss Lamour appears as a beautiful patrician girl, who is the beloved of a young lieutenant in the government forces and his best friend." When I read Frank S. Nugent's *New York Times* review (6/19/37) I am almost as astonished. He notes the lack of politics in this "glib little fiction" but for Nugent there was also no horror. "True, it speaks of the Spanish revolution, but merely as Hollywood has, in the past, regarded the melodramatic turmoils of Ruritania and Zenda." He calls the film "a pre-tested melodrama which should suit the average palate," and in his conclusion makes a joke: "Its sympathies, neither Loyalist nor Rebel, are clearly on the side of the Ruritanians."

Frank S. Nugent was not eight years old. Was Nugent's cynicism more appropriate than my horror? At eight, I ignored the silly romance at the film's center and registered only the panic of unmotivated murder. When I returned home after the Saturday matinee, I packed my lead toy soldiers with their flattish Great War helmets into a shoebox and tucked it deep in the long closet of my bedroom. I performed the ritual with so much solemnity that I might have played taps for background music. By this time I felt not panic but a sadness that would not relent, which may have derived from another melancholy that absorbed me that weekend. The film opened in New Haven on Saturday, July 10, 1937, while Amelia Earhart was missing over the Pacific. I remember playing outside the house, keeping the window open and a radio near the window; I remember a report that the Navy had spotted her plane on an atoll: I remember the correction of the report. In my mind's eye, Amelia Earhart circled continually, high in the air, the hum of the Lockheed's engine distant and plaintive, gas almost gone, the pilot in her leather helmet peering for land as she circled . . .

It must have been a month or two later, maybe a cool September day, that something on the radio or in a headline reminded me of the film. Spain and China were in the news. On that day, alone in the house, I carried my War Cards down cellar to the coal furnace. I was not allowed to open the furnace door but I opened it anyway and threw the War Cards onto the red coals. At first they smoldered and turned brown and I feared that they would not burn, would give me away when my father came home and fixed the furnace. Then one card burst into bright yellow flame, then another, then all together flared briefly in the shadow-and-red hellfire of the furnace on Ardmore Street.

Considerations

1. Hall describes watching a movie that profoundly affected him. If you have had a similar experience, describe both the time and the place where you saw the movie. Then explain your response to the movie. How did it change the way you thought or acted?
2. Compare the responses (in schools, at home, on the playground) to World War II Hall describes to the responses you remember observing or expe-

riencing during the 1991 war with Iraq. Do the differences or the similarities seem more striking? Explain.

3. Hall says, "A phenomenon like War Cards, as I remember them, makes it
   seem as if we were being prepared; as if *they* made sure that we grew up
   expecting to become soldiers, accepting the guns and the bombing" (paragraph 6). What is your response to this statement? To what extent do you
   believe that the purpose (or effect) of war toys is to prepare the new
   generation to fight wars?

4. Read Hall's evaluation of *Last Train from Madrid*. Describe the roles played
   by male characters and the roles played by female characters. Which male
   characters seem admirable? Which female characters seem admirable? Explain your response. Would you expect similar roles to be played by men
   and women living under similar circumstances today? Explain.

ERNEST HEMINGWAY (1899–1961)

A New Kind of War

> Born in Oak Park, Illinois, Ernest Hemingway grew up with a love of danger
> and adventure. Immediately following his high school graduation, he became a
> reporter. He then tried to enlist in the Army but was turned down because of
> an old eye injury. A few months later, he achieved his goal of serving in World
> War I by volunteering as an ambulance driver. He was gravely wounded dur-
> ing the war, both physically and emotionally. After the Armistice was signed,
> he returned home to the United States only briefly, choosing instead to live in
> Paris as part of a community of expatriates, many of whom, like Hemingway,
> were writers. In 1952, he received the Pulitzer Prize for The Old Man and
> the Sea, and in 1954 he was awarded the Nobel Prize for literature. As he
> grew older, Hemingway struggled increasingly with depression and alcoholism
> and in 1961 committed suicide. His best-known works include the novels The
> Sun Also Rises (1926), A Farewell to Arms (1929), and For Whom
> the Bell Tolls (1940).

Madrid.—The window of the hotel is open and, as you lie in bed, you hear the firing in the front line seventeen blocks away. There is a rifle fire all night long. The rifles go tacrong, capong, craang, tacrong, and then a ma-chine gun opens up. It has a bigger calibre and is much louder, rong, cara-rong, rong, rong. Then there is the incoming boom of a trench mortar shell and a burst of machine gun fire. You lie and listen to it and it is a great thing to be in bed with your feet stretched out gradually warming the cold foot of the bed and not out there in University City or Carabanchel. A man is singing hard-voiced in the street below and three drunks are arguing when you fall asleep.

In the morning, before your call comes from the desk, the roaring burst of a high explosive shell wakes you and you go to the window and look out to see a man, his head down, his coat collar up, sprinting desperately across the paved square. There is the acrid smell of high explosive you hoped you'd never smell again, and, in a bathrobe and bedroom slippers, you hurry down the marble stairs and almost into a middle-aged woman, wounded in the abdomen, who is being helped into the hotel entrance by two men in blue workmen's smocks. She has her two hands crossed below her big, old-style Spanish bosom and from between her fingers the blood is spurting in a thin stream. On the corner, twenty yards away, is a heap of rubble, smashed cement and thrown up dirt, a single dead man, his torn clothes dusty, and a great hole in the sidewalk from which the gas from a broken main is rising, looking like a heat mirage in the cold morning air.

"How many dead?" you ask a policeman.

"Only one," he says. "It went through the sidewalk and burst below. If it would have burst on the solid stone of the road there might have been fifty."

A policeman covers the top of the trunk, from which the head is   5
missing; they send for someone to repair the gas main and you go in to
breakfast. A charwoman, her eyes red, is scrubbing the blood off the marble
floor of the corridor. The dead man wasn't you nor anyone you know and
everyone is very hungry in the morning after a cold night and a long day the
day before up at the Guadalajara front.

"Did you see him?" asked someone else at breakfast.

"Sure," you say.

"That's where we pass a dozen times a day. Right on that corner."
Someone makes a joke about missing teeth and someone else says not to
make that joke. And everyone has the feeling that characterizes war. It wasn't
me, see? It wasn't me.

The Italian dead up on the Guadalajara front weren't you, although
Italian dead, because of where you had spent your boyhood, always seemed,
still, like our dead. No. You went to the front early in the morning in a
miserable little car with a more miserable little chauffeur who suffered visibly
the closer he came to the fighting. But at night, sometimes late, without
lights, with the big trucks roaring past, you came on back to sleep in a bed
with sheets in a good hotel, paying a dollar a day for the best rooms on the
front. The smaller rooms in the back, on the side away from the shelling,
were considerably more expensive. After the shell that lit on the sidewalk in
front of the hotel you got a beautiful double corner room on that side, twice
the size of the one you had had, for less than a dollar. It wasn't me they
killed. See? No. Not me. It wasn't me anymore.

Then, in a hospital given by the American Friends of Spanish Democ-   10
racy, located out behind the Morata front along the road to Valencia, they
said, "Raven wants to see you."

"Do I know him?"

"I don't think so," they said, "but he wants to see you."

"Where is he?"

"Upstairs."

In the room upstairs they are giving a blood transfusion to a man with   15
a very gray face who lay on a cot with his arm out, looking away from the
gurgling bottle and moaning in a very impersonal way. He moaned mechanically and at regular intervals and it did not seem to be him that made the
sound. His lips did not move.

"Where's Raven?" I asked.

"I'm here," said Raven.

The voice came from a high mound covered by a shoddy gray blanket.
There were two arms crossed on the top of the mound and at one end there
was something that had been a face, but now was a yellow scabby area with
a wide bandage cross where the eyes had been.

"Who is it?" asked Raven. He didn't have lips, but he talked pretty
well without them and with a pleasant voice.

"Hemingway," I said. "I came up to see how you were doing."   20

"My face was pretty bad," he said. "It got sort of burned from the grenade, but it's peeled a couple of times and it's doing better."

"It looks swell," I said. "It's doing fine."

I wasn't looking at it when I spoke.

"How are things in America?" he asked. "What do they think of us over there?"

"Sentiment's changed a lot," I said. "They're beginning to realize the government is going to win this war."

"Do you think so?"

"Sure," I said.

"I'm awfully glad," he said. "You know, I wouldn't mind any of this if I could just watch what was going on. I don't mind the pain, you know. It never seemed important really. But I was always awfully interested in things and I really wouldn't mind the pain at all if I could just sort of follow things intelligently. I could even be of some use. You know, I didn't mind the war at all. I did all right in the war. I got hit once before and I was back and rejoined the battalion in two weeks. I couldn't stand to be away. Then I got this."

He had put his hand in mine. It was not a worker's hand. There were no callouses and the nails on the long, spatulate fingers were smooth and rounded.

"How did you get it?" I asked.

"Well, there were some troops that were routed and we went over to sort of reform them and we did and then we had quite a fight with the fascists and we beat them. It was quite a bad fight, you know, but we beat them and then someone threw this grenade at me."

Holding his hand and hearing him tell it, I did not believe a word of it. What was left of him did not sound like the wreckage of a soldier somehow. I did not know how he had been wounded, but the story did not sound right. It was the sort of way everyone would like to have been wounded. But I wanted him to think I believed it.

"Where did you come from?" I asked.

"From Pittsburgh. I went to the University there."

"What did you do before you joined up here?"

"I was a social worker," he said. Then I knew it couldn't be true and I wondered how he had really been so frightfully wounded and I didn't care. In the war that I had known, men often lied about the manner of their wounding. Not at first; but later. I'd lied a little myself in my time. Especially late in the evening. But I was glad he thought I believed it, and we talked about books, he wanted to be a writer, and I told him about what happened north of Guadalajara and promised to bring some things from Madrid next time we got out that way. I hoped maybe I could get a radio.

"They tell me Dos Passos and Sinclair Lewis are coming over, too," he said.

"Yes," I said. "And when they come I'll bring them up to see you."

"Gee, that will be great," he said. "You don't know what that will mean to me."

"I'll bring them," I said.

"Will they be here pretty soon?"

"Just as soon as they come I'll bring them."

"Good boy, Ernest," he said. "You don't mind if I call you Ernest, do you?"

The voice came very clear and gentle from that face that looked like some hill that had been fought over in muddy weather and then baked in the sun.

"Hell, no," I said. "Please. Listen, old-timer, you're going to be fine. You'll be a lot of good, you know. You can talk on the radio."

"Maybe," he said. "You'll be back?"

"Sure," I said. "Absolutely."

"Goodbye, Ernest," he said.

"Goodbye," I told him.

Downstairs they told me he'd lost both eyes as well as his face and was also badly wounded all through the legs and in the feet.

"He's lost some toes, too," the doctor said, "but he doesn't know that."

"I wonder if he'll ever know it."

"Oh, sure he will," the doctor said. "He's going to get well."

And it still isn't you that gets hit but it is your countryman now. Your countryman from Pennsylvania, where once we fought at Gettysburg.

Then, walking along the road, with his left arm in an airplane splint, walking with the gamecock walk of the professional British soldier that neither ten years of militant party work nor the projecting metal wings of the splint could destroy, I met Raven's commanding officer, Jock Cunningham, who had three fresh rifle wounds through his upper left arm (I looked at them, one was septic) and another rifle bullet under his shoulder blade that had entered his left chest, passed through, and lodged there. He told me, in military terms, the history of the attempt to rally retiring troops on his battalion's right flank, of his bombing raid down a trench which was held at one end by the fascists and at the other end by the government troops, of the taking of this trench and, with six men and a Lewis gun, cutting off a group of some eighty fascists from their own lines, and of the final desperate defense of their impossible position his six men put up until the government troops came up and, attacking, straightened out the line again. He told it clearly, completely convincingly, and with a strong Glasgow accent. He had deep, piercing eyes sheltered like an eagle's, and, hearing him talk, you could tell the sort of soldier he was. For what he had done he would have had a V.C. in the last war. In this war there are no decorations. Wounds are the only decorations and they do not award wound stripes.

"Raven was in the same show," he said. "I didn't know he'd been hit. Ay, he's a good mon. He got his after I got mine. The fascists we'd cut off were very good troops. They never fired a useless shot when we were in that bad spot. They waited in the dark there until they had us located and then opened with volley fire. That's how I got four in the same place."

We talked for a while and he told me many things. They were all important, but nothing was as important as what Jay Raven, the social worker from Pittsburgh with no military training, had told me was true. This is a strange new kind of war where you learn just as much as you are able to believe.

Considerations

1. This essay, first published in April 1937, describes Hemingway's work as a correspondent during the Spanish civil war. From the details provided, what impressions do you get of this war? Why does Hemingway call it "a new kind of war"?

2. Hemingway writes the first part of the essay using second person ("you," as in "You lie and listen to it and it is a great thing to be in bed . . ."). Then he switches, mid-essay, to first person. ("I" or "me," as in "It wasn't me they killed.") What is the effect of this switch? How would the essay be different if Hemingway had chosen to use either first or second person throughout?

3. The essay relies heavily on dialogue, especially in the hospital scenes with Jay Raven. What do you learn about Raven from the dialogue? About Hemingway?

4. Why do you think Hemingway was skeptical about Raven's story when he first heard it? How does Jock Cunningham's description of the same incident relate to Raven's explanation?

5. From reading this essay, what conjectures can you make about Hemingway's attitude toward this war? Cite specific details on which you base your evaluation.

CONNECTIONS: WAR AND POWER

1. Considering any of the following works, discuss the implications of the way women's and men's roles in war have traditionally been defined: "The Things They Carried," "On the Other Side of the War: A Story," "I'm Your Horse in the Night," "Spoils of War," *Antigone*, "Mother and Poet," and "War Cards, Purpose, and Blame."

2. "On the Other Side of the War," "Spoils of War," *Picnic on the Battlefield*, "Guests of the Nation," and "The Man He Killed" suggest that defining the "enemy" isn't always easy. Discuss your response to the implications of these works.

3. Discuss the contrasting views of young and old, of those who go and those who wait, as suggested by "Spoils of War," "Dulce et Decorum

Est," "Mother and Poet," "War Cards, Purpose, and Blame," "A New Kind of War," *Antigone,* and *Picnic on the Battlefield.*

4. Consider the concepts of loyalty and duty as suggested by "Guests of the Nation," "The Things They Carried," "The End of the Duel," "The Conscientious Objector," "War Cards, Purpose, and Blame," *Picnic on the Battlefield,* and *Antigone.*

5. Choose any three works in this section, and compare or contrast your responses to these works with your responses to any war (or armed conflict) you have lived through (either as a participant or as an observer at home).

12

Death

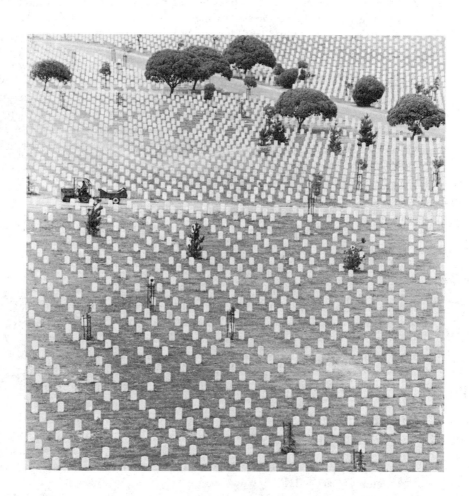

KATHERINE ANNE PORTER (1890–1980)

The Jilting of Granny Weatherall

Born in Indian Creek, Texas, Katherine Anne Porter knew early in her life that she wanted to be a writer. In 1911, she began work as a reporter in Chicago and Denver. Following a nearly fatal bout with influenza in 1918, Porter went to Mexico, where her studies of Aztec and Mayan art motivated her to begin writing short fiction. Her first collection of short stories, Flowering Judas and Other Stories, *in which "The Jilting of Granny Weatherall" appears, was published in 1930; she went on to write several short novels and her full-length novel,* Ship of Fools *(1962). In 1965, her* Collected Stories *won both the Pulitzer Prize and the National Book Award.*

She flicked her wrist neatly out of Doctor Harry's pudgy careful fingers and pulled the sheet up to her chin. The brat ought to be in knee breeches. Doctoring around the country with spectacles on his nose! "Get along now, take your schoolbooks and go. There's nothing wrong with me."

Doctor Harry spread a warm paw like a cushion on her forehead where the forked green vein danced and made her eyelids twitch. "Now, now, be a good girl, and we'll have you up in no time."

"That's no way to speak to a woman nearly eighty years old just because she's down. I'd have you respect your elders, young man."

"Well, Missy, excuse me." Doctor Harry patted her cheek. "But I've got to warn you, haven't I? You're a marvel, but you must be careful or you're going to be good and sorry."

"Don't tell me what I'm going to be. I'm on my feet now, morally speaking. It's Cornelia. I had to go to bed to get rid of her." 5

Her bones felt loose, and floated around in her skin, and Doctor Harry floated like a balloon around the foot of the bed. He floated and pulled down his waistcoat and swung his glasses on a cord. "Well, stay where you are, it certainly can't hurt you."

"Get along and doctor your sick," said Granny Weatherall. "Leave a well woman alone. I'll call for you when I want you. . . . Where were you forty years ago when I pulled through milk-leg and double pneumonia? You weren't even born. Don't let Cornelia lead you on," she shouted, because Doctor Harry appeared to float up to the ceiling and out. "I pay my own bills, and I don't throw my money away on nonsense!"

She meant to wave good-by, but it was too much trouble. Her eyes closed of themselves, it was like a dark curtain drawn around the bed. The pillow rose and floated under her, pleasant as a hammock in a light wind. She listened to the leaves rustling outside the window. No, somebody was swishing newspapers: no, Cornelia and Doctor Harry were whispering together. She leaped broad awake, thinking they whispered in her ear.

"She was never like this, *never* like this!" "Well, what can we expect?" "Yes, eighty years old. . . ."

Well, and what if she was? She still had ears. It was like Cornelia to   10
whisper around doors. She always kept things secret in such a public way.
She was always being tactful and kind. Cornelia was dutiful; that was the
trouble with her. Dutiful and good: "So good and dutiful," said Granny,
"that I'd like to spank her." She saw herself spanking Cornelia and making a
fine job of it.

"What'd you say, Mother?"

Granny felt her face tying up in hard knots.

"Can't a body think, I'd like to know?"

"I thought you might want something."

"I do. I want a lot of things. First off, go away and don't whisper."   15

She lay and drowsed, hoping in her sleep that the children would keep
out and let her rest a minute. It had been a long day. Not that she was tired.
It was always pleasant to snatch a minute now and then. There was always so
much to be done, let me see: tomorrow.

Tomorrow was far away and there was nothing to trouble about.
Things were finished somehow when the time came; thank God there was
always a little margin over for peace: then a person could spread out the plan
of life and tuck in the edges orderly. It was good to have everything clean
and folded away, with the hair brushes and tonic bottles sitting straight on
the white embroidered linen: the day started without fuss and the pantry
shelves laid out with rows of jelly glasses and brown jugs and white stone-
china jars with blue whirligigs and words painted on them: coffee, tea, sugar,
ginger, cinnamon, allspice: and the bronze clock with the lion on top nicely
dusted off. The dust that lion could collect in twenty-four hours! The box
in the attic with all those letters tied up, well she'd have to go through that
tomorrow. All those letters—George's letters and John's letters and her letters
to them both—lying around for the children to find afterwards made her
uneasy. Yes, that would be tomorrow's business. No use to let them know
how silly she had been once.

While she was rummaging around she found death in her mind and it
felt clammy and unfamiliar. She had spent so much time preparing for death
there was no need for bringing it up again. Let it take care of itself now.
When she was sixty she had felt very old, finished, and went around making
farewell trips to see her children and grandchildren, with a secret in her
mind: This is the very last of your mother, children! Then she made her will
and came down with a long fever. That was all just a notion like a lot of
other things, but it was lucky too, for she had once for all got over the idea
of dying for a long time. Now she couldn't be worried. She hoped she had
better sense now. Her father had lived to be one hundred and two years old
and had drunk a noggin of strong hot toddy on his last birthday. He told the
reporters it was his daily habit, and he owed his long life to that. He had
made quite a scandal and was very pleased about it. She believed she'd just
plague Cornelia a little.

"Cornelia! Cornelia!" No footsteps, but a sudden hand on her cheek.
"Bless you, where have you been?"

"Here, mother."   20

"Well, Cornelia, I want a noggin of hot toddy."

"Are you cold, darling?"

"I'm chilly, Cornelia. Lying in bed stops the circulation. I must have told you that a thousand times."

Well, she could just hear Cornelia telling her husband that Mother was getting childish and they'd have to humor her. The thing that most annoyed her was that Cornelia thought she was deaf, dumb, and blind. Little hasty glances and tiny gestures tossed around her and over her head saying, "Don't cross her, let her have her way, she's eighty years old," and she sitting there as if she lived in a thin glass cage. Sometimes Granny almost made up her mind to pack up and move back to her own house where nobody could remind her every minute that she was old. Wait, wait, Cornelia, till your own children whisper behind your back!

In her day she had kept a better house and had got more work done.   25
She wasn't too old yet for Lydia to be driving eighty miles for advice when one of the children jumped the track, and Jimmy still dropped in and talked things over: "Now, Mammy, you've a good business head, I want to know what you think of this? . . ." Old Cornelia couldn't change the furniture around without asking. Little things, little things! They had been so sweet when they were little. Granny wished the old days were back again with the children young and everything to be done over. It had been a hard pull, but not too much for her. When she thought of all the food she had cooked, and all the clothes she had cut and sewed, and all the gardens she had made— well, the children showed it. There they were, made out of her, and they couldn't get away from that. Sometimes she wanted to see John again and point to them and say, Well, I didn't do so badly, did I? But that would have to wait. That was for tomorrow. She used to think of him as a man, but now all the children were older than their father, and he would be a child beside her if she saw him now. It seemed strange and there was something wrong in the idea. Why, he couldn't possibly recognize her. She had fenced in a hundred acres once, digging the post holes herself and clamping the wires with just a negro boy to help. That changed a woman. John would be looking for a young woman with the peaked Spanish comb in her hair and the painted fan. Digging post holes changed a woman. Riding country roads in the winter when women had their babies was another thing: sitting up nights with sick horses and sick negroes and sick children and hardly ever losing one. John, I hardly ever lost one of them! John would see that in a minute, that would be something he could understand, she wouldn't have to explain anything!

It made her feel like rolling up her sleeves and putting the whole place to rights again. No matter if Cornelia was determined to be everywhere at once, there were a great many things left undone on this place. She would start tomorrow and do them. It was good to be strong enough for everything, even if all you made melted and changed and slipped under your hands, so that by the time you finished you almost forgot what you were working for. What was it I set out to do? she asked herself intently, but she could not remember. A fog rose over the valley, she saw it marching across the creek swallowing the trees and moving up the hill like an army of ghosts. Soon it would be at the near edge of the orchard, and then it was time to go in and light the lamps. Come in, children, don't stay out in the night air.

Lighting the lamps had been beautiful. The children huddled up to her and breathed like little calves waiting at the bars in the twilight. Their eyes followed the match and watched the flame rise and settle in a blue curve, then they moved away from her. The lamp was lit, they didn't have to be scared and hang on to mother any more. Never, never, never more. God, for all my life I thank Thee. Without Thee, my God, I could never have done it. Hail, Mary, full of grace.

I want you to pick all the fruit this year and see that nothing is wasted. There's always someone who can use it. Don't let good things rot for want of using. You waste life when you waste good food. Don't let things get lost. It's bitter to lose things. Now, don't let me get to thinking, not when I am tired and taking a little nap before supper. . . .

The pillow rose about her shoulders and pressed against her heart and the memory was being squeezed out of it: oh, push down the pillow, somebody: it would smother her if she tried to hold it. Such a fresh breeze blowing and such a green day with no threats in it. But he had not come, just the same. What does a woman do when she has put on the white veil and set out the white cake for a man and he doesn't come? She tried to remember. No, I swear he never harmed me but in that. He never harmed me but in that . . . and what if he did? There was the day, the day, but a whirl of dark smoke rose and covered it, crept up and over into the bright field where everything was planted so carefully in orderly rows. That was hell, she knew hell when she saw it. For sixty years she had prayed against remembering him and against losing her soul in the deep pit of hell, and now the two things were mingled in one and the thought of him was a smoky cloud from hell that moved and crept in her head when she had just got rid of Doctor Harry and was trying to rest a minute. Wounded vanity, Ellen, said a sharp voice in the top of her mind. Don't let your wounded vanity get the upper hand of you. Plenty of girls get jilted. You were jilted, weren't you? Then stand up to it. Her eyelids wavered and let in streamers of blue-gray light like tissue paper over her eyes. She must get up and pull the shades down or she'd never sleep. She was in bed again and the shades were not down. How could that happen? Better turn over, hide from the light, sleeping in the light gave you nightmares. "Mother, how do you feel now?" and a stinging wetness on her forehead. But I don't like having my face washed in cold water!

Hapsy? George? Lydia? Jimmy? No, Cornelia, and her features were   30
swollen and full of little puddles. "They're coming, darling, they'll all be here soon." Go wash your face, child, you look funny.

Instead of obeying, Cornelia knelt down and put her head on the pillow. She seemed to be talking but there was no sound. "Well, are you tongue-tied? Whose birthday is it? Are you going to give a party?"

Cornelia's mouth moved urgently in strange shapes. "Don't do that, you bother me, daughter."

"Oh, no, Mother, oh, no. . . ."

Nonsense. It was strange about children. They disputed your every word. "No what, Cornelia?"

"Here's Doctor Harry." 35

"I won't see that boy again. He just left five minutes ago."

"That was this morning, Mother. It's night now. Here's the nurse."

"This is Doctor Harry, Mrs. Weatherall. I never saw you look so young and happy!"

"Ah, I'll never be young again—but I'd be happy if they'd let me lie in peace and get rested."

She thought she spoke up loudly, but no one answered. A warm weight 40 on her forehead, a warm bracelet on her wrist, and a breeze went on whispering, trying to tell her something. A shuffle of leaves in the everlasting hand of God. He blew on them and they danced and rattled. "Mother, don't mind, we're going to give you a little hypodermic." "Look here, daughter, how do ants get in this bed? I saw sugar ants yesterday." Did you send for Hapsy too?

It was Hapsy she really wanted. She had to go a long way back through a great many rooms to find Hapsy standing with a baby on her arm. She seemed to herself to be Hapsy also, and the baby on Hapsy's arm was Hapsy and himself and herself, all at once, and there was no surprise in the meeting. Then Hapsy melted from within and turned flimsy as gray gauze and the baby was a gauzy shadow, and Hapsy came up close and said, "I thought you'd never come," and looked at her very searchingly and said, "You haven't changed a bit!" They leaned forward to kiss, when Cornelia began whispering from a long way off, "Oh, is there anything you want to tell me? Is there anything I can do for you?"

Yes, she had changed her mind after sixty years and she would like to see George. I want you to find George. Find him and be sure to tell him I forgot him. I want him to know I had my husband just the same and my children and my house like any other woman. A good house too and a good husband that I loved and fine children out of him. Better than I hoped for even. Tell him I was given back everything he took away and more. Oh, no, oh, God, no, there was something else besides the house and the man and the children. Oh, surely they were not all? What was it? Something not given back. . . . Her breath crowded down under her ribs and grew into a monstrous frightening shape with cutting edges; it bored up into her head, and the agony was unbelievable: Yes, John, get the doctor now, no more talk, my time has come.

When this one was born it should be the last. The last. It should have been born first, for it was the one she had truly wanted. Everthing came in good time. Nothing left out, left over. She was strong, in three days she would be as well as ever. Better. A woman needed milk in her to have her full health.

"Mother, do you hear me?"

"I've been telling you—" 45

"Mother, Father Connolly's here."

"I went to Holy Communion only last week. Tell him I'm not so sinful as all that."

"Father just wants to speak to you."

He could speak as much as he pleased. It was like him to drop in and inquire about her soul as if it were a teething baby, and then stay on for a cup of tea and a round of cards and gossip. He always had a funny story of some sort, usually about an Irishman who made his little mistakes and confessed them, and the point lay in some absurd thing he would blurt out in the confessional showing his struggles between native piety and original sin. Granny felt easy about her soul. Cornelia, where are your manners? Give Father Connolly a chair. She had her secret comfortable understanding with a few favorite saints who cleared a straight road to God for her. All as surely signed and sealed as the papers for the new Forty Acres. Forever . . . heirs and assigns forever. Since the day the wedding cake was not cut, but thrown out and wasted. The whole bottom dropped out of the world, and there she was blind and sweating with nothing under her feet and the walls falling away. His hand had caught her under the breast, she had not fallen, there was the freshly polished floor with the green rug on it, just as before. He had cursed like a sailor's parrot and said, "I'll kill him for you." Don't lay a hand on him, for my sake leave something to God. "Now, Ellen, you must believe what I tell you. . . ."

So there was nothing, nothing to worry about any more, except some- 50
times in the night one of the children screamed in a nightmare, and they both hustled out shaking and hunting for the matches and calling, "There, wait a minute, here we are!" John, get the doctor now, Hapsy's time has come. But there was Hapsy standing by the bed in a white cap. "Cornelia, tell Hapsy to take off her cap. I can't see her plain."

Her eyes opened very wide and the room stood out like a picture she had seen somewhere. Dark colors with the shadows rising towards the ceiling in long angles. The tall black dresser gleamed with nothing on it but John's picture, enlarged from a little one, with John's eyes very black when they should have been blue. You never saw him, so how do you know how he looked? But the man insisted the copy was perfect, it was very rich and handsome. For a picture, yes, but it's not my husband. The table by the bed had a linen cover and a candle and a crucifix. The light was blue from Cornelia's silk lampshades. No sort of light at all, just frippery. You had to live forty years with kerosene lamps to appreciate honest electricity. She felt very strong and she saw Doctor Harry with a rosy nimbus around him.

"You look like a saint, Doctor Harry, and I vow that's as near as you'll ever come to it."

"She's saying something."

"I heard you, Cornelia. What's all this carrying-on?"

"Father Connolly's saying—"   55

Cornelia's voice staggered and bumped like a cart in a bad road. It rounded corners and turned back again and arrived nowhere. Granny stepped up in the cart very lightly and reached for the reins, but a man sat beside her and she knew him by his hands, driving the cart. She did not look in his face, for she knew without seeing, but looked instead down the road where the trees leaned over and bowed to each other and a thousand birds were singing a Mass. She felt like singing too, but she put her hand in the bosom of her dress and pulled out a rosary, and Father Connolly murmured Latin in a very solemn voice and tickled her feet. My God, will you stop that nonsense? I'm a married woman. What if he did run away and leave me to face the priest by myself? I found another a whole world better. I wouldn't have exchanged my husband for anybody except St. Michael himself, and you may tell him that for me with a thank you in the bargain.

Light flashed on her closed eyelids, and a deep roaring shook her. Cornelia, is that lightning? I hear thunder. There's going to be a storm. Close all the windows. Call the children in. . . . "Mother, here we are, all of us." "Is that you, Hapsy?" "Oh, no, I'm Lydia. We drove as fast as we could." Their faces drifted above her, drifted away. The rosary fell out of her hands and Lydia put it back. Jimmy tried to help, their hands fumbled together, and Granny closed two fingers around Jimmy's thumb. Beads wouldn't do, it must be something alive. She was so amazed her thoughts ran round and round. So, my dear Lord, this is my death and I wasn't even thinking about it. My children have come to see me die. But I can't, it's not time. Oh, I always hated surprises. I wanted to give Cornelia the amethyst set—Cornelia, you're to have the amethyst set, but Hapsy's to wear it when she wants, and, Doctor Harry, do shut up. Nobody sent for you. Oh, my dear Lord, do wait a minute. I meant to do something about the Forty Acres, Jimmy doesn't need it and Lydia will later on, with that worthless husband of hers. I meant to finish the altar cloth and send six bottles of wine to Sister Borgia for her dyspepsia. I want to send six bottles of wine to Sister Borgia, Father Connolly, now don't let me forget.

Cornelia's voice made short turns and tilted over and crashed. "Oh, Mother, oh, Mother, oh, Mother. . . ."

"I'm not going, Cornelia. I'm taken by surprise. I can't go."

You'll see Hapsy again. What about her? "I thought you'd never come."   60
Granny made a long journey outward, looking for Hapsy. What if I don't find her? What then? Her heart sank down and down, there was no bottom to death, she couldn't come to the end of it. The blue light from Cornelia's lampshade drew into a tiny point in the center of her brain, it flickered and winked like an eye, quietly it fluttered and dwindled. Granny lay curled down within herself, amazed and watchful, staring at the point of light that was herself; her body was now only a deeper mass of shadow in an endless

darkness and this darkness would curl around the light and swallow it up. God, give a sign!

For the second time there was no sign. Again no bridegroom and the priest in the house. She could not remember any other sorrow because this grief wiped them all away. Oh, no, there's nothing more cruel than this—I'll never forgive it. She stretched herself with a deep breath and blew out the light.

Considerations

1. How appropriate is the title? Would you argue that it is more appropriate than, say, "The Death of Granny Weatherall"? Explain.
2. Compare the words Granny uses to describe her state of health to Doctor Harry with the words the author/narrator uses to describe Granny's physical and emotional feelings. Discuss the tone established by the contrast between the two descriptions. What does the discrepancy suggest about Granny's character?
3. Describe Granny's attitude toward death. In what ways does this attitude parallel (or contrast to) her approach to life?
4. Describe the relationships between Granny and her children. What significance do you see in the ways the children respond to their mother's old age and dying?
5. Describe Granny's response to the priest, then consider that response in relation to the final paragraph of the story.

WILLIAM FAULKNER (1879–1962)

A Rose for Emily

William Faulkner was born in New Albany, Mississippi, and lived most of his life in nearby Oxford, Mississippi. An erratic student, Faulkner did not graduate from high school, although he was granted special admission to the University of Mississippi and attended from 1919 to 1921. Faulkner had a profound love and fascination for his Southern heritage, yet he also questioned and challenged what he learned from his family's history. His forebears had owned slaves, fought in the Civil War, and lived through the difficult years of Reconstruction. In his works, Faulkner creates as his setting the imaginary Yoknapatawpha County, which he positions in northern Mississippi. Most of his short stories and novels examine the lives of people who live in his mythical county. Among his best-known novels are The Sound and the Fury *(1929),* Light in August *(1932), and* Absalom! Absalom! *(1936). "A Rose for Emily" originally appeared in his collection of short stories* These Thirteen *(1931). In 1950, he received the Nobel Prize for literature, declaring in his acceptance speech that it is "the problems of the human heart in conflict with itself which alone can make good writing."*

I

When Miss Emily Grierson died, our whole town went to her funeral: the men through a sort of respectful affection for a fallen monument, the women mostly out of curiosity to see the inside of her house, which no one save an old manservant—a combined gardener and cook—had seen in at least ten years.

It was a big, squarish frame house that had once been white, decorated with cupolas and spires and scrolled balconies in the heavily lightsome style of the seventies, set on what had once been our most select street. But garages and cotton gins had encroached and obliterated even the august names of that neighborhood; only Miss Emily's house was left, lifting its stubborn and coquettish decay above the cotton wagons and the gasoline pumps—an eyesore among eyesores. And now Miss Emily had gone to join the representatives of those august names where they lay in the cedar-bemused cemetery among the ranked and anonymous graves of Union and Confederate soldiers who fell at the battle of Jefferson.

Alive, Miss Emily had been a tradition, a duty, and a care; a sort of hereditary obligation upon the town, dating from that day in 1894 when Colonel Sartoris, the mayor—he who fathered the edict that no Negro woman should appear on the streets without an apron—remitted her taxes, the dispensation dating from the death of her father on into perpetuity. Not that Miss Emily would have accepted charity. Colonel Sartoris invented an involved tale to the effect that Miss Emily's father had loaned money to the town, which the town, as a matter of business, preferred this way of repaying. Only a man of Colonel Sartoris' generation and thought could have invented it, and only a woman could have believed it.

When the next generation, with its more modern ideas, became mayors and aldermen, this arrangement created some little dissatisfaction. On the first of the year they mailed her a tax notice. February came, and there was no reply. They wrote her a formal letter, asking her to call at the sheriff's office at her convenience. A week later the mayor wrote her himself, offering to call or to send his car for her, and received in reply a note on paper of an archaic shape, in a thin, flowing calligraphy in faded ink, to the effect that she no longer went out at all. The tax notice was also enclosed, without comment.

They called a special meeting of the Board of Aldermen. A deputation   5 waited upon her, knocked at the door through which no visitor had passed since she ceased giving china-painting lessons eight or ten years earlier. They were admitted by the old Negro into a dim hall from which a stairway mounted into still more shadow. It smelled of dust and disuse—a close, dank smell. The Negro led them into the parlor. It was furnished in heavy, leather-covered furniture. When the Negro opened the blinds of one window, they could see that the leather was cracked; and when they sat down, a faint dust rose sluggishly about their thighs, spinning with slow motes in the single sun-ray. On a tarnished gilt easel before the fireplace stood a crayon portrait of Miss Emily's father.

They rose when she entered—a small, fat woman in black, with a thin gold chain descending to her waist and vanishing into her belt, leaning on an ebony cane with a tarnished gold head. Her skeleton was small and spare; perhaps that was why what would have been merely plumpness in another was obesity in her. She looked bloated, like a body long submerged in motionless water, and of that pallid hue. Her eyes, lost in the fatty ridges of her face, looked like two small pieces of coal pressed into a lump of dough as they moved from one face to another while the visitors stated their errand.

She did not ask them to sit. She just stood in the door and listened quietly until the spokesman came to a stumbling halt. Then they could hear the invisible watch ticking at the end of the gold chain.

Her voice was dry and cold. "I have no taxes in Jefferson. Colonel Sartoris explained it to me. Perhaps one of you can gain access to the city records and satisfy yourselves."

"But we have. We are the city authorities, Miss Emily. Didn't you get a notice from the sheriff, signed by him?"

"I received a paper, yes," Miss Emily said. "Perhaps he considers himself   10 the sheriff . . . I have no taxes in Jefferson."

"But there is nothing on the books to show that, you see. We must go by the—"

"See Colonel Sartoris. I have no taxes in Jefferson."

"But, Miss Emily—"

"See Colonel Sartoris." (Colonel Sartoris had been dead almost ten years.) "I have no taxes in Jefferson. Tobe!" The Negro appeared. "Show these gentlemen out."

II

So she vanquished them, horse and foot, just as she had vanquished 15 their fathers thirty years before about the smell. That was two years after her father's death and a short time after her sweetheart—the one we believed would marry her—had deserted her. After her father's death she went out very little; after her sweetheart went away, people hardly saw her at all. A few of the ladies had the temerity to call, but were not received, and the only sign of life about the place was the Negro man—a young man then— going in and out with a market basket.

"Just as if a man—any man—could keep a kitchen properly," the ladies said; so they were not surprised when the smell developed. It was another link between the gross, teeming world and the high and mighty Griersons.

A neighbor, a woman, complained to the mayor, Judge Stevens, eighty years old.

"But what will you have me do about it, madam?" he said.

"Why, send her word to stop it," the woman said. "Isn't there a law?"

"I'm sure that won't be necessary," Judge Stevens said. "It's probably 20 just a snake or a rat that nigger of hers killed in the yard. I'll speak to him about it."

The next day he received two more complaints, one from a man who came in diffident deprecation. "We really must do something about it, Judge. I'd be the last one in the world to bother Miss Emily, but we've got to do something." That night the Board of Aldermen met—three gray-beards and one younger man, a member of the rising generation.

"It's simple enough," he said. "Send her word to have her place cleaned up. Give her a certain time to do it in, and if she don't . . . "

"Dammit, sir," Judge Stevens said, "will you accuse a lady to her face of smelling bad?"

So the next night, after midnight, four men crossed Miss Emily's lawn and slunk about the house like burglars, sniffing along the base of the brickwork and at the cellar openings while one of them performed a regular sowing motion with his hand out of a sack slung from his shoulder. They broke open the cellar door and sprinkled lime there, and in all the outbuildings. As they recrossed the lawn, a window that had been dark was lighted and Miss Emily sat in it, the light behind her, and her upright torso motionless as that of an idol. They crept quietly across the lawn and into the shadow of the locusts that lined the street. After a week or two the smell went away.

That was when people had begun to feel really sorry for her. People in 25
our town, remembering how old lady Wyatt, her great-aunt, had gone completely crazy at last, believed that the Griersons held themselves a little too
high for what they really were. None of the young men were quite good
enough for Miss Emily and such. We had long thought of them as a tableau,
Miss Emily a slender figure in white in the background, her father a sprad-
dled silhouette in the foreground, his back to her and clutching a horsewhip,
the two of them framed by the back-flung front door. So when she got to
be thirty and was still single, we were not pleased exactly, but vindicated;
even with insanity in the family she wouldn't have turned down all of her
chances if they had really materialized.

When her father died, it got about that the house was all that was left
to her; and in a way, people were glad. At last they could pity Miss Emily.
Being left alone, and a pauper, she had become humanized. Now she too
would know the old thrill and the old despair of a penny more or less.

The day after his death all the ladies prepared to call at the house and
offer condolence and aid, as is our custom. Miss Emily met them at the door,
dressed as usual and with no trace of grief on her face. She told them that
her father was not dead. She did that for three days, with the ministers calling
on her, and the doctors, trying to persuade her to let them dispose of the
body. Just as they were about to resort to law and force, she broke down, and
they buried her father quickly.

We did not say she was crazy then. We believed she had to do that. We
remembered all the young men her father had driven away, and we knew
that with nothing left, she would have to cling to that which had robbed
her, as people will.

III

She was sick for a long time. When we saw her again, her hair was cut
short, making her look like a girl, with a vague resemblance to those angels
in colored church windows—sort of tragic and serene.

The town had just let the contracts for paving the sidewalks, and in the 30
summer after her father's death they began the work. The construction company came with niggers and mules and machinery, and a foreman named
Homer Barron, a Yankee—a big, dark, ready man, with a big voice and eyes
lighter than his face. The little boys would follow in groups to hear him cuss
the niggers, and the niggers singing in time to the rise and fall of picks.
Pretty soon he knew everybody in town. Whenever you heard a lot of
laughing anywhere about the square, Homer Barron would be in the center
of the group. Presently we began to see him and Miss Emily on Sunday
afternoons driving in the yellow-wheeled buggy and the matched team of
bays from the livery stable.

At first we were glad that Miss Emily would have an interest, because
the ladies all said, "Of course a Grierson would not think seriously of a

Northerner, a day laborer." But there were still others, older people, who said that even grief could not cause a real lady to forget *noblesse oblige*°— without calling it *noblesse oblige*. They just said, "Poor Emily. Her kinsfolk should come to her." She had some kin in Alabama; but years ago her father had fallen out with them over the estate of old lady Wyatt, the crazy woman, and there was no communication between the two families. They had not even been represented at the funeral.

And as soon as the old people said, "Poor Emily," the whispering began. "Do you suppose it's really so?" they said to one another. "Of course it is. What else could . . . " This behind their hands; rustling of craned silk and satin behind jalousies closed upon the sun of Sunday afternoon as the thin, swift clop-clop-clop of the matched team passed: "Poor Emily."

She carried her head high enough—even when we believed that she was fallen. It was as if she demanded more than ever the recognition of her dignity as the last Grierson; as if it had wanted that touch of earthiness to reaffirm her imperviousness. Like when she bought the rat poison, the arsenic. That was over a year after they had begun to say "Poor Emily," and while the two female cousins were visiting her.

"I want some poison," she said to the druggist. She was over thirty then, still a slight woman, though thinner than usual, with cold, haughty black eyes in a face the flesh of which was strained across the temples and about the eye-sockets as you imagine a lighthouse-keeper's face ought to look. "I want some poison," she said.

"Yes, Miss Emily. What kind? For rats and such? I'd recom—"   35

"I want the best you have. I don't care what kind."

The druggist named several. "They'll kill anything up to an elephant. But what you want is—"

"Arsenic," Miss Emily said. "Is that a good one?"

"Is . . . arsenic? Yes, ma'am. But what you want—"

"I want arsenic."   40

The druggist looked down at her. She looked back at him, erect, her face like a strained flag. "Why, of course," the druggist said. "If that's what you want. But the law requires you to tell what you are going to use it for."

Miss Emily just stared at him, her head tilted back in order to look him eye for eye, until he looked away and went and got the arsenic and wrapped it up. The Negro delivery boy brought her the package; the druggist didn't come back. When she opened the package at home there was written on the box, under the skull and bones: "For rats."

IV

So the next day we all said, "She will kill herself"; and we said it would be the best thing. When she had first begun to be seen with Homer Barron,

---

noblesse oblige: The obligation of those holding high rank or social position to behave generously and courteously toward others.

we had said, "She will marry him." Then we said, "She will persuade him yet," because Homer himself had remarked—he liked men, and it was known that he drank with the younger men in the Elks' Club—that he was not a marrying man. Later we said, "Poor Emily" behind the jalousies as they passed on Sunday afternoon in the glittering buggy, Miss Emily with her head high and Homer Barron with his hat cocked and a cigar in his teeth, reins and whip in a yellow glove.

Then some of the ladies began to say that it was a disgrace to the town and a bad example to the young people. The men did not want to interfere, but at last the ladies forced the Baptist minister—Miss Emily's people were Episcopal—to call upon her. He would never divulge what happened during that interview, but he refused to go back again. The next Sunday they again drove about the streets, and the following day the minister's wife wrote to Miss Emily's relations in Alabama.

So she had blood-kin under her roof again and we sat back to watch developments. At first nothing happened. Then we were sure that they were to be married. We learned that Miss Emily had been to the jeweler's and ordered a man's toilet set in silver, with the letters H. B. on each piece. Two days later we learned that she had bought a complete outfit of men's clothing, including a nightshirt, and we said, "They are married." We were really glad. We were glad because the two female cousins were even more Grierson than Miss Emily had ever been.

So we were not surprised when Homer Barron—the streets had been finished some time since—was gone. We were a little disappointed that there was not a public blowing-off, but we believed that he had gone on to prepare for Miss Emily's coming, or to give her a chance to get rid of the cousins. (By that time it was a cabal, and we were all Miss Emily's allies to help circumvent the cousins.) Sure enough, after another week they departed. And, as we had expected all along, within three days Homer Barron was back in town. A neighbor saw the Negro man admit him at the kitchen door at dusk one evening.

And that was the last we saw of Homer Barron. And of Miss Emily for some time. The Negro man went in and out with the market basket, but the front door remained closed. Now and then we would see her at a window for a moment, as the men did that night when they sprinkled the lime, but for almost six months she did not appear on the streets. Then we knew that this was to be expected too; as if that quality of her father which had thwarted her woman's life so many times had been too virulent and too furious to die.

When we next saw Miss Emily, she had grown fat and her hair was turning gray. During the next few years it grew grayer and grayer until it attained an even pepper-and-salt iron-gray, when it ceased turning. Up to the day of her death at seventy-four it was still that vigorous iron-gray, like the hair of an active man.

From that time on her front door remained closed, save for a period of six or seven years, when she was about forty, during which she gave lessons

45

in china-painting. She fitted up a studio in one of the downstairs rooms, where the daughters and granddaughters of Colonel Sartoris' contemporaries were sent to her with the same regularity and in the same spirit that they were sent to church on Sundays with a twenty-five-cent piece for the collection plate. Meanwhile her taxes had been remitted.

Then the newer generation became the backbone and the spirit of the town, and the painting pupils grew up and fell away and did not send their children to her with boxes of color and tedious brushes and pictures cut from the ladies' magazines. The front door closed upon the last one and remained closed for good. When the town got free postal delivery, Miss Emily alone refused to let them fasten the metal numbers above her door and attach a mailbox to it. She would not listen to them. 50

Daily, monthly, yearly we watched the Negro grow grayer and more stooped, going in and out with the market basket. Each December we sent her a tax notice, which would be returned by the post office a week later, unclaimed. Now and then we would see her in one of the downstairs windows—she had evidently shut up the top floor of the house—like the carven torso of an idol in a niche, looking or not looking at us, we could never tell which. Thus she passed from generation to generation—dear, inescapable, impervious, tranquil, and perverse.

And so she died. Fell ill in the house filled with dust and shadows, with only a doddering Negro man to wait on her. We did not even know she was sick; we had long since given up trying to get any information from the Negro. He talked to no one, probably not even to her, for his voice had grown harsh and rusty, as if from disuse.

She died in one of the downstairs rooms, in a heavy walnut bed with a curtain, her gray head propped on a pillow yellow and moldy with age and lack of sunlight.

V

The Negro met the first of the ladies at the front door and let them in, with their hushed, sibilant voices and their quick, curious glances, and then he disappeared. He walked right through the house and out the back and was not seen again.

The two female cousins came at once. They held the funeral on the second day, with the town coming to look at Miss Emily beneath a mass of bought flowers, with the crayon face of her father musing profoundly above the bier and the ladies sibilant and macabre; and the very old men—some in their brushed Confederate uniforms—on the porch and the lawn, talking of Miss Emily as if she had been a contemporary of theirs, believing that they had danced with her and courted her perhaps, confusing time with its mathematical progression, as the old do, to whom all the past is not a diminishing road but, instead, a huge meadow which no winter ever quite touches, divided from them now by the narrow bottle-neck of the most recent decade of years. 55

Already we knew that there was one room in that region above stairs which no one had seen in forty years, and which would have to be forced. They waited until Miss Emily was decently in the ground before they opened it.

The violence of breaking down the door seemed to fill this room with pervading dust. A thin, acrid pall as of the tomb seemed to lie every-where upon this room decked and furnished as for a bridal: upon the valance curtains of faded rose color, upon the rose-shaded lights, upon the dressing table, upon the delicate array of crystal and the man's toilet things backed with tarnished silver, silver so tarnished that the monogram was obscured. Among them lay collar and tie, as if they had just been removed, which, lifted, left upon the surface a pale crescent in the dust. Upon a chair hung the suit, carefully folded; beneath it the two mute shoes and the discarded socks.

The man himself lay in the bed.

For a long while we just stood there, looking down at the profound and fleshless grin. The body had apparently once lain in the attitude of an embrace, but now the long sleep that outlasts love, that conquers even the grimace of love, had cuckolded him. What was left of him, rotted beneath what was left of the nightshirt, had become inextricable from the bed in which he lay; and upon him and upon the pillow beside him lay that even coating of the patient and biding dust.

Then we noticed that in the second pillow was the indentation of a   60 head. One of us lifted something from it, and leaning forward, that faint and invisible dust dry and acrid in the nostrils, we saw a long strand of iron-gray hair.

Considerations

1. Who is the narrator? What is his attitude toward Miss Emily? What values are reflected by his observations about Miss Emily and about the town and its citizens?

2. Reread the story, making note of details that mean more to you or that you had not noticed from your first reading. In addition, make a list of the events of the story in chronological order. How would the story be different if it were told according to the chronology you have outlined?

3. What is your response to the title? How does it relate to the story's action and themes?

4. What role does Tobe play in the story? Why does he leave when the townspeople enter Miss Emily's house?

5. Read the following commentary and then write your response to it. Does your understanding of or reaction to the story change after reading Faulk-ner's explanation of his process of writing? Explain.

Commentary

WILLIAM FAULKNER
On the Meaning of "A Rose for Emily"°

Q. What is the meaning of the title "A Rose for Emily"?

A. Oh, it's simply the poor woman had had no life at all. Her father had kept her more or less locked up and then she had a lover who was about to quit her, she had to murder him. It was just "A Rose for Emily"—that's all.

Q. I was wondering, one of your short stories, "A Rose for Emily," what ever inspired you to write this story . . . ?"

A. That to me was another sad and tragic manifestation of man's condition in which he dreams and hopes, in which he is in conflict with himself or with his environment or with others. In this case there was the young girl with a young girl's normal aspirations to find love and then a husband and a family, who was brow-beaten and kept down by her father, a selfish man who didn't want her to leave home because he wanted a housekeeper, and it was a natural instinct of—repressed which—you can't repress it—you can mash it down but it comes up somewhere else and very likely in a tragic form, and that was simply another manifestation of man's injustice to man, of the poor tragic human being struggling with its own heart, with others, with its environment, for the simple things which all human beings want. In that case it was a young girl that just wanted to be loved and to love and to have a husband and a family.

Q. And that purely came from your imagination?   5

A. Well, the story did but the condition is there. It exists. I didn't invent that condition, I didn't invent the fact that young girls dream of someone to love and children and a home, but the story of what her own particular tragedy was was invented, yes. . . .

Q. Sir, it has been argued that "A Rose for Emily" is a criticism of the North, and others have argued saying that it is a criticism of the South. Now, could this story, shall we say, be more properly classified as a criticism of the times?

A. Now that I don't know, because I was simply trying to write about people. The writer uses environment—what he knows—and if there's a symbolism in which the lover represented the North and the woman who murdered him represents the South, I don't say that's not valid and not there, but it was no intention of the writer to say, Now let's see, I'm going to write

Setting: From 1957 to 1958, William Faulkner served as writer-in-residence at the University of Virginia. The following commentary, which is an excerpt from *Faulkner in the University* (1959), edited by Frederick Gwynn and Joseph Blotner, records a question-and-answer session between Faulkner and University of Virginia students.

a piece in which I will use a symbolism for the North and another symbol for the South, that he was simply writing about people, a story which he thought was tragic and true, because it came out of the human heart, the human aspiration, the human—the conflict of conscience with glands, with the Old Adam. It was a conflict not between the North and the South so much as between, well you might say, God and Satan.

Q. Sir, just a little more on that thing. You say it's a conflict between God and Satan. Well, I don't quite understand what you mean. Who is—did one represent the—

A. The conflict was in Miss Emily, that she knew that you do not murder people. She had been trained that you do not take a lover. You marry, you don't take a lover. She had broken all the laws of her tradition, her background, and she had finally broken the law of God too, which says you do not take human life. And she knew she was doing wrong, and that's why her own life was wrecked. Instead of murdering one lover, and then to go and take another and when she used him up to murder him, she was expiating her crime.

Q. Was the "Rose for Emily" an idea or a character? Just how did you go about it?

A. That came from a picture of the strand of hair on the pillow. It was a ghost story. Simply a picture of a strand of hair on the pillow in the abandoned house.

ALICE WALKER (1944–   )

To Hell with Dying

"To Hell with Dying" appears in Alice Walker's anthology of short stories, In Love and Trouble: Stories of Black Women *(1967). For biographical information on Walker, see page 371.*

"To hell with dying," my father would say. "These children want Mr. Sweet!"

Mr. Sweet was a diabetic and an alcoholic and a guitar player and lived down the road from us on a neglected cotton farm. My older brothers and sisters got the most benefit from Mr. Sweet, for when they were growing up he had quite a few years ahead of him and so was capable of being called back from the brink of death any number of times—whenever the voice of my father reached him as he lay expiring. "To hell with dying, man," my father would say, pushing the wife away from the bedside (in tears although she knew the death was not necessarily the last one unless Mr. Sweet really wanted it to be). "These children want Mr. Sweet!" And they did want him, for at a signal from Father they would come crowding around the bed and throw themselves on the covers, and whoever was the smallest at the time would kiss him all over his wrinkled brown face and tickle him so that he would laugh all down in his stomach, and his mustache, which was long and sort of straggly, would shake like Spanish moss and was also that color.

Mr. Sweet had been ambitious as a boy, wanted to be a doctor or lawyer or sailor, only to find that black men fare better if they are not. Since he could become none of these things he turned to fishing as his only earnest career and playing the guitar as his only claim to doing anything extraordinarily well. His son, the only one that he and his wife, Miss Mary, had, was shiftless as the day is long and spent money as if he were trying to see the bottom of the mint, which Mr. Sweet would tell him was the clean brown palm of his hand. Miss Mary loved her "baby," however, and worked hard to get him the "li'l necessaries" of life, which turned out mostly to be women.

Mr. Sweet was a tall, thinnish man with thick kinky hair going dead white. He was dark brown, his eyes were squinty and sort of bluish, and he chewed Brown Mule tobacco. He was constantly on the verge of being blind drunk, for he brewed his own liquor and was not in the least a stingy sort of man, and was always very melancholy and sad, though frequently when he was "feelin' good" he'd dance around the yard with us, usually keeling over just as my mother came to see what the commotion was.

Toward all of us children he was very kind, and had the grace to be shy with us, which is unusual in grown-ups. He had great respect for my mother for she never held his drunkenness against him and would let us play with him even when he was about to fall in the fireplace from drink. Although Mr. Sweet would sometimes lose complete or nearly complete control of his

5

head and neck so that he would loll in his chair, his mind remained strangely acute and his speech not too affected. His ability to be drunk and sober at the same time made him an ideal playmate, for he was as weak as we were and we could usually best him in wrestling, all the while keeping a fairly coherent conversation going.

We never felt anything of Mr. Sweet's age when we played with him. We loved his wrinkles and would draw some on our brows to be like him, and his white hair was my special treasure and he knew it and would never come to visit us just after he had had his hair cut off at the barbershop. Once he came to our house for something, probably to see my father about fertilizer for his crops because, although he never paid the slightest attention to his crops, he liked to know what things would be best to use on them if he ever did. Anyhow, he had not come with his hair since he had just had it shaved off at the barbershop. He wore a huge straw hat to keep off the sun and also to keep his head away from me. But as soon as I saw him I ran up and demanded that he take me up and kiss me with his funny beard which smelled so strongly of tobacco. Looking forward to burying my small fingers into his woolly hair I threw away his hat only to find he had done something to his hair, that it was no longer there! I let out a squall which made my mother think that Mr. Sweet had finally dropped me in the well or something and from that day I've been wary of men in hats. However, not long after, Mr. Sweet showed up with his hair grown out and just as white and kinky and impenetrable as it ever was.

Mr. Sweet used to call me his princess, and I believed it. He made me feel pretty at five and six, and simply outrageously devastating at the blazing age of eight and a half. When he came to our house with his guitar the whole family would stop whatever they were doing to sit around him and listen to him play. He liked to play "Sweet Georgia Brown," that was what he called me sometimes, and also he liked to play "Caldonia" and all sorts of sweet, sad, wonderful songs which he sometimes made up. It was from one of these songs that I heard that he had had to marry Miss Mary when he had in fact loved somebody else (now living in Chi-ca-go, or De-stroy, Michigan). He was not sure that Joe Lee, her "baby," was also his baby. Sometimes he would cry and that was an indication that he was about to die again. And so we would all get prepared, for we were sure to be called upon.

I was seven the first time I remember actually participating in one of Mr. Sweet's "revivals"—my parents told me I had participated before, I had been the one chosen to kiss him and tickle him long before I knew the rite of Mr. Sweet's rehabilitation. He had come to our house, it was a few years after his wife's death, and was very sad, and also, typically, very drunk. He sat on the floor next to me and my older brother, the rest of the children were grown up and lived elsewhere, and began to play his guitar and cry. I held his woolly head in my arms and wished I could have been old enough to have been the woman he loved so much and that I had not been lost years and years ago.

When he was leaving, my mother said to us that we'd better sleep light that night for we'd probably have to go over to Mr. Sweet's before daylight. And we did. For soon after we had gone to bed one of the neighbors knocked on our door and called my father and said that Mr. Sweet was sinking fast and if he wanted to get in a word before the crossover he'd better shake a leg and get over to Mr. Sweet's house. All the neighbors knew to come to our house if something was wrong with Mr. Sweet, but they did not know how we always managed to make him well, or at least stop him from dying, when he was so often near death. As soon as we heard the cry we got up, my brother and I and my mother and father, and put on our clothes. We hurried out of the house and down the road for we were always afraid that we might someday be too late and Mr. Sweet would get tired of dallying.

When we got to the house, a very poor shack really, we found the   10 front room full of neighbors and relatives and someone met us at the door and said it was all very sad that old Mr. Sweet Little (for Little was his family name, although we mostly ignored it) was about to kick the bucket. My parents were advised not to take my brother and me into the "death room," seeing we were so young and all, but we were so much more accustomed to the death room than he that we ignored him and dashed in without giving his warning a second thought. I was almost in tears, for these deaths upset me fearfully, and the thought of how much depended on me and my brother (who was such a ham most of the time) made me very nervous.

The doctor was bending over the bed and turned back to tell us for at least the tenth time in the history of my family that, alas, old Mr. Sweet Little was dying and that the children had best not see the face of implacable death (I didn't know what "implacable" was, but whatever it was, Mr. Sweet was not!). My father pushed him rather abruptly out of the way saying, as he always did and very loudly for he was saying it to Mr. Sweet, "To hell with dying, man, these children want Mr. Sweet"—which was my cue to throw myself upon the bed and kiss Mr. Sweet all around the whiskers and under the eyes and around the collar of his nightshirt where he smelled so strongly of all sorts of things, mostly liniment.

I was very good at bringing him around, for as soon as I saw that he was struggling to open his eyes I knew he was going to be all right, and so could finish my revival sure of success. As soon as his eyes were open he would begin to smile and that way I knew that I had surely won. Once, though, I got a tremendous scare, for he could not open his eyes and later I learned that he had had a stroke and that one side of his face was stiff and hard to get into motion. When he began to smile I could tickle him in earnest because I was sure that nothing would get in the way of his laughter, although once he began to cough so hard that he almost threw me off his stomach, but that was when I was very small, little more than a baby, and my bushy hair had gotten in his nose.

When we were sure he would listen to us we would ask him why he was in bed and when he was coming to see us again and could we play his guitar, which more than likely would be leaning against the bed. His eyes would get all misty and he would sometimes cry out loud, but we never let it embarrass us, for he knew that we loved him and that we sometimes cried too for no reason. My parents would leave the room to just the three of us; Mr. Sweet, by that time, would be propped up in bed with a number of pillows behind his head and with me sitting and lying on his shoulder and along his chest. Even when he had trouble breathing he would not ask me to get down. Looking into my eyes he would shake his white head and run a scratchy old finger all around my hairline, which was rather low down, nearly to my eyebrows, and made some people say I looked like a baby monkey.

My brother was very generous in all this, he let me do all the revivaling—he had done it for years before I was born and so was glad to be able to pass it on to someone new. What he would do while I talked to Mr. Sweet was pretend to play the guitar, in fact pretend that he was a young version of Mr. Sweet, and it always made Mr. Sweet glad to think that someone wanted to be like him—of course, we did not know this then, we played the thing by ear, and whatever he seemed to like, we did. We were desperately afraid that he was just going to take off one day and leave us.

It did not occur to us that we were doing anything special; we had not   15
learned that death was final when it did come. We thought nothing of triumphing over it so many times, and in fact became a trifle contemptuous of people who let themselves be carried away. It did not occur to us that if our father had been dying we could not have stopped it, that Mr. Sweet was the only person over whom we had power.

When Mr. Sweet was in his eighties I was studying in the university many miles from home. I saw him whenever I went home, but he was never on the verge of dying that I could tell and I began to feel that my anxiety for his health and psychological well-being was unnecessary. By this time he not only had a mustache but a long flowing snow-white beard, which I loved and combed and braided for hours. He was very peaceful, fragile, gentle, and the only jarring note about him was his old steel guitar, which he still played in the old sad, sweet, down-home blues way.

On Mr. Sweet's ninetieth birthday I was finishing my doctorate in Massachusetts and had been making arrangements to go home for several weeks' rest. That morning I got a telegram telling me that Mr. Sweet was dying again and could I please drop everything and come home. Of course I could. My dissertation could wait and my teachers would understand when I explained to them when I got back. I ran to the phone, called the airport, and within four hours I was speeding along the dusty road to Mr. Sweet's.

The house was more dilapidated than when I was last there, barely a shack, but it was overgrown with yellow roses which my family had planted many years ago. The air was heavy and sweet and very peaceful. I felt strange walking through the gate and up the old rickety steps. But the strangeness left me as I caught sight of the long white beard I loved so well flowing down the thin body over the familiar quilt coverlet. Mr. Sweet!

His eyes were closed tight and his hands, crossed over his stomach, were thin and delicate, no longer scratchy. I remembered how always before I had run and jumped up on him just anywhere; now I knew he would not be able to support my weight. I looked around at my parents, and was surprised to see that my father and mother also looked old and frail. My father, his own hair very gray, leaned over the quietly sleeping old man, who, incidentally, smelled still of wine and tobacco, and said, as he'd done so many times, "To hell with dying, man! My daughter is home to see Mr. Sweet!" My brother had not been able to come as he was in the war in Asia. I bent down and gently stroked the closed eyes and gradually they began to open. The closed, wine-stained lips twitched a little, then parted in a warm, slightly embarrassed smile. Mr. Sweet could see me and he recognized me and his eyes looked very spry and twinkly for a moment. I put my head down on the pillow next to his and we just looked at each other for a long time. Then he began to trace my peculiar hairline with a thin, smooth finger. I closed my eyes when his finger halted above my ear (he used to rejoice at the dirt in my ears when I was little), his hand stayed cupped around my cheek. When I opened my eyes, sure that I had reached him in time, his were closed.

Even at twenty-four how could I believe that I had failed? that Mr. 20 Sweet was really gone? He had never gone before. But when I looked at my parents I saw that they were holding back tears. They had loved him dearly. He was like a piece of rare and delicate china which was always being saved from breaking and which finally fell. I looked long at the old face, the wrinkled forehead, the red lips, the hands that still reached out to me. Soon I felt my father pushing something cool into my hands. It was Mr. Sweet's guitar. He had asked them months before to give it to me; he had known that even if I came next time he would not be able to respond in the old way. He did not want me to feel that my trip had been for nothing.

The old guitar! I plucked the strings, hummed "Sweet Georgia Brown." The magic of Mr. Sweet lingered still in the cool steel box. Through the window I could catch the fragrant delicate scent of tender yellow roses. The man on the high old-fashioned bed with the quilt coverlet and the flowing white beard had been my first love.

Considerations

1. What is your response to Mr. Sweet? The mother and father in the story see him as a fine companion to accompany the growing years of their children. Do you agree? Explain.

2. What reasons does the narrator suggest for Mr. Sweet's life choices (including his many "deaths")? What is your response to these reasons?

3. What do the narrator and her brother learn from the many "rescues" they perform? Do you see these lessons as negative? Positive? A combination? Explain.

4. The narrator leaves her dissertation and her classes behind—assuming that her teachers will understand—to rush to the bedside of Mr. Sweet. If you were one of her professors, listening to her explanation, how would you respond? Explain your reasons.
5. What does the narrator learn from her final encounter with Mr. Sweet? Consider the way she sees her parents as well as the way she sees herself. What insights does she seem to have about the relationship between life and death?

AMY HEMPEL (1951–   )

In the Cemetery Where Al Jolson Is Buried°

*Amy Hempel was born in Chicago but grew up and went to school in Califor-
nia. Following graduation from San Francisco State College, she moved to
New York, worked at her writing, and became a contributing editor for* Vanity
Fair *magazine. Many of the short stories in her collection* Reasons to Live
*(in which "In the Cemetery Where Al Jolson Is Buried" appears) are set in
California and take their themes from Hempel's experiences with the death of
family members and from her difficult years as a struggling writer. In spite of
her serious themes, her gift for insight, humor, and irony makes hope and
resilience, rather than pain and suffering, dominate her fictional vision.*

"Tell me things I won't mind forgetting," she said. "Make it useless stuff
or skip it."

I began. I told her insects fly through rain, missing every drop, never
getting wet. I told her no one in America owned a tape recorder before Bing
Crosby did. I told her the shape of the moon is like a banana—you see it
looking full, you're seeing it end-on.

The camera made me self-conscious and I stopped. It was trained on
us from a ceiling mount—the kind of camera banks use to photograph
robbers. It played us to the nurses down the hall in Intensive Care.

"Go on, girl," she said. "You get used to it."

I had my audience. I went on. Did she know that Tammy Wynette had   5
changed her tune? Really. That now she sings "Stand by Your *Friends*"? That
Paul Anka did it too, I said. Does "You're Having *Our* Baby." That he got
sick of all that feminist bitching.

"What else?" she said. "Have you got something else?"

Oh, yes.

For her I would always have something else.

"Did you know that when they taught the first chimp to talk, it lied?
That when they asked her who did it on the desk, she signed back the name
of the janitor. And that when they pressed her, she said she was sorry, that it
was really the project director. But she was a mother, so I guess she had her
reasons."

"Oh, that's good," she said. "A parable."   10

"There's more about the chimp," I said. "But it will break your heart."

"No, thanks," she says, and scratches at her mask.

We look like good-guy outlaws. Good or bad, I am not used to the
mask yet. I keep touching the warm spot where my breath, thank God,

---

Al Jolson: (1886–1950) American entertainer; he starred in the first motion picture to feature
sound, *The Jazz Singer*, wearing black-face make-up.

comes out. She is used to hers. She only ties the strings on top. The other ones—a pro by now—she lets hang loose.

We call this place the Marcus Welby Hospital. It's the white one with the palm trees under the opening credits of all those shows. A Hollywood hospital, though in fact it is several miles west. Off camera, there is a beach across the street.

She introduces me to a nurse as the Best Friend. The impersonal article is more intimate. It tells me that *they* are intimate, the nurse and my friend.

"I was telling her we used to drink Canada Dry ginger ale and pretend we were in Canada."

"That's how dumb we were," I say.

"You could be sisters," the nurse says.

So how come, I'll bet they are wondering, it took me so long to get to such a glamorous place? But do they ask?

They do not ask.

Two months, and how long is the drive?

The best I can explain it is this—I have a friend who worked one summer in a mortuary. He used to tell me stories. The one that really got to me was not the grisliest, but it's the one that did. A man wrecked his car on 101 going south. He did not lose consciousness. But his arm was taken down to the wet bone—and when he looked at it—it scared him to death.

I mean, he died.

So I hadn't dared to look any closer. But now I'm doing it—and hoping that I will live through it.

She shakes out a summer-weight blanket, showing a leg you did not want to see. Except for that, you look at her and understand the law that requires *two* people to be with the body at all times.

"I thought of something," she says. "I thought of it last night. I think there is a real and present need here. You know," she says, "like for someone to do it for you when you can't do it yourself. You call them up whenever you want—like when push comes to shove."

She grabs the bedside phone and loops the cord around her neck.

"Hey," she says, "the end o' the line."

She keeps on, giddy with something. But I don't know with what.

"I can't remember," she says. "What does Kübler-Ross say comes after Denial?"

It seems to me Anger must be next. Then Bargaining, Depression, and so on and so forth. But I keep my guesses to myself.

"The only thing is," she says, "is where's Resurrection? God knows, I want to do it by the book. But she left out Resurrection."

She laughs, and I cling to the sound the way someone dangling above a ravine holds fast to the thrown rope.

"Tell me," she says, "about that chimp with the talking hands. What do they do when the thing ends and the chimp says, 'I don't want to go back to the zoo'?"

When I don't say anything, she says, "Okay—then tell me another animal story. I like animal stories. But not a sick one—I don't want to know about all the seeing-eye dogs going blind."

No, I would not tell her a sick one.

"How about the hearing-ear dogs?" I say. "They're not going deaf, but they are getting very judgmental. For instance, there's this golden retriever in New Jersey, he wakes up the deaf mother and drags her into the daughter's room because the kid has got a flashlight and is reading under the covers."

"Oh, you're killing me," she says. "Yes, you're definitely killing me."

"They say the smart dog obeys, but the smarter dog knows when to disobey."

"Yes," she says, "the smarter anything knows when to disobey. Now, for example."

She is flirting with the Good Doctor, who has just appeared. Unlike the Bad Doctor, who checks the IV drip before saying good morning, the Good Doctor says things like "God didn't give epileptics a fair shake." The Good Doctor awards himself points for the cripples he could have hit in the parking lot. Because the Good Doctor is a little in love with her, he says maybe a year. He pulls a chair up to her bed and suggests I might like to spend an hour on the beach.

"Bring me something back," she says. "Anything from the beach. Or the gift shop. Taste is no object."

He draws the curtain around her bed.

"Wait!" she cries.

I look in at her.

"Anything," she says, "except a magazine subscription."

The doctor turns away.

I watch her mouth laugh.

What seems dangerous often is not—black snakes, for example, or clear-air turbulence. While things that just lie there, like this beach, are loaded with jeopardy. A yellow dust rising from the ground, the heat that ripens melons overnight—this is earthquake weather. You can sit here braiding the fringe on your towel and the sand will all of a sudden suck down like an hourglass. The air roars. In the cheap apartments on-shore, bathtubs fill themselves and gardens roll up and over like green waves. If nothing happens, the dust will drift and the heat deepen till fear turns to desire. Nerves like that are only bought off by catastrophe.

"It never happens when you're thinking about it," she once observed. "Earthquake, earthquake, earthquake," she said.

"Earthquake, earthquake, earthquake," I said.

Like the aviaphobe who keeps the plane aloft with prayer, we kept it up until an aftershock cracked the ceiling.

That was after the big one in seventy-two. We were in college; our dormitory was five miles from the epi-center. When the ride was over and my jabbering pulse began to slow, she served five parts champagne to one part orange juice, and joked about living in Ocean View, Kansas. I offered to drive her to Hawaii on the new world psychics predicted would surface the next time, or the next.

I could not say that now—next.

Whose next? she could ask.   55

Was I the only one who noticed that the experts had stopped saying *if* and now spoke of *when?* Of course not; the fearful ran to thousands. We watched the traffic of Japanese beetles for deviation. Deviation might mean more natural violence.

I wanted her to be afraid with me. But she said, "I don't know. I'm just not."

She was afraid of nothing, not even of flying.

I have this dream before a flight where we buckle in and the plane moves down the runway. It takes off at thirty-five miles an hour, and then we're airborne, skimming the tree tops. Still, we arrive in New York on time.

It is so pleasant.   60

One night I flew to Moscow this way.

She flew with me once. That time she flew with me she ate macadamia nuts while the wings bounced. She knows the wing tips can bend thirty feet up and thirty feet down without coming off. She believes it. She trusts the law of aerodynamics. My mind stampedes. I can almost accept that a battle-ship floats when everybody knows steel sinks.

I see fear in her now, and am not going to try to talk her out of it. She is right to be afraid.

After a quake, the six o'clock news airs a film clip of first-graders yelling at the broken playground per their teacher's instructions.

"*Bad* earth!" they shout, because anger is stronger than fear.   65

But the beach is standing still today. Everyone on it is tranquilized, numb, or asleep. Teenaged girls rub coconut oil on each other's hard-to-reach places. They smell like macaroons. They pry open compacts like clam-shells; mirrors catch the sun and throw a spray of white rays across glazed shoulders. The girls arrange their wet hair with silk flowers the way they learned in *Seventeen.* They pose.

A formation of low-riders pulls over to watch with a six-pack. They get vocal when the girls check their tan lines. When the beer is gone, so are they—flexing their cars on up the boulevard.

Above this aggressive health are the twin wrought-iron terraces, painted flamingo pink, of the Palm Royale. Someone dies there every time the sheets are changed. There's an ambulance in the driveway, so the remaining residents line the balconies, rocking and not talking, one-upped.

The ocean they stare at is dangerous, and not just the undertow. You can almost see the slapping tails of sand sharks keeping cruising bodies alive.

If she looked, she could see this, some of it, from her window. She would be the first to say how little it takes to make a thing all wrong.

There was a second bed in the room when I got back to it!

For two beats I didn't get it. Then it hit me like an open coffin.

She wants every minute, I thought. She wants my life.

"You missed Gussie," she said.

Gussie is her parents' three-hundred-pound narcoleptic maid. Her attacks often come at the ironing board. The pillowcases in that family are all bordered with scorch.

"It's a hard trip for her," I said. "How is she?"

"Well, she didn't fall asleep, if that's what you mean. Gussie's great— you know what she said? She said, 'Darlin', stop this worriation. Just keep prayin', down on your knees'—me, who can't even get out of bed."

She shrugged. "What am I missing?"

"It's earthquake weather," I told her.

"The best thing to do about earthquakes," she said, "is not to live in California."

"That's useful," I said. "You sound like Reverend Ike—'The best thing to do for the poor is not to be one of them.'"

We're crazy about Reverend Ike.

I noticed her face was bloated.

"You know," she said, "I feel like hell. I'm about to stop having fun."

"The ancients have a saying," I said. "'There are times when the wolves are silent; there are times when the moon howls.'"

"What's that, Navaho?"

"Palm Royale lobby graffiti," I said. "I bought a paper there. I'll read you something."

"Even though I care about nothing?"

I turned to the page with the trivia column. I said, "Did you know the more shrimp flamingo birds eat, the pinker their feathers get?" I said, "Did you know that Eskimos need refrigerators? Do you know *why* Eskimos need refrigerators? Did you know that Eskimos need refrigerators because how else would they keep their food from freezing?"

I turned to page three, to a UPI filler datelined Mexico City. I read her MAN ROBS BANK WITH CHICKEN, about a man who bought a barbecued chicken at a stand down the block from a bank. Passing the bank, he got the idea. He walked in and approached a teller. He pointed the brown paper bag at her and she handed over the day's receipts. It was the smell of barbecue sauce that eventually led to his capture.

The story had made her hungry, she said—so I took the elevator down six floors to the cafeteria, and brought back all the ice cream she wanted. We lay side by side, adjustable beds cranked up for optimal TV-viewing, littering the sheets with Good Humor wrappers, picking toasted almonds out of the gauze. We were Lucy and Ethel, Mary and Rhoda, in extremis. The blinds were closed to keep light off the screen.

We watched a movie starring men we used to think we wanted to sleep with. Hers was a tough cop out to stop mine, a vicious rapist who went after cocktail waitresses.

"This is a good movie," she said when snipers felled them both.

I missed her already.

A Filipino nurse tiptoed in and gave her an injection. The nurse re-   95 moved the pile of popsicle sticks from the nightstand—enough to splint a small animal.

The injection made us both sleepy. We slept.

I dreamed she was a decorator, come to furnish my house. She worked in secret, singing to herself. When she finished, she guided me proudly to the door. "How do you like it?" she asked, easing me inside.

Every beam and sill and shelf and knob was draped in gay bunting, with streamers of pastel crepe looped around bright mirrors.

"I have to go home," I said when she woke up.

She thought I meant home to her house in the Canyon, and I had to   100 say No, *home* home. I twisted my hands in the time-honored fashion of people in pain. I was supposed to offer something. The Best Friend. I could not even offer to come back.

I felt weak and small and failed.

Also exhilarated.

I had a convertible in the parking lot. Once out of that room, I would drive it too fast down the Coast high-way through the crab-smelling air. A stop in Malibu for sangria. The music in the place would be sexy and loud. They'd serve papaya and shrimp and watermelon ice. After dinner I would shimmer with lust, buzz with heat, vibrate with life, and stay up all night.

Without a word, she yanked off her mask and threw it on the floor. She kicked at the blankets and moved to the door. She must have hated having to pause for breath and balance before slamming out of Isolation, and out of the second room, the one where you scrub and tie on the white masks.

A voice shouted her name in alarm, and people ran down the corridor.   105 The Good Doctor was paged over the intercom. I opened the door and the nurses at the station stared hard, as if this flight had been my idea.

"Where is she?" I asked, and they nodded to the supply closet.

I looked in. Two nurses were kneeling beside her on the floor, talking to her in low voices. One held a mask over her nose and mouth, the other rubbed her back in slow circles. The nurses glanced up to see if I was the doctor—and when I wasn't, they went back to what they were doing.

"There, there, honey," they cooed.

On the morning she was moved to the cemetery, the one where Al Jolson is buried, I enrolled in a "Fear of Flying" class. "What is your worst fear?" the instructor asked, and I answered, "That I will finish this course and still be afraid."

I sleep with a glass of water on the nightstand so I can see by its level 110 if the coastal earth is trembling or if the shaking is still me.

What do I remember?

I remember only the useless things I hear—that Bob Dylan's mother invented Wite-Out, that twenty-three people must be in a room before there is a fifty-fifty chance two will have the same birthday. Who cares whether or not it's true? In my head there are bath towels swaddling this stuff. Nothing else seeps through.

I review those things that will figure in the retelling: a kiss through surgical gauze, the pale hand correcting the position of the wig. I noted these gestures as they happened, not in any retrospect—though I don't know why looking back should show us more than looking *at*.

It is just possible I will say I stayed the night.

And who is there that can say that I did not? 115

I think of the chimp, the one with the talking hands.

In the course of the experiment, that chimp had a baby. Imagine how her trainers must have thrilled when the mother, without prompting, began to sign to her newborn.

Baby, drink milk.

Baby, play ball.

And when the baby died, the mother stood over the body, her wrin- 120 kled hands moving with animal grace, forming again and again the words: Baby, come hug, Baby, come hug, fluent now in the language of grief.

Considerations

1. Make a list of all the references to show business personalities, beginning with the reference to Al Jolson in the title. How do these references suggest possible themes for the story?
2. In the first section of the story, the Best Friend introduces the story of the chimp who learned to talk. Note other references to the chimp, and describe your response to the chimp's reappearance in the story's conclu-

sion. How do the actions of the mother chimp reflect the emotions of the narrator?

3. Create your own scenario explaining why the Best Friend has stayed away so long and why she says, as she leaves the hospital, "I could not even offer to come back".

4. Note the structure of the story. Rather than simply being split into paragraphs, it is split into many short sections, most consisting of three to ten very short paragraphs. What does this structure add to the story's tone and meaning?

5. How do earthquakes figure into the story? Note the various references to earthquakes, and suggest what they add to the characterization of the Best Friend and to the story's theme.

EDGAR ALLAN POE (1809–1849)
The Cask of Amontillado°

For biographical information about Edgar Allan Poe, see page 695.

The thousand injuries of Fortunato I had borne as I best could; but when he ventured upon insult, I vowed revenge. You, who so well know the nature of my soul, will not suppose, however, that I gave utterance to a threat. *At length* I would be avenged; this was a point definitively settled—but the very definitiveness with which it was resolved, precluded the idea of risk. I must not only punish, but punish with impunity. A wrong is unredressed when retribution overtakes its redresser. It is equally unredressed when the avenger fails to make himself felt as such to him who has done the wrong.

It must be understood, that neither by word nor deed had I given Fortunato cause to doubt my good-will. I continued, as was my wont, to smile in his face, and he did not perceive that my smile *now* was at the thought of his immolation.

He had a weak point—this Fortunato—although in other regards he was a man to be respected and even feared. He prided himself on his connoisseurship in wine. Few Italians have the true virtuoso spirit. For the most part their enthusiasm is adopted to suit the time and opportunity—to practice imposture upon the British and Austrian *millionaires.* In painting and gemmary° Fortunato, like his countrymen, was a quack—but in the matter of old wines he was sincere. In this respect I did not differ from him materially: I was skilful in the Italian vintages myself, and bought largely whenever I could.

It was about dusk, one evening during the supreme madness of the carnival season, that I encountered my friend. He accosted me with excessive warmth, for he had been drinking much. The man wore motley.° He had on a tight-fitting parti-striped dress, and his head was surmounted by the conical cap and bells. I was so pleased to see him, that I thought I should never have done wringing his hand.

I said to him: "My dear Fortunato, you are luckily met. How remark- 5
ably well you are looking to-day! But I have received a pipe° of what passes for Amontillado, and I have my doubts."

"How?" said he. "Amontillado? A pipe? Impossible! And in the middle of the carnival!"

"I have my doubts," I replied; "and I was silly enough to pay the full Amontillado price without consulting you in the matter. You were not to be found, and I was fearful of losing a bargain."

"Amontillado!"

Amontillado: A pale, dry sherry wine. *gemmary:* Scientific knowledge of gems. *motley:* garment of many colors. *pipe:* A large keg.

"I have my doubts."

"Amontillado!"

"And I must satisfy them." 10

"Amontillado!"

"As you are engaged, I am on my way to Luchesi. If any one has a critical turn, it is he: He will tell me—"

"Luchesi cannot tell Amontillado from Sherry."

"And yet some fools will have it that his taste is a match for your own." 15

"Come, let us go."

"Whither?"

"To your vaults."

"My friend, no; I will not impose upon your good nature. I perceive you have an engagement. Luchesi—"

"I have no engagement;—come." 20

"My friend, no. It is not the engagement, but the severe cold with which I perceive you are afflicted. The vaults are insufferably damp. They are encrusted with nitre."°

"Let us go, nevertheless. The cold is merely nothing. Amontillado! You have been imposed upon. And as for Luchesi, he cannot distinguish Sherry from Amontillado."

Thus speaking, Fortunato possessed himself of my arm. Putting on a mask of black silk, and drawing a *roquelaire*° closely about my person, I suffered him to hurry me to my palazzo.

There were no attendants at home; they had absconded to make merry in honor of the time. I had told them that I should not return until the morning, and had given them explicit orders not to stir from the house. These orders were sufficient, I well knew, to insure their immediate disappearance, one and all, as soon as my back was turned.

I took from their sconces two flambeaux,° and giving one to Fortunato, 25 bowed him through several suites of rooms to the archway that led into the vaults. I passed down a long and winding staircase, requesting him to be cautious as he followed. We came at length to the foot of the descent, and stood together on the damp ground of the catacombs° of the Montresors.

The gait of my friend was unsteady, and the bells upon his cap jingled as he strode.

"The pipe?" said he.

"It is farther on," said I; "but observe the white web-work which gleams from these cavern walls."

He turned toward me, and looked into my eyes with two filmy orbs that distilled the rheum° of intoxication.

"Nitre?" he asked, at length. 30

---

nitre: A white phosphate. *roquelaire:* Cloak. *flambeaux:* Torches. *catacombs:* Underground tunnels with recesses for graves. *rheum:* Watery discharge.

"Nitre," I replied. "How long have you had that cough?"

"Ugh! ugh! ugh!—ugh! ugh! ugh!—ugh! ugh! ugh!—ugh! ugh! ugh!—ugh! ugh! ugh!"

My poor friend found it impossible to reply for many minutes.

"It is nothing," he said, at last.

"Come," I said, with decision, "we will go back; your health is precious. You are rich, respected, admired, beloved; you are happy, as once I was. You are a man to be missed. For me it is no matter. We will go back; you will be ill, and I cannot be responsible. Besides there is Luchesi—" 35

"Enough," he said; "the cough is a mere nothing; it will not kill me. I shall not die of a cough."

"True—true," I replied; "and, indeed, I had no intention of alarming you unnecessarily; but you should use all proper caution. A draught of this Medoc° will defend us from the damps."

Here I knocked off the neck of a bottle which I drew from a long row of its fellows that lay upon the mould.

"Drink," I said, presenting him the wine.

He raised it to his lips with a leer. He paused and nodded to me familiarly, while his bells jingled. 40

"I drink," he said, "to the buried that repose around us."

"And I to your long life."

He again took my arm, and we proceeded.

"These vaults," he said, "are extensive."

"The Montresors," I replied, "were a great and numerous family." 45

"I forget your arms."

"A huge human foot d'or, in a field azure; the foot crushes a serpent rampant whose fangs are imbedded in the heel."

"And the motto?"

"*Nemo me impune lacessit.*"°

"Good!" he said. 50

The wine sparkled in his eyes and the bells jingled. My own fancy grew warm with the Medoc. We had passed through walls of piled bones, with casks and puncheons° intermingling, into the inmost recesses of the catacombs. I paused again, and this time I made bold to seize Fortunato by an arm above the elbow.

"The nitre!" I said; "see, it increases. It hangs like moss upon the vaults. We are below the river's bed. The drops of moisture trickle among the bones. Come, we will go back ere it is too late. Your cough—"

"It is nothing," he said; "let us go on. But first, another draught of the Medoc."

Medoc: A red wine. *Nemo . . . lacessit:* "No one can injure me with impunity." *puncheons:* Broad, heavy timbers.

I broke and reached him a flagon of De Grâve. He emptied it at a breath. His eyes flashed with a fierce light. He laughed and threw the bottle upward with a gesticulation I did not understand.

I looked at him in surprise. He repeated the movement—a grotesque one. 55

"You do not comprehend?" he said.

"Not I," I replied.

"Then you are not of the brotherhood."

"How?"

"You are not of the masons." 60

"Yes, yes," I said; "yes, yes."

"You? Impossible! A mason?"

"A mason," I replied.

"A sign," he said.

"It is this," I answered, producing a trowel from beneath the folds of 65
my *roquelaire*.

"You jest," he exclaimed, recoiling a few paces. "But let us proceed to the Amontillado."

"Be it so," I said, replacing the tool beneath the cloak, and again offering him my arm. He leaned upon it heavily. We continued our route in search of the Amontillado. We passed through a range of low arches, descended, passed on, and descending again, arrived at a deep crypt, in which the foulness of the air caused our flambeaux rather to glow than flame.

At the most remote end of the crypt there appeared another less spacious. Its walls had been lined with human remains, piled to the vault overhead, in the fashion of the great catacombs of Paris. Three sides of this interior crypt were still ornamented in this manner. From the fourth the bones had been thrown down, and lay promiscuously upon the earth, forming at one point a mound of some size. Within the wall thus exposed by the displacing of the bones, we perceived a still interior recess, in depth about four feet, in width three, in height six or seven. It seemed to have been constructed for no especial use within itself, but formed merely the interval between two of the colossal supports of the roof of the catacombs, and was backed by one of their circumscribing walls of solid granite.

It was in vain that Fortunato, uplifting his dull torch, endeavored to pry into the depth of the recess. Its termination the feeble light did not enable us to see.

"Proceed," I said; "herein is the Amontillado. As for Luchesi—" 70

"He is an ignoramus," interrupted my friend, as he stepped unsteadily forward, while I followed immediately at his heels. In an instant he had reached the extremity of the niche, and finding his progress arrested by the rock, stood stupidly bewildered. A moment more and I had fettered him to the granite. In its surface were two iron staples, distant from each other about two feet, horizontally. From one of these depended a short chain, from the other a padlock. Throwing the links about his waist, it was but the work of a few seconds to secure it. He was too much astounded to resist. Withdrawing the key I stepped back from the recess.

"Pass your hand," I said, "over the wall; you cannot help feeling the nitre. Indeed it is *very* damp. Once more let me *implore* you to return. No? Then I must positively leave you. But I must first render you all the little attentions in my power."

"The Amontillado!" ejaculated my friend, not yet recovered from his astonishment.

"True," I replied; "the Amontillado."

As I said these words I busied myself among the pile of bones of which 75
I have before spoken. Throwing them aside, I soon uncovered a quantity of building stone and mortar. With these materials and with the aid of my trowel, I began vigorously to wall up the entrance of the niche.

I had scarcely laid the first tier of the masonry when I discovered that the intoxication of Fortunato had in a great measure worn off. The earliest indication I had of this was a low moaning cry from the depth of the recess. It was *not* the cry of a drunken man. There was then a long and obstinate silence. I laid the second tier, and the third, and the fourth; and then I heard the furious vibrations of the chain. The noise lasted for several minutes, during which, that I might hearken to it with the more satisfaction, I ceased my labors and sat down upon the bones. When at last the clanking subsided, I resumed the trowel, and finished without interruption the fifth, the sixth, and the seventh tier. The wall was now nearly upon a level with my breast. I again paused, and holding the flambeaux over the mason-work, threw a few feeble rays upon the figure within.

A succession of loud and shrill screams, bursting suddenly from the throat of the chained form, seemed to thrust me violently back. For a brief moment I hesitated—I trembled. Unsheathing my rapier, I began to grope with it about the recess; but the thought of an instant reassured me. I placed my hand upon the solid fabric of the catacombs, and felt satisfied. I reapproached the wall. I replied to the yells of him who clamored. I re-echoed—I aided—I surpassed them in volume and in strength. I did this, and the clamorer grew still.

It was now midnight, and my task was drawing to a close. I had completed the eighth, the ninth, and the tenth tier. I had finished a portion of the last and the eleventh; there remained but a single stone to be fitted and plastered in. I struggled with its weight; I placed it partially in its destined position. But now there came from out the niche a low laugh that erected the hairs upon my head. It was succeeded by a sad voice, which I had difficulty in recognizing as that of the noble Fortunato. The voice said—

"Ha! ha! ha!—he! he!—a very good joke indeed—an excellent jest. We will have many a rich laugh about it at the palazzo—he! he! he!—over our wine—he! he! he!"

"The Amontillado!" I said. 80

"He! he! he!—he! he! he!—yes, the Amontillado. But is it not getting late? Will not they be awaiting us at the palazzo—the Lady Fortunato and the rest? Let us be gone."

"Yes," I said, "let us be gone."

"*For the love of God, Montresor!*"

"Yes," I said, "for the love of God!"

But to these words I hearkened in vain for a reply. I grew impatient. I called aloud: 85

"Fortunato!"

No answer. I called again:

"Fortunato!"

No answer still. I thrust a torch through the remaining aperture and let it fall within. There came forth in return only a tingling of the bells. My heart grew sick—on account of the dampness of the catacombs. I hastened to make an end of my labor. I forced the last stone into its position; I plastered it up. Against the new masonry I re-erected the old rampart of bones. For the half of a century no mortal has disturbed them. *In pace requiescat!*°

In pace requiescat: Rest in peace.

Considerations

1. Who is the listener as Montresor tells his story? Why do you think he has waited fifty years before revealing the details of his night in the catacombs?
2. Consider carefully the setting of the story. How is the carnival celebration (which is similar to Mardi Gras in New Orleans) significant to the plot as well as to the development of the story's characters and themes?
3. What are Montresor's motives for revenge against Fortunato? Consider how the family motto and the family crest relate to his anger. Consider also Fortunato's reactions when Montresor tells him about the crest.
4. As the tension mounts, this story becomes heavily fraught with irony. Identify several examples of irony, and explain what they contribute to the plot, the setting, and the development of the characters.
5. The final statement in the story, *In pace requiescat,* is a Latin phrase meaning "Rest in peace." Explain why you do or do not find this phrase a fitting conclusion for the story. If you wish, suggest an alternative ending.

ERNEST HEMINGWAY (1891–1961)

A Clean, Well-Lighted Place

For biographical information about Ernest Hemingway, see page 1116.

It was late and every one had left the café except an old man who sat in the shadow the leaves of the tree made against the electric light. In the daytime the street was dusty, but at night the dew settled the dust and the old man liked to sit late because he was deaf and now at night it was quiet and he felt the difference. The two waiters inside the café knew that the old man was a little drunk, and while he was a good client they knew that if he became too drunk he would leave without paying, so they kept watch on him.

"Last week he tried to commit suicide," one waiter said.

"Why?"

"He was in despair."

"What about?" 5

"Nothing."

"How do you know it was nothing?"

"He has plenty of money."

They sat together at a table that was close against the wall near the door of the café and looked at the terrace where the tables were all empty except where the old man sat in the shadow of the leaves of the tree that moved slightly in the wind. A girl and a soldier went by in the street. The street light shone on the brass number on his collar. The girl wore no head covering and hurried beside him.

"The guard will pick him up," one waiter said. 10

"What does it matter if he gets what he's after?"

"He had better get off the street now. The guard will get him. They went by five minutes ago."

The old man sitting in the shadow rapped on his saucer with his glass. The younger waiter went over to him.

"What do you want?"

The old man looked at him. "Another brandy," he said. 15

"You'll be drunk," the waiter said. The old man looked at him. The waiter went away.

"He'll stay all night," he said to his colleague. "I'm sleepy now. I never get into bed before three o'clock. He should have killed himself last week."

The waiter took the brandy bottle and another saucer from the counter inside the café and marched out to the old man's table. He put down the saucer and poured the glass full of brandy.

"You should have killed yourself last week," he said to the deaf man. The old man motioned with his finger. "A little more," he said. The waiter poured on into the glass so that the brandy slopped over and ran down the stem into the top saucer of the pile. "Thank you," the old man said. The waiter took the bottle back inside the café. He sat down at the table with his colleague again.

"He's drunk now," he said.

"He's drunk every night."

"What did he want to kill himself for?"

"How should I know."

"How did he do it?"

"He hung himself with a rope."

"Who cut him down?"

"His niece."

"Why did they do it?"

"Fear for his soul."

"How much money has he got?"

"He's got plenty."

"He must be eighty years old."

"Anyway I should say he was eighty."

"I wish he would go home. I never get to bed before three o'clock. What kind of hour is that to go to bed?"

"He stays up because he likes it."

"He's lonely. I'm not lonely. I have a wife waiting in bed for me."

"He had a wife once too."

"A wife would be no good to him now."

"You can't tell. He might be better with a wife."

"His niece looks after him."

"I know. You said she cut him down."

"I wouldn't want to be that old. An old man is a nasty thing."

"Not always. This old man is clean. He drinks without spilling. Even now, drunk. Look at him."

"I don't want to look at him. I wish he would go home. He has no regard for those who must work."

The old man looked from his glass across the square, then over at the waiters.

"Another brandy," he said, pointing to his glass. The waiter who was in a hurry came over.

"Finished," he said, speaking with that omission of syntax stupid people employ when talking to drunken people or foreigners. "No more tonight. Close now."

"Another," said the old man.

"No. Finished." The waiter wiped the edge of the table with a towel and shook his head.

The old man stood up, slowly counted the saucers, took a leather coin purse from his pocket and paid for the drinks, leaving half a peseta tip.

The waiter watched him go down the street, a very old man walking unsteadily but with dignity.

"Why didn't you let him stay and drink?" the unhurried waiter asked. They were putting up the shutters. "It is not half-past two."

"I want to go home to bed."

"What is an hour?"

"More to me than to him."   55

"An hour is the same."

"You talk like an old man yourself. He can buy a bottle and drink at home."

"It's not the same."

"No, it is not," agreed the waiter with a wife. He did not wish to be unjust. He was only in a hurry.

"And you? You have no fear of going home before your usual hour?"   60

"Are you trying to insult me?"

"No, hombre,° only to make a joke."

"No," the waiter who was in a hurry said, rising from pulling down the metal shutters. "I have confidence. I am all confidence."

"You have youth, confidence, and a job," the older waiter said. "You have everything."

"And what do you lack?"   65

"Everything but work."

"You have everything I have."

"No. I have never had confidence and I am not young."

"Come on. Stop talking nonsense and lock up."

"I am of those who like to stay late at the café," the older waiter said.   70
"With all those who do not want to go to bed. With all those who need a light for the night."

"I want to go home and into bed."

"We are of two different kinds," the older waiter said. He was now dressed to go home. "It is not only a question of youth and confidence although those things are very beautiful. Each night I am reluctant to close up because there may be some one who needs the café."

"Hombre, there are bodegas° open all night long."

"You do not understand. This is a clean and pleasant café. It is well lighted. The light is very good and also, now, there are shadows of the leaves."

"Good night," said the younger waiter.   75

"Good night," the other said. Turning off the electric light he continued the conversation with himself. It is the light of course but it is necessary that the place be clean and pleasant. You do not want music. Certainly you do not want music. Nor can you stand before a bar with dignity although that is all that is provided for these hours. What did he fear? It was not fear or dread. It was a nothing that he knew too well. It was all a nothing and a

hombre: Man. *bodegas:* Bars.

man was nothing too. It was only that and light was all it needed and a certain cleanness and order. Some lived in it and never felt it but he knew it all was nada y pues nada y nada y pues nada.° Our nada who art in nada, nada be thy name thy kingdom nada thy will be nada in nada as it is in nada. Give us this nada our daily nada and nada us our nada as we nada our nadas and nada us not into nada but deliver us from nada; pues nada. Hail nothing full of nothing, nothing is with thee. He smiled and stood before a bar with a shining steam pressure coffee machine.

"What's yours?" asked the barman.

"Nada."

"Otro loco mas,"° said the barman and turned away.

"A little cup," said the waiter.   80

The barman poured it for him.

"The light is very bright and pleasant but the bar is unpolished," the waiter said.

The barman looked at him but did not answer. It was too late at night for conversation.

"You want another copita?"° the barman asked.

"No, thank you," said the waiter and went out. He disliked bars and   85
bodegas. A clean, well-lighted café was a very different thing. Now, without thinking further, he would go home to his room. He would lie in the bed and finally, with daylight, he would go to sleep. After all, he said to himself, it is probably only insomnia. Many must have it.

---

nada y pues . . . nada: ". . . nothing and then nothing and nothing and then nothing." The lines that follow insert the Spanish word nada *("nothing") into the Lord's Prayer and the Hail Mary, creating a nihilistic parody.* Otro loco mas: *"Another crazy man."* copita: *Small cup.*

Considerations

1. Describe the relationship between the two waiters. How do you think their relationship might affect the way each views the old man?
2. Consider each of the three main characters (the waiters and the old man). What conflicts does each face? Based on what you learn from the story, explain how you think each will resolve (or fail to resolve) these conflicts.
3. What do you make of the parodies of the Lord's Prayer and the Hail Mary? What do these distortions contribute to the tone of the story and to its theme?
4. What is the significance of the title? Why is a "clean, well-lighted place" important to the older waiter and to the old man but not to the younger waiter? Do you have places equivalent to the "clean, well-lighted place"? Explain the importance of such places to you.

5. Write the scene that takes place in the café the next day when the two waiters report for work.

JOHN DONNE (1572–1631)

Death, be not proud

John Donne was forced to leave Oxford University without a degree because he refused to repudiate his Roman Catholic heritage at a time when anti-Catholic sentiment in England ran high. For years, he educated himself and struggled through prayer and reading to decide between the Roman Catholic and Anglican churches. During this time, he also became known as a witty, wise poet whose output varied from secular, erotic poems to holy sonnets. Finally, in 1615, Donne was ordained in the Anglican Church and became known as one of the greatest preachers of his time.

Death, be not proud, though some have called thee
Mighty and dreadful, for thou are not so;
For those whom thou think'st thou dost overthrow
Die not, poor Death, nor yet canst thou kill me.
From rest and sleep, which but thy pictures be,   5
Much pleasure; then from thee much more must flow,
And soonest our best men with thee do go,
Rest of their bones, and soul's delivery.
Thou art slave to fate, chance, kings, and desperate men,
And dost with poison, war, and sickness dwell,   10
And poppy or charms can make us sleep as well
And better than thy stroke; why swell'st thou then?
One short sleep past, we wake eternally
And death shall be no more; Death, thou shalt die.

Considerations

1. In this poem, the speaker directly addresses death. Death becomes personified, rather than remaining an abstract concept. Give a brief description of the character Death as pictured by the speaker.
2. Discuss the paradox (apparent contradiction) in the final line: "Death, thou shalt die." How can death die? What value system is implied by this statement?
3. Using the approach suggested here, plan a speech addressing an abstract concept: Love, Anger, Hope, Envy, Pride (or a concept of your choice).

e. e. cummings (1894–1962)
Buffalo Bill's

> *Edward Estlin Cummings was born in Cambridge, Massachusetts, and earned
> bachelor's and master's degrees from Harvard University before serving as a
> volunteer ambulance driver in France during World War I. His experimental
> punctuation, line division, and capitalization brought him wide attention and
> acclaim as an innovative and entertaining poet.*

Buffalo Bill's
defunct
    who used to
    ride a watersmooth-silver
                stallion   5
and break onetwothreefourfive   pigeons justlikethat
                               Jesus
he was a handsome man
              and what i want to know is
how do you like your blueeyed boy   10
Mister Death

Considerations

1. Consider the effect of the word "defunct" as opposed to these words:
   "dead," "deceased," "passed on," "gone to his just reward."
2. How would the poem be changed if the lines were printed as traditional
   sentences rather than in the arrangement cummings chose?
3. Three names are capitalized in this poem: Buffalo Bill, Jesus, Mister
   Death. Consider the possible significance of this choice. For example,
   what relationship among the three might be implied?

RUTH WHITMAN (1922–   )
Castoff Skin

> *Contemporary poet Ruth Whitman writes often on themes related to women's
> lives. In 1974, she received a grant from the National Endowment for the
> Humanities that enabled her to follow the westward trail from Illinois to Cali-
> fornia and thus to complete research for her book-length poem Tamsen Don-
> ner: A Woman's Journey (Alice James Books, 1977).*

She lay in her girlish sleep at ninety-six,
small as a twig.
Pretty good figure

for an old lady, she said to me once.
Then she crawled away, leaving   5
a tiny stretched transparence

behind her. When I kissed her paper cheek
I thought of the snake,
of his quick motion.

Considerations

1. What is the central metaphor of the poem? What does this metaphor
   suggest about the speaker's view of death?
2. What can you tell about the woman who is described by the poem?
3. What does the speaker imply about her view of the woman she
   describes?

JANE COOPER (1924–   )

In the House of the Dying

So once again, hearing the tired aunts
whisper together under the kitchen globe,
I turn away; I am not one of them.

At the sink I watch the water cover my hands
in a sheath of light. Upstairs she lies alone   5
dreaming of autumn nights when her children were born.

On the steps between us grows in a hush of waiting
the impossible silence between two generations.
The aunts buzz on like flies around a bulb.

I am dressed like them. Standing with my back turned   10
I wash the dishes in the same easy way.
Only at birth and death do I utterly fail.

For death is my old friend who waits on the stairs.
Whenever I pass I nod to him like the newsman
who is there every day; for them he is the priest.   15

While the birth of love is so terrible to me
I feel unworthy of the commonest marriage.
Upstairs she lies, washed through by the two miracles.

Considerations

1. What are the "two miracles" the speaker mentions in the final line of the poem? How does she see these "miracles" as related?
2. What can you infer about the relationship between the speaker and the woman who lies upstairs dying?
3. What view of death is suggested by this poem? Note particularly the contrast between the speaker's view and the view she ascribes to the aunts.

EMILY DICKINSON (1830–1886)

Born in Amherst, Massachusetts, Emily Dickinson was one of three children. She attended Mount Holyoke Seminary for Women for less than a year, rebelling against the evangelical revival and the spirit of fundamentalist Christianity that was sweeping the campus. Possibly because of her strong feelings about the religious atmosphere at Mount Holyoke, or possibly because of her father's strong desire to have her at home, she left school. After this time, she traveled very little and spent most of her life in her parents' home, where she tended to household duties, read, and wrote. In 1862, she began a literary correspondence with the critic T. W. Higginson, to whom she had sent some of her poems. Higginson responded to her innovative punctuation and verse structure by suggesting that she write more conventionally. Although Dickinson wrote more than one thousand lyrics, only seven of them were published in her lifetime, and these without her permission.

Apparently with no surprise

Apparently with no surprise
To any happy Flower
The Frost beheads it at its play—
In accidental power—
The blonde Assassin passes on—
The Sun proceeds unmoved
To measure off another Day
For an Approving God.

Considerations

1. Who or what might be represented by the "blonde Assassin"?
2. What is implied by the phrase "an Approving God"? Why not "the Approving God" or "our Approving God"? To what and why does this God give approval?
3. What view of death does the poem suggest?

I heard a Fly buzz—when I died—

I heard a Fly buzz—when I died—
The Stillness in the Room
Was like the Stillness in the Air—
Between the Heaves of Storm—

The Eyes around—had wrung them dry—   5
And Breaths were gathering firm
For the last Onset—when the King
Be witnessed—in the Room—

I willed my Keepsakes—Signed away
What portion of me be   10
Assignable—and then it was
There interposed a Fly—

With Blue—uncertain stumbling Buzz—
Between the light—and me—
And then the Windows failed—and then   15
I could not see to see—

The Bustle in a House

The Bustle in a House
The Morning after Death
Is solemnest of industries
Enacted upon Earth—

The Sweeping up the Heart   5
And putting Love away
We shall not want to use again
Until Eternity.

A. E. HOUSMAN (1859–1936)

To an Athlete Dying Young

For biographical information on A. E. Housman, see page 191.

The time you won your town the race
We chaired you through the market-place;
Man and boy stood cheering by,
And home we brought you shoulder-high.

To-day, the road all runners come,   5
Shoulder-high we bring you home,
And set you at your threshold down,
Townsman of a stiller town.

Smart lad, to slip betimes away
From fields where glory does not stay   10
And early though the laurel grows
It withers quicker than the rose.

Eyes the shady night has shut
Cannot see the record cut,
And silence sounds no worse than cheers   15
After earth has stopped the ears:

Now you will not swell the rout
Of lads that wore their honours out,
Runners whom renown outran
And the name died before the man.   20

So set, before its echoes fade,
The fleet foot on the sill of shade,
And hold to the low lintel up
The still-defended challenge-cup.

And round early-laurelled head   25
Will flock to gaze the strengthless dead,
And find unwithered on its curls
The garland briefer than a girl's.

THEODORE ROETHKE (1908–1963)

Elegy for Jane
My Student, Thrown by a Horse

For biographical information on Theodore Roethke, see page 24.

I remember the neckcurls, limp and damp as tendrils;
And her quick look, a sidelong pickerel smile;
And how, once startled into talk, the light syllables leaped for her,
And she balanced in the delight of her thought,
A wren, happy, tail into the wind,   5
Her song trembling the twigs and small branches.
The shade sang with her;
The leaves, their whispers turned to kissing;
And the mold sang in the bleached valleys under the rose.

Oh, when she was sad, she cast herself down into such a pure depth,   10
Even a father could not find her:
Scraping her cheek against straw;
Stirring the clearest water.

My sparrow, you are not here,
Waiting like a fern, making a spiny shadow.   15
The sides of wet stones cannot console me,
Nor the moss, wound with the last light.

WILLIAM STAFFORD (1914–   )

Traveling through the dark

Born in Kansas, William Stafford lived and worked in that state, earning bachelor's and master's degrees at the University of Kansas and a doctorate at the University of Iowa. Since 1948, he has taught literature and writing at Lewis and Clark College in Portland, Oregon. "Traveling through the Dark" appears in Stafford's collection Stories That Could Be True: New and Collected Poems *(1960).*

Traveling through the dark I found a deer
dead on the edge of the Wilson River road.
It is usually best to roll them into the canyon:
that road is narrow; to swerve might make more dead.

By glow of the tail-light I stumbled back of the car   5
and stood by the heap, a doe, a recent killing;
she had stiffened already, almost cold.
I dragged her off; she was large in the belly.

My fingers touching her side brought me the reason—
her side was warm; her fawn lay there waiting,   10
alive, still, never to be born.
Beside that mountain road I hesitated.

The car aimed ahead its lowered parking lights;
under the hood purred the steady engine.
I stood in the glare of the warm exhaust turning red;   15
around our group I could hear the wilderness listen.

I thought hard for us all—my only swerving—,
then pushed her over the edge into the river.

HARVEY FIERSTEIN (1954–   )

On Tidy Endings

*Born in Brooklyn to parents who had emigrated from eastern Europe, Harvey
Fierstein began his career in the theater early: at age eleven, he was a founding
actor in the Gallery Players Community Theater in Brooklyn. In addition, he
studied painting at New York's Pratt Institute and acted in several Broadway
plays before writing* Torch Song Trilogy *(1982), which won the Drama
Desk Award, the Theater World Award, and the Tony Award for best play.
He also won the Tony for best actor in the Broadway production of this play
and holds the distinction of being the first person to earn Tonys for both best
play and best actor for the same production. His plays present themes related to
the lives of gay men; Fierstein said of his success with* Torch Song Trilogy
*that the play demonstrated that "you could use a gay context and a gay expe-
rience and speak in universal truths." On Tidy Endings appears in* Safe Sex,
a collection of Fierstein's plays (1987).

Scene *The curtain rises on a deserted, modern Upper West Side apartment. In the
bright daylight that pours in through the windows we can see the living room of the
apartment. Far Stage Right is the galley kitchen, next to it the multilocked front door
with intercom. Stage Left reveals a hallway that leads to the two bedrooms and baths.*

    *Though the room is still fully furnished (couch, coffee table, etc.), there are boxes
stacked against the wall and several photographs and paintings are on the floor leaving
shadows on the wall where they once hung. Obviously someone is moving out. From
the way the boxes are neatly labeled and stacked, we know that this is an organized
person.*

    *From the hallway just outside the door we hear the rattling of keys and two
arguing voices:*

JIM *(Offstage)*: I've got to be home by four. I've got practice.
MARION *(Offstage)*: I'll get you to practice, don't worry.
JIM *(Offstage)*: I don't want to go in there.
MARION *(Offstage)*: Jimmy, don't make Mommy crazy, alright? We'll go
    inside, I'll call Aunt Helen and see if you can go down and play with
    Robbie.

    (The door opens. MARION *is a handsome woman of forty. Dressed in a
business suit, her hair conservatively combed, she appears to be going to
a business meeting.* JIM *is a boy of eleven. His playclothes are typical, but
someone has obviously just combed his hair.* MARION *recovers the key
from the lock.)*

JIM: Why can't I just go down and ring the bell?
MARION: Because I said so.

(As MARION steps into the room she is struck by some unexpected emotion. She freezes in her path and stares at the empty apartment. JIM lingers by the door.)

JIM: I'm going downstairs.

MARION: Jimmy, please.

JIM: This place gives me the creeps.

MARION: This was your father's apartment. There's nothing creepy about it.

JIM: Says you.

MARION: You want to close the door, please?

(JIM reluctantly obeys.)

MARION: Now, why don't you go check your room and make sure you didn't leave anything.

JIM: It's empty.

MARION: Go look.

JIM: I looked last time.

MARION *(Trying to be patient)*: Honey, we sold the apartment. You're never going to be here again. Go make sure you have everything you want.

JIM: But Uncle Arthur packed everything.

MARION *(Less patiently)*: Go make sure.

JIM: There's nothing in there.

MARION *(Exploding)*: I said make sure!

(JIM jumps, then realizing that she's not kidding, obeys.)

MARION: Everything's an argument with that one. *(She looks around the room and breathes deeply. There is sadness here. Under her breath:)* I can still smell you. *(Suddenly not wanting to be alone)* Jimmy? Are you okay?

JIM *(Returning)*: Nothing. Told you so.

MARION: Uncle Arthur must have worked very hard. Make sure you thank him.

JIM: What for? Robbie says, *(Fey mannerisms)* "They love to clean up things!"

MARION: Sometimes you can be a real joy.

JIM: Did you call Aunt Helen?

MARION: Do I get a break here? *(Approaching the boy understandingly)* Wouldn't you like to say good-bye?

JIM: To who?

MARION: To the apartment. You and your daddy spent a lot of time here together. Don't you want to take one last look around?

JIM: Ma, get a real life.

MARION: "Get a real life." *(Going for the phone)* Nice. Very nice.

JIM: Could you call already?

MARION *(Dialing)*: Jimmy, what does this look like I'm doing?

(JIM kicks at the floor impatiently. Someone answers the phone at the other end.)

MARION *(Into the phone)*: Helen? Hi, we're upstairs. . . . No, we just walked in the door. Jimmy wants to know if he can come down. . . . Oh, thanks.

(Hearing that, JIM breaks for the door.)

MARION *(Yelling after him)*: Don't run in the halls! And don't play with the elevator buttons!

(The door slams shut behind him.)

MARION *(Back to the phone)*: Hi. . . . No, I'm okay. It's a little weird being here. . . . No. Not since the funeral, and then there were so many people. Jimmy told me to get "a real life." I don't think I could handle anything realer. . . . No, please. Stay where you are. I'm fine. The door-man said Arthur would be right back and my lawyer should have been here already. . . . Well, we've got the papers to sign and a few other odds and ends to clean up. Shouldn't take long.

(The intercom buzzer rings.)

MARION: Hang on, that must be her.

(MARION goes to the intercom and speaks.) Yes? . . . Thank you.

(Back to the phone) Helen? Yeah, it's the lawyer. I'd better go. . . . Well, I could use a stiff drink, but I drove down. Listen, I'll stop by on my way out. Okay? Okay. 'Bye.

(She hangs up the phone, looks around the room. That uncomfortable feeling returns to her quickly. She gets up and goes to the front door, opens it and looks out. No one there yet. She closes the door, shakes her head knowing that she's being silly and starts back into the room. She looks around, can't make it and retreats to the door. She opens it, looks out, closes it, but stays right there, her hand on the doorknob.
The bell rings. She throws open the door.)

MARION: That was quick.

(JUNE LOWELL still has her finger on the bell. Her arms are loaded with contracts. MARION's contemporary, JUNE is less formal in appearance and more hyper in her manner.)

JUNE: *That* was quicker. What, were you waiting by the door?
MARION *(Embarrassed)*: No. I was just passing it. Come on in.
JUNE: Have you got your notary seal?
MARION: I think so.

JUNE: Great. Then you can witness. I left mine at the office and thanks to gentrification I'm double-parked downstairs. *(Looking for a place to dump her load)* Where?

MARION *(Definitely pointing to the coffee table)*: Anywhere. You mean you're not staying?

JUNE: If you really think you need me I can go down and find a parking lot. I think there's one over on Columbus. So, I can go down, park the car in the lot and take a cab back if you really think you need me.

MARION: Well . . . ?

JUNE: But you shouldn't have any problems. The papers are about as straightforward as papers get. Arthur is giving you power of attorney to sell the apartment and you're giving him a check for half the purchase price. Everything else is just signing papers that state that you know that you signed the other papers. Anyway, he knows the deal, his lawyers have been over it all with him, it's just a matter of signatures.

MARION *(Not fine)*: Oh, fine.

JUNE: Unless you just don't want to be alone with him . . . ?

MARION: With Arthur? Don't be silly.

JUNE *(Laying out the papers)*: Then you'll handle it solo? Great. My car thanks you, the parking lot thanks you, and the cab driver that wouldn't have gotten a tip thanks you. Come have a quick look-see.

MARION *(Joining her on the couch)*: There are a lot of papers here.

JUNE: Copies. Not to worry. Start here.

(MARION starts to read.)

JUNE: I ran into Jimmy playing Elevator Operator.

(MARION jumps.)

JUNE: I got him off at the sixth floor. Read on.

MARION: This is definitely not my day for dealing with him.

(JUNE gets up and has a look around.)

JUNE: I don't believe what's happening to this neighborhood. You made quite an investment when you bought this place.

MARION: Collin was always very good at figuring out those things.

JUNE: Well, he sure figured this place right. What, have you tripled your money in ten years?

MARION: More.

JUNE: It's a shame to let it go.

MARION: We're not ready to be a two-dwelling family.

JUNE: So, sublet it again.

MARION: Arthur needs the money from the sale.

JUNE: Arthur got plenty already. I'm not crying for Arthur.

MARION: I don't hear you starting in again, do I?

JUNE: Your interests and your wishes are my only concern.

MARION: Fine.

JUNE: I still say we should contest Collin's will.

MARION: June! . . .

JUNE: You've got a child to support.

MARION: And a great job, and a husband with a great job. Tell me what Arthur's got.

JUNE: To my thinking, half of everything that should have gone to you. And more. All of Collin's personal effects, his record collection . . .

MARION: And I suppose their three years together meant nothing.

JUNE: When you compare them to your sixteen-year marriage? Not nothing, but not half of everything.

MARION *(Trying to change the subject)*: June, who gets which copies?

JUNE: Two of each to Arthur. One you keep. The originals and anything else come back to me. *(Looking around)* I still say you should've sublet the apartment for a year and then sold it. You would've gotten an even better price. Who wants to buy an apartment when they know someone died in it. No one. And certainly no one wants to buy an apartment when they know the person died of AIDS.

MARION *(Snapping)*: June. Enough!

JUNE *(Catching herself)*: Sorry. That was out of line. Sometimes my mouth does that to me. Hey, that's why I'm a lawyer. If my brain worked as fast as my mouth I would have gotten a real job.

MARION *(Holding out a stray paper)*: What's this?

JUNE: I forgot. Arthur's lawyer sent that over yesterday. He found it in Collin's safety-deposit box. It's an insurance policy that came along with some consulting job he did in Japan. He either forgot about it when he made out his will or else he wanted you to get the full payment. Either way, it's yours.

MARION: Are you sure we don't split this?

JUNE: Positive.

MARION: But everything else . . . ?

JUNE: Hey, Arthur found it, his lawyer sent it to me. Relax, it's all yours. Minus my commission, of course. Go out and buy yourself something. Anything else before I have to use my cut to pay the towing bill?

MARION: I guess not.

JUNE *(Starting to leave)*: Great. Call me when you get home. *(Stopping at the door and looking back)* Look, I know that I'm attacking this a little coldly. I am aware that someone you loved has just died. But there's a time and place for everything. This is about tidying up loose ends, not holding hands. I hope you'll remember that when Arthur gets here. Call me.

(And she's gone.

MARION looks ill at ease to be alone again. She nervously straightens the papers into neat little piles, looks at them and then remembers:)

MARION: Pens. We're going to need pens.

(At last a chore to be done. She looks in her purse and finds only one. She goes to the kitchen and opens a drawer where she finds two more. She starts back to the table with them but suddenly remembers something else. She returns to the kitchen and begins going through the cabinets until she finds what she's looking for: a blue Art Deco teapot. Excited to find it, she takes it back to the couch.

Guilt strikes. She stops, considers putting it back, wavers, then:)

MARION *(To herself)*: Oh, he won't care. One less thing to pack.

(She takes the teapot and places it on the couch next to her purse. She is happier. Now she searches the room with her eyes for any other treasures she may have overlooked. Nothing here. She wanders off into the bedroom.

We hear keys outside the front door. ARTHUR *lets himself into the apartment carrying a load of empty cartons and a large shopping bag.*

ARTHUR *is in his mid-thirties, pleasant looking though sloppily dressed in work clothes and slightly overweight.*

ARTHUR *enters the apartment just as* MARION *comes out of the bedroom carrying a framed watercolor painting. They jump at the sight of each other.)*

MARION: Oh, hi, Arthur. I didn't hear the door.

ARTHUR *(Staring at the painting)*: Well hello, Marion.

MARION *(Guiltily)*: I was going to ask you if you were thinking of taking this painting because if you're not going to then I'll take it. Unless, of course, you want it.

ARTHUR: No. You can have it.

MARION: I never really liked it, actually. I hate cats. I didn't even like the show. I needed something for my college dorm room. I was never the rock star poster type. I kept it in the back of a closet for years until Collin moved in here and took it. He said he liked it.

ARTHUR: I do too.

MARION: Well, then you keep it.

ARTHUR: No. Take it.

MARION: We've really got no room for it. You keep it.

ARTHUR: I don't want it.

MARION: Well, if you're sure.

ARTHUR *(Seeing the teapot)*: You want the teapot?

MARION: If you don't mind.

ARTHUR: One less thing to pack.

MARION: Funny, but that's exactly what I thought. One less thing to pack. You know, my mother gave it to Collin and me when we moved in to our first apartment. Silly sentimental piece of junk, but you know.

ARTHUR: That's not the one.

MARION: Sure it is. Hall used to make them for Westinghouse back in the thirties. I see them all the time at antiques shows and I always wanted to buy another, but they ask such a fortune for them.

ARTHUR: We broke the one your mother gave you a couple of years ago. That's a reproduction. You can get them almost anywhere in the Village for eighteen bucks.

MARION: Really? I'll have to pick one up.

ARTHUR: Take this one. I'll get another.

MARION: No, it's yours. You bought it.

ARTHUR: One less thing to pack.

MARION: Don't be silly. I didn't come here to raid the place.

ARTHUR: Well, was there anything else of Collin's that you thought you might like to have?

MARION: Now I feel so stupid, but actually I made a list. Not for me. But I started thinking about different people; friends, relatives, you know, that might want to have something of Collin's to remember him by. I wasn't sure just what you were taking and what you were throwing out. Anyway, I brought the list. *(Gets it from her purse)* Of course these are only suggestions. You probably thought of a few of these people yourself. But I figured it couldn't hurt to write it all down. Like I said, I don't know what you are planning on keeping.

ARTHUR *(Taking the list)*: I was planning on keeping it all.

MARION: Oh, I know. But most of these things are silly. Like his high school yearbooks. What would you want with them?

ARTHUR: Sure. I'm only interested in his Gay period.

MARION: I didn't mean it that way. Anyway, you look it over. They're only suggestions. Whatever you decide to do is fine with me.

ARTHUR *(Folding the list)*: It would have to be, wouldn't it. I mean, it's all mine now. He did leave this all to me.

(MARION is becoming increasingly nervous, but tries to keep a light approach as she takes a small bundle of papers from her bag.)

MARION: While we're on the subject of what's yours. I brought a batch of condolence cards that were sent to you care of me. Relatives mostly.

ARTHUR *(Taking them)*: More cards? I'm going to have to have another printing of thank-you notes done.

MARION: I answered these last week, so you don't have to bother. Unless you want to.

ARTHUR: Forge my signature?

MARION: Of course not. They were addressed to both of us and they're mostly distant relatives or friends we haven't seen in years. No one important.

ARTHUR: If they've got my name on them, then I'll answer them myself.

MARION: I wasn't telling you not to, I was only saying that you don't have to.

ARTHUR: I understand.

(MARION picks up the teapot and brings it to the kitchen.)

MARION: Let me put this back.

ARTHUR: I ran into Jimmy in the lobby.

MARION: Tell me you're joking.

ARTHUR: I got him to Helen's.

MARION: He's really racking up the points today.

ARTHUR: You know, he still can't look me in the face.

MARION: He's reacting to all of this in strange ways. Give him time. He'll come around. He's really very fond of you.

ARTHUR: I know. But he's at that awkward age: under thirty. I'm sure in twenty years we'll be the best of friends.

MARION: It's not what you think.

ARTHUR: What do you mean?

MARION: Well, you know.

ARTHUR: No I don't know. Tell me.

MARION: I thought that you were intimating something about his blaming you for Collin's illness and I was just letting you know that it's not true. *(Foot in mouth, she braves on.)* We discussed it a lot and . . . uh . . . he understands that his father was sick before you two ever met.

ARTHUR: I don't believe this.

MARION: I'm just trying to say that he doesn't blame you.

ARTHUR: First of all, who asked you? Second of all, that's between him and me. And third and most importantly, of course he blames me. Marion, he's eleven years old. You can discuss all you want, but the fact is that his father died of a "fag" disease and I'm the only fag around to finger.

MARION: My son doesn't use that kind of language.

ARTHUR: Forget the language. I'm talking about what he's been through. Can you imagine the kind of crap he's taken from his friends? That poor kid's been chased and chastised from one end of town to the other. He's got to have someone to blame just to survive. He can't blame you, you're all he's got. He can't blame his father; he's dead. So, Uncle Arthur gets the shaft. Fine, I can handle it.

MARION: You are so wrong, Arthur. I know my son and that is not the way his mind works.

ARTHUR: I don't know what you know. I only know what I know. And all I know is what I hear and see. The snide remarks, the little smirks . . . And it's not just the illness. He's been looking for a scapegoat since the day you and Collin first split up. Finally he has one.

MARION *(Getting very angry now)*: Wait. Are you saying that if he's going to blame someone it should be me?

ARTHUR: I think you should try to see things from his point of view.

MARION: Where do you get off thinking you're privy to my son's point of view?

ARTHUR: It's not that hard to imagine. Life's rolling right along, he's having a happy little childhood, when suddenly one day his father's moving out. No explanations, no reasons, none of the fights that usually accompany such things. Divorce is hard enough for a kid to understand when he's listened to years of battles, but yours?

MARION: So what should we have done? Faked a few months' worth of fights before Collin moved out?

ARTHUR: You could have told him the truth, plain and simple.

MARION: He was seven years old at the time. How the hell do you tell a seven-year-old that his father is leaving his mother to go sleep with other men?

ARTHUR: Well, not like that.

MARION: You know, Arthur, I'm going to say this as nicely as I can: Butt out. You're not his mother and you're not his father.

ARTHUR: Thank you. I wasn't acutely aware of that fact. I will certainly keep that in mind from now on.

MARION: There's only so much information a child that age can handle.

ARTHUR: So it's best that he reach his capacity on the street.

MARION: He knew about the two of you. We talked about it.

ARTHUR: Believe me, he knew before you talked about it. He's young, not stupid.

MARION: It's very easy for you to stand here and criticize, but there are aspects that you will just never be able to understand. You weren't there. You have no idea what it was like for me. You're talking to someone who thought that a girl went to college to meet a husband. I went to protest rallies because I liked the music. I bought a guitar because I thought it looked good on the bed! This lifestyle, this knowledge that you take for granted, was all a little out of left field for me.

ARTHUR: I can imagine.

MARION: No. I don't think you can. I met Collin in college, married him right after graduation and settled down for a nice quiet life of Kids and Careers. You think I had any idea about this? Talk about life's little surprises. You live with someone for sixteen years, you share your life, your bed, you have a child together, and then you wake up one day and he tells you that to him it's all been a lie. A lie. Try that on for size. Here you are the happiest couple you know, fulfilling your every life fantasy and he tells you he's living a lie.

ARTHUR: I'm sure he never said that.

MARION: Don't be so sure. There was a lot of new ground being broken back then and plenty of it was muddy.

ARTHUR: You know that he loved you.

MARION: What's that supposed to do, make things easier? It doesn't. I was brought up to believe, among other things, that if you had love that was enough. So what if I wasn't everything he wanted. Maybe he wasn't exactly everything I wanted either. So, you know what? You count your blessings and you settle.

ARTHUR: No one has to settle. Not him. Not you.

MARION: Of course not. You can say, "Up yours!" to everything and
everyone who depends on and needs you, and go off to make yourself
happy.

ARTHUR: It's not that simple.

MARION: No. This is simpler. Death is simpler. *(Yelling out)* Happy now?

*(They stare at each other. MARION calms the rage and catches her breath.
ARTHUR holds his emotions in check.)*

ARTHUR: How about a nice hot cup of coffee? Tea with lemon? Hot
cocoa with a marshmallow floating in it?

MARION *(Laughs)*: I was wrong. You *are* a mother.

*(ARTHUR goes into the kitchen and starts preparing things. MARION
loafs by the doorway.)*

MARION: I lied before. He *was* everything I ever wanted.

*(ARTHUR stops, looks at her, and then changes the subject as he goes on
with his work.)*

ARTHUR: When I came into the building and saw Jimmy in the lobby I
absolutely freaked for a second. It's amazing how much they look alike.
It was like seeing a little miniature Collin standing there.

MARION: I know. He's like Collin's clone. There's nothing of me in him.

ARTHUR: I always kinda hoped that when he grew up he'd take after me.
Not much chance, I guess.

MARION: Don't do anything fancy in there.

ARTHUR: Please. Anything we can consume is one less thing to pack.

MARION: So you've said.

ARTHUR: So *we've* said.

MARION: I want to keep seeing you and I want you to see Jim. You're still
part of this family. No one's looking to cut you out.

ARTHUR: Ah, who'd want a kid to grow up looking like me anyway. I
had enough trouble looking like this. Why pass on the misery?

MARION: You're adorable.

ARTHUR: Is that like saying I have a good personality?

MARION: I think you are one of the most naturally handsome men I know.

ARTHUR: Natural is right, and the bloom is fading.

MARION: All you need is a few good nights' sleep to kill those rings under
your eyes.

ARTHUR: Forget the rings under my eyes, *(Grabbing his middle)* . . . how
about the rings around my moon?

MARION: I like you like this.

ARTHUR: From the time that Collin started using the wheelchair until he
died, about six months, I lost twenty-three pounds. No gym, no diet.
In the last seven weeks I've gained close to fifty.

MARION: You're exaggerating.

ARTHUR: I'd prove it on the bathroom scale, but I sold it in working order.

MARION: You'd never know.

ARTHUR: Marion, *you'd* never know, but ask my belt. Ask my pants. Ask my underwear. Even my stretch socks have stretch marks. I called the ambulance at five A.M., he was gone at nine and by nine-thirty, I was on a first-name basis with Sara Lee. I can quote the business hours of every ice-cream parlor, pizzeria and bakery on the island of Manhattan. I know the location of every twenty-four-hour grocery in the greater New York area, and I have memorized the phone numbers of every Mandarin, Szechuan and Hunan restaurant with free delivery.

MARION: At least you haven't wasted your time on useless hobbies.

ARTHUR: Are you kidding? I'm opening my own Overeater's Hotline. We'll have to start small, but expansion is guaranteed.

MARION: You're the best, you know that? If I couldn't be everything that Collin wanted then I'm grateful that he found someone like you.

ARTHUR *(Turning on her without missing a beat)*: Keep your goddamned gratitude to yourself. I didn't go through any of this for you. So your thanks are out of line. And he didn't find "someone like" me. It was me.

MARION *(Frightened)*: I didn't mean . . .

ARTHUR: And I wish you'd remember one thing more: He died in my arms, not yours.

(MARION is totally caught off guard. She stares disbelieving, openmouthed. ARTHUR walks past her as he leaves the kitchen with place mats. He puts them on the coffee table. As he arranges the papers and place mats he speaks, never looking at her.)

ARTHUR: Look, I know you were trying to say something supportive. Don't waste your breath. There's nothing you can say that will make any of this easier for me. There's no way for you to help me get through this. And that's your fault. After three years you still have no idea or understanding of who I am. Or maybe you do know but refuse to accept it. I don't know and I don't care. But at least understand, from my point of view, who you are: You are my husband's *ex*-wife. If you like, the mother of *my* stepson. Don't flatter yourself into thinking you're any more than that. And whatever you are, you're certainly not my friend.

(He stops, looks up at her, then passes her again as he goes back to the kitchen.
MARION is shaken, working hard to control herself. She moves toward the couch.)

MARION: Why don't we just sign these papers and I'll be out of your way.

ARTHUR: Shouldn't you say *I'll* be out of *your* way? After all, I'm not just
   signing papers, I'm signing away my home.
MARION *(Resolved not to fight, she gets her purse)*: I'll leave the papers here.
   Please have them notarized and returned to my lawyer.
ARTHUR: Don't forget my painting.
MARION *(Exploding)*: What do you want from me, Arthur?
ARTHUR *(Yelling back)*: I want you the hell out of my apartment! I want
   you out of my life! And I want you to leave Collin alone!
MARION: The man's dead. I don't know how much more alone I can
   leave him.

   *(ARTHUR laughs at the irony, but behind the laughter is something much
   more desperate.)*

ARTHUR: Lots more, Marion. You've got to let him go.
MARION: For the life of me, I don't know what I did, or what you think
   I did, for you to treat me like this. But you're not going to get away
   with it. You will not take your anger out on me. I will not stand here
   and be badgered and insulted by you. I know you've been hurt and I
   know you're hurting but you're not the only one who lost someone
   here.
ARTHUR *(Topping her)*: Yes I am! You didn't just lose him. I did! You lost
   him five years ago when he divorced you. This is not your moment of
   grief and loss, it's mine! *(Picking up the bundle of cards and throwing it
   toward her)* These condolences do not belong to you, they're mine.
   (Tossing her list back to her) His things are not yours to give away, they're
   mine! This death does not belong to you, it's mine! Bought and paid
   for outright. I suffered for it, I bled for it. I was the one who cooked
   his meals. I was the one who spoon-fed them. I pushed his wheelchair.
   I carried and bathed him. I wiped his backside and changed his diapers.
   I breathed life into and wrestled fear out of his heart. I kept him alive
   for two years longer than any doctor thought possible and when it was
   time I was the one who prepared him for death.
      I paid in full for my place in his life and I will *not* share it with
   you. We are not the two widows of Collin Redding. Your life was not
   here. Your husband didn't just die. You've got a son and a life somewhere else. Your husband's sitting, waiting for you at home, wondering,
   as I am, what the hell you're doing here and why you can't let go.

   *(MARION leans back against the couch. She's blown away. ARTHUR
   stands staring at her.)*

ARTHUR *(Quietly)*: Let him go, Marion. He's mine. Dead or alive; mine.

   *(The teakettle whistles. ARTHUR leaves the room, goes to the kitchen and
   pours the water as MARION pulls herself together.*
      *ARTHUR carries the loaded tray back into the living room and sets it
   down on the coffee table. He sits and pours a cup.)*

ARTHUR: One marshmallow or two?

(MARION *stares, unsure as to whether the attack is really over or not.*)

ARTHUR *(Placing them in her cup)*: Take three, they're small.

(MARION *smiles and takes the offered cup.*)

ARTHUR *(Campily)*: Now let me tell you how I *really* feel.

(MARION *jumps slightly, then they share a small laugh. Silence as they each gather themselves and sip their refreshments.*)

MARION *(Calmly)*: Do you think that I sold the apartment just to throw you out?

ARTHUR: I don't care about the apartment . . .

MARION: . . . Because I really didn't. Believe me.

ARTHUR: I know.

MARION: I knew the expenses here were too much for you, and I knew you couldn't afford to buy out my half . . . I figured if we sold it, that you'd at least have a nice chunk of money to start over with.

ARTHUR: You could've given me a little more time.

MARION: Maybe. But I thought the sooner you were out of here, the sooner you could go on with your life.

ARTHUR: Or the sooner you could go on with yours.

MARION: Maybe. *(Pauses to gather her thoughts)* Anyway, I'm not going to tell you that I have no idea what you're talking about. I'd have to be worse than deaf and blind not to have seen the way you've been treated. Or mistreated. When I read Collin's obituary in the newspaper and saw my name and Jimmy's name and no mention of you . . . *(Shakes her head, not knowing what to say)* You know that his secretary was the one who wrote that up and sent it in. Not me. But I should have done something about it and I didn't. I know.

ARTHUR: Wouldn't have made a difference. I wrote my own obituary for him and sent it to the smaller papers. They edited me out.

MARION: I'm sorry. I remember, at the funeral, I was surrounded by all of Collin's family and business associates while you were left with your friends. I knew it was wrong. I knew I should have said something but it felt good to have them around me and you looked like you were holding up . . . Wrong. But saying that it's all my fault for not letting go? . . . There were other people involved.

ARTHUR: Who took their cue from you.

MARION: Arthur, you don't understand. Most people that we knew as a couple had no idea that Collin was Gay right up to his death. And even those that did know only found out when he got sick and the word leaked out that it was AIDS. I don't think I have to tell you how stupid and ill-informed most people are about homosexuality. And AIDS . . . ? The kinds of insane behavior that word inspires? . . .

Those people at the funeral, how many times did they call to see how he was doing over these years? How many of them ever went to see him in the hospital? Did any of them even come here? So, why would you expect them to act any differently after his death?

So, maybe that helps to explain their behavior, but what about mine, right? Well, maybe there is no explanation. Only excuses. And excuse number one is that you're right, I have never really let go of him. And I am jealous of you. Hell, I was jealous of anyone that Collin ever talked to, let alone slept with . . . let alone loved.

The first year, after he moved out, we talked all the time about the different men he was seeing. And I always listened and advised. It was kind of fun. It kept us close. It kept me a part of his intimate life. And the bottom line was always that he wasn't happy with the men he was meeting. So, I was always allowed to hang on to the hope that one day he'd give it all up and come home. Then he got sick.

He called me, told me he was in the hospital and asked if I'd come see him. I ran. When I got to his door there was a sign, IN-STRUCTIONS FOR VISITORS OF AN AIDS PATIENT. I nearly died.

ARTHUR: He hadn't told you?

MARION: No. And believe me, a sign is not the way to find these things out. I was so angry . . . And he was so sick . . . I was sure that he'd die right then. If not from the illness then from the hospital staff's neglect. No one wanted to go near him and I didn't bother fighting with them because I understood that they were scared. I was scared. That whole month in the hospital I didn't let Jimmy visit him once.

You learn.

Well, as you know, he didn't die. And he asked if he could come stay with me until he was well. And I said yes. Of course, yes. Now, here's something I never thought I'd ever admit to anyone: had he asked to stay with me for a few weeks I would have said no. But he asked to stay with me until he was well and knowing there was no cure I said yes. In my craziness I said yes because to me that meant forever. That he was coming back to me forever. Not that I wanted him to die, but I assumed from everything I'd read . . . And we'd be back together for whatever time he had left. Can you understand that?

(ARTHUR *nods.*)

MARION (*Gathers her thoughts again*): Two weeks later he left. He moved in here. Into this apartment that we had bought as an investment. Never to live in. Certainly never to live apart in. Next thing I knew, the name Arthur starts appearing in every phone call, every dinner conversation.

"Did you see the doctor?"

"Yes. Arthur made sure I kept the appointment."

"Are you going to your folks for Thanksgiving?"

"No. Arthur and I are having some friends over."

I don't know which one of us was more of a coward, he for not telling or me for not asking about you. But eventually you became a given. Then, of course, we met and became what I had always thought of as friends.

(ARTHUR *winces in guilt.*)

MARION: I don't care what you say, how could we not be friends with something so great in common: love for one of the most special human beings there ever was. And don't try and tell me there weren't times when you enjoyed my being around as an ally. I can think of a dozen occasions when we ganged up on him, teasing him with our intimate knowledge of his personal habits.

(ARTHUR *has to laugh.*)

MARION: Blanket stealing? Snoring? Excess gas, no less? (*Takes a moment to enjoy this truce*) I don't think that my loving him threatened your relationship. Maybe I'm not being truthful with myself. But I don't. I never tried to step between you. Not that I ever had the opportunity. Talk about being joined at the hip! And that's not to say I wasn't jealous. I was. Terribly. Hatefully. But always lovingly. I was happy for Collin because there was no way to deny that he was happy. With everything he was facing, he was happy. Love did that. You did that.

He lit up with you. He came to life. I envied that and all the time you spent together, but more, I watched you care for him (sometimes *overcare* for him), and I was in awe. I could never have done what you did. I never would have survived. I really don't know how you did.

ARTHUR: Who said I survived?

MARION: Don't tease. You did an absolutely incredible thing. It's not as if you met him before he got sick. You entered a relationship that you knew in all probability would end this way and you never wavered.

ARTHUR: Of course I did. Don't have me sainted, Marion. But sometimes you have no choice. Believe me, if I could've gotten away from him I would've. But I was a prisoner of love.

(*He makes a campy gesture and pose.*)

MARION: Stop.

ARTHUR: And there were lots of pluses. I got to quit a job I hated, stay home all day and watch game shows. I met a lot of doctors and learned a lot of big words. (ARTHUR *jumps up and goes to the pile of boxes where he extracts one and brings it back to the couch.*) And then there was all the exciting traveling I got to do. This box has a souvenir from each one of our trips. Wanna see?

(MARION *nods. He opens the box and pulls things out one by one.*)

ARTHUR *(Continues) (Holding up an old bottle)*: This is from the house we rented in Reno when we went to clear out his lungs. *(Holding handmade potholders)* This is from the hospital in Reno. Collin made them. They had a great arts and crafts program. *(Copper bracelets)* These are from a faith healer in Philly. They don't do much for a fever, but they look great with a green sweater. *(Glass ashtrays)* These are from our first visit to the clinic in France. Such lovely people. *(A Bible)* This is from our second visit to the clinic in France. *(A bead necklace)* A Voodoo doctor in New Orleans. Next time we'll have to get there earlier in the year. I think he sold all the pretty ones at Mardi Gras. *(A tiny piñata)* Then there was Mexico. Black market drugs and empty wallets. *(Now pulling things out at random)* L.A., San Francisco, Houston, Boston . . . We traveled everywhere they offered hope for sale and came home with souvenirs. *(ARTHUR quietly pulls a few more things out and then begins to put them all back into the box slowly. Softly as he works:)*

Marion, I would have done anything, traveled anywhere to avoid . . . or delay . . . Not just because I loved him so desperately, but when you've lived the way we did for three years . . . the battle becomes your life. *(He looks at her and then away.)*

His last few hours were beyond any scenario I had imagined. He hadn't walked in nearly six months. He was totally incontinent. If he spoke two words in a week I was thankful. Days went by without his eyes ever focusing on me. He just stared out at I don't know what. Not the meals as I fed him. Not the TV I played constantly for company. Just out. Or maybe in.

It was the middle of the night when I heard his breathing become labored. His lungs were filling with fluid again. I knew the sound. I'd heard it a hundred times before. So, I called the ambulance and got him to the hospital. They hooked him up to the machines, the oxygen, shot him with morphine and told me that they would do what they could to keep him alive.

But, Marion, it wasn't the machines that kept him breathing. He did it himself. It was that incredible will and strength inside him. Whether it came from his love of life or fear of death, who knows. But he'd been counted out a hundred times and a hundred times he fought his way back.

I got a magazine to read him, pulled a chair up to the side of his bed and holding his hand, I wondered whether I should call Helen to let the cleaning lady in or if he'd fall asleep and I could sneak home for an hour. I looked up from the page and he was looking at me. Really looking right into my eyes. I patted his cheek and said, "Don't worry, honey, you're going to be fine."

But there was something else in his eyes. He wasn't satisfied with that. And I don't know why, I have no idea where it came from, I just heard the words coming out of my mouth, "Collin, do you want to die?" His eyes filled and closed, he nodded his head.

I can't tell you what I was thinking, I'm not sure I was. I slipped off my shoes, lifted his blanket and climbed into bed next to him. I helped him to put his arms around me, and mine around him, and whispered as gently as I could into his ear, "It's alright to let go now. It's time to go on." And he did.

Marion, you've got your life and his son. All I have is an intangible place in a man's history. Leave me that. Respect that.

MARION: I understand.

(ARTHUR *suddenly comes to life, running to get the shopping bag that he'd left at the front door.*)

ARTHUR: Jeez! With all the screamin' and sad storytelling I forget something. *(He extracts a bouquet of flowers from the bag.)* I brung you flowers and everything.

MARION: You brought *me* flowers?

ARTHUR: Well, I knew you'd never think to bring me flowers and I felt that on an occasion such as this somebody oughta get flowers from somebody.

MARION: You know, Arthur, you're really making me feel like a worthless piece of garbage.

ARTHUR: So what else is new? *(He presents the flowers.)* Just promise me one thing: Don't press one in a book. Just stick them in a vase and when they fade just toss them out. No more memorabilia.

MARION: Arthur, I want to do something for you and I don't know what. Tell me what you want.

ARTHUR: I want little things. Not much. I want to be remembered. If you get a Christmas card from Collin's mother, make sure she sent me one too. If his friends call to see how you are, ask if they've called me. Have me to dinner so I can see Jimmy. Let me take him out now and then. Invite me to his wedding.

(They both laugh.)

MARION: You've got it.

ARTHUR *(Clearing the table)*: Let me get all this cold cocoa out of the way. We still have the deed to do.

MARION *(Checking her watch)*: And I've got to get Jimmy home in time for practice.

ARTHUR: Band practice?

MARION: Baseball. *(Picking her list off the floor)* About this list, you do what you want.

ARTHUR: Believe me, I will. But I promise to consider your suggestions. Just don't rush me. I'm not ready to give it all away. (ARTHUR *is off to the kitchen with his tray and the phone rings. He answers it in the kitchen.)* Hello? . . . Just a minute. *(Calling out)* It's your eager Little Leaguer.

(MARION picks up the living room extension and ARTHUR hangs his up.)

MARION *(Into the phone)*: Hello, honey. . . . I'll be down in five minutes. No. You know what? You come up here and get me. . . . No, I said you should come up here. . . . I said I want you to come up here. . . . Because I said so. . . . Thank you.

(She hangs up the receiver.)

ARTHUR *(Rushing to the papers)*: Alright, where do we start on these?

MARION *(Getting out her seal)*: I guess you should just start signing everything and I'll stamp along with you. Keep one of everything on the side for yourself.

ARTHUR: Now I feel so rushed. What am I signing?

MARION: You want to do this another time?

ARTHUR: No. Let's get it over with. I wouldn't survive another session like this.

(He starts to sign and she starts her job.)

MARION: I keep meaning to ask you; how are you?

ARTHUR *(At first puzzled and then)*: Oh, you mean my health? Fine. No, I'm fine. I've been tested, and nothing. We were very careful. We took many precautions. Collin used to make jokes about how we should invest in rubber futures.

MARION: I'll bet.

ARTHUR *(Stops what he's doing)*: It never occurred to me until now. How about you?

MARION *(Not stopping)*: Well, we never had sex after he got sick.

ARTHUR: But before?

MARION *(Stopping but not looking up)*: I have the antibodies in my blood. No signs that it will ever develop into anything else. And it's been five years so my chances are pretty good that I'm just a carrier.

ARTHUR: I'm so sorry. Collin never told me.

MARION: He didn't know. In fact, other than my husband and the doctors, you're the only one I've told.

ARTHUR: You and your husband . . . ?

MARION: Have invested in rubber futures. There'd only be a problem if we wanted to have a child. Which we do. But we'll wait. Miracles happen every day.

ARTHUR: I don't know what to say.

MARION: Tell me you'll be there if I ever need you.

(Arthur gets up, goes to her and puts his arms around her. They hold each other. He gently pushes her away to make a joke.)

ARTHUR: Sure! Take something else that should have been mine.

MARION: Don't even joke about things like that.

(The doorbell rings. They pull themselves together.)

ARTHUR: You know we'll never get these done today.

MARION: So, tomorrow.

(ARTHUR goes to open the door as MARION gathers her things. He opens the door and JIMMY is standing in the hall.)

JIM: C'mon, Ma. I'm gonna be late.

ARTHUR: Would you like to come inside?

JIM: We've gotta go.

MARION: Jimmy, come on.

JIM: Ma!

(She glares. He comes in. ARTHUR closes the door.)

MARION *(Holding out the flowers)*: Take these for Mommy.

JIM *(Taking them)*: Can we go?

MARION *(Picking up the painting)*: Say good-bye to your Uncle Arthur.

JIM: 'Bye, Arthur. Come on.

MARION: Give him a kiss.

ARTHUR: Marion, don't.

MARION: Give your uncle a kiss good-bye.

JIM: He's not my uncle.

MARION: No. He's a hell of a lot more than your uncle.

ARTHUR *(Offering his hand)*: A handshake will do.

MARION: Tell Uncle Arthur what your daddy told you.

JIM: About what?

MARION: Stop playing dumb. You know.

ARTHUR: Don't embarrass him.

MARION: Jimmy, please.

JIM *(He regards his MOTHER's softer tone and then speaks)*: He said that after me and Mommy he loved you the most.

MARION *(Standing behind him)*: Go on.

JIM: And that I should love you too. And make sure that you're not lonely or very sad.

ARTHUR: Thank you.

(ARTHUR reaches down to the boy and they hug. JIM gives him a little peck on the cheek and then breaks away.)

MARION *(Going to open the door)*: Alright, kid, you done good. Now let's blow this joint before you muck it up.

(JIM rushes out the door. MARION turns to ARTHUR.)

MARION: A child's kiss is magic. Why else would they be so stingy with them. I'll call you.

(ARTHUR *nods understanding.* MARION *pulls the door closed behind her.* ARTHUR *stands quietly as the lights fade to black.*)

THE END

NOTE: *If being performed on film, the final image should be of* ARTHUR *leaning his back against the closed door on the inside of the apartment and* MARION *leaning on the outside of the door. A moment of thought and then they both move on.*

Considerations

1. Describe the relationship between Jim and Marion. Evaluate the way each responds to Collin's death and to the other's response to Collin's death.
2. June says, "Arthur got plenty already. I'm not crying for Arthur." What does she mean by this? What is your evaluation of Arthur's losses—and gains—from his relationship with Collin and from Collin's death?
3. Think about the title of the play. June warns Marion to "[tidy] up loose ends . . . when Arthur gets here." What is implied by a "tidy" ending or by "tidying up loose ends"? To what extent is the ending described "tidy"? How might the play's title be considered ironic?
4. Describe the relationship between Arthur and Marion. For whom do you have more sympathy? Explain.
5. What do the three main characters in the play (Arthur, Marion, and Jimmy) learn about themselves, about each other, about Collin, and—especially—about facing death (either their own or the death of others)?

JESSICA MITFORD (1917–   )

The American Way of Death

> *Born in England, Jessica Mitford, the sixth child of Lord and Lady Redesdale,*
> *was educated entirely at home. In the 1930s, Mitford left England for the*
> *United States and, in 1939, took up permanent residence. In the late 1950s,*
> *she began her career as an investigative journalist and has researched and ex-*
> *posed many examples of deception, fraud, and gullibility in American society.*
> *Her articles have appeared in such magazines as* The Nation, Esquire, *and*
> *the* Atlantic Monthly. *"The American Way of Death" is an excerpt from her*
> *book of the same title (1963).*

The drama begins to unfold with the arrival of the corpse at the
mortuary.

Alas, poor Yorick!° How surprised he would be to see how his counterpart of today is whisked off to a funeral parlor and is in short order
sprayed, sliced, pierced, pickled, trussed, trimmed, creamed, waxed, painted,
rouged, and neatly dressed—transformed from a common corpse into a
Beautiful Memory Picture. This process is known in the trade as embalming
and restorative art, and is so universally employed in the United States and
Canada that the funeral director does it routinely, without consulting corpse
or kin. He regards as eccentric those few who are hardy enough to suggest
that it might be dispensed with. Yet no law requires embalming, no religious
doctrine commends it, nor is it dictated by considerations of health, sanita-
tion, or even of personal daintiness. In no part of the world but in Northern
America is it widely used. The purpose of embalming is to make the corpse
presentable for viewing in a suitably costly container; and here too the funeral director routinely, without first consulting the family, prepares the body
for public display.

Is all this legal? The processes to which a dead body may be subjected
are after all to some extent circumscribed by law. In most states, for instance,
the signature of next of kin must be obtained before an autopsy may be
performed, before the deceased may be cremated, before the body may be
turned over to a medical school for research purposes; or such provision must
be made in the decedent's will. In the case of embalming, no such permission
is required nor is it ever sought. A textbook, *The Principles and Practices of*
Embalming, comments on this: "There is some question regarding the legality
of much that is done within the preparation room." The author points out
that it would be most unusual for a responsible member of a bereaved family
to instruct the mortician, in so many words, to "*embalm*" the body of a
deceased relative. The very term "embalming" is so seldom used that the

---

Alas, poor Yorick!: A reference to Shakespeare's *Hamlet;* in a comic scene, two gravediggers discover the skull of a man they knew, and Hamlet addresses his remains with these words.

mortician must rely upon custom in the matter. The author concludes that unless the family specifies otherwise, the act of entrusting the body to the care of a funeral establishment carries with it an implied permission to go ahead and embalm.

Embalming is indeed a most extraordinary procedure, and one must wonder at the docility of Americans who each year pay hundreds of millions of dollars for its perpetuation, blissfully ignorant of what it is all about, what is done, how it is done. Not one in ten thousand has any idea of what actually takes place. Books on the subject are extremely hard to come by. They are not to be found in most libraries or bookshops.

In an era when huge television audiences watch surgical operations in   5
the comfort of their living rooms, when, thanks to the animated cartoon, the geography of the digestive system has become familiar territory even to the nursery school set, in a land where the satisfaction of curiosity about almost all matters is a national pastime, the secrecy surrounding embalming can, surely, hardly be attributed to the inherent gruesomeness of the subject. Custom in this regard has within this century suffered a complete reversal. In the early days of American embalming, when it was performed in the home of the deceased, it was almost mandatory for some relative to stay by the embalmer's side and witness the procedure. Today, family members who might wish to be in attendance would certainly be dissuaded by the funeral director. All others, except apprentices, are excluded by law from the preparation room.

A close look at what does actually take place may explain in large measure the undertaker's intractable reticence concerning a procedure that has become his major *raison d'être.*° Is it possible he fears the public information about embalming might lead patrons to wonder if they really want this service? If the funeral men are loath to discuss the subject outside the trade, the reader may, understandably, be equally loath to go on reading at this point. For those who have the stomach for it, let us part the formaldehyde curtain. . . .

The body is first laid out in the undertaker's morgue—or rather, Mr. Jones is reposing in the preparation room—to be readied to bid the world farewell.

The preparation room in any of the better funeral establishments has the tiled and sterile look of a surgery, and indeed the embalmer-restorative artist who does his chores there is beginning to adopt the term "dermasurgeon" (appropriately corrupted by some mortician-writers as "demi-surgeon") to describe his calling. His equipment, consisting of scalpels, scissors, augurs, forceps, clamps, needles, pumps, tubes, bowls and basins, is crudely imitative of the surgeon's, as is his technique, acquired in a nine- or twelve-month post-high-school course in an embalming school. He is supplied by an advanced chemical industry with a bewildering array of fluids, sprays, pastes,

---

raison d'être: French term meaning "reason for being."

oils, powders, creams, to fix or soften tissue, shrink or distend it as needed, dry it here, restore the moisture there. There are cosmetics, waxes and paints to fill and cover features, even plaster of Paris to replace entire limbs. There are ingenious aids to prop and stabilize the cadaver: a Vari-Pose Head Rest, the Edwards Arm and Hand Positioner, the Repose Block (to support the shoulders during the embalming), and the Throop Foot Positioner, which resembles an old-fashioned stocks.

Mr. John H. Eckels, president of the Eckels College of Mortuary Science, thus describes the first part of the embalming procedure: "In the hands of a skilled practitioner, this work may be done in a comparatively short time and without mutilating the body other than by slight incision—so slight that it scarcely would cause serious inconvenience if made upon a living person. It is necessary to remove the blood, and doing this not only helps in the disinfecting, but removes the principal cause of disfigurements due to discoloration."

Another textbook discusses the all-important time element: "The earlier this is done, the better, for every hour that elapses between death and embalming will add to the problems and complications encountered. . . ." Just how soon should one get going on the embalming? The author tells us, "On the basis of such scanty information made available to this profession through its rudimentary and haphazard system of technical research, we must conclude that the best results are to be obtained if the subject is embalmed before life is completely extinct—that is, before cellular death has occurred. In the average case, this would mean within an hour after somatic death." For those who feel that there is something a little rudimentary, not to say haphazard, about this advice, a comforting thought is offered by another writer. Speaking of fears entertained in early days of premature burial, he points out, "One of the effects of embalming by chemical injection, however, has been to dispel fears of live burial." How true; once blood is removed, chances of live burial are indeed remote.

To return to Mr. Jones, the blood is drained out through the veins and replaced by embalming fluid pumped in through the arteries. As noted in *The Principles and Practices of Embalming,* "every operator has a favorite injection and drainage point—a fact which becomes a handicap only if he fails or refuses to forsake his favorites when conditions demand it." Typical favorites are the carotid artery, femoral artery, jugular vein, subclavian vein. There are various choices of embalming fluid. If Flextone is used, it will produce a "mild, flexible rigidity. The skin retains a velvety softness, the tissues are rubbery and pliable. Ideal for women and children." It may be blended with B. and G. Products Company's Lyf-Lyk tint, which is guaranteed to reproduce "nature's own skin texture . . . the velvety appearance of living tissue." Suntone comes in three separate tints: Suntan; Special Cosmetic Tint, a pink shade "especially indicated for young female subjects"; and Regular Cosmetic Tint, moderately pink.

About three to six gallons of a dyed and perfumed solution of formaldehyde, glycerin, borax, phenol, alcohol, and water is soon circulating

10

through Mr. Jones, whose mouth has been sewn together with a "needle directed upward between the upper lip and gum and brought out through the left nostril," with the corners raised slightly "for a more pleasant expression." If he should be bucktoothed, his teeth are cleaned with Bon Ami and coated with colorless nail polish. His eyes, meanwhile, are closed with flesh-tinted eye caps and eye cement.

The next step is to have at Mr. Jones with a thing called a trocar. This is a long, hollow needle attached to a tube. It is jabbed into the abdomen, poked around the entrails and chest cavity, the contents of which are pumped out and replaced with "cavity fluid." This done, and the hole in the abdomen sewn up, Mr. Jones's face is heavily creamed (to protect the skin from burns which may be caused by leakage of the chemicals), and he is covered with a sheet and left unmolested for a while. But not for long—there is more, much more, in store for him. He has been embalmed, but not yet restored, and the best time to start the restorative work is eight to ten hours after embalming, when the tissues have become firm and dry.

The object of all this attention to the corpse, it must be remembered, is to make it presentable for viewing in an attitude of healthy repose. "Our customs require the presentation of our dead in the semblance of normality . . . unmarred by the ravages of illness, disease or mutilation," says Mr. J. Sheridan Mayer in his *Restorative Art*. This is rather a large order since few people die in the full bloom of health, unravaged by illness and unmarked by some disfigurement. The funeral industry is equal to the challenge: "In some cases the gruesome appearance of a mutilated or disease-ridden subject may be quite discouraging. The task of restoration may seem impossible and shake the confidence of the embalmer. This is the time for intestinal fortitude and determination. Once the formative work is begun and affected tissues are cleaned or removed, all doubts of success vanish. It is surprising and gratifying to discover the results which may be obtained."

The embalmer, having allowed an appropriate interval to elapse, returns   15
to the attack, but now he brings into play the skill and equipment of sculptor and cosmetician. Is a hand missing? Casting one in plaster of Paris is a simple matter. "For replacement purposes, only a cast of the back of the hand is necessary; this is within the ability of the average operator and is quite adequate." If a lip or two, a nose or an ear should be missing, the embalmer has at hand a variety of restorative waxes with which to model replacements. Pores and skin texture are simulated by stippling with a little brush, and over this cosmetics are laid on. Head off? Decapitation cases are rather routinely handled. Ragged edges are trimmed, and head joined to torso with a series of splints, wires and sutures. It is a good idea to have a little something at the neck—a scarf or high collar—when time for viewing comes. Swollen mouth? Cut out tissue as needed from inside the lips. If too much is removed, the surface contour can easily be restored by padding with cotton. Swollen necks and cheeks are reduced by removing tissue through vertical incisions made down each side of the neck. "When the deceased is casketed, the

pillow will hide the suture incisions . . . as an extra precaution against leakage, the suture may be painted with liquid sealer."

The opposite condition is more likely to present itself—that of emaciation. His hypodermic syringe now loaded with massage cream, the embalmer seeks out and fills the hollowed and sunken areas by injection. In this procedure the backs of the hands and fingers and the under-chin area should not be neglected.

Positioning the lips is a problem that recurrently challenges the ingenuity of the embalmer. Closed too tightly they tend to give a stern, even disapproving expression. Ideally, embalmers feel, the lips should give the impression of being ever so slightly parted, the upper lip protruding slightly for a more youthful appearance. This takes some engineering, however, as the lips tend to drift apart. Lip drift can sometimes be remedied by pushing one or two straight pins through the inner margin of the lower lip and then inserting them between the two front upper teeth. If Mr. Jones happens to have no teeth, the pins can just as easily be anchored in his Armstrong Face Former and Denture Replacer. Another method to maintain lip closure is to dislocate the lower jaw, which is then held in its new position by a wire run through holes which have been drilled through the upper and lower jaws at the midline. As the French are fond of saying, *il faut souffrir pour être belle.*°

If Mr. Jones has died of jaundice, the embalming fluid will very likely turn him green. Does this deter the embalmer? Not if he has intestinal fortitude. Masking pastes and cosmetics are heavily laid on, burial garments and casket interiors are color-correlated with particular care, and Jones is displayed beneath rose-colored lights. Friends will say, "How *well* he looks." Death by carbon monoxide, on the other hand, can be rather a good thing from the embalmer's viewpoint: "One advantage is the fact that this type of discoloration is an exaggerated form of a natural pink coloration." This is nice because the healthy glow is already present and needs but little attention.

The patching and filling completed, Mr. Jones is now shaved, washed and dressed. Cream-based cosmetic, available in pink, flesh, suntan, brunette, and blond, is applied to his hands and face, his hair is shampooed and combed (and, in the case of Mrs. Jones, set), his hands manicured. For the horny-handed son of toil special care must be taken; cream should be applied to remove ingrained grime, and the nails cleaned. "If he were not in the habit of having them manicured in life, trimming and shaping is advised for better appearance—never questioned by kin."

Jones is now ready for casketing (this is the present participle of the   20 verb "to casket"). In this operation his right shoulder should be depressed slightly "to turn the body a bit to the right and soften the appearance of lying flat on the back." Positioning the hands is a matter of importance, and special rubber positioning blocks may be used. The hands should be cupped

---

il faut souffrir pour être belle: French term meaning "one must suffer to be beautiful."

slightly for a more lifelike, relaxed appearance. Proper placement of the body requires a delicate sense of balance. It should lie as high as possible in the casket, yet not so high that the lid, when lowered, will hit the nose. On the other hand, we are cautioned, placing the body too low "creates the impression that the body is in a box."

Jones is next wheeled into the appointed slumber room where a few last touches may be added—his favorite pipe placed in his hand or, if he was a great reader, a book propped into position. (In the case of little Master Jones a Teddy bear may be clutched.) Here he will hold open house for a few days, visiting hours 10 A.M. to 9 P.M.

Considerations

1. Although her topic in this essay is certainly serious, Mitford often uses humor. List several comments or observations you consider humorous and analyze the effect of humor on the tone of the essay. In addition, consider how Mitford's use of humor suggests her theme(s).
2. What are the benefits and disadvantages of embalming and restoration, according to Mitford? In her view, what values have caused these practices to be nearly universally adopted throughout the United States (as well as some other parts of the world)?
3. Note that Mitford frequently includes quotations from the professional journals and textbooks used by funeral directors. Why might she use this strategy? Analyze the effect of this strategy on your response to her essay.
4. What is the effect of Mitford's naming the corpse "Mr. Jones" rather than simply referring to "the body"?
5. Analyze Mitford's attitude toward American funeral practices. Then explain why you agree or disagree with the views she supports.

ELISABETH KÜBLER-ROSS (1924–   )

On the Fear of Death

A Swiss-American psychiatrist, Elisabeth Kübler-Ross has done extensive re-search on the topics of death and dying. Born in Zurich, Switzerland, she earned her doctorate from the University of Zurich and then came to the United States for her internship. Following her years as an intern and resident, she began her work with terminally ill patients while teaching psychiatry at the University of Chicago Medical School. "On the Fear of Death" comes from her first book, On Death and Dying *(1969).*

> *Let me not pray to be sheltered from*
> *dangers but to be fearless in facing*
> *them.*
> *Let me not beg for the stilling of*
> *my pain but for the heart to conquer it.*
> *Let me not look for allies in life's*
> *battlefield but to my own strength.*
> *Let me not crave in anxious fear to*
> *be saved but hope for the patience to*
> *win my freedom.*
> *Grant me that I may not be a*
> *coward, feeling your mercy in my*
> *success alone; but let me find the grasp*
> *of your hand in my failure.*

Rabindranath Tagore, *Fruit-Gathering*

Epidemics have taken a great toll of lives in past generations. Death in infancy and early childhood was frequent and there were few families who didn't lose a member of the family at an early age. Medicine has changed greatly in the last decades. Widespread vaccinations have practically eradi-cated many illnesses, at least in western Europe and the United States. The use of chemotherapy, especially the antibiotics, has contributed to an ever-decreasing number of fatalities in infectious diseases. Better child care and education has effected a low morbidity and mortality among children. The many diseases that have taken an impressive toll among the young and middle-aged have been conquered. The number of old people is on the rise, and with this fact come the number of people with malignancies and chronic diseases associated more with old age.

Pediatricians have less work with acute and life-threatening situations as they have an ever-increasing number of patients with psychosomatic dis-turbances and adjustment and behavior problems. Physicians have more peo-ple in their waiting rooms with emotional problems than they have ever had before, but they also have more elderly patients who not only try to live with their decreased physical abilities and limitations but who also face loneliness and isolation with all its pains and anguish. The majority of these people are not seen by a psychiatrist. Their needs have to be elicited and gratified by other professional people, for instance, chaplains and social workers. It is for them that I am trying to outline the changes that have taken place in the last few decades, changes that are ultimately responsible for the increased fear of death, the rising number of emotional problems, and the greater need for understanding of and coping with the problems of death and dying.

When we look back in time and study old cultures and people, we are impressed that death has always been distasteful to man and will probably always be. From a psychiatrist's point of view this is very understandable and can perhaps best be explained by our basic knowledge that, in our unconscious, death is never possible in regard to ourselves. It is inconceivable for our unconscious to imagine an actual ending of our own life here on earth, and if this life of ours has to end, the ending is always attributed to a malicious intervention from the outside by someone else. In simple terms, in our unconscious mind we can only be killed; it is inconceivable to die of a natural cause or of old age. Therefore death in itself is associated with a bad act, a frightening happening, something that in itself calls for retribution and punishment.

One is wise to remember these fundamental facts as they are essential in understanding some of the most important, otherwise unintelligible communications of our patients.

The second fact that we have to comprehend is that in our unconscious mind we cannot distinguish between a wish and a deed. We are all aware of some of our illogical dreams in which two completely opposite statements can exist side by side—very acceptable in our dreams but unthinkable and illogical in our wakening state. Just as our unconscious mind cannot differentiate between the wish to kill somebody in anger and the act of having done so, the young child is unable to make this distinction. The child who angrily wishes his mother to drop dead for not having gratified his needs will be traumatized greatly by the actual death of his mother—even if this event is not linked closely in time with his destructive wishes. He will always take part or the whole blame for the loss of his mother. He will always say to himself—rarely to others—"I did it, I am responsible, I was bad, therefore Mommy left me." It is well to remember that the child will react in the same manner if he loses a parent by divorce, separation, or desertion. Death is often seen by a child as an impermanent thing and has therefore little distinction from a divorce in which he may have an opportunity to see a parent again.

Many a parent will remember remarks of their children such as, "I will bury my doggy now and next spring when the flowers come up again, he will get up." Maybe it was the same wish that motivated the ancient Egyptians to supply their dead with food and goods to keep them happy and the old Amerian Indians to bury their relatives with their belongings.

When we grow older and begin to realize that our omnipotence is really not so omnipotent, that our strongest wishes are not powerful enough to make the impossible possible, the fear that we have contributed to the death of a loved one diminishes—and with it the guilt. The fear remains diminished, however, only so long as it is not challenged too strongly. Its vestiges can be seen daily in hospital corridors and in people associated with the bereaved.

A husband and wife may have been fighting for years, but when the partner dies, the survivor will pull his hair, whine and cry louder and beat his chest in regret, fear and anguish, and will hence fear his own death more than before, still believing in the law of talion—an eye for an eye, a tooth for a tooth—"I am responsible for her death, I will have to die a pitiful death in retribution."

Maybe this knowledge will help us understand many of the old customs and rituals which have lasted over the centuries and whose purpose is to diminish the anger of the gods or the people as the case may be, thus decreasing the anticipated punishment. I am thinking of the ashes, the torn clothes, the veil, the *Klage Weiber*° of the old days—they are all means to ask you to take pity on them, the mourners, and are expressions of sorrow, grief, and shame. If someone grieves, beats his chest, tears his hair, or refuses to eat, it is an attempt at self-punishment to avoid or reduce the anticipated punishment for the blame that he takes on the death of a loved one.

This grief, shame, and guilt are not very far removed from feelings of 10 anger and rage. The process of grief always includes some qualities of anger. Since none of us likes to admit anger at a deceased person, these emotions are often disguised or repressed and prolong the period of grief or show up in other ways. It is well to remember that it is not up to us to judge such feelings as bad or shameful but to understand their true meaning and origin as something very human. In order to illustrate this I will again use the example of the child—and the child in us. The five-year-old who loses his mother is both blaming himself for her disappearance and being angry at her for having deserted him and for no longer gratifying his needs. The dead person then turns into something the child loves and wants very much but also hates with equal intensity for this severe deprivation.

The ancient Hebrews regarded the body of a dead person as something unclean and not to be touched. The early American Indians talked about the evil spirits and shot arrows in the air to drive the spirits away. Many other cultures have rituals to take care of the "bad" dead person, and they all originate in this feeling of anger which still exists in all of us, though we dislike admitting it. The tradition of the tombstone may originate in the wish to keep the bad spirits deep down in the ground, and the pebbles that

---

Klage Weiber: Lamenting widows.

many mourners put on the grave are leftover symbols of the same wish. Though we call the firing of guns at military funerals a last salute, it is the same symbolic ritual as the Indian used when he shot his spears and arrows into the skies.

I give these examples to emphasize that man has not basically changed. Death is still a fearful, frightening happening, and the fear of death is a universal fear even if we think we have mastered it on many levels.

What has changed is our way of coping and dealing with death and dying and our dying patients.

Having been raised in a country in Europe where science is not so advanced, where modern techniques have just started to find their way into medicine, and where people still live as they did in this country half a century ago, I may have had an opportunity to study a part of the evolution of mankind in a shorter period.

I remember as a child the death of a farmer. He fell from a tree and   15 was not expected to live. He asked simply to die at home, a wish that was granted without question. He called his daughters into the bedroom and spoke with each one of them alone for a few moments. He arranged his affairs quietly, though he was in great pain, and distributed his belongings and his land, none of which was to be split until his wife should follow him in death. He also asked each of his children to share in the work, duties, and tasks that he had carried on until the time of the accident. He asked his friends to visit him once more, to bid goodbye to them. Although I was a small child at the time, he did not exclude me or my siblings. We were allowed to share in the preparations of the family just as we were permitted to grieve with them until he died. When he did die, he was left at home, in his own beloved home which he had built, and among his friends and neigh-bors who went to take a last look at him where he lay in the midst of flowers in the place he had lived in and loved so much. In that country today there is still no make-believe slumber room, no embalming, no false makeup to pretend sleep. Only the signs of very disfiguring illnesses are covered up with bandages and only infectious cases are removed from the home prior to the burial.

Why do I describe such "old-fashioned" customs? I think they are an indication of our acceptance of a fatal outcome, and they help the dying patient as well as his family to accept the loss of a loved one. If a patient is allowed to terminate his life in the familiar and beloved environment, it requires less adjustment for him. His own family knows him well enough to replace a sedative with a glass of his favorite wine; or the smell of a home-cooked soup may give him the appetite to sip a few spoons of fluid which, I think, is still more enjoyable than an infusion. I will not minimize the need for sedatives and infusions and realize full well from my own experience as a country doctor that they are sometimes life-saving and often unavoidable. But I also know that patience and familiar people and foods could replace many a bottle of intravenous fluids given for the simple reason that it fulfills the physiological need without involving too many people and/or individual nursing care.

The fact that children are allowed to stay at home where a fatality has struck and are included in the talk, discussions, and fears gives them the feeling that they are not alone in their grief and gives them the comfort of shared responsibility and shared mourning. It prepares them gradually and helps them view death as part of life, an experience which may help them grow and mature.

This is in great contrast to a society in which death is viewed as taboo, discussion of it is regarded as morbid, and children are excluded with the presumption and pretext that it would be "too much" for them. They are then sent off to relatives, often accompanied by some unconvincing lies of "Mother has gone on a long trip" or other unbelievable stories. The child senses that something is wrong, and his distrust in adults will only multiply if other relatives add new variations of the story, avoid his questions or suspicions, shower him with gifts as a meager substitute for a loss he is not permitted to deal with. Sooner or later the child will become aware of the changed family situation and, depending on the age and personality of the child, will have an unresolved grief and regard this incident as a frightening, mysterious, in any case very traumatic experience with untrustworthy grown-ups, which he has no way to cope with.

It is equally unwise to tell a little child who lost her brother that God loved little boys so much that he took little Johnny to heaven. When this little girl grew up to be a woman she never solved her anger at God, which resulted in a psychotic depression when she lost her own little son three decades later.

We would think that our great emancipation, our knowledge of science and of man, has given us better ways and means to prepare ourselves and our families for this inevitable happening. Instead the days are gone when a man was allowed to die in peace and dignity in his own home.

The more we are making advancements in science, the more we seem to fear and deny the reality of death. How is this possible?

We use euphemisms, we make the dead look as if they were asleep, we ship the children off to protect them from the anxiety and turmoil around the house if the patient is fortunate enough to die at home, we don't allow children to visit their dying parents in the hospitals, we have long and controversial discussions about whether patients should be told the truth—a question that rarely arises when the dying person is tended by the family physician who has known him from delivery to death and who knows the weaknesses and strengths of each member of the family.

I think there are many reasons for this flight away from facing death calmly. One of the most important facts is that dying nowadays is more gruesome in many ways, namely, more lonely, mechanical, and dehumanized; at times it is even difficult to determine technically when the time of death has occurred.

Dying becomes lonely and impersonal because the patient is often taken out of his familiar environment and rushed to an emergency room. Whoever has been very sick and has required rest and comfort especially may recall his experience of being put on a stretcher and enduring the noise of the ambulance siren and hectic rush until the hospital gates open. Only those who have lived through this may appreciate the discomfort and cold necessity of such transportation which is only the beginning of a long ordeal—hard to endure when you are well, difficult to express in words when noise, light, pumps, and voices are all too much to put up with. It may well be that we might consider more the patient under the sheets and blankets and perhaps stop our well-meant efficiency and rush in order to hold the patient's hand, to smile, or to listen to a question. I include the trip to the hospital as the first episode in dying, as it is for many. I am putting it exaggeratedly in contrast to the sick man who is left at home—not to say that lives should not be saved if they can be saved by a hospitalization but to keep the focus on the patient's experience, his needs and his reactions.

When a patient is severely ill, he is often treated like a person with no   25
right to an opinion. It is often someone else who makes the decision if and when and where a patient should be hospitalized. It would take so little to remember that the sick person too has feelings, has wishes and opinions, and has —most important of all—the right to be heard.

Well, our presumed patient has now reached the emergency room. He will be surrounded by busy nurses, orderlies, interns, residents, a lab technician perhaps who will take some blood, an electrocardiogram technician who takes the cardiogram. He may be moved to X-ray and he will overhear opinions of his condition and discussions and questions to members of the family. He slowly but surely is beginning to be treated like a thing. He is no longer a person. Decisions are made often without his opinion. If he tries to rebel he will be sedated and after hours of waiting and wondering whether he has the strength, he will be wheeled into the operating room or intensive treatment unit and become an object of great concern and great financial investment.

He may cry for rest, peace, and dignity, but he will get infusions, transfusions, a heart machine, or tracheotomy if necessary. He may want one single person to stop for one single minute so that he can ask one single question—but he will get a dozen people around the clock, all busily preoccupied with his heart rate, pulse, electrocardiogram or pulmonary functions, his secretions or excretions but not with him as a human being. He may wish to fight it all but it is going to be a useless fight since all this is done in the fight for his life, and if they can save his life they can consider the person afterwards. Those who consider the person first may lose precious time to save his life! At least this seems to be the rationale or justification behind all this—or is it? Is the reason for this increasingly mechanical, de-personalized approach our own defensiveness? Is this approach our own way to cope with and repress the anxieties that a terminally or critically ill patient evokes in us? Is our concentration on equipment, on blood pressure, our desperate attempt to deny the impending death which is so frightening and discomforting to us that we displace all our knowledge onto machines, since they are less close to us than the suffering face of another human being which would remind us once more of our lack of omnipotence, our own limits and failures, and last but not least perhaps our own mortality?

Maybe the question has to be raised: Are we becoming less human or more human? . . . it is clear that whatever the answer may be, the patient is suffering more—not physically, perhaps, but emotionally. And his needs have not changed over the centuries, only our ability to gratify them.

Considerations

1. What relationship do you see between the poem that serves as the introduction and the essay itself?
2. Consider the various examples and explanations the essay provides of children's reactions to death and then give your responses to the points Kübler-Ross makes.
3. Summarize briefly the story of the farmer's death. Evaluate the values and the attitudes toward death suggested by this story.
4. According to Kübler-Ross, why do humans find facing death or talking about death (particularly their own death) so difficult? Do you agree with her observations? Explain.
5. In paragraph 2, Kübler-Ross suggests particular readers she hopes to reach. Evaluate the essay, keeping these readers in mind. How successfully do you think she communicates to them? Cite specific passages from the essay to support your analysis.

CONNECTIONS: DEATH

1. Several works in this section depict death as an enemy to be faced and fought; others view death as a natural part of the life cycle, to be accepted and even welcomed. Respond to these opposing views of death, considering any or all of the following works: "The Jilting of Granny Weatherall," "To Hell with Dying," "Death, be not proud," "In the Cemetery Where Al Jolson Is Buried," "In the House of the Dying," "The American Way of Death," and "On the Fear of Death."
2. Compare the use of humor to address the serious subject of death as demonstrated in the following works: "To Hell with Dying," "In the

Cemetery Where Al Jolson Is Buried," *On Tidy Endings,* and "The American Way of Death."

3. Discuss the responses of—and the roles played by—those who are well and living as they face the dying and death of people close to them. Consider any or all of these works: "The Jilting of Granny Weatherall," "In the Cemetery Where Al Jolson Is Buried," "A Rose for Emily," *On Tidy Endings,* "In the House of the Dying," and "On the Fear of Death."

4. Consider the relationships suggested between love and death by any or all of the following works: "The Jilting of Granny Weatherall," "A Rose for Emily," and *On Tidy Endings.*

5. Explain the advice you think Elisabeth Kübler-Ross would give the following people: (1) The parents in "To Hell with Dying" during the time their young children were called on to act as resurrecting angels; (2) the family, doctor, and priest who wait at Granny Weatherall's bedside; and (3) the best friend in "In the Cemetery Where Al Jolson Is Buried."

13

Three American Poets

When Elizabeth Bishop was born in Worcester, Massachusetts, in 1911, Robert Frost, at age 37, was in the process of selling his farm in Derry, New Hampshire, and moving his family to Great Britain. Six years later, when Gwendolyn Brooks was born in Topeka, Kansas, Frost, faced by the onset of World War I, had returned to New England following the publication of two volumes of poetry and had begun teaching at Amherst College. At the time of Brooks's birth and Frost's return to the United States, Elizabeth Bishop had already lost her father to death and her mother to mental illness; she had moved from Massachusetts to Nova Scotia and back again to Massachusetts.

Although Frost began his career as a writer while Bishop and Brooks were still children, these three American poets are considered contemporaries whose works reflect the themes of loss, isolation, danger, displacement, courage, and survival that are typical of twentieth-century literature. The poetry of Frost, Bishop, and Brooks incorporates their diverse cultural backgrounds; each poet also demonstrates a complex understanding of poetic conventions and a canny, almost paradoxical, ability both to work with and to challenge traditional forms. All three poets see the dark side of life yet write with wit; in their poems, humor and irony often play off violent, ugly, or disturbing images.

The following selections, as well as the brief commentaries on the poets' lives and works, provide the opportunity for a closer look at how each writer saw the world. Their similarities, as well as their differences, open possibilities for thinking about their visions of the times and places they knew.

Timeline: Key Events in the Lives of Three American Poets
Robert Frost, Elizabeth Bishop, Gwendolyn Brooks

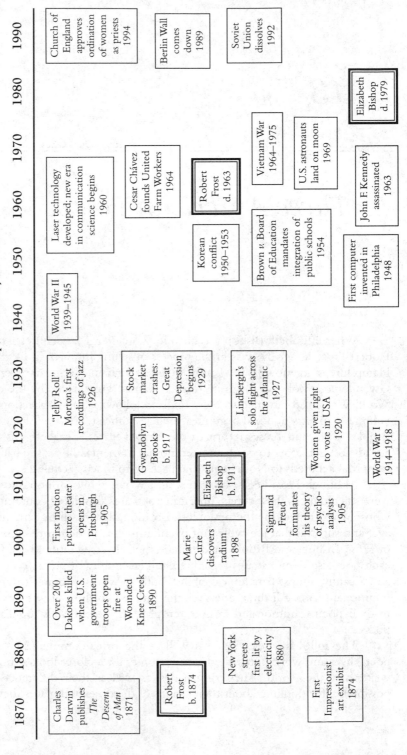

ROBERT FROST (1874–1963)

Robert Frost's father, William Frost, ventured out of his native New Hampshire to work as headmaster at a small private school in Pennsylvania. There he met and married the school's only teacher, Isabelle Moodie. After their marriage in 1873, William and Isabelle struck out for San Francisco, where their son Robert was born. Their marriage was apparently stormy, and Isabelle left William for a year during Robert's early childhood. During these years, William worked as a journalist for the San Francisco Bulletin. *He died in 1885 of tuberculosis, possibly complicated by alcoholism. Following her husband's last wishes, Isabelle and her children returned east with his body so that he might be buried in Lawrence, Massachusetts.*

Robert attended high school in Lawrence, proving himself an excellent student of classics and also becoming known as class poet. He shared the honor of being named class valedictorian with Elinor White, whom he resolved to marry. After attending Dartmouth for part of a semester, Frost dropped out and attempted to persuade Elinor to set the wedding date immediately. She, however, insisted on first completing her studies at St. Lawrence College, graduating in 1895 and agreeing to the marriage in the same year.

After supporting himself and Elinor at a variety of jobs while continuing to write poetry, Frost decided to return to college and in 1897 persuaded Harvard to accept him as a special student. In 1899, the Frosts moved to Derry, New Hampshire, living on a farm purchased for them by Frost's grandfather. The years in New Hampshire were difficult. By 1905, Elinor had given birth to five children, and the family faced constant economic problems. Frost acknowledged to friends that he had seriously contemplated suicide during this time. In 1906, however, his financial circumstances improved when he accepted a teaching position at Pinkerton Academy, where he was inspired to introduce creative innovations to the established curriculum, teaching drama and also writing most of the poems that he eventually published in his first book.

Because of his difficulty in finding an American publisher, Frost sold the farm in 1911 and moved his family to London. There he submitted his poems to the English publisher Alfred Nutt, who published the collection A Boy's Will *in 1913. The book won great acclaim in England, and as a result Frost became acquainted with many poets whose work he had long admired, including Ezra Pound, William Butler Yeats, and Amy Lowell. In 1915, World War I forced the Frost family to return to the United States. The success that Frost had enjoyed in England spread to the United States, and in 1917 he was invited to teach at Amherst College, where he remained for many years, occasionally spending time at other colleges and universities as visiting professor or poet-in-residence.*

Lawrence Thompson's biography of Frost, published between 1966 and 1976, presents convincing evidence that Frost was not simply the kindly, wise poet-farmer living the idyllic rural life that many of his admirers imagined; he was far more complex. He had suffered many personal tragedies, including the death, at age four, of his first-born son, the mental illness of his sister Jeanie, the death of his daughter Marjorie following childbirth in 1934, the estrangement and death of his wife (who refused to see him during her final illness) in 1938, and the suicide of his only living son in 1940. Thompson's research suggests that these troubles, combined with Frost's ambitions and vanity, often led to mean-spirited and even vindictive actions that alienated many of his friends and family members.

Whatever his personal failings may have been, he traveled widely, serving as a goodwill ambassador to South America and to what was then the Soviet Union. In 1961, he was recognized as one of America's strongest and most distinct voices when John F. Kennedy invited him to read a poem at the inauguration ceremonies. Frost continued to accept speaking engagements until his death at the age of eighty-eight on January 29, 1963.

Frost's poems often seem deceptively simple because he draws on familiar subjects, often depicting scenes from the natural world as well as people with easily recognized strengths and failings. Frost's language, while powerful and evocative, is easily accessible to most readers and so it is easy to overlook the way his poems often depend on ambiguity for their impact. His works offer many different possibilities, whether they focus on an image from nature (see, for example, the extended discussion of "The Road Not Taken" in Chapter 1, pages 5–10, as well as "Nothing Gold Can Stay," "Stopping by Woods on a Snowy Evening," and "Desert Places") or on a scene from daily life ("Mending Wall," "Home Burial," and "Out, Out—"). Frost's poetry can never be reduced to a formula; his work often surprises the reader. For example, "Acquainted with the Night" uses city images rather than the rural, country scenes many readers associate with his work. The selections offered here provide merely a glimpse at the variety that characterizes Frost's vast body of work.

Mending Wall

Something there is that doesn't love a wall,
That sends the frozen-ground-swell under it,
And spills the upper boulders in the sun;
And makes gaps even two can pass abreast.
The work of hunters is another thing: 5
I have come after them and made repair
Where they have left not one stone on a stone,
But they would have the rabbit out of hiding,
To please the yelping dogs. The gaps I mean,
No one has seen them made or heard them made,   10
But at spring mending-time we find them there.
I let my neighbor know beyond the hill;

And on a day we meet to walk the line
And set the wall between us once again.
We keep the wall between us as we go.   15
To each the boulders that have fallen to each.
And some are loaves and some so nearly balls
We have to use a spell to make them balance:
"Stay where you are until our backs are turned!"
We wear our fingers rough with handling them.   20
Oh, just another kind of outdoor game,
One on a side. It comes to little more:
There where it is we do not need the wall:
He is all pine and I am apple orchard.
My apple trees will never get across   25
And eat the cones under his pines, I tell him.
He only says, "Good fences make good neighbors."
Spring is the mischief in me, and I wonder
If I could put a notion in his head:
"*Why* do they make good neighbors? Isn't it   30
Where there are cows? But here there are no cows.
Before I built a wall I'd ask to know
What I was walling in or walling out,
And to whom I was like to give offense.
Something there is that doesn't love a wall,   35
That wants it down." I could say "Elves" to him,
But it's not elves exactly, and I'd rather
He said it for himself. I see him there
Bringing a stone grasped firmly by the top
In each hand, like an old-stone savage armed.   40
He moves in darkness as it seems to me,
Not of woods only and the shade of trees.
He will not go behind his father's saying,
And he likes having thought of it so well
He says again, "Good fences make good neighbors." 45

Home Burial°

He saw her from the bottom of the stairs
Before she saw him. She was starting down,
Looking back over her shoulder at some fear.
She took a doubtful step and then undid it
To raise herself and look again. He spoke   5

Home Burial: It was the custom until the early twentieth century for remote homes and farms to
have their own family burial ground.

Advancing toward her: "What is it you see
From up there always—for I want to know."
She turned and sank upon her skirts at that,
And her face changed from terrified to dull.
He said to gain time: "What is it you see,"   10
Mounting until she cowered under him.
"I will find out now—you must tell me, dear."
She, in her place, refused him any help
With the least stiffening of her neck and silence.
She let him look, sure that he wouldn't see,   15
Blind creature; and a while he didn't see.
But at last he murmured, "Oh," and again, "Oh."

"What is it—what?" she said.

                    "Just that I see."

"You don't," she challenged. "Tell me what it is."

"The wonder is I didn't see at once.   20
I never noticed it from here before.
I must be wonted to it—that's the reason.
The little graveyard where my people are!
So small the window frames the whole of it.
Not so much larger than a bedroom, is it?   25
There are three stones of slate and one of marble,
Broad-shouldered little slabs there in the sunlight
On the sidehill. We haven't to mind *those*.
But I understand: it is not the stones,
But the child's mound—"

                    "Don't, don't, don't, don't," she cried.   30

She withdrew, shrinking from beneath his arm
That rested on the banister, and slid downstairs;
And turned on him with such a daunting look,
He said twice over before he knew himself:
"Can't a man speak of his own child he's lost?"   35

"Not you!—Oh, where's my hat? Oh, I don't need it!
I must get out of here. I must get air.—
I don't know rightly whether any man can."

"Amy! Don't go to someone else this time.
Listen to me. I won't come down the stairs."   40

He sat and fixed his chin between his fists.
"There's something I should like to ask you, dear."

"You don't know how to ask it."

     "Help me, then."
Her fingers moved the latch for all reply.
"My words are nearly always an offense.   45
I don't know how to speak of anything
So as to please you. But I might be taught,
I should suppose. I can't say I see how.
A man must partly give up being a man
With womenfolk. We could have some arrangement   50
By which I'd bind myself to keep hands off
Anything special you're a-mind to name.
Though I don't like such things 'twixt those that love.
Two that don't love can't live together without them.
But two that do can't live together with them."   55
She moved the latch in a little. "Don't— don't go.
Don't carry it to someone else this time.
Tell me about it if it's something human.
Let me into your grief. I'm not so much
Unlike other folks as your standing there   60
Apart would make me out. Give me my chance.
I do think, though, you overdo it a little.
What was it brought you up to think it the thing
To take your mother-loss of a first child
So inconsolably—in the face of love.   65
You'd think his memory might be satisfied—"

"There you go sneering now!"

     "I'm not, I'm not!
You make me angry. I'll come down to you.
God, what a woman! And it's come to this,
A man can't speak of his own child that's dead."   70

"You can't because you don't know how to speak.
If you had any feelings, you that dug
With your own hand—how could you?—his little grave;
I saw you from that very window there,
Making the gravel leap and leap in air,   75
Leap up, like that, like that, and land so lightly
And roll back down the mound beside the hole.
I thought, Who is that man? I didn't know you.

And I crept down the stairs and up the stairs
To look again, and still your spade kept lifting.   80
Then you came in. I heard your rumbling voice
Out in the kitchen, and I don't know why,
But I went near to see with my own eyes.
You could sit there with the stains on your shoes
Of the fresh earth from your own baby's grave   85
And talk about your everyday concerns.
You had stood the spade up against the wall
Outside there in the entry, for I saw it."

"I shall laugh the worst laugh I ever laughed.
I'm cursed. God, if I don't believe I'm cursed."   90

"I can repeat the very words you were saying.
'Three foggy mornings and one rainy day
Will rot the best birch fence a man can build.'
Think of it, talk like that at such a time!
What had how long it takes a birch to rot   95
To do with what was in the darkened parlour.
You *couldn't* care! The nearest friends can go
With anyone to death, comes so far short
They might as well not try to go at all.
No, from the time when one is sick to death,   100
One is alone, and he dies more alone.
Friends make pretense of following to the grave,
But before one is in it, their minds are turned
And making the best of their way back to life
And living people, and things they understand.   105
But the world's evil. I won't have grief so
If I can change it. Oh, I won't, I won't!"

"There, you have said it all and you feel better.
You won't go now. You're crying. Close the door.
The heart's gone out of it: why keep it up?   110
Amy! There's someone coming down the road!"

"*You*—oh, you think the talk is all. I must go—
Somewhere out of this house. How can I make you—"

"If—you—do!" She was opening the door wider.
"Where do you mean to go? First tell me that.   115
I'll follow and bring you back by force. I *will!*—"

"Out, Out—"

The buzz saw snarled and rattled in the yard
And made dust and dropped stove-length sticks of wood,
Sweet-scented stuff when the breeze drew across it.
And from there those that lifted eyes could count
Five mountain ranges one behind the other   5
Under the sunset far into Vermont.
And the saw snarled and rattled, snarled and rattled,
As it ran light, or had to bear a load.
And nothing happened: day was all but done.
Call it a day, I wish they might have said   10
To please the boy by giving him the half hour
That a boy counts so much when saved from work.
His sister stood beside them in her apron
To tell them "Supper." At the word, the saw,
As if to prove saws knew what supper meant,   15
Leaped out at the boy's hand, or seemed to leap—
He must have given the hand. However it was,
Neither refused the meeting. But the hand!
The boy's first outcry was a rueful laugh,
As he swung toward them holding up the hand,   20
Half in appeal, but half as if to keep
The life from spilling. Then the boy saw all—
Since he was old enough to know, big boy
Doing a man's work, though a child at heart—
He saw all spoiled. "Don't let him cut my hand off—   25
The doctor, when he comes. Don't let him, sister!"
So. But the hand was gone already.
The doctor put him in the dark of ether.
He lay and puffed his lips out with his breath.
And then—the watcher at his pulse took fright.   30
No one believed. They listened at his heart.
Little—less—nothing!—and that ended it.
No more to build on there. And they, since they
Were not the one dead, turned to their affairs.

Nothing Gold Can Stay

Nature's first green is gold,
Her hardest hue to hold.
Her early leaf's a flower;
But only so an hour.

Then leaf subsides to leaf.   5
So Eden sank to grief,
So dawn goes down to day.
Nothing gold can stay.

Stopping by Woods on a Snowy Evening

Whose woods these are I think I know.
His house is in the village, though;
He will not see me stopping here
To watch his woods fill up with snow.

My little horse must think it queer   5
To stop without a farmhouse near
Between the woods and frozen lake
The darkest evening of the year.

He gives his harness bells a shake
To ask if there is some mistake.   10
The only other sound's the sweep
Of easy wind and downy flake.

The woods are lovely, dark and deep,
But I have promises to keep,
And miles to go before I sleep,   15
And miles to go before I sleep.

Acquainted with the Night

I have been one acquainted with the night.
I have walked out in rain—and back in rain.
I have outwalked the furthest city light.

I have looked down the saddest city lane.
I have passed by the watchman on his beat   5
And dropped my eyes, unwilling to explain.

I have stood still and stopped the sound of feet
When far away an interrupted cry
Came over houses from another street,

But not to call me back or say good-by;   10
And further still at an unearthly height
One luminary clock against the sky

Proclaimed the time was neither wrong nor right.
I have been one acquainted with the night.

Desert Places

Snow falling and night falling fast, oh, fast
In a field I looked into going past,
And the ground almost covered smooth in snow,
But a few weeds and stubble showing last.

The woods around it have it—it is theirs.   5
All animals are smothered in their lairs.
I am too absent-spirited to count;
The loneliness includes me unawares.

And lonely as it is that loneliness
Will be more lonely ere it will be less—   10
A blanker whiteness of benighted snow
With no expression, nothing to express.

They cannot scare me with their empty spaces
Between stars—on stars where no human race is.
I have it in me so much nearer home   15
To scare myself with my own desert places.

ELIZABETH BISHOP (1911–1979)

Elizabeth Bishop's childhood was turbulent and unstable. Her father, Thomas Bishop, a successful businessman and member of an affluent Worcester, Massachusetts, family, died when she was eight months old. Apparently unable to cope with this loss, her mother, Gertrude Bulmer, suffered bouts of mental illness and was permanently committed to a mental hospital when Elizabeth was five. After this time, Elizabeth never saw her mother again, and her later memories of her mother were uniformly bitter. During many of the years before her mother's commitment and for the year following, Elizabeth lived with her Bulmer grandparents in Great Village, a small town in Nova Scotia. She grew to love these grandparents and looked back on her time with them as one of the few happy periods in her life.

Her brief idyll came to an abrupt end when her Bishop grandparents insisted that she return to Worcester so that they could provide her with the advantages of wealth, particularly an expensive education. The six-year-old Elizabeth regarded this move as a terrible loss; she felt as though she had been kidnapped. In her misery, she became ill with asthma, an illness that was to afflict her for the rest of her life. During this time, as Elizabeth struggled with her feelings of isolation and loss, she accompanied her aunt, Florence Bishop, to the dentist's office. Her experiences there are reflected in "In the Waiting Room," (page 1227), and it is from this specific incident that Elizabeth herself dated her "feeling of irremediable estrangement from the world" (quoted in Brett Millier, Elizabeth Bishop, Life and the Memory of It, Berkeley: University of California Press, 1993).

Elizabeth stayed in Worcester for only nine months before moving to Boston to live with her Aunt Maud, her mother's sister. Her childhood and early adult years were characterized by her sense of having no home and of living primarily at a series of boarding schools and then at Vassar College. Her biographer, Brett Millier, notes that for Elizabeth "holidays became horrible trials . . . deciding where to spend them was a weighing of obligations and impositions, rarely of desires" (32). During her college years, she frequently spent vacations at a hotel in Boston rather than return to one of her family's houses, none of which she ever considered "home."

Even after her graduation from Vassar in 1934, rootlessness remained a feature of Bishop's life. Having begun her career as a poet while still in college, she moved to an apartment in Greenwich Village where she lived with Louise Crane, a classmate from Vassar. During these years, Bishop was introduced to Marianne Moore, a poet with whom she would have a long friendship and literary correspondence that ended only with Moore's death in 1972. Moore was the first of Bishop's poet-mentor-friends; others included Randall Jarrell, Robert Lowell, and May Swenson.

In 1938, Bishop and Louise Crane bought a house together in Key West (one of the "three loved houses" described in "One Art," page 1230). Bishop lived in Key West for nine years, working diligently on her poetry. A perfectionist, she would often revise a poem for years before finally judging it ready to be sent off for consideration by a publisher. In June 1945, she submitted her first book, North & South, *for the Houghton Mifflin Literary Fellowship. Her manuscript was chosen over those of 800 other entrants and won the prize of $1,000. The book was published in 1946, receiving outstanding reviews. In reviewing* North & South, *in which both "The Fish" (page 1223) and "The Man-Moth" (page 1222) appear, the poet Randall Jarrell described Bishop's work as "unusually personal and honest in its wit, perception, and sensitivity—and in its restrictions too; all her poems have written underneath, "I have seen it" (quoted by Robert Giroux, introduction,* One Art: Elizabeth Bishop, Letters, *Farrar, Straus, Giroux, 1994).*

In 1951, Bryn Mawr College awarded Bishop a fellowship of $2,500, which allowed her to follow a dream of circumnavigating the South American continent. In November of that year, she arrived in Brazil. She expected to stay in Rio de Janeiro with friends for two weeks, but instead she renewed her friendship with Maria Carlota Castellat de Macedo Soares (known as Lota), whom she had met briefly in New York in 1942. Lota asked Bishop to stay and live with her. Bishop later told friends that Lota's offer "was the first time anyone ever offered me a home, or so much" (Giroux, xiii). For the next 15 years, Elizabeth and Lota lived together as friends and lovers, in the other two "loved houses" of "One Art." During the early years of their relationship, Bishop wrote several stories related to her childhood memories, including "In the Village," a fictionalized version of her mother's insanity during Bishop's childhood years in Great Village, Nova Scotia. This story was published by the New Yorker *in 1953. In 1955, Bishop published her second volume of poetry, which combined twenty new poems along with the poems from* North & South; *this book won the Pulitzer Prize for poetry.*

Lota, in the meantime, was deeply involved in Brazilian politics. Following the 1960 election of a candidate whose campaign for governor she had supported, Lota was appointed to a position overseeing progressive city-planning reforms. She worked energetically until 1965, when changes in the political power structure undermined her efforts. In this same year, Bishop was offered a term as writer-in-residence at the University of Washington in Seattle. She took the position, regretting that Lota would not accompany her. When Bishop returned to Brazil, she found Lota much changed, and in 1967, Lota was diagnosed with arteriosclerosis. Lota seemed improved in late summer and joined Bishop in New York. The trip exhausted Lota physically and emotionally, however, and on the day after her arrival, she took an overdose of Valium and died the following day. After a heartbreaking trip back to Brazil to settle Lota's estate, Bishop moved to her house at Ouro Prêto, Brazil, where she lived unhappily for a brief time, struggling with her depression following Lota's suicide. During the next few years, Bishop alternated between living in Brazil, California, and Massachusetts, where she held the position of writer-in-residence at Harvard University. In 1972, she co-edited, with Emanuel Brasil, the Anthology of Twentieth-Century Brazilian Poetry, and in 1976 she won the Neustadt International Prize of Literature. She spent her remaining years traveling, writing poetry, and teaching. At the time of her death in 1979, she had just begun the fall term as a visiting professor of poetry at the Massachusetts Institute of Technology.

    Bishop's poems reflect a keen eye for description; she often begins with a concrete image—an object, person, animal, or place—and explores its nuances and implications. Some of her earlier poems, such as "The Man-Moth," reflect not only her playful fascination with the ambiguities of language but also her early interest in surrealism, in dreams that border on nightmare. Like many American writers, Bishop values a sense of moral force and purpose as reflected by both interior and exterior landscapes.

The Man-Moth°

Here, above,
cracks in the buildings are filled with battered moonlight.
The whole shadow of Man is only as big as his hat.
It lies at his feet like a circle for a doll to stand on,
and he makes an inverted pin, the point magnetized to the moon.   5
He does not see the moon; he observes only her vast properties,
feeling the queer light on his hands, neither warm nor cold,
of a temperature impossible to record in thermometers.

But when the Man-Moth
pays his rare, although occasional, visits to the surface,   10
the moon looks rather different to him. He emerges
from an opening under the edge of one of the sidewalks
and nervously begins to scale the faces of the buildings.
He thinks the moon is a small hole at the top of the sky,
proving the sky quite useless for protection.   15
He trembles, but must investigate as high as he can climb.

Up the façades,
his shadow dragging like a photographer's cloth behind him,
he climbs fearfully, thinking that this time he will manage
to push his small head through that round clean opening   20
and be forced through, as from a tube, in black scrolls on the light.
(Man, standing below him, has no such illusions.)
But what the Man-Moth fears most he must do, although
he fails, of course, and falls back scared but quite unhurt.

Then he returns   25
to the pale subways of cement he calls his home. He flits,

Man-Moth: "Newspaper misprint for 'mammoth'" (Bishop's note).

he flutters, and cannot get aboard the silent trains
fast enough to suit him. The doors close swiftly.
The Man–Moth always seats himself facing the wrong way
and the train starts at once at its full, terrible speed,   30
without a shift in gears or a gradation of any sort.
He cannot tell the rate at which he travels backwards.

        Each night he must
be carried through artificial tunnels and dream recurrent dreams.
Just as the ties recur beneath his train, these underlie   35
his rushing brain. He does not dare look out the window,
for the third rail, the unbroken draught of poison,
runs there beside him. He regards it as a disease
he has inherited the susceptibility to. He has to keep
his hands in his pockets, as others must wear mufflers.   40

        If you catch him,
hold up a flashlight to his eye. It's all dark pupil,
an entire night itself, whose haired horizon tightens
as he stares back, and closes up the eye. Then from the lids
one tear, his only possession, like the bee's sting, slips.   45
Slyly he palms it, and if you're not paying attention
he'll swallow it. However, if you watch, he'll hand it over,
cool as from underground springs and pure enough to drink.

The Fish

I caught a tremendous fish
and held him beside the boat
half out of water, with my hook
fast in a corner of his mouth.
He didn't fight.   5
He hadn't fought at all.
He hung a grunting weight,
battered and venerable
and homely. Here and there
his brown skin hung in strips   10
like ancient wallpaper,
and its pattern of darker brown
was like wallpaper:
shapes like full-blown roses
stained and lost through age.   15
He was speckled with barnacles,
fine rosettes of lime,

and infested
with tiny white sea-lice,
and underneath two or three   20
rags of green weed hung down.
While his gills were breathing in
the terrible oxygen
—the frightening gills,
fresh and crisp with blood,   25
that can cut so badly—
I thought of the coarse white flesh
packed in like feathers,
the big bones and the little bones,
the dramatic reds and blacks   30
of his shiny entrails,
and the pink swim bladder
like a big peony.
I looked into his eyes
which were far larger than mine   35
but shallower, and yellowed,
the irises backed and packed
with tarnished tinfoil
seen through the lenses
of old scratched isinglass.°   40
They shifted a little, but not
to return my stare.
—It was more like the tipping
of an object toward the light.
I admired his sullen face,   45
the mechanism of his jaw,
and then I saw
that from his lower lip
—if you could call it a lip—
grim, wet, and weaponlike,   50
hung five old pieces of fish-line,
or four and a wire leader
with the swivel still attached,
with all their five big hooks
grown firmly in his mouth.   55
A green line, frayed at the end
where he broke it, two heavier lines,
and a fine black thread
still crimped from the strain and snap

isinglass: Semitransparent substance sometimes used to make windows in early-model automobiles.

when it broke and he got away.   60
Like medals with their ribbons
frayed and wavering,
a five-haired beard of wisdom
trailing from his aching jaw.
I stared and stared   65
and victory filled up
the little rented boat,
from the pool of bilge
where oil had spread a rainbow
around the rusted engine   70
to the bailer rusted orange,
the sun-cracked thwarts,
the oarlocks on their strings,
the gunnels—until everything
was rainbow, rainbow, rainbow!   75
And I let the fish go.

First Death in Nova Scotia

In the cold, cold parlor
my mother laid out Arthur
beneath the chromographs:
Edward, Prince of Wales,
with Princess Alexandra,   5
and King George with Queen Mary.
Below them on the table
stood a stuffed loon
shot and stuffed by Uncle
Arthur, Arthur's father.   10

Since Uncle Arthur fired
a bullet into him,
he hadn't said a word.
He kept his own counsel
on his white, frozen lake,   15
the marble-topped table.
His breast was deep and white,
cold and caressable;
his eyes were red glass,
much to be desired.   20

"Come," said my mother,
"Come and say good-bye

to your little cousin Arthur."
I was lifted up and given
one lily of the valley
to put in Arthur's hand.
Arthur's coffin was
a little frosted cake,
and the red–eyed loon eyed it
from his white, frozen lake.   30

Arthur was very small.
He was all white, like a doll
that hadn't been painted yet.
Jack Frost had started to paint him
the way he always painted   35
the Maple Leaf (Forever).
He had just begun on his hair,
a few red strokes, and then
Jack Frost had dropped the brush
and left him white, forever.   40

The gracious royal couples
were warm in red and ermine;
their feet were well wrapped up
in the ladies' ermine trains.
They invited Arthur to be   45
the smallest page at court.
But how could Arthur go,
clutching his tiny lily,
with his eyes shut up so tight
and the roads deep in snow?   50

Sestina°

September rain falls on the house.
In the failing light, the old grandmother
sits in the kitchen with the child
beside the Little Marvel Stove,
reading the jokes from the almanac,   5
laughing and talking to hide her tears.

Sestina: A verse form in which the final words of the first six-line stanza must be used at the ends
of the lines in the next stanza in a rotating order; the final three lines must contain all six words.

25

She thinks that her equinoctial tears
and the rain that beats on the roof of the house
were both foretold by the almanac,
but only known to a grandmother.   10
The iron kettle sings on the stove.
She cuts some bread and says to the child,

It's time for tea now; but the child
is watching the teakettle's small hard tears
dance like mad on the hot black stove,   15
the way the rain must dance on the house.
Tidying up, the old grandmother
hangs up the clever almanac

on its string. Birdlike, the almanac
hovers half open above the child,   20
hovers above the old grandmother
and her teacup full of dark brown tears.
She shivers and says she thinks the house
feels chilly, and puts more wood in the stove.

It was to be, says the Marvel Stove.   25
I know what I know, says the almanac.
With crayons the child draws a rigid house
and a winding pathway. Then the child
puts in a man with buttons like tears
and shows it proudly to the grandmother.   30

But secretly, while the grandmother
busies herself about the stove,
the little moons fall down like tears
from between the pages of the almanac
into the flower bed the child   35
has carefully placed in the front of the house.

Time to plant tears, says the almanac.
The grandmother sings to the marvellous stove
and the child draws another inscrutable house.

In the Waiting Room

In Worcester, Massachusetts,
I went with Aunt Consuelo

to keep her dentist's appointment
and sat and waited for her
in the dentist's waiting room.   5
It was winter. It got dark
early. The waiting room
was full of grown-up people,
arctics and overcoats,
lamps and magazines.   10
My aunt was inside
what seemed like a long time
and while I waited I read
the *National Geographic*
(I could read) and carefully   15
studied the photographs:
the inside of a volcano,
black, and full of ashes;
then it was spilling over
in rivulets of fire.   20
Osa and Martin Johnson°
dressed in riding breeches,
laced boots, and pith helmets.
A dead man slung on a pole
—"Long Pig,"° the caption said.   25
Babies with pointed heads
wound round and round with string;
black, naked women with necks
wound round and round with wire
like the necks of light bulbs.   30
Their breasts were horrifying.
I read it right straight through.
I was too shy to stop.
And then I looked at the cover:
the yellow margins, the date.   35

Suddenly, from inside,
came an *oh!* of pain
—Aunt Consuelo's voice—
not very loud or long.
I wasn't at all surprised;   40
even then I knew she was
a foolish, timid woman.
I might have been embarrassed,

---

21 *Osa and Martin Johnson:* American adventurers and travel writers.   25 *"Long Pig":* Term for the human carcass.

but wasn't. What took me
completely by surprise   45
was that it was *me:*
my voice, in my mouth.
Without thinking at all
I was my foolish aunt,
I—we—were falling, falling,   50
our eyes glued to the cover
of the *National Geographic,*
February, 1918.

I said to myself: three days
and you'll be seven years old.   55
I was saying it to stop
the sensation of falling off
the round, turning world
into cold, blue-black space.
But I felt: you are an *I,*   60
you are an *Elizabeth,*
you are one of *them.*
Why should you be one, too?
I scarcely dared to look
to see what it was I was.   65
I gave a sidelong glance
—I couldn't look any higher—
at shadowy gray knees,
trousers and skirts and boots
and different pairs of hands   70
lying under the lamps.
I knew that nothing stranger
had ever happened, that nothing
stranger could ever happen.
Why should I be my aunt,   75
or me, or anyone?
What similarities—
boots, hands, the family voice
I felt in my throat, or even
the *National Geographic*   80
and those awful hanging breasts—
held us all together
or made us all just one?
How—I didn't know any
word for it—how "unlikely" . . .   85
How had I come to be here,
like them, and overhear

a cry of pain that could have
got loud and worse but hadn't?

The waiting room was bright   90
and too hot. It was sliding
beneath a big black wave,
another, and another.

Then I was back in it.
The War° was on. Outside,   95
in Worcester, Massachusetts,
were night and slush and cold,
and it was still the fifth
of February, 1918.

95 *The War:* World War I.

One Art

The art of losing isn't hard to master;
so many things seem filled with the intent
to be lost that their loss is no disaster.

Lose something every day. Accept the fluster
of lost door keys, the hour badly spent.   5
The art of losing isn't hard to master.

Then practice losing farther, losing faster:
places, and names and where it was you meant
to travel. None of these will bring disaster.

I lost my mother's watch. And look! my last, or   10
next-to-last, of three loved houses went.
The art of losing isn't hard to master.

I lost two cities, lovely ones. And, vaster,
some realms I owned, two rivers, a continent.
I miss them, but it wasn't a disaster.   15

—Even losing you (the joking voice, a gesture
I love) I shan't have lied. It's evident
the art of losing's not too hard to master
though it may look like (*Write* it!) like disaster.

GWENDOLYN BROOKS (1917–   )

Shortly after her birth in Kansas on June 7, 1917, Gwendolyn Brooks's family moved to Bronzeville, a predominantly black district in Chicago's South Side. There the Brooks family lived for all of Gwendolyn's childhood and adolescence. Living in this area provided Brooks with her sources, images, and direction as a poet. According to family lore, Brooks began writing poetry at the age of seven. Her mother, Keziah, found her filling a page with two-line verses, causing her family to predict that she would follow in the footsteps of renowned black poet Paul Laurence Dunbar. Brooks's mother, a former schoolteacher, encouraged her daughter to read widely and to continue writing. Her brother took over many of her household chores so that she would have time for her creative work. Her father, David, also provided inspiration: his habit of singing and reciting poetry filled the household with cadences that Brooks began to weave into her own lines and verses.

Brooks recalls that from the age of eleven she kept notebooks regularly, partly because of her family's encouragement but also because of her need for a private life of the mind to which she could escape from the harsh realities of her school days. She felt particularly keenly the taunting she received, from black classmates as well as white, because her skin was dark and her hair tightly curled. This theme surfaces in many of her poems and in her one novel, Maud Martha. *In her autobiography,* Report from Part One, *Brooks describes her experiences in elementary school:*

> One of the first "world" truths revealed to me when I at last became a member of SCHOOL was that to be socially successful, a little girl must be Bright (of skin). It was better if your hair was . . . at least Good Grade (Good Grade implied, usually, no involvement with the Hot Comb)—but Bright you marvelously needed to be. (37)

As she moved into her teenage years, Brooks found herself uncomfortable at parties and excluded from the whirl of social events and extracurricular activities that seemed the essential core of her peers' lives. In response, she spent nearly all her free hours alone in her room, writing, reading, and thinking deeply about the world she saw each day as well as about the inner world she developed through her growing intimate acquaintance with novels, poems, and essays. Her 1949 long poem "The Womenhood" (an excerpt of which appears on page 1234) reflects her perception that the young black men she met preferred black women whose skin was light and whose features were close to the "ideal image" of white women who appeared on the covers of popular magazines.

When she was sixteen, she wrote to poet James Weldon Johnson, sending him some of her poems to critique. He responded with encouragement and suggested that she read the works of modern poets such as T. S. Eliot, Ezra Pound, and e. e. cummings and continue her reading of the works of Langston Hughes, Countee Cullen, and Johnson himself. About a year later, Brooks met both Johnson and Hughes at poetry readings at local churches. Hughes was particularly supportive; reading her poems on the spot, he pronounced her talented and encouraged her to go on with her writing. Hughes continued to be a mentor and years later wrote reviews of her work and published her poems in a Chicago area publication for which he wrote a column.

Brooks graduated from Wilson Junior College in 1936; in the early 1940s she participated in a poetry workshop at the South Side Community Art Center, continuing her study of the major modernist poets whom Johnson had recommended to her and working on her own poetic technique. In 1939, she married Henry Blakely and later became the mother of two children. During the early years of their marriage, Blakely and Brooks lived in a two-room kitchenette apartment that Brooks acknowledged as a prime source for her poetry: "If you wanted a poem," she writes in her autobiography, "you had only to look out of a window. There was material always, walking or running, fighting or screaming or singing" (69). "kitchenette building" (page 1233), and "The Mother" (page 1233), which appeared in her first published book, A Street in Bronzeville *(1945), reflect this time.*

In 1949, Brooks published her second work, Annie Allen, *which was awarded the Pulitzer Prize in 1952. Considered her most experimental work, this long poem shows a young black woman as she comes of age, hoping to live out her childhood dreams, which are threatened by poverty and racism. Critics praised Brooks for her use of traditional poetic forms, such as the sonnet and ballad, that integrated the cadences of colloquial speech with the rhythms of formal language. Brooks herself, however, has ambivalent feelings about* Annie Allen, *noting that it is a book that appealed primarily to "certain academy-oriented critics" and that caused many aspiring young black poets to consider her "a tool of the Establishment" and to look on her "with admiration and anxiety" (quoted by Charles Whitaker in "Gwendolyn Brooks—A Poet for All Ages,"* Ebony, *June 1987, p. 214).*

The Bean Eaters, a collection published in 1960, contains some of Brooks's finest poems. Written during the height of the civil rights movement, the poems bring to life the people Brooks depicts. In the title poem (page 1235), for example, she shows an aging couple whose lives have grown predictable, yet who continue to find strength by "remembering . . . / Remembering, with twinklings and twinges."

Brooks marks 1967 as a pivotal year in her life. In Report from Part One, *she says, "It frightens me to realize that, if I had died before the age of fifty, I would have died a 'Negro' fraction" (45). She goes on to note, "Until 1967, my own blackness did not confront me with a shrill spelling of itself. I knew that I was what most people were calling 'a Negro'; I called myself that, although always the word fell awkwardly on a poet's ear" (83). Suddenly, however, Brooks confronted the concept of a New Black consciousness (the capital letters are hers) at the spring 1967 Fisk University Writers' Conference. Here the air was electric with New Black voices, and Brooks describes herself as walking around in amazement, listening, looking, and learning (84–85). Over the next few years, Brooks tried to define for herself a new awareness based not on an integrationist theme but on a separate vision of African-American culture. During those years, she said she worked at "trying to weave the coat that I shall wear" (85). She described her remarkable change in consciousness in these words:*

> *I—who have "gone the gamut" from an almost angry rejection of my dark skin by some of my brainwashed brothers and sisters to a surprised queenhood in the new black sun—am qualified to enter at least the kindergarten of new consciousness now. New consciousness and trudge-toward-progress. I have hopes for myself. (86)*

Since this watershed time, Brooks's career, poetry, and energies have taken many new directions. One example is her decision to allow only independent African-American presses to publish her work. Another is her determined support of young writers: since 1970, in her role as poet laureate of Illinois, she has funded out of her own pocket annual awards to young Illinois poetry writers. She continues to celebrate life, to assert hope, and to honor courage. Her 1986 poem "To the Young Who Want to Die" (page 1237) provides an example of her post-1967 poetic vision and demonstrates her conviction that "poetry is life distilled."

kitchenette building

We are things of dry hours and the involuntary plan,
Grayed in, and gray. "Dream" makes a giddy sound, not strong
Like "rent," "feeding a wife," "satisfying a man."

But could a dream send up through onion fumes
Its white and violet, fight with fried potatoes   5
And yesterday's garbage ripening in the hall,
Flutter, or sing an aria down these rooms

Even if we were willing to let it in,
Had time to warm it, keep it very clean,
Anticipate a message, let it begin?   10

We wonder. But not well! not for a minute!
Since Number Five is out of the bathroom now,
We think of lukewarm water, hope to get in it.

The Mother

Abortions will not let you forget.
You remember the children you got that you did not get,

The damp small pulps with a little or with no hair,
The singers and workers that never handled the air.
You will never neglect or beat   5
Them, or silence or buy with a sweet.
You will never wind up the sucking-thumb
Or scuttle off ghosts that come.
You will never leave them, controlling your luscious sigh,
Return for a snack of them, with gobbling mother-eye.   10

I have heard in the voices of the wind the voices of my dim killed children.
I have contracted. I have eased
My dim dears at the breasts they could never suck.
I have said, Sweets, if I sinned, if I seized
Your luck   15
And your lives from your unfinished reach,
If I stole your births and your names,
Your straight baby tears and your games,
Your stilted or lovely loves, your tumults, your marriages, aches, and your
    deaths,
If I poisoned the beginnings of your breaths,   20
Believe that even in my deliberateness I was not deliberate.
Though why should I whine,
Whine that the crime was other than mine?—
Since anyhow you are dead.
Or rather, or instead,   25
You were never made.
But that too, I am afraid,
Is faulty: oh, what shall I say, how is the truth to be said?
You were born, you had body, you died.
It is just that you never giggled or planned or cried.   30

Believe me, I loved you all.
Believe me, I knew you, though faintly, and I loved,
    I loved you all.

From "The Womanhood"

3

Stand off, daughter of the dusk,
And do not wince when the bronzy lads
Hurry to cream-yellow shining.
It is plausible. The sun is a lode.

True, there is silver under   5
The veils of the darkness.
But few care to dig in the night
For the possible treasure of stars.

The Bean Eaters

They eat beans mostly, this old yellow pair.
Dinner is a casual affair.
Plain chipware on a plain and creaking wood,
Tin flatware.

Two who are Mostly Good.   5
Two who have lived their day,
But keep on putting on their clothes
And putting things away.

And remembering . . .
Remembering, with twinklings and twinges,   10
As they lean over the beans in their rented back room that
    is full of beads and receipts and dolls and cloths,
        tobacco crumbs, vases and fringes.

the rites for Cousin Vit

Carried her unprotesting out the door.
Kicked back the casket-stand. But it can't hold her,
That stuff and satin aiming to enfold her,
The lid's contrition nor the bolts before.
Oh oh. Too much. Too much. Even now, surmise,   5
She rises in the sunshine. There she goes,
Back to the bars she knew and the repose
In love-rooms and the things in people's eyes.
Too vital and too squeaking. Must emerge.
Even now she does the snake-hips with a hiss,   10
Slops the bad wine across her shantung, talks
Of pregnancy, guitars and bridgework, walks
In parks or alleys, comes haply on the verge
Of happiness, haply hysterics. Is.

Of Robert Frost

There is a little lightning in his eyes.
Iron at the mouth.
His brows ride neither too far up nor down.

He is splendid. With a place to stand.

Some glowing in the common blood.   5
Some specialness within.

Boy Breaking Glass

TO MARC CRAWFORD FROM WHOM THE COMMISSION

Whose broken window is a cry of art
(success, that winks aware
as elegance, as a treasonable faith)
is raw: is sonic: is old-eyed première.
Our beautiful flaw and terrible ornament.   5
Our barbarous and metal little man.

"I shall create! If not a note, a hole.
If not an overture, a desecration."

Full of pepper and light
and Salt and night and cargoes.   10

"Don't go down the plank
if you see there's no extension.
Each to his grief, each to
his loneliness and fidgety revenge.

Nobody knew where I was and now I am no longer there."   15

The only sanity is a cup of tea.
The music is in minors.

Each one other
is having different weather.
"It was you, it was you who threw away my name!   20
And this is everything I have for me."

Who has not Congress, lobster, love, luau,
the Regency Room, the Statue of Liberty,
runs. A sloppy amalgamation.
A mistake.   25
A cliff.
A hymn, a snare, and an exceeding sun.

To the Young Who Want to Die

Sit down. Inhale. Exhale.
The gun will wait. The lake will wait.
The tall gall in the small seductive vial
will wait will wait:
will wait a week: will wait through April.   5
You do not have to die this certain day.
Death will abide, will pamper your postponement.
I assure you death will wait. Death has
a lot of time. Death can
attend to you tomorrow. Or next week. Death is   10
just down the street; is most obliging neighbor;
can meet you any moment.

You need not die today.
Stay here—through pout or pain or peskyness.
Stay here. See what the news is going to be tomorrow.   15

Graves grow no green that you can use.
Remember, green's your color. You are Spring.

CONNECTIONS: THREE AMERICAN POETS

1. Each of these poets was born in the United States. How does each poet's
   work represent (or fail to represent) your view of the "American" identity?
   In what ways do these poets' visions of American life affirm each other?
   In what ways do they extend or modify one another? In what ways do
   they contradict one another?

2. Do further research about the lives of one of the poets. Do biographers
   always agree? To what extent do any of the works included in this chapter
   impress you as autobiographical? How does knowing more about an author's life affect your interpretation of his or her work?

3. Considering the biographical details and the works included, focus on the topic of either gender or race as it is addressed (or not addressed) by these three poets. What similarities and differences do you observe?

4. Do some research into important social, cultural, or historical events or decisions that occurred during the time these poems were written. (The time line on page 1210 will provide some ideas.) In what ways do the poems reflect the era in which they were written?

5. Choose any poem in this book (other than those included in this chapter). Read the poem and write your response. Then do research on the author's life and times. Reread the poem and write your response, keeping in mind what you discovered as you researched. Then compare your initial response with your second response. Comment on the changes (or lack of changes) you observe.

6. Choose a poet from this text (other than the three poets represented in this chapter). Read a wide selection of his or her poems, and then select six you consider to be particularly intriguing, important, or representative of the poet's work. Do research on the poet's life and times, and use the information you find to write an introduction that will interest readers in the six poems you selected.

Appendix
MLA Documentation

Whenever you use someone else's words or ideas, either by paraphrasing or quoting directly, you must provide documentation to acknowledge your source. There are many different formats for providing such documentation. When you are writing a paper for a course in one of the humanities (art, literature, music, or history, for example), use the format established by the Modern Language Association (MLA).

USING AND DOCUMENTING QUOTATIONS FROM LITERARY WORKS

Quoting from Poems

1. When you quote one line from a poem or a verse play, run the line in with your own words and enclose it in quotation marks:

   The narrator urges his father, "Do not go gentle into that good night."

2. When you quote two or three lines of poetry, you may either run them in with your own words or set them off separately. When you run them in with your own words, enclose the quotation in quotation marks, and indicate line breaks with a slash. Space before and after the slash.

> The narrator in "Slipping" tells us, "Age comes to my father as a slow / slipping: the leg that weakens, will barely support him. . . ."

Note: The three dots at the end of the sentence (called an ellipsis) indicate that the line continues but that those words have been omitted here. The fourth dot is the period that would normally go at the end of the sentence.

3. When you quote more than three lines of poetry, you must set them apart from your own words by beginning a new line and indenting. *Do not use quotation marks with an indented quotation.*

The first stanza of Thomas's poem introduces its memorable images and rhythms:

> Do not go gentle into that good night,
> Old age should burn and rave at close of day;
> Rage, rage against the dying of the light.
>
> Though wise men at their end know dark is right,
> Because their words had forked no lightning they
> Do not go gentle into that good night.

Quoting from Plays

1. When you are quoting from a verse play, follow the guidelines for quoting poems.

2. When you are quoting from a play that is divided into acts, scenes, and lines, you should indicate this information in parentheses following the quotation (see the example that follows item 3).

3. When you are quoting no more than three lines, run them in with your own words.

> Hamlet reminds the Queen, "I must be cruel only to be kind" (III.IV.185).

Note: The traditional format uses roman numerals for the act and scene and arabic numbers for the line or lines. Some professors may prefer that you use arabic numbers for act, scene, and lines: (3.4.185). Note also that the parenthetical information comes *after* the quotation marks but *before* the period.

4. When you are quoting more than three lines from a play, you must set them off from your own words by spacing down two lines and indenting. In this case, do not enclose the quotation in quotation marks, and place the parenthetical information *after* the period.

Example from verse play

> Hamlet reminds the Queen:
>
> > I will bestow him, and will answer well
> > The death I gave him. So, again, good night.

I must be cruel only to be kind
Thus bad begins and worse remains behind. (III.iv.185)

Example from prose play

In Fierstein's *On Tidy Endings,* Arthur tells Marion:

> His things are not yours to give away, they're mine! This death
> does not belong to you, it's mine! Bought and paid for outright.
> I suffered for it, I bled for it. I was the one who cooked his meals.
> I was the one who spoon-fed them. I pushed his wheel-chair. I
> carried and bathed him. (868)

Note: Because this is a one-act play and does not have line designations, the citation is the page number on which the quotation appears in the book from which the play is taken.

Quoting from Fiction

1. When you are quoting no more than four lines, run them in with your own words.

   In Faulkner's "A Rose for Emily," the narrator calls Miss Emily "a fallen monument" (978).

Note: The citation is the page number on which the quotation appears in the book from which the story is taken. In a short paper that discusses only one or two stories, your professor may not require this citation.

2. When you are quoting more than three lines from a work of fiction, you must set them off from your own words by spacing down two lines and indenting. In this case, the quotation is not enclosed in quotation marks.

   William Faulkner opens his short story "A Rose for Emily" with the narrator's description of the town's response to Miss Emily's death:

   > When Miss Emily Grierson died, our whole town went to her
   > funeral: the men through a sort of respectful affection for a fallen
   > monument, the women mostly out of curiosity to see the inside
   > of her house, which no one save an old manservant . . . had seen
   > in at least ten years. (978)

Note: The citation is the page number on which the quotation appears in the book from which the story was taken. The three dots are an ellipsis indicating that words are omitted from the original quotation.

3. When you quote a passage from a work of fiction that contains dialogue, you must punctuate the dialogue as a quotation within a quotation.

Example of short passage with dialogue

> The narrator explains the problem of confronting Miss Emily by describing the reaction of an important town official. "'Dammit, sir,' Judge Stevens said, 'will you accuse a lady to her face of smelling bad?'" (980)

Note: The quotation is set off by regular (double) quotation marks; the dialogue within the quotation is set off by single quotation marks. The page number citation appears after the question mark because the question mark, unlike the period, remains inside the quotation marks.

Example of long passage (more than four lines) with dialogue

> The narrator's description of town gossip shows the difficulties Miss Emily faced in her new relationship with Homer:

>> At first we were glad that Miss Emily would have an interest, because the ladies all said, "Of course a Grierson would not think seriously of a Northerner, a day laborer." But there were still others, older people, who said that even grief could not cause a real lady to forget *noblesse oblige*—without calling it *noblesse oblige*. (981)

Note: With a long passage, the quotation is indented but not enclosed in quotation marks. The dialogue, therefore, is set off by standard quotation marks rather than the single quotation marks.

USING AND DOCUMENTING SOURCES

The following list suggests some ways of incorporating someone else's words or ideas into the body of your paper. Items 1 through 4 illustrate these ways by referring to the following source material by Nancie Atwell:

> Like writing, reading becomes meaningful only when it involves the particular response of an individual—one's own ways of perceiving reality through the prism of written language. And, like writing, reading generates its most significant meanings when the reader engages in a process of discovery, weaving and circling among the complex of behaviors that characterizes genuine participation in written language. (From *In the Middle* by Nancie Atwell, Boynton-Cook Publishers, Portsmouth, N.H., 1987, p. 155.)

Item 5 in the list refers to another original source:

> New evidence suggests that at least two theaters used during Shakespeare's time may have been uncovered at a London construction site. One theater, the Swan, is believed to be at least 350 years old. (From: "Shakespearean Theaters Reborn," *New York Times,* August 19, 1987, p. 56.)

1. A brief quotation, including the author's name.

> Nancie Atwell believes that meaningful reading and writing both require "the particular response of an individual" (155).

Because the author's name appears in the introduction to the quotation, document it simply by giving the page number where the original quotation appears. Place the page number in parentheses before the ending punctuation.

2. A brief quotation without the author's name.

> "The particular response of an individual" gives meaning to both reading and writing (Atwell 155).

Because the author's name does not appear in the text, you must provide it, along with the page number. Give the author's last name only. (However, if in your paper you cite two or more authors with the same last name, use both first and last name.) If you cite more than one source by the same author, use an abbreviated title (one or two significant words) to identify the work, for example, (Atwell, *Middle* 155).

3. A paraphrase or summary.

> Nancie Atwell suggests that both reading and writing gain meaning only when they involve the unique reaction of one person—an individual's special way of understanding his or her world through the prism of literature (155).

Even though Atwell's sentences and phrases are not directly cited, the writer uses this author's ideas. (Note particularly the use of the prism image.) Therefore, the source must be documented. Because Atwell's name is mentioned, only the page number (in parentheses, before the final punctuation) is required. When the author's name is not mentioned, his or her last name appears within the parentheses just before the page number, for example, (Atwell 155).

4. A long quotation.

> Those interested in the importance of the reader's response to literature should consider Nancie Atwell's thoughts:

> > Like writing, reading becomes meaningful only when it involves the particular response of an individual—one's own ways of perceiving reality through the prism of written language. And, like writing, reading generates its most significant meanings when the reader engages in a process of discovery, weaving and circling among the complex of behaviors that characterizes genuine participation in written language. (155)

When you quote four or more typed lines, indent the quotation 10 spaces from the left margin. Use the normal right margin. *Do not use quotation marks.* Provide documentation within parentheses *after* the final mark of punctuation.

If you do not cite the author's name in the introduction to the quotation, you must include it in the parenthetical documentation. If you do cite the author's name in the introduction to the quotation, provide only the page number.

5. A quotation from an unsigned source (for instance, an unsigned newspaper article).

> The *New York Times* noted that a theater uncovered at a construction site in London "is believed to be at least 350 years old" ("Shakespearean" 56).

> When the article has no author's byline, use an abbreviated title (often the first word other than "a," "an," or "the") and the page number in parentheses.

6. A source written by two or more people.

If the source is written by two or three people, use all authors' names. For instance, if your source is *No Man's Land* by Sandra Gilbert and Susan Gubar, you could cite it in either of these ways:

> The writer's pen may be considered by some to be "a metaphorical pistol" (Gilbert and Gubar 3).

> or

> Gilbert and Gubar note that some consider the writer's pen to be "a metaphorical pistol" (3).

If the source is written by four or more authors, give only the name of the first author, followed by "et al." Note that *et,* the Latin word for "and," is not an abbreviation and therefore requires no period. *Al.* is the abbreviation for the Latin *alia* (meaning "others") and does require a period. For instance, if the source is *Women's Ways of Knowing* by Mary Field Belenky, Blythe McVicker Clinchy, Nancy Rule Goldberger, and Jill Mattuck Tarule, you could cite it in either of these ways:

> Instructors should consider studies suggesting "that women cultivate their capacities for listening while encouraging men to speak" (Belenky et al. 45).

> or

> As Belenky et al. remind us, instructors should consider studies suggesting "that women cultivate their capacities for listening while encouraging men to speak" (45).

COMPILING A LIST OF WORKS CITED

Documentation in the text of a paper and in parenthetical citations leads readers to a list of works cited. This list appears at the end of the paper. Arrange entries in the list of works cited alphabetically so that the reader can find the full reference quickly.

Note: You may have previously learned the old MLA format, in which the list of works cited included *all* materials consulted, paraphrased, or quoted. In the new MLA format, the list includes only those works that are actually paraphrased or quoted.

The following list of sample entries illustrates the MLA bibliographic style. If you are using a type of source not included in this list, consult a more complete handbook or style guide.

1. Book by one author.

   Atwell, Nancie. *In the Middle.* Portsmouth: Boynton, 1987.

2. Book by two or three authors.

   Gilbert, Sandra M., and Susan Gubar. *No Man's Land.* New Haven: Yale UP, 1988.

3. Book by four or more authors.

   Belenky, Mary Field, et al. *Women's Ways of Knowing.* New York: Basic, 1986.

4. Book with an editor.

   Gill, Elaine, ed. *Mountain Moving Day: Poems by Women.* Trumans-burg: Crossing, 1973.

5. Two or more books by the same authors (list in alphabetical order by title).

   Gilbert, Sandra M., and Susan Gubar. *The Madwoman in the Attic.* New Haven: Yale UP, 1979.

   ———. *No Man's Land.* New Haven: Yale UP, 1988.

6. Works in an anthology or collection.

   Atwood, Margaret. "Fishbowl." *Mountain Moving Day: Poems by Women.* Ed. Elaine Gill. Trumansburg: Crossing, 1973.

7. Multivolume work.

   Graves, Robert. *The Greek Myths.* Vol 2. New York: Braziller, 1967. Vol. 2.

8. Article from a professional journal that paginates each issue separately (each new issue begins with page 1).

Johnson, Gale. "Ibsen's Tragic Comedies." *The Center Magazine* 12.2 (1979): 15–21.

9. Article from a professional journal that paginates issues continuously throughout the year. For instance, the first issue of 1991 might begin with page 1 and end with page 330. The second issue, then, would begin with page 331, and so on.

Heilman, Robert B. "Charlotte Brontë, Reason, and the Moon." *Nineteenth-Century Fiction* 14 (1960): 283–302.

10. Article in a newspaper.

Signed

Paulsen, Karen. "Poetry for the '90's." *Boston Globe* 12 Sept. 1990: A55.

Unsigned

"Shakespearean Theaters Reborn." *New York Times* 19 Aug. 1987: 56.

ASSEMBLING THE LIST OF WORKS CITED

Arrange the entries in the list of works cited alphabetically according to the first word of the entry. Here is how the examples listed above would appear in a list of works cited; note that the entries are double-spaced and that a double space appears between each entry:

Works Cited

Atwell, Nancie. *In the Middle*. Portsmouth: Boynton, 1987.

Atwood, Margaret. "Fishbowl." *Mountain Moving Day: Poems by Women*. Ed. Elaine Gill. Trumansburg: Crossing, 1973.

Belenky, Mary Field, et al. *Women's Ways of Knowing*. New York: Basic, 1986.

Gilbert, Sandra M., and Susan Gubar. *The Madwoman in the Attic*. New Haven: Yale UP, 1979.

———. *No Man's Land*. New Haven: Yale UP, 1988.

Gill, Elaine, ed. *Mountain Moving Day: Poems by Women*. Trumansburg: Crossing, 1973.

Graves, Robert. *The Greek Myths*. Vol. 2. New York: Braziller, 1967.

Heilman, Robert B. "Charlotte Brontë, Reason, and the Moon." *Nineteenth-Century Fiction* 14 (1960): 283–302.

Johnson, Gale. "Ibsen's Tragic Comedies." *The Center Magazine* 12.2 (1979):

15–21.

Paulsen, Karen. "Poetry for the '90's." *Boston Globe* 12 Sept. 1990: A55.

"Shakespearean Theaters Reborn." *New York Times* 19 Aug. 1987: 56.

GUIDELINES
Preparing the List of Works Cited

- Double-space entries.
- Double-space between entries.
- Begin the first line of each entry at the left margin.
- Indent the second and subsequent lines five spaces.
- Arrange entries in alphabetical order, according to the first word of the entry (excluding "a," "an," or "the").

INDEX OF FIRST LINES (alphabetical)

INDEX OF AUTHORS, TITLES, AND SUBJECTS